THE GROWTH
OF
PRESIDENTIAL
POWER

THE GROWTH
OF
PRESIDENTIAL
POWER

A DOCUMENTED HISTORY

by
WILLIAM M. GOLDSMITH
Brandeis University

with an Introductory Essay by
Arthur M. Schlesinger, jr.

Volume III
Triumph and Reappraisal

New York
CHELSEA HOUSE PUBLISHERS
in association with
R. R. BOWKER COMPANY
New York and London
1974

Project Editor: Deborah Weiss
Managing Editor: Roberta Morgan
Assistant Editor: Kathryn Hammell
Editorial Consultant: Leon Freidman

Published by Chelsea House Publishers in association
with R. R. Bowker Company (a Xerox Education Company)

Library of Congress Cataloging in Publication Data

Goldsmith, William M.
    The growth of Presidential power.
    Includes bibliographies.
    CONTENTS: v. 1. The formative years.—v. 2. Decline and resurgence.—
v. 3. Triumph and reappraisal.
    1. Executive power—United States—History.
2. Presidents—United States—History. I. Title.
JK511.G64   353.03'2   74-9623
ISBN 0-8352-0778-1

THE GROWTH
OF
PRESIDENTIAL POWER

Volume I
The Formative Years
Volume II
Decline and Resurgence
Volume III
Triumph and Reappraisal

Contents

VOLUME III
TRIUMPH AND REAPPRAISAL

III. ADMINISTRATIVE POWER RECAPTURED

IV. EXECUTIVE LEADERSHIP

V. THE PRESIDENT AS WORLD LEADER IN WAR AND PEACE

VI. LIMITS OF PRESIDENTIAL POWER REEXAMINED

VII. THE FUTURE OF
    PRESIDENTIAL POWER

I. The Progressive Impact
on the Presidency

THE PROGRESSIVE IMPACT
ON THE PRESIDENCY

Theodore Roosevelt and the
Roots of Progressivism

During the last three decades of the nineteenth century, major changes in American life placed increased burdens upon the national government, and particularly upon the office of the President. The population of the country almost doubled, but it by no means kept pace with industrial development, urbanization and immigration, all of which increased at phenomenal rates. Of these three, the rate of industrial development was the most important; indeed, the accelerated growth of American cities and the numbers of immigrants pouring into this country can be attributed to this fantastic expansion in technology and production. The completion of the national railway systems led the way, for without greatly expanded transportation facilities, the growth of the inland cities would have been impossible, and many of the opportunities which beckoned the continuing influx of immigrants would have been nonexistent. The confluence of all three of these developments during the last 30 years of the nineteenth century produced a period of unprecedented growth, accompanied by a wide range of problems which seriously challenged the American political system.

Industrial development was unquestionably quickened by the pressure of the Civil War, but in the years directly following that national tragedy, technological breakthroughs and a resourceful and strenuous search for new markets and new sources of capital, both here and abroad, greatly broadened the progress made during the war. While the population was increasing from close to 40,000,000 people in 1870 to almost 76,000,000 in 1900, production indices multiplied at many times that rate of increase. From 1863[1] to 1899 the index of manufacturing production rose by over 700 percent. The tonnage of coal mined expanded by slightly over 800 percent; the value of steel products increased by 400 percent; and oil production swelled from 221,000,000 to 2,672,000,000 gallons, an increase of slightly over 1200 percent. In 1860 the value of manufactured articles produced in the United States ranked fourth internationally, but by 1894 U.S. manufacturing had captured first place. By 1909 production in the United States equaled the combined output of Great Britain and Germany, her nearest rivals. Certainly from the point of view of industrial productivity, the United States came of age during this period.[2]

The dynamics of this industrial growth were everywhere reflected in the development of urbanized American life. Villiages became towns, towns became cities and cities became bursting metropolitan centers in the rush of economic and industrial expansion. As the railroads stretched farther across the country, cities like Pittsburgh, Cleveland, Chicago and St. Louis became transportation depots and new commercial market centers. The older coastal cities continued to grow too, remaining trading centers for both foreign and domestic products, centers of commerce and finance, since they retained significant control of the expanding industrial resources, and also centers of industry, because they were already established seats for marketing and transportation. In addition, as ports of debarkation, they were flooded with new arrivals into the country, who quickly became a readily available labor pool, eager to obtain employment, but not yet capable of doing very much about the terms under which they worked. Urbanization and immigration flourished in the wake of the incredible industrialization going on throughout the country. But poverty, death and disease always trailed closely behind this dynamic growth and development.

The end of the nineteenth century and the beginning of the twentieth was also a turning point of considerable significance to the office of the President of the United States. The early presidency had been marked by the emergence of men of singular character and influence. Immediately following the constitutional ratification conventions, George Washington was inaugurated and served for two decisive terms as Chief Executive, defining the basic role of the office, firmly grounding its prestige in the political system at home and in cautious contacts with the rest of the world. He handed on a tradition of integrity and national commitment which has never been overshadowed. Washington's successor, John Adams, maintained the austere integrity of the office, but he was not able to provide the national leadership that Washington's heroic stature and popularity with the American people had made possible.

Thomas Jefferson, the third President of the United States, made his unique contributions to the office and to its growing power and influence as the first political party leader to be elected President. He used this dual leadership role to initiate policy and to direct its conversion into legislative reality. Jefferson, contrary to some inaccurate assessments, turned out to be a very strong Executive leader in office. He was much more than a mere administrative arm of the legislature; rather he was a source of policy leadership in both the foreign and domestic fields, and probably the most gifted and brilliant man ever to hold the office. His Republican successors, James Madison, James Monroe and John Quincy Adams, all men who had made very significant contributions to the development of the early republic, failed to realize comparable effectiveness in the presidential office. Madison was too indecisive and allowed Congress to get the upper hand; Monroe served in a calmer period but he lacked the imagination and leadership qualities of his predecessors; and Adams was thwarted in his quite extensive policy plans by his inability to persuade men and to lead them to follow his counsel. Andrew Jackson restored vigorous presidential leadership after 20 years of virtual eclipse, enlarging the area of executive influence by his direct appeal to the people over the heads of the Congress. His policies did not always fulfill his ambitious democratic objectives, but he certainly established a bond between the Chief Executive and his constituents which later became one of the principal strengths of the office.

Jackson's success in broadening the base of presidential support and invigorating the presidency through his assertion of an active leadership role was not repeated, however, in the administrations of his immediate successors. His encroachments upon congressional power and prestige led to the heated attack by Clay, Webster and Calhoun upon the "usurpation of executive power"—a catchphrase which became the battle cry of the political party which replaced the Jacksonians in office in 1840. Although the crippling divisions between Whig majorities in both houses of the legislature and the Whig President prevented that party from carrying out its program of dismantling the powers of the Chief Executive, the Whig theory of legislative supremacy survived during the administrations of Taylor, Fillmore, Pierce and Buchanan, when for all practical purposes the party was already dead. Legislative supremacy was strengthened by the constitutional crisis of the Johnson administration, when impeachment almost succeeded, and when the connecting links of trust and communication between the two branches of government were severely damaged.

Although the Mexican and Civil Wars, which called forth the full exercise of the powers of the President as Commander in Chief, tended to emphasize the prerogatives of the office and the character of two very strong wartime Presidents, James Polk and Abraham Lincoln, immediately following these violent interruptions of the peaceful course of constitutional government, both through law (the Tenure of Office Act) and in practice, successive Congresses attempted and for the most part succeeded, throughout the nineteenth century, in greatly restricting the role and power of the President. "Congressional government" was the dominant theme of the last quarter of nineteenth-century politics in America.

The emergence of Theodore Roosevelt changed that pattern. His personality and his concept of the Executive office would not permit him to limit the role of the President in seeing to it that the laws passed by Congress were faithfully executed. Of course this is an essential responsibility of the President, and Roosevelt by no means ignored it, but he was not content to let it go at that. In almost every aspect of government in which the Chief Executive had any function to play, Roosevelt stretched the reach of presidential influence. Over and over again he reiterated his commitment to an active presidency. He argued that the Chief Executive could not "content himself with the negative merit of keeping his talents undamaged in a napkin," but that he was "a steward of the people bound actively and affirmatively to do all he could for the people."[3] Roosevelt felt that the President should not be restricted in his executive actions for the public welfare unless such actions were explicitly forbidden under the Constitution. He acknowledged that he was broadening the use of executive power but denied usurping it:

> In other words, I acted for the public welfare. I acted for the common well-being of all our people, whenever and in whatever manner was necessary, unless prevented by direct constitutional or legislative prohibition. I did not care a rap for the mere form and show of power; I cared immensely for the use that could be made of the substance.[4]

This was not idle rhetoric. There was no aspect of the presidential office which this active Chief Executive left untouched. He responded to what he considered were the needs of the people and the times, and he pursued his understanding of their problems intensely. Yet he never fully comprehended the complex nature of the problems, and did not understand the most effective manner in which they could be resolved; as a result he frequently failed to accomplish anywhere near as much as he seemed to be anxious to achieve. But these deficiencies were not from a lack of will or a commitment to act. They were born of critical shortcomings in his understanding of the nature of the complicated social and economic institutions which were developing in his time and of the need to effect change through more basic and substantive reforms of the institutional and behavior patterns of the whole society.

There can be little doubt that Theodore Roosevelt also extended the foreign policy leadership of the presidency far beyond the limits of any previous President from Washington through McKinley. That overreach for power was described carefully in Volume II of this series. Unlike some other activist Presidents who have tended to emphasize either domestic or foreign policy as their particular field of competence, Roosevelt characteristically chose both and appears to have exerted almost equal influence in each of these areas. John Morton Blum has successfully traced Roosevelt's early consolidation of political power in his own party as the major stepping-stone to controlling the presidential office.[5] The President understood well how vulnerable a Chief Executive could be to the restrictions imposed upon him by Congress if he did not assert and maintain political leadership within that body through effective leadership of his own political party. After his sweeping electoral victory in 1904 Roosevelt exerted all his political prowess in guiding the Hepburn Act through Congress. However, despite his successful battle to crush the rival power of Mark Hanna within the Republican party, followed by his strong victory in the election, Roosevelt still did not and could not lead a united Republican party in the Congress on all the elements of his program. He was not forced to abandon his party, however, but rather he plotted to exploit his influence within Republican ranks to its maximum, and then attempted to attract and if possible manipulate members of the opposition party whose interests from time to time coincided with his own.

Although he was somewhat hampered by deep ideological divisions within his own party in Congress on legislative matters, Roosevelt had few checks upon his power and influence in the area of executive leadership, into which he poured much of his boundless energy, imagination and conviction. He plowed new fields of presidential activity when he used his executive authority to initiate cases like the antitrust suits against the Northern Securities Corporation, the American Tobacco Corporation and the Standard Oil Company, and when he forced a settlement to the threatened anthracite coal strike, which could have shut down a considerable part of American industry and endangered the health of many millions of Americans who relied on that fuel to heat their homes; he most certainly broke new ground when he spelled out the responsibility of the President to protect the national environment, and vigorously pursued programs for soil conservation, the protection of the national forests and waterways, and flood control. In all such cases

Roosevelt had few or no precedents upon which to base his actions, or anything more than the constitutional principles contained in the general welfare clause and implied in other parts of the Constitution.

Most of this consummate activity was healthy and invigorating, and the public interest was well served by Roosevelt's actions. In some cases the President failed to go far enough and in others he seriously challenged what Congress considered to be its prerogatives; but in retrospect these presidential domestic efforts were exemplary, and strengthened the country and its institutions in very substantial ways. Much of the credit properly belongs to Roosevelt for his dynamic and imaginative use and development of the presidential office at a critical turning point in history. But it should also be noted that he was the benefactor of a number of converging historical forces which came together at that moment in time and triggered very widespread and dynamic responses on the part of individuals and groups who reacted to the scandalous neglect, oversight and exploitation which weak government and a paralyzed presidency had permitted to fester and grow throughout all levels of American society for too long. The net result was the creation of an irrevocable model for dynamic presidential leadership which would serve as a paradigm for the presidency in the twentieth century. Of course all twentieth century Presidents would not strictly pattern their behavior according to the clearly etched guidelines of this energetic example; nevertheless it remains as one of the most significant standards by which they are all ultimately judged.

I think it would be accurate to state that the achievements of industrial development, urbanization and immigration during the late nineteenth century were accomplished at the expense of other societal values which were sacrificed upon the altar of what William James called "the bitch goddess success." Individual income rose and more comforts were available to larger numbers of persons, but average incomes did not rise as rapidly as did the profits and power of those in control. The rate of expansion had much to do with the tragedies it frequently left in its wake. It was not only a rising birthrate, but also a continual influx of immigrants (in some cases actively recruited for purposes of exploitation) that accounted for a population increase which neither the rural or urban areas of the country were prepared to support. By this I do not mean that there was not enough land or work—both for some time were in plentiful supply. But the amount of land under cultivation increased too rapidly for a balanced and profitable agricultural economy, and the cities expanded before adequate housing and basic utilities and services were in sufficient supply for minimal standards of health, privacy and security to be available to the hundreds of thousands who flocked to their most crowded and disease-ridden centers.

The depressed conditions of agriculture throughout the country produced an early wave of agrarian protest—the populist movement—which challenged but never quite threatened the existing structure of economic and political power. The farmers' grievances were aggravated by their own unrestricted expansion of soil under cultivation, which obviously brought down the general price level of agricultural products. C. Vann Woodward determined that "the farmer got less for the 23,687,950 acres he planted in cotton in 1894 than for the 9,350,000 acres in 1873."[6] The southern farmer was particularly vulnerable because his was a one-crop economy, and he was dependent upon the price structure in other areas of the country for basic needs. The rapid expansion of the railroads throughout the nation encouraged the continuous flow of westward migration and the overpopulation of certain farm areas. Initially the railroads facilitated migration among all those who were not hardy enough to undertake the frontier invasion in the days of the covered wagon. The existence of available transportation created the possibility of marketing agricultural products beyond the confines of adjacent communities for the first time. Finally, however, the greed of the railroad interests mercilessly convinced Americans and foreign immigrants to move on to more fertile pastures, by painting roseate pictures of the riches and splendors which lay in store for the adventurous pioneers.

The original source of this highly developed and ultimately disastrous form of land exploitation was the huge unrestricted grants of free land awarded by the Congress to the railroads in order to encourage and expedite their rapid growth. A government estimate of the total area granted to the railroads was 130,401,606 acres, and this did not include initial grants which were forfeited by the railroads because of their failure to meet expected construction schedules. These initial grants had been close to 200,000,000 acres. Most of this land was given to the big transcontinental roads and was doled out in channels of land, five to ten miles wide and sometimes wider, which cut across the entire western region of the country. Having already obtained free land over which the railroad would run, there was an abundant amount on both sides to sell to prospective settlers for development. Obviously much of the best acreage in the nation went to the railroads at that time, for they had first choice, and land close to the only connecting link with the market was always at a premium.

It is difficult to imagine the magnitude of these areas. The Northern Pacific Railroad received total grants of 44,000,000 acres, the Southern Pacific, 24,000,000 and the Sante Fe 17,000,000. The Atchison, Topeka, and Santa Fe received 6400 acres for every mile of track they layed down. The total railroad land grants included one-fourth of the states of Minnesota and Washington, one-fifth of Wisconsin, Iowa, Kansas, North Dakota and Montana, one-seventh of Nebraska, one-eighth of California and one-ninth of Louisiana. In all it was an area of 242,000 square miles, larger than Germany or France. In addition, the states turned over 55,000,000 acres of land for railroad construction. The figures boggle the mind.[7]

Matthew Josephson describes how one major railroad head enticed European immigrants to settle on this land:

> [T]he new president made a tremendous effort to populate his railroad barony. He filled the entire world with his pictures, stereopticon slides and "literature" illustrating the Eden-like Northwestern territories. Hundreds of his immigration agents spread their dragnet throughout Europe and England, hauling the peasants from Germany and Sweden in by the thousands to Oregon and the Columbia Basin; depopulating sometimes whole villages in Russia. These vast migrations, which brought, in one instance a train of 6,000 wagons across the Rockies, were inspired of course by an excessive enthusiasm. In the case of the Scandinavians

especially, agents were reported to have deceived the peasant "by painting too bright a picture of the future awaiting him in the new land."[8]

The hopes and enthusiasm of these newcomers, as well as the discouraged Americans from barren and rocky sections of New England and parts of the South, were frequently crushed by unrewarding experiences in the new world. Often they ran into drought and other natural enemies, staking out farms in areas that simply would not yield a worthwhile crop; in other cases the railroads and the granaries took back from them more than they earned in their back-breaking labors. The farmer was powerless without the railroad in the West, for it was the only means of getting his crop to market; but the railroads bled him white, and what they could not take from him, the mortgage bankers, the feed and equipment dealers, the middleman at the wholesale market did. The hopeful immigrants and many of the easterners and southerners who ventured West had a difficult time making ends meet, and many finally returned East, or drifted into emerging urban areas, admitting their tragic defeat and looking desperately for a chance at survival. The overwhelming majority of farmers suffered most during the last three decades of the nineteenth century, when the government appeared to be indifferent to their plight.

As a result many turned to forms of radical politics, aimed at transforming what they had come to believe in as a worn out system which needed to be replaced with one more responsive to and protective of the needs of the people. The farmers organized in the West and in the South, first into the relatively moderate patrons of husbandry, a rural fraternal order, then into the granger movement and finally the more radical farmer's alliances.[9] Initially organized as social and educational organizations devoted to advancing the interests of farmers, the alliances developed a wide range of cooperative enterprises, storing and marketing agricultural products, but they increasingly turned their attention to more political objectives. They were strongly opposed to the exploiting roles adopted by the railroads and the banks, were interested in various forms of government regulation and ownership, and were determined to persuade the country to develop a more plentiful and flexible money system. For several years they operated as political independents, supporting mostly Democrats, Greenbackers and Independents who would respond to their demands, but in the early 1890s they developed their own "people's party," generally referred to as "populists," who met with astounding success, initially on the state level, yet polling over one million votes in the presidential election of 1892. Emphasizing the need for free and unlimited coinage of silver, the populists picked up allies in the mountain states, and by 1896 they nominated a pro-silver, populist-inclined Democratic party candidate for President, William Jennings Bryan, who most of the populists decided to support.

The nomination of Bryan and the combined threat to the populist-Democratic alliance frightened many conservative and gold-Democrats, however, and enabled the Republican party to win a resounding victory in 1896. The strong populist overtones accompanying the national election that year resulted in a sharp political cleavage, strengthening the conservative position in the country for the time being. But the long-range influence of the populist organization and ideas were felt for some time in America and were most directly reflected in the convergence of forces that surfaced at the turn of the century, forming one of the dominant strains of the "age of reform."

The Progressive era emerged after the collapse of populism. Basically it was a period of urban and middle class protest against many of the same forces of expanding industrialism and unrestrained finance capitalism that had plagued the rural population. The farmers had been outrageously exploited by the railroads and the financial institutions of a burgeoning industrial society. They had protested against unjust rate manipulation by the railroads, extortion of unjust charges by the granaries and storage facilities located in the growing industrial centers, against high mortgage rates, money and banking practices, and against the behemoth of the "trusts" which enveloped all of these institutions, including the manufacturing industries which produced the implements and products the farmer needed and bought with his hard-earned and inflated dollars. But by the late 1890s there were others in America who began to be alarmed by the inordinate power and corruption which they saw in business, industry and in the government(s) they seemed to control.

The last quarter of the nineteenth century had produced, among some upper and middle class Americans, a rising sense of outrage at the scandalous patronage of the political party machines, rooted in state and local organizations, but reaching into and influencing government on the national level. This was manifested in the long struggle for civil service reform (see Volume II of this series) by those who were called "mugwumps," essentially white, Anglo-Saxon Protestants of secure social standing in American society—ministers, doctors, lawyers, journalists and more traditionally oriented businessmen who reacted sharply against the aggressive tide of materialism. The heirs of this tradition, in some cases the sons and daughters of mugwump fathers and mothers, came to maturity in the last decade of the nineteenth and the first decade and a half of the twentieth century. For the most part they were cut from the same roots as their lineal and spiritual predecessors, but they tended to be much more successful, much more broadly based, and found allies among other groups in the society who were also reacting against the excesses of the "robber barons."

Part of the explanation for these developing new power vectors in American politics during the twentieth century is found in the significant demographic changes which took place within the society. The earlier social structure in America had been fundamentally rural with a few large cities and many more small towns and villages. This pattern began to change at the midpoint of the nineteenth century, but was in full retreat by the end of 1800s. In the early 1900s the number of Americans living in urban communities exceeded the number living in rural America for the first time. This shift has continued throughout this century, with major cities growing at a fantastic rate. The cities in the midwest led the way, becoming sprawling centers of trade and industry before they could develop any planning or social structures to absorb the growth. Chicago's population increased from 110,000 in 1860 to 2,185,000 in 1910. Cleveland grew from 43,000 people to well over one-half million in the same period; Detroit was just a few steps behind (46,000 to 466,000). Eastern seaboard cities like Boston and New York grew at a slower pace, but the character of their populations changed more radically.

Ten million immigrants poured into the United States during the last years of the nineteenth century, and another fourteen million arrived during the first 15 years of the twentieth century. Boston's population tripled and New York's quadrupled, and by the turn of the century, the number of foreign-born residents outnumbered the number of native-born Americans in both cities.

The nature and size of these population changes created many complex problems. None of these cities was equipped with adequate facilities to absorb that kind of growth. Housing was inadequate, health care very tenuous or nonexistent, water and sewage problems abounded; there were not adequate schools or law enforcement agencies to take care of these rapidly multiplying millions, many of whom were crowded, layer upon layer, into congested slums. Disease and poverty aggravated the severity of these conditions, and few had the time, patience or experience to work their way successfully through these mounting problems. The city rapidly became as potent a source of agitation for reform as the countryside had been in the 1880s and 1890s.

It has been said that the United States was born in the country and moved to the city, and that is pretty much the history not only of its major population shifts but also of the reform movement during the late nineteenth century and the beginning of the twentieth. During the 1890s and after the turn of the century there were increasing evidences of dissatisfaction among individuals and groups with the social and economic disorders which the combined effects of industrialization, urbanization and immigration had produced in this country. The inordinate growth of a number of major cities had not produced prosperity and happiness for their inhabitants, but rather misery, congestion, poverty, filth and disease. Immigrants who had swarmed to the United States with the dream of avoiding the poverty, hopelessness and in some cases the persecution they had experienced in the countries of their birth, frequently discovered that they were again confronted with these same conditions in this country, but here there appeared to be no escape from their dilemma.

The middle and upper class Americans who by the twentieth century were comfortably settled in these same communities, were also disturbed by what they saw developing all around them. Suffering a loss of power and prestige during the nineteenth century, they watched as the aggressive new leaders of business and industry emerged at the top of the heap in the struggle for economic gain, using their financial power to corrupt the institutions of local and national government in an effort to protect their interests by, in many cases, removing from office and power the established elites who had dominated the political structure of the country from the very beginning.

Much of this would have gone unnoticed if the problems of the poor had not impinged upon those better off. The filth, disease and crime which thrived in the poorer and more thickly settled areas of the city soon spread to the community outside, affecting the lives and values of the more fortunate. Upper and middle class taxpayers were critical of the waste and the graft which were part of the corrupt political machines running many of the thickly populated cities; they feared the disease and crime which appeared in other areas of their communities, and they resented their own lack of status and power within a system that permitted such "outrages." Reform started on the municipal level because it was closest at hand, and because the influence of the upper and middle class reformers was strongest among their immediate neighbors. Some few were motivated by humane concern for those who were enveloped in these impoverished conditions, but fear of disease and crime, frustration over graft and corruption and resentment at their loss of status and power were perhaps the more sustaining motives among the middle and upper class reformers. Roy Lubove writes:

> [T]he accomplishments of housing reformers after 1890 could be traced in part to public fear—fear of the slum's threat to the health and well-being of the entire city—. . . .[10]

But what one has most to understand about the Progressive era is that a number of individuals and groups converged around some critical interests to produce the most significant and powerful effort for reform that had yet appeared in American life. The initial thrust undoubtedly came from both sympathetic and horrified patricians, the successors to the "mugwumps," the "goo-goos" (standing for good government) as some referred to them, but the widespread impact of what Hofstadter has called the "Progressive impulse" came about because these patrician reformers were able to ally themselves with other groups in the society who could identify their interests with some of the same reforms, and to attract journalists, professionals and politicians to their ranks who could communicate the problems to an ever widening audience and provide the organizational strength to bring about significant change.

None of this happened overnight. It was a fascinating period, overflowing with good intentions, a developing sense of social conscience, widespread public education and discussion of the ills of the present order and energetic efforts to recapture old values which had eroded under the onslaught of the industrial expansion of the previous century. Certainly Hofstadter's "status revolution" was part of this response to the preeminence of materialism and the rise of the new men of wealth and power, but it was by no means the exclusive motivation. Hofstadter defined an important and perhaps the leading group of Progressives as

> men . . . [who] were Progressives not because of economic deprivations but primarily because they were victims of an upheaval of status that took place in the United States during the closing decades of the nineteenth and the early years of the twentieth century. Progressivism, in short, was to a very considerable extent led by men who suffered from the events of their time not through a shrinkage in their means but through the changed pattern in the distribution of deference and power.[11]

Despite the recent avalanche of criticism which the Hofstadter thesis has attracted, no one has disproven this descriptive analysis of what he claimed to be "a large and strategic section of Progressive leadership."[12] Certainly there were other leaders who were drawn to Progressivism for different reasons and for the "adherence of a heterogeneous public whose various segments responded to various needs," as Hofstadter himself took pains to point out.[13] The patrician and middle class Progressives would have been as unsuccessful as the "mugwumps" if they had not succeeded in attracting to their ranks, or perhaps better, allying with, other groups and classes who eventually swelled their numbers into the largest majority consensus yet to appear in a national presidential election in this country.

Hofstadter's general definition of Progressivism allows for this kind of latitude:

> [B]y "Progressivism" I mean something more than the Progressive (or Bull Moose) Party formed by the Republican insurgents who supported Theodore Roosevelt for the presidency in 1912. I mean rather that broader impulse toward criticism and change that was everywhere so conspicuous after 1900, when the already forceful stream of agrarian discontent was enlarged and redirected by the growing enthusiasm of middle-class people for social and economic reform. As all observant contemporaries realized, Progressivism in this larger sense was not confined to the Progressive Party but affected in a striking way all the major and minor parties and the whole tone of American political life. It was, to be sure, a rather vague and not altogether cohesive or consistent movement, but this was probably the secret of its considerable successes, as well as of certain of its failures. While Progressivism would have been impossible without the impetus given by several social grievances, it was not nearly so much the movement of any social class, or coalition of classes, against a particular class or group as it was a rather widespread and remarkably good-natured effort of the greater part of society to achieve some not very clearly specified self-reformation. Its general theme was the effort to restore a type of economic individualism and political democracy that was widely believed to have existed earlier in America and to have been destroyed by the great corporation and the corrupt political machine, and with that restoration to bring back a kind of morality and civic purity that was also believed to have been lost.[14]

One can agree with Peter Filene that the term "movement" is perhaps too pretentious for the loosely knit and shifting political and social coalitions which were activated to pursue different objectives during this period.[15] The panoply of Progressive causes, activities, legislation and diverse groups certainly defied any rigid ideological definition. Progressivism operated on both the local and national levels, in the East as well as in the West, and the significant economic, social and cultural differences between inhabitants of these areas, to say nothing of the character of the problems they confronted, were bound to splinter rather than unite different attitudes, goals and tactics. There is no doubt that Samuel Hay's finding about early 1900 Pittsburgh, where the reform movement was populated with businessmen from industries which had "developed and grown primarily within the past fifty years and had come to dominate the city's economic life," is accurate, but it should be understood that the social structure of Pittsburgh was quite different from that of New York or Boston, either in 1900 or 1850. It is doubtful whether an older patrician class and a professionally-oriented middle class, which definitely existed in those two cities and underwent substantial losses of political power during the nineteenth century, could find its counterpart in Pittsburgh during the same period.[16] Whatever Progressivism was or was not, it certainly could not duplicate in nineteenth or twentieth century Pittsburgh, the 200-year old highly stratified social structures of communities like Boston and New York.

The research of E. Daniel Potts in early twentieth century Iowa confirmed the thesis advanced by Hofstadter, George Mowry, Alfred D. Chandler, jr. and recently supported studies conducted in Massachusetts, Washington and Baltimore, that Progressive leaders tended to be overwhelmingly middle class, urban, native-born Protestants, college educated, self-employed in professions or modest-sized businesses and rather new to politics.[17] But Potts also discovered that the leaders of two different factions of Progressive leadership did not differ markedly from their "standpat" Republican opponents with respect to these same social characteristics. What then, asked Potts, motivated the Progressives but failed to make reformers out of those Republicans who possessed the same social characteristics? It is a good question, but it does not necessarily destroy the Hofstadter theory of status and power deprivation, although it weakens it as an overall explanation of the behavior and attitudes of national leadership. If the social characteristics of Progressives did not differ markedly from the social characteristics of non-Progressives, then the use of social characteristics as an explanation of Progressive social and political attitudes is certainly not convincing.

The Progressive "revisionists" have challenged the Hofstadter thesis from another perspective. Some recent research by Joseph Huthmacher and Michael Rogin, among others, has discovered substantial working class and lower income support for Progressive candidates, and even some deviations among its leaders from the almost universally accepted Progressive leadership profile.[18] When Filene adds to all this his findings of serious policy and ideological conflicts between many who have heretofore been accepted as Progressives, one has to be at least sympathetic to his argument that the label "Progressive Movement" ought to be retired. Such a term tends to obliterate rather than clarify significant differences in the American response to the forces of industrialization and urbanization, and precludes any meaningful understanding of this period in the future.[19]

Although the arguments and analyses of these Progressive "revisionist" historians are interesting and illuminating, they have not yet washed away the usefulness of defining the period or even the theories which attempted to explain its essential character. Granted that sufficient differences in attitudes, political behavior and policies existed to preclude categorizing it as a movement with a set of shared assumptions and very general objectives, there is still something as unique and distinctive about this period as there is about any other important period of American history. There were certainly significant enough ideological and social distinctions among groups in the American Revolution or New Deal periods to suggest, on the same grounds as the Progressive revisionists have advanced, that these historical categories be abandoned as meaningful descriptions of highly complex periods of history. Obviously it would be as difficult if not impossible to define the typical American Revolutionary or New Deal leader as it has been to profile the typical Progressive leader. Each of these periods is further differentiated by its stages of development, subject to wide social and political differences and even ideological conflicts, as the perspective of the viewer shifts in time from one region of the country to the other, from city to rural area, and even from issue to issue. There was a great difference between a western Pennsylvania farmer or yeoman and a Charleston planter, but both were American Revolutionaries.

There are even more refined distinctions as one applies a time line to political attitudes and behavior. So it is with the Tugwells and the Berles, the Johnsons and the Richbergs, the Corcorans and the Cohens in the New Deal period. All were patriotic American revolutionaries, all were New Dealers, but the differences between them were frequently greater and more significant than the assumptions and objectives they held in common. This is what makes them fascinating periods, so complex and profound in their richly contrasting profiles of experiences in American history.

What the recent historical studies tend to emphasize (to their credit) is that in its gradual development, the Progressive impulse enlarged its span of influence, deepened its grip upon much broader elements of the American people, and reflected its spirit in wide-ranging activities which encompassed municipal reform crusades throughout the country. Progressivism finally emerged in national politics and enlisted large segments of the American people, different in economic and social class, geographical and functional (urban and rural) location, in a broad base of support which stretched far beyond the contours of its initial base in the major urban centers. It was this developing stage of Progressivism into an American pluralist pattern which accounts for the current uproar, but also enlarges the lasting significance of Progressivism as an important social, political and economic development in American history.

Something must be said for the great missionaries of Progressivism—the muckrakers—who in the phenomenal development of investigative journalism and mass communication carried the Progressive message to all corners of the American continent. The muckrakers dramatized the significance and urgency of the Progressive message, and educated and persuaded most Americans to accept its basic objectives for society. They prompted Americans to enlist in the reform movements spawned in the Progressive period, and ultimately to reflect Progressive attitudes in their local and national political activity. This was an immense and important undertaking, and nothing like it in mass communication or mass public adult education has ever taken place before or since. The muckrakers brought home to their millions of readers the dramatic urgency of reform, necessary if the American dream was to be recaptured. As Hofstadter writes:

> To an extraordinary degree the work of the Progressive movement rested upon its journalism. The fundamental critical achievement of American Progressivism was the business of exposure, and journalism was the chief occupational source of its creative writers.[20]

The sheer magnitude of the expansion of the circulation of the daily newspapers and the popular magazines during the period was a phenomenon closely linked to the rise of Progressivism, for the muckrakers found an increasingly larger mass audience in those newspapers and magazines and this greatly increased the potential for reform politics. Hofstadter cites the dimensions of this growth in the last three decades of the nineteenth century and the first ten years of the twentieth:

In 1870 there were 574 daily newspapers in the country; by 1899 there were 1,610; by 1909 2,600. The circulation of daily newspapers increased over the same span of time from 2,800,000 to 24,200,000.[21]

The growth of the popular magazines was even more significant because most of the muckrakers published their exposés in these journals. The older and more respectable magazines—the *Atlantic, Harper's, Scribner's* and the *Century*—sold for 35 cents and reached a limited readership of essentially eastern, upper middle class readers, never numbering more than 130,000. The new popular magazines which appeared at the turn of the century—*McClure's, Ladies Home Journal, Everybody's, Collier's, Hampton's, The Outlook, Cosmpolitan, The Saturday Evening Post, The Independent, World's Work*—sold at 10, 12 or 15 cents a copy and circulated to audiences of several hundred thousand to up to a million readers.[22] And it was these individuals who generated the national mood for reform.

Richard Hofstadter brilliantly captured many of the complexities of this society in his absorbing treatment of the period. No other single work on the Progressive era has attracted so much attention, nor dramatized its spirit and its social and political tensions as well as *The Age of Reform*. Hofstadter has identified the strands of populist ideas which carried over into this very changed ambience, illuminated the striking contrasts and frequent similarities between the two periods and encouraged younger revisionists to probe more deeply to discover the questions left unanswered. Revisionism does not render useless Progressivism as a very meaningful historical category or insignificant a very imaginative interpretation of its dynamics. It appears to me that a very substantial core of the Hofstadter analysis of the Progressive era stands up firmly in the light of withering criticisms from his detractors. Hofstadter's study is after all a long, interpretative historical essay, and not a narrative history. Opting for what he believed to be most significant in the period—the passion for economic and political reform within the system—he saw the middle class urban reformers as the critical force in the initial Progressive impulse; he argued that the reformers were basically motivated by a sense of status and power deprivation which developed during the excesses of the Gilded Age. His central theme has not been successfully challenged. Although some of the recent criticism casts some doubt on this interpretation, no one has yet refuted it or brought to bear any substantial evidence which provides a serious alternative explanation.

Progressivism really hit its stride, however, when it became the focal point of presidential politics in the early part of the twentieth century. Theodore Roosevelt was the first President to sense the power of the Progressive impulse, and he succeeded to a great extent in harnessing its rather diffuse social power and transforming it into political support for his reform policies. Roosevelt first captured the imagination of the Progressives when he dramatically challenged the power of the Morgan and Harriman interests in the government's prosecution of the Northern Securities (Holding) Company. As Hofstadter points out with a nice balance of cynicism and idealism:

The government's suit encouraged everyone to feel at last that the President of the United States was really bigger and more powerful than

Morgan and the Morgan interests, that the country was governed from Washington and not from Wall Street. Roosevelt was immensely gratified when the dissolution [of the holding company] was finally upheld by the Supreme Court in 1904, and he had every right to be—not because he had struck a blow at business consolidation, for the decree was ineffective and consolidation went on apace, but because for the first time in the history of the presidency he had done something to ease the public mind on this vital issue. It was, he said, "one of the great achievements" of his first administration, "for through it we emphasized in signal fashion, as in no other way could be emphasized, the fact that the most powerful men in this country were held to accountability before the law." Henceforth, whatever he might do or say, a large part of the public persisted in thinking of him as a "trust-buster."[23]

There is enough irony in this passage to launch a dozen new revisionist historians, for Hofstadter appears to be arguing that Roosevelt won over the legitimate Progressive instincts against the concentrated power of the few by a grandstand play which really had no essential bearing upon the concentration of economic power in American life. Some writers like Gabriel Kolko have made a very good case for this point of view.[24] But I really do not think that either Hofstadter or Roosevelt was being totally cynical on this question. The fact was that the prosecution of the Northern Securities Company was not an effective curb on the Morgan and Harriman interests, or on further efforts to consolidate private economic power; but it did in fact establish the legal power of the government to move against such concentrations and it created an important public trust in the President, who had demonstrated if not his mastery of the complexities of effective antitrust action, his independence of the influence of the Morgans and the Harrimans, and his willingness to attempt to defend the public interest against encroachments such as theirs. Progressivism needed more than that to achieve its desired goals, but at least it was an interesting and an exhilarating beginning.

Theodore Roosevelt was a brilliant political leader who was able time and time again to capture the imagination of the public and enlist its support for his actions. In doing so he not only responded to the Progressive impulse, but he also gave it political direction and greatly expanded its popularity and its base. This was Roosevelt's greatest strength—he was an activist and a popularizer of great ideas. He never really got down to the difficult work of analyzing their complexities or mastering effective means of implementing them, yet he was such a supreme egoist that he was confident that once he had established his authority to act, he could persuade or manipulate those involved into "righteous action." He really believed he could control the power of the trusts and the huge corporations by holding the weapons of reprisal in his own hands and demanding compliance under threat. When he created the Bureau of Corporations he would not relinquish the personal power to decide in each case what the action of the government should be. But the problem was that he did not understand the nature of the economic structure of power sufficiently enough to know when and where to strike. As a result his potential power over the trusts was almost useless.

And yet when it came to questions of power, his understanding was always illuminating. In the agonizing period before the threatened anthracite coal strike, he complained to Henry Cabot Lodge:

> Unfortunately, the strength of my public position before the country is also its weakness. I am genuinely independent of the big monied men in all matters where I think the interests of the public are concerned, and probably I am the first President of recent times of whom this can be truthfully said. I think it right and desirable that this should be true of the President. But where I do not grant any favors to these big monied men which I do not think the country requires that they should have, it is out of the question for me to expect them to grant favors to me in return.[25]

He did succeed in obtaining Morgan's cooperation in settling the coal strike, but in all probability it was because the financier considered it in his interest to act as he did. The problem that neither Roosevelt nor, in the final analysis, the Progressives ever mastered was how to get "the malefactors of great wealth" to act when they did not consider it in their interest to do so. Roosevelt and other Progressives like Louis Dembitz Brandeis and Woodrow Wilson had different theories concerning how compliance with the public interest should be enforced, and these theories collided at what was undoubtedly the high point of the Progressive era—the presidential election of 1912—and then ironically merged in certain respects in the legislative reforms which were brought about as a result of that national decision.

Before turning to that election, however, a final word on Roosevelt's successful politicizing of the Progressive impulse is necessary. The early middle class reformers were first interested essentially in municipal government (e.g., Tom Johnson in Cleveland, Samuel "Golden Rule" Jones in Toledo and Louis Brandeis in Boston). In many of these early efforts the emphasis was on honesty and efficiency in public service, the initiative frequently coming from the local chamber of commerce, as Leonard White has demonstrated,[26] and the solution being more than likely a nonpolitical, city-manager type reorganization of municipal government. Much of the early muckraking also tended to expose local graft and corruption, but gradually the emphasis of many of these articles turned to national problems—the power of the trusts, corruption at the national level and the failure of the people to control their own political institutions.

The thrust of the Progressive reformers on the state level, men like Robert La Follette in Wisconsin and Hiram Johnson in California, was a good deal more radical than that of the municipal reformers, and confronted problems created by the railroads, the utilities and the trusts, all of which had their national parallels. In many instances these movements inherited much of the spirit and some of the same constituency of the populist movement.

Despite his denunciation of the muckrakers, for it was Roosevelt who hung that title on these crusading journalists in a derogatory swipe at their efforts, the President's activities frequently were in harmony with their objectives, for he dramatized the same problems and urged greater citizen participation in their solutions. Rather than side-stepping the Progressive impulse developing among the people independent of the national political parties and turning to nonpolitical solutions of essentially political problems, Roosevelt attempted to bring the Progressives into his political party, and to channel their efforts to reform of the national system. Of all the major national political figures of his day, Theodore Roosevelt was probably the most receptive to the rising tide of Progressivism. Robert La Follette and Hiram Johnson were still regional leaders in the early 1900s, but Roosevelt had a national constituency and he continued to broaden its base by his receptivity to Progressive ideas and his frequent leadership of Progressive causes. His struggle against the trusts, his fight for pure food and drug legislation, meat inspection, regulation of the railroads and for an employers liability law, for conservation and later for democratizing the political process not only endeared him to many political Progressives, but also brought many essentially non-politically oriented reformers into the political process. Theodore Roosevelt transformed the presidential office from its inert nineteenth century pattern into a veritable cockpit of political leadership for social reform. Or at least he appeared to do so, for he transformed what had generally been a local political and social protest effort into a national political context.

There is no question that Roosevelt became more radical in the course of his second term in office. He spent much of his energy consolidating political support within the Republican party during his first term, but in the second term he was ready to expend a good deal of the political capital he had accumulated once he was assured of his position in office. When many of his efforts were blocked or opposed by alarmed conservatives in his own party, the President leaned more heavily upon his newer allies in the insurgent-Progressive ranks of the party. His most radical statement came at the end of his second term in office when in a special message to Congress he charged that "the representatives of predatory wealth — of the wealth accumulated on a giant scale by all forms of iniquity, ranging from the oppression of wageworkers to unfair and unwholesome methods of crushing out competition, and to defrauding the public by stock jobbing and the manipulation of securities" were thwarting his program.[27] In summarizing the rest of the message, William H. Harbaugh writes:

> He upraided "decent citizens" for permitting "those rich men whose lives are evil and corrupt" to control the national destiny. He condemned those editors, lawyers, and politicians who had been "purchased" by corporations. He declared it a travesty on justice for the law to grant labor the right to organize and for the courts to override that right "under the guise of protecting property rights." Roosevelt censured the judiciary for failing "to stop the abuses of the criminal rich." Additional special messages amplified these and other themes, including the need to guarantee the workingman "a larger share of the wealth." If a fraction of the president's recommendations were put into law, said the New York *Commercial and Financial Chronicle*, "they would commit the country to a course of new experiments and make over the face of social creation."[28]

Such messages enhanced Roosevelt's reputation among the Progressives and stimulated many to believe that there was yet hope for substantial change within the system. In describing Roosevelt's impact on the California Progressives, Mowry observes:

> His name and his doctrines were grafted into the very origins of the movement, and his position in national affairs was repeatedly used by Californians as an effective answer to the charges of party treason raised against them. . . . He was a source of inspiration, a symbol of progressive virtues, and a protector at the highest court.[29]

But at the moment when his policies and the growing support of Progressives throughout the country gave promise to a brilliant reform program, Roosevelt's second term in the White House ended, and he went to Africa to hunt lions, leaving in his place in the White House his old friend and secretary of war, William Howard Taft, who was annointed by the country to be his Republican successor. Taft was more of a conservative than Roosevelt, and although he had been a loyal supporter of the latter's administration and policies, once called upon to lead himself, he responded more to his conservative instincts and to the conservative forces within the Republican party than to Roosevelt's Square Deal program. For a while Taft vacillated, attempting to straddle both the Progressive and the conservative wings of the party, pleasing neither by his conduct. In the end his instincts won out, and he aligned himself with many of Roosevelt's implacable foes. Misunderstanding between the two widened when Taft failed to appoint James R. Garfield to his cabinet, removed Roosevelt's famous chief forester, Gifford Pinchot, (although Pinchot warranted his own removal by his attacks upon the Taft administration) and joined with the conservatives in supporting the Payne-Aldrich Tariff. As the breach between Taft and the Progressives became less reconcilable, Roosevelt was urged to raise the Progressive standard and challenge Taft for the Republican presidential nomination in 1912.

Bryan, Wilson and Democratic Progressivism

The Democrats were not immune to the Progressive ferment in the country. The oldest American party, the party of Jefferson and Jackson, also had its Progressive wing, led by its perennial presidential candidate, the great commoner—William Jennings Bryan. Bryan had already made his mark on American history, despite his three defeats in the presidential campaigns of 1896, 1900 and 1908. He was perhaps one of the two or three unsuccessful candidates for that office who will be remembered long after some of their victorious opponents are forgotten.[30] Bryan's nomination in 1896 shifted the center of gravity and ultimately changed the character of the Democratic party. The Democrats were defeated that year because they drove their conservative supporters and financial backers out of their ranks by adopting Bryan and the populist free silver platform. They frightened many of the urban working class who were concerned that Bryan's election would bring on a depression and result in the loss of their jobs, and reinforced the division of the country along rural and urban lines and according to sections, just at the point when the city people were becoming more numerous than country folk and the population of the northeast was growing more rapidly than the South and West.

But in long-range terms the 1896 division led to the identification of the Democrats with the more Progressive outlook on American political and economic problems. Bryan predated Roosevelt and certainly Wilson in his support for most of the major Progressive issues—railroad regulation, control of the trusts, the federal income tax, currency reform and government control of the banks, tariff reform, prohibition of injunctions in labor disputes, the eight-hour day, women's suffrage, anti-imperialism, temperance and international arbitration. He even predated Roosevelt's support for the referendum and recall, although in Bryan's case it was because it was proposed on a state-wide basis. The Democratic party became so identified with these issues in the first decade and a half of the twentieth century that it challenged Roosevelt for the support of the Progressives in 1912, transformed Woodrow Wilson's narrow and muddled thinking on most of these questions and brought him to victory in the three-cornered race that same year.

Bryan was certainly not a great thinker; he came to be a defender of most of these issues because he felt the great surge of popular support in their behalf. When he first went to Congress in 1892 he accepted free silver as a platform because that was what his constituency wanted, and he made no bones about it:

> I don't know anything about free silver. The people of Nebraska are for free silver and I am for free silver. I will look up the arguments later.[31]

It is rather incredible that this unpretentious and rather lovable man could have had such a broad influence or anticipated so many of the intellectuals of his period. Perhaps no presidential candidate has been so demeaned for lack of intellect as Bryan. Oswald Garrison Villard described him as the most ignorant of all the men he had observed in 31 years of newspaper service. Note also the bitter comments of H. L. Mencken as he observed Bryan during the so-called "monkey" trial in Tennessee:

> He seemed only a poor clod like those around him, deluded by a childish theology, full of an almost pathological hatred for all human learning, all human dignity, all beauty, all fine and noble things. He was a peasant come home to the barnyard. Imagine a gentleman and you have imagined everything that he was not. What animated him from end to end of his grotesque career was simply ambition—the ambition of a common man to get his hands upon the collars of his superiors, or failing that, to get his thumb into their eyes. He was born with a roaring voice, and it had the trick of inflaming half-wits. His whole career was devoted to raising those half-wits against their betters, that he himself might shine.[32]

One can readily believe in the existence of two Americas as one becomes intoxicated by the flow of Mencken's words, but appalled at the cruelty of his invective. Bryan was one of the few "tribunes of the people" that this country has produced, and to caricature only his limitations, regardless of the skill with which it is done, means one fails to grasp the great wisdom of the people which he reflected, for he mixed much of this buncombe and hoopla with insight, and sometimes political sagacity far ahead of his times. Even Mencken granted Bryan his identity with the masses he represented so well:

> He knew every country town in the South and West, and he could crowd the most remote of them to suffocation by simply winding his horn. The city's proletariat, transiently flustered by him in 1896, quickly penetrated his buncombe and would have no more of him; the cockney gallery jeered him at every Democratic national convention for twenty-five years. But out where the grass grows high, and the horned cattle dream away the lazy afternoons, and men still fear the powers and principalities of the air—out there between the corn-rows he held his old puissance to the end. There was no need of beaters to drive in his game. For miles the flivver dust would choke the roads. And when he rose at the end of the day to discharge his Message there would be such breathless attention, such as rapt and enchanted ecstasy, such a sweet rustle of amens as the world had not known since Johann fell to Herod's ax.[33]

Describing Bryan in the twilight of his career at the Scopes trial, Mencken saw that he had not lost that great empathy with his people:

> He liked people who sweated freely, and were not debauched by the refinements of the toilet. Making his progress up and down the Main streets of little Dayton, surrounded by gaping primates from the upland valleys of the Cumberland Range, his coat laid aside, his bare arms and hairy chest shining damply, his bald head sprinkled with dust—so accoutred and on display he was obviously happy. He liked getting up early in the morning, to the tune of the cocks crowing on the dunghill. He liked the heavy, greasy victuals of the farmhouse kitchen. He liked country lawyers, country pastors, all country people. He liked the country sounds and country smells. I believe that this liking was sincere—perhaps the only sincere thing in the man. His nose showed no uneasiness when a hillman in faded overalls and hickory shirt accosted him on the street, and besought him for some light upon some mystery of Holy Writ. The simian gabble of the crossroads was not gabble to him, but wisdom of an occult and superior sort.[34]

What Mencken did not note was the fact that the period of political change which transformed so much of both rural and urban America began in the country with the populists and Bryan, who perceived long before their city cousins many of the ugly and unjust conditions which were developing in America. The rising tide of urbanism rejected this rural hero and smashed the populist upheaval, but not before it borrowed heavily from the populist-Bryan critique of the world, which the industrial revolution in America had created. Henry Steele Commager has placed Bryan's contribution much more in the focus of the historical perspective in which it belongs:

Bryan was the last great spokesman of the America of the nineteenth century—of the America of the Middle West and the South, the America of the farm and the country town, the America that read its Bible and went to Chautauqua, distrusted the big city and Wall Street, believed in God and the Declaration of Independence. He was himself one of these people. He thought their thoughts, and he spoke the words they were too inarticulate to speak. Above all, he fought their battles. He never failed to raise his voice against injustice, he never failed to believe that in the end justice would be done. Others of his generation served special interests or special groups—the bankers, the railroads, the manufacturers, the officeholders; he looked upon the whole population as his constituency.[35]

William Jennings Bryan and Woodrow Wilson had certain things in common. Both were Democrats, both were Presbyterians, they were both fine orators, a decisive factor in both their careers, and they were moralists to the very fibre of their bones. But in terms of personality and style they were oceans apart. Bryan was extremely outgoing, generous and forgiving. He was the type of preacher who enjoyed the hand-shaking rituals after prayer meetings, fried chicken and lemonade at church suppers, the sweaty and congested contact with crowds and followers. To the scholar, Wilson had a far more interesting inner life, passionate and complex, whereas his outward demeanor was correct and always above reproach. By no stretch of the imagination could Wilson be considered forgiving or even generous. He was a very good hater, he never forgave an act of disloyalty or a personal slight. One could be high in President Wilson's esteem for years, but a single disagreement could terminate that long relationship. Such was the case of Colonel House and the President. For years Wilson was as close to the colonel as two friends or a President and his closest advisor could be, and yet when for once Wilson assigned Colonel House to an active role requiring his personal discretion and judgment, the President cut him dead when a major disagreement came between them. He never shared his intimacy again. No, Woodrow Wilson was not a forgiving nor a particularly generous man. If one thinks of him as a preacher, which he was in some exalted sense, he was the dramatic outsider who whisks into the presence of the congregation, holds it spellbound and then slips away without ever pressing the flesh. Wilson was not a fleshy, physical person like Bryan.

Both Bryan and Wilson personified the evangelical tradition of christianity and politics. Both were deeply religious, and an abiding faith burned within them. They wanted to lead, to save, to crusade, and power was merely an instrument toward that end. Power as an end in itself was unthinkable. It needed to be clothed in a righteous cause; it needed to be the means to some higher goal. There is no question that Wilson denied that side of his character which might have hungered for power and fame. As Alexander and Juliette George have pointed out, Wilson suppressed such ambitions and encompassed his objectives in a larger and more rational frame of reference:

Wilson recoiled from recognizing that the motive behind his urge for leadership was highly personal; that wielding power in certain ways and seeking great accomplishment were devices for enhancing his self-esteem.

His stern Calvinist conscience forbade an unabashed pursuit or use of power for personal gratification. He could express his desire for power only insofar as he convincingly rationalized it in terms of altruistic service, and fused it with laudable social objectives.[36]

It is curious how circumstances finally threw the careers of these two great Americans together and even more curious how much the intellectual ivy league university president owed to the small town lawyer and stump speaker, who had graduated from a third-rate college and read precious few books while doing it. At the historic Democratic party convention in Baltimore in 1912, Bryan finally handed on the mantle of party leadership to Woodrow Wilson, but more than that, he handed on the leadership of the Progressive tradition in American politics, which Roosevelt had forfeited by leaving the presidency in 1908 and then trying hopelessly to regain it in 1912. Bryan never succeeded in getting himself placed in the White House, but he had an earlier and, by all odds, a better claim to that tradition than had Roosevelt. The hero of San Juan Hill could not stand the idea of Bryan any more than he could tolerate the writings of the muckrakers, but he built his career on Bryan and the muckrakers' critique of a decaying American society and the Progressive policies that were implicit in that critique. Of course Roosevelt never acknowledged this debt; his aristocratic class snobbery and his very partisan outlook made him contemptuous of the great commoner, but the emotional fervor and most of the ideas which emerged from Roosevelt's dramatic and very radical special message delivered almost as his swan song to the Congress in 1908, reflected much of Bryan's and the populist's critique of American institutions and many of their (albeit modified) remedies.

It is ironic that at the very moment when Roosevelt was revealing publicly how much of a convert he was to the great commoner's ideas, Wilson, who also rebuked and ridiculed Bryan in those days, was affirming his confidence in and support of the same trusts and malefactors of great wealth whom Bryan had always, and Roosevelt had only lately, come to denounce. In fact Wilson had been strongly opposed to Bryan and his followers in the Democratic party for many years, and this proved to be a considerable stumbling block to uniting their efforts to win a later election. The young Princeton professor of jurisprudence and political economy had attacked Bryan and his populist supporters as early as 1896, condemning the famous "Cross of Gold" speech with which Bryan swept the Democratic convention and won the nomination, as "ridiculous." He characterized the members of the farmers' alliances as possessing "crude and ignorant minds," and wound up by voting the "Gold Democratic" ticket.[37]

By 1904, Wilson's principal biographer, Arthur Link, writes, the young professor who was now president of the university had become convinced that Bryan's leadership of the party was a fatal mistake. He told a friend that Bryan had "no brains," and that it was a pity "that a man with his power of leadership should have no mental rudder."[38] He went further than that in an address to a southern audience meeting in New York City that same year; he demanded a rehabilitation of the Democratic party "on the only lines that can restore it to dignity and power."[39] Wilson charged that since 1896 the party had been invaded and used by a noisy minority, men who should never have been admitted to its councils. If they had campaigned under their proper designation as populists and radical theorists, they would have been reduced to insignificance in national politics. Wilson argued that it was time that the South, which had been humiliated by that group, "should demand that it be utterly and once and for all thrust out of Democratic counsels."[40] The country "will tolerate no party of discontent or radical experiment," but rather needs a party of conservative reform, acting within a framework of law and ancient institutions.[41]

Two years later a number of wealthy conservative Democrats began to think seriously of Wilson as the man to call on to lead the party away from Bryan and the Progressives and back to its more conservative center of gravity. The leader of this group, in fact its architect, was Colonel George Brinton McClellan Harvey, the president of the famous publishing firm of Harper and Brothers and also editor of the influential *Harpers Weekly*. Harvey was extremely active in Democratic party politics and hob-nobbed with the few wealthy angels who supported that party, people like August Belmont, William C. Whitney and Thomas Fortune Ryan. The New York editor and publisher enjoyed a position of eminence among American journalists, had widespread contacts among politicians and businessmen, and was itching to become a President-maker. He stimulated a great deal of interest in Wilson as a possible future Democratic presidential candidate, and in the meanwhile tried to convince the Princeton president to run for the Senate from New Jersey. Harvey was almost in a position to guarantee the support of the Democratic political machine in the state if Wilson accepted. After toying with the idea for some months, Wilson backed away from it when he realized it would involve a nasty public dispute with an old friend who was running for the office as a Democratic Progressive candidate against the bosses.

Harvey persisted in his activities to carve out a political career for the Princeton University president as a conservative alternative to Bryan. After Wilson had dined at Delmonico's with Harvey, Ryan and the editor of the *New York Sun*, William M. Laffan, they urged him to commit to paper his position on contemporary political and economic questions. Several months later Wilson responded with a concise statement which he titled "Credo"; Link summarizes it in his biography:

> . . . Wilson declared that the Constitution was the guarantee of American liberty and that it and the laws enacted under it were entirely adequate to remedy the wrongs that had corrupted modern business. On the important question of trust and business regulation, Wilson was unequivocal. Great trusts and combinations are . . . necessary, because [they are] the most convenient and efficient, instrumentalities of modern business . . . ; the vast bulk of their transactions are legitimate. Some businessmen violated the law, to be sure, . . . but they should be punished under the law which they violated, not by direct regulation of business by governmental commissions. Business practices in violation of good morals and sound business methods should be brought within the prohibitions of the civil and criminal law . . . ; the federal government, however, should not undertake the direct supervision and regulation of business. Proceeding next to a discussion of the labor problem, Wilson set himself firmly against the union movement. The constitution guarantees to every man

the right to sell his labor to whom he pleases for such price as he is willing to accept, . . . men who would abridge or abrogate the right of freedom of contract have neither the ideas nor the sentiments needed for the maintenance or for the enjoyment of liberty.[42]

With tongue in cheek Link adds that "there is every reason to believe that this remarkable pronouncement made a favorable impression upon Laffan, Ryan and Harvey."[43]

They could not have asked for anything better designed to please them; that was probably the author's intention. Ryan later agreed to finance Wilson's campaign when he decided to run for governor of New Jersey in 1910. But it is almost embarrassing to read such an ignorant statement over half a century later and to realize at the same time that it was made by the president of one of the outstanding universities in the country and a future President of the United States. To denounce Bryan for ignorance and to mouth such ill-informed platitudes in the middle of the Progressive era is almost unbelievable, unless one can speculate that Wilson was attempting to deceive his attentive elite audience. Other public statements in the same vein rule out such a possibility, as does any knowledge of Wilson's character. He had an unlimited capacity for self-delusion, but he was not a hypocrite.

Wilson continued to voice his meaningless moralisms for some time afterward, yet he had the audacity to criticize Bryan for his "vacuity," and avoided publicly endorsing him or even permitting him to speak on the Princeton campus during the election of 1908. Throughout the campaign he continued to preach morality, urging that the only remedy which could save America from the extremes of socialism and monopolistic capitalism was the adoption of a new morality, defined as a "social reunion and social reintegration which every man of station and character and influence in the country can in some degree and within the scope of his own life set afoot."[44] He implored the bankers of the country

to see to it that there be in his calling no class spirit, no feeling of antagonism to the people, to plain men whom the bankers, to their great loss and detriment, do not know. It is their duty to be intelligent, thoughtful, patriotic intermediaries between capital and the people at large; to understand and serve the general interest; to be public men serving the country as well as private men serving their depositors and the enterprises whose securities and notes they hold.[45]

These were noble sentiments, but the Progressives had been saying for some time that the moral ends of government could only be served by major reforms in the economic and political structure of the country. Woodrow Wilson had nothing to say about these reforms at that point in his still unlaunched political career.

Woodrow Wilson's conversion to Progressivism came shortly after he accepted the candidacy of the Democratic party for governor of New Jersey. It is more than possible that the two events were closely related. In the summer of 1910 Wilson was receptive to the idea of leaving Princeton, but it required a higher cause to win him away from his important duties at the university. His philosophical and religious view of life required nothing less for the full commitment of his energies. But he was undoubtedly upset by the loss of his highly emotional struggle with Dean West over the location of the graduate school, and although he still elicited strong support among a good number of the trustees of the university, his heart was no longer in it. He began looking for new fields to conquer, new triumphs to record. He literally knew nothing about New Jersey politics, but he was a quick learner, and when Colonel Harvey continued to insist that Wilson would be elected governor in 1910 and President two years thereafter, he began to weigh such predictions somewhat more seriously.

The Republican party gained control of state politics in New Jersey in the mid-nineties, and dominated the state political scene for the next 15 years. Republican leadership was wedded to big business and the utilities, and historian Arthur Link suggests that there was more business corruption in New Jersey politics than in any other state in the Union. The Progressives in New Jersey, most of whom were Republicans or independents, had been saying that for some time, but had received no support from the president of Princeton University. If Wilson were to run for governor, however, he would have to confront the concrete problems which the Progressives had pushed to the top of the political agenda. The New Jersey Progressives and independent voters would not be content with the vague moral generalities and bromides with which he had been filling his speeches for some time, and the political arithmetic of the situation strongly indicated that he could not be elected governor without drawing heavily from these two groups. In order to break the grip of the conservative, business-oriented Republican party Wilson would have to hold the regular Democratic supporters and attract the Progressives and independents to his side.

This was precisely what he did. The Democratic party nomination for governor was arranged through negotiations between Harvey and James Smith, jr., Democratic boss of Newark-Essex County and one of the major Democratic leaders in the state. Smith was able to convince several others of the powerful Democratic political leaders in the state to go along with the Wilson nomination, but before it was offered they wanted assurances that Wilson would accept, and that he would do nothing to break down the existing party organization in the state, over which Smith and the others presided and used to their own great personal advantage. When Harvey approached Wilson with these questions, he was informed by the future President that he would not go out of his way to obtain the nomination for governor. However when the New York editor and publisher countered with a second question soliciting Wilson's reaction should the nomination come to him "on a silver platter, without your turning a hand to obtain it" and without any requirement or suggestion of any pledges to the machine, Wilson jumped at the bait. "If the nomination for governor were to come to me in that way," Wilson replied, "I should regard it as my duty to give the matter very serious consideration."[46]

With Harvey, Smith and the other Democratic party leaders running interference, it was smooth sailing from that point on. Wilson's supporters were conscious of the fact that his national and statewide reputation would be a great asset in a state ridden with corruption and patronage politics. They also clearly recognized his strong potential as a presidential candidate in 1912, and the idea of becoming presidential kingmakers appealed to these primarily regional politicians. The most serious opposition to Wilson's candidacy came from the small band of Progressives in the Democratic party who saw the president of Princeton as the guileless pawn of the party's corrupt bosses; they worked feverishly to block his nomination. There were a few uncertain moments on the eve of the state convention, but patronage power paid off, and Wilson drove ahead to a first ballot victory without lifting a finger or making a single speech. It later appeared that his silence and politically independent reputation strengthened his appeal to many unpledged delegates.

In his acceptance speech delivered to the wildly cheering convention, Wilson reminded them that he had not sought the nomination, nor had he made any pledges "of any kind to prevent me from serving the people of the State with singleness of purpose."[47] The new candidate even announced that the organizational leaders of the party who had supported him had made no demands of pledges upon him in return for their support. He was a free and independent candidate and he intended to adhere to the Progressive-oriented party platform which was "sound, explicit and business-like."[48] Wilson obviously meant what he said. After almost a decade of ridiculing and occasionally attacking the Progressives, he had joined them on most questions.

Link indicates that such a broad change in his thinking had been crystallizing for over a year or more, and his now strong assertion of Progressivism was not an overnight conversion or pure opportunism. Yet no decision of this nature can be explained simply with regard to Woodrow Wilson. He demanded more exalted reasons for anything he decided to do. It was characteristic of him to suppress any admission of personal ambition and to express his goals in terms of higher moral objectives. He probably would have explained his espousal of Progressive ideas and policies as being the result of developing events and his own reflections upon these developments, ignoring the fact that Progressivism had so permeated the political environment that the only way a Democrat could be elected governor of New Jersey or President of the United States was to boldly support a Progressive program.

Within the general area of reform there was room for considerable difference of emphasis and method, and Wilson was free to stress his own brand of Progressivism; but from that point on there was no doubt of his determined commitment to political and economic reform. This came as shocking news to many of his earlier conservative and business supporters and especially to the political leaders who had made his nomination as governor possible. But it did not appear to disturb Wilson. The inner light of certainty confirmed all of his major decisions, and once he had made up his mind, he was convinced that he was right and nothing whatsoever could prevail upon him to retreat. Somehow and somewhere he had become convinced of the necessity of political reform along Progressive lines, and from that point on he would take second place to no one on the critical issues concerning all Progressives.

Wilson's campaign started slowly and the candidate revealed that he had not yet divorced himself from his old habit of sermonizing in broad generalities. That did not satisfy the Progressives, for they were quick to discover that his speeches lacked concrete discussion of existing evils or specific commitments to policies which would deal with them. One critic wrote:

> Dr. Wilson did not discuss a living State issue. All he did was to give his hearers a revamped edition of his speech on miscellaneous corporations, which he has been delivering, with variations, for five years. . . . Aside from that he pleaded that the ins be put out and the outs be put into control of the State machinery.[49]

The reaction of the Progressive leader George Record, who Link describes as "the intellectual and ideological architect of the Progressive movement in the State," was indicative of their disaffection. Record characterized the Wilson speeches as "extremely weak, and it is no wonder the independent minded hearers were disappointed."[50]

Fortunately the candidate was quick to sense the validity of these criticisms; he immediately set about remedying his errors. He began to strike out hard on concrete issues one month before the election and he embraced Progressive measures he had previously shunned or criticized. He supported the Progressive policy of direct nomination of all candidates by the people. He advocated a public service commission to regulate utility rates. He spoke in favor of a constitutional amendment to provide for the direct election of senators. In a public exchange of letters with Record, Wilson tackled, directly and candidly, a series of searching questions put to him by the Progressive leader and probably won the election by the able manner in which he declared his views. He was forced to spell out his precise level of commitment to every principle he advocated, even to the point of supporting the repeal of the County Board of Elections Law and the Hillery maximum tax law. The experienced New Jersey Progressives had been advocating these specific reforms for years and knew precisely what they wanted to achieve. They were amazed at the forthright manner in which the Democratic candidate for governor pledged himself explicitly to these same reforms.

The Progressives were stunned at the comprehensive nature of Wilson's conversion. He was in the process of seizing the Progressive leadership in the state of New Jersey, and threatened to enact what they had advocated without tangible hopes of enacting for many years. And Wilson was certainly not bluffing. As the campaign approached election day, he became more and more strident in his attack upon political and economic corruption, and openly condemned the bosses in his own party who had arranged for his nomination, as well as the corrupt politicians in the Republican party. He endeared himself to the independent voters because of this, and swept to a striking victory.

Arthur Link has described Wilson's tenure as governor of New Jersey with such marvelous attention to style and detail that it is possible to follow Wilson's political growth and ideas with the appreciation that this critical apprenticeship deserves. Link is an outstanding example of that rare and gifted biographer whose admiration for his subject does not allow him to emphasize only his positive and godlike qualities, but takes pain to document his weaknesses and mistakes, the full face profile, warts and all. He clearly reveals the opportunistic aspects of Wilson's conversion to Progressivism, but he also demonstrates that once having committed himself to the doctrine, Wilson became as fervent and effective a member of the faith as existed at that time anywhere in America.

Woodrow Wilson brought to the practice of Progressive politics a theoretical mastery of the art of political leadership. Ever since he had written a student essay on cabinet government at Princeton, Wilson had admired the clarity and dynamics of the parliamentary system and had been critical in his doctoral thesis and elsewhere of the sluggishness of the American system, tending to divide the powers of government and thus to weaken them, rather than concentrating power in the hands of a political leader, responsible to the legislature and ultimately to the people. In a position of political power in government for the first time in his life, Wilson turned to his theory of political leadership, only recently adapted to the American system, particularly in the presidency, in his Columbia lectures, where he rejected his earlier dismissal of the importance of that office and indicated that the President (or even a governor by substitution) could assert real power and become the instrument of the will of the people.

In his earlier analysis of American government, his Ph.D. thesis published in 16 editions under the title of *Congressional Government*, Wilson had lamented the dispersion of power within our system, absorbed mostly by the legislature, in fact by the standing committees of Congress. In his Columbia lectures delivered almost 25 years later, he discovered hidden resources of power in the office of the Chief Executive which could be marshalled by appealing first to public opinion, and after having won the confidence of the people, providing sufficiently strong executive leadership to dominate the legislature and govern in the public interest.[51] In a sense Wilson was imposing the British prime ministry upon the American presidency through the imaginative leadership of public opinion.

Almost as if to test this theory of leadership on the state level of government, Wilson proceeded to apply his theory to the circumstances in which he now found himself and to demonstrate its viability in his newly-won office. Before he could push ahead with his Progressive reform policies, however, he was confronted with a challenge that truly tested his recent conversion to reform. At the time of his selection as the candidate for governor, Wilson refused to pledge his support to the Democratic party leaders for any subsequent favors or patronage. As United States senators in New Jersey were still appointed by the state legislature, Wilson was canny enough to ask whether James Smith had any notion of being reappointed to the Senate. If there was anything which the New Jersey Progressives wanted less, it was that. Wilson received indirect assurances from Harvey and others that this was out of the question for many reasons, including the health of the Newark organizational leader.

Following his election victory, which had also swept into power a Democratic majority in the state legislature, Smith visited Wilson at Princeton and informed him that he now felt in better health and was considering returning to the senate. The newly-elected governor immediately realized that any such move would quickly end his honeymoon with his Progressive supporters and make a mockery of his campaign promises. Wilson tried to talk Smith out of his objective, but failing in that he promised to fight him to the death on any such move. Smith was not persuaded that the Princeton professor could block the immense statewide power he controlled within the Democratic party, so the struggle was joined. Wilson quickly demonstrated that he was not simply an armchair political philosopher, for he campaigned so effectively against Smith that he undermined the combined strength of the Democratic political bosses in the state legislature, weaning away their followers with threats of voter reprisals. He finally crushed Smith's campaign, but at the same time he confirmed the selection of the Progressive candidate who triumphed in the Democratic state primary.

For the remaining weeks of the session of the New Jersey legislature in 1911 Woodrow Wilson was unbeatable. He completely dominated the session, invading (despite protests) the Democratic legislative caucus, laying out his program and demanding the support of the members of his party, persuading, inspiring, and even threatening legislators into support of measures. New Jersey and the rest of the country had never seen anything like it. As governor, Wilson prepared and later had introduced into the legislature by friendly supporters, one piece of reform legislation after another until all of his major campaign promises had been achieved. He succeeded in guiding through the New Jersey legislature and signing an election reform bill, corrupt practices legislation, established of a public utilities commission with power to set rates and to impose other standards on behalf of the public and finally a workman's compensation law, thus completing the list of measures for which the governor had promised the voters and the Progressives he would fight.[52] Later in the session Wilson joined the battle for the Walsh-Leavitt Municipal Reform Act, another much sought after piece of Progressive legislation, which after a long campaign of taking the issue to the voters, the governor was able to sign.

Wilson's achievements in New Jersey did not go unnoticed in the rest of the country. He was besieged with invitations to appear and to speak in every section of the nation, and indeed, he did travel and speak frequently in the period between the close of the first session of the New Jersey legislature and the Democratic national convention held in Baltimore in the summer of 1912. There was increasing support from many quarters for his candidacy for President. Not indifferent to these overtures, in 1912 he campaigned in a dozen different states and made at least 40 different speeches in an effort to capture the nomination. He had, however, lost his initial supporters—the bankers and industrialists who Colonel Harvey had gathered together to support him as a conservative alternative to the Bryan-Progressive leadership of the Democratic party. Thomas Fortune Ryan would not be drawn to a presidential candidate who had just succeeded in ramming through his own state legislature measures which seriously restricted the role of corporations in the political process and regulated the activities of the utilities. Wilson also lost the confidence of the organizational leaders of the Democratic party who had initially arranged his nomination, but who he had made enemies of by his attacks on them and his support for legislation aimed at undermining their power in the political process.

But what Wilson lost by being abandoned by conservative businessmen and political bosses, he more than made up for in the enthusiastic reaction of Progressives, not only in New Jersey but throughout the country, to his dynamic leadership in the governor's office. Progressives had advocated the reforms Wilson pushed through for almost a decade in New Jersey, but until he was elected governor there had been no realistic chance of their passage, or anything like the dynamic political leadership he provided for Democratic and Republican Progressives alike. Even Bryan himself was convinced that Wilson was on the right track, particularly by Wilson's support of the popularly selected Progressive candidate for the Senate, James E. Martine, who opposed the political organization leader Smith. "The fact that you were against us in 1896 raised a question in my mind in regard to your views on public questions," Bryan wrote to Wilson, "but your attitude in the Senatorial case has tended to reassure me."[53] But still a little sceptical, the great commoner enclosed a worn copy of the 1908 Democratic platform, and requested that Wilson explain his position on the various planks. Bryan was gratified by Wilson's unequivocal endorsement, but he persisted in asserting his senior role as a "birthright" Progressive:

> I notice that you do not recommend the income tax. . . . I hope that you
> will see your way clear to send a message to the legislature on that
> subject, . . .[54]

Wilson quickly earned a further commendation from the Democratic elder statesman when three weeks later he sent a strong message to the legislature urging the adoption of the income tax amendment. Bryan was pleased and observed that Wilson was a governor who recognized "the responsibilities of his position."[55]

Wilson also was not stinting in his new appraisal of the leader of Progressivism within the Democratic party. After Mrs. Wilson brought the two men together for dinner at Princeton, the governor reflected:

> I feel that I can now say that I know him, and have a very different
> impression of him from that I had before seeing him thus close at hand. He
> has extraordinary force of personality, and it seems the force of sincerity
> and conviction. . . . A truly captivating man, I must admit.[56]

Nor was Wilson sparing in his public praise of Bryan at that stage of his political career. Speaking on the same platform with him at a Democratic rally at Burlington, New Jersey, Wilson was generous in his praise of the great commoner, and amazingly candid for the first time with regard to his own debt to Bryan's leadership:

> Mr. Bryan has borne the heat and burden of a long day; we have come in at
> a very much later time to reap the reward of the things that he has done.
> Mr. Bryan has shown the stout heart, which, in spite of the long years of
> repeated disappointments, has always followed in the star of hope, and it
> is because he has cried America awake that some other men have been able
> to translate into action the doctrines he has so diligently preached.[57]

But the eloquent Wilson was to rise to even greater heights of rhetoric when he again spoke from the same platform as Bryan at the festive occasion of the Jackson Day dinner held in the ballroom of the Raleigh Hotel in Washington in January 1912. By that time enemies of both Wilson and Bryan had done their best to sow the seeds of bad feeling between the two Democratic leaders by publishing a letter Wilson had written several years earlier to the president of a midwestern railroad and a trustee of Princeton University, in which the university president complimented the midwesterner on an anti-Bryan speech he had delivered in Kansas. Wilson had read the speech and agreed with its sentiments:

> I have read it with relish and entire agreement. Would that we could do something at once dignified and effective to knock Mr. Bryan once and for all into a cocked hat.[58]

The newspapers ate up the potential controversy and Bryan was obviously angered by his recollection of the old anti-Bryan Wilson. He told a reporter from the *New York Sun*, a strong anti-Bryan paper which had published the letter:

> [Y]ou may just say that if Mr. Wilson wanted to knock me into a cocked hat, he and the *Sun* are on the same platform. That's what the *Sun* has been trying to do to me since 1896.[59]

Bryan was in the company of Wilson's friend and later secretary of the navy, Josephus Daniels, when he read the story quoting the Wilson letter. When Wilson later asked him about Bryan's reaction, Daniels asked whether he would not rather hear first what he (Daniels) had said to pacify the great commoner. When Wilson agreed, Daniels recalled that he told Bryan: "You must give these college presidents time to catch up with us."[60]

The Jackson Day dinner took place in the aftermath of this flap, and when Wilson arose after midnight to reply to a toast, the ballroom hushed, realizing the awkwardness of Wilson's position with Bryan sitting on the same platform. It was a test, however, which the future President met magnificently, and it might well explain Bryan's last minute support of Wilson at the Democratic convention later that year. After a cursory discussion of the Democratic Progressive program, Wilson turned very dramatically to Bryan and said:

> We have differed as to measures; it has taken us sixteen years and more to come to any comprehension of our community of thought in regard to what we ought to do. What I want to say is that one of the most striking things in recent years is that with all the rise and fall of particular ideas, with all the ebb and flow of particular proposals, there has been one interesting fixed point in the history of the Democratic party, and that fixed point has been the character and the devotion and the preachings of William Jennings Bryan.
>
> I, for my part, never want to forget this: That while we have differed with Mr. Bryan upon this occasion and that in regard to the specific things to be done, he has gone serenely on pointing out to a more and more convinced people what it was that was the matter. He has had the steadfast vision all along of what it was that was the matter and he has, not any more than Andrew Jackson did, not based his career upon calculation, but has based it upon principle.
>
> Let us apologize to each other that we ever suspected or antagonized one another; let us join hands once more all around the great circle of

community of counsel and of interest which will show us at last to have been indeed the friends of our country and the friends of mankind.[61]

One can visualize that the Democrats, seated in the room and moved by these words of respect and admiration as well as their admission of error, were moved and felt at that moment that the Democratic party was indeed fortunate to possess two such capable leaders as Bryan and Wilson. For his part Bryan was obviously affected by this eloquent tribute and arose to acknowledge it, putting his hand affectionately on Wilson's shoulder, saying, "That was splendid, splendid."[62] Wilson responded by saying simply, "I am indeed fortunate that you think it so."[63]

Another observer overheard Bryan tell a friend after the dinner that "it was the greatest speech in American political history."[64] Henry Morgenthau, sr., who was in the audience, commented upon the interest of the audience:

> His speech revealed to these men a new power in the party. . . . The audience progressed from rapt attention to enthusiasm.[65]

Morgenthau later pledged $2,000 a month to help finance Wilson's campaign for the presidency.

Link reports that some of Wilson's friends and advisors thought that this speech was the turning point of Wilson's career. Supporters of Wilson and his major opponent for the Democratic nomination, the recently elected Democratic Speaker of the House of Representatives, James Beauchamp "Champ" Clark of Missouri, thought that the speech which Bryan subsequently delivered at the dinner signified his abdication of party leadership. Even if that is what it did not mean, it certainly must have occurred to Bryan and others that whether or not he continued in the active leadership of the party, his Progressive principles would survive and that there were good men at hand to carry on.

The details of the complicated struggles leading up to the Baltimore convention and the selection of Woodrow Wilson as the party's candidate on the 46th ballot, after trailing "Champ" Clark in the earlier voting, are related with masterful authority by Arthur Link. Wilson had correctly appraised the mood of the country and his own party, and by 1912 he had certainly convinced himself of the validity of Progressive policies. His conversion had not come too late, and his striking record during his first year as a reform governor of New Jersey goes down in history as one of the most remarkable political achievements during the entire Progressive era.

After the convention Wilson rested in the governor's summer mansion at Sea Girt, New Jersey, undoubtedly thinking very seriously about his future course. The Democratic candidates were favored highly because the Republicans were divided. Theodore Roosevelt had led a walkout from the Republican convention in Chicago and had launched an independent challenge to the Republican President, his former friend and advisor, William Howard Taft. The Roosevelt-inspired and -led Progressive party also challenged the Democratic candidate, for if the famed "trust-busting" two-term President could reawaken the tremendous popularity he formerly enjoyed among the American people and attract the Progressives in both parties, he might well outpoll both his opponents. Wilson's work was cut out for him if he hoped to be elected.

The Democratic candidate possessed some outstanding assets which he could apply in his pursuit of the presidency. Certainly he was intellectually qualified, having been a close student of political institutions all of his life, an outstanding teacher and a very successful author and speaker on political subjects. In addition he had many years of administrative experience as the president of one of the country's outstanding universities, where he had earned a national reputation as an innovating educational leader. He had gone from the university to executive leadership of a heavily industrial state, and had established an outstanding record of reform in this position. Observers were convinced that he was a man of firm and principled action, and moreover an effective political leader. He had also won the hearts and votes of many independents and Progressives by his unprecedented reform program, and in a period when Progressive ideas had permeated throughout all parties, all regions and all sections and classes of the population, this late but deserved reputation was a great asset. Finally Wilson was a lifelong regular Democrat, and despite the fact that he had turned on the party bosses who had been responsible for his nomination for governor, his belief in the principle of party regularity and responsible party government assured him of strong Democratic party support. His southern nativity would not hurt either in a political party which year in and year out maintained its center of popular support in the southern states.

Wilson's major problem in the campaign was finding a "political formula"[66] for delineating his Democratic Progressivism from Roosevelt's and convincing Republican, Democratic and independent Progressives throughout the country that the Progressive cause would be more effectively served by his presidency than by that of his Progressive party opponent, the former President. In political terms Wilson had to hold on to the loyal regular Democratic supporters and pick up enough additional independents and Progressives to exploit the potentially suicidal division in the Republican ranks. It was a comfortable political position to be in, the odds were in his favor; on the other hand strange things have happened in national presidential campaigns, and any serious errors on the part of the candidate could still prove to be disastrous. Wilson was in somewhat the same position as Lincoln in 1860, when then it was the Democratic party which was divided and the odds were in favor of the Republican candidate if he could hold on to the faithful in the North. But the two Progressive-oriented candidates in 1912 would be debating the best methods to achieve the shared objective of a more democratically controlled and just society. In his campaign Wilson would stress the need for the greatest range of freedom and opportunity for the individual and the enjoyment of the simpler values of a preindustrial America; while Roosevelt accepted what he considered to be the inevitable growth and size of industry, he placed his emphasis upon its control by stronger and more responsible government in the executive branch.

Theodore Roosevelt's campaign for the presidency probably began in the winter of 1911 when he was informed that the Taft administration had initiated an antitrust suit against the United States Steel Corporation based upon its purchase of the Tennessee Coal and Iron Company. The sale had taken place during the Roosevelt administration and had been approved by the President after he had discussed the matter with the heads of the steel corporation, because he did not believe that the acquisition of the southern corporation would give U. S. Steel any greater monopolistic control of the market. There was great pressure upon the

President to approve the merger at the time, because the manipulation of the stock of the Tennessee Coal and Iron Company had caused a major crisis which was about to break wide open and threaten the stability of the financial community. The stock of the corporation had been pledged against loans made by a number of brokerage houses, and when this became known, a run on the stock was expected as investors would hurry to unload their stock, thus inviting chaos in the financial community. At least that was the reasoning advanced by J. P. Morgan to the President when he requested that Roosevelt give unofficial prior approval to the merger.

Roosevelt was enraged that Taft, who he claimed had been consulted at the time as a member of the President's cabinet and had given his strong approval, would now repudiate the President's word and file an antitrust suit against U.S. Steel based primarily upon this merger. Roosevelt rushed into print, vigorously defended the decision he had made as President and attempted to demonstrate that despite the aquisition of the Tennessee company, the United States Steel Corporation during those years and up to the time of the suit, controlled a diminishing share of the steel market. But Roosevelt wanted to emphasize what he considered to be a more important point with respect to the effectiveness of antitrust suits by the government as a means of controlling the harmful effects of industrial and business power. He continued to defend the antitrust suits initiated by his administration, because

it was only these suits that made the great masters of corporate capital in America fully realize that they were the servants and not the masters of the people, that they were subject to the law and that they would not be permitted to be a law unto themselves; and the corporations against which we proceed [sic] had sinned, not merely by being big [which we did not regard as in itself a sin], but by being guilty of unfair practices towards their competitors, and by procuring unfair advantages from the railways.[67]

But Roosevelt now felt that the continuation of what he considered to be indiscriminate antitrust litigation was ineffective and pointless:

The Anti-Trust Law cannot meet the whole situation, nor can any modification of the principle of the Anti-Trust Law avail to meet the whole situation. The fact is that many of the men who have called themselves Progressives, and who certainly believe that they are Progressives, represent in reality in this matter not progress at all but a kind of sincere rural toryism. These men believe that it is possible by strengthening the Anti-Trust Law to restore business to the competitive conditions of the middle of the last century. Any such effort is foredoomed to end in failure, and, if successful, would be mischievous to the last degree. Business cannot be successfully conducted in accordance with the practices and theories of sixty years ago unless we abolish steam, electricity, big cities, and, in short, not only all modern business and modern industrial conditions, but all the modern conditions of our civilization. The effort to restore competition as it was sixty years ago, and to trust for justice solely to this proposed restoration of competition, is just as foolish as if we should go back to the flintlocks of Washington's Continentals as a substitute for modern weapons of precision. The effort to prohibit all combinations, good or bad, is bound to fail, and ought to fail; when made, it merely means that some of the worst combinations are not checked and that honest business is checked. Our purpose should be, not to strangle business as an incident of strangling combinations, but to regulate big corporations in thoroughgoing and effective fashion, so as to help legitimate business as an incident to thoroughly and completely safeguarding the interests of the people as a whole.[68]

In a speech delivered at the dedication ceremonies of John Brown's battlefield at Osawatomie, Kansas, in 1910, Roosevelt sketched out the body of principles upon which he was to make his last political stand in 1912. At that time, however, he had no intention of becoming a candidate again for the presidency. As a respected national leader he was making a statement of faith, rallying Progressive forces within his party to stand and fight for their point of view within the party. Roosevelt was disturbed at a number of things which President Taft had done (and some that he had not done) since taking over the reins of government in 1909. Open warfare had broken out within the Republican party by the summer of 1910, and as William Leuchtenburg has written, one of the objectives of Roosevelt's Osawatomie speech was to reassure his old Progressive comrades-in-arms that his absence in Africa and Europe for a year had not dampened his commitment to the Progressive cause.

The Progressives (or insurgents as they were then called within the ranks of the Republican party) at first misunderstood Roosevelt's position and intepreted his Kansas speech and other addresses he made that summer as the opening guns of a challenge to Taft for the candidacy of the Republican party in 1912. That was clearly not Roosevelt's intention at that point. He wanted to bring pressure upon Taft to heal the breach in the party by shifting his stance in the direction of Progressive principles. In the event that he had forgotten what they were, in that address Roosevelt spelled out his interpretation of Progressivism and introduced his new and encompassing slogan for reform—the New Nationalism. The speech at Osawatomie did not provide a detailed blueprint for all the reform policies for which the Progressive party under Roosevelt's leadership later campaigned in 1912, but it established the principles from which they would emerge. The Republican Progressives reacted to the speech enthusiastically, and immediately raised it as a battle cry against Taft. Pressures began to build up within the party for Roosevelt to challenge the President in the primaries to be held in the spring of 1912, but Roosevelt was not persuaded by either their enthusiasm or their entreaties, and he adamently refused to commit himself to such a struggle for the next year or more.

Theodore Roosevelt
"The New Nationalism"
Speech at Osawatomie, Kansas
August 31, 1910

Theodore Roosevelt, *The New Nationalism* (New York, 1961), 21-39.

We come here to-day to commemorate one of the epochmaking events of the long struggle for the rights of man—the long struggle for the uplift of humanity. Our country—this great republic—means nothing unless it means the triumph of a real democracy, the triumph of popular government, and, in the long run, of an economic system under which each man shall be guaranteed the opportunity to show the best that there is in him. That is why the history of America is now the central feature of the history of the world; for the world has set its face hopefully toward our democracy; and, O my fellow citizens, each one of you carries on your shoulders not only the burden of doing well for the sake of your own country, but the burden of doing well and of seeing that this nation does well for the sake of mankind.

There have been two great crises in our country's history: first, when it was formed, and then, again, when it was perpetuated; and, in the second of these great crises—in the time of stress and strain which culminated in the Civil War, on the outcome of which depended the justification of what had been done earlier, you men of the Grand Army, you men who fought through the Civil War, not only did you justify your generation, not only did you render life worth living for our generation, but you justified the wisdom of Washington and Washington's colleagues. If this republic had been founded by them only to be split asunder into fragments when the strain came, then the judgment of the world would have been that Washington's work was not worth doing. It was you who crowned Washington's work, as you carried to achievement the high purpose of Abraham Lincoln.

Now, with this second period of our history the name of John Brown will be forever associated; and Kansas was the theater upon which the first act of the second of our great national life dramas was played. It was the result of the struggle in Kansas which determined that our country should be in deed as well as in name devoted to both union and freedom; that the great experiment of democratic government on a national scale should succeed and not fail. In name we had the Declaration of Independence in 1776; but we gave the lie by our acts to the words of the Declaration of Independence until 1865; and words count for nothing except in so far as they represent acts. This is true everywhere; but, O my friends, it should be truest of all in political life. A broken promise is bad enough in private life. It is worse in the field of politics. No man is worth his salt in public life who makes on the stump a pledge which he does not keep after election; and, if he makes such a pledge and does not keep it, hunt him out of public life. [Roosevelt interpolated these words into the original version of his speech. The Kansas crowd greeted them with a tremendous shout. They were taken as an attack on President Taft who had pledged in 1908 to lower the tariff but had capitulated to Republican protectionalists who had passed the high Payne-Aldrich tariff in 1909. Footnote in Roosevelt.] I care for the great deeds of the past chiefly as spurs to drive us onward in the present. I speak of the men of the past partly that they may be honored by our praise of them, but more that they may serve as examples for the future.

It was a heroic struggle; and, as is inevitable with all such struggles, it had also a dark and terrible side. Very much was done of good, and much also of evil; and, as was inevitable in such a period of revolution, often the same man did both good and evil. For our great good fortune as a nation, we, the people of the United States as a whole, can now afford to forget the evil, or, at least, to remember it without bitterness, and to fix our eyes with pride only on the good that was accomplished. Even in ordinary times there are very few of us who do not see the problems of life as through a glass, darkly; and when the glass is clouded by the murk of furious popular passion, the vision of the best and the bravest is dimmed. Looking back, we are all of us now able to do justice to the valor and the disinterestedness and the love of the right, as to each it was given to see the right, shown both by the men of the North and the men of the South in that contest which was finally decided by the attitude of the West. We can admire the heroic valor, the sincerity, the self-devotion shown alike by the men who wore the blue and the men who wore the gray; and our sadness that such men should have had to fight one another is tempered by the glad knowledge that ever hereafter their descendants shall be found fighting side by side, struggling in peace as well as in war for the uplift of their common country, all alike resolute to raise to the highest pitch of honor and usefulness the nation to which they all belong. As for the veterans of the Grand Army of the Republic, they deserve honor and recognition such as is paid to no other citizens of the republic; for to them the republic owes its all; for to them it owes its very existence. It is because of what you and your comrades did in the dark years that we of to-day walk, each of us, head erect, and proud that we belong, not to one of a dozen little squabbling contemptible commonwealths, but to the mightiest nation upon which the sun shines.

I do not speak of this struggle of the past merely from the historic standpoint. Our interest is primarily in the application to-day of the lessons taught by the contest of half a century ago. It is of little use for us to pay lip loyalty to the mighty men of the past unless we sincerely endeavor to apply to the problems of the present precisely the qualities which in other crises enabled the men of that day to meet those crises. It is half melancholy and half amusing to see the way in which well-meaning people gather to do honor to the men who, in company with John Brown, and under the lead of Abraham Lincoln, faced and solved the great problems of the nineteenth century, while, at the same time, these same good people nervously shrink from, or frantically denounce, those who are trying to meet the problems of the twentieth century in the spirit which was accountable for the successful solution of the problems of Lincoln's time.

Of that generation of men to whom we owe so much, the man to whom we owe most is, of course, Lincoln. Part of our debt to him is because he forecast our present struggle and saw the way out. He said:—

I hold that while man exists it is his duty to improve not only his own condition, but to assist in ameliorating mankind.

And again:—

Labor is prior to, and independent of, capital. Capital is only the fruit of labor, and could never have existed if labor had not first existed. Labor is the superior of capital, and deserves much the higher consideration.

If that remark was original with me, I should be even more strongly denounced as a communist agitator than I shall be anyhow. It is Lincoln's. I am only quoting it; and that is one side; that is the side the capitalist should hear. Now, let the workingman hear his side.

Capital has its rights, which are as worthy of protection as any other rights. . . . Nor should this lead to a war upon the owners of property. Property is the fruit of labor; . . . property is desirable; is a positive good in the world.

And then comes a thoroughly Lincolnlike sentence:—

Let not him who is houseless pull down the house of another, but let him work diligently and build one for himself, thus by example assuring that his own shall be safe from violence when built.

It seems to me that, in these words, Lincoln took substantially the attitude that we ought to take; he showed the proper sense of proportion in his relative estimates of capital and labor, of human rights and property rights. Above all, in this speech, as in many others, he taught a lesson in wise kindliness and charity; an indispensable lesson to us of to-day. But this wise kindliness and charity never weakened his arm or numbed his heart. We cannot afford weakly to blind ourselves to the actual conflict which faces us to-day. The issue is joined, and we must fight or fail.

In every wise struggle for human betterment one of the main objects, and often the only object, has been to achieve in large measure equality of opportunity. In the struggle for this great end, nations rise from barbarism to civilization, and through it people press forward from one stage of enlightenment to the next. One of the chief factors in progress is the destruction of special privilege. The essence of any struggle for healthy liberty has always been, and must always be, to take from some one man or class of men the right to enjoy power, or wealth, or position, or immunity, which has not been earned by service to his or their fellows. That is what you fought for in the Civil War, and that is what we strive for now.

At many stages in the advance of humanity, this conflict between the men who possess more than they have earned and the men who have earned more than they possess is the central condition of progress. In our day it appears as the struggle of free men to gain and hold the right of self-government as against the special interests, who twist the methods of free government into machinery for defeating the popular will. At every stage, and under all circumstances, the essence of the struggle is to equalize opportunity, destroy privilege, and give to the life and citizenship of every individual the highest possible value both to himself and to the commonwealth. That is nothing new. All I ask in civil life is what you fought for in the Civil War. I ask that civil life be carried on according to the spirit in which the army was carried on. You never get perfect justice, but the effort in handling the army was to bring to the front the men who could do the job. Nobody grudged promotion to Grant, or Sherman, or Thomas, or Sheridan, because they earned it. The only complaint was when a man got promotion which he did not earn.

Practical equality of opportunity for all citizens, when we achieve it, will have two great results. First, every man will have a fair chance to make of himself all that in him lies; to reach the highest point to which his capacities, unassisted by special privilege of his own and unhampered by the special privilege of others, can carry him, and to get for himself and his family substantially what he has earned. Second, equality of opportunity means that the commonwealth will get from every citizen the highest service of which he is capable. No man who carries the burden of the special privileges of another can give to the commonwealth that service to which it is fairly entitled.

I stand for the square deal. But when I say that I am for the square deal, I mean not merely that I stand for fair play under the present rules of the game, but that I stand for having those rules changed so as to work for a more substantial equality of opportunity and of reward for equally good service. One word of warning, which, I think, is hardly necessary in Kansas. When I say I want a square deal for the poor man, I do not mean that I want a square deal for the man who remains poor because he has not the energy to work for himself. If a man who has had a chance will not make good, then he has got to quit. And you men of the Grand Army, you want justice for the brave man who fought, and punishment for the coward who shirked his work. Is not that so?

Now, this means that our government, national and state, must be freed from the sinister influence or control of special interests. Exactly as the special interests of cotton and slavery threatened our political integrity before the Civil War, so now the great special business interests too often control and corrupt the men and methods of government for their own profit. We must drive the special interests out of politics. That is one of our tasks to-day. Every special interest is entitled to justice—full, fair, and complete,—and, now, mind you, if there were any attempt by mob violence to plunder and work harm to the special interest, whatever it may be, that I most dislike, and the wealthy man, whomsoever he may be, for whom I have the greatest contempt, I would fight for him, and you would if you were worth your salt. He should have justice. For every special interest is entitled to justice, but not one is entitled to a vote in Congress, to a voice on the bench, or to representation in any public office. The Constitution guarantees protection to property, and we must make that promise good. But it does not give the right of suffrage to any corporation.

The true friend of property, the true conservative, is he who insists that property shall be the servant and not the master of the commonwealth; who insists that the creature of man's making shall be the servant and not the master of the man who made it. The citizens of the United States must effectively control the mighty commercial forces which they have themselves called into being.

There can be no effective control of corporations while their political activity remains. To put an end to it will be neither a short nor an easy task, but it can be done.

We must have complete and effective publicity of corporate affairs, so that the people may know beyond peradventure whether the corporations obey the law and whether their management entitles them to the confidence of the public. It is necessary that laws should be passed to prohibit the use of corporate funds directly or indirectly for political purposes; it is still more necessary that such laws should be thoroughly enforced. Corporate expenditures for political purposes, and especially such expenditures by public service corporations, have supplied one of the principal sources of corruption in our political affairs.

It has become entirely clear that we must have government supervision of the capitalization, not only of public service corporations, including, particularly, railways, but of all corporations doing an interstate business. I do not wish to see the nation forced into the ownership of the railways if it can possibly be avoided, and the only alternative is thoroughgoing and effective regulation, which shall be based on a full knowledge of all the facts, including a physical valuation of property. This physical valuation is not needed, or, at least, is very rarely needed, for fixing rates; but it is needed as the basis of honest capitalization.

We have come to recognize that franchises should never be granted except for a limited time, and never without proper provision for compensation to the public. It is my personal belief that the same kind and degree of control and supervision which should be exercised over public service corporations should be extended also to combinations which control necessaries of life, such as meat, oil, and coal, or which deal in them on an important scale. I have no doubt that the ordinary man who has control of them is much like ourselves. I have no doubt he would like to do well, but I want to have enough supervision to help him realize that desire to do well.

I believe that the officers, and, especially, the directors, of corporations should be held personally responsible when any corporation breaks the law.

Combinations in industry are the result of an imperative economic law which cannot be repealed by political legislation. The effort at prohibiting all combination has substantially failed. The way out lies, not in attempting to prevent such combinations, but in completely controlling them in the interest of the public welfare. For that purpose the Federal Bureau of Corporations is an agency of first importance. Its powers, and, therefore, its efficiency, as well as that of the Interstate Commerce Commission, should be largely increased. We have a right to expect from the Bureau of Corporations and from the Interstate Commerce Commission a very high grade of public service. We should be as sure of the proper conduct of the interstate railways and the proper management of interstate business as we are now sure of the conduct and management of the national banks, and we should have as effective supervision in one case as in the other. The Hepburn Act, and the amendment to the Act in the shape in which it finally passed Congress at the last session, represent a long step in advance, and we must go yet further.

There is a widespread belief among our people that, under the methods of making tariffs which have hitherto obtained, the special interests are too influential. Probably this is true of both the big special interests and the little special interests.

These methods have put a premium on selfishness, and, naturally, the selfish big interests have gotten more than their smaller, though equally selfish, brothers. The duty of Congress is to provide a method by which the interest of the whole people shall be all that receives consideration. To this end there must be an expert tariff commission, wholly removed from the possibility of political pressure or of improper business influence. Such a commission can find the real difference between cost of production, which is mainly the difference of labor cost here and abroad. As fast as its recommendations are made, I believe in revising one schedule at a time. A general revision of the tariff almost inevitably leads to log-rolling and the subordination of the general public interest to local and special interests.

The absence of effective state, and, especially, national, restraint upon unfair money getting has tended to create a small class of enormously wealthy and economically powerful men, whose chief object is to hold and increase their power. The prime need is to change the conditions which enable these men to accumulate power which it is not for the general welfare that they should hold or exercise. We grudge no man a fortune which represents his own power and sagacity, when exercised with entire regard to the welfare of his fellows. Again, comrades over there, take the lesson from your own experience. Not only did you not grudge, but you gloried in the promotion of the great generals who gained their promotion by leading the army to victory. So it is with us. We grudge no man a fortune in civil life if it is honorably obtained and well used. It is not even enough that it should have been gained without doing damage to the community. We should permit it to be gained only so long as the gaining represents benefit to the community. This, I know, implies a policy of a far more active governmental interference with social and economic conditions in this country than we have yet had, but I think we have got to face the fact that such an increase in governmental control is now necessary.

No man should receive a dollar unless that dollar has been fairly earned. Every dollar received should represent a dollar's worth of service rendered—not gambling in stocks, but service rendered. The really big fortune, the swollen fortune, by the mere fact of its size acquires qualities which differentiate it in kind as well as in degree from what is possessed by men of relatively small means. Therefore, I believe in a graduated income tax on big fortunes, and in another tax which is far more easily collected and far more effective—a graduated inheritance tax on big fortunes, properly safeguarded against evasion and increasing rapidly in amount with the size of the estate.

The people of the Unites States suffer from periodical financial panics to a degree substantially unknown among the other nations which approach us in financial strength. There is no reason why we should suffer what they escape. It is of profound importance that our financial system should be promptly investigated, and so thoroughly and effectively revised as to make it certain that hereafter our currency will no longer fail at critical times to meet our needs.

It is hardly necessary for me to repeat that I believe in an efficient army and a navy large enough to secure for us abroad that respect which is the surest guarantee of peace. A word of special warning to my fellow citizens who are as progressive as I hope I am. I want them to keep up their interest in our internal affairs; and I want them also continually to remember Uncle Sam's interests abroad. Justice and fair dealing among nations rest upon principles identical with those which control justice and fair dealing among the individuals of which nations are composed, with the vital exception that each nation must do its own part in international police work. If you get into trouble here, you can call for the police; but if Uncle Sam gets into trouble, he has got to be his own policeman, and I want to see him strong enough to encourage the peaceful aspirations of other peoples in connection with us. I believe in national friendships and heartiest good will to all nations; but national friendships, like those between men, must be founded on respect as well as on liking, on forbearance as well as upon trust. I should be heartily ashamed of any American who did not try to make the American government act as justly toward the other nations in international relations as he himself would act toward any individual in private relations. I should be heartily ashamed to see us wrong a weaker power, and I should hang my head forever if we tamely suffered wrong from a stronger power.

Of conservation I shall speak more at length elsewhere. Conservation means development as much as it does protection. I recognize the right and duty of this generation to develop and use the natural resources of our land; but I do not recognize the right to waste them, or to rob, by wasteful use, the generations that come after us. I ask nothing of the nation except that it so behave as each farmer here behaves with reference to his own children. That farmer is a poor creature who skins the land and leaves it worthless to his children. The farmer is a good farmer who, having enabled the land to support himself and to provide for the education of his children, leaves it to them a little better than he found it himself. I believe the same thing of a nation.

Moreover, I believe that the natural resources must be used for the benefit of all our people, and not monopolized for the benefit of the few, and here again is another case in which I am accused of taking a revolutionary attitude. People forget now that one hundred years ago there were public men of good character who advocated the nation selling its public lands in great quantities, so that the nation could get the most money out of it, and giving it to the men who could cultivate it for their own uses. We took the proper democratic ground that the land should be granted in small sections to the men who were actually to till it and live on it. Now, with the water power, with the forests, with the mines, we are brought face to face with the fact that there are many people who will go with us in conserving the resources only if they are to be allowed to exploit them for their benefit. That is one of the fundamental reasons why the special interests should be driven out of politics. Of all the questions which can come before this nation, short of the actual preservation of its existence in a great war, there is none which compares in importance with the great central task of leaving this land even a better land for our descendants than it is for us, and training them into a better race to inhabit the land and pass it on. Conservation is a great moral issue, for it involves the patriotic duty of insuring the safety and continuance of the nation. Let me add that the health and vitality of our people are at least as well worth conserving as their forests, waters, lands, and minerals, and in this great work the national government must bear a most important part.

I have spoken elsewhere also of the great task which lies before the farmers of the country to get for themselves and their wives and children not only the benefits of better farming, but also those of better business methods and better conditions of life on the farm. The burden of this great task will fall, as it should, mainly upon the great organizations of the farmers themselves. I am glad it will, for I believe they are all well able to handle it. In particular, there are strong reasons why the Departments of Agriculture of the various states, the United States Department of Agriculture, and the agricultural colleges and experiment stations should extend their work to cover all phases of farm life, instead of limiting themselves, as they have far too often limited themselves in the past, solely to the question of the production of crops. And now a special word to the farmer. I want to see him make the farm as fine a farm as it can be made; and let him remember to see that the improvement goes on indoors as well as out; let him remember that the farmer's wife should have her share of thought and attention just as much as the farmer himself.

Nothing is more true than that excess of every kind is followed by reaction; a fact which should be pondered by reformer and reactionary alike. We are face to face with new conceptions of the relations of property to human welfare, chiefly because certain advocates of the rights of property as against the rights of men have been pushing their claims too far. The man who wrongly holds that every human right is secondary to his profit must now give way to the advocate of human welfare, who rightly maintains that every man holds his property subject to the general right of the community to regulate its use to whatever degree the public welfare may require it.

But I think we may go still further. The right to regulate the use of wealth in the public interest is universally admitted. Let us admit also the right to regulate the terms and conditions of labor, which is the chief element of wealth, directly in the interest of the common good. The fundamental thing to do for every man is to give him a chance to reach a place in which he will make the greatest possible contribution to the public welfare. Understand what I say there. Give him a chance, not push him up if he will not be pushed. Help any man who stumbles; if he lies down, it is a poor job to try to carry him; but if he is a worthy man, try your best to see that he gets a chance to show the worth that is in him. No man can be a good citizen unless he has a wage more than sufficient to cover the bare cost of living, and hours of labor short enough so that after his day's work is done he will have time and energy to bear his share in the management of the community, to help in carrying the general load. We keep countless men from being good citizens by the conditions of life with which we surround them. We need comprehensive workmen's compensation acts, both state and national laws to regulate child labor and work for women, and, especially, we need in our common schools not merely education in book learning, but also practical training for daily life and work. We need to enforce better sanitary conditions for our workers and to extend the use of safety appliances for our workers in industry and commerce, both within and between the states. Also, friends, in the interest of the workingman himself we need to set our faces like flint against mob violence just as against corporate greed; against violence and injustice and lawlessness by wage workers just as much as against lawless cunning and greed and selfish arrogance of employers. If I could ask but one thing of my fellow countrymen, my request would be that, whenever they go in for reform, they remember the two sides, and that they always exact justice from one side as much as from the other. I have small use for the public servant who can always see and denounce the corruption of the capitalist, but who cannot persuade himself, especially before election, to say a word about lawless mob violence. And I have equally small use for a man, be he a judge on the bench, or editor of a great paper, or wealthy and influential private citizen, who can see clearly enough and denounce the lawlessness of mob violence, but whose eyes are closed so that he is blind when the question is one of corruption in business on a gigantic scale. Also remember what I said about excess in reformer and reactionary alike. If the reactionary man, who thinks of nothing but the rights of property, could have his way, he would bring about a revolution; and one of my chief fears in connection with progress comes because I do not want to see our people, for lack of proper leadership, compelled to follow men whose intentions are excellent, but whose eyes are a little too wild to make it really safe to trust them. Here in Kansas there is one paper which habitually denounces me as the tool of Wall Street, and at the same time frantically repudiates the statement that I am a Socialist on the ground that that is an unwarranted slander of the Socialists. [The *Appeal to Reason*, a widely circulated socialist paper edited by Julius Augustus Wayland, "The One Hoss Editor." It purveyed a peculiarly populistic brand of socialist doctrine. Footnote in Roosevelt.]

National efficiency has many factors. It is a necessary result of the principle of conservation widely applied. In the end it will determine our failure or success as a nation. National efficiency has to do, not only with natural resources and with men, but it is equally concerned with institutions. The state must be made efficient for the work which concerns only the people of the state; and the nation for that which concerns all the people. There must remain no neutral ground to serve as a refuge for lawbreakers, and especially for lawbreakers of great wealth, who can hire the vulpine legal cunning which will teach them how to avoid both jurisdictions. It is a misfortune when the national legislature fails to do its duty in providing a national remedy, so that the only national activity is the purely negative activity of the judiciary in forbidding the state to exercise power in the premises.

I do not ask for overcentralization; but I do ask that we work in a spirit of broad and far-reaching nationalism when we work for what concerns our people as a whole. We are all Americans. Our common interests are as broad as the continent. I speak to you here in Kansas exactly as I would speak in New York or Georgia, for the most vital problems are those which affect us all alike. The national government belongs to the whole American people, and where the whole American people are interested, that interest can be guarded effectively only by the national government. The betterment which we seek must be accomplished, I believe, mainly through the national government.

The American people are right in demanding that New Nationalism, without which we cannot hope to deal with new problems. The New Nationalism puts the national need before sectional or personal advantage. It is impatient of the utter confusion that results from local legislatures attempting to treat national issues as local issues. It is still more impatient of the impotence which springs from overdivision of governmental powers, the impotence which makes it possible for local selfishness or for legal cunning, hired by wealthy special interests, to bring national activities to a deadlock. This New Nationalism regards the executive power as the steward of the public welfare. It demands of the judiciary that it shall be interested primarily in human welfare rather than in property, just as it demands that the representative body shall represent all the people rather than any one class or section of the people.

I believe in shaping the ends of government to protect property as well as human welfare. Normally, and in the long run, the ends are the same; but whenever the alternative must be faced, I am for men and not for property, as you were in the Civil War. I am far from underestimating the importance of dividends; but I rank dividends below human character. Again, I do not have any sympathy with the reformer who says he does not care for dividends. Of course, economic welfare is necessary, for a man must pull his own weight and be able to support his family. I know well that the reformers must not bring upon the people economic ruin, or the reforms themselves will go down in the ruin. But we must be ready to face temporary disaster, whether or not brought on by those who will war against us to the knife. Those who oppose all reform will do well to remember that ruin in its worst form is inevitable if our national life brings us nothing better than swollen fortunes for the few and the triumph in both politics and business of a sordid and selfish materialism.

If our political institutions were perfect, they would absolutely prevent the political domination of money in any part of our affairs. We need to make our political representatives more quickly and sensitively responsive to the people whose servants they are. More direct action by the people in their own affairs under proper safeguards is vitally necessary. The direct primary is a step in this direction, if it is associated with a corrupt practices act effective to prevent the advantage of the man willing recklessly and unscrupulously to spend money over his more honest competitor. It is particularly important that all moneys received or expended for campaign purposes should be publicly accounted for, not only after election, but before election as well. Political action must be made simpler, easier, and freer from confusion for every citizen. I believe that the prompt removal of unfaithful or incompetent public servants should be made easy and sure in whatever way experience shall show to be most expedient in any given class of cases.

One of the fundamental necessities in a representative government such as ours is to make certain that the men to whom the people delegate their power shall serve the people by whom they are elected, and not the special interests. I believe that every national officer, elected or appointed, should be forbidden to perform any service or receive any compensation, directly or indirectly, from interstate corporations; and a similar provision could not fail to be useful within the states.

The object of government is the welfare of the people. The material progress and prosperity of a nation are desirable chiefly so far as they lead to the moral and material welfare of all good citizens. Just in proportion as the average man and woman are honest, capable of sound judgment and high ideals, active in public affairs,—but, first of all, sound in their home life, and the father and mother of healthy children whom they bring up well,—just so far, and no farther, we may count our civilization a success. We must have—I believe we have already—a genuine and permanent moral awakening, without which no wisdom of legislation or administration really means anything; and, on the other hand, we must try to secure the social and economic legislation without which any improvement due to purely moral agitation is necessarily evanescent. Let me again illustrate by a reference to the Grand Army. You could not have won simply as a disorderly and disorganized mob. You needed generals; you needed careful administration of the most advanced type; and a good commissary—the cracker line. You well remember that success was necessary in many different lines in order to bring about general success. You had to have the administration at Washington good, just as you had to have the administration in the field; and you had to have the work of the generals good. You could not have triumphed without that administration and leadership; but it would all have been worthless if the average soldier had not had the right stuff in him. He had to have the right stuff in him, or you could not get it out of him. In the last analysis, therefore, vitally necessary though it was to have the right kind of organization and the right kind of generalship, it was even more vitally necessary that the average soldier should have the fighting edge, the right character. So it is in our civil life. No matter how honest and decent we are in our private lives, if we do not have the right kind of law and the right kind of administration of the law, we cannot go forward as a nation. That is imperative; but it must be an addition to, and not a substitution for, the qualities that make us good citizens. In the last analysis, the most important elements in any man's career must be the sum of those qualities which, in the aggregate, we speak of as character. If he has not got it, then no law that the wit of man can devise, no administration of the law by the boldest and strongest executive, will avail to help him. We must have the right kind of character—character that makes a man, first of all, a good man in the home, a good father, a good husband—that makes a man a good neighbor. You must have that, and, then, in addition, you must have the kind of law and the kind of administration of the law which will give to those qualities in the private citizen the best possible chance for development. The prime problem of our nation is to get the right type of good citizenship, and, to get it, we must have progress, and our public men must be genuinely progressive.

The election of 1910, which swept Woodrow Wilson into office in New Jersey, was a disaster for the conservative Taft forces in the Republican party. The Democrats were remarkably successful throughout the country, but in the Democratic as well as the Republican party it was the Progressives who won and the conservatives who lost. In many areas like New Jersey, Republican Progressives deserted their party and supported the Democrats if their own candidate was not satisfactory. For the first time in 16 years the Democrats gained control of the House of Representatives, and the Republican margin was cut in the Senate so that marginal Progressive support for any measure was decisive to its victory or defeat. Such developments did not strengthen President Taft's prospects for reelection in 1912, and Senator La Follette was already in the field as a challenger.

But Roosevelt refused to respond to the pressures of Progressives to enter the race, and it was not until the Taft mistake of introducing the antitrust case against United States Steel in the fall of 1911 that he mounted his "New Nationalism" challenge to Taft in the spring primaries, capturing them by a better than 2 to 1 margin. Feeling they had been deprived of their proper representation and victory at the Republican convention in the summer of 1912, Roosevelt and his followers walked out and founded the Progressive party. La Follette withdrew from the race when his prospects diminished with Roosevelt's return to battle.

In the summer of 1912 Woodrow Wilson was confronted with the formidable problem of standing up to Theodore Roosevelt's Progressive "New Nationalism" program. His conversion to Progressivism was complete by that time, but he had not yet adjusted to or fully developed his thinking on national questions. His early speeches in the presidential race reflected some of the same vague generalities that had characterized his gubernatorial campaign in New Jersey before the Progressives forced him to become more explicit and to embrace their program. As Link observed: "He seemed undecided, searching about for some great issue to carry to the people."[69]

It was at that time that his historic meeting with Louis Dembitz Brandeis took place. The Boston attorney was a unique figure in American life. Born in Louisville, Kentucky of German-Jewish immigrant parents, the young Brandeis had studied both here and abroad and had graduated at the top of his class at the Harvard School of Law. In fact Brandeis established an academic record at that institution which was never equaled during his lifetime. He practiced law in Boston after spending one lackluster year in a law office in Louisville, and within a short time he was recognized as one of the leading attorneys in the country. For the most part Brandeis practiced corporation law, having as his clients some of the major firms in the northeast; but he increasingly demonstrated an interest in public affairs and earned an equal but very different reputation as a fearless champion of the public interest. At first in Boston but later in the country at large, Brandeis began devoting most of his time and legal talent to developing and defending important cases on an unpaid basis in the interest of the people and the community. In Boston he formed a group of like-minded lawyers and businessmen who tackled the public transportation interests and then the utilities, and won important battles in obtaining better-regulated public franchises and rate regulations.

On the national scene Brandeis continued his activities as the "people's attorney," chastising the monoplies, attacking the inefficiency, the improper financing and rate regulations of the railroads, exposing the shortcomings of the big insurance companies, defending laws reducing hours for women's employment and minimum wages before the Supreme Court, investigating working conditions and arbitrating labor disputes in the garment industry, establishing savings bank life insurance in Massachusetts and exposing violations of the public interest on the cabinet level in the Taft administration. Brandeis deservedly earned a powerful reputation for his skill as an investigative public interest attorney a half century or more before Ralph Nader began a somewhat similar career. He revolutionized the law through his development of the now famous "Brandeis brief," a copious compilation of economic, scientific and sociological information which he combined with legal precedents to present his arguments before the courts, congressional committees, regulatory commissions or wherever the public's business was being conducted.

Brandeis was also a Progressive, but a pragmatic one rather than a rigid idealogue. He brought to the reform movement a sensitive compassion for human suffering and injustice, but he was unique in his insistence upon making a thoroughgoing investigation of all the factual aspects of a problem before declaring his views on the subject. Deeply committed to the democratic process, he possessed a social imagination which could usually find a fresh solution to a problem within the framework of the existing political system. He tackled problems, as he put it, *in situ*, not on an elevated abstract level, but rather in the form and shape in which they arose in the marketplace of social and economic conflict. He was a doer as well as a thinker, and many of his legal and social views and actions changed the nature of American society.

In the summer of 1912 Brandeis was at the height of his career as a public interest advocate. He was better informed on the nature of corporation practices than almost anyone else in the country, and he had been working for some time with Senator La Follette and others to amend the antitrust laws and introduce other changes meant to restore greater economic freedom and opportunity in the country. Unlike Roosevelt he believed that the concentration of power and wealth in the great trusts and monopolies was not inevitable but was inefficient and destructive to the public interest. Their very size was a threat to the public interest in a democratic society, Brandeis thought, and he was interested in reducing their ability to control the market, set prices and protect what he considered to be their inefficient monopolistic power, which operated in conflict with the public interest.

Brandeis visited the Democratic candidate for President at his seashore gubernatorial summer home in August 1912, shortly after the Democratic convention. Wilson and Brandeis were meeting for the first time, but they got on famously and spent the lunch hour and most of the rest of the afternoon conferring on critical public issues, with regard to which Wilson was still searching for solutions. Link has noted the importance of this meeting to Wilson, who was floundering in an unsuccessful effort to come to grips with the problem of monopoly and the trusts. He encouraged Brandeis to help him to clarify his thinking on the subject, and to assist him in constructing his approach to the central issue of the campaign:

> [U]ntil his conferences with Brandeis—Wilson insisted that only by making corporation officials personally responsible for their monopolistic practices could the problem of trust control be met. It was a simple and totally innocuous approach to the problem, a carry-over from Wilson's reactionary phase; the truth was that he was dismally ignorant on the subject until Brandeis outlined his program for the regulation of competition to him. It was, moveover, a happy coincidence that Wilson's and Brandeis's fundamental objectives, the establishment of unhampered competition and the liberation of economic enterprise in the United States, were the same. It is not surprising, therefore, that Wilson time and

again went to him for advice with regard to the specific ways of regulating competition. He was an avid student and rapidly absorbed all that Brandeis taught him.[70]

Wilson, like many of the Progressive leaders, had poured forth a great amount of rhetoric in denouncing the excesses of monopoly and the abuses of freedom, but he had not thought through the implications of their critique and had not come up with any alternate scheme of economic organization, or even any substantial method of eliminating present abuses. The essence of the problem was the method of preventing monopoly and regulating free competition. In that area Wilson had clearly indicated an abysmal ignorance.

> Because Brandeis understood the problem thoroughly, because he was ready with a definite plan for the bridling of monopoly, he became the chief architect of Wilson's New Freedom. After his first interview with Brandeis, for example, Wilson spoke with new confidence on the subject. "Both of us have as an object the prevention of monopoly," he declared. "Monopoly is created by unregulated competition, by competition that overwhelms all other competitions, and the only way to enjoy industrial freedom is to destroy that condition."[71]

And then his biographer adds: "New words, these, for Woodrow Wilson!"[72]

Wilson lost no time putting these new ideas to work. Speaking several days after his meeting with Brandeis to 10,000 workers at a Labor Day rally in Buffalo, New York, he at once began to attack Roosevelt's position on this subject and to compare it with his own new approach to the problem. He asserted that Roosevelt "was a self-appointed divinity, whose proposal to legalize and regulate the trusts by a Board of Experts, which would inevitably be controlled by the trust leaders themselves, offered nothing for the wage slaves of the United States!"[73]

> As to the monopolies, which Mr. Roosevelt proposes to legalize and to welcome, I know that they are so many cars of juggernaut, and I do not look forward with pleasure to the time when the juggernauts are licensed and driven by commissioners of the United States. . . .
>
> And what has created these monopolies? Unregulated competition. It has permitted these men to do anything they choose to do to squeeze their rivals out and crush their rivals to the earth. We know the processes by which they have done those things. We can prevent these processes through remedial legislation, and so restrict the wrong use of competition that the right use of competition will destroy monopoly. Ours is a programme of liberty; theirs a programme of regulation.
>
> I want you workingmen to grasp that point, because I want to say to you right now that the programme I propose does not look quite so much like acting as a Providence for you as the other programme looks. I want frankly to say to you that I am not big enough to play Providence, and my objection to the other plan is that I do not believe there is any man who is big enough to play Providence. . . . If you want a great struggle for liberty, that will cost you blood, adopt the Roosevelt regulation programme, put

yourself at the disposal of a Providence resident at Washington, and then see what will come of it.[74]

Wilson then went on to compare his own program more favorably with that of his opponent:

My kind of leading will not be telling other people what they have got to do. By leading I mean finding out what the interests of the community are agreed to be, and then trying my level best to find the methods of solution by common counsel. That is the only feasible programme of social uplift that I can imagine.

When you have thought the whole thing out, therefore, you will find that the programme of the new party legalizes monopolies and systematically subordinates workingmen to them and the plans made by the Government, both with regard to employment and with regard to wages. By what means, except open revolt, could we ever break the crust of our life again and become free men, breathing an air of our own, choosing and living lives that we wrought out for ourselves? Perhaps this new all-conquering combination between money and government would be benevolent to us, perhaps it would carry out the noble programme of social betterment, which so many credulously expect of it, but who can assure us of that? Who will give bond that it will be general and gracious and pitiful and righteous? What man or set of men can make us more secure under it by their empty promise and assurance that it will take care of us and be good?[75]

But clearly the Democratic candidate needed more answers and information than he had yet acquired, and he turned again to Brandeis for more advice. He met with him in Boston on September 27, but immediately thereafter he wired Brandeis asking him to "set forth as explicitly as possible the actual measures by which competition can be effectively regulated. The more explicit we are on this point, the more completely will the enemies' guns be spiked."[76]

Brandeis quickly responded to Wilson's cry for more ammunition. The following day he sent him several articles he had written on the subject, and two days later he transmitted a much larger quantity of material, embodying the fruits of his prodigious research on the problem. Among them was a brilliant memorandum entitled "Suggestions for letter of Governor Wilson on Trusts," which is the most coherent, forceful and explicit statement of Brandeis' and subsequently Wilson's position on economic regulation of the trusts. It is probably one of the most important documents ever submitted by a private citizen to a presidential candidate, for it outlines not only the ideas for later campaign speeches on the subject, but constitutes a virtual blueprint or master plan for much of the regulatory legislation which was forthcoming in the first two years of the Wilson administration.

Louis Dembitz Brandeis
Memorandum Submitted to Woodrow Wilson,
Democratic Candidate for President
September 30, 1912

Melvin I. Urofsky and David W. Levy, eds., *Letters of Louis D. Brandeis* (Albany, New York, 1972) II, 688-94.

SUGGESTIONS FOR LETTER OF
GOVERNOR WILSON ON TRUSTS

You have asked me to state what the essential difference is between the Democratic Party's solution of the Trust Problem and that of the New Party; and how we propose to "regulate competition". My answer is this:

The two parties differ fundamentally regarding the economic policy which the country should pursue. The Democratic Party insists that competition can be and should be maintained in every branch of private industry; that competition can be and should be restored in those branches of industry in which it has been suppressed by the trusts; and that, if at any future time monopoly should appear to be desirable in any branch of industry, the monopoly should be a public one—a monopoly owned by the people and not by the capitalists. The New Party, on the other hand, insists that private monopoly may be desirable in some branches of industry, or at all events, inevitable, and that existing trusts should not be dismembered or forcibly dislodged from those branches of industry which they have already acquired a monopoly, but should be made "good" by regulation. In other words, the New Party declares that private monopoly in industry is not necessarily evil, but may do evil; and that legislation should be limited to such as should attempt merely to prevent the doing of evil. The New Party does not fear commercial power, however great, if only methods for regulation are provided. We believe that no methods of regulation ever have been or can be devised to remove the menace inherent in private monopoly and overweening commercial power.

This difference in the economic policy of the two parties is fundamental and irreconcilable. It is the difference between industrial liberty and industrial absolutism.

On the other hand, there is no fundamental difference between the two parties as to the means to be adopted or the machinery to be employed in order to "regulate" industry. The differences between the two parties in this respect would doubtless be found to be either differences in detail or such differences as necessarily result from the differences in the ends sought to be accomplished. The New Party, in its tolerance of private monopoly, would have no use for legal or administrative machinery by which existing trusts might be effectively disintegrated. The

Democratic Party, while preserving competition, would have no use for a price fixing board.

The Sherman Anti Trust Act has, in the past, been little more than a declaration of our economic policy. The experience gained in the twenty-two years since the Act was passed has, however, served some useful purpose. It has established the soundness of the economic policy which it embodies; and it has taught us what the defects in the statute are which have in large part prevented its effective operation. To make that Sherman law a controlling force—to preserve competition where it now exists, and to restore competition where it has been suppressed—additional and comprehensive legislation is necessary. The prohibitions upon combination contained in the act must be made more definite; the provisions for enforcing its provisions by the Courts must be improved; and they must be supplemented by other adequate machinery to be administered by a Federal Board or Commission.

The general character of this new legislation should be as follows:

First: Remove the Uncertainties in the Sherman Law.

This can be accomplished, in large measure, by making the prohibitions upon combinations more definite, somewhat as the LaFollette-Stanley Anti Trust bills propose. The Sherman Law, as interpreted by the United States Supreme Court, prohibits monopolies and combinations "unreasonably" in restraint of trade. Experience has taught us, in the main, what combinations are thus "unreasonable". They are the combinations which suppress competition; and experience has also taught us that competition is never suppressed by the greater efficiency of one concern. It is suppressed either by agreement to form a monopoly or by those excesses of competition which are designed to crush a rival. And experience has taught us, likewise, many of the specific methods or means by which the great trusts, utilizing their huge resources or particularly favored positions commonly crush rivals; for instance "cut throat" competition; discrimination against customers who would not deal exclusively with the combination; excluding competitors from access to essential raw material; espionage; doing business under false names or "fake independents"; securing unfair advantage through railroad debates; or acquiring, otherwise than through efficiency, such a control over the market as to dominate the trade. The time has come to utilize that experience and to embody its dictates in rules of positive law, which will instruct the many business men who desire to obey the statute, what they should avoid—and admonish those less conscientious what they must avoid. By making the prohibitions upon combinations thus definite, the uncertainty of the act about which business men most complain will be in large measure, removed, and the enforcement of the law will become simpler and more effective.

Second: Facilitate the Enforcement of the law by the Courts.

A great advance in regulating competition and preventing monopoly will result from making the judicial machinery efficient: and several measures, wisely framed to further this end are also embodied in the LaFollette-Stanley Anti Trust bills. Efficient judicial machinery will give relief to the people by effecting a real disintegration of those trusts which have heretofore suppressed competition and will also enable individuals who have suffered from illegal acts to secure adequate compensation. Efficient judicial machinery will be even more potent as a deterrent than as a cure; for inefficient judicial processes is the greatest encouragement to law-breaking. Despite the tolerance of trusts heretofore exhibited by the government, it is hardly conceivable that private monopoly would have acquired its present sway in America, if the judicial machinery for enforcing the prohibitions of the Sherman Law had been adequate; and it is certain that the lamentable failure of the proceedings against the Standard Oil and the Tobacco Trust could have been averted. For the failure of those proceedings is not due primarily to inability of Courts to prevent or to disintegrate illegal combinations. It is due to defects in judicial machinery or methods.

The failure of the decrees to restore competition is due mainly to the fact, that the Court in dividing the trust properties into injured person or corporation would have to institute entirely independent proceedings—proceedings exactly as if the Government had never acted. In other words the private litigant would derive no legal aid from the decree in favor of the Government.

This rule of general law has afforded to the trusts immunity for wrong done. Few injured individuals or concerns could afford to conduct the expensive litigation necessary to establish the illegality of the trusts. Few could, regardless of expense, obtain the evidence required for that purpose until it was disclosed in the proceeding instituted by the Government. But before the Government's protracted litigation closed, the Statute of Limitation would ordinarily bar any suits of individual concerns to recover compensation for the wrongs done.

The pending bills supply these gross defects in the judicial machinery by a very simple device. They provide in substance, that whenever in a proceeding instituted by the Government a final judgment is rendered declaring that the defendant has entered into a combination in unreasonable restraint of trade, that finding shall be conclusive as against the defendant in any other proceeding brought against the defendant by anyone, so that the injured person would thereafter merely have to establish the amount of the loss suffered; and the danger of losing the right to compensation (while awaiting the results of the Government suit) is averted by the further simple device of providing that the Statute of Limitations shall not run while the Government suit is pending.

These are a few of the many improvements in judicial machinery which, if adopted, would go far toward making the Sherman law a controlling force. It is largely by similar improvements in our judicial machinery, and not by the recall of judges, that the inefficiency of our courts will be overcome and a just administration of law be attained.

Third: Create a Board or Commission to Aid in Administering The Sherman Law.

The functions of Government should not be limited to the enactment of wise rules of action, and the providing of efficient judicial machinery, by which those guilty of breaking the law may be punished, and those injured, secure compensation. The several segments, did not make these segments separate and distinct;—but, on the contrary, provided that these segments should or might be owned (and necessarily controlled) by the same stockholders in the same proportions. Such a provision invited certain failure of the declared purpose of restoring competition. Actual disintegration of each of these trusts and absolute restoration of competitive conditions could have been attained if the decrees had made a proper distribution of the properties among the several concerns and had been provided that these segments should be, not nominally but actually, separate and distinct. That would have been accomplished if for a limited period no person had been permitted to own at the same time stock in more than one of the segments. The LaFollette-Stanley Anti Trust bills provide, among other things, for this radical change in the methods of "disintegration".

In another respect the Standard Oil and Tobacco Trust suits presents an even more glaring defect in judicial processes; namely, the failure to afford redress for wrongs done in the past. Each of these trusts had extorted hundreds of millions of dollars from the public and in the process had ruthlessly crushed hundreds and possibly thousands of independent business concerns. Upon the admitted facts the Supreme Court declared unanimously that the combinations and their acts were illegal, but the corporation was left in undisputed possession of their ill-gotten gains, and no reparation was made to anyone for the great wrong so profitably pursued by the trusts,—obviously a failure of justice destined to bring into disrepute not only the Sherman Law, but all law.

This failure is not inherent in judicial processes. It is due wholly to a surprising lack of effective legal method and machinery. The judicial determination of the illegality of the combination and its practices should result, under any proper system of law, as a matter of course, in compensation to the injured, and reparation to the public in some form for the profits wrongfully obtained. The Sherman Law contemplated in part such a result, for it provided that anyone injured by an illegal combination might recover three times the damages actually suffered. But that provision has been practically a dead letter; because under the general rules of law the decisions in proceedings instituted by the government do not enure in any respect to the individual benefit of those who have been injured. In order to get redress, the Government, at least where the general public is concerned, is charged with securing also compliance with the law. We need the inspector and the policeman, even more than we need the prosecuting attorney; and we need for the enforcement of the Sherman law and regulation of competition an administrative Board with broad powers. What the precise powers of such a Board should be is a subject which will require the most careful consideration of Congress. The bill introduced by Senator Newlands August 21, 1911 and the Federal Commission bill introduced later by Senator LaFollette, contain many suggestions of value. It is clear that the scope of the duties of any Board that may be created, should be broad; and it is probable that whatever powers are conferred upon the Board at the outset will be increased from time to time as we learn from experience as to some of the powers which may be safely conferred upon the Board. There is little room for difference of opinion.

1. The Board should have ample powers of investigation.

In the complicated questions involved in dealing with big business, the first requisite is knowledge, comprehensive, accurate, and up to date, of the details of operations of business.

The Bureau of Corporations has, to a slight extent, collected some such information in the past, and a part of it has been published with much benefit to the public. The current collection and prompt publication of such information concerning the various branches of business would prove of great value in preserving competition. The methods of destructive competition will not bear the light of day. The mere substitution of knowledge for ignorance—of publicity for secrecy—will go far toward preventing monopoly. But aside from the questions bearing specifically upon the Sherman law, the collection of this data would prove of inestimable advantage in the conduct of business.

2. The Board should co-operate with the Department of Justice in securing compliance with the Sherman Law. The comprehensive knowledge of the different branches of business systematically acquired by the Board would greatly facilitate and expedite the work of the Department of Justice and would enable it to supply the Court with that detailed and expert knowledge required to deal intelligently with the intricate commercial problems involved in administering the Sherman Law.

3. The Board should be empowered to aid in securing compliance with the law, not only in the interests of the general public, but at the request and for the benefit of those particular individuals or concerns who have been injured or fear injury by infractions of the law by others. The inequality between the great corporations with huge resources and the small competitor and others is such that "equality before the law" will no longer be secured merely by supplying adequate machinery for enforcing the law. To prevent oppression and injustice the Government must be prepared to lend its aid.

Brandeis' role was critical in the evolution of the "New Freedom" campaign of 1912, but Wilson's contribution should not be minimized. As William E. Leuchtenburg has put it, "If Brandeis supplied him with the special knowledge he needed, Wilson's success in turning the trust issue into a crusade to preserve fundamental liberties was wholly his own achievement."[77] One immediately grasps his sense of moral suasion upon reading any of the New Freedom campaign addresses. He swept through the country mesmerizing his listeners and reawakening much of the excitement and idealism of the long slumbering American dream. Wilson called for a rebirth of freedom and opportunity, the opening-up of politics to the public view, and a sense of pride and strength in the power of the ordinary people. And he said these things eloquently and with a sense of conviction that impressed many Americans; it was a very unusual presidential campaign.

Time and time again Wilson returned to the theme of the lost opportunities in American life:

American industry is not free, as it once was free; American enterprise is not free; the man with only a little capital is finding it harder to get into the field, more and more impossible to compete with the big fellow. Why? Because the laws of this country do not prevent the strong from crushing the weak. That is the reason, and because the strong have crushed the weak the strong dominate the industry and the economic life of this country. No man can deny that the lines of endeavor have more and more narrowed and stiffened; no man who knows anything about the development of industry in this country can have failed to observe that the larger kinds of credit are more and more difficult to obtain, unless you obtain them upon the terms of uniting your efforts with those who already control the industries of the country; and nobody can fail to observe that any man who tries to set himself up in competition with any process of manufacture which has been taken under the control of large combinations of capital will presently find himself either squeezed out or obliged to sell and allow himself to be absorbed. . . .

What this country needs above everything else is a body of laws which will look after the men who are on the make rather than the men who are already made. Because the men who are already made are not going to live indefinitely, and they are not always kind enough to leave sons as able and honest as they are.

The originative part of America, the part of America that makes new enterprises, the part into which the ambitious and gifted workingman makes his way up, the class that saves, that plans, that organizes, that presently spreads its enterprises until they have a national scope and character,—that middle class is being more and more squeezed out by the processes which we have been taught to call the processes of prosperity. Its members are sharing prosperity, no doubt; but what alarms me is that they are not *originating* prosperity. No country can afford to have its prosperity originated by a small controlling class. The treasury of America does not lie in the brains of a small body of men now in control of the great enterprises that have been concentrated under the direction of a very small number of persons. The treasury of America lies in those ambitions, those energies, that cannot be restricted to a special favored class. It depends upon the inventions of unknown men, upon the originations of unknown men, upon the ambitions of unknown men. Every country is renewed out of the ranks of the unknown, not out of the ranks of those already famous and powerful and in control.[78]

He spoke of the need to open up the political process so the people could understand the public business:

So I take it to be a necessity of the hour to open up all the processes of politics and of public business,—open them wide to public view; to make them accessible to every force that moves, every opinion that prevails in the thought of the people; to give society command of its own economic life again, not by revolutionary measures, but by a steady application of the principle that the people have a right to look into such matters and to control them; to cut all privileges and patronage and private advantage and secret enjoyment out of legislation.

Wherever any public business is transacted, wherever plans affecting the public are laid, or enterprises touching the public welfare, comfort or convenience go forward, wherever political programs are formulated, or candidates agreed on,—over that place a voice must speak, with the divine prerogative of a people's will, the words: "Let there be light."[79]

But he always returned to the theme of the strength of the people being called upon to recover the vitality of the society:

The flower does not bear the root, but the root the flower. Everything that blooms in beauty in the air of heaven draws its fairness, its vigor, from its roots. Nothing living can blossom into fruitage unless through nourishing stalks deep-planted in the common soil. The rose is merely the evidence of the vitality of the root; and the real source of its beauty, the very blush that it wears upon its tender cheek, comes from those silent sources of life that lie hidden in the chemistry of the soil. Up from that soil, up from the silent bosom of the earth, rise the currents of life and of energy. Up from the common soil, up from the quiet heart of the people, rise joyously to-day streams of hope and determination bound to renew the face of the earth in glory.[80]

And in a later speech:

I do not believe that America is securely great because she has great men in her now. America is great in proportion as she can make sure of having great men in the next generation. She is rich in her unborn children; rich, that is to say, if those unborn children see the sun in a day of opportunity, see the sun when they are free to exercise their energies as they will. If they open their eyes in a land where there is no special privilege, then we shall come into a new era of American greatness and American liberty; but if they open their eyes in a country where they must be employees or nothing, if they open their eyes in a land of merely regulated monopoly, where all the conditions of industry are determined by small groups of men, they will see an America such as the founders of this Republic would have wept to think of. The only hope is in the release of the forces which philanthropic trust presidents want to monopolize. Only the emancipation, the freeing and heartening of the vital energies of the people will redeem us.[81]

What a striking presidential campaign! Roosevelt with his charisma and his New Nationalism; Wilson articulating the fears and hopes of the silent and crushed Americans; Taft reassuring the solid and the complacent that all was well; and Eugene V. Debs challenging the very possibility that any of the dilemmas within the existing economic system could be resolved at all.

But the central issue remained the trusts and the distribution of economic and social power in the future of American society. Brandeis armed Wilson with a potent weapon of political appeal to match Roosevelt's strident theory of executive power and control. Wilson summed up what he had to say on this subject in what was probably his most important speech of the campaign—"Monopoly or Opportunity?"

Woodrow Wilson
"Monopoly, or Opportunity?"
Presidential Campaign Speech
1912

Woodrow Wilson, *The New Freedom* (Englewood Cliffs, New Jersey, 1961), 101-15.

Gentlemen say, they have been saying for a long time, and, therefore, I assume that they believe, that trusts are inevitable. They don't say that big business is inevitable. They don't say merely that the elaboration of business upon a great co-operative scale is characteristic of our time and has come about by the natural operation of modern civilization. We would admit that. But they say that the particular kind of combinations that are now controlling our economic development came into existence naturally and were inevitable; and that, therefore, we have to accept them as unavoidable and administer our development through them. They take the analogy of the railways. The railways were clearly inevitable if we were to have transportation, but railways after they are once built stay put. You can't transfer a railroad at convenience; and you can't shut up one part of it and work another part. It is in the nature of what economists, those tedious persons, call natural monopolies; simply because the whole circumstances of their use are so stiff that you can't alter them. Such are the analogies which these gentlemen choose when they discuss the modern trust.

I admit the popularity of the theory that the trusts have come about through the natural development of business conditions in the United States, and that it is a mistake to try to oppose the processes by which they have been built up, because those processes belong to the very nature of business in our time, and that therefore the only thing we can do, and the only thing we ought to attempt to do, is to accept them as inevitable arrangements and make the best out of it that we can by regulation.

I answer, nevertheless, that this attitude rests upon a confusion of thought. Big business is no doubt to a large extent necessary and natural. The development of business upon a great scale, upon a great scale of co-operation, is inevitable, and, let me add, is probably desirable. But that is a very different matter from the development of trusts, because the trusts have not grown. They have been artificially created; they have been put together, not by natural processes, but by the will, the deliberate planning will, of men who were more powerful than their neighbors in the business world, and who wished to make their power secure against competition.

The trusts do not belong to the period of infant industries. They are not the products of the time, that old laborious time, when the great continent we live on was undeveloped, the young nation struggling to find itself and get upon its feet amidst older and more experienced competitors. They belong to a very recent and very sophisticated age, when men knew what they wanted and knew how to get it by the favor of the government.

Did you ever look into the way a trust was made? It is very natural, in one sense, in the same sense in which human greed is natural. If I haven't efficiency enough to beat my rivals, then the thing I am inclined to do is to get together with my rivals and say: "Don't let's cut each other's throats; let's combine and determine prices for ourselves; determine the output, and thereby determine the prices: and dominate and control the market." That is very natural. That has been done ever since freebooting was established. That has been done ever since power was used to establish control. The reason that the masters of combination have sought to shut out competition is that the basis of control under competition is brains and efficiency. I admit that any large corporation built up by the legitimate processes of business, by economy, by efficiency, is natural; and I am not afraid of it, no matter how big it grows. It can stay big only by doing its work more thoroughly than anybody else. And there is a point of bigness,—as every business man in this country knows, though some of them will not admit it,—where you pass the limit of efficiency and get into the region of clumsiness and unwieldiness. You can make your combine so extensive that you can't digest it into a single system; you can get so many parts that you can't assemble them as you would an effective piece of machinery. The point of efficiency is overstepped in the natural process of development oftentimes, and it has been overstepped many times in the artificial and deliberate formation of trusts.

A trust is formed in this way: a few gentlemen "promote" it—that is to say, they got it up, being given enormous fees for their kindness, which fees are loaded on to the undertaking in the form of securities of one kind or another. The argument of the promoters is, not that every one who comes into the combination can carry on his business more efficiently than he did before; the argument is: we will assign to you as your share in the pool twice, three times, four times, or five times what you could have sold your business for to an individual competitor who would have to run it on an economic and competitive basis. We can afford to buy it at such a figure because we are shutting out competition. We can afford to make the stock of the combination half a dozen times what it naturally would be and pay dividends on it, because there will be nobody to dispute the prices we shall fix.

Talk of that as sound business? Talk of that as inevitable? It is based upon nothing except power. It is not based upon efficiency. It is no wonder that the big trusts are not prospering in proportion to such competitors as they still have in such parts of their business as competitors have access to; they are prospering freely only in those fields to which competition has no access. Read the statistics of the Steel Trust, if you don't believe it. Read the statistics of any trust. They are constantly nervous about competition, and they are constantly buying up new competitors in order to narrow the field. The United States Steel Corporation is gaining in its supremacy in the American market only with regard to the cruder manufactures of iron and steel, but wherever, as in the field of more advance manufactures of iron and steel, it has important competitors, its portion of the product is not increasing, but is decreasing, and its competitors, where they have a foothold, are often more efficient than it is.

Why? Why, with unlimited capital and innumerable mines and plants everywhere in the United States, can't they beat the other fellows in the market? Partly because they are carrying too much. Partly because they are unwieldy. Their organization is imperfect. They bought up inefficient plants along with efficient, and they have got to carry what they have paid for, even if they have to shut some of the plants up in order to make any interest on their investments; or, rather, not interest on their investments, because that is an incorrect word,—on their alleged capitalization. Here we have a lot of giants staggering along under an almost intolerable weight of artificial burdens, which they have put on their own backs, and constantly looking about lest some little pigmy with a round stone in a sling may come out and slay them.

For my part, I want the pigmy to have a chance to come out. And I foresee a time when the pigmies will be so much more athletic, so much more astute, so much more active, than the giants, that it will be a case of Jack the giant-killer. Just let some of the youngsters I know have a chance and they'll give these gentlemen points. Lend them a little money. They can't get any now. See to it that when they have got a local market they can't be squeezed out of it. Give them a chance to capture that market and then see them capture another one and another one, until these men who are carrying an intolerable load of artificial securities find that they have got to get down to hard pan to keep their foothold at all. I am willing to let Jack come into the field with the giant, and if Jack has the brains that some Jacks that I know in America have, then I should like to see the giant get the better of him, with the load that he, the giant, has to carry,—the load of water. For I'll undertake to put a water-logged giant out of business any time, if you will give me a fair field and as much credit as I am entitled to, and let the law do what from time immemorial law has been expected to do,—see fair play.

As for watered stock, I know all the sophistical arguments, and they are many, for capitalizing earning capacity. It is a very attractive and interesting argument, and in some instances it is legitimately used. But there is a line you cross, above which you are not capitalizing your earning capacity, but capitalizing your control of the market, capitalizing the profits which you got by your control of the market, and didn't get by efficiency and economy. These things are not hidden even from the layman. These are not half-hidden from college men. The college men's days of innocence have passed, and their days of sophistication have come. They know what is going on, because we live in a talkative world, full of statistics, full of congressional inquiries, full of trials of persons who have attempted to live independently of the statutes of the United States; and so a great many things have come to light under oath, which we must believe upon the credibility of the witnesses who are, indeed, in many instances very eminent and respectable witnesses.

I take my stand absolutely, where every progressive ought to take his stand, on the proposition that private monopoly is indefensible and intolerable. And there I will fight my battle. And I know how to fight it. Everybody who has even read the newspapers knows the means by which these men built up their power and created these monopolies. Any decently equipped lawyer can suggest to you statutes by which the whole business can be stopped. What these gentlemen do not want is this: they do not want to be compelled to meet all comers on equal terms. I am perfectly willing that they should beat any competitor by fair means; but I know the foul means they have adopted, and I know that they can be stopped by law. If they think that coming into the market upon the basis of mere efficiency, upon the mere basis of knowing how to manufacture goods better than anybody else and to sell them cheaper than anybody else, they can carry the immense amount of water that they have put into their enterprises in order to buy up rivals, then they are perfectly welcome to try it. But there must be no squeezing out of the beginner, no crippling his credit; no discrimination against retailers who buy from a rival; no threats against concerns who sell supplies to a rival; no holding back of raw material from him; no secret arrangements against him. All the fair competition you choose, but no unfair competition of any kind. And then when unfair competition is eliminated, let us see these gentlemen carry their tanks of water on their backs. All that I ask and all I shall fight for is that they shall come into the field against merit and brains everywhere. If they can beat other American brains, then they have got the best brains.

But if you want to know how far brains go, as things now are, suppose you try to match your better wares against these gentlemen, and see them undersell you before your market is any bigger than the locality and make it absolutely impossible for you to get a fast foothold. If you want to know how brains count, originate some invention which will improve the kind of machinery they are using, and then see if you can borrow enough money to manufacture it. You may be offered something for your patent by the corporation,—which will perhaps lock it up in a safe and go on using the old machinery; but you will not be allowed to manufacture. I know men who have tried it, and they could not get the money, because the great money lenders of this country are in the arrangement with the great manufacturers of this country, and they do not propose to see their control of the market interfered with by outsiders. And who are outsiders? Why, all the rest of the people of the United States are outsiders.

They are rapidly making us outsiders with respect even of the things that come from the bosom of the earth, and which belong to us in a peculiar sense. Certain monopolies in this country have gained almost complete control of the raw material, chiefly in the mines, out of which the great body of manufactures are carried on, and they now discriminate, when they will, in the sale of that raw material between those who are rivals of the monopoly and those who submit to the monopoly. We must soon come to the point where we shall say to the men who own these essentials of industry that they have got to part with these essentials by sale to all citizens of the United States with the same readiness and upon the same terms. Or else we shall tie up the resources of this country under private control in such fashion as will make our independent development absolutely impossible.

There is another injustice that monopoly engages in. The trust that deals in the cruder products which are to be transformed into the more elaborate manufactures often will not sell these crude products except upon the terms of monopoly,—that is to say, the people that deal with them must buy exclusively from them. And so again you have the lines of development tied up and the connections of development knotted and fastened so that you cannot wrench them apart.

Again, the manufacturing monopolies are so interlaced in their personal relationships with the great shipping interests of this country, and with the great railroads, that they can often largely determine the rates of shipment.

The people of this country are being very subtly dealt with. You know, of course, that, unless our Commerce Commissions are absolutely sleepless, you can get rebates without calling them such at all. The most complicated study I know of is the classification of freight by the railway company. If I wanted to make a special rate on a special thing, all I should have to do is to put it in a special class in the freight classification, and the trick is done. And when you reflect that the twenty-four men who control the United States Steel Corporation, for example, are either presidents or vice-presidents or directors in 55 per cent. of the railways of the United States, reckoning by the valuation of those railroads and the amount of their stock and bonds, you know just how close the whole thing is knitted together in our industrial system, and how great the temptation is. These twenty-four gentlemen administer that corporation as if it belonged to them. The amazing thing to me is that the people of the United States have not seen that the administration of a great business like that is not a private affair; it is a public affair.

I have been told by a great many men that the idea I have, that by restoring competition you can restore industrial freedom, is based upon a failure to observe the actual happenings of the last decades in this country; because, they say, it is just free competition that has made it possible for the big to crush the little.

I reply, it is not free competition that has done that; it is illicit competition. It is competition of the kind that the law ought to stop, and can stop,—this crushing of the little man.

You know, of course, how the little man is crushed by the trusts. He gets a local market. The big concerns come in and undersell him in his local market, and that is the only market he has; if he cannot make a profit there, he is killed. They can make a profit all through the rest of the Union, while they are underselling him in his locality, and recouping themselves by what they can earn elsewhere. Thus their competitors can be put out of business, one by one, wherever they dare to show a head. Inasmuch as they rise up only one by one, these big concerns can see to it that new competitors never come into the larger field. You have to begin somewhere. You can't begin in space. You can't begin in an airship. You have got to begin in some community. Your market has got to be your neighbors first and those who know you there. But unless you have unlimited capital (which of course you wouldn't have when you were beginning) or unlimited credit (which these gentlemen can see to it that you shan't get), they can kill you out in your local market any time they try, on the same basis exactly as that on which they beat organized labor; for they can sell at a loss in your market because they are selling at a profit everywhere else, and they can recoup the losses by which they beat you by the profits which they make in fields where they have beaten other fellows and put them out. If ever a competitor who by good luck has plenty of money does break into the wider market, then the trust has to buy him out, paying three or four times what the business is worth. Following such a purchase it has got to pay the interest on the price it has paid for the business, and it has got to tax the whole people of the United States, in order to pay the interest on what it borrowed to do that, or on the stocks and bonds it issued to do it with. Therefore the big trusts, the big combinations, are the most wasteful, the most uneconomical, and, after they pass a certain size, the most inefficient, way of conducting the industries of this country.

A notable example is the way in which Mr. Carnegie was bought out of the steel business. Mr. Carnegie could build better mills and make better steel rails and make them cheaper than anybody else connected with what afterward became the United States Steel Corporation. They didn't dare leave him outside. He had so much more brains in finding out the best processes; he had so much more shrewdness in surrounding himself with the most successful assistants; he knew so well when a young man who came into his employ was fit for promotion and was ripe to put at the head of some branch of his business and was sure to make good, that he could undersell every mother's son of them in the market for steel rails. And they bought him out at a price that amounted to three or four times,—I believe actually five times,—the estimated value of his properties and of his business, because they couldn't beat him in competition. And then in what they charged afterward for their product,—the product of his mills included,—they made us pay the interest on the four or five times the difference.

That is the difference between a big business and a trust. A trust is an arrangement to get rid of competition, and a big business is a business that has survived competition by conquering in the field of intelligence and economy. A trust does not bring efficiency to the aid of business; it *buys efficiency out of business*. I am for big business, and I am against the trusts. Any man who can survive by his brains, any man who can put the others out of the business by making the thing cheaper to the consumer at the same time that he is increasing its intrinsic value and quality, I take off my hat to, and I say: "You are the man who can build up the United States, and I wish there were more of you."

There will not be more, unless we find a way to prevent monopoly. You know perfectly well that a trust business staggering under a capitalization many times too big is not a business that can afford to admit competitors into the field; because the minute an economical business, a business with its capital down to hard pan, with every ounce of its capital working, comes into the field against such an overloaded corporation, it will inevitably beat it and undersell it; therefore it is to the interest of these gentlemen that monopoly be maintained. They cannot rule the markets of the world in any way but by monopoly. It is not surprising to find them helping to found a new party with a fine program of benevolence, but also with a tolerant acceptance of monopoly.

There is another matter to which we must direct our attention, whether we like it or not. I do not take these things into my mouth because they please my palate; I do not talk about them because I want to attack anybody or upset anything; I talk about them because only by open speech about them among ourselves shall we learn what the facts are.

You will notice from a recent investigation [A House subcommittee, the Pujo committee, launched an investigation of the "money trust" in 1912. With Samuel Untermyer as its counsel, the committee revealed the concentration of control of credit in the hands of a few men. Footnote in Wilson.] that things like this take place: A certain bank invests in certain securities. It appears from evidence that the handling of these securities was very intimately connected with the maintenance of the price of a particular commodity. Nobody ought, and in normal circumstances nobody would, for a moment think of suspecting the managers of a great bank of making such an investment in order to help those who were conducting a particular business in the United States maintain the price of their commodity; but the circumstances are not normal. It is beginning to be believed that in the big business of this country nothing is disconnected from anything else. I do not mean in this particular instance to which I have referred, and I do not have in mind to draw any inference at all, for that would be unjust; but take any investment of an industrial character by a great bank. It is known that the directorate of that bank interlaces in personnel with ten, twenty, thirty, forty, fifty, sixty boards of directors of all sorts, of railroads which handle commodities, of great groups of manufacturers which manufacture commodities, and of great merchants who distribute commodities; and the result is that every great bank is under suspicion with regard to the motive of its investments. It is at least considered possible that it is playing the game of somebody who has nothing to do with banking, but with whom some of its directors are connected and joined in interest. The ground of unrest and uneasiness, in short, on the part of the public at large, is the growing knowledge that many large undertakings are interlaced with one another, are indistinguishable from one another in personnel.

Therefore, when a small group of men approach Congress in order to induce the committee concerned to concur in certain legislation, nobody knows the ramifications of the interests which those men represent; there seems no frank and open action of public opinion in public counsel, but every man is suspected of representing some other man and it is not known where his connections begin or end.

I am one of those who have been so fortunately circumstanced that I have had the opportunity to study the way in which these things come about in complete disconnection from them, and I do not suspect that any man has deliberately planned the system. I am not so uninstructed and misinformed as to suppose that there is a deliberate and malevolent combination somewhere to dominate the government of the United States. I merely say that, by certain processes, now well known, and perhaps natural in themselves, there has come about an extraordinary and very sinister concentration in the control of business in the country.

However it has come about, it is more important still that the control of credit also has become dangerously centralized. It is the mere truth to say that the financial resources of the country are not at the command of those who do not submit to the direction and domination of small groups of capitalists who wish to keep the economic development of the country under their own eye and guidance. The great monopoly in this country is the monopoly of big credits. So long as that exists, our old variety and freedom and individual energy of development are out of the question. A great industrial nation is controlled by its system of credit. Our system of credit is privately concentrated. The growth of the nation, therefore, and all our activities are in the hands of a few men who, even if their action be honest and intended for the public interest, are necessarily concentrated upon the great undertakings in which their own money is involved and who necessarily, by very reason of their own limitations, chill and check and destroy genuine economic freedom. This is the greatest question of all, and to this statesmen must address themselves with an ernest determination to serve the long future and the true liberties of men.

This money trust, or, as it should be more properly called, this credit trust, of which Congress has begun an investigation, is no myth; it is no imaginary thing. It is not an ordinary trust like another. It doesn't do business every day. It does business only when there is occasion to do business. You can sometimes do something large when it isn't watching, but when it is watching, you can't do much. And I have seen men squeezed by it; I have seen men who, as they themselves expressed it, were put "out of business by Wall Street,"because Wall Street found them inconvenient, and didn't want their competition.

Let me say again that I am not impugning the motives of the men in Wall Street. They may think that that is the best way to create prosperity for the country. When you have got the market in your hand, does honesty oblige you to turn the palm upside down and empty it? If you have got the market in your hand and believe that you understand the interest of the country better than anybody else, is it patriotic to let it go? I can imagine them using this argument to themselves.

The dominating danger in this land is not the existence of great individual combinations,—that is dangerous enough in all conscience,—but the combination of the combinations,—of the railways, the manufacturing enterprises, the great mining projects, the great enterprises for the development of the natural water-powers of the country, threaded together in the personnel of a series of boards of directors into a "community of interest"more formidable than any conceivable single combination that dare appear in the open.

The organization of business has become more centralized, vastly more centralized, than the political organization of the country itself. Corporations have come to cover greater areas than states; have come to live under a greater variety of laws than the citizen himself, have excelled states in their budgets and loomed bigger than whole commonwealths in their influence over the lives and fortunes of entire communities of men. Centralized business has built up vast structures of organization and equipment which overtop all states and seem to have no match or competitor except the federal government itself.

What we have got to do,—and it is a colossal task not to be undertaken with a light head or without judgment,—what we have got to do is to disentangle this colossal "community of interest." No matter how we may purpose dealing with a single combination in restraint of trade, you will agree with me in this, that no single, avowed, combination is big enough for the United States to be afraid of; but when all the combinations are combined and this final combination is not disclosed by any process of incorporation or law, but is merely an identity of personnel, or of interest, then there is something that even the government of the nation itself might come to fear,—something for the law to pull apart, and gently, but firmly and persistently, dissect.

You know that the chemist distinguishes between a chemical combination and an amalgam. A chemical combination has done something which I cannot scientifically describe, but its molecules become intimate with one another and have practically united, whereas an amalgam has a mere physical union created by pressure from without. Now, you can destroy that mere physical contact without hurting the individual elements, and this community of interest is an amalgam; you can break it up without hurting any one of the single interests combined. Not that I am particularly delicate of some of the interests combined,—I am not under bonds to be unduly polite to them,—but I am interested in the business of the country, and believe its integrity depends upon this dissection. I do not believe any one group of men has vision enough or genius enough to determine what the development of opportunity and the accomplishment by achievement shall be in this country.

The facts of the situation amount to this: that a comparatively small number of men control the raw material of this country; that a comparatively small number of men control the water-powers that can be made useful for the economical production of the energy to drive our machinery; that that same number of men largely control the railroads; that by agreements handed around among themselves they control prices, and that that same group of men control the larger credits of the country.

When we undertake the strategy which is going to be necessary to overcome and destroy this far-reaching system of monopoly, we are rescuing the business of this country, we are not injuring it; and when we separate the interests from each other and dismember these communities of connection, we have in mind a greater community of interest, a vaster community of interest, the community of interest that binds the virtues of all men together, that community of mankind which is broad and catholic enough to take under the sweep of its comprehension all sorts and conditions of men; that vision which sees that no society is renewed from the top but that every society is renewed from the bottom. Limit opportunity, restrict the field of originative achievement, and you have cut out the heart and root of all prosperity.

The only thing that can ever make a free country is to keep a free and hopeful heart under every jacket in it. Honest American industry has always thriven, when it has thriven at all, on freedom; it has never thriven on monopoly. It is a great deal better to shift for yourselves than to be taken care of by a great combination of capital. I, for my part, do not want to be taken care of. I would rather starve a free man than be fed a mere thing at the caprice of those who are organizing American industry as they please to organize it. I know, and every man in his heart knows, that the only way to enrich America is to make it possible for any man who has the brains to get into the game. I am not jealous of the size of any business that has grown to that size. I am not jealous of any process of growth, no matter how huge the result, provided the result was indeed obtained by the processes of wholesome development, which are the processes of efficiency, of economy, of intelligence, and of invention.

When all the winged words had spent their fury, Wilson won the election easily, although like Lincoln, he polled a minority of the votes cast. The final tally awarded 6,293,019 popular votes to Woodrow Wilson; he received 435 electoral votes. Roosevelt had a popular vote of 4,119,507 and took 88 electoral votes. William

Howard Taft, the incumbent, received 3,484,956 popular votes and 8 electoral votes; Eugene V. Debs collected 901,873 votes but only 1 electoral vote.[82] Taft, the regular Republican candidate, was only able to carry two states, Vermont and Utah. If one totals the combined votes of Wilson, Roosevelt and Debs, all three advocates of Progressive policies, over 75 percent of the American people who voted endorsed Progressivism of one variety or another. It was certainly the most sweeping mandate for political, social and economic change in American history. It will be interesting to trace its impact on the existing institutional framework of industry and government in the next sections.

Some complained during the campaign that Wilson had inspired men's interests and emotions, but had not clarified the problems at hand. One critic observed:

> His mind is like a light which destroys the outlines of what it plays upon; there is much illumination, but you see very little.[83]

One could distinguish between the principle of Roosevelt's views and the principle of Wilson and Brandeis' position, but what concrete steps the new President would take to restrict monopoly and the trusts, and recover freedom of opportunity for "the man on the make" remained to be seen. Leuchtenburg observes that Wilson "gave to the trust question in 1912 a spirit of elevated thought and action men had rarely heard before, but he left many of his contemporaries and two generations of historians bewildered about precisely what he did propose to do about the trusts."[84] Whether or not Progressivism was more than good intentions, more than a national outpouring of moral outrage and exalted hopes and aspirations now remained to be seen.

Regardless of the specific details of the new policies, however, it became clear in the revolutionary presidential campaign of 1912 that the office of the presidency had attained a new importance in the American political system. The impact of Theodore Roosevelt's energy and resourcefulness in the previous decade left a legacy of executive precedents which stretched the limits of presidential power beyond previous boundaries. After almost half a century of humiliating emasculation at the hands of a strident and too easily corruptible Congress, the twentieth century presidency emerged as the focal point of dynamic leadership in the national government, the center of initiative and policymaking in domestic as well as foreign affairs. From that point on, the personal character, the social and economic values, the leadership qualities of the individual inhabiting the White House would become crucial, for the fate of the nation would frequently hang in the balance of the quality of leadership which would emerge from 1600 Pennsylvania Avenue.

NOTES

1. Figures were not always readily available for the exact comparative periods; when they were not, the closest approximation was used.

2. Comparative population figures were taken from the U.S. Bureau of the Census, *Historical Statistics of the United States: Colonial Times to 1957* (Washington, D.C., 1960). The comparative foreign and domestic manufacturing statistics come from Harold Underwood Faulkner, *American Economic History* (New York, 1949), 402. Other figures were drawn from Robert Higgs, *The Transformation of the American Economy, 1865-1914* (New York, 1971), 19, 21, 34, 46; and Edward Chase Kirkland, *Industry Comes of Age: Business, Labor and Public Policy, 1860-1897* (Chicago, 1967), 400.

3. Theodore Roosevelt, *An Autobiography* (New York, 1913), 389.

4. Roosevelt, 389.

5. John Morton Blum, *The Republican Roosevelt* (New York, 1963).

6. C. Vann Woodward, *Origins of the New South, 1877-1913* (Baton Rouge, Louisiana, 1971), 185.

7. These figures were compiled from material in Thomas C. Cochran and William Miller, *The Age of Enterprise: A Social History of Industrial America* (New York, 1961), 108, 131-33; Faulkner, 489-92; and Kirkland, 57-68.

8. Matthew Josephson, *The Robber Barons* (New York, 1962), 243.

9. In the northwest it was the National Farmer's Alliance; in the South, the National Farmer's Alliance and Industrial Union and the Colored Farmer's Alliance. The growth and development of these organizations is traced in John D. Hicks, *The Populist Revolt* (Lincoln, Nebraska, 1971).

10. Roy Lubove, *The Progressives and the Slums: Tenement House Reform in New York City, 1890-1917* (Pittsburgh, Pennsylvania, 1962), 88.

11. Richard Hofstadter, *The Age of Reform* (New York, 1955), 135.

12. Hofstadter, *Age of Reform*, 135.

13. Hofstadter, *Age of Reform*, 135.

14. Hofstadter, *Age of Reform*, 5.

15. Peter Filene, "An Obituary for the Progressive Movement," in Barton J. Bernstein and Allen J. Matusow, eds., *Twentieth Century America* (New York, 1972), 37-51.

16. Samuel Hays, "The Politics of Reform in Municipal Government in the Progressive Era," in *Pacific Northwest Quarterly*, LV (October 1964), 157-68.

17. E. Daniel Potts, "The Progressive Profile in Iowa," in *Mid America*, XLVII (October 1965), 257-68. The Mowry findings are summarized in his essay "The Urban Gentry On the Defensive," in Arthur E. Mann, ed., *The Progressive Era* (New York, 1963), 28-39. Chandler's research appears in Elting E. Morison, ed., *The Letters of Theodore Roosevelt* (Cambridge, Massachusetts, 1954) VIII, 1462-65. Research on the cities of Boston, Washington, D.C. and Baltimore can be found in Richard B. Sherman, "The Status Revolution and Massachusetts Progressive Leadership," in *Political Science Quarterly*, LXXVIII (March 1965), 59-65.

18. J. Joseph Huthmacher, "Urban Liberalism and the Age of Reform," in Bernstein and Matusow, 7-16. See also Michael Paul Rogin, *The Intellectuals and McCarthy: The Radical Specter* (Cambridge, Massachusetts, 1967), 116-20.

19. William T. Kerr, jr., "The Progressives of Washington, 1910-1912," in *Pacific Northwest Quarterly*, LV (January 1964), 16-27. See also James B. Crooks, *Politics and Progress: The Rise of Urban Progressivism in Baltimore, 1895-1911* (Baton Rouge, Louisiana, 1968), Chapter VIII.

20. Hofstadter, *Age of Reform*, 185.

21. Hofstadter, *Age of Reform*, 187.

22. Hofstadter, *Age of Reform*, 191.

23. Hofstadter, *Age of Reform*, 235-36.

24. Gabriel Kolko, *The Triumph of Conservatism* (Chicago, 1967).

25. Morison, III, 332.

26. Leonard White, *The City Manager* (Chicago, 1927).

27. James D. Richardson, ed., *Messages and Papers of the Presidents* (New York, 1897) XV, 7135.

28. William H. Harbaugh, "The Republican Party: 1893-1932," in Arthur M. Schlesinger, jr., ed., *History of U.S. Political Parties* (New York, 1973) III, 2085. Roosevelt wrote to his son, Kermit, that he had put his "deepest and most earnest convictions" into this special message. Elting Morison observed that in it the President anticipated nearly every reform which was to be passed in the Taft and Wilson administrations, and a few which would have to wait for the New Deal for their enactment. (George Mowry, *The Era of Theodore Roosevelt: 1910-1912* [New York, 1962], 222.)

29. Harbaugh, "The Republican Party," 2085.

30. Henry Clay and perhaps Adlai Stevenson in this century belong in this category.

31. Richard Hofstadter, *The American Political Tradition* (New York, 1948), 190.

32. H. L. Mencken, "In Memoriam: W. J. B.," in George F. Whicher, ed., *William Jennings Bryan and the Campaign of 1896* (Lexington, Massachusetts, 1953), 84.

33. Mencken, 83.

34. Mencken, 83.
35. Henry Steele Commager, "William Jennings Bryan," in Whicher, 89.
36. Alexander L. and Juliette L. George, *Woodrow Wilson and Colonel House: A Personality Study* (New York, 1956), 116-17.
37. Arthur S. Link, *Wilson: The Road to the White House* (Princeton, New Jersey, 1947), 25.
38. Quoted in Link, 96.
39. Quoted in Link, 96.
40. Quoted in Link, 96.
41. Quoted in Link, 96.
42. Quoted in Link, 111-12.
43. Quoted in Link, 111-12.
44. Quoted in Link, 121.
45. Quoted in Link, 121.
46. Quoted in Link, 142.
47. Quoted in Link, 167.
48. Quoted in Link, 167.
49. Quoted in Link, 178.
50. Quoted in Link, 178.
51. Woodrow Wilson, *Constitutional Government in the United States* (New York, 1908), see especially 68-74.
52. Link examines the provisions contained in all of this legislation in *Wilson*, 245-67, and compares it favorably with reform legislation passed in some of the most Progressive states in the Union. For example the Geran Elections Reform Act mandated direct primary elections for all elected officials and delegates to national conventions.
     Candidates for the legislature were required to declare, before the primaries were held, whether they would support the senatorial candidate endorsed by the voters at the party primary. Officials of the district election boards were to be chosen by the Civil Service Commission on the basis of examination, while the election and appointment of local election officials was to be made under the supervision of the courts. The state convention was also reconstituted by the law as a convention of party nominees and the governor only, which should meet for the single purpose of writing the party platform. The Geran law, moreover, incorporated the following provisions which one would normally expect to find in a corrupt practices act, aimed at election reform: personal registration was required of voters in general elections in cities over 5,000; sample ballots were to be mailed to all voters before a general election; an official ballot was to be substituted for the old party ballot which had previously been used and had been the source of much corruption. (Link, 257-58.)
53. Quoted in Link, 317.
54. Quoted in Link, 317.
55. Quoted in Link, 317.
56. Quoted in Link, 318.
57. Quoted in Link, 318.
58. Quoted in Link, 353.
59. Quoted in Link, 355.
60. Quoted in Ray Stannard Baker, *Woodrow Wilson: Life and Letters* (New York, 1931) III, 261.
61. Quoted in Link, 356.
62. Quoted in Link, 356.
63. Quoted in Link, 356.
64. Quoted in Baker, III, 266.
65. Quoted in Baker, III, 265.
66. See my discussion of this term as introduced by Gaetano Mosca in *The Growth of Presidential Power*, Volume II, section one.
67. Theodore Roosevelt, "The Trusts, the People, and the Square Deal," reprinted in Edwin C. Rozwenc, ed., *Roosevelt, Wilson and the Trusts* (Boston, 1968), 47.
68. Roosevelt, "The Trusts, the People, and the Square Deal," 49.
69. Link, 488.
70. Link, 489.
71. Link, 489.
72. Link, 489.
73. Link, 489-90.
74. Quoted in Link, 490.
75. Quoted in Link, 490-91.

76. Quoted in Link, 491.
77. William E. Leuchtenburg, "Woodrow Wilson and *The New Freedom*," in Woodrow Wilson, *The New Freedom* (Englewood Cliffs, New Jersey, 1961), 5.
78. Wilson, *The New Freedom* 25-26.
79. Wilson, *The New Freedom*, 86.
80. Wilson, *The New Freedom*, 63.
81. Wilson, *The New Freedom*, 166.
82. Arthur M. Schlesinger, jr., ed., *The Coming to Power* (New York, 1972), 519.
83. Leuchtenburg, "Wilson and *The New Freedom*," 7.
84. Leuchtenburg, "Wilson and *The New Freedom*," 7.

Bibliography

Baker, Ray Stannard. *Woodrow Wilson: Life and Letters.* Vol. III. Garden City, New York: Doubleday, Page and Company, 1927.

Bernstein, Barton J. and Matusow, Allen J., eds. *Twentieth Century America.* New York: Harcourt, Brace and World, Inc., 1969.

Blum, John Morton. *The Republican Roosevelt.* Cambridge, Massachusetts: Harvard University Press, 1961.

Cochran, Thomas C. and Miller, William. *The Age of Enterprise: A Social History of Industrial America.* New York: Harper and Row Publishers, 1961.

Crooks, James B. *Politics and Progress: The Rise of Urban Progressivism in Baltimore, 1895-1911.* Chapter VIII. Baton Rouge, Louisiana: Louisiana State University Press, 1968.

Faulkner, Harold Underwood. *American Economic History.* New York: Harper and Row Publishers, 1949.

George, Alexander L. and Juliette L. *Woodrow Wilson and Colonel House: A Personality Study.* New York: The John Day Company, 1956.

Hays, Samuel. "The Politics of Reform in Municipal Government in the Progressive Era." *Pacific Northwest Quarterly.* LV (October 1964).

Hicks, John D. *The Populist Revolt.* Lincoln, Nebraska: University of Nebraska Press, 1971.

Higgs, Robert. *The Transformation of the American Economy, 1865-1914.* New York: John Wiley and Sons, 1971.

Hofstadter, Richard. *The Age of Reform.* New York: Alfred A. Knopf, 1955.

———. *The American Political Tradition.* New York: Alfred A. Knopf, 1948.

Josephson, Matthew. *The Robber Barons.* New York: Harcourt, Brace and World, Inc., 1962.

Kerr, William T., jr. "The Progressives in Washington, 1910-1912." *Pacific Northwest Quarterly.* LV (January 1964).

Kirkland, Edward Chase. *Industry Comes of Age: Business, Labor and Public Policy, 1860-1897.* Chicago: Quadrangle Books, 1967.

Kolko, Gabriel. *The Triumph of Conservatism.* Chicago: Quadrangle Books, 1963.

Link, Arthur S. *Wilson: The Road to the White House.* Princeton, New Jersey: Princeton University Press, 1947.

Lubove, Roy. *The Progressives and the Slums: Tenement House Reform in New York City, 1890-1917.* Pittsburgh, Pennsylvania: University of Pittsburgh Press, 1962.

Mann, Arthur E. *The Progressive Era.* New York: Holt, Rinehart and Winston, Inc., 1963.

Morison, Elting E., ed. *The Letters of Theodore Roosevelt.* Cambridge, Massachusetts: Harvard University Press, 1951.

Mowry, George. *The Era of Roosevelt: 1910-1912.* New York: Harper and Row Publishers, 1962.

Potts, E. Daniel. "The Progressive Profile in Iowa." *Mid America.* XLVII (October, 1965).

Richardson, James D., ed. *Messages and Papers of the Presidents of the United States.* New York: Bureau of National Literature, 1897.

Rogin, Michael Paul. *The Intellectuals and McCarthy: The Radical Specter.* Cambridge, Massachusetts: M.I.T. Press, 1967.

Roosevelt, Theodore. *An Autobiography.* New York: The Macmillan Company, 1913.

Rozwenc, Edwin C., ed. *Roosevelt, Wilson and the Trusts.* Boston: D. C. Heath and Company, 1968.

Schlesinger, Arthur M., jr., ed. *History of U.S. Political Parties.* Vol. III. New York: Chelsea House Publishers/R. R. Bowker Company, 1973.

., ed. *The Coming To Power.* New York: Chelsea House Publishers/McGraw-Hill, 1972.

White, Leonard D. *The City Manager.* Chicago: The University of Chicago Press, 1927.

Whicher, George F., ed. *William Jennings Bryan and the Campaign of 1896.* Boston: D. C. Heath and Company, 1953.

Wilson, Woodrow. *Constitutional Government in the United States.* New York: Columbia University Press, 1908.

    . *The New Freedom.* Englewood Cliffs, New Jersey: Prentice-Hall, Inc., 1961.

Woodward, C. Vann. *Origins of the New South, 1877-1913.* Baton Rouge, Louisiana: Louisiana State University Press, 1951.

II. Presidential Legislative Leadership

PRESIDENTIAL LEGISLATIVE LEADERSHIP

Woodrow Wilson Takes the Helm

During the early days of the republic and in fact throughout most of the nineteenth century, Presidents rarely had anything to do with the proposing or framing of legislation. This was probably due in part to the pervasiveness of Whig principles at mid-century and thereafter to the crippling impact of the impeachment proceedings against Andrew Johnson, the persistence of the Tenure of Office Act and the general domination of the Executive by Congress in the latter part of the century. During this period Presidents rarely applied the veto power, nor did they otherwise traffic in the legislative process. Certainly the leadership and organization of Congress were beyond their purview. Writing in 1884, Woodrow Wilson observed that "from whatever point we view the relations of the executive and the legislature, it is evident that the power of the latter has steadily increased at the expense of the prerogatives of the former, and that the degree in which the one of these great branches of government is balanced against the other is a very insignificant degree indeed."[1]

The one major exception to this rule was Thomas Jefferson, who served the country well before most of these influences set in, and who dominated every aspect of the legislative process while he was in office. Jefferson was the acknowledged intellectual and political leader of his party, and during his two terms in the White House, he not only drafted legislation, but he reached into the august halls of Congress itself, where he was instrumental in organizing his party's legislative forces, recruiting and selecting its leaders and generally directing the actions of the Republican party on all critical questions confronting the legislature.

Conscious of Jefferson's example, Woodrow Wilson entered the White House, convinced of the necessity of making the presidency a dynamic center of legislative activity. At first thought this appeared strange, for Wilson wrote 29 years earlier.

> The business of the President, occasionally great, is usually not much above routine. Most of the time it is *mere* administration, mere obedience of directions from the masters of policy, the Standing Committees. Except in so far as his power of veto constitutes him a part of the legislature, the President might, not inconveniently, be a permanent officer; the first official of a carefully-graded and impartially regulated civil service system, through whose sure series of merit-promotions the youngest clerk might rise even to the chief magistracy. He is part of the official rather than of the political machinery of the government, and his duties call rather for

training than for constructive genius. If there can be found in the official systems of the States a lower grade of service in which men may be advantageously drilled for Presidential functions, so much the better. The States will have better governors, the Union better Presidents, and there will have been supplied one of the most serious needs left unsupplied by the Constitution,—the need for a proper school in which to rear federal administrators.[2]

Woodrow Wilson always believed in strong executive leadership, but his negative views of the presidency in the last part of the nineteenth century emerged from his study of the eclipse of that office in the time of an overbearing Congress. The young Wilson greatly admired the architectonic structure and style of the British parliamentary system, particularly the clear-cut leadership of the Prime Minister in Parliament. The fundamental thrust of his criticisms of American politics was that it had diffused and dissipated much of its power by its confusing lack of leadership at the center of government, while the British system both clearly defined the executive and cabinet functions and based them both in the legislature. The Prime Minister and the cabinet were responsible for introducing and defending governmental policy decisions, and stayed in power only so long as Parliament and the people supported those decisions. In other words he had never been opposed to executive power as such, but argued that the American presidency, at least during the latter third of the nineteenth century, was a poor substitute for that kind of parliamentary leader.

Wilson's first attempt to improve this condition, which he thought had diminished and enfeebled American statesmanship, was to argue for a transformation of the American political system into a quasi-parliamentary form of government, which he called "cabinet government." In an article he wrote while still an undergraduate at Princeton, he proposed some minor constitutional revisions which would have resulted in major functional changes in the operating principles of the American system. The President would be required to appoint members of his cabinet from both houses of Congress, and they in turn would serve as administration leaders in Congress. Able to introduce legislation drafted by the executive branch and supported by the Chief Executive, they would advocate it in congressional debates and guide its passage through the Congress, standing or falling upon its success as a unified administration effort.

Expectedly much of the youthful Wilson's proposal was characterized by a certain naive purity of purpose and execution, and there were many flaws in his recommendations. Wilson wanted the legislative cabinet members to resign when measures they supported were defeated, and he saw no insuperable obstacle in making opposition party representatives members of the President's cabinet when the opposing party controlled the Congress. What was impressive about the proposal was not the specific recommendations, many of which were utopian and unworkable, but rather the rationale of the basic transformation of government which Wilson was trying to bring about. He not only despaired at the quality of leadership in both houses, but he and many other observers began to become pessimistic about the American political system and its current dysfunctional performance. Wilson realized that government could not be representative unless the conditions of politics were open and not shrouded behind the closed doors of executive sessions of the standing committees. Political policies and the discussions of them also needed to be clear, coherent, and dramatic enough to arouse the people's interest and to stimulate them into action:

> The main objective of a representative assembly, therefore, should be the discussion of public business. They should legislate as if in the presence of the whole country, because they come under the closest scrutiny and fullest criticism of all the representatives of the country speaking in open and free debate. Only in such an assembly, only in such an atmosphere of publicity, only by means of such a vast investigating machine, can the different sections of a great country learn each other's feelings and interests. It is not enough that the general course of legislation is known to all. Unless during its progress it is subject to a thorough, even a tediously prolonged, process of public sifting, to the free comment of friend and foe alike, to the ordeal of battle among those upon whose vote its fate depends, an act of open legislation may have its real intent and scope completely concealed by its friends and undiscovered by its enemies, and may be as fatally mischievous as the darkest measure of an oligarchy or a despot.[3]

Wilson had tremendous faith in the power of rational debate as a means of informing the public, illuminating public issues and generally invigorating the political process. He was a rationalist but also a dialectician, for he relied upon the dialectical process to enliven and clarify public issues so that the public could capture the "sense of the meeting" and be able to articulate and implement its own interests. His purpose in outlining a possible transformation of the American government was to produce this kind of vigorous dialogue at the center of the system so that the people would become informed and perhaps even enlightened by the very process of government, and the system would become more responsive to their needs and interests. Woodrow Wilson called this responsible government:

> [D]ebate is the essential function of a popular representative body. In the severe, distinct, and sharp enunciation of underlying principles, the unsparing examination and telling criticism of opposite positions, the careful, painstaking unravelling of all the issues involved, which are incident to the free discussion of questions of public policy, we see the best, the only effective means of educating public opinion.[4]

Those words were written by an undergraduate in college late in the nineteenth century, yet they reflect a piercing insight into the desirable and functional operation of a democratic political system, and they remained as an implicit guideline of the style and conduct of Woodrow Wilson as he became governor of New Jersey and President of the United States. In later political works written as a graduate student and as a university professor and president, Wilson greatly modified his earlier proposal and attempted to work within the framework of existing institutions and practices, but he never abandoned this fundamental dialectical concept of the purpose and possibility of representative government.[5] As a state governor and later as a President, he demonstrated that with inspired leadership his ideal could almost be realized.

Woodrow Wilson was sworn in as Executive head of the government of the United States on March 4, 1913, and it rapidly became very clear that he had extensive legislative plans in mind. He had met previously with party leaders in Trenton, and with the assistance of his advisors he had already thought through several major legislative proposals which would implement promises made during his "New Freedom" campaign for the presidency. By that time Wilson's concept of the office of Chief Executive had changed radically from the views expressed above, which had been written in 1884 in his doctoral dissertation. In a lecture delivered at Columbia University in 1907, Woodrow Wilson argued for a different kind of President:

> Greatly as the practice and influence of Presidents has varied, there can be no mistaking the fact that we have grown more and more inclined from generation to generation to look to the President as the unifying force in our complex system, the leader both of his party and of the nation.[6]

> The nation as a whole has chosen him, and is conscious that it has no other political spokesman. His is the only national voice in affairs. Let him once win the admiration and confidence of the country, and no other single force can withstand him, no combination of forces will easily overpower him. His position takes the imagination of the country. He is the representative of no constituency, but of the whole people. When he speaks in his true character, he speaks for no special interest. If he rightly interpret the national thought and boldly insist upon it, he is irresistible; and the country never feels the zest of action so much as when its President is of such insight and calibre. Its instinct is for unified action, and it craves a single leader. It is for this reason that it will often prefer to choose a man rather than a party. A President whom it trusts can not only lead it, but form it to his own views.[7]

> The President is at liberty, both in law and conscience, to be as big a man as he can. His capacity will set the limit; and if Congress be overborne by him, it will be no fault of the makers of the Constitution,—it will be from no lack of constitutional powers on its part, but only because the President has the nation behind him, and Congress has not. He has no means of compelling Congress except through public opinion.[8]

Arthur Link believes that events between 1907 and 1913, namely the continued success of Theodore Roosevelt and the failure of William Taft as a popular leader, strengthened Wilson's new view of the presidency. Close to the eve of his inauguration in 1913, Woodrow Wilson wrote:

> [The President] is expected by the Nation to be the leader of his party as well as the Chief Executive officer of the Government, and the country will take no excuses from him. He must play the part and play it successfully or lose the country's confidence. He must be prime minister, as much

concerned with the guidance of legislation as with the just and orderly execution of law, . . .[9]

As President, Wilson rapidly set about demonstrating the validity of his assertions. He was extremely fortunate in that his ideas about presidential legislative leadership were first tested at a time when political circumstances were particularly ripe for this kind of development. Wilson reaped the benefits of the muckraking and political reform movements which had begun at the turn of the century and had shattered party alignments. He inherited a climate of public opinion which basically supported his intentions to seek tariff reform, establish national control of the monetary and banking system of the country and regulate industrial and monopolistic practices, which had become repugnant to most Americans.

Republican party unity had been torn asunder by these issues, but Wilson felt he could count on the support of Republican Progressives like Senator Robert La Follette in his struggles to remedy these problems, remembering that he had enlisted their support in his New Jersey triumphs. Furthermore, the President benefited from recent political developments in Congress, where the long standing dynasty of the Republican leader in the House, Speaker Joseph G. Cannon from Illinois, was overthrown by a revolt in his own party, depriving him of control of the routing of bills and committee appointments, and crippling his future power as an opposition leader. In addition, the composition of Congress shifted in the 1912 election, and Wilson came into power as the head of a party which had 290 members out of a total of 435 in the House, and 51 out of 96 in the Senate. Better still, 114 of the Democratic members of the House were in Congress for their first term and were eager to please their more seasoned colleagues in order to establish eligibility for presidential patronage, which they knew was necessary for reelection.

Wilson quickly capitalized upon these conditions and immediately began to assert his leadership in the legislative area. His first victory was the tariff reform bill. Before this bill was introduced the President had been active in working with members of his party in both houses to reorganize their structure and leadership. Even with Democratic majorities in both houses, under the old seniority system the important committee positions would have gone to conservatives; but by-passing this method of selecting leaders, Progressive supporters of the President with little or no seniority were promoted to key leadership roles.

The former senator from Pennsylvania, Joseph F. Clark, in a speech delivered to the Senate in the winter of 1963, described some of the changes that took place in the Congress. Some of his information was being made public for the first time, because he discovered it as he read the minutes of the Democratic caucus, which are kept under lock and key in the Capitol, and open only to the inspection of members of the Senate and possibly their staff. Senator Clark described the circumstances under which these changes took place:

> In all, the progressives of the three parties had a very slim majority in the Senate of 1913, but that majority was sufficient, and it enabled the Democratic Senators, with the aid of their Progressive colleagues and of their friends in the Republican Party, to set aside the seniority system in

the Senate, to displace senior committee chairmen, to replace the senior committee chairmen with young men, some of whom had not served in the Senate for more than 2 years; and, as a result of quiet meetings during different evenings in Washington they took over the Senate, reconstituted the membership of all committees, got rid of all the senior chairmen, and put their own men in.

A conference was held at Senator Luke Lea's home, to decide on a caucus leader, one who would be able to reconcile the differences with the conservative faction of the party and keep it united in the Senate with the progressive faction. Thirty Senators were present at that meeting at Senator Lea's home, and they agreed on John W. Kern, a Senator from Indiana with only 2 years' tenure in the Senate. Positions on certain important committees were given to men who deserved them because of seniority, but the memberships of various committees were packed with progressives, regardless of their seniority, and on several occasions the committee chairmen were themselves replaced. The old Senate procedures were changed to prevent a committee chairman from halting legislation arbitrarily. Instead of only the chairman, a majority of the committee might call the committee together at any time for consideration of a pending bill.[10]

Having carefully prepared for the struggle, President Wilson launched his campaign for tariff reform. He conferred with Representative Oscar Underwood, chairman of the House Ways and Means Committee, in Trenton at the end of December 1912. Underwood assured the President that his committee would complete work on a tariff reform bill by the middle of the following March. He was as good as his word. The House Democratic caucus appointed to the Ways and Means Committee new members who were favorable to the legislation, and the committee finished work on a tariff reform bill on March 17, 1913. The chairman sent the bill immediately to the White House for the perusal of the President. Studying the measure carefully, Wilson conferred with Underwood frequently during the following days and outlined his objections to the committee's draft. The President insisted that the compromises which the committee had negotiated with representatives from southern and western states, concerned with holding the line on present tariff rates for food products, sugar, leather, and wool, would have to be eliminated. He demanded that the bill be rewritten to incorporate these changes.

There was strong public support for drastic tariff reduction, and although the President was aware that various domestic interests, such as those of the sugar and wool growers, were determined to put up a strong fight to maintain high tariffs, he was initially confident that he would succeed in defeating them, as he had triumphed over pressure groups in his reform battles as governor of New Jersey. The only compromise he was willing to make in this sweeping ultimatum was to maintain a one percent duty on sugar, instead of the proposed 1.9 percent. The Ways and Means Committee complied with the President's request, and rewrote the measure according to his specifications. When the Louisiana sugar interests failed to endorse it, the sugar tariff was eliminated entirely, but later incorporated as a compromise figure.

Congress was called into special session on April 7, 1913, and the President appeared in person the next day to argue in support of the Underwood bill. This was a significant precedent in itself, since no President since John Adams had appeared before Congress to speak in favor of legislation. Wilson was struck by the dramatic impact of this precedent-shattering action. He wrote to a friend on the day of the speech:

> Today I break another precedent by reading my message to Congress in person. The town is agog about it. It seems I have been smashing precedents almost daily ever since I got here, chiefly no doubt because I did not know how it has been the custom to do so and was not particularly careful to inquire, and proceeded to do it in the most simple and natural way—which is always and everywhere contrary to precedent. The President has not addressed Congress in person since John Adams' day—and yet what [could be] more natural and dignified? And a President is likely to read his own message rather better than a clerk would.[11]

There was initially considerable adverse reaction among members of Congress, but rather than risk a debate over a resolution calling for a joint session to hear the address (which required unanimous consent), the Vice President ruled it a question of "high privilege on which unanimous consent was not required."[12]

> When Wilson arrived in the Capitol, the atmosphere was tense. "Members of Congress," one cabinet member later wrote, "appeared to be a trifle nervous. . . . Some . . . had a sullen look."[13]

But when the speech was over the reaction was favorable; Mrs. Wilson remarked to her husband as they were driving back to the White House that that was the kind of thing Theodore Roosevelt would have liked to do. Wilson is reported to have replied with a laugh: "Yes, I think I put one over on Teddy."[14]

President Woodrow Wilson
Address to Congress on
The Underwood Tariff Reform Bill
April 8, 1913

James D. Richardson, ed., *Messages and Papers of the Presidents* (New York, 1897) XVI, 7871-73.

Mr. Speaker, Mr. President, Gentlemen of the Congress: I am very glad indeed to have this opportunity to address the two Houses directly and to verify for myself the impression that the President of the United States is a person, not a mere department of the Government hailing Congress from some isolated island of jealous power, sending messages, not speaking naturally and with his own voice—that he is a human being trying to cooperate with other human beings in a common service. After this pleasant experience I shall feel quite normal in all our dealings with one another.

I have called the Congress together in extraordinary session because a duty was laid upon the party now in power at the recent elections which it ought to perform promptly, in order that the burden carried by the people under existing law may be lightened as soon as possible and in order, also, that the business interests of the country may not be kept too long in suspense as to what the fiscal changes are to be to which they will be required to adjust themselves. It is clear to the whole country that the tariff duties must be altered. They must be changed to meet the radical alteration in the conditions of our economic life which the country has witnessed within the last generation. While the whole face and method of our industrial and commercial life were being changed beyond recognition the tariff schedules have remained what they were before the change began or have moved in the direction they were given when no large circumstance of our industrial development was what it is to-day. Our task is to square them with the actual facts. The sooner that is done the sooner we shall escape from suffering from the facts and the sooner our men of business will be free to thrive by the law of nature (the nature of free business) instead of by the law of legislation and artificial arrangement.

We have seen tariff legislation wander very far afield in our day—very far indeed from the field in which our prosperity might have had a normal growth and stimulation. No one who looks the facts squarely in the face or knows anything that lies beneath the surface of action can fail to perceive the principles upon which recent tariff legislation has been based. We long ago passed beyond the modest notion of "protecting" the industries of the country and moved boldly forward to the idea that they were entitled to the direct patronage of the Government. For a long time—a time so long that the men now active in public policy hardly remember the conditions that preceded it—we have sought in our tariff schedules to give each group of manufacturers or producers what they themselves thought that they needed in order to maintain a practically exclusive market as against the rest of the world. Consciously or unconsciously, we have built up a set of privileges and exemptions from competition behind which it was easy by any, even the crudest, forms of combination, to organize monopoly; until at last nothing is normal, nothing is obliged to stand the tests of efficiency and economy, in our world of big business, but everything thrives by concerted arrangement. Only new principles of action will save us from a final hard crystallization of monopoly and a complete loss of the influences that quicken enterprise and keep independent energy alive.

It is plain what those principles must be. We must abolish everything that bears even the semblance of privilege or of any kind of artificial advantage, and put our business men and producers under the stimulation of a constant necessity to be efficient, economical, and enterprising, masters of competitive supremacy, better workers and merchants than any in the world. Aside from the duties laid upon articles which we do not, and probably can not, produce, therefore, and the duties laid upon luxuries and merely for the sake of the revenues they yield, the object of the tariff duties henceforth laid must be effective competition, the whetting of American wits by contest with the wits of the rest of the world.

It would be unwise to move toward this end headlong, with reckless haste, or with strokes that cut at the very roots of what has grown up amongst us by long process and at our own invitation. It does not alter a thing to upset it and break it and deprive it of a chance to change. It destroys it. We must make changes in our fiscal laws, in our fiscal system, whose object is development, a more free and wholesome development, not revolution or upset or confusion. We must build up trade, especially foreign trade. We need the outlet and the enlarged field of energy more than we ever did before. We must build up industry as well, and must adopt freedom in the place of artificial stimulation only so far as it will build, not pull down. In dealing with the tariff the method by which this may be done will be a matter of judgment, exercised item by item. To some not accustomed to the excitements and responsibilities of greater freedom our methods may in some respects and at some points seem heroic, but remedies may be heroic and yet be remedies. It is our business to make sure that they are genuine remedies. Our object is clear. If our motive is above just challenge and only an occasional error of judgment is chargeable against us, we shall be fortunate.

We are called upon to render the country a great service in more matters than one. Our responsibility should be met and our methods should be thorough, as thorough as moderate and well considered, based upon the facts as they are, and not worked out as if we were beginners. We are to deal with the facts of our own day, with the facts of no other, and to make laws which square with those facts. It is best, indeed it is necessary, to begin with the tariff. I will urge nothing upon you now at the opening of your session which can obscure that first object or divert our energies from that clearly defined duty. At a later time I may take the liberty of calling your attention to reforms which should press close upon the heels of the tariff changes, if not accompany them, of which the chief is the reform of our banking and currency laws; but just now I refrain. For the present, I put these matters on one side and think only of this one thing—of the changes in our fiscal system which may best serve to open once more the free channels of prosperity to a great people whom we would serve to the utmost and throughout both rank and file.

I thank you for your courtesy.

The Democratic caucus in the House met for ten days and debated every tariff schedule, but the leadership remained in firm control and beat down any efforts to weaken the bill. In the end only 13 Democrats refused to be bound by caucus discipline. On May 8, 1913, the House approved the measure by a vote of 281 to 139 with only 5 Democrats defecting.

This first legislative victory for the President and his party was substantial. Overall tariff schedules were reduced from the average *ad valorem* rate of between 37 and 40 percent, established by the Republican Payne-Aldrich tariff, to 29 percent. But this percentage reduction did not reveal the full impact of the bill, for the measure also substantially expanded the free trade list. Furthermore, the House added as an amendment to the Underwood bill a personal and corporate income tax designed to raise an additional $100,000,000 of tax revenue. The rates were low (one percent on personal and corporate income over $4000 and an additional one percent surtax on income between $20,000 and $50,000; a two percent tax was added on incomes between $50,000 and $100,000), but the long-range significance of this triumph was tremendous. Wilson had succeeded in identifying the measure as a party and presidential issue, and he did not allow the egalitarian aspects of this legislation to be lost on the general public.

The struggle in the Senate was more difficult. There was formidable opposition from the committee stage right through to the final vote. Again the President was extremely active in leading the fight. He met with members of the Senate in the President's room of the Capitol and succeeded in persuading many of them to his point of view; he corresponded with other senators, urging them to stand fast in the face of strong pressure from local constituents and other interests who were seeking special protection in the tariff schedules. At the time he was credited by the newspapers with having had considerable success in influencing a number of senators not to bolt the party, despite considerable adverse pressure.

But the interest groups affected by the downward revision of the tariff schedules in the Underwood bill were not idle either, and they mounted an impressive campaign on Capitol Hill to hinder the President's progress. One reporter wrote:

> The Senate is the target for the attacks of the accredited and adequately equipped agents of the interests that have decreed the humiliation of the Party in control of the Upper House. . . . Every skillful trick known to the underground workers in the lobby has been brought into play; every influence that can be commanded by the combination of interests and trained by them upon the ninety-six Senators has been called into action. Coercion, denunciation, threats of future punishment and promises baited with cajolery of prospective political advancement have been covertly held out to secure enough Democratic votes to obstruct the reduction of the tariff on fostered industries.[15]

The President observed that there were so many lobbyists active in Washington at that time that "a brick couldn't be thrown without hitting one of them."[16] Wilson threw the most effective brick at his disposal by making an appeal to the country on this issue.

President Woodrow Wilson
Appeal to the Country on Tariff Reform
May 26, 1913

Arthur S. Link, *Wilson: The New Freedom* (Princeton, New Jersey, 1956), 187.

I think that the public ought to know the extraordinary exertions being made by the lobby in Washington to gain recognition for certain alterations of the tariff bill. Washington has seldom seen so numerous, so industrious, or so insidious a lobby. The newspapers are being filled with paid advertisements calculated to mislead the judgment of public men not only, but also the public opinion of the country itself. There is every evidence that money without limit is being spent to sustain this lobby, and to create an appearance of a pressure of public opinion antagonistic to some of the chief items of the tariff bill.

It is of serious interest to the country that the people at large should have no lobby and be voiceless in these matters, while great bodies of astute men seek to create an artificial opinion and to overcome the interests of the public for their private profit. It is thoroughly worth the while of the people of this country to take knowledge of this matter. Only public opinion can check and destroy it.

The Government in all its branches ought to be relieved from this intolerable burden and this constant interruption to the calm progress of debate. I know that in this I am speaking for the members of the two houses, who would rejoice as much as I would, to be released from this unbearable situation.

The first reaction to this blast was not encouraging. The public was confused, and the press accused the President of shooting from the hip without evidence and mistaking for lobbying the legitimate activities of interested parties in presenting their case to Congress. The Republicans seized upon this moment to counter-attack, feeling that the President had pulled a "boner" which they could capitalize upon. "It would seem as if the Administration and Members of Congress were engaged in an effort to create a public opinion which should be inimical to all business interests," charged former President Taft.[17] The Republican leaders in the Senate, hoping to put Wilson on the spot and expose his charges as false, introduced a resolution to create a select committee of five members of the Senate to investigate the alleged lobby and to receive testimony from senators and the President.

The Democrats were troubled by this move and uncertain as to how to react to it, until they discovered that the President welcomed the hearings and felt confident that they would strengthen the case for the tariff reform bill. Believing that, the Democratic leadership then agreed to support the resolution. The committee hearings got off to a slow start, and in the first days produced nothing sensational, but when the senators got around to interrogating the representatives of the sugar interests, testimony was obtained regarding the expenditure of millions of dollars over the years by the beet sugar industry to fund a vast campaign directed at influencing newspapers, businessmen, bankers and railroad executives in their fight against free sugar. No violations of law were uncovered, but the hearings adequately demonstrated the validity of the President's charges of interference on the part of the sugar interests, and, further, kept both the Senate and the tariff bill in the public's mind throughout the period. Senator Robert La Follette, the Republican Progressive "war horse" from Wisconsin, was impressed with the results, and reflected the attitude of much of the public when he commented:

> The country is indebted to President Wilson for exploding the bomb that blew the lid off the congressional lobby. He hurled his short-fuse missile directly at the insidious interference with tariff legislation. . . . Congress sneered. The interests cried demagogue. The public believed. The case is proved.[18]

With the wind of public opinion blowing strongly behind them, the Democratic leaders moved into caucus and onto the floor of the Senate to push the legislation through. They were able to eliminate all opposition to unequivocal tariff reform, and by the time the bill went to the floor of the Senate for debate, 47 of the 49 Democratic senators pledged their votes in support of the Underwood bill, which had undergone even more downward revisions of tariff schedules at the hands of the Senate Finance Committee. Debate on the measure droned on all that summer, with many of the western Republicans, including some Progressives, battling to win exemptions favoring their local constituents. The Democrats remained firm, however, and when the tariff bill was passed in the Senate in early September by a vote of 44 to 37, the *ad valorem* rates had been reduced four percent below the rates proposed in the House bill.

This was well beyond what any seasoned observer might have predicted the previous spring, and much of the credit belonged to the President, who supplied very active and inspired leadership throughout the battle. He was involved in every step of the process—the early drafting, committee hearings, committee negotiations and revisions, the actual floor fights—and of course figured prominently in the public discussion of the measure. Operating sometimes from his executive office and frequently in the President's room right off the Senate chamber, he argued, cajoled, compromised and persuaded members of his party to hold the line. With the exception of Jefferson, no previous President had been so thoroughly and so successfully involved in leading his party in a legislative campaign, and the effort made an indelible mark on the efficacy of the presidential office.

Wilson was delighted with the result of this first important endeavor, but even while the tariff fight was still going on, the President was also deeply involved in establishing the groundwork for an overhaul of the banking and currency situation in the country. By 1913 no one was satisfied with the obsolete and disorganized state of the banking community in the United States, any more than they were satisfied with the inflexible supply of money. For years William Jennings Bryan had espoused the virtue of removing the control of the banking and credit in the country from Wall Street, and developing a national currency controlled by the government. Many political conservatives and businessmen were horrified by Bryan's "radical" ideas, but in 1913 the country was receptive to change and anxious to see what kind of monetary and banking reform the new President would recommend.

Although Wilson claimed to be ignorant of such subjects, it later became clear that his overall grasp of the principles involved in banking and currency reform was not only adequate, but he had for some years read widely into the history of banking and monetary policy in this country, and had included that topic in his reading lists and in class discussions at Princeton. Bryan was at first suspicious of Wilson's views on the subject, but the new Democratic standard-bearer was able to allay the great commoner's fears by throwing his support behind Bryan's proposed plank on banking legislation in the Democratic platform. Even before his inauguration Wilson began planning and negotiating the substance of the reform, measures he would introduce in this area. He considered that his overwhelming election was a mandate for banking and currency reform, particularly when the Progressive party had also promised reforms in that area.

The first major figure involved in the planning was Congressman Carter Glass from Virginia who was the new chairman of the House banking committee, and Dr. H. Parker Willis, his staff advisor on banking matters. Glass was a printer and a newspaper publisher, but having had no background in banking or economics before coming to the Congress, Willis did most of the work in drafting revisions of the proposed legislation. Glass and Willis were conservatives and quite sympathetic to the smaller businessmen and bankers. The first proposal they submitted to Wilson while he was still governor of New Jersey was a bill which provided for a highly decentralized, privately controlled system of 20 or more independent reserve banks. The clear intent of the bill was to oppose the emphasis put upon centralization and Wall Street control which was reflected in another proposal initiated by Republican Senator Nelson W. Aldrich of Rhode Island. The draft of the bill that Congressman Glass showed to the President-elect veered far away from the Bryan schemes of cheap money as well.

Wilson was not wholly satisfied with Willis' and Glass' handiwork. He was searching for some coordinating instrument which could serve the purpose of a central bank without any of its disadvantages. He persuaded Glass and Willis to reconsider their draft and to incorporate into the next version some kind of a central governing board, which did not assume the trappings and practical attributes of a central bank. In truth Wilson had stumbled upon a brilliant solution to what appeared to be an irreconcilable conflict—"the progressive demand for decentralization with the practical necessity for centralized control."[19] A month later they began to piece together the outline of the structure which would eventually emerge as the Federal Reserve System. In this second draft bill Glass proposed "a reserve system of fifteen or more regional banks, owned and controlled by member banks, which would hold a portion of member banks' reserves, perform other central banking functions and issue currency against commercial assets and gold. Controlling the entire system was a powerful Federal Reserve Board composed of six public members and three bankers chosen indirectly by the directors of the regional banks."[20] It was a good beginning, but there were very deep shoals that lay ahead. Neither Bryan, who was now secretary of state in Wilson's cabinet, nor any of the Progressives in Congress had seen or approved of the proposed statute, and when they were consulted serious objections were raised.

Bryan and the Progressives were not exactly novices in the banking and finance field, and although many conservatives, bankers and businessmen considered them "dangerous radicals" on the subject (and one could include the pre-1910 Wilson in this group), their thinking and analysis was devoid of the self-serving advice and criticism that had been forthcoming from those engaged in banking, and their concern was directed towards the protection of public rather than private interests. Bryan was upset when Wilson first outlined to him the newly-drafted provisions of the Glass bill, and then asked for his support. Bryan later recalled his reply:

> I called his attention to the fact that our party had been committed by
> Jefferson and Jackson and by recent platforms to the doctrine that the

issue of money is a function of government and should not be surrendered to banks, and that I was so committed to the doctrine that I could not consistently indorse the authorization of more bank notes and that to do so would forfeit the confidence of those who trusted me—this confidence being my only political asset, the loss of which would deprive me of any power to assist him.

I also pointed out my objection to a divided control and argued in favor of making the entire board of control appointive by the President, so that the government would have complete and undisputed authority over the issue of the government notes which, in my judgment, should be substituted for the contemplated bank notes.[21]

I assured him that if I felt compelled to dissent from any part of the plan, I would accompany the dissent with an explicit statement of confidence in the disinterestedness of his intention and make my dissent as mild as conditions would permit.[22]

Wilson advisedly took Bryan's warning seriously. The secretary of state was soon joined by his old comrade-in-arms, Senator Robert L. Owen, chairman of the Senate banking committee, who not only had reservations about the Glass bill, but also resented the fact that he had not been consulted in the initial drafting of the legislation. Apprehensive about a possible division within his own party before the bill was even reported to the Congress, Secretary of the Treasury William Gibbs McAdoo, who became Wilson's son-in-law the following year, stepped into the picture and introduced his own proposal designed to overcome some of the objections raised. It had the opposite effect, however, for it was far more radical than the Glass measure; it called for the establishment of a "National Reserve" or central bank within the Treasury Department itself, with 15 branches throughout the country. The "National Reserve" system was to be controlled by a "National Reserve Board," consisting entirely of political appointees. The "National Reserve" or central bank would be empowered to issue the entire supply of paper money in circulation, based upon gold and commercial assets and be administered by a National Currency Commission, which was also meant to function from within the United States Treasury.

Congressman Glass was appalled by the McAdoo plan and quickly rallied banker pressures upon the White House in sufficient strength to convince the President to get McAdoo to withdraw his proposal. McAdoo later claimed that he was never serious about it, but had thrown it into the controversy in order to frighten the bankers into softening their opposition to the more decentralized Glass scheme. But before the Glass bill would be acceptable to Bryan, Owen and the Progressives, major changes had to be made. Bryan and Owen insisted that the minimal conditions necessary for their support would be a board of governors who would be appointed by the President and would represent the public interest, and United States Treasury control of the circulation of money.

At that point Wilson again called upon his trusted advisor, Louis Brandeis, and requested his considered opinion on the matter. Brandeis' advice was concise and to the point, and he fully agreed with Bryan:

The power to issue currency should be vested exclusively in Government officials, even when the currency is issued against commerical paper. The American people will not be content to have the discretion necessarily involved vested in a Board composed wholly or in part of bankers; for their judgment may be biased by private interests or affiliation. . . . The conflict between the policies of the Administration and the desires of the financiers and of big business, is an irreconcilable one. Concessions to the big business interests must in the end prove futile.[23]

Brandeis did recommend that Wilson appoint an advisory council of bankers, but he warned:

While we must give the most careful consideration to their recommendations and avail ourselves of their expert knowledge, it is extremely dangerous to follow their advice even in a field technically their own.[24]

The Boston attorney also warned the President against passing legislation in order to avoid "panic conditions," but to wait until he made sure that the changes embodied in the statute would really serve the public interest.[25] Wilson took this counsel and acted upon it. The results were revealed in the Federal Reserve Act of 1913. Shortly thereafter the President called Glass, McAdoo and Owen to the White House and informed them that he had decided in favor of Bryan's minimum conditions for support of the bill: governmental control of the Federal Reserve Board and the issuance of Federal Reserve notes as the obligation of the United States Treasury. Historian Link explains that the latter concession was somewhat deceptive, for it did not accomplish all that the Progressives desired; they wanted the government to issue all paper money and to retire all other bank notes in circulation. When Glass pointed this out to the President, who he thought had missed this point, Wilson quickly indicated that he was quite aware of it:

Exactly so, Glass. Every word you say is true; the government liability is a mere thought. And so, if we can hold to the substance of the thing and give the other fellow the shadow, why not do it, if thereby we may save our bill?[26]

Having hammered out all of the major differences between the critical groups supporting the legislation, Wilson once again called the Congress together for a special reading of a second message concerning the proposal of the Glass bill, which with its new-found modifications was then introduced into the House and later the Senate. Although there remained some last ditch opposition from Republicans and a handful of recalcitrant Democrats, Wilson again guided the struggle and did not let up until he had the completed legislation on his desk. Bryan came to his rescue at the most critical moment, urging his friends to "stand by the President and assist in securing the passage of this measure at the earliest possible moment."[27]

The New Freedom was becoming a reality; a unique instance when campaign promises were being realized once in office. Kolko's evidence of some banker support for the measure[28] does not negate its impact upon the nature of the society. By 1913 there was almost universal support for some form of national reorganization of the banking and monetary structure of the country, but as interesting and detailed as the discussion of the reception of the reforms within the banking community is, it does not demonstrate that the President and other political forces were not in absolute control of the agenda for reform. The truth is that there was sharp division within their ranks on all these questions; but the most enlightened bankers were prepared to live with the Wilson reforms, waiting in their attempt to influence them at a later time.

President Woodrow Wilson
Special Message to Congress
On Banking and Currency Reform
June 23, 1913

Richardson, XVI, 7879-81.

Mr. Speaker, Mr. President, Gentlemen of the Congress: It is under the compulsion of what seems to me a clear and imperative duty that I have a second time this session sought the privilege of addressing you in person. I know, of course, that the heated season of the year is upon us, that work in these chambers and in the committee rooms is likely to become a burden as the season lengthens, and that every consideration of personal convenience and personal comfort, perhaps, in the cases of some of us, considerations of personal health even, dictate an early conclusion of the deliberations of the session; but there are occasions of public duty when these things which touch us privately seem very small; when the work to be done is so pressing and so fraught with big consequence that we know that we are not at liberty to weigh against it any point of personal sacrifice. We are now in the presence of such an occasion. It is absolutely imperative that we should give the business men of this country a banking and currency system by means of which they can make use of the freedom of enterprise and of individual initiative which we are about to bestow upon them.

We are about to set them free; we must not leave them without the tools of action when they are free. We are about to set them free by removing the trammels of the protective tariff. Ever since the Civil War they have waited for this emancipation and for the free opportunities it will bring with it. It has been reserved for us to give it to them. Some fell in love, indeed, with the slothful security of their dependence upon the Government; some took advantage of the shelter of the nursery to set up a mimic mastery of their own within its walls. Now both the tonic and the discipline of liberty and maturity are to ensue. There will be some readjustments of purpose and point of view. There will follow a period of expansion and new enterprise, freshly conceived. It is for us to determine now whether it shall be rapid and facile and of easy accomplishment. This it can not be unless the resourceful business men who are to deal with the new circumstances are to have at hand and ready for use the instrumentalities and conveniences of free enterprise which independent men need when acting on their own initiative.

It is not enough to strike the shackles from business. The duty of statesmanship is not negative merely. It is constructive also. We must show that we understand what business needs and that we know how to supply it. No man, however casual and superficial his observation of the conditions now prevailing in the country, can fail to see that one of the chief things business needs now, and will need increasingly as it gains in scope and vigor in the years immediately ahead of us, is the proper means by which readily to vitalize its credit, corporate and individual, and its originative brains. What will it profit us to be free if we are not to have the best and most accessible instrumentalities of commerce and enterprise? What will it profit us to be quit of one kind of monopoly if we are to remain in the grip of another and more effective kind? How are we to gain and keep the confidence of the business community unless we show that we know how both to aid and to protect it? What shall we say if we make fresh enterprise necessary and also make it very difficult by leaving all else except the tariff just as we found it? The tyrannies of business, big and little, lie within the field of credit. We know that. Shall we not act upon the knowledge? Do we not know how to act upon it? If a man can not make his assets available at pleasure, his assets of capacity and character and resource, what satisfaction is it to him to see opportunity beckoning to him on every hand, when others have the keys of credit in their pockets and treat them as all but their own private possession? It is perfectly clear that it is our duty to supply the new banking and currency system the country needs, and it will need it immediately more than it has ever needed it before.

The only question is, When shall we supply it—now, or later, after the demands shall have become reproaches that we were so dull and so slow? Shall we hasten to change the tariff laws and then be laggards about making it possible and easy for the country to take advantage of the change? There can be only one answer to that question. We must act now, at whatever sacrifice to ourselves. It is a duty which the circumstances forbid us to postpone. I should be recreant to my deepest convictions of public obligation did I not press it upon you with solemn and urgent insistence.

The principles upon which we should act are also clear. The country has sought and seen its path in this matter within the last few years—sees it more clearly now than it ever saw it before—much more clearly than when the last legislative proposals on the subject were made. We must have a currency, not rigid as now, but readily, elastically responsive to sound credit, the expanding and contracting credits of everyday transactions, the normal ebb and flow of personal and corporate dealings. Our banking laws must mobilize reserves; must not permit the concentration anywhere in a few hands of the monetary resources of the country or their use for speculative purposes in such volume as to hinder or impede or stand in the way of other more legitimate, more fruitful uses. And the control of the system of banking and of issue which our new laws are to set up must be public, not private, must be vested in the Government itself, so that the banks may be the instruments, not the masters, of business and of individual enterprise and initiative.

The committees of the Congress to which legislation of this character is referred have devoted careful and dispassionate study to the means of accomplishing these objects. They have honored me by consulting me. They are ready to suggest action. I have come to you, as the head of the Government and the responsible leader of the party in power, to urge action now, while there is time to serve the country deliberately and as we should, in a clear air of common counsel. I appeal to you with a deep conviction of duty. I believe that you share this conviction. I therefore appeal to you with confidence. I am at your service without reserve to play my part in any way you may call upon me to play it in this great enterprise of exigent reform which it will dignify and distinguish us to perform and discredit us to neglect.

The prevention of a major cleavage in the Democratic and Progressive ranks before the Glass bill was introduced by no means prevented extended debate and opposition to the measure as it slowly made its way through the two houses of Congress during the next few months. The defection of a small group of Democratic senators who held powerful positions in the Senate Banking and Currency Committee cost the administration many worried hours, and some earlier opposition in the House from southern and western agrarians was also cause for concern. But by far the strongest opposition to the bill appeared to come from conservative bankers and Republican diehards who predicted disaster for the American way of life if the measure became law. Paul M. Warburg, who earlier authored the Aldrich plan and later became a member of the first Federal Reserve Board and was considered the intellectual leader of the New York banking community, strongly denounced the bill publicly and attacked it privately in a letter to Colonel House, Wilson's most intimate advisor:

> I need not tell you how mortified I am that after all your and my trouble there are still in the Glass-Owen bill issue of notes by the government, *12* reserve banks, and practically management by the government. If such a bill passes, history will write President Wilson as a complete failure and Bryan will once more have ruined the chances of the Democratic Party.[29]

Senator Nelson Aldrich was even more emphatic in arguing that if the bill passed, it would represent a triumph for Bryanism, which the voters of the country and the majority of the Democratic party had rejected:

> Mr. Bryan will have achieved the purpose for which he has been contending for a decade. It would be difficult to find in history an occasion where a political dogma which had never found a permanent place in the tenets of the dominant [Democratic] party and which had been rejected by unanimous verdict of the civilized world could be successfully injected into a great legislative measure as the price for the support of a faction.[30]

But Wilson was not disturbed by these charges. He accepted the Bryan conditions primarily because he thought they were right, and history has certainly demonstrated the validity of his judgment. He handled the long struggle for the Federal Reserve Bill with the sure hand of a veteran Executive leader, and the measure became law shortly before Christmas in 1913. In the interim period Wilson's mood vacillated from a confident satisfaction with the system and a pride in his own leadership to weary and exasperated complaints and disillusionment with the obstacles placed in his path. One day during the bank struggle he wrote to a close friend:

> Editorially the papers which are friendly (and some which are not) represent me, in the most foolish way, as master of the situation here, bending Congress to my indomitable individual will. That is, of course, silly. Congress is made up of thinking men who want the party to succeed as much as I do, and who wish to serve the country effectively and intelligently. They have found out that I am honest and that I have no personal purpose of my own to serve (except that "If it be a sin to covet honour, then I am the most offending soul alive!") and accept my guidance because they see that I am attempting only to mediate their own thoughts and purposes. I do not know how to wield a big stick, but I do know how to put my mind at the service of others for the accomplishment of a common purpose. They are using me; I am not driving them. . . . And what a pleasure it is, what a deep human pleasure, to work with strong men, who do their own thinking and know how to put things in shape! Why a man should wish to be the whole show and surround himself with weak men, I cannot imagine! How dull it would be! How tiresome to watch a plot which was only the result of your own action and every part of which you could predict before it was put on the boards! That is not power. Power consists in one's capacity to link his will with the purpose of others, to lead by reason and a gift for cooperation. It is a multiple of combined brains.[31]

Only a week after he had written the above, Wilson reacted entirely differently to what he considered to be the Senate's resistance to this same leadership:

> The struggle goes on down here without intermission. Why it should *be* a struggle it is hard (cynicism put on one side) to say. Why *should* public men, senators of the United States, have to be led and stimulated to what all the country knows to be their duty! Why should they see less clearly, apparently, than anyone else what the straight path of service is! To whom are they listening? Certainly not to the voice of the people, when they quibble and twist and hesitate. They have strangely blunted perceptions, and exaggerate themselves in the most extraordinary degree. Therefore it *is* a struggle and must be accepted as such. A man of my temperament and my limitations will certainly wear himself out in it; but that is a small matter; the danger is that he may lose his patience and suffer the weakness of exasperation. It is against these that I have to constantly guard myself. How does the game look to you, and the actors in it, as you sit at a distance and look on at it? It is more important to me to know how it looks outside of Washington than how it looks inside. The men who think *in Washington* only cannot think for the country. It is a place of illusions. The disease is that men think of themselves and not of their tasks of service, and are more concerned with what will happen to them than what

will happen to the country. I am not complaining or scolding or holding myself superior; I am only analyzing, as a man will on Sunday, when the work pauses and he looks before and after. My eye is no better than theirs; it is only fresher, and was a thoughtful spectator of these very things before it got on the inside and tried to see straight there.[32]

The passage of the Federal Reserve Act was an important milestone in the Wilson administration. Link calls it "the greatest single piece of constructive legislation of the Wilson era and one of the most important domestic Acts in the nation's history."[33] Wilson was pleased with his triumph: "I feel that I have had a part in completing a work which I think will be of lasting benefit to the business of the country."[34] *The New York Times* accurately credited the President with the legislative leadership that accomplished this achievement:

> It is without the slightest question the powerful and unyielding pressure from the White House, in behalf of the sound and prompt recasting of the original measure, which made possible the enactment of the present law. . . .[35]

Link also observes that many of the contemporary critics of the Federal Reserve Act were right in pointing out some of its deficiencies and flaws. The Federal Reserve Board was not delegated sufficient authority to discharge the functions of a central bank. The money supply, as the radicals had complained, was left largely in the hands of private bankers; by basing the supply of money on gold and commercial paper, the government tied its hands, preventing it from relieving serious and prolonged periods of deflation. The law was not a perfect solution to the multiple problems which confronted the American financial system, but it was a significant beginning. Many like Glass, Bryan and Owen made major contributions to its substance along the way, but it was Wilson who supplied the drive and power that put the measure across:

> Not only had he courageously risked disrupting his party, mediated among the rival factions, and imposed a solution that satisfied both Democratic conservatives and Bryanites; he had also withstood the powerful assaults of private bankers, and had maintained unrelenting pressure upon both houses of Congress until the final victory was achieved. He had given the American people perhaps their best example of responsible leadership in action.[36]

After the tariff and banking measures were enacted, Wilson turned his attention to antitrust activity and legislation. Here again the election campaign of 1912 had consolidated strong public opinion in support of significant reform. Link points out that there "was no important argument over the virtues or dangers of industrial monopoly and the restraint of competition by private groups; all major spokesmen agreed that competition in industry must be preserved when possible."[37] Where the controversy arose was over what means should be chosen to achieve and maintain economic freedom. One group, which was broadly representative of large business interests and conservative opinion, favored relying on the Sherman Act and the Supreme Court's interpretation of what constituted a "contract, combination in the form of trust or otherwise, or conspiracy in restraint of trade."[38] A second group made up of former-President Theodore Roosevelt and a number of Progressives favored a system which would encourage the formation of efficient combinations under strict federal control. The third group, best characterized by its intellectual leader, Louis D. Brandeis, wanted a thoroughgoing amendment of the Sherman Act, which would be aimed at the destruction of giant monopolies and interlocking directorates, and the reconstruction of free competition. Wilson was won over to this point of view during the campaign, and his "New Freedom" speeches reflected its outlook. He intended to support a legislative program designed to achieve those objectives, and he leaned heavily again on Brandeis and his associates when working out the details.

Before launching this third major legislative effort, however, the President rested for a few weeks over the Christmas and New Year holidays at Pass Christian, Mississippi. He was able to recover much of the energy expended in months struggling over the tariff and banking legislation, and to fortify his determination to continue in his striking legislative leadership of what was developing into the most unprecedented and successful example of such guidance since the Jefferson administration. Presidential initiatives in the legislative area are commonplace today, but Theodore Roosevelt had been the first President in almost 100 years to strike out boldly in this direction, and even he had not been too successful in passing all of his major programs. He never led a united majority party, and he was constantly forced to compromise and to seek alliances with the opposition in order to obtain anything approaching a victory. Then in the course of a few short months Woodrow Wilson was able to transform the presidential office into a position of party leadership, developing that role to a fine art as he drove the major policies of his electoral platform through Congress.

Rested and refurbished Wilson returned to Washington on January 13, 1914, where he quickly took up the struggle for antitrust legislation. Once again he called both houses of Congress together and laid out his program for their consideration. It contained the major elements of the "New Freedom" concept which he had popularized during the campaign.

President Woodrow Wilson
Special Address to Congress
On Control of Trusts and Monopolies
January 20, 1914

Richardson, XVI, 7913-18.

Gentlemen of the Congress: In my report "on the state of the Union," which I had the privilege of reading to you on the 2d of December last, I ventured to reserve for discussion at a later date the subject of additional legislation regarding the very difficult and intricate matter of trusts and monopolies. The time now seems opportune to turn to that great question; not only because the currency legislation, which absorbed your attention and the attention of the country in December, is now disposed of, but also because opinion seems to be clearing about us with singular rapidity in this other great field of action. In the matter of the currency it cleared suddenly and very happily after the much-debated Act was passed; in respect of the monopolies which have multiplied about us and in regard to the various means by which they have been organized and maintained it seems to be coming to a clear and all but universal agreement in anticipation of our action, as if by way of preparation, making the way easier to see and easier to set out upon with confidence and without confusion of counsel.

Legislation has its atmosphere like everything else, and the atmosphere of accommodation and mutual understanding which we now breathe with so much refreshment is matter of sincere congratulation. It ought to make our task very much less difficult and embarrassing than it would have been had we been obliged to continue to act amidst the atmosphere of suspicion and antagonism which has so long made it impossible to approach such questions with dispassionate fairness. Constructive legislation, when successful, is always the embodiment of convincing experience, and of the mature public opinion which finally springs out of that experience. Legislation is a business of interpretation, not of origination; and it is now plain what the opinion is to which we must give effect in this matter. It is not recent or hasty opinion. It springs out of the experience of a whole generation. It has clarified itself by long contest, and those who for a long time battled with it and sought to change it are now frankly and honorably yielding to it and seeking to conform their actions to it.

The great business men who organized and financed monopoly and those who administered it in actual everyday transactions have year after year, until now, either denied its existence or justified it as necessary for the effective maintenance and development of the vast business processes of the country in the modern circumstances of trade and manufacture and finance; but all the while opinion has made head against them. The average business man is convinced that the ways of liberty are also the ways of peace and the ways of success as well; and at last the masters of business on the great scale have begun to yield their preference and purpose, perhaps their judgment also, in honorable surrender.

What we are purposing to do, therefore, is, happily, not to hamper or interfere with business as enlightened business men prefer to do it, or in any sense to put it under the ban. The antagonism between business and government is over. We are now about to give expression to the best business judgment of America, to what we know to be the business conscience and honor of the land. The Government and business men are ready to meet each other half way in a common effort to square business methods with both public opinion and the law. The best informed men of the business world condemn the methods and processes and consequences of monopoly as we condemn them; and the instinctive judgment of the vast majority of business men everywhere goes with them. We shall now be their spokesmen. That is the strength of our position and the sure prophecy of what will ensue when our reasonable work is done.

When serious contest ends, when men unite in opinion and purpose, those who are to change their ways of business joining with those who ask for the change, it is possible to effect it in the way in which prudent and thoughtful and patriotic men would wish to see it brought about, with as few, as slight, as easy and simple business readjustments as possible in the circumstances, nothing essential disturbed, nothing torn up by the roots, no parts rent asunder which can be left in wholesome combination. Fortunately, no measures of sweeping or novel change are necessary. It will be understood that our object is *not* to unsettle business or anywhere seriously to break its established courses athwart. On the contrary, we desire the laws we are now about to pass to be the bulwarks and safeguards of industry against the forces that have disturbed it. What we have to do can be done in a new spirit, in thoughtful moderation, without revolution of any untoward kind.

We are all agreed that "private monopoly is indefensible and intolerable," and our programme is founded upon that conviction. It will be a comprehensive but not a radical or unacceptable programme and these are its items, the changes which opinion deliberately sanctions and for which business waits:

It waits with acquiescence, in the first place, for laws which will effectually prohibit and prevent such interlockings of the *personnel* of the directorates of great corporations—banks and railroads, industrial, commercial, and public service bodies—as in effect result in making those who borrow and those who lend practically one and the same, those who sell and those who buy but the same persons trading with one another under different names and in different combinations, and those who affect to compete in fact partners and masters of some whole field of business. Sufficient time should be allowed, of course, in which to effect these changes of organization without inconvenience or confusion.

Such a prohibition will work much more than a mere negative good by correcting the serious evils which have arisen because, for example, the men who have been the directing spirits of the great investment banks have usurped the place which belongs to independent industrial management working in its own behoof. It will bring new men, new energies, a new spirit of initiative, new blood, into the management of our great business enterprises. It will open the field of industrial development and origination to scores of men who have been obliged to serve when their abilities entitled them to direct. It will immensely hearten the young men coming on and will greatly enrich the business activites of the whole country.

In the second place, business men as well as those who direct public affairs now recognize, and recognize with painful clearness, the great harm and injustice which has been done to many, if not all, of the great railroad systems of the country by the way in which they have been financed and their own distinctive interests subordinated to the interests of the men who financed them and of other business enterprises which those men wished to promote. The country is ready, therefore, to accept, and accept with relief as well as approval, a law which will confer upon the Interstate Commerce Commission the power to superintend and regulate the financial operations by which the railroads are henceforth to be supplied with the money they need for their proper development to meet the rapidly growing requirements of the country for increased and improved facilities of transportation. We can not postpone action in this matter without leaving the railroads exposed to many serious handicaps and hazards; and the prosperity of the railroads and the prosperity of the country are inseparably connected. Upon this question those who are chiefly responsible for the actual management and operation of the railroads have spoken very plainly and very earnestly, with a purpose we ought to be quick to accept. It will be one step, and a very important one, toward the necessary separation of the business of production from the business of transportation.

The business of the country awaits also, has long awaited and has suffered because it could not obtain, further and more explicit legislative definition of the policy and meaning of the existing antitrust law. Nothing hampers business like uncertainty. Nothing daunts or discourages it like the necessity to take chances, to run the risk of falling under the condemnation of the law before it can make sure just what the law is. Surely we are sufficiently familiar with the actual processes and methods of monopoly and of the many hurtful restraints of trade to make definition possible, at any rate up to the limits of what experience has disclosed. These practices, being now abundantly disclosed, can be explicitly and item by item forbidden by statute in such terms as will practically eliminate uncertainty, the law itself and the penalty being made equally plain.

And the business men of the country desire something more than that the menace of legal process in these matters be made explicit and intelligible. They desire the advice, the definite guidance and information which can be supplied by an administrative body, an interstate trade commission.

The opinion of the country would instantly approve of such a commission. It would not wish to see it empowered to make terms with monopoly or in any sort to assume control of business, as if the Government made itself responsible. It demands such a commission only as an indispensable instrument of information and publicity, as a clearing house for the facts by which both public mind and the managers of great business undertakings should be guided, and as an in-strumentality for doing justice to business where the processes of the courts or the natural forces of correction outside the courts are inadequate to adjust the remedy to the wrong in a way that will meet all the equities and circumstances of the case.

Producing industries, for example, which have passed the point up to which combination may be consistent with the public interest and the freedom of trade, can not always be dissected into their component units as readily as railroad companies or similar organizations can be. Their dissolution by ordinary legal process may oftentimes involve financial consequences likely to overwhelm the security market and bring upon it breakdown and confusion. There ought to be an administrative commission capable of directing and shaping such corrective processes, not only in aid of the courts but also by independent suggestion, if necessary.

Inasmuch as our object and the spirit of our action in these matters is to meet business half way in its processes of self-correction and disturb its legitimate course as little as possible, we ought to see to it, and the judgment of practical and sagacious men of affairs everywhere would applaud us if we did see to it, that penalties and punishments should fall, not upon business itself, to its confusion and interruption, but upon the individuals who use the instrumentalities of business to do things which public policy and sound business practice condemn. Every act of business is done at the command or upon the initiative of some ascertainable person or group of persons. These should be held individually responsible and the punishment should fall upon them, not upon the business organization of which they make illegal use. It should be one of the main objects of our legislation to divest such persons of their corporate cloak and deal with them as with those who do not represent their corporations, but merely by deliberate intention break the law. Business men the country through would, I am sure, applaud us if we were to take effectual steps to see that the officers and directors of great business bodies were prevented from bringing them and the business of the country into disrepute and danger.

Other questions remain which will need very thoughtful and practical treatment. Enterprises, in these modern days of great individual fortunes, are oftentimes interlocked, not by being under the control of the same directors, but by the fact that the greater part of their corporate stock is owned by a single person or group of persons who are in some way intimately related in interest. We are agreed, I take it, that holding *companies* should be prohibited, but what of the controlling private ownership of individuals or actually co-operative groups of individuals? Shall the private owners of capital stock be suffered to be themselves in effect holding companies? We do not wish, I suppose, to forbid the purchase of stocks by any person who pleases to buy them in such quantities as he can afford, or in any way arbitrarily to limit the sale of stocks to bona fide purchasers. Shall we require the owners of stock, when their voting power in several companies which ought to be independent of one another would constitute actual control, to make election in which of them they will exercise their right to vote? This question I venture for your consideration.

There is another matter in which imperative considerations of justice and fair play suggest thoughtful remedial action. Not only do many of the combinations effected or sought to be effected in the industrial world work an injustice upon the public in general; they also directly and seriously injure the individuals who are put out of business in one unfair way or another by the many dislodging and exterminating forces of combination. I hope that we shall agree in giving private individuals who claim to have been injured by these processes the right to found their suits for redress upon the facts and judgments proved and entered in suits by the Government where the Government has upon its own initiative sued the combinations complained of and won its suit, and that the statute of limitations shall be suffered to run against such litigants only from the date of the conclusion of the Government's action. It is not fair that the private litigant should be obliged to set up and establish again the facts which the Government has proved. He can not afford, he has not the power, to make use of such processes of inquiry as the Government has command of. Thus shall individual justice be done while the processes of business are rectified and squared with the general conscience.

I have laid the case before you, no doubt as it lies in your own mind, as it lies in the thought of the country. What must every candid man say of the suggestions I have laid before you, of the plain obligations of which I have reminded you? That these are new things for which the country is not prepared? No; but that they are old things, now familiar, and must of course be undertaken if we are to square our laws with the thought and desire of the country. Until these things are done, conscientious business men the country over will be unsatisfied. They are in these things our mentors and colleagues. We are now about to write the additional articles of our constitution of peace, the peace that is honor and freedom and prosperity.

In his campaign memorandum to Wilson,[39] Brandeis had set forth three major characteristics which he thought antitrust legislation ought to embody: the removal of uncertainties in the Sherman Anti-Trust Act, the facilitation of the enforcement of the law by the courts and the creation of a board or a commission to aid in administering the law. Brandeis was convinced that both litigation in the courts and industrial experience over the previous 25 years had delineated precisely what "unreasonable" restraint of trade and "unreasonable" combinations actually were. He considered that additional legislation spelling out these specific violations of the principle of antitrust would enable the government and the courts to administer the act more effectively. He was also convinced that these violations were not attributable to efforts to achieve greater efficiency on the part of a company or companies, but rather they involved the misuse of considerable economic and material resources in attempting to crush rivals or create a monopoly. Such practices included " 'cut throat' competition; discrimination against customers who would not deal exclusively with the combination; excluding competitors from access to essential raw material; espionage; doing business under false names or 'fake independents'; securing unfair advantage through railroad rebates; or acquiring otherwise than through efficiency, such control over the market as to dominate the trade."[40] Brandeis argued:

> The time has come to utilize that experience [obtained in attempting to combat monopolistic practices] and to embody its dictates in rules of positive law, which will instruct the many businessmen who desire to obey the statute, what they should avoid—and admonish those less conscientious what they must avoid. By making the prohibitions upon combinations thus definite, the uncertainty of the act about which businessmen most complain will be in large measure removed, and the enforcement of the law will become simpler and more effective.[41]

Wilson attempted to carry this strategy out and threw his support behind a bill initiated by Congressman Henry D. Clayton of Alabama, chairman of the House Judiciary Committee. In its original form the bill enumerated and outlawed specific violations of unfair trade practices. There was an early argument about adding an amendment which would outlaw any antitrust action against labor unions; and Samuel Gompers succeeded in organizing considerable support for the inclusion of such an amendment into the bill, although Wilson did not support him in that. The labor amendment was incorporated, however, and the amended bill passed the House by a healthy margin, only to run into real difficulty in the Senate Finance Committee. Conservatives on that committee debated the practicality of spelling out all the possible methods of restraining trade and finally wound up eliminating most of those restrictions and cutting the heart out of the bill. Link attributes this setback to Wilson, who for reasons of his own, virtually ignored the Clayton bill in the Senate, and allowed its opposition to gain the upper hand. Although this was one of the foundations of the Brandeis-Wilson antitrust program, the President allowed the most effective sections of the legislation to die in the Senate, and the Clayton Act never loomed very large on the antitrust horizon again.

One of the reasons that Wilson lost interest in the Clayton Act was that he shifted his antitrust strategy in midstream, and put his faith in the third part of the Brandeis program—the creation of a Federal Trade Commission which would administer or police both the Sherman and Clayton Acts. The proposed Federal Trade Commission (FTC) would be a five-member body, modeled after the Interstate Commerce Commission and appointed by the President for terms of seven years. The critical section of the bill empowered the commission to investigate and prevent unfair competition by the issuance of cease and desist orders, which would be enforced by the federal district courts. This strengthened power of the commission emerged in a new bill which the President supported—a measure introduced by Representative Raymond B. Stevens of New Hampshire at the instigation of a New York lawyer, George Rublee, who was working closely with Brandeis and was at that time serving as his liaison with various congressional committees. Rublee had been a member of Roosevelt's Progressive party and was critical of certain elements of the New Freedom program, particularly the attempt to enumerate in law the specific examples of unfair trade practices and combinations.

Rublee was the architect of the dramatic change of strategy which the President finally adopted. In explaining his reasoning on the question, Rublee concluded:

> There were a number of other bills besides the Clayton Bill in which monopolistic practices were defined. I had noticed that in most of these bills at the end of the list of forbidden practices there was a general clause prohibiting all other forms of unfair competition. The same general clause appeared at the end of the lists of specific practices enjoined in various decrees of Federal Courts in cases arising under the Sherman Law. . . . It therefore appeared that the phrase "unfair competition" had a recognized meaning in the terminology of anti-trust law. So I suggested to Mr. Stevens that the right way to legislate would be to strike out of the Clayton Act the objectionable and insufficient definitions and instead to declare unfair competition to be unlawful and give the Trade Commission power to prevent it. I drafted a bill on the general lines of the Committee's bill with the addition of a section declaring unfair competition to be unlawful and authorizing the Commission to issue complaints and make cease and desist orders.[42]

Unfortunately Brandeis was involved in very complicated railroad questions at that particular time and was not as influential as he might have been. There is no reason to believe that he changed his mind with regard to his initial proposal stressing both specific legal prohibitions and a trade commission. The unexpressed premise involved in Rublee's argument was that the Federal Trade Commission would be made up of men determined to implement its broad provisions, which, in turn would be sustained by the courts. Neither turned out to be true in practice; if the heart of the Clayton bill's specific prohibitions against unfair trade practices had not been eliminated, the commission would have received its mandate to act. How different things might have been if Wilson had not been frustrated in his initial effort to appoint Brandeis as attorney general or secretary of commerce. With Brandeis constantly at his side as a member of his official family and as a constitutional advisor to the President, the serious revision of his original strategy might not have taken place. Even though the revision was instigated by one of his own associates, the history of the Federal Trade Commission might have been very different indeed.

But Wilson acted upon Rublee's advice and placed all of his hopes in a considerably strengthened Federal Trade Commission. The earlier Covington bill was replaced by the Stevens bill and the President again exerted his full power and influence to overcome considerable opposition to the bill. Wilson apparently did not realize that his new antitrust strategy was almost an adoption of the argument which he had rejected during the 1912 campaign; in pinning all of his hopes on a presidentially appointed commission, he was reconciling himself to a critical aspect of the "New Nationalsim" views which Theodore Roosevelt had expressed during the same campaign. Furthermore, in order to obtain the votes necessary to pass the Stevens bill, the President was forced to accept an amendment which considerably broadened the powers of the courts to review the Federal Trade Commission's cease and desist decrees, a provision which further weakened the antitrust position. The courts later seized upon this provision to very effectively weaken the activity and force of the commission, and ultimately to betray the objectives of Progressivism and the New Freedom.

Nevertheless, Wilson's record as a legislative leader had been brilliant. In every respect save this last compromise and change in strategy he had relentlessly pursued the objective set forth in his spirited campaign for the presidency; he transformed into law many of the key goals of the Progressive era, and demonstrated not only the great resilience and influence of the presidential office, but restored the discipline and effectiveness of party government to the United States. He was even successful in getting the Democrats in the House to adopt a rule binding members to support the administration's policies. It was a remarkable achievement, regardless of its shortcomings and any future problems, for no President in American history had done more to elevate the Executive office to the position of power, influence and integrity which it enjoyed during those fruitful years.

But with all of this institutional achievement there were certain ominous signs of future problems and limitations in accomplishing the basic goals of Progressivism. Perhaps the trouble was rooted not simply in political or administrative strategies or methods of achieving the New Freedom, but rather in the too narrow definition of New Freedom itself. Walter Lippmann suggested as much when he wrote at that time:

> The New Freedom means the effort of small business men and farmers to use the government against the larger collective organization of industry. Wilson's power comes from them; his feeling is with them; his thinking is for them. Never a word of understanding for the new type of administrator, the specialist, the professionally trained business man; practically no mention of the consumer—even the tariff is for the business

man; no understanding of the new demands of labor, its solidarity, its aspiration for some control over the management of business; no hint that it may be necessary to organize the fundamental industries in the country on some definite plan so that our resources may be developed by scientific method instead of by men "on the make"; no friendliness for the larger, collective life upon which the world is entering, only a constant return to the commercial chances of young men trying to set up in business. That is the push and force of this New Freedom, a freedom for the little profiteer, but no freedom for the nation from the narrowness, the poor incentives, the limited vision of small competitors,—no freedom from clamorous advertisement, from wasteful selling, from duplication of plants, from unnecessary enterprise, from the chaos, the welter, the strategy of industrial war.[43]

There was also the sense that the achievement of desired legislative goals was tantamount to resolving these deepest problems. In late October 1914 Wilson wrote to a friend:

The situation is just this: the reconstructive legislation which for the last two decades the opinion of the country has demanded . . . has now been enacted. That program is practically completed.[44]

That was undoubtedly true. Wilson had succeeded in guiding through Congress not only the tariff revision and Federal Reserve Act, but a modified Clayton Bill,[45] the strengthened Federal Trade Commission and the Rayburn Bill, a measure which gave the Interstate Commerce Commission authority over the issuance of new railroad securities,—a power which Brandeis also strongly recommended, particularly in the wake of the New York, New Haven and Hartford Railroad scandal. The scope of this legislative program was breathtaking. In his State of the Union Message in 1914 the President reported to the Congress:

Our program of legislation with regard to the regulation of business is now virtually complete. It has been put forth, as we intended, as a whole and leaves no conjecture as to what is to follow. The road at least lies clear and firm before business. It is a road which it can travel without fear or embarrassment.[46]

But it was not simply laws, but the effective administration of those laws which would indicate the success or failure of the Progressive goals. Laws have to be administered by men, and in the selection of these administrators and in providing them with the guidance of clear directions as to how they should interpret those laws Wilson and the Progressive New Freedom program would be tested. In this critical area the anti-Progressives had incredible staying-power and experience, and they could and did salvage much comfort from the astute maneuvers they directed in subsequent days. Even such an inveterate opponent of the Federal Reserve Bill as Nelson Aldrich could advise one of his allies:

Whether the bill will work or not depends entirely, as I stated, upon the character and the wisdom of the men who will control the various organizations, especially the Federal Reserve Board. There is undoubtedly a general disposition to make the best of the legislation with the hope that it will turn out all right. . . .

The general effect of the act has unquestionably been helpful. While I have some doubts about the ultimate results, it seems to me no good purpose would be subserved by expressing publicly any doubts upon the subject.[47]

Satisfied at having achieved what he considered to be a total victory, President Wilson was content to retire gracefully from the field and leave to his advisors, Colonel House and his son-in-law McAdoo, the task of healing the wounds of the banking community (many of whom, however, viewed the new law with approval) by due consideration in the appointment process. A number of bankers or former bankers were offered posts and Wilson finally appointed Paul M. Warburg as one of the five commissioners of the Federal Reserve Board (the secretary of the treasury served as an *ex officio* member of the board) and made several other appointments which pleased the banking community.

But the men who the President appointed to the Federal Trade Commission were even more critical, for in that case the policy options available were more open-ended, and the personnel of the commission would largely determine how and even if the law was to be properly administered. The Federal Trade Commission Act, unfortunately, was passed during a period when the economy was undergoing one of its periodic declines, and many interpreted the mild depression as a reaction to the reforms introduced by the new Democratic administration, basing their concern around a degree of uncertainty about what lay ahead for the business community. One can discern in Wilson's speeches and actions at that time the feeling that he was sensitive to these feelings, and attempted to assure the business community that he had exhausted his reform agenda and that his administration was desirous of cooperating with business in nurturing a more productive economic climate. What better way for the President to provide such assurance than to appoint businessmen the leaders of the new Federal Trade Commission, and encourage overtures to the business community seeking their cooperation in defining and carrying out the objectives of the new law?

That was precisely what the President did, appointing Edward N. Hurley of Chicago as vice chairman of the commission. Hurley was a Chicago manufacturer and former head of the Illinois Manufacturers Association. Most of the other appointments were also drawn from the business community, and obviously when the commission finally got down to the job of defining its role under the new statute, it adopted methods and approaches which were sympathetic to the business community. Wilson appointed Rublee to the first commission, but the Senate refused to approve the appointment; as a result the commission lacked a strong and independent leader who could interpret the law objectively and impartially. The absence of the specific definitions of unfair trade practices stricken from the Clayton Act relieved the commission of the obligation of holding to explicit definitions of practices or what constituted their clear violation of law; instead the commission adopted the role of a friendly advisor, informing and instructing the business community as to the advisability and legality of certain actions, but rarely investigating and ordering violators to cease and desist. Rublee and Brandeis opposed this interpretation of the Federal Trade Commission Act, but Brandeis was not a member of the commission and Rublee served only for a short time in an interim appointment while Congress was not in session.

Gabriel Kolko has perceptively examined and documented this significant shift in attitude and direction on the part of the FTC in his study, *The Triumph of Conservatism.* The book makes too much of the clamor for governmental intervention and antitrust legislation on the part of business before Wilson's program was passed. There was support for these measures, but there was also very strong opposition, and much bewilderment as well. Frequently big business was divided by industry on tariff questions, and by size, industry and even region with respect to banking and monetary reform and industrial regulation. But once the Progressive legislation was on the books, the ranks of business solidified and made the most out of what some considered to be a bad bargain. Joseph E. Davies, the first chairman of the FTC, and his second-in-command, Vice Chairman Hurley, succeeded brilliantly in watering down the compulsory and punitive potential of the act, and in stressing the cooperative and consultative role of the commission. In fact, against Brandeis and Rublee's advice, the commission transformed itself into a quasi-judicial body, interpreting different aspects of the range of antitrust laws, providing companies and corporations with "expert" advice as to whether or not their policies and projected policies were in compliance with the law. The commission considered the business community as its clients, and it offered its services as a highly-informed and authoritative counsel. Instead of serving primarily as a law-enforcing body, the early Federal Trade Commission became the governmental representative of the interests of business, and used much of its energy and resources in helping to keep business and industrial organizations out of trouble. Even the President recognized and endorsed this role:

> [T]he Federal Trade Commission was established so that men would have some place where they could take counsel as to what the law was and what the law permitted.[48]

The assistant chairman argued that other agencies in the government were looking out for the interests of their clientele, and the Federal Trade Commission had been created to perform a similar function for business:

> Through a period of years the government has been gradually extending its machinery of helpfulness to different classes and groups upon whose prosperity depends in a large degree the prosperity of the country [e.g. farmers, railroads, labor, etc.]. . . . To do for general business that which these other agencies do for the groups to which I have referred was the thought behind the creation of the trade commission.[49]

Even later critics of the Federal Trade Commission assumed that this was one of its statutory functions:

> At its creation in 1914, the FTC was designed primarily to deal with *antitrust* problems—the Federal Trade Commission Act and the Clayton Act were considered together by Congress as extensive (sic) to the

Sherman Antitrust Act. And under the FTC Act, Congress intended the FTC to perform several functions in connection with antitrust problems. These included data gathering and informing businessmen (it was thought that the antitrust laws lacked "certainty," a deficiency that the FTC could remedy by advising businessmen on the legality of proposed business activities), as well as enforcement. . . .[50]

But this concept of the commission's function was completely foreign to its initial architect, Louis D. Brandeis. Shortly after the commission was organized it invited Brandeis to sit down with its members one morning in a private session and explain his ideas regarding the basic operating principles of the commission. Reading the 44-page typescript report of this meeting, one is reminded of a group of eager students seated around an admired teacher in a seminar discussion. The members of the commission raised the critical questions that were on their minds, and Brandeis lectured to them in his clear, precise and at times eloquent manner. Regarding the problem of giving prior advice to businessmen who wanted to know whether or not their procedures were in compliance with the law, Brandeis indicated that he was emphatically opposed to the commission's adopting such a practice, that the law did not authorize it and if the commission indulged in that practice it would find itself in great difficulties. Brandeis' statement on this question, although only an informal opinion and certainly not a presidential policy, is, however, of considerable importance, since he was the advisor who first proposed the New Freedom program to the President and in that proposal first sketched out the concept of a trade commission.

Louis D. Brandeis
Recorded Minutes (Extract) of a Meeting
With the Federal Trade Commission
April 30, 1915

Typescript record of the meeting, Louis D. Brandeis Papers, University of Louisville Law School Library, Louisville, Kentucky. (Marked File 8006-5-1.)

BEFORE THE FEDERAL TRADE COMMISSION

Commerce Building, Washington, D.C.
Friday, April 30th, 1915, 9 A.M.

Present:
  Hon. Edward N. Hurley, Acting Chairman
  Hon. William J. Harris
  Hon. William H. Parry
  Hon. George Rublee, and
  Hon. Louis D. Brandeis.

(Mr. Brandeis, on invitation of the Commission, appeared, and made the following statement:)

THE ACTING CHAIRMAN: Mr. Brandeis, we are very glad to have you with us this morning.

MR. BRANDEIS: If there are any matters in your mind, or anything that I can throw any light on, I shall be glad to talk over the things in which you are most interested.

COMMISSIONER PARRY: He might tell the things he has in his mind.

MR. BRANDEIS: Perhaps you had better bring up matter in your mind.

COMMISSIONER RUBLEE: That would be the most practical way of proceeding.

THE ACTING CHAIRMAN: The great thing I have in mind is as to the powers that we have, and how we should proceed, and the manner in which we should keep in touch with business, and as to the best method of procedure in connection with our organization.

COMMISSIONER HARRIS: I would like to hear him along the question as to our authority in going beyond a certain point in giving advice.

MR. BRANDEIS: What do you specifically have in mind?

COMMISSIONER HARRIS: A party came to us and wanted us to authorize him, practically, to do a certain thing—

MR. BRANDEIS: Bringing up a question in the Sherman Law.

COMMISSIONER PARRY: We understood that they wanted us to grant them license to do something that might be in contravention of the Sherman Law, but their contention now is that it is the Clayton Law, section 7. We have had a great many questions like this.

MR. BRANDEIS: The question, broadly, then, is whether this Commission had power practically to construe in advance actions, and to advise people what they could do and what they could not do. That, really, is the question.

COMMISSIONER HARRIS: Their claim is that the Interstate Commerce Commission did that really before the law definitely gave them the authority.

COMMISSIONER RUBLEE: The law has never given them the authority.

COMMISSIONER HARRIS: They are urging that we act just as the Interstate Commerce Commission.

MR. BRANDEIS: That question which they bring up is a question which has been very much discussed as, on the one hand, a thing that was desirable, and, on the other hand, as a thing that was dangerous. I remember, when coming down to Washington in the Roosevelt administration, eight years ago, Seth Low, of the National Civic Federation, was down here with his committee, and they had up a draft of the bill which was submitted to me at that time for consideration, which would have expressly given this power to somebody, whether it was given to the Attorney General, or the Commissioner of Corporations, or somebody else,—the power to practically decide in advance whether certain action men wished to take was or was not within the prohibition of the Sherman Act. Now that was very much discussed then, and has been discussed almost ever since, whenever any effort has been made to bring this question up. The problem was under consideration by the Clapp Committee in 1911 or 1912, when they went into the trust matters so extensively; and it was brought up here in order to get the legislation now. From the business standpoint, it is desirable. It would be a very convenient thing if a man could come before your body and say, "Here are the facts; is this right? Can we do this, or can we do that?" It sounds very alluring. I believe it to be absolutely impossible of proper application, and for this Commission, I think it would be one of the most dangerous powers that it could possibly assume.

Now, take this situation. In the first place, whether a thing is within the prohibition of the law, or is not, is a legal question. Ultimately, it has got to be decided, if the question does come up, by the Supreme Court of the United States. It is a very difficult problem. It has tested the learning and the ability of the best lawyers. Now, this is a commission of business men—you have three business men and two lawyers; and the lawyers are not selected because they are to determine the law for the Board; they are elected as an aid. It never was intended, in the composition of the Board, and certainly not in the legislation, for you to exercise this power. That was very much discussed, and the only strong argument that was put up against the Trade Commission was the danger of giving to the Commission just such power as this; that it was almost inevitable that if that power were given the public would be tricked; I mean, that the Commission, with the best of intent, would be hoodwinked; and it is really inevitable that it should be. For just see this situation—see just what this situation is. The difficulty in deciding any question that comes up is really the difficulty in getting at the facts. Most men can decide any problem correctly if all of the facts be properly set before them. The difficulty in this situation of you passing upon this condition is twofold. In the first place, the facts do not exist yet. You are to determine in advance, largely as prophets, what is going to happen. Assuming absolutely good faith on the part of the people who come before you, you are to determine whether that which they are planning to do is going to result in an improper restraint of trade. You can not decide that fact because you do not know what the facts are going to be, nor the conditions to which they are going to apply them, because they do not even know; because they are going to act, and even in good faith, upon the circumstances as they arise from time to time. For you to say in advance, even if you get a full and fair statement from all of these people as to what they were planning to do, is to predict things on a state of facts which you do not know, because they are in the future.

But the other point is, and that is the point that we lawyers have to deal with more frequently, and which is constantly impressed upon us, no statement of facts, however honest your people may be, can be relied upon until it has been subjected to the careful study and criticism of people who have a different point of view. Now, these people may be perfectly honest in laying this matter before you. They see it from their side. They do not know the whole field. They only see the difficulties which they have got and which they are trying to overcome. They do not see the other side—the evils which may attend their doing of this act. If we are going to get anywhere near the truth and justice in this action you have got to have the other side fully represented, and that never can be done in advance because the people who are going to be affected by this are not available. They may not exist, I mean. They may not be in existence as an industry or as a commercial force. But even if they are, they can not be summoned here to take action, and you cannot possibly have the knowledge which would make you wise enough to deal with that situation in such a way as to make it safe. Everybody who has undertaken to deal with this in the past ten years has been confronted with that situation—the practical certainty that if any board—if the Attorney General—or if any board of any kind undertook to deal with this situation the community would get tricked, even with the best of intent on the part of the government agency.

Brandeis' advice was ignored, however, and the commission pursued its honeymoon with the American business community, frequently acting more as an advocate and consultant than as a serious regulator of free trade. Of course there are those who argued that even if Brandeis' advice had been followed and the Federal Trade Commission had maintained an essential distance from the business community, its efforts to restrain unfair trade practices might have been frustrated anyway, or that Brandeis' theory of attempting to regulate competition would not have produced a better and more just society either. But all the evidence certainly indicates that with the emasculation of the specific prohibitions against most of the unfair trade practices contained in the original Clayton bill, combined with the transformation of the regulatory agency into a public arm and advocate of the business community, Brandeis' concept of the New Freedom did not fail—it was never tried.

There is general agreement among the serious students of the Progressive era that its accomplishments fell far short of its rhetorical objectives. Progressives wanted not only to recapture the lost moral tone of American society; they believed in the purification of democratic institutuions, the restoration of freedom and competition in economic areas and the renewal of American ideals and values at all levels of American life. Both Theodore Roosevelt and Woodrow Wilson captured their own and quite different concepts of the thrust of Progressive ideas and objectives, and transformed them into viable political programs. Wilson was the more successful of the two in guiding his Progressive policies through Congress, demonstrating a dynamic quality of legislative leadership that could only be compared to that of Thomas Jefferson. In a little over a year's time he succeeded in ushering through Congress a comprehensive program of reform legislation, unequaled in all of previous American history. If Wilson never accomplished another political objective, he would still go down in history as one of the most able and effective Presidents to serve in the office. From a technical point of view the legislative leadership he demonstrated in his first two years in office has probably never been surpassed.

But the question must be raised as to what avail all his accomplishments served. Wilson's Progressivism was not, as some have claimed, all rhetoric and void of the energizing juices of life and reality. He was not simply a naive university president, an enthusiastic idealogue and an impractical reformer. He was a political realist, a brilliant political leader, who could inspire multitudes as well as he could muster votes. But his commitment to Progressivism was not only late, but somewhat shallow and opportunistic. He was captivated by the beauty and simplicity of Brandeis' social and economic philosophy, and had been impressed earlier by the power and influence of Bryan's strength in the Democratic party. But he was not a "birthright" Progressive; he never really reacted strongly to the severe injustices imposed by the economic exploitation and manipulation of the giant trusts—he never had a "gut" response to the great social disruption brought about by America's industrial revolution. Brandeis' program for a New Freedom appealed to him because it filled a glaring gap in his bland presidential campaign; it was consistent with his new allegiance to Progressivism and its principles of freedom and liberty appealed to his basic philosophy of nineteenth century liberalism. Unlike La Follette and Brandeis, he did not resent the power exerted by the robber barons of the turn of the century or feel contemptuous of their knowledge of their own business empires, rather he wanted to restrain their ability to prevent other young Americans from rising into their ranks.

Wilson's limited commitment to and understanding of Progressive ideals allowed him to virtually abandon the struggle once the legislative goals of his administration were achieved. Having established a formal legal framework of statutes within which the industrial and business community was forced to operate, Wilson considered his major task accomplished, and he relaxed his leadership and lost interest in implementing his policies. The mild depression which accompanied his tenure in office caused him to be oversensitive to the complaints of business, but the outbreak of war in Europe distracted his interest in domestic affairs. Beyond those factors which certainly contributed to his attitude, the President was satisfied that he had made his contribution to reform politics and that once finished, it was time to pull in his horns and adopt a more conservative posture.

Apart from Wilson's attitude towards reform, the more basic question remained: did the Progressives fully understand the nature of the problems with which they were wrestling, and were their solutions adequate to bring about the goals they desired? This is too broad a question to open up in the midst of an institutional analysis of presidential power, but it cannot be avoided if the success and failure of the Progressive era is to be properly evaluated. Although his general line of analysis is often too severe and biased, I most certainly have considerable sympathy for Gabriel Kolko's summary of the Progressive failure:

> To have been successful, a movement of fundamental change would have had to develop a specific diagnosis of existing social dynamics and, in particular, the variable nature and consequences of political intervention in the economy. It would have, in short, required a set of operating premises radically different than any that were formulated in the Progressive Era or later. . . . No socially or politically significant group tried to articulate an alternative means of organizing industrial technology in a fashion that permitted democratic control over centralized power, or participation in routine, much less crucial, decisions in the industrial process. No party tried to develop a program that suggested democracy could be created only by continuous mass involvement in the decisions that affected their lives, if the concentration of actual power in the hands of an elite was to be avoided. In brief, the Progressive Era was characterized by a paucity of alternatives to the status

quo, a vacuum that permitted political capitalism to direct the growth of industrialism in America, to shape its politics, to determine the ground rules for American civilization in the twentieth century, and to set the stage for what was to follow.[51]

The reformers of the Progressive period, as well as the later architects of the New Deal, lacked the basic understanding of the dynamics of the economic system they were attempting to change, and for this reason both their analysis of the problems involved and the solutions they offered fell short of any conclusive resolution. Of course this criticism is advanced with the arrogance of hindsight, for there was no one in public or private life at that time who had the insight and vision to bring about lasting solutions to these vexing problems. Perhaps only with the advanced theories of John Maynard Keynes, his deep and pervasive understanding of capitalism and the business mentality, could Americans even begin to cope with the power and complexity of the system that the new technology and the other converging social and economic forces had wrought. But this is getting ahead of our story.

What also need to be stated are the peculiar limitations of the narrow legislative approach to problems of this dimension. Legislation can only be the beginning of the long and complex process of dealing with monopoly, inordinate concentrations of economic and social power and abuses of the public trust. A law simply establishes the framework within which many more actions and decisions have to be made. The reformer who does not understand this, and who considers the battle won once the President's signature is engraved on the bill, does not understand the nature of social and political change, and the extraordinary obstacles that are always blocking the road to progress in any area. The Progressives not only lacked the comprehensive understanding of the economic and technological system they were attempting to shape, but they also did not possess sufficient understanding of the dynamics of change to have achieved their ultimate goals. Of course they were successful in many ways, and they unquestionably left their mark on the American experience. But more decisive and comprehensive changes would have to await greater understanding of the problems, and a better grasp of the process of fundamental change in the society by the American people and their policymakers.

This is, of course, no final assessment of the impact of Progressivism. It was more of a mood, a thrust and approach to problems than an organized and coherent program or movement. It was rooted in its commitment to the early American values of freedom and individual dignity rather than any clear vision of the future or an effective strategy for realizing its aims. Its accomplishments, nevertheless, were significant, not only in a material sense, but perhaps more important, the Progressives lifted the sagging spirits of many Americans who had been crushed or orphaned by the technological and industrial revolutions of the late nineteenth century.

Wilson's legislative achievements in this context were substantial; they established a new scaffolding for the American economy, a scaffolding which had greater potential than that originally constructed and created a more humane and responsible framework for economic progress in the future. The Progressive upsurge also encouraged such striking reforms as the popular election of United States senators and witnessed the fantastic growth of the labor movement, workmen's compensation, child labor reform and women's suffrage. But Progressivism represented a beginning, not an end. It was an unfinished and indeterminate agenda rather than a comprehensive program for reform; a moral statement rather than a final solution to complex problems which much stronger forces in the society controlled.

The Emerging Pattern of Presidential Legislative Leadership

It is almost 30 years since Professor Lawrence Chamberlain published his landmark study, *The President, Congress and Legislation.*[52] In it he surveyed and evaluated the influence of the Chief Executive in the legislative process over a period of 60 years—from 1880 to 1940. His study covered not only the early years when Theodore Roosevelt and Woodrow Wilson were asserting the legislative role of the presidency, but also the major period of the New Deal, when executive influence was at its height. It is not surprising then that his findings reveal that the Chief Executive played a significant role in a good deal of the legislation that became law during this period. His conclusions are quite familiar to most political scientists, and have often been cited by students of American government as a prime empirical source for the analysis of the relation between the Executive and Congress in the legislative process. Briefly, he found that despite increased participation by the Executive, particularly during this century, it was Congress which continued to play the predominant role in the legislative process, accounting independently for 40 percent of the important laws passed between 1880 and 1940, with another 30 percent the result of combined congressional-Executive cooperation. And with respect to the 20 percent of the legislation which could be attributed primarily to presidential influence, Chamberlain pointed out that many of these laws evolved only after long periods of debate and consideration in the Congress before they were adopted by the Chief Executive.

Over three decades have elapsed since the conclusion of Chamberlain's study. Other limited accounts of the President's legislative role have been provided since, but no one has employed Chamberlains' method to test the relevance of his conclusions for the post-World War II period. The following represents an effort to apply similar criteria to major legislative measures passed in the mid-century period, beginning with the presidency of Harry Truman at the end of World War II through the tragically shortened term of John Fitzgerald Kennedy in the 1960s.

Chamberlain's Methods and Conclusions

The Chamberlain study analyzes the legislative histories of 90 significant laws passed during the period from 1880 to 1940. In each case the author has made a judgment as to whether the President, the Congress, the President and Congress together, or outside interest groups were primarily responsible for the passage of the law. In selecting statutes, Professor Chamberlain adhered to no rigid criteria but attempted to pick the most significant legislation and measures which embodied major changes in governmental policy. In assigning responsibility, he pointed out a number of subtle factors that had to be considered. Initiation of the proposal was by no means a sufficient criterion. By the time a bill passes both houses, its terms may well be completely transformed, making it into something quite different and perhaps even quite inconsistent with the original proposal. Initiation, although important, may not be important enough to guarantee passage, and the intervention of the other branch may well be of decisive importance. In short, each piece of legislation had to be studied carefully and judged on the basis of its individual legislative history, sometimes going back for several years or more as it passed slowly through the discussion and planning stages in the executive departments, or the committee stage in the legislature.

Chamberlain did, to be sure, recognize the fact that any such judgments, by their very nature, tended to be influenced by subjective factors. To minimize their tendency to be arbitrary he adopted a rule of thumb, formulated as follows: "Unless the impact of the Executive and Congress, judged in terms of its total effect upon the form, substance and operation of the statute in question, is sufficiently clear-cut to remove reasonable doubt, the dilemma has been avoided by classifying the act as joint. If this method is defective," he went on to explain, "because it fails to accord sufficient weight to the more subtle factors which are at work in all legislative activity, it has the merit of removing doubtful allocations from the area of controversy and of restricting conclusions to those statutes about whose origins the facts are relatively well agreed."[53]

At the conclusion of the Chamberlain study a final tabulation was made of the 90 legislative measures he analyzed.[54] The results are shown below:

1890-1940 Analysis

Presidential Influence Preponderant

Agriculture:	1	Agricultural Adjustment Act of 1933.
Banking:	3	Silver Purchase Repeal Act of 1893; Emergency Banking Act of 1933; Gold Reserve Act of 1934.
Business:	3	Securities Act of 1933; Securities and Exchange Act of 1934; Public Utilities Holding Company Act of 1935.
Credit:	3	War Finance Corporation Act of 1918; Reconstruction Finance Corporation Act of 1932; Home Owners' Loan Corporation Act of 1933.

Immigration: 0

Labor: 1   Second Employers' Liability Act of 1908.

National Defense: 6   Militia Act of 1903; General Staff Act
                                     of 1903; Selective Service Act of 1917;
                                     Naval Construction Acts of 1901-1905;
                                     Naval Construction Act of 1916; Navy
                                     Act of 1938.

Natural Resources: 0

Railroads Tariff: 2   Underwood Act of 1913; Reciprocal Trade
                           ___   Agreements Act of 1934.
                           19

Congressional Influence Preponderant

Agriculture: 2   Capper-Volstead Act of 1922; McNary-
                                     Haugen bills, 1924-1928.

Banking: 6   Currency Acts of 1873; 1878; 1890; 1900;
                                     1908; Glass-Steagall Act of 1933.

Business: 1   Sherman Act of 1890.

Credit: 3   Federal Farm Loan Act of 1916; War
                                     Finance Corporation Revival Act of 1921;
                                     Agricultural Credits Act of 1923.

Immigration: 9   Chinese Exclusion Act of 1882; Chinese
                                     Exclusion Act of 1892; General Immigra-
                                     tion Acts of 1882; 1903; 1907; 1913; 1917;
                                     1921; 1924.

Labor: 3   Department of Labor Act of 1913; Second
                                     Child Labor Act of 1919; Norris-LaGuardia
                                     Act of 1932.

National Defense: 4   National Defense Act of 1916; National
                                     Defense Act of 1920; Selective Service
                                     Act of 1940; Naval Disarmament Act of
                                     1920-21.

Natural Resources: 2   Carey Act of 1894; Act of 1897.

Railroads: 3   Interstate Commerce Act of 1887; Valuation
                                     Act of 1913; Transportation Act of 1920.

Tariff: 2   Wilson Act of 1894; Payne-Aldrich Act
                           ___   of 1909.
                           35

Joint Presidential-Congressional Influence

Agriculture:	3	Agriculture Marketing Act of 1929; Soil Conservation Act of 1936; Agricultural Adjustment Act of 1938.
Banking:	4	Federal Reserve Act of 1913; Thomas Silver Amendment of 1933; Silver Purchase Act of 1934; Banking Act of 1935.
Business:	2	Clayton Act of 1914; National Industrial Recovery Act of 1933.
Credit:	2	Federal Home Loan Bank Act of 1932; Emergency Farm Mortgage Act of 1933.
Labor:	4	First Employers' Liability Act of 1906; First Child Labor Act of 1916; National Labor Relations Act of 1935; Wages and Hours Act of 1938.
National Defense:	3	Army Act of 1901; Naval Construction Act of 1929; Naval Construction Act of 1934.
Natural Resources:	7	General Revision Act of 1891; Newlands Act of 1902; Weeks Act of 1911; Migratory Bird Act of 1913; Migratory Bird Treaty Act of 1918; Migratory Bird Refuge Act of 1929; Taylor Grazing Act of 1934.
Railroads:	4	Hepburn Act of 1906; Mann-Elkins Act of 1910; Emergency Railroad Transportation Act of 1933; Transportation Act of 1940.
Tariff:	0	
	29	

Pressure Group Influence Preponderant

Labor:	1	Railway Labor Disputes Act of 1926.
Natural Resources:	1	Clarke-McNary Act of 1924.
Railroads:	1	Elkins Act of 1903.
Tariff:	4	McKinley Tariff Act of 1890; Dingley Tariff Act of 1897; Fordney-McCumber Tariff Act of 1922; Hawley-Smoot Tariff Act of 1930.
	7	

Of the 90 major legislative measures used in the survey, approximately 20 percent (19) were credited to the primary influence of the President; roughly 40 percent (35) to Congress; a little over 30 percent (29) were the result of combined presidential-congressional efforts; and slightly less than 10 percent (7) were assigned to the influence of external interest groups.[55]

The Chamberlain research ended at the terminus of the New Deal period. The popular lore then and now indicates that in this period Congress was overwhelmed by the driving force of Franklin Roosevelt's personality and political wizardry, and throughout his first two peacetime terms, played very much of a second fiddle to the President in the legislative process. The research confirmed the fact that presidential influence was more effective during that period than in the previous 40 years. In fact in that time span (which covered less than one-fifth of the total period), almost one-half of the bills credited to presidential sponsorship were passed. But Chamberlain was quick to point out that even during that high point of executive leadership, Congress still played a very important legislative role. Of the 23 selected laws passed during Roosevelt's two terms, the President was credited with major responsibility for 8, the Congress with 2, and the other 13 were accounted for as joint presidential-congressional products. However, Chamberlain insisted that "when the backgrounds of these laws are examined . . . the contribution of Congress assumes substantial proportions."[56]

To demonstrate the validity of his argument, Chamberlain cited the example of the Agricultural Adjustment Act of 1933, which was classified in his tabulation as falling under the rubric of presidential responsibility. Yet he wrote:

> [T]he struggle for farm legislation which virtually monopolized the attention of several sessions of Congress during the twenties had left its mark. The almost continuous series of hearings had provided a clearing house for the various agencies, governmental and private, which were seeking new formulae for putting the farmer back on his feet. The domestic allotment plan of 1933 did not spring into being overnight. Its lineal ancestry can be traced directly back to the earlier plans of the McNary-Haugen era. Congress acted in response to executive pressure in its speedy approval of the agricultural adjustment bill, and it did so in spite of the opposition of the two committee chairmen, because the congressional mood at this time was one of cooperation. In this sense the priority of presidential influence was incontrovertible. On the other hand, the influence of previous congressional activity upon the substance of the bill requested by the President, while impossible to measure or weigh in exact terms, was no less important.[57]

It was also significant to note that of "the entire ninety laws, no less than seventy-seven trace their ancestry directly to bills which originally had been introduced without administration support."[58] Of the 19 laws attributed to presidential influence, 12 had been originally introduced by Congress and had been subject to extensive debate. Of the 29 laws credited to joint presidential-congressional influence, no less than 26 had been previously introduced in Congress without presidential assistance and had also been discussed and analyzed in committee meetings and in floor debate.

Rejecting the image of congressional impotence during the New Deal era, Chamberlain concluded:

> These figures do not support the thesis that Congress is unimportant in the formulation of major legislation. Rather, they indicate not that the President is less important than is generally supposed but that Congress is more important.[59]

He interprets his research as demonstrating "the joint character of the American legislative process." This is hardly a controversial conclusion in our period, when Congress has played such a decisive role in the successes and failures of the postwar administrations. But at the time the book was written, in the wake of the New Deal leadership of FDR, the proposition appeared somewhat more dubious until Chamberlain's evidence was presented.

Present Study and Findings

It is essential to follow Chamberlain's same rules of thumb in a follow-up study of his conclusions; otherwise any attempt to compare results would be useless. It would have been of considerable comparative advantage to have been able to continue Chamberlain's same legislative categories, but this proved to be unrealistic, for the obvious reason that postwar legislative activity occurred in many areas that had been untouched in the prewar period. In fact the new categories themselves reveal important shifts in the political, social and economic priorities of postwar life in the United States. Foreign policy and social welfare legislation (particularly housing) head this list, but there were also marked legislative developments in civil rights, atomic energy and space. Considerable legislative activity has continued in the fields of agriculture, immigration, labor, national defense, tariffs, and to some degree in the areas of railroads, business and natural resources (all original Chamberlain categories), but there had been little or nothing in the areas of banking and currency (except on an international level) or government credit.

Chamberlain eliminated governmental reorganization legislation because he felt it was in a class by itself, although he included the General Staff Act of 1903, which was essentially a bill to reform the organizational structure of the army. Because of this I felt justified in including the National Security Act of 1947 and its major revision in 1949, for both were essentially reorganizations of the structure of the military establishment. Tax legislation was left out, Chamberlain stipulated, because it was far too complex to include in a study of this scope. Individual legislative measures such as the T.V.A. and the Social Security Act were not included because the author felt that "they did not fall into any well defined category in which there has been a continuous stream of legislation." Here I have more or less split the difference with Chamberlain, leaving out public power legislation, but including amendments to the Social Security Act when they represented significant changes, along with other social welfare legislation which was too important to exclude and which also met the other two tests imposed by Chamberlain. I have also felt compelled to leave out the two very important statehood acts because there were five such laws passed in the period between 1880-1940 and none were included in the Chamberlain sample. Finally, foreign policy legislation, as distinguished from treaty-making, was too important to exclude. In fact, the legislative nature of much of our foreign policy in the postwar era is a significant development in our political system in and of itself.[60]

Like Chamberlain's method and his thesis, this analysis does not rely upon a highly "systematic" criterion of selection and classification. I have followed a rule which defies precision: The law in question must in my judgment be an important piece of legislation in its own right, embodying a significant change in governmental policy. In assigning responsibility, the President, Congress, or the interest groups must be clearly in command of the legislation or it is classified as joint congressional-Executive.

These are matters of individual judgment. For example I have included the Mutual Defense Assistance Act of 1949 because it extended military aid to the NATO countries for the first time, the Foreign Aid Act of 1951 because it incorporated both economic and military aid (in sizable amounts) for the first time, and the Foreign Aid Act of 1964, because it went through the Congress without any substantial reductions, and it did reverse the history of legislation in that field from 1951 until that time. The foreign aid statutes from 1952 to 1963 were all excluded because they followed the pattern (more or less) of the 1951 law in which the Congress inflicted substantial cuts in the President's proposals. The Civil Rights Acts of 1957 and 1964 were selected, while the Civil Rights Acts of 1960 was not, because the former two marked the development of new policies while the latter did not. It was unfortunately necessary to eliminate the Agricultural Act of 1949, a very good example of congressional law-making and an interesting demonstration of a newly elected Democratic Congress turning on the President and defeating his farm program (and incidentally his platform), the Congress' action constituting business as usual, while the President's program was the radical departure. Hopefully, in balance, such inclusions and exclusions were compensatory and permitted a soundly based comparison with Chamberlain's findings.

The problem of assigning responsibility is more difficult, however; but there are certain things to look for that make the task somewhat easier. One has to be mindful of the complexity of the legislative process and the difficulty of accurately assigning the responsibility of the passage of a law to any single action or pressure. However, presidential intervention in the form of a recommendation, a special message, the testimony of cabinet officers or other administrative aides, statements in the State of the Union, economic or budget messages, or a bill drafted in an executive department, are all signs that the President must necessarily be included in the overall responsibility, if his objectives are not later reversed by the legislature. If the legislature's role in the passage of a law is simply to accept methodically such leads, the law can obviously be assigned to presidential responsibility. If on the other hand the Congress wages a considerable battle over the bill, modifies it to any real extent or otherwise imposes its own real imprimatur upon the finished legislation, the bill must be classified in the joint presidential-legislative category. A congressional law is one which is clearly the work of the Congress, passed without presidential assistance or in some instances in the face of his vigorous opposition. The laws for which interest groups have been assigned responsibility were the most difficult to delineate. Since pressure groups are active at all times, they have had decisive influence only on those rare occasions when they have mounted an extraordinary offensive, usually in the face of congressional indifference.

Of importance, but not necessarily a decisive factor, is the question of where the original bill was drafted. This indicates at least an initial interest in the statute, but this interest can be blunted or destroyed if the content of the measure is seriously altered during its legislative journey. An example of this was the Displaced Persons Act of 1948, strongly supported by President Truman and his secretary of state in the early stages of consideration but assailed and vetoed at a later date after certain allegedly discriminatory amendments were added to the original bill by Congress.

However a long period of germination in the Congress is not always the decisive consideration in assigning priority of influence. A bill that originally emerges in the Congress may have absolutely no chance of passing until adopted or sometimes changed by the President. The Area Redevelopment Act was a good example of this. The bill was the brain child of Senator Paul Douglas, who piloted it through the tortuous seas of congressional infighting two different times only to have it vetoed on both occasions by President Eisenhower. On the third time around the bill failed to pass both houses. During the presidential primary in West Virginia (an area badly in need of redevelopment), candidate Kennedy revived the bill and promised all-out support of the measure if he were to be elected in November. After his election he was good to his word and appointed a special redevelopment committee headed by Paul Douglas to meet during the interregnum to prepare proposals for legislation in the forthcoming session of Congress. With Paul Douglas leading the fight in the Senate and the President providing direction among administration leaders in the House, the bill was passed in short order. Credit must be divided here between the President and Congress, but it is certainly clear that the bill would never have passed without the intervention of the President.

Although the Chamberlain study uses 1940 as the cut-off date, I have decided to focus my analysis on the nearly 20-year period following the end of World War II (from mid-1945 to the end of 1964), eliminating the war years because this extended period was exceptional and would tend to emphasize the role of the wartime Commander in Chief in the legislative process. Analysis of the postwar period thus insures greater continuity with the earlier period and enhances the validity of comparative judgments that can be made.

It is impossible to include the full legislative histories of all the laws studied as Chamberlain has done in his book, but I have, with the assistance of my students, analyzed the legislative history of the postwar period and made as careful and as comparatively accurate judgments as possible.[61] After the most significant laws were selected, each was again thoroughly analyzed and evaluated for its major influence. The results will indicate the general drift of the postwar relationship between the President and Congress in the legislative process.

Mid-Century Analysis

Presidential Influence Preponderant

1946	1	British Loan.
1947	2	Presidential Succession Act; National Security Act of 1947.
1948	1	Selective Service Act of 1948.
1949	2	Trade Agreement Extension Act of 1949; Amendments to the National Security Act of 1947.
1950	2	Social Security Act Amendments of 1950; Defense Production Act of 1950.
1951	1	Civil Defense Act of 1951.
1954	3	Agricultural Act of 1954; The Atomic Energy Act of 1954; Social Security Amendments of 1954.
1955	1	Joint Resolution on Pescadores Islands and Formosa.
1957	1	Middle East Joint Resolution.
1958	2	Agricultural Act of 1958.
1961	4	Arms Control and Disarmament Act of 1961; The Peace Corps; Housing Act of 1961; Communications Satellite Act.
1962	1	Trade Expansion Act.
1963	2	Medical School Act; Mental Health Act.
1964	4	Economic Opportunity Act of 1964; Urban Mass Transportation Act of 1964; Foreign Aid Law of 1964; Land and Water Conservation Fund.
	26	

Joint Presidential-Congressional Influence

1946	4	Federal Aid for Airports; Federal Aid for Hospitals; Employment Act of 1946; Atomic Energy Act of 1946.
1947	1	Assistance to Greece and Turkey.
1948	1	Foreign Assistance Act of 1948.
1949	3	The National Housing Act of 1949; Mutual Defense Assistance Act; Fair Labor Standards Amendments.
1950	3	Housing Act of 1950; National Science Foundation; Displaced Persons Act of 1950.

1951	2	Universal Military Training Act of 1951; Mutual Security Act of 1951.
1953	1	Submerged Lands Act.
1954	1	St. Lawrence Seaway.
1956	1	Federal-Aid Highway Act.
1957	1	Civil Rights Act of 1957.
1958	1	National Aeronautics and Space Administration; National Defense Education Act.
1959	2	Labor-Management Reporting and Disclosure Act; Social Security Amendments.
1961	1	Area Redevelopment Act.
1962	3	Drug Amendments to Food and Drug Act; Joint Resolution on Relations with Cuba; Manpower Retraining Act of 1962.
1963	1	Higher Educational Facilities Act of 1963.
1964	1	Civil Rights Act of 1964.
	28	

Congressional Influence Preponderant

1947	1	Labor-Management Relations Act (Taft-Hartley).
1948	2	Displaced Persons Act of 1948, Amendments to the Reciprocal Trade Act of 1934.
1950	1	Internal Security Act of 1950 (McCarran Act).
1951	1	Amendments to the Reciprocal Trade Act of 1934.
1952	1	Immigration and Nationality Act of 1952.
1956	1	Amendments to the 1948 Water Pollution Control Act.
	7	

Interest Group Influence Preponderant

1948	1	Amendments to the Interstate Commerce Act (Reed-Bulwinkle Act).
1952	1	Amendments to the Federal Trade Commission Act (Fair Trade Price Acts).
	2	

Comparisons

The figures for the postwar period indicate important changes took place in the legislative process. First of all the amount of significant legislation increased. The Chamberlain study selected 90 different statutes over a period of 60 years. I found it necessary to include 63 laws which were passed in a time span of 20 years, one-third the time of the earlier period, and I have listed my laws by year rather than by special category because the number of categories has increased so.

The most dramatic change, however, was in the number of laws attributed to independent congressional influence. In the earlier sample these accounted for 40 percent of the total legislation. In such cases the statute would in all probability not only have been drafted in either one of the legislative houses, but the major role in its passage would have come from the Congress, with little or no executive intervention. In fact in some instances the law would have been passed over a presidential veto. In the mid-century period the number of these laws dropped sharply to less than 11 percent (6), three of which were passed over a presidential veto. This 10 percent, when compared with 40 percent during the Chamberlain period, represents a decline of 75 percent in statutes initiated by and supported primarily by the Congress.

Laws that can basically be identified with presidential influence have increased from 20 percent (19) in the 1880-1940 period to 41 percent (26) in the more recent time span, an increase of more than 100 percent. Joint presidential-congressional influence in lawmaking has also increased from approximately 30 percent (29) in the early period to 44 percent (28) in the recent selection. Finally, interest groups were the dominant influence in the passage of 3 percent (2) of the laws, as compared to 10 percent (7) in the previous 60 years.

Perhaps the statistic of greatest comparative significance is that in the Chamberlain sample 47 percent (42) of the measures became law without presidential intervention, while at mid-century only 14 percent (8) could claim to have done so. Included in that category of laws is one that was quickly reversed by subsequent action of the Congress (Displaced Persons Act of 1948) and two others that have proved to be unenforceable (Internal Security Act of 1950 and the Fair Trade Price Act of 1952). That left the Taft-Hartley Act, the Reed-Bulwinkle Act and two amended versions of the Reciprocal Trade Act (which have long since been radically changed by subsequent legislation) as the unassailable symbols of congressional lawmaking during the 20-year mid-century period.[63]

These statistics reveal that the President has indeed become a major partner in the legislative process, and that very little significant legislation is now passed that either does not emanate from the executive branch, or is not significantly influenced by executive action at some stage of its legislative history. In the Chamberlain period the President was involved in less than half the significant laws which were passed, while in the later period which I have analyzed, only 12 percent of the statutes singled out for consideration became law without significant presidential intervention. That means that the President played an important role in the passage of almost 90 percent of this legislation.[64]

This is certainly an institutional development of major proportions, and its effect upon the American political system has not been sufficiently recognized. Chamberlain acknowledged the increasing importance of the President's role in the legislative process, but the development since his study was made has been so overwhelming that the relationship between the President and Congress must be seen in this new light. A recent evaluation of legislation passed during the period between 1961 and 1966 concludes:

> Members of Congress could retard, accelerate, or deflect those [legislative] impulses, and they could expand, limit, or modify the specific proposals initiated from the White House. But they could not set in motion the legislative steam itself. Constitutionally, they had every right to do so. Theoretically, perhaps, they had the opportunity. Practically, they did not.[65]

Chamberlain also stressed the long period of legislative gestation in which the Congress became quite familiar, perhaps even expert, in the intricacies of a particular law. He refers specifically to the lengthy prenatal legislative period which transpired before the Agricultural Adjustment Act, the Tennessee Valley Authority and the Reciprocal Trade Agreement were hatched. Such periods, I would contend, are not necessarily related to the subsequent passage of the laws. Many, many bills simply die in the Congress because of insufficient support (and in many cases they should). No one has yet demonstrated a causal relationship between the long prenatal legislative period and the ultimate success and quality of a law. In fact many of our most effective and successful laws have emerged from consideration during a single session of Congress. The bills that languished for long periods in the Congress, either without majority support or, if strongly opposed by the President, without the two-thirds majority necessary to override his veto, were not pulled together by legislative leadership and driven through the Congress. Nor did the careful analysis and debate they prompted tend to educate or win over additional senators, congressmen, or the public, to their standards. If they finally became laws, the chances were that it was because they won the support of a strong executive leader who pulled them out of the committee pigeonhole where they rested almost forgotten and built support for them among the general public and also in the Congress. What was more important than those protracted periods of gestation was what rallied the political power to transform them from either executive or legislative proposals into law.

Obviously there is another side to the coin. Although few important laws are passed without presidential influence, many important presidential proposals are defeated on the floor of the Congress or waylaid and pigeonholed in the powerful standing committees. Although President Kennedy's supporters argue that Congress passed over 85 percent of his administration's bills that came up for a record vote on the floor of both houses in 1962, 37.9 percent of his proposals never got out of their respective committees and were as dead as the proposals that were defeated on the floor by the end of the session.[66]

This does not detract from, but rather reinforces, the argument that the legislative process is a joint undertaking with a very clear division of both labor and power. Divided political control of the Congress and the presidency obviously inhibits the power and influence of each. A President who cannot call upon at least a nominal majority of his partisans in both houses must negotiate with Congress from a position of weakness rather than strength. David Truman has clearly demonstrated that this cuts both ways, for the congressional party is very much weaker when one of its own is not in the White House.[67] But these are the acknowledged conditions within which the American political system has always operated. They make the practice of organic unity at the center of the legislative process more difficult, but not impossible.

Conclusions

The drift of the argument, supported by these more recent indices of legislative influence, is not that Congress is an inferior partner in the legislative process, but that joint presidential-congressional lawmaking has become institutionalized in the last several decades. This development was officially recognized as early as 1934 by President Franklin D. Roosevelt when he established a legislative "clearinghouse" within the ill-fated National Emergency Council. Its purpose was to coordinate legislative proposals coming from various departments and agencies within the administration. As the Emergency Council withered on the vine, the Bureau of the Budget moved into the vacuum and assumed responsibility for legislative clearance after the Brownlow Report in the winter of 1937. By 1939 the Bureau was processing agency reports on 2,448 pending public bills, and handled 438 drafts of proposed legislation sponsored by various departments or agencies of the executive branch.[68] Richard Neustadt has called this executive legislative role "by far the oldest, best intrenched, most thoroughly institutionalized of the President's coordinative instruments. . . ."[69]

The postwar emergence of the President's legislative program was another institutional development of the office "of no mean proportions," and was additional evidence of the increasing importance of the President's role in the legislative process.[70] Starting with Harry Truman, every successive President of the United States presented a legislative program to the Congress on an annual basis, and much of the following legislative session was involved in the consideration of those proposals.

Chamberlain's findings were really not inconsistent with these developments, but his conclusion that the role of Congress was more important than that of the President in the legislative process appears no longer to be true. A bill may well germinate for several decades in the Congress, but if it does not have strong executive support, it has little chance of becoming a law. Even if the Congress girds itself and mobilizes sufficient strength to pass a bill in both houses without presidential approval, it still faces the possibility of a presidential veto; Congress has been able to overcome such a veto on only a handful of important occasions in the last three decades. It makes no sense, however, to continue to argue which is the more important partner. By definition one must assume that the function of the legislature is necessary and essential to legislation. But recent experience has clearly demonstrated, in both Republican and Democratic administrations, that executive leadership, initiative and influence are equally essential elements in the legislative process.

More general recognition of this basic political fact of life should lead to certain fundamental changes in the rhetoric of our politics and in the habits of both the national electorate and the political leadership which it installs in office. The literature and journalism of political science have for too long promoted the image of the relationship of the President and Congress in terms of adversaries. Granted that at times they take on this character, the evidence of recent legislative history indicates that the more basic institutional function of the legislative process is, and should be, a joint undertaking. The concept of the separation of powers is constitutionally inaccurate and practically disastrous. The political rhetoric that beckons America back to such a "faith of our fathers" is a fraud on its face. The constitutional provisions that provide for cooperation between the President and Congress in the appointing process, in treaty-making, and in recommending and vetoing procedures of the legislative process clearly reveal the absurdity of the term "separation."

This has not always been recognized, even by the occupant of the presidential office himself. In describing President Dwight Eisenhower's concept of the proper relationship between the President and Congress, Emmet Hughes relates:

> Quite frequently, he would murmur that Franklin D. Roosevelt had "usurped" powers of the Legislature and that the Congress understandably had felt "deprived" of its "rightful role" for two decades. From this, he inferred a sense of obligation, as President, to redress matters by "restoring" some power to the Legislature.... Such Presidential solicitude plainly implied a sense of the *separateness* of the two branches that forbade any political trespassing.[71]

And yet this same President took the legislative initiative in 1954 and pushed through the Congress more of his "program" than any mid-century President, with the exception of the unexpired term of John F. Kennedy that was filled by Lyndon Johnson.[72]

The conclusion one is forced to draw from the evidence collected is that over the past three decades or more, in practice if not in theory, the presidency has become an integral and decisive part of the legislative process. That does not mean that the function of Congress is in any way downgraded by such a development. On the contrary, such a notion is based upon an erroneous concept of the proper role of the legislature. The independent formulation of legislation is not the only, nor even the best or most efficient, way in which Congress can lay claim to its constitutionally delegated powers. One encounters in John Stuart Mill's famous chapter on the "Proper Functions of a Representative Assembly" the argument that control rather than sole determination of legislation is the responsibility that a representative assembly can best discharge. This is what Mill had in mind when he wrote that it should be recognized that

in legislation as well as in administration, the only task to which a representative assembly can possibly be competent is *not that of doing the work, but of causing it to be done.*[73]

The complexities of modern government, the problems with which it is faced and the sheer magnitude of the legislative work load guarantee that no modern legislature can properly perform the tasks of independently formulating, analyzing, refining and amending legislation, even in a 12-month session. It is physically and intellectually impossible, as well as politically undesirable. The executive branch, on the other hand, can at least expand in response to the multiple problems and demands with which it is confronted, and direct specialized talents and efforts to preparing a legislative program without sacrificing its central authority or responsibility to the general welfare. A legislature of over 500 representatives, however, cannot afford such a luxury, even if it is able to expand its staff services limitlessly. In the final analysis it must reformulate, analyze and evaluate everything that has been done for it by staff work that cannot be properly responsible to a collective body.

Congress is much better equipped to examine carefully and to analyze thoughtfully proposals that have been prepared by an Executive who is free from its parochial limitations. By this I do not mean to denigrate concerns and interests. They play, and they should play, a vitally important role as one set of conditions that go into the making of a law which is to apply to the whole country. If they are allowed to dominate the entire legislative procedure, however, the common interest and ultimately the constituent elements of that common interest, the special interests, will suffer too—in fact, suffer all the more. There is a great need for a division of labor in the legislative process, based upon an organic understanding of limited but essential functions of all of its component parts.

I am certainly not suggesting that, in everything but name, the American system has taken on the functional operating methods of the British parliamentary system, or that it should. With respect to the legislative process our system is more representative and flexible and our legislature far more important and more functionally effective than its British counterpart. The Congress always has the option to override a presidential veto. It can and occasionally does introduce bills of importance without any prior consultation with administration personnel. Its standing committees and subcommittees have far more power and perform more significant work than do the British committees. The voice of Congress—its opinions and decisions—is considerably more influential than the more or less automatic approval of a parliamentary government majority. Yet in the relationship between Executive and legislature, both with respect to executive (or in the British case, cabinet) initiative and influence, the American system in mid-century is closer to the parliamentary system than it ever has been before. When one considers the successful history of that aspect of the British system, why should there be any apprehension about this?

In brief I am suggesting that mid-century conditions have brought about a de facto legislative arrangement in which both branches of our divided, but not separated, political system are forced to operate (under optimal conditions, i.e., one-party "control" of both branches) in a manner best suited to both their special and very different responsibilities and capacities. Only if the President proposes too little or the Congress disposes of too much does the system really break down.

If in reality this is the pattern of the mid-century relationship between the President and Congress in the legislative process, then there must be a greater recognition of it on the part of all parties concerned and a considerable effort to bring existing, and in many instances archaic, political habits and procedures into line with prevailing conditions. Perhaps the priority of public discussion ought to be the need for the reorganization of the political structure, rather than the further strengthening of the office of the presidency. Included on the agenda for change might be the irrational electoral ticket-splitting (which still goes on) between candidates for the presidency and Congress; perhaps a constitutional amendment to expand the term served in the House of Representatives from two to four years (expiring in a presidential election year), and developing better methods for creating joint presidential-congressional party policies and more effective means for implementing these policies in the legislative procedures of Congress would be viable alternatives. Walter Lippmann has suggested that the rules of Congress ought to be changed in order to make the consideration of all presidential legislative proposals by both houses mandatory. Ultimately such public discussion ought to involve a thoroughgoing analysis and hopefully a major reorganization of the machinery of our splintered and centrifugal party system, where allegiances to local leaders and interests are often given priority over the general welfare in national elections. Most of these proposals are already being given some consideration in Washington and throughout the country at large, essentially not because they constitute logical, theoretical or even partisan solutions to basic problems in the American system, but because they represent pragmatic responses to realities that have been long in the making, and that have emerged in the course of the give and take of the political process.

The problem of the relationship of the President to Congress, however, arises not only in the legislative field, but, as we have observed, exists in all the other areas of executive responsibility as well. A number of altogether too simple solutions have been proposed to correct this complex problem—solutions such as weakening the presidential office, creating assistant Presidents, making the presidency a collective office and bringing members of Congress into the President's cabinet. All of these proposals address themselves to an attempt to limit the President's power and to diffuse his authority and control. They may look acceptable on an organizational chart, but such suggestions fly in the face of the history of the growth of presidential power.

This growth and development has not been accomplished by any one President, in any one area, or in any specific period. It has been, for the most part, a steady, relentless, almost inevitable development, rooted in and paralleling the growth of the country and its continuing need for the political institutions to reflect its growth and to respond to the needs and problems it has created.

What seems to be needed is not some constitutional check on arbitrary presidential power, or some statutory limitation on the President's functions or responsibilities. These functions and responsibilities, as we have seen, have been hewn out of the crucible of experience and have greater pragmatic justification for their existence than would any law limiting their power. The real check on executive, or for that matter, congressional power has been the wrath or conviction of mobilized, inflamed, sometimes ill-informed, public opinion. In a later section I will discuss some instances where public opinion has either forced or prevented presidential action. But in the broadest sense the key to the acquisition of political power in the American political system is the struggle for the support of the majority of the people, and when that support is clearly evident, the President is in the driver's seat. Under these circumstances no formal constitutional or statutory limitation can constitute a real barrier for any prolonged period of time.

Congress is the obvious political instrument for the application of effective constraints upon the President, but it is at present badly equipped to challenge the President in the vital zone of public discussion. Much congressional activity takes place behind the closed doors of committee rooms in executive sessions, and those portions of its deliberations which take place in public hearings and on the floor of Congress itself are frequently irrelevant and confusing. Rarely does the majority or even the minority in either house mobilize its efforts sufficiently so that its voice can be heard above the din. Rarely is an important issue clearly joined between Congress and the President, nor is the position of the Senate, the House or a majority of either articulated in the public press or other communications media. Many of our mid-century Presidents have mastered the techniques of eloquently dramatizing their decisions and policies to the American people, and, all other things being equal, the public usually responds and supports them. It is rare indeed when the Congress is able to communicate with its constituents on as effective a level and solicit the support necessary for the success of its policies.

This is not to say that Congress is impotent in dealing with the President on nonlegislative matters. It possesses the power of advice and consent in major administrative appointments and in the treaty-making process; its "power of the purse" makes it a senior partner in determining the level of the national budget; and it usually finds other ways and means of bringing pressure to bear on the Chief Executive or his administrative departments. Richard Neustadt directs our attention to three recent developments whereby Congress has utilized its strategic position to effectively curtail presidential power and at the same time advance its own interests.[74]

Although civil service reform has succeeded in depoliticizing most of the green pastures of patronage from early times, Congress has recently invaded the realm of nontenured civil service appointments—the so-called "schedule C" positions. In the appointment of jobs on the levels of assistant to assistant secretaries, where the department or the President usually has some influence, congressmen have pressed their claims on reluctant administrators and the President himself, using as their bargaining weapons their support for administration legislative or appropriation objectives. Congress has also exploited the device of limiting appropriations to one year, affording it the opportunity of bargaining annually with the President for its support of more than one-fourth of the federal budget items. A third method of controlling presidential power is the device of writing into the enabling statute a provision for prior consultation on the part of the administrators of a particular program with members of appropriate congressional committees. This gives

Congress the opportunity of further harassing the President with respect to programs and policies already endorsed by a formal act of Congress. It also weakens his control over his own administrative family, who are forced to cater to and negotiate with appropriate committees continually, and to appease not one but two masters.

These inhibiting devices are part of the secret phase of government that takes place behind closed doors, and which the public rarely hears about. These activities can limit, even cripple, the President's power to act in the development of continuing, long-range social and economic programs, but they have little impact upon crisis management, in limiting presidential power in situations where his executive, foreign policy or commander in chief powers are employed to influence, control or to initiate major policies or changes. Here public opinion is decisive, and the lack of an articulate congressional opinion or voice concerning these questions permits an effective President to command the field by default. This condition, which results in the absence of a healthy and instructive dialectic at the center of the political system, produces a situation in the country at large which is devoid of political resonance and encourages apathy and ignorance leading to later frustration and doubt. If the opposition party in Congress would assume a responsible educational role in the legislative as well as the nonlegislative areas, when there was a decided difference of policy between the two parties mounting an intelligent attack upon the President's actions and proposals, the dialectical clash of these two positions would (hopefully) clarify the controversy and produce sufficient political resonance within the country at large to develop an informed and ultimately an articulate and effective public opinion. Such a process suggests not only the proper limitations of presidential power, but the development of a political environment, a political culture, which could reflect a higher level of politics and government in the future.

Presidential Power
And the Economy

Roosevelt's New Deal Sets a Precedent

When the eminent British economist, John Maynard Keynes, visited the United States during the Depression in 1934, he was appalled by the general ignorance of economics in this country, and he was particularly surprised at the lack of understanding of the subject on the part of the Chief Executive. He told Frances Perkins, who was President Roosevelt's secretary of labor, that he had "supposed the President was more literate, economically speaking";[73] and he was a good deal more candid with Alvin Johnson when he complained that "I don't think your President Roosevelt knows anything about economics."[76] The confused and at times contradictory economic policies of the New Deal tended to give weight to

Keynes' assessment, and almost three decades would pass before an American President would redeem himself in the eyes of the followers of Keynes, who came to dominate the field of economics in this country as well as in Europe in the middle years of the twentieth century.

In the early days of the republic the nature of economic problems and the demands upon Presidents for economic leadership were simpler and more limited. Alexander Hamilton, as Washington's secretary of the treasury, convinced the first President of the constitutionality and advisability of governmental intervention in economic affairs when the interest of the nation was at stake. Andrew Jackson, Martin Van Buren, Grover Cleveland and other nineteenth century Presidents were also forced to confront major economic problems and to develop economic policies in response to them. But none of those leaders appeared to have developed any systematic understanding of the nature of economics, nor had they taken the leadership in the development of overall economic policy. Their efforts were confined to responding to particular problems with specific policy recommendations.

The complexity of twentieth century economic and social problems brought about a significant change in those responses. It was no longer simply solving a tariff question or handling a monetary crisis, but rather a broader spectrum of economic problems and dislocations with which Presidents were confronted. In the election of 1912 the national debate centered around economic policy, and all of the candidates developed or were forced to develop broad-ranged platforms on these issues. But the total collapse of the American economy in 1929, its catastrophic and pervasive impact on the society and its persistent duration, called for a level of understanding of the nature of the economic system and proposals designed to correct its shortcomings that went considerably beyond the scope of the problems faced by previous Presidents. Although he had taken a few undergraduate courses in economics and economic history at Harvard, and had also been a member of the Progressive Wilson administration, Franklin D. Roosevelt was hardly prepared to deal adequately with the deepset nature of the problems which confronted him in March 1933. When Roosevelt assumed the presidential office, three and one-half years of depression had disfigured the American economy beyond recognition, and had affected every American family, many to the point of almost complete starvation. The inspiring inaugural address and the declaration of the bank holiday gave rise to guarded optimism and hope, but those were mere promissory notes; the real job of coming to grips with the crisis still lay ahead.

The New Deal period has never received the serious economic study it deserves. There is no work of economic analysis comparable to Arthur Schlesinger, jr.'s superb political history of that era.[77] Schlesinger and most economists agree that John Maynard Keynes had only a modest and rather late influence in the development of economic policies during that period. The major New Deal innovations came before Keynes' seminal work, *The General Theory of Employment, Interest and Money*, appeared in 1936, and it was only in the twilight of what Schlesinger has called the "Second New Deal" and during World War II that people strongly influenced by Keynes came into positions of power and influence in the Roosevelt administration. Keynes' ideas were voiced around

Washington even in the early 1930s, but, although he urged the President to spend his way out of the Depression, and there were people in the Roosevelt administration who responded to his suggestion, consciously and unconsciously, it is clear that Roosevelt did not take Keynes' advice; budget deficits remained relatively small and the President continued to worry about balancing the budget. The New Deal was not firmly guided by any clear economic doctrine, Keynesian or otherwise, and the record of both its achievements and failures substantially supports this judgment.

Nevertheless Roosevelt made his own creative contribution to the growth of presidential power in the economic and human welfare areas. The radical departures of the New Deal were not part of any systematic economic theory. There simply was none, but Roosevelt was willing to use the power of the presidential office and the federal government to try to alleviate economic suffering and blight. Previous Presidents had concerned themselves with questions that touched various aspects of the national economy, but no other President had attempted to utilize the full strength of the federal agencies to draw together all of its independent strands of latent power to attack the economic ills of the country.

Keynes recognized the courage involved in these innovating efforts, even if he did not approve of the unsystematic and nontheoretical approach to the problem. At the end of 1933 he wrote to Roosevelt:

> You have made yourself the trustee for those in every country who seek to mend the evils of our condition by reasoned experiment within the framework of the existing social system.
>
> If you fail, rational change will be gravely prejudiced throughout the world leaving orthodoxy and revolution to fight it out.
>
> But, if you succeed, new and bolder methods will be tried everywhere, and we may date the first chapter of the new economic era from your accession to office.[78]

Keynes very prophetically indicated at an early date what the overall impact of the New Deal would be.

Once the bank crisis was relieved (see section four of this volume), Roosevelt moved in a number of other directions, seemingly all at the same time. He shored up the wavering relief situation by rushing through Congress a half-billion dollar appropriation to be channeled through the faltering and almost bankrupt state and local relief organizations. He got the Congress to approve a Civilian Conservation Corps, whose goal it was to employ a quarter of a million unemployed young men by that summer, working at various conservation projects throughout the country. Before the program was ended, two and one-half million Americans were involved, and they had done much to rehabilitate many of the neglected roads and forests of the country, and also in many cases their own health and personal faith in the future.

In rapid succession he proposed, and saw passed, three agricultural statutes: the Agricultural Adjustment Act, the Emergency Farm Mortgage Act and the Farm Credit Act. All three were designed to relieve the farmers' major problems by restoring farm income, protecting the farmer from mortgage foreclosures and making available essential credit. For labor and business Roosevelt introduced a complex program—the National Industrial Recovery Act, popularly known as the

NRA or the Blue Eagle—where codes were set up in each industry in an attempt to eliminate price cutting and to provide work for many unemployed. In addition Section 7a of this act asserted for the first time by law of the United States that labor had the right to organize into unions of its own choice. There were monetary reforms (Roosevelt quickly went off the gold standard); these included the Homeowners Loan Act, providing federal support for the refinancing of home mortgages; a series of banking and securities investment statutes, attempting to protect the depositor and the investor by regulation and insurance of bank deposits; and strict regulation of the security and stock markets. The Tennessee Valley Authority was launched with an ambitious program for the development of public power, flood control and scientific agricultural advances for depressed areas. Later on there were vast public works projects, social security legislation, a minimum wage law and the National Labor Relations Act, which was considered the magna carta for the industrial trade union movement and created an institutional framework for labor-management relations. The list is long and impressive, and represents a fantastic effort by the American President to mobilize the resources of the federal government to combat the severe effects of the Depression, to get the American economy moving again, and moreover, to get it moving in the direction of a more just and equitable distribution of the goods and resources of the society.

The general criticism of the New Deal, which the record appears to bear out, is that despite the tremendous effort to prop up the economic system and to overcome the industrial stagnation which had set in, the American economy was not basically affected by these activities. Keynesian economists maintain that their principles were never applied during the New Deal. Although the overall governmental outlays appeared to be large by comparison with other periods, they were in no way large enough, and increased national, state and local taxation negated their impact.[79] "For the most part, the Federal government engaged in a salvaging program and not in a program of national expansion."[80] Although some substantial improvements were made in a number of areas, real recovery came only after America's entry into World War II. Five years after Roosevelt became President, unemployment was still at the incredibly high rate of 19 percent, and dropped only 4.4 percent in the remaining two prewar years.[81] There were almost nine million men unemployed right up to the outbreak of the war.

This is not to say that the New Deal was a failure. If the economy was not turned right end up, at least people were fed, conditions did improve and the country was strengthened in thousands of ways by the creative use of resources, manpower and government funds during the period. Roosevelt and his associates were feeling their way, as Keynes observed, into a new economic era, an era where frequent depressions, mass unemployment, hunger and human misery could be eliminated if the imagination and determination to achieve those results were strongly present. Roosevelt was able to demonstrate dramatically that in an advanced industrial nation the population did not have to sit back and accept economic adversity with resignation, but could be mobilized by governmental activity and spending to meet immediate needs and to improve conditions, without disturbing the political and economic underpinnings of the society.

That was the beginning of the welfare state in this country, when the political leaders began or perhaps were forced to consider it their obligation to intervene in the affairs of men when those affairs were not providing the great masses of the people with a sufficient amount of material goods and services for a decent standard of living. The presidency emerged as a political office which took charge of forcefully directing such an effort, acquiring ideas, preparing legislation, enlisting support and mobilizing resources to accomplish the task. Even if the systematic economic theory to translate the principle of the state's responsibility in the area of human welfare into immediate tangible results was missing, no future President of the United States could ignore these new responsibilities. The Great Depression and the leadership of Franklin D. Roosevelt combined to create a new agenda for American politics—an agenda that not every successive President would admirably live up to, but one which all future Presidents would be forced to recognize and respond to on the level of their own understanding, abilities and political support. As the London *Economist* put it, "Mr. Roosevelt may have given the wrong answers to many of his problems, but he is at least the first President of modern America who has asked the right questions."[82]

The New Dealers were men of action who wanted to test their ideas in the exacting arena of everyday affairs. They lacked an overall economic theory and a comprehensive ideology; their total lack of a systematic philosophy of politics aroused even the contemptuous judgment of Leon Trotsky: "Your President abhors 'systems' and 'generalities.' Your philosophic method is even more antiquated than your economic system." Trotsky was identifying what Schlesinger has pointed to as the

great central source of its [the New Deal] energy . . . the instinctive contempt of practical, energetic, and compassionate people for dogmatic absolutes. Refusing to be transfixed by abstractions or to be overawed by ideology, the New Dealers responded by doing things.[83]

John Kenneth Galbraith suggested that Roosevelt possessed "what was more important than theory, and surely far more useful than bad theory, a set of intelligent economic attitudes."[84] However, the lack of a sound theoretical understanding of their own economic system prevented the New Dealers from taking the steps necessary to bring the country's major problems to a real solution. The President's wife, Eleanor Roosevelt, told the American Youth Congress that "the things that have been done . . . helped but they did not solve the fundamental problems."[85] Roosevelt's interesting and controversial secretary of agriculture, Henry A. Wallace, summed up the situation rather eloquently in Biblical terms:

We are children of the transition—we have left Egypt but we have not yet arrived at the Promised Land.[86]

John Maynard Keynes

The man who was to lead not only the United States but the rest of the industrialized free world into the economic Promised Land was John Maynard Keynes, the leading economic thinker of his century, perhaps of any century. Future generations will undoubtedly honor Keynes as the one most responsible for the amazing economic recovery of the western democracies in the aftermath of World War II. Economist Robert Lekachman wrote that the relationship between Keynesian doctrine and the New Deal was one of "tepid affection," but by the end of World War II, Keynes' reputation and influence in both academic and government circles had skyrocketed, and on the basis of his own and his followers' wartime performance in both Britain and the United States, Keynesian economists and Keynesian principles were firmly entrenched in Washington agencies and groups who were working on postwar economic planning.[87]

In his major work, *The General Theory of Employment, Interest and Money*, Keynes set out to examine and analytically reconstruct the basic principles upon which the free enterprise or capitalistic system operated. In so doing he had to reject many of the fundamental premises of classical economics. One of the most important of these was the *idée fixe* that there was no such thing as involuntary unemployment, that indeed when involuntary unemployment existed it was merely a transitory phenomenon. The experience of the Depression in the United States and Europe seemed to refute such a contention, but classical economics considered all unemployment either seasonal, frictional or voluntary. There was a theoretical wage, its protagonists argued, where it was marginally profitable for the manufacturer to expand his business and hire enough labor for increased production. Theoretically there was a wage figure which could allow all labor willing to be employed to be put to work, and an equilibrium which could be established between supply and demand within the system. Hence there could not be any involuntary employment, because the system could offer full employment at some wage, theoretical as it was.

Keynes realized how dubious this time-honored theory was, for it belied the evidence which the real world all around him could supply. There were millions of men unemployed, and that unemployment was anything but voluntary. The classical economists tried to explain such unemployment by the existence of the friction between trade unions and the monopoly or oligopoly, which interfered with the wage and price market and prevented equilibrium. Keynes recognized that such frictions did exist, that they did interfere normally with the free wage and price market, but that they hardly were responsible for producing the mass unemployment that existed during the 1930s.

He contended that an equilibrium did indeed exist between supply and demand, but there was nothing to dictate that that equilibrium could only be reached at a full employment level. The principal reason that the classical economists held to this theory was that in a free market atmosphere, they argued, there were no slippages. Everything that went into the economy, in terms of supply, was taken out in terms of demand. The fact that many businessmen and some laborers set aside part of their earnings for savings offered no difficulties for them, for savings were simply delayed purchases, investment and consumption of future goods in preference to present consumption. In fact savings were necessary in order to finance the expansion of capital. But Keynes persisted in his attack, and pointed out that the theory that all savings the economy could generate at full employment were automatically invested was in flat contradiction of everyday experience.

Investment was geared to many mercurial factors governing the human psyche, among other elements, which increased or decreased according to the day to day expectations of the investor. In fact he went on to postulate that it was the rate of investment that governed the whole equilibrium of the system and led either to full or underemployment. When subjective and objective factors governing investment were promising, savings were drawn into the investment field, business thrived and expanded and employment was high. When the same factors tended to discourage investment, all of these factors worked in reverse to decrease profits, reduce the level of employment and in general to lower the state of equilibrium of the market considerably below the level of full employment.

If this reasoning was valid, then the objective of a society which wanted to maintain full employment was to see to it that aggregate spending (including investment) remained at a high enough level to stretch the total economy to its maximum point of equilibrium. The national government, Keynes maintained, was the instrument, and the only possible instrument, for directing and controlling such economic activity, because it was the only institution in the society which was both devoted to the general welfare and powerful enough to perform this function.

The argument between Keynes and the classical economists during the Great Depression was based upon the postulates contained in this analysis. Some classical economists argued that the return to equilibrium (and hence full employment) could only be stimulated by further reduction of wages, so that the market would reach a point where it became profitable to employ every man willing to work. Keynes pointed out that the major fallacy in such thinking was that while it might be theoretically valid in a single case and an individual employer might continue to reduce the cost of labor so that it became profitable both to produce more goods and to hire more labor, when such reductions were introduced throughout the entire economy, it resulted in a general depression of aggregate demand, producing a regressive effect upon the market and more rather than less unemployment.

Keynes' solution, then, for a society that wanted to maintain full employment, was to scrap the concept of attempting to reach a frictionless mythical equilibrium through the automatic operation of a so-called free market, an equilibrium which incidentally did not even in theory guarantee full employment at the lowest possible wage, and to opt for sufficient economic controls by the state to maintain a high level of aggregate demand. This could be achieved partially through monetary policy or the adjusting of national interest rates (what the British called the Bank rate), but would also need to rely upon fiscal policy, which involved changes in tax rates and public investment. After 1945 very few of Keynes' basic postulates were in serious dispute among major economists. The question was rather the degree to which any particular government was willing to refine and apply these principles to its day to day economic policy.

The major advance in the role of the science of economics and of the economists who practiced it in the policymaking councils of government in this country did not come during the New Deal, but with the passage of the Full Employment Act of 1946. President Truman remarked on the occasion of the statute's tenth anniversary that there "is almost no other piece of domestic legislation enacted while I was President to which I would attach equal significance."[88] The law as it was passed, however, was a marked departure from the initial proposal, which was a clear and forthright effort to introduce Keynesian concepts into the decision-making level of the structure of the American government.

The initial draft of the Full Employment Act was permeated with the Keynesian viewpoint of governmental responsibility in maintaining full employment. In the declaration of policy introducing the specific implementation clauses of the bill, the following objectives appeared, among others:

> All Americans able to work and seeking work have the right to useful, remunerative, regular, and full-time employment, and it is the policy of the United States to assure the existence at all times of sufficient employment opportunities to enable all Americans who have finished their schooling and who do not have full-time housekeeping responsibilities freely to exercise this right.[89]
>
> . . . it is the responsibility of the Federal Government to pursue such consistent and openly arrived at economic policies and programs as will stimulate and encourage the highest feasible levels of employment opportunities through private and other non-Federal investment and expenditure; (e) To the extent that continuing full employment cannot otherwise be achieved, it is the further responsibility of the Federal Government to provide such volume of Federal investment and expenditure as may be needed to assure continuing full employment.[90]

To implement these objectives, the bill proposed an annual "National Production and Employment Budget" which would be presented to the Congress at the beginning of each session and would provide a forecast of the sizes of the labor force, private investment, government expenditure and consumer expenditure during the coming year. On the basis of those estimates, it was then incumbent upon the President to "set forth in such a Budget a general program for preventing inflationary economic dislocations, or diminishing the aggregate volume of investment and expenditure to the level required to assure a full employment volume of production or both."[91] There were, of course, the expected genuflections to the home, the hearth and the private enterprise system, but it was clear that if the private sector failed to maintain the maximum level of employment, the federal government should be prepared to assume the burden.

In the course of a two year struggle to guide the bill through the Congress (realistically described in Stephen Bailey's *Congress Makes A Law*), its cutting edge was substantially blunted by an effectively mobilized opposition of special interest groups—the law which emerged in 1946 was an emasculated version of the original proposal. It substituted for the national full employment budget, an annual report to be presented to the Congress by the President—a report which was to review and analyze current economic conditions and to outline governmental measures consistent with a new definition of goals which had a very different emphasis than the original objectives:

The Congress hereby declares that it is the CONTINUING policy and

responsibility of the Federal Government TO USE ALL PRAC-
TICABLE MEANS *consistent with its needs and obligations and other
essential considerations of national policy* WITH THE ASSISTANCE
AND COOPERATION of industry, agriculture, labor and State and
local governments, TO COORDINATE AND UTILIZE ALL ITS
PLANS, FUNCTIONS, AND RESOURCES FOR THE PURPOSE OF
CREATING AND MAINTAINING, IN A MANNER CALCU-
LATED to foster and PROMOTE free competitive enterprise and the
general welfare, CONDITIONS UNDER WHICH THERE WILL BE
AFFORDED *useful employment*, FOR THOSE able, WILLING, and
seeking to work, *and* TO PROMOTE *maximum* EMPLOYMENT,
PRODUCTION, AND PURCHASING POWER.[92]

The simple but powerful concept of the federal government's responsibility for
full employment was obviously seriously modified in the compromise statute, and
the notion of an annual full employment budget, complete with proposals for
government expenditures (when necessary) was removed. The qualifications which
defined the contours of the annual economic report were quite different than the
abandoned concept of a full employment budget. The new bill did, however, create
a Council of Economic Advisors (CEA) to the President, whose very presence
within the Executive office would in time at least partially compensate for the loss of
stronger language in the 1946 law. The council was to be composed of individuals
each of "Whom Shall Be A Person Who, As A Result Of His Training, Experience
And Attainments, Is Exceptionally Qualified To Analyze And Interpret Economic
Developments, to appraise programs and activities of the Government" in the light
of the objectives of the law, and "To Formulate And Recommend National
Economic Policy To Promote Employment, Production And Purchasing Power
Under Free Competitive Enterprise."[93] A determined President, acting on the
advice of such professional economic advisors, could and ultimately would restore
vitality to the concept of full employment in the guise of a more comprehensive and
sophisticated concept—full economic growth. A President could use this advice to
transform the economic report into a charter for a revision of economic thinking
and an outline of governmental policies designed to achieve new objectives. But it
took almost 20 years to accomplish this change.

The council got off to a somewhat slow start under its first chairman, Edwin G.
Nourse, a moderately conservative economist who had spent most of his working
years in Washington with the Brookings Institution. Nourse held a restricted view
of the role of the council, arguing that it should limit itself to providing the President
with economic analysis and advice with respect to policy formation. He was
strongly opposed to the council involving itself in policymaking or formulating
policy decisions per se, an action which broadened strictly economic questions into
social and political considerations. He was also strongly opposed to members of the
council testifying before congressional committees, with the exception of the
Appropriations Committee of the House. The other two members of the original
council, John D. Clark and Leon H. Keyserling, both of whom were activists,
disagreed sharply with Nourse on his views with regard to the limited function of the

council in making and defending presidential economic policy, and also with many other of his conservative views.

These disagreements finally led to an open break, with Nourse resigning after three difficult years of presiding over a divided council. The disagreement itself, however, was critical to the future influence of the Council of Economic Advisors, and it is significant that Keyserling and Clark's functional definition of the role of the council prevailed. Nourse later expressed his views on the question as follows:

> The sharpest difference between me and my colleagues was that I differentiated clearly between economic analysis and political synthesis. Keyserling and Clark wanted to be policymakers. But I saw the Council as an apex of economic thought, with us processing problems for the President's consideration. Our role is to give the President a notion of how professional economic thought was dividing on a question, and then give him our best judgment on it. If the President, for political considerations, formulated a policy that led to bad economic policy, the role of the Council was then to show him the least bad way to apply bad policy. . . .
>
> [T]he economist must be spiritually capable of bringing the choicest pearls of scientific work to cast before the politically motivated and politically conditioned policy makers of the executive branch. He must be prepared to see these carefully fabricated materials rejected or distorted, and still carry on the same process of preparation and submission again tomorrow, unperturbed and unabashed. He must all the while be aware that his professional brethren and the public will hold him accountable for the final compromised product while he, by virtue of his relationship with the Executive office, is estopped from saying anything in explanation or vindication of his own workmanship.[94]

Testifying before the Joint Committee on the Economic Report of the President, Keyserling gave his very different view of the role of members of the council as far as participating in public discussion of the President's policies was concerned:

> [A]fter the Presidential message in question and the recommendations contained therein are sent to the Congress . . . it has been practically the universal custom and is entirely appropriate for those officials whose statutory responsibility makes it clear that they have been advisors to the President in the field covered by such Presidential message and recommendations to appear before such congressional committees, to discuss and analyze the matters involved, and in fact to amplify and support recommendations made by the President and the analysis underlying it. In addition, it has been almost the universal custom and entirely appropriate for such officials to appear before congressional committees, and to make analyses and give advice in the fields in which they operate under statute, even when this has not been preceded by a Presidential message.
>
> . . . That this construction of the Council's role is correct is supported by the legislative history of the Employment Act, by the expressed views of

some of the sponsors of the Act, by the fact that the Joint Committee on the Economic Report and other congressional committees have frequently invited the members of the Council to appear before them for this purpose, and by the fact that doing so is in accord with the Council's responsibilities as defined by the President. More important, it is in accord with the whole tenor of the American system of government, and I believe it a good and healthy thing that public officials should be subjected to the questioning and testing of their views by congressional committees, particularly when these public officials have been appointed and confirmed under acts of Congress to deal with the very subject matters which these committees are considering and to help in the preparation of the very reports and recommendations which the President sends to these committees.

. . . I believe that members of the Council of Economic Advisors are in exactly the same position, with respect to expressing themselves frankly and fully before congressional committees, as any other agency heads of integrity who have advised the President in important fields in which the President makes recommendations to the Congress. Under our system, no responsible official in such a position, while working for the President, parades before the public or before congressional committees the differences of viewpoint that there may be between himself and the President on matters under consideration by the Congress. If these differences are minor in character, the responsible public official does not feel entitled to the luxury of self-satisfaction of having the President agree with him in every detail; government could not function if that were expected. But if the President, in his recommendations to the Congress, were to depart from the analysis and advice given him by the official in question to the extent that it would be regarded as a fundamental repudiation of that official's views, the official of integrity should resign where under all the circumstances he believes it in the national interest to do so.[95]

The problems of the early council were further complicated by Nourse's inability to communicate with President Truman. Edward Flash, jr., in his detailed study of the council from its inception, indicates that Nourse's contacts with the President were infrequent, off-hand, indirect and generally unsatisfactory. Nourse pointed out that he had no trouble obtaining an appointment with the President, but was unhappy about what took place after he arrived in the Oval Office:

[T]he President was always very gracious, friendly and nice—too nice, in fact. He wasn't business-like enough. He'd tell me what had happened on his walk that morning, or tell me chit-chat about his family—wasting minutes of this precious appointment. As I think back, I can honestly say that I think I never had a real intellectual exchange with the President, that I was opening my mind to analysis with him, that he was following me. And the situation wasn't much better when I sent him reports. On the occasion when we turned in a majority and minority report the President took them and said, "Thank you for making this report. I'll study it with great care." But the next day he saw Clark Clifford [a presidential assistant] in the morning and he said, "Well, I asked these guys for a report, and they gave me two reports. You take them and see if you can make anything out of them." You see, that was the frustrating part of it. I felt there was little opportunity to become more effective.[96]

Once again Keyserling had very different ideas on the subject:

Dr. Nourse was simply unable to adjust himself to the nature and the problems of the Presidency. He could never understand that the President of the United States has too many things to do to engage in long bull sessions on economics of the kind that took place at The Brookings Institution. He could never understand that the President must delegate, must have confidence in his principal officers, and that these officers have not just cause for complaint when the President not only remains accessible to them but also accepts practically everything that they recommend to him.[97]

After three trying years Nourse resigned and was replaced as chairman by Keyserling. It is ironic, in view of the discussion above, that the events that led up to his resignation involved a number of public speeches he made in which he was critical of the economic policies of the Truman administration. After he left however, the council was cohesive and enjoyed considerable influence and success.

The outbreak of the Korean War presented a real opportunity for the expansion of economic policy, but Truman's loss of public support during the steel crisis and his dwindling political capital in his last months in office, steadily weakened the power and influence of his economic advisors.

Despite the Truman accolade ten years later, he has only one slight reference to the council in his two-volume, 1000-page *Memoirs*. Histories of the Truman administration, like that of Cabell Phillips, make only the briefest of references to it, and in general its accomplishments were minimal. Under Nourse very little was accomplished, but in the second period under the leadership of Keyserling it did have a great impact upon wartime economic planning and activities, such as wage and price controls, excess profit taxes and mobilization problems. But neither the Nourse or Keyserling councils was really part of the magic White House circle, and Flash's considered judgment that the council was welcomed, on balance, more as a distant cousin than as an established member of the family seems accurate.

President Eisenhower appointed another conservative as his council chairman, Professor Arthur F. Burns of Columbia University. Burns was an extremely able man, who developed a very close and confidential relationship with Eisenhower during his over four years as chairman of the CEA, but as an economist, he was classified as empirical or inductive, with a strong anti-Keynesian bent. Both he and the President shared a more or less liberal conservative outlook, and Burns' position was fortified by his professional competence and standing within the profession, lending a certain prestige to an administration which was heavily populated with men of little academic or governmental experience.

Despite Burns' relatively influential role in policymaking, he tended to adapt his proposals to the prevailing sentiments of not only Eisenhower but also his big-business-oriented cabinet. He conceived of his role more as that of a top level source of accurate, detailed, and up to the minute economic data, than as a policy innovator with determined theories and proposals of his own. The overall by-word during Burns' tenure as chairman, and that of his successor, fellow Columbia and Barnard economics professor, J. Raymond Saulnier, was "caution." These two economic advisors to President Eisenhower recommended a cautious approach to the recessions of 1953-54 and 1957, and the mild period of inflation in 1956 and early 1957. Burns himself was extremely candid and objective in evaluating the role of the council in the recovery from the recession of 1954-55. With reference to a series of very modest proposals for accelerated federal spending which the administration adopted, Burns later wrote:

> The rescheduling of expenditures for the fiscal year 1955 was delayed in execution and became effective when no longer needed.[98]

In short the Burns and Saulnier era was one in which the council developed a very close and responsible relationship with the Chief Executive, and a modest but significant influence in recommending proposals which were fundamentally in line with the prevailing economic views of the major figures in the administration. No really innovative measures were introduced, but Burns and his successor were able to claim that they had succeeded in preventing recessions from lengthening into full-fledged depressions and holding inflation to within reasonable limits. This period was not one of dynamic economic growth and development, but was marked by the steady increase of unemployment, as well as the continued limited use and development of existing industrial facilities.

Burns' major impact as chairman of the CEA was in giving the "President's program unity," within the framework of their jointly held "basic and inseparable" tenets of restricted government interference, i.e.,

> the relative efficiency of competitive markets, compared with government directives, for organizing production and consumption; widely shared confidence as a prerequisite to the generation of jobs and income; maximum encouragement to and minimum interference with the private economy on the part of the federal government; reliance in anticyclical policy upon indirect influence on private behavior rather than direct control; federal government collaboration with the states in promoting research and providing public facilities; and federal assistance in cooperation with states and localities in helping "less fortunate citizens" with problems of unemployment, illness, old age and blighted neighborhoods.[99]

President Kennedy Leads an Economic Revolution

In the administration of John F. Kennedy both Keynes and the Council of

Economic Advisors came into their own. For the first time in our history the White House was inhabited by a President who was willing (and able) to sit down and learn modern post-Keynesian economics, and though his progress was slow and his convictions hesitant, he finally threw his support behind an economic policy which was based upon advanced modern economic theory, and in practice was successful in securing an unprecedented period of economic growth in our domestic economy.

Kennedy's CEA chairman, Walter Heller, came to the White House from the chairmanship of the department of economics at the University of Minnesota, where he had earned a reputation in his field as a tax specialist, as one interested in operations as opposed to theory, and a firm believer in aggregate demand as a means of achieving economic growth and full employment. Heller was quite familiar with governmental operations, having been in and out of governmental service several times during his teaching career, and having served as a consultant to a number of important governmental and quasi-governmental committees. His associates, James Tobin and Kermit Gordon, were also academic economists, but both had also held previous government positions and were active consultants to governmental bureaus and private foundations operating in the field of economic development and research. All three had outstanding reputations among their peers, the country's professional economists, and although their special interests varied—Tobin being primarily interested in theory, while Gordon was inclined towards practical operations—they shared a strong conviction concerning the active role of government in fostering economic growth through the development of aggregate demand. If their predecessors were characterized as liberal Conservatives, perhaps Heller, Tobin and Gordon could be described as conservative Liberals.

When Kennedy assumed office he was faced with serious economic problems. The country was in the throes of its third recession within 10 years, and the unemployment rate had skyrocketed to an abnormal 6.8 percent of the labor force. On top of that the United States was experiencing an unfavorable balance of payments crisis which imposed certain limitations upon the measures that could be used in combating the recession. During the 1960 presidential campaign Kennedy presented both a simplified conception and solution of the domestic economic problem by constantly referring to the slow rate of economic growth during the Eisenhower years and urging the American voter that "we must get moving again." Indeed there was a decided drop in the rate of economic growth during the years immediately preceding the 1960 campaign—2.3 percent compared with the Truman period of 1947-53, which had a growth rate of 4.6 percent. However, there were explanations for such a significant differential.[100]

Economic growth is measured by gain in the gross national product (GNP) from year to year. If the period selected had been from 1945 to 1953 instead of 1947-53, the growth rate would have been seen to drop considerably because of the cutback in military production, dating from the end of World War II. By 1947 industrial production was beginning to catch up with the renewed demand for civilian goods created by the austerity of the war years, both in this country and Western Europe. The British Loan and the Marshall Plan further stimulated production, while the Korean War continued to pump additional stimulus into the domestic economy. It is no wonder that at the end of the Korean War the gross national product returned to a more modest annual rate of gain. It was simply Eisenhower's misfortune to inherit this condition. When compared with the average rate of gain based on the overall industrial performance in this century, the 1953-59 period was fairly standard.

What had changed, however, were the population, which boomed in this country after World War II, and the radical developments of automation. To keep up with both these developments, considerably more than the normal rate of economic growth was essential, and Eisenhower and his economic advisors failed to deal decisively or imaginatively with that problem. Their cautious measures perhaps blunted the more destructive aspects of the three Eisenhower recessions, but by no means came to terms with the fundamental causes of these periodic crises, which got progressively more serious and lengthy and created each time a higher residue of unemployment. Furthermore the American economic growth rate during that period lagged considerably behind that of most of the other industrial nations of the world, and it was estimated to be close to one-third the rate of growth of the Soviet economy.[101] For all of these reasons Kennedy made the economy one of the central points of his campaign, referring to it in over 20 speeches; once in office he was, of course, anxious to do something significant about it.

For all of his bravado on the issue of economic growth during his campaign, Kennedy was not completely convinced that his Keynesian economic advisors had all the answers and could pull off the necessary miracle of doubling the economic growth rate in order to take up the slack in the economy and to cut back the mounting rate of unemployment. The President had earned only a C grade[102] in his single economics course at Harvard (taught, incidentally, by a man who later became a left-wing CIO union official), and his friend, Seymour Harris, chairman of the economics department at Harvard, indicated that Kennedy "at first seemed allergic to modern economics."[103] Kennedy in his senatorial days once confided to Theodore Sorensen "that he could remember the difference between fiscal policy, dealing with budgets and taxes, and monetary policy, dealing with money and credit, only by reminding himself that the name of the man most in charge of monetary policy, Federal Reserve Board Chairman William McChesney Martin, jr., began with an "M" as in "monetary."[104] On his first meeting with Walter Heller during the 1960 campaign Kennedy asked him skeptically:

Do you really think we can make good on that promise . . . of a five per cent rate of growth?[105]

But as President, Kennedy became an apt pupil of the outstanding economists who surrounded him. In addition to his able Council of Economic Advisors, he received a good deal of advice from Paul Samuelson of MIT, Seymour Harris of Harvard, and, of course, John Kenneth Galbraith, who was his ambassador to India, but who continued to bombard him with economic analysis and advice. All of these men were modern Keynesian or post-Keynesian economists, but rather unusually, most of them had considerable interest and experience in both politics and government, and they realized that logical and sound economic policy frequently had to be tempered by political considerations beyond the power of the President to control.

Kennedy, as Sorensen has pointed out, was "confronted with a delicate and dangerous imbalance of payments, an 'independent' Federal Reserve Board, and a conservative coalition in Congress." In addition he had a Republican secretary of the treasury, Douglas Dillon, who had been appointed, at least in part, in an attempt to instill confidence in the new administration within the business community. Finally he was thoroughly aware of the marginal nature of his campaign victory, and rightly or wrongly he did not believe he could go too far too quickly.

In the interregnum, Kennedy, as President-elect, appointed a special task force headed by Samuelson to provide him with a report on the economy. In his first State of the Union Message the President used the Samuelson report as background for a series of proposals he made three days later in a comprehensive economic message. In his State of the Union Message the President reported:

> The present state of our economy is disturbing. We take office in the wake of seven months of recession, three and one half years of slack, seven years of diminished economic growth, and nine years of falling farm income. . . .
>
> Save for a brief period in 1958, insured unemployment is at the highest peak in our history. Of some five and one-half million Americans who are without jobs, more than one million have been searching for work for more than four months. . . .
>
> In short, the American economy is in trouble. The most resourceful industrialized country on earth ranks among the last in the rate of economic growth. Since last spring our economic growth rate has actually receded. Business investment is in a decline. Profits have fallen below predicted levels. Construction is off. A million unsold automobiles are in inventory. Fewer people are working, and the average work week has shrunk well below forty hours. . . .
>
> This Administration does not intend to stand helplessly by . . . to waste idle hours and empty plants while awaiting the end of the recession. . . .[106]

Samuelson and most of his colleagues were probably convinced that a substantial tax cut and a public works program would give the economy the shot in the arm it needed, but they did not propose such radical remedies at that time. Fully aware of the President's political situation and appreciative of the limitations on the options available to him, the MIT economist recommended a series of measures aimed at increasing aggregate demand without necessarily creating a budget deficit. The new President's predecessor had so thoroughly inundated the American public with his strong emphasis upon the desirability of a balanced budget (although his administration set a peacetime record in deficits—$12.9 billion in 1959) that it would have taken extremely strong convictions with regard to deficit financing for Kennedy to challenge that principle immediately. President Kennedy had no such convictions when he entered the White House; in fact he was inclined to favor a balanced budget, all other things being equal. Nor was he eager to propose a deficit in his first budget, and he shied away from measures which would lead to it. The Samuelson report, however, was revolutionary in the sense that the President had called upon a number of the nation's leading economists to analyze the state of the economy and to recommend policies at the outset of his administration. These were economists who were very frankly Keynesian in their approach, and who were willing to emphasize the long-term importance of economic growth and to restore the almost forgotten concept of the late 1940s—full employment.

Samuelson initially outlined what he termed "first line of defense policies," measures justified on their own merit and in need of immediate attention and action by the administration "to bring the recession to an end, to reinstate a condition of expansion and recovery" and to make sure that such expansion "would not after a year or two peter out at levels of activity far below our true potential."[107] Samuelson's "second line of defense policies" dealt essentially with longer-range policies, in particular, a tax cut recommendation. Under the former he included the expansion and development of broader and more adequate unemployment compensation, more education programs (which included school construction, higher rates of pay for teachers, construction of college dormitories, etc.), urban renewal projects, useful public works, aid to depressed areas, development and conservation of national resources, residential housing construction, and making available, at lower rates of interest, long-term credit. "The second line of defense policies" focused exclusively on a temporary tax cut of four or five percent in the event that economic indices continued to decline in the early months of 1961 and unemployment continued to rise. Under those conditions the Samuelson report urged a temporary tax cut in March or April, with authorization for the President to extend the period for one or two 3-6 month periods if necessary.[108]

The Kennedy administration accepted most of the first line of defense proposals in the Samuelson report, and a month later in his economic message to the Congress the President recommended a series of stop-gap measures which would pump more money into the flagging economy and meet some of the immediately critical human needs of those in distress. He proposed legislation "(1) to add a temporary thirteen week supplement to unemployment benefits; (2) to extend aid to the children of unemployed workers; (3) to redevelop distressed areas; (4) to increase Social Security payments and encourage earlier retirement; (5) to raise the minimum wage and broaden its coverage; (6) to provide emergency relief to feed grain farmers; and (7) to finance a comprehensive home-building and slum clearance program."[109] Sorensen observes that those measures resulted in additional governmental expenditures of over one and one-half billion dollars, and the creation of an estimated 420,000 construction jobs.[110]

The President, without congressional approval and under his own executive authority,

> directed all Federal agencies to accelerate their procurement and construction, particularly in labor surplus areas. He compressed a long range program of post office construction into the first six months, released over a billion dollars in state highway funds ahead of schedule, raised farm price supports and advanced their payment, and speeded up the distribution of tax refunds and GI life insurance dividends. To expand credit and stimulate building, he ordered a reduction in the maximum

permissible interest rate on FHA-insured loans, lowered the interest rate on Small Business Administration loans in distressed areas, expanded its available credit and liberalized lending by the Federal Home Loan Banks. To aid the unemployed, he broadened the distribution of surplus food, directed that preference be given distressed areas in defense contracts, created a "pilot" Food Stamp program for the needy and expanded the services of the U.S. Employment Offices. Finally, he encouraged the Federal Reserve Board to keep long-term interest rates low through the purchase of long-term government issues.[111]

The cumulative impact of these measures was, in all probability, significant towards developing the mild recovery that became noticeable in the spring of 1961. But it was also clear that Kennedy had not yet embraced the new economics whole-heartedly, that he was willing to utilize and expand existing programs, and in some instances initiate supplementary efforts to already established institutional activities and approaches by pumping additional federal money into the economy; yet he was still reluctant to fully accept the broader implications of Keynesian doctrines. Samuelson's second line had included a tax cut, but Kennedy backed away from this kind of Keynesian proposal. In fact during the summer of 1961 he came "dangerously close" to introducing a tax increase to offset the increased domestic expenditures and additional military appropriations prompted by the Berlin Crisis.[112] Such a policy was in sharp contradiction with the advice of Heller and the council, who along with Samuelson favored a tax cut from the beginning, and were appalled by Kennedy's references throughout the year to the attempt of the administration to stay within the limits of a balanced budget. Walter Heller concludes that "judged only in terms of policies actually proposed and adopted, modern economics established a firm beachhead on the New Frontier, but not much more, in 1961."[113]

Kennedy's early timidity in proposing the more extreme remedies of the new economics was a by-product of his essentially conservative or cautious temperament (after all his favorite biography was Lord Cecil's study of Melbourne), his marginal political victory, and his still hesitant attitude toward the new economics. He was determined to act with great restraint if the recession could be arrested within the framework of accepted policy. Writing of Kennedy's attitude, Heller quoted Norton Long, who long ago pointed out that

> both the limits of popular knowledge and the relation of popularly accepted values to permissible practice are basic conditions defining the politically feasible.[114]

Heller and his colleagues on the Council of Economic Advisors were very much aware of the political limits of economic policymaking, but they were anxious to attack the lag in economic growth by stimulating the economy to greater expansion while it was struggling to recover, rather than waiting until the danger signals of another recession appeared. Kennedy, on the other hand, restrained by his cautious Republican secretary of the treasury, Douglas Dillon, was reluctant to use this unfamiliar weapon unless the need was urgent—urgent enough to build the political support essential to its passage. Moreover, during the first year in office, the President lacked sufficient confidence in modern economic theory and practice to risk everything on the projections of theoretical estimates and conjectures.

But several things happened in the spring and summer of 1962 which led the President to revise his initial objections. The first was the crisis brought about by the increase in the price of steel and the subsequent breach between the business community and the administration. This was followed in several months by a rapid decline in the stock market, triggered by the dramatic crash of May 28, 1962, the worst day on the stock exchange since 1929. No causal relationship is to be inferred by linking these events. They simply highlighted the "pause" in the economic recovery during this period and caused the President and his secretary of the treasury to look with more favor on the proposals of his economic advisors, which they had ignored for more than a year.

Increased public concern over the plight of the economy and mounting pressures for a tax cut from the AFL-CIO and economists outside of government like Samuelson and his colleague, Robert Solow, created a general climate of agonizing reappraisal, during which Sorensen indicates the President sceptically and perhaps even reluctantly decided on a tax cut for 1963 in early June of 1962. But he did that only after Dillon and other critics had been appeased by the combination of the proposal with plans for major tax revisions. Kennedy had invited the powerful chairman of the House Ways and Means Committee (Wilbur Mills) to sit in on the decisive meetings with his economic advisors in August, and Mills had insisted on tax reform in return for his support for a tax cut in 1963. The President believed that a tax "package" of this nature would better satisfy the Congress, although he was also extremely sceptical about its chances of passing. He was not yet completely convinced of the necessity of an immediate cut, feeling that the economic indicators were too indecisive, and that such a proposal without first building public support would run the risk of a disastrous defeat in Congress.

While he agonized over this problem he delivered a remarkable commencement address at Yale University, which must go down as the most brilliant and illuminating statement on economic problems ever made by a President of the United States. In it he dealt with the myths which hinder the public and the business ccommunity from really understanding the nature of the economy and its problems. Those myths, the President indicated, "relate not to basic clashes of philosophy or ideology but to ways and means of reaching common goals—to research for sophisticated solutions to complex and obstinate issues."[115] He spoke of the myth and fear of the size and shape of government, of budget deficits, of the public debt, of public confidence. The speech, Walter Heller has written, "put Presidential economic discourse on a wholly new plane," and his economic advisors were agreed that it "marked a new era in American economic policy."[116]

They were right. The President profited from his tutorials and memoranda from his council; in return he was attempting to educate his constituents, the American people, to a level of economic understanding requisite for acting responsibly on economic questions in mid-twentieth century America.

President John F. Kennedy
The Yale Address
1962

Public Papers of the Presidents: John F. Kennedy, 1962 (Washington, D.C., 1963), 470-75.

President Griswold, members of the faculty, graduates and their families, ladies and gentlemen: Let me begin by expressing my appreciation for the very deep honor that you have conferred upon me. As General de Gaulle occasionally acknowledges America to be the daughter of Europe, so I am pleased to come to Yale, the daughter of Harvard. It might be said now that I have the best of both worlds, a Harvard education and a Yale degree.

I am particularly glad to become a Yale man because as I think about my troubles, I find that a lot of them have come from other Yale men. Among businessmen, I have had a minor disagreement with Roger Blough, of the law school class of 1931, and I have had some complaints, too, from my friend Henry Ford, of the class of 1940. In journalism I seem to have a difference with John Hay Whitney, of the class of 1926—and sometimes I also displease Henry Luce of the class of 1920, not to mention also William F. Buckley, Jr., of the class of 1950. I even have some trouble with my Yale advisers. I get along with them, but I am not always sure how they get along with each other.

I have the warmest feelings for Chester Bowles of the class of 1924, and for Dean Acheson of the class of 1915, and my assistant, McGeorge Bundy, of the class of 1940. But I am not 100 percent sure that these three wise and experienced Yale men wholly agree with each other on every issue.

So this administration which aims at peaceful cooperation among all Americans has been the victim of a certain natural pugnacity developed in this city among Yale men. Now that I, too, am a Yale man, it is time for peace. Last week at West Point, in the historic tradition of that Academy, I availed myself of the powers of Commander in Chief to remit all sentences of offending cadets. In that same spirit, and in the historic tradition of Yale, let me now offer to smoke the clay pipe of friendship with all of my brother Elis, and I hope that they may be friends not only with me but even with each other.

In any event, I am very glad to be here and as a new member of the club, I have been checking to see what earlier links existed between the institution of the Presidency and Yale. I found that a member of the class of 1878, William Howard Taft, served one term in the White House as preparation for becoming a member of this faculty. And a graduate of 1804, John C. Calhoun, regarded the Vice Presidency, quite naturally, as too lowly a status for a Yale alumnus—and became the only man in history to ever resign that office.

Calhoun in 1804 and Taft in 1878 graduated into a world very different from ours today. They and their contemporaries spent entire careers stretching over 40 years in grappling with a few dramatic issues on which the Nation was sharply and emotionally divided, issues that occupied the attention of a generation at a time: the national bank, the disposal of the public lands, nullification or union, freedom or slavery, gold or silver. Today these old sweeping issues very largely have disappeared. The central domestic issues of our time are more subtle and less simple. They relate not to basic clashes of philosophy or ideology but to ways and means of reaching common goals—to research for sophisticated solutions to complex and obstinate issues. The world of Calhoun, the world of Taft had its own hard problems and notable challenges. But its problems are not our problems. Their age is not our age. As every past generation has had to disenthrall itself from an inheritance of truisms and stereotypes, so in our own time we must move on from the reassuring repetition of stale phrases to a new, difficult, but essential confrontation with reality.

For the great enemy of the truth is very often not the lie—deliberate, contrived, and dishonest—but the myth—persistent, persuasive, and unrealistic. Too often we hold fast to the cliches of our forebears. We subject all facts to a prefabricated set of interpretations. We enjoy the comfort of opinion without the discomfort of thought.

Mythology distracts us everywhere—in government as in business, in politics as in economics, in foreign affairs as in domestic affairs. But today I want to particularly consider the myth and reality in our national economy. In recent months many have come to feel, as I do, that the dialog between the parties— between business and government, between the government and the public—is clogged by illusion and platitude and fails to reflect the true realities of contemporary American society.

I speak of these matters here at Yale because of the self-evident truth that a great university is always enlisted against the spread of illusion and on the side of reality. No one has said it more clearly than your President Griswold: "Liberal learning is both a safeguard against false ideas of freedom and a source of true ones." Your role as university men, whatever your calling, will be to increase each new generation's grasp of its duties.

There are three great areas of our domestic affairs in which, today, there is a danger that illusion may prevent effective action. They are, first, the question of the size and the shape of government's responsibilities; second, the question of public fiscal policy; and third, the matter of confidence, business confidence or public confidence, or simply confidence in America. I want to talk about all three, and I want to talk about them carefully and dispassionately—and I emphasize that I am concerned here not with political debate but with finding ways to separate false problems from real ones.

If a contest in angry argument were forced upon it, no administration could shrink from response, and history does not suggest that American Presidents are totally without resources in an engagement forced upon them because of hostility in one sector of society. But in the wider national interest, we need not partisan wrangling but common concentration on common problems. I come here to this distinguished university to ask you to join in this great task.

Let us take first the question of the size and shape of government. The myth here is that government is big, and bad—and steadily getting bigger and worse. Obviously this myth has some excuse for existence. It is true that in recent history each new administration has spent much more money that its predecessor. Thus President Roosevelt outspent President Hoover, and with allowances for the special case of the Second World War, President Truman outspent President Roosevelt. Just to prove that this was not a partisan matter, President Eisenhower then outspent President Truman by the handsome figure of $182 billion. It is even possible, some think, that this trend may continue.

But does it follow from this that big government is growing relatively bigger? It does not—for the fact is for the last 15 years, the Federal Government—and also the Federal debt—and also the Federal bureaucracy—have grown less rapidly than the economy as a whole. If we leave defense and space expenditures aside, the Federal Government since the Second World War has expanded less than any other major sector of our national life—less than industry, less than commerce, less than agriculture, less than higher education, and very much less than the noise about big government.

The truth about big government is the truth about any other great activity—it is complex. Certainly it is true that size brings dangers—but it is also true that size can bring benefits. Here at Yale which has contributed so much to our national progress in science and medicine, it may be proper for me to mention one great and little noticed expansion of government which has brought strength to our whole society—the new role of our Federal Government as the major patron of research in science and in medicine. Few people realize that in 1961, in support of all university research in science and medicine, three dollars out of every four came from the Federal Government. I need hardly point out that this has taken place without undue enlargement of Government control—that American scientists remain second to none in their independence and in their individualism.

I am not suggesting that Federal expenditures cannot bring some measure of control. The whole thrust of Federal expenditures in agriculture have been related by purpose and design to control, as a means of dealing with the problems created by our farmers and our growing productivity. Each sector, my point is, of activity must be approached on its own merits and in terms of specific national needs. Generalities in regard to Federal expenditures, therefore, can be misleading—each case, science, urban renewal, education, agriculture, natural resources, each case must be determined on its merits if we are to profit from our unrivaled ability to combine the strength of public and private purpose.

Next, let us turn to the problem of our fiscal policy. Here the myths are legion and the truth hard to find. But let me take as a prime example the problem of the Federal budget. We persist in measuring our Federal fiscal integrity today by the conventional or administrative budget—with results which would be regarded as absurd in any business firm—in any country of Europe—or in any careful assessment of the reality of our national finances. The administrative budget has sound administrative uses. But for wider purposes it is less helpful. It omits our special trust funds and the effect that they have on our economy; it neglects changes in assets or inventories. It cannot tell a loan from a straight expenditure—and worst of all it cannot distinguish between operating expenditures and long term investments.

This budget, in relation to the great problems of Federal fiscal policy which are basic to our economy in 1962, is not simply irrelevant; it can be actively misleading. And yet there is a mythology that measures all of our national soundness or unsoundness on the single simple basis of this same annual administrative budget. If our Federal budget is to serve not the debate but the country, we must and will find ways of clarifying this area of discourse.

Still in the area of fiscal policy, let me say a word about deficits. The myth persists that Federal deficits create inflation and budget surpluses prevent it. Yet sizeable budget surpluses after the war did not prevent inflation, and persistent deficits for the last several years have not upset our basic price stability. Obviously deficits are sometimes dangerous—and so are surpluses. But honest assessment plainly requires a more sophisticated view than the old and automatic cliche that deficits automatically bring inflation.

There are myths also about our public debt. It is widely supposed that this debt is growing at a dangerously rapid rate. In fact, both the debt per person and the debt as a proportion of our gross national product have declined sharply since the Second World War. In absolute terms the national debt since the end of World War II has increased only 8 percent, while private debt was increasing 305 percent, and the debts of State and local governments—on whom people frequently suggest we should place additional burdens—the debts of State and local governments have increased 378 percent. Moreover, debts, public and private, are neither good nor bad, in and of themselves. Borrowing can lead to over-extension and collapse—but it can also lead to expansion and strength. There is no single, simple slogan in this field that we can trust.

Finally, I come to the problem of confidence. Confidence is a matter of myth and also a matter of truth—and this time let me take the truth of the matter first.

It is true—and of high importance—that the prosperity of this country depends on the assurance that all major elements within it will live up to their responsibilities. If business were to neglect its obligations to the public, if labor were blind to all public responsibility, above all, if government were to abandon its obvious—and statutory—duty of watchful concern for our economic health—if any of these things should happen, then confidence might well be weakened and the danger of stagnation would increase. This is the true issue of confidence.

But there is also the false issue—and its simplest form is the assertion that any and all unfavorable turns of the speculative wheel—however temporary and however plainly speculative in character—are the result of, and I quote, "a lack of confidence in the national administration." This I must tell you, while comforting, is not wholly true. Worse, it obscures the reality—which is also simple. The solid ground of mutual confidence is the necessary partnership of government with all of the sectors of our society in the steady quest for economic progress.

Corporate plans are not based on a political confidence in party leaders but on an economic confidence in the Nation's ability to invest and produce and consume. Business had full confidence in the administrations in power in 1929, 1954, 1958, and 1960—but this was not enough to prevent recession when business lacked full confidence in the economy. What matters is the capacity of the Nation as a whole to deal with its economic problems and its opportunities.

The stereotypes I have been discussing distract our attention and divide our effort. These stereotypes do our Nation a disservice, not just because they are exhausted and irrelevant, but above all because they are misleading—because they stand in the way of the solution of hard and complicated facts. It is not new that past debates should obscure present realities. But the damage of such a false dialogue is greater today than ever before simply because today the safety of all the world—the very future of freedom—depends as never before upon the sensible and clearheaded management of the domestic affairs of the United States.

The real issues of our time are rarely as dramatic as the issues of Calhoun. The differences today are usually matters of degree. And we cannot understand and attack our contemporary problems in 1962 if we are bound by traditional labels and wornout slogans of an earlier era. But the unfortunate fact of the matter is that our rhetoric has not kept pace with the speed of social and economic change. Our political debates, our public discourse—on current domestic and economic issues— too often bear little or no relation to the actual problems the United States faces.

What is at stake in our economic decisions today is not some grand warfare of rival ideologies which will sweep the country with passion but the practical management of a modern economy. What we need is not labels and cliches but more basic discussion of the sophisticated and technical questions involved in keeping a great economic machinery moving ahead.

The national interest lies in high employment and steady expansion of output, in stable prices, and a strong dollar. The declaration of such an objective is easy; their attainment in an intricate and interdependent economy and world is a little more difficult. To attain them, we require not some automatic response but hard thought. Let me end by suggesting a few of the real questions on our national agenda.

First, how can our budget and tax policies supply adequate revenues and preserve our balance of payments position without slowing up our economic growth?

Two, how are we to set our interest rates and regulate the flow of money in ways which will stimulate the economy at home, without weakening the dollar abroad? Given the spectrum of our domestic and international responsibilities, what should be the mix between fiscal and monetary policy?

Let me give several examples from my experience of the complexity of these matters and how political labels and ideological approaches are irrelevant to the solution.

Last week, a distinguished graduate of this school, Senator Proxmire, of the class of 1938, who is ordinarily regarded as a liberal Democrat, suggested that we should follow in meeting our economic problems a stiff fiscal policy, with emphasis on budget balance and an easy monetary policy with low interest rates in order to keep our economy going. In the same week, the Bank for International Settlement in Basel, Switzerland, a conservative organization representing the central bankers of Europe suggested that the appropriate economic policy in the United States should be the very opposite; that we should follow a flexible budget policy, as in

Europe, with deficits when the economy is down and a high monetary policy on interest rates, as in Europe, in order to control inflation and protect goals. Both may be right or wrong. It will depend on many different factors.

The point is that this is basically an administrative or executive problem in which political labels or cliches do not give us a solution.

A well-known business journal this morning, as I journeyed to New Haven, raised the prospects that a further budget deficit would bring inflation and encourage the flow of gold. We have had several budget deficits beginning with a $12½ billion deficit in 1958, and it is true that in the fall of 1960 we had a gold dollar loss running at $5 billion annually. This would seem to prove the case that a deficit produces inflation and that we lose gold, yet there was no inflation following the deficit of 1958 nor has there been inflation since then.

Our wholesale price index since 1958 has remained completely level in spite of several deficits, because the loss of gold has been due to other reasons: price instability, relative interest rates, relative export-import balances, national security expenditures—all the rest.

Let me give you a third and final example. At the World Bank meeting in September, a number of American bankers attending predicted to their European colleagues that because of the fiscal 1962 budget deficit, there would be a strong inflationary pressure on the dollar and a loss of gold. Their predictions of inflation were shared by many in business and helped push the market up. The recent reality of noninflation helped bring it down. We have had no inflation because we have had other factors in our economy that have contributed to price stability.

I do not suggest that the Government is right and they are wrong. The fact of the matter is in the Federal Reserve Board and in the administration this fall, a similar view was held by many well-informed and disinterested men that inflation was the major problem that we would face in the winter of 1962. But it was not. What I do suggest is that these problems are endlessly complicated and yet they go to the future of this country and its ability to prove to the world what we believe it must prove.

I am suggesting that the problems of fiscal and monetary policies in the sixties as opposed to the kinds of problems we faced in the thirties demand subtle challenges for which technical answers, not political answers, must be provided. These are matters upon which government and business may and in many cases will disagree. They are certainly matters that government and business should be discussing in the most sober, dispassionate, and careful way if we are to maintain the kind of vigorous economy upon which our country depends.

How can we develop and sustain strong and stable world markets for basic commodities without unfairness to the consumer and without undue stimulus to the producer? How can we generate the buying power which can consume what we produce on our farms and in our factories? How can we take advantage of the miracles of automation with the great demand that it will put upon highly skilled labor and yet offer employment to the half million of unskilled school dropouts each year who enter the labor market, eight million of them in the 1960's?

How do we eradicate the barriers which separate substantial minorities of our citizens from access to education and employment on equal terms with the rest?

How, in sum, can we make our free economy work at full capacity—that is, provide adequate profits for enterprise, adequate wages for labor, adequate utilization of plant, and opportunity for all?

These are the problems that we should be talking about—that the political parties and the various groups in our country should be discussing. They cannot be solved by incantations from the forgotten past. But the example of Western Europe shows that they are capable of solution—that governments, and many of them are conservative governments, prepared to face technical problems without ideological preconceptions, can coordinate the elements of a national economy and bring about growth and prosperity—a decade of it.

Some conversations I have heard in our own country sound like old records, long-playing, left over from the middle thirties. The debate of the thirties had its great significance and produced great results, but it took place in a different world with different needs and different tasks. It is our responsibility today to live in our own world, and to identify the needs and discharge the tasks of the 1960's.

If there is any current trend toward meeting present problems with old cliches, this is the moment to stop it—before it lands us all in a bog of sterile acrimony.

Discussion is essential; and I am hopeful that the debate of recent weeks, though up to now somewhat barren, may represent the start of a serious dialog of the kind which has led in Europe to such fruitful collaboration among all the elements of economic society and to a decade of unrivaled economic progress. But let us not engage in the wrong argument at the wrong time between the wrong people in the wrong country—while the real problems of our own time grow and multiply, fertilized by our neglect.

Nearly 150 years ago Thomas Jefferson wrote, "The new circumstances under which we are placed call for new words, new phrases, and for the transfer of old words to new objects." New words, new phrases, the transfer of old words to new objects—that is truer today than it was in the time of Jefferson, because the role of this country is so vastly more significant. There is a show in England called "Stop the World, I Want to Get Off." You have not chosen to exercise that option. You are part of the world and you must participate in these days of our years in the solution of the problems that pour upon us, requiring the most sophisticated and technical judgment; and as we work in consonance to meet the authentic problems of our times, we will generate a vision and an energy which will demonstrate anew to the world the superior vitality and the strength of the free society.

Two months after the Yale address President Kennedy spoke to the American people over television and officially announced the tax cut he would propose in his economic message the following January. But he still lacked enthusiasm for the measure, and his attitude came through in a lackluster performance. Despite attempts by Sorensen and others to brighten it up by charts and real-life human-interest examples, the speech still came off, in the words of the President, as a "C-minus performance."[117] His lack of enthusiasm continued during the fall when he was totally distracted by the Cuban missile crisis, but by December, Sorensen reported, his interest quickened again, and he convinced his listeners at The Economics Club of New York, a gathering of primarily Republican businessmen, that the impending tax bill would create a favorable business climate. Kenneth Galbraith complained that it was the "most Republican speech since McKinley," but Kennedy's loyal assistant and alter-ego (Sorensen) insisted that although "it sounded like Hoover, . . . it was actually Heller."[118]

Kennedy's economic advisors worked hard with their pupil to raise his "consciousness" and confidence in the new economics. There were many tutorials in the Oval Office, and Heller estimates that the Council of Economic Advisors supplied the President with 300 memoranda on economic questions during his 34 months in the White House. They surrounded him with post-Keynesian prophets, going so far as to arrange for Paul Samuelson to fly from Massachusetts to Washington with the President when he was in the process of making up his mind on the tax cut. But the education finally took hold, and Heller was proud of his honors student:

> What was pleasing to his economic advisors, and fortunate for the country, was his responsiveness to *analysis*, the force of economic logic and fact; to *analogy*, the demonstrated success of Keynesian policies abroad; and to *anomaly*, the continued sacrifice of human and material resources on the altar of false concepts of "sound finance."[119]

In the New York Economic Club speech, Kennedy demonstrated his new convictions:

> Our true choice is not between tax reduction, on the one hand, and the avoidance of large Federal deficits on the other. It is increasingly clear that no matter what party is in power, so long as our national security needs keep rising, an economy hampered by restrictive tax rates will never produce enough revenue to balance our budget just as it will never produce enough jobs or enough profits. Surely the lesson of the last decade is that budget deficits are not caused by wild-eyes spenders but by slow economic growth and periodic recession, and any new recession would break all deficit records.
>
> In short, it is a paradoxical truth that tax rates are too high today and tax revenues are too low and the soundest way to raise the revenues in the long run is to cut the rates now. The experiences of a number of European countries and Japan have borne this out. This country's own experience with tax reduction in 1954 has borne this out. And the reason is that only full employment can balance the budget, and tax reduction can pave the way to that employment. The purpose of cutting taxes now is not to incur a budget deficit, but to achieve the more prosperous, expanding economy which can bring a budget surplus.[120]

The long period of indecisiveness and uncertainty finally ended with the economic report delivered to the Congress on January 21, 1963. The statement outlined Heller's Keynesian "tax drag" theory, saying that the present tax rate withdrew too many dollars from the national economy to promote the necessary demand, the necessary markets, which in turn would stimulate the necessary incentive for investment to move the economy to maximum production and full employment. The message stated clearly that the present economy was not faltering, and that the tax cut was not simply a gimmick to arrest a developing recession. By all relative standards the national economy was blossoming, moving ahead at a rising rate of gross national product (GNP) (a $61 billion, or better than 12 percent, increase over the previous year), and even experiencing a "sizable drop" in the rate of unemployment. Yet even this "gratifying recovery" was not great enough to fully absorb the nation's resources, maximize production and operate on a full employment basis. Nothing less than a maximum utilization of effort and resources would produce the necessary goal of full employment. And without full employment the economy was always in danger, the recovery always short of satisfactory and the competitive position of the United States vulnerable in relation to most of the countries of Europe, which had reached that objective. President Kennedy's Council of Economic Advisors finally convinced him that nothing short of a full recovery and a maximum economic growth rate could strengthen the economy sufficiently to avoid the frequent and increasing recessions which had hobbled the American economy in the postwar world. And they also convinced him that a sizable across-the-board tax cut was the most efficient mechanism for rapidly achieving their desirable level of growth.

President John F. Kennedy
Economic Message (Extract) to Congress
January 21, 1963

Public Papers of the Presidents, John F. Kennedy, 1963 (Washington, D.C., 1964), 57-66.

. . . [Concerning the] Employment Act of 1946, I report to you

—that the "economic condition" of the United States in 1962 was one of continued advances in "employment, production, and purchasing power;"

—that the "foreseeable trends" in 1963 point to still further advances;

—that more vigorous expansion of our economy is imperative to gain the heights of "maximum employment, production, and purchasing power" specified in the Act and to close the gap that has persisted since 1957 between the "levels . . . obtaining" and the "levels needed" to carry out the policy of the Act;

—that the core of my 1963 "program for carrying out" the policy of the Act is major tax reduction and revision, carefully timed and structured to speed our progress toward full employment and faster growth, while maintaining our recent record of price stability and balance of payments improvement.

The state of the economy poses a perplexing challenge to the American people. Expansion continued throughout 1962, raising total wages, profits, consumption, and production to new heights. This belied the fears of those who predicted that we were about to add another link to the ominous chain of recessions which were more and more frequently interrupting our economic expansions—in 1953-54 after 45 months of expansion, in 1957-58 after 35 months, in 1960-61 after 25 months. Indeed, 22 months of steady recovery have already broken this melancholy sequence, and the prospects are for further expansion in 1963.

Yet if the performance of our economy is high, the aspirations of the American people are higher still—and rightly so. For all its advances the Nation is still falling substantially short of its economic potential—a potential we must fullfill both to then, necessarily couples pride in our achievements with a sense of challenge to master the job as yet undone. No nation, least of all ours, can rest easy

—when, in spite of a sizable drop in the unemployment rate (seasonally adjusted) from 6.7 percent as 1961 began to 5.6 percent as 1962 ended, the unemployment rate has fallen below 5 percent in but 1 month in the past 5 years, and there are still 4 million people unemployed today;

—when, in spite of a gratifying recovery which raised gross national product (GNP) from an annual rate of $501 billion as 1961 began to $562 billion as 1962 ended, $30-40 billion of usable productive capacity lies idle for lack of sufficient markets and incentives;

—when, in spite of a recovery growth rate of 3.6 percent yearly from 1960 to 1962, our realized growth trend since 1955 has averaged only 2.7 percent annually as against Western European growth rates of 4, 5, and 6 percent and our own earlier postwar growth rate of 4½ percent;

—when, in spite of achieving record corporate profits before taxes of $51 billion in 1962, against a previous high of $47 billion in 1959, our economy could readily generate another $7-8 billion of profits at more normal rates of capacity use;

—when, in spite of a rise of $28 billion in wages and salaries since the trough of the recession in 1961—with next-to-no erosion by rising prices—the levels of labor income could easily be $18-20 billion higher at reasonably full employment.

We cannot now reclaim the opportunities we lost in the past. But we can move forward to seize the even greater possibilities of the future. The decade ahead presents a most favorable gathering of forces for economic progress. Arrayed before us are a growing and increasingly skilled labor force, accelerating scientific and technological advances, and a wealth of new opportunities for innovation at home and for commerce in the world. What we require is a coherent national determination to lift our economy to a new plane of productivity and initiative. It is in this context and spirit that we examine the record of progress in the past 2 years and consider the means for achieving the goals of the Employment Act of 1946.

The 1961-62 Record

As I took office 24 months ago, the Nation was in the grip of its third recession in 7 years; the average unemployment rate was nearing 7 percent; $50 billion of potential output was running to waste in idle manpower and machinery.

In these last 2 years, the Administration and the Congress have taken a series of important steps to promote recovery and strengthen the economy:

1. Early in 1961 vigorous antirecession measures helped get recovery off to a fast start and gave needed assistance to those hardest hit by the recession.

2. In 1961 and 1962 new measures were enacted to redevelop chronically depressed areas; to retrain the unemployed and adapt manpower to changing technology; to enlarge social security benefits for the aged, the unemployed and their families; to provide special tax incentives to boost business capital spending; to raise the wages of underpaid workers; to expand housing and urban redevelopment; to help agriculture and small business—these and related measures improved the structure and functioning of the economy and aided the recovery.

3. Budgetary policy was designed to facilitate the expansion of private demand—to avoid the jolting shift from stimulus to restriction that did much to cut short recovery in 1958-60. The resulting fiscal shift in 1960-61 was much milder. In addition to increases in defense and space programs, measures of domestic improvement, such as the acceleration of public works, reinforced demand in the economy.

4. Monetary conditions were also adjusted to aid recovery within the constraints imposed by balance of payments considerations. While long-term interest rates rose by one-third in 1958-60, they changed little or actually declined in 1961-62. And the money supply grew much more rapidly in the present expansion than in the preceding one.

These policies facilitated rapid recovery from recession in 1961 and continuing expansion in 1962—an advance that carried total economic activity onto new high ground. The record rate of output of $562 billion in the final quarter of 1962 was, with allowance for price changes, 10 percent above the first quarter of 1961 and 8 percent above the last recovery peak in the second quarter of 1960. The industrial production index last month was 16 percent above the low point in January 1961 and 7 percent above the last monthly peak in January 1960.

These gains in output brought with them a train of improvements in income, employment, and profits, while the price level held steady and our balance of payments improved. In the course of the 1961-62 expansion:

1. Personal income rose by $46 billion to $450 billion, 12 percent above its peak in the previous expansion. Net income per farm rose by $330 as farm operators' net income from farming increased by $800 million. Total after-tax income of American consumers increased by 8 percent; this provided a $400 per year increase in living standards (1962 prices) for a family of four.

2. Civilian nonfarm employment increased by 2 million while the average factory work week was rising from 39.3 to 40.3 hours.

3. Corporate profits, as noted, reached a record $51 billion for 1962.

4. Wholesale prices remained remarkably stable, while consumer prices rose by only 1.1 percent a year—a better record of price stability than that achieved by any other major industrial country in the world, with the single exception of Canada.

5. This improving competitive situation, combined with closer international financial cooperation and intensive measures to limit the foreign currency costs of defense, development assistance, and other programs, has helped to bring about material improvements in our balance of payments deficit—from $3.9 billion in 1960 to $2.5 billion in 1961 and now to about $2 billion in 1962.

These are notable achievements. But a measure of how far we have come does not tell us how far we still have to go.

A year ago, there was widespread consensus that economic recovery in 1962, while not matching the swift pace of 1961, would continue at a high rate. But the pace slackened more than expected as the average quarterly change in GNP was only $6 billion in 1962 against $13 billion in 1961. The underlying forces in the private economy—no longer buttressed by the exuberant demand of the postwar decade, yet still thwarted by income tax rates bred of war and inflation—failed to provide the stimulus needed for more vigorous expansion. While housing and government purchases rose about as expected and consumer buying moved up rather well relative to income, increases in business investment fell short of expectations.

Yet, buttressed by the policies and programs already listed, the momentum of the expansion was strong enough to carry the economy safely past the shoals of a sharp break in the stock market, a drop in the rate of inventory accumulation, and a wave of pessimism in early summer. As the year ended, the economy was still moving upward.

The Outlook For 1963

The outlook for continued moderate expansion in 1963 is now favorable:

1. Business investment, responding in part to the stimulus of last year's depreciation reform and investment tax credit and to the prospect of early tax reduction and reform, is expected to rise at least modestly for 1963 as a whole.

2. Home construction should continue at about its 1962 level.

3. Government purchases—Federal, State, and local combined—are expected to rise at a rate of $2 billion a quarter.

4. Consumer purchases should rise in line with gains in business and Government activity.

These prospects, taking into account the proposed tax reduction, lead to the projection of a gross national product for 1963 of $578 billion, understood as the midpoint of a $10 billion range.

I do not expect a fifth postwar recession to interrupt our progress in 1963. It is not the fear of recession but the fact of 5 years of excessive unemployment, unused capacity, and slack profits—and the consequent hobbling of our growth rate—that constitutes the urgent case for tax reduction and reform. And economic expansion in 1963, at any reasonably predictable pace, will leave the economy well below the Employment Act's high standards of maximum employment, production, and purchasing power:

We end 1962 with an unemployment rate of 5.6 percent. That is not "*maximum employment.*" It is frustrating indeed to see the unemployment rate stand still even though the output of goods and services rises. Yet past experience tells us that only sustained major increases in production can reemploy the jobless members of today's labor force, create job opportunities for the 2 million young men and women entering the labor market each year, and produce new jobs as fast as technological change destroys old ones.

We end 1962 with U.S. output of goods and services running some $30-40 billion below the economy's capacity to produce. That is not *"maximum production."* And the prospective pace of expansion for 1963 promises little if any narrowing of the production gap until tax reduction takes hold. Our growing labor force and steadily rising productivity raise our capacity to produce by more than $20 billion a year. We need to run just to keep pace and run swiftly to gain ground in our race to full utilization.

We end 1962 with personal income, wages and salaries, and corporate profits also setting new records. But even this favorable record does not represent *"maximum purchasing power,"* as the figures I have already cited clearly demonstrate.

In summary: The recovery that was initiated shortly after I took office 2 years ago now stands poised at a moment of decision. I do not believe the American people will be—or should be—content merely to set new records. Private initiative and public policy must join hands to break the barriers built up by the years of slack since 1957 and bring the Nation into a new period of sustained full employment and rapid economic growth. This cannot be done overnight, but it can be done. The main block to full employment is an unrealistically heavy burden of taxation. The time has come to remove it.

Tax Reduction and Reform in 1963

We approach the issue of tax revision, not in an atmosphere of haste and panic brought on by recession or depression, but in a period of comparative calm. Yet if we are to restore the healthy glow of dynamic prosperity to the U.S. economy and avoid a lengthening of the 5-year period of unrealized promise, we have no time to lose. Early action on the tax program outlined in my State of the Union Message— and shortly to be presented in detail in my tax message—will be our best investment in a prosperous future and our best insurance against recession.

The Responsible Citizen and Tax Reduction

In this situation, the citizen serves his country's interest by supporting income tax reductions. For through the normal processes of the market economy, tax reduction can be the constructive instrument for harmonizing public and private interests:

—The taxpayer as *consumer*, pursuing his own best interest and that of his family, can turn his tax savings into a higher standard of living, and simultaneously into stronger markets for the producer.

—The taxpayer as *producer*—businessman or farmer—responding to the profit opportunities he finds in fuller markets and lower tax rates, can simultaneously create new jobs for workers and larger markets for the products of other factories, farms, and mines.

Tax reduction thus sets off a process that can bring gains for everyone, gains won by marshalling resources that would otherwise stand idle—workers without jobs and farm and factory capacity without markets. Yet many taxpayers seem prepared to deny the nation the fruits of tax reduction because they question the financial soundness of reducing taxes when the Federal budget is already in deficit. Let me make clear why, in today's economy, fiscal prudence and responsibility call for tax reduction even if it temporarily enlarges the Federal deficit—why reducing taxes is the best way open to us to increase revenues.

Our choice is not the oversimplified one sometimes posed, between tax reduction and a deficit on one hand and a budget easily balanced by prudent management on the other. If the projected 1964 Federal cash deficit of $10.3 billion did not allow for a $2.7 billion loss in receipts owing to the new tax program, the projected deficit would be $7.6 billion. We have been sliding into one deficit after another through repeated recessions and persistent slack in our economy. A planned cash surplus of $0.6 billion for the fiscal year 1959 became a record cash deficit of $13.1 billion, largely as the result of economic recession. A planned cash surplus of $1.8 billion for the current fiscal year is turning into a cash deficit of $8.3 billion, largely as the result of economic slack. If we were to slide into recession through failure to act on taxes, the cash deficit for next year would be larger *without* the tax reduction than the estimated deficit *with* tax reduction. Indeed, a new recession could break all peace-time deficit records. And if we were to try to force budget balance by drastic cuts in expenditures—necessarily at the expense of defense and other vital programs—we would not only endanger the security of the country, we would so depress demand, production, and employment that tax revenues would fall and leave the government budget still in deficit. The attempt would thus be self-defeating.

So until we restore full prosperity and the budget-balancing revenues it generates, our practical choice is not between deficit and surplus but between two kinds of deficits: between deficits born of waste and weakness and deficits incurred as we build our future strength. If an individual spends frivolously beyond his means today and borrows beyond his prospects for earning tomorrow, this is a sign of weakness. But if he borrows prudently to invest in a machine that boosts his business profits, or to pay for education and training that boosts his earning power, this can be a source of strength, a deficit through which he builds a better future for himself and his family, a deficit justified by his increased potential.

As long as we have large numbers of workers without jobs, and producers without markets, we will as a Nation fall into repeated deficits of inertia and weakness. But, by comparison, if we enlarge the deficit temporarily as the by-product of our positive tax policy to expand our economy this will serve as a source of strength, not a sign of weakness. It will yield rich *private* dividends in higher output, faster growth, more jobs, higher profits and incomes; and, by the same token, a large *public* gain in expanded budget revenues. As the economy returns to full employment, the budget will return to constructive balance.

This would not be true, of course, if we were currently straining the limits of our productive capacity, when the dollars released by tax reduction would push against unyielding bottlenecks in industrial plant and skilled manpower. Then, tax reduction would be an open invitation to inflation, to a renewed price-wage spiral, and would threaten our hard-won balance of payments improvement. Today, however, we not only have unused manpower and idle plant capacity; new additions to the labor force and to plant capacity are constantly enlarging our productive potential. We have an economy fully able and ready to respond to the stimulus of tax reduction.

Our need today, then, is

—to provide *markets* to bring back into production underutilized plant and equipment;

—to provide *incentives* to invest, in the form both of wider markets and larger profits—investment that will expand and modernize, innovate, cut costs;

—most important, by means of stronger markets and enlarged investment, to provide *jobs* for the unemployed and for the new workers streaming into the labor force during the sixties—and, closing the circle, the new jobholders will generate still larger markets and further investment.

It was in direct response to these needs that I pledged last summer to submit proposals for a top-to-bottom reduction in personal and corporate income taxes in 1963—for reducing the tax burden on private income and the tax deterrents to private initiative that have for too long held economic activity in check. Only when we have removed the heavy drag our fiscal system now exerts on personal and business purchasing power and on the financial incentives for greater risk-taking and personal effort can we expect to restore the high levels of employment and high rate of growth that we took for granted in the first decade after the war.

Taxes and Consumer Demand

In order to enlarge markets for consumer goods and services and translate these into new jobs, fuller work schedules, higher profits, and rising farm incomes, I am proposing a major reduction in individual income tax rates. Rates should be cut in three stages, from their present range of 20 to 91 percent to the more reasonable range of 14 to 65 percent. In the first stage, beginning July 1, these rate reductions will cut individual liabilities at an annual rate of $6 billion. Most of this would translate immediately into greater take-home pay through a reduction in the basic withholding rate. Further rate reductions would apply to 1964 and 1965 incomes, with resulting revenue losses to be partially offset by tax reforms, thus applying a substantial additional boost to consumer markets.

These revisions would directly increase the annual rate of disposable after-tax incomes of American households by about $6 billion in the second half of 1963, and some $8 billion when the program is in full effect, with account taken of both tax reductions and tax reform. Taxpayers in all brackets would benefit, with those in the lower brackets getting the largest proportional reductions.

American households as a whole regularly spend between 92 and 94 percent of the total after-tax (disposable) incomes they receive. And they generally hold to this range even when income rises and falls; so it follows that they generally spend about the same percentage of dollars of income added or subtracted. If we cut about $8 billion from the consumer tax load, we can reasonably expect a direct addition to consumer goods markets of well over $7 billion.

A reduction of corporate taxes would provide a further increment to the flow of household incomes as dividends are enlarged; and this, too, would directly swell the consumer spending stream.

The direct effects, large as they are, would be only the beginning. Rising output and employment to meet the new demands for consumer goods will generate new income—wages, salaries, and profits. Spending from this extra income flow would create more jobs, more production, and more incomes. The ultimate increases in the continuing flow of incomes, production, and consumption will greatly exceed the initial amount of tax reduction.

Even if the tax program had no influence on investment spending—either directly or indirectly—the $8-9 billion added directly to the flow of consumer income would call forth a flow of at least $16 billion of added consumer goods and services.

But the program will also generate direct and indirect increases in investment spending. The production of new machines, and the building of new factories, stores, offices, and apartments add to incomes in the same way as does production of consumer goods. This too sets off a derived chain reaction of consumer spending, adding at least another $1 billion of output of consumer goods for every $1 billion of added investment.

Taxes and Investment

To raise the Nation's capacity to produce—to expand the quantity, quality, and variety of our output—we must not merely replace but continually expand, improve, modernize, and rebuild our productive capital. That is, we must invest, and we must grow.

The past half decade of unemployment and excess capacity has led to inadequate business investment. In 1962, the rate of investment was almost unchanged from 1957 though gross national product had risen by almost 16 percent, after allowance for price changes. Clearly it is essential to our employment and growth objectives as well as to our international competitive stance that we stimulate more rapid expansion and modernization of America's productive facilities.

As a first step, we have already provided important new tax incentives for productive investment. Last year the Congress enacted a 7-percent tax credit for business expenditures on major kinds of equipment. And the Treasury, at my direction, revised its depreciation rules to reflect today's conditions. Together, these measures are saving business over $2 billion a year in taxes and significantly increasing the net rate of return on capital investments.

The second step in my program to lift investment incentives is to reduce the corporate tax rate from 52 percent to 47 percent, thus restoring the pre-Korean rate. Particularly, to aid small businesses, I am recommending that effective January 1, 1963, the rate on the first $25,000 of corporate income be dropped from 30 to 22 percent while the 52 percent rate on corporate income over $25,000 is retained. In later stages, the 52 percent rate would drop to 47 percent. These changes will cut corporate liabilities by over $2.5 billion before structural changes.

The resulting increase in profitability will encourage risk-taking and enlarge the flow of internal funds which typically finance a major share of corporate investment. In recent periods, business *as a whole* has not been starved for financial accommodation. But global totals mask the fact that thousands of small or rapidly growing businesses are handicapped by shortage of investible funds. As the total impact of the tax program takes hold and generates pressures on existing capacity, more and more companies will find the lower taxes a welcome source of finance for plant expansion.

The third step toward higher levels of capital spending is a combination of structural changes to remove barriers to the full flow of investment funds, to sharpen the incentives for creative investment, and to remove tax-induced distortions in resource flow. Reduction of the top individual income tax rate from 91 to 65 percent is a central part of this balanced program.

Fourth, apart from *direct* measures to encourage investment, the tax program will go to the heart of the main deterrent to investment today, namely, inadequate markets. Once the sovereign incentive of high and rising sales is restored, and the businessman is convinced that today's new plant and equipment will find profitable use tomorrow, the effects of the directly stimulative measures will be doubled and redoubled. Thus—and it is no contradiction—the most important single thing we can do to stimulate investment in today's economy is to raise consumption by major reduction of individual income tax rates.

Fifth, side-by-side with tax measures, I am confident that the Federal Reserve and the Treasury will continue to maintain, consistent with their responsibilities for the external defense of the dollar, monetary and credit conditions favorable to the flow of savings into long-term investment in the productive strength of the country.

Given a series of large and timely tax reductions and reforms, as I have proposed, we can surely achieve the balanced expansion of consumption and investment so urgently needed to overcome a half decade of slack and to capitalize on the great and growing economic opportunities of the decade ahead.

The impact of my tax proposals on the budget deficit will be cushioned by the scheduling of reductions in several stages rather than a single large cut; the careful pruning of civilian expenditures for fiscal 1964—those other than for defense, space, and debt service—to levels below fiscal 1963; the adoption of a more current time schedule for tax payments of large corporations, which will at the outset add about $1½ billion a year to budget receipts; the net offset of $3½ billion of revenue loss by selected structural changes in the income tax; most powerfully, in time, by the accelerated growth of taxable income and tax receipts as the economy expands in response to the stimulus of the tax program.

Impact on the Debt

Given the deficit now in prospect, action to raise the existing legal limit on the public debt will be required.

The ability of the Nation to service the Federal debt rests on the income of its citizens whose taxes must pay the interest. Total Federal interest payments as a fraction of the national income have fallen, from 2.8 percent in 1946 to 2.1 percent last year. The gross debt itself as a proportion of our GNP has also fallen steadily— from 123 percent in 1946 to 55 percent last year. Under the budgetary changes scheduled this year and next, these ratios will continue their decline.

It is also of interest to compare the rise in Federal debt with the rise in other forms of debt. Since the end of 1946, the Federal debt held by the public has risen by $12 billion; net State-local debt, by $58 billion; net corporate debt, by $237 billion; and net total private debt, by $518 billion.

Clearly, we would prefer smaller debts than we have today. But this does not settle the issue. The central requirement is that debt be incurred only for constructive purposes and at times and in ways that serve to strengthen the position of the debtor. In the case of the Federal Government, where the Nation is the debtor, the key test is whether the increase serves to strengthen or weaken our economy. In terms of jobs and output generated without threat to price stability— and in terms of the resulting higher revenue—the debt increases foreseen under my tax program clearly pass this test.

Monetary and debt management policies can accommodate our debt increase in 1963—as they did in 1961 and 1962—without inflationary strain or restriction of private credit availability.

Impact on Prices and the Balance of Payments

The Administration tax program for 1963 can strengthen our economy within a continuing framework of price stability and an extension of our hard-won gains in the U.S. balance of payments position.

Rising prices from the end of the war until 1958 led the American people to expect an almost irreversible upward trend of prices. But now prices have been essentially stable for 5 years. This has broken the inflationary psychology and eased the task of assuring continued stability.

We are determined to maintain this stability and to avoid the risk of either an inflationary excess of demand in our markets or a renewed price-wage spiral. Given the excess capacities of our economy today, and its large latent reserves of productive power, my program of fiscal stimulus need raise no such fears. The new discipline of intensified competition in domestic and international markets, the abundant world supplies of primary products, and increased public vigilance all lend confidence that wage-price problems can be resolved satisfactorily even as we approach our full-employment target.

Indeed, in many respects the tax program will contribute to continued price stability. Tax reduction and reform will increase productivity and tend to cut unit labor costs by stimulating cost-cutting investment and technological advance, and reducing distortions in resource allocation. As long as wage rate increases stay within the bounds of productivity increases, as long as the push for higher profit margins through higher prices is restrained—as long as wage and price changes reflect the "guideposts" that were set out a year ago and are reaffirmed in the accompanying Report of the Council of Economic Advisers—the outlook for stable prices is excellent.

Price stability has extra importance today because of our need to eliminate the continuing deficit in the international balance of payments. During the past 2 years we have cut the over-all deficit, from nearly $4 billion in 1960 to about $2 billion in 1962. But we cannot relax our efforts to reduce the payments deficit still further. One important force working strongly in our favor is our excellent record of price stability. Since 1959, while U.S. wholesale prices have been unchanged, those in every major competing country (except Canada) have risen appreciably. Our ability to compete in foreign markets—and in our own—has accordingly improved.

We shall continue to reduce the overseas burden of our essential defense and economic assistance programs, without weakening their effectiveness—both by reducing the foreign exchange costs of these programs and by urging other industrial nations to assume a fairer share of the burden of free world defense and development assistance.

But the area in which our greatest effort must now be concentrated is one in which Government can provide only leadership and opportunity; private business must produce the results. Our commercial trade surplus—the excess of our exports of goods and services over imports—must rise substantially to assure that we will reach balance of payments equilibrium within a reasonable period.

Under our new Trade Expansion Act, we are prepared to make the best bargains for American business that have been possible in many years. We intend to use the authority of that act to maximum advantage to the end that our agricultural and industrial products have more liberal access to other markets—particularly those of the European Economic Community.

With improved Export-Import Bank facilities and the new Foreign Credit Insurance Association, our exporters now have export financing comparable to that of our major competitors. As an important part of our program to increase exports, I have proposed a sharp step-up in the export expansion program of the Department of Commerce. Funds have been recommended both to strengthen our overseas marketing programs and to increase the Department's efforts in the promotion of an expanded interest in export opportunities among American firms.

In the meantime, we have made and will continue to make important progress in increasing the resistance of the international monetary system to speculative attack. The strength and the stability of the payments system have been consolidated during the past year through international cooperation. That cooperation successfully met rigorous tests in 1962—when a major decline occurred in the stock markets of the world; when the Canadian dollar withstood a run in June; and when the establishment of Soviet bases in Cuba threatened the world. Through direct cooperation with other countries the Unites States engaged in substantial operations in the forward markets for other currencies and held varying amounts of other currencies in its own reserves; the Federal Reserve engaged in a wide circle of swap arrangements for obtaining other currencies; and the Treasury initiated a program of borrowings denominated in foreign currencies. And with the approval by Congress of the necessary enabling legislation, the United States joined other major countries in strengthening the International Monetary Fund as an effective bulwark to the payments system.

With responsible and energetic public and private policies, and continued alertness to any new dangers, we can move now to revitalize our domestic economy without fear of inflation or unmanageable international financial problems—indeed, in the long run, a healthy balance of payments position depends on a healthy economy. As the Organization for Economic Cooperation and Development has emphatically stated in recent months, a prosperous American economy and a sound balance of payments position are not alternatives between which we must choose;

rather, expansionary action to bolster our domestic growth—with due vigilance against inflation—will solidify confidence in the dollar.

Impact on State and Local Governments

The Federal budget is hard pressed by urgent responsibilities for free world defense and by vital tasks at home. But the fiscal requirements laid upon our States, cities, school districts, and other units of local government are even more pressing. It is here that the first impacts fall—of rapidly expanding populations, especially at both ends of the age distribution; of mushrooming cities; of continuing shift to new modes of transportation; of demands for more and better education; of problems of crime and delinquency; of new opportunities to combat ancient problems of physical and mental health; of the recreational and cultural needs of an urban society.

To meet these responsibilities, the total of State and local government expenditures has expanded 243 percent since 1948—in contrast to 166 percent for the Federal Government; their debts by 334 percent—in contrast to 18 percent for the Federal Government.

The Federal budget has helped to ease the burdens on our States and local governments by an expanding program of grants for a multitude of purposes, and inevitably it must continue to do so. The Federal tax reductions I propose will also ease these fiscal burdens, chiefly because greater prosperity and faster growth will automatically increase State and local tax revenues at existing rates.

Tax Reduction and Future Fiscal Policy

While the basic purpose of my tax program is to meet our longer run economic challenges, we should not forget its role in strengthening our defenses against recession. Enactment on schedule of this program which involves a total of over $10 billion of net income tax reduction annually would be a major counterforce to any recessionary tendencies that might appear.

Nevertheless, when our calendar of fiscal legislation is lighter than it is in 1963, it will be important to erect further defenses against recession. Last year, I proposed that the Congress provide the President with limited standby authority (1) to initiate, subject to Congressional veto, temporary reductions in individual income tax rates and (2) to accelerate and initiate properly timed public capital improvements in times of serious and rising unemployment.

Work on the development of an acceptable plan for quick tax action to counter future recessions should continue; with the close cooperation of the Congress, it should be possible to combine provision for swift action with full recognition of the Constitutional role of the Congress in taxation.

The House and the Senate were unable to agree in 1962 on standby provisions for temporary speed-ups in public works to help fight recession. Nevertheless, recognizing current needs for stepped-up public capital expenditures, the Congress passed the very important Public Works Acceleration Act (summarized in Appendix A of the Report of the Council of Economic Advisers). I urge that the Congress appropriate the balance of funds authorized for programs under the Public Works Acceleration Act. Initial experience under this program offers promise that rapid temporary acceleration of public projects at all levels of government, under a stand-by program, can be an effective instrument of flexible antirecession policy. Further evaluation of experience should aid in the development of an effective stand-by program which would allow the maximum room for swift executive action consistent with effective Congressional control.

The tax cut was not enacted until after President Kennedy's assassination, but the heart of the matter was the proposal itself, coming at a time of a budget deficit and in the midst of a rising, although slowly, rate of economic growth. It dramatized as nothing else could, the conversion of the President of the United States to basic Keynesian doctrine, and led to an unprecedented period of stability and growth in the American economy.[121] The income tax cut which was finally enacted in 1964 amounted to 11 billion dollars at 1963 income levels ($14 billion at 1965 levels) and a $6 million corporate income tax cut.[122] The loss of this vast amount of government revenue resulted in the predicted upsurge in the vigor of the national economy. From the first quarter of 1961 to the first quarter of 1966, the gross national product advanced by 218 billion dollars, thus doubling the growth rate of the economy as compared to the Eisenhower years (2.25 percent to 4.50 percent). Seven million new jobs were created during that period, reducing the unemployment rate from almost seven percent to under four percent. During the same period, corporate profits doubled (after taxes), and total real compensation for all employees rose about 30 percent.[123]

All of this was not the direct result of the tax cut enacted in 1964, but the promise of such a reduction in the summer of 1962 and the achievement of this goal in 1964 provided both a psychological and material stimulus to the economy for most of that period. The Keynesians' advice was heeded, although much later than it was offered, but the results suggested that economic decision-making would never again be quite the same.

President Kennedy's role in this remarkable achievement has been pointed out by many who were close to and involved in the decision-making process. The Harvard economist, friend and frequent advisor of the President, Seymour Harris, was amazed at the amount of time and interest the President spent in thinking about economic problems in the face of his heavy responsibilities in the area of national security:

> What astonishes me is how much time the President nevertheless devotes to economic problems, how interested he is in them and how much he has learned in the last two years. He is now by far the most knowledgeable President of all time in the general area of economics.[124]

Harris later wrote that Kennedy had "become the most literate of all presidents in his understanding of modern economics and revealed great courage in his willingness to risk political losses in putting his economics to the test of the market place."[125] The former "C"-student in economics had become an honors student in the graduate school of the White House.

Of greater overall importance, however, was the impact of the tax cut on the future thinking and practice of the government's role and responsibilities in the national economy. Walter Heller is convinced:

> The tax cut has opened minds and let new ideas in. It has led to a growing consensus—at a higher level of understanding—on the active use of government economic tools to manage prosperity. Even though politics will at times blunt the use of these tools, the level of economic debate, and hence the quality of economic policy decisions, has been permanently raised.[126]

Robert Lekachman is also certain that

> [e]ven though in shape the new program favored established interests, a new principle of economic policy had indeed won through, a rare event in human affairs. . . . It is as certain as such things can be that never again will an American government profess helplessness in the face of un-employment, recession, and lagging economic growth. Rational fiscal policy expressed in the use of taxes as stabilizing agents and the acceptance of deficits without guilt may be a belated achievement but not the less treasurable because it comes a generation after the birth of the doctrine which justifies the public action.[127]

It would have been difficult to convince the supporters of a stronger full employment bill in 1946 that 20 years later the Council of Economic Advisors, conceived more or less as an afterthought in a watered down and much amended version of the original proposal, could have developed the influence it commanded in the Kennedy administration. Yet there is very little doubt that Walter Heller and his associates were primarily responsible for convincing President Kennedy of the validity of their arguments by means of the over 300 detailed memoranda which the council submitted to him. Their professional analysis of the economy and their policy proposals based upon that anyalsis were his soundest guides in planning a program of dynamic economic growth and development for the country.

During its 20 years of postwar existence the Council of Economic Advisors became a respected and vital source of both objective information and persuasive influence in the decision-making process of the executive branch of government. The very pervasiveness of economic problems and their always critical nature perforce brought this new administrative staff agency into the rarified atmosphere of the corridors of power. Though the council possessed only the power of its knowledge and experience and its ability to persuade an increasingly sensitive and informed Executive, the rising importance of economic policy in both domestic and foreign affairs made its role a critical one. But, of course, all of this enhanced the power and influence of the President himself, and closely and continuously involved him not only as an administrator, but as an initiator of policy in areas where life and death, starvation and affluence, and growth and decline of the national economy were involved. For the mid-century presidency this was an extremely important responsibility. The creation of the Council of Economic Advisors provided the President with an effective administrative staff agency which could enlighten him and assist him in the formulation and implementation of economic policy, but when the President was ready or even forced to act, he had to draw upon his executive or legislative powers to translate policy into reality.

The tax cut was only one of the solutions which modern economics offered as an antidote to the recurring recessions and underemployment that plagued the American economy in the post-World War II era. John Kenneth Galbraith was continuously critical of the Council of Economic Advisors' methods of stimulating expanded economic growth:

> The expansion produced by tax-cutting, he argued to Kennedy toward the end of 1962, would be an expansion of consumer goods; and these the American people already had in abundance. But it was "in the area of public needs, notably schools, colleges, hospitals, foreign policy that our need for growth is greatest." Tax-cutting, as he later put it, was "reactionary" Keynesianism, providing the things the country least needed at the expense of the things it most needed. "I am not sure," he said, "what the advantage is in having a few more dollars to spend if the air is too dirty to breathe, the water too polluted to drink, the commuters are losing out on the struggle to get in and out of the cities, the streets are filthy, and the schools so bad that the young, perhaps wisely, stay away, and hoodlums roll citizens for some of the dollars they saved in taxes." Moreover, fiscal and monetary policy could not immediately help those who entered the labor market under handicaps—the semi-literate, the undereducated, the unskilled young and the Negro.[128]

During the Kennedy administration this argument was resolved in favor of the fiscal policy supported by the Council of Economic Advisors. It was decided primarily upon political considerations; the President considered the Galbraith approach out of the question and his political judgment was probably correct. If a public works program had been proposed to the Congress at that time, the chances are that it would have gone down the drain long before the President's assassination. The more conservative tax cut was revolutionary enough for him, and indeed the manner in which he presented it to the Congress spoke more directly to the major economic problems of our time than anything said by any of his predecessors.

But as Robert Lekachman has indicated, the application of modern fiscal policy is no longer the issue. This has already been resolved.

> It has been superseded by a much harder set of choices dependent on social valuations more complex than the simple preference of prosperity to depression, growth to stagnation, and progress to retrogression. These are the choices which were foreshadowed by the controversy in the Kennedy administration over the best way to stimulate the American economy. When a President and a Congress acknowledge the need for fiscal stimulus, *how* should this stimulus be supplied? The practical choice, the major social valuation, and the continuing political argument focus upon the two routes to economic expansion which are open, the twentieth century liberal route and the twentieth century conservative alternative.[129]

Granted that the Congress will eventually have to make this kind of a social value judgment, the modern presidency with its vast new responsibility to the continued maintenance of full employment and economic growth will have to provide the guidance in such a choice. The American people will no longer accept anything less from their political system.

Still to be tested, however, will be the influence of the advice of the Council of Economic Advisors and other outstanding economists outside of government when they advocate an increase in taxes in the face of an inflationary spiral and a condition of high, perhaps too high, aggregate demand. A tax increase has more severe political consequences than the relatively few drawbacks of a popular tax cut, and it remains to be seen whether a future President can educate the public sufficiently to have them absorb a substantial tax increase in response to appeals that such a costly item for them will benefit the national economy.

NOTES

1. Woodrow Wilson, *Congressional Government: A Study in American Politics* (Boston, 1885), 51-52.
2. Wilson, *Congressional Government*, 253-54.
3. Woodrow Wilson, "Cabinet Government in the United States," in Arthur S. Link, ed., *The Papers of Woodrow Wilson* (Princeton, New Jersey, 1966) I, 493-510.
4. Wilson, "Cabinet Government," 1, 500.
5. See "Government by Debate: Being a Short View of Our National Government As It Is and As It Might Be," a previously unpublished essay in Link, *The Papers of Woodrow Wilson*, II, 159-275.
6. Woodrow Wilson, *Constitutional Government in the United States* (New York, 1908), 60.
7. Wilson, *Constitutional Government in the United States*, 68.
8. Wilson, *Constitutional Government in the United States*, 70-71.
9. Arthur S. Link, *Wilson: The New Freedom* (Princeton, New Jersey, 1956), 147.
10. Quoted in Joseph S. Clark, et al., *The Senate Establishment* (New York, 1963), 26-27.
11. From an introduction to Fred L. Israel, ed., *The State of the Union Messages of the Presidents* (New York, 1966) I, xvi.
12. Quoted in Israel, I, xvi.
13. Quoted in Israel, I, xvi.
14. Quoted in Israel, I, xvii.
15. Quoted from the New York *World* in Link, *Wilson*, 186-87.
16. Quoted from the New York *World* in Link, *Wilson*, 187.
17. Quoted in Link, *Wilson*, 187-88.
18. Quoted in Link, *Wilson*, 190.
19. Link, *Wilson*, 204.
20. Quoted in Link, *Wilson*, 205.
21. Ray Stannard Baker, *The Life and Letters of Woodrow Wilson* (Garden City, New York, 1927) IV, 160.
22. Quoted in Link, *Wilson*, 206-07.
23. Quoted in Link, *Wilson*, 212.
24. Baker, IV, 163.
25. Baker, IV, 163-64.
26. Quoted in Link, *Wilson*, 213 (footnote)
27. Quoted in Link, *Wilson*, 222.
28. Gabriel Kolko, *The Triumph of Conservatism* (Chicago, 1967), Chapter 9.
29. Quoted in Link, *Wilson*, 225.
30. Quoted in Link, *Wilson*, 236.
31. Baker, IV, 183.

32. Baker, IV, 184.
33. Link, *Wilson*, 238.
34. Quoted in Link, *Wilson*, 238.
35. Baker, IV, 201.
36. Link, *Wilson*, 240.
37. Link, *Wilson*, 423.
38. Henry Steele Commager, ed., *Documents of American History*, 5th ed. (New York, 1949) II, 136.
39. See Volume III, section one of *The Growth of Presidential Power*. See also Melvin I. Urofsky and David W. Levy, eds., *The Letters of Louis D. Brandeis* (Albany, New York, 1972) II, 688-94.
40. Urofsky and Levy, II, 690.
41. Urofsky and Levy, II, 695.
42. Link, *Wilson*, 437.
43. Walter Lippmann, *Drift and Mastery* (Englewood Cliffs, New Jersey, 1961), 83-84.
44. Quoted in Kolko, 269.
45. Link, *Wilson*, 444.
46. Kolko, 269.
47. Quoted in Kolko, 248.
48. Kolko, 273.
49. Kolko, 274.
50. Edward F. Cox, Robert C. Fellmuth and John E. Schulz, *"The Nader Report" on the Federal Trade Commission* (New York, 1969), 215.
51. Kolko, 304-05.
52. Lawrence Chamberlain, *The President, Congress and Legislation* (New York, 1946).
53. See James A. Robinson, *Congress and Foreign Policy Making: A Study in Legislative Influence and Initiative* (Homewood, Illinois, 1962), 8-9. Robinson takes Chamberlain to task for his "unsystematic" method of selecting statutes, and also for bypassing foreign policy legislation. There is something to be said for both criticisms, but on the other hand Robinson's own approach both to Chamberlain's study and to foreign policy decisions is extremely "unsystematic." He apparently has not analyzed the content of Chamberlain's book very carefully for he extends the scope of the study five years beyond that which Chamberlain used for his study and then projects this same advanced date onto the chart when there is obviously no data to support the configurations he represents.

   In his study of foreign policy decisions (not all of which are legislative), Robinson admits that his own criterion for selecting examples is extremely "unscientific," since he incorporated into his study the analysis of judgments of 22 different individuals who are by no means in complete agreement with respect to methodology, objectives and systematic or unsystematic analysis of their material. The problem is then compounded by imposing upon this conglomeration of data a Lasswellian analytical framework, in which the decision-making process is broken down into seven component elements: intelligence function, recommendation, prescription, invocation, application, appraisal, termination.

   It appears that in breaking down the legislative process this way into its component decision-making elements and evaluating these functions separately, one runs the risk of missing the forest by concentrating on the trees. Furthermore Robinson expects a "yes or no" answer. Unlike Chamberlain and Dahl (Robert A. Dahl, *Congress and Foreign Policy* [New York, 1964]), he does not allow for the possibility of joint executive-legislative collaboration, but insists upon limiting the answer to either one or the other. Using this method he virtually eliminates the Congress from the vital pressure points of decision-making in the process of formulating and developing foreign policy legislation. This not only oversimplifies the complexity of the legislative process, it also distorts the relative influence of both branches in the procedure. His evaluation of the Congress' role in the Foreign Assistance Act of 1948 is a good example of how his method can lead one astray.
54. Chamberlain, 450-52.
55. Chamberlain, 453.
56. Chamberlain, 454.
57. Chamberlain, 454-55.
58. Chamberlain, 454.
59. Chamberlain, 454.
60. I refer here not only to the plethora of foreign aid legislation which has been a major focus of American foreign policy in the postwar era and which has involved both houses of Congress, but also to such legislative actions as the joint policy resolutions vis à vis the Pescadores Islands and Formosa, the Middle East and Cuba.

61. The preliminary analysis of the individual statutes was conducted by members of a seminar on the President and Congress (Politics 21a) in the politics department of Brandeis University in the fall semester of 1965. The students did a superb job, and I would like to thank them again for all their hard work. I reviewed all of the case studies carefully and did further research where necessary.

The task was made immeasurably easier by the increasingly able analysis and record maintained by the *Congressional Quarterly*. There are also a number of superb case studies which are helpful additions to the already rather full record, as well as some shorter monographs. (See bibliography.)

62. Amendments to the 1948 Water Pollution Act have been included in this category despite the fact that President Eisenhower called for a renewal of this legislation in his special message to the Congress on health legislation. The Congress had added several important amendments including a $50,000,000 federal support program for grants-in-aid to local communities to build sewage treatment plants. The President was so opposed to this feature of the bill that he considered vetoing it, but he did not. The unique features of this amendment qualify it for this special consideration.

63. Completed some ten years ago, this research has recently been reevaluated in an article by Ronald C. More and Steven C. Teel, "Congress as Policy-Maker: A Necessary Reappraisal," in *Political Science Quarterly*, LXXXV, No. 3 (September 1970). In it the authors present a forceful case for challenging the argument that the President has come to dominate the legislative process. They provide substantial evidence to demonstrate that this is not the case. I think they are right in saying that the President does not *control* the legislative process, but that Congress still plays an important, frequently a crucial, role in that process. The point of my argument is that the President does this as well. Legislation which these authors identify as having originated in the Congress (all legislation does so in a formal sense, but much of it was initially drafted outside of Congress by the executive departments or by the White House), such as the Atomic Energy Act of 1946 and the Area Development Act (1961), would never have become law without the strong intervention and leadership of the President. Since the end of World War II and certainly in the New Deal period, the Chief Executive has become deeply involved in all aspects of the legislative process, and his acceptance or rejection of a measure is frequently decisive in whether or not a bill does become law or not.

This was true when this study was made and it is also true today. The arguments advanced by Hugh G. Gallagher, which are based upon no apparent new research but rely on the Noe and Till data, are far too sweeping and, more importantly, they go beyond the claims that these authors make. Gallagher's statement that "Congress legislates, and, except in rare instances, the President has had little to say about it" is simply contrary to fact. Constitutionally the President always has been, and is increasingly, an integral part of the legislative process. See Hugh G. Gallagher, "Presidents, Congress and Legislative Functions," in Rexford G. Tugwell and Thomas E. Cronin, eds., *The Presidency Reappraised* (New York, 1974).

64. The percentage would be even higher if the study were extended to include the post-Kennedy years when the role of the President did anything but recede.

65. James L. Sundquist, *Politics and Policy: The Eisenhower, Kennedy and Johnson Years* (Washington, D.C., 1973), 489.

66. These figures were extrapolated from the presidential scoreboard prepared by the editors of the *Congressional Quarterly Almanac* for 1962, 82-91. The *Congressional Quarterly* gives President Kennedy an overall batting average of 44.6 percent, or credit for having gotten 133 of his 298 legislative proposals passed. The difference between the administration's claimed successes and the *Quarterly's* percentage is explained by the following factors. First, the Kennedy administration's arithmetic dealt only with those of their proposals which reached the floor of both houses for a record vote. Second, they differed in their definitions of what constituted an administration proposal. *Congressional Quarterly* broke down the President's special messages and draft bills into specific proposals, whereas the administration was content to arrive at their percentage figures on the basis of general or overall programs, which in many cases had been significantly modified in the course of their legislative history. Of the 165 administration proposals which did not become law in 1962, 113 never were presented to both houses of Congress for a vote. They died in congressional committees.

67. David B. Truman, *The Congressional Party* (New York, 1959), 316-17.

68. Richard E. Neustadt, "Presidency and Legislation: The Growth of Central Clearance," in *American Political Science Review*, XLVIII, No. 3 (September 1954), 653.

69. Neustadt, "The Growth of Central Clearance," 642.

70. Richard E. Neustadt, "Presidency and Legislation: Planning the President's Program," in *American Political Science Review*, XLIX, No. 4 (December 1955), 981.

71. Emmet John Hughes, *The Ordeal of Power* (New York, 1963), 128.
72. "President Eisenhower may have flirted, in moments of weariness, with the Whig notion that the legislative branch should legislate and the executive branch should execute—although in practice he sent to Capitol Hill a legislative program virtually as complete . . . as that of any other president. . . ." (Sundquist, 489.)
73. John Stuart Mill, *Representative Government* (London, 1910), 237. (My emphasis.)
74. Richard E. Neustadt, "Politicians and Bureaucrates," in David B. Truman, ed., *The Congress and the Future* (Englewood Cliffs, New Jersey, 1965), 105-06.
75. Quoted in Arthur M. Schlesinger, jr., *The Coming of the New Deal* (Boston, 1958), 406.
76. Schlesinger, *The Coming of the New Deal*, 406.
77. See Arthur M. Schlesinger, jr., *The Crisis of the Old Order* (Boston, 1957); *The Coming of the New Deal*; and *The Politics of Upheaval* (Boston, 1960).
78. Quoted in Schlesinger, *The Politics of Upheaval*, 656.
79. E. Cary Brown has demonstrated this in a definitive article published in the *American Economic Review*, XLVI, No. 5 (December 1936), 866.
80. Quoted in Brown, 866.
81. Robert Lekachman, *The Age of Keynes* (New York, 1966), 142.
82. William Leuchtenburg, *Franklin D. Roosevelt and the New Deal* (New York, 1963), 326.
83. Schlesinger, *The Politics of Upheaval*, 647.
84. Schlesinger, *The Politics of Upheaval*, 650.
85. Leuchtenburg, 347-48.
86. Leuchtenburg, 347.
87. See Lekachman, Chapter Seven, "Keynes in the Postwar World."
88. Quoted in Gerhart Colm, "The Executive Office and Fiscal and Economic Policy," in *Law and Contemporary Problems*, XXIV, No. 4 (Autumn 1956), 715.
89. Bailey, 243.
90. Bailey, 244.
91. Bailey, 246.
92. Bailey, 228.
93. Bailey, 229.
94. Quoted in Corrinne Silverman, *The President's Economic Advisors*, Inter-University Program #48 (Indianapolis, Indiana, 1959), 13.
95. Silverman, 11-12.
96. Silverman, 13-14.
97. Quoted in Edward Flash, jr., *Economic Advice and Presidential Leadership* (New York, 1965), 25.
98. Quoted in Flash, 156.
99. Flash, 159.
100. Seymour E. Harris, *The Economics of the Political Parties* (New York, 1962), 45.
101. Lekachman, 200; 212.
102. Theodore C. Sorensen, *Kennedy* (New York, 1965), 394. Schlesinger, on the other hand, reports that it was a "B," and the highest mark he received in his freshman year at Harvard. See Arthur M. Schlesinger, jr., *A Thousand Days, John F. Kennedy in the White House* (Boston, 1965), 626.
103. Quoted in Walter Heller, *New Dimensions of Political Economy* (Cambridge, Massachusetts, 1966), 30.
104. Sorensen, 394.
105. Schlesinger, *A Thousand Days*, 626. The honest answer to the question raised was probably "no." Economists like Paul Samuelson who were influential as advisors to Kennedy did not believe a five percent rate of economic growth could be maintained for any period of time. Experience bore out this prognosis, for even by the late sixties when the slack in the economy was overcome, the growth rate only climbed to 4.5 percent.
106. Quoted in Sorensen, 396.
107. *The New York Times*, January 6, 1961.
108. *The New York Times*, January 6, 1961.
109. Sorensen, 397.
110. Sorensen, 397.
111. Sorensen, 397.
112. Sorensen, 400.
113. Heller, 30.

114. Quoted in Heller, 27.
115. *Public Papers of the Presidents: John F. Kennedy, 1962* (Washington, D.C., 1963), 470-71.
116. Heller, 33; 37.
117. Sorensen, 427.
118. Sorensen, 430.
119. Heller, 35.
120. Quoted in Sundquist, 44.
121. See Heller and James Tobin, "The Intellectual Revolution in U.S. Economic Policy-Making," Second Noel Buxton Lecture of the University of Essex (London, 1966).
122. Heller, 71.
123. Heller, 77. It is unfortunate that Congress failed to grant President Kennedy the standby authority to (1) initiate, subject to congressional veto, temporary reduction in individual income tax rates, and (2) to accelerate and initiate properly timed public capital improvements in times of serious and rising unemployment. There is an excellent discussion of this proposal in Louis Fisher, *President and Congress* (New York, 1972), 155-73.
124. Sorensen, 395.
125. Seymour Harris, *Economics of the Kennedy Years* (New York, 1964), 258.
126. Heller, 40-41.
127. Lekachman, 284-84.
128. Schlesinger, *A Thousand Days*, 648-49.
129. Lekachman, 286.

Bibliography

Bailey, Stephen K. *Congress Makes a Law*. New York: Columbia University Press, 1950.

Baker, Ray Stannard. *Woodrow Wilson: His Life and Letters*. Vols. I-III. Garden City, New York: Doubleday, Page and Company, 1927.

Berman, Daniel. *A Bill Becomes a Law: The Civil Rights Act of 1960*. New York: The Macmillan Company, 1962.

Chamberlain, Lawrence H. *The President, Congress and Legislation*. New York: Columbia University Press, 1946.

Clark, Joseph S., et. al. *The Senate Establishment*. New York: Hill and Wang, 1963.

Commager, Henry Steele, ed. *Documents of American History.* Fifth ed. New York: Appleton-Century-Crofts, 1949.

Congressional Quarterly Almanac. 87th Cong., 2d sess., 1962 Vol. XVIII.

Dahl, Robert A. *Congress and Foreign Policy*. New York: Norton Library, 1964.

Davis, C. Cullomo. "The Transformation of the Federal Trade Commission, 1914-1929. *Mississippi Valley Historical Review*. XLIX. No. 3 (December 1962).

Fisher, Louis. *President and Congress*. New York: Macmillan Free Press, 1972.

Harris, Richard. *The Real Voice*. New York: The Macmillan Company, 1964.

Harris, Seymour E. *Economics of the Kennedy Years*. New York: Harper and Row, 1964.

Hughes, Emmet John. *The Ordeal of Power*. New York: Atheneum, 1963.

Israel, Fred L., ed. *The State of the Union Messages of the Presidents*. Vol. I. New York: Chelsea House Publishers, 1966.

Jones, Joseph Marion. *The Fifteen Weeks*. New York: The Viking Press, 1955.

Kolko, Gabriel. *The Triumph of Conservatism*. Chicago: Quadrangle Paperbacks, 1967.

Link, Arthur S. *Wilson: The New Freedom*. Princeton, New Jersey: Princeton University Press, 1956.

———, ed. *The Papers of Woodrow Wilson*. Vol. I. Princeton, New Jersey: Princeton University Press, 1966.

Lippmann, Walter. *Drift and Mastery*. Englewood Cliffs, New Jersey: Prentice-Hall, Inc., 1961.

McAdams, Alan K. *Power and Politics in Labor Legislation*. New York: Columbia University Press, 1964.

Mill, John Stuart. *Representative Government*. London: Oxford University Press, 1910.

More, Ronald C. and Teel, Steven C. "Congress as Policy-Maker: A Necessary Reappraisal." *Political Science Quarterly*. LXXXV. No. 3 (September 1970).

Neustadt, Richard E. "Politicians and Bureaucrats" David B. Truman, ed. *The Congress and America's Future*. Englewood Cliffs, New Jersey: Prentice-Hall, Inc., 1965.

———. "Presidency and Legislation: Planning the President's Program." *The American Political Science Review*. XLIX. No. 4 (December 1955).

———. "Presidency and Legislation: The Growth of Central Clearance." *The American Political Science Review*. XLVIII. No. 3 (September 1954).

Richardson, James D., ed. *Messages and Papers of the Presidents*. Vol. XVI. New York: Bureau of National Literature, 1897.

Robinson, James A. *Congress and Foreign Policy Making: A Study in Legislative Influence and Initiative*. Homewood, Illinois: Dorsey Press, 1962.

Sundquist, James L. *Politics and Policy: The Eisenhower, Kennedy, and Johnson Years*. Washington, D.C.: The Brookings Institution, 1973.

Truman, David B. *The Congressional Party*. New York: John Wiley and Sons, 1959.

U.S. Congress. *Presidential Vetoes*. List of bills vetoed and action taken thereon by the Senate and the House of Representatives from the 1st through the 86th

Cong., 1798 to 1961. Senate Library. Washington, D.C.: U.S. Government Printing Office, 1961.

Wilson, Woodrow. *Congressional Government: A Study in American Politics.* Boston: Houghton Mifflin, 1885.

　　　Constitutional Government in the United States. New York: Columbia University Press, 1908.

III. Administrative Power Recaptured

ADMINISTRATIVE POWER RECAPTURED

The Removal Power in
The Twentieth Century

The majority opinion in the Myers v. United States case, written by Chief Justice William Howard Taft, was an anticlimax in the long struggle over the President's removal power. The problem had been largely forgotten for 40 years when Taft's strident and all-encompassing opinion, written in 1926, stirred up the temporarily calm political waters. While the action of the Congress in repealing the Tenure of Office Act in 1885 had eliminated the immediate obstacle to the President's removal power, it did not protect future Chief Executives from a congressional restoration of a like statute. In fact the Congress continued to limit the President's power to remove some federal officials through stipulations of tenure or other conditions in the legislation creating federal offices and the procedures by which they were to be filled.

These were the conditions which surrounded the appointment and dismissal of Frank S. Myers, named a first-class postmaster by President Woodrow Wilson in 1917 in Portland, Oregon. On January 20, 1920, his resignation was requested, and when he refused to comply less than a month later, on February 2, 1920, he was removed from office by order of the postmaster general, acting under the direction of President Wilson. Myers protested his removal and continued to do so until the end of his four-year term. According to the Act of Congress of July 12, 1876, under whose authority he was appointed to his post, removal of a first-class postmaster by the President could be effective only with the advice and consent of Congress. President Wilson did not request or receive that consent in his removal of Myers. It was for that reason that the Portland postmaster continued to fight his removal, and that after his death, when his four-year term had expired, his heirs sued in the Court of Claims for loss of earnings for the duration of his official term. The claims court ruled against Myers, and the case went to the Supreme Court on appeal.

Ex-President Taft, sitting as chief justice of the Supreme Court, was anxious to tackle the full scope of the question which the *Myers* case presented. He wanted a sweeping dictum to uphold the President's independent removal power, and when he failed to achieve unanimity at the court conference in which the case was discussed, he invited the five justices he knew he could count on (Van Devanter, Sutherland, Butler, Sanford and Stone) for a Sunday afternoon meeting at his home, at which time he was assured of their support in a majority opinion and thought it "well not to make any concession."[1] It is interesting to note that after these eminent judges made up their minds as to the outcome of the case, they argued among themselves to determine the constitutional principles with which to support their decision. It took Taft a full year to draft and polish up his decision, and during this period he reported that five reliable judges stood firm, although Stone seemed "a little bit fuzzy and captious in respect to form of statement, and [betrayed] in some degree a little of the legal school master."[2] Stone, Butler and Van Devanter were all pressed into service to assist the chief justice in revising his initial draft, but Stone proved to be the most stubborn and incisive critic. Had Taft followed Stone's views, the final majority opinion would probably have been briefer and based almost entirely upon the implied powers rooted in the general grant of executive power in the Constitution.

Chief Justice Taft, however, based his argument primarily upon the fact that the question had arisen at the first session of the First Congress, that it had been thoroughly discussed by its members, many of whom had been present at the Constitutional Convention, and that they had decided then that the President should possess the removal power. He admitted that in the beginning "it might have been decided either way, but it was decided in favor of the view that the Constitution vested the executive power of removal in the President, with only the exceptions that appear in the instrument itself."[3] To Taft the controlling argument was

> not because a congressional conclusion on a constitutional issue is conclusive, but first because of our agreement with the reasons upon which it was avowedly based, second because this was the decision of the First Congress on a question of primary importance in the organization of the Government made within two years after the Constitutional Convention and within a much shorter time after its ratification, and third because that Congress numbered among its leaders those who had been members of the Convention.[4]

> It was the Congress that launched the Government. It was the Congress that rounded out the Constitution itself by the proposing of the first ten amendments which had in effect been promised to the people as a consideration for the ratification. It was the Congress in which Mr. Madison, one of the first in the framing of the Constitution, led also in the organization of the Government under it. It was a Congress whose constitutional decisions have always been regarded as of the greatest weight in the interpretation of that fundamental instrument.[5]

The chief justice argued that this construction was accepted and acted upon by both the executive and legislative branches for 73 years, despite the "heat of political differences between the Executive and the Senate in President Jackson's time."[6]

> This Court has repeatedly laid down the principle that a contemporaneous legislative exposition of the Constitution when the founders of our Government and framers of our Constitution were actively participating in public affairs, acquiesced in for a long term of years, fixes the construction to be given to its provisions.[7]

In the course of his long, rambling decision, Taft indicated from time to time why he agreed with James Madison and Andrew Jackson in their strong defense of the President's independent removal power. He endorsed Madison's view that the President's responsibility to execute the laws was impossible without such power, for he must "execute them by the assistance of subordinates" for whom he was responsible. He also accepted the argument that the power to remove was incident to the power to appoint, against Stone's advice to drop this questionable theory, since it presented an opportunity for Congress to deprive the President of his patronage power and cripple him politically by vesting the appointment of all minor officials with the heads of departments. Clearly, however, the experience of the chief justice as President of the United States was always uppermost in his mind, and he wrote Justice Butler a year before he completed the decision:

> My experience in the executive office satisfies me that it would be a great mistake to change that view [majority opinion] and give to the Senate any greater power of hampering the President and tying him down. . . .[8]

Commenting on the decision in the *New Republic*, Professor Thomas Reed Powell of the Harvard Law School wrote:

> The opinion of the majority of the court was written by ex-president Taft.[9]

The *Myers* decision concluded by holding unconstitutional the Act of 1876, which stipulated that the Senate must join with the President in the removal of first-class postmasters, and the Tenure of Office Act, which had already been repealed, but had extended this procedure to all presidential appointments. The sweeping claims of the decision triggered immediate reactions from distinguished students of the Court. Professor Powell wrote:

> The logic is so lame, the language so inconclusive, the history so far from compelling, that I venture to think that the mainspring of the decision and its only conceivable justification are to be found in the judgment of the majority that the result is one that ought to be reached.[10]

The National Municipal League was so appalled by the implications of the decision with respect to civil service reform that it commissioned Professor Corwin to write a book on the removal power; in it he argued that the opinion "was decidedly vulnerable on both historical and logical grounds."[11] In a later analysis, the Princeton professor attacked Taft's construction of the inherent powers of the President based upon the opening words of Article II: "The executive power shall be vested in a President of the United States."

> Not only is this an entirely novel canon of constitutional interpretation, it is one which, if it were applied to the "general welfare" clause of Article I of the Constitution, would pave the way for a complete revolution in our system by converting the National Government from one of "enumerated" powers into one of plenary power.[12]

Of the three dissenting opinions, the arguments advanced by Mr. Justice Louis D. Brandeis were the most comprehensive and decisive. Brandeis' law clerk at that time, James M. Landis, who later became dean of the Harvard Law School and a member of a number of government regulatory commissions, has pointed out that he believed that Brandeis' dissent "exhibits more research than any other opinion in the law books."[13] Embarrassed by its length (56 pages), Justice Brandeis offered to pay for its printing but Taft would not consider it.[14]

Justice Oliver Wendell Holmes in his dissent relied upon McReynolds' (the third dissenter) and Brandeis' "exhaustive research," and characterized Taft's inferences from the general grants of executive power in the Constitution "spiders' webs inadequate to control the dominant theory." He refused to address himself to the larger question and concluded:

> We have to deal with an office that owes its existence to Congress and that Congress may abolish tomorrow. Its duration and the pay attached to it while it lasts depend upon Congress alone. Congress alone confers on the President the power to appoint to it and at any time may transfer that power to other hands. With such power over its own creation I have no more trouble in believing that Congress has power to prescribe a term of life for it free from any interference that I have in accepting the undoubted power of Congress to decree its end. I have equally little trouble in accepting its power to prolong the tenure of the incumbent until Congress or the Senate shall have assented to his removal. The duty of the President to see that the laws be executed is a duty that does not go beyond the laws or require him to achieve more than Congress sees fit to leave within his power.[15]

Brandeis did not challenge the validity of the proposition that the President must possess the removal power in order to control and influence his heads of departments and senior political officers, but he insisted that that was not at issue in the case. He maintained that the only question the Court could properly decide was whether the President was justified in removing Myers, a first-class postmaster in Portland, Oregon. He summoned a number of powerful arguments against the action of the President. First, Brandeis concluded, President Wilson had appointed Myers to his post under the statute then under fire and had raised no objections as to its constitutionality at that time; neither had the half a dozen other Presidents who appointed postmasters under the provisions of that law. He asked:

> May the President, having acted under the statute in so far as it creates the office and authorized the appointment, ignore, while the Senate is in session, the provision which prescribes the condition under which the removal may take place?[16]

Brandeis quickly went to the heart of the larger question which Chief Justice Taft raised in the majority opinion when he declared the statute of 1879, along with the Tenure of Office Act, unconstitutional. The question was whether the Congress was powerless to make the consent of the Senate a condition for any removal of an official by the President from an executive office. Taft had, of course, answered in the affirmative, basing his argument generally on the construction of the Constitution established by the First Congress. Brandeis challenged Taft's interpretation of that construction both on historical and constitutional grounds. He argued that the decision in 1789 was made with respect to the removal power of the President in cases of special cabinet officers or department heads (like the secretary of state), which was the subject of particular statutes passed at that time, but which did not apply to all other executive officers appointed by the President. Furthermore he showed that those representatives and senators who voted for the measure (with not even a majority in the Senate, without the vote of the Vice President who broke the tie) were divided among themselves with respect to whether or not the Constitution implied that the President had the independent power to remove all appointed executive officials. Brandeis demonstrated that the written record of the debate indicated that only a minority were convinced of this, hence the vote at that time could not be considered a clear endorsement of the principle.

Justice Brandeis also pointed out that almost from the beginning of the republic, Congress had prescribed conditions for the appointment to office, the creation of offices and definitions of their functions, had established tenure and had even stipulated conditions for the removal of officers. These were legitimate legislative functions, Brandeis maintained, and they could not be constitutionally negated by the claim that the general grant of executive power to the President overrode or assumed precedence with respect to removals over any such statutory conditions. Not even a good case for expedience could be made for that power, the justice argued, since the President had the constitutional power to suspend any executive official if the Congress was not in session, and to bring him to its attention when it reconvened.

Both opinions invoked constant but learned quotations from important historical figures and from previous court decisions, in an effort by each side to refute each other's opinions and support its own arguments. Taft was disturbed by a passing reference made by Brandeis, in which Chief Justice Marshall, in the landmark decision in Marbury v. Madison, indicated his agreement with Marbury's right to his job, regardless of the President's power. Of course it was a case of *obiter dictum*, yet Taft was unhappy until he found a quotation in Marshall's *Life of Washington* which conflicted with that dictum insofar as it acknowledged the established patterns by recognizing the President's independent removal power. Justice Stone tried to get Taft to simply fault Marshall with an error in judgment or an oversight in the *Marbury* case, but Taft dared not assert himself "where angels fear to tread."

As is true in most judicial conflicts, there was right on both sides. Taft in my opinion had the better understanding of the role of the presidency in history, realizing, undoubtedly from first hand experience, how important, even psychologically, the removal power was to a frequently beleaguered President, pressured on all sides, and unable even to control his own administrative family. He realized that a limited defense of the removal power was vulnerable to increasing legislative attack, since once the principle of the necessity of the removal power to the maintenance of executive administrative responsibility was waived, there would be little or no basis for defending it in other instances. He felt it was a case of "all or nothing." Brandeis, on the other hand, had a tighter legal case, based on what he considered to be the narrow question before the Court. He felt that Taft's opinion was a serious judicial encroachment upon legislative prerogatives, an assault upon the Founding Fathers' efforts to protect the government from autocratic power. In the closing paragraph of his opinion Brandeis argued:

> In America, as in England, the conviction prevailed that the people must look to representative assemblies for the protection of their liberties. And protection of the individual, even if he be an official, from the arbitrary or capricious exercise of power was then believed to be an essential of free government.[17]

In order to defend the principle of the President's removal power, Taft enlarged the scope of his argument far beyond the reasonable needs of executive responsibility, while Brandeis, insensitive to the history of the presidency in the latter half of the nineteenth century, failed to acknowledge that the legislature had exploited its doctrine of the removal power, not simply to maintain the cherished separation of powers, but to cripple the Executive and render him impotent, to serve its own greedy interests. If Chief Justice Taft had followed Justice Stone's advice and confined his argument to the implicit needs of the executive power, then, as Professor Hart has pointed out, "to class a power as executive means no more than to say it must be located in executive officers."[18] But he did not limit or protect the Court in that manner, and as a result the *Myers* decision provided a potential issue for future Courts to reexamine, possibly reverse or restrict its application.

That was precisely what the succeeding Court under the leadership of Charles Evans Hughes did in the next ten years. In a case arising during the first administration of FDR, the Court was asked to review the argument of the former chairman of the Federal Trade Commission, William E. Humphrey, the bête noire of the Progressives and the New Dealers,[19] who had been removed from office by the President, not for any actions reflecting upon his character or malfeasance in office, but because Roosevelt indicated that "the aims and purposes of the Administration with respect to the work of the Commission can be carried out most effectively with personnel of my own selection."[20] The President had asked Humphrey to resign, believing that:

> I do not feel that your mind and my mind go along together on either the policies or the administering of the Federal Trade Commission, and, frankly, I think it best for the people of this country that I should have a full confidence.[21]

Yet Humphrey refused, and Roosevelt fired him. The commissioner ignored the President's dismissal, continued to claim the possession and benefits of the office and later sued the government for his salary covering the period of time which would have remained of his appointment (after his death his heirs continued the battle).

Humphrey had been first appointed by President Calvin Coolidge and then reappointed by Herbert Hoover; he was not only out of step with the objectives and programs of the New Deal, but the President was convinced that there were perfectly legitimate grounds for his removal, as he had failed to carry out the rules and statutory requirements of the law in his capacity as chairman of the FTC. But Roosevelt was convinced by his advisor, James M. Landis, that there was no need to invite difficulty by raising the issue of Humphrey's conduct in office, because the breadth and scope of the *Myers* decision was quite adequate to allow Humphrey's dismissal on purely political grounds. Taft had argued in his decision that the President had the power to remove even executive officers of a "quasi-judicial character . . . whose decisions . . . the President cannot in a particular case properly influence or control. But even in such a case,"[22] Taft decided

> he may consider the decision after its rendition as a reason for removing the officer, on the ground that the discretion regularly entrusted to that officer by statute has not been on the whole intelligently or wisely exercised.[23]

That was going too far for the antipresidential mood of the Hughes Court, and in the *Humphrey* case Justice Sutherland wrote a unanimous decision establishing certain limits upon the *Myers* doctrine. The enabling legislation which created the Federal Trade Commission had not only defined the quasi-judicial functions of that body, but the Congress had also prescribed justifiable reasons or causes for the dismissal of its members.[24] The problem that the Court faced was whether or not the *Myers* decision empowered the President to go beyond those reasons to remove a commissioner, and indeed whether the removal power of the President applied to such officials as served on quasi-judicial boards and commissions created by the legislature.

Justice Sutherland, after carefully analyzing the language of the statute and reviewing the discussion in Congress when the law was first enacted, rejected the government's reliance on the *Myers* decision and ruled that the removal of a member of the commission could only be upheld if the dismissal was based upon the causes outlined in the Federal Trade Commission Act:

> [T]he language of the Act, the legislative reports, and the general purposes of the legislation as reflected by the debates, all combine to demonstrate the congressional intent to create a body of experts who shall gain experience by length of service; a body which shall be independent of Executive authority, *except in its selection*, and free to exercise its judgment without leave or hindrance of any other official or any department of the Government. To the accomplishment of these purposes, it is clear that Congress was of the opinion that length and certainty of tenure would vitally contribute. And to hold that, nevertheless the members of the Commission continue in office at the mere will of the President, might be to thwart, in large measure, the very ends which Congress sought to realize by definitely fixing the term of office.

> We conclude that the intent of the Act is to limit the Executive power of removal to the causes enumerated, the existence of none of which is claimed here.[25]

Continuing, Sutherland then dealt with the second question of whether or not the removal doctrine in *Myers* indeed applied to officials who served on quasi-judicial boards or commissions such as the FTC:

> The Federal Trade Commission is an administrative body created by Congress to carry into effect legislative policies embodied in the statute in

accordance with the legislative standard therein prescribed, and to perform other specified duties as a legislative or as a judicial aid. Such a body cannot in any proper sense be characterized as an arm or an eye of the Executive. Its duties performed without Executive leave and in the contemplation of the statute, must be free from Executive control. . . .

We think it plain under the Constitution that illimitable power of removal is not possessed by the President in respect of officers of the character of those just named. The authority of Congress, in creating quasi-legislative or quasi-judicial agencies, to require them to act in discharge of their duties independently of Executive control cannot well be doubted; and that authority includes, as an appropriate incident, power to fix the period during which they shall continue, and to forbid their removal except for cause in the meantime. For it is quite evident that one who holds his office only during the pleasure of another cannot be depended upon to maintain an attitude of independence against the latter's will.

The result of what we now have said is this: Whether the power of the President to remove an officer shall prevail over the authority of Congress to condition the power by fixing a definite term and precluding a removal except for cause will depend upon the character of the office; the Myers decision, affirming the power of the President alone to make the removal, is confined to purely executive officers; and as to officers of the kind here under consideration, we hold that no removal can be made during the prescribed term for which the officer is appointed except for one or more of the causes named in the applicable statute.[26]

Over 20 years later a decision in another case which came before the Supreme Court confirmed the restricted scope of the President's removal power. The question was brought to the Court in a suit filed by Wiener, who had been appointed as one of three members of the War Claims Commission, and had been removed from that office after President Eisenhower was inaugurated, because the new President wished to fill the position "with personnel of my own selection." Justice Frankfurter, after reviewing the doctrine of the removal power of the President as it had evolved from the *Myers* decision to the *Humphrey's Executor* case, stated that the opinion of the Court was that the War Claims Commission fell within the same category as the Federal Trade Commission, and that the previous judgment of the Court should apply in this case as well:

Judging the matter in all the nakedness in which it is presented, namely, the claim that the President could remove a member of an adjudicatory body like the War Claims Commission merely because he wanted his own appointees on such a Commission, we are compelled to conclude that no such power is given to the President directly by the Constitution, and none is impliedly conferred upon him by statute simply because Congress said nothing about it. The philosophy of *Humphrey's Executor*, in its explicit language as well as its implications, precludes such a claim.[27]

At mid-century, then, the President had consolidated his power to remove executive officers without the approval of the Senate, but definite limits had been placed upon that power with regard to presidential appointees in the quasi-legislative, quasi-judicial commissions and boards within which an increasing number of the important decisions of government are made. But although this legal reasoning neatly separated the personnel of the quasi-legislative, quasi-judicial regulatory agencies from the interference of the executive branch of the government, it by no means resolved the serious problems which they posed. If, in fact, it was necessary that they retain their "independent" character, it would mean that they should be independent of the pressures of the Congress and the powerful private industry and interest groups with which they had to deal on a continuing basis, as well as maintaining their independence of the executive branch. How was such "independence" to be established and protected? Was it desirable?

Although the word had a nice pure ring to it, did it not in reality mean that unless the agencies were capable of operating in an environment similar to that of the judicial branch of the government that "independence" would really be a myth, and that their severance from the politically responsible executive branch would leave them vulnerable to the most powerful interests, which could concentrate their influence in their own directions and in their own behalf?

The logical and constitutional legal reasoning of Justices Brandeis, Sutherland and Frankfurter did not supply answers to this vexing problem. The ambience of the regulatory agencies constituted a vast empire of power which demanded attention and control to serve the public interest. These decisions by the Court weakened the influence of the President to make the agency decision-makers answerable to him and ultimately to public opinion. Perhaps it was a necessary and desirable development. But it raised more questions than it answered, and provided a legal rather than a social and political resolution to a very serious problem emerging in the complex realm of American government. The President's Committee on Administrative Management, which will be discussed in the following chapter, proposed that the commissions be realigned with the executive branch, but Congress once again rebuked that solution, leaving the problem of the regulatory agencies and their responsibilities to the public interest a festering dilemma for American government.

Administrative Reorganization of
The Executive Branch

The ambiguity of the Constitution permitted, in fact invited, the long struggle between the legislative and executive branches with respect to the appointment and removal powers, and almost from the beginning Congress exploited its constitutional authority to influence and often to control policy and decision-making in the various administrative departments of the executive branch. Its powers in this area were both implicitly and explicitly spelled out in the Constitution, and nowhere in our system is there less "separation of powers" than in the administration of the government.

Through the implicit thrust of the provision "to make all Laws which shall be necessary and proper for carrying into Execution the foregoing powers [referring to all of the stipulated powers of both houses], and all other powers vested by this Constitution in the Government of the United States, or in any Department or Officer thereof," Congress has created all of the administrative departments of the government, and has the right to reorganize them when "necessary." Through the "power of the purse," its specific responsibilities in the raising of tax revenue and in the authorization and appropriation of funds to operate the departments and to meet the expenditures of the government, it possesses additional power, which it has used effectively throughout the history of this country, to play a major controlling role in the administration of the executive branch.

Benjamin Franklin and others warned the Constitutional Convention of the threat to liberty which an all-powerful Executive, as well as an all-powerful legislature would constitute. In response, the delegates wrote into the Constitution a number of safeguards to protect the new government from the domination of its President, while attempting at the same time to protect the Executive from an overbearing Congress. Opponents of presidential power had been weaned on the struggle between the King and Parliament in Britain, and the most sophisticated among them, like Franklin, were well aware that the Crown's access to almost unlimited patronage had enabled the British monarch to control Parliament for many years. They were convinced that the legislative branch, with its close rapport with and accountability to its constituents, should be armed with full authority to appropriate all funds, making it the central responsibility of its legislating function. The powers of a legislature to appropriate funds, to determine how, when and where they should be used, were and continue to be formidable weapons with which to worry and perhaps to control the Executive.

Recognizing this the Founding Fathers established this principle as the law of the land, stating explicitly in the Constitution that no funds could be expended without having been authorized by Congress, and that all money bills must originate in the House of Representatives. It is and was possible to interpret such provisions loosely or flexibly, allowing the Chief Executive and his department heads a considerable degree of discretion with respect to decisions governing the expenditure of properly appropriated funds. There are factors of time, place and condition which can redirect the initial course, but Congress, especially during the nineteenth century, was usually very adamant in its attempts to hold the executive branch tightly in rein. During that period Congress frequently exploited its powerful prerogatives and asserted its claims at the expense of the Executive.

Throughout most of the nineteenth century Congress labored diligently to limit the power of the executive branch by preventing the various departments from shifting appropriations for one purpose to another, from trying to hold on to their surpluses, or allocating funds for purposes not decreed by Congress, and from over-spending and expecting Congress to cover any deficits by supplementary appropriations. Albert Gallatin, a Swiss-born Republican from Pennsylvania, was the first congressman to mount a full-scale campaign against these procedures. He published a book analyzing existing practices, or malpractices as he considered them. In *A Sketch of the Finances of the United States*, he charged:

> [I]f, therefore, the moneys specifically appropriated to one head of service are applied to another head, they are not applied and accounted for pursuant, but contrary, to law. Such a mode is undoubtedly liable to great abuses; it deceives the Legislature, who, when appropriating one hundred thousand dollars for the defensive protection of the frontiers, did not think that the Treasury would assume a power to apply them to the quartermaster or any other department. It deprives the Legislature from any control, not only over the distribution of the moneys among the several heads of service, but even over the total sum to be expended. For the million and a half dollars appropriated for the annual support of six thousand men, the nominal establishment, may be spent in the same time, and in fact has actually been expended within fourteen months for the 3,500 men who constituted the effective establishment. The same abuse has, for a considerable time, prevailed in England, where it has, at several periods, been taken notice of, and did lately produce a motion of impeachment against the Ministers.[28]

Gallatin finally succeeded in passing legislation aimed at restricting the transfer of funds problem, but it did not wholly eliminate the practice. As Jefferson's secretary of the treasury, he persisted in his efforts to control these "loose" procedures, and he was responsible for urging the President to include in his First Annual Message a plea that the appropriations should be "in specific sums for each specific purpose, *of susceptible definition*"[29] and that transfers of appropriated money from one purpose to another be prohibited and contingency funds be reduced. A noted student of these matters has written that Congress has always sought

> to control the Executive through the device of highly specific appropriations rather than by consideration of the requirements of an effective budgetary process. These controls have never worked satisfactorily and have broken down at times when it is important for the budget process to be effective. Yet when the Congress wishes to assert its authority over the Executive, it returns to restrictions on the use of appropriations with unvarying monotony.[30]

Congress' major complaint against the executive branch was the never-ending problem of supplementary appropriations, which were the result of inaccurate estimates, overspending or the refusal of the legislature to appropriate sufficient funds for the department's needs. A solution to this practice was finally attempted in 1906. A measure, sponsored by the chairman of the House Appropriations Committee, Congressman James A. Tawney, which forbade supplementary requests except in situations of imperative necessity, with a full explanation of the need, along with the reasons why the item was not included in the regular appropriations request, was introduced. Apparently this measure met with some success in the period immediately following its passage. But Congress was sufficiently alarmed at the continuance of this practice to act again three years later by tacking on a rider to a sundry appropriations supplement. That action began the movement to restore the President to a position of equal footing with Congress in the administration of the executive branch of the government. Though not the intent of the rider, it appeared to be its result. In an effort to bring the annual estimates (submitted to the secretary of the treasury by the individual department heads) into line with the annual revenues, Congress proposed that in the event that the estimates for continuing and permanent appropriations exceeded the estimated revenue,

> the Secretary of Treasury shall transmit the estimates to Congress as heretofore required by law and at once transmit a detailed statement of all of said estimates to the President, to the end that he may, in giving Congress information of the state of the Union and in recommending to their consideration such measures as he may judge necessary, advise the Congress how in his judgment the estimated appropriations could with the least injury to the public service be reduced so as to bring the appropriations within the estimated revenues, or, if such reduction be not in his judgment practicable without undue injury to the public service, that he may recommend to Congress such loans or new taxes as may be necessary to cover the deficiency.[31]

This law brought the President back into the financial operation of the government after many years of exile and laid the groundwork for a more important role for him in the future.

In the period when the office of the presidency was eclipsed by the aggressive posture of the legislature, the powers asserted by Congress (as described in Volume II of this series)—control of the appointing process and of the removal power, and organizational and financial control of the executive departments—all converged to diminish the power and function of the President as a leader in the American political system. In domestic affairs from William Henry Harrison to Grover Cleveland (with the exceptions of Polk during the Mexican War and Lincoln during the Civil War), the presidency receded into the back seat of history, the captive of policies created by Congress. This was the period characterized by Woodrow Wilson as the era of "Congressional Government."

The crucial struggle against congressional power waged by Hayes and Garfield had brought some degree of balance back into the system, and the triumphs of the presidency in the administrations of Cleveland and Theodore Roosevelt made the problem of presidential control within the executive branch of the government more acute. However, with its powers of authorizing policies and programs, appropriating funds, creating and organizing executive departments, and monitoring and investigating those departments, Congress had arrived at the point where those same departments and their directing officers considered themselves more responsible to the chairmen of their related special House and Senate committees than they did to the President of the United States, whose chief advisors and cabinet members they were.

The Major Contributions
Of the Taft Commission

The Appropriations Act of 1909 created a new role for the President in the appropriations procedure and opened up new opportunities for the development of very much needed and long overdue functions for the Chief Executive in the administrative affairs of his own executive departments. Congress had long recognized the President's often independent role in the foreign relations field and as Commander in Chief of the Armed Forces, but had fought jealously to isolate him from influence in the administrative affairs of the executive branch. This center of governmental power shifted significantly during Theodore Roosevelt's administration, and although his successor, William Howard Taft, differed fundamentally with Roosevelt with respect to the executive prerogatives of the presidential office, he inherited a position which already had begun to consolidate considerably more power in the hands of the Chief Executive than had been held in the previous century.[32] Taft's secretary of the treasury, Franklin McVeagh, expressed the hope that both the legislative and executive branches could reorganize themselves along systematic lines to develop the administrative machinery necessary for coordinating an efficient budget system:

> [S]omething should be done to organize the divided consideration now given the expenditures of the Government and the interrelation of its income and outgo. The responsibilities relative to estimates, appropriations and revenues are extremely scattered and disintegrated. The vast sums that pass through the Treasury coming and going are without any centralized study or recommendation such as other countries find it necessary to give to their Government finances. We shall have to continue to divide this important work between the executive and the legislative departments of the Government. There should, however, be found a way to organize work done in the executive department and to organize the work done in the legislative department, and then to establish a responsible cooperation between the two. To map out a new system will require thorough study; and to arrange for this it would seem to be necessary for the Congress to appoint a commission representative of the executive and legislative departments of the Government. And I hope Congress may be interested enough to appoint such a commission during its present session.[33]

Congress acted by granting the President's request for $100,000 to finance a commission of this type, and Taft appointed "The President's Commission on Economy and Efficiency" on March 8, 1911. Frederick Cleveland of the Bureau of Municipal Research was appointed chairman of the group, and he submitted a 568-page report to the President the following year. In that report the commission pointed out the shortcomings of the amended appropriations bill of 1909 which first brought the President back into the picture, because it assumed that his participation would begin only *after* the initial figures were submitted to the Congress, and only *if* the estimated expenditures were out of line with the estimated revenues. The report also revealed that there was no "executive officer or any official person or group or any branch of the Government required by law to consider the estimates from the viewpoint of the needs of the country or with the idea of bringing the estimated expenditures within the estimated revenue before submission to the Congress as a request for appropriation.[34]

The report went on to state:

The broad theory of the Constitution is that the Congress shall have the power to determine questions of policy which involve the expenditure of money, i.e., what shall be done, and what organization, what equipment, and what funds shall be provided; that the President shall have the power to execute and shall be held responsible for the economy and efficiency with which plans and policies adopted by Congress are executed. In this constitutional plan the courts were to have practically no part unless some right of an individual or of a State might be involved in the action taken by the legislative or the executive branch.

This underlying constitutional theory has, however, been widely departed from in practice. The legislative branch has not only assumed to settle questions of policy but also, through appropriations and minuteness of detail in organic law, has deprived the executive branch (the administration) of the exercise of discretion with respect to a large part of the public business. While the purpose has been to prevent the misuse of power, the effect has been to relieve administrative officers of responsibility for waste and inefficiency in the service. The underlying motive which has transformed monarchial to constitutional forms of government has been to make the executive branch more responsible. In this country monarchy, as a form, was overthrown by revolution. This having been accomplished, the legislative branch has proceeded on a theory which has operated to make the administration irresponsible—in other words, to defeat one of the primary purposes of the Constitution.[35]

In order to overcome this disorderly irresponsibility, the commission made six recommendations:

1. That the President, as the Constitutional head of the executive branch of the Government, shall each year submit to the Congress, not later than the first Monday after the beginning of the regular session, a budget.

2. That the budget so submitted shall contain:

(a) *A budgetary message*, setting forth in brief the significance of the proposals to which attention is invited.

(b) *A summary financial statement*, setting forth in very summary form: (1) The financial condition; (2) a statement of the condition of appropriations and other data pertaining to the "general fund" as well as to the other funds of the Government; (3) an account of revenues and expenditures for the last completed fiscal year; and (4) a statement showing the effect of past financial policy as well as of budget proposals on the general-fund surplus.

(c) *A summary of expenditures*, classified by objects, setting forth the contracting and purchasing relations of the Government.

(d) *Summaries of estimates*, setting forth: (1) The estimated revenues for a period of years; (2) estimated expenditures compared with actual expenditures for a period of years.

(e) *A summary of changes in law*, setting forth what legislation it is thought should be enacted in order to enable the administration to transact public business with greater economy and efficiency, i.e., changes in organic law which, if enacted, would affect appropriations as well as the character of work to be done.

3. That the Secretary of the Treasury be required to submit to the Congress the following detailed reports supporting the general summaries and executive conclusions or recommendations contained in the budget, as follows:

(a) *A book of estimates*, containing the supporting details to the summaries of estimates of expenditure contained in the budget.

(b) *A consolidated financial report*, containing a detailed statement of revenues and a consolidated statement of expenditures for the last five fiscal years, with such explanatory matter as is necessary to give information with respect to increases or decreases in revenue or expenditure or other relations to which it is thought that the attention of the executive and legislative branches is to be given.

4. That the head of each department and independent establishment should be required to submit to the Secretary of the Treasury and to the Congress annual reports which, among other things, would contain detailed accounts of expenditures so classified as to show amounts of increases or decreases in stores, equipment, property, etc., including lands, buildings, and other improvements, as well as such other data or operative statistics and comment in relation thereto as may be necessary to show results obtained and the economy and efficiency of doing Government work, as well as of contracting and purchasing.

5. That the President and heads of departments issue orders which will require that such accounts be kept, such reports be made, and such estimates be prepared as will enable them to obtain the information needed to consider the different conditions, relations, above enumerated before the estimates are submitted; that the President recommend to the Congress the enactment of such laws as will enable the administration to comply with the requirements of the Congress.

6. That the President recommend for the consideration of the Congress such changes in the form of appropriation bills as will enable the Government to avail itself of the benefits of the exercise of discretion on

the part of the executive in the transaction of current business in order that the Government may do work and accomplish results with economy and efficiency as will definitely fix responsibility for failure so to exercise such discretion.[36]

The report attempted to explain and justify its recommendations with over 500 pages of words and statistics. Central to the argument was the concept of executive responsibility:

One of the fundamental purposes of establishing constitutional government is to secure responsible government. The reason for urging that the budget should be submitted by the President is that the President is the only person who under the Constitution is responsible for the acts of the executive branch of what is known as "the administration." Under the British constitutional system the titular executive is the Crown. The effective head of "the administration," or, as it is called, in accordance with British usage, "the Government," however, is the cabinet. In other words, the cabinet, at the head of which is the prime minister, is made responsible for the execution of laws and for the administration of public business. It is the "administration's" proposals and the "administration's" acts which are considered by the Parliament.

Frequently it is said that our form of government is defective in that no provision has been made for the location of executive responsibility; that the President, in the nature of things, cannot be held responsible for the business of the various departments and establishments throughout the service; that the business of the Government must be attended to by others who are appointed by the President, by and with the advice and consent of the Senate. The commission believes that such a conclusion is unwarranted from a constitutional point of view, although it may be supported historically. Constitutionally, the President is the Prime Minister of the United States; constitutionally the President is chosen by a "college of electors," who in turn are chosen by the vote of the people instead of being chosen by Congress, who are in turn chosen by the vote of the people. The mere difference in the method of choosing the President on the one hand and the prime minister on the other does not warrant the conclusion, therefore, that the executive branch of our Government can not be made responsible.

In the opinion of the Commission the establishment of executive responsibility for the manner in which business is transacted in each of the departments and establishments is essential to obtaining results with economy and efficiency.[37]

The argument continued:

The constructive recommendations of the Commission are to the effect that the President shall each year get before the country what it is that the administration desires to do; shall indicate in a budget message wherein action is necessary to enable the administration adequately to meet the public needs; shall indicate what definite legislation is desired and what funds are needed; shall lay the foundation for such cooperation between the legislative branch and the executive branch as will enable the Government most efficiently to provide for the welfare of the people. As an incident to such procedure it is suggested that the President shall indicate wherein limitations are placed upon executive officers which relieve them from responsibility which they must necessarily bear if they are to give to the country the benefit of intelligent administrative direction and control.

The adoption of the recommendation of the Commission that the President of the United States shall submit the budget would have for its effect to make him responsible for knowing what the estimates contain before submission; to make him aware of financial conditions; to bring before him for consideration the changes desired. The recommendation that the Secretary of the Treasury shall prepare the Book of Estimates containing the detail items in support of the summaries contained in the budget would have for its effect to make the Secretary of the Treasury not only the official editor of the estimates prepared in departments (which he now is) and the ministerial agent for their transmission to Congress, but also an effective assistant to the President in bringing together the data and in presenting them in such form that their significance can be readily understood and considered, thereby enabling the President and his Cabinet to act intelligently. To this end there would be worked out as a result of conference, and stated in summary form, a definite administrative program to be presented by the President as the head of the administration in the consideration of which each member of the Cabinet would arrange the details of his estimates in such manner as to support this program.

The further concrete proposal is that the budget shall be transmitted with a special message to the Congress, setting forth briefly what the proposals of the administration are to which attention is specially invited. In other words, it is assumed that the President as the one officer of Government who represents the people as a whole is in the best position to lay before the Congress and to state to the people what the Government is doing and what it proposes to do; that the President, under the powers given to him by the Constitution, is in a better position than anyone else to dramatize the work of the Government—to so impress this upon the attention of the people, through the public press, by means of a budgetary message as to arouse discussion and elicit comment such as will keep the Congress as well as the administration in touch with public opinion when deciding whether or not the proposals are such as will best meet welfare demands.[38]

In proposing such a revolutionary change, the President's commission argued that in assigning administrative discretion to the executive branch and providing the President with the power and responsibility of coordinating a budget for congressional consideration, the foundations would be established for a new era of cooperation and mutual confidence between the executive and legislative branches. This marked a significant change from what existed at that time:

> The present procedure is one which induces the Congress and the administration to deal with each other on a plane of lack of mutual confidence—for each to be in the attitude of trying to deceive the other—but the administration itself and its several branches and divisions are handled in the same way. Each Secretary is carrying on his business with little or no information given to the other Secretaries or the President with respect to what he is doing. Each bureau and division chief under the Secretary is in like manner carrying on the business under his control. For it, he alone assumes responsibility. He gives to the Secretary and to his fellow chiefs only such information as seems to be necessary in order to get along. He has assumed a responsibility which can not be enforced. He goes directly to the Congress and deals directly through its members for his funds (he may not even be known to the Committee on Appropriations, preferring rather to get someone else to represent him). He may obtain funds for purposes against the wishes of his superior, and even against the written recommendations of the President. Each member of the administration is in the attitude of "dealing in the dark," so far as other members of the administration and the Congress are concerned.[39]

Finally, the commission argued that the creation of an annual budget which would be publicly presented, not simply to the Congress but also to the American public, would provide a background of information for public thought and discussion, and the development of an informed public opinion.

> One of the most important features of the commission's recommendation is that which requires that every plan to be executed be made an open book, to be read by the Congress, by officers of the administration, and by the public. Any committee of Congress wishing to know what is being done, what organization is provided for doing the work, what moneys are being expended, how they are being expended, how it is proposed that they shall be expended in the future, can obtain this information at once without waiting for the dilatory and slow results of the special inquiry. The power of legislative control over an administration under such circumstances would be great; but the greatest power to enforce responsibility would be through the possibility of making the acts of officers public.[40]

The fact is that both the executive and legislative branches of our Government are highly sensitive to expressions of public opinion. The adoption of the recommendations of the commission would make this influence many times more powerful than at present. As has been said, provision would be made whereby not only each branch of the Government would be taken into the confidence of the other branches, but also the plans and activities of all branches would be kept constantly before the people. Recognizing in the President not only the constitutional power, but also the possibility of getting before the country in a most effective way the proposals of the administration and of supporting these proposals with such details of fact as will enable the public press and citizen welfare organizations to discuss them intelligently; recognizing in the Congress the constitutional power to consider these proposals in determining questions of policy; recognizing the desirability of having the details of business determined by those who must transact it—the concrete recommendations of the commission provide for giving publicity to each act of each group of officers or agents and for basing this publicity on complete, accurate, and prompt statements of fact.[41]

President Taft submitted the commission's report with a strong endorsement, indicating that it was his desire that "the President and the Congress may cooperate—the one in laying before the Congress and the country a clearly expressed administrative program to be acted on; the other in laying before the President a definite enactment to be acted on by him."[42]

The report of the President's commission was a real breakthrough and a landmark in the field of budgetary reform. It also eventually led to the strengthening and reorganization of the executive branch. But these things did not happen immediately. Taft submitted the first executive budget in 1913 just before he went out of office, but a hostile Democratic Congress ignored it. In his message of submittal he argued:

In a Government such as ours, in which the legislative branch is made up of some 500 members, it is not to be assumed that each member or any committee of such a body is familiar with the many details which go to make up the public business. The increasing need for an Executive account of stewardship is apparent. The President is the constitutional head of an organization that is continental in the scope of its operations. Executive officers under him for whom he is responsible must manage and direct the details of hundreds of essentially different businesses that are highly complex and technical in their requirements. These officers must be held accountable for efficiency as managers; they must be held accountable for economy in the expenditure of public funds; they must be made to feel responsible for the fidelity of employees who are charged with money transactions aggregating more than $5,000,000,000 each year, or $16,000,000 each business day.[43]

Taft passed over any question of additional legislative authorization needed by the President to submit a budget, arguing that an obligation to do so was implied in his executive responsibilities as Chief Administrator, although he noted that no previous President had made use of this prerogative:

In the discharge of duties the President has submitted annual reviews of the conditions affecting the national welfare and also many special recommendations for legislation; but the Chief Executive has never undertaken to lay before the Congress the facts necessary to the determination of questions of policy pertaining to that phase of public business which is his special responsibility, namely, the carrying on of the work of the Government during the succeeding year. [44]

Two years after the report was submitted to Congress Taft complained in a speech at Columbia University that "dust is accumulating on the Commission's reports."[45] Yet the idea of a presidential budget persisted, and although Congress took no concrete action, and the resident of the White House, Woodrow Wilson, gave no clear indication of his interest in it, the proposal was still very much alive; year after year legislation was introduced to bring such a change into effect.

The Budget and Accounting Act of 1921

The impetus for Congress' real interest in the proposals presented by the Taft Commission came on the heels of the adoption of the executive budget by a number of states after 1913, particularly the law passed in Illinois in 1917. In 1918 Representative Medill McCormick of Illinois introduced legislation which eventually led, although in a different form, to the Budget and Accounting Act of 1921. Hearings were held in 1919 by the House Select Committee on "The Need for a Budget System." The committee was chaired by Congressman James Good of Iowa, who was responsible for piloting the final measure through the House, and was the major force in its becoming a law. In the initial House bill, passed by an overwhelming margin of 285 to 3, provision was made for an executive budget to be drawn up by a new office, the Bureau of the Budget, which was to serve as a staff agency to the Chief Executive. The Senate, however, failed to consider the measure that year because of the debate over the Versailles Treaty.

In his State of the Union Message in 1920 President Wilson entered the fray for the first time and urged legislative action on an executive budget, and also recommended that a special appropriations committee be created in each house to centralize the now fantastically dispersed activity of more than a dozen different committees which passed on appropriations. When the matter came up for Senate consideration the following year, the now Senator McCormick introduced his own bill in place of the House measure. That bill proposed that the secretary of the treasury, rather than the President, be responsible for the budget. In the McCormick bill the Bureau of the Budget was also placed within the Treasury Department. The conference committee which reported out the compromise bill returned the responsibility for preparing the budget to the President, but Wilson vetoed the measure because McCormick had also inserted a clause which provided that the comptroller general, who was to head up a new general accounting office, would be removable only by concurrent resolution of the Congress.

The Budget and Accounting Act finally became law in 1921, when the Congress partially satisfied the President's objections by changing the removal clause requiring a concurrent resolution (which did not need the signature of the President to be valid) to a joint resolution requiring the President's approval. But basically the law carried through, in the most significant sense, the major part of the Taft Commission recommendations. First of all, it called for a comprehensive executive budget, which assigned to the President the fundamental responsibility for coordinating an overall estimate of the needs of his administration, and the responsibility of preparing an estimate of the probable revenues the government could expect to collect during the coming fiscal year. Secondly, it provided the President with much needed professional assistance in the establishment of the Bureau of the Budget, which, although formally assigned to the Treasury Department, was clearly intended to serve as the President's staff agency to aid in the preparation of the budget and to strengthen his authority over his administrative family. Finally, it created the General Accounting Agency under the comptroller general, who was answerable to the Congress with respect to expenditure of appropriated funds. These were mainly formal and structural changes, but they possessed tremendous potential for very significant functional and substantive reforms in the operation of the presidential office as well as the whole system of American government.

The anachronism of an executive head of state who had virtually no authority with respect to the allocation of expenditures of the government over which he presided became a relic of the past, and the President finally began to emerge as a central and invigorated force in the administrative functions of the government. Of course he had to share many aspects of the role with the powerful fiscal committees of the Congress, such as the House Ways and Means Committee, and with the bureaucratic agency heads who had for so long dealt directly with the Congress; but paralleling his growing influence as an initiating force in the legislative area, the President was then able to assert significant authority and direction in administrative affairs, power that had been denied him in the nineteenth century. Richard E. Neustadt has written that "no other single innovation has so markedly enlarged the practical importance of the Presidency to the whole executive establishment; those sponsors got more than they bargained for."[46]

The Budget and Accounting Act of 1921
June 10, 1921

United States Statutes at Large, 67th Cong., XLII, Part I, 20-27.

Title I—Definitions

Section 1
   This Act may be cited as the "Budget and Accounting Act, 1921."

Sec. 2
      When used in this Act—
      The terms "department and establishment" and "department or establishment"

mean any executive department, independent commission, board, bureau, office, agency, or other establishment of the Government, including the municipal government of the District of Columbia, but do not include the Legislative Branch of the Government or the Supreme Court of the United States;

The term "the Budget" means the Budget required by section 201 to be transmitted to Congress;

The term "Bureau" means the Bureau of the Budget;

The term "Director" means the Director of the Bureau of the Budget; and

The term "Assistant Director" means the Assistant Director of the Bureau of the Budget.

Title II—The Budget

Sec. 201

The President shall transmit to Congress on the first day of each regular session, the Budget, which shall set forth in summary and in detail:

(a) Estimates of the expenditures and appropriations necessary in his judgment for the support of the Government for the ensuing fiscal year; except that the estimates for such year for the Legislative Branch of the Government and the Supreme Court of the United States shall be transmitted to the President on or before October 15th of each year, and shall be included by him in the Budget without revision;

(b) His estimates of the receipts of the Government during the ensuing fiscal year, under (1) laws existing at the time the Budget is transmitted and also (2) under the revenue proposals, if any, contained in the Budget;

(c) The expenditures and receipts of the Government during the last completed fiscal year;

(d) Estimates of the expenditures and receipts of the Government during the fiscal year in progress;

(e) The amount of annual, permanent, or other appropriations, including balances of appropriations for prior fiscal years, available for expenditure during the fiscal year in progress, as of November 1 of such year;

(f) Balanced statements of (1) the condition of the Treasury at the end of the last completed fiscal year, (2) the estimated condition of the Treasury at the end of the fiscal year in progress, and (3) the estimated condition of the Treasury at the end of the ensuing fiscal year if the financial proposals contained in the Budget are adopted;

(g) All essential facts regarding the bonded and other indebtedness of the Government; and

(h) Such other financial statements and data as in his opinion are necessary or desirable in order to make known in all practicable detail the financial condition of the Government.

Sec. 202

(a) If the estimated receipts for the ensuing fiscal year contained in the Budget, on the basis of laws existing at the time the Budget is transmitted, plus the estimated amounts in the Treasury at the close of the fiscal year in progress, available for expenditure in the ensuing fiscal year, are less than the estimated expenditures for the ensuing fiscal year contained in the Budget, the President in the Budget shall make recommendations to Congress for new taxes, loans, or other appropriate action to meet the estimated deficiency.

(b) If the aggregate of such estimated receipts and such estimated amounts in the Treasury is greater than such estimated expenditures for the ensuing fiscal year, he shall make such recommendations as in his opinion the public interests require.

Sec. 203

(a) The President from time to time may transmit to Congress supplemental or deficiency estimates for such appropriations or expenditures as in his judgment (1) are necessary on account of laws enacted after the transmission of the Budget, or (2) are otherwise in the public interest. He shall accompany such estimates with a statement of the reasons therefor, including the reasons for their omission from the Budget.

(b) Whenever such supplemental or deficiency estimates reach an aggregate which, if they had been contained in the Budget, would have required the President to make a recommendation under subdivision (a) of section 202, he shall thereupon make such recommendation.

Sec. 204

(a) Except as otherwise provided in this Act, the contents, order, and arrangement of the estimates of appropriations and the statements of expenditures and estimated expenditures contained in the Budget or transmitted under section 203, and the notes and other data submitted therewith, shall conform to the requirements of existing law.

(b) Estimates for lump-sum appropriations contained in the Budget or transmitted under section 203 shall be accompanied by statements showing, in such detail and form as may be necessary to inform Congress, the manner of expenditure of such appropriations and of the corresponding appropriations for the fiscal year in progress and the last completed fiscal year. Such statements shall be in lieu of statements of like character now required by law.

Sec. 205

The President, in addition to the Budget, shall transmit to Congress on the first Monday in December, 1921, for the service of the fiscal year ending June 30, 1923, only, an alternative budget, which shall be prepared in such form and amounts and according to such system of classification and itemization as is, in his opinion, most appropriate, with such explanatory notes and tables as may be necessary to show where the various items embraced in the Budget are contained in such alternative budget.

Sec. 206

No estimate or request for an appropriation and no request for an increase in an item of any such estimate or request, and no recommendation as to how the revenue needs of the Government should be met, shall be submitted to Congress or any committee thereof by any officer or employee of any department or establishment, unless at the request of either House of Congress.

Sec. 207

There is hereby created in the Treasury Department a Bureau to be known as the Bureau of the Budget. There shall be in the Bureau a Director and an Assistant Director, who shall be appointed by the President and receive salaries of $10,000 and $7,500 a year, respectively. The Assistant Director shall perform such duties as the Director may designate, and during the absence or incapacity of the Director or during a vacancy in the office of Director he shall act as Director. The Bureau, under such rules and regulations as the President may prescribe, shall prepare for him the Budget, the alternative Budget, and any supplemental or deficiency estimates, and to this end shall have authority to assemble, correlate, revise, reduce, or increase the estimates of the several departments or establishments.

Sec. 208

(a) The Director, under such rules and regulations as the President may prescribe, shall appoint and fix the compensation of attorneys and other employees and make expenditures for rent in the District of Columbia, printing, binding, telegrams, telephone service, law books, books of reference, periodicals, stationery, furniture, office equipment, other supplies, and necessary expenses of the office, within the appropriations made therefor.

(b) No person appointed by the Director shall be paid a salary at a rate in excess of $6,000 a year, and not more than four persons so appointed shall be paid a salary at a rate in excess of $5,000 a year.

(c) All employees in the Bureau whose compensation is at a rate of $5,000 a year or less shall be appointed in accordance with the civil-service laws and regulations.

(d) The provisions of law prohibiting the transfer of employees of executive departments and independent establishments until after service of three years shall not apply during the fiscal years ending June 30, 1921, and June 30, 1922, to the transfer of employees to the Bureau.

(e) The Bureau shall not be construed to be a bureau or office created since January 1, 1916, so as to deprive employees therein of the additional compensation allowed civilian employees under the provisions of section 6 of the Legislative, Executive, and Judicial Appropriation Act for the fiscal years ending June 30, 1921, and June 30, 1922, if otherwise entitled thereto.

Sec. 209

The Bureau, when directed by the President, shall make a detailed study of the departments and establishments for the purpose of enabling the President to determine what changes (with a view of securing greater economy and efficiency in the conduct of the public service) should be made in (1) the existing organization, activities, and methods of business of such departments or establishments, (2) the appropriations therefor, (3) the assignment of particular activities to particular services, or (4) the regrouping of services. The results of such study shall be embodied in a report or reports to the President, who may transmit to Congress such report or reports or any part thereof with his recommendations on the matters covered thereby.

Sec. 210

The Bureau shall prepare for the President a codification of all laws or parts of laws relating to the preparation and transmission to Congress of statements of receipts and expenditures of the Government and of estimates of appropriations. The President shall transmit the same to Congress on or before the first Monday in December, 1921, with a recommendation as to the changes which, in his opinion, should be made in such laws or parts of laws.

Sec. 211

The powers and duties relating to the compiling of estimates now conferred and imposed upon the Division of Bookkeeping and Warrants of the office of the Secretary of the Treasury are transferred to the Bureau.

Sec. 212

The Bureau shall, at the request of any committee of either House of Congress having jurisdiction over revenue or appropriations, furnish the committee such aid and information as it may request.

Sec. 213

Under such regulations as the President may prescribe, (1) every department and establishment shall furnish to the Bureau such information as the Bureau may from time to time require, and (2) the Director and the Assistant Director, or any employee of the Bureau when duly authorized, shall, for the purpose of securing such information, have access to, and the right to examine, any books, documents, papers, or records of any such department or establishment.

Sec. 214

(a) The head of each department and establishment shall designate an official thereof as budget officer therefor, who, in each year under his direction and on or before a date fixed by him, shall prepare the departmental estimates.

(b) Such budget officer shall also prepare, under the direction of the head of the department or establishment, such supplemental and deficiency estimates as may be required for its work.

Sec 215

The head of each department and establishment shall revise the departmental estimates and submit them to the Bureau on or before September 15 of each year. In case of his failure so to do, the President shall cause to be prepared such estimates and data as are necessary to enable him to include in the Budget estimates and statements in respect to the work of such department or establishment.

Sec. 216

The departmental estimates and any supplemental or deficiency estimates submitted to the Bureau by the head of any department or establishment shall be prepared and submitted in such form, manner, and detail as the President may prescribe.

Sec. 217

For expenses of the establishment and maintenance of the Bureau there is appropriated, out of any money in the Treasury not otherwise appropriated, the sum of $225,000, to continue available during the fiscal year ending June 30, 1922.

Title III—General Accounting Office

Sec. 301

There is created an establishment of the Government to be known as the General Accounting Office, which shall be independent of the executive departments and under the control and direction of the Comptroller General of the United States. The offices of Comptroller of the Treasury and Assistant Comptroller of the Treasury are abolished, to take effect July 1, 1921. All other officers and employees of the office of the Comptroller of the Treasury shall become officers and employees in the General Accounting Office at their grades and salaries on July 1, 1921, and all books, records, documents, papers, furniture, office equipment and other property of the office of the Comptroller of the Treasury shall become the property of the General Accounting Office. The Comptroller General is authorized to adopt a seal for the General Accounting Office.

Sec. 302

There shall be in the General Accounting Office a Comptroller General of the United States and an Assistant Comptroller General of the United States, who shall be appointed by the President with the advice and consent of the Senate, and shall receive salaries of $10,000 and $7,500 a year, respectively. The Assistant Comptroller General shall perform such duties as may be assigned to him by the Comptroller General, and during the absence or incapacity of the Comptroller General, or during a vacancy in that office, shall act as Comptroller General.

Sec. 303

Except as hereinafter provided in this section, the Comptroller General and the Assistant Comptroller General shall hold office for fifteen years. The Comptroller General shall not be eligible for reappointment. The Comptroller General or the Assistant Comptroller General may be removed at any time by joint resolution of Congress after notice and hearing, when, in the judgment of Congress, the Comptroller General or Assistant Comptroller General has become permanently incapacitated or has been inefficient, or guilty of neglect of duty, or of malfeasance in office, or of any felony or conduct involving moral turpitude, and for no other cause and in no other manner except by impeachment. Any Comptroller General or Assistant Comptroller General removed in the manner herein provided shall be ineligible for reappointment to that office. When a Comptroller General or Assistant Comptroller General attains the age of seventy years, he shall be retired from his office.

Sec. 304

All powers and duties now conferred or imposed by law upon the Comptroller of the Treasury or the six auditors of the Treasury Department, and the duties of the Division of Bookkeeping and Warrants of the Office of the Secretary of the Treasury relating to keeping the personal ledger accounts of disbursing and collecting officers, shall, so far as not inconsistent with this Act, be vested in and imposed upon the General Accounting Office and be exercised without direction from any other officer. The balances certified by the Comptroller General shall be final and conclusive upon the executive branch of the Government. The revision by the Comptroller General of settlements made by the six auditors shall be discontinued, except as to settlements made before July 1, 1921.

The administrative examination of the accounts and vouchers of the Postal Service now imposed by law upon the Auditor for the Post Office Department shall be performed on and after July 1, 1921, by a bureau in the Post Office Department to be known as the Bureau of Accounts, which is hereby established for that purpose. The Bureau of Accounts shall be under the direction of a Comptroller, who shall be appointed by the President with the advice and consent of the Senate, and shall receive a salary of $5,000 a year. The Comptroller shall perform the administrative duties now performed by the Auditor for the Post Office Department and such other duties in relation thereto as the Postmaster General may direct. The appropriation of $5,000 for the salary of the Auditor for the Post Office Department for the fiscal year 1922 is transferred and made available for the salary of the Comptroller, Bureau of Accounts, Post Office Department. The officers and employees of the Office of the Auditor for the Post Office Department engaged in the administrative examination of accounts shall become officers and employees of the Bureau of Accounts at their grades and salaries on July 1, 1921. The appropriations for salaries and for contingent and miscellaneous expenses and tabulating equipment for such office for the fiscal year 1922, and all books, records, documents, papers, furniture, office equipment, and other property shall be apportioned between, transferred to, and made available for the Bureau of Accounts and the General Accounting Office, respectively, on the basis of duties transferred.

Sec. 305

Section 236 of the Revised Statutes is amended to read as follows:

"Sec. 236. All claims and demands whatever by the Government of the United States or against it, and all accounts whatever in which the Government of the United States is concerned, either as debtor or creditor, shall be settled and adjusted in the General Accounting Office."

Sec. 306

All laws relating generally to the administration of the departments and establishments shall, so far as applicable, govern the General Accounting Office. Copies of any books, records, papers, or documents, and transcripts from the books and proceedings of the General Accounting Office, when certified by the Comptroller General or the Assistant Comptroller General under its seal, shall be admitted as evidence with the same effect as the copies and transcripts referred to in sections 882 and 886 of the Revised Statutes.

Sec. 307

The Comptroller General may provide for the payment of accounts or claims adjusted and settled in the General Accounting Office, through disbursing officers of the several departments and establishments, instead of by warrant.

Sec. 308

The duties now appertaining to the Division of Public Moneys of the Office of the Secretary of the Treasury, so far as they relate to the covering of revenues and repayments into the Treasury, the issue of duplicate checks and warrants, and the certification of outstanding liabilities for payment, shall be performed by the Division of Bookkeeping and Warrants of the Office of the Secretary of the Treasury.

Sec. 309

The Comptroller General shall prescribe the forms, systems, and procedure for administrative appropriation and fund accounting in the several departments and establishments, and for the administrative examination of fiscal officers' accounts and claims against the United States.

Sec. 310

The offices of the six auditors shall be abolished, to take effect July 1, 1921. All other officers and employees of these offices except as otherwise provided herein shall become officers and employees of the General Accounting Office at their grades and salaries on July 1, 1921. All books, records, documents, papers, furniture, office equipment, and other property of these offices, and of the Division of Bookkeeping and Warrants, so far as they relate to the work of such division transferred by section 304, shall become the property of the General Accounting Office. The General Accounting Office shall occupy temporarily the rooms now occupied by the office of the Comptroller of the Treasury and the six auditors.

Sec. 311

(a) The Comptroller General shall appoint, remove, and fix the compensation of such attorneys and other employees in the General Accounting Office as may from time to time be provided for by law.

(b) All such appointments, except to positions carrying a salary at a rate of more than $5,000 a year, shall be made in accordance with the civil-service laws and regulations.

(c) No person appointed by the Comptroller General shall be paid a salary at a rate of more than $6,000 a year, and not more than four persons shall be paid a salary at a rate of more than $5,000 a year.

(d) All officers and employees of the General Accounting Office, whether transferred thereto or appointed by the Comptroller General, shall perform such duties as may be assigned to them by him.

(e) All official acts performed by such officers or employees specially designated therefor by the Comptroller General shall have the same force and effect as though performed by the Comptroller General in person.

(f) The Comptroller General shall make such rules and regulations as may be necessary for carrying on the work of the General Accounting Office, including rules and regulations concerning the admission of attorneys to practice before such office.

Sec. 312

(a) The Comptroller General shall investigate, at the seat of government or elsewhere, all matters relating to the receipt, disbursement, and application of public funds, and shall make to the President when requested by him, and to Congress at the beginning of each regular session, a report in writing of the work of the General Accounting Office, containing recommendations concerning the legislation he may deem necessary to facilitate the prompt and accurate rendition and settlement of accounts and concerning such other matters relating to the receipt, disbursement, and application of public funds as he may think advisable. In such regular report, or in special reports at any time when Congress is in session, he shall make recommendations looking to greater economy or efficiency in public expenditures.

(b) He shall make such investigations and reports as shall be ordered by either House of Congress or by any committee of either House having jurisdiction over revenue, appropriations, or expenditures. The Comptroller General shall also, at the request of any such committee, direct assistants from his office to furnish the committee such aid and information as it may request.

(c) The Comptroller General shall specially report to Congress every expenditure or contract made by any department or establishment in any year in violation of law.

(d) He shall submit to Congress reports upon the adequacy and effectiveness of the administrative examination of accounts and claims in the respective departments and establishments and upon the adequacy and effectiveness of departmental inspection of the offices and accounts of fiscal officers.

(e) He shall furnish such information relating to expenditures and accounting to the Bureau of the Budget as it may request from time to time.

Sec. 313

All departments and establishments shall furnish to the Comptroller General such information regarding the powers, duties, activities, organization, financial transactions, and methods of business of their respective offices as he may from time to time require of them; and the Comptroller General, or any of his assistants or employees, when duly authorized by him, shall, for the purpose of securing such information, have access to and the right to examine any books, documents, papers, or records of any such department or establishment. The authority contained in this section shall not be applicable to expenditures made under the provisions of section 291 of the Revised Statutes.

Sec. 314

The Civil Service Commission shall establish an eligible register for accountants for the General Accounting Office, and the examinations of applicants for entrance upon such register shall be based upon questions approved by the Comptroller General.

Sec. 315

(a) All appropriations for the fiscal year ending June 30, 1922, for the offices of the Comptroller of the Treasury and the six auditors, are transferred to and made available for the General Accounting Office, except as otherwise provided herein.

(b) During such fiscal year the Comptroller General, within the limit of the total appropriations available for the General Accounting Office, may make such changes in the number and compensation of officers and employees appointed by him or transferred to the General Accounting Office under this Act as may be necessary.

(c) There shall also be transferred to the General Accounting Office such portions of the appropriations for rent and contingent and miscellaneous expenses, including allotments for printing and binding, made for the Treasury Department for the fiscal year ending June 30, 1922, as are equal to the amounts expended from similar appropriations during the fiscal year ending June 30, 1921, by the Treasury Department for the offices of the Comptroller of the Treasury and the six auditors.

(d) During the fiscal year ending June 30, 1922, the appropriations and portions of appropriations referred to in this section shall be available for salaries and expenses of the General Accounting Office, including payment for rent in the District of Columbia, traveling expenses, the purchase and exchange of law books, books of reference, and for all necessary miscellaneous and contingent expenses.

Sec. 316

The General Accounting Office and the Bureau of Accounts shall not be construed to be a bureau or office created since January 1, 1916, so as to deprive employees therein of the additional compensation allowed civilian employees under the provisions of section 6 of the Legislative, Executive, and Judicial Appropriation Act for the fiscal year ending June 30, 1922, if otherwise entitled thereto.

Sec. 317

The provisions of law prohibiting the transfer of employees of executive departments and independent establishments until after service of three years shall not apply during the fiscal year ending June 30, 1922, to the transfer of employees to the General Accounting Office.

Sec. 318

This Act shall take effect upon its approval by the President: *Provided,* That sections 301 to 317, inclusive, relating to the General Accounting Office and the Bureau of Accounts, shall take effect July 1, 1921.

The Budget and Accounting Act of 1921 provided the framework for making basic changes in the existing fragmented administrative system, but it did not accomplish those changes in and of itself. Some of the bill's supporters, like Congressman Good, foresaw the real potential for the broad reconstruction of the administrative role of the Executive and for the reorganization of the whole executive branch; however, the legislative debates demonstrated that many others viewed the reform primarily as a means of effecting savings and introducing efficiency into the operation of the executive branch. Nicholas Murray Butler, a powerful member of the Republican party and president of Columbia University, supported Congressman Good's concept. He had told the Senate committee which was conducting hearings on the bill

> My point of view, Senator, is that the introduction of a properly formulated national budget is not an end in itself, but a means, and a very important means, to improving the whole administrative organization of the National Government. As I read our political and governmental history, we have patched and amended our administrative machinery to meet emergencies and conditions for about 125 years, but we have never really taken up the question of its reorganization from the standpoint of the governmental needs and business methods of today, when our Federal Government has become, of course, the largest business undertaking in the world.[47]

A young assistant secretary of the navy, Franklin D. Roosevelt, testifying at the same hearing, forecast the role of the budget director as the chief administrative staff officer to the President, with all that such a function implies, and although he believed this development would be some time in coming, he felt "that the budget system is the opening wedge."[48]

But the new director of the budget under President Harding, General Charles G. Dawes, had a more limited view of his role. He was firmly committed to the belief that efficiency in order to realize savings was the almost exclusive objective of the new structure. On the other hand he had a clear view of the organizational leverage necessary to execute that minimal goal, and made a significant contribution by establishing the operating procedures and the structure necessary to achieve it.

Dawes was very conscious of the sensitive position of the bureau's placement within the Treasury Department, and was much aware of the possibility of its having a restrictive effect upon his activities. He was happy to discover that the stature of the secretary, Andrew W. Mellon, prevented this from happening. Dawes confided to his diary:

A small or jealous man in his place would make the Budget Director's life miserable and his work largely ineffectual. . . . The effectiveness of the Budget machinery depends upon its complete dependence upon the President.[49]

At another time Dawes pointed out that the secretary had walked upstairs to his office, a trip which the director characterized as "an historic walk in the annals of the Budget Bureau."[50] The new budget director lost no time in taking advantage of Mellon's cooperation, and he acted to "devise means to stop this terrible waste in the utilization of government facilities."[51] He created new coordinating agencies which centralized the functions of purchasing, supplying, and providing other services for the various government departments, which were staffed by delegated officials from the departments involved, and directed by a chief coordinator appointed by the President. The organizational structure was modeled on General Pershing's plan for coordinating the American Expeditionary Forces in World War I; most of the coordinators pressed into service were former military colleagues of General Dawes. Economy and elimination of waste were the bywords of this effort, and the rationale behind it was that in centralizing purchasing and common service efforts, savings would be achieved, if from nothing else than from the sheer magnitude and bargaining power of the buyer.

All of this was channeled in a direction very dear to the hearts of Congress, the elimination of waste and the introduction of modern business techniques to achieve efficiency and savings. To accomplish this, Dawes called upon President Harding to firm up his position and power vis-à-vis the department and bureau heads, and drafted two strong directives, signed by the President, which spelled out in greater detail what the functions and responsibilities of the Bureau of the Budget were to be.

President Warren G. Harding
Directive on the Bureau of the Budget
September 21, 1921

Richardson, XVII, 8996-97.

EXECUTIVE ORDER

[The Budget]

The White House,
September 21, 1921

By virtue of the authority vested in me by the Budget and Accounting Act, 1921, approved June 10, 1921, I hereby prescribe the following rules and regulations with regard to the preparation and submission of the Budget and the conduct of the Bureau of the Budget:

Revision of the Estimates

Pursuant to the provisions of section 207 of the Budget and Accounting Act, the Bureau of the Budget, under the supervision of the Director and subject to review and determination by the President, shall assemble, revise, reduce or increase the estimates of the departments or establishments as submitted to the Bureau. The Director of the Budget shall determine the plan as to the contents, order and arrangement of the estimates. In increasing or decreasing the estimates of the appropriations necessary for any department or establishment he shall take into consideration any proper reduction in working forces, reduction in compensation, and the elimination of unnecessary activities. Estimates, however, in respect to the principal or interest of the public debt shall be subject to revision only with the concurrence of the Secretary of the Treasury. For the purpose of assisting the President with information in the formation of business policy for the Government the estimates of appropriations and of expenditures and receipts, when assembled and revised by the Bureau, shall be transmitted by the Director to the President as soon as possible after their receipt from the departments and establishments by the Bureau, in the form of a consolidated statement of estimated revenue and expenditure, with supporting schedules.

Warren G. Harding

President Warren G. Harding
Directive on the Bureau of the Budget
November 8, 1921

Richardson, XVII, 9007-10.

Preparation and Submission
of the Budget

The White House
November 8, 1921

I hereby prescribe the following rules and regulations with regard to the preparation and submission of the Budget and the conduct of the Bureau of the Budget.

Revision of the Estimates

Pursuant to the provisions of section 207 of the Budget and Accounting Act, the Bureau of the Budget, under the supervision of the Director and subject to review and determination by the President, shall assemble, revise, reduce or increase the estimates of the departments or establishments as submitted to the Bureau. The Director of the Budget shall determine the plan as to the contents, order and arrangements of the estimates. In increasing or decreasing the estimates of the appropriations necessary for any department or establishment he shall take into consideration any proper reduction in working forces, reduction in compensation, and the elimination of unnecessary activities. Estimates, however, in respect to the principal or interest of the public debt shall be subject to revision only with the concurrence of the Secretary of the Treasury. For the purpose of assisting the President with information in the formation of business policy for the Government the estimates of appropriations and of expenditures and receipts, when assembled and revised by the Bureau, shall be transmitted by the Director to the President as soon as possible after their receipt from the departments and establishments by the Bureau, in the form of a consolidated statement of estimated revenue and expenditure, with supporting schedules.

2. Concurrently with the transmission of the estimates by the Director of the Bureau of the Budget to the President, the Secretary of the Treasury shall transmit a statement, for the information of the President, showing, from the point of view of the Treasury, the relation between the estimated appropriations and expenditures and the estimated receipts of the Government. This statement shall contain all necessary memoranda and tables, together with such other comments as may be pertinent to the subject matter of the Budget, including suggestions and recommendations as to how the revenue needs of the Government may be met. The Secretary of the Treasury shall, at the same time, prepare and transmit to the President, for incorporation in the budget, the figures for the actual expenditures of the Government for the last completed fiscal year, the figures for the actual and estimated receipts for the last, the current and the ensuing fiscal years, required by sub-divisions (b), (c), and (d) of section 201 of the Budget and Accounting Act, and also the financial statements required by the provisions of sub-divisions (f), (g), and (h) of the same section. The Secretary of the Treasury shall, if the estimated receipts for the ensuing fiscal year, on the basis of laws existing at the time the budget is transmitted, plus the estimated amounts in the Treasury at the close of the fiscal year in progress available for expenditure in the ensuing fiscal year, are less than the estimated expenditures for the ensuing fiscal year, make recommendations to the President for new taxes, loans, or other appropriate action to meet the estimated deficiency. If, on the other hand, the aggregate of such estimated receipts and such estimated amounts in the Treasury is greater than such estimated expenditures for the ensuing fiscal year, the Secretary, for the information of the President, shall make such recommendations and suggest such financial measures as in his opinion the public interest may require. The Director of the Budget shall make available to the Secretary of the Treasury at his request any information in the possession of the Bureau or any of its employees in respect to the receipts and expenditures of the Government and any other matters that may be pertinent to the business of the Treasury. The Secretary of the Treasury shall make available to the Director of the Budget at his request any information in the possession of the Treasury or any of its employees in respect to the receipts and expenditures of the Government and any other matters that may be pertinent to the business of the Budget.

3. The Director of the Budget, in gathering information for the use of the President, acts for the President, and his calls upon the Chiefs of Bureaus and other

Administrative Officers for purposes of consultation or information take precedence over the Cabinet Head of a Department, or any head of an independent organization.

4. The Budget Officer in each department, being appointed by the Cabinet head, will present to the Director of the Budget the views of the Cabinet head upon the wisdom of conclusions drawn by the Director of the Budget, for the use of the Chief Executive and Congress; but, as in the case of Bureau Chiefs and other officers, the call of the Director of the Budget for their presence and advice takes precedence over the Cabinet head.

5. The coordinating agencies established by the Executive are for the purpose of enabling the President, in matters of routine business, to so coordinate the activities of the different departments and establishments as will insure the most economical and efficient expenditure of moneys appropriated by Congress. They provide the machinery through which, with the minimum of obstruction and delay, the Executive may impose a unified plan of governmental routine business. The Director of the Bureau of the Budget shall have general supervision over the work of the coordinating agencies heretofore created by Executive Order, subject to such instructions as may hereafter be issued by the President.

6. The Chief Coordinator, General Supply, appointed under the provisions of Executive Order of July 27, 1921, shall exercise general supervision, subject to the Director of the Budget, over the coordination of the routine business activities of the governmental organization, with particular attention to methods of purchasing, liquidiation of supplies, specification of materials, advertising, warehousing, employment, manufacturing, disbursing and other ordinary business activities of the Government.

7. The decision of the Chief Coordinator, in all matters of coordination, shall be transmitted to the heads of departments or independent establishments concerned and shall be final, except that such heads may appeal to the Director of the Budget within four days after the receipt of notice of the coordinating order, and if not sustained by the Director of the Budget may appeal to the President of the United States within six days after the decision of the Director of the Budget. If such appeal is not taken or is not sustained the decision in question shall stand, and shall be published to those affected by the heads of the departments concerned.

8. The heads of departments and subordinate officials will retain all present responsibility with respect to individual business transactions, subject to such policies as may be imposed in the manner indicated above.

9. All persons heretofore or hereafter appointed to duty under the Chief Coordinator, either in Washington or in the Corps Areas of the country, shall be regarded as so appointed or detailed by the President of the United States, and they shall not be subject to reassignment by department heads except as authorized by Executive Order. Such persons shall not be required to submit any report to any department except such as may be required as to their location or assignment or for purposes of pay, the intention being to prevent any interference with their direct responsibility to the President of the United States and his agents, the Director of the Budget and the Chief Coordinator. The above does not apply to departmental

representatives on the various coordinating boards, and, in case of those detailed to coordinating duty in addition to other duties, it applies only with respect to such coordinating duty.

10. All Bureau chiefs and employees of the executive Government are directed to furnish any available information desired for purposes of coordination, or to attend any conference on coordination, at the request of the Chief Coordinator. It shall not be necessary for any duly authorized representative of the Director of the Budget, of the Chief Coordinator or any coordinating authority established by Executive Order, to secure the approval of the head of a department or military or naval authority of a request for information for use in connection with the activities of the coordinating bodies. The duly authorized agents of the Director of the Budget, of the Chief Coordinator, or of the coordinating boards, shall have access to all books and papers of the various departments and independent establishments which contain any information pertinent to the subject under consideration for coordination.

11. All departments and establishments must be so organized for the transaction of matters of routine business as to facilitate their proper cooperation with the general coordinating agencies. Where the existing form of the organization of the routine business of the departments and establishments, or the form of reorganization suggested by the head of the department or establishment does not, in the judgment of the Director of the Bureau of the Budget, properly meet the requirements of the situation, the Director of the Bureau of the Budget shall recommend to the President the form which, in his judgment, such departmental organization should take to that end. In his final determination of the form of organization the President will then consider the recommendations of the department head or head of the independent establishment concurrently with those of the Director of the Budget.

12. All coordinating agencies made subject by Executive Order to the supervision of the Director of the Budget shall make quarterly reports to him of their activities for transmission by him to the President.

Warren G. Harding

These presidential directives further clarified the potential powers the Budget and Accounting Act had placed in the hands of the President of the United States and through him, in his director of the Bureau of the Budget. These powers were used by the early directors to establish routine budget procedures and economy efforts, but in time they were directed towards more significant objectives, for example, executive departmental reorganization, policy planning and legislative clearance. Seeds of a considerable number of elements of the power of the modern presidency were planted by the Budget and Accounting Act of 1921 and the two executive orders which followed close behind.

A later Budget Bureau director concluded that the "early years of the Bureau of the Budget were spent in overcoming the customs and concepts developed in the previous century. General Dawes . . . had to resort to threatening recalcitrant bureau chiefs with a letter from President Harding promising prompt dismissal from the government service of all such persons refusing to comply with the requests of the Bureau of the Budget."[52] These early victories increased both the power and prestige of the bureau, although at that time it was decided to use that power and prestige to achieve limited goals. Despite the limited nature of their goals, however, "the budget system and the facilities of the Bureau enabled the President once again to assume leadership of the Executive branch and to find out what was being done by the many administrative agencies."[53] One perceptive student of the period has written:

> Under Dawes and his successors . . . economy was to be secured primarily through the efficient conduct of "routine business" or housekeeping service. In relation to the standards of private industry, in 1921 there was, no doubt, much room for greater economy and efficiency in procurement, office procedure, space utilization, etc., in the federal government. Since policy matters and questions as to the substance of programs, according to Dawes, were not to be considered by the Budget Bureau, the review of the estimates was looked upon primarily as a job of budget mechanics and therefore of secondary importance. Nevertheless, the programs of the departments and establishments were submitted for the President regarding the substance of those programs.[54]

Significant increments in the future power and dynamics of the administrative aspect of the presidential office were latent in this routine and unexploited side of the budgetary system.

Franklin D. Roosevelt's Committee On Administrative Management

Those who envisaged a great future for the new Bureau of the Budget were few and far between in the 1920s, and fewer still were those who saw it emerging as the central nervous system of the executive branch of the government. In the mid-1930s its staff had still not increased beyond 45 employees, and its power and prestige were not yet apparent. It was not until 1938 that the bureau established the small Division of Research and Investigation, which began to concern itself with implementing Section 209 of the Budget and Accounting Act, which was concerned with analysis of the administrative structure and the operation of the existing government. But by that time Roosevelt's Committee on Administrative Management was well under way with its proposals in that area; they would eventually strengthen the presidential office and make research and investigation an integral part of the bureau's regular operations.

The New Deal created additional administrative problems for the President of the United States, because in his efforts to cope with the Depression, Franklin Roosevelt established a considerable number of emergency agencies which operated outside of the framework of the regular administrative departments. In order to coordinate policies and guidelines in this rapidly expanding establishment, Roosevelt created a temporary Executive Council which consisted of members of his cabinet, along with the heads of the new independent agencies (plus several others, including the director of the budget and members of the President's staff). The council met weekly on one of the days usually allotted to a cabinet meeting. An executive secretary to this group was appointed by the President and in time the council began to spawn its own subordinates (e.g., an economic advisor), and form its own subcommittees, each of which had its own secretariat. Six months later the President created the National Emergency Council, which was conceived to be a working secretariat for the Executive Council. It was composed of some of the key members of the larger group and was designed to provide staff assistance and continuity with the other meetings, maintain records of the Executive Council, carry on systematic exchange of information between the multiple programs and agencies with regard to the emergency activities of each and all, and also to inform the general public of developments in these areas.

As if these assignments were not beyond the limits of human possibility for a group of its size, the Emergency Council also very quickly assumed operational responsibility by appointing directors in each state to carry through a program of coordination among the multiple agencies on the state level. This process of administrative procreation continued for several years, working effectively in some instances, but making hopelessly more complicated the already complex network of agencies and coordinating groups which came under the general jurisdiction of the President.

By 1936 Roosevelt was becoming more sympathetic to the advice of many of his advisors; he began to think seriously of bringing his new "floating" agencies under the rubric of the existing departmental structure. He was extremely interested in plans for the overall reorganization of the executive branch, for he was faced with the complex problem of proliferating bureaucracies on the one hand, and with limited staff assistance with which to direct and control those agencies and their quickly multiplying list of employees on the other. At a White House meeting in the fall of 1935 Roosevelt asked one of his old friends and advisors, Dr. Charles E. Merriam of the University of Chicago, who was a member of the National Resources Planning Board (a New Deal advisory group), to prepare a memorandum on the subject of reorganizing the management of his burgeoning administrative family. Merriam prepared the memo, which he called "a plan for a plan," in which he urged:

> The organization, development, and position of the American Executive is one of the great contributions of American genius; and the continuance and development of this agency is one of the brightest prospects of modern democracy. It is important, however, that the Executive office be developed on the side of management and administrative supervision as well as on the political side if its full possibilities can be realized in our national affairs.

... It would be possible to make a thorough study of this whole problem as it develops in American public life—a study directed toward the institutional arrangements, general understandings and practices which would most effectively aid the Executive in the double task of management plus political leadership and direction.[55]

Professor Merriam suggested that the public administration committee of the Social Science Research Council might undertake such a study, and that its chairman, Louis Brownlow, was well qualified to direct it. Merriam and Brownlow were both members of an interlocking directorate which connected most of the major academic and public administration groups in the country. Merriam was a professor of political science at the University of Chicago, past president of the American Political Science Association, vice chairman of President Hoover's Research Committee on Social Trends, one of the principal founding members of the Social Science Research Council, director of the Spelman Fund of the Rockefeller Foundation, and one of the three members of the National Planning Board. Brownlow's career was less organizational but equally interesting. He had been a reporter, a city editor, a writer, a state senator in Tennessee, a city commissioner in Washington, D.C., a city manager in two other American cities, and was at that time the director of the Public Administration Clearing House in Chicago.

Both men had made significant and unique contributions to American politics, Merriam as a pioneer in bringing together the skills of the social scientist and the realities of practical politics, and Brownlow as an intimate observer of the Washington scene and a professionally oriented American in politics, who struggled for a lifetime in various capacities in an attempt to improve the quality and efficiency of American government on the local and national level. As plans for their study developed, Merriam and Brownlow brought a third member into their group, Luther H. Gulick, director of the National Institute of Public Administration, who possessed some of the technical skills and experience which the other two lacked. The three—Merriam, Brownlow and Gulick—made up a formidable team for the attack on this critical problem, and the results of their labor were an accurate reflection of their eminent qualifications for the positions to which they were appointed.

President Roosevelt did not immediately agree to all aspects of the Merriam proposal, although he considered them carefully. He rejected Merriam's suggestion that the study be financed by money from the Rockefeller Foundation, because he thought it would be politically inexpedient. He also wanted the study expanded so that it encompassed the problem of reorganizing the growing maze of executive departments, commissions and other agencies. His immediate reaction to Brownlow and his administrative committee of the Social Science Research Council was positive, but he thought that government funds ought to support the undertaking. The President was firm on one other question; he did not want the report to appear before the 1936 elections, expressing the hope that the proposals which would come from the study could be considered on a non-political basis after the election.

Despite Roosevelt's initially positive reaction, final approval for the study was not forthcoming in 1935. Dr. Merriam met again with the President in early 1936 and Roosevelt indicated that it was his intention to submit a request to the Congress for the support of their study toward the end of the session. He asked for an outline of the proposal to aid him in drafting the message to Congress, and it was generally agreed that the work would be funded through the National Resources Committee, but that it be conducted by the Brownlow group or perhaps an independent committee which would include Brownlow, Merriam and other members of the advisory committee of the National Resources Committee.

In his one-page draft of a memorandum for the President, written in pencil on Florida Hotel stationery, Brownlow proposed

> What is needed is a careful study of the managerial and administrative relationships of the President to *all* the far flung and complicated agencies of the Federal government. After all the President is responsible in fact if not always in law for all of them and cannot escape the responsibility. The recognition of this central fact makes it impossible to devolve his prerogative.
>
> In its exercise he must work with and through staff agencies for the control and direction of fiscal, personnel, planning, legal aspects of *all* agencies (including those charged with performing staff functions). This relationship may differ in its mechanics as among (1) staff, (2) operating, (3) regulatory agencies; and again as the administration of each is (1) centralized, (2) regionalized, (3) decentralized with or to the states or other selective and non-national agencies.
>
> Over-all management requires coordination of all these relationships to make effective the President's responsible control but without depriving him of coordinated information and recommendations and without adding to his burdens and by diminishing the number of agencies reporting directly to him.[56]

Just about that time Brownlow was approached by Senator Harry Byrd of Virginia, who had just been appointed chairman of a special Senate committee on the reorganization of the executive agencies. Byrd asked Brownlow to serve as chairman of its advisory committee; but while Brownlow explained to Byrd his prior commitment to the President, at that early stage of discussion, neither saw any serious conflict between the two undertakings. Byrd was a friendly supporter of the President during that period, and amicable discussions ensued between the two groups for some time.

This state of affairs continued until the end of the year. Brownlow remained chairman of the senator's advisory committee, but the essential research study was assigned to the Brookings Institution. Although Byrd had also wanted Luther Gulick to join Brownlow in overseeing his committee's work, Gulick was soon named as one of the three members of what came to be known as the President's Committee on Administrative Management. In the spring of 1936 an agreement was reached, dividing the research labors between the Brookings group and the President's Committee. The President's Committee would study executive management from the point of view of the President's control of government operations, while the Byrd or Brookings group would concentrate upon bringing greater efficiency and savings to government operations by eliminating overlapping operations and duplication within the administrative structure of the executive branch.

This distinction was clear in theory, but in practice the research efforts of the two groups began to overlap and impinge upon one another. The conflict was almost inevitable, for the Brookings study was by necessity oriented towards the interests and concerns of its sponsoring agency, the United States Senate, while the Brownlow committee looked at the problem from the perspective of the President and his concern with his own control over the executive branch. Relations were further exacerbated by Senator Byrd's break with the President over spending policies and deficit finance, and the senator's annoyance at not being shown the Brownlow report before it was too late to initiate changes in it. The hostility which developed between the two groups was rather costly in political terms, for the loss of Senator Byrd's support, upon which the Brownlow committee had originally counted, and the actual hostile opposition it encountered, probably accounted for the defeat of the committee's proposals in 1937 and 1938.

It should be emphasized that in planning the study on administrative management, President Roosevelt was not hoodwinked by this group of well-meaning professional reformers. He was fully involved in the discussions once the parameters of the study were agreed upon, and he contributed substantially to their refinement. As indicated above, he was the one to introduce the problem of reorganization and to insist upon its inclusion in the study; he also made a number of other very cogent suggestions. Speaking on the function of the Bureau of the Budget in an early conversation at the White House, he told Brownlow that

> the Bureau of the Budget had never exercised its functions with respect to continuing examinations of the organization because it had been led astray by General Dawes' decision that the Budget Bureau should keep a small staff and thereby be an example of economy to other bureaus; that this precedent established by Dawes had been followed by all of the other budget directors, and that the Bureau of the Budget never had been adequately staffed to enable it to do the work it does undertake, much less to undertake the other job.[57]

President Roosevelt announced the appointment of the Committee on Administrative Management on March 22, 1936, and shortly thereafter the committee began gathering an extremely capable staff and plotting out its agenda for the next nine months. Brownlow and Merriam were already committed to be in Europe for most of that summer, but they appointed a staff before their departure. Upon their return they really got down to work and produced one of the most readable and effective reports ever written by a presidential, or for that matter, congressional, advisory committee or commission.

The President had exacted a promise from Brownlow that the report would not be made available to the public, or even to him, until after the elections. Brownlow and Gulick brought it to him on November 14, 1936, and he was sufficiently enthusiastic about it to cry out "One hundred per cent,"[58] banging his fist on the table with each word. When he got down to details he expressed some disappointment with the committee's proposal for regulatory agencies, and suggested that the reorganization proposal would have to be limited to two years. He recommended several other modifications but on the whole, it was just what the President had wanted, and he gave the committee the go-ahead signal to finish the report. On January 12, 1937 he submitted the report to the Congress, along with an enthusiastic letter of transmittal.

In the letter he unequivocally endorsed the proposals and pleaded for serious consideration of them by the legislature. "The plain fact is," he explained

> that the present organization and equipment of the executive branch of the Government defeats the constitutional intent that there be a single responsible Chief Executive to coordinate and manage the departments and activities in accordance with the laws enacted by the Congress. Under these conditions the Government cannot be thoroughly effective in working, under popular control, for the common good.[59]

President Franklin D. Roosevelt
Letter of Transmittal to Congress Submitted
With the Report on Administrative Management
January 12, 1937

The President's Committee on Administrative Management, *Report of the Committee with Studies of Administrative Management in the Federal Government;* Submitted to the President and to the Congress in Accordance with Public Law 739, 74th Cong., 2nd sess. (Washington, D.C., 1937), iii-v.

To the Congress of the United States: I address this message to the Congress as one who has had experience as a legislator, as a subordinate in an executive department, as the chief executive of a State, and as one on whom, as President, the constitutional responsibility for the whole of the executive branch of the Government has lain for 4 years.

Now that we are out of the trough of the depression, the time has come to set our house in order. The administrative management of the Government needs overhauling. We are confronted not alone by new activities, some of them temporary in character, but also by the growth of the work of the Government matching the growth of the Nation over more than a generation.

Except for the enactment of the Budget and Accounting Act of 1921, no extensive change in management has occurred since 1913, when the Department of Labor was established. The executive structure of the Government is sadly out of date. I am not the first President to report to the Congress that antiquated machinery stands in the way of effective administration and of adequate control by the Congress. Theodore Roosevelt, William H. Taft, Woodrow Wilson, and Herbert Hoover made repeated but not wholly successful efforts to deal with the problem. Committees of the Congress have also rendered distinguished service to the Nation through their efforts from time to time to point the way to improvement of governmental management and organization.

The opportunity and the need for action now comes to you and to me. If we have faith in our republican form of government and in the ideals upon which it has rested for 150 years, we must devote ourselves energetically and courageously to the task of making that Government efficient. The great stake in efficient democracy is the stake of the common man.

In these troubled years of world history a self-government cannot long survive unless that government is an effective and efficient agency to serve mankind and carry out the will of the Nation. A government without good management is a house builded on sand.

In striving together to make our Government more efficient, you and I are taking up in our generation the battle to preserve that freedom of self-government which our forefathers fought to establish and hand down to us. They struggled against tyranny, against nonrepresentative controls, against government by birth, wealth, or class, against sectionalism. Our struggle now is against confusion, against ineffectiveness, against waste, against inefficiency. This battle, too, must be won, unless it is to be said that in our generation national self-government broke down and was frittered away in bad management.

Will it be said "Democracy was a great dream, but it could not do the job?" Or shall we here and now, without further delay, make it our business to see that our American democracy is made efficient so that it will do the job that is required of it by the events of our time?

I know your answer, and the answer of the Nation, because, after all, we are a practical people. We know good management in the home, on the farm, and in business, big and little. If any nation can find the way to effective government, it should be the American people through their own democratic institutions.

Over a year ago it seemed to me that this problem of administrative management of the executive branch of the Government should be a major order of business of this session of the Congress. Accordingly, after extended discussions and negotiations, I appointed a Committee on Administrative Management, to examine the whole problem broadly and to suggest for my guidance and your consideration a comprehensive and balanced program for dealing with the overhead organization and management of the executive branch as it is established under the Constitution.

The Committee has now completed its work, and I transmit to you its report, Administrative Management in the Government of the United States. I have examined this report carefully and thoughtfully, and am convinced that it is a great document of permanent importance. I think that the general program presented by the Committee is adequate, reasonable, and practical, and that it furnishes the basis for immediate action. The broad facts are known; the need is clear; what is now required is action.

The Committee on Administrative Management points out that no enterprise can operate effectively if set up as is the Government today. There are over 100 separate departments, boards, commissions, corporations, authorities, agencies, and activities through which the work of the Government is being carried on.

Neither the President nor the Congress can exercise effective supervision and direction over such a chaos of establishments, nor can overlapping, duplication, and contradictory policies be avoided.

The Committee has not spared me; they say, what has been common knowledge for 20 years, that the President cannot adequately handle his responsibilities; that he is overworked; that it is humanly impossible, under the system which we have, for him fully to carry out his constitutional duty as Chief Executive, because he is overwhelmed with minor details and needless contacts arising directly from the bad organization and equipment of the Government. I can testify to this. With my predecessors who have said the same thing over and over again, I plead guilty.

The plain fact is that the present organization and equipment of the executive branch of the Government defeats the constitutional intent that there be a single responsible Chief Executive to coordinate and manage the departments and activities in accordance with the laws enacted by the Congress. Under these conditions the Government cannot be thoroughly effective in working, under popular control, for the common good.

The Committee does not spare the Comptroller General for his failure to give the Congress a prompt and complete audit each year, totally independent of administration, as a means of holding the Executive truly to account; nor for his unconstitutional assumption of executive power; nor for the failure to keep the accounting system of the Government up to date to serve as the basis of information, management, and control.

The Committee criticizes the use of boards and commissions in administration, condemns the careless use of "corporations" as governmental instrumentalities, and points out that the practice of creating independent regulatory commissions, who perform administrative work in addition to judicial work, threatens to develop a "fourth branch" of the Government for which there is no sanction in the Constitution. Nor does the Committee spare the inadequacy of the civil-service system.

To meet this situation and bring our administrative management up to date, the Committee presents an integrated five-point program, which you will find set out in its report. It includes these major recommendations:

1. Expand the White House staff so that the President may have a sufficient group of able assistants in his own office to keep him in closer and easier touch with the widespread affairs of administration, and to make the speedier clearance of the knowledge needed for Executive decision.

2. Strengthen and develop the managerial agencies of the Government, particularly those dealing with the budget and efficiency research, with personnel and with planning, as management-arms of the Chief Executive.

3. Extend the merit system upward, outward, and downward to cover practically all non-policy-determining posts; reorganize the civil-service system as a part of management under a single, responsible administrator,

and create a citizen board to serve as the watch dog of the merit system; and increase the salaries of key posts throughout the service so that the Government may attract and hold in a career service men and women of ability and character.

4. Overhaul the 100 independent agencies, administrations, authorities, boards, and commissions, and place them by Executive order within one or the other of the following 12 major executive departments: State, Treasury, War, Justice, Post Office, Navy, Conservation, Agriculture, Commerce, Labor, Social Welfare, and Public Works; and place upon the Executive continuing responsibility for the maintenance of effective organization.

5. Establish accountability of the Executive to the Congress by providing a genuine independent postaudit of all fiscal transactions by an auditor general, and restore to the Executive complete responsibility for accounts and current transactions.

As you will see, this program rests solidly upon the Constitution and upon the American way of doing things. There is nothing in it which is revolutionary, as every element is drawn from our own experience either in government or large-scale business.

I endorse this program and feel confident that it will commend itself to you also with your knowledge of government, and to the vast majority of the citizens of the country who want and believe in efficient self-government.

No important advance can be made toward the major objectives of the program without the passage by the Congress of the necessary legislation.

It will be necessary to provide for the establishment of two new departments, a Department of Social Welfare and a Department of Public Works, for the assignment by the President of all the miscellaneous activities to the 12 major departments thus provided, for reorganization of the civil-service system, for modernizing and strengthening the managerial agencies of the Executive, and for making the Executive more strictly accountable to the Congress. By the creation of two new departments nearly 100 agencies now not under regular departments can be consolidated as to their administrative functions under a total of 12 regular departments of the Government.

The remaining elements of the five-point program, though they must await your action on the basic legislation, may be initiated through appropriations and Executive orders.

In placing this program before you I realize that it will be said that I am recommending the increase of the powers of the Presidency. This is not true. The Presidency as established in the Constitution of the United States has all of the powers that are required. In spite of timid souls in 1787 who feared effective government the Presidency was established as a single strong Chief Executive Office in which was vested the entire executive power of the National Government, even as the legislative power was placed in the Congress, and the judicial in the Supreme Court. What I am placing before you is not the request for more power, but for the tools of management and the authority to distribute the work so that the President can effectively discharge those powers which the Constitution now places upon him. Unless we are prepared to abandon this important part of the Constitution, we must equip the Presidency with authority commensurate with his responsibilities under the Constitution.

The Committee on Administrative Management, after a careful examination of recent attempts to reorganize the Government and of State reorganizations carried out so ably by Gov. Frank O. Lowden in Illinois, Gov. Alfred E. Smith in New York, Gov. Harry F. Byrd in Virginia, Gov. William Tudor Gardiner in Maine, and by other governors, accepts the view held by my distinguished predecessors that the detailed work of reorganization is, as President Theodore Roosevelt said over 30 years ago, "essentially executive in its nature." The Committee accordingly recommends that reorganization should be a continuing duty and authority of the Chief Executive on the basis of standards set by the Congress. To make this safe, the Committee insists, however, that the Congress keep a watchful eye upon reorganization both through the annual budget and through the maintenance of strict executive accountability to the Congress under the independent audit of all financial transactions by an Auditor General. Under the proposed plan the Congress must by law establish the major departments and determine in advance the general principles which shall guide the President in distributing the work of the Government among these departments, and in this task the President is to act on the basis of careful research by the Bureau of the Budget and after conference with those primarily affected. Reorganization is not a mechanical task, but a human task, because government is not a machine, but a living organism. With these clear safeguards, and in view of our past muddling with reorganization, one cannot but accept the logic and wisdom of the recommendations.

I would not have you adopt this five-point program, however, without realizing that this represents an important step in American history. If we do this, we reduce from over 100 down to a dozen the operating executive agencies of the Government, and we bring many little bureaucracies under broad coordinated democratic authority

But in so doing, we shall know that we are going back to the Constitution, and giving to the executive branch modern tools of management and an up-to-date organization which will enable the Government to go forward efficiently. We can prove to the world that American Government is both democratic and effective.

In this program I invite your cooperation, and pledge myself to deal energetically and promptly with the executive responsibilities of reorganization and administrative management, when you shall have made this possible by the necessary legislation.

Franklin D. Roosevelt

The report is too long and too complex to reprint in its entirety, but several sections of it are of immediate relevance to the growth of presidential power. It begins with a brief introduction which attempts to set the presidency in the perspective of American history, and to spell out the principles of effective management of public affairs which the report applies in its consideration of the administrative functions of the presidential office. It also summarizes the five principal recommendations of the study, two of which I will deal with in detail, and the others, which are not quite so relevant to the institution of the presidency, are referred to in passing.

Introduction to the Report of
The President's Committee on Administrative Management
January 12, 1937

The President's Committee on Administrative Management, *Report*, 1-4.

The government of the United States is the largest and most difficult task undertaken by the American people, and at the same time the most important and the noblest. Our Government does more for more men, women, and children than any other institution; it employs more persons in its work than any other employer. It covers a wider range of aims and activities than any other enterprise; it sustains the frame of our national and our community life, our economic system, our individual rights and liberties. Moreover, it is a government of, by, and for the people—a democracy that has survived for a century and a half and flourished among competing forms of government of many different types and colors, old and new.

From time to time the decay, destruction, and death of democracy has been gloomily predicted by false prophets who mocked at us, but our American system has matched its massive strength successfully against all the forces of destruction through parts of three centuries.

Our American Government rests on the truth that the general interest is superior to and has priority over any special or private interest, and that final decision in matters of common interest to the Nation should be made by free choice of the people of the Nation, expressed in such manner as they shall from time to time provide, and enforced by such agencies as they may from time to time set up. Our goal is the constant raising of the level of the happiness and dignity of human life, the steady sharing of the gains of our Nation, whether material or spiritual, among those who make the Nation what it is.

We are too practical a people to be satisfied by merely looking forward to glittering goals or with mere plans, talk, and pledges. By democracy we mean getting things done that we, the American people, want done in the general interest. Without results we know that democracy means nothing and ceases to be alive in the minds and hearts of men. With us the people's will is not merely an empty phrase; it denotes a grave and stern determination in the major affairs of our Nation—a determination which we propose to make good as promptly and firmly as may be necessary and appropriate—a determination which does not intend to be baffled in its basic plans and purposes by any cluttering or confusion in the machinery for doing what it has been deliberately decided to do.

After the people's judgment has been expressed in due form, after the representatives of the Nation have made the necessary laws, we intend that these decisions shall be promptly, effectively, and economically put into action.

The American Executive

The need for action in realizing democracy was as great in 1789 as it is today. It was thus not by accident but by deliberate design that the founding fathers set the American Executive in the Constitution on a solid foundation. Sad experience under the Articles of Confederation, with an almost headless Government and committee management, had brought the American Republic to the edge of ruin. Our forefathers had broken away from hereditary government and pinned their faith on democratic rule, but they had not found a way to equip the new democracy for action. Consequently, there was grim purpose in resolutely providing for a Presidency which was to be a national office. The President is indeed the one and only national officer representative of the entire Nation. There was hesitation on the part of some timid souls in providing the President with an election independent of the Congress; with a longer term than most governors of that day; with the duty of informing the Congress as to the state of the Union and of recommending to its consideration "such Measures as he shall judge necessary and expedient"; with a two-thirds veto; with a wide power of appointment; and with military and diplomatic authority. But this reluctance was overcome in the face of need and a democratic executive established.

Equipped with these broad constitutional powers, reenforced by statute, by custom, by general consent, the American Executive must be regarded as one of the very greatest contributions made by our Nation to the development of modern democracy—a unique institution the value of which is as evident in times of stress and strain as in periods of quiet.

As an instrument for carrying out the judgment and will of the people of a nation, the American Executive occupies an enviable position among the executives of the states of the world, combining as it does the elements of popular control and the means for vigorous action and leadership—uniting stability and flexibility. The American Executive as an institution stands across the path of those who mistakenly assert that democracy must fail because it can neither decide promptly nor act vigorously.

Our Presidency unites at least three important functions. From one point of view the President is a political leader—leader of a party, leader of the Congress, leader of a people. From another point of view he is head of the Nation in the ceremonial sense of the term, the symbol of our American national solidarity. From still another point of view the President is the Chief Executive and administrator within the Federal system and service. In many types of government these duties are divided or only in part combined, but in the United States they have always been united in one and the same person whose duty it is to perform all of these tasks.

Your Committee on Administrative Management has been asked to investigate and report particularly upon the last function; namely, that of administrative management—the organization for the performance of the duties imposed upon the President in exercising the executive power vested in him by the Constitution of the United States.

Improving the Machinery of Government

Throughout our history we have paused now and then to see how well the spirit and purpose of our Nation is working out in the machinery of everyday government with a view to making such modifications and improvements as prudence and the spirit of progress might suggest. Our Government was the first to set up in its formal Constitution a method of amendment, and the spirit of America has been from the beginning of our history the spirit of progressive changes to meet conditions shifting perhaps more rapidly here than elsewhere in the world.

Since the Civil War, as the tasks and responsibilities of our Government have grown with the growth of the Nation in sweep and power, some notable attempts have been made to keep our administrative system abreast of the new times. The assassination of President Garfield by a disappointed office seeker aroused the Nation against the spoils system and led to the enactment of the civil-service law of 1883. We have struggled to make the principle of this law effective for half a century. The confusion in fiscal management led to the establishment of the Bureau of the Budget and the budgetary system in 1921. We still strive to realize the goal set for the Nation at that time. And, indeed, many other important forward steps have been taken.

Now we face again the problem of governmental readjustment, in part as the result of the activities of the Nation during the desperate years of the industrial depression, in part because of the very growth of the Nation, and in part because of the vexing social problems of our times. There is room for vast increase in our national productivity and there is much bitter wrong to set right in neglected ways of human life. There is need for improvement of our governmental machinery to meet new conditions and to make us ready for the problems just ahead.

Facing one of the most troubled periods in all the troubled history of mankind, we wish to set our affairs in the very best possible order to make the best use of all of our national resources and to make good our democratic claims. If America fails, the hopes and dreams of democracy over all the world go down. We shall not fail in our task and our responsibility, but we cannot live upon our laurels alone.

We seek modern types of management in National Government best fitted for the stern situations we are bound to meet, both at home and elsewhere. As to ways and means of improvement, there are naturally sincere differences of judgment and opinion, but only a treasonable design could oppose careful attention to the best and soundest practices of government available for the American Nation in the conduct of its heavy responsibilities.

The Foundations of
Governmental Efficiency

The efficiency of government rests upon two factors: the consent of the governed and good management. In a democracy consent may be achieved readily, though not without some effort, as it is the cornerstone of the constitution. Efficient management in a democracy is a factor of peculiar significance.

Administrative efficiency is not merely a matter of paper clips, time clocks, and standardized economies of motion. These are but minor gadgets. Real efficiency goes much deeper down. It must be built into the structure of a government just as it is built into a piece of machinery.

Fortunately the foundations of effective management in public affairs, no less than in private, are well known. They have emerged universally wherever men have worked together for some common purpose, whether through the state, the church, the private association, or the commercial enterprise. They have been written into constitutions, charters, and articles of incorporation, and exist as habits of work in the daily life of all organized peoples. Stated in simple terms these canons of efficiency require the establishment of a responsible and effective chief executive as the center of energy, direction, and administrative management; the systematic organization of all activities in the hands of a qualified personnel under the direction of the chief executive; and to aid him in this, the establishment of appropriate managerial and staff agencies. There must also be provision for planning, a complete fiscal system, and means for holding the Executive accountable for his program.

Taken together, these principles, drawn from the experience of mankind in carrying on large-scale enterprises, may be considered as the first requirement of good management. They comprehend the subject matter of administrative management as it is dealt with in this report. Administrative management concerns itself in a democracy with the executive and his duties, with managerial and staff aides, with organization, with personnel, and with the fiscal system because these are the indispensable means of making good the popular will in a people's government.

Modernizing our
Governmental Management

In the light of these canons of efficiency, what must be said of the Government of the United States today? Speaking in the broadest terms at this point, and in detail later on, we find in the American Government at the present time that the effectiveness of the Chief Executive is limited and restricted, in spite of the clear intent of the Constitution to the contrary; that the work of the Executive Branch is badly organized; that the managerial agencies are weak and out of date; that the public service does not include its share of men and women of outstanding capacity and character; and that the fiscal and auditing systems are inadequate. These weaknesses are found at the center of our Government and involve the office of the Chief Executive itself.

While in general principle our organization of the Presidency challenges the admiration of the world, yet in equipment for administrative management our Executive Office is not fully abreast of the trend of our American times, either in business or in government. Where, for example, can there be found an executive in any way comparable upon whom so much petty work is thrown? Or who is forced to see so many persons on unrelated matters and to make so many decisions on the basis of what may be, because of the very press of work, incomplete information? How is it humanly possible to know fully the affairs and problems of over 100 separate major agencies, to say nothing of being responsible for their general direction and coordination?

These facts have been known for many years and are so well appreciated that it is not necessary for us to prove again that the President's administrative equipment is far less developed than his responsibilities, and that a major task before the American Government is to remedy this dangerous situation. What we need is not a new principle, but a modernizing of our managerial equipment.

This is not a difficult problem in itself. In fact, we have already dealt with it successfully in State governments, in city governments, and in large-scale private industry. Gov. Frank O. Lowden in Illinois, Gov. Alfred E. Smith in New York, Gov. Harry F. Byrd in Virginia, and Gov. William Tudor Gardiner in Maine, among others, have all shown how similar problems can be dealt with in large governmental units. The Federal Government is more extensive and more complicated, but the principles of reorganization are the same. On the basis of this experience and our examination of the Executive Branch we conclude that the following steps should now be taken:

1. To deal with the greatly increased duties of executive management falling upon the President the White House staff should be expanded.

2. The managerial agencies of the Government, particularly those dealing with the budget, efficiency research, personnel, and planning, should be greatly strengthened and developed as arms of the Chief Executive.

3. The merit system should be extended upward, outward, and downward to cover all non-policy-determining posts, and the civil service system should be reorganized and opportunities established for a career system attractive to the best talent of the Nation.

4. The whole Executive Branch of the Government should be overhauled and the present 100 agencies reorganized under a few large departments in which every executive activity would find its place.

5. The fiscal system should be extensively revised in the light of the best governmental and private practice, particularly with reference to financial records, audit, and accountability of the Executive to the Congress.

These recommendations are explained and discussed in the following sections of this report.

The Purpose of Reorganization

In proceeding to the reorganization of the Government it is important to keep prominently before us the ends of reorganization. Too close a view of machinery must not cut off from sight the true purpose of efficient management. Economy is not the only objective, though reorganization is the first step to savings; the elimination of duplication and contradictory policies is not the only objective, though this will follow; a simple and symmetrical organization is not the only objective, though the new organization will be simple and symmetrical; higher salaries and better jobs are not the only objectives, though these are necessary; better business methods and fiscal controls are not the only objectives, though these too are demanded. There is but one grand purpose, namely, to make democracy work today in our National Government; that is, to make our Government an up-to-date, efficient, and effective instrument for carrying out the will of the Nation. It is for this purpose that the Government needs thoroughly modern tools of management.

As a people we congratulate ourselves justly on our skill as managers—in the home, on the farm, in business big and little—and we properly expect that management in government shall be of the best American model. We do not always get these results, and we must modestly say "we count not ourselves to have attained", but there is a steady purpose in America to press forward until the practices of our governmental administration are as high as the purpose and standards of our people. We know that bad management may spoil good purposes, and that without good management democracy itself cannot achieve its highest goals.

The first section of the report dealt with staffing the White House with presidential assistants. At first sight the addition of a mere half dozen employees to a federal bureaucracy already consisting of hundreds of thousands of persons hardly seems significant enough to mention. But these new men were to be the President's men, possessed of "high competence, great physical vigor, and a passion for anonymity," the last being a phrase Brownlow picked up in England from Tom Jones, who played such an anonymous role during World War I to Prime Minister Lloyd George. These assistants, the report went on to specify,

> would have no power to make decisions or issue instructions in their own right. . . . They would not be assistant presidents in any sense. Their function would be, when any matter was presented to the President for action affecting any part of the administrative work of the Government, to assist him in obtaining quickly and without delay all pertinent information possessed by any of the executive departments so as to guide him in making his responsible decisions; and then when the decisions had been made, to assist him in seeing to it that every administrative department and agency affected is promptly informed.[60]

They were to work in the interstices of the executive departments where the machinery of government frequently broke down and where it was physically and mentally impossible for the President to operate. They were to expand the antennae of the Chief Executive, reading, listening, moving about, and devouring for him information that he might need, but which he would not have time to obtain himself. Giving their full time and attention to very special and critical problems, they would coordinate all of the information and personnel involved and boil it all down to the point where the problem could be laid out in terms of concrete and specific options, thus facilitating a presidential decision. They were in a position to follow through on any problem, policy, or decision, to see whether or not it was carried out on the department or bureau level, and if not, to find out why not.

These presidential assistants would be troubleshooters, crisis managers, coordinators, even creative forces, as long as they retained their "passion for anonymity." Their own names and powers were unimportant and insignificant as long as they spoke in the name of the President. In time they would specialize in limited areas, so that their background and know-how would amount to a built-in expertise in the decision-making process. In short, these assistants would extend and intensify the range of the President's information and contact without in any way diminishing his responsibility to decide or his power to act. They were there to make that responsibility more realistic, that power more effective.

Report on Administrative Management
Recommendations on Presidential Assistants
January 12, 1937

The President's Committee on Administrative Management, *Report*, 5-6.

In this broad program of administrative reorganization the White House itself is involved. The President needs help. His immediate staff assistance is entirely inadequate. He should be given a small number of executive assistants who would be his direct aides in dealing with the managerial agencies and administrative departments of the Government. These assistants, probably not exceeding six in number, would be in addition to his present secretaries, who deal with the public, with the Congress, and with the press and the radio. These aides would have no power to make decisions or issue instructions in their own right. They would not be interposed between the President and the heads of his departments. They would not be assistant presidents in any sense. Their function would be, when any matter was presented to the President for action affecting any part of the administrative work of the Government, to assist him in obtaining quickly and without delay all pertinent information possessed by any of the executive departments so as to guide him in making his responsible decisions; and then when decisions have been made, to assist him in seeing to it that every administrative department and agency affected is promptly informed. Their effectiveness in assisting the President will, we think, be directly proportional to their ability to discharge their functions with restraint. They would remain in the background, issue no orders, make no decisions, emit no public statements. Men for these positions should be carefully chosen by the President from within and without the Government. They should be men in whom the President has personal confidence and whose character and attitude is such that they would not attempt to exercise power in their own account. They should be possessed of high competence, great physical vigor, and a passion for anonymity. They should be installed in the White House itself, directly accessible to the President. In the selection of these aides the President should be free to call on departments from time to time for the assignment of persons who, after a tour of duty as his aides, might be restored to their old positions.

This recommendation arises from the growing complexity and magnitude of the work of the President's office. Special assistance is needed to insure that all matters coming to the attention of the President have been examined from the over-all managerial point of view, as well as from all standpoints that would bear on policy and operation. It also would facilitate the flow upward to the President of information upon which he is to base his decisions and the flow downward from the President of the decisions once taken for execution by the department or departments affected. Thus such a staff would not only aid the President but would also be of great assistance to the several executive departments and to the managerial agencies in simplifying executive contacts, clearance, and guidance.

The President should also have at his command a contingent fund to enable him to bring in from time to time particular persons possessed of particular competency for a particular purpose and whose services he might usefully employ for short periods of time.

The President in his regular office staff should be given a greater number of positions so that he will not be compelled, as he has been compelled in the past, to use for his own necessary work persons carried on the pay rolls of other departments.

If the President be thus equipped he will have but the ordinary assistance that any executive of a large establishment is afforded as a matter of course.

In addition to this assistance in his own office the President must be given direct control over and be charged with immediate responsibility for the great managerial functions of the Government which affect all of the administrative departments, as is outlined in the following sections of this report. These functions are personnel management, fiscal and organizational management, and planning management. Within these three groups may be comprehended all of the essential elements of business management.

The development of administrative management in the Federal Government requires the improvement of the administration of these managerial activities, not only by the central agencies in charge, but also by the departments and bureaus. The central agencies need to be strengthened and developed as managerial arms of the Chief Executive, better equipped to perform their central responsibilities and to provide the necessary leadership in bringing about improved practices throughout the Government.

The three managerial agencies, the Civil Service Administration, the Bureau of the Budget, and the National Resources Board should be a part and parcel of the Executive Office. Thus the President would have reporting to him directly the three managerial institutions whose work and activities would affect all of the administrative departments.

The budgets for the managerial agencies should be submitted to the Congress by the President as a part of the budget for the Executive Office. This would distinguish these agencies from the operating administrative departments of the Government, which should report to the President through the heads of departments who collectively compose his Cabinet. Such an arrangement would materially aid the President in his work of supervising the administrative agencies and would enable the Congress and the people to hold him to strict accountability for their conduct.

Perhaps the most significant recommendation of the Report on Administrative Management, certainly in terms of its historical impact, was its reconstruction or better perhaps, its transformation of the role of the Bureau of the Budget. President Roosevelt had earlier clearly grasped the bureau's potential effectiveness, and the Budget and Accounting Act had written into law far greater power and influence than the agency had ever before been permitted to assume. But more than a decade and a half went by without any systematic effort on the part of its various directors or its small staff to expand its functions and fulfill its destiny. No previous President had encouraged its growth or shown any ability to exploit its latent power effectively. When Roosevelt revealed both his interest and enthusiasm for expanding its influence the committee recommended a staff role for the bureau that pervaded into almost every aspect of the Chief Executive's administrative responsibilities. "At no time," the writers of the report argued, "has the Bureau of the Budget achieved or even approximated its maximum possible usefulness and effectiveness as an instrument of administrative management."[61] The report attempted to correct that situation by outlining an administrative role for the bureau which resulted in the more than tenfold multiplication of its staff, and the development of its functions along a broad spectrum of activity which transformed it into the administrative "right arm" of the President of the United States. It rapidly became the nerve center of an intricate system of departments, bureaus and governmental agencies, which both monitored and coordinated this vast and complex network.

Report on Administrative Management
Section on Budgeting and Administrative Control
January 12, 1937

The President's Committee on Administrative Management, *Report*, 16-20.

The creation in 1921 of the Bureau of the Budget was a major step in the direction of effective administrative management in the Federal Government. It placed upon the President responsibility for the preparation of a comprehensive annual budget and recognized the need for executive discretion and leadership in preparing and submitting to the Congress a program of revenue and expenditure. At the same time it provided the President with one of the primary instruments needed for effective over-all management of the executive establishment. The Director at the head of the Bureau is appointed by the President and, though within the Department of the Treasury, reports directly to the President. Through him the President can review and control the effectiveness of governmental agencies.

Purpose of the Budget System

It is the purpose of the budget system to provide in financial terms for planning, information, and control. Through the budget the spending agencies are required to translate their work programs in advance into fiscal terms, so that each activity may be brought into balance and proportion with all other activities, and with the revenues and resources of the Government, and in harmony with long-range and general economic policies. The budget not only serves as the basis of information for the Congress and the public with regard to the past work and future plans of the Administration, but also as the means of control of the general policy of the Government by the Legislative Branch and of the details of administration by the Executive. The Bureau of the Budget was therefore set up as the right arm of the President for the central fiscal management of the vast administrative machine and to enable him to submit regularly to the Congress a complete report on past activities and a future program for advance approval by the Legislative Branch.

In addition to its duties in the preparation of the annual budget, the Bureau of the Budget was given administrative research functions of outstanding importance. It was charged with the responsibility of making a continuous study of the organization, operation, and efficiency of the Executive Branch of the Government. Through its control over budgeting the Bureau is in a key position to detect weaknesses in the organization and functioning of the various departments and agencies and is the appropriate agency continuously to investigate administrative problems and to make recommendations to the President and the departments in the interest of economy and efficiency.

Substantial progress has been achieved through the Bureau of the Budget during its 15 years of operation. A spotlight has been thrown on national fiscal problems. The Executive has been placed in a better position to plan and control the fiscal program, for which he is held responsible in the public mind. It has been possible to scrutinize departmental needs in detail, and the departments have been assisted in improving their budgetary practices. The Congress has been presented not only with a more intelligible picture of the Nation's finances and financial problems but with a clear comparison between estimates and actual expenditures for the particular governmental activities. Substantial advances in improving governmental operation and in coordinating activities have been effected through the agency of the Bureau. Its staff has aided the President in the performance of many difficult administrative duties. The technical phases of budget making have been constantly improved and refined.

At no time, however, has the Bureau of the Budget achieved or even approximated its maximum possible usefulness and effectiveness as an instrument of administrative management. Because of its small operating appropriation, the

Bureau has failed to develop an adequate staff of the highest attainable competence. Such a staff is necessary if it is to cope with the problems raised by a rapid growth in the magnitude and complexity of governmental organization and expenditures. It has not perfected its own organization and methods as a directing and controlling agency of the President. Rather, the Bureau has emphasized the task of preparing the Budget to the distinct disadvantage of its important complementary functions. It has only partially developed supervision over the execution of the Budget by the spending agencies.

The administrative research functions placed upon the Bureau are practically undeveloped; it is in this respect that the Bureau has missed its greatest opportunity. The Budget and Accounting Act of 1921 specifically authorized the Bureau to make detailed studies of the administrative departments and establishments for the purpose of advising the President intelligently as to changes that should be made in their organization and methods, in the grouping of services, and in the appropriations for various activities. The Bureau of Efficiency was abolished by an act of Congress, approved March 3, 1933, mainly on the grounds that it duplicated work that the law required the Bureau of the Budget to do. Its records and files were transferred to the Bureau of the Budget, but adequate provisions for carrying on its work are still to be made. Research in administrative organization has been negligible. Recommendations for reorganization have been conspicuously absent.

Staffing of the
Bureau of the Budget

One obtains a vivid realization of the inadequate staff of the Bureau of the Budget from the fact that its appropriation for the current fiscal year (ending June 30, 1937) amounted to only $187,000—a sum considerably less than is spent by a single finance and accounting division of some of the great Government departments, and less than 3 percent of the amount required to audit the expenditures. It has a total personnel of only 45 and, aside from the statutory positions of Director and Assistant Director, has only two positions compensated in excess of $6,000 per annum. Only $18,700 was provided for "research, surveys, and assistance." Yet this small staff is charged with preparing a budget of billions and with aiding the President in the exercise of his vast responsibility for the over-all management of the huge and intricate Federal administrative machine.

If the Bureau of the Budget is to be developed into a serviceable tool for administrative management to aid the President in the exercise of over-all control, it needs greater resources and better techniques. If continuing power is given the President to transfer and consolidate executive establishments, he will need adequate information, based on analyses of the greatest competence, as a guide to action. The Bureau of the Budget is the logical staff agency for the performance of this service. It should be given appropriations and a staff commensurate with the magnitude of the assignment. A relatively small sum invested in strengthening the Bureau of the Budget as a staff agency of the President will yield enormous returns in the increased efficiency of Government operation. It is with this in mind that recommendations regarding the Bureau of the Budget are presented.

The Director of the Bureau of the Budget is one of the few Government officers in a position to advise the President from an over-all, as opposed to a bureau or departmental, point of view. He should therefore be relieved to the greatest possible extent from the minor details of administration. He should be released for duties of maximum importance to the President and freed so that he may attend important conferences of Cabinet officers and planning groups, where programs are being considered that may eventually result in appropriation requests or in changes in governmental organization or procedure. In accordance with suggestions made elsewhere in this report, the salary of the Director should be increased. It should be possible for the President to select a Director from the career service, though he should continue, of course, to have the right to appoint a man of his own choosing.

The position of Assistant Director of the Bureau of the Budget should be filled under civil-service rules, preferably by promotion from the career service. It should be a high permanent post to which career men should be encouraged to aspire. Continuity in office is important if the Assistant Director is to have the necessary background from which to advise a new Director concerning the techniques of budget making and the intricacies of Government machinery and if he is to be skilled in the execution of policies and programs. Breadth of experience, depth of knowledge, and broad vision are needed in this office; these can be obtained only through intensive training and long experience in the Government itself. The Assistant Director should maintain the ordinary contacts with the administrative and budget officers of the departments as well as with the heads of other over-all management agencies such as the civil-service establishment. He should direct the activities of the several divisions of the Bureau of the Budget and in every possible way should assume responsibilities that would leave the Director free to concern himself with matters of major policy and program.

If the Bureau of the Budget is to perform effectively its functions of fiscal and over-all management it must be staffed with an adequate personnel. Division chiefs of high competence should be appointed from the career service. It should continue to have a career man as administrative assistant to attend to the institutional needs of the Bureau, such as personnel, appropriations, organization, financial records, and general services. The Director should have the authority to appoint a number of special assistants from inside or outside the service for special assignments and to retain consultants from business and the professions on a temporary basis for investigations or conferences in technical fields. The right to transfer or detail personnel from other Government agencies is of particular importance to the Bureau of the Budget and this should be authorized. For long-term periods the Bureau should reimburse the departments from which the personnel are borrowed. In turn, the Bureau should be permitted to accept reimbursement from Government agencies when it undertakes studies of organization and procedure at their request.

Activities of the Bureau: Estimates

The preparation and execution of the Budget are essentially executive tasks. The Bureau of the Budget as a managerial agency of the President should therefore be made responsible for the execution, as well as the formulation, of the budget as a national fiscal plan. The task of scrutinizing and passing upon departmental estimates and of exercising some measure of continuing direction over the execution of the budget should be assigned to a special division in the Bureau. The highly important task of budgeting requires a staff of unusual competence, breadth of vision, keen insight into governmental problems, and long acquaintance with the work of the Government. Only a staff having these qualifications can be of assistance to the President, the Congress, and the departments in the preparation and consideration of a budget. Well-considered and informed central direction of budgeting is essential; arbitrary, uninformed, and undiscriminating decisions must be avoided.

The staff in charge of budget estimates must keep in constant touch with the entire administrative machine for the purpose of developing and executing both short-term fiscal plans. Through this staff the President may exercise effective control over the formulation and execution of fiscal plans and policies and may review carefully and wisely the departmental estimates. In this manner fiscal planning may assume its proper relationship to the economic and social planning for which the Nation holds the President responsible.

Administrative Research and Other Managerial Activities

The President needs a research agency to investigate the broad problems involved in the administrative management of the Government—problems of administrative organization, finance, coordination, procedures and methods of work, and the many technical aspects of management. The function of investigation and research into administrative problems should be developed as an aid to over-all executive management.

Economy and efficiency in government require constant investigation and reorganization of the administrative structure. It is a mistake to assume that the Government can be reorganized once for all. Continuous study of the administrative organization of the huge Federal machine is necessary; new activities are constantly emerging and old activities are constantly changing, increasing, decreasing, or disappearing. Unless there is a special agency equipped to investigate problems of organization, new activities are set up without careful attention to where they should be located and what kind of organization is required. This results in costly mistakes and confusion. On the other hand, when the need for certain governmental activities declines or disappears, unless there is a special agency constantly studying the organizational requirements, adjustments are made later or not at all.

A division of administrative research in the Bureau of the Budget is the logical place to develop these functions which were authorized in the act of 1921. It should stimulate the continuous study of organization, methods, and procedures at the departmental or bureau level by the departments and bureaus themselves. It should engage in such studies on its own initiative where necessary, but should follow the policy of aiding and encouraging the departments to study their own organizational and procedural problems. It should endeavor to develop principles of organization that have general applicability and to act as a clearing house and consultation center for administrative research carried on in the departments. It should not undertake studies in fields in which other agencies of the Government are more competent or for which they are better equipped. Above all, persons engaged in administrative research should be freed from detailed routine duties involved in handling budget estimates.

The administrative research activities should be concentrated in a separate division of the Bureau of the Budget. It should be headed by a permanent chief possessing in unusual degree imagination, vision, creativeness, and analytical insight, as well as intimate acquaintanceship with both the practices of government and the principles of public administration. The research division must be staffed with persons of unusually high competence. Important research assignments upon administrative problems can be carried out successfully only by highly trained and experienced persons familiar with the organization and techniques of public administration. Flexible staff arrangements are necessary to permit the use of specialists drawn from the Government and from business for temporary periods.

A division of information should be established to serve as a central clearing house for the correlation and coordination of the administrative policies of the several departments in the operation of their own informational services, and to perform related duties. The United States Information Service might well be transferred to this division. It might also develop into a service which would supervise and foster regional associations of executive officers of the Government and other activities for coordination of the field services. The Director of the Bureau has been authorized by law to approve the use of printing and binding appropriations for the periodicals and journals published by Government agencies; the chief of the division of information could assist him in carrying out this duty.

The President has turned to the Bureau of the Budget for assistance in carrying out a number of important executive duties placed upon him. By reason of its close contact with the operating departments and with the President as a managerial agency, the Bureau is better able to perform these activities than are other administrative units.

One of the most important of these activities is the preparation, consideration, and clearance of Executive orders. Executive orders have been used since the early days of the Government, and, with the great increase in size and complexity of the governmental machine, have been utilized to an ever-increasing extent. They are particularly necessary in periods of emergency when there is rapid change in governmental policies and organization. Executive direction and control of national administration would be impossible without the use of this device. The activity of the Bureau of the Budget as a clearing agency in the issuance and amendment of Executive orders should be continued and strengthened by the development of a more adequate and expert staff. It should be equipped to aid the President in the consideration of administrative problems and to draft the necessary Executive orders.

Wider use could be made of Executive orders to establish uniform codes regulating management throughout the Government. These codes might well cover such matters as budgetary and other financial practices and controls, personnel, supplies, coordination, and other matters related to general organization and management. Such regulations should be promulgated after careful consideration by the departments. They could be arranged in suitable codes and would be of material assistance in guiding administrative officers.

Departmental regulations governing internal organization and management might also be cleared with the Bureau of the Budget. The purpose would not be formal approval or disapproval, but to give to the departments such assistance as the experts of the Bureau might be able to render and to enable the Bureau to inform the President upon any matters which should be brought to his attention. This clearance would result in the establishment of a greater degree of uniformity in the departmental management practices in matters in which uniformity is desirable. It would provide a desirable pooling of the experience of the several departments in many management activities. The Bureau of the Budget should be equipped to assist the departments, at their request, in preparing regulations relating to their internal management.

Another important activity of the Bureau of the Budget as a staff aid to the President is in connection with proposed legislation arising within the executive departments and establishments. In addition to his position as the head of the Executive Branch, the President is charged by the Constitution with important legislative duties, including the duty to advise the Congress "from time to time" of such "Measures as he shall judge necessary and expedient." As Chief Executive he may require "the principal Officer in each of the executive Departments" to give him an "Opinion, in writing, . . . upon any subject relating to the Duties of their respective Offices." Though the final authority for all legislative acts rests with the Congress and the President, it is the duty of the executive departments to supply the Congress with information and advice concerning the laws which they administer.

Inasmuch as a large part of the legislation is concerned with the structure and functioning of administrative departments and the creation and modification of administrative powers, the Congress is entitled, in the consideration of such legislation, to have from the administrative departments the benefit of their experience and special knowledge. All legislation recommended by the Executive Branch of the Government should be carefully considered before presentation to the Congress. The administrative, financial, legal, international, and other effects and implications of all such proposals should be thoroughly examined and the proposed legislation should be carefully drafted. Conflicts and differences between administrative departments concerning proposed legislation, whether of major policies or details, should, so far as possible, be adjusted before such bills are presented to the Congress. Though the ultimate decision in all such conflicts rests with the Congress, its work is hindered by differences between departments. These ordinarily should be adjusted within the Executive Branch of the Government in accordance with the constitutional concept of a single, and not a plural, Executive.

During recent years the Bureau of the Budget has functioned as an agency for the President in the clearance of the fiscal aspects of legislative measures proposed by the executive departments. This clearance is of value to the Congress and to the departments and is essential to the exercise of the authority and responsibility of the

President. It should be applied to all legislation proposed by the executive departments and agencies and should not be limited to fiscal considerations. The Bureau of the Budget could well take over the present duties of the National Emergency Council in this respect.

To aid the President in carrying out this responsibility the Bureau of the Budget should develop a staff equipped to act as a clearance agency on all aspects of proposed legislation and to provide the departments with expert and technical assistance. This would enable the Administration to prepare more expertly proposed legislative measures and to insure that ill-considered measures are not submitted to the Congress.

Recommendations

Our recommendations regarding budgeting and administrative control may be briefly summarized as follows:

1. The Director of the Bureau of the Budget should be relieved from routine duties and thus enabled to devote himself to problems of fiscal policy and planning. Provision should be made for an adequate permanent staff of the highest competence, implemented by special assistants on assignment from the operating agencies and by temporary consultants and specialists recruited from business and industry for special assignments.

2. The execution, as well as the preparation, of the budget should be supervised by the Bureau of the Budget and should be closely correlated with fiscal programs and plans.

3. The administrative research function of the Bureau of the Budget should be adequately developed to aid the President in his duties as head of the executive establishment. The Bureau should carry on constructive studies in public administration for the constant improvement of Government organization and procedure and should also stimulate continuous study of these problems by departments and bureaus.

4. The information function of the Bureau of the Budget should be developed and improved. The United States Information Service should be transferred to it, as should other appropriate activities in the coordination of the field services of the Government.

5. The Bureau of the Budget should serve in various ways as an agency of the President. Improvement should be made in its facilities for the clearance of Executive orders and the establishment of uniform codes of management in the Government. It should assist the departments in their regulations governing internal organization. It could render important service to the President and to the Congress in coordinating and clearing legislative recommendations which originate in the Executive Branch.

In my selective sampling of the Report of the President's Committee on Administrative Management, a great deal has been left out, including some things of considerable importance. My criterion for selection has been to emphasize those recommendations which most directly affected the presidential office, and also those which survived the legislative onslought and the test of time and experience in future years.

The Brownlow group also recommended rather drastic changes in personnel management. It sought a thoroughgoing expansion of the civil service to include all government positions. Such expansion would cover all jobs which did not fall into the "policy determining" category. Finding the operation of the existing Civil Service Commission "slow, cumbersome, wasteful and ineffective," the committee recommended it be replaced by a highly professional civil service administrator who would have full power to direct the central personnel agency.[62] The administrator would be provided with a non-salaried board of eminent citizens who would periodically examine the operation of the agency and advise the director and the President on federal employment policies and problems. Finally the committee found top salaries in the federal service to be out of line with comparable positions in industry, universities and public service foundations, and urged that they be raised in order to attract first-rate personnel to critical positions within the federal government.

The Budget and Accounting Act of 1921 had created a comptroller general who was directed to set up and supervise uniform accounting systems throughout the various administrative departments, and also to audit all expenditures of the federal government. The committee found the accounting systems still fragmented and unsatisfactory, and recommended that the responsibility for establishing such a system be assumed by the Treasury Department. The comptroller general, on the other hand, would become an auditor-general, concentrating his efforts and those of his staff upon the complex assignment of auditing all governmental expenditures.

The committee also recommended the establishment of a permanent planning body in the Executive office of the President. A temporary planning agency, the National Resources Board, had been created during the New Deal by executive order, but its activity had been hampered by its lack of a permanent professional staff and its relatively low level of influence within the framework of the federal government. The Brownlow group now proposed that a five-member, non-salaried National Resources Board be created as "a central planning agency under the President," with a full-time director and a staff "equal to the performance of the heavy tasks imposed upon it."[63]

The National Resources Board was to serve first as a clearinghouse for other planning efforts being conducted on the state and regional level and directed towards preventing the waste of our natural and human resources, and to the improvement of the quality of American life. Many such decentralized efforts were already underway, but the lack of a central coordinating agency for planning was a major obstacle to their success. Such an agency would have no operational responsibilities, but would conduct studies and pursue planning on a national level. Acting as "a general staff" for the President, it would provide him with relevant information and policy recommendations for the development and the preservation of the nation's natural resources as well as the development of the essential equilibrium of equally valuable human resources in American life.

Finally, the President's Committee on Administrative Management proposed a general reorganization of the permanent and "temporary" administrative departments and agencies of the federal government. That, of course, would be a monumental undertaking. At the time that the report was prepared there were over 100 separately organized establishments reporting to the President, including ten regular executive departments and many additional boards, commissions, administration authorities, corporations and agencies which were theoretically under the President's jurisdiction but not in a specific executive department. There were also more than a dozen so-called independent regulatory commissions. The aim of the President's Committee was to "reduce to a manageable compass the number of agencies reporting to the President."[64]

What was proposed was a general reorganization of the entire network of agencies into 12 major departments, which would include the existing departments of State, War, Navy, Treasury, Justice, Post Office, Agriculture, Commerce, Interior and Labor, and two new departments—Social Welfare and Public Works. In the general reshuffling all existing and future agencies would be located under the general administrative jurisdiction of these basic departments, so there would at least be a line of authority starting with the President and flowing down to their chief officers and divisional heads. Clearly some of these agencies would be nearly autonomous within the framework of the department under which they operated, yet the line of authority and policy enforcement would be clear and direct.

The most controversial aspect of this proposal related to the future of the independent regulatory commissions. They had been created by the Congress to perform a wide range of regulatory functions, which included quasi-legislative rule-making for entire industries (e.g., the Interstate Commerce Commission and the railroads), and also quasi-judicial functions with respect to determining individual and corporate liability in cases arising from regulations under their jurisdiction. Apart from their overall accountability to Congress and/or the President, confusion frequently arose over this kind of hybrid role, where an impartial performance of their judicial functions was threatened by their discretionary role as administrators:

> Pressures and influences properly enough directed toward officers responsible for formulating and administering policy constitute an unwholesome atmosphere in which to adjudicate private rights. But the mixed duties of the commissions render escape from these subversive influences impossible.
>
> Furthermore, the same men are obliged to serve as prosecutors and as judges. This not only undermines judicial fairness; it weakens public confidence in that fairness. Commission decisions affecting private rights and conduct lie under the suspicion of being rationalizations of the preliminary findings which the commission, in the role of a prosecutor, presented to itself.

The independent commission, in short, provides the proper working conditions neither for administration nor for adjudication. It fails to provide responsibility for the first; it does not provide complete independence for the second.[65]

The committee proposed transferring the administrative functions of the commissions to a bureau or a division of a regular executive department where its chief officer would be responsible to the department secretary and through him to the President, while the section performing judicial or quasi-judicial functions would retain wholly independent status, although it would also be placed within the framework of an existing department for purely administrative functions (supply, services, etc.).

The proposed method of congressional review was one of the more innovative aspects of the President's program. If, for example, a reorganization plan submitted by the President was defeated by a resolution in both houses of Congress and the President vetoed the resolution, a two-thirds majority would be necessary to defeat the measure.

The Reorganization Act of 1939

President Roosevelt submitted these proposals to the Congress in early January 1937, after a preliminary meeting with congressional leaders, who, in many cases, were not too happy with what they heard. Their main objections were to the transfer of the regulatory commissions to the executive branch, and they also responded negatively to the salary increases for cabinet members. The administration had very unwisely failed to consult with them during the earlier stages of drafting the report, and the legislators, now faced with a *fait accompli*, reacted as if something were being put over on them. Roosevelt did not always exhibit the tact for which he was so famous. When the extremely popular and powerful House leader Sam Rayburn asked the President if the Interstate Commerce Commission might be permitted to remain outside of the executive branch, the President replied firmly: "There will be no exceptions, not one."[66] Later the President remarked to Brownlow:

> You see, Louis, what I am up against. This was quite a little package to give them this afternoon. Every time they recovered from a blow I socked them on the jaw with another.[67]

The year 1937 was not Roosevelt's most popular with the American people, nor was it a high point of legislative accomplishment in Congress. On the contrary it was a period of economic recession, the year of the Court fight in which almost every New Deal measure was either defeated or emasculated by a Congress in which the President's party controlled three-fourths of the votes. The proposal to reorganize the Supreme Court probably caused the greatest uproar among citizens in general, and newspapers and organized opposition groups, such as the Committee to Uphold Constitutional Government, in particular (see section six of this volume). The Court "packing" proposal came several weeks after the reorganization plan was submitted to Congress, but the furor it aroused literally swamped any immediate considerations of the Brownlow committee proposals. The strong opposition of Senator Byrd was another negative factor of significant proportions.

At a time when the Supreme Court proposal seemed to illustrate the inflated ambitions of the President for increased power, a plan for concentrating a great deal more administrative power and resources in the Chief Executive's hands would be bound to run into trouble. The death of the Democratic Senate leader, a trusted disciple of FDR, Senator Joseph Robinson of Arkansas, who was also chairman of the joint committee considering the bill and its Senate sponsor, further crippled the efforts to push the measure through before the end of the session. The Senate bill itself was a somewhat watered-down version of the original proposal, bypassing those provisions to which the Senate and House leaders had initially taken exception. There was, for example, no provision for salary increases, and nine of the independent regulatory commissions, plus the Corps of Engineers and the Mississippi River Commission were exempted from administrative reorganization. But the Senate did accept the concept of greater staff assistance for the President, the general proposal for reorganization (agreeing to a Department of General Welfare, but not of Public Works), setting up a civil service commissioner and providing for a genuine audit. However, a combination of all the distracting factors mentioned above prevented any reorganization measure from coming to a vote that year. The House did somewhat better, passing two different measures; the first one approved six presidential assistants, and the second endorsed presidentially initiated administrative reorganization and a new Department of Welfare, but exempted, like the Senate, a number of regulatory agencies. Without Senate approval, however, none of these measures became law during the 1937 session of Congress.

In 1938 the situation reversed itself, for a reorganization bill passed in the Senate but was defeated in the House. The bill's endorsement by a small majority in the Senate, however, was a pyrrhic victory. The prolonged fight in the upper chamber widened divisions within the President's party, which helped defeat the measure in the House, and support came from some senators only after certain critical elements of the reorganization proposal were removed from the bill.

Opposition to the bill came from some of the groups which were first allied in the Court battle—conservative, anti-New Deal Democrats and Republicans were joined by some solid New Deal supporters who were strongly opposed to certain aspects of the bill, but did not oppose reorganization in principle. Senator Edward Burke, a Democrat from Nebraska, reflected the conservative opposition in his statement that "I am not willing, in the search for efficient management, to establish one-man rule in this country."[68] On the other hand, a strong New Dealer like Senator Robert Wagner of New York voted against the bill, because he wanted to retain the Civil Service Commission, and because he was opposed to the proposed method of congressional review of executive reorganization proposals in the Senate bill. Father Coughlin's well-organized opposition to the bill also built up pressure against it among the senator's large Catholic constituency. Over 100,000 telegrams inundated Washington from all over the nation, largely in response to the Royal Oak, the Michigan priest's fervent appeals and well-organized opposition from the Committee to Uphold Constitutional Government. Another blow to the hopes of achieving reorganization in 1938 came when the Senate failed to substitute its bill as an amendment to the earlier House measure, a parliamentary maneuver which would have allowed the bill to go to a conference committee without further debate in the House.

Despite a 225-member Democratic majority in the House of Representatives, reorganization was defeated in the House in 1938 by an eight-vote margin, regardless of the fact that the administration had already accepted many deletions and changes in the hopes of winning. Roosevelt continued in his temporary lapse of popularity and public support in early 1938, and this accounted for most of the success of the opposition. He did not move effectively to win popular support for reorganization, and the majority of the public was unconcerned, while an aroused minority was extremely outspoken and effective in opposition.

A reorganization bill finally passed both houses in 1939, but it was hardly an endorsement of the Brownlow committee's proposals of 1937. The new law consisted of a title empowering the President to submit reorganization proposals, subject to their rejection within 60 days by a majority vote in both houses, and another title authorizing six administrative staff assistants for the President. The statute also exempted independent establishments from reorganization, including the Maritime Commission, the Interstate Commerce Commission, the Federal Communications Commission, the Federal Power Commission, etc.

Nevertheless, the new law did give the President certain leverage that he had not previously possessed. He could not bring about the kind of transformation of the executive branch that his learned advisors had counselled, but he made progress by establishing inroads with which he could develop greater cohesiveness and, in fact, more effective management control in his own departments than he had previously possessed. By 1939 the mercurial pendulum of public opinion swung back in the President's direction. In a more receptive climate, both in the Congress and the nation, Roosevelt faced the possibility of accomplishing at least some of the objectives of the President's Committee on Administrative Management, by skillful administrative moves rather than by bold and straightforward legislative proposals.

The Reorganization Act of 1939
April 3, 1939

United States Statutes at Large, 76th Cong., 1st sess., LIII, Part 2, 561-66.

TITLE I—REORGANIZATION

Part I

Section 1

(a) The Congress hereby declares that by reason of continued national deficits beginning in 1931 it is desirable to reduce substantially Government expenditures and that such reduction may be accomplished in some measure by proceeding immediately under the provisions of this Act. The President shall investigate the organization of all agencies of the Government and shall determine what changes therein are necessary to accomplish the following purposes:

(1) To reduce expenditures to the fullest extent consistent with the efficient operation of the Government;

(2) To increase the efficiency of the operations of the Government to the fullest extent practicable within the revenues;

(3) To group, coordinate, and consolidate agencies of the Government, as nearly as may be, according to major purposes;

(4) To reduce the number of agencies by consolidating those having similar functions under a single head, and to abolish such agencies as may not be necessary for the efficient conduct of the Government; and

(5) To eliminate overlapping and duplication of effort.

(b) The Congress declares that the public interest demands the carrying out of the purposes specified in subsection (a) and that such purposes may be accomplished in great measure by proceeding immediately under the provisions of this title, and can be accomplished more speedily thereby than by the enactment of specific legislation.

Sec. 2

When used in this title, the term "agency" means any executive department, commission, independent establishment, corporation owned or controlled by the United States, board, bureau, division, service, office, authority, or administration, in the executive branch of the Government.

Sec. 3

No reorganization plan under section 4 shall provide—

(a) For the abolition or transfer of an executive department or all the functions thereof or for the establishment of any new executive department;

(b) In the case of the following agencies, for the transfer, consolidation, or abolition of the whole or any part of such agency or of its head, or of all or any of the functions of such agency or of its head: Civil Service Commission, Coast Guard, Engineer Corps of the United States Army, Mississippi River Commission, Federal Communications Commission, Federal Power Commission, Federal Trade Commission, General Accounting Office, Interstate Commerce Commission, National Labor Relations Board, Securities and Exchange Commission, Board of Tax Appeals, United States Employees' Compensation Commission, Veterans' Administration, National Mediation Board, National Railroad Adjustment Board, Railroad Retirement Board, the Federal Deposit Insurance Corporation, or the Board of Governors of the Federal Reserve System; or

(c) For changing the name of any executive department or the title of its head, or for designating any agency as "Department" or its head as "Secretary"; or

(d) For the continuation of any agency beyond the period authorized by law for the existence of such agency; or

(e) For the continuation of any function of any agency beyond the period authorized by law for the exercise of such function; or

(f) For authorizing any agency to exercise any function which is not expressly authorized by law.

Sec. 4

Whenever the President, after investigation, finds that—

(a) the transfer of the whole or any part of any agency or the functions thereof to the jurisdiction and control of any other agency; or

(b) the consolidation of the functions vested in any agency; or

(c) the abolition of the whole or any part of any agency which agency or part (by reason of transfers under this Act or otherwise, or by reason of termination of its functions in any manner) does not have, or upon the taking effect of the reorganizations specified in the reorganization plan will not have, any functions, is necessary to accomplish one or more of the purposes of section 1 (a), he shall—

(d) prepare a reorganization plan for the making of the transfers, consolidations, and abolitions, as to which he has made findings and which he includes in the plan. Such plan shall also—

(1) designate, in such cases as he deems necessary, the name of any agency affected by a reorganization and the title of its head;

(2) make provision for the transfer or other disposition of the records, property (including office equipment), and personnel affected by such transfer, consolidation, or abolition;

(3) make provision for the transfer of such unexpended balances of appropriations available for use in connection with the function or agency transferred or consolidated, as he deems necessary by reason of the transfer or consolidation for use in connection with the transferred or consolidated functions, or for the use of the agency to which the transfer is made, but such unexpended balances so transferred shall be used only for the purposes for which such appropriation is originally made;

(4) make provision for winding up the affairs of the agency abolished; and

(e) transmit such plan (bearing an identifying number) to the Congress, together with a declaration that, with respect to each transfer, consolidation, or abolition referred to in paragraph (a), (b), or (c) of this section and specified in the plan, he has found that such transfer, consolidation, or abolition is necessary to accomplish one or more of the purposes of section 1 (a). The delivery to both Houses shall be on the same day and shall be made to each House while it is in session.

The President, in his message transmitting a reorganization plan, shall state the reduction of expenditures which it is probable will be brought about by the taking effect of the reorganizations specified in the plan.

Sec. 5

The reorganizations specified in the plan shall take effect in accordance with the plan:

(a) Upon the expiration of sixty calendar days after the date on which the plan is transmitted to the Congress, but only if during such sixty-day period there has not been passed by the two Houses a concurrent resolution stating in substance that the Congress does not favor the reorganization plan.

(b) If the Congress adjourns sine die before the expiration of the sixty-day period, a new sixty-day period shall begin on the opening day of the next succeeding regular or special session. A similar rule shall be applicable in the case of subsequent adjournments sine die before the expiration of sixty days.

Sec. 6

No reorganization under this title shall have effect—

(a) of continuing any agency or function beyond the time when it would have terminated if the reorganization had not been made; or

(b) of continuing any function beyond the time when the agency in which it was vested before the reorganization would have terminated if the reorganization had not been made; or

(c) of authorizing any agency to exercise any function which is not expressly authorized by law.

Sec. 7

For the purposes of this title any transfer, consolidation, abolition, designation, disposition, or winding up of affairs, referred to in section 4 (d), shall be deemed a "reorganization".

Sec. 8

(a) All orders, rules, regulations, permits, or other privileges made, issued, or granted by or in respect of any agency or function transferred to, or consolidated with, any other agency or function under the provisions of this title, and in effect at the time of the transfer or consolidation, shall continue in effect to the same extent as if such transfer or consolidation had not occurred, until modified, superseded, or repealed.

(b) No suit, action, or other proceeding lawfully commenced by or against the head of any agency or other officer of the United States, in his official capacity or in relation to the discharge of his official duties, shall abate by reason of any transfer of authority, power, and duties from one officer or agency of the Government to another under the provisions of this title, but the court, on motion or supplemental petition filed at any time within twelve months after such transfer takes effect, showing a necessity for a survival of such suit, action, or other preceeding to obtain a settlement of the questions involved, may allow the same to be maintained by or against the head of the agency or other officer of the United States to whom the authority, powers, and duties are transferred.

(c) All laws relating to any agency or function transferred to, or consolidated with, any other agency or function under the provisions of this title, shall, insofar as such laws are not inapplicable, remain in full force and effect.

Sec. 9

The appropriations or portions of appropriations unexpended by reason of the operation of this title shall not be used for any purpose, but shall be impounded and returned to the Treasury.

Sec. 10

(a) Whenever the employment of any person is terminated by a reduction of personnel as a result of a reorgnization effected under this title, such person shall thereafter be given preference, when qualified, whenever an appointment is made in the executive branch of the Government, but such preference shall not be effective for a period longer than twelve months from the date the employment of such person is so terminated.

(b) Any transfer of personnel under this title shall be without change in classification or compensation, except that this requirement shall not operate after the end of the fiscal year during which the transfer is made to prevent the adjustment of classification or compensation to conform to the duties to which such transferred personnel may be assigned.

Sec. 11

If the reorganizations specified in a reorganization plan take effect, the reorganization plan shall be printed in the Statutes at Large in the same volume as the public laws, and shall be printed in the Federal Register.

Sec. 12

No reorganization specified in a reorganization plan shall take effect unless the plan is transmitted to the Congress before January 21, 1941.

Part 2

Sec. 21

The following sections of this part are enacted by the Congress:

(a) As an exercise of the rule-making power of the Senate and the House of Representatives, respectively, and as such they shall be considered as part of the rules of each House, respectively, but applicable only with respect to the procedure to be followed in such House in the case of resolutions (as defined in section 22); and such rules shall supersede other rules only to the extent that they are inconsistent therewith; and

(b) With full recognition of the constitutional right of either House to change such rules (so far as relating to the procedure in such House) at any time, in the same manner and to the same extent as in the case of any other rule of such House.

Sec. 22

As used in this part, the term "resolution" means only a concurrent resolution of the two Houses of Congress, the matter after the resolving clause of which is as follows: "That the Congress does not favor the reorganization plan numbered   transmitted to Congress by the President on   , 19   .", the blank spaces therein being appropriately filled; and does not include a concurrent resolution which specifies more than one reorganization plan.

Sec. 23

A resolution with respect to a reorganization plan shall be referred to a committee (and all resolutions with respect to the same plan shall be referred to the same committee) by the President of the Senate or the Speaker of the House of Representatives, as the case may be.

Sec. 24

(a) If the committee to which has been referred a resolution with respect to a reorganization plan has not reported it before the expiration of ten calendar days after its introduction (or,   the case of a resolution received from the other House, ten calendar days after its receipt), it shall then (but not before) be in order to move either to discharge the committee from further consideration of such resolution, or to discharge the committee from further consideration of any other resolution with respect to such reorganization plan which has been referred to the committee.

(b) Such motion may be made only by a person favoring the resolution, shall be highly privileged (except that it may not be made after the committee has reported a resolution with respect to the same reorganization plan), and debate thereon shall be limited to not to exceed one hour, to be equally divided between those favoring and those opposing the resolution. No amendment to such motion shall be in order, and it shall not be in order to move to reconsider the vote by which such motion is agreed to or disagreed to.

(c) If the motion to discharge is agreed to or disagreed to, such motion may not be renewed, nor may another motion to discharge the committees be made with respect to any other resolution with respect to the same reorganization plan.

Sec. 25

(a) When the committee has reported, or has been discharged from further consideration of, a resolution with respect to a reorganization plan, it shall at any time thereafter be in order (even though a previous motion to the same effect has been disagreed to) to move to proceed to the consideration of such resolution. Such motion shall be highly privileged and shall not be debatable. No amendment to such motion shall be in order and it shall not be in order to move to reconsider the vote by which such motion is agreed to or disagreed to.

(b) Debate on the resolution shall be limited to not to exceed ten hours, which shall be equally divided between those favoring and those opposing the resolution. A motion further to limit debate shall not be debatable. No amendment to, or motion to recommit, the resolution shall be in order, and it shall not be in order to move to reconsider the vote by which the resolution is agreed to or disagreed to.

Sec. 26

(a) All motions to postpone, made with respect to the discharge from committee, or the consideration of, a resolution with respect to a reorganization plan, and all motions to proceed to the consideration of other business, shall be decided without debate.

(b) All appeals from the decisions of the Chair relating to the application of the rules of the Senate or the House of Representatives, as the case may be, to the procedure relating to a resolution with respect to a reorganization plan shall be decided without debate.

Sec. 27

If, prior to the passage by one House of a resolution of that House with respect to a reorganization plan, such House receives from the other House a resolution with respect to the same plan, then—

(a) If no resolution of the first House with respect to such plan has been referred to committee, no other resolution with respect to the same plan may be reported or (despite the provisions of section 24 (a)) be made the subject of a motion to discharge.

(b) If a resolution of the first House with respect to such plan has been referred to committee—(1) the procedure with respect to that or other resolutions of such House with respect to such plan which have been referred to committee shall be the same as if no resolution from the other House with respect to such plan had been received; but (2) on any vote on final passage of a resolution of the first House with respect to such plan the resolution from the other House with respect to such plan shall be automatically substituted for the resolution of the first House.

TITLE II—BUDGETARY CONTROL

Sec. 201

Section 2 of the Budget and Accounting Act, 1921 (U. S. C., 1934 edition, title 31, sec. 2), is amended by inserting after the word "including" the words "any independent regulatory commission or board and".

TITLE III—ADMINISTRATIVE ASSISTANTS

Sec. 301

The President is authorized to appoint not to exceed six administrative assistants and to fix the compensation of each at the rate of not more than $10,000 per annum. Each such administrative assistant shall perform such duties as the President may prescribe.

The threat of an impending war produced a soberness among the Congress and the American people, and the Reorganization Act of 1939 was followed by a quick approval of Reorganization Plan I, which established the Executive Office of the President, transferred the Bureau of the Budget and the National Resources Planning Board into it, created the Federal Security Agency, the Federal Works Agency and the Federal Loan Agency, and transferred related bureaus under their jurisdiction. Reorganization Plan II followed Plan I by a week, but involved only interdepartmental transfers of a noncontroversial nature. Four months later the President issued an executive order (No. 8248) which spelled out in greater detail what the function of the staff agencies and assistants would be. The changes were mild indeed, and all the hullabaloo raised about the concentration of power in the Executive and talk of "a dictator in the White House" appeared to have been very wide of the mark. Roosevelt regained some of his lost popularity, and more people looked with confidence to a strong leader in times of awful doubts and upheavals. He demonstrated once again his ability to ascertain the limits of political change, and prepared to utilize fully his new and considerably enchanced administrative structure.

The Reorganization Act of 1939 did not bring about all of the reforms that Brownlow, Merriam and Gulick desired, but it had a revolutionary impact upon the presidency in its administrative capacity. Previous twentieth-century Presidents had been crippled by the absence of trained staff assistance and the lack of the power and organizational structure to control their own administrative subordinates. The first budget director under the new structure pointed out that

> [i]f the President does not have the means to carry out his executive functions, he becomes a chief of state something like the Dalai Lama, a venerated ruler in whose name all ministerial actions are taken but who is carefully shielded from reality.[69]

The major accomplishment of the reorganization effort was to create a presidential office capable of performing its administrative responsibilities. The most important and unique contribution of the Brownlow report was to make this accomplishment possible through its creative definition of the administrative role of the President. No one had succeeded in that effort prior to that time but from that point on all future administrative developments in the presidential office would be mere extensions of their brilliant formulation.

The key to the development of the President's capacity to deal with his enlarged administrative responsibilities was the transfer of the Bureau of the Budget to the Executive Office of the White House and its rapid growth as a "general staff" to the entire executive branch. Within several years the bureau increased its pre-1939 personnel roster of about 45 to 15 times that number. It no longer limited itself to assisting executive departments in submitting budget estimates, but expanded the scope of its operation to perform many other diverse functions. Its reach into the departments and other agencies became more pervasive. Programs were analyzed more carefully and related to estimates for appropriations. As the new director put it:

> Budgetary control requires more than a periodical examination of expenditures of departments. The services carried on, the units of work performed, and the accomplishments under the various programs of the departments must be related to expenditures.[70]

The growth of the bureau's legislative clearance function was another index of its expanding influence. Neustadt has shown that the increase began even before the transfer of the agency to the Executive Office of the President, stimulated by the arguments brought out in the Brownlow report, but it especially continued to increase after the 1939 law was passed. In 1939 the bureau "processed agency reports on 2,448 pending public bills," an increase of 800 percent.[71] The Division of Administrative Management was also established at that time to fulfill a mandate of the Budget and Accounting Act calling for the bureau to carry out studies of the "organization, activities and methods of business" of the departments and other agencies, "with a view to securing greater efficiency and economy in the conduct of the public service." Fully aware of the confusion bordering upon chaos existing in the various systems of statistics, forms, statements, etc., used by different agencies throughout the federal government, a Statistical Standards Division was created to improve and coordinate all federal statistical services.

The Bureau of the Budget has been likened to a centralized nervous system, the chief characteristic distinguishing the higher from the lower species of animal.

> Man can think because what he hears, and what he feels are conveyed to a single center for classification, comparison, decision, and action. The Bureau of the Budget, along with the other divisions of the Executive Office of the President, provides a system by which information can be collected, classified, compared and transmitted for decision by the Chief Executive. Processing of departmental estimates, study of fiscal policies, follow through on departmental programs, coordination of statistics, organization and management surveys, clearing of legislation and executive orders—these are senses by which the President is enabled, under modern conditions, to do the job entrusted to him by the Constitution: namely to get from the various departments information about "the duties of their respective offices," and to transmit to Congress his recommendation of such "measure as he shall judge necessary and expedient."[72]

This was written only about a year after the real growth of the Bureau of the Budget had begun. In recent years all of these functions have continued to expand, and the bureau has developed greater and more far-reaching influence in the highest circles of government. The increased size of the federal establishment and the national budget, and the greater complexity of governmental affairs during World War II and in the postwar period have resulted in the continued growth of the power and status of the Bureau of the Budget as the right arm of the President as he attempts to control the steadily expanding executive branch of the government.

The creation of six executive assistants to the President also proved to be of great advantage to President Roosevelt and his hard-pressed successors. It is difficult to picture Roosevelt without the services of Harry Hopkins, Judge Samuel Rosenman, or Stephen Early; Harry Truman without Clark Clifford, Judge Vinson or John Steelman; Dwight Eisenhower without Sherman Adams; or John F. Kennedy without Theodore Sorensen and Lawrence O'Brien, all of whom served as presidential assistants at one time. They were frequently able to give single-minded attention to critical problems in domestic or foreign affairs, serve as special troubleshooters, advisors and representatives of the President, and they were able to expedite the decision-making process by providing the President with clear, concise and comprehensive breakdowns of problems, and to outline for him alternative solutions or options from which he could choose.[73]

At that time there was no real apprehension that in the not too distant future these presidential assistants would multiply like the proverbial loaves and fish, and even then they would be like an iceberg, the visible element of a greatly expanding (some would even suggest "swelling") Executive Office of the President. There was also no thought given then to the problem that these assistants might become so powerful and influential in their own right that they would gradually assume presidential prerogatives, acting in the name of the President in situations of which the President was not fully informed; initiating, coordinating and even deciding questions which the President had not even considered.

Presidential assistants normally reflected the character of the administration in which they served; the tone and style of their operating procedure being set by the inhabitant of the White House at that particular time. An important aspect of the evaluation of the quality of an individual President is how well or how poorly he used his "staff assistants," to what extent he retained the control of this staff and whether or not the staff enhanced the objective of obtaining greater "responsibility" on the part of the President or whether instead he was isolated further from those individuals and groups to whom he should have been "responsible?" If, indeed, a mid-century President should overextend the potential of the Executive office, to multiply staff at geometric, as opposed to mathematical, multiples, to delegate too much authority to staff assistants, then these very valuable staff assistants to the President, backed up by the substantial resources of the White House, might easily become a problem of serious magnitude in the age of what Schlesinger calls the "Imperial Presidency."

In some of the cases the carry-over from the President's report was not so successful. The National Resources Planning Board which had been transferred into the Executive Office of the President was wiped out by Congress in 1943, but some of its important functions were later assumed by the Council of Economic Advisors which emerged from the Full Employment Act of 1946. Reorganization continued to stimulate great interest and controversy, and many shifts and consolidations were accomplished during and after the war. The legislative veto, however, introduced by the Reorganization Act of 1939, worked very successfully for Roosevelt, but backfired in Truman's case, when he was confronted with a Republican-dominated Congress.

From the beginning Congress successfully excluded the regulatory commissions from integration into the existing executive departments, thus defeating a vital recommendation of the Committee on Administrative Management. This attitude persisted into the 1970s. James M. Landis, a former dean of the Harvard Law School and a former member of three different regulatory commissions, recommended, in a brilliant report written for President John F. Kennedy after his election in 1960, a division between the operating and judicial functions of the commissions and the incorporation of the operating functions into the executive branch, in a reorganization move similar to that proposed by the Brownlow group more than 20 years earlier, but Congress was no more willing to accept that arrangement in 1961 than it had been in 1930.[74] The Landis proposal was all the more interesting because he savagely attacked the Brownlow committee's analysis of the commissions in a book published the year after the report was issued.[75]

The work of the two Hoover commissions, the first in 1947 and the second in 1955, essentially continued in detail the thrust and principles laid down by the Brownlow group. The objective was to unify the executive branch and to strengthen the President's leadership. Further consolidation of agencies was proposed along with departmental management reforms aimed at firming up a central line of control running from the President through his departmental secretary to the bureau or section heads. Extensive proposals were made for attracting and holding career public servants and generally improving the quality of personnel in the government service.

When the original alarmists and extremists lost their struggle to defeat all of the President's Committee's proposals in 1939, responsible criticism of the major reforms which were enacted was not widespread. Professor Lindsay Rogers of Columbia University, who was an original advisory member of the Brownlow group, was one of the negative voices who criticized the committee for not incorporating into its proposal his suggestion borrowed from the British cabinet. Rogers proposed a secretariat modelled after the British cabinet experience, adapted, of course, to the American system with one man at the head of it. Roosevelt was adamantly opposed to this idea, and he apparently convinced or persuaded the committee members to his point of view. Rogers was convinced that they had simply given in to him, and he accused them of "selling out." On the contrary Brownlow argued that Rogers did not fully consider the possibility that Roosevelt had convinced his committee that he was right, which is just what he had done.

A more eminent critic, Edward S. Corwin, was most unhappy with the proposals for the independent regulatory commissions, because they stemmed from what he considered to be an invalid assumption regarding administrative practice.

Of course, the advocates of the President's plan strongly urge the claims of administrative *unity* and *efficiency*. But are the two things necessarily synonymous in the case of so vast an organization as the national government? It seems to me clearly not; but rather that efficient administration must in such a case always depend to an important extent upon the expert knowledge and pride in his job of the largely independent bureaucrat. In other words, administration in the sense of the daily task of carrying out the laws and performing the public services for which they provide is a *pluralistic*, not a *monistic* universe; and to imagine the President as a sort of boss of the works under whose all-seeing eye everything takes place, is merely to imagine something that does not exist and never will. To be sure, such considerations do not dispose entirely of the argument for the President's plan; and no one would care to deny that administrative set-up must be constantly tinkered with to keep it at all efficient.[76]

In his classic work on the presidency, Professor Corwin returned to the subject again, but still focused his criticism of the 1937 study on its proposals regarding the regulatory commissions which, after all, were not accepted. There is not a favorable or even a critical word regarding any of the other major recommendations which were accepted, nor any recognition by Corwin of the role of the report in defining and strengthening the administrative role of the President of the United States.

One must not lose sight of the fact that the reorganization of the executive branch in the American political system has been and should be a continuing process. There must always be a continuing adjustment of the administrative machinery of the government as it reacts to the pressures and changes which are taking place in the political, social and economic environment in which it is operating. It is to the credit of the President's Committee on Administrative Management that they understood this, and proposed a "*continuing* Presidential authority over a *continuing* problem."[77] Testifying before the Joint Congressional Committee on Government Organization, Louis Brownlow pointed out that

> [i]f the Archangel Michael could come down and arrange it perfectly by the 1st day of March 1937, by the last day of March 1938 you would need another Archangel to come down and adjust it.[78]

The basic principles underlying Professor Lindsay Rogers' criticism of the Report of the President's Committee on Administrative Management were heard again and again as the years went on, advanced in somewhat changed form, frequently by different individuals. Rogers and others who have followed in his wake wanted to see the presidency strengthened and its administrative control tightened, and reiterated over and over again that the President needs a chief of staff, or, as the second Hoover commission urged, two appointed Vice Presidents who would assume chief of staff responsibilities in the area of foreign policy-national security and in domestic affairs. Nelson Rockefeller, chairman of the President's Advisory Committee on Government Organization in the Eisenhower administration, followed this line of reasoning, designating two subordinates as the first secretary (in charge of foreign affairs-national security) and executive assistant to the President for domestic affairs.[79] President Dwight Eisenhower actually put this concept into practice in the domestic area, for Sherman Adams carried the title of assistant to the President and was for all intents and purposes an assistant President or chief of staff, for all papers, appointments, policies and decisions flowed through his office on their way to the President. In describing his understanding with the President as to what his duties and responsibilities were, Adams wrote:

As I have said, when Eisenhower asked me to be the Assistant to the President he never specifically defined my responsibilities or outlined their limits. He never gave me, nor did I ever seek, a delegation of presidential power and authority, as so many capital correspondents and politicians have assumed. I realize that the columnists referred to me as "The Assistant President" and "the second most powerful executive in the government" because my duties in the White House were too broad and general to be described precisely. Eisenhower simply expected me to manage a staff that would boil down, simplify and expedite the urgent business that had to be brought to his personal attention and to keep as much work of secondary importance as possible off his desk. Any power or authority that I exercised while carrying out this appointed task was solely on a *de facto* basis and, except when I was acting on an explicit directive from the President, my duties and responsibilities were implied rather than stated.[80]

Such power is awesome, and such ambiguity about its limits and responsibilities somewhat frightening. Eisenhower's successor rejected this staff structure, returning to a more flexible and diffused organizational pattern in which the President did not delegate to any one chief of staff anything comparable to the decision-making powers Adams exercised (either explicitly or implicitly) in determining and implementing the flow of information, problems and decisions both to and from the President. In a staff paper written for the Jackson Committee on National Policy Machinery, Richard Neustadt argued, even before Kennedy replaced Eisenhower in the White House, that the new "super-cabinet" officer would add to, rather than ease, the congestion in the present system.

At first glance, the proposal may appear an answer to current difficulties in the operation of the policy machinery. The First Secretary would be expected to encompass the whole range of national security problems. He would be charged with giving committee coordinating mechanisms the stiffening of authoritative direction. Theoretically, he would be no mere White House staff assistant but a super-Cabinet member, thus able to direct fellow Cabinet members in a way that ordinary Presidential aides cannot. Theoretically he would relieve a President of many burdens both within the Government and in negotiations with other Chiefs of Government. . . .

Careful analysis of the First Secretary proposal, however, reveals serious shortcomings and limitations. . . .

Giving a man the title of "First Secretary" does not thereby give him power. Under this proposal, the Secretaries of State and Defense and other Cabinet officers would retain their present statutory functions and authority. These officials would continue to be accountable to the Congress for the proper performance of their statutory duties. They would equally continue to be responsible to the President.

Being responsible to the President, the Secretaries of State and Defense and other Cabinet officers would report directly to him. They would be bound to question the decisions of a First Secretary; his placement between them and the President would inevitably generate friction and resentment. The First Secretary could gain the power he needed only if the President consistently accepted the First Secretary's judgment over that of his department heads.

But if the President were consistently so deferential to his First Secretary who then would be President? And who would be willing to be Cabinet officers?[81]

The real limitation of this approach to administrative reform is that the problem is merely compounded when the proposal seeks to relieve the President of power and decision-making which his constitutional obligations and executive control require him to possess. Neustadt neatly sums it up by stating flatly:

Our governmental system has no place for a first Secretary. He is thought of as a mediator and a judge of the conflicting ... policies advocated by the major departments, the Congress and its committees and private groups. But in the American system only one official has the constitutional and political power required to assume that role and maintain it. That official is the President of the United States. He cannot be relieved of his burdens by supplying him with a "deputy" to do what only he can do.[82]

Central to continuing efforts towards administrative reorganization, however, is and will be the objective not of increasing the President's power at the expense of the Congress or of the bureaucrats who head the administrative agencies, so as to be in a position of dominating either, but rather to provide the President with sufficient power and assistance to enable him to carry out the awesome responsibilities of managing his constantly growing administrative "household," so that he shall indeed be able to "take Care that the Laws be faithfully executed." When, however, efforts at administrative reorganization become attempts to short-circuit or isolate the Chief Executive from other centers of power within the government, or, if the President himself attempts to undercut those centers in order to draw more power into his own hands, then administrative reorganization merely denigrates the presidency, making it a frightening and destructive agent of government.

NOTES

1. Quoted from a letter in Alpheus T. Mason, *William Howard Taft: Chief Justice* (New York, 1965), 224.
2. Quoted in Mason, *William Howard Taft*, 225.
3. Quoted in Alpheus T. Mason, *Harlan Fiske Stone* (New York, 1956), 224 footnote.
4. *Myers* v. *United States*, 272 U.S. 136 (1926).
5. *Myers* v. *United States*, 272 U.S. 175.
6. *Myers* v. *United States*, 272 U.S. 174-75.
7. *Myers* v. *United States*, 272 U.S. 175.
8. Mason, *Harlan Fiske Stone*, 224 footnote.
9. Thomas Reed Powell, "Spinning Out the Executive Power," in *New Republic*, November 17, 1926, 369.

10. Powell, 369.
11. Edward S. Corwin, *The President's Removal Power Under the Constitution* (New York, 1957), vi.
12. Edward S. Corwin, *The President: Office and Powers, 1787-1957* (New York, 1957), 4.
13. James M. Landis, "Mr. Justice Brandeis: A Law Clerk's View," an address delivered at the Fifty-Fifth Annual Meeting of the American Jewish Historical Society, Brandeis University, Waltham, Massachusetts, on February 16, 1957. Later printed in the *American Jewish Historical Society Publication*, XLVI, No. 4 (June 1957), 471.
14. William Leuchtenburg, "The Contentious Commissioner: Humphrey's Executor *v.* United States," in Harold M. Hyman and Leonard W. Levy, eds., *Freedom and Reform: Essays in Honor of Henry Steele Commager* (New York, 1967), 294.
15. *Myers* v. *United States,* 272 U.S. 177.
16. *Myers* v. *United States,* 272 U.S. 241.
17. *Myers* v. *United States,* 272 U.S. 294.
18. James Hart, *Tenure of Office Under the Constitution* (Baltimore, Maryland, 1930), 304.
19. See the attacks upon Humphrey by Senators Thomas J. Walsh, William E. Borah and George Norris in G. Cullom Davis, "The Transformation of the Federal Trade Commission," in *Mississippi Valley Historical Review*, XLIX, No. 3 (December 1962).
20. *Humphrey's Executor* v. *United States,* 295 U.S. (1935).
21. *Humphrey's Executor* v. *United States,* 295 U.S.
22. *Myers* v. *United States,* 272 U.S. 135.
23. *Myers* v. *United States,* 272 U.S. 135.
24. *Humphrey's Executor* v. *United States,* 295 U.S.
25. *Humphrey's Executor* v. *United States,* 295 U.S.
26. *Humphrey's Executor* v. *United States,* 295 U.S.
27. *Wiener* v. *United States,* 357 U.S. (1958).
28. Quoted in Lucius Wilmerding, jr., *The Spending Power: A History of the Efforts of Congress to Control Expenditures* (New Haven, Connecticut, 1943), 37. The full text of this fascinating document is reprinted in Henry Adams, ed., *The Writings of Albert Gallatin* (Philadelphia, Pennsylvania, 1879) III, 73-201.
29. Quoted in Wilmerding, 51.
30. Arthur Smithies, *The Budgetary Process in the United States* (New York, 1955), 49.
31. Quoted in William Franklin Willoughby, *The Problem of the National Budget* (New York, 1918), 137.
32. Although Roosevelt introduced revolutionary changes with respect to the executive and foreign policy functions of the presidency, his efforts to shake up the administrative machinery of the government through the appointment of the Keep Commission resulted only in proposals for minor administrative reforms, which Congress failed to support. See Harold T. Pinkett, "The Keep Commission, 1905-1909: A Rooseveltian Effort for Administrative Reform," in *Journal of American History*, III, No. 2 (September 1965), 297-312.
33. Willoughby, 141-42.
34. "The Need for a National Budget," Message from the President of the United States on the Report of the Commission on Economy and Efficiency, *House Doc. No. 854,* 62nd Cong., 2nd sess. (Washington, D.C., 1912), 21.
35. "The Need for a National Budget," 72.
36. "The Need for a National Budget," 7-8.
37. "The Need for a National Budget," 143.
38. "The Need for a National Budget," 144-45.
39. "The Need for a National Budget," 221.
40. "The Need for a National Budget," 221
41. The Need for a National Budget," 222.
42. "The Need for a National Budget," 5.
43. "Message of the President Submitting a Budget for the Fiscal Year 1914," *Senate Doc. No. 1113,* 62nd Cong., 3rd sess. (Washington, D.C., 1913).
44. "Submitting a Budget for 1914," *Senate Doc. No. 1113,* 62nd Cong., 3rd sess.
45. Quoted in Henry F. Pringle, *The Life and Times of William Howard Taft* (New York, 1939) II, 607.
46. Richard E. Neustadt, "Politicians and Bureaucrats," in David Truman, ed., *The Congress and America's Future* (Englewood Cliffs, New Jersey, 1965), 110.
47. Quoted in Fritz Morstein Marx, "The Bureau of the Budget: Its Evolution and Present Role," in *American Political Science Review*, XXXIX (August 1945), 667.
48. Marx, 668.
49. Quoted in Marx, 671.

1540

50. Marx, 672.
51. Marx, 672.
52. Harold D. Smith, "The Bureau of the Budget," in *Public Administration Review*, I, No. 2 (Winter 1940-41), 109.
53. Smith, 109.
54. Norman Pearson, "The Budget Bureau: From Routine Business to General Staff," in *Public Administration Review,* III (Spring 1943), 132.
55. Quoted in Louis Brownlow, *A Passion for Anonymity: The Autobiography of Louis Brownlow* (Chicago, 1958), 327.
56. Brownlow, 334-35.
57. Brownlow, 338.
58. Brownlow, 378.
59. The President's Committee on Administrative Management, *Report of the Committee with Studies of Administrative Management in the Federal Government*; Submitted to the President and to the Congress in Accordance with Public Law No. 739, 74th Cong., 2nd sess. (Washington, D.C., 1937), iv.
60. The President's Committee on Administrative Management, *Report*, 5.
61. The President's Committee on Administrative Management, *Report*, 16.
62. The President's Committee on Administrative Management, *Report*, 9-12.
63. The President's Committee on Administrative Management, *Report*, 29.
64. The President's Committee on Administrative Management, *Report*, 31.
65. The President's Committee on Administrative Management, *Report*, 40.
66. Quoted in Richard Polenberg, *Reorganizing Roosevelt's Government: The Controversy Over Executive Reorganization, 1936-1939* (Cambridge, Massachusetts, 1966), 44.
67. Quoted in Polenberg, 42.
68. Quoted in Polenberg, 126.
69. Quoted in Smith, 107.
70. Smith, 111.
71. Richard E. Neustadt, "Presidency and Legislation: The Growth of Central Clearance," in *American Political Science Review*, XLVIII (September 1954), 653.
72. Smith, 114-15.
73. Presidents from Andrew Jackson on had always relied greatly upon informal advisors and assistants who helped write speeches, prepare drafts of proposed legislation and assisted with the critical problems of one sort or another with which all Presidents are burdened. Often they were placed in nondemanding positions in governmental departments so they could receive subsistance while they helped and advised the President; others gave of their time freely, if it was financially possible. But this new arrangement regularized and strengthened what had frequently been a difficult, sometimes awkward and even embarrassing arrangement, as Presidents became dependent upon voluntary assistance from outsiders in order to fulfill their constitutional responsibilities.
74. James M. Landis, *Report on Regulatory Agencies to the President-Elect* (Washington, D.C., 1960).
75. James M. Landis, *The Administrative Process* (New Haven, Connecticut, 1938), 4-5.
76. Edward S. Corwin, "The President as Administrative Chief," in *Journal of Politics*, I, No. 1 (February 1939), 44.
77. Herbert Emmerich, *Essays on Federal Reorganization* (Birmingham, Alabama, 1959), 86.
78. Emmerich, 85-86.
79. See Nelson A. Rockefeller's testimony before the Subcommittee on National Policy Machinery of the Committee on Government Operations of the United States Senate (Jackson Committee), "Organizing for National Security," Part VII, July 1, 1960, 941-87.
80. Sherman Adams, *First Hand Report: The Story of the Eisenhower Administration* (New York, 1961), 50.
81. Senate Subcommittee on National Policy Machinery, Staff Report on "Super-Officers and Superstaff," November 16, 1960, 3-4.
82. "Super-Officers and Superstaff," 5.

Bibliography

Adams, Charles Francis. *Appeal to the Whigs* (a pamphlet). Boston: n.p., 1835.

Adams, Sherman. *First Hand Report: The Story of the Eisenhower Administration.* New York: Harper and Brothers, 1961.

Bailey, Stephen Kemp. *Congress Makes a Law: The Story Behind the Employment Act of 1946.* New York: Columbia University Press, 1950.

Basler, Roy P., ed. *The Collected Works of Abraham Lincoln.* Vol. VIII. New Brunswick, New Jersey: Rutgers University Press, 1953.

Bassett, John Spencer, ed. *Correspondence of Andrew Jackson.* Vol. V. Washington, D.C.: Carnegie Institution of Washington, 1931.

Benton, Thomas Hart. *Thirty Years View; or, A History of the Working of the American Government For Thirty Years, From 1820 to 1850.* New York: D. Appleton and Company, 1854.

Binkley, Wilfred E. *President and Congress.* Third revised ed. New York: Vintage Books, 1962.

Blaine, James. *Twenty Years in Congress.* Vol. II. Norwich, Connecticut: The Henry Bill Publishing Company, 1886.

Brown, E. Carey. "Fiscal Policy in the Thirties." *American Economic Review.* XLVI. No. 5 (December 1936).

Brownlow, Louis. *A Passion for Anonymity: The Autobiography of Louis Brownlow.* Chicago: University of Chicago Press, 1958.

"The Budget and Accounting Act of 1921," *United States Statutes at Large* 67th Cong. XLII. Part I.

Catterall, Ralph C. H. *The Second Bank of the United States.* Chicago: University of Chicago Press, 1903.

Cleveland, Grover. *Presidential Problems.* New York: The Century Company, 1904.

Colm, Gerhard. "The Executive Office and Fiscal and Economic Policy." *Law and Contemporary Problems.* XXIV. No. 4 (Autumn 1956).

1542

Colton, Calvin, ed. *The Works of Henry Clay*. Vols. VII, VIII. New York: G. P. Putnam's Sons, 1904.

Commager, Henry Steele, ed. *Documents of American History*. Fifth ed. New York: Appleton-Century-Crofts, Inc., 1949.

Congressional Globe, January 11, 1869.

Corwin, Edward S. "The President as Administrative Chief." *The Journal of Politics*. I. No. 1 (February 1939).

_____ . *The President's Removal Power Under the Constitution*. New York: National Municipal League, 1927.

Cox, Lawanda and John H. *Politics, Principle, and Prejudice, 1865-1866*. Glencoe, Illinois: Free Press of Glencoe, 1963.

DeWitt, David Miller. *The Impeachment and Trial of Andrew Johnson*. New York: The Macmillan Company, 1903.

Dillard, Dudley. *The Economics of John Maynard Keynes: The Theory of a Monetary Economy*. London: Crosby Lockwood and Son, Ltd., 1958.

Donald, David. *The Politics of Reconstruction, 1863-1867*. Baton Rouge, Louisiana: Louisiana University Press, 1965.

Duane, William J. *Narrative and Correspondence Concerning the Removal of Deposites [sic] and Occurrences Connected Therewith*. Philadelphia, Pennsylvania, 1838.

Emmerich, Herbert. *Essays on Federal Reorganization*. Birmingham, Alabama: University of Alabama Press, 1950.

Flash, Edward S., jr. *Economic Advice and Presidential Leadership*. New York: Columbia University Press, 1965.

Gales, Joseph, ed. *Debates and Proceedings in the Congress of the United States*. Vol. I. Washington, D.C.: Gales and Seaton, 1834.

Hammond, Bray. *Banks and Politics in America, From the Revolution to the Civil War*. Princeton, New Jersey: Princeton University Press, 1957.

Harris, Seymour. *The Economics of Political Parties*. New York: The Macmillan Company, 1962.

_____ . *The Economics of the Kennedy Years and a Look Ahead*. New York: Harper and Row, 1964.

Hart, James. *Tenure of Office Under the Constitution*. Baltimore, Maryland: The Johns Hopkins Press, 1930.

Heller, Walter. *New Dimensions of Political Economy*. Cambridge, Massachusetts: Harvard University Press, 1966.

Hesseltine, William B. *Ulysses S. Grant, Politician*. New York: Frederick Ungar Publishing Company, 1957.

Hobbs, Edward H. *Behind the President: A Study of Executive Office Agencies*. Washington, D.C.: Public Affairs Press, 1954.

Humphrey's Executor v. *United States*, 295 U.S. 62 (1934).

Kennedy, John F. *Profiles in Courage*. New York: Harper and Brothers, 1955.

Landis, James M. *The Administrative Process*. New Haven, Connecticut: Yale University Press, 1938.

_____. "Mr. Justice Brandeis: A Law Clerk's View." An address delivered at the Fifty-Fifth Annual Meeting of the American Jewish Historical Society, Brandeis University, Waltham, Massachusetts, February 16, 1957. Later printed by the *American Jewish Historical Society Publication*. XLVI. No. 4 (June 1957).

Lekachman, Robert. *The Age of Keynes*. New York: Random House, 1966.

Leuchtenburg, William. "The Contentious Commissioner: Humphrey's Executor v. United States." eds., Harold M. Hyman and Leonard W. Levy, *Freedom and Reform: Essays in Honor of Henry Steele Commager*. New York: Harper and Row, 1967.

_____. *Franklin D. Roosevelt and the New Deal*. New York: Harper Torchbooks, 1963.

Marx, Fritz Morstein. "The Bureau of the Budget: Its Evolution and Present Role." *American Political Science Review* XXXIX (August 1945)

Mason, Alpheus Thomas. *Harlan Fiske Stone*. New York: The Viking Press, 1956.

_____. *William Howard Taft: Chief Justice*. New York: Simon and Schuster, 1965.

"Message of the President Submitting a Budget for the Fiscal Year 1914." *Senate Doc. No. 1113*. 62nd Cong., 3rd sess. Washington, D.C.: U.S. Government Printing Office, 1913.

1544

Milton, George Fort. *The Age of Hate: Andrew Johnson and the Radicals.* New York: Coward-McCann, Inc., 1930.

Morganston, Charles. *The Appointing and Removal Power of the President of the United States.* Washington, D.C.: U.S. Government Printing Office, 1929.

Myers v. *United States,* 272 U.S. 136 (1926).

"The Need for a National Budget." Message from the President of the United States on the Report of the Commission on Economy and Efficiency. *House Doc. No. 854.* 62nd Cong., 2nd sess. Washington, D.C.: U.S. Government Printing Office, 1912.

Neustadt, Richard E. "Presidency and Legislation: The Growth of Central Clearance." *American Political Science Review.* XLVIII (September 1954).

"Organizing for National Security." Hearings Before the Subcommittee on National Policy Machinery of the Committee on Government Operations of the United States Senate, July 1, 1960.

Pearson, Norman. "The Budget Bureau: From Routine Business to General Staff." *Public Administration Review.* III (Spring 1943).

Pinkett, Harold T. "The Keep Commission, 1905-1909: A Rooseveltian Effort for Administrative Reform." *Journal of American History.* LII. No. 2 (September 1965).

Polenberg, Richard. *Reorganizing Roosevelt's Government: The Controversy Over Executive Reorganization, 1936-1939.* Cambridge, Massachusetts: Harvard University Press, 1966.

Powell, Thomas Reed. "Spinning Out the Executive Power." *New Republic.* November 17, 1926.

The President's Committee on Administrative Management. *Report of the Committee with Studies of Administrative Management in the Federal Government.* Submitted to the President and to the Congress in Accordance with Public Law 739, 74th Cong., 2nd sess. Washington, D.C.: U.S. Government Printing Office, 1937.

Pringle, Henry F. *The Life and Times of William Howard Taft.* Vol. II. New York: Farrar and Rinehart, Inc., 1939.

Public Papers of the Presidents: John F. Kennedy, 1962-1963. Washington, D.C.: U.S. Government Printing Office, 1963.

"Report on Regulatory Agencies to the President-Elect." Submitted by the Chairman of the Subcommittee on Administrative Practice and Procedure to the Committee on the Judiciary of the United States Senate, December, 1960. Washington, D.C.: U.S. Government Printing Office, 1960.

"The Reorganization Act of 1939." *United States Statutes at Large.* 76th Cong., 1st sess. LIII. Part 2.

Richardson, James D., ed. *Messages and Papers of the Presidents.* Vols. III, VIII-X, XVII. New York: Bureau of National Literature, 1897.

Rowan, Hobart. *The Free Enterprisers: Kennedy, Johnson, and the Business Establishment.* New York: G. P. Putnam's Sons, 1964.

Samuelson, Paul A. *Economics: An Introductory Analysis.* Sixth ed. New York: McGraw-Hill, 1964.

_____. "Prospects and Policies for the 1961 American Economy." *New York Times.* January 6, 1961.

Schlesinger, Arthur M., jr. *The Coming of the New Deal.* Boston: Houghton Mifflin Company, 1958.

_____. *The Crisis of the Old Order.* Boston: Houghton Mifflin Company, 1957.

_____. *The Politics of Upheaval.* Boston: Houghton Mifflin Company, 1960.

_____. *A Thousand Days: John F. Kennedy in the White House.* Boston: Houghton Mifflin Company, 1965.

Sherman, John. *John Sherman's Recollections of Forty Years in the House, Senate and Cabinet.* Vol. II. Chicago: Werner, 1895.

Shores, Venila Lovina. *The Hayes-Conkling Controversy, 1877-1879.* John Spencer Bassett and Sidney Bradshaw Fay, eds., *Smith College Studies in History.* IV. No. 4 (July 1919).

Smith, Harold D. "The Bureau of the Budget." *Public Administration Review.* I. No. 2 (Winter 1940-41).

Smithies, Arthur. *The Budgetary Process in the United States.* New York: McGraw-Hill, 1955.

Sorensen, Theodore C. *Kennedy.* New York: Harper and Row, 1965.

Statutes at Large, Treaties and Proclamations of the United States of America. XIV.

Stryker, Lloyd Paul. *Andrew Johnson: A Study in Courage.* New York: The Macmillan Company, 1930.

"Super-Officers and Superstaffs." Staff Report of Subcommittee on National Policy Machinery of Committee on Government Operations of the United States Senate, November 16, 1960.

Thach, Charles C., jr. *The Creation of the Presidency, 1775-1789.* Baltimore, Maryland: The Johns Hopkins Press, 1922.

Tobin, James. "The Intellectual Revolution in U.S. Economic Policy-Making." Second Noah Buxton Lecture of the University of Essex. London, 1966.

Webster, Daniel. *The Writings and Speeches of Daniel Webster.* Vol. VII. Boston: Little, Brown and Company, 1903.

Welles, Gideon. *Diary of Gideon Welles.* Vol. III. Boston: Houghton Mifflin Company, 1911.

White, Leonard D. *The Jeffersonians.* New York: The Macmillan Company, 1959.

Williams, Charles Richard, ed. *Diary and Letters of Rutherford B. Hayes.* Vol. III. Columbus, Ohio: Ohio State Archaeological and Historical Society, 1924.

Willoughby, William Franklin. *The Problem of a National Budget.* New York: D. Appleton and Company, 1918.

Wilmerding, Lucius, jr. *The Spending Power: A History of the Efforts of Congress to Control Expenditures.* New Haven, Connecticut: Yale University Press, 1943.

Wilson, Woodrow. *Congressional Government.* New York: Meridian Books, Inc., 1956.

IV. Executive Leadership

EXECUTIVE LEADERSHIP

When speaking of the executive powers of the President one generally asserts a very broad definition of those powers. Indeed in the previous two volumes of this series this has been the interpretation upon which I have based my study of the Executive. Yet it was not until the turn of the twentieth century, during the administration of Theodore Roosevelt, that such a definition found its expression in the social and economic policies advanced by the President. Underlying this broad interpretation of executive power, however, are certain assumptions about the office of the presidency itself. Even the narrowest conception of executive power acknowledges the duty of the President "to take care that the laws are faithfully executed," but nothing like a consensus exists to support the President's role as the social conscience of the nation.

Many Presidents have denied this responsibility both in word and deed, and although these have on the whole tended to be the more obvious failures in office, at least several "adequate" Chief Executives have harbored a strong reticence and an active opposition to the intrusion of the President into the legislative, social and economic realms. Presidents like Franklin Pierce and Warren Harding abstained out of indifference and inadequacy, but others like John Adams and William Howard Taft were opposed to the broad construction of executive power on constitutional and philosophical grounds. Taft stated the case most forcefully when he argued:

> The true view of the Executive function is, as I conceive it, that the President can exercise no power which cannot be fairly and reasonably traced to some specific grant of power or justly implied and included within such express grant as proper and necessary to its exercise. Such specific grant must be either in the Federal Constitution or in an act of Congress passed in pursuance thereof. There is no undefined residum of power which he can exercise because it seems to him to be in the public interest, and there is nothing in the Neagle case [see Volume II of this series] and its definition of a law of the United States, or in other precedents, warranting such an inference. The grants of Executive power are necessarily in general terms in order not to embarrass the Executive within the field of action plainly marked for him, but his jurisdiction must be justified and vindicated by affirmative constitutional or statutory provision, or it does not exist.[1]

But Taft was speaking for the presidency of an early period in American life. The nineteenth century had thrown up a large number of Presidents—Federalists, Whigs, Republicans and Democrats—who agreed with Taft, but even as he wrote this passage he must have been aware that the currents of history were running strongly against such a limited concept of executive responsibility. The tradition of an enlarged view of presidential power and responsibility was established in the nineteenth century of the Jefferson, Jackson and Lincoln administrations. In the twentieth century Theodore Roosevelt and Woodrow Wilson set the standards of public responsibility and presidential power against which all Presidents who followed were to be judged.

In both their actions and their words Roosevelt and Wilson stood as dynamic refutations of the narrow concept of executive power. The strong and great Presidents who followed them heeded not the warnings of Taft, but rather the admonitions of Roosevelt:

> The most important factor in getting the right spirit in my Administration, next to the insistence upon courage, honesty, and a genuine democracy of desire to serve the plain people, was my insistence upon the theory that the executive power was limited only by specific restrictions and prohibitions appearing in the Constitution or imposed by Congress under its Constitutional powers. My view was that every executive officer, and above all every executive officer in high position, was a steward of the people bound actively and affirmatively to do all he could for the people, and not to content himself with the negative merit of keeping his talents undamaged in a napkin. I declined to adopt the view that what was imperatively necessary for the Nation could not be done by the President unless he could find some specific authorization to do it. My belief was that it was not only his right but his duty to do anything that the needs of the Nation demanded unless such action was forbidden by the Constitution or by the laws. Under this interpretation of executive power I did and caused to be done many things not previously done by the President and the heads of the departments. I did not usurp power, but I did greatly broaden the use of executive power. In other words, I acted for the public welfare, I acted for the common well-being of all our people, whenever and in whatever manner was necessary, unless prevented by direct constitutional or legislative prohibition.[2]

With the same emphasis in mind, Wilson argued that the President

> has become the leader of his party and the guide of the nation in political purpose, and therefore in legal action. . . .
> . . . If he rightly interprets the national thought and boldly insists upon it, he is irresistible, and the country never feels the zest of action so much as when its President is of such insight and calibre.[3]

Franklin D. Roosevelt
Confronts an Emergency

The Constitution does not specify the responsibilities of the President (nor for that matter of the Congress) in a national emergency, but the logic of the situation clearly indicates that the Chief Executive must act in some way, particularly when the Congress is not in session. Such action bears the imprimatur of John Locke, certainly one of the writers who most influenced the thinking of the Founding Fathers on the subject of government:

> [The] power to act according to discretion for the public good, without the prescription of the law, and sometimes even against it, is that which is called prerogative; for since in some governments the law-making power is not always in being, and is usually too numerous, and so too slow for the dispatch requisite to execution, and because, also, it is impossible to foresee and so by laws to provide for all accidents and necessities that may concern the public, or make such laws as will do no harm, if they are executed with an inflexible rigour on all occasions and upon all persons that may come in their way, therefore, there is a latitude left to the executive power to do many things of choice which the laws do not prescribe.[4]

The bank holiday of 1933 provides an excellent example of the President's reliance upon the Lockian "prerogative" in order to act swiftly to prevent an almost certain and total economic disaster. The last few weeks of the Hoover administration in 1933 were an economic nightmare. The chain of bank failures had reached astronomical proportions and as far back as October 1932, the governor of Nevada had called for a bank holiday. The groundswell really began to rise, however, when the Detroit banks closed down in February after their largest depositor, Henry Ford, refused to come to their assistance. There was no alternative available to the governor of the state but to proclaim a bank holiday, setting off a chain reaction which brought the grand total of states declaring bank holidays to 38 by the time of the inauguration of Franklin Delano Roosevelt on March 4, 1933.

During the last desperate days of the Hoover administration his secretary of commerce, Ogden Mills, and Eugene Meyer of the Federal Reserve Board urged the President to call a national bank holiday. Hoover refused to act without the concurrence of the new President. Yet Mills warned him that controls on the price of gold in the international exchanges and in the limitation of gold withdrawals would be necessary. The secretary of commerce was certain that that could be accomplished under the power granted in the Trading with the Enemy Act of World War I. Hoover, however, was reluctant to act on his own initiative and passed the buck to the Federal Reserve Board. When the board refused to make a decision, Mills urged Hoover to act under his war powers. But no action was forthcoming. Hoover's attorney general, William D. Mitchell, questioned the legality of such an action, and Roosevelt refused to assume responsibility for any action before being sworn in as President.

Several weeks earlier Hoover had written to the President-elect, trying to persuade him to issue a statement to calm the fears of the country. What is more, he had suggested that Roosevelt endorse Hoover's policies of "sound finance" and reject his own promised "New Deal." Roosevelt indicated to a friend that he thought the proposition was "cheeky." "I am equally concerned with you in regard to the gravity of the present banking situation," he wrote the Republican President, "but my thought is that it is so deepseated that the fire is bound to spread in spite of anything that is done by way of mere statements."[5]

The end was not long in coming. Agnes Meyer wrote in her diary that the world was "literally rocking beneath our feet. Hard on H to go out of office to the sound of crashing banks."[6] In February 1933 a number of state banks shut down for short periods, but in March the bottom dropped out. Looking backward Roosevelt reflected:

> By Inauguration Day practically every other bank in the country had either been closed or placed under restrictions by State Proclamations. Federal Reserve banks observed the State holidays, and were also closed on March 4th. All the leading exchanges ceased operations. It can be said that financial and banking business in the United States had stopped.
>
> I had come to the conclusion, after consultation with Senator Thomas J. Walsh, who had been slated to be the Attorney General in the new Cabinet, until the date of his death on March 2, 1933, that the "Trading with the Enemy Act" of October 6, 1917, as amended September 24, 1918, was still in effect. This Act gave the President power to regulate or prohibit transactions in foreign exchange and in gold and silver, and also to prohibit the hoarding of gold, silver coin, bullion, and paper currency. I determined to use this power to close all the banks in order to prevent complete chaos on the Monday following Inauguration Day, which was a Saturday.[7]

Watching the inaugural parade, the critic and then reporter for the *New Republic*, Edmund Wilson, wrote:

> If the parade went on any longer, it would be too dark to see, too cold to stay out. And you are glad when it is over, anyway. The America it represented has burst with the bursting of the boom, and you realized, as you watched the marchers, how abysmally silly it was. This delirium is the ghost it has given up.[8]

But the inaugural message, not the parade, was the important symbol of that clear March day. The new President spelled out his indictment and his intentions in unmistakable language:

> Plenty is at our doorstep, but a generous use of it languishes in the very sight of the supply. Primarily this is because the rulers of the exchange of mankind's goods have failed through their own stubbornness and their own incompetence, have admitted their failure and abdicated. Practices of the unscrupulous money changers stand indicted in the court of public opinion, rejected by the hearts and minds of men.
>
> True they have tried, but their efforts have been cast in the pattern of an outworn tradition. Faced by failure of credit, they have proposed only the lending of more money. Stripped of the lure of profit by which to induce our people to follow their false leadership, they have resorted to exhortations, pleading tearfully for restored confidence. They know only

the rules of a generation of self-seekers. They have no vision, and when there is no vision the people perish.

The money changers have fled from their high seats in the temple of our civilization. We may now restore that temple to the ancient truths. The measure of that restoration lies in the extent to which we apply social values more noble than mere monetary profit.[9]

His determination to halt the debacle was equally clear and uncompromising:

It is hoped that the normal balance of Executive and legislative authority may be wholly adequate to meet the unprecedented task before us. But it may be that an unprecedented need for undelayed action may call for temporary departure from that normal balance of public procedure.

I am prepared under my constitutional duty to recommend the measures that a stricken Nation in the midst of a stricken world may require. These measures, or such measures as the Congress may build out of its own experience and wisdom, I shall seek, within my constitutional authority, to bring to speedy adoption.

But in the event that the Congress shall fail to take one of these two courses, and in the event that a national emergency is still critical, I shall not evade the clear course of duty that will then confront me. I shall ask the Congress for the one remaining instrument to meet the crisis—broad Executive power to wage a war against the emergency, as great as the power that would be given to me if we were in fact invaded by a foreign foe.[10]

After taking the oath of office, Roosevelt lost no time in translating his intentions into action. That very evening he put the final touches on two presidential proclamations, one calling Congress back into session and the other announcing a national bank holiday. They were issued the following day. Four days later he introduced the Emergency Banking Bill providing for a number of immediate steps to place the full resources of the Federal Reserve System behind the faltering banks and, even more important, to restore the confidence of the people in the banking system. Within eight hours the bill was passed and signed by the President. Three days later he spoke to the country in his first fireside chat, in which he explained what he had done and why he had done it. There is little doubt that the overwhelming majority of his listeners learned more about the complexities and problems of our banking system that evening in 12 short minutes, than they ever had learned before, or ever would learn subsequently.

President Franklin D. Roosevelt
Bank Holiday Proclamation
March 6, 1933

Samuel Rosenman, ed., *The Public Papers and Addresses of Franklin D. Roosevelt* (New York, 1938) II, 24-26.

Whereas there have been heavy and unwarranted withdrawals of gold and currency from our banking institutions for the purpose of hoarding; and

Whereas continuous and increasingly extensive speculative activity abroad in foreign exchange has resulted in severe drains on the Nation's stocks of gold; and

Whereas those conditions have created a national emergency; and

Whereas it is in the best interests of all bank depositors that a period of respite be provided with a view to preventing further hoarding of coin, bullion or currency or speculation in foreign exchange and permitting the application of appropriate measures to protect the interests of our people; and

Whereas it is provided in Section 5 (b) of the Act of October 6, 1917 (40 Stat. L. 411), as amended, "That the President may investigate, regulate, or prohibit, under such rules and regulations as he may prescribe, by means of licenses or otherwise, any transactions in foreign exchange and the export, hoarding, melting, or earmarkings of gold or silver coin or bullion or currency . . ."; and

Whereas it is provided in Section 16 of the said Act "That whoever shall willfully violate any of the provisions of this Act or of any license, rule, or regulation issued thereunder, and whoever shall willfully violate, neglect, or refuse to comply with any order of the President issued in compliance with the provisions of this Act, shall, upon conviction, be fined not more than $10,000, or, if a natural person, imprisoned for not more than ten years, or both . . .";

Now, therefore, I, Franklin D. Roosevelt, President of the United States of America, in view of such national emergency and by virtue of the authority vested in me by said Act and in order to prevent the export, hoarding, or earmarking of gold or silver coin or bullion or currency, do hereby proclaim, order, direct and declare that from Monday, the Sixth day of March, to Thursday, the Ninth day of March, Nineteen Hundred and Thirty-three, both dates inclusive, there shall be maintained and observed by all banking institutions and all branches thereof located in the United States of America, including the territories and insular possessions, a bank holiday, and that during said period all banking transactions shall be suspended. During such holiday, excepting as hereinafter provided, no such banking institution or branch shall pay out, export, earmark, or permit the withdrawal or transfer in any manner or by any device whatsoever, of any gold or silver coin or bullion or currency or take any other action which might facilitate the hoarding thereof; nor shall any such banking institution or branch pay out deposits, make loans or discounts, deal in foreign exchange, transfer credits from the United States to any place abroad, or transact any other banking business whatsoever.

During such holiday, the Secretary of the Treasury, with the approval of the President and under such regulations as he may prescribe, is authorized and empowered (a) to permit any or all of such banking institutions to perform any or all of the ususal banking functions, (b) to direct, require or permit the issuance of clearing house certificates or other evidences of claims against assets of banking institutions, and (c) to authorize and direct the creation in such banking institutions of special trust accounts for the receipt of new deposits which shall be subject to withdrawal on demand without any restriction or limitation and shall be kept separately in cash or on deposit in Federal Reserve Banks or invested in obligations of the United States.

As used in this order the term "banking institutions" shall include all Federal Reserve Banks, national banking associations, banks, trust companies, savings banks, building and loan associations, credit unions, or other corporations, partnerships, associations or persons, engaged in the business of receiving deposits, making loans, discounting business paper, or transacting any other form of banking business.

President Franklin D. Roosevelt
First Fireside Chat
March 12, 1933

Rosenman, II, 61-65.

I want to talk for a few minutes with the people of the United States about banking—with the comparatively few who understand the mechanics of banking but more particularly with the overwhelming majority who use banks for the making of deposits and the drawing of checks. I want to tell what has been done in the last few days, why it was done, and what the next steps are going to be. I recognize that the many proclamations from State capitols and from Washington, the legislation, the Treasury regulations, etc., couched for the most part in banking and legal terms, should be explained for the benefit of the average citizen. I owe this in particular because of the fortitude and good temper with which everybody has accepted the inconvenience and hardships of the banking holiday. I know that when you understand what we in Washington have been about I shall continue to have your cooperation as fully as I have had your sympathy and help during the past week.

First of all, let me state the simple fact that when you deposit money in a bank the bank does not put the money into a safe deposit vault. It invests your money in many different forms of credit—bonds, commercial paper, mortgages and many other kinds of loans. In other words, the bank puts your money to work to keep the wheels of industry and of agriculture turning around. A comparatively small part of the money you put into the bank is kept in currency—an amount which in normal times is wholly sufficient to cover the cash needs of the average citizen. In other words, the total amount of all the currency in the country is only a small fraction of the total deposits in all of the banks.

What, then, happened during the last few days of February and the first few days of March? Because of undermined confidence on the part of the public, there was a general rush by a large portion of our population to turn bank deposits into currency or gold—a rush so great that the soundest banks could not get enough currency to meet the demand. The reason for this was that on the spur of the moment it was, of course, impossible to sell perfectly sound assets of a bank and convert them into cash except at panic prices far below their real value.

By the afternoon of March 3d scarcely a bank in the country was open to do business. Proclamations temporarily closing them in whole or in part had been issued by the Governors in almost all the States.

It was then that I issued the proclamation providing for the nationwide bank holiday, and this was the first step in the Government's reconstruction of our financial and economic fabric.

The second step was the legislation promptly and patriotically passed by the Congress confirming my proclamation and broadening my powers so that it became possible in view of the requirement of time to extend the holiday and lift the ban of that holiday gradually. This law also gave authority to develop a program of rehabilitation of our banking facilities. I want to tell our citizens in every part of the Nation that the national Congress—Republicans and Democrats alike—showed by this action a devotion to public welfare and a realization of the emergency and the necessity for speed that it is difficult to match in our history.

The third stage has been the series of regulations permitting the banks to continue their functions to take care of the distribution of food and household necessities and the payment of payrolls.

This bank holiday, while resulting in many cases in great inconvenience, is affording us the opportunity to supply the currency necessary to meet the situation. No sound bank is a dollar worse off than it was when it closed its doors last Monday. Neither is any bank which may turn out not to be in a position for immediate opening. The new law allows the twelve Federal Reserve Banks to issue additional currency on good assets and thus the banks which reopen will be able to meet every legitimate call. The new currency is being sent out by the Bureau of Engraving and Printing in large volume to every part of the country. It is sound currency because it is backed by actual, good assets.

A question you will ask is this: why are all the banks not to be reopened at the same time? The answer is simple. Your Government does not intend that the history of the past few years shall be repeated. We do not want and will not have another epidemic of bank failures.

As a result, we start tomorrow, Monday, with the opening of banks in the twelve Federal Reserve Bank cities—those banks which on first examination by the Treasury have already been found to be all right. This will be followed on Tuesday by the resumption of all their functions by banks already found to be sound in cities where there are recognized clearing houses. That means about 250 cities of the United States.

On Wednesday and succeeding days banks in smaller places all through the country will resume business, subject, of course, to the Government's physical ability to complete its survey. It is necessary that the reopening of banks be extended over a period in order to permit the banks to make applications for necessary loans, to obtain currency needed to meet their requirements and to enable the Government to make common sense checkups.

Let me make it clear to you that if your bank does not open the first day you are by no means justified in believing that it will not open. A bank that opens on one of the subsequent days is in exactly the same status as the bank that opens tomorrow.

I know that many people are worrying about State banks not members of the Federal Reserve System. These banks can and will receive assistance from member banks and from the Reconstruction Finance Corporation. These State banks are following the same course as the National banks except that they get their licenses to resume business from the State authorities, and these authorities have been asked by the Secretary of the Treasury to permit their good banks to open up on the same schedule as the national banks. I am confident that the State Banking Departments will be as careful as the national Government in the policy relating to the opening of banks and will follow the same broad policy.

It is possible that when the banks resume a very few people who have not recovered from their fear may again begin withdrawals. Let me make it clear that the banks will take care of all needs—and it is my belief that hoarding during the past week has become an exceedingly unfashionable pastime. It needs no prophet to tell you that when the people find that they can get their money—that they can get it when they want it for all legitimate purposes—the phantom of fear will soon be laid. People will again be glad to have their money where it will be safely taken care of and where they can use it conveniently at any time. I can assure you that it is safer to keep your money in a reopened bank than under the mattress.

The success of our whole great national program depends, of course, upon the cooperation of the public—on its intelligent support and use of a reliable system.

Remember that the essential accomplishment of the new legislation is that it makes it possible for banks more readily to convert their assets into cash than was the case before. More liberal provision has been made for banks to borrow on these assets at the Reserve Banks and more liberal provision has also been made for issuing currency on the security of these good assets. This currency is not fiat currency. It is issued only on adequate security, and every good bank has an abundance of such security.

One more point before I close. There will be, of course, some banks unable to reopen without being reorganized. The new law allows the Government to assist in making these reorganizations quickly and effectively and even allows the Government to subscribe to at least a part of new capital which may be required.

I hope you can see from this elemental recital of what your Government is doing that there is nothing complex, or radical, in the process.

We had a bad banking situation. Some of our bankers had shown themselves either incompetent or dishonest in their handling of the people's funds. They had used the money entrusted to them in speculations and unwise loans. This was, of course, not true in the vast majority of our banks, but it was true in enough of them to shock the people for a time into a sense of insecurity and to put them into a frame of mind where they did not differentiate, but seemed to assume that the acts of a comparative few had tainted them all. It was the Government's job to straighten out this situation and do it as quickly as possible. And the job is being performed.

I do not promise you that every bank will be reopened or that individual losses will not be suffered, but there will be no losses that possibly could be avoided; and there would have been more and greater losses had we continued to drift. I can even promise you salvation for some at least of the sorely pressed banks. We shall be engaged not merely in reopening sound banks but in the creation of sound banks through reorganization.

It has been wonderful to me to catch the note of confidence from all over the country. I can never be sufficiently grateful to the people for the loyal support they have given me in their acceptance of the judgment that has dictated our course, even though all our processes may not have seemed clear to them.

After all, there is an element in the readjustment of our financial system more important than currency, more important than gold, and that is the confidence of the people. Confidence and courage are the essentials of success in carrying out our plan. You people must have faith; you must not be stampeded by rumors or guesses. Let us unite in banishing fear. We have provided the machinery to restore our financial system; it is up to you to support and make it work.

It is your problem no less than it is mine. Together we cannot fail.

Frances Perkins, Roosevelt's secretary of labor and the first woman to serve in any cabinet, has described the incredible effect Roosevelt had upon his listening audience:

When he talked on the radio, he saw them gathered in the little parlor, listening with their neighbors. He was conscious of their faces and hands, their clothes and homes.

His voice and his facial expression as he spoke were those of an intimate friend. After he became President, I often was at the White House when he broadcast, and I realized how unconscious he was of the twenty or thirty of us in that room and how clearly his mind was focused on the people listening at the other end. As he talked his head would nod and his hands would move in simple, natural, comfortable gestures. His face would smile and light up as though he were actually sitting on the front porch or in the parlor with them. People felt this, and it bound them to him in affection.

I have sat in those little parlors and on those porches myself during some of the speeches, and I have seen men and women gathered around the radio, even those who didn't like him or were opposed to him politically, listening with a pleasant, happy feeling of association and friendship. The exchange between them and him through the medium of the radio was very real. I have seen tears come to their eyes as he told them of some tragic episode, of the sufferings of the persecuted people in Europe, of the poverty during unemployment, of the sufferings of the homeless, of the sufferings of people whose sons had been killed in the war, and they were tears of sincerity and recognition and sympathy.

. . . The quality of his being one with the people, of having no artificial or natural barriers between him and them, made it possible for him to be a leader without ever being or thinking of being a dictator. I don't think he fully appreciated this aspect of his nature as a part of his leadership, but he intuitively used it. It was this quality that made the people trust him and do gladly what he explained was necessary for them to do. While some of his political enemies said that these were merely the signs and marks of a slick politician, the more one associated with him the more one knew that however political he might be, and he certainly did have great political skill, this quality was not a political device at all.[11]

These were the executive powers put into action to protect the national welfare. In word and in deed, Franklin D. Roosevelt moved quickly and decisively to stem the tidal wave of disaster and despair, finding constitutional justification in the broad implications of the executive power.

Harry Truman Takes a Stand

Since the founding of the republic, American Presidents have virtually ignored the problem of the Black man in society and have done precious little to relieve the great burdens placed upon him by the racism that has existed from its very beginning. During the slavery period Blacks were taken for granted as mere instruments of labor. They were brought to this country not to enjoy freedom, but to be imprisoned within the institution of slavery. Even after the legal overthrow of slavery, the racism which existed both in the North and in the South prohibited or made it next to impossible for Blacks to achieve any real sense of social and economic equality, not to mention equality before the law. This is America's original sin, and she has never really atoned for that sin; she has failed to correct 300 years of injustice to an entire race, or to compensate for all the neglect, the dishonor and the deprivations which that experience has involved.

If Lincoln had lived to serve out his second term in office there is some chance that his conscience would have driven him to make a real start towards emancipating the Black man in mind and spirit, as well as in body. He may have tried to urge upon the country laws and institutions which would have made the great sacrifices of the Civil War more intelligible and more meaningful. Lincoln was not committed to full equality for the Negro, but he had an amazing capacity for learning and growing in knowledge and sensitivity. Before he could confront the problem, however, he was assassinated, and his successors failed to rise to the challenge to complete the emancipation process. Not only in the nineteenth century, but in the twentieth century as well, Presidents of the United States ignored the problem and in most instances exacerbated it.

In recent years the society, ignited and driven by the Black revolution, has started out on the hard road to self-recognition and reconstruction, taking the earliest steps towards what could eventually become a truly integrated multi-racial society. But America is still a long way from that objective, and she was still farther away from it in 1946 when Harry S. Truman, certainly a most unlikely President for the historical role he was to assume, set in motion the governmental machinery which began to examine this problem and recommend the first major steps towards its ultimate resolution.

Harry S. Truman was an unlikely candidate for this important role because there was nothing in his career previous to that time which indicated the concern and interest which he would evidence. Truman was born and spent his entire lifetime in a small town in the border state of Missouri, where racial prejudice was prevalent—deeply rooted in the past and firmly imbedded in the social structure. It was natural for him to absorb the local mores, yet Truman also grew in the presidency. Margaret Truman, the President's daughter, records a response which Truman made to a group of southerners who visited him before the 1948 Democratic Convention, when they "practically pledged the support of the Dixiecrats if Dad would only 'soften' his views on civil rights."[12] The President replied:

> My forbears were Confederates. I come from a part of the country where Jim Crowism is as prevalent as it is in New York or Washington. Every factor and influence in my background—and my wife's for that matter—would foster the personal belief that you were right.
>
> But my very stomach turned over when I learned that Negro soldiers, just back from overseas, were being dumped out of army trucks in Mississippi and beaten.
>
> Whatever my inclinations as a native of Missouri might have been, as President I know this is bad. I shall fight to end evils like this.[13]

Harry Truman was never a social integrationist, and to his dying day, according to the compiler of his oral biography, he used the objectionable term "nigger" when referring to Black people. But he was brought up on the Constitution, and he believed that the full protection of the law must be extended to every American, regardless of race, creed or national origin. He demonstrated this commitment more than once in his almost eight years in the White House.

It is not difficult to find fault with Truman's civil rights record if it is judged by the criteria of the enlightened liberalism of a later day. He was slow to act, he needed constant pressure to take an action, and when he did move the results were meager. But Harry Truman was at heart a small-town, middle-American, complete with many limitations attributable to middle-America, as well as the considerable strength of character which is frequently observed among such individuals. When Truman first went to Washington as a senator, he was classified as a moderate on racial issues. During the war he voted for the Fair Employment Practices Commission, signed a petition to cut off a filibuster against an anti-poll tax bill, and also agreed to direct his special wartime committee investigating waste and inefficiency in defense industries to report racial discrimination in plants which had received defense contracts, and also in the army. It was always a question of rights, however and not one of social integration. Truman argued:

> I am not appealing for social equality of the Negro. The Negro himself knows better than that. . . . Negroes want justice, not social relations.[14]

Truman never said one thing in Washington and another back in Missouri. Speaking before an all-white audience of farmers in Sedalia, Missouri, in 1940, "many of them ex-Ku Kluxers," Truman spoke out in favor of protecting the constitutional rights of Blacks, defending the way he had voted in Washington:

> I believe in the brotherhood of man, not merely the brotherhood of white men but the brotherhood of all men before the law.
>
> I believe in the Constitution and Declaration of Independence. In giving Negroes the rights that are theirs we are only acting in accord with our own ideals of a true democracy.
>
> If any class or race can be permanently set apart from, or pushed down below the rest in political and civil rights, so may any other class or race when it shall incur the displeasure of its more powerful associates, and we may say farewell to the principles on which we count our safety.
>
> In the years past, lynching and mob violence, lack of schools, and countless other unfair conditions hastened the progress of the Negro from the country to the city. In these centers the Negroes never had much chance in regard to work or anything else. By and large they went to work mainly as unskilled laborers and domestic servants.
>
> They have been forced to live in segregated slums, neglected by the authorities. Negroes have been preyed upon by all types of exploiters from the installment salesmen of clothing, pianos, and furniture to the venders of ice.
>
> The majority of our Negro people find cold comfort in shanties and tenements. Surely, as freemen, they are entitled to something better than this. . . . It is our duty to see that Negroes in our locality have increased opportunity to exercise their privilege as freemen.[15]

One can, of course, write such speeches off as smart politics, because in 1940 he was appealing to a growing number of Black voters in his state, but the feeling behind his statements ran much deeper than whatever possible political advantages were involved. Harry Truman's mother was such a confirmed "Confederate" that she refused to sleep in Lincoln's bed when he teased her by telling her it was the only one available in the White House; she chided him for placing a wreath at the Lincoln Memorial in Washington, D.C. Coming from that kind of a background, Truman's words and deeds on the constitutional issue of civil rights had to be rooted in something far deeper than personal political advantage. Of course, it is never clear whether such statements did not lose Truman more white votes than it gained him Black supporters.

As President, Truman's problem was how to advance the interests and constitutional protections of Blacks without driving the southern Democrats out of the party. He never really solved this problem because many southerners walked out during his 1948 campaign.

But once elected President Truman realized that he had many major problems to confront. He inherited a war that was already won when he became President, but peace was still a long way off; also a part of the legacy was domestic inferno, rather than blissful tranquility. All of the pent up frustrations and antagonisms which lay beneath the surface of the society (and in some cases they were hardly below the surface) burst forth at the end of the war, and Truman was the man called upon to deal with them. Very little tangible progress was made during the period of the New Deal and the war towards the advancement of civil rights for American Blacks. In the White House it was Eleanor Roosevelt, the President's wife, rather than the President, who was the sympathetic supporter of the Black community, and while she provided sympathy, an attentive ear and in the final instance, access to the President, she did not necessarily influence his presidential actions.

During those years Mrs. Roosevelt grew in stature, identifying more and more with the oppressed and forgotten in the society. The President sometimes used her as a lightning rod to ground the shock waves that were increasing throughout the society on this issue. He, too, was sympathetic in his patrician manner, but he never quite understood nor did he identify with the suffering and humiliation which Black people experienced. Possibly personal tragedy and humiliation in her own life had much to do with her intimate and deeply felt empathy, but although she used her influence with the President to good purpose in some very critical situations, the net effect for Black citizens was miserably small. A few high level appointments, a local committee to investigate conditions, a statement of protest or reassurance sometimes resulted in clearing the air, but they did not basically change the lot of Black people in the society. Very little of a concrete nature was done in this respect. Barton Bernstein argues that the Blacks' "advance during the depression had been marked by more promise than by substance."[16]

In defense of Roosevelt, it must be said that he was dealing with catastrophe on all sides during this period, and after almost ten years of battling the worst economic depression in our entire history, he was confronted with the most threatening international conflict in the American experience. In restoring confidence in the American political system, feeding the hungry, attempting to develop jobs for the unemployed and in a thousand ways trying to upgrade the lives of all Americans, he considered he was doing the best he could for Black Americans as well. When the war came the jobs in defense industries were opened to Blacks and integration of the armed forces and other minimal goals increased, but they were counteracted by the pressures of the world crisis itself; the difficulty of achieving broad social objectives while fighting a war and attempting to produce the materials to make winning that war possible was profound. Roosevelt made some concessions; he set up by presidential directive the Fair Practices Employment Committee to work on jobs for minorities in government and defense industries (in order to forestall a threatened march on Washington), but he had time for very little else, and he avoided doing any more than he was literally forced to do. He and his advisors agreed that the social revolution would have to take a back seat to winning the war. They rejected the argument advanced by Blacks that this was what the war was all about.

Truman's situation from the beginning was entirely different. He had neither a depression nor a war to use as a basis for avoiding or postponing action, and as the pressure increased, he did act. He was particularly outraged at the indignities and the atrocities that befell returning Black servicemen, and at a certain point, regardless of the political consequences, he decided to move. It should not be inferred that the political consequences of his actions were all negative, however, for along with the racists he would be losing through any such action, he stood to gain hundreds of thousands of militant liberals and Blacks who would be impressed by his honesty and courage. In fact it was these supporters who constituted the marginal majority in his uphill victory in 1948.

Presidential Commissions

It was earlier observed that twentieth century Presidents beginning with Theodore Roosevelt increasingly made use of the device of the presidential commission or investigating committee in order to gather information and to rivet public attention upon a particular problem. (See Volume II of this series.) Theodore Roosevelt named a number of such commissions, placing particular emphasis on conservation and the protection of the natural environment. Herbert Hoover expanded the use of presidential commissions, broadening their scope to the point that he even appointed one such commission to study social trends; Franklin Roosevelt transformed the structure of the executive branch of the government on the basis of recommendations obtained from his President's Committee on Administrative Management (see section three of this volume). The only serious study of these commissions records that some 100 commissions were appointed up to 1940.[17] Another study reveals that 44 more commissions were appointed between 1945 and 1970.[18] Hoover was by far the most extravagant advocate of this particular form of information gathering; he appointed 62 presidential commissions in the first 16 months of his single term in office. Obviously their importance and prestige did not improve with their sheer number, and such widespread overexpansion was bound to deflate their usefulness, if only temporarily.

When challenged regarding their authority to appoint such commissions, Presidents have fallen back on general grants of power assigned to them in the Constitution, providing the President was not authorized to create them directly by Congress, as has sometimes been the case. President John Tyler was the first to be called upon to justify naming such an advisory body (in that case it was a commission to investigate corruption in the New York Customhouse); when a House resolution raised the question of his authority, he answered promptly:

> I have to state that the authority for instituting the commission . . . is the authority vested in the President of the United States to "take care that the laws be faithfully executed, and to give to Congress from time to time information on the state of the Union, and to recommend to their consideration such measures as he shall judge necessary and expedient." The expediency, if not the necessity, of inquiries into the transactions of our customs-houses, especially in cases where abuses and malpractices are alleged, must be obvious to Congress. . . .[19]

President Tyler made clear to the House that the information which the commission was gathering was for his own use as President, although he conjectured that in all probability it would contain much material that he would later make public and probably incorporate into proposals for the Congress. This constitutional justification has stood up over the years, although the various presidential commissions and the propensity of certain Presidents to increase their number have been severely criticized.[20]

Although it has generally been agreed that Presidents do have the power to establish such commissions, and, indeed, to appoint their members, it is perhaps preferable to first seek congressional approval so that funds will be forthcoming to support their investigations. The Chief Executive has no nonappropriated funds with which to support a commission; he must either seek an appropriation from Congress, find support for its work by going to the private sector and obtaining a private grant[21] or it must operate on a purely voluntary basis without any staff assistance. This last option would be difficult or impossible since the staffs of most presidential commissions do the work of research and writing, and then the members of the commission supervise the overall operation and review the staff's work and conclusions. Early in the century $25,000 or $50,000 was assumed to be a reasonable grant for a presidential commission, today their cost has sky-rocketed by geometric proportions.[22]

Presidential commissions have played significant roles in a number of different problem areas and activities. The major distinction between the function of each commission is one of objective. Some are appointed for the purpose of gathering information with the ultimate objective of proposing legislation in an area which the President has already determined requires governmental attention. Not having sufficient knowledge, information, data or background to formulate such legislation, the commissions set out to gather it. In other instances the data may be available, but the general public may be unaware of the problem or the information regarding it, and the commission and particularly its report(s) is used to illuminate and broaden its understanding in the area. Frequently such commissions function in both capacities; they explore a problem thoroughly and provide new information on the subject, and at the same time they educate the public as to the significance of this information or problem. Clearly such commissions are as good or as bad as their creators are either capable or intend to make them. When a President is sympathetic to a particular objective, his selection of the personnel of such a commission and his charge to it can predictably insure the quality of its work and the nature of its conclusions. In other instances the President might be searching for guidance in an area of general ignorance to him and the nation, and here again the high level commission can perform a very useful public service.

The President's Committee on Civil Rights

An entirely different category of presidential commission has been that considered as "administrative," namely those committees concerned with investigations and studies which affect the administrative process of government. Here again there are a number of different types of commissions within this general category. Some are primarily created to investigate the administration of an ongoing governmental administrative operation, such as the commission to investigate the New York Customhouse, or President Hoover's commission to study and review United States policy in Haiti. In his capacity of Commander in Chief the President has sometimes appointed a commission to administrate broad policy in an area of his jurisdiction. President William McKinley indicated the broad responsibilities of such a presidential commission in his definition of the goals of the (first) Philippine Commission, created "in order to facilitate the most humane, pacific, and effective extension of authority through these Islands, and to secure with the least possible delay, the benefits of a wise and generous protection of life and property of the inhabitants. . . ."[23] This commission recommended (predictably) continued United States control of the Philippines and created the (second) Philippine Commission to serve as a civil governing agency there.

Presidents have also appointed administrative commissions to inquire into areas of administrative responsibility where the public is concerned and apprehensive, such as the Roberts Commission to investigate the disaster at Pearl Harbor and the Warren Commission on the assassination of President Kennedy. More common have been the very effective commissions set up to examine and recommend reforms in the administrative structure of the executive branch of the government. The work of the Taft Commission and the Brownlow Committee (see section three in this volume) have radically changed the structure of the modern presidency, and the two Hoover Commissions in the Truman and Eisenhower administrations continued this work. At its best the presidential commission can provide essential functions which no other branch of the government can perform. As President Herbert Hoover observed:

> It is necessary that we make the fullest use of the best brains and the best judgment and the best leadership in our country before we determine upon policies which effect the welfare of a hundred and twenty million people.[24]

But beyond the assistance that such presidential commissions can render to a particular President, by providing background information for possible legislation, such commissions can also perform a vital role in public education, through its exploration and illumination of critical issues and questions of the public domain. The British Royal Commissions have performed this function for two centuries and changed the nature of British society in the process. Supreme Court Justice Felix Frankfurter argued, "The History of British democracy might in considerable measure by written in terms of the history of successive Royal Commissions."[25] The potential for expanding the social and political consciousness of both the public and the government is unlimited if properly approached. Commenting on the work of the royal commissions, Harold Laski wrote: "The aid that device has given to clarity in both policy and Administration is literally beyond estimation."[26] A presidential commission can draw upon the best minds in the country—from the academy, the professions, the sciences, business, etc.—and it can provide them with resources that cannot be duplicated anywhere else. Many future outstanding public servants have had their first experience with government as members of or as staff consultants to such commissions, and the process has also benefited from the talents and experience of former governmental officials no longer in public life.

But presidential commissions also have their perplexing problems, and the record indicates that most Presidents have not known how or been able to make the most efficient and effective use of them. In some cases, Hoover being a glaring example, the concept was overtaxed; he appointed so many commissions that there was no chance of their being able to communicate their findings coherently to either the public or to the Congress, even if they had succeeded. Many presidential commissions have been too partisan, others have lacked adequate staffs and funding, and still others have had to fight congressional opposition from their very inception. On the whole, presidential commissions have never mastered the art of communicating their information and policy recommendations effectively enough. Many of their reports do little but gather dust on library shelves. They seem not to have read Marshall McLuhan or discovered the world of television. Little or no time has been spent in orchestrating their presentation. They have not followed the career of Franklin D. Roosevelt very carefully.[27]

There are other more fundamental difficulties in the work of the commissions themselves. Recent presidential commissions have fallen into the habit of allowing staff personnel to conduct the major part of their work, and the commission members have merely reviewed and evaluated these investigations and have sometimes held public hearings. These commissions appoint a staff director, meet infrequently and for the most part are quite remote from much of the material they are actually examining. Edward Jay Epstein has brilliantly documented this case in his criticisms of the conduct of the Warren Commission on the Assassination of President Kennedy, and although some of his charges are controversial, the substance of his descriptive analysis of the commission's conduct appears to be undeniable.[28]

Harry Truman's Committee on Civil Rights miraculously escaped many of these pitfalls. The President was visited by a committee of prominent Black and white liberals in the fall of 1946, and they begged him to do something to halt the outbreak of lynchings that had been taking place in Georgia and Louisiana. They had hoped for a strong statement that "would make real news," and a commitment to use the power of his office to bring such terror to a halt. Truman appeared to be shocked by the dimension of the crimes about which they informed him, but a serious student of the incident has written that the President already had plans to act before his interview with the committee. Several of his top advisors had also urged him to appoint such a committee. While the committee was bound to incur the wrath of diehard southern racists, it was calculated to build the President's stature in the liberal and minority communities in the North. Whatever the motive, Harry Truman announced the creation of the top-level Committee on Civil Rights on December 5, 1946, made up of a number of outstanding Americans, with a strong liberal bias. Although the selection process tended to predetermine the findings of the group, in this case the President could do little else, once he had made up his mind to name such a committee. The problem was to protect the civil rights of Black Americans; to appoint members of a commission who did not believe in protecting such rights would have been hypocritical and certainly counterproductive. All

Americans who supported the Constitution were obliged to support the principles of civil rights for all Americans, and it would have been absurd for the President to go out of his way to appoint some individuals to the commission who interpreted the Constitution through highly-colored glasses and misconstrued its basic constitutional guarantees.

In his *Memoirs*, Truman explained why he had appointed the committee and what he had expected it to accomplish:

> I took this action because of the repeated anti-minority incidents immediately after the war in which homes were invaded, property was destroyed, and a number of innocent lives were taken. I wanted to get the facts behind these incidents of disregard for individual and group rights which were reported in the news with alarming regularity, and to see that the law was strengthened, if necessary, so as to offer adequate protection and fair treatment to all of our citizens.[29]

The executive order establishing the committee pointed out that the action of "individuals who take the law into their own hands and inflict summary punishment and wreak personal vengeance is subversive of our democratic system of law enforcement and public criminal justice, and gravely threatens our form of government."[30] It was instructed "to inquire into and to determine whether and in what respect current law-enforcement measures and the authority and means possessed by Federal, State, and local governments may be strengthened and improved to safeguard the civil rights of the people."[31] The prestigious character of the committee was reflected in its members who included the president of General Electric, the presidents of Dartmouth College and the University of North Carolina, and a number of other leading citizens. Within the Truman administration the committee was referred to as "Noah's Ark," because it included two Blacks, two women, two Catholics, two Jews, two businessmen, two southerners, two labor leaders and two college presidents.[32] Speaking to the members of the committee shortly after its formation, Truman told them:

> I want our Bill of Rights implemented in fact. We have been trying to do this for 150 years. We are making progress, but we are not making progress fast enough. This country could very easily be faced with a situation similar to the one with which it was faced in 1922.[33]

Truman went on in the *Memoirs* to explain that by his reference to 1922, he was referring "to the revival of terrorism in that year by the Ku Klux Klan."[34]

President Harry S. Truman
Executive Order 9308 Establishing
The President's Committee on Civil Rights
December 5, 1946

To Secure These Rights: The Report of the President's Committee on Civil Rights (New York, 1947), viii.

Whereas the preservation of civil rights guaranteed by the Constitution is essential to domestic tranquility, national security, the general welfare, and the continued existence of our free institutions; and

Whereas the action of individuals who take the law into their own hands and inflict summary punishment and wreak personal vengeance is subversive of our democratic system of law enforcement and public criminal justice, and gravely threatens our form of government; and

Whereas it is essential that all possible steps be taken to safeguard our civil rights:

Now, therefore, by virtue of the authority vested in me as President of the United States by the Constitution and the statutes of the United States, it is hereby ordered as follows:

1. There is hereby created a committee to be known as the President's Committee on Civil Rights, which shall be composed of the following-named members, who shall serve without compensation:

Mr. C. E. Wilson, chairman; Mrs. Sadie T. Alexander, Mr. James B. Carey, Mr. John S. Dickey, Mr. Morris L. Ernst, Rabbi Roland B. Gittelsohn, Dr. Frank P. Graham, The Most Reverend Francis J. Haas, Mr. Charles Luckman, Mr. Francis P. Matthews, Mr. Franklin D. Roosevelt, Jr., The Right Reverend Henry Knox Sherrill, Mr. Boris Shishkin, Mrs. M. E. Tilly, Mr. Channing H. Tobias.

2. The Committee is authorized on behalf of the President to inquire into and to determine whether and in what respect current law-enforcement measures and the authority and means possessed by Federal, State, and local governments may be strengthened and improved to safeguard the civil rights of the people.

3. All executive departments and agencies of the Federal Government are authorized and directed to cooperate with the Committee in its work, and to furnish the Committee such information or the services of such persons as the Committee may require in the performance of its duties.

4. When requested by the Committee to do so, persons employed in any of the executive departments and agencies of the Federal Government shall testify before the Committee and shall make available for the use of the Committee such documents and other information as the Committee may require.

5. The Committee shall make a report of its studies to the President in writing, and shall in particular make recommendations with respect to the adoption or establishment, by legislation or otherwise, of more adequate and effective means

and procedures for the protection of the civil rights of the people of the United States.

6. Upon rendition of its report to the President, the Committee shall cease to exist, unless otherwise determined by further Executive Order.

Harry S. Truman

Ten months later the President's Committee returned with a very comprehensive report on the critical problem areas of civil rights in the country. Nothing comparable to its scope and authority had ever been forthcoming from the executive branch of the government. The report identified problems and conditions requiring significant and immediate attention, and the committee made a number of recommendations covering a wide range of situations from the protection of the security of the person to segregation in education, health and housing. Positive recommendations were made to the President to act immediately to implement the report; this he proceeded to do.

Most of this quite readable report is taken up with identifying and analyzing the critical areas where, without equal treatment under the law, and, as the report put it, without equality of opportunity, "freedom becomes an illusion." It begins by defining what the committee decided were the four most basic rights "essential to the well-being of the individual and to the progress of the society":

1. *The right to safety and security of the person.* This would include protection from lawless violence (e.g. lynching), arbitrary arrest and punishment and involuntary servitude of all kinds and varieties.
2. *The right to citizenship and its privileges.* The essential right which was denied to many Americans was the right to vote.
3. *The right to freedom of conscience and expression.*
4. *The right to equality of opportunity.* This included the largest areas of deprivation—employment, housing, education, health, recreation and transportation.[35]

The body of the report explored the physical reality in which these basic rights were denied Americans for one reason or another, and made specific recommendations for governmental action, either in the form of legislation or through administrative policy or structural changes through which these rights could be extended and reinforced. Problems such as lynching, police brutality, illegal arrests, unequal administration of the law, particularly the criminal law, the right to vote, equal opportunities and integration of the armed services, the inequities which existed in the areas of education, housing, acceptance in labor unions, job opportunities, health services (both public and private), recreational facilities were all covered in the report. A special section was devoted to the gross inequities in all these areas which existed in the national capital in Washington, D.C.

Although four out of five of the cases which the committee investigated involved discrimination or deprivation of rights or privileges of Black Americans, the committee also examined and was concerned that measures be taken to protect the rights and privileges of American Indians, Mexican-Americans, Japanese-Americans, Puerto Ricans, Filipinos and American Jews. Different patterns of discrimination existed in different sections of the country, and the committee was concerned that steps be taken to end all forms of deprivations of rights and privileges, regardless of group or section.

What was significant about the report was that in addition to collecting information for the President and Congress on this problem, the report was printed and widely publicized throughout the country. A presidentially-appointed committee was attempting to inform all Americans that Blacks and other minorities were being victimized by lynchings and police brutality; they were frequently denied equal protection of the law, barred from many professions and many regular job opportunities, segregated in the armed forces and required to perform menial functions and denied equal opportunities in education, housing, health services and recreational facilities. Beyond this, the committee told the American people and their government that they must do something about these scandalous conditions. This was the revolutionary aspect of the report, which had originated in the executive branch of the government.

To Secure These Rights:
The Report of the President's Committee on Civil Rights
1947

To Secure These Rights, 149-75.

Mr. President: Your Committee has reviewed the American heritage and we have found in it again the great goals of human freedom and equality under just laws. We have surveyed the flaws in the nation's record and have found them to be serious. We have considered what government's appropriate role should be in the securing of our rights, and have concluded that it must assume greater leadership.

We believe that the time for action is now. Our recommendations for bringing the United States closer to its historic goal follow.

THE COMMITTEE'S
RECOMMENDATIONS

I. To strengthen the machinery
for the protection of civil rights,
the President's Committee recommends:

1. The reorganization of the Civil Rights Section of the Department of Justice to provide for:

The establishment of regional offices;

A substantial increase in its appropriation and staff to enable it to engage
   in more extensive research and to act more effectively to prevent civil
   rights violations;
An increase in investigative action in the absence of complaints;
The greater use of civil sanctions;
Its elevation to the status of a full division in the Department of Justice.

The creation of regional offices would enable the Civil Rights Section to
provide more complete protection of civil rights in all sections of the country. It
would lessen its present complete dependence upon United States Attorneys and
local FBI agents for its work in the field. Such regional offices should be established
in eight or nine key cities throughout the country, and be staffed with skilled
personnel drawn from the local areas. These offices should serve as receiving points
for complaints arising in the areas, and as local centers of research, investigation,
and preventive action. Close cooperation should be maintained between these
offices, local FBI agents, and the United States Attorneys.

The Department of Justice has suggested that heads of these regional offices
should have the status of Assistant United States Attorneys, thereby preserving the
centralization of federal criminal law enforcement. The President's Committee is
fearful that under this plan the goal of effective, courageous, and nonpolitical civil
rights protection in the field will not be reached unless satisfactory measures are
taken to prevent these assistants from becoming mere political subordinates within
the offices of the United States Attorneys.

Additional funds and personnel for research and preventive work would free
the Civil Rights Section from its present narrow status as a prosecutive agency.
Through the use of properly developed techniques and by the maintenance of
continuous checks on racial and other group tensions, much could be done by the
Section to reduce the number of lynchings, race riots, election irregularities, and
other civil rights violations. Troublesome areas, and the activities of organizations
and individuals who foment race tensions could be kept under constant scrutiny.

A larger staff and field-office facilities would also make it possible for the
Section to undertake investigations of suspected civil rights violations, without
waiting for the receipt of complaints. There are many problems, such as the possible
infringement of civil rights resulting from practices used in committing persons to
mental institutions, which might be so studied. These investigations in the absence
of complaints could also be combined with educational and mediation efforts to
check chronic incidents of police brutality or persistent interferences with the right
to vote.

The difficulty of winning convictions in many types of criminal civil rights
cases is often great. The Committee believes that the Civil Rights Section should be
granted increased authority, by Congress if necessary, to make appropriate use of
civil sanctions, such as suits for damages or injunctive relief, suits under the
Declaratory Judgment Act, and the right of intervention by means of briefs amicus
curiae in private litigation where important issues of civil rights law are being
determined.

Finally, the Committee urges congressional action raising the Civil Rights
Section to full divisional status in the Department of Justice under the supervision
of an Assistant Attorney General. We believe this step would give the federal civil

rights enforcement program prestige, power, and efficiency that it now lacks. Moreover, acceptance of the above recommendations looking toward increased activity by the Civil Rights Section and the passage by Congress of additional civil rights legislation would give this change added meaning and necessity.

2. The establishment within the FBI of a special unit of investigators trained in civil rights work.

The creation of such unit of skilled investigators would enable the FBI to render more effective service in the civil rights field than is now possible. At the present time, its investigators are concerned with enforcement of all federal criminal statutes. In some instances, its agents have seemingly lacked the special skills and knowledge necessary to effective handling of civil rights cases, or have not been readily available for work in this area.

These special agents should work in close harmony with the Civil Rights Section and its regional offices.

3. The establishment by the state governments of law enforcement agencies comparable to the federal Civil Rights Section.

There are large areas where, because of constitutional restrictions, the jurisdiction of the federal government as a protector of civil rights is either limited or denied. There are civil rights problems, unique to certain regions and localities, that can best be treated and solved by the individual states. Furthermore, our review of the work of the Civil Rights Section has persuaded us of the cardinal importance of developing specialized units for the enforcement of civil rights laws. We believe that this is true at the state level too. States which have, or will have, civil rights laws of their own, should buttress them with specially designed enforcement units. These would have the further effect of bringing the whole program closer to the people. They would also facilitate systematic local cooperation with the federal Civil Rights Section, and they would be able to act in the areas where it has no authority.

Here and elsewhere the Committee is making recommendations calling for remedial action by the states. The President's Executive Order invited us to consider civil rights problems falling within state as well as federal jurisdiction. We respectfully request the President to call these recommendations to the attention of the states and to invite their favorable consideration.

4. The establishment of a permanent Commission on Civil Rights in the Executive Office of the President, preferably by Act of Congress;
And the simultaneous creation of a Joint Standing Committee on Civil Rights in Congress.

In a democratic society, the systematic, critical review of social needs and public policy is a fundamental necessity. This is especially true of a field like civil rights, where the problems are enduring, and range widely. From our own efforts, we have learned that a temporary, sporadic approach can never finally solve these problems.

Nowhere in the federal government is there an agency charged with the continuous appraisal of the status of civil rights, and the efficiency of the machinery with which we hope to improve that status. There are huge gaps in the available information about the field. A permanent Commission could perform an invaluable function by collecting data. It could also carry on technical research to improve the fact-gathering methods now in use. Ultimately, this would make possible a periodic audit of the extent to which our civil rights are secure. If it did this and served as a clearing house and focus of coordination for the many private, state, and local agencies working in the civil rights field, it would be invaluable to them and to the federal government.

A permanent Commission on Civil Rights should point all of its work towards regular reports which would include recommendations for action in the ensuing periods. It should lay plans for dealing with broad civil rights problems, such as those arising from the technological displacement and probable migration of southern Negroes to cities throughout the land. It should also investigate and make recommendations with respect to special civil rights problems, such as the status of Indians and their relationship to the federal government.

The Commission should have effective authority to call upon any agency of the executive branch for assistance. Its members should be appointed by the President with the approval of the Senate. They should hold a specified number of regular meetings. A full-time director should be provided with an adequate appropriation and staff.

Congress, too, can be aided in its difficult task of providing the legislative ground work for fuller civil rights. A standing committee, established jointly by the House and the Senate, would provide a central place for the consideration of proposed legislation. It would enable Congress to maintain continuous liaison with the permanent Commission. A group of men in each chamber would be able to give prolonged study to this complex area and would become expert in its legislative needs.

5. *The establishment by the states of permanent commissions on civil rights to parallel the work of the federal Commission at the state level.*

The states should create permanent civil rights commissions to make continuing studies of prejudice, group tensions, and other local civil rights problems; to publish educational material of a civil rights nature; to evaluate existing legislation; and to recommend new laws. Such commissions, with their fingers on their communities' pulses, would complement at the state level the activities of a permanent federal Commission on Civil Rights.

6. *The increased professionalization of state and local police forces.*

The Committee believes that there is a great need at the state and local level for the improvement of civil rights protection by more aggressive and efficient enforcement techniques. Police training programs, patterned after the FBI agents' school and the Chicago Park District Program, should be instituted. They should be oriented so as to indoctrinate officers with an awareness of civil rights problems. Proper treatment by the police of those who are arrested and incarcerated in local jails should be stressed. Supplemented by salaries that will attract and hold competent personnel, this sort of training should do much to make police forces genuinely professional.

II. To strengthen the right to
safety and security of the person,
the President's Committee recommends:

1. The enactment by Congress of new legislation to supplement Section 51 of Title 18 of the United States Code which would impose the same liability on one person as is now imposed by the statute on two or more conspirators.

The Committee believes that Section 51 has in the past been a useful law to protect federal rights against encroachment by both private individuals and public officers. It believes the Act has great potential usefulness today. Greater efforts should be made through court tests to extend and make more complete the list of rights safeguarded by this law.

2. The amendment of Section 51 to remove the penalty provision which disqualifies persons convicted under the Act from holding public office.

There is general agreement that this particular penalty creates an unnecessary obstacle to the obtaining of convictions under the Act and that it should be dropped.

3. The amendment of Section 52 to increase the maximum penalties that may be imposed under it from a $1,000 fine and a one-year prison term to a $5,000 fine and a ten-year prison term, thus bringing its penalty provisions into line with those in Section 51.

At the present time the Act's penalties are so light that it is technically a misdemeanor law. In view of the extremely serious offenses that have been and are being successfully prosecuted under Section 52, it seems clear that the penalties should be increased.

4. The enactment by Congress of a new statute, to supplement Section 52, specifically directed against police brutality and related crimes.

This Act should enumerate such rights as the right not to be deprived of property by a public officer except by due process of law; the right to be free from personal injury inflicted by a public officer; the right to engage in a lawful activity without interference by a public officer; and the right to be free from discriminatory law enforcement resulting from either active or passive conduct by a public officer.

This statute would meet in part the handicap in the use of Section 52 imposed by the Supreme Court in *Screws v. United States*. This was the case in which the Court required prosecutors to establish that defendants had willfully deprived victims of a "specific constitutional right." In later prosecutions, the Civil Rights Section has found it very difficult to prove that the accused acted in a "willful" manner. By spelling out some of the federal rights which run against public officers, the supplementary statute would relieve the Civil Rights Section of this extraordinary requirement.

The Committee considered and rejected a proposal to recommend the enactment of a supplementary statute in which an attempt would be made to include a specific enumeration of all federal rights running against public officers. Such an enumeration would inevitably prove incomplete with the passage of time and might prejudice the protection of omitted rights. However, the committee believes that a new statute, such as the one here recommended, enumerating the rights for the protection of which Section 52 is now most commonly employed, is desirable.

5. *The enactment by Congress of an antilynching act.*

The Committee believes that to be effective such a law must contain four essential elements. First, it should define lynching broadly. Second, the federal offense ought to cover participation of public officers in a lynching, or failure by them to use proper measures to protect a person accused of a crime against mob violence. The failure or refusal of public officers to make proper efforts to arrest members of lynch mobs and to bring them to justice should also be specified as an offense.

Action by private persons taking the law into their own hands to mete out summary punishment and private vengeance upon an accused person; action by either public officers or private persons meting out summary punishment and private vengeance upon a person because of his race, color, creed or religion—these too must be made crimes.

Third, the statute should authorize immediate federal investigation in lynching cases to discover whether a federal offense has been committed. Fourth, adequate and flexible penalties ranging up to a $10,000 fine and a 20-year prison term should be provided.

The constitutionality of some parts of such statute, particularly those providing for the prosecution of private persons, has been questioned. The Committee believes that there are several constitutional bases upon which such a law might be passed and that these are sufficiently strong to justify prompt action by Congress.

6. *The enactment by Congress of a new criminal statute on involuntary servitude, supplementing Sections 443 and 444 of Title 18 of the United States Code.*

This statute should make full exercise of congressional power under the Thirteenth Amendment by defining slavery and involuntary servitude broadly. This would provide a basis for federal prosecutions in cases where individuals are deliberately deprived of their freedom by public officers without due process of law or are held in bondage by private persons. Prosecution under existing laws is limited to the narrow, technical offense of peonage or must be based upon the archaic "slave kidnaping" law, Section 443.

7. *A review of our wartime evacuation and detention experience looking toward the development of a policy which will prevent the abridgment of civil rights of any person or groups because of race or ancestry.*

We believe it is fallacious to assume that there is a correlation between loyalty and race or national origin. The military must be allowed considerable discretionary power to protect national security in time of war. But we believe it is possible to establish safeguards against the evacuation and detention of whole groups because of their descent without endangering national security. The proposed permanent Commission on Civil Rights and the Joint Congressional Committee might well study this problem.

8. Enactment by Congress of legislation establishing a procedure by which claims of evacuees for specific property and business losses resulting from the wartime evacuation can be promptly considered and settled.

The government has acknowledged that many Japanese American evacuees suffered considerable losses through its actions and through no fault of their own. We cannot erase all the scars of evacuation; we can reimburse those who present valid claims for material losses.

III. To strengthen the right
to citizenship and its privileges,
the President's Committee recommends:

1. Action by the states or Congress to end poll taxes as a voting prerequisite.

Considerable debate has arisen as to the constitutionality of a federal statute abolishing the poll tax. In four times passing an anti-poll tax bill, the House of Representatives has indicated its view that there is a reasonable chance that it will survive a court attack on constitutional grounds. We are convinced that the elimination of this obstacle to the right of suffrage must not be further delayed. It would be appropriate and encouraging for the remaining poll tax states voluntarily to take this step. Failing such prompt state action, we believe that the nation, either by act of Congress, or by constitutional amendment, should remove this final barrier to universal suffrage.

2. The enactment by Congress of a statute protecting the right of qualified persons to participate in federal primaries and elections against interference by public officers and private persons.

This statute would apply only to federal elections. There is no doubt that such a law can be applied to primaries which are an integral part of the federal electoral process or which affect or determine the result of a federal election. It can also protect participation in federal election campaigns and discussions of matters relating to national political issues. This statute should authorize the Department of Justice to use both civil and criminal sanctions. Civil remedies should be used wherever possible to test the legality of threatened interferences with the suffrage before voting rights have been lost.

3. The enactment by Congress of a statute protecting the right to qualify for, or participate in, federal or state primaries or elections against discriminatory action by state officers based on race or color, or depending on any other unreasonable classification of persons for voting purposes.

This statute would apply to both federal and state elections, but it would be limited to the protection of the right to vote against discriminatory interferences based on race, color, or other unreasonable classification. Its constitutionality is clearly indicated by the Fourteenth and Fifteenth Amendments. Like the legislation suggested under (2) it should authorize the use of civil and criminal sanctions by the Department of Justice.

4. The enactment by Congress of legislation establishing local self-government for the District of Columbia; and the amendment of the Constitution to extend suffrage in presidential elections, and representation in Congress to District residents.

The American tradition of democracy requires that the District of Columbia be given the same measure of self-government in local affairs that is possessed by other communities throughout the country. The lack of congressional representation and suffrage in local and national elections in the District deprives a substantial number of permanent Washington residents of a voice in public affairs.

5. The granting of suffrage by the States of New Mexico and Arizona to their Indian citizens.

These states have constitutional provisions which have been used to disfranchise Indians. In New Mexico, the constitution should be amended to remove the bar against voting by "Indians not taxed." This may not be necessary in Arizona where the constitution excludes from the ballot "persons under guardianship." Reinterpretation might hold that this clause no longer applies to Indians. If this is not possible, the Arizona constitution should be amended to remove it.

6. The modification of the federal naturalization laws to permit the granting of citizenship without regard to the race, color, or national origin of applicants.

It is inconsistent with our whole tradition to deny on a basis of ancestry the right to become citizens to people who qualify in every other way.

7. The repeal by the states of laws discriminating against aliens who are ineligible for citizenship because of race, color, or national origin.

These laws include the alien land laws and the prohibition against commercial fishing in California. The removal of race as a qualification for naturalization would remove the structure upon which this discriminatory legislation is based. But if federal action on Recommendation 6 is delayed, state action would be eminently desirable.

8. The enactment by Congress of legislation granting citizenship to the people of Guam and American Samoa.

This legislation should also provide these islands with organic acts containing guarantees of civil rights, and transfer them from naval administration to civilian control. Such legislation for Guam and American Samoa has been introduced in the present Congress.

9. The enactment by Congress of legislation, followed by appropriate administrative action, to end immediately all discrimination and segregation based on race, color, creed, or national origin, in the organization and activities of all branches of the Armed Services.

The injustice of calling men to fight for freedom while subjecting them to humiliating discrimination within the fighting forces is at once apparent. Furthermore, by preventing entire groups from making their maximum contribution to the national defense, we weaken our defense to that extent and impose heavier burdens on the remainder of the population.

Legislation and regulations should expressly ban discrimination and segregation in the recruitment, assignment, and training of all personnel in all types of military duty. Mess halls, quarters, recreational facilities and post exchanges should be nonsegregated. Commissions and promotions should be awarded on considerations of merit only. Selection of students for the Military, Naval, and Coast Guard academies and all other service schools should be governed by standards from which considerations of race, color, creed, or national origin are conspicuously absent. The National Guard, reserve units, and any universal military training program should all be administered in accordance with these same standards.

The Committee believes that the recent unification of the armed forces provides a timely opportunity for the revision of present policy and practice. A strong enunciation of future policy should be made condemning discrimination and segregation within the armed services.

10. The enactment by Congress of legislation providing that no member of the armed forces shall be subject to discrimination of any kind by any public authority or place of public accommodation, recreation, transportation, or other service or business.

The government of a nation has an obligation to protect the dignity of the uniform of its armed services. The esteem of the government itself is impaired when affronts to its armed forces are tolerated. The government also has a responsibility for the well-being of those who surrender some of the privileges of citizenship to serve in the defense establishments.

IV. To strengthen the right to
freedom of conscience and expression
the President's Committee recommends:

1. The enactment by Congress and the state legislatures of legislation requiring all groups, which attempt to influence public opinion, to disclose the pertinent facts about themselves through systematic registration procedures.

Such registration should include a statement of the names of officers, sources of financial contributions, disbursements, and the purposes of the organization. There is no question about the power of the states to do this. Congress may use its taxing and postal powers to require such disclosure. The revenue laws should be changed so that tax returns of organizations claiming tax exemption show the suggested information. These returns should then be made available to the public.

The revenue laws ought also to be amended to require the same information from groups and organizations which claim to operate on a non-profit basis but which do not request tax exemption. The Committee also recommends further study by appropriate governmental agencies looking toward the application of the disclosure principle to profit-making organizations which are active in the market place of public opinion.

Congress ought also to amend the postal laws to require those who use the first-class mail for large-scale mailings to file disclosure statements similar to those now made annually by those who use the second-class mail. The same requirement should be adopted for applicants for metered mail permits. Postal regulations ought also to require that no mail be carried by the Post Office which does not bear the name and address of the sender.

2. Action by Congress and the executive branch clarifying the loyalty obligations of federal employees, and establishing standards and procedures by which the civil rights of public workers may be scrupulously maintained.

The Committee recognizes the authority and the duty of the government to dismiss disloyal workers from the government service. At the same time the Committee is equally concerned with the protection of the civil rights of federal workers. We believe that there should be a public enunciation by responsible federal officials of clear, specific standards by which to measure the loyalty of government workers.

It is also important that the procedure by which the loyalty of an accused federal worker is determined be a fair, consistently applied, stated "due process." Specific rules of evidence should be laid down. Each employee should have the right to a bill of particular accusations, representation by counsel at all examinations or hearings, the right to subpoena witnesses and documents, a stenographic report of proceedings, a written decision, and time to prepare a written brief for an appeal. Competent and judicious people should have the responsibility for administering the program.

The Attorney General has stated to the Committee in a letter, "It is my firm purpose, insofar as my office has control over this program, to require substantial observance of the safeguards recommended by the President's Committee."

V. To strengthen the right
to equality of opportunity,
the President's Committee recommends:

1. In general:

The elimination of segregation, based on race, color, creed, or national origin, from American life.

The separate but equal doctrine has failed in three important respects. First, it is inconsistent with the fundamental equalitarianism of the American way of life in that it marks groups with the brand of inferior status. Secondly, where it has been followed, the results have been separate and unequal facilities for minority peoples. Finally, it has kept people apart despite incontrovertible evidence that an environment favorable to civil rights is fostered whenever groups are permitted to live and work together. There is no adequate defense of segregation.

The conditioning by Congress of all federal grants-in-aid and other forms of federal assistance to public or private agencies for any purpose on the absence of discrimination and segregation based on race, color, creed, or national origin.

We believe that federal funds, supplied by taxpayers all over the nation, must not be used to support or perpetuate the pattern of segregation in education, public housing, public health services, or other public services and facilities generally. We recognize that these services are indispensable to individuals in modern society and to further social progress. It would be regrettable if federal aid, conditioned on nonsegregated services, should be rejected by sections most in need of such aid. The Committee believes that a reasonable interval of time may be allowed for adjustment to such a policy. But in the end it believes that segregation is wrong morally and practically and must not recieve financial support by the whole people.

A minority of the Committee favors the elimination of segregation as an ultimate goal but opposes the imposition of a federal sanction. It believes that federal aid to the states for eduction, health, research and other public benefits should be granted provided that the states do not discriminate in the distribution of the funds. It dissents, however, from the majority's recommendation that the abolition of segregation be made a requirement, until the people of the states involved have themselves abolished the provisions in their state constitutions and laws which now require segregation. Some members are against the non-segregation requirement in educational grants on the ground that it represents federal control over education. They feel, moreover, that the best way ultimately to end segregation is to raise the educational level of the people in the states affected; and to inculcate both the teachings of religion regarding human brotherhood and the ideals of our democracy regarding freedom and equality as a more solid basis for genuine and lasting acceptance by the peoples of the states.

2. For employment:

The enactment of a federal Fair Employment Practice Act prohibiting all forms of discrimination in private employment, based on race, color, creed, or national origin.

A federal Fair Employment Practice Act prohibiting discrimination in private employment should provide both educational machinery and legal sanctions for enforcement purposes. The administration of the act should be placed in the hands of a commission with power to receive complaints, hold hearings, issue cease-and-desist orders and seek court aid in enforcing these orders. The Act should contain definite fines for the violation of its procedural provisions. In order to allow time for voluntary adjustment of employment practices to the new law, and to permit the establishment of effective enforcement machinery, it is recommended that the sanction provisions of the law not become operative until one year after the enactment of the law.

The federal act should apply to labor unions and trade and professional associations, as well as to employers, insofar as the policies and practices of these organizations affect the employment status of workers.

The enactment by the states of similar laws;

A federal fair employment practice statute will not reach activities which do not affect interstate commerce. To make fair employment a uniform national policy, state action will be needed. The successful experiences of some states warrant similar action by all of the others.

The issuance by the President of a mandate against discrimination in government employment and the creation of adequate machinery to enforce this mandate.

The Civil Service Commission and the personnel offices of all federal agencies should establish on-the-job training programs and other necessary machinery to enforce the nondiscrimination policy in government employment. It may well be desirable to establish a government fair employment practice commission, either as a part of the Civil Service Commission, or on an independent basis with authority to implement and enforce the Presidential mandate.

3. For education:

Enactment by the state legislatures of fair educational practice laws for public and private educational institutions, prohibiting discrimination in the admission and treatment of students based on race, color, creed, or national origin.

These laws should be enforced by independent administrative commissions. These commissions should consider complaints and hold hearings to review them. Where they are found to be valid, direct negotiation with the offending institution should be undertaken to secure compliance with the law. Wide publicity for the commission's findings would influence many schools and colleges sensitive to public opinion to abandon discrimination. The final sanction for such a body would be the cease-and-desist order enforceable by court action. The Committee believes that educational institutions supported by churches and definitely identified as denominational should be exempted.

There is a substantial division within the Committee on this recommendation. A majority favors it.

4. For housing:

The enactment by the states of laws outlawing restrictive covenants;
Renewed court attack, with intervention by the Department of Justice, upon restrictive covenants.

The effectiveness of restrictive covenants depends in the last analysis on court orders enforcing the private agreement. The power of the state is thus utilized to bolster discriminatory practices. The Committee believes that every effort must be made to prevent this abuse. We would hold this belief under any circumstances; under present conditions, when severe housing shortages are already causing hardship for many people of the country, we are especially emphatic in recommending measures to alleviate the situation.

5. For health services:

The enactment by the states of fair health practice statutes forbidding discrimination and segregation based on race, creed, color, or national origin, in the operation of public or private health facilities.

Fair health practice statutes, following the pattern of fair employment practice laws, seem desirable to the Committee. They should cover such matters as the training of doctors and nurses, the admission of patients to clinics, hospitals and other similar institutions, and the right of doctors and nurses to practice in hospitals. The administration of these statutes should be placed in the hands of commissions, with authority to receive complaints, hold hearings, issue cease-and-desist orders and engage in educational efforts to promote the policy of these laws.

6. For public services:

The enactment by Congress of a law stating that discrimination and segregation, based on race, color, creed, or national origin, in the rendering of all public services by the national government is contrary to public policy;
The enactment by the states of similar laws;

The elimination of discrimination and segregation depends largely on the leadership of the federal and state governments. They can make a great contribution toward accomplishing this end by affirming in law the principle of equality for all, and declaring that public funds, which belong to the whole people, will be used for the benefit of the entire population.

The establishment by act of Congress or excutive order of a unit in the federal Bureau of the Budget to review the execution of all government programs, and the expenditures of all government funds, for compliance with the policy of nondiscrimination;

Continual surveillance is necessary to insure the nondiscriminatory execution of federal programs involving use of government funds. The responsibility for this task should be located in the Bureau of the Budget which has the duty of formulating the executive budget and supervising the execution of appropriation acts. The Bureau already checks the various departments and agencies for compliance with announced policy. Administratively, this additional function is consistent with its present duties and commensurate with its present powers.

The enactment by Congress of a law prohibiting discrimination or segregation, based on race, color, creed, or national origin, in interstate transportation and all the facilities thereof, to apply against both public officers and the employees of private transportation companies;

Legislation is needed to implement and supplement the Supreme Court decision in *Morgan v. Virginia*. There is evidence that some state officers are continuing to enforce segregation laws against interstate passengers. Moreover, carriers are still free to segregate such passengers on their own initiative since the

Morgan decision covered only segregation based on law. Congress has complete power under the Constitution to forbid all forms of segregation in interstate commerce. We believe it should make prompt use of it.

> The enactment by the states of laws guaranteeing equal access to places of public accommodation, broadly defined, for persons of all races, colors, creeds, and national origins.

Since the Constitution does not guarantee equal access to places of public accommodation, it is left to the states to secure that right. In the 18 states that have already enacted statutes, we hope that enforcement will make practice more compatible with theory. The civil suit for damages and the misdemeanor penalty have proved to be inadequate sanctions to secure the observance of these laws. Additional means, such as the revocation of licenses, and the issuance of cease-and-desist orders by administrative agencies are needed to bring about wider compliance. We think that all of the states should enact such legislation, using the broadest possible definition of public accommodation.

7. *For the District of Columbia:*

> The enactment by Congress of legislation to accomplish the following purposes in the District;
> Prohibition of discrimination and segregation, based on race, color, creed, or national origin, in all public or publicly-supported hospitals, parks, recreational facilities, housing projects, welfare agencies, penal institutions, and concessions on public property;
> The prohibition of segregation in the public school system of the District of Columbia;
> The establishment of a fair educational practice program directed against discrimination, based on race, color, creed, or national origin, in the admission of students to private educational institutions;
> The establishment of a fair health practice program forbidding discrimination and segregation by public or private agencies, based on race, color, creed, or national origin, with respect to the training of doctors and nurses, the admission of patients to hospitals, clinics, and similar institutions, and the right of doctors and nurses to practice in hospitals;
> The outlawing of restrictive covenants;
> Guaranteeing equal access to places of public accommodation, broadly defined, to persons of all races, colors, creeds, and national origins.

In accordance with the Committee's division on antidiscrimination laws with respect to private education, the proposal for a District fair education program was not unanimous.

Congress has complete power to enact the legislation necessary for progress toward full freedom and equality in the District of Columbia. The great majority of these measures has been recommended in this report to Congress and to the states to benefit the nation at large. But they have particular meaning and increased urgency with respect to the District. Our nation's capital, the city of Washington, should serve as a symbol of democracy to the entire world.

8. *The enactment by Congress of legislation ending the system of segregation in the Panama Canal Zone.*

The federal government has complete jurisdiction over the government of the Panama Canal Zone, and therefore should take steps to eliminate the segregation which prevails there.

VI. To rally the American people
to the support of a continuing
program to strengthen civil rights,
the President's Committee recommends:

A long term campaign of public education to inform the people of the civil rights to which they are entitled and which they owe to one another.

The most important educational task in this field is to give the public living examples of civil rights in operation. This is the purpose of our recommendations which have gone before. But there still remains the job of driving home to the public the nature of our heritage, the justification of civil rights and the need to end prejudice. This is a task which will require the cooperation of the federal, state, and local governments and of private agencies. We believe that the permanent Commission on Civil Rights should take the leadership in serving as the coordinating body. The activities of the permanent Commission in this field should be expressly authorized by Congress and funds specifically appropriated for them.

Aside from the education of the general public, the government has immediate responsibility for an internal civil rights campaign for its more than two million employees. This might well be an indispensable first step in a large campaign. Moreover, in the armed forces, an opportunity exists to educate men while in service. The armed forces should expand efforts, already under way, to develop genuinely democratic attitudes in officers and enlisted men.

As the Committee concludes this Report we would remind ourselves that the future of our nation rests upon the character, the vision, the high principle of our people. Democracy, brotherhood, human rights—these are practical expressions of the eternal worth of every child of God. With His guidance and help we can move forward toward a nobler social order in which there will be equal opportunity for all.

The report of the President's Committee was greeted by the liberal community with extravagant praise. James. R. Newman in the *New Republic* expressed a widely held point of view:

For those who cherish liberty, freedom and forebearance; for those sickened by the sight of reaction riding the land; for those who feel alone and for those who are afraid, here is a noble reaffirmation of the principles that made America.[36]

Despite some division within the committee on a few of the more sensitive issues, there was no equivocation on the "separate but equal" doctrine which had dominated so many of these questions since the Plessy v. Ferguson decision of the Supreme Court. Striking out hard against this theory of equality, the report stated:

> Segregation has become the cornerstone of the elaborate structure of discrimination against some American citizens. Theoretically this system simply duplicates educational, recreational and other public services, according facilities to the two races which are "separate but equal." In the Committee's opinion this is one of the outstanding myths of American history for it is almost always true that while indeed separate, these facilities are far from equal. Throughout the segregated public institutions, Negroes have been denied an equal share of tax-supported services and facilities.[37]

President Truman's views did not go that far, however. He was what one might call a Plessy v. Ferguson constitutionalist on this issue. Perhaps political considerations prevented him from embracing the pure doctrine of full equality on a social as well as a political and economic level, but in postwar America during the 1940s, the achievement of eliminating unjust discrimination and establishing full equality for the Black citizen with regard to all aspects of public rights and services was going considerably beyond what the Congress and certainly large segments of the American people were willing to do. For this Missouri-born, small town ex-haberdasher and (as his mother used to think of him) dirt farmer, whose mother never lowered the Confederate flag, it was a substantial jump. Truman never paraded himself as a social integrationist, but he appeared to be sincere in seeking full equality before the law for every American. He pursued this objective at a greater risk than any President who held the office.

In February 1948 Truman sent a special message on civil rights to the Congress, requesting the passage of legislation to implement practically all of the proposals of the committee. Left out were any suggestions for social integration, except with regard to interstate transportation, where segregation resulted directly and overtly in inequities in services available.[38] Many of us wanted more than this from the government, for if Congress had enacted the full Truman program, this country would have taken so many more strides forward than it did, it would have moved into the second half of the century so much closer to its cherished constitutional goals of freedom and equality for all Americans that there is simply no predicting how much brighter the tortured 1950s and 1960s might have been. Once major change really begins to move, incremental improvements are not all that difficult. But the country was not yet ready for even this minimal program of reform, and the major portions of the President's proposals were never implemented.

President Harry S. Truman
Special Message to Congress
On Civil Rights
February 2, 1948

Public Papers of the Presidents: Harry S. Truman, 1948 (Washington, D.C., 1964), 121-26.

To the Congress of the United States: In the State of the Union Message on January 7, 1948, I spoke of five great goals toward which we should strive in our constant effort to strengthen our democracy and improve the welfare of our people. The first of these is to secure fully our essential human rights. I am now presenting to the Congress my recommendations for legislation to carry us forward toward that goal.

This Nation was founded by men and women who sought these shores that they might enjoy greater freedom and greater opportunity than they had known before. The founders of the United States proclaimed to the world the American belief that all men are created equal, and that governments are instituted to secure the inalienable rights with which all men are endowed. In the Declaration of Independence and the Constitution of the United States, they eloquently expressed the aspirations of all mankind for equality and freedom.

These ideals inspired the peoples of other lands, and their practical fulfillment made the United States the hope of the oppressed everywhere. Throughout our history men and women of all colors and creeds, of all races and religions, have come to this country to escape tyranny and discrimination. Millions strong, they have helped build this democratic Nation and have constantly reinforced our devotion to the great ideals of liberty and equality. With those who preceded them, they have helped to fashion and strengthen our American faith—a faith that can be simply stated:

We believe that all men are created equal and that they have the right to equal justice under law.

We believe that all men have the right to freedom of thought and of expression and the right to worship as they please.

We believe that all men are entitled to equal opportunities for jobs, for homes, for good health and for education.

We believe that all men should have a voice in their government and that government should protect, not usurp, the rights of the people.

These are the basic civil rights which are the source and the support of our democracy.

Today, the American people enjoy more freedom and opportunity than ever before. Never in our history has there been better reason to hope for the complete realization of the ideals of liberty and equality.

We shall not, however, finally achieve the ideals for which this Nation was founded so long as any American suffers discrimination as a result of his race, or religion, or color, or the land of origin of his forefathers.

Unfortunately, there still are examples—flagrant examples—of discrimination which are utterly contrary to our ideals. Not all groups of our population are free from the fear of violence. Not all groups are free to live and work where they please or to improve their conditions of life by their own efforts. Not all groups enjoy the full privileges of citizenship and participation in the government under which they live.

We cannot be satisfied until all our people have equal opportunities for jobs, for homes, for education, for health, and for political expression, and until all our people have equal protection under the law.

One year ago I appointed a committee of fifteen distinguished Americans and asked them to appraise the condition of our civil rights and to recommend appropriate action by Federal, state and local governments.

The committee's appraisal has resulted in a frank and revealing report. This report emphasizes that our basic human freedoms are better cared for and more vigilantly defended than ever before. But it also makes clear that there is a serious gap between our ideals and some of our practices. This gap must be closed.

This will take the strong efforts of each of us individually, and all of us acting together through voluntary organizations and our governments.

The protection of civil rights begins with the mutual respect for the rights of others which all of us should practice in our daily lives. Through organizations in every community—in all parts of the country—we must continue to develop practical, workable arrangements for achieving greater tolerance and brotherhood.

The protection of civil rights is the duty of every government which derives its powers from the consent of the people. This is equally true of local, state, and national governments. There is much that the states can and should do at this time to extend their protection of civil rights. Wherever the law enforcement measures of state and local governments are inadequate to discharge this primary function of government, these measures should be strengthened and improved.

The Federal Government has a clear duty to see that Constitutional guarantees of individual liberties and of equal protection under the laws are not denied or abridged anywhere in our Union. That duty is shared by all three branches of the Government, but it can be fulfilled only if the Congress enacts modern, comprehensive civil rights laws, adequate to the needs of the day, and demonstrating our continuing faith in the free way of life.

I recommend, therefore, that the Congress enact legislation at this session directed toward the following specific objectives:

1. Establishing a permanent Commission on Civil Rights, a Joint Congressional Committee on Civil Rights, and a Civil Rights Division in the Department of Justice.

2. Strengthening existing civil rights statutes.

3. Providing Federal protection against lynching.

4. Protecting more adequately the right to vote.

5. Establishing a Fair Employment Practice Commission to prevent unfair discrimination in employment.

6. Prohibiting discrimination in interstate transportation facilities.

7. Providing home-rule and suffrage in Presidential elections for the residents of the District of Columbia.

8. Providing Statehood for Hawaii and Alaska and a greater measure of self-government for our island possessions.

9. Equalizing the opportunities for residents of the United States to become naturalized citizens.

10. Settling the evacuation claims of Japanese-Americans.

Strengthening the Government Organization

As a first stop, we must strengthen the organization of the Federal Government in order to enforce civil rights legislation more adequately and to watch over the state of our traditional liberties.

I recommend that the Congress establish a permanent Commission on Civil Rights reporting to the President. The Commission should continuously review our civil rights policies and practices, study specified problems, and make recommendations to the President at frequent intervals. It should work with other agencies of the Federal Government, with state and local governments, and with private organizations.

I also suggest that the Congress establish a Joint Congressional Committee on Civil Rights. This Committee should make a continuing study of legislative matters relating to civil rights and should consider means of improving respect for and enforcement of those rights.

These two bodies together should keep all of us continuously aware of the condition of civil rights in the United States and keep us alert to opportunities to improve their protection.

To provide for better enforcement of Federal civil rights laws, there will be established a Division of Civil Rights in the Department of Justice. I recommend that the Congress provide for an additional Assistant Attorney General to supervise this Division.

Strengthening Existing Civil Rights Statutes

I recommend that the Congress amend and strengthen the existing provisions of Federal law which safeguard the right to vote and the right to safety and security of person and property. These provisions are the basis for our present civil rights enforcement program.

Section 51 of Title 18 of the United States Code, which now gives protection to citizens in the enjoyment of rights secured by the Constitution or Federal laws, needs to be strengthened in two respects. In its present form, this section protects persons only if they are citizens, and it affords protection only against conspiracies by two or more persons. This protection should be extended to all inhabitants of the United States, whether or not they are citizens, and should be afforded against infringement by persons acting individually as well as in conspiracy.

Section 52 of Title 18 of the United States Code, which now gives general protection to individuals against the deprivation of Federally secured rights by public officers, has proved to be inadequate in some cases because of the generality of its language. An enumeration of the principle rights protected under this section is needed to make more definite and certain the protection which the section affords.

Federal Protection Against Lynching

A specific Federal measure is needed to deal with the crime of lynching—against which I cannot speak too strongly. It is a principle of our democracy, written into our Constitution, that every person accused of an offense against the law shall have a fair, orderly trial in an impartial court. We have made great progress toward this end, but I regret to say that lynching has not yet finally disappeared from our land. So long as one person walks in fear of lynching, we shall not have achieved equal justice under law. I call upon the Congress to take decisive action against this crime.

Protecting the Right to Vote

Under the Constitution, the right of all properly qualified citizens to vote is beyond question. Yet the exercise of this right is still subject to interference. Some individuals are prevented from voting by isolated acts of intimidation. Some whole groups are prevented by outmoded policies prevailing in certain states or communities.

We need stronger statutory protection of the right to vote. I urge the Congress to enact legislation forbidding interference by public officers or private persons with the right of qualified citizens to participate in primary, special and general elections in which Federal officers are to be chosen. This legislation should extend to elections for state as well as Federal officers insofar as interference with the right to vote results from discriminatory action by public officers based on race, color, or other unreasonable classification.

Requirements for the payment of poll taxes also interfere with the right to vote. There are still seven states which, by their constitutions, place this barrier between their citizens and the ballot box. The American people would welcome voluntary action on the part of these states to remove this barrier. Nevertheless, I believe the Congress should enact measures insuring that the right to vote in elections for Federal officers shall not be contingent upon the payment of taxes.

I wish to make it clear that the enactment of the measures I have recommended will in no sense result in Federal conduct of elections. They are designed to give qualified citizens Federal protection of their right to vote. The actual conduct of elections, as always, will remain the responsibility of State governments.

Fair Employment Practice Commission

We in the United States believe that all men are entitled to equality of opportunity. Racial, religious and other invidious forms of discrimination deprive the individual of an equal chance to develop and utilize his talents and to enjoy the rewards of his efforts.

Once more I repeat my request that the Congress enact fair employment practice legislation prohibiting discrimination in employment based on race, color, religion or national origin. The legislation should create a Fair Employment

Practice Commission with authority to prevent discrimination by employers and labor unions, trade and professional associations, and government agencies and employment bureaus. The degree of effectiveness which the war-time Fair Employment Practice Committee attained shows that it is possible to equalize job opportunity by government action and thus to eliminate the influence of prejudice in employment.

Interstate Transportation

The channels of interstate commerce should be open to all Americans on a basis of complete equality. The Supreme Court has recently declared unconstitutional state laws requiring segregation on public carriers in interstate travel. Company regulations must not be allowed to replace unconstitutional state laws. I urge the Congress to prohibit discrimination and segregation, in the use of interstate transportation facilities, by both public officers and the employees of private companies.

The District of Columbia

I am in full accord with the principle of local self-government for residents of the District of Columbia. In addition, I believe that the Constitution should be amended to extend suffrage in Presidential elections to the residents of the District.

The District of Columbia should be a true symbol of American freedom and democracy for our own people, and for the people of the world. It is my earnest hope that the Congress will promptly give the citizens of the District of Columbia their own local, elective government. They themselves can then deal with the inequalities arising from segregation in the schools, and other public facilities, and from racial barriers to places of public accommodation which now exist for one-third of the District's population.

The present inequalities in essential services are primarily a problem for the District itself, but they are also of great concern to the whole Nation. Failing local corrective action in the near future, the Congress should enact a model civil rights law for the Nation's Capital.

Our Territories and Possessions

The present political status of our Territories and possessions impairs the enjoyment of civil rights by their residents. I have in the past recommended legislation granting statehood to Alaska and Hawaii, and organic acts for Guam and American Samoa including a grant of citizenship to the people of these Pacific Islands. I repeat these recommendations.

Furthermore, the residents of the Virgin Islands should be granted an increasing measure of self-government, and the people of Puerto Rico should be allowed to choose their form of government and their ultimate status with respect to the United States.

Equality in Naturalization

All properly qualified legal residents of the United States should be allowed to become citizens without regard to race, color, religion or national origin. The

Congress has recently removed the bars which formerly prevented persons from China, India and the Philippines from becoming naturalized citizens. I urge the Congress to remove the remaining racial or nationality barriers which stand in the way of citizenship for some residents of our country.

Evacuation Claims of the Japanese-Americans

During the last war more than one hundred thousand Japanese-Americans were evacuated from their homes in the Pacific states solely because of their racial origin. Many of these people suffered property and business losses as a result of this forced evacuation and through no fault of their own. The Congress has before it legislation establishing a procedure by which claims based upon these losses can be promptly considered and settled. I trust that favorable action on this legislation will soon be taken.

The legislation I have recommended for enactment by the Congress at the present session is a minimum program if the Federal Government is to fulfill its obligation of insuring the Constitutional guarantees of individual liberties and of equal protection under the law.

Under the authority of existing law, the Executive branch is taking every possible action to improve the enforcement of the civil rights statutes and to eliminate discrimination in Federal employment, in providing Federal services and facilities, and in the armed forces.

I have already referred to the establishment of the Civil Rights Division of the Department of Justice. The Federal Bureau of Investigation will work closely with this new Division in the investigation of Federal civil rights cases. Specialized training is being given to the Bureau's agents so that they may render more effective service in this difficult field of law enforcement.

It is the settled policy of the United States Government that there shall be no discrimination in Federal employment or in providing Federal services and facilities. Steady progress has been made toward this objective in recent years. I shall shortly issue an Executive Order containing a comprehensive restatement of the Federal non-discrimination policy, together with appropriate measures to ensure compliance.

During the recent war and in the years since its close we have made much progress toward equality of opportunity in our armed services without regard to race, color, religion or national origin. I have instructed the Secretary of Defense to take steps to have the remaining instances of discrimination in the armed services eliminated as rapidly as possible. The personnel policies and practices of all the services in this regard will be made consistent.

I have instructed the Secretary of the Army to investigate the status of civil rights in the Panama Canal Zone with a view to eliminating such discrimination as may exist there. If legislation is necessary, I shall make appropriate recommendations to the Congress.

The position of the United States in the world today makes it especially urgent that we adopt these measures to secure for all our people their essential rights.

The peoples of the world are faced with the choice of freedom or enslavement, a choice between a form of government which harnesses the state in the service of the individual and a form of government which chains the individual to the needs of the state.

We in the United States are working in company with other nations who share our desire for enduring world peace and who believe with us that, above all else, men must be free. We are striving to build a world family of nations—a world where men may live under governments of their own choosing and under laws of their own making.

As a part of that endeavor, the Commission on Human Rights of the United Nations is now engaged in preparing an international bill of human rights by which the nations of the world may bind themselves by international covenant to give effect to basic human rights and fundamental freedoms. We have played a leading role in this undertaking designed to create a world order of law and justice fully protective of the rights and the dignity of the individual.

To be effective in those efforts, we must protect our civil rights so that by providing all our people with the maximum enjoyment of personal freedom and personal opportunity we shall be a stronger nation—stronger in our leadership, stronger in our moral position, stronger in the deeper satisfactions of a united citizenry.

We know that our democracy is not perfect. But we do know that it offers a fuller, freer, happier life to our people than any totalitarian nation has ever offered.

If we wish to inspire the peoples of the world whose freedom is in jeopardy, if we wish to restore hope to those who have already lost their civil liberties, if we wish to fulfill the promise that is ours, we must correct the remaining imperfections in our practice of democracy.

We know the way. We need only the will.

Harry S. Truman

The President paid a high price for initiating his civil rights program and aligning himself with northern liberals in the Democratic party to fight for a strong civil rights platform at the 1948 Democratic Convention. He described this decision and its consequences in a memorable passage in his *Memoirs*.

Harry S. Truman
Reflections on his Civil Rights Program
1958

Harry S. Truman, *Memoirs* (New York, 1958) II, 180-85.

The beginning of this splinter opposition dated all the way back to December 5, 1946, when I had appointed a committee to investigate and report on the status of civil rights in America. I took this action because of the repeated anti-minority incidents immediately after the war in which homes were invaded, property was destroyed, and a number of innocent lives were taken. I wanted to get the facts behind these incidents of disregard for individual and group rights which were reported in the news with alarming regularity, and to see that the law was strengthened, if necessary, so as to offer adequate protection and fair treatment to all of our citizens.

I directed that the committee's survey should not be confined to the problem of any one minority group but should extend to all areas of racial and religious discrimination. It was a simple approach to one of the oldest problems of a democratic society, yet the leaders of "white supremacy" began at once their campaign of demagoguery to attempt to nullify my efforts to develop federal safeguards against racial discrimination. It was this movement which culminated in the bolt of part of the southern bloc in 1948 under the misleading name of States' Rights Democrats.

The Fair Employment Practices Committee had been established by an Executive Order of President Roosevelt on June 25, 1941, "to encourage full participation in the national defense program by all citizens . . . regardless of race, creed, color or national origin." The committee was continued until June 30, 1946, under the National War Agency Appropriations Act and was terminated at that time against my wishes. The FEPC had shown that, in the majority of wartime cases, discriminatory practices by employers and unions could be reduced or eliminated by simple negotiation when the work of the negotiator was backed by a firm national policy.

Nevertheless, there were many unresolved cases handled by the FEPC which indicated to me that executive authority was not enough to insure compliance in the face of organized opposition. I saw that legislative authority would be required to put an end to such un-American practices. The Committee on Civil Rights was set up to get the facts and to publicize as widely as possible the need for legislation.

In the Executive Order creating the committee, I pointed out that the nation was losing ground in civil rights and that the preservation of the liberties was the duty of every branch of government and every public official—state, federal, and local. The constitutional guarantees of individual liberties and of equal protection under the law clearly place on the federal government the duty to act when state or local authorities abridge or fail to uphold these guarantees. I felt that the federal government was hampered, however, by inadequate civil-rights statutes and that the Department of Justice lacked the tools to enforce such statutes as there were. This was a condition that I wanted to see corrected.

Speaking to the fifteen members of the Committee on Civil Rights at the White House on January 15, 1947, I said: "I want our Bill of Rights implemented in fact. We have been trying to do this for 150 years. We are making progress, but we are not making progress fast enough. This country could very easily be faced with a situation similar to the one with which it was faced in 1922." I was referring, of course, to the revival of terrorism in that year by the Ku Klux Klan.

Six months later I restated the motives of my civil-rights program in an address to the annual convention of the National Association for the Advancement of

Colored People on June 29, 1947. "As Americans," I asserted, "we believe that every man should be free to live his life as he wishes. He should be limited only by his responsibility to his fellow countrymen. If this freedom is to be more than a dream, each man must be guaranteed equality of opportunity. The only limit to an American's achievement should be his ability, his industry and his character."

In October of the same year the Civil Rights Committee delivered its report, which showed that a positive need existed for legislation to secure the rights of American minority groups. The report listed ten important recommendations, as follows:

(1) Establishing a permanent Commission on Civil Rights, a joint Congressional Committee on Civil Rights, and a Civil Rights Division in the Department of Justice. (2) Strengthening existing civil-rights statutes. (3) Providing federal protection against lynching. (4) Protecting more adequately the right to vote. (5) Establishing a Fair Employment Practices Commission to prevent unfair discrimination in employment. (6) The modification of the federal naturalization laws to permit the granting of citizenship without regard to the race, color, or national origin of applicants. (7) Providing home rule and suffrage in presidential elections of the residents of the District of Columbia. (8) Providing statehood for Hawaii and Alaska and a greater measure of self-government for our island possessions. (9) Equalizing the opportunities for residents of the United States to become naturalized citizens. (10) Settling the evacuation claims of Japanese Americans.

I asked for specific civil-rights legislation in my message to the Congress on February 2, 1948, to enact these recommendations into law. At the same time I urged the abolition of segregation and discrimination in the use of transportation facilities by both public officers and the employees of private companies throughout the country. And later I incorporated these recommendations into the 1948 platform of the Democratic party.

The platform of a political party is a promise to the public. Unless a man can run on his party's platform—and try to carry it out, if elected—he is not an honest man. All campaign oratory that is not based on principles and issues represented in a definite platform is sheer demagoguery. When a party has no principles and issues on which to stand, it invariably turns to personalities and to the use of the "big lie" technique, ignoring the only basis upon which a political campaign can be logically conducted.

I was one of those who had helped write the Democratic party platform in my own state during the 1934, 1938, and 1942 campaigns and the national platform in 1936, 1940, and 1944. I believed in the principles these platforms advanced, and when I was elected President, I tried to carry out the platform promises that had been made. The basic principle in all of those platforms was the benefit of the average man who has no pull in Washington. To me, party platforms are contracts with the people, and I always looked upon them as agreements that had to be carried out. That is why I was perfectly willing to risk defeat in 1948 by sticking to the civil-rights plank in my platform.

There were people around me, of course, who were anxious to prevent any sort of split in the Democratic party, and efforts were made to soften the approach to the civil-rights issue. I would not stand for any double talk on this vital principle, however, and insisted on plain language being used. Members of the Cabinet and others warned me that I was riding to a defeat if I stuck to my FEPC orders and if I did not let up on the battle for civil-rights legislation. But I wanted to win the fight by standing on my platform, or lose it the same way.

I was reasonably sure, far in advance of the convention, that there would be a splintering off of the South or at least a portion of it. The attitude which had been taken by Southerners toward the policy of integration in the armed forces was well known. Practically all of the training camps in World War II were located in the South because of climate conditions, and the idea of integration, therefore, encountered strong resistance. The Southerners were especially bothered by integration among construction workers, who were employed without discrimination as to race for the purpose of building the government's training camps, and they were not happy over the orders on fair employment. I expected trouble, and it developed promptly at the 1948 convention.

The military establishment—particularly the Navy—had been strongly opposed to my policy of integration in the armed services, but I had forced it into practice. Then they discovered that no difficulty resulted from integration after all. Integration is the best way to create an effective combat organization in which the men will stand together and fight. Experience on the front has proved that the morale of troops is strengthened where Jim Crow practices are not imposed.

I felt also that any other course would be inconsistent with international commitments and obligations. We could not endorse a color line at home and still expect to influence the immense masses that make up the Asian and African peoples. It was necessary to practice what we preached, and I tried to see that we did it.

Every Democratic platform since 1932 has stressed the devotion of our party to the constitutional ideal of civil rights. But what aroused many Southerners now was that I meant to put this pledge into practice. When the Southerners saw in 1948 that I meant to put it into effect, they bolted the party. When J. Strom Thurmond, the governor of South Carolina, who headed the revolt, made his dramatic departure from the convention floor in Philadelphia with his followers, he was asked by a reporter to clarify his position.

"President Truman is only following the platform that Roosevelt advocated," the reporter pointed out.

"I agree," Thurmond replied, "but Truman really *means* it."

Despite the clarity with which the Civil Rights Committee had expressed its findings and recommendations, and the wide publicity which I had encouraged on the subject, the program which I insisted be included in the platform was shamefully distorted and misrepresented by political demagogues and press propaganda. My appeal for equal economic and political rights for every American citizen had nothing at all to do with the personal or social relationships of individuals or the right of every person to choose his own associates. The basic constitutional privilege which I advocated was deliberately misconstrued to include or imply racial miscegenation and intermarriage. My only goal was equal opportunity and security under the law for all classes of Americans.

The States' Rights Democrats claimed that this was not a bolt from the Democratic party. They said they represented the true Democrats of the Southland. It was a bolt. It also was a manifestation of prejudice. I had seen at first hand a similar reaction in 1928, when Al Smith ran for the Presidency on the Democratic ticket. I was very active in Jackson County politics at that time and did everything I could to carry the county for him. Still, because of anti-Catholic prejudice, our traditionally Democratic county voted Smith down by thirty thousand votes. Because of the success of that prejudice the belief was then stated that no Catholic, Jew, or Negro could ever hold high public office again. That was twenty-five years ago, and the prejudice has now become much less apparent, although it has yet to be overcome. Hitler's persecution of the Jews did much to awaken Americans to the dangerous extremes to which prejudice can be carried if allowed to control government actions.

I never did believe that the great mass of Southerners had the same viewpoint as the minority Dixiecrat contingent. I was raised amidst some violently prejudiced Southerners myself, and I believe the vast majority of good Southerners understand that the blind prejudices of past generations cannot continue in a free republic. Much progress in civil rights has been made voluntarily by the South itself, and it was to help and to speed this progress that my program was designed. It was because they understood this that the reasoning people of the eleven states that had once formed the Confederacy did not withdraw from the Democratic convention and join with the splinter party.

I did not discount the handicap which the loss of a "Solid South" presented as far as my chances of winning the election were concerned. I knew that it might mean the difference between victory and defeat in November. I knew, too, that if I deserted the civil-liberties plank of the Democratic party platform I could heal the breach, but I have never traded principles for votes, and I did not intend to start the practice in 1948 regardless of how it might affect the election.

I was confident that the voters would see that the Dixiecrats were trying in vain to build a platform on an issue that was not a reality but a fiction. With this confidence—which few of those around me seemed to share—I was willing to take the risk imposed on my chances of being elected President in my own right.

Although many candidates for the presidency have had to cope with splits within their parties, the situation which I faced in 1948 was without a comparable precedent in the history of American politics. I was confronted not with one major defection in the Democratic party but with two bolts of sizable proportions. In addition to the faction which was preparing to withdraw its support from me and to pick an alternate candidate on the platform of States' Rights Democrats, there were the so-called Progressives under the leadership of another Democrat, Henry Wallace.

Under President Roosevelt, Wallace had served as one of the best Secretaries of Agriculture this country ever had, and he enjoyed considerable personal prestige as Vice-President during Roosevelt's third term. He was not an opponent to be discounted, and it was predicted that he would get a large vote.

After I became President I found it necessary to part with Henry Wallace when I found him interfering with my conduct of foreign policy. I felt then that he cherished an idealistic notion that he would be able to stir up a following in the country that could elect him President. The creation of the Progressive party in 1948 was an attempt on the part of Wallace and his supporters to materialize that aspiration.

Some honest and well-meaning agitators for peace with Russia at any price found in Wallace a spokesman for their point of view. He had consistently maintained that I was too rough in dealing with the Soviets and that peace could be obtained if we were more conciliatory in our approach. He had made many trips for Roosevelt—to China, South America, and Russia, including Siberia—and these activities had given him a world prominence and contributed to the development of a considerable and enthusiastic following for him.

There was, however, a sinister aspect to the Wallace movement. It provided a front for the Communists to infiltrate the political life of the nation and spread confusion. Without the conscious knowledge of many members of the new Progressive party, the Reds were working swiftly and skillfully to gain control of the nominating convention and to dominate party committees and the platform.

Wallace himself, who seemed to have been transformed into a mystic with a zeal that verged on fanaticism, was apparently unaware of the purposes to which the Communists were putting his "progressive" movement. I always felt that he was an honest man and a faithful public servant but that he simply did not understand what was happening.

I knew from personal experience with the Russians that Wallace's dream of appeasement was futile and that, if allowed to materialize, it would be tragic. I had learned that the Russians understood only force. Wallace did not think this was true, but he did not have the experience with the Soviets that had been mine.

I realized that the Progressives would cost me votes, but, like the Dixiecrats, they stood for principles which I knew I must reject.

My nomination for the presidency by the Democratic party in 1948 was also challenged by a third movement within the ranks. This threatened to develop at any time during the spring into a full-fledged boom for General Dwight D. Eisenhower.

Among the chief agitators who claimed that I was not perpetuating the New Deal policies of President Roosevelt were the late President's sons, James and Elliott, former Cabinet members James F. Byrnes and Harold Ickes, and Senator Claude Pepper of Florida. There were many others who felt that because the press and the polls made it appear that my chances of success in the campaign were falling away to almost nothing someone else should get the Democratic party nomination.

Truman did not exaggerate the bitterness which was stirred up, reflected not only by the states' rightists who walked out of the convention, but also among many of the regulars who remained in the party. Lyndon Johnson, who was running "scared" for the Senate in 1948, denounced the program in no uncertain terms:

> My feelings are well known in my district and in Washington. And Harry
> Truman knows I am against him on this program. I just don't think

Congress should try to cram his program down the throats of Southern states. . . .[39]

He called the program

a farce and a sham—an effort to set up a police state in the guise of liberty. . . . I am opposed to the anti-lynching bill because the federal government has no more business enacting a law against one kind of murder than another. I am against the FEPC [Fair Employment Practices Commission] because if a man can tell you whom you must hire, he can tell you whom you cannot employ.[40]

That was the straight southern Democratic line against Truman's civil rights program in 1948, and it was echoed by the man who would eventually lead the Democratic party in enacting an even more liberal program in the 1950s and 1960s. Lyndon Johnson learned well and he grew in his considerations of this issue as the country also began to move. But before any of this that took place, Harry Truman took a stand, long before the country was ready for it, and at a high personal cost to himself as well.

Of course, it is true that Truman was also pressured from the Left by Henry Wallace and his Progressive party, but Truman took his initial steps before Wallace's party was formed. He may well have picked up more electoral votes in the North than those he lost in the South because of his strong stand on civil rights, but that is one of the ironies of politics. Truman was not a full-fledged advocate of integration. He drew the line on social "mixing" of the races, and he was not at all adept at or even enthusiastic about pushing his legislative program once announced, but in 1946 and 1948 when it was a difficult thing to do, he stood up to be counted for a broader civil rights program than had been proposed by any previous President in American history. Americans still had a long and tempestuous road ahead in resolving this question, which threatened at times to rip the country apart; but it should be noted, with full recognition of the ambivalence and qualifications involved, that as President, Harry Truman set the nation's course back in the right direction after a century of neglect and drift.

President Eisenhower Equivocates
And a Constitutional Crisis
Develops in Little Rock

On May 20, 1954, three days after the Supreme Court's historic school desegregation decision (Brown v. Board of Education of Topeka), the six-member School Board of Little Rock, Arkansas, issued a statement indicating that they would comply with the Court's ruling. The following year a plan for integrating the city's schools was approved. The timetable outlined in the plan called for the integration of the high schools in 1957, the junior high schools in the following two or three years and the elementary schools by 1963. The school board's integration plan was challenged as not being rapid enough by the parents of 33 Black children in the winter of 1956. They were represented by counsel from the National Association for the Advancement of Colored People, and filed suit against the school board in the federal district court in Little Rock. The school board's plan was upheld, first in the district court, and then, on appeal in the United States Court of Appeals. The suit was then dropped.

Little Rock appeared to be preparing for the desegregation of its schools in a calm and deliberate fashion. Superintendent of Schools Virgil T. Blossom conducted a campaign of appearances before over 150 different community groups, urging acceptance of the plan on the grounds that the law required it and that it would "provide as little integration for as long as possible." General community acceptance seemed evident when two members of the school board (elected on a staggered system) won an election over two avowed segregationists by an almost 2-to-1 margin.

But Little Rock is part of a state, as well as being a city in its own right, and the question of integrating the city's schools began to concern the state government. In the November election of 1956, 44 percent of the state's voters endorsed a resolution calling for an amendment to the United States Constitution prohibiting the federal government from exercising any control over the public schools in the country, and they also voted for an amendment to the state constitution requiring the Arkansas legislature to oppose the Supreme Court's decision by every constitutional means. The balloting in Little Rock for these two measures was three times as heavy as in the school board election, but the results that time were equally divided. The state legislature quickly complied with the resolution, passing a handful of laws, one of which made it illegal to require any child to enroll in or attend any school in which both white and Black children were registered.

Segregationist activity in Little Rock built up as the deadline for integrating the high schools approached. The city was visited and its segregationist elements were harangued against by the die-hard governor of Georgia and his ally, the leader of the Georgia White Citizen's Council. A group of Little Rock mothers petitioned Arkansas Governor Orval Faubus "to prevent forcible integration of the Little Rock schools as now planned by the School Board." Meanwhile, registration and careful screening by the superintendent and principals of the high schools had eliminated most of the Black children who had applied for transfer to the all-white school, and left only nine "eligibles," all of whom were near the top of their class at the all-Black high school.

On August 29 the newly formed mothers' group entered a suit against the Little Rock School Board in the state chancery court, seeking to prevent the integration plan from going into effect. The grounds for the injunction were that the school board plan was in violation of the new state law. The court granted the order preventing the integration plan from going into effect. The judge, placing great weight on the testimony of Governor Faubus and others, decided that "through certain events over which the School Board has no control public sentiment has undergone a swift change and that a probability of violence and civil commotion exists."[41] Governor Faubus testified that he personally knew that revolvers had been taken from Black and white students, but he never revealed the source of his information.[42]

Attorneys for the school board then quickly filed a motion before Federal Judge Davies in the district court requesting that he rule the chancery court injunction invalid. This he promptly did, citing their lack of jurisdiction in the case and following it up by enjoining all persons "from interfering with and preventing the opening of integrated high schools on September 3, 1957."

It was at that point that the governor went into action. Without any request from the Little Rock School Board, its superintendent, the mayor of the city, or even the chief of police, and without consulting any of those officials, Governor Faubus called out the state militia and surrounded Central High School on Monday evening, September 2, 1957. In the proclamation authorizing the action, he explained that "it has been made known to me, as Governor, from many sources, that there is imminent danger of tumult, riot, and breach of the peace and the doing of violence to persons and property in Pulaski County [Little Rock], Arkansas."[43]

An hour later he went on television to explain his reasons for calling out the troops. He said that a telephone campaign was underway to mobilize the mothers of the white children at Central High the following morning, that there were indications that automobile caravans from outside the city were due to arrive at the same time, that the sale of weapons had increased in the past few days, and that revolvers had been taken from both Black and white youngsters. He continued:

> This is a decision I have reached prayerfully. It has been made after conferences with dozens of people and after the checking and the verification of as many of the reports as possible.
>
> The mission of the State Militia is to maintain or restore order and to protect the lives and property of citizens. They will act not as segregationists or integrationists, but as soldiers called to active duty to carry out their assigned tasks.
>
> But I must state here in all sincerity, that it is my opinion—yes, even a conviction, that it will not be possible to restore or to maintain order and protect the lives and property of the citizens if forcible integration is carried out tomorrow in the schools of this community. The inevitable conclusion, therefore, must be that the schools in Pulaski County, for the time being, must be operated on the same basis as they have been operated in the past.[44]

The mayor of the city contradicted this report vehemently:

> The Governor has called out the National Guard to put down trouble where none existed. He did so without a request from those of us who are directly responsible for preservation of peace and order. The only effect is to create tension where none existed. I call the Governor's attention to the fact that after almost a week of sensational developments brought about by his own actions, the Little Rock police have not had a single case of interracial violence. This is clear evidence that the Governor's excuse for calling out the Guard is simply a hoax.[45]

Mrs. Daisy Bates, president of the Arkansas State Conference of Branches of the National Association for the Advancement of Colored People (NAACP), who was counseling the nine black students, later described the speech as contributing "to the mass hysteria that was to grip the city of Little Rock for several months."[46]

The school board returned to the federal judge for instructions, and after a ten-minute hearing Judge Davies reaffirmed his earlier opinion to integrate on schedule. The mayor indicated that he thought it would be illegal to attempt to bring the Black students through the National Guard without a federal escort; on the first day, September 3, 1957, the Black students made no attempt to enter Central High School.

That afternoon the attention of the country, and a good part of the world, which was watching the Little Rock drama intently, turned to the presidential press conference in Washington for some indication of what the President intended to do in the face of this violation of a federal court injunction. The President was not very helpful:

> My speaking will be always in this subject, as I have always done, urging Americans to recognize what America is, the concepts on which it is based, and to do their part so far as they possibly can to bring out the kind of America that was visualized by our forebears. . . .
>
> Now it is for this reason, because I know this is a slow process, the Supreme Court in its decision of 1954 pointed out that emotional difficulties that would be encountered by a Negro, even if given—or by Negroes if given—equal but separate schools, and I think, probably their reasoning was correct, at least I have no quarrel with it.
>
> But there are very strong emotions on the other side, people that see a picture of mongrelization of the race, they call it. They are very strong emotions, and we are going to whip this thing in the long run by Americans being true to themselves and not merely by law.[47]

This was not the first unclear statement that President Eisenhower had made on this question since the Supreme Court decision of 1954. In a later account of his years in the White House, he explained his failure to speak up in favor of the decision during his two terms in office:

> After the Supreme Court's 1954 ruling, I refused to say whether I either approved or disapproved of it. The Court's judgment was law, I said, and I would abide by it. This determination was one of principle. I believed that if I should express, publicly, either approval or disapproval of a Supreme Court decision in one case, I would be obliged to do so in many, if not all, cases. Inevitably I would eventually be drawn into a public statement of disagreement with some decision, creating a suspicion that my vigor of enforcement would, in such cases, be in doubt. Moreover, to indulge in a practice of approving or criticizing Court decisions, could tend to lower the dignity of government, and would, in the long run, be hurtful. In this case I definitely agreed with the unanimous decision.[48]

Despite the reasonable tone of this defense written almost ten years later, it was not always clear to those around the President at the time that these were his views. His assistant and speechwriter for several years, Emmett John Hughes, records a quite different private attitude. Before delivering his first campaign speech in 1956, President Eisenhower told Hughes:

> I am convinced that the Supreme Court decision *set back* progress in the South *at least fifteen years.* . . . It's all very well to talk about school integration—if you remember, you may be also talking about social *dis*integration. Feelings are deep on this, especially where children are involved. . . . We can't demand *perfection* in these moral questions. All we can do is to keep working toward a goal and keep it high. And the fellow who tries to tell me that you can do these things by *force* is just plain *nuts.*[49]

Three years had elapsed since the Supreme Court had decided the *Brown* case, yet during this period of executive impotence and indifference in implementing its clear directives, the President had allowed the forces hostile to the decision to gain valuable time to organize their resistance to it throughout the South. White citizens' councils had organized in every southern state, and hearing of the Little Rock crisis they flocked to rally in the climate of hatred, advocating "bloodshed if necessary" to keep the Black children out of the white schools.[50] Time is always an important factor in such complex federal-state confrontations, and President Eisenhower's failure to speak out in support of the Supreme Court's decision, and to act to implement it was extremely costly to the achievement of equal rights and the maintenance of community peace and order.

Harry Golden has pointed out that immediately following the *Brown* decision, a number of southern and border-state governors spoke out courageously in favor of compliance with the law. The governor of Arkansas at that time, Francis Cherry, was among them. He stated unequivocally that "Arkansas will obey the law."[51] He was strongly supported by the governors of Kentucky, Tennessee, Oklahoma and Maryland. Even the governor of Virginia promised in the beginning that he would call a meeting of all local and state officials to "work toward a plan which shall be acceptable to our citizens and in keeping with the edict of the court."[52] But there was no signal and definitely no public support for these moves from the conspicuously quiet White House, and in the social and political vacuum into which the decision dropped, the extremists rapidly took over.

Back in Little Rock Mrs. Bates readied plans for the children's first day at the high school. The presence of the troops appeared only to have attracted a larger and more bitter mob of segregationists, but the children were eager to attempt to enter the school in spite of those obstacles and they called upon local white and Black ministers to accompany them. While the details of their approach to the school were being arranged, one of the children, Elizabeth Eckford, who had not been informed of any change of plans or where the children and the ministers had arranged to meet, went on alone and walked the gauntlet bravely all by herself. Her description of what she encountered exposes one of the most disgraceful chapters in American history, but unfortunately it was the kind of occurrence which has happened and will continue to happen time and time again before the racial crisis is over.

You remember the day before we were to go in, we met Superintendent Blossom at the school board office. He told us what the mob might say and do but he never told us we wouldn't have any protection. He told our parents not to come because he wouldn't be able to protect the children if they did.

That night I was so excited I couldn't sleep. The next morning I was about the first one up. While I was pressing my black and white dress—I had made it to wear on the first day of school—my little brother turned on the TV set. They started telling about a large crowd gathered at the school. The man on TV said he wondered if we were going to show up that morning. Mother called from the kitchen, where she was fixing breakfast, "Turn that TV off!" She was so upset and worried. I wanted to comfort her, so I said, "Mother, don't worry."

Dad was walking back and forth, from room to room, with a sad expression. He was chewing on his pipe and he had a cigar in his hand, but he didn't light either one. It would have been funny, only he was so nervous.

Before I left home Mother called us into the living-room. She said we should have a word of prayer. Then I caught the bus and got off a block from the school. I saw a large crowd of people standing across the street from the soldiers guarding Central. As I walked on, the crowd suddenly got very quiet. Superintendent Blossom had told us to enter by the front door. I looked at all the people and thought, "Maybe I will be safer if I walk down the block to the front entrance behind the guards."

At the corner I tried to pass through the long line of guards around the school so as to enter the grounds behind them. One of the guards pointed across the street. So I pointed in the same direction and asked whether he meant for me to cross the street and walk down. He nodded "yes." So, I walked across the street conscious of the crowd that stood there, but they moved away from me.

For the moment all I could hear was the shuffling of their feet. Then someone shouted, "Here she comes, get ready!" I moved away from the crowd on the sidewalk and into the street. If the mob came at me I could then cross back over so the guards could protect me.

The crowd moved in closer and then began to follow me, calling me names. I still wasn't afraid. Just a little bit nervous. Then my knees started to shake all of a sudden and I wondered whether I could make it to the center entrance a block away. It was the longest block I ever walked in my whole life.

Even so, I still wasn't too scared because all the time I kept thinking that the guards would protect me.

When I got right in front of the school, I went up to a guard again. But this time he just looked straight ahead and didn't move to let me pass him. I didn't know what to do. Then I looked and saw that the path leading to the front entrance was a little further ahead. So I walked until I was right in front of the path to the front door.

I stood looking at the school—it looked so big! Just then the guards let some white students go through.

The crowd was quiet. I guess they were waiting to see what was going to happen. When I was able to steady my knees, I walked up to the guard who had let the white students in. He too didn't move. When I tried to squeeze past him, he raised his bayonet and then the other guards closed in and they raised their bayonets.

They glared at me with a mean look and I was very frightened and didn't know what to do. I turned around and the crowd came toward me.

They moved closer and closer. Somebody started yelling, "Lynch her! Lynch her!"

I tried to see a friendly face somewhere in the mob—someone who maybe would help. I looked into the face of an old woman and it seemed a kind face, but when I looked at her again, she spat on me.

They came closer, shouting, "No nigger bitch is going to get in our school. Get out of here!"

I turned back to the guards but their faces told me I wouldn't get help from them. Then I looked down the block and saw a bench at the bus stop. I thought, "If I can only get there I will be safe." I don't know why the bench seemed a safe place to me, but I started walking toward it. I tried to close my mind to what they were shouting, and kept saying to myself, "If I can only make it to the bench I will be safe."

When I finally got there, I don't think I could have gone another step. I sat down and the mob crowded up and began shouting all over again. Someone hollered, "Drag her over to this tree! Let's take care of the nigger." Just then a white man sat down beside me, put his arm around me and patted my shoulder. He raised my chin and said, "Don't let them see you cry."

Then a white lady—she was very nice—she came over to me on the bench. She spoke to me but I don't remember now what she said. She put me on the bus and sat next to me. She asked me my name and tried to talk to me but I don't think I answered. I can't remember much about the bus ride but the next thing I remembered I was standing in front of the School for the Blind, where Mother works.

I thought, "Maybe she isn't here. But she has to be here!" So I ran upstairs, and I think some teachers tried to talk to me, but I kept running until I reached Mother's classroom.

Mother was standing at the window with her head bowed, but she must have sensed I was there because she turned around. She looked as if she had been crying, and I wanted to tell her I was all right. But I couldn't speak. She put her arms around me and I cried.[53]

The other eight children also attempted to enter the school accompanied by four clergymen, but they were also refused and finally returned to their homes. Meanwhile, Governor Faubus attempted to explain and justify his decision to call out the National Guard to the President of the United States. The President responded quickly, reminding the governor that he would act according to his constitutional duties.

President Dwight D. Eisenhower
Reply to Governor Orval Faubus' Telegram
September 5, 1957

Southern School News, October 1957, 2.

Your telegram received, requesting my assurance of, understanding of, and cooperation in the course of action you have taken on school integration recommended by the Little Rock School Board and ordered by the United States District Court pursuant to the mandate of the United States Supreme Court.

When I became President, I took an oath to support and defend the Constitution of the United States. The only assurance I can give you is that the federal Constitution will be upheld by me by every legal means at my command.

There is no basis of fact to the statements you make in your telegram that federal authorities have been considering taking you into custody or that telephone lines to your executive mansion have been tapped by any agency of the federal government.

At the request of Judge Davies, the Department of Justice is presently collecting facts as to interference with or failure to comply with the district's court order. You and other state officials—as well as the National Guard which is, of course, uniformed, armed and partially sustained by the government   will, I am sure, give full cooperation to the United States District Court.

The next day Governor Faubus replied to the President's telegram, blandly ignoring the implications of the President's message:

Thank you for your telegram in reply to my appeal for your understanding and cooperation in connection with my efforts to preserve the public peace and good order in this community. I have notified the United States District Attorney and the FBI that my personal counsel, William J. Smith, and the director of Arkansas State Police, Herman Lindsey, are available to discuss certain evidence upon which I acted to preserve the public peace. I shall cooperate in upholding the Constitution of Arkansas and the nation.[54]

At the end of the week the Black children were still not in school, and more legal steps were underway. The school board petitioned Judge Davies for a delay in his integration order, and the NAACP attorneys replied by quoting the language of Brown v. Board of Education of Topeka: "the vitality of these constitutional principles cannot be allowed to yield simply because of disagreement with them." Over the weekend the governor was supported by a statement signed by eight of the ten Little Rock aldermen, who more than counterbalanced Mayor Mann, who was to leave office in November. The aldermen said that they were aware

> that there was, and still exists, racial tension between our people because of the United States Supreme Court's decision concerning our schools. We believe that Gov. Faubus took the proper course in calling out the Arkansas National Guard in this crisis to protect the lives and property of all our people.[55]

The following week the federal government was requested to enter the case as a friend of the court (*amicus curiae*) by Judge Davies after he had read a 400-page report on conditions in Little Rock, placed in his hands by the attorney general of the United States. He also directed the government to file a petition for a restraining order against the governor and the commanders of the National Guard units on duty at the school, preventing them from interfering with the execution of the integration order. The hearing on this petition was set for September 20, 1957.

The next weekend intermediaries brought Governor Faubus and President Eisenhower together at the President's summer White House in Newport, Rhode Island, in the hope that face-to-face contact between the two would result in a settlement of the conflict. Congressman Brooks Hays, a liberal who represented the Little Rock district, and Sherman Adams, assistant to the President, initiated the idea of the meeting and made the arrangements. Attorney General Herbert Brownell told the President that he doubted the value of a meeting with the governor, but Congressman Hays argued "that Faubus was not essentially a segregationist, that his son attended an integrated college" and that the governor believed that desegregation should be introduced first in the primary grades in grammar school.[56]

President Eisenhower finally decided to see the governor after Faubus agreed to request the meeting, assuring the President that he was willing to comply with the federal court order. Eisenhower later claimed that subtle changes in the wording of the request for an interview were made by Faubus after agreement had been reached on the text. Faubus had originally agreed to state:

> It is certainly my intention to comply with the order . . . by the District Court.

The actual message that the President received read:

> It is certainly my intention to comply with the order . . . *consistent with my responsibilities under the Constitution of the United States and that of Arkansas.*[57]

But the meeting was already set by that time, so the President went through with it. The two men talked privately for fifteen minutes, and for another two hours with their advisors present.

Most of the time of the meeting was taken up by both Eisenhower and Faubus' attempts to explain the background of their positions to each other. Faubus wanted to convince the President that he was not an out-and-out segregationist and that if everyone demonstrated sufficient patience the problem could be solved. The governor was playing for time, while the President realized there could be no interminable delays. It could mean an open invitation to defiance all over the South. Faubus protested that he was a loyal citizen, who recognized the supremacy of the federal courts. He told the President he would withdraw the National Guard, if necessary, but Eisenhower, sharp and to the point—for once—told him not to withdraw them but to give them different orders:

> [T]he Guard should continue to preserve order but allow the Negro children to attend Central High School.[58]

The meeting was inconclusive. Both the President and the governor were at least partially convinced that each had gotten the other to understand his point of view. But there was no agreement about precisely what would happen in Little Rock. Apparently Eisenhower thought that Faubus would abide by the court's orders and cooperate in seeing that they were carried out peacefully, while Faubus thought that the President had understood his plight, and would instruct the Department of Justice to cooperate by delaying any final decision. Both were wrong, and events within the next few days proved as much.

Eisenhower Finally Acts

The Department of Justice under the resolute leadership of Attorney General Herbert Brownell moved steadfastly ahead and gave no indication that it would delay the legal maneuvers. Faubus, on the other hand, convinced that the President was pushing him into a corner, did nothing to prevent, and in fact in some ways continued to encourage, the onrushing debacle. Judge Davies issued the injunction restraining the governor and the state units of the National Guard that were involved (and anyone under their orders) from interfering with the integration of Central High. Attorneys for the governor and the guard excused themselves from the federal court before the judgment was rendered, denying the right of the court to question the judgment of the chief executive of the state when he was acting in pursuit of his constitutional duties. Three hours later the units of the guard were withdrawn from the vicinity of Central High School.

The subsequent events are quite familiar. The following Monday morning the largest crowd yet gathered around Central High in an angry mood. While waiting for the Black students to appear, some members of the crowd caught sight of four Black newspaper reporters, chased them and pummeled them severely as they tried to escape. While this was going on and attracting the attention of the main body of the crowd in front of the school, the students succeeded in quietly entering the side door under the protection of the local police force, which was out in full strength. Some white students promptly walked out of the school, and the crowd continued to agitate outside for the rest of the morning. It was estimated by a rather heroic chief of police that the situation was terribly close to getting out of hand. In order to prevent any further violence the Black students were sent home around midday; in the afternoon President Eisenhower, describing the morning's events as disgraceful, issued the following proclamation to the citizens of Little Rock.

President Dwight D. Eisenhower
Proclamation to the Citizens of Little Rock
to Cease from Obstructing Enforcement of
A Federal Court Order
September 23, 1957

Proclamation No. 3203, 22 Federal Register 7573.

Whereas certain persons in the State of Arkansas, individually and in unlawful assemblages, combinations, and conspiracies, have wilfully obstructed the enforcement of orders of the United States District Court for the Eastern District of Arkansas with respect to matters relating to enrollment and attendance at public schools, particularly at Central High School, located in Little Rock School District, Little Rock, Arkansas; and

Whereas such wilful obstruction of justice hinders the execution of the laws of that State and of the United States, and makes it impracticable to enforce such laws by the ordinary course of judicial proceedings; and

Whereas such obstruction of justice constitutes a denial of the equal protection of the laws secured by the Constitution of the United States and impedes the course of justice under those laws:

Now, therefore, I, Dwight D. Eisenhower, President of the United States, under and by virtue of the authority vested in me by the Constitution and statutes of the United States, including Chapter 15 of Title 10 of the United States Code, particularly sections 332, 333 and 334 thereof, do command all persons engaged in such obstruction of justice to cease and desist therefrom, and to disperse forthwith.

In witness whereof, I have hereunto set my hand and caused the Seal of the United States of America to be affixed.

Done at the City of Newport, Rhode Island this twenty-third day of September in the year of our Lord Nineteen hundred and fifty-seven and of the Independence of the United States of America the one hundred and eighty-second.

Dwight D. Eisenhower

By the President:
John Foster Dulles, *Secretary of State*

The following morning Little Rock Mayor Woodrow Wilson Mann was in frequent contact with the White House, reporting on the reaction of the mob to the President's proclamation. Almost as large a crowd returned the second day, and although no actual rioting had broken out and it had been clearly announced that the Black students would not attempt to enter the school that day, the crowd refused to disperse, ignored the President's proclamation and continued to press police lines around the school. In the middle of the morning the President decided to take the final step; he issued Executive Order 10730, "Providing Assistance for the Removal of an Obstruction to Justice Within the State of Arkansas," under the same statute used by Washington in the Whiskey Rebellion, although amended and considerably strengthened since then.

President Dwight D. Eisenhower
Executive Order Authorizing the Use of
Military Forces to Enforce the Court Order
September 24, 1957

Executive Order No. 10730, 22 Federal Register 7628.

Whereas on September 23, 1957, I issued Proclamation No. 3204 reading in part as follows:

"Whereas certain persons in the State of Arkansas, individually and in unlawful assemblages, combinations, and conspiracies, have willfully obstructed the enforcement of orders of the United States District Court for the Eastern District of Arkansas with respect to matters relating to enrollment and attendance at public schools, particularly at Central High School, located in Little Rock School District, Little Rock, Arkansas; and

"Whereas such wilful obstruction of justice hinders the execution of the laws of that State and of the United States, and makes it impracticable to enforce such laws by the ordinary course of judicial proceedings; and

"Whereas such obstruction of justice constitutes a denial of the equal protection of the laws secured by the Constitution of the United States and impedes the course of justice under those laws:

"Now, therefore, I, Dwight D. Eisenhower, President of the United States, under and by virtue of the authority vested in me by the Constitution and Statutes of the United States, including Chapter 15 of Title 10 of the United States Code, particularly sections 332, 333 and 334 thereof, do command all persons engaged in such obstruction of justice to cease and desist therefrom, and to disperse forthwith;" and

Whereas the command contained in that Proclamation has not been obeyed and wilful obstruction of enforcement of said court orders still exists and threatens to continue:

Now, therefore, by virtue of the authority vested in me by the Constitution and Statutes of the United States, including Chapter 15 of Title 10, particularly sections 332, 333 and 334 thereof, and section 301 of Title 3 of the United States Code, it is hereby ordered as follows:

Section 1. I hereby authorize and direct the Secretary of Defense to order into the active military service of the United States as he may deem appropriate to carry out the purposes of this Order, any or all of the units of the National Guard of the United States and of the Air National Guard of the United States within the State of

Arkansas to serve in the active military service of the United States for an indefinite period and until relieved by appropriate orders.

Sec. 2. The Secretary of Defense is authorized and directed to take all appropriate steps to enforce any orders of the United States District Court for the Eastern District of Arkansas for the removal of obstruction of justice in the State of Arkansas with respect to matters relating to enrollment and attendance at public schools in the Little Rock School District, Little Rock, Arkansas. In carrying out the provisions of this section, the Secretary of Defense is authorized to use the units, and members thereof, ordered into the active military service of the United States pursuant to Section 1 of this Order.

Sec. 3. In furtherance of the enforcement of the aforementioned orders of the United States District Court for the Eastern District of Arkansas, the Secretary of Defense is authorized to use such of the armed forces of the United States as he may deem necessary.

Sec. 4. The Secretary of Defense is authorized to delegate to the Secretary of the Army or the Secretary of the Air Force, or both, any of the authority conferred upon him by this Order.

Dwight D. Eisenhower

In his proclamation and later in the executive order addressed to certain persons in the state of Arkansas, President Eisenhower referred to "unlawful assemblages, combinations, and conspiracies" which "wilfully obstructed the enforcement of orders of the United States District Court for the Eastern District of Arkansas." He charged that "such obstruction of justice constituted a denial of the equal protection of the laws secured by the Constitution of the United States and impeded the course of justice under those laws." This was an enlargement of the view taken by Washington, Jefferson, Jackson, and even Cleveland, for it introduced the concept of "equal protection of the laws" to all citizens, in addition to the enforcement of a federal law or court order.

The President cited the Constitution of the United States and Chapter 15 of Title 10, particularly sections 332, 333, and 334 thereof, and section 301 of Title 3 of the *United States Code* as the legal basis for his executive order. Section 332 is based upon the laws of 1795 and 1807, and another revision in 1861, which only amounted to a minor change in language, but strengthened the statute somewhat. But Section 333 is based upon one of the civil rights laws of 1871 (April 20, 1871, Chapter 22-3, Statute 14). This law made it a crime not only to conspire to obstruct the law, or to overthrow the government of the United States, but also for any person

> under color of any law, statute, ordinance, regulation, custom, or cause to be subjected, any person within the jurisdiction of the United States to the deprivation of any rights, privileges, or immunities secured by the Constitution of the United States.[59]

Furthermore, the 1871 statute went on to stipulate that the President's responsibilities required him to act if "the constituted authorities of such State shall either be unable to protect, or shall, from any cause, fail in or refuse protection of the people in such rights."[60]

That statute had not been brought to bear upon a civil rights disorder up to that time, but it would be cited as precedent by Eisenhower's successors from that point on. It is also noteworthy that the Eisenhower proclamation and subsequent executive order, in emphasizing the denial of "equal protection of the law" to Blacks in the situation, made a significant advance in the implementation of the protection of constitutional rights to all citizens. The law cited by the President constituted a strong affirmation of the Chief Executive's obligation to protect principles long since forgotten and rights long since ignored, particularly in the South. The section of the *United States Code* which the President cited was revised in 1956, incorporating new provisions without objections from the southern states.

Revised *United States Code*
Responsibilities of the President
In Dealing with an Insurrection
1956

United States Code, 1958 Edition, II, Title 10, Chapter 15, 972-73.

CHAPTER 15
INSURRECTION

Sec.
331. Federal aid for State governments.
332. Use of militia and armed forces to enforce Federal authority.
333. Interference with State and Federal law.
334. Proclamation to disperse.

Sec. 331. Federal aid for State governments
Whenever there is an insurrection in any State against its government, the President, may, upon the request of its legislature or of its governor if the legislature cannot be convened, call into Federal service such of the militia of the other States, in the number requested by that State, and use such of the armed forces, as he considers necessary to suppress the insurrection. (August 10, 1956, ch. 1041, 70A Stat. 15.)

Historical and Revision Notes

Revised section	Source (U.S. Code)	Source (Statutes at Large)
331	50:201.	R. S. 5297.

The words "armed forces" are substituted for the words "land or naval forces of the United States". The word "governor" is substituted for the word "executive". The word "may" is substituted for the words "It shall be lawful . . . to". The words "into Federal service" are substituted for the word "forth" for uniformity and clarity.

Cross References

Army National Guard in Federal service, call, see section 3500 of this title.
Use of Army and Air Force as posse comitatus, see section 1385 of Title 18, Crimes and Criminal Procedure.

Sec. 332. Use of militia and armed forces to enforce Federal authority
Whenever the President considers that unlawful obstructions, combinations, or assemblages, or rebellion against the authority of the United States, make it impracticable to enforce the laws of the United States in any State or Territory by the ordinary course of judicial proceedings, he may call into Federal service such of the militia of any State, and use such of the armed forces, as he considers necessary to enforce those laws or to suppress the rebellion. (Aug. 10, 1956, ch. 1041, 70A Stat. 15.) . . .

Historical and Revision Notes

Revised Section	Source (U.S. Code)	Source (Statutes at Large)
332	50:202.	R. S. 5298.

Sec. 333. Interference with State and Federal law
The President, by using the militia or the armed forces, or both, or by any other means, shall take such measures as he considers necessary to suppress, in a State, and insurrection, domestic violence, unlawful combination, or conspiracy, if it—

(1) so hinders the execution of the laws of that State, and of the United States within the State, that any part or class of its people is deprived of a right, privilege, immunity, or protection named in the Constitution and secured by law, and the constituted authorities of that State are unable, fail, or refuse to protect that right, privilege, or immunity, or to give that protection; or
(2) opposes or obstructs the execution of the laws of the United States or impedes the course of justice under those laws.

In any situation covered by clause (1), the State shall be considered to have denied the equal protection of the laws secured by the Constitution. (Aug. 10, 1956, ch. 1041, 70A Stat. 15.)

Historical and Revision Notes

Revised section	Source (U.S. Code)	Source (Statutes at Large)
333	50:203.	R. S. 5299.

The words "armed forces" are substituted for the words "land or naval forces of the United States". The word "shall" is substituted for the words "It shall be lawful for . . . and it shall be his duty".

Sec. 334. Proclamation to disperse

Whenever the President considers it necessary to use the militia or the armed forces under this chapter, he shall, by proclamation, immediately order the insurgents to disperse and retire peaceably to their abodes within a limited time. (Aug. 10, 1956, ch. 1041, 70A Stat. 16.)

Historical and Revision Notes

Revised section	Source (U.S. Code)	Source (Statutes at Large)
334	50:204.	R. S. 5300

The words "militia or the armed forces" are substituted for the words "military forces" for clarity and to conform to sections 331, 332, and 333 of this title.

The right of the United States Government to act under the statute upon which the present code is based was upheld by the Supreme Court in a case it reviewed in 1879 (*Ex parte Siebold*, 100 U.S. 371). In that instance the State of Maryland argued that when federal marshals sought to enforce the federal electoral laws within a state, they violated the right of the state to maintain its own police powers. In the majority opinion rejecting their argument, Mr. Justice Bradley wrote:

It is argued that the preservation of peace and good order in society is not within the powers confided in the government of the United States, but belongs exclusively to the States. Here again we are met with the theory that the government of the United States does not rest upon the soil and territory of the country. We think this theory is founded upon an entire misconception of the nature and powers of that government. We hold it to be an incontrovertible principle, that the government of the United States may, by means of physical force, exercise through its official agents, execute on every foot of American soil the powers and functions that belong to it. This necessarily involves the power to command obedience to its laws, and hence the power to keep the peace to that extent.[61]

On the same day that he issued his executive order President Eisenhower spoke to the nation over television. He attempted to describe the events at Central High School which had necessitated his extraordinary action, and also to review the responsibilities of the Chief Executive "to see that the laws are carried out."

President Dwight D. Eisenhower
Radio and Television Address
Explaining the Little Rock Situation
September 24, 1957

Public Papers of the Presidents of the United States: Dwight D. Eisenhower, 1957 (Washington, D.C., 1958), 689-94.

Good Evening, my fellow citizens: For a few minutes this evening I want to speak to you about the serious situation that has arisen in Little Rock. To make this talk I have come to the President's office in the White House. I could have spoken from Rhode Island, where I have been staying recently, but I felt that, in speaking from the house of Lincoln, of Jackson and of Wilson, my words would better convey both the sadness I feel in the action I was compelled today to take and the firmness with which I intend to pursue this course until the orders of the Federal Court at Little Rock can be executed without unlawful interference.

In that city, under the leadership of demagogic extremists, disorderly mobs have deliberately prevented the carrying out of proper orders from a Federal Court. Local authorities have not eliminated that violent opposition and, under the law, I yesterday issued a Proclamation calling upon the mob to disperse.

This morning the mob again gathered in front of the Central High School of Little Rock, obviously for the purpose of again preventing the carrying out of the Court's order relating to the admission of Negro children to that school.

Whenever normal agencies prove inadequate to the task and it becomes necessary for the Executive Branch of the Federal Government to use its powers and authority to uphold Federal Courts, the President's responsibility is inescapable.

In accordance with that responsibility, I have today issued an Executive Order directing the use of troops under Federal authority to aid in the execution of Federal law at Little Rock, Arkansas. This became necessary when my Proclamation of yesterday was not observed, and the obstruction of justice still continues.

It is important that the reasons for my action be understood by all our citizens.

As you know, the Supreme Court of the United States had decided that separate public educational facilities for the races are inherently unequal and therefore compulsory school segregation laws are unconstitutional.

Our personal opinions about the decision have no bearing on the matter of enforcement; the responsibility and authority of the Supreme Court to interpret the Constitution are very clear. Local Federal Courts were instructed by the Supreme Court to issue such orders and decrees as might be necessary to achieve admission to public schools without regard to race—and with all deliberate speed.

During the past several years, many communities in our Southern States have instituted public school plans for gradual progress in the enrollment and attendance of school children of all races in order to bring themselves into compliance with the law of the land.

They thus demonstrated to the world that we are a nation in which laws, not men, are supreme.

I regret to say that this truth—the cornerstone of our liberties—was not observed in this instance.

It was my hope that this localized situation would be brought under control by city and State authorities. If the use of local police powers had been sufficient, our traditional method of leaving the problems in those hands would have been pursued. But when large gatherings of obstructionists made it impossible for the decrees of the Court to be carried out, both the law and the national interest demanded that the President take action.

Here is the sequence of events in the development of the Little Rock school case.

In May of 1955, the Little Rock School Board approved a moderate plan for the gradual desegregation of the public schools in that city. It provided that a start toward integration would be made at the present term in the high school, and that the plan would be in full operation by 1963. Here I might say that in a number of communities in Arkansas integration in the schools has already started and without violence of any kind. Now this Little Rock plan was challenged in the courts by some who believed that the period of time as proposed in the plan was too long.

The United States Court at Little Rock, which has supervisory responsibility under the law for the plan of desegregation in the public schools, dismissed the challenge, thus approving a gradual rather than an abrupt change from the existing system. The court found that the school board had acted in good faith in planning for a public school system free from racial discrimination.

Since that time, the court has on three separate occasions issued orders directing that the plan be carried out. All persons were instructed to refrain from interfering with the efforts of the school board to comply with the law.

Proper and sensible observance of the law then demanded the respectful obedience which the nation has a right to expect from all its people. This, unfortunately, has not been the case at Little Rock. Certain misguided persons, many of them imported into Little Rock by agitators, have insisted upon defying the law and have sought to bring it into disrepute. The orders of the court have thus been frustrated.

The very basis of our individual rights and freedoms rests upon the certainty that the President and the Executive Branch of Government will support and insure the carrying out of the decisions of the Federal Courts, even, when necessary with all the means at the President's command.

Unless the President did so, anarchy would result.

There would be no security for any except that which each one of us could provide for himself.

The interest of the nation in the proper fulfillment of the law's requirements cannot yield to opposition and demonstrations by some few persons.

Mob rule cannot be allowed to override the decisions of our courts.

Now, let me make it very clear that Federal troops are not being used to relieve local and state authorities of their primary duty to preserve the peace and order of the community. Nor are the troops there for the purpose of taking over the responsibility of the School Board and the other responsible local officials in running Central High School. The running of our school system and the maintenance of peace and order in each of our States are strictly local affairs and the Federal Government does not interfere except in a very few special cases and when requested by one of the several States. In the present case the troops are there, pursuant to law, solely for the purpose of preventing interference with the orders of the Court.

The proper use of the powers of the Executive Branch to enforce the orders of a Federal Court is limited to extraordinary and compelling circumstances. Manifestly, such an extreme situation has been created in Little Rock. This challenge must be met and with such measures as will preserve to the people as a whole their lawfully-protected rights in a climate permitting their free and fair exercise.

The overwhelming majority of our people in every section of the country are united in their respect for observance of the law—even in those cases where they may disagree with that law.

They deplore the call of extremists to violence.

The decision of the Supreme Court concerning school integration, of course, affects the South more seriously than it does other sections of the country. In that region I have many warm friends, some of them in the city of Little Rock. I have deemed it a great personal privilege to spend in our Southland tours of duty while in the military service and enjoyable recreational periods since that time.

So from intimate personal knowledge, I know that the overwhelming majority of the people in the South—including those of Arkansas and of Little Rock—are of good will, united in their efforts to preserve and respect the law even when they disagree with it.

They do not sympathize with mob rule. They, like the rest of our nation, have proved in two great wars their readiness to sacrifice for America.

A foundation of our American way of life is our national respect for law.

In the South, as elsewhere, citizens are keenly aware of the tremendous disservice that has been done to the people of Arkansas in the eyes of the nation, and that has been done to the nation in the eyes of the world.

At a time when we face grave situations abroad because of the hatred that Communism bears toward a system of government based on human rights, it would be difficult to exaggerate the harm that is being done to the prestige and influence, and indeed to the safety, of our nation and the world.

Our enemies are gloating over this incident and using it everywhere to misrepresent our whole nation. We are portrayed as a violator of those standards of conduct which the peoples of the world united to proclaim in the Charter of the United Nations. There they affirmed "faith in fundamental human rights" and "in the dignity and worth of the human person" and they did so "without distinction as to race, sex, language or religion."

And so, with deep confidence, I call upon the citizens of the State of Arkansas to assist in bringing to an immediate end all interference with the law and its processes. If resistance to the Federal Court orders ceases at once, the further presence of Federal troops will be unnecessary and the City of Little Rock will return to its normal habits of peace and order and a blot upon the fair name and high honor of our nation in the world will be removed.

Thus will be restored the image of America and of all its parts as one nation, indivisible, with liberty and justice for all.

Good night, and thank you very much.

The next day the Black students were brought to school under the protection of a paratroop escort, and the crowd was finally dispersed under point of bayonets. The paratroopers remained on duty at Central High for several months, and the National Guard for the rest of the school year. Eight of the nine Black students finished out the year (one was expelled), under continual harassment from other students. Many unpleasant but no further violent incidents occurred.

Although the federal government, its laws, and the orders of the federal courts were finally vindicated by the President's use of his ultimate weapon under the executive powers of the Constitution, in retrospect it seems clear that this showdown could have been avoided had the President been willing to use his full power and influence much earlier in the Little Rock situation. A great deal was at stake there. As Richard Neustadt has written, "Eisenhower could no longer stay his hand in Little Rock without yielding to every Southern Governor the right—even the duty—to do what Faubus did."[62] Irrespective of his personal attitudes on the question of the Supreme Court decision, and his publicly stated reluctance to use federal troops to enforce the law, his position as President of the United States demanded that he protect his power by enforcing the law, and that he also guard his options carefully so as to avoid a situation where options no longer existed. Ultimately he had no alternative but to use his last resort, federal troops. In fact Neustadt argues that the very things Eisenhower did limited his options and strengthened the governor's will to resist him.

> Among others: Eisenhower's influence with Faubus was diminished by his earlier statements to the press and by his unconditional agreement to converse in friendly style at Newport.[63]

It was much worse than that. The President had allowed a vacuum to arise all over the South by his failure to speak out decisively on the problem and to spell out what the consequences of defiance of the law would entail. As a result the extreme segregationists rapidly came to the fore, filled the vacuum, and brought pressure on neutral governors such as Faubus, who might have resisted at some point if he had had strong backing from the President and thought that he could stay alive politically if he did so. When no such backing was forthcoming, and while there was still time to be effective and to salvage his political career, Faubus backslid. When he finally sat down with the President, there was really nothing Eisenhower could do or say that could persuade him to pull the President's chestnuts out of the fire.

The governor would take that action which would best serve his interests, and in this case it meant letting the President assume all further responsibility.

Eisenhower was forced to make this unfortunate but necessary decision primarily because he tried to avoid making any decision at all with respect to the problem, not only in Little Rock, but throughout the country. His equivocal position on the Supreme Court decision which had set the Little Rock situation in motion, compounded further by his questionable press conference comments about his determination not to use troops under any circumstances, had the effect of undermining the confidence and courage of those who wanted to see the law carried out, or who were at least willing to comply with it, and of encouraging those who wanted to destroy it. From Goliath to Hitler, the strategy of appeasing the bully has proven to be a counsel of despair, an invitation to disaster. For a President of the United States to attempt to avoid dealing with the lawless elements who were determined to prevent the application of the Brown v. Board of Education of Topeka decision before it eliminated segregated schools in the South, marked a shameful chapter in the history of the executive responsibilities of the Chief of State.

Of course there was really no way of avoiding the showdown and at the same time continuing to maintain a society of law and order, as Eisenhower finally realized and said in his speech of September 24. In attempting to avoid and postpone that showdown, however, he only built up the arrogance and false confidence of the mob, making it doubly hard to deal with them and suppress their lawless actions when the crisis occurred. Eisenhower's original ambivalence and indecisiveness encouraged the mob to grow, emboldened their actions and ultimately created the conditions which led to the violence that the President wanted above all to avoid. The inaction, passivity and indecision displayed were certainly not in the great tradition of the strong and effective use of the executive prerogative.

A technical comparison of the Little Rock crisis with Andrew Jackson's relationship with the South Carolina nullifiers illuminates the importance of clarity, strength and decisiveness in an executive crisis. Jackson allowed no doubt to arise as to his opinion with respect to the defiance of the law by the South Carolinians, nor his actions if they continued to defy the federal government. From the very beginning of the crisis he kept himself well informed with regard to the actions and the plans of the "nullifiers," and he accomplished this without the assistance of the F.B.I. or an immense federal bureaucracy. Throughout the crisis he communicated his position with respect to the enforcement of the law to the would-be offenders, and he made no secret of his own preparations to support his authority with all the manpower and resources at his command. Without the benefit of telephone, telegraph or any other form of telecommunication, and separated from the crisis center by many days journey, Jackson never was at a loss for information about what was going on, and he in turn communicated quickly, directly and clearly to the South Carolinian rebels precisely what was on his mind. As a result of this clear communication and understanding on both sides and because of his firm approach to the problem, Jackson was able to maintain the rule of law and to crush the opposition without any bloodshed or violence.

By contrast, the Little Rock crisis was muddled almost from beginning to end. There was never any clear understanding of where the President stood on the question, nor of what he would do if the court order was challenged. Despite the advantages of instant communication, it is to no avail if there is no source of clear and accurate information with which to communicate. It is evident that Governor Faubus had no real idea of what the President's response to his lawless action would be, and under pressure he gambled. The President, on the other hand, after months of relaying inadequate and misleading signals, was forced to employ more executive power domestically than had any President of the United States in many decades. It was a tragic example of too little, too late, and then too much. Reflecting upon the incident some years later, his predecessor in the White House, Harry Truman, remarked:

> If the fella that succeeded me had just given people a little leadership, there wouldn't have been all that difficulty over desegregating the schools, but he didn't do it. He didn't use the powers of the office of the President to uphold a ruling of the Supreme Court of the United States, and I never did understand that.
>
> If he'd got out in front and told people they had to uphold the law of the land, it's my opinion that they'd have done it. But he didn't; he shillyshallied around, and that's the reason we're in the fix we're in now.[64]

That is as good a definition of presidential leadership as there is.

But to the credit of President Eisenhower, in the final analysis he did act in the Little Rock crisis, firmly and without turning back. The rights of American citizens were upheld by the federal government and enforced by its Executive without equivocation. A mid-century precedent was established in terms of supporting the order of the federal court, and it would be difficult, if not impossible, for future Presidents to ignore or step back from such a strong federal interest in what was essentially a local matter, except for the violations of federal rights.

There was also the happier side of the long-term resolution of the problem. For many years Little Rock underwent a series of crises in school desegregation, and it looked at times as if the struggle had all been in vain. Several times the feeble steps forward made with such turmoil were all but erased, and at one time Central High School was completely shut down, along with all the high schools in the city for an entire year. But today if one looks back on the events, the effort seems to have been very worthwhile. First of all, the immediate children involved in the initial crisis appear to have all profited from their education and have gone on to initiate very useful careers.[65] And today the school system in Little Rock is completely integrated through the 12 grades of elementary, junior high and high school. The city is not without race problems and its school system is still improving, but there is an air of progress and determination there that a visitor cannot fail to observe. But then again, perhaps it is because the people of Little Rock can compare the years of violence, international disgrace and the subsequent educational and economic hardships their racial problems have cost them with the sense of progress, well being and hope to which their present policies have led. A contingent of 800 Little Rock citizens (Black and white) who volunteer their time as school aides is part of the reason for the success. Little Rock has weathered its worst crises, and is more integrated, possesses more social stability and a more determined sense of its future destiny than the cities of New York or Boston. That is the wonder of the Little Rock story.

The Civil Rights Apprenticeship
Of John Fitzgerald Kennedy

After studying the racial attitudes and policies of American Presidents from Lincoln to Theodore Roosevelt, George Sinkler concluded (as Lincoln often said of McClellan) that they had the "slows."[66] That is not to say that they revealed bitter anti-Black prejudice. In most instances they were racist only in their belief that whites were superior to Blacks. They possessed no overt hostility towards Black people. In fact Sinkler argues that their "expressed intentions" were good; it was their lack of positive action that was to be deplored:

> If the Presidents of this period are judged only on their expressed intentions in matters of race, they make a good showing. When measured by actual accomplishment, with one or two notable exceptions, their record is one of stark failure to enforce the federal laws involving matters of race, and an extreme reluctance to champion an unreserved racial equality in the full spirit of American democracy. When it came to a choice between vigorous action or inaction in matters of race the Presidents were paralyzed.[67]

John Fitzgerald Kennedy intended that this pattern be changed. When he announced his candidacy for the presidency he made a remarkable speech, calling for presidential leadership of the highest calibre. ". . . [T]he White House," Kennedy urged, "is not only the center of *political* leadership."

> It must be the center of *moral* leadership—a "bully pulpit," as Theodore Roosevelt described it. For only the President represents the national interest. And upon him alone converge all the needs and aspirations of all parts of the country, all departments of the Government, all nations of the world.
>
> It is not enough merely to represent prevailing sentiment—to follow McKinley's practice, as described by Joe Cannon, "of keeping his ear so close to the ground he got it full of grasshoppers." We will need in the sixties a President who is willing and able to summon his national constituency to its finest hour—to alert the people to our dangers and our opportunities—to demand of them the sacrifices that will be necessary.

Despite the increasing evidence of a lost national purpose and a soft national will, F.D.R.'s words in his first inaugural still ring true: "In every dark hour of our national life, a leadership of frankness and vigor has met with that understanding and support of the people themselves which is essential to victory."[68]

Senator John F. Kennedy
"The Challenges of the Modern Presidency"
Address to the National Press Club
January 14, 1960

Arthur M. Schlesinger, jr. and Fred L. Israel, eds., *History of American Presidential Elections, 1789-1968* (New York, 1971) IV, 3536-40.

The modern presidential campaign covers every issue in and out of the platform from cranberries to creation. But the public is rarely alerted to a candidate's views about the central issue on which all the rest turn. That central issue—and the point of my comments this noon—is not the farm problem or defense or India. It is the Presidency itself.

Of course a candidate's views on specific policies are important, but Theodore Roosevelt and William Howard Taft shared policy views with entirely different results in the White House. Of course it is important to elect a good man with good intentions, but Woodrow Wilson and Warren G. Harding were both good men of good intentions; so were Lincoln and Buchanan; but there is a Lincoln Room in the White House and no Buchanan Room.

The history of this Nation—its brightest and its bleakest pages—has been written largely in terms of the different views our Presidents have had of the Presidency itself. This history ought to tell us that the American people in 1960 have an imperative right to know what any man bidding for the Presidency thinks about the place he is bidding for, whether he is aware of and willing to use the powerful resources of that Office; whether his model will be Taft or Roosevelt, Wilson or Harding.

Not since the days of Woodrow Wilson has any candidate spoken on the Presidency itself before the votes have been irrevocably cast. Let us hope that the 1960 campaign, in addition to discussing the familiar issues where our positions too often blur, will also talk about the Presidency itself, as an instrument for dealing with those issues, as an Office with varying roles, powers, and limitations.

During the past 8 years, we have seen one concept of the Presidency at work. Our needs and hopes have been eloquently stated—but the initiative and follow-through have too often been left to others. And too often his own objectives have been lost by the President's failure to override objections from within his own party, in the Congress or even in his Cabinet.

The American people in 1952 and 1956 may have preferred this detached, limited concept of the Presidency after 20 years of fast-moving, creative Presidential rule. Perhaps historians will regard this as necessarily one of those frequent periods of consolidation, a time to draw breath, to recoup our national energy. To quote the state of the Union message: "No Congress . . . on surveying the state of the Nation, has met with a more pleasing prospect than that which appears at the present time."

Unfortunately this is not Mr. Eisenhower's last message to the Congress, but Calvin Coolidge's. He followed to the White House Mr. Harding, whose sponsor declared very frankly that the times did not demand a first-rate President. If true, the times and the man met.

But the question is what do the times—and the people—demand for the next 4 years in the White House?

They demand a vigorous proponent of the national interest—not a passive broker for conflicting private interests. They demand a man capable of acting as the commander in chief of the Grand Alliance, not merely a bookkeeper who feels that his work is done when the numbers on the balance sheet come out even. They demand that he be the head of a responsible party, not rise so far above politics as to be invisible—a man who will formulate and fight for legislative policies, not be a casual bystander to the legislative process.

Today a restricted concept of the Presidency is not enough. For beneath today's surface gloss of peace and prosperity are increasingly dangerous, unsolved, long-postponed problems—problems that will inevitably explode to the surface during the next 4 years of the next administration—the growing missile gap, the rise of Communist China, the despair of the underdeveloped nations, the explosive situations in Berlin and in the Formosa Straits, the deterioration of NATO, the lack of an arms control agreement, and all the domestic problems of our farms, cities, and schools.

This administration has not faced up to these and other problems. Much has been said—but I am reminded of the old Chinese proverb: "There is a great deal of noise on the stairs but nobody comes into the room."

The President's state of the Union message reminded me of the exhortation from "King Lear" that goes: "I will do such things—what they are I know not . . . but they shall be the wonders of the earth."

In the decade that lies ahead—in the challenging revolutionary sixties—the American Presidency will demand more than ringing manifestoes issued from the rear of the battle. It will demand that the President place himself in the very thick of the fight, that he care passionately about the fate of the people he leads, that he be willing to serve them at the risk of incurring their momentary displeasure.

Whatever the political affiliation of our next President, whatever his views may be on all the issues and problems that rush in upon us, he must above all be the Chief Executive in every sense of the word. He must be prepared to exercise the fullest powers of his Office—all that are specified and some that are not. He must master complex problems as well as receive one-page memorandums. He must originate action as well as study groups. He must reopen the channels of communication between the world of thought and the seat of power.

Ulysses Grant considered the President "a purely administrative officer." If he administered the Government departments efficiently, delegated his functions smoothly, and performed his ceremonies of state with decorum and grace, no more was to be expected of him. But that is not the place the Presidency was meant to have in American life. The President is alone, at the top—the loneliest job there is, as Harry Truman has said.

If there is destructive dissension among the services, he alone can step in and straighten it out—instead of waiting for unanimity. If administrative agencies are not carrying out their mandate—if a brushfire threatens some part of the globe—he alone can act, without waiting for the Congress. If his farm program fails, he alone deserves the blame, not his Secretary of Agriculture.

"The President is at liberty, both in law and conscience, to be as big a man as he can." So wrote Prof. Woodrow Wilson. But President Woodrow Wilson discovered that to be a big man in the White House inevitably brings cries of dictatorship.

So did Lincoln and Jackson and the two Roosevelts. And so may the next occupant of that office, if he is the man the times demand. But how much better it would be, in the turbulent sixties, to have a Roosevelt or a Wilson than to have another James Buchanan, cringing in the White House, afraid to move.

Nor can we afford a Chief Executive who is praised primarily for what he did not do, the disasters he prevented, the bills he vetoed—a President wishing his subordinates would produce more missiles or build more schools. We will need instead what the Constitution envisioned: a Chief Executive who is the vital center of action in our whole scheme of Government.

This includes the legislative process as well. The president cannot afford—for the sake of the Office as well as the Nation—to be another Warren G. Harding, described by one backer as a man who "would, when elected, sign whatever bill the Senate sent him—and not send bills for the Senate to pass." Rather he must know when to lead the Congress, when to consult it and when he should act alone.

Having served 14 years in the legislative branch, I would not look with favor upon its domination by the Executive. Under our government of "power as the rival of power," to use Hamilton's phrase, Congress must not surrender its responsibilities. But neither should it dominate. However large its share in the formulation of domestic programs, it is the President alone who must make the major decisions of our foreign policy.

That is what the Constitution wisely commands. And, even domestically, the President must initiate policies and devise laws to meet the needs of the Nation. And he must be prepared to use all the resources of his office to insure the enactment of that legislation—even when conflict is the result.

By the end of his term Theodore Roosevelt was not popular in the Congress—particularly when he criticized an amendment to the Treasury appropriation which forbade the use of Secret Service men to investigate Congressmen.

And the feeling was mutual, Roosevelt saying: "I do not much admire the Senate, because it is such a helpless body when efficient work is to be done."

And Woodrow Wilson was even more bitter after his frustrating quarrels. Asked if he might run for the Senate in 1920, he replied: "Outside of the United States, the Senate does not amount to a damn. And inside the United States the Senate is most despised. They haven't had a thought down there in 50 years."

But, however bitter their farewells, the facts of the matter are that Roosevelt and Wilson did get things done—not only through their Executive powers but through the Congress as well. Calvin Coolidge, on the other hand, departed from

Washington with cheers of Congress still ringing in his ears. But when his World Court bill was under fire on Capitol Hill he sent no messages, gave no encouragement to the bill's leaders, and paid little or no attention to the whole proceeding—and the cause of world justice was set back.

To be sure, Coolidge had held the usual White House breakfasts with congressional leaders—but they were aimed, as he himself said, at "good fellowship," not a discussion of "public business." And at his press conferences, according to press historians, where he preferred to talk about the local flower show and its exhibits, reporters who finally extracted from him a single sentence—"I'm against that bill"—would rush to file tongue-in-cheek dispatches, proclaiming that: "President Coolidge, in a fighting mood, today served notice on Congress that he intended to combat, with all the resources at his command, the pending bill. . . ."

But in the coming years we will need a real fighting mood in the White House— a man who will not retreat in the face of pressure from his congressional leaders— who will not let down those supporting his views on the floor. Divided Government over the past 6 years has only been further confused by this lack of legislative leadership. To restore it next year will help restore purpose to both the Presidency and the Congress.

The facts of the matter are that legislative leadership is not possible without party leadership, in the most political sense—and Mr. Eisenhower prefers to stay above politics (although a weekly news magazine last fall reported the startling news, and I quote, that "President Eisenhower is emerging as a major political figure"). When asked, early in his first term, how he liked the "game of politics," he replied with a frown that his questioner was using a derogatory phrase. "Being President," he said, "is a very great experience . . . but the word 'politics' . . . I have no great liking for that."

But no President, it seems to me, can escape politics. He has not only been chosen by the Nation—he has been chosen by his party. And if he insists that he is "President of all the people" and should, therefore, offend none of them—if he blurs the issues and differences between the parties—if he neglects the party machinery and avoids his party's leadership—then he has not only weakened the political party as an instrument of the democratic process—he has dealt a blow to the democratic process itself.

I prefer the example of Abe Lincoln, who loved politics with the passion of a born practitioner. For example, he waited up all night in 1863 to get the crucial returns on the Ohio governorship. When the Unionist candidate was elected, Lincoln wired: "Glory God in the highest. Ohio has saved the Nation."

But the White House is not only the center of political leadership. It must be the center of moral leadership—a "bully pulpit," as Theodore Roosevelt described it. For only the President represents the national interest. And upon him alone converge all the needs and aspirations of all parts of the country, all departments of the Government, all nations of the world.

It is not enough merely to represent prevailing sentiment—to follow McKinley's practice, as described by Joe Cannon, of "keeping his ear so close to the ground he got it full of grasshoppers." We will need in the sixties a President who is willing and able to summon his national constituency to its finest hour—to alert the people to our dangers and our opportunities—to demand of them the sacrifices that will be necessary. Despite the increasing evidence of a lost national purpose and a soft national will, F.D.R.'s words in his first inaugural still ring true: "In every dark hour of our national life, a leadership of frankness and vigor has met with that understanding and support of the people themselves which is essential to victory."

Roosevelt fulfilled the role of moral leadership. So did Wilson and Lincoln, Truman and Jackson and Teddy Roosevelt. They led the people as well as the Government—they fought for great ideals as well as bills. And the time has come to demand that kind of leadership again.

And so, as this vital campaign begins, let us discuss the issues the next President will face—but let us also discuss the powers and tools with which we must face them.

For we must endow that office with extraordinary strength and vision. We must act in the image of Abraham Lincoln summoning his wartime Cabinet to a meeting on the Emancipation Proclamation. That Cabinet has been carefully chosen to please and reflect many elements in the country. But "I have gathered you together," Lincoln said, "to hear what I have written down. I do not wish your advice about the main matter—that I have determined for myself."

And later, when he went to sign after several hours of exhausting and handshaking that had left his arm weak, he said to those present: "If my name goes down in history, it will be for this act. My whole soul is in it. If my hand trembles when I sign this proclamation, all who examine the document hereafter will say: 'He hesitated.' "

But Lincoln's hand did not tremble. He did not hesitate. He did not equivocate. For he was the President of the United States.

It is in this spirit that we must go forth in the coming months and years.

While Kennedy wanted progress in the area of civil rights as much as he did in any other domestic field, it took a certain period of apprenticeship in the White House to strengthen his determination (and also that of his brother, the attorney general) to do the things that were necessary to accomplish his purpose. He had to want progress enough to put his political capital—a good deal of it—on the line. The price of pursuing too aggressive a policy in the area of civil rights could cost the young President the next election and also weaken his influence in Congress, on both domestic and foreign policy priorities. His electoral victory had been too close and the strength of his civil rights supporters had been too marginal to risk an early showdown. Yet Kennedy confronted a number of related problems in the early months of his presidency.

Kennedy and his advisors had decided, even before the election, that if he was successful in his quest for the office, he would not move immediately for further legislation in the civil rights area. But it did not mean that his administration would be inactive concerning these problems. Kennedy deplored President Eisenhower's equivocation with regard to the *Brown* decision; as a result he wanted to make clear that he considered it the law of the land and that he intended to enforce it and other federal laws protecting the civil rights of Black Americans. But how, to what extent, in what particular areas were the questions with which he was faced.

These questions were gradually resolved during the course of the first two years of his administration. He put the legislative route aside for the time being, judging it to be too costly and too politically risky, and he argued in turn that much more could be done by firmly implementing laws already on the books. The Congress had passed a civil rights law in 1957 and another in 1960, strengthening the authority of the attorney general's office in dealing with voting registration cases. The newly-elected President maintained that through effective executive implementation of these and other laws, substantial progress could be made without new legislation. Probably one of the principal reasons the President put his brother in the office of attorney general was because he was well aware of the vigor with which Robert Kennedy pursued the objectives which he was determined to achieve. When asked to spell out his strategy in more detail, the President replied:

> [T]here is a good deal that can be done by the Executive branch without legislation. For example, the President could sign an Executive order ending discrimination in housing tomorrow. Second, the President could compel all companies which do business with the Government, and after all that is nearly every American company, to practice open, fair hiring of personnel without regard to race, creed or color. . . . In addition, the Department of Justice can pursue the right to vote with far more vigor. . . . So I would say that the greater opportunity is in the Executive branch without Congressional action.[69]

This strategy was primarily attributable to one of Kennedy's key civil rights advisors, Harris Wofford, jr., a remarkable young lawyer who had served on the staff of the Civil Rights Commission and later taught at the Law School at Notre Dame; he had a long background as an activist in the civil rights field. But with all of his enthusiasm for this approach to the problem, Wofford stated very candidly in the spring of 1961, after he had been appointed special civil rights advisor to the President:

> I do not mean that the new avenue of executive action will be easy. This course has plenty of contradictions and it will not . . . resolve the built-in political contradictions. The need for the enactment of vital measures for the general welfare . . . may still at any given moment have to be weighed against other actions to advance Civil Rights. Since these social measures have the most direct impact on our racial minorities, so many of whom are at the bottom of our economic ladder, the weighing process is sometimes painful. You may on occasion disagree with the result of the weighing of priorities. But for your disagreement to be effective you will need to look at the process through a political lens that takes into account the major contradictions shaping this problem.[70]

If this caution was not fully understood by all who embraced this new "executive approach" to the old problems in the civil rights area, they soon learned that a considerable number of obstacles restricted progress in that respect as well. When, for example, the President decided against initiating civil rights legislation because it would antagonize southern Democratic votes which he needed in

Congress, he soon realized that these same senators and congressmen would be just as angry over any overt executive actions taken by the President. Kennedy delayed the famous "stroke of the pen" on the housing order for almost two years after he became President, so as not to alienate their support for other priorities. This caused much concern in the civil rights-liberal activist camp. There were other delays and ineffective efforts in the early months which tended to reinforce this disillusionment among some. Time seemed to be running out, and the Kennedy administration had not established a record that came near to fulfilling promises made during the campaign.

It is fair to say that legitimate obstacles accounted for some of this tardiness. It takes time to conduct investigations into voting restrictions and procedures, to litigate such cases and to grind ahead in asserting national prerogatives in the complex web of federalism within which the attorney general and his talented civil rights staff were forced to operate.[71] Kennedy did initiate some immediate and significant changes, however. He appointed a civil rights advisor, Harris Wofford, to coordinate efforts to stimulate activity within the various executive departments of the government, and also to maintain contact with the leaders of the civil rights movement outside of government. Wofford presided over a subcabinet of officials who met regularly to press for reforms within their departments; they succeeded in achieving some top level appointments and general improvements in departmental and agency hiring practices, and did their best to encourage the principle of equal opportunity wherever it could be pursued. There were also many symbolic gestures, such as the resignations of Robert Kennedy, Angier Biddle Duke, George Cabot Lodge and Charles Bartlett, all members of the Kennedy inner circle, from the Metropolitan Club in Washington because it discriminated against Blacks. Vice President Lyndon B. Johnson was pressed into service as the chairman of the new President's Committee on Equal Employment Opportunity which pressured private corporations doing business with the government to adopt the principle of equal opportunity in their hiring practices.

But the major emphasis of the Kennedy administration in the civil rights area was in the increased effort to expedite the voter registration procedure for Black citizens throughout the South, enabling them to engage in the political process. Under the provisions of the Civil Rights Act of 1957 and the amendments added to it in 1960, the Eisenhower administration had moved, as Alexander M. Bickel of the Yale Law School put it, "with about the vigor and imagination displayed by William McKinley in enforcing the Sherman Anti-Trust Act of 1890."[72] In the course of three years the attorney general under Eisenhower filed six voting suits, settled one and tried two others. Three of the six were filed too late to come to trial before President Eisenhower's retirement.

The Kennedy administration sought to improve this dismal record. The civil rights division was strengthened under the direction of Burke Marshall, who came to the government from a partnership in a prestigious Washington law firm; he was a quiet, self-effacing but relentless champion of Black equality before the law. The small civil rights division was increased many times over, and it was engaged, day in and day out, in the arduous task of investigating, collecting, and evaluating evidence of violations of the right to vote, bringing suit when the evidence warranted it and attempting, frequently through persuasion and even pressure, to bring about compliance to the law without resorting to legal action. In 1962 Alex Bickel reported the staff had increased to almost 50 persons and was still growing; by 1963 58 law suits had been filed and many more were in the process of preparation.

But despite all of this effort, the results hardly came up to expectations. As Bickel wrote, "Observers, admiring the moving of mountains, fear the production, in the end, of mice."[73] Fleming concluded: "Notwithstanding these accelerated governmental and private efforts, it soon became apparent that Negro registration was growing at a hopelessly slow pace."[74] The Justice Department suits had resulted in impressive breakthroughs in a number of "black belt" counties, but "generally progress was frustrated by the repressive climate of the rural South and the interminable delays of litigation."[75] Burke Marshall pessimistically argued in 1964:

> The federal government has demonstrated a seeming inability to make significant advances, in seven years' time, since the 1957 law, in making the right to vote real for Negroes in Mississippi, large parts of Alabama and Louisiana, and in scattered counties in other states. . . . Does this mean that this basic problem is beyond solution and the simple right beyond realization?
>
> The experience of the Justice Department to date would not justify this conclusion. . . . Discrimination in the registration process has been eliminated, through the normal channels of judicial action, in Macon and Bullock counties, Alabama, the heart of the Deep South. It has probably been eliminated in other places, for example, Terrel County, Georgia, with results being not visible as yet because of the absence of effective registration efforts by local Negroes. If this has been done in these counties, failures elsewhere can be attributed not to the flaws in the system, but to flaws in courts and men and to a lack of time. And these are defects that can be remedied with enough money, enough energy, enough lawyers, and enough months or years.
>
> The harder question is whether the tempo of the civil rights movement has not quickened to such a degree that there is not enough time left. . . . The only tangible result in the near future will be a mass of litigation in the federal courts which will take months or years to resolve. And that in itself will be divisive between Negroes and whites, between state and federal governments, with racial issues continuing to be a prime political factor in any election.[76]

This failure of what Victor S. Navasky defined as "federalism,"[77] the approach used by John F. Kennedy, his attorney general and his entire staff in their attempt to eliminate racial discrimination during his early period in office, was disappointing. The method was flawless, Burke Marshall affirmed, and the results were predictable if you could "hang in there" long enough. The problem was that the over 20 million Blacks in the United States were tired of waiting and were frustrated enough to begin to take control of events on their own. James Meredith of Kosciusko, Mississippi was one of these impatient and ambitious Blacks. His proved to be the case where the process of federalism broke down completely, forcing a reexamination of its premises and a shift in the tactics which it dictated. These changes had significant implications for the executive power of the President of the United States, yet to understand how these changes came about, it is also necessary to understand the nature of the dynamics of the situation as it developed. Of specific concern to the case of James Meredith is the precise level of President Kennedy's commitment to the civil rights cause and the results of that commitment. In this and other instances the level of emotional involvement was decisive to the success or failure of the executive policy taken.

Two Historic Telephone Calls

There is no evidence that either John F. Kennedy or his brother Robert was seriously concerned or involved in civil rights questions much before the presidential campaign of 1960. In Congress John F. Kennedy voted most often with the northern liberal wing of the Democratic party, but his assistant and close advisor, Theodore Sorensen, recalls that "he knew and cared comparatively little about the problems of civil rights and civil liberties" during those years.[78] When he became a serious candidate for the presidency, Kennedy, with the guidance and encouragement of Sorensen, Wofford and others, began to talk to civil rights leaders in the spring of 1960. Although he advocated measures of which they approved, Martin Luther King probably summed up their attitude most accurately when he reported, after a breakfast with Kennedy at the Hotel Carlyle in New York before the 1960 convention, that the senator from Massachusetts "displayed a definite concern but . . . not what I would call a 'depthed' understanding"[79] of their problems. Having lost any hopes for the major part of the southern vote by his refusal to side-step the *Brown* decision and the need for civil rights legislation, Kennedy needed the Black vote to secure the White House.

In November he received a solid percentage of that vote. The Gallup and Harris polls put the figure at between 68 and 78 percent. Schlesinger observed that if only whites had voted in that election, Kennedy would have been beaten solidly by Richard M. Nixon. Critical states like Illinois, South Carolina, Michigan and others were carried by the margin provided by the Black vote.[80] Much has been made of the fascinating telephone calls made by Kennedy and his brother during the campaign; the first was to Mrs. Martin Luther King, who was pregnant at the time her husband was jailed in DeKalb County, Georgia, for violation of a driving ordinance, and later when Robert Kennedy called the judge involved in the case and was credited with having persuaded him to free the civil rights leader. News of these calls leaked out to the press, and in short time hundreds of thousands of leaflets describing the events were distributed in the Black communities throughout the country. The fact that this incident occurred just before the November election is considered by Theodore White, Theodore Sorensen, Arthur Schlesinger, jr., and others to have had a decisive impact on the outcome of the election. It probably did, but the full story behind these calls has, to my knowledge, yet to be told.

With minor errors in details, the story was repeated in Theodore H. White's

The Making of a President: 1960 and Anthony Lewis' *Portrait of a Decade*, but neither of these descriptions or any others that I have seen relates the real drama that was played out in Atlanta, Washington and on the campaign trail with both candidates just two weeks before the election of 1960. The importance of the details involved in this story and their influence upon later attitudes and events shared by President John F. Kennedy and his brother in the civil rights area are, in my view, critical to the understanding of their slow and at times painful pilgrimage to a greater understanding of the civil rights problem. Both brothers were great competitors, eager and quick to exploit opportunities, but neither one was yet fully committed to the real struggle for civil rights, and nothing illustrates that better than their conduct in this episode.

The familiar descriptions of the situation relate the fact that Martin Luther King was arrested with a group of 51 other Blacks, most of whom were students, for conducting a sit-in in the eating facilities of Rich's, downtown Atlanta's most prestigious department store. King himself was arrested in the posh Magnolia Room, where many of the so-called "power elite" in the city met for luncheon. Mayor William Hartsfield referred to it as the holy of holies. The students had been meeting in Atlanta to plan further actions in support of the wave of sit-ins that was sweeping the South. They were determined to desegregate the white eating places in Atlanta, none of which served Blacks. Ironically, Rich's sold merchandise to Blacks, but would not serve them food. The owner of the store, Dick Rich, was friendly with King and had contributed large sums to Black colleges and other causes in the Black community. But the State of Georgia and the city of Atlanta enforced ordinances requiring segregation in eating facilities, and Rich's went along with the law and with custom. Accordingly, Blacks could not try on hats without placing tissue paper around the lining, nor shoes without first slipping on "footlets," to prevent contact with their stockings. King, on moving to Atlanta from Montgomery, must have purchased a lot of household furnishings at Rich's, because he once remarked that he spent $4500 there one year, but they refused to sell him a cup of coffee.

All of the Blacks who were arrested refused bond and remained in jail for the next three days while furious negotiations went on between Rich and powerful Atlanta merchants, the mayor and the Black leaders of the community. Mayor Hartsfield, an Atlanta booster of incomparable charm and folksy wisdom, was trying as he did on many occasions, to reduce the emotional level of the confrontation and work out a compromise that would be in the best interests of his city. He was attempting to negotiate a 30 to 60 day cooling-off period in which both parties involved in the dispute would sit down and try to work out a solution to the total problem. That was the Hartsfield way, as it was also characteristic of his successor, Ivan Allen. Both were superb practitioners of the art of politics.

On the third day of these hectic negotiations, Harris Wofford, who was serving as an advisor to Kennedy during the campaign and specialized in civil rights issues, called Morris Abram, an Atlanta attorney of considerable influence, particularly with the mayor, to inquire as to King's status. Abram could tell him only that negotiations were under way at city hall, but that he was hurrying down there and would call to inform him of King's situation later. Wofford had been close to King since the Montgomery bus boycott and had helped arrange a small grant from the American Friends Service Committee to finance a trip to India for King so he could acquire greater understanding of the philosophy of nonviolence practiced by Ghandi. Later that day Abram called Wofford back, and then put Mayor Hartsfield on the line; he told the Kennedy advisor that he was going to release King and the others, and was also going to announce that he was doing it at Kennedy's instigation. Wofford was stunned by this news, and begged the mayor to wait until he could get in touch with the Kennedys, who were campaigning in the midwest at that time. But the old man who had served as Atlanta's mayor for a quarter of a century pooh-poohed his objections, told Wofford he knew more about politics than anyone in the Kennedy organization, and that such an announcement would get Kennedy a "heap of votes" in Atlanta and elsewhere in the country.

Later that day the prisoners were released and Hartsfield suggested to the press that "a representative of the Kennedy camp in Georgia had asked him to get King out of jail."[81] There was a great deal of speculation as to who that might have been in the press and there were references to a "mystery man." Hartsfield finally indicated that it was not really anyone in Georgia, but someone up in Washington, obviously Wofford.[82]

In the meantime Wofford was desperately trying to get in touch with the Kennedys to alert them to the developments in Atlanta. He finally made contact with Bobby Kennedy sometime that evening. In an interview with this author, Wofford indicated that he had never heard such language in his life. Robert Kennedy apparently reacted violently, accused Wofford of losing the election for his brother and did not calm down for some time. It had nothing to do with King or his troubles; Kennedy evaluated the situation solely with respect to its effect upon the campaign for President. In this case, however, once Robert Kennedy's initial anger and reactions had time to simmer, something of a fierce and almost last ditch debate must have taken place in the Kennedy camp. Being partially committed at least, they attempted to weigh the pros and cons of intervening further.

Events took over before a decision could be made or soundings taken as to the reaction of both Black and white, northern and southern Democrats, to the situation in Atlanta. When Coretta King arrived at the party hastily called to celebrate the prisoners' release from jail Saturday night in Atlanta, she discovered that her husband was not among them. Dr. King had been taken into custody by the sheriff of DeKalb County for technical violation of a parole. Some months earlier he had been found guilty of driving a motor vehicle without a license, and placed on probation for a year, plus a $25.00 fine. Now DeKalb County Judge Oscar Mitchell wanted King arrested for violation of that parole. The judge ruled the next week that King had violated the good behavior provision of his parole by his arrest in Atlanta, and he quickly sentenced him to Reidsville state prison, some 300 miles from the court, to serve a term of four months. This extraordinarily harsh sentence shocked even the *Atlanta Constitution*, which, although sympathetic to the objectives of the civil rights movement, had criticized the tactics of the sit-ins, arguing that

> to seek change by violating the storekeeper's legal rights and bodily
> disrupting his business—not only as a symbol of discontent, but

repeatedly as an instrument of force—can only breed resentment, not reason in this reasonable and sympathetic city.[83]

Now the *Constitution* was shocked by Judge Mitchell's sentence and protested against it in its editorial column. Others throughout the country were also upset by this obvious display of discrimination and injustice, and telegrams of protest poured into Georgia in support of King.[84] In Washington aides of President Eisenhower in the Justice Department prepared an important statement on the King case for the President to issue. The statement read:

> It seems to me fundamentally unjust that a man who has just peacefully attempted to establish his right to equal treatment, free from racial discrimination should, be imprisoned on an unrelated charge, in itself insignificant. Accordingly, I have asked the Attorney General to take all proper steps to join with Dr. Martin Luther King in an appropriate application for his release.[85]

It was a strong and moving statement, and had the President or the Vice President released it at the time, the course of history might have been somewhat different. Certainly it could have increased the margin of Richard Nixon's votes among the critical marginal Black voters, who ultimately accounted for John F. Kennedy's victory the following week. Mayor Hartsfield was aware of the fact that Black Republican leaders in Georgia had been desperately attempting to get either Eisenhower or Nixon to issue such a statement while King was still in jail in Atlanta; that was the major reason why he jumped the gun against Wofford's warning when he released the sit-ins from jail. Hartsfield, rather than the Kennedys or their advisors, first grasped the political value of coming to King's assistance.

King languished in the Atlanta jail for five days until he was bound over to the DeKalb county jail for the hearing before Judge Mitchell. During that period his attorney, Donald Hollowell, worked feverishly to vacate the county judge's action, but to no avail. After King was sentenced on Tuesday, October 25, Hollowell returned to the DeKalb County Courthouse at 8 a.m. and attempted to obtain a writ of habeas corpus. It was only then that he was informed that Dr. King had been transferred during the night (actually at 3 a.m. in the morning) to the Reidsville state prison hundreds of miles away. It was at that point that Hollowell filed a motion appealing the decision and requesting that the prisoner be released on bail, pending the hearing of the appeal. It was in the form of a bill of exception, requesting release of the prisoner on bail, a routine procedure in a case involving a misdemeanor. He was also prepared to file a similar request in the state supreme court in the event that Judge Mitchell failed to comply with his motion. Judge Mitchell's conduct in quickly sentencing King to four months in prison and whisking him off overnight to the state prison simply would not stand up under any kind of review, and Hollowell was confident that his legal efforts would eventually succeed, but he was concerned in the meantime with his client's safety.

It was at that point that the Kennedys intervened. The climate had been carefully tested, King had already been in jail for a week and public opinion appeared to be crystallizing in his favor. It was clear that there had been a good deal of communication between the Democratic candidate, his brother, Kennedy's brother-in-law, Sargent Shriver, Wofford, Abram, Hartsfield and others. The governor of Georgia, hard pressed to keep his state in the Democratic column, entered the picture and admitted having talked to Senator Kennedy, but he denied that he had been instrumental in Hartsfield's release of the sit-ins the previous week. The governor reported that in his conversation with Senator Kennedy the Democratic presidential candidate had told him that "he had no authority to interfere nor any desire or intention of interfering."[86] The mayor finally confirmed that conversation, after having probably been leaked by somebody high in the Kennedy headquarters. Hartsfield confirmed Vandiveer's claim, stating to the newspaper that "Kennedy is taking no part in this."[87] And he probably did not interfere, at least in public, but that very evening he called Martin Luther King's wife to console her in the absence of the jailed civil rights leader. According to Mrs. King, the senator told her:

> I want to express to you my concern about your husband. I know this must be very hard for you. I understand you are expecting a baby, and I just wanted you to know that I was thinking about you and Dr. King. If there is anything I can do to help, please feel free to call on me.[88]

Mrs. King thanked him for his concern and told Kennedy she would appreciate anything he could do. The following day his brother called Judge Mitchell and questioned him as to the legality of refusing bail to Dr. King, who was only charged with a misdemeanor. There is no question that these telephone calls, which were quickly reported to the press, though not by the Kennedys, increased the pressure on Judge Mitchell to release King. But there is no basis for determining that either one was decisive in the final action. The judge had no valid legal grounds for holding the civil rights leader in jail when the case was under appeal and bail was available. If he had held to his stand, the probability of a quick reversal by a superior court was inevitable.

Judge Mitchell may have been under far more severe economic and political pressure to release King from those whose power he probably held in far greater awe than that of Robert Kennedy, who held no official position in Georgia or anywhere else. The most powerful figures in the Democratic party in the state wanted the case out of the newspapers because it was not helping their electoral possibilities one bit. The major economic interests in Atlanta, always extremely sensitive to public impressions which damaged the image of their city, realized the difficulty involved in explaining that the injustice imposed upon Dr. King emanated from a semirural county outside of Atlanta and had little to do with King's activities in that city. All of these forces converged upon Judge Mitchell, along with the probability or perhaps certainty that an unfavorable ruling would be quickly overturned anyway. Whatever the real explanation, Senator Kennedy and his brother profited from their last minute, but very cautious, intervention. The candidate for President called King's pregnant wife and the candidate's brother, the judge, and millions of Americans who sensed some of the potential power of the Kennedys were convinced that these actions accounted for King's release.

Perhaps it is a digression to discuss in such detail this rather small incident, but it seems to me it rather sharply points up the ambivalence that characterized Kennedy's position on civil rights questions during his candidacy and in his first two years in the White House. The hearts of John and Robert Kennedy were increasingly moved by the plight of their Black fellow citizens, and more and more they were determined to use their prestige and power to come to their aid. But their respect for the status quo, so clearly described in the brilliant chapter on federalism by Victor Navaky in his book on Robert Kennedy, and their instinctive political caution, frequently prevented them from doing as much as they ought to have done. Their efforts in this case were absolutely minimal; their rewards maximum. The proper action would have been to make a strong statement similar to the one drafted for Eisenhower, a statement which publicly condemned the action as contemptible and contrary to the right of every citizen to gain equal justice before the law.

If the Kennedys were overly cautious in risking their political futures in this instance, President Eisenhower and the Republican candidate, Nixon, were suicidal in ignoring a great opportunity. Martin Luther King and his family were more than generous to the Democratic candidate in the praise they extended to him for his thoughtful action, fully aware of the political implications of such statements. Mrs. King promptly released the story of Senator Kennedy's telephone call, indicating how reassuring it had been, and her husband told his father's congregation that evening that he was very grateful to the senator for his action. But it was Martin Luther "Daddy" King, sr. who topped this historic incident with the statement that later made history. With his son back at his side as his assistant in the Thanksgiving prayer meeting at the Ebenezer Baptist Church that evening, "Daddy" King told his parishioners:

> It took courage to call my daughter-in-law at a time like this. Kennedy has the moral courage to stand up for what he knows is right.[89]

It is understood that "Daddy" King had earlier backed Nixon, simply on the grounds of supporting a Protestant against a Catholic, but that evening in his church he cast away any such thought and gave Kennedy what was probably the strongest endorsement he had yet received from a Black citizen:

> If I had a suitcase full of votes, I'd take them all and place them at Senator Kennedy's feet.[90]

Georgia Democratic leaders tried to counteract whatever negative effect these events and statements would have on Georgia white voters, Governor Vandiver going so far as to lament that it was "a sad commentary on the year 1960 and its political campaign when the Democratic nominee for the Presidency makes a call to the home of the foremost radical in the country."[91] But he wound up declaring that the Democratic presidential ticket would still carry the state, and to compensate for Kennedy's phone call he reminded Georgia voters that the Republican presidential candidate was a member of the NAACP, and their vice presidential candidate, Henry Cabot Lodge, had publicly stated that if the Republicans were elected a Black man would be appointed to the cabinet. Nixon never endorsed this statement. These statements reflect something of what Kennedy was up against when he attempted privately to press the governor and others to use their influence to free King.

Shortly thereafter Mayor Hartsfield dropped the trespassing charges against King and the other 51 sit-in protesters; the vacating of those charges, of course, removed any basis for the parole violation in DeKalb County. The Sunday before election day hundreds of thousand of leaflets were distributed at Black churches and in Black communities throughout the country, featuring "Daddy" King's message, and alluding to Richard Nixon's silence during the incident. The rest is history.

James Meredith Asserts his Rights

It was indeed somewhat surprising that John Fitzgerald Kennedy, being very much aware of the recent history of failure and disillusionment in Little Rock, followed so closely in Oxford and Jackson, Mississippi, the pattern of indecision which led to rioting and violence at Central High School in 1957. Kennedy, of course, was never equivocal about his own attitude towards the Supreme Court decision, but he did fail in his initial test to communicate successfully to the officials of the State of Mississippi and the lawless mobs who rioted on the night of September 30, 1962, his determination to enforce the law. His efforts to temporize with outright violations of law by the governor, the lieutenant governor and other Mississippi state officials encouraged the mob to imitate their defiance of the law and ultimately to resort to violence, in the hope of preventing the registration of a single Black student at the University of Mississippi.

Kennedy, like Eisenhower, should have anticipated such a showdown. It was bound to come; in fact there was no way to avoid it. By 1961 those southern schools and institutions of higher learning which had not yet begun to integrate remained adamant about complying with the 1954 court decision, and it was inevitable that a mid-century President would come face-to-face with a situation in which the attempt of a Black student or students to enroll in a previously all-white school would provoke a crisis. In fact President Kennedy, before Oxford, had experienced several such incidents on the lower school levels. James Meredith's attempt to enter the University of Mississippi, however, was his first real civil rights crisis. It demonstrated without a doubt that the good faith, caution and restraint with which the President and his brother, the new attorney general, entered into negotiations with southern governors and other officials in order to encourage state compliance with the laws of the land, and state cooperation in maintaining law while Black citizens sought the protection of their rights under that law, were not adequate to protect those citizens or to insure that their rights would be protected. President Eisenhower had not even tried to exert presidential leadership in this critical area. President Kennedy tried very hard, but in the initial stages of his effort, he allowed the complex obstacles of federalism to inhibit his actions and to work to the advantage of those who would impede the law.

James Meredith was a 29-year old native of Mississippi, born and raised on a cotton farm in a rural area about 100 miles south of Oxford, Mississippi, the home of the University of Mississippi (Ole Miss). Meredith was one of ten children, all of whom graduated from high school, and seven of whom went on to college in a state which has the third highest rate of illiteracy in the nation. His grandfather had been a slave, and his father had been forced to discontinue his education at the fourth grade. Meredith entered the United States Army Air Force after graduating from high school, and was discharged as a staff sergeant after nine years in the service. While in the service he had taken a number of college courses in different university towns and cities in which he was stationed. When he returned home to Mississippi with his wife and child after many years absence, he was determined to advance his education as far as possible, and although he registered and studied during the interim at an all-Black college, Jackson State, he was determined to transfer to the best institution of higher learning in the state.

While at Jackson, Meredith wrote a paper which broadly reflected his state of mind at that time. It is worth examining that paper to begin to understand the formidable young man with whom the racial bigots in Mississippi were going to have to deal.

Meredith applied to the University of Mississippi in February 1961, inspired by the election of John F. Kennedy and confident that the new President would ensure the rights and privileges of Black citizens under the law. To Meredith this meant that he relied upon the support of the government and the President in what he expected to be a struggle to enter the university. He sent for an application form, proceded to fill it out and attached to it a covering letter in which he introduced himself to the registrar of the university, acquainted him with the fact that he was a Black citizen of the state, that he possessed the necessary qualifications and that he was looking forward to an early admission to the University of Mississippi.

> With all the presently occurring events regarding changes in our old educational system taking place in our country in this new age, I feel certain that this letter does not come as a surprise to you. I certainly hope that this matter will be handled in a manner that will be complimentary to the University and the state of Mississippi.[92]

It was clear from Meredith's letter that he was prepared to be challenged by the university officials, but he in turn was prepared to challenge them if they attempted to prevent him from obtaining the best education his home state could offer. Mississippi would probably have been quite willing to finance Meredith's education in an out-of-state institution of his choice, as was the practice in Mississippi and many other states when pressured by qualified Blacks, but Meredith was after something more than his own education. Besides, he loved Mississippi in his own way and saw no reason why the state should not be responsive to his needs. In his book about his three-year struggle for an education, Meredith writes very lyrically of his attachment to the Mississippi earth:

> Always, without fail, regardless of the number of times I enter Mississippi, it creates within me feelings that are felt at no other time. There is the feeling of joy. Joy because I have once again lived to enter the land of my fathers, the land of my birth, the only land in which I feel at home. It also inspires a feeling of hope because where there is life there is also a hope, a chance. At the same time, there is a feeling of sadness. Sadness because I am immediately aware of the special subhuman role that I must play, because I am a Negro, or die. Sadness because it is the home of the greatest number of Negroes outside of Africa, yet my people

suffer from want of everything in a rich land of plenty, and, most of all, they must endure the inconvenience of indignity.

Then, there is the feeling of love. Love of the land. To me, Mississippi is the most beautiful country in the world, during all seasons. In the spring, all is green and fresh, the air is clean and sweet, and everything is healthy. As a boy I knew that any running stream of water was fit to drink. I feel love because I have always felt that Mississippi belonged to me and one must love what is his.

In the summer there is maturity. The grass begins to level off and seed. A feeling of repose overcomes you. You have the urge to pull alongside the road and take a cowpath up into the bushes and lie down under a big tree. The effect of the heat shows everywhere. Blackberries begin to ripen; muscadine vines begin to hang from the burden of a good crop; and a black snake is likely to cross the road at any moment. Since the crops are nearly all laid by, the whole state takes on a relaxed and idle atmosphere. Summer is also the most suitable season for a lynching.[93]

Meredith was very concerned that members of the Black community, particularly Black students, understand precisely what he was doing and why he did it. Early on in his struggle he prepared a paper on this subject which he sent to students and communities throughout the state.

James H. Meredith
"Why I Plan to Go to the
University of Mississippi"
March 24, 1961

James Meredith, *Three Years in Mississippi* (Bloomington, Indiana, 1966), 87-90.

I wish to explain why I plan to go to the University of Mississippi because I want the people of our society to know my reasons, since I believe that there are many false conceptions about them among the Negroes of Mississippi.

First, there are my constitutional rights. It has been duly decided that no citizen of the United States can be denied the privilege of getting an education because of his race. The fact that no Negro has ever attended the school in question indicates to me that this right to an education has not been acknowledged.

My birthplace dictates to me the school of my choice. I think here of President Kennedy's statement, "If Africa is not for the Africans, then who is it for." I sincerely believe that Mississippi education is for the citizens of Mississippi; therefore, the only question is whether or not the Negro of Mississippi is a citizen. If he is not a citizen, then he is not entitled to this education; if he is a citizen, then he is entitled to this education.

The Negro has his own educational facilities! My only answer to this statement is that there is a limit to the number of teachers that can be utilized in the state and a greater limit to the number of preachers needed, in addition to the fact that not every young Negro seeking to gain a position of leadership desires to be a teacher or a preacher. Furthermore, I feel that it is a great injustice to force all our Negro male college graduates to serve as privates in the armed forces, without giving them the privilege of obtaining a commission through the ROTC program as can the white graduates of Mississippi schools and all other students in the U.S. This situation is not only detrimental to the individuals concerned, but to our country as a whole, because of the need to place the most capable persons in positions of leadership and work.

Problems. The greatest problem we face today, as I see it, is to stop the trend of our young Negroes toward an attitude of hopelessness. This is a demoralizing trend and will prove detrimental both to Mississippi and the nation if it is not stopped. It will truly be hard for others to conceive of the fears and inferior feelings that prevail among our people. Our young people, to the detriment of themselves, the state, the nation, and the world, are willing to give up what is theirs by right and nature for what they consider to be the only alternative they have.

I have read widely and have traveled a good deal, and I am firmly convinced that the American nation is truly the greatest among nations. From reports and from personal observation I feel that during the past three or so years the peoples of the world have begun to question our greatness because of our inability to solve the problem of unequal treatment of our citizens. The Negro is not by any means the only example of this unequal treatment, but I think that it is true that we are the greatest example. And Mississippi ranks first in the unequal treatment of its Negro citizens. I believe this is true, not because Mississippi has the worst group of people by natural endowment, but because the state has now, and has always had, the greatest number of Negroes in proportion to the number of whites. For this reason, the whites have been able to excite the hates and fears of the masses in order to hamper our progress. If the United States is to maintain its position of leadership, then it must solve its problem of unequal treatment of its citizens. And Mississippi must start progressing toward this end.

Why do I feel that I am the one individual to take direct action? I do not. I have no choice in the matter. I have seen very clearly all the faults in the society in which I live, and I am powerless to restrain myself from seeking to correct conditions that need to change for the benefit of all. Probably my greatest single reason to act is my son. He is only one year old, and yet I have already spent countless sleepless nights, trying to answer this question of my conscience, "When he grows up and sees all of the injustices and learns the illogical justifications upon which they are built, he will ask me, 'What have you done to correct these conditions?' What will I give as an answer?" I do not think that "Shut up, boy" will be an appropriate one.

Fears of the so-called Negro leadership. "I'm goin' to lose my job." They might have closed schools in Prince Edward County, Virginia, where only a handful of students were involved, but Mississippi schools will never be closed. Of all the unreasonable acts I hold against the powers-that-be in Mississippi, committing the inhumane act of closing the schools and denying hundreds of thousands of children the right to secure an education is one thing that I am positive that no respectable citizen of this state would even seriously consider. If the schools of Mississippi are not closed, then Negro teachers will be teaching Negro students here long after all of us are gone.

White position. Most white people to whom I have talked, and I have talked to all with whom I have had the opportunity—from the man who installed my telephone to banking officials, agree that Mississippi carries segregation to unreasonable limits.

Most of my contact with white Mississippians was during my service in the armed forces. I did not meet any white Mississippian in the Air Force with whom I could not work to complete our assigned task together. One of my greatest inspirations came from an Air Force colonel, who was born and raised in Mississippi and told me that he was a personal friend of the then governor. When I sought my last promotion in service, I had to meet a board of three colonels. Normally the questions asked an applicant are about his job and military procedures, but I was asked about the race question. They wanted to know how I felt about Mississippi and Mississippians, what my parents thought, and what other Negroes thought. When they had finished and I started out, the colonel from Mississippi, who was president of the board, called me back to tell me that, when he had checked my record, he had noticed that I was a Negro from Mississippi and he had persuaded the board to interrogate me in this unusual manner. He made this statement, "We are with you, but the degree of success attained in this new move to unify the potentials of our country will depend on you." "You" I interpreted to mean the Negro.

I have also talked with many white students in Mississippi. None of them seems to want or expect any radical changes, but all agree that certain changes will have to be made before there can be any progress in the state.

Am I afraid? This is somehow the most asked question. Before answering it, we must answer the question, "Afraid of what?" Am I afraid of failing to attain the goal of reducing the unequal treatment of our people? Yes. No one has ever gone into outer space and returned alive. [This was written shortly before the Russians sent their first cosmonaut into space.] When the day comes that we make our first attempt, I suspect that there will be many doubts as to its success. No Negro has gone to a school in Mississippi heretofore proclaimed for whites only, and for this reason I realize that I too might fail. Am I afraid of something happening to me? Or to my family or to my friends? By any logical interpretation, to my knowledge I seek to commit no crime, to break no law, or to infringe upon the rights of anyone; therefore, if this is the case, and something is to happen to me, then surely something has already happened to me.

Finally, I plan to enter the University of Mississippi for the good of my people, my country, my state, my family, and myself.

J. H. Meredith

Four days after Meredith mailed his application to the university, he received a letter from the registrar stating that the application would not be considered because the university had found it necessary to cut off all applications filed after January 25, 1961, an arbitrary date not previously announced. This was the beginning of the long and tortuous struggle in which Meredith never faltered or complained. He came back time and again, refusing to be discouraged by any obstacles placed in his path. Several days after receiving the note from the registrar, he wrote to the Department of Justice in Washington, indicating that the university had neither accepted nor rejected his application, but was using delaying tactics to discourage his ultimate admission to the university. After reviewing his reasons for wanting to study at Mississippi, Meredith set forth very candidly and forthrightly what he thought the Department of Justice's responsibilities were in his case:

> What do I want from you? I think that the power and influence of the federal government should be used where necessary to insure compliance with the laws as interpreted by the proper authority. I feel that the federal government can do more in this area if it chooses and I feel that it should choose to do so. In view of the above information I simply ask that the federal agencies use the power and prestige of their positions to insure the full rights of citizenship for our people.[94]

Meredith spent the next two years of his life attempting to persuade the Department of Justice and, ultimately, the President of the United States, to live up to his definition of responsibility. Paraphrasing Kennedy's words, he was "summoning" the national leadership "to its finest hour"; asking it to be true to its constitutional purpose by demonstrating that this is a society of laws and not of men (and prejudice). It is arguable whether the national leadership responded to that call as clearly and as forthrightly as it was issued. Ultimately there was no question that Meredith would win his fight if he could persevere long enough to enjoy his victory. But as someone has written, "ultimately we are all dead." That or a number of other as undesirable solutions could materialize if the President, the attorney general and all the power they could command did not or could not establish a climate where the decision of the courts, if necessary the highest court, could prevail. When a climate of lawful authority is threatened, delayed, ridiculed and ultimately rebuked, the society of laws is in more danger than even the champions of civil rights were during those often fearful but frequently inspiring days.

Meredith was the perfect hero for the stark drama that was unfolding. A loner, an individual of incomparable courage and will power, he never once deviated from his purpose or weakened in his determination to push the machinery of the law to the point where it would protect his rights. It must be understood that from the time of the *Brown* case on through to Meredith seven years later, the executive branch did not actively enforce the Supreme Court ruling, but rather the situation existed where its enforcement was the burden of individual citizens, groups and voluntary organizations like the NAACP Legal Defense and Educational Fund, to bring the issue *in situ*, as Brandeis would say, to the courts for adjudication. If complaints were not filed by citizens who were denied their rights, and suits were not introduced to obtain equal justice before the law, the government was limited to certain actions rather narrowly defined by statute, allowing something very close to the status quo to prevail. That, at least, was the interpretation of federalism which the attorney general and his eminent legal advisors advanced.

The problem was that the evidence of flagrant violations of the law and the abuse of individual rights was apparent for all to see, and it was difficult to explain to the injured citizen why it was his responsibility to risk his life to force the government to act to protect his rights. If a climate of physical and psychological force was maintained, not only by local vigilantes, but by the local and state political and law enforcement agencies themselves, it was the responsibility of the federal government to intervene on its own initiative to reestablish an environment where the law of the land was respected, and if not respected, at least obeyed. Was it not? Yet, while legal scholars at the law schools were pondering these questions, James Meredith went to the courts to seek justice under the law. Through attorneys provided by the Legal Defense and Education Fund, Meredith appeared in the federal district court in Meridian, Mississippi and filed suit against the trustees of the University of Mississippi for admission to the university. He lost the first round in a decision handed down six months later by a segregationist federal judge, who ruled that the university had not rejected Meredith on the basis of his race. He based his decision on the testimony of the trustees and the administrative officers of the university that no consideration or mention of Meredith's race had entered into their denial of his admission. Meredith's lawyers promptly filed in the Fifth Circuit Court of Appeals for a temporary injunction to overrule the district judge's decision, enabling the plaintiff to begin school immediately at the beginning of the winter-spring semester.

The Fifth Circuit Court, a remarkable panel of judges,[95] turned down Meredith's motion because they felt that the record of the lower court was unclear and confusing; they proposed a prompt full trial on the merits of the case in the district court. The majority opinion revealed substantial sympathy for many of the arguments presented by Meredith, however, and there was hope that the Fifth Circuit Court of Appeals would ultimately rule in his favor. In June of that same year, in a memorable decision which carefully traced the history of the case and examined in detail the fraudulent arguments used to hide the discriminatory decision made by the university, Meredith won his first court battle. Rarely has such a careful and deliberate analysis been given to the incredible hypocrisy and the deliberate fabrication of a supposedly reputable and honorable group of men, entrusted to conduct the affairs of the highest institution of learning in the state of Mississippi. This is such a distinguished decision that it probably belongs alongside of Brown v. Board of Education of Topeka. It also clearly belongs in a documented history of presidential power because it provides the substance of the arguments that presidential power should be used to protect the rights of citizens against unconstitutional, hypocritical subterfuge. It is a stunning piece of evidence for the case that American society is one of laws and not of men.

Decision of the Fifth Circuit Court
Admitting James H. Meredith to
The University of Mississippi
June 25, 1962

305 F. 2d 343 (5th Cir. 1962).

The Meredith matter is before us again. This time the appeal is from a final judgment after a trial on the merits. The judgment denies James H. Meredith, a Mississippi Negro in search of an education, an injunction to secure his admission to the University of Mississippi. We reverse with directions that the injunction issue.

A full review of the record leads the Court inescapably to the conclusion that from the moment the defendants discovered Meredith was a Negro they engaged in a carefully calculated campaign of delay, harassment, and masterly inactivity. It was a defense designed to discourage and to defeat by evasive tactics which would have been a credit to Quintus Fabius Maximus.

After the trial on the merits, the district judge found "as a fact, that the University is not a racially segregated institution." He found that the state had no policy of segregation. He did find that segregation was the custom *before* Brown v. Board of Education . . . was decided in May 1954. But, he held, "there is no custom or policy now, nor was there any at the time of the plaintiff's application, which excluded Negroes from entering the University." This about-face in policy, news of which may startle some people in Mississippi, could have been accomplished only by telepathic communication among the University's administrators, the Board of Trustees of State Institutions of Higher Learning. As the trial judge pointed out in his opinion, "nearly every member of the Board of Trustees, testified unequivocally and definitely that at no time had the question of race of a party ever been discussed at a meeting of the Board of Trustees or at any other place and that so far as the Board of Trustees was concerned, all policies and regulations were adopted and followed without regard to race, creed or color."

In our previous opinion in this case, . . . on the appeal from a denial of the preliminary injunction, it seemed to us that "what everybody knows the court must know." We took "judicial notice that the state of Mississippi maintains a policy of segregation in its schools and colleges." (We find nothing now in this case reaching the dignity of proof to make us think we were wrong to take judicial notice of Mississippi's policy of segregation.) Nevertheless, on that appeal, giving the University the benefit of the doubt, it seemed to us that a trial on the merits would be in the interest of justice: for reasons not attributable to the endeavors or competency of counsel, it was impossible to determine from the record whether there were valid, non-discriminatory grounds for the University's refusing Meredith's admission.

The district judge found no reason in the trial on the merits to change his earlier findings of fact and conclusions of law. He held that the evidence "shows clearly that there was no denial of admission because of his race and color." In reaching this conclusion the trial judge adopted the findings of fact in his earlier opinion on the motion for a preliminary injunction. It is necessary therefore to review the case from the beginning. Such whole-case review has the advantage of enabling the Court to consider the various contentions in context and to determine whether the pieces fit together to make a pattern of unlawful discrimination.

I

James H. Meredith was born in 1933 near Kosciusko, in Attala County, one of the rural counties in Mississippi. After graduating from high school in 1950 he volunteered for service in the United States Air Force. When his hitch was over he reenlisted. In the Air Force he rose to the rank of staff sergeant. He was discharged in the summer of 1960. He was never in trouble with civilian or military authorities. Meredith received an honorable discharge and the Good Conduct Medal.

Meredith got his education the hard way. Sometime in 1953 he decided to improve himself. He turned first to "Fundamentals of Speech" and "Composition and Literature," extension courses of the University of Kansas. In 1954 he enrolled in a course in "Government of the United States" at Washburn University in Topeka. He received the grade of "C" in each of these subjects. From 1954 to 1960 he took advantage of college level courses of the United States Armed Forces Institute, for which Jackson State College credited him with fifty-seven quarter hours credit. Meredith's most fruitful years, educationally, were the two years he spent in Japan just before leaving the service. He attended the Far East Division of the University of Maryland. He tackled difficult courses such as "Russian," and he carried a heavy schedule. In 1958-1959 he had 5 "B's"; in 1959-1960 he had 3 "B's" and 3 "A's". The University of Maryland credited him with thirty-four semester hours for twelve courses.

Promptly after returning home, Meredith registered at Jackson State College, a "Negro" college in Hinds County, Mississippi. He moved to Jackson with his wife and child. At Jackson State his grades were almost all "A's" and "B's". In January 1961 he applied for admission to the University of Mississippi. When asked on the witness stand why he wished to transfer, he said Jackson State was "substandard."

These facts raise a doubt as to the defendants' good faith in asserting that Meredith was not in good faith in applying for admission to the University of Mississippi. That Meredith's transfer would mean the loss of credits and possibly the loss of some G.I. Benefits, that he was in his late twenties, that he might find the University of Mississippi considerably more difficult than Jackson State College, demonstrate his perseverance and fit in with the character of a man who is having a hard time getting a college education but is willing to pay the price exacted of a Negro for admission to the University of Mississippi.

II

The defendants' Fabian policy of planned discouragement and discrimination by delay is evident from the correspondence between Meredith and the University.

Sometime in January 1961 Meredith wrote the Registrar for application forms. He received a prompt reply thanking him for his interest and enclosing the forms. January 31 he wrote the Registrar, enclosing the executed forms. In this letter Meredith expressly informed the University that he was a Negro. This was not a gesture of defiance—the forms require a photograph and an indication of race—but a predicate for pointing out that although he could not furnish the names of alumni who reside in his county and have known him for at least two years, he was submitting certificates regarding his moral character from Negro citizens who had known him in the county of his birthplace. As is apparent from the letter, Meredith was "hopeful that the complications [would] be as few as possible." We read this letter as showing no chip on the shoulder and no evidence of such abnormal concern as to support the defendants' contention that from the start Meredith's letters indicate he was "belligerent," a "trouble-maker," and had psychological problems. We think it not unreasonable for a Negro to have some concern over his reception on the "Ole Miss" campus.

February 4, 1961, two days before registration began for the second semester, the Registrar telegraphed Meredith:

"For your information and guidance it has been found necessary to discontinue consideration of all applications for admission or registration for the second semester which were received after January 25, 1961. Your application was received subsequent to such date and thus we must advise you not to appear for registration."

In his holding on the preliminary injunction, the trial judge found as a fact that this first refusal of admissions was a proper refusal because of "overcrowded conditions." In February 1961, however, there were only 2500 to 2600 male students on the campus. As of September 1961, as the Director of Student Personnel testified, there were about 3000 male students on the campus.

February 20 Meredith wrote the Registrar requesting that his application be treated as a continuing application for admission during the summer session. He called attention to his transcripts having been forwarded from the Universities he attended. He concluded, "Again, I would like to express my gratitude for the respectable and humane manner in which you are handling this matter and I am very hopeful that this procedure will continue." The next day his room deposit of ten dollars was returned.

February 23 Meredith returned the ten dollars, explaining that he had requested his application be considered for the summer session. After waiting a month for an answer Meredith wrote the Registrar again. This time he requested that his application be considered as a continuing one for the summer session and for the fall session. He inquired whether his transcripts had been received and whether there were "any further prerequisites to admission." After waiting eight days for an answer, and apparently thoroughly alarmed by eloquent silence from the University, Meredith again wrote the Registrar. It is the letter of a man of perseverance, but a man of patience and politeness. He asked the Registrar to please let him have the University's evaluation of his credits acceptable to the University "if it [were] appropriate at [that] time." He enclosed five certificates certifying to his good moral character and recommending him for admission to the University; the earlier letters were silent on the subject of recommending him. He said that he "realize[d] that [he was] not a usual applicant to the University of Mississippi, and that some timely items might need to be considered."

Another month went by. Still no answer. April 12 Meredith wrote the Dean of the College of Liberal Arts at the University. In laconic style, barren of comment, Meredith told of his application and his unanswered letters. He concluded:

"When I forwarded my application to Mr. Ellis on January 31, 1961, I stated in a letter to him and in my application that I am a Negro citizen of Mississippi. Because of my failure to hear from Mr. Ellis since his telegram to me of February 4, 1961, I have concluded that Mr. Ellis has failed to act upon my application solely because of my race and color, especially since I have attempted to comply with all of the admission requirements and have not been advised of any deficiencies with respect to same.

"I am, therefore, requesting you to review my case with the Registrar and advise me what admission requirements, if any, I have failed to meet, and to give me some assurance that my race and color are not the basis for my failure to gain admission to the University."

The Dean did not reply to this letter. Belatedly, May 9, the Registrar replied, advising Meredith that "the maximum credit which could be allowed is forty-eight semester hours [for the 90 hours submitted] if your application for admission as a transfer student should be approved." The letter asked Meredith to "please advise if you desire your application to be treated as a pending application."

Meredith took this as a good omen. May 15 he wrote that he wished to attend the first term of the session starting in June, and that it was imperative he be informed with respect to his admission because he would have to make arrangements for his family. He enclosed a letter to the Director of Men's Housing, applying for an apartment appropriate for his family size—a wife and small child. Not having received an answer by May 21, Meredith wrote again. He said that since the Registrar had asked if his application should be considered as pending, he had "assumed by the nature of [the] request that [his] application was entirely complete and that [he had] met all of the pre-registration requirements."

The axe fell May 25, 1961. On that date the Registrar closed his correspondence file on the application and returned the money Meredith had deposited. He gave the following reasons for returning admission:

"The University cannot recognize the transfer of credits from the institution which you are now attending since it is not a member of the Southern Association of Colleges and Secondary Schools. Our policy permits the transfer of credits only from member institutions of regional associations. Furthermore, students may not be accepted by the University from those institutions whose programs are not recognized. As I am sure you realize, your application does not meet other requirements for admission. Your letters of recommendation are not sufficient for either a resident or a nonresident applicant. I see no need for mentioning any other deficiencies."

We pause in narrating the facts to observe that the explanation is inadequate on its face. (1) It ignores the credits from Washburn, Kansas, and Maryland. (2) The "programs" from those institutions are of course "recognized" by Mississippi. As for Jackson State, its program was established and is supervised by the identical

Board of Trustees supervising the program at the University of Mississippi. (3) The letters of recommendation refer to the requirement of alumni certificates, a patently discriminatory device.

Up to this point the University had successfully avoided decisive action on the 1961 Fall term. And, because of the lateness of hour, the University was in a favorable position to resist the expected assaults on the summer sessions.

III

May 31, 1961, Meredith filed a complaint in the United States District Court for the Southern District of Mississippi. The defendants were the Board of Trustees of the State Institutions of Higher Learning, the Chancellor of the University of Mississippi, the Dean of the College of Liberal Arts, and the Registrar of the University. The Governor of Mississippi appoints the Board with the consent of the state senate. The Board, a constitutional body, is vested with the management and control of all Mississippi's colleges and universities, including the Negro colleges.

The complaint is filed as a class action. It alleges that the defendants are pursuing a state policy, state practice, state custom, and state usage of maintaining and operating separate state institutions of higher learning for the white and Negro citizens of Mississippi; that under this policy Meredith was denied admission to the University solely because of race and color. At the first hearing the plaintiff was denied permission to introduce evidence relating to other colleges and universities in Mississippi. (In view of the theory of the complaint that segregation was a state policy being carried out by the Board charged with administering all of the state's institutions of higher learning, this ruling was clearly erroneous.) The evidence, therefore, relates only to the University.

At the time the complaint was filed counsel for Meredith sought a restraining order; the summer term was about to begin. The trial judge denied the order.

The case was set for a hearing on the plaintiff's motion for a preliminary injunction, June 12, 1961. This was four days *after* commencement of the summer session. About 3:30 p.m. on the afternoon of the hearing the trial judge stopped the trial and continued the case on the ground that because of his crowded docket he had set aside only one day to hear the case. The case was continued until July 10, 1961, at which time, according to the court, the entire case would be heard since, in the interim, the answer would be filed, the issues "definitely framed and we can begin the case and finish it." In practice, in almost all cases, a hearing on a motion for a preliminary injunction is held before an answer is filed.

The case was not heard on July 10 because of a scheduled three-judge court case which required the presence of the trial judge below and involved counsel for both parties. Meredith's counsel therefore filed, June 29, another motion for a preliminary injunction, since the second summer term would commence July 17. The motion was fixed for a hearing on July 11. On July 10 the chief counsel for the defendants, Assistant Attorney General Shands, was ill. His illness caused the case to be continued to August 10, 1961. By that time any possibility of attending the second summer session had gone winging.

June 9 and 30, 1961, and again July 27, July 28, and August 4, 1961 Meredith's counsel sought to take the Registrar's deposition. The efforts were singularly unsuccessful. The trial judge denied the first motion on the ground that the deposition could not be taken prior to the expiration of twenty days from the filing of the complaint. . . . The second notice of taking was suspended and stayed by the court on the ground of Mr. Shands' poor health, June 27, two weeks before the July 10 postponement of the trial. August 1 the trial judge vacated the other three notices on the ground that the court was "in the process of trial on plaintiff's motion for Temporary Injunction, and the exercise of [the] court's discretion." This appears to us to have been a clear abuse of judicial discretion.

Counsel for Meredith filed a motion that the University produce records of all students admitted to the February 1961 term, the 1961 summer terms, and the September 1961 term for inspection July 1 to July 7. The motion, filed June 20, was not heard until July 27, because of Mr. Shands' ill health and because of the crowded court calendar. August 1 the district court ordered the records produced for inspection, but limited inspection of records to applications for undergraduate enrollment in the 1961 summer terms, and to applications to the graduate schools. This order was manifestly erroneous and was one of the causes for the poor state of the record in the hearing for the preliminary injunction.

July 10 the trial judge announced that the hearing on August 10 would be a trial on the merits. August 1 this ruling was reversed; the trial judge ruled that the August 10 hearing would be a continuation of the June 12 hearing on the preliminary injunction.

July 19 the defendants filed their answer. The answer supplemented the Registrar's letter of May 25 by giving a large number of additional reasons, many of them trivial, for the University's having refused Meredith admission. The answer emphasizes the following reasons. (1) Meredith failed or refused to submit the requisite alumni certificates. (2) Meredith "was not seeking admission to the University of Mississippi in good faith for the purpose of securing an education," considering all of the circumstances and particularly the fact that as a consequence of transferring to the University he would lose credits and G.I. benefits. (3) Meredith's fear that his application might be denied because of his race "shocked, surprised and disappointed" the Registrar. It was so "rash" and "unjustified" that it raised grave questions as to Meredith's "ability to conduct himself as a normal person and a harmonious student on the campus of the University of Mississippi." The Registrar, for himself and the other defendants, all of whom adopted his answer, denied that "he understands and interprets the policy of the State of Mississippi as being that Negroes and whites are educated in separate institutions of higher learning."

August 10 the hearing on the motion for a preliminary injunction, which commenced and was adjourned June 12, was resumed. But on August 11, it was recessed again. Mr. Shands had to appear in another court August 14 on motions he had filed in another suit. The hearing resumed August 15 and concluded August 16.

At the end of this hearing, the trial judge gave the defendants until September 5 to file their brief, and the plaintiff ten days thereafter to file a reply brief.

The last date to register for the fall semester was September 28. The trial judge did not decide the case until December 12. He entered an order in favor of the defendants December 14, 1961. That shot the first semester of 1961-62. The commencement of the second semester was not far off—February 6. Immediately following entry of the order, Meredith's counsel filed a notice of appeal and moved this Court for an order advancing the appeal. This Court heard the appeal January 9 and rendered its decision January 12. We affirmed the district court's denial of the motion for a preliminary injunction. We suggested that the district court proceed promptly with a full trial on the merits.

In that decision we disposed of one of the reasons the University stressed in rejecting Meredith—the requirement that he furnish alumni certificates. We held that such a requirement is a denial of equal protection of the laws in its application to Negro candidates for admission. Again we pause, this time to say that if there is any question as to the scope of that ruling, we now hold that the requirement of recommendations, whether from alumni or from citizens generally, attesting to an applicant's good moral character, or recommending an applicant for admission, is unconstitutional when, as this case demonstrates, the burden falls more heavily on the Negroes than on whites. This is not to say, of course, that good moral character is not a reasonable test for admission.

We held that on "the muddy record" before us it was "impossible to determine whether there were valid, nondiscriminatory grounds for the University's refusing Meredith's admission." We made certain observations for the guidance of the district judge presiding at the trial. We emphasized that, "*Within proper legal bounds*, the plaintiff should be afforded a fair, unfettered, and unharassed opportunity to prove his case."

The trial on the merits set for January 15, 1962, commenced January 16. At 2:00 p.m. on that date it was postponed until 3:00 p.m. January 17, to give the defendants' counsel an opportunity to confer with the defendants. At 3:00 p.m. January 17 the defendants' counsel moved for a continuance on account of Mr. Shands' illness; he was hospitalized. The two special assistants stated to the court that they were not prepared to proceed with the trial. The district court continued the case until 2:00 p.m. January 24, 1962.

Before the trial, the district court quashed that part of a subpoena requiring the Registrar to produce admission records for the February 1961 term; the Registrar was required to produce only records commencing with the first summer term. This holding, seriously handicapping plaintiff's counsel, apparently overlooked our ruling in the earlier opinion: "The limitation of evidence to that pertaining to the summer session of 1961 is clearly erroneous. It is erroneous since the policy and practice of the University in admissions were at issue."

February 5, 1962, the district judge entered an order denying all relief requested and dismissing the complaint. The same day, the plaintiff appealed to this Court and also filed a motion for a preliminary injunction pending appeal on the ground that unless Meredith were admitted to the February 1962 term, the case would become moot. This Court heard the motion February 10. A majority of the Court, Chief Judge Tuttle dissenting, denied the motion February 12. . . . Still anxious to give this case full study on an adequate record, we held that the appeal would not necessarily be moot; that Meredith could avoid the mootness by attending Jackson State College for one quarter of the school year or by being permitted to choose courses not necessarily leading to his graduation. Meredith pursued the latter course.

The net effect of all these delays was that the February 1961 term, the two summer terms of 1961, and the two regular terms of 1961-62 slipped by before the parties litigant actually came to a showdown fight. Some of these delays, as in any litigation, were inevitable. Some are attributable to continuances of doubtful propriety and to unreasonably long delays by the trial judge. We refer, for example, to the delay between the end of the trial, August 16, and the entry of the district court's order, December 14. Many of the delays resulted from the requests of defendants. We do not question Mr. Shands' good faith or the fact of his illness, but the Attorney General's Office is well-staffed. And—there are plenty of lawyers in Mississippi ready, able, and more than willing to represent the University. We draw the inference that not a few of the continuances and the requests for time in which to write briefs were part of the defendants' delaying action designed to defeat the plaintiff by discouragingly high obstacles that would result in the case carrying through his senior year. It almost worked.

As a matter of law, the principle of "deliberate speed" has no application at the college level; time is of the essence. In an action for admission to a graduate or undergraduate school, counsel for all the litigants and trial judges too should be sensitive to the necessity for speedy justice. . . .

IV

We turn now to the reasons the University gave in its letter of May 25 for rejecting Meredith.

A. Alumni Certificates—Letters of Recommendation

1. One of the most obvious dodges for evading the admission of Negroes to "white" colleges is the requirement that an applicant furnish letters or alumni certificates. The Board established the requirement by resolution, November 18, 1954, just a few months after the Supreme Court decided Brown v. Board of Education. We mention it again at this point in the opinion because its adoption and incorporation in current Bulletins (Catalogues) of the University show affirmative action by the Board to evade desegregation. The action unquestionably was part of conscious University and State policy. It was action that must have been preceded by discussion among members of the Board.

The University's continued use of the requirement seems completely unjustifiable in view of decisions denying the use of such certificates at Louisiana State University and at the University of Georgia. Since at least 1958, . . . the Board has been on notice that the courts construe such a requirement as an unconstitutional discrimination against Negroes. If the Board has any doubt about it, that doubt should have been resolved in 1959 when a similar requisite of the University of Georgia was held to be unconstitutional. . . . We regard the continued insistence on the requirement as demonstrable evidence of a State and University policy of segregation that was applied to Meredith.

2. Although defendants' counsel deny that the alumni certificates were for discriminatory purposes or had discriminatory effects, they assert that the enabling resolution of the Board was an administrative order having the effect of a state statute. For this reason, they say that a three-judge court should have passed on the constitutionality of the certificates. (This position is, of course, inconsistent with the defendants' we-still-say-its-scissors denial of any state policy of segregation in Mississippi's colleges.) We hold that the Board resolution was an administrative order having an effect similar to a statute, and that it constituted a broad State policy and University policy. We hold, however, that its manifest unconstitutionality makes a three-judge court unnecessary. . . .

3. The evidence also shows that the requirement of alumni certificates was discriminatorily applied to Meredith. The Registrar testified that the files of white transfer students admitted to the 1961 summer session contained letters of recommendation which did not mention good moral character. He explained that such students were permitted to register pending the receipt of all required certificates. No such latitude was extended Meredith.

B. The University's Policy Regarding Transfer Students from Non-Member Colleges of Regional Associations

February 7, 1961, just six days after the University received Meredith's application, the Board adopted the following resolution:

"[T]hat all state-supported Institutions of Higher Learning may accept transfer students from other state supported Institutions of Higher Learning, private colleges or denomination colleges only when the previous program of the transferring college is acceptable to the receiving Institution, and the program of studies completed by the student, and the quality of the student's work in said transferring college is acceptable to the receiving Institution and to the Board of Trustees."

This resolution stiffens the policy as stated in the University Bulletin, General Catalogue, Issue 1960:

"ADMISSION FOR TRANSFER STUDENTS: ADVANCED STANDING. Students may be admitted from *other approved institutions* of higher learning upon presentation of official transcripts of credits which certify honorable dismissal and eligibility for immediate readmission." (Emphasis supplied.)

The May 25 letter advised Meredith that he was denied admission because "students may not be accepted by the University from those institutions whose programs are not recognized." Translating, the Registrar said this means that Meredith could not transfer to the University because Jackson State College was not a member of the Southern Association of Colleges and Secondary Schools. It also means that the Board, which runs Jackson State too, could set up at Jackson State and other Negro colleges a program inherently incapable of ever being approved.

But this reason is no longer valid. December 16, 1961, Jackson State was admitted to membership in the Association.

The reason was never valid, and again demonstrates a conscious pattern of unlawful discrimination.

Before December 1961, as the Registrar testified, not one of the three Negro colleges was a member of the Association. They were, however, on the Association's *approved* list of Negro Colleges. At the time Meredith applied for admission, the University catalogue, as quoted, provided that transfer students might be accepted from another "approved Institution of Higher Learning." The College Accrediting Commission of the State of Mississippi . . . has approved Jackson State College.

In defending its position, the University draws a distinction between "accepting" credits and "recognizing" credits, a distinction that eludes the Court. The defendants' explanation is that "the justification for only recognition was the fact that the appellant could not transfer from Jackson State College." Any reasonable interpretation of the resolution would limit its effect to transfer students with credits only from non-approved or non-accredited colleges. It seems to us indefensible to ignore Meredith's attendance at such accredited universities as Maryland, Kansas, and Washburn on the excuse that his last college was Jackson State.

At the trial, plaintiff's counsel inspected 214 files of students denied admission to the Summer Sessions of 1961, the September Session of 1961, and the February Session of 1962. Not one was a student who had credits from both accredited and non-accredited colleges. Thus, Meredith was not in the same category with any other student *denied* admission for lack of credits. There were six instances of students denied transfer from non-accredited schools; these students, of course, had no credits to transfer. In five instances the applicant had attended only the one non-accredited school from which he requested transfer. One was in the same academic class as the plaintiff, in the sense that he had attended an accredited school, Bucknell. Unlike Meredith's transcripts, his Bucknell transcript states: "Permitted to withdraw. Academic status unsatisfactory." At the time of his application he was taking a course in English composition at an un-accredited junior college and taking a remedial reading class somewhere else. Even so, in spite of his miserable record, the Registrar advised the boy's mother that the University of Mississippi would admit him on probation if he were eligible to return to Bucknell and if he maintained a "D" average. Thus, Meredith was not treated the same as another in the same category but with an inferior record.

In short, the transfer policy was both discriminatorily applied and irrationally construed in order to bar Meredith's admission.

C. *Transfer of Credits from Jackson State*

May 9, 1961, the Registrar wrote Meredith a letter in which he evaluated Meredith's 90 semester credits at 48 semester hours. Six days later, just ten days before the axe fell on May 25, the Committee on Admissions adopted a policy of accepting "credits only from institutions which are members of a regional accrediting association or a recognized professional accrediting association."

Jackson State's admission as a member of the Southern Association of Colleges and Secondary Schools removes this policy as a bar to accepting Meredith's credits from that school. At the trial the Registrar testified that the policy operated to preclude acceptance of only the Jackson State credits. It is impossible to understand, therefore, why in the letter of May 25 the Registrar gave as the first reason for turning Meredith down that the University cannot *recognize* the transfer of credits from [an] institution which . . . is not a member of the Southern Association of Colleges and Secondary Schools." On the Registrar's own evaluation, Meredith had enough credits to be transferred as a sophomore. There is no suggestion in any of the correspondence that Meredith insisted on being transferred as a junior or that the University recognize all his credits.

We draw the inference again that the assigned reason for rejecting Meredith was a trumped-up excuse without any basis except to discriminate.

Thus far, we have covered all of the specific reasons given in the May 25 letter. On the record, as of May 25, 1961, the University had no valid, non-discriminatory grounds for refusing to accept Meredith as a student.

V

A college registrar is entitled to take advantage of play in the joints in administering an office frequently requiring deliberate ambiguity and conscious confusion in order not to offend the delicate sensibilities of some college student and his parents. We recognize the necessity for such latitude and the sagacity of the final clause in the Registrar's letter of May 25, "I see no need for mentioning any other deficiencies." But the reasonable discretion permissible in an admissions policy cannot be exercised to bring about unlawful discrimination.

We take up now the ex post facto rationalization of the turndown. It may be debatable whether the Court should consider any newly originated reasons and any post-May 25 evidence, but we sit as a court of equity. Consideration of such matters cuts both ways; the plaintiff seeks to take advantage of the new status of Jackson State College. In an analogous situation, in labor cases, evidence of a discriminatory discharge or other unfair labor practice occurring after the filing of the charge upon which the complaint is based may be considered by the National Labor Relations Board and the reviewing court. . . .

A. *The Alleged False Registration: A Frivolous Defense*

The defendants attempted to show Meredith swore falsely before the Circuit Clerk of Hinds County in making application to register as a voter, swearing that he was a citizen of Hinds County when he knew he was a citizen of Attala County. In his opinion on the merits, the district judge declined to make a finding of fact on this point "since these facts were not known to the Registrar at the time the application was rejected," and "concluded that this testimony should not be considered" in reaching his conclusions. In his opinion on the motion for a preliminary injunction the district court said that the *defendants* "brought out on cross examination that after [Meredith] entered Jackson State . . . he swore falsely that he was a citizen of Hinds County." The district court made no finding on the alleged "false swearing," although it found that Meredith "was and is now a citizen of Attala County, Mississippi."

The complaint alleges that Meredith is a resident of Hinds County. Jackson State College is in Hinds County. Meredith registered to vote in Hinds County. That is where he lived with his wife and child. J.R. McLeod, Deputy Clerk of Hinds

County registered Meredith after he received complete and accurate information from Meredith with regard to his residence. He testified that Meredith was properly registered and was "qualified to vote" in Hinds County.

Section 251 of the Mississippi Constitution prohibits registration of an elector in the four months preceding any election at which he offers to vote. But "no person who, in respect to age and residence would become entitled to vote within the said four months, shall be excluded from registration on account of his want of qualification at the time of registration."

Meredith's residence in Hinds County with his wife and child began September 1960. He registered in Hinds County February 2, 1961, which he had a right to do under Section 251 of the state constitution. As McLeod testified, "he had moved into Hinds County in time to have been qualified to have voted in 1961 (sic) since he moved in prior to the general election of 1960 . . . and on that basis I registered him." He said: Meredith "had stayed there past the general election on Tuesday after the first Monday of November which put him past one general election, and then he would have lived there a year before the next ensuing general election which would be Tuesday after the first Monday in November of '61. . . . *Yes, he was qualified to vote in Hinds County.*"

There is no false statement in the registration application Meredith filled out except the date. This he inadvertently wrote "February 2, 1960" when it was in fact February 2, 1961; the Poll Tax Exemption Certificate for Service Men, which McLeod filled out for Meredith at the same time he registered is properly dated February 2, 1961. Meredith correctly gave September 30, 1960, as the date his residence began in Jackson, in Hinds County. There can be no question therefore of any deception on his part. He stated that his prior place of residence was Kosciusko. It seems clear to us that he was open and straightforward. Meredith testified:

"I told him [the deputy clerk, McLeod] that I had been in the service [in order to qualify for a Poll Tax Exemption Certificate]. I told him that I had never lived in Hinds County. [He had not previously; the application shows the date his residence in Jackson commenced.] I told him that I had always lived in Attala County. [True enough, and necessary as a predicate for the poll tax exemption] . . . I was going to Jackson State College and wanted to register and vote in [Jackson] Hinds County, as the voting place most convenient and closest [to his residence]. . . . I explained my whole situation to the man when I went up to register to vote."

The testimony of the deputy fully supports Meredith's testimony and the correctness of the statements in the sworn affidavit.

There is confusion in some of the testimony. Mr. Shands caused some of the confusion by repeatedly referring to the Poll Tax Exemption Certificate as the registration application. (Meredith had taken his certificate out of his pocket and was holding it in his hands during the examination.) The plaintiff caused some of the confusion by polite "Yes Sir's" to some of Mr. Shands' leading questions (e.g., "You knew it was untrue"). In the printed record these "Yes Sir's" appear at first glance to be admissions of false statements. Examining the record closer, it is evident that Meredith made no admissions of any false statements; the "Yes Sir's" simply indicating Meredith was attentive and following the questions.

We hold that the contention is frivolous. We have gone into the facts in detail only because they show a determined policy of discrimination by harassment.

B. *Meredith a Troublemaker*

The Registrar, relying on his interpretation of Meredith's character from the correspondence and from the testimony, testified that he would have to deny Meredith admission *now*. He said, Meredith "would be a very bad influence" at the University: item one Meredith was "a man who has got a mission in life to correct all of the ills of the world." The defendants rely more importantly on excerpts from admittedly incomplete Air Force records to support their conclusion that Meredith was "a trouble maker" who has "psychological problems in connection with his race."

Taken out of context, some portions of Meredith's record lend support to the defendants' position. The most damaging bit is a psychiatry report dated April 29, 1960:

"This is a 26 year old Negro S Sgt who complains of tension, nervousness and occasional nervous stomach. Patient is extremely concerned with the 'racial problem' and his symptoms are intensified whenever there is a heightened tempo in the racial problems in the US and Africa. Patient feels he has a strong need to fight and defy authority and this he does in usually a passive procrastinating way. At times he starts a crusade to get existing rules and regulations changed. He loses his temper at times over minor incidents both at home and elsewhere. No evidence of a thinking disorder. Diagnosis: Passive aggressive reaction, chronic, moderate. Recommendations: No treatment recommended. Patient declined any medication."

It is certainly understandable that a sensitive Negro, especially one overseas, might have a nervous stomach over the racial problem. There must be a good many Negroes stateside with similar abdominal reactions. We find it significant that the psychiatrist found "no evidence of a thinking disorder," that he found Meredith's "strong need to fight and defy authority" took a "passive" form, and that no treatment was recommended. Meredith, incidentally, voluntarily went to the psychiatrist.

The defendants expressly admit in their brief that Meredith had a good record during his first enlistment. They count on a general deterioration of attitude allegedly demonstrated in his last efficiency report. This report is for the period November 3, 1959 to July 18, 1960 at San Francisco, California, although the reporting official who made out the fitness report had directly supervised Meredith only two months. The reporting official's comments should be compared with the comments in the report dated May 22, 1959. It furnishes no basis for down-grading Meredith as a psychological risk on the campus. The rating official thought that Meredith had a "negative attitude toward most of the jobs assigned him" (he was leaving the service in a couple of months); that Meredith "exercises no tact or diplomacy in dealing with persons of equal or higher rank, thus causing unnecessary friction"; that he needs improvement in his outlook on the world, more allegiance to his squadron in the Air Force, less of an "antagonistic attitude" and more of a "spirit of cooperation." But he also wrote: "Sgt. Meredith has taken advantage of many opportunities to further his own education, and has counseled and encouraged many airmen to do likewise. He has a quick mind, [is] capable of clear thinking, and is not content to merely ride with the tide".... He (the reporting official, a sergeant) did not recommend Meredith for promotion. But Meredith's immediate supervisor, the Adjutant, a lieutenant, and the Unit Commander, a major, disagreed. They recommended Meredith for promotion "along with other airmen of equal service and experience."

One short answer to the defendants' contention is the Good Conduct Medal. Another short answer is that Meredith's record shows just about the type of Negro who might be expected to try to crack the racial barrier at the University of Mississippi: a man with a mission and with a nervous stomach.

C. Bad Character Risk

The defendants are scraping the bottom of the barrel in asserting that the University should not now admit Meredith because he is a bad character risk. They rely on (1) the frivolous charge of false swearing, previously discussed, (2) alleged misrepresentation by Meredith in obtaining letters of recommendation from Negroes who knew him in Attala County before he entered the Service, and (3) certain trivia.

At the trial on the merits defendants' counsel introduced affidavits from four of the five Negroes who had written letters of recommendation for Meredith. These affidavits purport to show that Meredith obtained his letters by misrepresentation. The affidavits were obtained by one of the Assistant Attorney Generals of counsel in this case. He testified:

"The affiants were requested to come to the law office of Mr. John Clark Love, which they did on their voluntariness—they came of their own volition. When they arrived there, they were interviewed in the presence of the Justice of the Peace and in one instance by the Notary who was there present. They were asked various questions as to the good moral character of the plaintiff. They were asked under what conditions had the previous or the first certificates which accompanied the application—under what conditions were they asked. And they replied that he stated that he was attempting to get a job and that was the reason the certificates were asked."

Mr. Love is a man of stature in the community. He is a State Senator and a former member of the State Sovereignty Commission.

There is no evidence of coercion. But the affidavits were drawn by the defendants' attorney and were taken in the presence of persons representing, to a country Negro, the power and prestige of The Establishment of Attala County and the State of Mississippi. The statements would have carried more weight had the affiants testified as witnesses in open court protected by the safeguards our system of law extends to witnesses. The defendants give no explanation for failing to call these affiants as witnesses.

None of the affiants alleges that Meredith is a person of bad moral character. Only two of the four allege that Meredith represented that he needed the certificate to help obtain a job. Each alleges that the affiant did not know the certificate was to be used for admission to the University. Each alleges that the affiant had seen very little of Meredith since he left Kosciusko in 1949; that the affiant could not now certify to his good character nor recommend him for admission to the University of Mississippi.

An unsigned affidavit from the fifth affiant, the plaintiff's cousin, states: "At the time of the signing of this statement (the recommendation) I knew full well and was aware of the purpose for which such certificate was to be executed." This unsigned statement, unlike the executed affidavits, significantly is the only one that contains the following declaration: "I am not now nor have I ever been in any serious trouble or convicted of any crime or misdemeanor."

In sum, we consider it unreasonable to attach any substantial weight to these affidavits. They do not carry enough weight in themselves nor in connection with the evidence as a whole of Meredith's character to justify a reasonable belief that Meredith is a bad moral risk as a University student.

The other asserted "evidences" of bad moral character are trivia. The defendants contend that:

1. Meredith was "adamant [in] refus[ing] to properly get and send to the Registrar certificates from Alumni as to his good moral character"; further, "those certificates which he sent in lieu of the Alumni certificates never were valid certificates as they are absolutely silent as to the position or standing of the certifiers in the community."

2. Meredith admitted that he brought stationery with him from the Air Force. (This refers to a few sheets of surplus stationery. This question as to his honesty led to inquiries as to government property being in his possession and required the production of the serial number of a typewriter purchased after his discharge.)

3. "Appellant was not a good character risk for he refused to list Wayne University in his application to the University, when the application required that the prospective applicant list all universities and colleges attended." (Meredith attended Wayne for two weeks only.)

These are on a par with the defense, asserted in the complaint, that one of the reasons for rejecting the application was that "all letters received by [the Registrar] from plaintiff were sent registered mail return receipt requested." Or with the defense, argued even now, that his application is incomplete because "appellant has not seen fit to forward a supplemental transcript from Jackson State." This transcript was introduced into evidence and is in the record. Meredith repeatedly asked the Registrar to advise him whether there was anything further he needed to do to complete his application.

The triviality of these and other of the defendants' contentions is a proper consideration for the Court in reviewing the whole case to determine whether the University barred Meredith for good and valid reasons or in fact barred him because he was a Negro.

Conclusion

There are cases when discrimination is purposeless but unlawful because of its effect. In this case the essence of the complaint is purposeful discrimination against Negroes as a class. The inquiry into purpose makes it especially appropriate for the Court:

(1) To study the case as a whole, weighing all of the evidence and rational inferences in order to reach a net result;

(2) To consider the immediate facts in the light of the institution's past and present policy on segregation, as reflected not only in statutes and regulations, history and common knowledge;

(3) To measure sincerity of purpose against unreasonable delays and insubstantial reasons asserted for the institution's actions;

(4) To compare the actions taken with regard to the plaintiff with actions taken with regard to others in the same category;

(5) To pierce the veil of innocuity when a statute, regulation, or policy necessarily discriminates unlawfully or is applied unlawfully to accomplish discrimination.

The defendants fail the test. There are none so blind as those that will not see.

The defendants' answer asserts and the Registrar testified that the State of Mississippi has no policy of educating Negroes and whites in separate institutions. This is in the teeth of statutes, only a few of which need be cited for illustration. It is contrary to official state publications with which every college official in Mississippi must be familiar. It defies history and common knowledge.

Similarly, the defendants assert that there is no policy of excluding Negroes at the University. The district judge found that there was a policy of segregation *before* Brown v. Board of Education was decided in 1954. The trustees and the principal officials of the University testified that *after* 1954 there has been no change in policy with respect to the admission of Negroes. They testified that the admission of Negroes had never been discussed in any meeting of the Board or in any meeting of the administrative staff. In spite of the enormous publicity given to this case by the newspapers, some of which are in evidence, the trustees and other personal defendants said that none of the officials of the University discussed Meredith's application in an official capacity. Even the Registrar had not discussed Meredith's application with anyone except with the Dean of the College of Liberal Arts, who had merely referred Meredith's letter to the Registrar, and with the Director of Development who agreed that Meredith was planning to file suit. The hard fact to get around is that no person known to be a Negro has ever attended the University. In a similar situation involving the University of Alabama the district court made the finding, which we affirmed, that:

"There is no written policy or rule excluding prospective students from admission to the University on account of race or color. However, there is a tacit policy to that effect". . . .

The policy admittedly existed when, even under the Plessy v. Ferguson doctrine, . . . Negroes were being admitted to other state universities because the facilities ("programs" here) of the Negro colleges were not equal to the facilities of white colleges. . . . By an ironic twist, the defendants, *after* Plessy v. Ferguson has been overruled, seize upon the inferiority of the facilities—programs of Negro colleges as reason for excluding Negroes at Mississippi's white colleges and universities.

Reading the 1350 pages in the record as a whole, we find that James H. Meredith's application for transfer to the University of Mississippi was turned down solely because he was a Negro. We see no valid, non-discriminatory reason for the University's not accepting Meredith. Instead, we see a well-defined pattern of delays and frustrations, part of a Fabian policy of worrying the enemy into defeat while time worked for the defenders.

The judgment of the district court is Reversed and the case Remanded with directions that the district court issue the injunction as prayed for in the complaint, the district court to retain jurisdiction.

Armed with this decision, one would have expected the Chief Executive to put an end to the obstruction of justice and to act promptly to prevent any further obstructions of the orders of the court. But such was not the case—at least not yet. The university proceded to obtain several stays to the decision, stays which were issued by an unsympathetic judge who was also a member of the fifth circuit panel. But when their delaying tactics consumed the entire summer and prevented Meredith from enrolling in the summer semester, Justice Hugo Black of the United States Supreme Court vacated all of the stay orders and joined the appeals court in instructing the university to accept Meredith as a student.

At that point Mississippi Governor Ross R. Barnett issued a proclamation advising state elected and appointed officials in charge of education that they were responsible for carrying out the state's segregation laws, and actually instructing them "to interpose" the sovereignty of the state and themselves between the people and "any body politic seeking to usurp such power." This doctrine of "interposition," based upon the false premise that "Mississippi, as a Sovereign State, has the right under the Federal Constitution to determine for itself what the Federal Constitution has reserved to it," had arisen often in the early history of the republic, but two great Presidents, Andrew Jackson in the Nullification Crisis of 1832 and Abraham Lincoln in the Civil War, had fairly thoroughly put it to rest.[96] But as it emerged again as a viable basis upon which to determine the policy of a state, the federal government knew it must be repudiated quickly if the nation was to avoid considerable dislocation and possible bloodshed.

It was at that point that the United States Government, the Department of Justice in particular, became very much involved in the case. The department had filed an *amicus curiae* memorandum with Justice Black at his request, advising him to vacate the stay orders of Judge Cameron of the fifth district.[97] Several days after Justice Black's action the Department of Justice officially entered the case for the first time. Kennedy and his staff were convinced that the State of Mississippi would ignore the court's orders without more active federal intervention; and accordingly, the Department of Justice went directly to both the federal district court in Meridian and to the fifth circuit in order to obtain permission to enter the case. The district court remained adamant and refused the request, but the fifth circuit welcomed the government's intervention. It considerably strengthened the hand of the law, for Barnett and the trustees of the university would have to confront the combined efforts of a United States Circuit Court of Appeals and the full force of the United States Government in their attempt to enforce segregation. This did indeed change the nature of the confrontation.

But the questions in many peoples' minds were why such an intervention had not come earlier, and when it did come, why the federal presence was not more emphatic? The department had followed this case from the very beginning and it should have been able to recognize, as the Fifth Circuit Court had, that the officials of the university were clearly flaunting the meaning of the law of the land. The delay by the federal government in actively entering the case allowed university and state officials to entertain false hopes of avoiding the full force of the law, and also permitted a climate of hate and resistance to build up over a year's time. The results of this time lag proved disastrous.

In the meantime the Mississippi legislature had hastily passed a bill providing that no person could be eligible for admission to a state institution of higher learning if he had a criminal charge of moral turpitude pending against him in any Mississippi state or federal court. On the same day that the governor signed the bill, Meredith was conveniently tried *in absentia* by a state court, charged with swearing to a false statement on a voter registration application. He was promptly sentenced to a year in jail and fined $500. The Department of Justice quickly filed a motion before the federal district court in Meridian and in the Fifth District Court of Appeals for a stiff injunction prohibiting the enforcement of the Mississippi law, but also enjoining all state, county and municipal employees from any action which would have the purpose or effect of interfering with the enrollment and continued attendance of James Meredith at the University of Mississippi. Even the district court in Meridian went along with the government, in the face of the order handed down by the appeals court. The circuit court injunction was so broad that it covered every possible obstruction conceivable. And it took pains to point out:

> This was not the Government instituting a suit or intervening on behalf of private litigants to vindicate the civil rights of private suitors. It was the sovereign's intervening in the sovereign's court to uphold and maintain the sovereign's rule of law [98]

The Department of Justice's reluctance to intervene actively before this moment was based upon the best advice that President Kennedy and his brother received from the coterie of top-notch lawyers who served in staff positions in the civil rights division of the Department of Justice. Burke Marshall headed up the division and was perhaps the most forceful advocate of what Victor Navasky calls the "code of the Ivy League Gentlemen," a cautious and respectful approach to federalism:

> These men, who for the most part were graduated from the elite law academies of the Forties, brought with them the code of the Ivy League Gentlemen, which involved, among other things, the assumption that negotiation and settlement are preferable to litigation; the idea that winning in a higher court is preferable—for precedential purposes—to winning in a lower court; the notion that reasonable men can always work things out; patience at the prospect of endlessly protracted litigation; the preference for defined structures, for order. They were oriented toward corporate enterprise. Anti-trust lawyers like Burke Marshall and Ramsey

Clark (who had attended the University of Chicago Law School, "the Yale of the Middle West") had experienced settling many a case with a plea of *nolo contendere* in exchange for a cease-and-desist order. Tax lawyers like Louis Oberdorfer were used to talking things over, working things out in advance, with the Internal Revenue Service. Despite their residence at Yale, which espoused the rhetoric of legal realism (a rebellion against the formalistic approach of Harvard) men like Katzenbach and White were products of the case method of instruction which is (a) preoccupied with matters of legal doctrine and formal analysis (even though Yale taught that such abstract formulations should be put in the service of social causes), and (b) focused on the development of law at the appeals level to the exclusion of the actual trial level. As one scholar has noted, "This method . . . tends to ignore the relationship of theory to fact." Without disputing the dynamism, good will, ingenuity or capacity of these men, without underestimating the unique benefits of an Ivy League education, without suggesting that they were genteel assembly-line products who thought and felt alike, one can still argue that the system by which they defined themselves predisposed them to peaceful co-existence with present injustice—especially where they could see light at the end of the appellate tunnel.[99]

In his brilliant chapter on federalism Navasky uses extracts from the actual transcripts of the many telephone conversations between Governor Barnett and Attorney General Kennedy, and the effect of reading them interspersed between his devastating analysis of the legal approach to the civil rights problem produces the effect of a vivid passage of contrapuntal music. Marshall's concept of federalism, Navasky argues

seemed to accept the Edmund Burkean notion that the nation-state had some kind of organic reality over and above its parts and that to disrupt the fabric of the nation-state was greater evil than not to protect the human rights that the federal system was supposed to guarantee in the first place. It was typical of an Ivy League intellectual to have elaborated such a theory with Marshall's relentless reason. Its ultimate logic, of course, was the preservation of the existing social, economic and political arrangements for the black minority. To the extent that the free-lance pragmatists did their job, they patched the existing social framework and postponed radical reconstruction.[100]

Perhaps more to the point and less theoretical was another Justice Department official's assessment of their goals and accomplishments. John Nolan, who had single-handedly prevented a riot at Gadsden, Alabama, explained:

We weren't trying to solve the Civil Rights problems of the United States of America. We were just trying to keep people from getting hurt. We wanted to prevent bloodshed. They were lid-keeping operations.[101]

Alas the lid was not kept on very successfully in the Meredith confrontation.

On September 20, 1962, James Meredith, armed with a federal court of appeals order directing the university authorities (the trustees had by that time adopted a resolution giving Governor Barnett full authority to deal with the admission of James Meredith) to accept him as a student, and accompanied by a representative of Department of Justice, John Doar, and the chief United States marshal, Joseph McShane, Meredith arrived at the campus at Oxford with the full intention of registering as a student. He was met by a mob of students, state and city police and finally Governor Barnett, who blocked his entry into the university and refused to register him as a student.

On Monday of the following week the trustees were ordered to appear before the circuit court of appeals in New Orleans, at which time they agreed to comply with the court orders and to register Meredith under threat of conviction of contempt of a federal court. They were also ordered to rescind their earlier resolution naming the governor as their agent with respect to Meredith's admission to the university. The following day, Meredith, Doar and McShane went to the trustees' office in Jackson, only to be met by the governor again, who still adamantly refused to register Meredith, or even accept the papers Doar and McShane attempted to serve him with. *Time* magazine described the confrontation:

> Doar: Governor Barnett, I'm John Doar of the Justice Department, sir. These papers, Governor, I'd like to present you with these papers.
>
> The other man, James McShane, Chief U. S. Marshal, fumblingly tried to hand Barnett a sheaf of court orders. In a sonorous drawl, Barnett said that as a matter of "policy" he could not accept any court orders.
>
> Doar: I want to remind you, that the Court of Appeals of the Fifth Circuit entered a temporary restraining order at 8:30 this morning enjoining you from interfering in any way with the registration of James Meredith at the University of Mississippi. We'd like to get on now, Governor, to the business of registering Mr. Meredith.
>
> Barnett: (reading a "proclamation" addressed to Meredith) To preserve the peace, dignity and tranquillity of the state, I hereby finally deny you admission to the University of Mississippi
>
> The palaver went on for a while longer, with Doar getting more and more plaintive. Finally he made one last, limp try:
>
> Doar: Do you refuse to permit us to come in the door?
>
> Barnett: Yes, sir.
>
> Doar: All right. Thank you.
>
> Barnett: I do that politely.
>
> Doar: Thank you. We leave politely.
>
> As the three men left the building and walked back to the car, the waiting crowd erupted in gleeful yells.
>
> A teen-age boy: Goddam dirty nigger bastard, get out of here and stay out.[102]

The next day, Wednesday, September 26, the United States Government tried once again to register James Meredith at the University of Mississippi. Meredith appeared with his two government companions in Oxford and attempted to enter the university grounds. On that occasion Governor Barnett was not present, because his plane had been grounded in Jackson by bad weather. In his place was Lieutenant Governor Paul Johnson, who just as quietly but resolutely blocked their entrance. Not being able to persuade Johnson to step aside, McShane, a former Golden Gloves welterweight champion from New York City and also a former policeman, decorated several times for heroism, tried to shoulder his way past Johnson and his guard of state troopers. Lieutenant Governor Johnson told McShane, "We are going to block you and if there is any violence it will be on your part."[103] Once again the trio failed, and once again the court orders, the law, and the representatives of the executive department of the United States Government had been defeated by a handful of state officials backed up by a couple of dozen state troopers.

The government caravan set out the following day, again headed for Oxford, but this time they were accompanied by some two dozen United States marshals. They were ordered back to Memphis when they were just 20 miles from Oxford by Attorney General Kennedy, when he learned of the angry mood of the formidable mob then gathered around the admissions center of the university. Apparently his representatives in Oxford reported that the situation was ripe for a riot, and later events proved that that was probably no idle prediction.

While both the governor and the lieutenant governor were now in contempt of a federal circuit court order, and the trustees of the university were virtually out of the picture, Meredith was still not one wit closer to his registration than he had been in preceding weeks and months. Furthermore the television audiences of the nation had witnessed the drama at Oxford and Jackson, and had seen the representatives of the President of the United States ignored and shoved back in an illegal fashion by the local officials. Perhaps this had a positive effect upon some areas of the country, provoking sympathy and support for Meredith's courage and determination and the President's plight, but among the die-hard racists in Mississippi and elsewhere it was a stimulating shot in the arm and a call to the colors. Extremists like former Major General Edwin A. Walker, who was retired from the United States Army after an investigation found that he was foisting John Birch Society literature on his enlisted men in Germany, rushed to the scene, eager for action and thirsty for blood. He appealed over the radio to citizens of all states to march to Barnett's aid. On arriving in Oxford the day before the impending riot, Walker labeled the court orders supporting Meredith as part of the "conspiracy of the crucifixion by anti-Christ conspirators of the Supreme Court."[104] Ironically, Walker had been the United States Army officer in charge of the troops sent to Little Rock in 1957, to quell the disorders there. Before arriving in Oxford Walker appealed to other segregationists over a Texas radio station:

> Now is the time to be heard. Ten thousand strong from every state in the Union. Rally to the cause of freedom. The battle cry of the Republic. Barnett, yes; Castro, no. Bring your flags, your tents and your skillets. . . . The last time in such a situation I was on the wrong side. . . . This time I am out of uniform and I am on the right side, and I will be there.[105]

By the weekend the President no longer had any options. Despite the fact that both the governor and the lieutenant governor were found to be in contempt of the

Fifth Circuit Court of Appeals, committed to the custody of the attorney general of the United States, and ordered to pay a fine of $10,000 and $5,000 a day respectively, until they complied with the court order, neither one indicated any willingness to register Meredith at Oxford. United States troops and 167 United States marshals were waiting in readiness at Memphis Air Base, and reinforcements were on their way from various other parts of the country.

President Kennedy was haunted by a remark he had made during the 1960 campaign, in reference to Little Rock, "There is more power in the Presidency than to let things drift and then suddenly call out the troops." He, like Eisenhower, or any other sane man, wanted to avoid the use of troops and the violence that would make such a step necessary. But it was rapidly becoming clear that the situation had deteriorated to the point where this final step would be mandatory. Whatever else, he wanted to avoid the charge of having let things drift.

On Saturday, September 29, 1962, President Kennedy prepared for a showdown. He personally put through the first of several calls to Governor Barnett and tried to get him to commit himself as to whether he would admit Meredith to the university immediately and take the responsibility for protecting him and keeping the peace. Barnett stalled. He proposed several plans which would allow him to save face, and yet settle the problem. One idea was for Barnett to rush from Jackson to Oxford ostensibly to block Meredith's registration, while Meredith would be quietly registering in Jackson. The President finally agreed to this plan, but later in the evening Barnett reneged. The President then decided to act. After midnight he issued orders federalizing the Mississippi National Guard, ordered other army units to Memphis and announced a radio and television address for Sunday evening.

Sunday morning when Barnett learned that the President was preparing to reveal that the governor had repudiated his agreement to register Meredith in Jackson while he sped to Oxford as a decoy, he quickly proposed an alternative plan. It was a football weekend away from Oxford, and Barnett now proposed to bring Meredith quickly to the campus that afternoon. He would issue an outraged statement from his office in Jackson, but meanwhile Meredith could be registered. Moreover he argued that since the President had announced his radio-television address for Sunday evening, everyone would expect that he was going to announce the federal government's intention to register Meredith on the following Monday, and Meredith could be registered and established on campus before the mob could mobilize. This appeared to be the best idea yet, and the President bought it, but only after the governor's aides promised police protection for Meredith on the campus. Not taking any chances, Kennedy flew over 500 United States marshals into Oxford, armed with steel helmets, tear gas and sidearms. When Meredith arrived there were no Mississippi state police on hand to guard him, and those who later loitered on the outskirts of the mob did nothing to control it or break it up.

Meredith was taken secretly to a dormitory and left with a guard of 12 marshals (later increased to 24), while other marshals, under the direction of Chief McShane and Deputy Attorney General Katzenbach, took their stand at the Lyceum, an imposing antebellum building which was the administrative center of the university. They were heckled by large crowds, mostly of students, in the early afternoon, but by later afternoon, the composition of the mob changed and it developed an ugly mood. Toward evening a still larger crowd began to collect outside of the Lyceum, and under cover of darkness taunted the marshals with threats and oaths, and peppered them with bricks and bottles. As the crowd increased, the attack became more violent. The record is slightly confusing after that point. A reporter on the spot for *U. S. News and World Report* indicates there were 300 marshals present, while President Kennedy used the figure "between four or five hundred" in a television interview, and Sorensen states that the number "reached 550 in the end." There is more general agreement on the number of wounded and injured.[106]

The battle continued all night. It was a holocaust. The mob roamed through the campus burning and pillaging, attacking the marshals at the Lyceum almost continuously. It is difficult to portray the degree of violence that was manifested; the marshals were forced to use tear gas to repel the charging mobs, but the continuing encounter was very costly for them. No less than 35 marshals were shot, and more than another 150 were given medical treatment. Two people were killed by hidden snipers—a French newspaperman and a local TV repairman. The mob commandeered first a bulldozer and then a fire engine and tried to ram the marshals and the building with them, but fortunately the vehicles faltered at the right moment. Someone else took an automobile and sent it driverless in the direction of the marshals, but it swerved out of the way and rammed into a tree.

Back in Washington the President paced his office, frantically trying to find out why the regular army troops that were ordered to Oxford had not yet arrived. He kept getting reports that they were on their way, But the first contingent did not arrive until three o'clock in the morning. A local unit of the National Guard which had been federalized arrived earlier, but was quickly brushed aside by the angry mob. All this took place while the state police either disappeared or stood on the outskirts of the mob doing nothing. After they had left the scene for the second time, President Kennedy demanded that the governor bring them back; before Barnett could sputter out an excuse, the President hung up on him. Barnett issued a series of press releases during the evening, aimed more at covering up his role in the affair than condemning the riot. In his first statement he complained that Meredith had been sneaked in by helicopter without his knowledge (although of course it was at his suggestion), but later on he ranted that Mississippi would never surrender.

If the President had relied completely on the governor's promise to protect Meredith and maintain law and order, not only would Meredith have been lynched, but probably dozens of others would have been killed in the confusion. The casualties among the marshals were costly, but their courageous conduct held off the mob until the regular army units arrived to buttress the laws and principles that were under attack. Meredith started classes under heavy military escort the next day, and graduated a year later, a wiser but sadder human being. And Governor Barnett, none the wiser, continued to pander the accusation that "trigger happy" marshals were responsible for the riot, while the official government records show that at least eight marshals suffered injuries before the tear gas was fired.

Law and order had once again prevailed, and the President had succeeded in asserting the priority of federal power, but the cost was astronomical. I am not referring to a financial sum alone here, although it was high; the real price was paid in the loss of human life, in increased resentment, in weakened political strength and in the loss of status and prestige. It cannot be overlooked, however, that the

Meredith case also involved a huge government expenditure to pay for 17 months of litigation in federal and state courts (and that only covered the period before the riot), the mobilization of 16,000 troops (both National Guard and regular army), and the time and efforts of hundreds of others, including the United States marshals, representatives of the Department of Justice and others who became intimately involved with the developments. It would also be impossible to calculate the cost of personal anguish suffered by Meredith himself, which he was forced to undergo in order to obtain his University of Mississippi diploma.

In the long run the impact of the events at Oxford may have had a salutary effect upon the civil rights struggle, but it was difficult to come to that conclusion in the period immediately following the riot. The final victory came so late, the voices of hate had reached such a shrill pitch and the pleading tone of the President over radio and television was so subdued (to the point of being almost compromising) that it appeared at the time that the lesson, if indeed there was one, was lost in the dust and thunder of the agony. Certainly the mob neither heard nor heeded its words.

I can remember sitting up until the early hours of the morning with James Baldwin and Martin Luther King in a Boston railway station shortly thereafter, listening to their despairing reactions to these events. It was not only the clumsiness and hesitancy with which the whole business was handled that depressed them, but the lack of moral conviction in the President's remarks as he spoke patronizingly of war heroes and football stars to the rioting students and yahoos in Oxford that awful Sunday night. It was the wrong speech, to the wrong group, in the wrong tone, at the wrong time. President Kennedy was nothing if not an honest and self-disparaging critic of his own mistakes, and he once gave a "C minus" to a major speech delivered earlier that summer, explaining to the American people why he was postponing the tax cut until the following year. If the tax-cut speech in August only rated a "C-minus," the Oxford speech in September flunked the course. And that was a course that neither President Kennedy nor the American people could afford to fail.

President John F. Kennedy
Radio and Television Address on
The Situation in Mississippi
September 30, 1962

Public Papers of the Presidents of the United States   John F. Kennedy, 1962, 726-28.

Good evening, my fellow citizens: The orders of the court in the case of Meredith versus Fair are beginning to be carried out. Mr. James Meredith is now in residence on the campus of the University of Mississippi.

This has been accomplished thus far without the use of National Guard or other troops. And it is to be hoped that the law enforcement officers of the State of Mississippi and the Federal marshals will continue to be sufficient in the future.

All students, members of the faculty, and public officials in both Mississippi and the Nation will be able, it is hoped, to return to their normal activities with full confidence in the integrity of American law.

This is as it should be, for our Nation is based on the principle that observance of the law is the eternal safeguard of liberty and defiance of the law is the surest road to tyranny. The law which we obey includes the final rulings of the courts, as well as the enactments of our legislative bodies. Even among law-abiding men few laws are universally loved, but they are uniformly respected and not resisted.

Americans are free, in short, to disagree with the law but not to disobey it. For in a government of laws and not of men, no man, however prominent or powerful, and no mob, however unruly or boisterous, is entitled to defy a court of law. If this country should ever reach the point where any man or group of men by force or threat of force could long defy the commands of our court and our Constitution, then no law would stand free from doubt, no judge would be sure of his writ, and no citizen would be safe from his neighbors.

In this case in which the United States Government was not until recently involved, Mr. Meredith brought a private suit in Federal court against those who were excluding him from the University. A series of Federal courts all the way to the Supreme Court repeatedly ordered Mr. Meredith's admission to the University. When those orders were defied, and those who sought to implement them threatened with arrest and violence, the United States Court of Appeals consisting of Chief Judge Tuttle of Georgia, Judge Hutcheson of Texas, Judge Rives of Alabama, Judge Jones of Florida, Judge Brown of Texas, Judge Wisdom of Louisiana, Judge Gewin of Alabama, and Judge Bell of Georgia, made clear the fact that the enforcement of its order had become an obligation of the United States Government. Even though this Government had not originally been a party to the case, my responsibility as President was therefore inescapable. I accept it. My obligation under the Constitution and the statutes of the United States was and is to implement the orders of the court with whatever means are necessary, and with as little force and civil disorder as the circumstances permit.

It was for this reason that I federalized the Mississippi National Guard as the most appropriate instrument, should any be needed, to preserve law and order while United States marshals carried out the orders of the court and prepared to back them up with whatever other civil or military enforcement might have been required.

I deeply regret the fact that any action by the executive branch was necessary in this case, but all other avenues and alternatives, including persuasion and conciliation, had been tried and exhausted. Had the police powers of Mississippi been used to support the orders of the court, instead of deliberately and unlawfully blocking them, had the University of Mississippi fulfilled its standard of excellence by quietly admitting this applicant in conformity with what so many other southern State universities have done for so many years, a peaceable and sensible solution would have been possible without any Federal intervention.

This Nation is proud of the many instances in which Governors, educators, and everyday citizens from the South have shown to the world the gains that can be made by persuasion and good will in a society ruled by law. Specifically, I would like to take this occasion to express the thanks of this Nation to those southerners who have contributed to the progress of our democratic development in the entrance of students regardless of race to such great institutions as the State-supported universities of Virginia, North Carolina, Georgia, Florida, Texas, Louisiana, Tennessee, Arkansas, and Kentucky.

I recognize that the present period of transition and adjustment in our Nation's Southland is a hard one for many people. Neither Mississippi nor any other southern State deserves to be charged with all the accumulated wrongs of the last 100 years of race relations. To the extent that there has been failure, the responsibility for that failure must be shared by us all, by every State, by every citizen.

Mississippi and her University, moreover, are noted for their courage, for their contribution of talent and thought to the affairs of this Nation. This is the State of Lucius Lamar and many others who have placed the national good ahead of sectional interest. This is the State which had four Medal of Honor winners in the Korean war alone. In fact, the Guard unit federalized this morning, early, is part of the 155th Infantry, one of the 10 oldest regiments in the Union and one of the most decorated for sacrifice and bravery in 6 wars.

In 1945 a Mississippi sergeant, Jake Lindsey, was honored by an unusual joint session of the Congress. I close therefore with this appeal to the students of the University, the people who are most concerned.

You have a great tradition to uphold, a tradition of honor and courage won on the field of battle and on the gridiron as well as the University campus. You have a new opportunity to show that you are men of patriotism and integrity. For the most effective means of upholding the law is not the State policeman or the marshals or the National Guard. It is you. It lies in your courage to accept those laws with which you disagree as well as those with which you agree. The eyes of the Nation and of all the world are upon you and upon all of us, and the honor of your University and State are in the balance. I am certain that the great majority of the students will uphold that honor.

There is in short no reason why the books on this case cannot now be quickly and quietly closed in the manner directed by the court. Let us preserve both the law and the peace and then healing those wounds that are within we can turn to the greater crises that are without and stand united as one people in our pledge to man's freedom.

Thank you and good night.

[In addition to the President's address, the White House released the following papers:

1. On September 29 an announcement that the President had talked to Governor Ross Barnett of Mississippi on three occasions; that the President was unable to receive satisfactory assurances that law and order could or would be maintained in Oxford during the coming week; that the President was therefore federalizing units of the Mississippi National Guard; and that the units would be available for service on October 1.

2. On September 29 the text of Proclamation 3497, ordering persons engaged in obstructing justice in Mississippi to cease and desist therefrom and to disperse and retire peaceably forthwith.

3. On September 30 the text of Executive Order 11053 directing the Secretary of Defense to take all appropriate steps to enforce the court orders, including the calling into active service of units of the Mississippi National Guard.

4. On September 30 the text of the President's telegram to Governor Barnett referring to his two telephone conversations with the Governor on September 30, and requesting replies by the evening of September 30 to three questions as to the course of action the Governor intended to follow.][107]

It is interesting to note that both the Kennedy proclamation and the executive order lack the direct reference to the denial of equal rights under the law that was expressed in his predecessor's proclamation and order at Little Rock.

President John F. Kennedy
Proclamation Directing a Halt to
Obstructions of Justice in Mississippi
September 30, 1962

Proclamation No. 3497, 27 Federal Register 9681.

Obstructions of Justice in the State of Mississippi

Whereas the Governor of the State of Mississippi and certain law enforcement officers and other officials of that State, and other persons, individually and in unlawful assemblies, combinations and conspiracies, have been and are willfully opposing and obstructing the enforcement of orders entered by the United States District Court for the Southern District of Mississippi and the United States Court of Appeals for the Fifth Circuit; and

Whereas such unlawful assemblies, combinations and conspiracies oppose and obstruct the execution of the laws of the United States, impede the course of justice under those laws and make it impracticable to enforce those laws in the State of Mississippi by the ordinary course of judicial proceedings; and

Whereas I have expressly called the attention of the Governor of Mississippi to the perilous situation that exists and to his duties in the premises, and have requested but have not received from him adequate assurances that the orders of the courts of the United States will be obeyed and that law and order will be maintained;

Now, therefore, I, John F. Kennedy, President of the United States, under and by virtue of the authority vested in me by the Constitution and laws of the United States, including Chapter 15 of Title 10 of the United States Code, particularly sections 332, 333 and 334 thereof, do command all persons engaged in such obstructions of justice to cease and desist therefrom and to disperse and retire peacefully forthwith.

In witness whereof, I have hereunto set my hand and caused the seal of the United States of America to be affixed.

Done at the city of Washington this 30th day of September in the year of our Lord Nineteen Hundred and Sixty-Two, and of the independence of the United States of America the One Hundred and Eighty-Seventh.

John F. Kennedy

President John F. Kennedy
Executive Order Providing Assistance
To Enforce the Orders of the Court
September 30, 1962

Executive Order No. 11053, 27 Federal Register 9693.

Providing assistance for the removal of unlawful obstructions of justice in the State of Mississippi.

Whereas on September 30, 1962, I issued proclamation No. 3497 reading in part as follows [quoted in entirety above] and

Whereas the commands contained in that proclamation have not been obeyed and obstruction of enforcement of those court orders still exist and threatens to continue.

Now, therefore, by virtue of the authority vested in me by the Constitution and laws of the United States, including Chapter 15 of Title 10, particularly sections 332, 333 and 334 thereof, and section 301 of Title 3 of the United States Code, it is hereby ordered as follows:

Section 1. The Secretary of Defense is authorized and directed to take all appropriate steps to enforce all orders of the United States District Court for the Southern District of Mississippi and the United States Court of Appeals for the Fifth Circuit and to remove all obstructions of justice in the state of Mississippi.

Section 2. In furtherance of the enforcement of the aforementioned orders of the United States District Court for the Southern District of Mississippi and the United States Court of Appeals for the Fifth Circuit, the Secretary of Defense is authorized to use such of the armed forces of the United States as he may deem necessary.

Section 3. I hereby authorize the Secretary of Defense to call into the active military service of the United States, as he may deem appropriate to carry out the purposes of this order, any or all of the units of the Army National Guard and of the Air National Guard of the State of Mississippi to serve in the active military service of the United States for an indefinite period and until relieved by appropriate orders. In carrying out the provisions of Section 1, the Secretary of Defense is authorized to use the units, and members thereof, ordered into active military service of the United States pursuant to this section.

Section 4. The Secretary of Defense is authorized to delegate to the Secretary of the Army or the Secretary of the Air Force, or both, any of the authority conferred upon him by this order.

John F. Kennedy

In enunciating his "stewardship" theory of the presidency, Theodore Roosevelt repudiated the post-Civil War era of decline in presidential power, a period which a young political scientist at Johns Hopkins, Woodrow Wilson, characterized as one of congressional government. Roosevelt began to reassert certain executive prerogatives, dormant since the administrations of Jefferson, Jackson and Lincoln. But he accomplished something considerably more than that in his own right. He initiated a reconstruction or a reinterpretation of presidential power in this century in terms of the new social and economic problems which arose as a result of the intensive industrial and economic development which took place in this country during the latter part of the nineteenth century. Other significant twentieth-century Presidents who succeeded him would modify some of his assertions of executive power, and extend and transform others. But Theodore Roosevelt brought the American presidency nearly full-grown into the twentieth century, set the precedents and the style for its later development and left a legacy of accomplishments almost impossible to overestimate. This legacy left innumerable advantages to the future development of the office and the political system of which it is such a critical center of power.

Kennedy had certain obvious qualities in common with Theodore Roosevelt. One was age, Roosevelt being the youngest man ever to become President (42), and Kennedy the youngest man to be elected to the presidency (43). Both were vigorous, attractive men, possessed of great energy. Both inherited considerable wealth, and engaged in full-time political activity very early in their lives, and both shared a Harvard education. Before his election Kennedy identified himself with the Jacksonian-Roosevelt school of the presidency, asserting the need for executive energy and leadership:

> In the decade that lies ahead—in the challenging revolutionary sixties—the American Presidency will demand more than ringing manifestoes issued from the rear of the battle. It will demand that the President place himself in the very thick of the fight, that he care passionately about the fate of the people he leads, that he be willing to serve them at the risk of incurring their momentary displeasure.
>
> Whatever the political affiliation of our next President, whatever his views may be on all the issues and problems that rush in upon us, he must above all be the Chief Executive in every sense of the word. . . .[108]

The Meredith crisis in Oxford, Mississippi did not reveal all of the qualities of executive and moral leadership which John F. Kennedy had so eloquently called for in this preelection speech, but the following year, when he was faced with a somewhat similar crisis in Alabama, he rose to his finest hour and admirably fulfilled the exacting and challenging role which he himself had earlier spelled out.

A Lesson Well Learned

The following year brought about significant changes in the civil rights climate in America. In the past the significant surges forward of racial events had seemed to be related, at least partially, to the seasons of the year. There was a distinctive climatic rhythm to their development. A situation would begin boiling up in the spring, reaching something of a fever pitch by June and July. When people could move out of doors, when students were free from school, the limitations imposed by segregation became more unbearable and the protests more intense.

In 1963 the civil rights season started early with the campaign against segregation in Birmingham, Alabama, led by the Reverend Martin Luther King, jr. The savage tactics of Commissioner of Public Safety Eugene "Bull" Connor and his use of police dogs made the case for federal intervention stronger than it had ever been before. When the horrifying bombing of the Negro Baptist Church, killing seven innocent children and injuring many more, took place in the same city, a wave of disgust with southern racist elements spread from one end of the country to the other, then quickly around the world, quickening the pulse for new civil rights legislation and increasing protests from the North.

By late spring of 1963 the President's position had hardened on this issue, and when challenged again by another southern governor, George C. Wallace of Alabama, he was ready to mobilize and assert his full executive powers from the very start of the crisis. Although Wallace was a more formidable opponent than the aging and senile governor of Mississippi, he quickly caught the tempo of the President's mood, and went only far enough to save his face before capitulating to federal power. The confrontation arose over the applications of three Black students to enter the University of Alabama which, like "Ole Miss" had enrolled only white students up to that time. That policy was challenged in 1956 by Autherine Lucy, who succeeded under court order in enrolling in the university, but later was driven from the campus by rioting students. There was no effort on the part of the Eisenhower administration to employ federal law enforcement agencies to suppress the rioting, or to protect the student from the violence that continuously threatened her during the short period she was on the university campus. Nor did Eisenhower even mention the situation in his two volume, 1200-page history of his two administrations.

The Autherine Lucy case, however, established the right of a qualified Black applicant to a University of Alabama education, and it was inevitable that the issue would be joined again when other qualified Blacks applied for admission. In his campaign for the governorship Wallace vowed on repeated occasions that he would fight integration of the schools "to the point of standing in the school house door" to block the entry of any Black students. Despite this background of conflict James Hood and Vivian Malone processed their application forms for admission to the University of Alabama at Tuscaloosa, and Dave Mack McGlathery applied for night classes in advanced mathematics at the university extension at Huntsville. This action was taken in the early spring of 1963. In May of that year the federal district court ruled that the injunction obtained by Autherine Lucy against the dean of admissions of the university was applicable in the present case. The court held that the current dean of admissions was bound by the same court order as his predecessor to admit qualified Black students.

By that time Governor Wallace, repeating his campaign pledge, had promised on several occasions to block the entry of the Black students when they came to register at the university. Attorney General Robert Kennedy met privately with him, but they apparently came to no agreement. Both men continued to reiterate their original positions; Wallace of course threatening to prevent the Blacks from registering, and the attorney general vowing that he would uphold the law. There was no equivocation from Washington this time, however, about the role of the federal government in seeing to it that the federal court's orders were carried out; and there were no efforts to temporize or accommodate the Alabama officials. Wallace stated that he would see to it that no violence occurred, but the President refused to rely on such a promise. Plans were drawn up and adequate preparations made to alert sufficient Alabama National Guard units and federal troops to enforce the court order under all circumstances.

On the basis of Governor Wallace's public threat to personally block the registration of the students, the federal district court issued an injunction against the governor and his "agents, employees, subordinates, successors and all persons in active concert with them" from "blocking, or interfering with" the enrollment of the students at the university. Such an injunction gave the President the option of either arresting Wallace for interfering with the students' registration, removing him and registering them, or of issuing a presidential proclamation after the governor defied the court order, calling upon him to cease and desist from his unlawful activity, and authorizing the use of sufficient troops to enforce the order.

The drawbacks to using the first alternative were considerable. The problems of actually jailing the highest executive officer of a state were tremendous and could easily run into severe legal complications. Moreover such a move would be bound to stimulate even greater hostility, both at the university and throughout the state. The second alternative would avoid all of these difficulties, but might lead to violence if the governor did not back off after having his hour before the nation's television cameras. The President decided to accept the risks involved in the second plan, and Attorney General Robert Kennedy and his assistants, Burke Marshall and Nicholas Katzenbach, made all the preparations for setting it in motion. A command headquarters was set up in the attorney general's office in Washington, complete with four maps of the Tuscaloosa area, an open telephone line to Katzenbach who was in command of the field headquarters in Tuscaloosa, radio telephone communication with the field staff when they were in moving vehicles or on the university grounds, and finally a television set and radio to follow the press coverage of developing events.

There were no hitches in the plans. The governor arrived at the administration building of the university on the morning Vivian Malone and James Hood were scheduled to register; they set up a lecturn to hold his papers, placed a microphone around his neck, and waited for the students and their federal escort to appear. Katzenbach arrived without the students, was stopped by the governor and forced to listen to him read a five-page proclamation denouncing the "unwarranted and illegal" action of the federal government. "I stand here today," the governor said, "as Governor of this sovereign state, and refuse to willingly submit to illegal usurpation of power by the central government." When he was finished Assistant Attorney General Katzenbach said:

> "I take it from that statement that you are going to stand in the door and that you are not going to carry out the orders of the court?"
> "I stand according to my statement," replied Mr. Wallace.
> "Governor, I am not interested in a show," Mr. Katzenbach went on. "I don't know what the purpose of this show is. I am interested in the orders of these courts being enforced."[109]

The federal official then told the governor that he had no choice but to comply.

> "I would ask you once again to responsibly step aside," said Mr. Katzenbach. "If you do not, I'm going to assure that the orders of these courts will be enforced.
> "From the outset, Governor, all of us have known that the final chapter of this history will be the admission of these students."[110]

With that Katzenbach left under the silent, scornful stare of the governor and immediately telephoned the attorney general, who conferred in turn with the White House. Shortly thereafter, the President's proclamation (No. 3542) was issued, reiterating the same line of reasoning as the Oxford statement. An executive order followed, authorizing the use of federal troops and the nationalization of the Alabama units of the National Guard to enforce the law.

President John F. Kennedy
Proclamation Directing a Halt to
Obstructions of Justice in Alabama
June 11, 1963

Public Papers of the Presidents: John F. Kennedy, 1963, 467-68.

Unlawful Obstructions
of Justice and Combinations
in Alabama

Whereas on June 5, 1963, the United States District Court for the Northern District of Alabama entered an order enjoining the Governor of the State of Alabama, together with all persons acting in concert with him, from blocking or interfering with the entry of certain qualified Negro students to the campuses of the University of Alabama at Tuscaloosa and Huntsville, Alabama, and from preventing or seeking to prevent by any means the enrollment or attendance at the University of Alabama of any person entitled to enroll in or attend the University pursuant to the order of the court of July 1, 1955, in the case of *Lucy v. Adams*; and

Whereas both before and after the entry of the order of June 5, 1963, the Governor of the State of Alabama has declared publicly that he intended to oppose and obstruct the orders of the United States District Court relating to the enrollment and attendance of Negro students at the University of Alabama and would, on June 11, 1963, block the entry of two such students to a part of the campus of the University of Alabama at Tuscaloosa; and

Whereas I have requested but have not received assurances that the Governor and forces under his command will abandon this proposed course of action in violation of the orders of the United States District Court and will enforce the laws of the United States in the State of Alabama; and

Whereas this unlawful obstruction and combination on the part of the Governor and others against the authority of the United States will, if carried out as threatened, make it impracticable to enforce the laws of the United States in the State of Alabama by the ordinary course of judicial proceedings; and

Whereas this unlawful combination opposes the execution of the laws of the United States and threatens to impede the course of justice under those laws;

Now, Therefore, I, John F. Kennedy, President of the United States of America, under and by virtue of the authority vested in me by the Constitution and statutes of the United States, including Chapter 15 of Title 10 of the United States Code, particularly sections 332, 333 and 334 thereof, do command the Governor of the State of Alabama and all other persons engaged or who may engage in unlawful obstructions of justice, assemblies, combinations, conspiracies or domestic violence in that State to cease and desist therefrom.

In Witness Whereof, I have hereunto set my hand and caused the Seal of the United States of America to be affixed.

Done at the City of Washington this eleventh day of June in the year of our Lord nineteen hundred and sixty-three, and of the Independence of the United States of America the one hundred and eighty-seventh.

John F. Kennedy

By the President:

Dean Rusk, *Secretary of State*

[On the same day the President also issued Executive Order 11111 directing the Secretary of Defense to take all appropriate steps to enforce the laws of the United States in Alabama, including the calling into active service of units of the National Guard (28 F.R. 5709; 3 CFR 1963 Supp.).][111]

Some four and one-half hours later Katzenbach returned to the campus, armed with the President's proclamation and accompanied by members of the 31st Infantry Division of the Alabama State National Guard. Their commander ordered the governor (sadly) to step aside so that the order of the court could be accomplished. Wallace read a final statement, got into his car and drove away. Katzenbach then conducted the students into the building; they were registered and returned to their dormitories without any further delays. Forty-eight hours later Dave Mack McGlathery registered for his evening courses in mathematics at the extension in Huntsville without any commotion whatsoever. The governor did not turn up, and the local authorities took pains to discourage any possibility of a violent demonstration.

The night of the Tuscaloosa confrontation, President Kennedy went on radio and television once again, and more than made up for his previously unimpressive performance. He spoke this time from the heart as well as the head, framing the basic question of full equality for Black people in its proper historical and moral perspective, urging the American people to examine their consciences and to work harder at securing its resolution. At the same time he announced that he was about to send to the Congress his recommendation for the most far-reaching civil rights legislation yet conceived in our time. The Tuscaloosa situation had not only demonstrated the effective application of executive power to enforce civil rights, but also marked a turning point in the long struggle for human equality.

President John F. Kennedy
Radio and Television Address
To the Nation on Civil Rights
June 11, 1963

Public Papers of the Presidents: John F. Kennedy, 1963, 468-71.

Good evening, my fellow citizens: This afternoon, following a series of threats and defiant statements, the presence of Alabama National Guardsmen was required on the University of Alabama to carry out the final and unequivocal order of the United States District Court of the Northern District of Alabama. That order called for the admission of two clearly qualified young Alabama residents who happened to have been born Negro.

That they were admitted peacefully on the campus is due in good measure to the conduct of the students of the University of Alabama, who met their responsibilities in a constructive way.

I hope that every American, regardless of where he lives, will stop and examine his conscience about this and other related incidents. This Nation was founded by men of many nations and backgrounds. It was founded on the principle that all men are created equal, and that the rights of every man are diminished when the rights of one man are threatened.

Today we are committed to a worldwide struggle to promote and protect the rights of all who wish to be free. And when Americans are sent to Viet-Nam or West Berlin, we do not ask for whites only. It ought to be possible, therefore, for

American students of any color to attend any public institution they select without having to be backed up by troops.

It ought to be possible for American consumers of any color to receive equal service in places of public accommodation, such as hotels and restaurants and theaters and retail stores, without being forced to resort to demonstrations in the street, and it ought to be possible for American citizens of any color to register and to vote in a free election without interference or fear of reprisal.

It ought to be possible, in short, for every American to enjoy the privileges of being American without regard to his race or his color. In short, every American ought to have the right to be treated as he would wish to be treated, as one would wish his children to be treated. But this is not the case.

The Negro baby born in America today, regardless of the section of the Nation in which he is born, has about one-half as much chance of completing a high school as a white baby born in the same place on the same day, one-third as much chance of completing college, one-third as much chance of becoming a professional man, twice as much chance of becoming unemployed, about one-seventh as much chance of earning $10,000 a year, a life expectancy which is 7 years shorter, and the prospects of earning only half as much.

This is not a sectional issue. Difficulties over segregation and discrimination exist in every city, in every State of the Union, producing in many cities a rising tide of discontent that threatens the public safety. Nor is this a partisan issue. In a time of domestic crisis men of good will and generosity should be able to unite regardless of party or politics. This is not even a legal or legislative issue alone. It is better to settle these matters in the courts than on the streets, and new laws are needed at every level, but law alone cannot make men see right.

We are confronted primarily with a moral issue. It is as old as the scriptures and is as clear as the American Constitution.

The heart of the question is whether all Americans are to be afforded equal rights and equal opportunities, whether we are going to treat our fellow Americans as we want to be treated. If an American, because his skin is dark, cannot eat lunch in a restaurant open to the public, if he cannot send his children to the best public school available, if he cannot vote for the public officials who represent him, if, in short, he cannot enjoy the full and free life which all of us want, then who among us would be content to have the color of his skin changed and stand in his place? Who among us would then be content with the counsels of patience and delay?

One hundred years of delay have passed since President Lincoln freed the slaves, yet their heirs, their grandsons, are not fully free. They are not yet freed from the bonds of injustice. They are not yet freed from social and economic oppression. And this Nation, for all its hopes and all its boasts, will not be fully free until all its citizens are free.

We preach freedom around the world, and we mean it, and we cherish our freedom here at home, but are we to say to the world, and much more importantly, to each other that this is a land of the free except for the Negroes; that we have no second-class citizens except Negroes; that we have no class or cast system, no ghettoes, no master race except with respect to Negroes?

Now the time has come for this Nation to fulfill its promise. The events in Birmingham and elsewhere have so increased the cries for equality that no city or State or legislative body can prudently choose to ignore them.

The fires of frustration and discord are burning in every city, North and South, where legal remedies are not at hand. Redress is sought in the streets, in demonstrations, parades, and protests which create tensions and threaten violence and threaten lives.

We face, therefore, a moral crisis as a country and as a people. It cannot be met by repressive police action. It cannot be left to increased demonstrations in the streets. It cannot be quieted by token moves or talk. It is a time to act in the Congress, in your State and local legislative body and above all, in all of our daily lives.

It is not enough to pin the blame on others, to say this is a problem of one section of the country or another, or deplore the fact that we face. A great change is at hand, and our task, our obligation, is to make that revolution, that change, peaceful and constructive for all.

Those who do nothing are inviting shame as well as violence. Those who act boldly are recognizing right as well as reality.

Next week I shall ask the Congress of the United States to act, to make a commitment it has not fully made in this century to the proposition that race has no place in American life or law. The Federal judiciary has upheld that proposition in a series of forthright cases. The executive branch has adopted that proposition in the conduct of its affairs, including the employment of Federal personnel, the use of Federal facilities, and the sale of federally financed housing.

But there are other necessary measures which only the Congress can provide, and they must be provided at this session. The old code of equity law under which we live commands for every wrong a remedy, but in too many communities, in too many parts of the country, wrongs are inflicted on Negro citizens and there are no remedies at law. Unless the Congress acts, their only remedy is in the street.

I am, therefore, asking the Congress to enact legislation giving all Americans the right to be served in facilities which are open to the public—hotels, restaurants, theaters, retail stores, and similar establishments.

This seems to me to be an elementary right. Its denial is an arbitrary indignity that no American in 1963 should have to endure, but many do.

I have recently met with scores of business leaders urging them to take voluntary action to end this discrimination and I have been encouraged by their response, and in the last 2 weeks over 75 cities have seen progress made in desegregating these kinds of facilities. But many are unwilling to act alone, and for this reason, nationwide legislation is needed if we are to move this problem from the streets to the courts.

I am also asking Congress to authorize the Federal Government to participate more fully in lawsuits designed to end segregation in public education. We have succeeded in persuading many districts to desegregate voluntarily. Dozens have admitted Negroes without violence. Today a Negro is attending a State-supported institution in every one of our 50 States, but the pace is very slow.

Too many Negro children entering segregated grade schools at the time of the Supreme Court's decision 9 years ago will enter segregated high schools this fall, having suffered a loss which can never be restored. The lack of an adequate education denies the Negro a chance to get a decent job.

The orderly implementation of the Supreme Court decision, therefore, cannot be left solely to those who may not have the economic resources to carry the legal action or who may be subject to harassment.

Other features will be also requested, including greater protection for the right to vote. But legislation, I repeat, cannot solve this problem alone. It must be solved in the homes of every American in every community across our country.

In this respect, I want to pay tribute to those citizens North and South who have been working in their communities to make life better for all. They are acting not out of a sense of legal duty but out of a sense of human decency.

Like our soldiers and sailors in all parts of the world they are meeting freedom's challenge on the firing line, and I salute them for their honor and their courage.

My fellow Americans, this is a problem which faces us all—in every city of the North as well as the South. Today there are Negroes unemployed, two or three times as many compared to whites, inadequate in education, moving into the large cities, unable to find work, young people particularly out of work without hope, denied equal rights, denied the opportunity to eat at a restaurant or lunch counter or go to a movie theater, denied the right of a decent education, denied almost today the right to attend a State university even though qualified. It seems to me that these are matters which concern us all, not merely Presidents or Congressmen or Governors, but every citizen of the United States.

This is one country. It has become one country because all of us and all the people who came here had an equal chance to develop their talents.

We cannot say to 10 percent of the population that you can't have the right; that your children can't have the chance to develop whatever talents they have; that the only way that they are going to get their rights is to go into the streets and demonstrate. I think we owe them and we owe ourselves a better country than that.

Therefore, I am asking for your help in making it easier for us to move ahead and to provide the kind of equality of treatment which we would want ourselves; to give a chance for every child to be educated to the limit of his talents.

As I have said before, not every child has an equal talent or an equal ability or an equal motivation, but they should have the equal right to develop their talent and their ability and their motivation, to make something of themselves.

We have a right to expect that the Negro community will be responsible, will uphold the law, but they have a right to expect that the law will be fair, that the Constitution will be color blind, as Justice Harlan said at the turn of the century.

This is what we are talking about and this is a matter which concerns this country and what it stands for, and in meeting it I ask the support of all our citizens.

Thank you very much.

Kennedy Defends the People
Against the Steel Industry

On the afternoon of April 11, 1962, President John F. Kennedy marched into the State Department auditorium in an unusually angry mood. With obviously rising, although controlled emotion, he told the Washington correspondents who had gathered for his news conference: "I have several announcements to make."

The President had good reason to be furious on that spring afternoon. From the day that he took office Kennedy had been wrestling with a series of economic problems which cast a perpetual cloud of impending disaster over his administration. He had inherited from President Eisenhower a serious business recession, marked by rising unemployment and an increasingly unfavorable balance of payments causing a continuing drain on United States gold reserves. To meet these emergencies Kennedy had increased the flow of federal funds into the economy by a series of executive actions and legislative proposals, and had tried to encourage capital investment by various tax inducements for industry.

In order to avoid inflationary price and wage increases which might have been generated by these activities, he attempted to persuade both industry and labor to adhere to basic price and wage guidelines in their collective bargaining agreements. He was still wary of utilizing the major fiscal weapons at his command—a significant income tax reduction or large appropriation bills for public works—because of the narrow margin of popular confidence his recent electoral victory had indicated. He was not yet sure that he enjoyed sufficient public support (as distinguished from popularity, which he had in large measure, according to the polls) to initiate such large-scale spending or innovating programs. Historically, no American President had proposed public works programs of any real magnitude in the absence of a major depression, nor had any President ever drastically cut taxes in the midst of a recession, and Kennedy was not at all sure at that point that such moves were necessary, or that the general public had sufficiently mastered the intricacies of Keynesian economics to understand the rationale for such measures.[112] So, for a full year he had been laboring with a series of more modest efforts, one of which was an attempt to hold prices and wages down by convincing business and labor to adhere to his suggested guidelines.

An increase in the price of a basic commodity, such as steel, could be expected to throw the delicate mechanism of this economic program into serious jeopardy. American price schedules were already so high that businessmen and industrialists in this country were finding it more and more difficult to compete with foreign-made products. This, of course, seriously influenced the unfavorable balance of payments, and the President had assigned a very high priority to correcting this imbalance. Furthermore the threat of inflation was always imminent. Consequently the President continued in his efforts to persuade major labor unions to hold any new wage or increased fringe benefits demands to a minimum in order to prevent industry from passing on increased costs in the form of substantial price increases. Steel price increases normally advanced well beyond the figure necessary to cover the entire cost of the collective bargaining agreement.

With this clearly in mind, it is easy to understand why President Kennedy was extremely concerned during the winter of 1961-62 when the United Steelworkers of America and the various steel companies were negotiating a new collective bargaining agreement. He wanted the union leaders to restrict their contract demands to a figure that was within the range of the general productivity increase in the industry. That would allow the steel companies to grant an increase without resorting to a steel price boost to pay for it. The President directed his secretary of labor, Arthur Goldberg, former steelworkers' union general counsel, to intervene with his old employers and convince them of the reasonableness and advisability of the President's request. In addition President Kennedy met personally at the White House with representatives of the steel industry and the union, and urged the noninflationary wage contract. Earlier in the year the President had pressed the industry not to introduce a price increase when the automatic wage increase, which was part of the previous contract, came due; he had succeeded in that effort.

The steelworkers' union and the major steel companies came to a contract agreement at the end of March 1962. The settlement was well within the limits of the figure that the President's economic advisors indicated the steel companies could absorb, on the basis of increased productivity, without having to raise the price of steel. This was the first contract achieved without a strike since 1954, and would cost the steel companies less than one-third the amount of the average settlement signed during the previous 20 years. Obviously the intervention of President Kennedy and Secretary Goldberg was significant in affecting the unusual restraint shown by the steelworkers' union, and it was also clear that this new contract would not serve as justification for a subsequent price increase, as was the usual pattern.

However on the afternoon of April 11 it was obvious that something had gone wrong with this scenario. There was no written agreement between the President and the steel corporations that a price increase would be deferred at that time; however, it was certainly Kennedy's understanding that if he succeeded in persuading the union to pull in its horns, and to agree to a much smaller wage settlement than usual, the steel companies would hold up their end of the bargain by indefinitely delaying any price increase, at least until general economic conditions improved. The President was abruptly disabused of that idea by the arrival at the White House at approximately 6 p.m. on April 10, 1962 (the evening before the news conference mentioned earlier) of Roger Blough, chairman of the board of the United States Steel Corporation. Blough handed the President a press statement, which was due to be released in New York to the wire services in ten minutes, announcing that U.S. Steel would raise the price of steel products by an average of six dollars per ton, an increase of 3.5 percent, or three-tenths of a cent per pound.

President Kennedy glanced briefly over the release and rang immediately for Secretary Goldberg, who arrived at the White House in a matter of minutes. A sharp exchange of words followed between the former labor attorney and Mr.

Blough. The secretary of labor first accused Blough of discourtesy in informing the President ten minutes before the public announcement was to be made, presenting him, in other words, with a *fait accompli*. Goldberg proceeded to lambaste Blough, informing him that the increase would be a blow to the national economy and damaging to U.S. Steel and, in effect, accused the industry leader of doublecrossing the President. Kennedy was probably too stunned to say very much, and in a few minutes Blough left quietly for New York. The news, however, ignited the White House. President Kennedy immediately called in his executive assistants on domestic affairs, and together with members of the council of economic advisors and several cabinet members, he began plotting the strategy of how they would meet this challenge head on.[113] It was on this occasion that the President made his now-famous remark:

> My father always told me . . . that steel men were sons-of-bitches, but I never realized till now how right he was.[114]

At the White House meeting, however, little time was wasted on recriminations. Assignments were quickly ticked off, and the lights burned most of the night at 1600 Pennsylvania Avenue as well as in other offices in Washington. The President had to change into his dinner jacket and hurry to a White House reception for Congress. The previous year this same party was ruined for him by the Bay of Pigs debacle, and President Kennedy remarked on this second occasion, "I'll never have another Congressional reception."[115]

The President, personally affronted by U.S. Steel's action, and quite aware of the impact that the price increase would have on the economy and on the prestige of the office of the presidency, prepared to fight. The initial strategy called for an immediate effort to halt or delay the other steel companies from falling in line with U.S. Steel, the giant of the industry. The economists set to work collecting information necessary to make the case to the public explaining why the price increase was nonessential, and to document the harmful effects it would have upon the national economy. The Justice Department was alerted to focus its attention upon the possibility of collusion in fixing prices in restraint of trade, and the Senate and House antitrust subcommittees were also consulted and their chairmen persuaded to issue press statements challenging the action and calling their groups together quickly to explore any possible violations of law. The President also discussed with his secretaries of defense and of the treasury the current commercial relations between the Defense Department and U.S. Steel, and the possibilities of breaking any such agreements. And finally several of his assistants were instructed to begin work on a statement for the press conference the next day.

The following morning the second largest steel corporation in America, Bethlehem Steel Company, announced a similar price increase, and it was followed by the other giants of the industry Republic, Youngstown, and Jones and Loughlin. By afternoon additional smaller companies such as Wheeling had fallen in line. When the President went before the television cameras for his press conference on Wednesday afternoon, April 11, 1962, he was confronted with a bloc of companies representing 86 percent of the steel production of the country, all of which had raised their prices in line with the lead taken by the United States Steel Corporation. His angry reaction was designed to give them something to think about.

President John F. Kennedy
News Conference (Extract) on Steel Price Increases
April 11, 1962

Public Papers of the Presidents: John F. Kennedy, 1962, 315-17.

I have several announcements to make.

. . . Simultaneous and identical actions of United States Steel and other leading steel corporations increasing steel prices by some $6 a ton constitute a wholly unjustifiable and irresponsible defiance of the public interest. In this serious hour in our Nation's history, when we are confronted with grave crises in Berlin and Southeast Asia, when we are devoting our energies to economic recovery and stability, when we are asking reservists to leave their homes and families for months on end and servicemen to risk their lives—and four were killed in the last 2 days in Viet-Nam—and asking union members to hold down their wage requests at a time when restraint and sacrifice are being asked of every citizen, the American people will find it hard, as I do, to accept a situation in which a tiny handful of steel executives whose pursuit of private power and profit exceeds their sense of public responsibility can show such utter contempt for the interests of 185 million Americans.

If this rise in the cost of steel is imitated by the rest of the industry, instead of rescinded, it would increase the cost of homes, autos, appliances, and most other items for every American family. It would increase the cost of machinery and tools to every American businessman and farmer. It would seriously handicap our efforts to prevent an inflationary spiral from eating up the pensions of our older citizens, and our new gains in purchasing power.

It would add, Secretary McNamara informed me this morning, an estimated $1 billion to the cost of our defenses, at a time when every dollar is needed for national security and other purposes. It would make it more difficult for American goods to compete in foreign markets, more difficult to withstand competition from foreign imports, and thus more difficult to improve our balance of payments position, and stem the flow of gold. And it is necessary to stem it for our national security, if we're going to pay for our security commitments abroad. And it would surely handicap our efforts to induce other industries and unions to adopt responsible price and wage policies.

The facts of the matter are that there is no justification for an increase in steel prices. The recent settlement between the industry and the union, which does not even take place until July 1st, was widely acknowledged to be noninflationary, and the whole purpose and effect of this administration's role, which both parties understood, was to achieve an agreement which would make unnecessary any increase in prices. Steel output per man is rising so fast that labor costs per ton of steel can actually be expected to decline in the next 12 months. And in fact, the Acting Commissioner of the Bureau of Labor Statistics informed me this morning that, and I quote, "employment costs per unit of steel output in 1961 were essentially the same as they were in 1958."

The cost of the major raw materials, steel scrap and coal, has also been declining, and for an industry which has been generally operating at less than two-thirds of capacity, its profit rate has been normal and can be expected to rise sharply this year in view of the reduction in idle capacity. Their lot has been easier than that of one hundred thousand steel workers thrown out of work in the last 3 years. The industry's cash dividends have exceeded $600 million in each of the last 5 years, and earnings in the first quarter of this year were estimated in the February 28th Wall Street Journal to be among the highest in history.

In short, at a time when they could be exploring how more efficiency and better prices could be obtained, reducing prices in this industry in recognition of lower costs, their unusually good labor contract, their foreign competition and their increase in production and profits which are coming this year, a few gigantic corporations have decided to increase prices in ruthless disregard of their public responsibilities.

The Steelworkers Union can be proud that it abided by its responsibilities in this agreement, and this Government also has responsibilities which we intend to meet. The Department of Justice and the Federal Trade Commission are examining the significance of this action in a free, competitive economy. The Department of Defense and other agencies are reviewing its impact on their policies of procurement. And I am informed that steps are under way by those members of the Congress who plan appropriate inquiries into how these price decisions are so quickly made and reached and what legislative safeguards may be needed to protect the public interest.

Price and wage decisions in this country, except for a very limited restriction in the case of monopolies and national emergency strikes, are and ought to be freely and privately made. But the American people have a right to expect, in return for that freedom, a higher sense of business responsibility for the welfare of their country than has been shown in the last 2 days.

Some time ago I asked each American to consider what he would do for his country and I asked the steel companies. In the last 24 hours we had their answer.

At the White House and in various administrative offices down Pennsylvania Avenue, a veritable storm of activity was set in motion. As already mentioned, the council of economic advisors, supplemented by three economists from the Department of Labor, were burning the midnight oil in order to put together a damning economic indictment which would clearly demonstrate that the price increase was an unnecessary reaction to the contract settlement. Senator Estes Kefauver, chairman of the Senate Antitrust Subcommittee, and Congressman Emanuel Cellar, chairman of the parallel committee in the House, both publicly questioned the increase and promised to hold hearings of their committees to investigate the events leading the steel companies' action. They were then joined by other powerful voices in the Senate and House; Democratic majority leader, Senator Mike Mansfield, and his whip, Senator Hubert Humphrey, Speaker John McCormack of the House and his Republican colleagues, Congressman John W. Byrnes, chairman of the Republican Policy Committee, Congressman Henry Reuss and others, all denounced the price increase and questioned the reasoning behind it. The antitrust division of the Department of Justice, under the whiplash of Attorney General Robert Kennedy, was already investigating evidence of collusion in the actions of the other companies which followed U.S. Steel's lead. The Department of Justice also announced that a grand jury had been convened to explore possible violations of criminal law in the industry's efforts to fix the steel prices. It was also charged that the department was investigating the expense accounts of steel executives, until "the President restrained his brother."[116]

The president of Bethlehem Steel was quoted in the newspapers on Wednesday morning as having stated at a stockholders meeting the day before that there should not be a price increase in the steel industry. Early Thursday morning a number of the reporters who had quoted this statement in their stories the previous day were (in some cases) awakened by F.B.I. agents and interrogated as to the validity of the statement. Much criticism was unleashed upon this particular action, and charges of "gestapo" tactics were hurled at the attorney general, but it appears to have been a tempest in a teapot. The evening previous to the early morning awakening, the responsible officials in the Department of Justice requested that the F.B.I. question those reporters who were present at the six o'clock press conference. Their instructions were to provide the Justice Department with the information before 7 a.m. the following morning. Why it took eight hours for the F.B.I. to locate the reporters has never been disclosed.[117]

The Federal Trade Commission also announced that it was looking into the affair and, at the request of the President, Solicitor General Archibald Cox was set to work drafting possible legislation to roll back steel prices. Cox was convinced that the present antitrust laws were inadequate, and new legislation in the form of a steel price emergency act or amendments to the Defense Production Act would be necessary.

These activities undoubtedly created a good deal of apprehension within the steel industry, and they obviously had some impact upon public opinion as well, but the most effective tack the President took was his private effort to split the industry by encouraging a small group of reasonably large companies not to go along with the price increase. The most important of these was Inland Steel, a Chicago based, family-owned company. The head of the firm, Joseph Block, was an administration supporter and a friend of Arthur Goldberg. Edward C. Gudeman, undersecretary of commerce and a former Sears-Roebuck vice president, happened to be a boyhood chum of another member of the Block family who was an executive of the company. Goldberg, Gudeman and others appealed to Inland Steel's executives with a low-pressure approach aimed at delaying a decision on a price increase. They argued that United States Steel's action jeopardized the national interest and that Inland should at least delay its decision until its key executives had had enough time to think through the national and international implications. Joseph Block was vacationing in Japan at the time of the steel crisis, but he kept closely in touch with developments by phone, and announced his final decision in Kyoto on Friday morning. Inland would not go along with the increase. "We did not feel," Block explained, "that it was in the national interest to raise prices at this time. We felt this very strongly."[118] Shortly thereafter the four other smaller companies which had not yet acted announced that they too would hold the line. Kennedy won his first battle of the fight, but only an industry-wide rollback could be considered a victory; this had not yet been achieved.

The pressure mounted as Secretary of Defense Robert S. McNamara announced that the United States Government would buy steel only from those firms offering the best competitive price, and he also indicated that the government might seek to develop a synthetic substitute for steel. Throughout the week the President's representatives—first Goldberg, and later, when it appeared he was getting nowhere, Washington attorney Clark Clifford—met secretly with United States Steel vice president, Robert Tyson, aboard a company-owned plane in the Washington airport. On Friday, as Goldberg and Clifford were flying to New York City for a meeting with Blough, the news reached them that Bethlehem had caved in and rescinded its increase. At that point it was only a matter of time before Blough gave up; the crisis was over when U.S. Steel announced its price rollback at 5:28 that same afternoon.

There is a good deal to be learned from this situation which bears heavily on the potential power and limits of the office of the presidency. In the steel crisis Kennedy was faced with a situation that he could not easily avoid, because of its serious implications for the national economy and because he had already publicly implicated the presidency in the earlier wage negotiations. He later reflected as to whether, in retrospect, he thought he should have acted so vigorously.

President John F. Kennedy
Reflections on his Actions
During the Steel Crisis
December 17, 1962

Public Papers of the Presidents: John F. Kennedy, 1962, 895.

. . . I think it would have been a serious situation if I had not attempted with all my influence to try to get a rollback, because there was an issue of good faith involved. The steel union had accepted the most limited settlement that they had had since the end of the second war, they had accepted it 3 or 4 months ahead, they did it in part, I think, because I said that we could not afford another inflationary spiral, that it would affect our competitive position abroad, so they signed up. Then when their last contract was signed, which was the Friday or Saturday before, then steel put its prices up immediately. It seemed to me that the question of good faith was involved, and that if I had not attempted, after asking the unions to accept the noninflationary settlement, if I had not attempted to use my influence to have the companies hold their prices stable, I think the union could have rightfully felt that they had been misled. In my opinion it would have endangered the whole bargaining between labor and management, would have made it impossible for us to exert any influence from the public point of view in the future on these great labor-management disputes which do affect the public interest. So I have no regrets. The fact is, we were successful.

Now, supposing we had tried and made a speech about it, and then failed. I would have thought that would have been an awful setback to the office of the Presidency. Now, I just think, looking back on it, that I would not change it at all. There is no sense in raising hell, and then not being successful. There is no sense in putting the office of the Presidency on the line on an issue, and then being defeated. Now, an unfortunate repercussion of that was the strong feeling that the Government might interfere in a good many labor-management matters, or that it might interfere in the whole question of the free enterprise system. It was regrettable that the general conclusion was drawn in this particular incident. Given the problem that I had on that Tuesday night, I must say I think we had to do everything we could to get it reversed.

It was, of course, a stunning victory for the President over a powerful corporation which had previously won every other showdown it had had with other Presidents in the century (e.g., Taft and Truman, among others). And President Kennedy had scored his victory without any executive precedents or statutory weapons which he could use to achieve his ends. He was forced to collect all of the formal and informal sources of influence around him, and direct them towards a single objective. In this sense it was a significant triumph. But at the same time, it was a costly victory, for it alienated much of the support the President had previously gained in the business community, and increased the opposition to his later economic and tax proposals. If one were to apply Neustadt's criteria of presidential intervention,[119] that is, the ability to protect one's options while influencing the decision in favor of presidential policy, then the error arose in failing to gain a firm written commitment from the steel industry at the time of the wage negotiations, in return for administration pressure on the union to hold demands well within the limits of the increased industry-wide productivity. Without such a written commitment, the President was vulnerable to the events which took place— the surprise announcement of the price increase which he lacked the legal power to prevent.

The risk was too great because it foreclosed any options the President possessed for dealing with either the union or management. Once the President publicly lent his prestige to persuade the union to restrict its demands, on the assumption that the companies would not force a price increase if the union would come to reasonable terms, his prestige and hence his future power rested on the fulfillment of that act of good faith. But a President has no business exposing the prestige and power of his office to the good faith of the board of directors of the United States Steel Corporation. Kennedy made this error, but recovered miraculously by a display of power and persuasion seldom, if ever, equalled by a President in dealing with an industrial organization as complex as the American steel industry. Although this display of presidential executive power produced certain unwelcome by-products, the institutional power of the presidency was reaffirmed and enhanced in the area of the domestic economy on a level not previously attained.

To ignore the dangers in this kind of "crisis politics," however, would be irresponsible. Perhaps, in the final analysis, weighing the public interest against the rights of the private individuals and corporations involved, it may appear that the administration did not overstep the limits of executive power in this instance, and acted quite properly to harness the full force of the government to protect the common good. But there are great risks involved when the emphasis upon policy objectives overrides the careful and restrained selection of means. The process of weighing such considerations is always critical. In the case of the federal protection of individual constitutional rights threatened by mob and state violation of both, the Executive frequently acted too hesitantly and with too great a caution with respect to the means employed. In this case, however, the reverse appears to be true. Here, the President's policy and the President's power were directly challenged, and very little caution or concern with respect to the means employed was reflected in the actions taken. This is not a criticism of the actions per se, because under the circumstances they were probably necessary to achieve the desired goal. But in Neustadt's terms, the loss of the possibility of alternative actions can be blamed upon the inadequacy of prior decisions, and, indeed, created the necessity for the display of maximum executive power, which is always threatening to individual rights in a free society.

Perhaps Charles Reich's assessment that such "use of power, whether its objectives are good or bad, is dangerous," is justified. His admonition that the "very immensity of government power demands . . . that it be used in a disinterested manner," should also be seriously considered.[120] But the responsibility for the abuse of presidential power does not lie exclusively with the Chief Executive alone, but normally reflects significant dislocations in the political process itself, which have created conditions and circumstances where it becomes clear that nothing short of an overwhelming mustering of presidential power and influence can correct the balance of public and private interests.

Perhaps at this point it is possible to delineate the executive power of the President with greater clarity than at the beginning of the section. Central to all of his executive responsibilities is the requirement that the laws be executed. It is the President's responsibility to see that this is done, normally in a routine, administrative manner, but occasionally, as we have seen, under certain circumstances, the full power at the disposal of the national government has had to be mobilized to accomplish the objective. These were proud moments (in most cases) for Americans, although the events which led to the use of the enforcement powers were usually tragic historical misunderstandings or oversights, in which long-festering social or economic grievances suddenly ignited public rebellion or disorder. In these situations the President was forced by events to utilize his full power to maintain law and order, and to protect the very foundations of the political system, but—and this is a big exception—no one should be deluded into thinking that the threat or the actual use of force brought to any satisfactory solution the problems which first led to the abandonment of the normal political processes and the resort to illegal and at times violent action. Such problems and frequently the resentment and frustration they created, remained long after the tumult of the crisis had subsided, and it is there that the more subtle resources of presidential leadership—executive and otherwise—must be mobilized and directed towards solutions.

More of this aspect of the Executive—I think impulse would be the proper term—is reflected in the ability of the President to anticipate social, political and economic problems, and to utilize presidential power and leadership in solving them before they erupt into explosions which require military or other extraordinary actions to suppress. This becomes one of the most exacting responsibilities of the modern presidency, as everything becomes magnified in size and scope, and compressed in terms of time and distance. The President who does not have his ear to the ground, who is not sensitive to the signs and indices of economic, social and political disorder, contributes to the combustion of social disorder and anarchy, even when these events do not necessarily come to a boil during his administration. The presidency during the 1920s and the 1950s was of this genre—the delusive and treacherous calm before the storm. But for the sensitive national leader who was in touch with reality, who had any real understanding of the economic and social order, there were many signs during these periods which pointed towards the impending economic and social explosions which came in the 1930s and 1960s.

The modern President must be tuned into these significant warnings of trouble and disorder, and must respond to the problems, the needs and the frustrations which stimulate them. It is to be assumed that the modern President will use the full power of his office and the considerable military resources at his command to maintain law and order once they are seriously challenged; he will mobilize the considerable economic and political power of the office to respond to the challenge of a stubborn and profit-greedy industry, or a general economic collapse such as Roosevelt faced in 1932. The great Presidents of the future, however, will be distinguished not by such crisis leadership, but by their intuitive ability to prevent such crises from developing, by their understanding and their response to the national needs before they erupt into riot and rebellion, and by their acting to direct the nation toward the solution of its problems within the framework of the political process. But the Presidents who will carry out this role will utilize more than the executive powers in order to accomplish these objectives.

NOTES

1. William Howard Taft, *Our Chief Magistrate and His Powers* (New York, 1916), 139-40.
2. Theodore Roosevelt, *An Autobiography* (New York, 1913), 388-89.

3. Woodrow Wilson, *Constitutional Government in the United States* (New York, 1961), 60; 68.
4. John Locke, "An Essay Concerning the True Original Extent and End of Civil Government" (sometimes referred to as the "Second Treatise on Government"), in *Great Books of the Western World* (Chicago, 1952) XXXV, paragraph 160, 62.
5. Quoted in Arthur M. Schlesinger, jr., *The Crisis of the Old Order* (Cambridge, Massachusetts, 1959), 477. In a recently published fourth volume of a multi-volume biography of Roosevelt, Frank Freidel indicates that Hoover sent a second letter, but that the President-elect refused to take official action until he was formally inaugurated. (Frank Freidel, *Franklin D. Roosevelt: Launching the New Deal* [Boston, 1973] IV, 188-89, and Chapter 11.)
6. Quoted in William Leuchtenburg, *Franklin D. Roosevelt and the New Deal* (New York, 1963), 39.
7. Samuel Rosenman, ed., *The Public Papers and Addresses of Franklin D. Roosevelt* (New York, 1938) II, 27-28.
8. Edmund Wilson, *The American Earthquake* (New York, 1958), 483.
9. Rosenman, II, 11-12.
10. Rosenman, II, 15.
11. Frances Perkins, *The Roosevelt I Knew* (New York, 1946), 72-73.
12. Margaret Truman, *Harry S. Truman* (New York, 1973), 429.
13. M. Truman, 429.
14. Quoted in Barton J. Bernstein, "The Ambiguous Legacy: The Truman Administration and Civil Rights," in Barton J. Bernstein, ed., *Politics and Policies of the Truman Administration* (Chicago, 1970), 272.
15. Quoted in Merle Miller, *Plain Speaking: An Oral Biography of Harry S. Truman* (New York, 1973), 155.
16. Bernstein, 270.
17. Quoted in Carl Marcy, *Presidential Commissions* (New York, 1973), 8.
18. Frank Popper, *The President's Commissions* (New York, 1970), 66-67.
19. Marcy, 8.
20. Hoover's extravagance was referred to as his "sins of commission."
21. Marcy indicates that President Hoover raised, conservatively, $2,000,000 in private funds for his commissions.
22. Congress balked at appropriating $25,000 for the Keep Committee on Departmental Methods; it finally made $5,000 available to them. (Marcy, 19.)
23. Marcy, 60.
24. Marcy, 2.
25. Popper, 51.
26. Popper, 51.
27. Daniel Bell, in an interesting article describing the activities of the National Commission on Technology, Automation and Economic Progress, reports pessimistically on the disparity between the scope and the intensity of the work performed by the commission, and the reception and publication of its report by the White House. In this case the White House played down the report because it was judged to be too controversial for public consumption, and the issues which it explored were no longer at the cutting edge of public concern, as they had been when the commission was first created. But frequently no reasons at all are necessary for such failures. The White House simply fails to understand the potential of such reports, or it is not competent enough to deal properly with them. (Daniel Bell, "Government by Commission," in Thomas E. Cronin and Sanford D. Greenberg, eds., *The Presidential Advisory System* [New York, 1969], 117-23.)
28. *Inquest: The Warren Commission and the Establishment of Truth* (New York, 1966).
29. Harry S. Truman, *Memoirs* (New York, 1958) II,180.
30. *To Secure These Rights:* Report of the President's Committee on Civil Rights (New York, 1947), viii.
31. *To Secure These Rights*, viii.
32. H. S. Truman, 181.
33. H. S. Truman, 181.
34. H. S. Truman, 181.
35. Summarized in *To Secure These Rights.*
36. Alonzo L. Hamby, *Beyond the New Deal: Harry S. Truman and American Liberalism* (New York, 1973), 189.
37. *To Secure These Rights,* 81-82.
38. It should be noted that in December 1947 Truman's Department of Justice intervened with an *amicus curiae* brief in a restrictive covenant decision of the lower court being reviewed by the

Supreme Court. The solicitor general of the United States, Philip J. Perlman, made it clear at that time that the action marked the beginning of governmental intervention in important civil rights cases, a recommendation, incidentally, which had been made by the President's Committee on Civil Rights. (Hamby, 189.)

39. Quoted in Rowland Evans and Robert Novak, *Lyndon B. Johnson: The Exercise of Power* (New York, 1966), 5.
40. Quoted in Evans and Novak, 120.
41. *Southern School News,* September 1957, 6.
42. Quoted in Wilson and Jane Cassels Record, eds., *Little Rock U.S.A.* (San Francisco, California, 1960), 32.
43. *Race Relations Law Reporter,* II, No. 5 (October 1957), 937.
44. Part of the television speech of Governor Faubus, as reported in the *Southern School News,* October 1957, 1. It was reprinted in Record, 37.
45. Quoted in Corinne Silverman, "The Little Rock Story," in Edwin A. Bock and Alan K. Campbell, eds., *Case Studies in American Government* (Englewood Cliffs, New Jersey, 1962), 10.
46. Daisy Bates, *The Long Shadow of Little Rock* (New York, 1962), 61.
47. *The New York Times,* September 5, 1957. A transcript of the President's press conference appears in excerpt form in Silverman, 11.
48. Dwight D. Eisenhower, *The White House Years,* vol. II, *Waging Peace, 1956-1961* (New York, 1965), 150.
49. Quoted in Emmet John Hughes, *The Ordeal of Power* (New York, 1963), 201. Hughes also points out that Eisenhower publicly created doubt that he would ever backup a court order by force: "I can't imagine any set of circumstances that would induce me to send federal troops . . . into any area to enforce the orders of a federal court, because I believe that the common sense of America will never require it. . . . I would never believe it would be a wise thing to do." (Hughes, 243.)
50. Harry Golden, *Mr. Kennedy and the Negroes* (Cleveland, Ohio, 1964), 107. See also Record, 42.
51. Quoted in Golden, 107.
52. Quoted in Golden, 107.
53. Bates, 72-76.
54. Quoted in *Southern School News,* October 1957, 2.
55. Quoted in Record, 42.
56. Eisenhower, 165.
57. Eisenhower, 165-66.
58. Eisenhower, 166.
59. *United States Statutes at Large,* XVII, Chap. 22, 13.
60. *United States Statutes at Large,* XVII, Chap. 22, 13.
61. *Ex parte Siebold,* 100 U.S. 394-95 (1879).
62. Richard E. Neustadt, *Presidential Power: The Politics of Leadership* (New York, 1960), 3.
63. Neustadt, 57.
64. Quoted in Miller, 259-60.
65. The "Little Rock Nine," who volunteered to participate in the original integration of Central High School in 1957, all graduated from high school and in most cases went on to college; several finished up with graduate degrees. Ernest Green was the first Black student to graduate from Central High School in 1958. He studied at Michigan State University and left there with a graduate degree in sociology in 1964. At present he is married and lives in Brooklyn, New York, with his wife and two children. He is the executive director of the Brooklyn-based joint apprenticeship program of the Workers Defense League, a one and one-half million dollar program which recruits and trains young Blacks and Puerto Ricans for entry into the building and construction trade and the building-construction unions, once the last bastion of white exclusiveness in the trade union movement. The program is financed by funds from the Department of Labor and the Ford and Taconic Foundations.

Elizabeth Eckford, the unhappy young girl who was not notified of the change in plans on the first day of school in Little Rock and walked into the National Guard and the racist mob alone, is now specialist 55/c in the Women's Army Corps. She attended Knox University in Galesburg, Illinois, for one year and then transferred to Central State College in Wilberforce, Ohio. Melba Patillo Beals studied journalism and graduated from San Francisco State College; she has one daughter and works as a free lance writer.

Mrs. Thelma Mothershed Wair majored in education at Southern Illinois University and now teaches at Rock Junior High School in East St. Louis. Jefferson Thomas is also married, has one son and is now assistant manager of the credit department at the Mobil Oil Corporation in Los

Angeles. He received a bachelors' degree at California State University at Los Angeles. He also owns his own record shop in that city. Minnie Jean Brown attended Southern Illinois University with Thelma Mothershed and is now raising a family in Canada. Terrance Roberts, after attending the University of California at Los Angeles, is employed as a social worker in Los Angeles; Gloria Ray attended Illinois Institute of Technology, married a native of Sweden and is now living in that country.

All nine graduated from high school, although only four finished at Central High; and every one either graduated or studied for an undergraduate or graduate degree after leaving high school. (This rundown is compiled from information contained in "Whatever Happened to the Little Rock 9?" in *Ebony*, XXVII, February 1972, 136-38; "Looking Back," in *New Yorker*, May 8, 1971, 30-31; and in Bates, 217-18.)

66. George Sinkler, *The Racial Ideas of American Presidents: From Lincoln to Theodore Roosevelt* (Garden City, New York, 1971), 376.
67. Sinkler, 346.
68. Arthur M. Schlesinger, jr. and Fred L. Israel, eds., *History of American Presidential Elections, 1789-1968* (New York, 1971) IV, 3539. (My emphasis.)
69. Harold Fleming, "The Federal Executive and Civil Rights, 1961-1965," in *Daedalus*, Fall 1965, 922.
70. Fleming, 929.
71. It was particularly difficult because the teeth of the enforcement provisions of Title III of the 1957 Civil Rights Act, which would have given the attorney general injunctive powers to enforce school desegregation and other civil rights, had been stricken from the bill with the tacit approval of President Eisenhower.
72. Alexander M. Bickel, "Civil Rights: The Kennedy Record," in *New Republic*, December 15, 1962, 12.
73. Bickel, 12.
74. Fleming, 938.
75. Fleming, 938-39.
76. Burke Marshall, *Federalism and Civil Rights* (New York, 1964), 37-38.
77. Victor S. Navasky, *Kennedy Justice* (New York, 1971).
78. Theodore C. Sorensen, *Kennedy* (New York, 1965), 17.
79. Arthur M. Schlesinger, jr., *A Thousand Days: John F. Kennedy In the White House* (Boston, 1965), 847.
80. This conjecture is made on the basis of the margins of victory in those states, as compared with the number of Blacks voting. For example, in Illinois, Kennedy won by a mere 8,858 votes, while it is estimated that 250,000 Blacks voted in the election; in South Carolina the margin was 10,000 votes, with an estimated 40,000 Blacks voting; in Michigan the figure was 67,000 votes with 250,000 Blacks who went to the polls. See White, 323.
81. *Atlanta Constitution*, October 25, 1960, 1.
82. *Atlanta Constitution*, October 25, 1960, 1.
83. From an editorial in *Atlanta Constitution*, October 21, 1960.
84. One such telegram of protest came from Eleanor Roosevelt and was addressed to Mayor Hartsfield.
85. Quoted in David Lewis, *King: A Critical Biography* (New York, 1970), 127.
86. *Atlanta Constitution*, October 25, 1960, 1.
87. *Atlanta Constitution*, October 25, 1960, 1.
88. Quoted in Coretta Scott King, *My Life with Martin Luther King, Jr.* (New York, 1969), 196.
89. Lenwood G. Davis, *I Have A Dream . . . The Life and Times of Martin Luther King, Jr.* (Chicago, 1969), 105.
90. Davis, 105.
91. Jim Bishop, *The Days of Martin Luther King, Jr.* (New York, 1971), 240-41.
92. James H. Meredith, *Three Years in Mississippi* (Bloomington, Indiana, 1966), 57-58.
93. Meredith, 5.
94. Meredith, 61.
95. The remarkable role of the Fifth Circuit Court of Appeals in the civil rights crisis is discussed by Shirely Fingerhood, "The Fifth Circuit Court of Appeals," in Leon Friedman, ed., *Southern Justice* (New York, 1965), 214-27. The fifth district included the district courts in Florida, Georgia, Louisiana, Alabama, Mississippi and Texas, the section of the South which has most bitterly opposed the federal law on the question of the rights of Black citizens.
96. Quoted in Walter Lord, *The Past That Would Not Die* (New York, 1965), 140.

97. Judge Cameron of the fifth district issued a stay order for the decision to grant Meredith's request for an injunction, but Justice Black vacated this and other attempts by Cameron to stay the orders of the Fifth Circuit Court of Appeals in this case.

98. Lord, 149.

99. Navasky, 163-64.

100. Navasky, 185.

101. Quoted in Navasky, 205.

102. *Time*, LXXX, No. 14 (October 5, 1962), 15.

103. *The New York Times*, September 27, 1962, 1.

104. *The New York Times*, September 30, 1962, 69.

105. Schlesinger, *A Thousand Days,* 943.

106. After studying official records, Lord puts the figure at 541 persons wounded and injured on both sides.

107. *Public Papers of the Presidents: John F. Kennedy, 1962* (Washington, D.C., 1963), 728.

108. From a speech delivered to the National Press Club in Washington, D.C., by Senator John F. Kennedy, on January 14, 1960. See Schlesinger and Israel, *American Presidential Elections,* IV, 3537.

109. *The New York Times*, June 12, 1963, 20.

110. *The New York Times*, June 12, 1963, 20.

111. *Public Papers of the Presidents: John F. Kennedy, 1963* (Washington, D.C., 1964), 468.

112. See section two of this volume.

113. Before this meeting adjourned, participants in it included such White House regulars as the President's brother, Attorney General Robert Kennedy, Chairman Walter Heller of the Council of Economic Advisors, presidential assistants Theodore Sorensen, Richard Goodwin, Kenneth O'Donnell; also McGeorge Bundy, special assistant for national security affairs, the secretary of defense, the chairman of the Federal Trade Commission, the secretaries of labor and commerce and several subcabinet-level people. It was a real "crisis council."

114. Sorensen, 449.

115. Sorensen, 449.

116. Henry Fairlie, *The Kennedy Promise: The Politics of Expectation* (Garden City, New York, 1973), 220.

117. Navasky, 353.

118. Quoted in Hobart Rowen, *The Free Enterprisers: Kennedy, Johnson and the Business Establishment* (New York, 1974), 102.

119. See Neustadt.

120. Quoted in Fairlie, 204.

Bibliography

Atlanta Constitution. October 25, 1960.

Bates, Daisy. *The Long Shadow of Little Rock*. New York: David McKay Company, Inc., 1962.

Bernstein, Barton J., ed. *Politics and Policies of the Truman Administration*. Chicago: Quadrangle Books, 1970.

Bishop, Jim. *The Days of Martin Luther King, Jr.* New York: G. P. Putnam's Sons, 1971.

Cronin, Thomas E. and Greenberg, Sanford D., eds. *The Presidential Advisory System*. New York: Harper and Row, 1969.

Davis, Lenwood G. *I Have A Dream . . . The Life and Times of Martin Luther King, Jr.* Chicago: Adams Press, 1969.

Elsenhower, Dwight D. *The White House Years*. Vol. II, *Waging Peace, 1956-61* New York: Doubleday and Company, Inc., 1965.

Evans, Rowland and Novak, Robert. *Lyndon B. Johnson: The Exercise of Power*. New York: New American Library, 1966.

Ex parte Siebold, 100 U.S. 371 (1879).

Fairlie, Henry. *The Kennedy Promise: The Politics of Expectations*. Garden City, New York: Doubleday and Company, Inc., 1973.

Freidel, Frank *Franklin D. Roosevelt: Launching the New Deal*. Vol. IV. Boston: Little, Brown and Company, 1973.

Friedman, Leon, ed. *Southern Justice*. New York: Pantheon Books, Inc., 1965.

Golden, Harry. *Mr. Kennedy and the Negroes*. Cleveland, Ohio: The World Publishing Company, 1964.

Hamby, Alonzo L. *Beyond the New Deal: Harry S. Truman and American Liberalism*. New York: Columbia University Press, 1973.

Hughes, Emmet John. *The Ordeal of Power*. New York: Atheneum, 1963.

Inaugural Addresses of the Presidents of the United States, From George Washington 1789 to John F. Kennedy 1961. 87th Cong., 1st sess., House Doc. No. 218. Washington, D.C.: U.S. Government Printing Office, 1961.

King, Coretta Scott. *My Life with Martin Luther King, Jr.* New York: Holt, Rinehart and Winston, 1969.

Koenig, Louis, ed. *The Truman Administration, Its Principles and Practices.* New York: New York University Press, 1956.

Leuchtenburg, William E. *Franklin D. Roosevelt and the New Deal.* New York: Harper and Company, 1963.

Lewis, Anthony and The New York Times. "Little Rock." *Portrait of a Decade: Second American Revolution.* New York: Random House, 1964.

Lewis, David. *King: A Critical Biography.* New York: Frederick A. Praeger, 1969.

Locke, John. "Concerning Civil Government, Second Essay." *The Great Books of the Western World.* Chicago: Encyclopaedia Britannica, 1952.

"Looking Back." *The New Yorker.* May 8, 1971.

Lord, Walter. *The Past That Would Not Die.* New York: Harper and Row, 1965.

Marcy, Carl. *Presidential Commissions.* New York: Da Capo Press, 1973.

Marshall, Burke. *Federalism and Civil Rights.* New York: Columbia University Press, 1964.

McConnell, Grant. *Steel and the Presidency—1962.* New York: W. W. Norton and Company, 1963.

Meredith, James H. *Three Years in Mississippi.* Bloomington, Indiana: Indiana University Press, 1966.

Miller, Merle. *Plain Speaking: An Oral Biography of Harry S. Truman.* New York: Berkley Publishing Company/G. P. Putnam's Sons, 1973.

Navasky, Victor S. *Kennedy Justice.* New York: Atheneum, 1971.

Neustadt, Richard E. *Presidential Power: The Politics of Leadership.* New York: John Wiley and Sons, Inc., 1960.

Perkins, Francis. *The Roosevelt I Knew.* New York: The Viking Press, 1947.

Popper, Frank. *The President's Commissions.* New York: Twentieth Century Fund, 1970.

Public Papers of the Presidents of the United States: Dwight D. Eisenhower, 1957. Washington, D.C.: U.S. Government Printing Office, 1958.

Public Papers of the Presidents of the United States: John F. Kennedy, 1962. Washington, D.C.: U.S. Government Printing Office, 1963.

Public Papers of the Presidents of the United States: John F. Kennedy, 1963. Washington, D.C.: U.S. Government Printing Office, 1964.

Public Papers of the Presidents of the United States: Harry S. Truman, 1947. Washington, D.C.: U.S. Government Printing Office, 1948.

Race Relations Law Reporter. II. No. 5 (October 1957).

Race Relations Law Reporter. VII. (September 1962).

Record, Wilson, and Record, Jane Cassels. *Little Rock U.S.A.* San Francisco, California: Chandler Publishing Company, 1960.

Rosenman, Samuel, ed. *The Public Papers and Addresses of Franklin D. Roosevelt.* Vol. II. New York: Random House, 1938

Rowen, Hobart. *The Free Enterprisers, Kennedy, Johnson and the Business Establishment.* New York: G. P. Putnam's Sons, 1964.

Schlesinger, Arthur M., jr. *A Thousand Days: John F. Kennedy in the White House.* Boston: Houghton Mifflin Company, 1965.

──────. *The Crisis of the Old Order.* Cambridge, Massachusetts: Houghton Mifflin Company (The Riverside Press), 1957.

──────. *The Coming of the New Deal* Cambridge, Massachusetts. Houghton Mifflin Company (The Riverside Press), 1958.

──────. and Israel, Fred L., eds. *History of American Presidential Elections, 1789-1968.* Vol. IV. New York: Chelsea House Publishers/McGraw-Hill, 1971.

Sinkler, George. *The Racial Ideas of American Presidents: From Lincoln to Theodore Roosevelt.* Garden City, New York: Doubleday and Company, 1972.

Silverman, Corinne. "The Little Rock Story." Edwin A. Bock and Alan K. Campbell, eds., *Case Studies in American Government*. Englewood Cliffs, New Jersey: Prentice-Hall, Inc., 1962.

Sorensen, Theodore C. *Kennedy*. New York: Harper and Row, 1965.

Southern School News. September and October 1957.

Taft, William Howard. *Our Chief Magistrate and His Powers*. New York: Columbia University Press, 1916.

Time. LXXX. No. 14 (October 5, 1962).

To Secure These Rights: Reports of the President's Committee on Civil Rights. New York: Simon and Schuster, 1947.

Truman, Harry S. *Memoirs*. Vols. II, III. Garden City, New York: Doubleday and Company, 1956.

Truman, Margaret. *Harry S. Truman*. New York: William Morrow and Company, 1973.

United States Code. 1958 edition. Vol. II, Title 10, Chap. 15.

United States Statutes at Large. Vol. XVII, Chap. 22.

"Whatever Happened to the Little Rock 9?" *Ebony*. XXVII. February 1972.

Wilson, Edmund. *The American Earthquake*. New York: Anchor Books, 1964.

V. The President as World Leader in War and Peace

THE PRESIDENT AS
WORLD LEADER IN WAR AND PEACE

In the nineteenth century the President's responsibilities in the conduct of foreign affairs and his role as Commander in Chief were generally held separate. The Louisiana Purchase and the Monroe Doctrine were clear excercises in diplomacy, although it is true that both Presidents Polk and Monroe were guilty of confusing those roles during the course of their "diplomatic" efforts. With Theodore Roosevelt in the twentieth century, and with most of his successors, however, the thin line that once separated these two executive responsibilities rapidly disappeared, for the President frequently had to back up his diplomatic efforts with the threat, if not the actual deployment of force.

The world became smaller in the twentieth century; the time lag between distance and events diminished with the advent of new and more rapid forms of transportation and communication; and with these developments, the division between Chief Diplomat and Commander in Chief soon became a relic of the nineteenth century. It became particularly true during and after World War II, but it was already apparent, perhaps because of the international scope of the President's responsibilities, in World War I. Woodrow Wilson was first a man of peace, who was always greatly interested in the conduct of foreign affairs, but as President of the United States during the international conflict in which the United States became involved, he reluctantly assumed the responsibilities of civilian head of the armed forces, a role he executed effectively if not willingly. But even as early as 1917 the execution of the war powers overlapped into what were for him the more interesting and worthwhile problems of international diplomacy. Fortunately, he was able to delegate successfully most of his responsibilities on the battlefield to competent and effective military commanders. But later in the century, the war and peace roles of the Chief Executive became far more complex and interrelated, and mid-century Presidents were not easily able to divest themselves of constant attention to these responsibilities. This was true to such an extent that in Volume III of *The Growth of Presidential Power* it is no longer possible or useful to treat these roles as separate and distinct from one other, but rather they must be considered simultaneously under the rubric of the President as a world leader in war and peace.

Total War in the Twentieth Century

The fantastic economic growth of the nineteenth and twentieth centuries placed new demands upon the "war powers" of the President of the United States.

The development of such new weapons as the machine gun, the tank, the hand grenade, the aerial bomb, and later toxic gases, the flame thrower, the atom and hydrogen bombs and germ warfare, accompanied by terrifying new means of delivering death and destruction—the airplane, the submarine and the radar-guided rocket and supersonic jet planes—all have made the competitive struggle for war production even more of a decisive factor in the economy than ever before. Furthermore the mass scale of warfare, employing millions of fighting men backed up by many more supporting troops and civilian personnel, imposes taxing logistical demands upon the modern industrial system. To fight this kind of a "total war"[1] successfully, it has been necessary to organize and control the industrial economy and coordinate the transportation and communication industries so that they are geared to meet the requirements of a large scale military commitment.

These measures would have been a bit premature when the Council for National Defense was established in the summer of 1916, because this country was not yet at war and the American people would not have accepted such controls. But the National Defense Act of 1916 which created the council was designed to prepare the nation for any eventuality, and, especially, to improve planning and coordination, for war production. The council was made up of the secretaries of war, navy, interior, agriculture, commerce and labor. The principal burden of its mobilizing efforts was to rest upon an advisory commission consisting of seven business, labor and professional leaders with expert knowledge in special fields and presiding over a network of committees in the various basic fields (i.e., transportation, raw materials, etc.).

Bernard Baruch, who served on the advisory commission, was disappointed in the legislation authorizing the creation of the council, because he saw from the outset that it "lacked specific authority beyond the making of investigations and recommendations. At best it might serve to make a beginning at coordinating the preparedness effort."[2] An attempt to improve the situation was made in the summer of 1917, after Baruch and others had proposed reorganization to Wilson. The President sent a memorandum to Secretary of War Baker on July 17, recommending a number of changes aimed at simplifying the council's procedures and organization.

President Woodrow Wilson
Memorandum to Secretary of War Baker
On Reorganizing the Council for National Defense
July 17, 1917

Ray Stannard Baker, *Woodrow Wilson: Life and Letters* (New York, 1939) VII, 168-69.

To Secretary Baker, addressed to him in his capacity as chairman of the Council of National Defense:

I have, as you know, been giving a great deal of thought to the plan of reorganization submitted to me some time ago by the Council of National Defense.

The more I think of it the more it seems to me that the organization can be still more simplified greatly to its advantage. My suggestion,—a suggestion which I hope you will be kind enough to lay before the Council,—is that the three persons to whom will be entrusted the direction of purchases of raw materials, the purchases of finished products, and the arrangement of priorities of purchase and of shipment shall themselves be members of the War Industries Board, together with Mr. Frayne and representatives of the War and Navy Departments, under the chairmanship of Mr. Scott; that the War Industries Board serve as a clearing house for the determination of the immediate needs of the Government and the sequence of those needs; and that the three officials I have named, those charged, namely, with the purchase of raw materials, with the purchase of finished products, and with the determination of priorities, shall in association with Mr. Hoover in the matter of the purchase of foodstuffs be the executive agency through which all purchases are arranged for. It seems to me that in this way we shall get rid of what might be in danger of being a complicated piece of machinery without in any way interfering with the independence and energy of the three active officials mentioned.

There would then be a free field for these three officials to use the various committees now associated with the Council of National Defense for the fullest information and for any kind of assistance which they can properly render, and it would be within their choice, of course, to employ assistants or lieutenants as systematically as seemed necessary.

I would be obliged if I might have an early opinion from the Council on this suggestion.

In August the advisory commission was transformed into the War Industries Board of the Council on National Defense. But again, as Baruch pointed out, "this new agency, lacking authority, proved inadequate to the task."[3] Not until the spring of the following year, when a third reorganization took place, was the problem solved. That time the President named Baruch as chairman of the new War Industries Board, and delegated to him sufficient power to accomplish what was necessary.

President Woodrow Wilson
Letter to Bernard Baruch Naming him
Chairman of the War Industries Board
March 4, 1918

Baker, VII, 32-33.

Dear Mr. Baruch: I am writing to ask if you will not accept appointment as Chairman of the War Industries Board, and I am going to take the liberty at the same time of outlining the functions, the constitution, and action of the Board as I think they should now be established.

The functions of the new Board should be—

(1) The creation of new facilities and the disclosing and, if necessary, the opening up of new or additional sources of supply;

(2) The conversion of existing facilities, where necessary, to new uses;

(3) The studious conversion of resources and facilities by scientific, commercial, and industrial economies;

(4) Advice to the several purchasing agencies of the Government with regard to the prices to be paid;

(5) The determination, wherever necessary, of production and of delivery and of the proportions of any given article to be made immediately accessible to the several purchasing agencies when the supply of that article is insufficient, either temporarily or permanently;

(6) The making of purchases for the Allies.

The Board should be constituted as at present and should retain, so far as necessary and so far as consistent with the character and purpose of the reorganization, its present advisory agencies; but the ultimate decision of all questions, except the determination of prices, should rest always with the chairman, the other members acting in a cooperative and advisory capacity. The further organization of advice I will indicate below.

In the determination of priorities of production when it is not possible to have full supply of any article that is needed procured at once, the chairman should be assisted and, so far as practicable, guided by the present priorities organization or its equivalent.

In the determination of priorities of delivery, when they must be determined, he should be assisted when necessary, in addition to the present priorities organization, by the advice and cooperation of a committee constituted for the purpose and consisting of official representatives of the Food Administration, the Fuel Administration, the Railway Administration, the Shipping Board, and the War Trade Board, in order that when a priority of delivery has been determined there may be common, consistent, and concerted action to carry it into effect.

In the determination of prices the chairman should be governed by the advice of a committee consisting, besides himself, of the members of the Board immediately charged with the study of raw materials and of manufactured products, of the labor member of the Board, of the chairman of the Federal Trade Commission, the chairman of the Tariff Commission, and the Fuel Administrator.

The chairman should be constantly and systematically informed of all contracts, purchases, and deliveries, in order that he may have always before him a schematized analysis of the progress of business in the several supply divisions of the Government in all departments.

The duties of the chairman are—

(1) To act for the joint and several benefits of all of the supply departments of the Government;

(2) To let alone what is being successfully done and interfere as little as possible with the present normal processes of purchase and delivery in the several departments;

(3) To guide and assist wherever the need for guidance and assistance may be revealed; for example, in the allocation of contracts, in obtaining access to materials in any way preempted, or in disclosure of sources of supply;

(4) To determine what is to be done when there is any competitive or other conflict of interest between departments in the matter of supplies; for example, when there is not a sufficient immediate supply for all and there must be a decision as to priority of needs or delivery, or when there is a competition for the same source of manufacture or supply, or when contracts have not been placed in such a way as to get advantage of the full productive capacity of the country;

(5) To see that contracts and deliveries are followed up to where such assistance as is indicated under (3) and (4) above has proved to be necessary;

(6) To anticipate the prospective needs of the several supply departments of the Government and their feasible adjustment to the industry of the country as far in advance as possible, in order that as definite an outlook and opportunity for planning as possible may be afforded the business men of the country.

In brief, he should act as the general eye of all supply departments in the field of industry.

Cordially and sincerely, yours,

Woodrow Wilson

With such a heady delegation of power, Baruch could have easily operated as the industrial czar of the nation, perhaps in some ways he did, but apparently he was quick to delegate adequate power to his assistants on the board. One of his colleagues has written that although Baruch alone possessed the power, "in practice every functionary of the Board wielded whatever powers he needed."[4] In Baruch's opinion the most important "instrument of control" the board possessed was "the power to determine priority—the power to determine who gets what and when."[5]

> Through the use of priority rulings, WIB [War Industries Board] was able to direct, restrain, or stimulate war production as the ever-changing situation required. Priority allowed us to allocate scarce materials where they were needed most, to curtail less essential production, to break bottlenecks, to end reckless and chaotic competition and hoarding, to conserve fuel, to save shipping space, to pool and ration. Priority also became a potent factor in dispersal of war plants, in the regulation of transportation, and in controlling prices.[6]

It is interesting to note that both President Wilson and Bernard Baruch grasped, at least in some rudimentary form, the tremendous implications of such overall planning and control for a peacetime as well as a war economy. When he appointed the first members of the advisory committee of the Council for National Defense in 1917, the President told them that "he foresaw that such a Council might become an important adjunct in the development of American efficiency during peace time. . . .and that their work was to unite the forces of the country 'for the victories of peace as well as those of war.' "[7] In retrospect Baruch made this point even more explicitly:

> But the lessons to be learned from WIB were not confined to questions of war. The WIB experience had a great influence upon the thinking of business and government. WIB had demonstrated the effectiveness of industrial cooperation and the advantages of government planning and direction. We helped inter the extreme dogmas of *laissez-faire*, which had for so long molded American economic and political thought. Our experience taught that government direction of the economy need not be inefficient or undemocratic, and suggested that in time of danger it was imperative. This lesson was applied fifteen years later when the New Deal drew upon the experience of the WIB to mobilize the economic resources of the nation to meet the emergency of the great depression.[8]

The major difference between the wartime presidency of Woodrow Wilson, and that of his outstanding predecessor Abraham Lincoln (apart from the industrial and economic organization and control, described above) was, as E. S. Corwin has pointed out, that Lincoln relied largely on the executive war powers while Wilson, whenever possible, sought delegated power from the Congress. Wilson did not rely exclusively upon statutory power for everything he did, however. Having been stymied by a filibuster from obtaining authorization to arm American merchant vessels, he went ahead and armed them anyway, knowing full well that he possessed the constitutional power to do so. He also acted on the basis of his constitutional authority in creating the Committee on Public Information, the War Industries Board and several other emergency agencies, as well as in setting up cable censorship and directives for control of German firms in this country. But he obtained delegations of power from the Congress "to take over and operate the railroads and water systems, to regulate or commandeer all ship-building facilities in the United States, to regulate and prohibit exports, to raise an army by conscription, to allocate priorities in transportation, to regulate the conduct of resident enemy aliens, to take over and operate the telegraph and telephone systems, to redistribute functions among the executive agencies of the federal government, to control the foreign language press, and to censor all communications to and from foreign countries."[9]

Under a single delegation of power from the Congress in 1917 in the form of the Lever Act, the President was authorized to regulate through whatever agencies he wished to establish

> the importation, manufacture, storage, mining, and distribution of any necessaries; [he] could requisition foods, fuels, and other supplies necessary for any public use connected with national defense; could purchase, store and sell certain foods; could fix a reasonable guaranteed price for wheat, based on a statutory minimum; could take over and operate factories and mines, packing houses, pipe lines and similar industrial institutions important to national defense; could fix the price of

coal and coke and regulate their production, sale, shipment, distribution, and storage; and could regulate or even forbid the use of food materials in the manufacture of intoxicants.[10]

But once having obtained such extraordinary power Wilson divested himself of everything but ultimate responsibility, appointing competent administrators like Bernard Baruch (industry), Herbert Hoover (food) and William Gibbs McAdoo (railroads) to carry through on day-to-day problems and decisions.

These huge grants of power were not bestowed by a supine Congress, eager to unload all responsibility upon the President. There was considerable resistance and even an effort to write into the Lever Act a provision for a "Joint Committee on Expenditures in the Conduct of the War," a watch-dog provision somewhat similar to that with which the radicals saddled Lincoln during the Civil War. When the Senate wrote this amendment into the bill, Wilson attacked it strongly. He argued that if it was enacted it would "render my task of conducting the war practically impossible."[11] He also charged that it would constitute an assumption of the executive functions on the part of the legislature, and referred to the ominous record of a similar committee which had attempted to harass Lincoln during the Civil War. There was already existing and sufficient machinery in the possession of the Congress, the President pointed out, to investigate the effective enforcement of his administrative responsibility.[12]

President Woodrow Wilson
Letter (Extract) to Representative Lever
On the Proposed Senate Amendment
July 24, 1917

Baker, VII, 185-86.

To Representative A. F. Lever, who had sent the President a copy of the Food bill as it passed the Senate:

Section 23 is not only entirely foreign to the subject matter of the Food Administration Bill in which it is incorporated but would, if enacted into law, render my task of conducting the war practically impossible. I cannot believe that those who proposed this section scrutinized it with care or analyzed the effects which its operation would necessarily have. The constant supervision of executive action which it contemplates would amount to nothing less than an assumption on the part of the legislative body of the executive work of the administration.

There is a very ominous precedent in our history which shows how such a supervision would operate. I refer to the committee on the conduct of the war constituted by the Congress during the administration of Mr. Lincoln. It was the cause of constant and distressing harassment and rendered Mr. Lincoln's task all but impossible.

I am not, I beg you to believe, in any way questioning what might be the motives or the purpose of the members of such a committee: I am ready to assume that they would wish to cooperate in the most patriotic spirit, but cooperation of that kind is not practicable in the circumstances. The responsibility rests upon the administration. There are abundant existing means of investigation and of the effective enforcement of that responsibility. I sincerely hope that upon the reconsideration of this matter both Houses of Congress will see that my objections rest upon indisputable grounds and that I could only interpret the final adoption of Section 23 as arising from a lack of confidence in myself.

The bill went to the House-Senate Conference Committee; by standing firm and convincing administration supporters on the committee to do the same, the President was able to get the watch-dog committee amendment killed. He won a second victory by eliminating another feature of the bill he was strongly opposed to—a food control board in place of the single administrator (Herbert Hoover) already responsible to him. Not only was the President extremely proficient at this kind of legislative politics, but he also proved to be something of a prophet, as he had written several days previously to a friend who had requested an appointment for a cousin to the proposed Board; "there ain't going to be no Food Control Board."[13]

The idea of strong executive and legislative leadership was, as we have seen, not a new concept with Wilson. For Congress now to challenge this concept and to suggest that his model of responsible executive leadership should be modified was to attack one of the fundamental principles of Wilson's theory of government, and he correctly realized he would have to fight against it and win.

The pattern of war leadership which Wilson established was far more significant than anything he did in the military vein. Modern warfare was becoming far too massive and complex for a President to assume as direct a role in the development of strategy and tactics as Polk and Lincoln had, but the overall control and direction of the huge economic and industrial complex that undergirded the modern war effort was established through the outstanding legislative leadership of Woodrow Wilson, and implemented by equally successful administrative appointments such as Baruch, Hoover and McAdoo. It was in that respect that Wilson made an important contribution to the evolution of the power of the President as a wartime leader.

Wilson—Delegation of Military Leadership

On paper, Woodrow Wilson was not a likely prospect as a wartime Commander in Chief. As a very young boy he observed the wounded Confederate soldiers being brought into his father's church in Georgia, which served as a temporary army hospital, and he later referred to the Civil War as a "dark chapter in history." As President he did not exactly welcome nor understand the function and thinking of the professional army before this country became entangled in World War I. One day the acting secretary of war, Henry Breckinridge, was summoned to the White

House, where he found Wilson "trembling and white with passion." The President was holding in his hand a copy of the *Baltimore Sun*, and he pointed out a story which indicated that the general staff was preparing plans in the event of war with Germany. Breckinridge could not tell the President whether or not the story was accurate, so Wilson directed him to investigate, and if he found it to be true, to relieve every officer on the general staff and order them out of Washington.[14]

However, perhaps his early antipathy to the military and war resulted in a more creditable performance as Commander in Chief, for realizing that his abhorrence of war rendered him generally deficient in knowledge of military logistics and strategy, he wisely delegated almost all such decisions to his military leaders. On the other hand Wilson insisted that the principle of civilian control of the military be respected. In the few times when he did intervene in a question of overall military strategy, he expected quick compliance with his decision, and was intolerant of any protracted show of disagreement or defiance. Arthur Link describes such a situation when Wilson, early in his first term, turned down certain recommendations by the Joint Board of the Army and Navy (made up of the navy's general board and the army's general staff) regarding fleet maneuvers in the Pacific. In conveying his decision to his secretary of the navy, Wilson said:

> The Joint Board has of course presented the military aspect of the situation as it sees it and it may be right, but we are considering this matter with another light, on the diplomatic side, and must determine the policy.[15]

Then the joint board protested in a memorandum to the secretary of the navy, recommending an alternate plan rather similar to their first proposal. Wilson was astonished at the board's presumption in challenging the President's decision, and he told the secretary of the navy that the board had no right even to discuss these matters, once the President had decided:

> When a policy has been settled by the Administration and when it is communicated to the Joint Board, they have no right to be trying to force a different course, and I wish you would say to them that if this should occur again, there will be no General or Joint Boards. They will be abolished.[16]

Although Wilson was rigid on the question of civilian supremacy in matters involving political and diplomatic considerations, he more or less applied the same rule in reverse when it came to military decisions, giving his professional military leaders close to complete autonomy in wartime. He personally selected General John J. Pershing to head up the American Expeditionary Force in Europe, making him responsible to the President, rather than to a chief of staff in Washington. Pershing was ushered into the President's office in the White House on May 24th, 1917, for his first and only meeting with Wilson before leaving for France. After discussing some problems of shipping with the secretary of war, who accompanied the general, the President turned to Pershing. "General," he said, "we are giving you some difficult tasks these days." Pershing replied that that was what he was "trained to expect."[17] The President then spoke of the recent Mexican expedition and inquired about Pershing's acquaintance with France, but he said nothing about the part the American army should play in the war. When Pershing, upon leaving, expressed appreciation for his appointment, the President replied: "General, you were chosen entirely on your record and I have every confidence you will succeed."[18] That was the extent of their conversation during the entire period of the war.

Before leaving General Pershing received written orders signed by Secretary of War Newton D. Baker and approved by the President. At the same time for some reason he was also given a letter of instructions from the army's acting chief of staff, Major General Tasker E. Bliss, which reiterated what was said in the President's letter, but the former instructions included certain critical points that were not in General Bliss' letter. Those directions referred to the manner in which the American army should cooperate with the armed forces of the other nations involved. There was some small discrepancy between the two sets of instructions, but Pershing later wrote that the question of the organizational nature of the cooperative action that followed was dictated by circumstances rather than by the precise wording of an executive order which was general in nature and far removed from the field of battle. Just before sailing Secretary Baker told Pershing that "he would only give him two orders, 'one to go to France and the other to come home'; in the meantime, Pershing's authority in France would be supreme. He added: 'If you make good, the people will forgive almost any mistake. If you do not make good, they will probably hang us both on the first lamp-post they can find.' "[19]

Secretary of War Newton D. Baker
Memorandum to Major General J. J. Pershing on his
Command, Authority and Duties in Europe
May 26, 1917

John J. Pershing, *My Experiences in the World War* (New York, 1931), 38.

War Department
Washington
May 26, 1917

Secret
From: The Secretary of War
To: Major General J. J. Pershing, U.S. Army
Subject: Command, Authority and Duties in Europe

The President directs me to communicate to you the following:

1. The President designates you to command all the land forces of the United States operating in Continental Europe and in the United Kingdom of Great Britain and Ireland, including any part of the Marine Corps which may be detached for service there with the Army. From your command are excepted the Military Attachés and others of the Army who may be on duty directly with our several embassies.

2. You will proceed with your staff to Europe. Upon arrival in Great Britain, France or any other of the countries at war with the Imperial German Government, you will at once place yourself in communication with the American Embassy and through its agency with the authorities of any country to which the forces of the United States may be sent.

3. You are invested with the authority and duties devolved by the laws, regulations, orders and customs of the United States upon the commander of an army in the field in time of war and with the authority and duties in like manner devolved upon department commanders in peace and war, including the special authorities and duties assigned to the commander of the Philippine Department in so far as the same are applicable to the particular circumstances of your command.

4. You will establish, after consultation with the French War Office, all necessary bases, lines of communication, depots, etc., and make all the incidental arrangements essential to active participation at the front.

5. In military operations against the Imperial German Government, you are directed to cooperate with the forces of the other countries employed against that enemy; but in so doing the underlying idea must be kept in view that the forces of the United States are a separate and distinct component of the combined forces, the identity of which must be preserved. This fundamental rule is subject to such minor exceptions in particular circumstances as your judgment may approve. The decision as to when your command, or any of its parts, is ready for action is confided to you, and you will exercise full discretion in determining the manner of cooperation. But, until the forces of the United States are in your judgment sufficiently strong to warrant operations as an independent command, it is understood that you will cooperate as a component of whatever army you may be assigned to by the French Government.

6. You will keep the Department fully advised of all that concerns your command, and will communicate your recommendations freely and directly to the Department. And in general you are vested with all necessary authority to carry on the war vigorously in harmony with the spirit of these instructions and towards a victorious conclusion.

Newton D. Baker

Acting Chief of Staff Major General T. H. Bliss Memorandum to Major General J. J. Pershing on his Command, Authority and Duties in Europe
May 26, 1917

Pershing, 39.

War Department
Office of the Chief of Staff
Washington, D.C.
May 26, 1917

Secret

Dear General Pershing: In compliance with the orders of the President assigning you to the command of the United States forces in France, the Secretary of War directs that you proceed, with the necessary staff, to Paris, France, via England.

The Secretary of War further directs that, upon your arrival in France, you establish such relations with the French Government and the military representatives of the British Government now serving in France as will enable you effectively to plan and conduct active operations in conjunction and in cooperation with the French armies operating in France against Germany and her allies.

As a preliminary step, the Secretary of War deems it desirable that you have a thorough study made of the available bases, lines of communication and camps of instruction, so that you may direct preparations for the arrival of successive contingents of our troops in France. The equipment and training for active service of the troops under your command in the trenches or on the firing line should be carried on as rapidly as possible. While the entrance of our forces into the theater of active operations will be left entirely to your judgment, it should not be unduly hastened. Yet it is believed that the purpose of your presence in France will be materially advanced by the appearance of our troops upon the firing line.

The Secretary of War desires that you keep the department fully advised of all questions of importance concerning the operations of your troops and that you submit your views from time to time upon such questions, as well as upon matters pertaining to the general situation in Europe. He also expects that, as the superior military representative of the United States in France, you will exercise such general authority as will best contribute to the fulfillment of your mission in France.

Very sincerely,

Tasker H. Bliss, Major General
Acting Chief of Staff

Both President Wilson and Secretary Baker lived up to their word. They let General Pershing direct his army from his command post in France, and only in rare instances, always touching on problems which involved larger political or diplomatic considerations, did they venture to intervene. Wilson maintained more or less the same relationship with his permanent chief of staff on the home front, General Peyton C. March, although March's proximity to the White House obviously facilitated consultation. General March indicates that the President only "interfered twice with the operations of the War Department while I was Chief of Staff, and both times he was wrong."[20] He was referring to the Archangel expedition in the summer of 1919 and the Siberian expedition in the winter of 1920. The inclusion of American troops in both instances was agreed to by the President at the insistence of America's Allies on the Supreme War Council, and in each instance the President overruled his chief of staff for political rather than military reasons.

The creation of the Supreme War Council was in fact the most important development in the structure of military power and control during the war. American soldiers had fought outside the borders of the United States in three of the five wars in which they had been involved, but World War I was the first time an American army fought in Europe, as part of a grand coalition of nations. This presented a range of new problems for the country and the President as Commander in Chief, for the President was no longer free to organize the American military effort autonomously, to adopt the strategy and tactics he chose, but rather he had to integrate American and Allied efforts to achieve a collective victory over the German army and navy.

This both simplified some problems and complicated others. It simplified the normally troublesome question of where the battles should be fought, because by the time the United States entered the war, the battle areas were well defined, and the logistics determined by three years of previous struggle. How America could rapidly train, equip and transport millions of new recruits to this costly and destructive war, and then how those troops could be best used in battle alongside the British and the French, presented the complex aspects of the problem.

On November 13, 1917 Colonel House wired President Wilson:

> France, England, and Italy have agreed to form a Supreme War Council and believe that it is imperative that we should be represented in it because of the moral effect here. . . . I would advise not having a representative on the civil end . . . but would strongly urge having General Bliss on the military end.[21]

Three days later the President replied to House, telling him that he not only agreed, but insisted upon such an arrangement, and indicated that the war could not be carried on successfully without such a council. He also asked Colonel House to take part in the preliminary deliberations, and appointed General Tasker H. Bliss, formerly army chief of staff, to be the American member of the Permanent Committee of Military Advisors. That same evening Colonel House issued a statement in Paris, more or less making the arrangement official, and indicating that it was the intention of the United States to participate not only in the joint planning for a military victory, but also "in order to achieve a just and lasting peace."[22] This of course was a major departure from traditional American isolation from European politics, and it also marked a development in American military policy, where for the first time in the history of the republic, American men and arms were made subject to the control of a collective body not directly responsible to their political leader.

Under that arrangement President Wilson had greater difficulty avoiding active participation in the major military decisions of the war. However General Bliss' extraordinary tact helped forestall any situations where the two military representatives of the President might be in conflict, and Wilson be forced to intervene. The major problem which arose was over the deployment of American troops. The French argued strongly for the integration of American regiments into badly depleted French divisions, while General Pershing resisted such amalgamation, feeling that it would weaken the effectiveness of his army, and in the long run, be destructive to overall Allied strength. Wilson was very sympathetic to this position. General Pershing was embarrassed by what he considered the inadequate flow of American troops to France and their unreadiness for battle without further training. He finally agreed to American units training with French commands, and later in the spring of 1918, when the German advance in the Somme region threatened to divide the British and French armies, he went much further and offered American troops for any emergency duty proposed by the Allies. Later he allowed a number of American divisions, which were transported to Europe on British ships, to serve temporarily with the British army.

The problem became more acute when a unified Allied command was named in reaction to the powerful German attack in the spring of 1918. Theoretically the dual authority of Pershing and Bliss was now extended to Supreme Allied Commander Marshal Ferdinand Foch. Pershing could appeal to Wilson if he found himself in disagreement with a decision of the supreme commander, but the President was reluctant to go back on his public commitment to support the Allied effort to the hilt. He was finally forced to redefine the chain of command in his own military establishment, in order to insure his formal authority over Pershing, in the event of a serious conflict between the Commanding General of the American Expeditionary Army and the supreme commander of the Allied forces. This was achieved by permitting General Peyton March to issue a general order in Washington that the army chief of staff "takes rank and precedence over all officers of the Army," indicating, as General March pointed out, "that the Chief of Staff was the military superior of General Pershing."[23] Wilson thus shored up his chain of command in order to be better able to control his farflung military arm in the event of a serious crisis or dispute. Pershing proved to be shrewd enough to avoid such a showdown, and was able, albeit with encouragement from Washington from time to time, to work out his disagreements with Marshal Foch. Both General March and General Pershing were opposed to the Archangel and Siberian expeditions, so was Wilson himself for that matter, but the President finally agreed for diplomatic reasons, rather than on the basis of military considerations.

There seems to be considerable evidence to support the argument that in addition to his instinctive distaste for the responsibilities of Commander in Chief,

Woodrow Wilson abjured an active role in such a capacity for important policy considerations. First of all, as a "Johnny-come-lately" in World War I, the United States was forced to serve as a junior partner. On the basis of a commitment and sacrifices considerably smaller than that of her Allies, she was in no position to play a commanding role in the Supreme War Council. More important to Wilson was the argument that even if he could have imposed his influence more vigorously within the wartime Allied councils, he could only have done so at the expense of weakening his bargaining power at the peace table, which was the objective with which he was really concerned. "From the first day of the war to the last, all that Wilson sought was a peace that could be secured by a League of Nations, a peace that would make the world safe for democracy. He refused to act as Commander in Chief because to do so would have jeopardized this aim."[24] This assessment by Ernest R. May is perhaps an overstatement of the case, since there were negative as well as positive reasons for Wilson's reluctance to assert his prerogatives as Commander in Chief. But he designated such powers to others wisely, and preserved his influence and talents for what he considered more important activities. Perhaps it was the short duration of the war and the distance of the battlefields which permitted such remote controls to be effective.

A Critical Supreme Court Decision:
United States v. *Curtiss-Wright Export Corporation*

A Supreme Court decision made in 1936 contributed substantially towards establishing a firm constitutional basis for the expanded powers in the areas of foreign relations which the President would assert during World War II and in the period following it. Ironically the case itself involved only a very trivial incident, but it raised major questions to which the Court addressed itself. The Government of the United States brought suit against the Curtiss-Wright Export Corporation for violating a presidential proclamation placing an embargo on "the sale of arms and munitions of war in the United States to those countries now engaged in armed conflict in the Chaco," an area over which Bolivia and Paraguay were then at war. The President's proclamation had been authorized under an earlier joint resolution of both houses of Congress, which had delegated to him the power to decide when such an embargo should be put into effect. Curtiss-Wright, the defendant in the case, argued that the Congress had "abdicated its essential functions" in delegating to the President the power to make such a discretionary judgment, hence the restrictions set forth by the President should not be binding upon the parties involved. The United States, as prosecutor, maintained that the Curtiss-Wright Corporation had violated a law clearly established by Congress and implemented by the President.

The Court, in a majority decision written by Justice George Sutherland, addressed itself to the basic constitutional problems which the case raised, rather than to dispense with the immediate litigation on very narrow or legalistic grounds. It could have for example dismissed the appeal on the grounds that the Congress in its resolution was quite properly acting in accordance with its constitutional authority to regulate foreign commerce, and that justified the delegation of discretionary power to the President by virtue of the so-called "elastic clause" of the Constitution which authorizes Congress

> [t]o make all laws which shall be necessary and proper for carrying into Execution the foregoing powers, and all other powers vested by this Constitution in the Government of the United States, or in any Department or Officer thereof.

But obviously the Court felt that the appeal of the litigants raised substantial questions regarding the powers of the President in the area of foreign affairs, questions about which perhaps the Constitution itself was somewhat misleading, and they also obviously felt that there was a real need for the Court to speak, to try to define rather explicitly what those powers were and to delineate their constitutional basis and justification, and also their limitations. Indeed, this had been an ancient preoccupation of Justice Sutherland's. Some would later claim that the Court was engaging in a clear and dangerous exploration in *obiter dictum* in taking on such an assignment and was violating its own proper constitutional limits by "expanding" upon the narrower limits of the case and question at hand. But regardless of the merit of these objections, United States v. Curtiss-Wright Export Corporation[25] provides students of the American presidency with a very clear and illuminating discussion of the source and breadth of the President's power in the area of foreign affairs.

Mr. Justice Sutherland was considered a strong member of the conservative wing of the Court, and his opinion in this case certainly was not rooted in any deep conviction of the validity of executive primacy in the ordinary affairs of the republic. His decision in the Humphrey's Executor v. United States case handed down in the previous sitting of the Court clearly indicated his zeal—perhaps his overzealousness—in limiting the power of the President in domestic affairs.[26] But Justice Sutherland had long been a strong advocate of the important distinction between the sources of governmental power in domestic and foreign affairs, and indeed had written an article on this subject as early as 1909.[27] Acknowledging the Constitution as the decisive arbiter between state and national rights and power, Sutherland argued 25 years before he passed judgment in the *Curtiss-Wright* case that in the Declaration of Independence the "*United* Colonies" severed their ties to the sovereign British Crown, and from that point on assumed full sovereignty over their external affairs. He insisted that these powers were derived not from the individual colonies or states, which never possessed them, but rather from the act of creating an independent and sovereign and "*United*" nation. In 1909 Sutherland wrote:

> Much of the confusion [concerning the true nature of the powers of the government] has resulted from a failure to distinguish between our *internal* and our *external* relations. . . .
>
> It is clear from a consideration of the events leading up to and surrounding the adoption of the Constitution that the primary purpose of the specific enumeration of the powers of the General Government over

internal matters was to preclude any encroachment of that Government upon those powers which it was deemed the state governments should exclusively possess. . . . The effect of the enumeration is therefore quite as much to *affirm* the possession of these enumerated powers to the several States, as it is to *deny* them to the General Government. Over its internal affairs the state government possesses every power not delegated to the General Government, or prohibited by the Constitution of the United States or the state constitution. It will therefore be seen that, in this way, every power which any government in the world possesses over its *internal* affairs, is vested either in the *United* States or in the *several* States, unless affirmatively prohibited. . . . Is it not reasonable to conclude that it was likewise within the contemplation of the framers of the Constitution that every necessary and proper power possessed by foreign governments over their *external* affairs should be exercised by the Government of the United States over our external affairs? . . . They were anxious to keep for the people of each State in the fullest measure their right of local self-government, but there was not shown anywhere a disposition to curtail the power of the National Government in its external relations. On the contrary, there was clearly manifest a desire to make such power, in the words of the Annapolis recommendation, "adequate to the exigencies of the Union." The Declaration of Independence asserted it when that great instrument declared that the *United Colonies* as free and independent States (that is, as *United* States, not as separate States) "have full power to levy war, conclude peace, contract alliances, establish commerce, and *to do all other acts and things which independent States may of right do.*"

And so national sovereignty inhered in the United States from the beginning. Neither the Colonies nor the States which succeeded to them ever separately exercised authority over foreign affairs. Prior to the Revolution the Colonies were independent of each other, but all owed common allegiance to the Crown of Great Britain. They were invested with and exercised in subordination to the Crown certain governmental functions of a purely local and internal character, but so far as foreign relations were concerned the Imperial Government exercised plenary authority. When they severed their connection with Great Britain, they did not do so as *separate* Colonies, but as the *United* States of America and they declared not the *several* Colonies, but the *United* Colonies to be free and independent States—not New York or Georgia, or South Carolina severally—but all the Colonies in their *united* and *collective capacity*. This declaration was an assertion of and constituted the first step toward nationality. . . . These powers [over external affairs] were never delegated by the States; they were never possessed by the States, and the States could not delegate something which they did not have.[28]

In the *Curtiss-Wright* case the Court restricted its judgment to questions dealing with legislative and executive power in the area of foreign affairs, not wishing to pass at that time on "Whether, if the Joint Resolution had related solely to internal affairs it would be open to challenge that it constituted an unlawful delegation of legislative power to the Executive."[29] As a prelude to its views on these questions, however, the Court felt the need to sharply delineate the differences "between the powers of the federal government in respect of foreign or external affairs."[30] As Justice Sutherland indicated, the two "classes of powers are different both in respect to their origin and nature."[31] The powers of the federal government with respect to internal affairs are defined and limited by the specific provisions of the Constitution, including such implied powers as are necessary and proper to carry these powers into effect. The powers of the federal government with respect to external affairs, however, the Court argued, were not based upon or even limited by the Constitution, but existed even prior to the Constitution, being rooted in the acts which established the sovereignty of the American colonies as a nation.

The union of these communities, independent and sovereign, existed before they formed the federal government in 1789, and the sovereign power "to declare and wage war, to conclude peace, to make treaties, to maintain diplomatic relations with other sovereignties was possessed by that Confederation which served as their government until the Constitution of the United States was written and ratified."[32] This sovereignty was created when the colonies declared their independence from Great Britain, and was recognized in the community of nations when Great Britain negotiated a treaty of peace in 1783 with the "United States of America." Even earlier than this (1778) a treaty was negotiated with France which stipulated, among other things, that

> His Most Christian majesty guarantees on his part to the United States their liberty, sovereignty and independence, absolute and unlimited, as well in matters of government as commerce, and also their possessions, and the additions or conquests that their confederation may obtain during the war.[33]

For several years before the Declaration of Independence the colonies conducted their external affairs through a central agency—the Continental Congress. The limits that were then acknowledged by this sovereign power in its dealing with other sovereign powers were the practices or customs of international law generally acknowledged within the family of nations.

After seeking to establish the principle that this nation's power in dealing with external or foreign affairs was based not upon a constitutional grant, but rather upon its sovereign existence as a nation, Justice Sutherland went on to define the President's role, as the Executive head of this sovereign state, when acting on questions of external policy. Here the argument shifted back to the Constitution, for while the Court was saying that the nation's power in foreign affairs was not created by the Constitution, it relied upon constitutional provisions to delineate the Executive's powers in that realm. The Constitution spells out some of these responsibilities when it refers to the President's role in the treaty-making procedure and his power to appoint and receive ambassadors.

Firm action and statements from the very beginning by Washington, Jefferson and John Marshall, fortified this principle once in operation. Marshall argued on the floor of the House of Representatives that the "President is the sole organ of the nation in its external relations, and its sole representative with foreign nations."[34] As early as 1816 the Senate Committee on Foreign Relations had also attempted to define the President's responsibilities in this area:

> The President is the constitutional representative of the United States with regard to foreign nations. He manages our concerns with foreign nations and must necessarily be most competent to determine when, how, and upon what subjects negotiations may be urged with the greatest prospect of success. For his conduct he is responsible to the Constitution. The committee considers this responsibility the surest pledge for the faithful discharge of his duty. They think the interference of the Senate in the direction of foreign negotiations calculated to diminish that responsibility and thereby to impair the best security for the national safety. The nature of transactions with foreign nations, moveover, requires caution and unity of design, and their success frequently depends on secrecy and dispatch.[35]

Sutherland was quick to point out that in such delineations of presidential power, both Marshall and the Foreign Relations Committee were discussing "the very delicate, plenary and exclusive power of the President as the sole organ of the federal government in the field of international relations—a power which does not require as a basis for its exercise an act of Congress. . . ."[36] But the justice went on to point out that when the President operates in this sensitive international area, in order to avoid serious embarrassment, "congressional legislation which is to be made effective through negotiation and inquiry within the international field must often accord to the President a degree of discretion and freedom from statutory restriction which would not be admissable were domestic affairs alone involved."[37]

Only Justice McReynolds dissented from the opinion of the Court, although Justice Harlan Fiske Stone was ill and did not participate in the decision. Stone's later remark that he "always regarded it something of a misfortune that I was foreclosed from expressing myself in . . . the Curtiss-Wright case . . . because I was ill and away from the Court when it was decided,"[38] indicates that he might well have joined McReynolds in dissenting, or tried to temper the strong thrust of the decision.

Justice George Sutherland
The *Curtiss-Wright* Decision
1936

299 U.S. 304 (1936).

On January 27, 1936, an indictment was returned in the court below, the first count of which charges that appellees, beginning with the 29th day of May, 1934, conspired to sell in the United States certain arms of war, namely fifteen machine guns, to Bolivia, a country then engaged in armed conflict in the Chaco, in violation of the Joint Resolution of Congress approved May 28, 1934, and the provisions of a proclamation issued on the same day by the President of the United States pursuant to authority conferred by § 1 of the resolution. In pursuance of the conspiracy, the commission of certain overt acts was alleged, details of which need not be stated. The Joint Resolution (c. 365, 4S Stat. 811) follows:

> *Resolved by the Senate and House of Representatives of the United States of America in Congress assembled,* That if the President finds that the prohibition of the sale of arms and munitions of war in the United States to those countries now engaged in armed conflict in the Chaco may contribute to the reestablishment of peace between those countries, and if after consultation with the governments of other American Republics and with their cooperation, as well as that of such other governments as he may deem necessary, he makes proclamation to that effect, it shall be unlawful to sell, except under such limitations and exceptions as the President prescribes, any arms or munitions of war in any place in the United States to the countries now engaged in that armed conflict, or to any person, company, or association acting in the interest of either country, until otherwise ordered by the President or by Congress.
>
> Sec. 2. Whoever sells any arms or munitions of war in violation of section 1 shall, on conviction, be punished by a fine not exceeding $10,000 or by imprisonment not exceeding two years, or both.

The President's proclamation (48 Stat. 1744), after reciting the terms of the Joint Resolution, declares:

> Now, therefore, I, Franklin D. Roosevelt, President of the United States of America, acting under and by virtue of the authority conferred in me by the said joint resolution of Congress, do hereby declare and proclaim that I have found that the prohibition of the sale of arms and munitions of war in the United States to those countries now engaged in armed conflict in the Chaco may contribute to the reestablishment of peace between those countries, and that I have consulted with the governments of other American Republics and have been assured of the cooperation of such governments as I have deemed necessary as contemplated by the said joint resolution; and I do hereby admonish all citizens of the United States and every person to abstain from every violation of the provisions of the joint resolution above set forth, hereby made applicable to Bolivia and Paraguay, and I do hereby warn them that all violations of such provisions will be rigorously prosecuted.
>
> And I do hereby enjoin upon all officers of the United States charged with the execution of the laws thereof, the utmost diligence in preventing violations of the said joint resolution and this my proclamation issued thereunder, and in bringing to trial and punishment any offenders against the same.
>
> And I do hereby delegate to the Secretary of State the power of prescribing exceptions and limitations to the application of the said joint resolution of May 28, 1934, as made effective by this my proclamation issued thereunder.

On November 14, 1935, this proclamation was revoked (49 Stat. 3480), in the following terms:

> Now, therefore, I, Franklin D. Roosevelt, President of the United States
> of America, do hereby declare and proclaim that I have found that the
> prohibition of the sale of arms and munitions of war in the United States
> to Bolivia or Paraguay will no longer be necessary as a contribution to the
> reestablishment of peace between those countries, and the above-
> mentioned Proclamation of May 28, 1934, is hereby revoked as to the sale
> of arms and munitions of war to Bolivia or Paraguay from and after
> November 29, 1935, provided, however, that this action shall not have the
> effect of releasing or extinguishing any penalty, forfeiture or liability
> incurred under the aforesaid Proclamation of May 28, 1934, or the Joint
> Resolution of Congress approved by the President on the same date; and
> that the said Proclamation and Joint Resolution shall be treated as
> remaining in force for the purpose of sustaining any proper action or
> prosecution for the enforcement of such penalty, forfeiture or liability.

Appellees severally demurred to the first count of the indictment on the grounds (1) that it did not charge facts sufficient to show the commission by appellees of any offense against any law of the United States; (2) that this count of the indictment charges a conspiracy to violate the joint resolution and the Presidential proclamation, both of which had expired according to the terms of the joint resolution by reason of the revocation contained in the Presidential proclamation of November 14, 1935, and were not in force at the time when the indictment was found. The points urged in support of the demurrers were, first, that the joint resolution effects an invalid delegation of legislative power to the executive; second, that the joint resolution never became effective because of the failure of the President to find essential jurisdictional facts; and third, that the second proclamation operated to put an end to the alleged liability under the joint resolution.

The court below sustained the demurrers upon the first point, but overruled them on the second and third points. 14 F. Supp. 230. The government appealed to this court under the provisions of the Criminal Appeals Act of March 2, 1907, 34 Stat. 1246, as amended, U.S.C. Title 18, § 682. That act authorized the United States to appeal from a district court direct to this court in criminal cases where, among other things, the decision sustaining a demurrer to the indictment or any count thereof is based upon the invalidity or construction of the statute upon which the indictment is found.

First. It is contended that by the Joint Resolution, the going into effect and continued operation of the resolution was conditioned (a) upon the President's judgment as to its beneficial effect upon the reestablishment of peace between the countries engaged in armed conflict in the Chaco; (b) upon the making of a proclamation, which was left to his unfettered discretion, thus constituting an attempted substitution of the President's will for that of Congress; (c) upon the making of a proclamation putting an end to the operation of the resolution, which again was left to the President's unfettered discretion; and (d) further, that the extent of its operation in particular cases was subject to limitation and exception by the President, controlled by no standard. In each of these particulars, appellees urge that Congress abdicated its essential functions and delegated them to the Executive.

Whether, if the Joint Resolution had related solely to internal affairs it would be open to the challenge that it constituted an unlawful delegation of legislative power to the Executive, we find it unnecessary to determine. The whole aim of the resolution is to affect a situation entirely external to the United States, and falling within the category of foreign affairs. The determination which we are called to make, therefore, is whether the Joint Resolution, as applied to that situation, is vulnerable to attack under the rule that forbids delegation of the law-making power. In other words, assuming (but not deciding) that the challenged delegation, if it were confined to internal affairs, would be invalid, may it nevertheless be sustained on the ground that its exclusive aim is to afford a remedy for a hurtful condition within foreign territory?

It will contribute to the elucidation of the question if we first consider the differences between the powers of the federal government in respect of foreign or external affairs and those in respect of domestic or internal affairs. That there are differences between them, and that these differences are fundamental, may not be doubted.

The two classes of powers are different, both in respect of their origin and their nature. The broad statement that the federal government can exercise no powers except those specifically enumerated in the Constitution, and such implied powers as are necessary and proper to carry into effect the enumerated powers, is categorically true only in respect of our internal affairs. In that field, the primary purpose of the Constitution was to carve from the general mass of legislative powers *then possessed by the states* such portions as it was thought desirable to vest in the federal government, leaving those not included in the enumeration still in the states. *Carter* v. *Carter Coal Co.,* 298 U.S. 238, 294. That this doctrine applies only to powers which the states had, is self evident. And since the states severally never possessed international powers, such powers could not have been carved from the mass of state powers but obviously were transmitted to the United States from some other source. During the colonial period, those powers were possessed exclusively by and were entirely under the control of the Crown. By the Declaration of Independence, "the Representatives of the United States of America" declared the United [not the several] Colonies to be free and independent states, and as such to have "full Power to levy War, conclude Peace, contract Alliances, establish Commerce and to do all other Acts and Things which Independent States may of right do."

As a result of the separation from Great Britain by the colonies acting as a unit, the powers of external sovereignty passed from the Crown not to the colonies severally, but to the colonies in their collective and corporate capacity as the United States of America. Even before the Declaration, the colonies were a unit in foreign affairs, acting through a common agency—namely the Continental Congress, composed of delegates from the thirteen colonies. That agency exercised the powers of war and peace, raised an army, created a navy, and finally adopted the Declaration of Independence. Rulers come and go; governments end and forms of government change; but sovereignty survives. A political society cannot endure without a supreme will somewhere. Sovereignty is never held in suspense. When, therefore, the external sovereignty of Great Britain in respect of the colonies ceased, it immediately passed to the Union. *See Penhallow* v. *Doane,* 3, Dall. 54, 80-81. That fast was given practical application almost at once. The treaty of peace, made on September 23, 1783, was concluded between his Brittanic Majesty and the "United States of America." 8 Stat.—European Treaties—80.

The Union existed before the Constitution, which was ordained and established among other things to form "a more perfect Union." Prior to that event, it is clear that the Union, declared by the Articles of Confederation to be "perpetual," was the sole possessor of external sovereignty and in the Union it remained without change save in so far as the Constitution in express terms qualified its exercise. The Framers' Convention was called and exerted its powers upon the irrefutable postulate that though the states were several their people in respect of foreign affairs were one. Compare *The Chinese Exclusion Case,* 130 U.S. 581, 604, 606. In that convention, the entire absence of state power to deal with those affairs was thus forcefully stated by Rufus King:

> "The states were not 'sovereigns' in the sense contended for by some. They did not possess the peculiar features of sovereignty,—they could not make war, nor peace, nor alliances, nor treaties. Considering them as political beings, they were dumb, for they could not speak to any foreign sovereign whatever. They were deaf, for they could not hear any propositions from such sovereign. They had not even the organs or faculties of defence or offence, for they could not of themselves raise troops, or equip vessels for war. 5 Elliott's Debates 212.

It results that the investment of the federal government with the powers of external sovereignty did not depend upon the affirmative grants of the Constitution. The powers to declare and wage war, to conclude peace, to make treaties, to maintain diplomatic relations with other sovereignties, if they had never been mentioned in the Constitution, would have vested in the federal government as necessary concomitants of nationality. Neither the Constitution nor the laws passed in pursuance of it have any force in foreign territory unless in respect of our own citizens (see *American Banana Co.* v. *United Fruit Co.,* 213 U.S. 347, 356); and operations of the nation in such territory must be governed by treaties, international understandings and compacts, and the principles of international law. As a member of the family of nations, the right and power of the United States in that field are equal to the right and power of the other members of the international family. Otherwise, the United States is not completely sovereign. The power to acquire territory by discovery and occupation (*Jones* v. *United States,* 137 U.S. 202, 212), the power to expel undesirable aliens (*Fong Yue Ting* v. *United States,* 149 U.S. 698, 705 *et seq.*), the power to make such international agreements as do not constitute treaties in the constitutional sense (*Altman & Co.* v. *United States,* 224 U.S. 583, 600-601; Crandall, Treaties, Their Making and Enforcement, 2d ed., p. 102 and note 1), none of which is expressly affirmed by the Constitution, nevertheless exist as inherently inseparable from the conception of nationality. This the court recognized, and in each of the cases cited found the warrant for its conclusions not in the provisions of the Constitution, but in the law of nations.

In *Burnet* v. *Brooks*, 288 U.S. 378, 396, we said, "As a nation with all the attributes of sovereignty, the United States is vested with all the powers of government necessary to maintain an effective control of international relations." Cf. *Carter* v. *Carter Coal Co., supra*, p. 295.

Not only, as we have shown, is the federal power over external affairs in origin and essential character different from that over internal affairs, but participation in the exercise of the power is significantly limited. In this vast external realm, with its important, complicated, delicate and manifold problems, the President alone has the power to speak or listen as a representative of the nation. He *makes* treaties with the advice and consent of the Senate; but he alone negotiates. Into the field of negotiation the Senate cannot intrude; and Congress itself is powerless to invade it. As Marshall said in his great argument of March 7, 1800, in the House of Representatives, "The President is the sole organ of the nation in its external relations, and its sole representative with foreign nations." Annals. 6th Cong., col. 613. The Senate Committee on Foreign Relations at a very early day in our history (February 15, 1816), reported to the Senate, among other things, as follows:

> The President is the constitutional representative of the United States with regard to foreign nations. He manages our concerns with foreign nations and must necessarily be most competent to determine when, how, and upon what subjects negotiation may be urged with the greatest prospect of success. For his conduct he is responsible to the Constitution. The committee consider this responsibility the surest pledge for the faithful discharge of his duty. They think the interference of the Senate in the direction of foreign negotiations calculated to diminish that responsibility and thereby to impair the best security for the national safety. The nature of transactions with foreign nations, moreover, requires caution and unity of design, and their success frequently depends on secrecy and dispatch. U.S. Senate, Reports, Committee on Foreign Relations, vol. 8. p. 24.

It is important to bear in mind that we are here dealing not alone with an authority vested in the President by an exertion of legislative power, but with such an authority plus the very delicate, plenary and exclusive power of the President as the sole organ of the federal government in the field of international relations—a power which does not require as a basis for its exercise an act of Congress, but which, of course, like every other governmental power, must be exercised in subordination to the applicable provisions of the Constitution. It is quite apparent that if, in the maintenance of our international relations, embarrassment—perhaps serious embarrassment—is to be avoided and success for our aims achieved, congressional legislation which is to be made effective through negotiation and inquiry within the international field must often accord to the President a degree of discretion and freedom from statutory restriction which would not be admissible were domestic affairs alone involved. Moreover, he, not Congress, has the better opportunity of knowing the conditions which prevail in foreign countries, and especially is this true in time of war. He has his confidential sources of information.

He has his agents in the form of diplomatic, consular and other officials. Secrecy in respect of information gathered by them may be highly necessary, and the premature disclosure of it productive of harmful results. Indeed, so clearly is this true that the first President refused to accede to a request to lay before the House of Representatives the instructions, correspondence and documents relating to the negotiation of the Jay Treaty—a refusal the wisdom of which was recognized by the House itself and has never since been doubted. In his reply to the request, President Washington said:

> The nature of foreign negotiations requires caution, and their success must often depend on secrecy; and even when brought to a conclusion a full disclosure of all the measures, demands, or eventual concessions which may have been proposed or contemplated would be extremely impolitic; for this might have a pernicious influence on future negotiations, or produce immediate inconveniences, perhaps danger and mischief, in relation to other powers. The necessity of such caution and secrecy was one cogent reason for vesting the power of making treaties in the President, with the advice and consent of the Senate, the principle on which that body was formed confining it to a small number of members. To admit, then, a right in the House of Representatives to demand and to have as a matter of course all the papers respecting a negotiation with a foreign power would be to establish a dangerous precedent. 1 Messages and Papers of the Presidents, p. 194.

The marked difference between foreign affairs and domestic affairs in this respect is recognized by both houses of Congress in the very form of their requisitions for information from the executive departments. In the case of every department except the Department of State, the resolution *directs* the official to furnish the information. In the case of the State Department, dealing with foreign affairs, the President is *requested* to furnish the information "if not incompatible with the public interest." A statement that to furnish the information is not compatible with the public interest rarely, if ever, is questioned.

When the President is to be authorized by legislation to act in respect of a matter intended to affect a situation in foreign territory, the legislator properly bears in mind the important consideration that the form of the President's action—or, indeed, whether he shall act at all—may well depend, among other things, upon the nature of the confidential information which he has or may thereafter receive, or upon the effect which his action may have upon our foreign relations. This consideration, in connection with what we have already said on the subject, discloses the unwisdom of requiring Congress in this field of governmental power to lay down narrowly definite standards by which the President is to be governed. As this court said in *Mackenzie* v. *Hare*, 239 U.S. 299, 311, "As a government, the United States is invested with all the attributes of sovereignty. As it has the character of nationality it has the powers of nationality, especially those which concern its relations and intercourse with other countries. *We should hesitate long before limiting or embarrassing such powers.*" (Italics supplied.)

In the light of the foregoing observations, it is evident that this court should not be in haste to apply a general rule which will have the effect of condemning legislation like that under review as constituting an unlawful delegation of legislative power. The principles which justify such legislation find overwhelming support in the unbroken legislative practice which has prevailed almost from the inception of the national government to the present day.

Let us examine, in chronological order, the acts of legislation which warrant this conclusion:

The Act of June 4, 1794, authorized the President to lay, regulate and revoke embargoes. He was "authorized" "whenever, in his opinion, the public safety shall so require" to lay the embargo upon all ships and vessels in the ports of the United States, including those of foreign nations "under such regulations as the circumstances of the case may require, and to continue or revoke the same, whenever he shall think proper." C. 41, 1 Stat. 372. A prior joint resolution of May 7, 1794 (1 Stat. 401), had conferred *unqualified* power on the President to grant clearances, notwithstanding an existing embargo, to ships or vessels belonging to citizens of the United States bound to any port beyond the Cape of Good Hope.

The Act of March 3, 1795 (c. 53. 1 Stat. 444), gave the President authority to permit the exportation of arms, cannon and military stores, the law prohibiting such exports to the contrary notwithstanding, the only prescribed guide for his action being that such exports should be in "cases connected with the security of the commercial interest of the United States, and for public purposes only."

By the Act of June 13, 1798 (c. 53, § 5, 1 Stat. 566), it was provided that if the government of France "shall clearly disavow, and shall be found to refrain from the aggressions, depredations and hostilities" theretofore maintained against vessels and property of the citizens of the United States, "in violation of the faith of treaties, and the laws of nations, and shall thereby acknowledge the just claims of the United States to be considered as in all respects neutral, . . . it shall be lawful for the President of the United States, being well ascertained of the premises, to remit and discontinue the prohibitions and restraints hereby enacted and declared; and he shall be, and is hereby authorized to make proclamation thereof accordingly."

By § 4 of the Act of February 9, 1799 (c. 2, 1 Stat. 615), it was made "lawful" for the President, "if he shall deem it expedient and consistent with the interest of the United States," by order to remit certain restraints and prohibitions imposed by the act with respect to the French Republic, and also to revoke any such order "whenever, in his opinion, the interest of the United States shall require."

Similar authority, qualified in the same way, was conferred by § 6 of the Act of February 7, 1800, c. 10, 2 Stat. 9.

Section 5 of the Act of March 3, 1805 (c. 41, 2 Stat. 341), made it lawful for the President, whenever an armed vessel entering the harbors or waters within the jurisdiction of the United States and required to depart therefrom should fail to do so, not only to employ the land and naval forces to compel obedience, but "if he shall think it proper, it shall be lawful for him to forbid, by proclamation, all intercourse with such vessel, and with every armed vessel of the same nation, and the officers and crew thereof; to prohibit all supplies and aid from being furnished them" and to do various other things connected therewith. Violation of the President's proclamation was penalized.

On February 28, 1806, an act was passed (c. 9, 2 Stat. 351) to suspend commercial intercourse between the United States and certain parts of the Island of St. Domingo. A penalty was prescribed for its violation. Notwithstanding the positive provisions of the act, it was by § 5 made "lawful" for the President to remit and discontinue the restraints and prohibitions imposed by the act at any time "if he shall deem it expedient and consistent with the interests of the United States" to do so. Likewise in respect of the Non-intercourse Act of March 1, 1809, (c. 24, 2 Stat. 528); the President was "authorized" (§ 11, p. 530), in case either of the countries affected should so revoke or modify her edicts "as that they shall cease to violate the neutral commerce of the United States," to proclaim the fact, after which the suspended trade might be renewed with the nation so doing.

Practically every volume of the United States Statutes contains one or more acts or joint resolutions of Congress authorizing action by the President in respect of subjects affecting foreign relations, which either leave the exercise of the power to his unrestricted judgment, or provide a standard far more general than that which has always been considered requisite with regard to domestic affairs. Many, though not all, of these acts are designated in the footnote. [Editor's Note: The footnote referred to, here enclosed in brackets, is as follows: Thus, the President has been broadly "authorized" to suspend embargo acts passed by Congress, "if in his judgment the public interest should require it" (Act of December 19, 1806, c.1, § 3, 2 Stat. 411), or if, "in the judgment of the President," there has been such suspension of hostilities abroad as may render commerce of the United States sufficiently safe. Act of April 22, 1808, C. 52, 2 Stat. 490. See, also, Act of March 3, 1817, c. 39, § 2, 3 Stat. 361. Compare, but as to reviving an embargo act, the Act of May 1, 1810, c. 39, § 4, 2 Stat. 605.

[Likewise, Congress has passed numerous acts laying tonnage and other duties on foreign ships, in retaliation for duties enforced on United States vessels, but providing that if the President should be satisfied that the countervailing duties were repealed or abolished, then he might by proclamation suspend the duties as to vessels of the nation so acting. Thus, the President has been "authorized" to proclaim the suspension. Act of January 7, 1824, c. 4, § 4, 4 Stat. 3; Act of May 24, 1828, c. 111, 4 Stat. 308; Act of July 24, 1897, c. 13, 30 Stat. 214. Or it has been provided that the suspension should take effect whenever the President "shall be satisfied" that the discriminating duties have been abolished. Act of March 3, 1815, c. 77, 3 Stat. 224; Act of May 31, 1830, c. 219, § 2, 4 Stat. 425. Or that the President "may direct" that the tonnage duty shall cease to be levied in such circumstances. Act of July 13, 1832, c. 207, § 3, 4 Stat. 578. And compare Act of June 26, 1884, c. 121, § 14, 23 Stat. 53, 57.

[Other acts, for retaliation against discriminations as to United States commerce, have placed broad powers in the hands of the President, "authorizing" even the total exclusion of vessels of any foreign country so offending (Act of June 19, 1886, c. 421, § 17, 24 Stat. 79, 83), or the increase of duties on its goods or their total exclusion from the United States Act of June 17, 1930, c. 497, § 388, 46 Stat. 590, 704), or the exclusion of its goods or the detention, in certain circumstances, of its vessels, or the exclusion of its vessels or nationals from privileges similar to those which it has denied to citizens of the United States (Act of September 8, 1916, c. 463, §§ 804-806, 39 Stat. 756, 799-800). As to discriminations by particular countries, it has been made lawful for the President, by proclamation, which he "may in his discretion, apply . . . to any part or all" of the subjects named, to exclude certain goods of the offending country, or its vessels. Act of March 3, 1887, c. 339, 24 Stat. 475. And compare Act of July 26, 1892, c. 248, 27 Stat. 267. Compare, also, authority given the Postmaster General to reduce or enlarge rates of foreign postage, among other things, for the purpose of counteracting any adverse measures affecting our postal intercourse with foreign countries. Act of March 3, 1851, c. 20, § 2, 9 Stat. 587, 589.

[The President has been "authorized" to suspend an act providing for the exercise of judicial functions by ministers, consuls and other officers of the United States in the Ottoman dominions and Egypt whenever he "shall receive satisfactory information" that the governments concerned have organized tribunals likely to secure to United States citizens the same impartial justice enjoyed under the judicial functions exercised by the United States officials. Act of March 23, 1874, c. 62, 18 Stat. 23.

[Congress has also passed acts for the enforcement of treaties or conventions, to be effective only upon proclamation of the President. Some of them may be noted which "authorize" the President to make proclamation when he shall be "satisfied" or shall receive "satisfactory evidence" that the other nation has complied: Act of August 5, 1854, c. 269, §§ 1, 2, 10 Stat. 587; Act of March 1, 1873, c. 213, §§ 1, 2, 17 Stat. 482; Act of August 15, 1876, c. 290, 19 Stat. 200; Act of December 17, 1903, c. 1, § 1, 33 Stat. 3. *Cf.* Act of June 11, 1864, c. 116, § 1, 13 Stat. 121; Act of February 21, 1893, c. 150, 27 Stat. 472.

[Where appropriate, Congress has provided that violation of the President's proclamations authorized by the foregoing acts shall be penalized. See, *e.g.*, Act of June 19, 1886; Act of March 3, 1887; Act of September 8, 1916; Act of June 17, 1930—all *supra*.]

It well may be assumed that these legislative precedents were in mind when Congress passed the joint resolutions of April 22, 1898, 30 Stat. 739; March 14, 1912, 37 Stat. 630; and January 31, 1922, 42 Stat. 361, to prohibit the export of coal or other war material. The resolution of 1898 authorized the President "in his discretion, and with such limitations and exceptions as shall seem to him expedient" to prohibit such exportations. The striking identity of language found in the second resolution mentioned above and in the one now under review will be seen upon comparison. The resolution of March 14, 1912, provides:

> That whenever the President shall find that in any American country conditions of domestic violence exist which are promoted by the use of arms or munitions of war procured from the United States, and shall make proclamation thereof, it shall be unlawful to export except under such limitations and exceptions as the President shall prescribe any arms or munitions of war from any place in the United States to such country until otherwise ordered by the President or by Congress.
> Sec. 2. That any shipment of material hereby declared unlawful after such a proclamation shall be punishable by fine not exceeding ten thousand dollars, or imprisonment not exceeding two years, or both.

The third resolution is in substantially the same terms, but extends to any country in which the United States exercises extraterritorial jurisdiction, and provides for the President's action not only when conditions of domestic violence exist which *are* promoted, but also when such conditions *may* be promoted, by the use of such arms or munitions of war.

We had occasion to review these embargo and kindred acts in connection with an exhaustive discussion of the general subject of delegation of legislative power in a recent case, *Panama Refining Co.* v. *Ryan*, 293 U.S. 388, 421-422, and in justifying such acts, pointed out that they confided to the President "an authority which was cognate to the conduct by him of the foreign relations of the government."

The result of holding that the joint resolution here under attack is void and unenforceable as constituting an unlawful delegation of legislative power would be to stamp this multitude of comparable acts and resolutions as likewise invalid. And while this court may not, and should not, hesitate to declare acts of Congress, however many times repeated, to be unconstitutional if beyond all rational doubt it finds them to be so, an impressive array of legislation such as we have just set forth, enacted by nearly every Congress from the beginning of our national existence to the present day, must be given unusual weight in the process of reaching a correct determination of the problem. A legislative practice such as we have here, evidenced not by only occasional instances, but marked by the movement of a steady stream for a century and a half of time, goes a long way in the direction of proving the presence of unassailable ground for the constitutionality of the practice, to be found in the origin and history of the power involved, or in its nature, or in both combined.

In *The Laura*, 114 U.S. 411, 416, this court answered a challenge to the constitutionality of a statute authorizing the Secretary of the Treasury to remit or mitigate fines and penalties in certain cases, by repeating the language of a very early case (*Stuart* v. *Laird*, 1 Cranch 299, 309) that the long practice and acquiescence under the statute was a "practical exposition . . . too strong and obstinate to be shaken or controlled. Of course, the question is at rest, and ought not now to be disturbed." In *Burrow-Giles Lithographic Co.* v. *Sarony*, 111 U.S. 53, 57, the constitutionality of R.C. § 4952, conferring upon the author, inventor, designer or proprietor of a photograph certain rights, was involved. Mr. Justice Miller, speaking for the court, disposed of the point by saying: "The construction placed upon the Constitution by the first act of 1790, and the act of 1802, by the men who were contemporary with its formation, many of whom were members of the convention which framed it, is of itself entitled to very great weight, and when it is remembered that the rights thus established have not been disputed during a period of nearly a century, it is almost conclusive."

In *Field* v. *Clark*, 143 U.S. 649, 691, this court declared that " . . . the practical construction of the Constitution, as given by so many acts of Congress, and embracing almost the entire period of our national existence, should not be overruled, unless upon a conviction that such legislation was clearly incompatible with the supreme law of the land." The rule is one which has been stated and applied many times by this court. As examples, see *Ames* v. *Kansas*, 111 U.S. 449, 469; *McCulloch* v. *Maryland*, 4 Wheat, 316, 401; *Downes* v. *Bidwell*, 182 U.S. 244, 286.

The uniform, long-continued and undisputed legislative practice just disclosed rests upon an admissible view of the Constitution which, even if the practice found far less support in principle than we think it does, we should not feel at liberty at this late day to disturb.

We deem it unnecessary to consider, *seriatim*, the several clauses which are said to evidence the unconstitutionality of the Joint Resolution as involving an unlawful delegation of legislative power. It is enough to summarize by saying that, both upon principle and in accordance with precedent, we conclude there is sufficient warrant for the broad discretion vested in the President to determine whether the enforcement of the statute will have a beneficial effect upon the reestablishment of peace in the affected countries; whether he shall make proclamation to bring the resolution into operation; whether and when the resolution shall cease to operate and to make proclamation accordingly; and to prescribe limitations and exceptions to which the enforcement of the resolution shall be subject.

Second. The second point raised by the demurrer was that the Joint Resolution never became effective because the President failed to find essential jurisdictional facts; and the third point was that the second proclamation of the President operated to put an end to the alleged liability of appellees under the Joint Resolution. In respect of both points, the court below overruled the demurrer, and thus far sustained the government.

The government contends that upon an appeal by the United States under the Criminal Appeals Act from a decision holding an indictment bad, the jurisdiction of the court does not extend to questions decided in favor of the United States, but that such questions may only be reviewed in the usual way after conviction. We find nothing in the words of the statute or in its purposes which justifies this conclusion. The demurrer in the present case challenges the validity of the statute upon three separate and distinct grounds. If the court below had sustained the demurrer without more, an appeal by the government necessarily would have brought here for our determination all of these grounds, since in that case the record would not have disclosed whether the court considered the statute invalid upon one particular ground or upon all of the grounds alleged. The judgment of the lower court is that the statute is invalid. Having held that this judgment cannot be sustained upon the particular ground which that court assigned, it is now open to this court to inquire whether or not the judgment can be sustained upon the rejected grounds which also challenge the validity of the statute and, therefore, constitute a proper subject of review by this court under the Criminal Appeals Act. *United States* v. *Hastings*, 296 U.S. 188, 192.

In *Langnes* v. *Green*, 282, U.S. 531, where the decree of a district court had been assailed upon two grounds and the circuit court of appeals had sustained the attack upon one of such grounds only, we held that a respondent in certiorari might nevertheless urge in this court in support of the decree the ground which the intermediate appellate court had rejected. That principle is applicable here.

We proceed, then, to a consideration of the second and third grounds of the demurrers which, as we have said, the court below rejected.

1. The Executive proclamation recites, "I have found that the prohibition of the sale of arms and munitions of war in the United States to those countries now

engaged in armed conflict in the Chaco may contribute to the reestablishment of peace between those countries and that I have consulted with the governments of other American Republics *and have been assured of the cooperation of such governments as I have deemed necessary as contemplated by the said joint resolution*." This finding satisfies every requirement of the Joint Resolution. There is no suggestion that the resolution is fatally uncertain or indefinite; and a finding which follows its language, as this finding does, cannot well be challenged as insufficient.

But appellees, referring to the words which we have italicized above, contend that the finding is insufficient because the President does not declare that the cooperation of such governments as he deemed necessary included any American republic and, therefore, the recital contains no affirmative showing of compliance in this respect with the Joint Resolution. The criticism seems to us wholly wanting in substance. The President recites that he has consulted with the governments of other American republics, and that he has been assured of the cooperation of such governments as he deemed necessary *as contemplated by the joint resolution*. These recitals, construed together, fairly include within their meaning American republics.

2. The second proclamation of the President, revoking the first proclamation, it is urged, had the effect of putting an end to the Joint Resolution, and in accordance with a well-settled rule, no penalty could be enforced or punishment inflicted thereafter for an offense committed during the life of the Joint Resolution in the absence of a provision in the resolution to that effect. There is no doubt as to the general rule or as to the absence of a saving clause in the Joint Resolution. But is the case presented one which makes the rule applicable?

It was not within the power of the President to repeal the Joint Resolution; and his second proclamation did not purport to do so. It "revoked" the first proclamation; and the question is, did the revocation of the proclamation have the effect of abrogating the resolution or of precluding its enforcement in so far as that involved the prosecution and punishment of offenses committed during the life of the first proclamation? We are of opinion that it did not.

Prior to the first proclamation, the Joint Resolution was an existing law, but dormant, awaiting the creation of a particular situation to render it active. No action or lack of action on the part of the President could destroy its potentiality. Congress alone could do that. The happening of the designated events—namely, the finding of certain conditions and the proclamation by the President—did not call the law into being. It created the occasion for it to function. The second proclamation did not put an end to the law or affect what had been done in violation of the law. The effect of the proclamation was simply to remove for the future, a condition of affairs which admitted of its exercise.

We should have had a different case if the Joint Resolution had expired by its own terms upon the issue of the second proclamation. Its operative force, it is true, was limited to the period of time covered by the first proclamation. And when the second proclamation was issued, the resolution ceased to be a rule for the future. It did not cease to be the law for the antecedent period of time. The distinction is clearly pointed out by the Superior Court of Judicature of New Hampshire in

Stevens v. *Dimond*, 6 N.H. 330, 332, 333. There, a town by-law provided that if certain animals should be found going at large between the first day of April and the last day of October, etc., the owner would incur a prescribed penalty. The trial court directed the jury that the by-law, being in force for a year only, had expired so that the defendant could not be called upon to answer for a violation which occurred during the designated period. The state appellate court reversed, saying that when laws "expire by their own limitation, or are repealed, they cease to be the law in relation to the past, as well as the future, and can no longer be enforced in any case. No case is, however, to be found in which it was ever held before that they thus ceased to be law, unless they expired by express limitation in themselves, or were repealed. It has never been decided that they cease to be law, merely because the time they were intended to regulate had expired.... A very little consideration of the subject will convince any one that a limitation of the time to which a statute is to apply, is a very different thing from the limitation of the time a statute is to continue in force."

The first proclamation of the President was in force from the 28th day of May, 1934, to the 14th day of November, 1935. If the Joint Resolution had in no way depended upon Presidential action, but had provided explicitly that, at any time between May 28, 1934, and November 14, 1935, it should be unlawful to sell arms or munitions of war to the countries engaged in armed conflict in the Chaco, it certainly could not be successfully contended that the law would expire with the passing of the time fixed in respect of offenses committed during the period.

The judgment of the court below must be reversed and the cause remanded for further proceedings in accordance with the foregoing opinion.

Reversed

This authoritative validation of presidential power in the area of foreign affairs provided additional reinforcement for functions and responsibilities which strong Presidents had previously asserted, but which had frequently been challenged as usurpations of legislative power. The *Curtiss-Wright* decision was followed by another opinion written by Justice Sutherland, United States *v.* Belmont, in which the Court further enhanced the President's powers of independent judgment and responsibility in external affairs. In that case an executive agreement or understanding with a foreign nation (the Soviet Union) was upheld by the Court as binding upon the government; Justice Sutherland argued that such agreements do not necessarily "require the advice and consent of the Senate":

A treaty signifies "a compact made between two or more independent nations with a view to the public welfare." *Altman & Co.* v. *United States*, 224 U.S. 583, 600. But an international compact, as this was, is not always a treaty which requires the participation of the Senate. There are many such compacts, of which a protocol, a *modus vivendi*, a postal convention, and agreements like that now under consideration are illustrations. See 5 Moore, Int. Law Digest, 210-221. The distinction was pointed out by this court in the *Altman* case, *supra*, which arose under § 3 of the Tariff Act of 1897, authorizing the President to conclude commercial agreements with foreign countries in certain specified matters. We held that although this might not be a treaty requiring ratification by the Senate, it was a compact negotiated and proclaimed under the authority of the President, and as such was a "treaty" within the meaning of the Circuit Court of Appeals Act.[39]

In the light of these decisions and by virtue of the pressures imposed upon the Chief Executive by the changing nature of this country's role in world affairs, future Presidents could make far greater use of executive agreements as an integral foreign policy function. The *Curtiss-Wright* and *Belmont* decisions laid down the constitutional foundations for the far more independent, aggressive, and expanded use of the President's power as a leader in the sensitive field of international diplomacy.

The Destroyer Deal: Harbinger of a New Era

There is a well-cultivated myth that Franklin D. Roosevelt and his secretary of state, Cordell Hull, quite early in the 1930s perceived the ultimate designs of Hitler and the Japanese militarists and worked tirelessly to bring the American people around to their advanced views, despite the fact that, largely speaking, most Americans were committed to isolationism and the quest for peace. In a State Department publication *War and Peace: United States Foreign Policy, 1931-1941*—the myth takes concrete form:

> During a large part of the period with which this volume deals (1931-1941), much of public opinion in this country did not accept the thesis that a European war could vitally affect the security of the United States or that an attack on the United States by any of the Axis powers was possible. In this respect it differed from the President and the Secretary of State, who early became convinced that the aggressive policies of the Axis powers were directed toward an ultimate attack on the United States and that, therefore, our foreign relations should be so conducted as to give all possible support to the nations endeavoring to check the march of Axis aggression.[40]

There is very little in the public record to support such a myth. In fact, Roosevelt, as well as others who later joined his administration, rejected the reopening of the case for the entry of the United States into the League of Nations as far back as the preelection campaign in 1932. That is not to say that Roosevelt or his advisors were isolationists in the accepted sense of the term, nor that they lacked the proper dedication to international cooperation, which as a matter of fact they continued to acclaim all during the 1930s. But the public record clearly does not portray them as pre-1940 interventionists, nor as possessing any of the remarkable foresight exhibited by Winston Churchill as he steadfastly berated the House of Commons with Cassandralike accuracy and fervor during the ominous prewar years, ridiculing the gullibility of his government's policies, and warning again and again of the threat which Hitler and Fascism constituted to the life and security of Britain and the whole of western civilization.

During that same period the American President was primarily concerned with domestic problems, and in the few instances when he did intervene in European affairs, he was quick to point out that the United States would not back up any proposal with a commitment of armed force. The decade of the 1930s was a time when most of the American people and their leaders indulged themselves in the false security of inaccurately analyzing the causes of World War I, and hopefully wishing that caution, inaction and withdrawal would allow the country to avoid the horrors of another war. The President, although not a leader of this exercise in daydreaming, was certainly a victim of it, and even if he wanted to do more, there is precious little evidence that he translated such intentions into policy proposals.

His actions and statements during the period, particularly in a time of crisis, such as the threatened Italian invasion of Ethiopia, reflected the shock and anger of a decent man as he appealed to nations to respect the principles of international law, but he suggested no further commitment on the part of his country to see those principles enforced. When sanctions against the Mussolini government and arms support for the beleaguered little nation of Ethiopia were proposed by some nations, the President of the United States could only express "the hope of the people and the Government of the United States than an amicable solution will be found. . . ."[41] When war actually broke out Roosevelt invoked an embargo on the shipment of arms to either side, and later declared that "This Government is determined not to become involved in the controversy and is anxious for the restoration and maintenance of peace."[42]

The one major deviation of the Roosevelt administration from its policy of noninvolvement before World War II came in October 1937 when the President made his famous "quarantine the aggressors" speech in Chicago. But by that time the German armies had marched into the Rhineland in violation of the Versailles Treaty, Mussolini had invaded Ethiopia, the Nazis and the Fascists had come to the support of General Franco's legions in Spain and the Japanese army had invaded China.

All this went on while the United States watched with a concerned eye, but without offering any significant resistance to the aggressors or any concrete aid to the victims. In his *Memoirs* Cordell Hull describes in great detail his painstaking efforts to interject the moral force of the American government in hopes of preventing these events from taking place, but the difficulty was that neither Hitler, Mussolini, Franco or the Japanese respected this moral force and were not at all influenced by its opposition to their actions. They understood and respected another language—force—and when exhortations for peace were not backed up by the hard currency of troops and guns, they were unmoved by these well intentioned but ineffective efforts. In the Chicago speech, President Roosevelt strongly attacked the aggressor nations:

> The peace, the freedom and the security of ninety percent of the population of the world is being jeopardized by the remaining ten percent who are threatening a breakdown of all international order and law.

Surely the ninety percent who want to live in peace under law and in accordance with moral standards that have received almost universal acceptance through the centuries, can and must find some way to make their will prevail.[43]

Secretary Hull was shocked to hear these passages, for they had not been part of the original draft of the speech prepared by the State Department.

As I saw it, this had the effect of setting back for at least six months our constant educational campaign intended to create and strengthen public opinion toward international cooperation. Those of us who had been carrying on this campaign, through speeches, statements, and actions wherever possible, had been working as actively as we could; but we were always careful not to go too far lest a serious attack by the isolationist element throw us farther back than we were before. If we proceeded gradually and did not excite undue opposition, our words and actions, although not so dynamic or far-reaching as we might wish, had more effect on the world at large than if we made startling statements or took precipitate action and then, because of the bitter reaction we aroused, presented the world with the spectacle of a nation divided against itself.[44]

Immediate reaction was favorable, but the delayed backlash was severe. Two congressmen threatened to have the President impeached, and six pacifist organizations complained that he was leading the American people to world war.[45] Even the AFL and CIO were apprehensive, and a poll of Congress showed a two to one opposition to any cooperative efforts with the League of Nations to restrain Japan in the Far East. A diplomatic history of this period indicates that the address "did in fact produce a strong and country-wide protest, among Democrats as among Republicans, which serves well as evidence of the popular aversion to any program of common action with other nations."[46] The American people had not been prepared by their leaders for such a policy and they would not yet accept it.

The President correctly read the smoke signals and for the time being back-pedaled. A week after the Chicago speech he reassured the country that no sanctions would be used against Japan.[47] Not until the shooting war was underway was there any further attempt to publicly denounce the aggressor nations, and in any way to threaten to halt their forward march. By that time it was too late; Europe was already in flames.

By 1939, however, it is clear that Roosevelt was thoroughly alarmed by the turn of events in Europe and was beginning to attack the root of American impotence, its relatively weak military establishment. The Munich debacle, Germany's subsequent behavior and the manner in which the dictators summarily dismissed America's last minute diplomatic moves to prevent war in Europe must have convinced him that the United States could no longer afford its self-imposed arms limitations. In his State of the Union Message to Congress in January 1939, the President indicated that changed world conditions called for a very different policy than that which the country had pursued during the previous two decades:

There comes a time in the affairs of men when they must prepare to defend, not their homes alone, but the tenets of faith and humanity on which their churches, their governments and their very civilization are founded. . . .

We know what might happen to us of the United States if the new philosophies of force were to encompass the other continents and invade our own. We, no more than other nations, can afford to be surrounded by the enemies of our faith and our humanity. . . .

But the world has grown so small and weapons of attack so swift that no nation can be safe in its will to peace so long as any other powerful nation refuses to settle its grievances at the council table.

For if any government bristling with implements of war insists on policies of force, weapons of defense give the only safety.

In our foreign relations we have learned from the past what not to do. From new wars we have learned what we must do. . . .

We have learned that survival cannot be guaranteed by arming after the attack begins—for there is new range and speed to offense. . . .

We have learned that God-fearing democracies of the world which observe the sanctity of treaties and good faith in their dealings with other nations cannot safely be indifferent to international lawlessness anywhere. They cannot forever let pass, without effective protest, acts of aggression against sister nations—acts which automatically undermine all of us.

Obviously they must proceed along practical, peaceful lines. But the mere fact that we rightly decline to intervene with arms to prevent acts of aggression does not mean that we must act as if there were no aggression at all. Words may be futile, but war is not the only means of commanding a decent respect for the opinions of mankind. There are many methods short of war, but stronger and more effective than mere words, of bringing home to aggressor governments the aggregate sentiments of our people.

At the very least, we can and should avoid any action, or any lack of action, which will encourage, assist or build up an aggressor. We have learned that when we deliberately try to legislate neutrality, our neutrality laws may operate unevenly and unfairly—may actually give aid to an aggressor and deny it to the victim. The instinct of self-preservation should warn us that we ought not to let that happen any more.

And we have learned something else—the old, old lesson that probability of attack is mightily decreased by the assurance of an ever ready defense. Since 1931, nearly eight years ago, world events of thunderous import have moved with lightening speed. During those eight years many of our people clung to the hope that the innate decency of mankind would protect the unprepared who showed their innate trust in mankind. Today we are all wiser—and sadder.[48]

Roosevelt attempted to implement the promise of the speech by submitting a military budget to the Congress over 50 percent greater than that of the previous year. The Congress only reduced the President's figure by approximately $55 million.

Another popular myth about the prewar decade is that the President had the wisdom to understand what was happening in Europe, and the vision to prepare the country to cope with the situation, but that the Congress was constantly frustrating his efforts. President Truman reflected on this notion when he discussed the causes of World War II in a press conference in 1945. Commenting on the failure of the United States to prepare adequately during the 1930s, Truman agrued:

> Every time the President made an effort to get a preparedness program through the Congress, it was stifled.[49]

Once again, however, the facts do not bear out such a charge. During President Roosevelt's previous two terms the Congress had only once reduced the proposed military budget by a figure as high as $50 million. The executive estimates (as the proposed budgets are called) were low, and the final appropriations were low. They rarely differed by a figure that totaled as high as three percent of the total appropriations.[50] There was absolutely no basis for arguing that the Congress prevented the President from developing the kind of military establishment that would have made the country fully prepared for any eventuality in the 1940s. It was just not true. When the President finally awoke to the great dangers to which our relatively small army and navy exposed us, the Congress went right along with and consented to a series of escalating military budgets beginning in 1939.

The 1939 State of the Union Message marked the turning point in Roosevelt's six-year effort to reason with the dictatorships. They had continually rejected his efforts and publicly humiliated his attempts to conciliate their demands. Hitler's continued success in victimizing first Austria and then Czechoslovakia must have convinced Roosevelt that he would have to be stopped by force and that the United States, in one way or another, would have to support or perhaps even be part of that force. It would take time to convince the American people of that necessity, but it is clear in the 1939 speech that Roosevelt was now ready to revamp his policies and to prepare for the worst.

President Franklin D. Roosevelt
Annual Message to Congress
January 4, 1939

Rosenman, VIII, 1-7

Mr. Vice President, Mr. Speaker, Members of the Senate and the Congress:
In reporting on the state of the nation, I have felt it necessary on previous occasions to advise the Congress of disturbance abroad and of the need of putting our own house in order in the face of storm signals from across the seas. As this Seventy-sixth Congress opens there is need for further warning.

A war which threatened to envelop the world in flames has been averted; but it has become increasingly clear that world peace is not assured.

All about us rage undeclared wars—military and economic. All about us grow more deadly armaments—military and economic. All about us are threats of new aggression—military and economic.

Storms from abroad directly challenge three institutions indispensable to Americans, now as always. The first is religion. It is the source of the other two—democracy and international good faith.

Religion, by teaching man his relationship to God, gives the individual a sense of his own dignity and teaches him to respect himself by respecting his neighbors.

Democracy, the practice of self-government, is a covenant among free men to respect the rights and liberties of their fellows.

International good faith, a sister of democracy, springs from the will of civilized nations of men to respect the rights and liberties of other nations of men.

In a modern civilization, all three—religion, democracy and international good faith—complement and support each other.

Where freedom of religion has been attacked, the attack has come from sources opposed to democracy. Where democracy has been overthrown, the spirit of free worship has disappeared. And where religion and democracy have vanished, good faith and reason in international affairs have given way to strident ambition and brute force.

An ordering of society which relegates religion, democracy and good faith among nations to the background can find no place within it for the ideals of the Prince of Peace. The United States rejects such an ordering, and retains its ancient faith.

There comes a time in the affairs of men when they must prepare to defend, not their homes alone, but the tenets of faith and humanity on which their churches, their governments and their very civilization are founded. The defense of religion, of democracy and of good faith among nations is all the same fight. To save one we must now make up our minds to save all.

We know what might happen to us of the United States if the new philosophies of force were to encompass the other continents and invade our own. We, no more than other nations, can afford to be surrounded by the enemies of our faith and our humanity. Fortunate it is, therefore, that in this Western Hemisphere we have, under a common ideal of democratic government, a rich diversity of resources and of peoples functioning together in mutual respect and peace.

That Hemisphere, that peace, and that ideal we propose to do our share in protecting against storms from any quarter. Our people and our resources are pledged to secure that protection. From that determination no American flinches.

This by no means implies that the American Republics disassociate themselves from the nations of other continents. It does not mean the Americas against the rest of the world. We as one of the Republics reiterate our willingness to help the cause of world peace. We stand on our historic offer to take counsel with all other nations of the world to the end that aggression among them be terminated, that the race of armaments cease and that commerce be renewed.

But the world has grown so small and weapons of attack so swift that no nation can be safe in its will to peace so long as any other powerful nation refuses to settle its grievances at the council table.

For if any government bristling with implements of war insists on policies of force, weapons of defense give the only safety.

In our foreign relations we have learned from the past what not to do. From new wars we have learned what we must do.

We have learned that effective timing of defense, and the distant points from which attacks may be launched are completely different from what they were twenty years ago.

We have learned that survival cannot be guaranteed by arming after the attack begins—for there is new range and speed to offense.

We have learned that long before any overt military act, aggression begins with preliminaries of propaganda, subsidized penetration, the loosening of ties of good will, the stirring of prejudice and the incitement to disunion.

We have learned that God-fearing democracies of the world which observe the sanctity of treaties and good faith in their dealings with other nations cannot safely be indifferent to international lawlessness anywhere. They cannot forever let pass, without effective protest, acts of aggression against sister nations—acts which automatically undermine all of us.

Obviously they must proceed along practical, peaceful lines. But the mere fact that we rightly decline to intervene with arms to prevent acts of aggression does not mean that we must act as if there were no aggression at all. Words may be futile, but war is not the only means of commanding a decent respect for the opinions of mankind. There are many methods short of war, but stronger and more effective than mere words, of bringing home to aggressor governments the aggregate sentiments of our own people.

At the very least, we can and should avoid any action, or any lack of action, which will encourage, assist or build up an aggressor. We have learned that when we deliberately try to legislate neutrality, our neutrality laws may operate unevenly and unfairly—may actually give aid to an aggressor and deny it to the victim. The instinct of self-preservation should warn us that we ought not to let that happen any more.

And we have learned something else—the old, old lesson that probability of attack is mightily decreased by the assurance of an ever ready defense. Since 1931, nearly eight years ago, world events of thunderous import have moved with lightning speed. During these eight years many of our people clung to the hope that the innate decency of mankind would protect the unprepared who showed their innate trust in mankind. Today we are all wiser—and sadder.

Under modern conditions what we mean by "adequate defense"—a policy subscribed to by all of us—must be divided into three elements. First, we must have armed forces and defenses strong enough to ward off sudden attack against strategic positions and key facilities essential to ensure sustained resistance and ultimate victory. Secondly, we must have the organization and location of those key facilities so that they may be immediately utilized and rapidly expanded to meet all needs without danger of serious interruption by enemy attack.

In the course of a few days I shall send you a special message making recommendations for those two essentials of defense against danger which we cannot safely assume will not come.

If these first two essentials are reasonably provided for, we must be able confidently to invoke the third element, the underlying strength of citizenship—the self-confidence, the ability, the imagination and the devotion that give the staying power to see things through.

A strong and united nation may be destroyed if it is unprepared against sudden attack. But even a nation well armed and well organized from a strictly military standpoint may, after a period of time, meet defeat if it is unnerved by self-distrust, endangered by class prejudice, by dissension between capital and labor, by false economy and by other unsolved social problems at home.

In meeting the troubles of the world we must meet them as one people—with a unity born of the fact that for generations those who have come to our shores, representing many kindreds and tongues, have been welded by common opportunity into a united patriotism. If another form of government can present a united front in its attack on a democracy, the attack must and will be met by a united democracy. Such a democracy can and must exist in the United States.

A dictatorship may command the full strength of a regimented nation. But the united strength of a democratic nation can be mustered only when its people, educated by modern standards to know what is going on and where they are going, have conviction that they are receiving as large a share of opportunity for development, as large a share of material success and of human dignity, as they have a right to receive.

Our nation's program of social and economic reform is therefore a part of defense, as basic as armaments themselves.

Against the background of events in Europe, in Africa and in Asia during these recent years, the pattern of what we have accomplished since 1933 appears in even clearer focus.

For the first time we have moved upon deep-seated problems affecting our national strength and have forged national instruments adequate to meet them.

Consider what the seemingly piecemeal struggles of these six years add up to in terms of realistic national preparedness.

We are conserving and developing natural resources—land, water power, forests.

We are trying to provide necessary food, shelter and medical care for the health of our population.

We are putting agriculture—our system of food and fibre supply—on a sounder basis.

We are strengthening the weakest spot in our system of industrial supply—its long smouldering labor difficulties.

We have cleaned up our credit system so that depositor and investor alike may more readily and willingly make their capital available for peace or war.

We are giving to our youth new opportunities for work and education.

We have sustained the morale of all the population by the dignified recognition of our obligations to the aged, the helpless and the needy.

Above all, we have made the American people conscious of their interrelationship and their interdependence. They sense a common destiny and a common need of each other. Differences of occupation, geography, race and religion no longer obscure the nation's fundamental unity in thought and in action.

We have our difficulties, true—but we are a wiser and a tougher nation than we were in 1929, or in 1932.

Never have there been six years of such far-flung internal preparedness in our history. And this has been done without any dictator's power to command, without conscription of labor or confiscation of capital, without concentration camps and without a scratch on freedom of speech, freedom of the press or the rest of the Bill of Rights.

We see things now that we could not see along the way. The tools of government which we had in 1933 are outmoded. We have had to forge new tools for a new role of government operating in a democracy—a role of new responsibility for new needs and increased responsibility for old needs, long neglected.

Some of these tools had to be roughly shaped and still need some machining down. Many of those who fought bitterly against the forging of these new tools welcome their use today. The American people, as a whole, have accepted them. The Nation looks to the Congress to improve the new machinery which we have permanently installed, provided that in the process the social usefulness of the machinery is not destroyed or impaired.

All of us agree that we should simplify and improve laws if experience and operation clearly demonstrate the need. For instance, all of us want better provision for our older people under our social security legislation. For the medically needy we must provide better care.

Most of us agree that for the sake of employer and employee alike we must find ways to end factional labor strife and employer-employee disputes.

Most of us recognize that none of these tools can be put to maximum effectiveness unless the executive processes of government are revamped—reorganized, if you will—into more effective combination. And even after such reorganization it will take time to develop administrative personnel and experience in order to use our new tools with a minimum of mistakes. The Congress, of course, needs no further information on this.

With this exception of legislation to provide greater government efficiency, and with the exception of legislation to ameliorate our railroad and other transportation problems, the past three Congresses have met in part or in whole the pressing needs of the new order of things.

We have now passed the period of internal conflict in the launching of our program of social reform. Our full energies may now be released to invigorate the processes of recovery in order to preserve our reforms, and to give every man and woman who wants to work a real job at a living wage.

But time is of paramount importance. The deadline of danger from within and from without is not within our control. The hour-glass may be in the hands of other nations. Our own hour-glass tells us that we are off on a race to make democracy work, so that we may be efficient in peace and therefore secure in national defense.

The 1939 message revealed that Roosevelt had really confirmed some ideas in his own mind and no longer needed to talk like a neutralist. He identified American interests with those of the beleaguered democracies, and admitted that the existing

Neutrality Act of 1935 played into the hands of the dictators and even encouraged acts of aggression. The act had been passed at the height of isolationism and on the heels of an investigation conducted by Senator Gerald Nye from Nebraska, which had convinced many Americans that the United States was seduced into World War I by British propaganda and the greed and determination of munitions makers ready to ply their trade and bankers eager to protect their international investments and loans. Commenting on the fallacies of the American policy of neutrality during the thirties, Roosevelt later wrote:

> The aggressor nations knew that under our arms embargo the peace-loving nations of the world, which had not piled up as much armament as the aggressors had, were prevented from buying any war materials from us. The aggressors knew that as soon as they would declare war upon their victims, their victims would be shut off from obtaining implements of war from neutral nations. Of course, the aggressors had spent many years and a large portion of their wealth in piling up armaments, and did not have to buy materials outside. The victims of their aggression, however, who had not built up armament to the same extent, would have to look to neutral nations to sell the implements of war to them. It was clear, therefore, that so long as our arms embargo statute prevented the United States from helping all belligerents, the aggressor nations were given a tremendous advantage by it, and to that extent, were actually encouraged by our laws, to make war upon their neighbors. . . .
>
> That is why I was so anxious in July, 1939, for the Congress to repeal the arms embargo provisions of the neutrality law. For such a repeal would, in effect, say to the aggressor nations that if they did declare war they would find that their enemies would be able to obtain the needed war supplies here in America. I knew that the sale of arms by the United States could and would help the weaker nations resist attack from those nations which had built up these vast offensive striking forces.[51]

Prior to this speech, with the exception of the moments of deviation noted above, Roosevelt had not been confident enough to swim upstream against the powerful current of thinking which prevailed in the country at that time. The deep isolationist mood that pervaded much of American society during the 1930s was not easy to overcome. It was not centered in any one segment of the population but had significant roots in American history, especially in the populist movement of the late nineteenth century, in the era of reaction initiated by a handful of revisionist historians exposing the alleged motives for American's role in World War I and in the sympathy of certain ethnic groups in this country for the aspirations, or in other cases the harassments, of their mother countries. These groups had difficulty finding common ground and joining in any coordinated activity, but their numbers were not small and their mood and influence had a corrosive effect upon the feeble attempts of internationally-minded leaders like Roosevelt and Hull to move very dramatically or forcefully into action in the international arena.

The philosophy of isolating American politics from the nucleus of Europe's intense continental rivalries can be traced back as far as Washington's Farewell

Address, but even at the end of the nineteenth century and in the early decades of the twentieth century, many Americans still distrusted the unfamiliar and seemingly cosmopolitan culture of Europe; even more pointedly, they mistrusted the motives of other Americans' interest in and their desire to cultivate closer ties with Europe. This policy served American interests well in the formative stages of her history, but it was something of an anachronism in the highly industrialized twentieth century.

Much isolationist thinking was based upon an ideological gap between wealthy, generally upper-class, urban and east coast business and financial interests, who were generally internationally minded, and the middle-west and western, primarily rural, middle- and lower-class "populist" outlook which was instinctively isolationist. The populists distrusted the goals of the eastern capitalist gold standard "establishment," and even when that ill-fated party was long since dead, the attitude lived on in the flaming rhetoric of the La Follettes, the Wheelers, the Borahs and the Nyes,[52] and their millions of supporters throughout the country. Starting from a somewhat different perspective, the revisionist writers of the 1920s—John Maynard Keynes, Charles A. Beard, Walter Millis and others— created among intellectuals, many academicians and those of a liberal and radical persuasion, a distrust of the idealistic explanations of America's entry into World War I. The revelations of American financial and trade interests in the Allied nations, the role of the munitions-makers in selling arms to the combatants and the ruthless Machiavellian conquest policies pursued by the European leaders were exposed by these writers and were further supported by the publication of the diplomatic archives of the period. The munitions inquiry of the Nye Committee merely exacerbated these feelings. Thousands of undergraduates joined the Veterans of Future Wars, a sight frequently seen on the nation's campuses during the 1930s.

Many German Americans who were not necessarily sympathetic to the "lebensraum" goals of the Third Reich but who were more interested in American neutrality so as not to pit the United States against their homeland, were bitterly opposed to the internationalists and to the Jews, who, they alleged, sought to encourage America in more active opposition to the Nazis. Of course, there were active segments of the German-American community who were, secretly and publicly, extremely sympathetic to Hitler and his goals. A uniformed German-American Bund, replete with storm trooper elite guards who drilled in military formations and held what they hoped would become mass rallies and demonstrations, intensified emotions in this country. The Italian-American community was laced with its own pro- and anti-Fascist groups, but the larger percentage of Italian Americans desired U.S. neutrality in preference to support for the other side. Many Americans of Irish extraction or birth, although they had no particular sympathies for either Hitler or Mussolini, were so hostile to the British that they too recoiled at active American support for the United Kingdom and her allies. The propaganda broadcasts of the crusading priest from the shrine of the Little Flower in Michigan—Father Coughlin—orchestrated this theme continuously, interwoven with his own admixture of populism and anti-Semitism.

There were other sources of isolationism—sincere pacifists, figures of the stature of John L. Lewis and certain intellectuals and church leaders who feared the consequences of United States involvement in another world conflict. These groups supported the traditional isolationists in the Congress like Wheeler and Borah, Nye and Shipstead, and they were successful in preventing the government or its leaders from doing much apart from offering messages of reassurance to those nations caught up in the path of the totalitarian regimes, almost to the end of the decade. They were not powerful enough to dictate any exclusion policies with the exception of the neutrality legislation, but they were strong enough to prevent the internationalists from acting in any significant manner to discourage the outbreak of World War II. The fact of their very strong veto power set the tone of foreign policy during the 1930s.

Congress also was not quite in step with the President. Despite the fact that the Nazis had violated the infamous Munich pact and occupied all of Czechoslovakia in March 1939, and the Italians marched into Albania in April, Congress delayed and procrastinated in moving to repeal the Neutrality Act. The administration handled the matter awkwardly, and the congressional leaders on the measure, Senator Key Pittman and Congressman Sol Bloom, did not provide very effective direction. An unsatisfactory bill, which in effect retained the embargo on "arms and ammunition," but permitted shipment of "instruments of war," passed the House of Representatives at the end of June, but the measure died in the Senate Foreign Relations Committee in July before Congress adjourned.[53]

The defeat in the committee was largely due to the strength and influence of isolationists like Senator Borah, who in a famous meeting with the President and the secretary of state, disregarded their warnings of the imminence of war in Europe with his own prediction that there would be no war. He confessed, "I have my own sources of information which I have provided for myself, and on several occasions I've found them more reliable than the State Department."[54] This defeat had a very detrimental effect in the capitals in Europe, and once again reduced the President's arsenal to pure rhetoric. Meanwhile, Prime Minister Chamberlain gave a guarantee to Poland that Britain would come to its defense if invaded, partly in reaction to his embarrassment over Hitler's violation of the Munich Pact. War appeared imminent, but the Congress went home and the President was left to cope with the dictators again with mere words.

War came to Europe in September and the President quickly called Congress back into session, urging the revision of the existing neutrality law. Roosevelt wanted to return to the general principles of international law and to recover the right of a neutral nation to supply arms to belligerents. Emphasizing the urgency of such action, he proposed a number of measures aimed at appeasing the isolationists and further protecting America and Americans from becoming involved in incidents which might lead the United States to war. The President's message was very carefully drawn, avoiding any discussion of massive aid to the Allies (perhaps with tongue in check), and reminding America that changes in policy could help her to remain at peace. A revised neutrality law calling for cash-and-carry purchases in this country by belligerent nations was finally passed on November 3, 1939, and signed by the President the following day. He was then in a position to bolster both the morale and fighting efficiency of the embattled Allies, but events rapidly demonstrated that more than the purchase of cash-and-carry arms would be needed before long.

The initial fighting front of the war was Poland, but resistance there was overcome quickly and the Polish army was liquidated in a matter of weeks. The Nazis did not immediately follow up that victory with an attack on the western front, but they continued to build up their forces during the winter of 1939-40. During that period the Soviets attacked Finland, but despite the Finns' incredible resistance, when several times they hurled the Russian armies back, they were forced to sue for peace on Soviet terms in March. In April German divisions occupied Denmark and rapidly overcame the small but gallant Norwegian army. Finally in May the Nazis began their major offensive on the western front, rapidly invading the low countries with their motorized divisions. Within three weeks the Belgian army was forced to capitulate, and that was followed by the debacle at Dunkirk and the defeat of the French in June. This long list of Allied disasters evoked much sympathy and apprehension in the United States, but the President was not able to affect appreciably any of these events; and his efforts at diplomacy during that hopeless period were crowned with failure.

In the summer of 1940 Britain stood alone in defiance to the apparently invincible German army, and although the main body of its army and air force was still intact, the navy had suffered great losses and the British divisions on the continent, which had been evacuated at Dunkirk, were badly mauled. At the last minute Italy had entered the war, just before France fell, and the Japanese, linked by treaty to Germany and Italy, were making ominous preparations in the Pacific, threatening both British and American interests. In the face of it all, Winston Churchill and his countrymen remained steadfast, but they turned desperately to the United States for assistance. Britain needed the support of American industry to supply planes, guns, tanks and ammunition; it needed American moral support to reinforce its courageous decision to fight on, but of even more concern, it immediately needed additional sea power to prevent the Nazis from sweeping the English Channel while preparing to launch an invasion.

Churchill first mentioned his high priority needs when he corresponded with the President after becoming Prime Minister, before Dunkirk and the fall of France. That was the beginning of a very extensive correspondence between the Prime Minister and the President, which continued until Mr. Roosevelt's death in 1945. Churchill described the scope and mechanics involved in these communications in the second volume of his history of the Second World War.

Winston S. Churchill
Account of his War Correspondence
With President Franklin D. Roosevelt
1940-45

Winston S. Churchill, *The Second World War*, vol. II, *Their Finest Hour*, (London, 1949), 22-23.

Any account of the methods of government which developed under the National Coalition would be incomplete without an explanation of the series of personal messages which I sent to the President of the United States and the heads of other foreign countries and the Dominion Governments. This correspondence must be described. Having obtained from the Cabinet any specific decisions required on policy, I composed and dictated these documents myself, for the most part on the basis that they were intimate and informal correspondence with friends and fellow-workers. One can usually put one's thought better in one's own words. It was only occasionally that I read the text to the Cabinet beforehand. Knowing their views, I used the ease and freedom needed for the doing of my work. I was of course hand-in-glove with the Foreign Secretary and his Department, and any differences of view were settled together. I circulated these telegrams, in some cases after they had been sent, to the principal members of the War Cabinet, and, where he was concerned, to the Dominions Secretary. Before despatching them I, of course, had my points and facts checked departmentally, and nearly all military messages passed through Ismay's hands to the Chiefs of Staff. This correspondence in no way ran counter to the official communications or the work of the Ambassadors. It became, however, in fact the channel of much vital business, and played a part in my conduct of the war not less, and sometimes even more, important than my duties as Minister of Defence.

The very select circle, who were entirely free to express their opinion, were almost invariably content with the drafts and gave me an increasing measure of confidence. Differences with American authorities, for instance, insuperable at the second level, were settled often in a few hours by direct contact at the top. Indeed, as time went on, the efficacy of this top-level transaction of business was so apparent that I had to be careful not to let it become a vehicle for ordinary departmental affairs. I had repeatedly to refuse the requests of my colleagues to address President Roosevelt personally on important matters of detail. Had these intruded unduly upon the personal correspondence, they would soon have destroyed its privacy and consequently its value.

My relations with the President gradually became so close that the chief business between our two countries was virtually conducted by these personal interchanges between him and me. In this way our perfect understanding was gained. As Head of the State as well as Head of the Government, Roosevelt spoke and acted with authority in every sphere; and, carrying the War Cabinet with me, I represented Great Britain with almost equal latitude. Thus a very high degree of concert was obtained, and the saving in time and the reduction in the number of people informed were both invaluable. I sent my cables to the American Embassy in London, which was in direct touch with the President at the White House through special coding machines. The speed with which answers were received and things settled was aided by clock-time. Any message which I prepared in the evening, night, or even up to two o'clock in the morning, would reach the President before he went to bed, and very often his answer would come back to me when I woke the next morning. In all, I sent him nine hundred and fifty messages and received about eight hundred in reply. I felt I was in contact with a very great man who was also a warm-hearted friend and the foremost champion of the high causes which we served.

The first communication between Churchill as the new British Prime Minister and the President of the United States involved requests for immediate military and naval aid in the form of tanks, weapons, planes and destroyers. Churchill wrote that he closed all of his wartime communications to the President with a very special *nom de plume*—"Former Naval Person"—to add to the intimacy of their correspondence.

Winston S. Churchill
First Letter to President Roosevelt
Upon Becoming British Prime Minister
May 15, 1940

Churchill, II, 24-25.

Although I have changed my office, I am sure you would not wish me to discontinue our intimate private correspondence. As you are no doubt aware, the scene has darkened swiftly. The enemy have a marked preponderance in the air, and their new technique is making a deep impression upon the French. I think myself the battle on land has only just begun, and I should like to see the masses engage. Up to the present Hitler is working with specialised units in tanks and air. The small countries are simply smashed up, one by one, like matchwood. We must expect, though it is not yet certain, that Mussolini will hurry in to share the loot of civilisation. We expect to be attacked here ourselves, both from the air and by parachute and air-borne troops, in the near future, and are getting ready for them. If necessary, we shall continue the war alone, and we are not afraid of that.

But I trust you realise, Mr. President, that the voice and force of the United States may count for nothing if they are withheld too long. You may have a completely subjugated, Nazified Europe established with astonishing swiftness, and the weight may be more than we can bear. All I ask now is that you should proclaim non-belligerency, which would mean that you would help us with everything short of actually engaging armed forces. Immediate needs are, first of all, the loan of forty or fifty of your older destroyers to bridge the gap between what we have now and the large new construction we put in hand at the beginning of the war. This time next year we shall have plenty. But if in the interval Italy comes in against us with another hundred submarines we may be strained to breaking-point. Secondly, we want several hundred of the latest types of aircraft, of which you are now getting delivery. These can be repaid by those now being constructed in the United States for us. Thirdly, anti-aircraft equipment and ammunition, of which again there will be plenty next year, if we are alive to see it. Fourthly, the fact that our ore supply is being compromised from Sweden, from North Africa, and perhaps from Northern Spain, makes it necessary to purchase steel in the United States. This also applies to other materials. We shall go on paying dollars for as long as we can, but I should like to feel reasonably sure that when we can pay no more you will give us the stuff all the same. Fifthly, we have many reports of possible German parachute or airborne descents in Ireland. The visit of a United States squadron to Irish ports, which might well be prolonged, would be invaluable. Sixthly, I am looking to you to keep the Japanese quiet in the Pacific, using Singapore in any way convenient. The details of the material which we have in hand will be communicated to you separately.

With all good wishes and respect . . .

The President replied affirmatively to all of Churchill's requests except one involving the transfer of the obsolete destroyers.

> As you know a step of this kind could not be taken except with the specific authorization of the Congress, and I am not certain that it would be wise for that suggestion to be made to the Congress at this moment. Furthermore, it seems to me doubtful, from the point of view of our own defense requirements, which must be inevitably linked with the defense requirements of this hemisphere and with our obligations in the Pacific, whether we could dispose even temporarily of these destroyers. Furthermore, even if we were able to take the step you suggest, it would be at least 6 or 7 weeks as a minimum, as I see it, before these vessels could undertake active service under the British flag. . . .[55]

As a master politician, Roosevelt sensed the political problems which might prevent the Congress from approving of such a step, and he was completely convinced at that point that it would be illegal to move without the statutory approval of Congress. But the pressure on him continued to mount. Both Ickes and Morgenthau in his cabinet favored more aid to Britain, and in the next few days the battle news from Europe became worse and worse. Ickes reported that the President was haunted by another nightmare, the thought that Hitler might force England to surrender her fleet. He thought out loud in the presence of the secretary of the interior one day:

> Suppose Hitler says to England, "I will give you the most generous terms that a victor has ever offered to a conquered people. You may keep control of the British Isles (without any commitments as to colonies or independent dominions) but you made us destroy our fleet after the last war and now you must replace that fleet by surrendering yours. If you do not do this, we will move into England, take it over, and run it with Germans in every country." In such a situation what would England do?[56]

Ickes replied: "And if England should surrender the fleet where would we find ourselves?"

> The President only shrugged his shoulders. Of course, the Germans could go farther than this. If the fleet should set out for Canada, Hitler could say to England, "Bring back your fleet and surrender it or we will bomb England from end to end for sixty days." Under such a threat, and

with not only the ability but the capacity of Hitler to carry it out, it might be impossible for England not to order back her fleet for the purpose of handing it over to Hitler. Of course, those in command of the fleet might refuse to go back; they might be moved even to scuttle their ships, but a threat that could even force surrender could also be effective to prevent any scuttling.

There is no doubt in my mind that this country is in the most critical situation since we won our independence. The people are beginning to wake up, but even today there are few who can envisage all the dreadful possibilities that are involved.[57]

The President must have expressed the same doubts to the British ambassador in Washington, Lord Lothian, for Churchill cabled a reply to the questions plagueing the President's mind on May 20, 1940.

Prime Minister Winston S. Churchill
Cable to President Roosevelt
"Britain Will Persevere"
May 20, 1940

U.S. Department of State, *Foreign Relations of the United States, 1940* (Washington, D.C., 1959) III, 49.

London, May 20, 1940—1 p.m.
[Received May 20—8:40 a.m.]

Secret and personal for the President from Former Naval Person: Lothian has reported his conversation with you. I understand your difficulties but I am very sorry about the destroyers. If they were here in 6 weeks they would play an invaluable part. The battle in France is full of danger to both sides. Though we have taken heavy toll of enemy in the air and are clawing down two or three to one of their planes, they have still a formidable numerical superiority. Our most vital need is therefore the delivery at the earliest possible date of the largest possible number of Curtiss P-40 fighters now in course of delivery to your Army.

With regard to the closing part of your talk with Lothian, our intention is whatever happens to fight on to the end in this Island and, provided we can get the help for which we ask, we hope to run them very close in the air battles in view of individual superiority. Members of the present administration would likely go down during this process should it result adversely, but in no conceivable circumstances will we consent to surrender. If members of the present administration were finished and others came in to parley amid the ruins, you must not be blind to the fact that the sole remaining bargaining counter with Germany would be the fleet, and if this country was left by the United States to its fate no one would have the right to blame those then responsible if they made the best terms they could for the surviving inhabitants. Excuse me, Mr. President, putting this nightmare bluntly. Evidently I could not answer for my successors who in utter despair and helplessness might well have to accommodate themselves to the German will. However there is happily no need at present to dwell upon such ideas. Once more thanking you for your good will.

There was no further communication between Roosevelt and Churchill about the destroyers until after Dunkirk, when the Prime Minister pursued the question with renewed emphasis. He was encouraged by the President's speech at the University of Virginia, where he publicly denounced the isolationist position:

> Some indeed still held to the now somewhat obvious delusion that we in the United States can safely permit the United States to become a lone island, a lone island in a world dominated by the philosophy of force.
>
> Such an island may be the dream of those who still talk and vote as isolationists. Such an island represents to me and to the overwhelming majority of Americans today a helpless nightmare of a people without freedom—the nightmare of a people lodged in prison, handcuffed, hungry, and fed through the bars from day to day by the contemptuous, unpitying master of other continents.[58]

In the course of the speech Roosevelt also castigated the Italian last-minute entry into the war, declaring that "the hand that held the dagger has struck it into the back of its neighbor."[59] Hearing that, Churchill exploited the occasion to press the President once again for the destroyers.

Prime Minister Winston S. Churchill
Telegraph to President Roosevelt
Requesting American Destroyers
June 11, 1940

Foreign Relations, 1940, III, 52.

We all listened to you last night and were fortified by the grand scope of your declaration. Your statement that material aid of the United States will be given to the Allies in their struggle is a strong encouragement in a dark but not unhopeful hour. Everything must be done to keep France in the fight and to prevent any idea of the fall of Paris, should it occur, becoming the occasion of any kind of parley. The hope with which you inspired them may give them strength to persevere. [They should] continue to defend every yard of their soil and use full fighting force of their army. Hitler thus baffled of quick results will turn upon us and we are preparing ourselves to resist his fury and defend our Island. Having saved British Expeditionary Forces we do not lack troops at home and as soon as Divisions can be equipped on much higher scale needed for Continental service they will be despatched to France. Our intention is to have a strong army fighting in France for campaign of 1941. I have already cabled you about aeroplanes including flying boats which are so needful to us in the impending struggle for the life of Great Britain. But even more pressing is the need for destroyers. Italian outrage makes it necessary for us to cope with much larger number of submarines which may come out into the Atlantic and perhaps be based on Spanish ports. To this the only counter is destroyers. Nothing is so important as for us to have 30 or 40 old destroyers you have already had reconditioned. We can fit them very rapidly with our asdics and they will bridge over the gap of 6 months before our wartime new construction comes into play. We will return them or their equivalents to you without fail at 6 months notice if at any time you need them. The next 6 months are vital. If while we have to guard the East Coast against invasion new heavy German and Italian submarine attack is launched against our commerce the strain may be beyond our resources; and ocean traffic by which we live may be strangled. Not a day should be lost. I send you my heartfelt thanks and those of my colleagues for all you are doing and seeking to do for what we may now indeed call a common cause.

The French cabinet of Paul Reynaud resigned on the evening of June 16, 1940; before midnight a new cabinet under Marshal Henri Philippe Pétain was formed and they proceeded to negotiate an armistice with the Germans. The British were left to stand alone against the Germans, and pressures increased for substantial aid from the United States. One of the journalists in Washington who actively sought greater American participation in the war was Joseph Alsop, a well-known syndicated columnist and a distant cousin of FDR. After receiving important information from the British embassy of the desperate plight of the British navy, Alsop was able to persuade Benjamin Cohen, a close presidential advisor, to prepare a memorandum for the President, explaining that there were no real legal impediments to prohibit the transfer of destroyers to the British. The President had doubts about Cohen's arguments, but he sent the memo to Frank Knox, the new secretary of the navy, with the following comments. They reflect the President's concerns at that time. It is clear that he was struggling to find a legal and politically realistic way to make the transfer, but he was still convinced that it would require congressional action.

President Franklin D. Roosevelt
Memorandum to Secretary of the Navy Knox
Reconsidering the Transfer of Destroyers
July 22, 1940

Elliot Roosevelt, ed., *F. D. R.: His Personal Letters, 1928-1945* (New York, 1950) II, 1048-49.

The White House
July 22, 1940

Memorandum for the Secretary of the Navy: This memorandum from Ben Cohen is worth reading. In view of the clause in the big authorization bill I signed last Saturday which is intended to be a complete prohibition of sale, I frankly doubt if Cohen's memorandum would stand up.

Also I fear Congress is in no mood at the present time to allow any form of sale.

You might, however, think over the possibility at a little later date of trying to get Congressional action to allow the sale of these destroyers to Canada on condition that they be used solely in American Hemisphere defense, i.e., from Greenland to British Guiana including Bermuda and the West Indies. It is obvious that this would be of great assistance as it would release other ships for other purposes and would relieve the United States of a part of the responsibility for maintaining our present patrol.

F.D.R.

Isolationist sentiment played a major role during the 1930s, but at this critical moment in world history, when the fate of European civilization literally was in the hands of the beleagured citizens of the British Isles, another group—the internationalists—smaller and better organized than the isolationists, and also conscious of deep underlying support among substantial numbers of the inactive American public, were ignited into energetic, almost frenetic, activities to aid Great Britain in its hour of peril. The movers among this group were a small number of very influential, highly educated members of the American establishment—leaders of the communications media, the universities, the church and the foreign policy advisory groups, which would soon play an increasingly influential role in the formulation of policy and in the recruitment of policymakers. Since the struggle over the Versailles Treaty and the League of Nations, most of these individuals had sought a more involved and influential role for America in the councils of world politics; now, shocked by the collapse of international peacekeeping machinery, the outbreak of war on the continent and the unexpected fall of France, they rushed to do something effective as quickly as possible.

On June 2, 1940, a small group of friends met at the pleasant country home of Francis and Helen Hill Miller in Fairfax, Virginia, just outside of Washington. They all classified themselves as "internationalists" for they felt the United States had a major stake in the outcome of the present war in Europe and were anxious for the country to come to the aid of the British. There were civil servants, academicians, journalists and lawyers, and most were members of the influential Foreign Policy Association and the National Policy Committee, two organizations which prepared research papers and other information on policy matters for governmental and public consumption. They conversed all day, and an historian of this period, Mark Lincoln Chadwin, has summarized the conclusions upon which they agreed at the end of the day:

> All agreed that the preservation of the British fleet was crucial to American security. They noted the continuing activity of Nazi agents in this country and the growing number of news stories concerning designs on Greenland, Brazil, and most recently, Uruguay. They agreed that if French possessions in Africa fell into German hands, and if the British fleet were sunk or captured in a Nazi invasion of England, the Western hemisphere would be vulnerable to German subversion and invasion. Such intrusions might come either by a southerly route running from west Africa to the hump of Brazil or by a northerly one with Britain, Iceland, and Greenland as staging points. All were convinced that democracy in North America could not long survive if the totalitarians dominated the rest of the world.[60]

This small group rapidly fanned out to reach their counterparts in other parts of the country, and within several weeks the "Century group" was formed. They took their name from the famous private club in mid-town Manhattan where many of the original luncheon and dinner meetings were held when they first organized. Each member of the group contacted a handful of individuals known to her or him, nearly all of whom were also individuals who held special status in government or were influential in shaping public opinion. Among those who quickly became involved were several outspoken college and university presidents, editorial writers on important daily newspapers, the most powerful news magazine publisher in the country, newspapers columnists, influential businessmen, ministers and theologians, academicians and a few retired civil servants.[61]

The success of the Century group, when compared with other and much larger organizations pursuing somewhat similar objectives, is probably attributable not only to their general intelligence and sophistication in the methods and history of American policymaking and their positions of influence within their respective fields, but also to their incredible zeal, their effective and at times frenzied activity and finally because they directed their energies to specific policy goals. They were not interested in rhetorical gestures or utopian ends. By contrast, the isolationists were frequently long on rhetoric and lacked proper organization and familiarity with the politics of influence in policymaking. Their strength was fundamentally as populist agitators, their influence among the long stemmed orators of the House and Senate; the internationalists associated with the Century group, on the other hand, concentrated upon influencing top-level policymakers in the executive branch and presented their message in the most important and widely read newspapers and weekly journals of opinion.

It is, of course, impossible to assess accurately the achievements of these "hawks of World War II," as their historian, Mark Chadwin, has called them. Exactly what the precise influence of the Luce publications was or the importance of editorials in the *Herald Tribune*, the Louisville *Courier-Journal*, the opinions of Joseph Alsop, Walter Lippmann and George Fielding Eliot in newspapers throughout the country or of Elmer Davis on his CBS news commentary, is a matter of speculation. For that matter, gauging the effect of the letter to *The New York Times* signed by prominent members of the bar who presented publicly for the first time some of the legal arguments which the attorney general would use in advising the President that he had the authority to transfer the destroyers, is not easy, nor in all probability accurate. What is known is that this active and articulate band of "influentials" came to the support of an administration which very much wanted to move in the same direction as they, but was confronted with political problems which at times seemed impossible to overcome and from which they all too frequently in the past had backed off. Without question the Century group helped Roosevelt make up his mind on the transfer of the 50 obsolete destroyers to the British, as well as continuing to push the President and the American people closer to total involvement in the war.[62]

In a memorandum which they prepared for the President, the Century group urged that as part of the deal Britain make available to the United States certain "naval and air concessions in British possessions in the Western Hemisphere. . . ." They also suggested, as an alternative proposal, "that the United States should receive some guarantee that the British fleet should neither be scuttled nor surrendered, but in case of a successful German invasion of England, should operate thereafter from Canadian and/or American bases. . . ."[63]

Probably informed by his embassy in Washington that consideration of the transfer of the destroyers was heating up again, Churchill again cabled the President, emphasizing the urgency of the transaction.

Prime Minister Winston S. Churchill Cable to President Roosevelt Urging The Immediate Transfer of Destroyers
July 31, 1940

Foreign Relations, 1940, III, 57-58.

London
July 31, 1940—6 p.m.
[Received 6:37 p.m.]

Strictly secret and personal for the President from Former Naval Person: It is some time since I ventured to cable personally to you, and many things both good and bad have happened in between. It has now become most urgent for you to let us have the destroyers, motor boats and flying boats for which we have asked. The Germans have the whole French coastline from which to launch U-boats, divebomber attacks upon our trade and food, and in addition we must be constantly prepared to repel by sea action threatened invasion in the narrow waters, and also to deal with breakouts from Norway towards Ireland, Iceland, Shetlands and Faroes. Besides this we have to keep control of the exit from the Mediterranean, and if possible the command of that inland sea itself, and thus to prevent the war spreading seriously into Africa.

Point 2. We have a large construction of destroyers and anti-U-boat craft coming forward, but the next 3 or 4 months open the gap of which I have previously told you. Latterly, the air attack on our shores has become injurious. In the last 10 days we have had the following destroyers sunk: *Brazen, Codrington, Delight, Wren*; and the following damaged: *Beagle, Boreas, Brilliant, Griffin, Montrose, Walpole, Whitshed*, total 11. All this in the advent of any attempt which may be made at invasion. Destroyers are frightfully vulnerable to air bombing, and yet they must be held in the air bombing area to prevent seaborne invasion. We could not keep up the present rate of casualties for long, and if we cannot get a substantial reinforcement, the whole fate of the war may be decided by this minor and easily remediable factor.

This is a frank account of our present situation and I am confident, now that you know exactly how we stand, that you will leave nothing undone to ensure that 50 or 60 of your oldest destroyers are sent to me at once. I can fit them very quickly with asdics and use them against U-boats on the western approaches and so keep the more modern and better gunned craft for the narrow seas against invasion. Mr. President, with great respect I must tell you that in the long history of the world, this is a thing to do now. Large construction is coming to me in 1941, but the crisis will be reached long before 1941. I know you will do all in your power but I feel entitled and bound to put the gravity and urgency of the position before you. . . .

A Roosevelt cabinet meeting on August 2 considered the problem, and the President left a record of the discussion in his own words—an extremely rare exercise on his part. Apparently, at that time, he was convinced that enabling legislation would be next to impossible to secure without careful preliminary preparations, which included convincing his Republican opponent in the 1940 presidential race, Wendell Willkie, to agree to back the legislation and to join with him in rallying bipartisan support. The President also thought that an effort should be made to obtain British government assurances on the disposition of the British fleet in the event of a successful Nazi invasion.

President Franklin D. Roosevelt
Notes on a Cabinet Discussion of Possible Ways
To Secure the Transfer of Destroyers
August 2, 1940

E. Roosevelt, II, 1050-51.

At Cabinet meeting, in afternoon, long discussion in regard to devising ways and means to sell directly or indirectly fifty or sixty World War old destroyers to Great Britain. It was the general opinion, without any dissenting voice, that the survival of the British Isles under German attack might very possibly depend on their getting these destroyers.

It was agreed that legislation to accomplish this is necessary.

It was agreed that such legislation if asked for by me without any preliminaries would meet with defeat or interminable delay in reaching a vote.

It was agreed that the British be approached through Lord Lothian to find out if they would agree to give positive assurance that the British Navy, in the event of German success in Great Britain, would not under any conceivable circumstances fall into the hands of the Germans and that if such assurances could be received and made public, the opposition in the Congress would be greatly lessened. I suggested that we try to get further assurance from the British that the ships of their Navy would not be sunk, but would sail for North American or British Empire ports where they would remain afloat and available.

It was agreed that I would call up William Allen White, who has recently talked with Willkie on this subject; ask White to come to Washington at once to see Hull, Knox and Stimson and after that to see me; then returning to see Willkie and seek to get, with Willkie's approval, the support of Joe Martin and Charlie McNary for such a plan. It was agreed that if this procedure went through successfully that I would, at once, send a definite request to the Congress for the necessary legislation.

I stressed the point that in all probability the legislation would fail if it had substantially unanimous Republican opposition—and that the crux of the matter lay in the vote of the Republican minority in each house. I stressed the importance of having the issue acted on without regard to party politics in any way.

At 8:30 P.M., I talked with William Allen White, who was in Estes Park, Colorado; explained the above to him and asked him to come East.

He told me that he was sure that Willkie's attitude in the matter was the same as mine. I explained to him that that was wholly insufficient, and that Willkie's attitude was not what counted but that the Republican policy in Congress was the one essential.

White told me he would get in touch with Willkie and let me know at the earliest possible moment.

Members of the Century group promised the President that they would attempt to convince the Republican candidate to join with him in endorsing legislation authorizing the transfer of the destroyers. The group dispatched two of their key Republicans, Lewis Douglas and Russell Davenport, along with William Allen White, head of the Committee to Defend America by Aiding the Allies, to Colorado where Willkie was vacationing; there they attempted to get him to go along with the President. Willkie, however, was reluctant to make such a commitment. He was reminded by isolationist Arthur Krock of *The New York Times* that Roosevelt, before he was inaugurated, had established something of a precedent by refusing to cooperate with Hoover in 1933 on policies in the banking crisis, claiming that he was not fully informed of the background of the situation, and if he acted, he would be interfering with the legislative freedom of the Republican members of Congress. Krock also charged that "the high military command of the Navy Department opposes the transfer of these vessels," although this was later to be proved unfounded, for the existing legislation required the certification of the chief of naval operations before the ships could be transferred.[64] Despite the strong pleas by the influential Republican internationalists, Willkie refused them and issued this public statement:

> My general views on foreign policy and the vital interests of the United States in the present international situation are well known, having been stated by me publicly several times. As to specific executive or legislative proposals, I do not think it appropriate for me to enter into advance commitments and understandings. If the National Administration, through any of its accredited representatives, publicly takes any given position with reference to our foreign policy, I may on appropriate occasion comment thereon.[65]

Taking his cue from Krock, Willkie also alluded to Roosevelt's conduct in 1933. The President was, of course, locked into an election battle at that time with the Republican standard-bearer, but he was undoubtedly more interested in Willkie's influence upon the Republicans in Congress than in gaining his personal support. A recent revelation by one of the President's closest advisors at that time, Benjamin Cohen, indicates that the President was informed by an intermediary, Senator Claude Pepper of Florida, that the Republican minority leader in the Senate, Charles McNary, observed

> that his past commitments would make it difficult for him to support the transfer if it would require Senate approval before the election, but he, McNary, would make no objection if plausible grounds were found for proceeding without Senate action.[66]

The Century group persisted in its efforts to convince the Roosevelt administration and the American people that the immediate transfer of the destroyers was in their interest, despite presidential candidate Willkie's refusal to support congressional approval of the plan. Agreeing with the President that the likelihood of congressional approval would either be long in coming or not forthcoming at all, they directed their efforts towards urging the President to act without congressional approval and getting the American people to accept such an arrangement as vital to their own national defense. The broadcast by General Pershing was designed to expedite the latter objective, and his was followed by a speech by Colonel William J. "Wild Bill" Donovan, the popular former commander of New York's famous "Fighting 69th" Regiment. He had particular appeal to the Irish-Americans who were wary of being drawn into a war "to pull the British chestnuts out of the fire."

But the major obstacle to the destroyer transfer remained the President's reluctance to act on his own without congressional approval. This fear had been fortified by the attorney general's ruling earlier in the summer that several World War I statutes prevented this country from permitting the sale by private builders of some newly constructed torpedo boats, even if the purchase had the approval of the United States Navy. Additional legislation passed in the latter part of June 1940, appeared to strengthen the restrictions, requiring certification by the respective heads of the two services that any military or naval ships, tanks or equipment were unnecessary to the defense of the United States before they could be sold, transferred or otherwise discarded. In the face of these obstacles, how indeed could the President act on his own to authorize the transfer of the destroyers?

The Century committee decided to meet these objections head on by getting one of their number, Dean Acheson, together with three other well-known members of the national bar, to write a detailed letter to *The New York Times*, explaining the arguments pertaining to legal obstacles to the transfer of the destroyers. It proved to be the most effective step the group had yet taken—the lawyers did their work so well that they not only convinced the President, but also the attorney general and many of the apprehensive public. Seldom has a letter to a newspaper had such significant results.

The attorneys in question, Charles C. Burlingham, Thomas D. Thatcher and George Rublee, in addition to Acheson, were all members of the District of Columbia bar and had been advisors to previous Republican and Democratic administrations. Reaffirming the great urgency that action be taken immediately if Great Britain and her navy were to be saved and advocating that this constituted the first line of American defense, the lawyers proceeded to demolish the arguments that any existing statutes prevented such a transfer. They pointed out that the statute referred to in the attorney general's ruling—(Section 3 of Title V of the Espionage Act of June 15, 1917 - c.30 40 Stat. 222, U. S. C., Title 18, sec. 33); or possibly Section 23 of Title 18 of the United States Code—had no bearing on the transfer of the destroyers because the statute prevented the sale or transfer of ships or weapons which were built on order, or in other words with the intent of supplying a belligerent power. Since the obsolete destroyers were obviously not built for that purpose, the attorneys argued the statute was not applicable.

The more recent statute which was thought also to restrict the transfer was again considered no obstacle, for the chief of naval operations could quickly certify such a transfer if he fully understood that the *quid pro quo* in the deal involved the United States' obtaining a series of critical air and naval bases from Britain, located in a perimeter off the east coast. Assuming the agreement of the chief of naval operations, the lawyers urged that

> [t]here is no reason for us to put a strained or unnecessary interpretation on our own statutes contrary to our own national interests. . . .
>
> When vital interests of the United States are at stake, when the sentiment of the country is clear, the Government should not hesitate to exercise powers under existing law. To seek an unnecessary reaffirmation from Congress now would be to run a serious danger of delay and by delay possibly to endanger the vital interests of the people in keeping war from our own shores.[67]

It is clear that the letter had an immediate and reassuring influence on policymakers in the government and also upon the public at large. Secretary of War Henry Stimson remarked, "This adds a little speck of light to the situation," and many of the arguments were later reflected in the attorney general's opinion on the transfer, which he prepared for the President.[68]

By August 13, 1940, President Roosevelt had apparently made up his mind to go through with the destroyer deal, although it is not clear whether or not he had yet decided to abandon all efforts to obtain statutory authorization from the Congress. He cabled the Prime Minister, outlining two conditions for reaching agreement between the two countries.

President Franklin D. Roosevelt
Cable to Prime Minister Churchill
Enumerating Conditions for the Destroyer Transfer
August 13, 1940

Foreign Relations, 1940, III, 65-66.

Please deliver as soon as possible the following message from the President to the former naval person: I have been studying very carefully the message transmitted to me through the British Ambassador in Washington on August 8, and I have also been considering the possibility of furnishing the assistance in the way of releases and priorities contained in the memorandum attached to your message.

It is my belief that it may be possible to furnish to the British Government as immediate assistance at least 50 destroyers, the motor torpedo boats heretofore referred to, and, insofar as airplanes are concerned, five planes of each of the categories mentioned, the latter to be furnished for war testing purposes. Such assistance, as I am sure you will understand, would only be furnished if the American people and the Congress frankly recognized that in return therefor the national defense and security of the United States would be enhanced. For that reason it would be necessary, in the event that it proves possible to release the matériel above mentioned, that the British Government finds itself able and willing to take the two following steps:

1. Assurance on the part of the Prime Minister that in the event that the waters of Great Britain become untenable for British ships of war, the latter would not be turned over to the Germans or sunk, but would be sent to other parts of the Empire for continued defense of the Empire.

2. An agreement on the part of Great Britain that the British Government would authorize the use of Newfoundland, Bermuda, the Bahamas, Jamaica, St. Lucia, Trinidad and British Guiana as naval and air bases by the United States in the event of an attack on the American hemisphere by any non-American nation; and in the meantime the United States to have the right to establish such bases and to use them for training and exercise purposes with the understanding that the land necessary for the above could be acquired by the United States through purchase or through a 99-year lease.

With regard to the agreement suggested in point 2 above, I feel confident that specific details need not be considered at this time and that such questions as the exact locations of the land which the United States might desire to purchase or lease could be readily determined upon subsequently through friendly negotiation between the two Governments.

With regard to your reference to publicity concerning the contingent destination of the British fleet, I should make it clear that I have not had in mind any public statement by you but merely an assurance to me along the lines indicated, as for example, reiteration to me of your statement to Parliament on June 4.

I should welcome a reply as soon as may be possible.

American ambassador to Great Britain, Joseph Kennedy, later cabled the President that the Prime Minister was somewhat taken aback by the American terms, remarking, but not in an unfriendly way, "Isn't it a rather hard bargain for you to drive?"[69] There was no problem about the President's request that the Prime Minister give assurance on the transfer of the fleet, for Roosevelt had promised Churchill that no public announcement of that agreement would be made. But the Prime Minister wanted to protect himself from criticism which might focus on his gullibility in trading rights to land of inestimable value for 50 obsolete destroyers, worth (according to the President) about $40,000 or $50,000 apiece. Furthermore, the number of bases suggested by the President exceeded the number the British had initially had in mind. Disliking the whole idea of a trade or a deal, Churchill went ahead and announced to Parliament on August 20, without first consulting the President, that Britain would lease some bases to the United States and that the British and American democracies "will have to be somewhat mixed up together in some of their affairs for mutual and general advantage." He also stated that in the event that Britain were seized by Germany, the government would provide for the naval security of Canada and the Dominions and made sure that they would carry on the struggle.[70]

The Prime Minister's unilateral announcement upset plans in Washington and almost dissuaded the President from going ahead with the transfer. Roosevelt's keen political judgment convinced him that the only way the Congress and the American public could really be sold on the transfer of the destroyers was to convince them that their President had pulled off a shrewd Yankee horse trade, getting the better of the deal. Churchill's precipitate announcement almost eliminated the possibility of such an impression.

As a matter of fact the British suspected that this was the President's plan, and they did not much like it. Ambassador Kennedy quoted Lord Beaverbrook (British defense minister) as saying:

> If we are going to make a gift, well and good; if we are going to make a bargain, I don't want to make a bad one, and this is definitely a bad one.[71]

Kennedy went on to comment that "another opinion has been advanced that the President will make political capital out of getting these valuable bases for destroyers that are worth nothing to anybody except England for a few months and if this is the case, then England should stand out for a better deal."

> Don't misunderstand me, England never gets the impression they are licked and therefore they can never understand why they should not get the best of a trade.[72]

A great deal of complicated bargaining during the next two weeks finally resulted in a compromise settlement which in some sense satisfied both sides. To eliminate the possibility of criticism for having been taken in a horse trade, Churchill insisted that his government grant as a gift the lease of space for bases on the Avalon Peninsula, the southern coast of Newfoundland and on the east coast, the Great Bay of Bermuda. Leases on the rest of the bases were exchanged for naval and military equipment to be transferred from the United States to Great Britain.[73] The President persisted in his efforts to convince the public and hostile political critics that he was making an exceedingly advantageous swap. He wrote to Senator David I. Walsh, a confirmed isolationist and chairman of the Naval Affairs Committee, to try and convince him that the "deal" was a good one, and necessary to our national defense. He wanted to persuade Walsh that among other things the deal was not politically disastrous, which was apparently one of the senator's convictions, but that it should be understood as an action of the Commander in Chief, acting in the interest of national defense, and above partisan politics.

President Franklin D. Roosevelt
Letter to Senator David I. Walsh
Explaining the Destroyer Deal
August 22, 1940

E. Roosevelt, II, 1056-57.

The White House,
Aug. 22, 1940

Dear Dave: Here is the real meat in the coconut as expressed to me by a Dutchess County farmer yesterday morning. I told him the gist of the proposal which is, in effect, to buy ninety-nine year leases from Great Britain for at least seven naval and air bases in British Colonial possessions—not including the Dominion of Canada, which is a separate study on my part. The farmer replied somewhat as follows:

"Say, ain't you the Commander-in-Chief? If you are and own fifty muzzle-loadin' rifles of the Civil War period, you would be a chump if you declined to exchange them for seven modern machine guns—wouldn't you?"

Frankly, my difficulty is that as President and as Commander-in-Chief I have no right to think of politics in the sense of being a candidate or desiring votes. You and I know that our weakness in the past has lain in the fact that from Newfoundland to Trinidad our sole protection offshore lies in the three contiguous Islands of Porto Rico, St. Thomas and St. Croix. That, in the nature of modern warfare, is a definite operating handicap. If for fifty ships, which are on their last legs anyway, we can get the right to put in naval and air bases in Newfoundland, Bermuda, the Bahamas, Jamaica, St. Lucia, Trinidad and British Guiana, then our operating deficiency is largely cured.

Naturally, knowing the situation in all of these places intimately, I do not want the United States to assume control over the civilian populations on these Islands. In the first place, they do not want to live under the American Flag, and, in the second place, the civilian populations would be a drain on the national treasury, would create all kinds of tariff involvements in the Senate and House, and give future generations of Americans a headache.

Honestly, Dave, these Islands are of the utmost importance to our national defense as naval and air operating bases.

In regard to German retaliation, I think you can rest quietly on that score. If Germany, at the conclusion of this war or before that, wants to fight us, Germany will do so on any number of trumped-up charges.

Finally, I hope you will not forget that the founder of the Democratic Party purchased Louisiana from a belligerent nation, France, while France was at war with England. He did this without even consulting the Congress. He put the deal through and later on he asked the House Committee on Appropriations to put $15,000,000 into the appropriation bill.

By the way, the fifty destroyers are the same type of ship which we have been from time to time striking from the naval list and selling for scrap for, I think, $4,000 or $5,000 per destroyer. On that basis, the cost of the right to at least seven naval and air bases is an extremely low one from the point of view of the United States Government—i.e., about $250,000!

I do hope you will not oppose the deal which, from the point of view of the United States, I regard as being the finest thing for the nation that has been done in your lifetime and mine. I am absolutely certain that this particular deal will not get us into war and, incidentally, that we are not going into war anyway unless Germany wishes to attack us.

I hope to see you very soon.

    Always sincerely,

A brilliant opinion written by Attorney General Robert H. Jackson, dated August 27, 1940, probably added the final link in the argument that convinced the President to act. The opinion is a magnificent *tour de force* and an important watershed in the development of presidential power in the mid-century period. Not only does Jackson expertly dispose of the problem of statutory restrictions to the deal, but he asserts a modern construction of presidential power which from that point on guided its wartime and postwar development. Moreover the attorney general's (he later became a Supreme Court justice) opinion was the first important statement since Alexander Hamilton's *Pacificus* papers were published in 1793 to justify an action based upon the combined powers of the President as Commander in Chief and Chief Diplomat. Lincoln had not tapped this rich dual vein of power in any of his wartime activities, and even Wilson had not relied upon it in his postwar efforts to win support for the Versailles Treaty.

In his opinion the attorney general referred to the "plenary powers of the President as Commander-in-Chief of the Army and Navy and as the head of the state in its relations with foreign countries," asserting that the sweep of these combined powers provided adequate constitutional authority for the President to negotiate the destroyer deal without the authorization of Congress. His arguments rested heavily upon the then recent United States *v.* Curtiss Wright Export Corporation decision by the Supreme Court, which defined executive power in the area of foreign affairs more broadly than it had ever before been defined in American history. The decision referred to "the very delicate, plenary and exclusive power of the President as the sole organ of the Federal Government in the field of international relations—a power which does not require for its exercise an Act of Congress. . . ."[74]

Attorney General Jackson cited the statutes and decisions which certified such actions, and then turned to the more technical and legal problems involved in the transfer of the destroyers and the other implements of war specified by the British Prime Minister. He outlined very simple procedures whereby the transaction could be made in compliance with existing statutes and rulings of the courts. He recommended finally:

(a) That the proposed arrangement may be concluded as an Executive agreement, effective without awaiting ratification.

(b) That there is Presidential power to transfer title and possession of the proposed considerations upon certification of appropriate officers. . . .[75]

When one added to this sweeping definition of the power of the President as Commander in Chief of the Armed Forces, there was hardly any impediment to his right to transfer 50 obsolete navy destroyers and certain other obsolescent military weapons and equipment to Great Britain in exchange for air and naval bases vital to our national security. The power of the President to act as the official charged with the chief responsibility for national security, complimented with his role as the principle organ of foreign affairs, totally encompassed the action he took.

Attorney General Robert H. Jackson
Decision Submitted to President Roosevelt
Asserting the Legality of Certain Presidential Actions
August 27, 1940

Rosenman, IX, 394-405.

My Dear Mr. President: In accordance with your request I have considered your constitutional and statutory authority to proceed by Executive agreement with the British Government immediately to acquire for the United States certain off-shore naval and air bases in the Atlantic Ocean without awaiting the inevitable delays which would accompany the conclusion of a formal treaty.

The essential characteristics of the proposal are:

(a) The United States to acquire rights for immediate establishment and use of naval and air bases in Newfoundland, Bermuda, the Bahamas, Jamaica, St. Lucia, Trinidad, the British Guiana; such rights to endure for a period of 99 years and to include adequate provisions for access to, and defense of, such bases and appropriate provisions for their control.

(b) In consideration it is proposed to transfer to Great Britain the title and possession of certain over-age ships and obsolescent military materials now the property of the United States, and certain other small patrol boats which though nearly completed are already obsolescent.

(c) Upon such transfer all obligation of the United States is discharged. The acquisition consists only of rights, which the United States may exercise or not at its option, and if exercised may abandon without consent. The privilege of maintaining such bases is subject only to limitations necessary to reconcile United States use with the sovereignty retained by Great Britain. Our Government assumes no responsibility for civil administration of any territory. It makes no promise to erect structures, or maintain forces at any point. It undertakes no defense of the possessions of any country. In short it acquires optional bases which may be developed as Congress appropriates funds therefor, but the United States does not assume any continuing or future obligation, commitment, or alliance.

The questions of constitutional and statutory authority, with which alone I am concerned, seem to be these:

First. May such an acquisition be concluded by the President under an Executive agreement or must it be negotiated as a Treaty subject to ratification by the Senate?

Second. Does authority exist in the President to alienate the title to such ships and obsolescent materials, and if so, on what conditions?

Third. Do the statutes of the United States limit the right to deliver the so-called mosquito boats now under construction or the over-age destroyers by reason of the belligerent status of Great Britain?

I

There is, of course, no doubt concerning the authority of the President to negotiate with the British Government for the proposed exchange. The only questions that might be raised in connection therewith are (1) whether the arrangement must be put in the form of a treaty and await ratification by the Senate or (2) whether there must be additional legislation by the Congress. Ordinarily (and assuming the absence of enabling legislation) the question whether such an agreement can be concluded under Presidential authority or whether it must await ratification by a two-thirds vote of the United States Senate involves consideration of two powers which the Constitution vests in the President.

One of these is the power of the Commander in Chief of the Army and Navy of the United States, which is conferred upon the President by the Constitution but is not defined or limited. Happily, there has been little occasion in our history for the interpretation of the powers of the President as Commander in Chief of the Army and Navy. I do not find it necessary to rest upon that power alone to sustain the present proposal. But it will hardly be open to controversy that the vesting of such a function in the President also places upon him a responsibility to use all constitutional authority which he may possess to provide adequate bases and stations for the utilization of the naval and air weapons of the United States at their highest efficiency in our defense. It seems equally beyond doubt that present world conditions forbid him to risk any delay that is constitutionally avoidable.

The second power to be considered is that control of foreign relations which the Constitution vests in the President as a part of the Executive function. The nature and extent of this power has recently been explicitly and authoritatively defined by Mr. Justice Sutherland, writing for the Supreme Court. In 1936, in *United States* v. *Curtiss-Wright Export Corp., et al.* (299 U.S. 304), he said:

> It is important to bear in mind that we are here dealing not alone with an authority vested in the President by an exertion of legislative power, but with such an authority plus the very delicate, plenary, and exclusive power

of the President as the sole organ of the Federal Government in the field of international relations—a power which does not require as a basis for its exercise an act of Congress, but which, of course, like every other governmental power, much be exercised in subordination to the applicable provisions of the Constitution. It is quite apparent that if, in the maintenance of our international relations, embarrassment—perhaps serious embarrassment—is to be avoided and success for our aims achieved, congressional legislation which is to be made effective through negotiation and inquiry within the international field must often accord to the President a degree of discretion and freedom from statutory restriction which would not be admissible were domestic affairs alone involved. Moreover, he, not Congress, has the better opportunity of knowing the conditions which prevail in foreign countries, and especially is this true in time of war. He has his confidential sources of information. He has his agents in the form of diplomatic, consular, and other officials. Secrecy in respect of information gathered by them may be highly necessary, and the premature disclosure of it productive of harmful results.

The President's power over foreign relations while "delicate, plenary, and exclusive" is not unlimited. Some negotiations involve commitments as to the future which would carry an obligation to exercise powers vested in the Congress. Such Presidential arrangements are customarily submitted for ratification by a two-thirds vote of the Senate before the future legislative power of the country is committed. However, the acquisitions which you are proposing to accept are without express or implied promises on the part of the United States to be performed in the future. The consideration, which we later discuss, is completed upon transfer of the specified items. The Executive agreement obtains an opportunity to establish naval and air bases for the protection of our coast line but it imposes no obligation upon the Congress to appropriate money to improve the opportunity. It is not necessary for the Senate to ratify an opportunity that entails no obligation.

There are precedents which might be cited, but not all strictly pertinent. The proposition falls far short in magnitude of the acquisition by President Jefferson of the Louisiana Territory from a belligerent during a European war, the Congress later appropriating the consideration and the Senate later ratifying a treaty embodying the agreement.

I am also reminded that in 1850, Secretary of State Daniel Webster acquired Horse Shoe Reef, at the entrance of Buffalo Harbor, upon condition that the United States would engage to erect a lighthouse and maintain a light but would erect no fortification thereon. This was done without awaiting legislative authority. Subsequently, the Congress made appropriations for the lighthouse, which was erected in 1856. *Malloy, Treaties and Conventions* (Vol. I, p. 663).

It is not believed, however, that it is necessary here to rely exclusively upon your constitutional power. As pointed out hereinafter (in discussing the second question), I think there is also ample statutory authority to support the acquisition of these bases, and the precedents perhaps most nearly in point are the numerous acquisitions of rights in foreign countries for sites of diplomatic and consular establishments—perhaps also the trade agreements recently negotiated under statutory authority and the acquisition in 1903 of the coaling and naval stations and rights in Cuba under the act of March 2, 1901 (h. 803, 31 Stat. 895, 898). In the last-mentioned case the agreement was subsequently embodied in a treaty but it was only one of a number of undertakings, some clearly of a nature to be dealt with ordinarily by treaty, and the statute had required "that by way of further assurance the Government of Cuba will embody the foregoing provisions in a permanent treaty with the United States."

The transaction now proposed represents only an exchange with no statutory requirement for the embodiment thereof in any treaty and involving no promises or undertakings by the United States that might raise the question of the propriety of incorporation in a treaty. I therefore advise that acquisition by Executive agreement of the rights proposed to be conveyed to the United States by Great Britain will not require ratification by the Senate.

II

The right of the President to dispose of vessels of the Navy and unneeded naval material finds clear recognition in at least two enactments of the Congress and a decision of the Supreme Court—and any who assert that the authority does not exist must assume the burden of establishing that both the Congress and the Supreme Court meant something less than the clear import of seemingly plain language.

By section 5 of the act of March 3, 1883 (c. 141, 22 Stat. 582, 599-600 (U. S. C., title 34, sec. 492)), the Congress placed restrictions upon the methods to be followed by the Secretary of the Navy in disposing of naval vessels, which have been found unfit for further use and stricken from the naval registry, but by the last clause of the section recognized and confirmed such a right in the President free from such limitations. It provides:

> But no vessel of the Navy shall hereafter be sold in any other manner than herein provided, or for less than such appraised value, *unless the President of the United States shall otherwise direct in writing.* [Italics supplied]

In *Levinson* v. *United States* (258 U.S. 198, 201), the Supreme Court said of this statute that "the power of the President to direct a departure from the statute is not confined to a sale for less than the appraised value but extends to the manner of the sale," and that "the word 'unless' qualifies both the requirements of the concluding clause."

So far as concerns this statute, in my opinion it leaves the President as Commander-in-Chief of the Navy free to make such disposition of naval vessels as he finds necessary in the public interest, and I find nothing that would indicate that the Congress has tried to limit the President's plenary powers to vessels already stricken from the naval registry. The President, of course, would exercise his powers only under the high sense of responsibility which follows his rank as Commander-in-Chief of his Nation's defense forces.

Furthermore, I find in no other statute or in the decisions any attempted limitations upon the plenary powers of the President as Commander-in-Chief of the Army and Navy and as the head of the state in its relations with foreign countries to enter into the proposed arrangements for the transfer to the British Government of certain over age destroyers and obsolescent military materials except the limitations recently imposed by section 14 (a) of the act of June 28, 1940 (Public, No. 671). This section, it will be noted, clearly recognizes the authority to make transfers and seeks only to impose certain restrictions thereon. The section reads as follows:

> Sec. 14. (a) Notwithstanding the provision of any other law, no military or naval weapon, ship, boat, aircraft, munitions, supplies, or equipment, to which the United States has title, in whole or in part, or which have been contracted for, shall hereafter be transferred, exchanged, sold, or otherwise disposed of in any manner whatsoever unless the Chief of Naval Operations in the case of naval material, and the Chief of Staff of the Army in the case of military material, shall first certify that such material is not essential to the defense of the United States.

Thus to prohibit action by the constitutionally created Commander-in-Chief except upon authorization of a statutory officer subordinate in rank is of questionable constitutionality. However, since the statute requires certification only of matters as to which you would wish, irrespective of the statute, to be satisfied, and as the legislative history of the section indicates that no arbitrary restriction is intended, it seems unnecessary to raise the question of constitutionality which such a provision would otherwise invite.

I am informed that the destroyers involved here are the survivors of a fleet of over 100 built at about the same time and under the same design. During the year 1930, 58 of these were decommissioned with a view toward scrapping and a corresponding number were recommissioned as replacements. Usable material and equipment from the 58 vessels removed from the service were transferred to the recommissioned vessels to recondition and modernize them, and other usable material and equipment were removed and the vessels stripped. They were then stricken from the Navy Register, and 50 of them were sold as scrap for prices ranging from $5,260 to $6,800 per vessel, and the remaining 8 were used for such purposes as target vessels, experimental construction tests, and temporary barracks. The surviving destroyers now under consideration have been reconditioned and are in service, but all of them are over age, most of them by several years.

In construing this statute in its application to such a situation it is important to note that this subsection as originally proposed in the Senate bill provided that the appropriate staff officer shall first certify that "such material is not essential to and cannot be used in the defense of the United States." Senator Barkley and others objected to the subsection as so worded on the ground that it would prevent the release and exchange of surplus or used planes and other supplies for sale to the British and that it would consequently nullify the provisions of the bill (see sec. 1 of the act of July 2, 1940, H.R. 9850, Public, No. 703) which the Senate had passed several days earlier for that very purpose. Although Senator Walsh stated that he did not think the proposed subsection had that effect, he agreed to strike out the words "and cannot be used." Senator Barkley observed that he thought the modified language provided "a much more elastic term." Senator Walsh further stated that he would bear in mind in conference the views of Senator Barkley and others, and that he had "no desire or purpose to go beyond the present law, but to have some certificate filed as to whether the property is surplus or not" (Congressional Record, June 21, 1940, pp. 13370-13371).

In view of this legislative history it is clear that the Congress did not intend to prevent the certification for transfer, exchange, sale, or disposition of property merely because it is still used or usable or of possible value for future use. The statute does not contemplate mere transactions in scrap, yet exchange or sale except as scrap would hardly be possible if confined to material whose usefulness is entirely gone. It need only be certified as not essential, and "essential," usually the equivalent of vital or indispensable, falls far short of "used" or "usable."

Moreover, as has been indicated, the congressional authorization is not merely of a sale, which might imply only a cash transaction. It also authorizes equipment to be "transferred," "exchanged," or "otherwise disposed of"; and in connection with material of this kind for which there is no open market value is never absolute but only relative—and chiefly related to what may be had in exchange or replacement.

In view of the character of the transactions contemplated, as well as the legislative history, the conclusion is inescapable that the Congress has not sought by section 14 (a) to impose an arbitrary limitation upon the judgment of the highest staff officers as to whether a transfer, exchange, or other disposition of specific items would impair our essential defenses. Specific items must be weighed in relation to our total defense position before and after an exchange or disposition. Any other construction would be virtual prohibition of any sale, exchange, or disposition of material or supplies so long as they were capable of use, however ineffective, and such a prohibition obviously was not, and was not intended to be, written into the law.

It is my opinion that in proceeding under section 14 (a) appropriate staff officers may and should consider remaining useful life, strategic importance, obsolescence, and all other factors affecting defense value, not only with respect to what the Government of the United States gives up in any exchange or transfer, but also with respect to what the Government receives. In this situation good business sense is good legal sense.

I therefore advise that the appropriate staff officers may, and should, certify under section 14 (a) that ships and material involved in a sale or exchange are not essential to the defense of the United States if in their judgment the consummation of the transaction does not impair or weaken the total defense of the United States, and certainly so where the consummation of the arrangement will strengthen the total defensive position of the Nation.

With specific reference to the proposed agreement with the Government of Great Britain for the acquisition of naval and air bases, it is my opinion that the Chief of Naval Operations may, and should, certify under section 14 (a) that the destroyers involved are not essential to the defense of the United States if in his judgment the exchange of such destroyers for such naval and air bases will strengthen rather than impair the total defense of the United States.

I have previously indicated that in my opinion there is statutory authority for the acquisition of the naval and air bases in exchange for the vessels and material. The question was not more fully discussed at that point because dependent upon the statutes above treated and which required consideration in this section of the opinion. It is to be borne in mind that these statutes clearly recognize and deal with the authority to make dispositions by sale, transfer, exchange, or otherwise; that they do not impose any limitations concerning individuals, corporations, or governments to which such dispositions may be made; and that they do not specify or limit in any manner the considerations which may enter into an exchange. There is no reason whatever for holding that sales may not be made to or exchanges made with a foreign government or that in such a case a treaty is contemplated. This is emphasized when we consider that the transactions in some cases may be quite unimportant, perhaps only dispositions of scrap, and that a domestic buyer (unless restrained by some authorized contract or embargo) would be quite free to dispose of his purchase as he pleased. Furthermore, section 14 (a) of the act of June 28, 1940, supra, was enacted by the Congress in full contemplation of transfers for ultimate delivery to foreign belligerent nations. Possibly it may be said that the authority for exchange of naval vessels and material presupposes the acquisition of something of value to the Navy or, at least, to the national defense. Certainly I can imply no narrower limitation when the law is wholly silent in this respect. Assuming that there is, however, at least the limitation which I have mentioned, it is fully met in the acquisition of rights to maintain needed bases. And if, as I hold, the statute law authorizes the exchange of vessels and material for other vessels and material or, equally, for the right to establish bases, it is an inescapable corollary that the statute law also authorizes the acquisition of the ships or material or bases which form the consideration for the exchange.

Whether the statutes of the United States prevent the dispatch to Great Britain, a belligerent power, of the so-called "mosquito boats" now under construction or the over-age destroyers depends upon the interpretation to be placed on section 3 of title V of the act of June 15, 1917 (c. 30, 40 Stat. 217, 222). This section reads:

> During a war in which the United States is a neutral nation, it shall be unlawful to send out of the jurisdiction of the United States any vessel, built, armed, or equipped as a vessel of war, or converted from a private vessel into a vessel of war, with any intent or under any agreement or contract, written or oral, that such vessel shall be delivered to a belligerent nation, or to an agent, officer, or citizen of such nation, or with reasonable cause to believe that the said vessel shall or will be employed in the service of any such belligerent nation after its departure from the jurisdiction of the United States.

This section must be read in the light of section 2 of the same act and the rules of international law which the Congress states that it was its intention to implement (H. Rept. No. 30, 65th Cong., 1st sess., p. 9). So read, it is clear that it is inapplicable to vessels, like the overage destroyers, which were not built, armed, equipped as, or converted into, vessels of war with the intent that they should enter the service of a belligerent. If the section were not so construed, it would render meaningless section 2 of the act which authorizes the President to detain any armed vessel until he is satisfied that it will not engage in hostile operations before it reaches a neutral or belligerent port. The two sections are intelligible and reconcilable only if read in light of the traditional rules of international law. These are clearly stated by Oppenheim in his work on International Law (5th ed., vol. 2, sec. 334, pp. 574-576):

> Whereas a neutral is in nowise obliged by his duty of impartiality to prevent his subjects from selling armed vessels to the belligerents, such armed vessels being merely contraband of war, a neutral is bound to employ the means at his disposal to prevent his subjects from building, fitting out, or arming, to the order of either belligerent, vessels intended to be used as men-of-war, and to prevent the departure from his jurisdiction of any vessel which, by order of either belligerent, has been adopted to warlike use. The difference between selling armed vessels to belligerents and building them to order is usually defined in the following way:
>
> An armed ship, being contraband of war, is in nowise different from other kinds of contraband, provided that she is not manned in a neutral port, so that she can commit hostilities at once after having reached the open sea. A subject of a neutral who builds an armed ship, or arms a merchantman, not to the order of a belligerent, but intending to sell her to a belligerent, does not differ from a manufacturer of arms who intends to sell them to a belligerent. There is nothing to prevent a neutral from allowing his subjects to sell armed vessels, to deliver them to belligerents, either in a neutral port or in a belligerent port. . . .
>
> On the other hand, if a subject of a neutral builds armed ships to the order of a belligerent, he prepares the means of naval operations, since the ships, on sailing outside the neutral territorial waters and taking in a crew and ammunition, can at once commit hostilities. Thus, through the carrying out of the order of the belligerent, the neutral territory has been made the base of naval operations; and as the duty of impartiality includes an obligation to prevent either belligerent from making neutral territory the base of military or naval operations, a neutral violates his neutrality by not preventing his subjects from carrying out an order of a belligerent for the building and fitting out of men-of-war. This distinction, although of course logically correct, is hairsplitting. But as, according to the present law, neutral States need not prevent their subjects from supplying arms and ammunition to belligerents, it will probably continue to be drawn.

Viewed in the light of the above, I am of the opinion that this statute does prohibit the release and transfer to the British Government of the so-called mosquito boats now under construction for the United States Navy. If these boats were released to the British Government, it would be legally impossible for that Government to take them out of this country after their completion, since to the extent of such completion at least they would have been built, armed, or equipped with the intent, or with reasonable cause to believe, that they would enter the service of a belligerent after being sent out of the jurisdiction of the United States.

This will not be true, however, with respect to the overage destroyers, since they were clearly not built, armed, or equipped with any such intent or with reasonable cause to believe that they would ever enter the service of a belligerent.

In this connection it has been noted that during the war between Russia and Japan in 1904 and 1905, the German Government permitted the sale to Russia of torpedo boats and also of ocean liners belonging to its auxiliary navy. See Wheaton's International Law, 6th ed. (Keith), vol. 2, p. 977.

IV

Accordingly, you are respectfully advised:

(a) That the proposed arrangement may be concluded as an Executive agreement, effective without awaiting ratification.

(b) That there is Presidential power to transfer title and possession of the proposed considerations upon certification by appropriate staff officers.

(c) That the dispatch of the so-called "mosquito boats" would constitute a violation of the statute law of the United States, but with that exception there is no legal obstacle to the consummation of the transaction, in accordance, of course, with the applicable provisions of the Neutrality Act as to delivery.

Respectfully submitted.

Robert H. Jackson
Attorney General

In a message to Congress on September 3, 1940, the President announced an exchange of notes between the representatives of Great Britain and the United States. The notes signified an executive agreement whereby the President, acting on his own authority, transferred the 50 destroyers to Great Britain in exchange for 99-year leases on air and naval bases on the islands of Newfoundland, Bermuda, the Bahamas, Jamaica, St. Lucia, Trinidad and Antigua. Roosevelt pointed out, as Churchill had insisted, that the bases on Newfoundland and Bermuda were gifts of the British government, while the other leases were exchanged for the destroyers. The exchange of letters between the two governments authenticated that agreement.

British Ambassador Lord Lothian
Letter to Secretary of State Cordell Hull
On the Exchange of Destroyers for Bases
September 2, 1940

Rosenman, IX, 392-93.

British Embassy,
Washington, D.C.
September 2, 1940

The Honourable Cordell Hull,
Secretary of State of the United States,
Washington, D.C.

Sir: I have the honour under instructions from His Majesty's Principal Secretary of State for Foreign Affairs to inform you that in view of the friendly and sympathetic interest of His Majesty's Government in the United Kingdom in the national security of the United States and their desire to strengthen the ability of the United States to cooperate effectively with other nations of the Americas in the defence of the Western Hemisphere, His Majesty's Government will secure the grant to the Government of the United States, freely and without consideration, of the lease for immediate establishment and use of naval and air bases and facilities for entrance thereto and the operation and protection thereof, on the Avalon Peninsula and on the southern coast of Newfoundland, and on the east coast and on the Great Bay of Bermuda.

Furthermore, in view of the above and in view of the desire of the United States to acquire additional air and naval bases in the Caribbean and in British Guiana, and without endeavouring to place a monetary or commercial value upon the many tangible and intangible rights and properties involved, His Majesty's Government will make available to the United States for immediate establishment and use naval and air bases and facilities for entrance thereto and the operation and protection thereof, on the eastern side of the Bahamas, the southern coast of Jamaica, the western coast of St. Lucia, the west coast of Trinidad in the Gulf of Paria, in the island of Antigua and in British Guiana within fifty miles of Georgetown, in exchange for naval and military equipment and material which the United States Government will transfer to His Majesty's Government.

All the bases and facilities referred to in the preceding paragraphs will be leased to the United States for a period of ninety-nine years, free from all rent and charges other than such compensation to be mutually agreed on to be paid by the United States in order to compensate the owners of private property for loss by expropriation or damage arising out of the establishment of the bases and facilities in question.

His Majesty's Government, in the leases to be agreed upon, will grant to the United States for the period of the leases all the rights, power, and authority within the bases leased, and within the limits of the territorial waters and air spaces adjacent to or in the vicinity of such bases, necessary to provide access to and defence of such bases, and appropriate provisions for their control.

Without prejudice to the above-mentioned rights of the United States authorities and their jurisdiction within the leased areas, the adjustment and reconciliation between the jurisdiction of the authorities of the United States within these areas and the jurisdiction of the authorities of the territories in which these areas are situated, shall be determined by common agreement.

The exact location and bounds of the aforesaid bases, the necessary seaward, coast and antiaircraft defences, the location of sufficient military garrisons, stores, and other necessary auxiliary facilities shall be determined by common agreement.

His Majesty's Government are prepared to designate immediately experts to meet with experts of the United States for these purposes. Should these experts be unable to agree in any particular situation, except in the case of Newfoundland and Bermuda, the matter shall be settled by the Secretary of State of the United States and His Majesty's Secretary of State for Foreign Affairs.

I have the honour to be, with the highest consideration, Sir,

Your most obedient, humble servant,

Lothian

Secretary of State Cordell Hull
Reply to British Ambassador Lord Lothian
On the Exchange of Destroyers for Bases
September 2, 1940

Rosenman, IX, 394.

Department of State,
Washington, September 2, 1940

His Excellency the Right Honorable
The Marquess of Lothian, C.H.,
British Ambassador

Excellency: I have received your note of September 2, 1940.

I am directed by the President to reply to your note as follows:

The Government of the United States appreciates the declarations and the generous action of His Majesty's Government as contained in your communication

which are destined to enhance the national security of the United States and greatly
to strengthen its ability to cooperate effectively with the other nations of the
Americas in the defense of the Western Hemisphere. It therefore gladly accepts the
proposals.

The Government of the United States will immediately designate experts to
meet with experts designated by His Majesty's Government to determine upon the
exact location of the naval and air bases mentioned in your communication under
acknowledgment.

In consideration of the declarations above quoted, the Government of the
United States will immediately transfer to His Majesty's Government fifty United
States Navy destroyers generally referred to as the twelve hundred-ton type.

Accept, Excellency, the renewed assurances of my highest consideration.

Cordell Hull

The academic authorities were divided in their opinions as to the legality of the
attorney general's arguments and the President's subsequent decision to act. One
editor of the *American Journal of International Law* was convinced that "the
President has ample statutory authority to dispose of destroyers under the
conditions which existed, and he has ample authority under the Constitution to
acquire naval bases by the method of executive agreement."[76] Another editor of the
same journal was in complete disagreement, arguing that "the transaction was
sustained under statutes which hardly bear the construction placed upon them."[77]

Most of the arguments involved technicalities in the statutes cited in the
attorney general's opinion as well as various questions of international law. But
neither Jackson nor Roosevelt was at all interested in those questions. The attorney
general later revealed that his position was simply that Hitler's repeated violations
of international law justified retaliatory action by the United States, even at the cost
of risking our neutral status.[78] History has vindicated that decision, Charles A.
Beard notwithstanding, but in searching for the constitutional basis to authorize the
action, Jackson grafted two areas of executive responsibility into a third and more
awesome power which has since been seen reflected time and time again in the hot
and cold war actions of the mid-century Presidents.

Edward S. Corwin was so alarmed by this Hamiltonian resurgency of the
theory of executive prerogative that he described it as "an argument which
empowers the President, as Commander-in-Chief—and as organ of foreign
relations—to ride high, wide, and handsome over the legislative powers of the
Nation whenever he deems it desirable to do so."[79] In an earlier letter to *The New
York Times*, Corwin levelled even more serious charges against the President and
his attorney general:

> As a departure from neutral status, the President's action was a step
> toward belligerent status—a step toward war—and as such was an
> invasion of Congress's constitutional "power to declare war."
>
> Finally, as the President's action confronts us today it purports to be

justified by an opinion of the Attorney General which bases the President's action upon his vague, undefined powers as the Commander-in-Chief of the armed forces and as the organ of foreign relations and which impliedly represents those powers as capable of setting at naught the specifically delegated constitutional powers of Congress.

This opinion is thus an endorsement of unrestrained autocracy in the field of our foreign relations, neither more nor less. No such dangerous opinion was ever before penned by an Attorney General of the United States.[80]

Corwin, I think, ignores the inevitable and necessary evolution of presidential power and the growth of political institutions in the mid-twentieth century, which were based upon and also justified by certain general technological and social developments in society. World War II continued these developments and gave birth to a series of technological and social revolutions which show no sign of abating. Political institutions and practices which were satisfactory in the nineteenth century and even in the early part of the twentieth century were no longer adequate to cope with the hydrogen bomb and the worldwide social revolution in progress. Foreign affairs and military power became central foci of executive responsibility in this period, and wishful or nostalgic thinking could not eliminate the realities of the situation. Political restraints upon absolute power are essential, but the mid-century Presidents, unlike their nineteenth century predecessors, had to make almost instantaneous decisions, followed by immediate actions, frequently in the area of foreign affairs or national security—decisions and actions that were unthinkable and unnecessary in an earlier period. The Jackson opinion in the destroyer deal articulated the political and constitutional framework within which these developments in presidential practice could take place.

And yet Professor Corwin raised serious questions which continue to haunt us in the present decades. Even if Roosevelt's decision was the right one and the circumstances justified his extraordinary decision, it was undoubtedly the beginning of a period in which the continuous and incremental expansion of presidential power and the concomitant erosion of congressional power and responsibility, let loose grave problems for the future. In the past, Roosevelt had been very conscious of the importance of obtaining congressional support in situations when new areas of activity were being considered, or departures from normal operating procedures were contemplated. In this instance, however, the precarious state of British defenses and the near certainty of an attempted Nazi invasion prompted the President to circumvent all obstacles which might have led to further delays. A protracted congressional debate on the question during the weeks before the national presidential election would have further divided the country in a period when unity of purpose in the face of Hitler's threat was not only essential to national security, but also a *sine qua non* for the continued and courageous resistance of the British.

As the growth of presidential power increased during the next few decades, this broad and forceful interpretation of the combined powers of the Commander in Chief and the leader of foreign affairs would indeed, at times, exceed its proper constitutional limits. The desired "balance of powers" which the Founding Fathers sought to create would be violated time and again, as the same "necessary," but not anywhere near as justifiable, circumstances, would be advanced as reasons for its abandonment. At some point a stricter adherence to constitutional limits would have to be recognized and enforced if a balanced political system was to be kept from being transformed into a presidential monarchy. But where and how that line should be drawn is the continuing focus of this study.

Perhaps the solution lies not simply in imposing firmer restrictions on the power of the President, but rather in restoring the effectiveness of Congress in playing its constitutional role in a more balanced political system. In the final analysis it was not the thirst for or the improper aggrandizement of power on the part of the Executive which led to its inordinate use, but rather the complexity of problems in the world society to which, at times, the President was the only power capable of responding. If this is true, then it is not sufficient to focus entirely upon the growth and limits of presidential power, but one must, at the same time, explore the malfunctions of the political system which encourage such misuse of power.

The destroyer deal was unquestionably an important factor in the "Battle of Britain" during the dark days of 1940, when Britain stood alone and much of her naval strength had been destroyed or disabled. It is impossible to assess the destroyers' defensive value in purely naval terms, for certainly the destroyer deal gave the British a tremendous psychological boost at a time when it was badly needed. It was also a clear indication to the Axis powers of a greater and more significant commitment on the part of the United States to the defense of Britain. As Churchill told the House of Commons on September 5, 1940:

> I have no doubt Herr Hitler will not like this transference of destroyers, and I have no doubt that he will pay the United States out if he ever gets the chance. That is why I am very glad that the army, air, and naval frontiers of the United States have been advanced along a wide arc into the Atlantic Ocean, and this will enable them to take danger by the throat while it is still hundreds of miles from their homeland.[81]

Churchill's words were, of course, prophetic. The United States continued to advance her frontiers and ultimately her role as Britain's supporter, moving inexorably and irresistibly to the point of full participation in World War II. There was no conspiracy or immoral deception involved, as some have suggested, but simply a recognition on the part of the President, belated as it was, but also a good deal ahead of many of his countrymen, that the United States could not tolerate an Axis victory. It would have directly threatened our national security and challenged our national values. President Roosevelt honestly, but perhaps mistakenly, tried to defeat the Axis powers without direct intervention, but from the summer of 1940 on he took a number of decisive steps, beginning with the destroyer deal and followed by the Lend-Lease Act, on March 21, 1941, which not only committed this country to an Axis defeat, but, in hindsight, made our involvement in the war inevitable.

This was followed by the seizure of 65 Axis ships in American ports on March 30, 1941; an agreement with the Danish minister to the United States to occupy Greenland for defense purposes; an appeal to the French people not to support the

Nazi-dominated Vichy government, May 15, 1941; the declaration of a national "unlimited emergency," May 27, 1941. (He had previously declared a limited emergency on September 8, 1939 and ordered American naval ships to "sink on sight" any foreign submarine sighted in American "defensive waters.") All assets of Axis powers on deposit in the United States were frozen and an agreement with the government of Iceland for the United States to take over Great Britain's role as the defender of that island country for the remainder of the emergency was announced. Roosevelt proceeded to meet with Churchill at sea where they announced the "Atlantic Charter," postwar peace aims of Great Britain and the United States, August 14, 1941; announced that "henceforth American patrols would defend the freedom of the seas by striking first at all Axis raiders ("Rattlesnakes of the Atlantic") operating within American defense areas, September 11, 1941; shooting orders were issued to United States warships in the Atlantic to destroy any German or Italian sea or air forces encountered, in retaliation for the shelling and torpedoing of American ships in the North Atlantic by Nazi submarines, October 8, 1941; promised lend-lease aid to the Soviet Union on the basis that the defense of the Russians against the Nazi invaders was essential to the defense of the United States. [These actions, among others, are cited by Edward S. Corwin, *Total War and the Constitution* (New York, 1947), 29-31.] The 1941 declaration of war by Congress, following the Japanese attack on Pearl Harbor, was not the real beginning of the war, but rather an ending to a series of courageous and necessary executive actions which history is bound to justify rather than condemn.

Throughout the prewar period and certainly during the war itself, the President of the United States continued to utilize and sometimes to expand the newly fused powers of Commander in Chief and Chief Diplomat. [See Corwin, *Total War and the Constitution* and also his "Some Aspects of the Presidency," in *Public Policy in a World at War*, Annals of the American Academy of Political and Social Science, Vol. 218, November 1941. In both instances Corwin is very pessimistic about the escalation of the war and, subsequently, the peace powers of the President. His warnings had a prescient character to them as subsequent developments have indicated.] The Jackson rationale was an important point of departure and a continuing source of support for reinforcing this concept, but of even greater significance were the increased and more complex pressures and responsibilities placed upon the nation and its President by virtue of the new role of world leadership which these events made inevitable.

Franklin D. Roosevelt — The Ultimate Decision-Maker

In World War I, American troops fought on European soil and, at least theoretically, under Allied command. In World War II this precedent was expanded considerably when American divisions saw action on four of the five continents, American vessels waged war against the Axis on every major body of water on the face of the globe and once again American armies, ships and aircraft operated under the Supreme Allied Command. This time however the United States was not inhibited by or apologetic for its late entry into the war, nor was it humbled in the councils of the Allies by the comparative meagerness of its human and material sacrifices and commitment. In fact the very size of its contribution guaranteed the United States a leading, if not a controlling, voice in the critical decisions of strategy and tactics to be made in the course of the war. The sheer magnitude of these decisions and their far reaching implications, military and political, brought about significant changes in the military establishment and its relationship to the Commander in Chief.

During the approximately 20-year period between the two World Wars, the army and the navy receded into the background position they had always occupied in American life. They remained small, professional and materially and technically undernourished. After the collapse of Wilson's idealistic peace plans American society reverted to its historic super-nationalism and isolationism, and these attitudes somewhat intensified as the war clouds developed in Europe. The New Deal administration which came into power in 1933 made some contributions to the neglected state of the military establishment during the Depression years, channelling relief funds and labor to rebuild and develop some of the larger military and naval bases. President Franklin D. Roosevelt, an ex-assistant secretary of the navy and a student of naval history, developed an easygoing, cooperative relationship with the leading figures in both services, a relationship that served the country in good stead during the war, but did not compensate during the interim for the lack of funds and personnel that would have kept the military services abreast of the Axis countries.

As the war clouds burst into conflict in Europe, the President characteristically responded by devious, yet well thought-out and essentially sound actions. Ever since the reforms introduced by Secretary of War Elihu Root in 1903, there had been, at least theoretically, a military coordinating agency, the Joint Army-Navy Board. President Wilson had summarily eliminated it in his first term in office, but the board was revived in the thirties, although it had certainly not developed into a dynamic center of interservice planning on a coordinated scale. But by 1939 President Roosevelt was fully aware that war was imminent, and taking advantage of the newly established Executive Office of the President, a catch-all presidential administrative blanket, he brought the joint board under his own direct supervision. That gave the President direct access to and control over the top military commanders of each of the services, and spurred them forward to engage in more significant planning and development on an interservice basis. On questions of military strategy and tactics the civilian secretaries of the services were usually bypassed by the President, and in the prewar period he tended to take a very strong hand in making overall policy decisions, frequently against the advice of his military leaders. In this period, as William Emerson has written, "Jealous of his powers and deeply sensitive to the swirling political tides within Washington and the country, Roosevelt was ever unwilling to share his authority. He meant to exercise his powers as commander in chief."[82]

In its new preferred position the joint board began to play a more important role in combined army and navy planning. Strategic plans were developed encompassing joint operations for both services in preparation for any eventuality; a Joint Intelligence Committee was created, though unfortunately, only on the eve of Pearl Harbor. It is now clear however that by 1939 and 1940 Roosevelt had discerned the full dimensions of the inherent threat to American freedom that a Nazi victory would have meant, and that he was moving steadily in the direction of leading the American people to understand the implications of this threat and what was necessary to confront it.

In 1939, 1940 and even in 1941, the United States was just beginning to awaken from a long period of complacency in international affairs; it was intellectually and spiritually, as well as militarily, unprepared to confront the realities of its world. The military was not that far ahead of the civilian population, but by 1940 leaders like General George C. Marshall were apprehensive about developments in the war in Europe, and were anxious that the United States prepare for any eventuality. Marshall, as chief of staff, undertook to educate the President on the current state of the American military establishment. The revival of the joint board and the importance placed upon it by the President and the military leaders was another sign of their reaction to the rapidly developing events in Europe. Largely through that mechanism, many months before Pearl Harbor, top American staff officers met secretly with their British counterparts and developed very preliminary hypothetical plans for potential Allied action against the Axis powers.

Several days after the Japanese attack on Pearl Harbor, British Prime Minister Winston Churchill sailed for the United States, accompanied by his top military leaders. They arrived at Hampton Roads, Virginia, some eight days later and went immediately to the White House, where several weeks of intensive military and political discussion was scheduled.

That was the famous Acadia Conference where many of the critical decisions that determined the fate of the world for the next few years were made. The overall objectives and priorities of the war were determined at that time, and it was also agreed that a combined military command with headquarters in Washington would be created, which, subject to the approval of the President and the British war cabinet, would have supreme control of all Allied troops, ships and planes in the war against the Axis powers. Once this Combined Chiefs of Staff (CCS) was created, the Americans realized with acute embarrassment that their own military house was not in order, or at least not in the kind of order in which the British military leaders, who were now committed to coordinate their planning and their fighting with the Americans, operated.

General George Marshall, chief of staff of the American army, was tremendously impressed with the superior and smoothly coordinated staff work that the British air, ground and naval forces exhibited at the Acadia Conference. To a large extent this was a result of the British Joint Chiefs of Staff organization, which was a coordinated military command responsible to the war cabinet. Shortly after the conference the Americans created their own Joint Chiefs of Staff to match their British counterparts and to jointly assume command over the Allied forces throughout the world. The American Joint Chiefs of Staff (JCS) was made up of Marshall, General H. H. "Hap" Arnold, Commanding General of the Army Air Forces, and Admirals Ernest J. King, commander in chief of the United States fleet, and Harold R. Stark, chief of naval operations. Admiral Stark was later shifted to London, and the JCS operated with three members until the President appointed

Admiral William D. Leahy, chief of staff to the President, in June 1942. Admiral Leahy served as the principal liaison officer between the Joint Chiefs and the President and also as nonvoting chairman of the JCS.

President Roosevelt relied heavily upon his military leaders for the major strategic and tactical decisions of the war. He listened carefully to their advice, and for the most part accepted it. Churchill was much more apt to overrule his military advisors and to involve himself deeply in the intricate, day-by-day decisions of the war. But that is not to say that President Roosevelt kept himself aloof from the military conduct of the war. He met regularly with the Joint Chiefs of Staff, and communicated with them daily through the active participation of Admiral Leahy. It would also be inaccurate to say that any influence moved entirely in one direction. The extremely close relationship between Roosevelt and the JCS throughout the war, particularly the mutual high respect and friendship which the President, General Marshall and Admiral Leahy enjoyed, enabled the Joint Chiefs to understand fully Roosevelt's overall concepts of the war and to plan and work within those clearly defined limitations. On several occasions the President disagreed with his military staff, and in those instances the President's decision prevailed. Perhaps the most important of these was the decision on *Torch*, the code name for the North African landing in 1942, first called 'Gymnast.'

When Prime Minister Churchill arrived in the United States for the Acadia Conference just about two weeks after Pearl Harbor, he carried with him and presented to the President three papers which he had prepared during his trip, and which more or less outlined his concept of the overall strategy of the war. The first paper in Churchill's words "assembled the arguments why our main objective for the campaign of 1942 in the European theatre should be the occupation of the whole coastline of Africa and of the Levant from Dakar to the Turkish frontier by British and American forces."[83] His other two papers dealt with the war in the Pacific and the ultimate invasion and liberation of Europe. All three were remarkably able military and political analyses, in many ways they were prophetic of events to come. Of particular concern were Churchill's efforts to convince Roosevelt and his chiefs of staff that a large scale Allied offensive in North and West Africa was essential in 1942, not simply to frustrate further German penetration into those areas, but in order to control the North African coastline from Tunis to Egypt to protect free passage of British and American ships through the Mediterranean to the Suez Canal and the Levant. In order to achieve this objective Churchill suggested that in addition to the considerable British forces then fighting in North Africa, 55,000 more British troops and "not less than 150,000 American men during the next six months" should be landed in African Atlantic ports.[84]

The Acadia Conference gave tentative approval to the North African operation for the spring of 1942 (it was given the code name 'Gymnast'), but it was only one of a multitude of general decisions about the war made at the conference, covering activities in almost every part of the world; the details for these campaigns were passed on to the various staffs for more rigorous analysis and planning. In the face of the severe losses of ships in the North Atlantic during the winter of 1941-42 and the need to divert shipping to both the Indian and Pacific Oceans because of the successes of the Japanese in that part of the world, 'Gymnast' was temporarily shelved early in 1942. At about the same time the American War Plans Division, headed by General Dwight D. Eisenhower, was drawing up a master plan for the invasion of Northern France by a direct assault across the channel. Having given the defeat of Germany top priority in the list of Allied objectives, the American military leaders were anxious to engage the enemy as soon as possible at a point where their maximum strength could be concentrated and exerted. They were also terribly anxious to move the rapidly expanding American army into action so they could begin to obtain the experience under fire so necessary to an army before sustaining a long, hard campaign. In addition to these considerations, it was also felt by the American planners that such an invasion in 1942 would take some of the pressure off the badly pressed Russian army on the eastern front.

Roosevelt dispatched Marshall and Harry Hopkins to London in April to attempt to get the support of Churchill and the British chiefs of staff for the American plan. Hopkins played an extraordinary role as a special emissary of the President throughout the war. During the New Deal he had been the chief troubleshooter, heading up one emergency agency after another, and finally going into the cabinet as secretary of commerce. Before 1940 Roosevelt had seriously been grooming Hopkins to succeed him, and at that time Hopkins himself had presidential ambitions. Roosevelt did all that was humanly possible to boost Hopkins' political popularity, without any real success. The former social worker from Grinnell, Iowa, had received too much public abuse throughout the years, abuse that was oftentimes directed at him because he was easier to get at than the President, and also because he had a sharp tongue and had made a great number of enemies, some of whom were newspaper columnists. It soon became clear that Hopkins would not make an ideal running mate, and he selflessly stepped aside and continued to work in behalf of Roosevelt's nomination and election. Shortly after the election he resigned from the President's official family, but was soon back in the White House as a member of Roosevelt's private family, complete with bed and board. He actually assumed the position of one of the new administrative assistants to the President.

As the war progressed Roosevelt relied more and more on Hopkins for top-level assignments in expediting production goals in industry on the home front and in conducting face-to-face conferences with Churchill and Stalin abroad. In fact, Hopkins' presence at such conferences was an assurance of Roosevelt's personal concern and attention, and something of a guarantee that the matter under discussion would get immediate and capable top-level attention. When Hopkins first travelled to Moscow shortly after Hitler's attack on the Soviet Union, Roosevelt wrote a personal note to Stalin saying, "I ask you to treat Mr. Hopkins with the identical confidence you would feel if you were talking directly to me,"[85] and he meant it. In this important role Hopkins made no small contribution to the successful development of the coordinated military command and to the success of the war. Churchill once dubbed him "Lord Root of the Matter" for his down-to-earth, concrete approach to problems.

After several days of conferences Marshall and Hopkins succeeded in convincing the British to endorse the series of plans which had been proposed by the American War Planning Board. The initial plans for the invasion (code-named

'Roundup,' later changed to 'Overlord') called for 30 American and 18 British divisions. The tremendous logistical task of building up the required invasion force went under the code name of 'Bolero,' and a conditional operation ('Sledgehammer'), a smaller landing was scheduled for the fall of 1942 if the plight of the Russian armies on the eastern front demanded such a diversion, or if the German defenses in Western Europe became so weakened by the drain of manpower to other fronts that they invited such an attack. Hopkins sensed that the British were convinced that 'Sledgehammer' would be suicidal if attempted that year regardless of the provocation, but that they had gone along with the idea anyway, hoping that this would soon become apparent to the Americans. What was more essential to the British than anything was to get the United States actively committed to a Europe-first policy in the war. And this principle was clearly established at the Acadia Conference.

'Gymnast,' the North African invasion, remained prominent in Prime Minister Churchill's mind, however, and as Secretary of War Henry Stimson reported, it was still the President's "secret baby." But the American chiefs of staff thought otherwise. As the number of American troops who had completed basic training increased, and as Marshall and the other American military leaders became somewhat anxious to confront the enemy and to test their forces under battle conditions, some strong differences of opinion began to develop between the American military and Prime Minister Churchill and his chiefs of staff. Six weeks after Marshall and Hopkins returned from Britain with a firm agreement to move ahead with all aspects of 'Overlord,' the Americans began to feel that the British were stalling and were determined to delay any invasion of the French channel ports that year. Eisenhower returned from a trip to Britain with the definite impression that mobilization for an invasion was not proceeding at a fast enough rate even for a successful invasion of the continent in 1943. A telegram from Churchill to the President confirmed these suspicions, when the Prime Minister added to his message the cryptic remark, "Do not lose sight of 'Gymnast.' "[86] To complicate matters further, the suggestion fell on rather receptive ears, for, as indicated above, 'Gymnast' had always appealed to the President, not only because he recognized its strategic value. He also understood that it would be a more or less independent American action which not only would provide the trial by fire that the generals were looking for, but also promised a badly needed, identifiable victory in a reasonable period of time (incidentally during an election year), which of course would have a healthy effect upon public morale.

Churchill was back in the United States for continued talks in June 1942, and this time the battle over 'Sledgehammer' came out into the open. Robert Sherwood has reconstructed the arguments from Hopkins' papers:

> Churchill had stated his conception of the problems in writing to the President when they first met at Hyde Park. In this letter he said that all arrangements were proceeding to enable six or eight divisions to be landed on the coast of Northern France in September, 1942. But, though all preparations were being made, the British Government would not be in favor of undertaking a limited operation in 1942 if it were likely to lead to disaster. An unsuccessful operation, he argued, would not help the

Russians, would expose the French population to Nazi vengeance and would gravely delay the main operation in 1943. He expressed the view of the British Government that the Allies should not make any substantial landing in France in 1942 unless they were going to stay there. He said that the British military staffs had been unable to devise any plan for a landing in September, 1942, which had any chance of success. Churchill then went on to put a number of pointed questions. Had the American staffs devised such a plan? If so, what was it? What forces would be employed? At what points would they strike? What landing craft and shipping were available? Who was the general who was prepared to command the enterprise? What British forces and assistance would be required? If there were a plan which offered a reasonable prospect of success, the British Government would welcome it and share to the full the risks and sacrifices which it involved. But if there was no plan which commanded the confidence of any responsible authority, and if no substantial landing could be made in France in September, 1942, could the Allies afford to stand idle in the Atlantic theater during the whole of that year? Ought they not to be preparing some other operation, by which they might gain advantage and take some of the weight off Russia? It was in this setting, Churchill concluded, that the operation *Gymnast* should be studied.

Here, then, was the argument that the proponents of the Second Front had feared: the revival of *Gymnast*, the North African operation, instead of *Sledgehammer*, the trans-Channel assault in 1942. Stimson noted that Churchill had "taken up *Gymnast*, knowing full well I am sure that it was the President's great secret baby." It may be said that neither Stimson nor Marshall had serious objection to the North American operation in itself; it was considered feasible and there were many strategic points in its favor; but mounting it and maintaining it would involve the diversion of such a vast amount of shipping as well as naval and air forces and troops to the Mediterranean area that the *Bolero* build-up could not possibly be continued at a sufficient rate through the summer and autumn of 1942 and even through the following winter. Thus, if *Gymnast* were decided on, adequate strength for a full-force invasion of the Continent could not be established in the United Kingdom in time for the spring of 1943.[87]

Churchill employed his "matchless prose" in defense of 'Gymnast,' but he was opposed by Marshall, Hopkins and even Roosevelt, who remained firm to his commitment to his military leaders. And while the argument continued bad news continued to pour in from the Middle East and from the southern Russian front. Churchill confessed later that despite the hospitality of his American hosts, he had been the unhappiest Englishman in North America since General Burgoyne.

The argument raged back and forth at both Hyde Park and Washington for several days, completely disrupting the planned staff talks before they could be started. Because of the bad news of Rommel's triumphs in the Middle East, Churchill was forced to fly back to London to face a vote of censure in the House of Commons, based upon the defeat of the British army in the desert fighting. No final decisions were made, and Marshall and his colleagues were so discouraged by the

British attitudes about an early second front in Europe that they began making radical revisions in their earlier firm decision to defend Europe first; they commenced consideration of plans for a major offensive against Japan in the Pacific in 1942 and 1943. Such a development would have committed the bulk of the American forces to action in the Pacific, rather than in the European theater—a drastic change in the overall strategy and logistics of the war.

At that point the Commander in Chief intervened, calling such a proposal a "red herring," and indicating that its use to force British compliance with American strategy was a little like threatening to "take up your dishes and go home." There is no clear evidence as to whether or not the whole situation was a bluff, but President Roosevelt asserted his authority as Commander in Chief and scratched the plan at its inception. The ever faithful Hopkins made careful notes of a dinner conversation with the President the night before he and Marshall flew again to England to settle the issue of 'Sledgehammer' and 'Gymnast' once and for all with the British. Roosevelt was emphatic that the United States could not under any circumstances renege on its "Europe first" commitment, even if a second front in Europe could not be opened up in 1942. The President was not eager to abandon the 'Sledgehammer' operation, and wanted Hopkins to sound out Eisenhower and the other Americans in Britain to see if they agreed with the estimates of the British leaders, but he was willing to postpone it if necessary to consider seriously the North African invasion in the fall as a viable substitute. In a memorandum to Hopkins, Marshall and Admiral King which amounted to instructions on policy to be followed at their London conference, he outlined his plans in no uncertain terms, leaving no alternative to the two chiefs of staff who were going to the conference but to carry out the orders of their Commander in Chief.

Although this was one of only two known instances where the President directly overruled his chiefs of staff during the entire war, it clearly indicates that he was far from a silent partner in the determination of really significant questions of policy, and although there was full agreement between them most of the time, it is obvious that such agreement was based upon mutual understanding and restraint on the part of the chiefs as well as their Commander in Chief.

Honorable Harry L. Hopkins
Notes of Dinner Conversation with President Roosevelt
On the Eve of the London Conference
July 15, 1942

Robert E. Sherwood, *Roosevelt and Hopkins: An Intimate History* (New York, 1948), 602-03.

I cannot agree that if it be impossible to develop *Bolero* in 1942 that we should turn our faces away from Germany and toward Japan.

In the first place I am not content with the British Cabinet position. I want to know what our men on the ground—Eisenhower, Spaatz, Clark and Stark—think. Do they agree with the British Cabinet? Can you get a confidential report from them?

Even though we must reluctantly agree to no *Sledgehammer* in 1942, I still think we should press forward vigorously for the 1943 enterprise. I see nothing in the message from England to indicate any luke-warmness on their part for the 1943 enterprise. I am somewhat disturbed about this readiness to give up 1942. Will they also give up 1943?

But my main point is that I do not believe we can wait until 1943 to strike at Germany. If we cannot strike at *Sledgehammer*, then we must take the second best—and that is not the Pacific. There we are conducting a successful holding war. Troops and air alone will not be decisive at once—it requires the increasing strength of our Navy—which takes time.

If *Sledgehammer* cannot be launched then I wish a determination made while you are in London as to a specific and definite theatre where our ground and sea forces can operate against the German ground forces in 1942.

The theatres to be considered are North Africa and the Middle East.

Gymnast has the great advantage of being a purely American enterprise, it would secure Western Africa and deny the ports to the enemy, it would offer the beginning of what should be the ultimate control of the Mediterranean—it is the shortest route to supply. The other theatre is the Middle East; here we would possibly have no resistance—we can use our forces either in Egypt or from the head of the Persian Gulf. Both Russia and England are sorely pressed in this area.

Either of the above operations will require a substantial reduction in *Bolero* for the next three months. I am prepared to accept this.

Under any circumstances I wish *Bolero* and *Roundup* to remain an essential objective even though it must be interrupted.

I am prepared to consider in event *Sledgehammer* is not mounted—an appropriate transfer of air and landing craft to the Southwest Pacific.

President Franklin D. Roosevelt
Memorandum to Hopkins, Marshall and King
Instructions for the London Conference
July 16, 1942

Sherwood, 603-05.

MEMORANDUM FOR
      Hon. Harry L. Hopkins
      General Marshall
      Admiral King
SUBJECT: Instructions for London Conference—July, 1942.

1. You will proceed immediately to London as my personal representatives for the purpose of consultation with appropriate British authorities on the conduct of the war.

2. The military and naval strategic changes have been so great since Mr. Churchill's visit to Washington that it became necessary to reach immediate agreement on joint operational plans between the British and ourselves along two lines:

(a) Definite plans for the balance of 1942.

(b) Tentative plans for the year 1943 which, of course, will be subject to change in the light of occurrences in 1942, but which should be initiated at this time in all cases involving preparation in 1942 for operations in 1943.

3. (a) The common aim of the United Nations must be the defeat of the Axis Powers. There cannot be compromise on this point.

(b) We should concentrate our efforts and avoid dispersion.

(c) Absolute coordinated use of British and American forces is essential.

(d) All available U.S. and British forces should be brought into action as quickly as they can be profitably used.

(e) It is of the highest importance that U.S. ground troops be brought into action against the enemy in 1942.

4. British and American materiel promises to Russia must be carried out in good faith. If the Persian route of delivery is used, preference must be given to combat material. This aid must continue as long as delivery is possible and Russia must be encouraged to continue resistance. Only complete collapse, which seems unthinkable, should alter this determination on our part.

5. In regard to 1942, you will carefully investigate the possibility of executing *Sledgehammer*. Such an operation would definitely sustain Russia this year. It might be the turning point which would save Russia this year. *Sledgehammer* is of such grave importance that every reason calls for accomplishment of it. You should strongly urge immediate all-out preparations for it, that it be pushed with utmost vigor, and that it be executed whether or not Russian collapse becomes imminent. In the event Russian collapse becomes probable *Sledgehammer* becomes not merely advisable but imperative. The principal objective of *Sledgehammer* is the positive diversion of German Air Forces from the Russian Front.

6. Only if you are completely convinced that *Sledgehammer* is impossible of execution with reasonable chances of serving its intended purpose, inform me.

7. If *Sledgehammer* is finally and definitely out of the picture, I want you to consider the world situation as it exists at that time, and determine upon another place for U.S. Troops to fight in 1942.

It is my present view of the world picture that:

(a) If Russia contains a large German force against her, *Roundup* becomes possible in 1943, and plans for *Roundup* should be immediately considered and preparations made for it.

(b) If Russia collapses and German air and ground forces are released, *Roundup* may be impossible of fulfillment in 1943.

8. The Middle East should be held as strongly as possible whether Russia collapses or not. I want you to take into consideration the effect of losing the Middle East. Such loss means in series:

(1) Loss of Egypt and the Suez Canal.

(2) Loss of Syria.

(3) Loss of Mosul oil wells.

(4) Loss of the Persian Gulf through attacks from the north and west, together with access to all Persian Gulf oil.

(5) Joining hands between Germany and Japan and the probable loss of the Indian Ocean.

(6) The very important probability of German occupation of Tunis, Algiers, Morocco, Dakar and the cutting of the ferry route through Freetown and Liberia.

(7) Serious danger to all shipping in the South Atlantic and serious danger to Brazil and the whole of the East Coast of South America. I include in the above possibilities the use by the Germans of Spain, Portugal and their territories.

(8) You will determine the best methods of holding the Middle East. These methods include definitely either or both of the following:

(a) Sending aid and ground forces to the Persian Gulf, to Syria and to Egypt.

(b) A new operation in Morocco and Algiers intended to drive in against the backdoor of Rommel's armies. The attitude of French Colonial troops is still in doubt.

9. I am opposed to an American all-out effort in the Pacific against Japan with the view to her defeat as quickly as possible. It is of the utmost importance that we appreciate that defeat of Japan does not defeat Germany and that American concentration against Japan this year or in 1943 increases the chance of complete German domination of Europe and Africa. On the other hand, it is obvious that defeat of Germany, or the holding of Germany in 1942 or in 1943 means probable, eventual defeat of Germany in the European and African theatres and in the Near East. Defeat of Germany means the defeat of Japan, probably without firing a shot or losing a life.

10. Please remember three cardinal principles—speed of decision on plans, unity of plans, attack combined with defense but not defense alone. This affects the immediate objective of U.S. ground forces fighting against Germans in 1942.

11. I hope for total agreement within one week of your arrival.

> *Franklin D. Roosevelt*
> Commander-in-Chief

An Unnecessary American Tragedy

On February 19, 1942, President Roosevelt signed Executive Order No. 9066, which the American Civil Liberties Union later characterized as "the worst single wholesale violation of civil rights of American citizens in our history."[88] Presidential scholar James MacGregor Burns described the forced evacuation of approximately 112,000 Americans of Japanese ancestry, naturalized Japanese immigrants and Japanese nationals brought about by the order as "one of the sorriest episodes in American history."[89] The President had little to do with the actual evacuation, but in his capacity as Commander in Chief he approved the order and must bear the responsibility for its application.

Executive Order No. 9066 came some weeks after Pearl Harbor, shortly after the capture of Manila and the fall of Singapore. At the time the President was preoccupied with the urgent problems of America's entry into the war then raging all over the world; he had delegated a good deal of authority to the Department of Justice to work out "arrangements" for dealing with possible enemy aliens in the United States. The F.B.I. quickly rounded up all Germans, Italians and Japanese known to have been associated with previous subversive or alleged subversive activities, but the sneak attack on Pearl Harbor by the Japanese and their rapid follow-up victories in the Pacific quickly led the public particularly on the west coast, to clamor for stringent measures by the government.

Morton Grodzins has made a careful study of the events leading to this unfortunate decision and has absolved the President from an active role in preparing the plans for the evacuation, but he also indicates that Roosevelt never seriously questioned the army's recommendation; neither did he appear to be concerned over its implicit threat to the rights of an American citizen to due process of law. Japanese citizens and noncitizens alike, were classified as potentially dangerous enemies simply on the basis of their race or ethnic origin.[90] Grodzins' study indicates that the evacuation program was a response to frantic but strictly minority group pressure upon the army and the government to institute that policy. Much of the fear and paranoia which led to the evacuation and subsequent internment was instigated by racist organizations of long standing—the Native Sons and Daughters of the Golden West and the California Joint Immigration Committee. They were joined by national, state and local groups of the American Legion, the Los Angeles and other west coast cities Chambers of Commerce and, perhaps the most active and effective of all, a number of trade organizations engaged in competitive economic activity with large numbers of Japanese and Japanese-Americans—the Western Growers Protective Association, a cooperative organization of row crop vegetable growers, the Grower-Shipper Vegetable Association, the California Farm Bureau Federation and the Merchants and Manufacturers Association. These groups were not only frightened of Japanese invasion and the dangers of a fifth column supported by their countrymen, but they also stood to gain from the elimination of competition from Nesei farmers, florists and small businessmen. In addition many of these groups were heavy contributors to California politicians. Thus there was tremendous pressure exerted upon national and state figures to press for prompt evacuation.

Many of the more influential newspapers were slow to commit themselves to the campaign for evacuation, but nearly all west coast papers supported the President's action by the time it was taken. Even the balanced and renowned national columnist Walter Lippmann was an all-out supporter of immediate evacuation. There was hardly a defense of loyal Nesei and other Japanese. Major public figures like California's attorney general, Earl Warren, later to become the chief justice of the Supreme Court, and California governor, Cuthbert Oleson, joined the wolf pack. Only Senator Sheridan Downey and two members of the huge California congressional delegation, Congressmen Coffee and Voorhis, urged a policy of moderation amidst the lynch mob uproar.

Attorney General Francis Biddle, who was originally in charge of the alien security problem, was not sympathetic to any wholesale evacuation program, and he reports that the army commander in the area, Lieutenant General John L. De Witt, was not enthused about it either. De Witt, Biddle writes "kept his head at first and resisted suggestions that the Japanese be herded out of the coastal territory. . . ."[91] The general explained to the provost marshal general, Allen W. Gullion:

> An American citizen after all is an American citizen, and while they may not all be loyal, I think we can weed the disloyal out of the loyal and lock them up if necessary.[92]

This calm and objective attitude soon disappeared as the pressure campaign for evacuation went into high gear. Not too many weeks after he made the above statement, General De Witt recommended evacuation to the President as a military necessity. He had been pressured unmercifully by the California groups, and there was certainly reason to suspect the threat of invasion. The location of the Japanese fleet was unknown, the American fleet was badly crippled from the attack at Pearl Harbor and a Japanese submarine had shelled the California coast at Santa Barbara. But none of it justifies the necessity for an evacuation based upon purely racial criteria, ignoring totally any investigation of individuals involved or suspected crimes committed. De Witt's later explanations for the wholesale character of the evacuation, however, go a long way towards explaining his quick submission to the racist and frightened pressures placed upon him. In his recommendation for evacuation, he argued:

> The Japanese race is an enemy race and while many second and third generation Japanese born on United States soil, possessed of United States citizenship, have become "Americanized," the racial strains are undiluted. . . . It therefore follows that along the Pacific Coast over 112,000 potential enemies, of Japanese extraction, are at large today.[93]

Testifying the following year before the House Naval Affairs Subcommittee, General De Witt repeated this racist argument:

> A Jap's a Jap. They are a dangerous element, whether loyal or not. There's no way to determine their loyalty. . . . It makes no difference whether he is an American theoretically, he is still Japanese and you can't change him. . . . You can't change him by giving him a piece of paper.[94]

An army general holding such views was not going to hold out too long against the crescendo of well-financed and articulate pressure groups, even if surveys indicated that public opinion in the rest of the country was generally opposed to such a drastic step.[95] What was missing was an active and articulate leadership to remind Americans of the contradiction of embracing racism when in the midst of a war fought against the principle of racism. The attorney general and the Department of Justice attempted to play a moderating role, but Biddle was inexperienced and unsure of himself in his new position, and the President and the secretary of war were preoccupied with the vast plans to train and deploy a military and naval force that would number over 12 million before the war ended. Under these circumstances the army took over. They permitted the decision on the west coast to be made by the experienced military commander in charge, yet they understood the high cost of holding out against the pressure groups demanding evacuation; they were unwilling to pay the price of raising such a divisive issue. It was simpler to accept the argument of military necessity on the word of the responsibly military authority involved, without demanding any evidence or explanatory arguments. Without ever discussing the matter at a cabinet meeting or consulting with advisors, the President instructed the War Department to prepare an evacuation plan, including citizens, even before General De Witt's formal recommendations were received. He admonished the military planners only to "be as reasonable as you can."[96] After receiving these instructions, the assistant secretary of war reported, "We have *carte blanche* to do what we want as far as the President is concerned."[97]

The sad story of the forced migration and subsequent internment of over 100,000 people, at least 60 percent of whom were native-born American citizens who had no cause to be under suspicion of espionage or sabotage, has been related in detail elsewhere.[98] It was a shameful business, and all the more alarming because no really strong national figures spoke out against the outrage once it was underway. Wars are difficult upon friend and foe alike and one does not expect absolute and total protection of usual rights and privileges once the shooting begins. But the distinguishing hallmark of a free nation which respects due process under the law is its willingness to defend this principle under the most trying and difficult circumstances.

There were some positive aspects of this generally depressing episode, however. At a later date efforts were made to single out those loyal Nesei who had no sympathy for Japan, and to transfer them out of the camps and into jobs and unfettered existence in the interior. By the end of the war thousands had taken advantage of this relocation policy, while other thousands of Nesei young men had served with distinction in the United States armed forces and in the merchant marine. Many were toughened by the experience, and although they were very bitter at first, their overall experiences, writes a sympathetic student of racial equality, propelled them into more active and aggressive democratic activity than they were capable of before.[99] But there were many who remained bitter, some being repatriated in Japan, and there were also those Nesei who were not anxious to forget and forgive.

It is interesting to note that Hawaii, which was actually subjected to an all-out aerial attack by Japan, had a population in which 34.2 percent were Japanese or of Japanese ancestry as compared with 1.2 percent in California. Fifteen hundred miles closer to Japan and far more vulnerable to its sea and air forces, Hawaii never invoked anything like the extreme evacuation policy imposed by the mainland, yet no major acts of sabotage were discovered there. There is no question that more sensitive military information, communication technology and machinery were available in Hawaii than in California, yet "military necessity" did not require the removal to concentration camps of the entire Japanese population. To be accurate, martial law was in full force in Hawaii for more than two years after Pearl Harbor, but from a constitutional point of view, equal limitations upon the freedom of all citizens through military rule is certainly preferable to the total limitation of freedom of only some.

The President's initial executive order provided a general authorization for the evacuation policies that followed, but they were developed and supervised by the army. A second executive order about a month later created the War Relocation Authority designed to implement and supervise the removal and, subsequently, the conduct of the internment program.[100] Congress cooperated by passing legislation reinforcing the executive orders and providing legal penalties for their violation. Seven days before the President's first executive order was issued, Attorney General Biddle went on record by informing the secretary of war that "the Army could legally evacuate all persons in a specified territory if such action was deemed essential from a military point of view; but that American citizens of Japanese origin could not 'be singled out of an area and evacuated with other Japanese.' "[101] That was Biddle's last gesture of defiance, however. After the President had decided to act, it was "a matter of military judgment. I did not think I should oppose it any further," he said.[102]

President Franklin D. Roosevelt
Executive Order Authorizing the Secretary of War
To Prescribe Military Areas for National Defense
February 19, 1942

Federal Register, VII, No. 38 (February 25, 1942), 1407.

Whereas the successful prosecution of the war requires every possible protection against espionage and against sabotage to national-defense material, national-defense premises, and national-defense utilities as defined in Section 4, Act of April 20, 1918, 40 Stat. 533, as amended by the Act of November 30, 1940, 54 Stat. 1220, and the Act of August 21, 1941, 55 Stat. 655 (U.S.C., Title 50, Sec. 104):

Now, therefore, by virtue of the authority vested in me as President of the United States, and Commander in Chief of the Army and Navy, I hereby authorize and direct the Secretary of War, and the Military Commanders whom he may from time to time designate, whenever he or any designated Commander deems such action necessary or desirable, to prescribe military areas in such places and of such extent as he or the appropriate Military Commander may determine, from which any or all persons may be excluded, and with respect to which, the right of any person to enter, remain in, or leave shall be subject to whatever restrictions the Secretary of War or the appropriate Military Commander may impose in his discretion. The Secretary of War is hereby authorized to provide for residents of any such area who are excluded therefrom, such transportation, food, shelter, and other accommodations as may be necessary, in the judgment of the Secretary of War or the said Military Commander, and until other arrangements are made, to accomplish the purpose of this order. The designation of military areas in any region or locality shall supersede designations of prohibited and restricted areas by the Attorney General under the Proclamations of December 7 and 8, 1941, and shall supersede the responsibility and authority of the Attorney General under the said Proclamations in respect of such prohibited and restricted areas.

I hereby further authorize and direct the Secretary of War and the said Military Commanders to take such other steps as he or the appropriate Military Commander may deem advisable to enforce compliance with the restrictions applicable to each Military area hereinabove authorized to be designated, including the use of Federal troops and other Federal Agencies, with authority to accept assistance of state and local agencies.

I hereby further authorize and direct all Executive Departments, independent establishments and other Federal Agencies, to assist the Secretary of War or the said Military Commanders in carrying out this Executive Order, including the furnishing of medical aid, hospitalization, food, clothing, transportation, use of land, shelter, and other supplies, equipment, utilities, facilities, and services.

This order shall not be construed as modifying or limiting in any way the authority heretofore granted under Executive Order No. 8972, dated December 12, 1941, nor shall it be construed as limiting or modifying the duty and responsibility of the Federal Bureau of Investigation, with respect to the investigation of alleged acts of sabotage or the duty and responsibility of the Attorney General and the Department of Justice under the Proclamations of December 7 and 8, 1941, prescribing regulations for the conduct and control of alien enemies, except as such duty and responsibility is superseded by the designation of military areas hereunder.

Franklin D. Roosevelt

Public Law Providing Penalties for Violations Of Restrictions for Civilians in Military Areas
March 21, 1942

Public Law 503 (H.R. 6758), *United States Statutes at Large*, LVI, Part 1, 77th Cong., 2nd sess.

AN ACT

To provide a penalty for violation of restrictions or orders with respect to persons entering, remaining in, leaving, or committing any act in military areas or zones.

Be it enacted by the Senate and House of Representatives of the United States of America in Congress assembled, That whoever shall enter, remain in, leave, or commit any act in any military area or military zone prescribed, under the authority of an Executive order of the President, by the Secretary of War, or by any military commander designated by the Secretary of War, contrary to the restrictions applicable to any such area or zone or contrary to the order of the Secretary of War or any such military commander, shall, if it appears that he knew or should have known of the existence and extent of the restrictions or order and that his act was in violation thereof, be guilty of a misdemeanor and upon conviction shall be liable to a fine of not to exceed $5,000 or to imprisonment for not more than one year, or both, for each offense.

President Franklin D. Roosevelt
Executive Order Establishing the War Relocation Authority
March 18, 1942

Rosenman, XI, 174-76.

By virtue of the authority vested in me by the Constitution and statutes of the United States, as President of the United States and Commander in Chief of the Army and Navy, and in order to provide for the removal from designated areas of persons whose removal is necessary in the interests of national security, it is ordered as follows:

1. There is established in the Office for Emergency Management of the Executive Order of the President the War Relocation Authority, at the head of which shall be a Director appointed by and responsible to the President.

2. The Director of the War Relocation Authority is authorized and directed to formulate and effectuate a program for the removal, from the areas designated from time to time by the Secretary of War or appropriate military commander under the authority of Executive Order No. 9066 of February 19, 1942, of the persons or classes of persons designated under such Executive Order, and for their relocation, maintenance, and supervision.

3. In effectuating such program the Director shall have authority to—

(a) Accomplish all necessary evacuation not undertaken by the Secretary of War or appropriate military commander, provide for the relocation of such persons in appropriate places, provide for their needs in such manner as may be appropriate, and supervise their activities.

(b) Provide, insofar as feasible and desirable, for the employment of such persons at useful work in industry, commerce, agriculture, or public projects, prescribe the terms and conditions of such public employment, and safeguard the public interest in the private employment of such persons.

(c) Secure the cooperation, assistance, or services of any governmental agency.

(d) Prescribe regulations necessary or desirable to promote effective execution of such program, and, as a means of coordinating evacuation and relocation activities, consult with the Secretary of War with respect to regulations issued and measures taken by him.

(e) Make such delegations of authority as he may deem necessary.

(f) Employ necessary personnel, and make such expenditures, including the making of loans and grants and the purchase of real property, as may be necessary, within the limits of such funds as may be made available to the Authority.

4. The Director shall consult with the United States Employment Service and other agencies on employment and other problems incident to activities under this Order.

5. The Director shall cooperate with the Alien Property Custodian appointed pursuant to Executive Order No. 9095 of March 11, 1942, in formulating policies to govern the custody, management, and disposal by the Alien Property Custodian of property belonging to foreign nationals removed under this Order or under Executive Order No. 9066 of February 19, 1942; and may assist all other persons removed under either of such Executive Orders in the management and disposal of their property.

6. Departments and agencies of the United States are directed to cooperate with and assist the Director in his activities hereunder. The Departments of War and Justice, under the direction of the Secretary of War and the Attorney General, respectively, shall insofar as consistent with the national interest provide such protective, police, and investigational services as the Director shall find necessary in connection with activities under this Order.

7. There is established within the War Relocation Authority the War Relocation Work Corps. The Director shall provide, by general regulations, for the enlistment in such Corps, for the duration of the present war, of persons removed under this Order or under Executive Order No. 9066 of February 19, 1942, and shall prescribe the terms and conditions of the work to be performed by such Corps, and the compensation to be paid.

8. There is established within the War Relocation Authority a Liaison Committee on War Relocation, which shall consist of the Secretary of War, the Secretary of the Treasury, the Attorney General, the Secretary of Agriculture, the Secretary of Labor, the Federal Security Administrator, the Director of Civilian Defense, and the Alien Property Custodian, or their deputies, and such other persons or agencies as the Director may designate. The Liaison Committee shall meet at the call of the Director and shall assist him in his duties.

9. The Director shall keep the President informed with regard to the progress made in carrying out this Order, and perform such related duties as the President may from time to time assign to him.

10. In order to avoid duplication of evacuation activities under this Order and Executive Order No. 9066 of February 19, 1942, the Director shall not undertake any evacuation activities within military areas designated under said Executive Order No. 9066, without the prior approval of the Secretary of War or the appropriate military commander.

11. This Order does not limit the authority granted in Executive Order No. 8972 of December 12, 1941; Executive Order No. 9066 of February 19, 1942; Executive Order No. 9095 of March 11, 1942; Executive Proclamation No. 2525 of December 7, 1941; Executive Proclamation No. 2526 of December 8, 1941; Executive Proclamation No. 2527 of December 8, 1941; Executive Proclamation No. 2533 of December 29, 1941; or Executive Proclamation No. 2537 of January 14, 1942; nor does it limit the functions of the Federal Bureau of Investigation.

The Supreme Court reviewed the constitutionality of these measures in a case in which an American citizen of Japanese descent, Korematsu, was convicted in a federal court of violating the order issued by General De Witt excluding all persons of Japanese ancestry from the area in which he lived and worked, San Leandro, California. In an opinion written by Justice Black, the Court upheld the judgment. It denied that Korematsu was order to be imprisoned "in a concentration camp because of his ancestry, without evidence or inquiry concerning his loyalty and good disposition towards the United States."[103]

> He was excluded because we are at war with the Japanese Empire, because the properly constituted military authorities feared an invasion of our West Coast and felt constrained to take proper security measures, because they decided that the military urgency of the situation demanded that all citizens of Japanese ancestry be segregated from the West Coast temporarily, and finally, because Congress, reposing its confidence in this time of war in our military leaders—as inevitably it must—determined that they should have the power to do just this. There was evidence of disloyalty on the part of some, the military authorities considered that the need for action was great, and time was short. We cannot—by availing ourselves of the calm perspective of hindsight—now say that at the time these actions were unjustified.[104]

Of course the top military authority involved was the Commander in Chief, and was the statute passed by the Congress, although strengthening by law the President's edict merely reinforced his war powers. As happens in many Supreme Court decisions, the dissenting opinions in this instance are of greater significance to the future and to the question of presidential power than the majority decision of the Court. They delineate constitutional limits to the actions taken by the President in his capacity as Commander in Chief, to his military subordinates and to the Congress in violating the basic rights of American citizens. In his dissent, Justice Owen J. Roberts argued:

> I dissent because I think the indisputable facts exhibit a clear violation of Constitutional rights, . . . it is the case of convicting a citizen as a punishment for not submitting to imprisonment in a concentration camp, based on his ancestry, and solely because of his ancestry, without evidence or inquiry concerning his loyalty and good disposition towards the United States. If this be a correct statement of the facts disclosed by this record, and facts of which we take judicial notice, I need hardly labor the conclusion that Constitutional rights have been violated.[105]

In his dissenting opinion, Mr. Justice Frank Murphy struck out against the racist presumptions inherent in the President's orders and the legislative statute, but he was first careful to establish the rationale for the legitimate invocation of the principle of "military necessity":

> In dealing with matters relating to the prosecution and progress of a war, we must accord great respect and consideration to the judgments of the military authorities who are on the scene and who have a knowledge of the military facts. The scope of their discretion must, as a matter of

necessity and common sense, be wide. And their judgments ought not be overruled lightly by those whose training and duties ill-equip them to deal intelligently with matters so vital to the physical security of the nation.

At the same time, however, it is essential that there be definite limits to military discretion, especially where martial law has not been declared. Individuals must not be left impoverished of their constitutional rights on a plea of military necessity that has neither substance nor support. Thus other claims conflicting with the asserted constitutional rights of the individual, the military claim must subject itself to the judicial process of having its reasonableness determined and its conflicts with other interests reconciled. "What are the allowable limits of military discretion, and whether or not they have been overstepped in a particular case, are judicial questions." (Sterling *v.* Constantin, 287 U.S. 378, 401.)

The judicial test of whether the Government, on a plea of military necessity, can validly deprive an individual of any of his constitutional rights is whether the deprivation is reasonably related to a public danger that is so "imminent, and impending" as not to admit of delay and not to permit the intervention of ordinary constitutional processes to alleviate the danger. . . .

. . . It must be conceded that the military and naval situation in the spring of 1942 was such as to generate a very real fear of invasion of the Pacific Coast accompanied by fears of sabotage and espionage in that area. The military command was therefore justified in adopting all reasonable means necessary to combat these dangers. . . .[106]

He then examined the evidence which alone could have justified such an extraordinary deprivation of constitutional rights, and found it to be nonexistent:

No adequate reason is given for the failure to treat these Japanese Americans on an individual basis by holding investigations and hearings to separate the loyal from the disloyal, as was done in the case of persons of German and Italian ancestry. . . . It is asserted merely that the loyalties of this group "were unknown and time was of the essence." Yet nearly four months elapsed after Pearl Harbor before the first exclusion order was issued; nearly eight months went by until the last order was issued; and the last of these "subversive" persons was not actually removed until almost eleven months had elapsed. Leisure and deliberation seem to have been more of the essence than speed. And the fact that conditions were not such as to warrant a declaration of martial law adds strength to the belief that the factors of time and military necessity were not as urgent as they have been represented to be.

Moreover, there was no adequate proof that the Federal Bureau of Investigation and the military and naval intelligence services did not have the espionage and sabotage situation well in hand during this long period. Nor is there any denial of the fact that not one person of Japanese ancestry was accused or convicted of espionage or sabotage after Pearl Harbor while they were still free, a fact which is some evidence of the loyalty of the vast majority of these individuals and of the effectiveness of the established methods of combatting these evils. It seems incredible that under these circumstances it would have been impossible to hold loyalty hearings for the mere 112,000 persons—or at least for the 70,000 American citizens—especially when a large part of this number represented children and elderly men and women. Any inconvenience that may have accompanied an attempt to conform to procedural due process cannot be said to justify violations of constitutional rights of individuals.

I dissent, therefore, from this legalization of racism. Racial discrimination in any form and in any degree has no justifiable part whatever in our democratic way of life. It is unattractive in any setting but it is utterly revolting among a free people who have embraced the principles set forth in the Constitution of the United States. All residents of this nation are kin in some way by blood or culture to a foreign land. Yet they are primarily and necessarily a part of the new and distinct civilization of the United States. They must accordingly be treated at all times as the heirs of the American experiment and as entitled to all rights and freedoms guaranteed by the Constitution.[107]

After Justice Murphy's eloquent denunciation, it was left to Justice Robert H. Jackson to assert the authority of the Constitution and the primacy of the law over military expediency. Jackson, like Murphy, was convinced that racism was behind the military orders, yet he shied away from arguing the case on military or lack of military criteria. He suggested that perhaps the Court was incapable of preventing the military from violating the Constitution, but he insisted that it was the Court's obligation to assert the primacy of the principle nonetheless:

... I cannot say, from any evidence before me, that the orders of General De Witt were not reasonably expedient military precautions, nor could I say that they were. But even if they were permissible military procedures, I deny that it follows that they are constitutional. If, as the Court holds, it does follow, then we may as well say that any military order will be constitutional and have done with it.

The limitations under which courts always will labor in examining the necessity for a military order are illustrated by this case. How does the Court know that these orders have a reasonable basis in necessity? No evidence whatever on the subject has been taken by this or any other court. There is sharp controversy as to the credibility of the De Witt report. So the Court having no real evidence before it, has no choice but to accept General De Witt's own unsworn, self-serving statement, untested by any cross-examination, that what he did was reasonable. And thus it will always be when courts try to look into the reasonableness of a military order.

In the very nature of things, military decisions are not susceptible of intelligent judicial appraisal. They do not pretend to rest on evidence, but are made upon information that often would not be admissable and on assumptions that could not be proved. Information in support of an order could not be disclosed to courts without danger that it would reach the enemy. Neither can courts act on communications made in confidence. Hence courts can never have any real alternative to accepting the mere declaration of the authority that issued the order that it was reasonably necessary from a military point of view.

Much is said of the danger to liberty from the Army program for deporting and detaining these citizens of Japanese extraction. But a judicial construction of the due process clause that will sustain this order is a far more subtle blow to liberty than the promulgation of the order itself. A military order, however unconstitutional, is not apt to last longer than the military emergency. Even during that period a succeeding commander may revoke it all. But once a judicial opinion rationalizes such an order to show that it conforms to the Constitution, or rather rationalizes the Constitution to show that the Constitution sanctions such an order, the Court for all time has validated the principle of racial discrimination in criminal procedure and of transplanting American citizens. The principle then lies about like a loaded weapon ready for the hand of any authority that can bring forward a plausible claim for an urgent need. Every repetition imbeds that principle more deeply in our law and thinking and expands it to new purposes. All who observe the work of courts are familiar with what Judge Cardozo described as "the tendency of a principle to expand itself to the limit of its logic." A military commander may overstep the bounds of constitutionality, and it is an incident. But if we review and approve, that passing incident becomes the doctrine of the Constitution. There it has a generative power of its own, and all that it creates will be in its own image. Nothing better illustrates this danger than does the Court's opinion in this case. . . .

I should hold that a civil court cannot be made to enforce an order which violates constitutional limitations even if it is a reasonable exercise of military authority. The courts can exercise only the judicial power, can apply only law, and must abide by the Constitution, or they cease to be civil courts and become instruments of military policy.[108]

The implications of these strong dissenting opinions are quite difficult, but essential. At least three of the nine justices of this distinguished Court are saying that the evacuation and internment of the 112,000 Japanese and Americans of Japanese descent was not only a racist but also an unconstitutional action. What is perhaps even more frightening and difficult to accept is Justice Jackson's wise conclusion that the people cannot rely upon the courts to protect them from this kind of disaster, if they let "command of the war power fall into irresponsible and unscrupulous hands."[109] Rossiter supports this opinion when he argues that the decision in this case must be "convincing proof that the courts of the United States, from highest to lowest, can do nothing to restrain and next to nothing to mitigate an arbitrary presidential-military program suspending the liberties of the civilian population. . . ."[110] In short, no court, no law, not even the Constitution can protect our freedoms and liberties if we allow the political process to degenerate to the point where it no longer can provide the checks and balances to hold the Executive accountable to the people and true to the ideals upon which the republic was founded.

Clearly, this places the responsibility to evolve a sensitive understanding of our constitutional principles upon leaders and citizens alike, to insure restraint, not only under normal and favorable circumstances, but also in times of great stress, including wartime. There is no escape in a constitutional democracy from this level of accountability. The discipline of moral and intellectual commitment to the principles of liberty and freedom, and particularly to due process under our Constitution, can only be effective if the political process prepares the public and raises its level of understanding to the point where it can impose such restraints. Constitutional law is not only the great edifice of precedent which guides this process, but the illuminating dissents to the decisions of the Court can also have a significant role in terms of public education. The clarity of Justice John Marshall Harlan in Plessy v. Ferguson and of Justice Louis D. Brandeis and Justice Oliver Wendell Holmes in their classical dissents, have frequently had more impact on the future than the majority decisions. It is the sharp dialectic of the adversary process which clears the air and illuminates the problem for all to grasp, including, if necessary, later generations.

The President as
A World Leader

The wartime death of Franklin D. Roosevelt in the spring of 1945 elevated Vice President Harry S. Truman to the Commander in Chief's role in a period pregnant with change and innovation. Truman inherited the office as the country teetered on the threshold of an entirely new era of history, and many changes, long in preparation, were brought to fruition during his administration. That is not to say that Harry Truman did not bring to the presidential office his own unique qualities, concepts of the office, and style and character, but many of the developments which happened so quickly and with such apparent smoothness and efficiency during his nearly two terms in office had been planned and prepared for by the previous administration. As World War II came to a close problems crowded in upon the new President, demanding his attention. In each case the circumstances required the use and the joint application of the foreign policy and the Commander in Chief powers of the President, as outlined and justified in Attorney General Jackson's opinion, prepared for President Roosevelt in the destroyer deal with Britain in 1940.

The first of these problem developments was the atomic bomb, about which Truman knew absolutely nothing before entering the White House as President. He was forced to make the decision about dropping a bomb on Hiroshima a few short months after he first learned of its existence. At almost the same time he became at once the first President to lead the country as a member of the newly-formed United

Nations; the first President to negotiate an open treaty of military alliance with foreign powers (NATO); the first peacetime President to assign American troops to serve overseas under a joint command in accordance with such an alliance; the first President to commit American military manpower to carry out a mandate of the United Nations; and the first American President to assume full responsibility for the economic reconstruction of a good part of an entire continent (Europe, under the Marshall Plan). All of these innovations had considerable impact upon the growth of presidential power and were also significant historical landmarks.

Certainly the advent of the bomb changed the rules of war and dramatized the power and responsibility of the President. United States membership in the United Nations opened up a whole new set of options as well as problems, for the exercise of presidential power; and the new alliance and the economic aid program brought with them grave decisions and responsibilities with which a pre-World War II President had not been burdened. But the Truman Doctrine, first enunciated in a speech in 1947 to a joint session of Congress which had gathered to hear the President's request for aid to Greece and Turkey, may have led to the expansion of presidential power beyond the limits of all of the others mentioned above, and obviously drew the country into unprecedented political, economic and military roles which would eventually commit its power and prestige beyond the limits of even its tremendous capacities. It is this fact which justifies the selection of the Truman Doctrine as one of the critical watersheds in the evolution of presidential power.

The cruel circumstances of history made any satisfactory settlement of the political problems in postwar Europe next to impossible. There had been too much suffering, too much destruction and a much too widespread distrust of the prewar social, economic and political order to expect a normal resumption of the status quo. Many believed that much of the despair and the hopeless conditions of these countries after the war were traceable to that same social and political order, and the challenge to their peaceful reconstruction would come from internal as well as external forces.

The Union of Soviet Socialist Republics emerged from the rubble of World War II stronger than ever and actively encouraged this disbelief and distrust in the status quo, while continuing to stimulate and contribute to the sense of unrest and instability which already existed. A complex combination of almost paranoid fear and insecurity among Soviet leaders of the threats from within and without their society, and their overreaching revolutionary ideological interest in expanding their political base, insured their active postwar efforts to extend their influence considerably beyond the limits of prewar territorial borders.

Other European powers including Great Britain were hardly in a position to resist such expansion. For centuries Great Britain had manipulated the fulcrum of the balance of power on the continent, but the war had taken its toll, not only in human lives, but in economic resources and political cohesion. At the war's end the British Empire was in the process of dissolution, and even the Commonwealth was moving into an era of much greater independence. British capital, both at home and abroad, had been largely liquidated by the high cost of the war, and the British people were tired, their energies spent. Germany had been crushed and was in the process of being divided; France was very slowly recovering from her humiliating defeat and collapse. No European power was strong enough, or even willing, to accept the Soviet challenge.

It rapidly became clear that if the Russians were not to engulf Europe totally, the United States would have to exert its considerable power and influence as a countervailing force. This awareness did not come about quickly, nor without considerable soul-searching. The American people were hardly prepared to assume this major role in world affairs, particularly after almost two centuries of relative isolation from the controversies of Europe. But before President Truman's initial term was over, the United States had become, for the first time in its history, the dominant world power, and the President had emerged as the most powerful individual leader in the area of international affairs. This transformation inevitably left its mark upon the institution of the presidency. By the time Harry Truman left the White House in 1953, the role of the President as an international leader had become firmly established, and was developing into a more and more critical responsibility of this continually expanding office.

The American wartime President, Franklin Delano Roosevelt, appeared to have sensed some of the burden of these inevitable postwar responsibilities, but certainly not the full complexity and immediacy of their demands. He realized, more than most of his countrymen, how American isolationism during the 1920s and 30s had contributed to the circumstances which led to World War II, and he had experienced close enough contact with the Russians and the British during the war to realize the divergent views each country would hold as to the possible political and economic reconstruction of Europe after the war ended. But a combination of the compelling imperatives of daily military decisions, a certain naiveté concerning the complexity and amorality of international diplomacy, and his deteriorating health, marked by rapidly ebbing physical and mental energy, made Roosevelt somewhat vulnerable to the calculating *Realpolitik* so successfully pursued by Stalin and the Soviet leaders in the period towards the close of the war. The problems were so widespread, so numerous, so complex—the time, the energy, and the resources necessary to deal with them so demanding—that it is no wonder the dying man was not able to comprehend fully their urgency or their possible solutions.

Roosevelt was convinced, however, that a radical change from American prewar isolationism was necessary. He did not believe that the old order in Europe could be restored, nor that Soviet influence and power could be restricted within her prewar geographical borders. Moreover he had an unusual relationship with Stalin which could have eliminated some of the Soviet suspicion and distrust and contributed to direct and frank negotiations concerning growing problems. On the other hand, although Roosevelt thought he had struck an effective bargain at Yalta, he was quite aware of and incensed at the Russians' efforts to exploit these agreements to their own advantage. On his last day in Washington before he went to Warm Springs where he died, this problem greatly agitated the President; banging his fists on the table he remarked to a luncheon guest:

> Averell is right; we can't do business with Stalin. He has broken every one of the promises he made at Yalta.[111]

However, for the reasons suggested above, Roosevelt was not fully prepared to deal with the scope and the magnitude of the problems that emerged as the Nazi war machine began to collapse, and the Allied armies recaptured territories in Eastern and Western Europe which had been occupied during the war by the German army. Events moved too rapidly, and he was too remote from the day-to-day scene even to speculate how he could possibly have checkmated the Soviet political moves in Eastern Europe, backed up as they were by Russian military power very much at the scene.

Winston Churchill, on the other hand, was aware of the problem much earlier, and was justifiably concerned that Roosevelt and other American leaders did not fully comprehend the dimensions of their responsibilities in Europe, which grew proportionately with the decline of British power. Churchill saw the collapse of the German army as only the beginning of the problem of restoring order and freedom to Europe, and he considered the sweeping advance of the powerful Soviet army as another threat which had to be acknowledged realistically and effectively resisted. This was not a matter of a holy crusade against communism, but rather a considered judgment based upon his long political experience. Churchill understood and was sympathetic to the Soviet's distrust and fear of the West, but he was not sufficiently sympathetic to welcome a total Soviet takeover in Eastern Europe. Such a major shift in the "balance of power" was wholly unacceptable to him. Based upon his concept of national and western democratic interests, he saw the emergence of a Soviet-controlled Eastern Europe as a significant threat to peace and stability on that continent.

As the Russian armies advanced into the Balkans in 1944, Churchill was anxious to lay down some ground rules and work out reasonable areas of western and eastern influence. Roosevelt was unwilling to stir up this political hornet's nest before the November presidential election, and so Churchill travelled alone to Moscow for a confrontation with Marshal Stalin. He has described what took place immediately after they sat down and commenced their first meeting:

> The moment was apt for business, so I said, "Let us settle about our affairs in the Balkans. Your armies are in Rumania and Bulgaria. We have interests, missions, and agents there. Don't let us get at cross-purposes in small ways. So far as Britain and Russia are concerned, how would it do for you to have ninety per cent predominance in Rumania, for us to have ninety per cent of the say in Greece, and go fifty-fifty about Yugoslavia?"
> While this was being translated I wrote out on a half-sheet of paper:

Rumania
    Russia 90%
    The Others 10%
Greece
    Great Britain 90%
    (in accord with USA)
    Russia 10%
Yugoslavia 50-50%
Hungary 50-50%

Bulgaria
Russia 75%
The Others 25%

I pushed this across to Stalin, who had by then heard the translation. There was a slight pause. Then he took his blue pencil and made a large tick upon it, and passed it back to us. It was all settled in no more time than it takes to set down.

Of course we had long and anxiously considered our point, and were only dealing with immediate war-time arrangements. All larger questions were reserved on both sides for what we then hoped would be a peace table when the war was won.

After this there was a long silence. The pencilled paper lay in the centre of the table. At length I said, "Might it not be thought rather cynical if it seemed we had disposed of these issues, so fateful to millions of people, in such an offhand manner? Let us burn the paper." "No, you keep it," said Stalin.[112]

Churchill thought in political as well as military terms, and when he unsuccessfully urged Supreme Allied Commander Eisenhower to push his army as far east as possible before joining forces with the Russians, his political concern took precedence over his military objective. In fact, the notion that the military objectives of the war should be subordinated to political ends distinguished both Churchill and Stalin from their American counterparts, Roosevelt and Truman, who, by and large, permitted their military leaders' logistics to determine their objectives without political interference.

President Roosevelt's death was a great blow to the British-American alliance because although Churchill and Roosevelt had differed on the question of postwar settlements, their great intimacy and close cooperation during the war had enhanced their ability to communicate with and understand each other and usually to resolve their differences satisfactorily. Dealing with the new President, Harry Truman, was a different matter entirely. He was psychologically unprepared for the shock of his succession to the office, and the transition period was difficult for him. For some time he was extremely cautious in dealing with questions of international affairs and quite dependent upon Roosevelt's trusted counselors for advice and information. Churchill's dispute with Eisenhower during the last weeks of the war was a case in point. The British Prime Minister, recognizing the political implications of the rapid advance of Russian units into Eastern Europe, wanted the supreme allied commander to push his own operations eastward so that the meeting point of the Soviet army with British-American troops would be as far to the east as practicable, possibly in areas including most of Germany (especially Berlin), Czechoslovakia and part of Poland. Eisenhower refused even to consider seriously such "political" maneuvering, basing his planning strictly upon military considerations. Even when Churchill appealed over his head to the Commander in Chief, the field commander was supported in his judgment by the President. Churchill was so disturbed by the apparent American intransigence on this problem that several days after the German surrender he sent a desperate appeal to

Washington, of which he later said: "Of all the public documents I have written on this issue, I would rather be judged by this":

I am profoundly concerned about the European situation. I learn that half the American Air Force in Europe has already begun to move to the Pacific theatre. The newspapers are full of the great movements of the American armies out of Europe. Our armies also are, under previous arrangements, likely to undergo a marked reduction. The Canadian Army will certainly leave. The French are weak and difficult to deal with. Anyone can see that in a very short space of time our armed power on the Continent will have vanished, except for moderate forces to hold down Germay.

Meanwhile what is to happen about Russia? I have always worked for friendship with Russia, but, like you, I feel deep anxiety because of their misinterpretation of the Yalta decisions, their attitude towards Poland, their overwhelming influence in the Balkans, excepting Greece, the difficulties they make about Vienna, the combination of Russian power and the territories under their control or occupied, coupled with the Communist technique in so many other countries, and above all their power to maintain very large armies in the field for a long time. What will be the position in a year or two, when the British and American Armies have melted and the French has not yet been formed on any major scale, when we may have a handful of divisions, mostly French, and when Russia may choose to keep two or three hundred on active service?

An iron curtain is drawn down upon their front. We do not know what is going on behind. There seems little doubt that the whole of the regions east of the line Lubeck-Trieste-Corfu will soon be completely in their hands. To this must be added the further enormous area conquered by the American armies between Eisenach and the Elbe, which will, I suppose, in a few weeks be occupied, when the Americans retreat, by the Russian power. All kinds of arrangements will have to be made by General Eisenhower to prevent another immense flight of the German population westward as this enormous Muscovite advance into the centre of Europe takes place. And then the curtain will descend again to a very large extent, if not entirely. Thus a broad band of many hundreds of miles of Russian-occupied territory will isolate us from Poland.

Meanwhile the attention of our peoples will be occupied in inflicting severities upon Germany, which is ruined and prostrate, and it would be open to the Russians in a very short time to advance if they chose to the waters of the North Sea and the Atlantic.

Surely it is vital now to come to an understanding with Russia, or see where we are with her, before we weaken our armies mortally or retire to the zones of occupation. This can only be done by a personal meeting. I should be most grateful for your opinion and advice. Of course we may take the view that Russia will behave impeccably, and no doubt that offers the most convenient solution. To sum up, this issue of a settlement with Russia before our strength has gone seems to me to dwarf all others.[113]

But no major settlement or understanding between the East and the West was immediately forthcoming. It was several months before Truman was able to adjust to the vectors of power that were at this command as President of the United States. As a matter of fact some time would elapse before this country would demonstrate in word and in deed that it recognized the full obligations of its role in the new postwar world, and that it was prepared to provide the material wealth and power to meet those responsibilities. Truman did not want to deviate from what he understood Roosevelt's role and plans in world affairs had been, and he tried for a while to become something of a broker between Churchill and Stalin. He refused to meet with Churchill before the Potsdam Conference because he did not want to give Stalin the impression that the Anglo-American leaders were "ganging up on him." Churchill, who had exchanged over 1700 messages and had 9 different meetings encompassing 120 days during the war with Roosevelt, detected a distinctly different attitude in his successor, but the wartime Prime Minister did not remain in office for a sufficient period himself to do much about it.

Actually there was at least some basis for Churchill's apprehensions even before Roosevelt's death. Arthur Schlesinger, jr., has delineated the basic American ambivalence, reflected in Roosevelt's continued allegiance to an idealistic-Wilsonian vision of the postwar world, accompanied by a characteristic hard-boiled and realistic appraisal of each sitution as it arose.[114] Both Roosevelt and Secretary of State Cordell Hull (another confimed Wilsonian) were suspicious of Churchill and his "imperialistic" objectives. James Forrestal, then secretary of the navy, records the wartime President as humorously suggesting "that the British were perfectly willing for the United States to have a war with Russia at any time and that, in his opinion, to follow the British program would be to proceed toward that end."[115] Before Yalta and immediately afterwards Roosevelt was convinced that if the Russians could experience a genuinely cooperative attitude on the part of Britain and America, as well as seeing a clear recognition of legitimate Soviet rights and interests, then their suspicions and hostility towards the western democracies might be modified and postwar cooperation between the wartime Allies made easier.[116] But his was a hope, not a prediction, and towards the end of his life the President realized that his hope had not been realized in Russia's post-Yalta activities.

The cloud of revisionist Cold War historical critique hangs over this period in such a threatening fashion that it can hardly be ignored in an examination of the role of the President during the postwar era. Robert Osgood has written that "historical revisionism—the reinterpretation of events to refute the conventional view of the past—is a recurrent phenomenon in America, particularly in the aftermath of unpopular wars." Certainly the major claim of this statement is true, however I would not place special emphasis upon American revisionist studies came only after unpopular wars, because for one thing there have been few unpopular wars in American history. But wars and their leaders, popular and unpopular, have been raked over by schools of revisionist historians. Arthur Schlesinger has observed:

> Every war in American history has been followed in due course by skeptical reassessments of supposedly sacred assumptions. So the War of

1812, fought at the time for the freedom of the seas, was in later years ascribed to the expansionist ambitions of Congressional Warhawks; so the Mexican War became a slaveholder's conspiracy. So the Civil War has been pronounced a "needless war," and Lincoln has ever been accused of maneuvering the rebel attack on Fort Sumter. So too the Spanish-American War and the first and second World Wars have, each in its turn undergone revisionist critiques. It is not to be supposed that the Cold War would remain exempt.[117]

The immediate pre-constitutional period, the Jacksonian revolution, slavery, the age of the robber barons, the Progressive era and the New Deal are some of the other more important periods in American history that have come under fire from revisionist historians. The challenges to conventional wisdom in such cases have usually been invigorating and useful, not because the newer interpretation is necessarily more correct, but because such challenges have always forced careful reexamination of the sources and interpretations of each event. Frequently, this reexamination has resulted in significant modifications and fresh insights, while at the same time strengthening the inherent validity of aspects of the initial theses.

The revisionist historians of the cold war period have at least partially fulfilled this role, having succeeded in stirring up substantial controversy by forcing a necessary and rewarding reexamination of the period. Yet there is something about the current avalanche of cold war revisionist histories and interpretations, most of which have been the work of Marxist-oriented New Left critics of American policy which does not ring true to the best traditions of earlier schools of revisionism. They appear to be not simply independent scholars searching for the truth in a terribly complex period of history, but rather an embattled group of aggressive and organized idealogues, placing the craft of history at the service of the "inevitable revolution." More unfortunately, there appears to have been considerable reluctance on the part of many of the cold war revisionists to engage in serious discussion of criticisms of their historical methodology, their use of documentary sources and the *a priori* assumptions which have encouraged much of their work. This is not the place for a full statement of this argument; however, a discussion of some of the basic reservations with the revisionist approach is appropriate here.

Robert James Maddox has distinguished between what he terms "soft" and "hard" cold war revisionists. He argues that both are "more or less identified with the New Left," focusing their criticism not only upon the more conventional historical accounts of the origins of the cold war, but "on the very nature of the American system."[118] The "soft" revisionists emphasize what they consider to be a sharp break between the wartime policies and postwar plans of Franklin D. Roosevelt, and the postwar policies of his successor, Harry S. Truman and his secretary of state, James F. Byrnes. These revisionists allege that Truman and Byrnes decided to reject Roosevelt's attitude of cooperation with the Russians and replace it by a tough, unyielding and militaristic, diplomatic offensive. In some cases their scholarship in defense of this thesis is shoddy, and normally their speculative penchant is extensive. Schlesinger illustrates such an instance, citing the situation when a strained effort was made to indicate that after Roosevelt's death, Ambassador Harriman tried to persuade the new President that a "reconsideration of Roosevelt's policy was necessary."[119] The revisionist author, Gar Alperowitz, viewing that case cites as the basis for the description of the ambassador's argument, a conversation between Harriman and the new President, quoted in Truman's *Memoirs*. But if one takes the trouble to check the passage in the *Memoirs* it is quite obvious that it reflects an altogether different point of view on the part of the ambassador:

> Before leaving, Harriman took me aside and said, "Frankly, one of the reasons that made me rush back to Washington was the fear that you did not understand, *as I had seen Roosevelt understand*, that Stalin is breaking his agreements. My fear was inspired by the fact that you could not have had time to catch up with all the recent cables. But I must say that I am greatly relieved to discover that you have read them all and that we see eye to eye on the situation."[120]

The "hard" revisionists, as Maddox puts it, "raise more fundamental issues":

> To these scholars the Cold War was the inevitable result of the American system as it developed over the years. Based upon what American leaders perceived as the need for continuous economic expansion abroad, the corporate structure itself shaped foreign policies. Whatever personal differences existed among individuals, all American policymakers were dedicated to creating an American-dominated world order which would permit the system to expand unhindered. When Russia refused to acquiesce in American world hegemony, particularly in Eastern Europe, the preforce came to be defined as the enemy. Although the "hard" revisionists themselves emphasize the events of World War II and its immediate aftermath, they see this era merely as a phase—the latest being the American intervention in Vietnam—of the ongoing struggle between a conservative capitalist order and world revolution. They reject completely the notion that American-Russian relations would have evolved very differently had F.D.R. lived, or had someone other than Truman taken his place.[121]

Both "soft" and "hard" revisionist theories of the origins of the cold war are interesting hypotheses and clearly should be tested most rigorously in the light of all available information before being accepted or rejected. Unfortunately the rigorous testing and examination of alternative explanations of historical causation have not proceeded apace with the reiteration of the "soft" and "hard" theories. In the haste to establish a school centered upon these points of view, revisionists have spent more time denouncing their critics *ad hominem* than in attempting to join issue on the very substantial criticisms and reservations which have been raised. Only by coherent dialogue can our understanding of this period advance.

This was a difficult and terribly complex period in American history. Frequently its statesmen reacted clumsily, sometimes rashly and in a contradictory fashion, to the crises with which they were confronted. The American evaluation of Soviet actions and objectives during this period was characterized by these same vacillating attitudes. Both Roosevelt and Truman wanted to think and act otherwise but events often forced their hands. There was a genuine breakdown in communication and understanding. Harriman, one of Truman's advisors who most consistently advocated a "hard line" on Soviet policy, advised the President:

> It may be difficult for us to believe, but it still may be true that Stalin and Molotov considered at Yalta that by our willingness to accept a general wording of the declaration on Poland and liberated Europe, by our recognition of the need of the Red Army for security behind its lines, and of the predominant interest of Russia in Poland as a friendly neighbor and as a corridor to Germany, we understood and were ready to accept Soviet policies already known to us.[122]

But such mutual distrust and misunderstanding, coupled with a certain clumsiness and inexperience in the realities of "power politics" on an international scale, is far from the picture of Truman and Byrnes that the "revisionists" present. And it is not simply that they have blundered into their conclusions.

If they miss the subtlety and complexity of the problems which confronted the world leaders during this period, this oversight is rooted in a more serious myopic disorder—their basic misunderstanding of the nature of the Soviet state. Viewing Soviet society as a typical nation-state, they tend to interpret Russian territorial claims and political intervention as a very normal phenomenon, motivated exclusively by national self-interest. Their sympathy with Soviet arguments for protective security have led them to embrace balance-of-power diplomacy, where the world is divided into spheres of influence, and the dominant nations are justified in taking any necessary measures within their own areas to insure their continued security. American influence and/or control in the western hemisphere is used as a justification for the exertion of similar Soviet influence in the areas in Eastern Europe and the Balkans. There is just enough truth to the situations which this analogy attempts to embrace to provide a superficial validation, but beneath that surface lie a number of tortuous questions which expose its critical weakness.

Arthur Schlesinger, in his brilliant and exceedingly fair appraisal of the cold war revisionists, admits that some immediate postwar actions by the United States could have caused the Soviets to be apprehensive, and that both sides confused and misinterpreted enough of each other's signals to lead to a substantial misunderstanding. Truman's classic *gaffe* in his abrupt cancellation of lend-lease aid and the government's incredible duplicity surrounding Russia's request for a $6,000,000 loan, increased the Soviets' suspicion and confirmed some of their greatest fears. Such diplomatic mishaps do not necessarily fall into the conspiratorial pattern, however. On the other hand, Schlesinger points out that what the revisionists omit from their analysis is the significant fact that "the Soviet Union was not a traditional national state."[123] Indeed, the facts are that it was and is "a totalitarian state, endowed with an all-explanatory, all-consuming ideology, committed to the infallibility of government and party, still in a somewhat messianic mood, equating dissent with treason, and ruled by a dictator who, for all his quite extraordinary abilities, had his paranoid moments."[124]

Marxism-Lenism gave the Russian leaders a view of the world according to which all societies were inexorably destined to proceed along appointed roads by appointed stages until they achieve the classless nirvana. Moreover, given the resistance of the capitalists to this development, the existence of any non-communist was *by definition* a threat to the Soviet Union. "As long as capitalism and socialism exist," Lenin wrote, "we cannot live in peace: in the end, one or the other will triumph—a funeral dirge will be sung either over the Soviet Republic or over world capitalism."

Stalin and his associates, whatever Roosevelt or Truman did or failed to do, were bound to regard the United States as the enemy, not because of this deed or that, but because of the primordial fact that America was the leading capitalist power and thus, by Leninist syllogism, unappeasably hostile, driven by the logic of its system to oppose, encircle and destroy Soviet Russia. Nothing the United States could have done in 1944-45 would have abolished this mistrust, required and sanctified as it was by Marxist gospel—nothing short of the conversion of the United States into a Stalinist despotism; and even this would not have sufficed, as the experience of Jugoslavia and China soon showed, unless it was accompanied by total subservience to Moscow. So long as the United States remained a capitalist democracy, no American policy, given Moscow's theology, could hope to win basic Soviet confidence, and every American action was poisoned from the source. So long as the Soviet Union remained a messianic state, ideology compelled a steady expansion of communist power.[125]

Robert James Maddox has been one of the most strident critics of the New Left-cold war revisionists. He suggests the revisionists have no interest in writing "objective" history, but are convinced that American history "begins and ends with ideology," and therefore it is the historian's task "to create a version of the past which can be used to help achieve the goals his ideological preferences dictate."[126] For the "soft" revisionist this takes the form of attempting to influence present policy by demonstrating past errors; for the "hards" it represents the challenge "to show the need for a radical restructuring of the existing system."[127]

Maddox points to the employment of double-standards by the revisionists, justifying or explaining Russia's actions by reference to national security or *Realpolitik*, and measuring western actions against some ideal standard; there is little or no effort on their part, he argues, to search for evidence that might invalidate an hypothesis. Rather there is a constant exploitation of any evidence which remotely supports their contentions, describing the motives, and goals of the Soviets as "frank" and "sincere" (and presenting Stalin's actions in the most favorable light), while disclaiming any attempt to deal systematically with Soviet foreign policy. But these are shortcomings which are common at times to both sides of the controversy, Maddox grants. His major criticism of the revisionists is the charge that they "have revised the evidence itself."[128]

Granting a generous allowance for mere carelessness . . . these books [the works of seven of the leading New Left revisionists] *without exception* are based upon persuasive misusages of the source materials. Although the frequency varies from volume to volume, even the best fails to attain the most flexible definition of scholarship. Stated briefly, the most striking characteristic of revisionist historiography has been the extent to which the New Left authors have revised the evidence itself. And if the component parts of historical interpretations are demonstrably false, what can be said about the interpretations? They may yet be valid, but in the works examined they are often irrelevant to the data used to support them. Until this fact is recognized, there can be no realistic assessment of which elements of revisionism can justifiably be incorporated into new syntheses and which must be discarded altogether.[129]

Other criticisms of the cold war revisionists have been couched in more reserved academic language and have tended to deal with value judgments and conclusions rather than to directly attack their use of historical data. Charles S. Maier has charged the revisionists with analyzing "specific historical issues on the basis of *a priori* values about the political system that most strongly affects the controversies their writings have touched off."

> For the revisionists . . . the key issues hinge not upon facts or evidence but upon assessments as to how repressive or non-repressive contemporary liberal institutions are. These judgments in turn must be made within ground rules that allow only polar alternatives for evaluating political action. What is non-revolutionary must be condemned as counter-revolutionary, and reformist political aspirations are dismissed in advance. Similarly the foreign policies of Western powers cannot escape the stigma of imperialism, for imperialism and exploitation are defined by the revisionists as virtually inherent in any economic intercourse between industrialized and less developed states, or just between unequals.[130]

Another critic of the cold war revisionists, J. L. Richardson, has emphasized the polemical character of much of their work and the conflict between their commitment to social and political points of view and their responsibilities to the disciplines of historical scholarship:

> What we have, then, is not so much Cold War history as Cold War polemic. The narrowness of vision appears to stem from the values and assumptions of the writers. As to values, the revisionist writings exemplify certain dangers in the current trend in favor of "commitment" in the social sciences. What is overlooked is that scholarship is itself a value, as well as a discipline, and that its demands represent the essential commitment of the scholar, which may conflict with his other social and political commitments. Revisionists are very conscious of this in commenting on views opposed to their own. . . . There is value in what may be termed the naive commitment of the historians to follow his material regardless of where it may lead him: Historians often dislike what happened or wish that it had happened differently. There is nothing they can do about it. They have to state the truth as they see it without worrying whether this shocks or confirms existing prejudices. The revisionists, however, give the

impression of quarrying purposefully for material to fit a structure fully designed in advance.[131]

A more sympathetic critic writes:

Whereas the radical critic clearly sees—indeed, too clearly sees—the calculation and self-interest that have marked American foreign policy, he persistently ignores the deeper sources of collective self-aggrandizement. Even if it were true that America's security in this century has been totally unconditioned by events occurring beyond our frontiers, it would not follow that our expansion must be attributed to forces generated by a particular socio-economic structure. There may be few reliable lessons that the study of state relations reveals. But one is surely that the identification of the collective self with something greater than the self is so endemic a trait in the case of great states that it may be considered to form part of their natural history. The radical attempt to find the roots of America's expansion primarily in her institutional forms dismisses this lesson. It necessarily denies that it is power itself, more than a particular form of power, which prompts expansion.

Thus radical criticism will not confront the eternal and insoluble problems inordinate power creates, just as it will not acknowledge that men possessed of this power are always ready to use it if only in order to rule over others. In the radical *weltanschauung* there is little, if any, appreciation that dominion is its own reward and that men may sacrifice material interest in order to rule (or, for that matter, to be emulated). There is also little, if any, appreciation that expansion may be rooted in an insecurity that is not simply self-generated. It is no doubt true that America's expansion is in large measure the result of an expansive concept of security and that this concept is, in part, related to the nature of America's institutions. It is not true that America's security in this century has been unconditioned by events occurring beyond our frontier and that, in consequence, to the extent our security has been compromised it has been the result of our own persistent expansionism and aggressiveness.[132]

None of the above is intended to undercut the amazing energy and influence of this new school of historians who have already made an incredible impact, particularly upon the present student generation; rather it is a challenge to them to meet these criticisms head-on, to join issue with the detailed criticisms like those quoted above. These evaluations will stand or fall on their ability to substantiate their conclusions as well. The *ad hominem* attacks but otherwise relative silence the Maddox book received is not an encouraging harbinger of what could undoubtedly be an illuminating dialogue.

We have all profited from the stimulating challenge of the revisionists; it is now time for them to take note of their thoughtful critics, no matter how harsh, and to respond in depth.

During the period just before the end of the war, and immediately thereafter, Roosevelt and Truman were kept well informed of Soviet attitudes and developments by the very able American ambassador, Averell Harriman, and his second in command, George Kennan. Harriman believed that the continued "generous and considerate attitude" adopted by the United States was considered by the Soviets as a sign of weakness:

> I cannot list the almost daily affronts and total disregard which the Soviets evince in matters of interest to us. . . .[133]

He urged effective reprisals, choosing "one or two cases where their actions are intolerable and [making] them realize that they cannot continue their present attitude except at great cost to themselves."[134]

Kennan was more eloquent and discursive in his lengthy and perceptive messages sent back to the United States in 1944 and 1945. As early as September 1944, he wrote a 35-page essay entitled "Russia—Seven Years Later," in which he carefully examined the mainsprings of Soviet policy. He later commented that "In it I poured forth, as in nothing else I ever wrote, the essence of what I knew about Russia generally, and Stalin's Russia in particular, as a phenomenon on the horizon of American policy makers."[135]

> It would be useful to the Western World to realize that despite all the vicissitudes by which Russia has been afflicted since August 1939, the men in the Kremlin have never abandoned their faith in the program of territorial and political expansion which had once commended itself so strongly to Tsarist diplomats, and which underlay the German-Russian Nonagression Pact of 1939.[136]

But Kennan was pessimistic about what the American response would be to such a frank appraisal:

> There will be much talk about the necessity for "understanding Russia"; but there will be no place for the American who is really willing to undertake this disturbing task. The apprehension of what is valid in the Russian world is unsettling and displeasing to the American mind. He who would undertake this apprehension will not find his satisfaction in the achievement of anything practical for his people, still less in any official or public appreciation for his efforts. The best he can look forward to is the lonely pleasure of one who stands at long last on a chilly and inhospitable mountaintop where few have been before, where few can follow, and where few will consent to believe that he has been.[137]

The cold war revisionists dismiss Harriman and Kennan as hardline anti-Soviets; William Appleman Williams went so far as to indicate that the basis for Harriman's antagonism was his failure during the 1920s to gain control of the world's manganese supplies through a deal with the Russians.[138] But over 20 years later the reports of these two diplomats have a prophetic ring. The general euphoria which accompanied the last days of the war and the subsequent Allied victory postponed any possibility of immediate reactions to their warnings until it was too late to change Soviet policy in areas where the Russian army had taken physical possession of the land. No subsequent information or analysis has undermined or refuted Harriman and Kennan's appraisals of Soviet policy during that period, however, and the suspicion lingers that if their advice had been heeded earlier rather than later, the overreaction which finally took place in American policy as the country responded to its frustration at its inability to inhibit Soviet moves in Eastern Europe would not have occurred.

The Soviets wasted no time in politically consolidating their control in the territory into which their armies marched during World War II. The list began with Estonia, Latvia, Lithuania and part of Poland, which they laid claim to at the time of the Nazi-Soviet Pact; by the end of the war the list included Bulgaria, Hungary and Rumania. Yugoslavia, Czechoslovakia and the rest of Poland were slated for similar "liberations," and Austria, Germany, Greece, Turkey and Iran were probably the ultimate objectives in this general Soviet political design. Soviet ideology considered national socialism in Germany as the last gasp of capitalist imperialism and looked toward the end of the war as the point when a more general breakdown of both capitalism and colonial imperialism would be universal. There was certainly considerable evidence supporting such an historical prediction in 1945 and 1946, and Soviet Russia was determined to exploit the impending crisis with every weapon in its revolutionary arsenal. On the other hand, the Russian people were exhausted and could not be quickly or easily summoned again to the battlefields to support another war outside of their homeland. With hindsight one can conclude that Churchill's admonitions were correct, that Soviet pressure in Eastern Europe should have been resisted earlier rather than later, and some basic understanding reached at that time among the three Allies about the political structure of postwar Europe, and, indeed, of the rest of the world.

American policy in world affairs during 1945 suffered from two major misconceptions of the problems at hand—one was military and the other political. The basic military error was fostered by the erroneous judgment of most of the military leaders that an invasion of Japan would be necessary before the war in the Pacific could be terminated. If indeed that was true, then the immediate entry of Soviet Russia into the war was a military *sine qua non*. The movement of a number of Russian divisions into Manchuria, so the theory continued, tying up hundreds of thousands of Japanese troops, would be a great help to the American invading army. It would prevent serious reinforcement of the defending troops already in Japan, and would probably save thousands of American lives. It also might prevent the necessity of an American invasion of the Chinese mainland.

If on the other hand such a costly invasion of Japan was not necessary and the war was just about won, the introduction at that point of the Russian army into the Pacific area of operations would not have been timely and definitely not in America's military and political interest. It guaranteed Russia a voice in all Asian postwar settlements, provided the Soviets with a base of operations in China and Korea, and a justifiable future naval and military role in the Pacific.

It turned out that the additional troops were not necessary. The Japanese sued for peace after the second atomic raid on Nagasaki, but even before that happened their defenses were so badly battered that when the 21st Bomber Command of the 20th Air Force put 896 planes in a regular bombing mission over Japan, they returned to their bases on Guam, Tinian and Saipon without the loss of a single plane. The Japanese lacked fuel and planes and could not possibly have held out against many more such raids, regardless of the atomic bombs dropped on Hiroshima and Nagasaki. In other words Japan was beaten before and without the entry of the Soviet Union into the war—and for that matter before and without the dropping of the atomic bombs. The last minute involvement of the Russians proved costly in terms of later political and military problems in the Pacific area, and the explosion of the two atomic bombs over Hiroshima and Nagasaki was a tragedy of epic proportions. Also the immediate deployment of hundreds of planes and troops from the European theater weakened the American military, hence political, negotiating position there after the war. Here was another clear demonstration of the American reliance on the priority of military, as opposed to political values.

But this is the judgment of hindsight, made under circumstances free from the terrifying pressures which weighed heavily on those responsible for making the decisions at the time. Although there were considerable differences of opinion among both the military and civilian advisors to the President as to what would be necessary to bring about a Japanese surrender, it was almost universally agreed that some small-scale invasion of the southern Japanese island of Kyushu was necessary either for a successful naval blockade (with estimated initial casualties of 30,000) or for properly preparing for and staging a large-scale invasion of the Tokyo Plain, which both of the highest ranking army generals with authority in that theater, Marshall and MacArthur, thought would eventually be necessary. From beginning to end the Joint Chiefs of Staff continued to urge Russian entry into the war at the earliest possible moment, hoping to contribute to the defeat of Japan militarily and psychologically

The second misconception which lay at the basis of the American outlook and policy was the Roosevelt and early Truman belief that the Russians were most concerned about their territorial vulnerability to hostile neighboring nations, and that their paranoia on that subject would subside once they were convinced of America's and Britain's innately fair and unselfish postwar objectives in Europe. Roosevelt and his key advisors were convinced that the terrible trauma of the war had forged a lasting alliance within which the Allies could hammer out all misunderstandings and meet to resolve conflicting interests around a conference table. They also counted upon the evident exhaustion of the Russian people and their armies, and upon the strong internal pressures on the Soviet leaders to avoid further warfare. Assuming conflicting political interests existed between Great Britain and the Soviet Union, the Americans conceived of themselves as mediators who could intervene to smooth ruffled waters and negotiate successful solutions to any conflicts which might arise. This simplistic view of Soviet policy objectives completely overlooked the Soviet Union's ideological picture of the world and its continuing commitment to revolutionary objectives.

While the Americans were looking for ways to implement this formula for a peaceful world, Russian military strategy and political tactics were being geared to achieving virtual political control in as many bordering and adjacent countries as possible. When the mopping up operation in Lithuania, Latvia and Estonia was completed, governments subservient to the Soviets were established in Rumania, Hungary and Bulgaria. Despite the agreements at Yalta between the three powers, the presence of the Red Army and Soviet political agents in these areas made the subsequent elections and shuffling of governments merely a facade for Soviet control. The same was true in Poland, where the British and the Americans put up more sustained resistance, and somewhat delayed a complete communist takeover. Only in Germany and Austria, which had been divided into zones for each occupying army, were the British and the Americans able to restrain Soviet hegemony and encourage the inhabitants to defy Soviet pressure.

Soviet territorial ambitions were not restricted to Eastern Europe. Before the end of the war the Russians developed a systematic campaign of military and diplomatic pressure upon Iran with the obvious intention of reducing this small country to a satellite status. Iran had been occupied simultaneously by British and Russian troops in August 1941 in an effort to prevent Nazi influence and to insure a direct line of communication by rail from the Persian Gulf to the Russian border. A treaty was signed in 1942 among Russia, Great Britain and Iran, permitting the presence of Allied troops in the country for the duration of the fighting, but promising to evacuate them six months after the war was over. American troops joined the British and Soviets during the war to transport precious supplies in increasing quantities on the Allied-operated Trans-Iranian railroad.

Even before the war's end the Soviets responded to this wartime hospitality and assistance by a series of moves similar to their activities in Eastern Europe, where they had reduced a number of previously independent governments to puppet status. Under the protection of their troops in the northern provinces of Iran, they encouraged and protected the growth of a pro-Soviet Iranian communist organization, the Tudeh party. When the Iranian government flatly turned down Russian demands for exclusive rights to the rich oil and mineral deposits in the northern provinces, the Soviets set the Tudeh to work, demonstrating and rioting to bring down the existing government. Their immediate objective was to obtain political autonomy (but not independence) for the northern province of Azerbaijan, where, under the protection of Soviet troops, the Tudeh party officially dissolved and transferred its membership to a so-called democratic party, or front. Just after the end of the war, it was reported that arms were distributed by reinforced Soviet troops to democratic party members and peasants, and a rebellion against the central government was set in motion. Soviet troops prevented military units of the central government from quelling the rebellion, and in December 1945, under Soviet protection, a rebel and autonomous government was declared in Azerbaijan, under the leadership of a former Tudeh party leader.

The question of Russian intervention in the affairs of Iran was raised at the foreign ministers conference in Moscow in December 1945, without any satisfactory results. The Iranian government, having protested vainly to Moscow, brought the question before the Security Council of the United Nations in London in January 1946, but Soviet Foreign Minister André Vishinsky frustrated any efforts to discuss the question, arguing it was a matter for the Soviets and the Iranians to settle by themselves. Meanwhile American resistance was beginning to stir. President Truman ordered an early evacuation of American troops from Iran, hoping to force or embarrass the Russians to follow suit. This again reflected American naiveté in dealing with the Russians. When Secretary of State Byrnes returned from the Moscow meeting of foreign ministers, Truman was alarmed at the lack of information from Byrnes with respect to the progress of those meetings and at the background information from State Department representatives detailing Soviet activities. The President was upset by the Soviet moves in Iran, and he instructed Byrnes to take a stronger position in resistance to what he then considered obvious Russian efforts to reduce Iran to a Soviet satellite.

President Harry S. Truman
Letter to Secretary of State Byrnes
Concerning Soviet Activities in Iran
January 5, 1946

Truman, I, 551-52.

My dear Jim: I have been considering some of our difficulties. As you know, I would like to pursue a policy of delegating authority to the members of the Cabinet in their various fields and then back them up in the results. But in doing that and in carrying out that policy I do not intend to turn over the complete authority of the President nor to forgo the President's prerogative to make the final decision.

Therefore it is absolutely necessary that the President should be kept fully informed on what is taking place. This is vitally necessary when negotiations are taking place in a foreign capital, or even in another city than Washington. This procedure is necessary in domestic affairs and it is vital in foreign affairs. At San Francisco no agreements or compromises were ever agreed to without my approval. At London you were in constant touch with me and communication was established daily if necessary. I only saw you for a possible thirty minutes the night before you left after your interview with the Senate committee.

I received no communication from you directly while you were in Moscow. The only message I had from you came as a reply to one which I had Under Secretary Acheson send you about my interview with the Senate Committee on Atomic Energy.

The protocol was not submitted to me, nor was the communiqué. I was completely in the dark on the whole conference until I requested you to come to the *Williamsburg* and inform me. The communiqué was released before I ever saw it.

Now I have infinite confidence in you and in your ability but there should be a complete understanding between us on procedure. Hence this memorandum.

For the first time I read the Ethridge letter this morning. It is full of information on Rumania and Bulgaria and confirms our previous information on those two police states. I am not going to agree to the recognition of those governments unless they are radically changed.

I think we ought to protest with all the vigor of which we are capable against the Russian program in Iran. There is no justification for it. It is a parallel to the program of Russia in Latvia, Estonia and Lithuania. It is also in line with the high-handed and arbitrary manner in which Russia acted in Poland.

At Potsdam we were faced with an accomplished fact and were by circumstances almost forced to agree to Russian occupation of Eastern Poland and the occupation of that part of Germany east of the Oder River by Poland. It was a high-handed outrage.

At the time we were anxious for Russian entry into the Japanese War. Of course we found later that we didn't need Russia there and that the Russians have been a headache to us ever since.

When you went to Moscow you were faced with another accomplished fact in Iran. Another outrage if I ever saw one.

Iran was our ally in the war. Iran was Russia's ally in the war. Iran agreed to the free passage of arms, ammunition and other supplies running into the millions of tons across her territory from the Persian Gulf to the Caspian Sea. Without these supplies furnished by the United States, Russia would have been ignominiously defeated. Yet now Russia stirs up rebellion and keeps troops on the soil of her friend and ally—Iran.

There isn't a doubt in my mind that Russia intends an invasion of Turkey and the seizure of the Black Sea Straits to the Mediterranean. Unless Russia is faced with an iron fist and strong language another war is in the making. Only one language do they understand—"how many divisions have you?"

I do not think we should play compromise any longer. We should refuse to recognize Rumania and Bulgaria until they comply with our requirements; we should let our position on Iran be known in no uncertain terms and we should continue to insist on the internationalization of the Kiel Canal, the Rhine-Danube waterway and the Black Sea Straits and we should maintain complete control of Japan and the Pacific. We should rehabilitate China and create a strong central government there. We should do the same for Korea.

Then we should insist on the return of our ships from Russia and force a settlement of the Lend-Lease debt of Russia.

I'm tired of babying the Soviets.

Soviet pressure upon Turkey at the end of the war and during the immediate postwar period was very similar to the pattern of activity directed against the neighboring country of Iran. During the days of the Nazi-Soviet Pact the Russians had unsuccessfully demanded land and sea bases in the Turkish Straits. Hitler and Von Ribbentrop had virtually ignored that and other Russian attempts to obtain a stronger foothold in the Black Sea area. Before the end of the war, in March 1945, the Soviets abruptly abandoned their 20-year treaty of friendship with Turkey and offered to sign a new treaty only if the Turks ceded certain areas near the Turkish-Russian border to them, granted permission for Soviet bases in the straits and placed the straits under joint Soviet-Turkish control. The Russians also demanded that Turkey abandon her long and peaceful association with Great Britain. As an indication of their serious intentions, the Soviets massed 25 divisions on the southern border of the Caucasus. When the Turks refused to accept those humiliating conditions, Russia and her new Eastern European satellites conducted a propaganda war of nerves on the Turkish government and attempted to stimulate a campaign for the separation of Armenia from Turkey. In the summer of 1946 the Soviet government renewed its demands for joint control of the straits in a formal note, copies of which were sent to the British and American governments.

For over a year in office President Truman had been gradually assessing the drift of international affairs and carefully studying and judging both the objectives and methods of Russian policy. Both he and his advisors had become increasingly alarmed by the growing Soviet truculence and the continuous pressure for Soviet control of territory and political hegemony over governments outside of the Soviet borders. The new "sphere of Soviet influence" encompassed almost all of Eastern Europe and Manchuria; their aggressive appetite for new territories appeared to be insatiable. Truman and his advisors were slowly moving away from their earlier sympathetic and tolerant attitude, and were beginning to stiffen their resistance to growing Soviet demands.

By the summer of 1946 the American government was in no mood to accede to further Soviet pressure involving additional territorial acquisitions. Truman had proposed free access for all countries to the world's strategic waterways at the Potsdam Conference, but the latest Soviet demands indicated its attempt to strengthen its position in the Middle and Near East by gaining control of Turkey and the straits, moving simultaneously into Greece, and then on to engulf Iran and Iraq. Should the Russians succeed in this venture, it would given them a commanding position from which they could move on into Arabia to control the land bridge between Europe and Asia and Africa and Asia. These Russian objectives were clearly dictated by motives other than mere fear and insecurity, and President Truman and his advisors prepared to move in order to frustrate their "imperialistic" design.

At that time the National Security Council had not yet come into existence, but informal meetings were being held among the secretaries of state, war, and navy, joined by the chiefs of staff and experts on the Mediterranean and Middle East. Already a naval task force had been ordered to the Mediterranean, and estimates of military and naval needs and capacities were hastily gathered in order to prepare to support the Turks. The President's advisors were sufficiently apprehensive about the implications of Soviet control of Turkey and subsequently of Greece that there was general agreement concerning a recommendation to oppose the Soviet proposal firmly, realizing that the United States would be obligated in the final analysis to back up such a position by force.

At a meeting at the White House in which the President accepted the recommendations of his policy advisors, General Eisenhower questioned him sharply as to whether he really understood the implications of the Soviet threat. It has been reported that the President pulled from his desk a worn map of the Middle East area and proceeded to deliver what observers have recalled as a "masterful" lecture upon the historical background of the area, and its current strategic significance. Much to the enjoyment of those present, General Eisenhower good-naturedly admitted that he was convinced that the President understood. Truman was a dedicated student of history all of his life, and frequently surprised the unsuspecting with the thoroughness of his background knowledge of important problems.

The Turkish Straits problem temporarily subsided as a consequence of the strong stand taken by Turkey, Britain and the United States, but pressure building up in Greece soon invoked serious American attention. The collapse of Italy in September 1943 had permitted the Allies to transfer considerable quantities of arms to the various guerilla bands in Greece, who had fought the Italians and had later confronted their German replacements. The Nazis had succeeded in regaining control of the major cities, but the guerillas dominated large areas of the country, and, supplied with increasing British and American arms and communications, they presented a formidable threat to the invaders. The politics of the guerilla armies were complex and fratricidal, and as early as October 1943, fighting broke out between the two principal bands—the National People's Liberation Army (in Greek letters, ELAS) and the Greek National Democratic League (EDES). The former was a left-wing, communist-oriented group, by far the largest in number; the latter, initially non-communist and republican, gradually absorbed conservative and monarchist elements. The British played a strong hand in Greece from the outset, and although they were primarily interested in driving the Nazis out of the country, they were reluctant to sit by and observe a communist-dominated state emerge.

The British were able to negotiate joint EAM (the political arm of ELAS)-EDES support of a provisional government in late 1944, but fighting broke out again in the winter of 1944-45, and British troops in Athens were hard pressed to defend the central sections of the city. After shipping in reinforcements the British were able to negotiate a settlement with the EAM-ELAS, in which the rebels agreed to disband their private army and support the government. The British in turn promised a plebiscite on the question of the return of the King and the establishment of a constitutional monarch within the framework of a democratic parliamentary government.

The provisional arrangements lasted for a year or more, but an election was finally held in the spring of 1946 under international supervision, and the King returned in September as a result of the plebiscite. But during the winter of 1946-47 increased EAM-ELAS guerilla activity broke out again, apparently organized and well supplied from outside the country. Internally, Greece faced a drastic economic crisis, and in February Britain announced the retirement of half the garrison of British regulars stationed primarily in Athens. British military activity in Greece had drawn increased criticism from labor party backbenchers in the House of Commons, and the disintegrating condition of British financial resources made such a move necessary.

On the afternoon of February 21, 1947, the British ambassador in Washington telephoned the Department of State to request an immediate appointment. The new secretary of state, General George Catlett Marshall, World War II chief of staff of the United States Army, had just left his office on his way to Princeton University to deliver an important address, but the under-secretary, Dean Acheson, arranged for a meeting between the ambassador and the secretary for the following Monday. He requested that a formal note be delivered in the meantime so that it could be studied by the State Department staff in preparation for that meeting. When delivered, the message revealed that the situation in Greece was desperate. There was a real possibility that the democratically elected political regime was in danger of being overthrown by an invading army of Greek guerillas who had been supplied with arms in neighboring communist countries. And there was an equal danger that the regime would collapse from within because of an economic crisis of monumental proportions. Turkey was not in quite as bad shape, but if Greece fell, Turkey would soon follow. An official British study of the economic situation in that country and of the condition of the Turkish army indicated that Turkey also needed considerable economic and military aid at once if she was going to be able to maintain and defend her political independence. Great Britain had come to the end of the road; she revealed her total incapacity to deal with the situation and asked the United States what she proposed to do about it. All British troops were to be withdrawn from Greece within a short period, and economic aid would be terminated at the end of March. The British hoped that the United States would be able to assume those burdens, having earlier declared (with Britain) its strong interest in seeing that neither nation fell under communist control.

The response in Washington to the British proposal was immediate and positive. Both the Greeks and the Turks had asked for help earlier, and a large Greek loan had been under consideration for some time. Specialists in the State Department had made careful studies of the condition of the Greek economy, had assessed its strengths and weaknesses and were ready to recommend where funds could be effectively spent. Several presidential appointees had recently returned from a special economic mission to Greece, and they documented further the near-panic condition of the Greek economy and the shaky status of the political structure. State Department officials realized that if the United States did not act and act promptly, the collapse of constitutional government in Greece was imminent. High-level meetings were called which brought together officials from the State Department and the Departments of War and the Navy. Plans for rushing not only economic, but also military, aid to the Greeks were discussed. Within five days of the initial telephone call from the British embassy, and barely three days after Secretary Marshall's discussion with the British ambassador, the Near Eastern Affairs staff had produced a set of comprehensive proposals embodied in a paper entitled "Position and Recommendations of the Department of State Regarding Immediate Aid to Greece and Turkey."[139] The proposals were based upon the principle that the political and territorial integrity of Greece and Turkey should be maintained, and that every effort should be extended to insure the democratic character and the sound economic foundations of their governments.

To implement these objectives, proposals were made to extend immediate export-import bank credits to the two governments without the normal inhibiting restrictions, and to submit legislation for longer rate financing; it was also suggested that military supplies be made available under existing legislation, recommending additional legislation to authorize the additional supplies needed; finally they proposed to authorize the assignment of professionally trained civilian personnel for economic, administrative and financial assignments with the Greek government—personnel who would be able to supervise proper utilization of American financial and technical aid.

These proposals were subsequently changed, amended and even enlarged upon in the course of the many revisions by the highest echelons of both the State Department and the White House. Within days they were incorporated into a special message to be delivered to a joint session of Congress by the President. Before this, the message was discussed at a meeting which the President held at the White House for congressional leaders of both parties, most of whom were lukewarm to the proposal until Dean Acheson arose and held everyone spellbound with his incisive analysis of the threat of a communist takeover in both these countries. When Acheson finished there was not a negative vote in the room, and American foreign policy was well on its way to an important turning point, perhaps as significant as the changes executed in 1939 or during the first administration of Theodore Roosevelt at the turn of the century.

President Truman delivered his special message on aid to Greece and Turkey to a joint session of Congress on March 12, 1947. He requested an immediate appropriation of $400 million—$250 million for Greece and $150 million for Turkey—and authorization for the assignment of American civilian and military personnel "to assist in the tasks of reconstruction and for supervising the use of such financial and material assistance as may be furnished."[140] The Congress responded quickly, and a bill authorizing the President's recommendations passed the Senate before the end of April and the House in early May. That in itself was a revolutionary departure from past practice, for rarely did Congress rush through and vote on an almost half a billion dollar program of that nature in such a short period of time. Furthermore, it was not a loan but an "aid" program, the money was being appropriated directly for the use of people outside of the continental limits of the United States and to governments outside of this hemisphere. There was no peacetime precedent in American history for such a program.

But those were not the only revolutionary departures occurring at that time. In his speech to the joint session of Congress, President Truman enunciated a new foreign policy for the United States, a policy which came to be known as the "Truman Doctrine." Arguing that World War II had been fought to create conditions in which nations would be able to work out their own ways of life free from coercion, the President affirmed that that was one of "the primary objectives of foreign policy of the United States . . . ,"[141] and one of the reasons why this country took a leading part in the establishment of the United Nations. He observed, however, that "the peoples of a number of countries of the world [had] recently had totalitarian regimes forced upon them against their will."[142] He mentioned Poland, Rumania and Bulgaria as examples, indicating that the political regimes in those countries had been established by coercion and intimidation "in violation of the Yalta agreement,"[143] and under protest from the United States. The economic and military aid programs for Greece and Turkey were being established, he explained, to help those countries protect themselves from similar attempts at intimidation.

But above and beyond his specific proposals for aid to Greece and Turkey the President asserted:

> I believe that it must be the policy of the United States to support free peoples who are resisting attempted subjugation by armed minorities or by outside pressures.

I believe that we must assist free peoples to work out their own destinies in their own way.[144]

Such a declaration, in the context of the President's candid indictment of Soviet intimidation in Poland, Rumania and Bulgaria, and his charge of communist insurrections in Greece mounted on its borders by Soviet-oriented nations, clearly indicated a stiffening of American policy with respect to Soviet political and military intervention in the Balkans and in Eastern Europe. It was not the beginning of the "cold war," but it certainly was the first major American response to the aggressive Soviet actions which had been taking place in Europe since the end of the "hot" war.

President Harry S. Truman
The Truman Doctrine—Special Message
To Congress on Aid to Greece and Turkey
March 12, 1947

Public Papers of the Presidents: Harry S. Truman, 1947, 176-80.

[As delivered in person before a joint session.]

Mr. President, Mr. Speaker, Members of the Congress of the United States: The gravity of the situation which confronts the world today necessitates my appearance before a joint session of the Congress.

The foreign policy and the national security of this country are involved.

One aspect of the present situation, which I present to you at this time for your consideration and decision, concerns Greece and Turkey.

The United States has received from the Greek Government an urgent appeal for financial and economic assistance. Preliminary reports from the American Economic Mission now in Greece and reports from the American Ambassador in Greece corroborate the statement of the Greek Government that assistance is imperative if Greece is to survive as a free nation.

I do not believe that the American people and the Congress wish to turn a deaf ear to the appeal of the Greek Government.

Greece is not a rich country. Lack of sufficient natural resources has always forced the Greek people to work hard to make both ends meet. Since 1940, this industrious, peace loving country has suffered invasion, four years of cruel enemy occupation, and bitter internal strife.

When forces of liberation entered Greece they found that the retreating Germans had destroyed virtually all the railways, roads, port facilities, communications, and merchant marine. More than a thousand villages had been burned. Eighty-five percent of the children were tubercular. Livestock, poultry, and draft animals had almost disappeared. Inflation had wiped out practically all savings.

As a result of these tragic conditions, a militant minority, exploiting human want and misery, was able to create political chaos which, until now, has made economic recovery impossible.

Greece is today without funds to finance the importation of those goods which are essential to bare subsistence. Under these circumstances the people of Greece cannot make progress in solving their problems of reconstruction. Greece is in desperate need of financial and economic assistance to enable it to resume purchases of food, clothing, fuel and seeds. These are indispensable for the subsistence of its people and are obtainable only from abroad. Greece must have help to import the goods necessary to restore internal order and security so essential for economic and political recovery.

The Greek Government has also asked for the assistance of experienced American administrators, economists and technicians to insure that the financial and other aid given to Greece shall be used effectively in creating a stable and self-sustaining economy and in improving its public administration.

The very existence of the Greek state is today threatened by the terrorist activities of several thousand armed men, led by Communists, who defy the government's authority at a number of points, particularly along the northern boundaries. A Commission appointed by the United Nations Security Council is at present investigating disturbed conditions in northern Greece and alleged border violations along the frontier between Greece on the one hand and Albania, Bulgaria, and Yugoslavia on the other.

Meanwhile, the Greek Government is unable to cope with the situation. The Greek army is small and poorly equipped. It needs supplies and equipment if it is to restore authority to the government throughout Greek territory.

Greece must have assistance if it is to become a self-supporting and self-respecting democracy.

The United States must supply this assistance. We have already extended to Greece certain types of relief and economic aid but these are inadequate.

There is no other country to which democratic Greece can turn.

No other nation is willing and able to provide the necessary support for a democratic Greek government.

The British Government, which has been helping Greece, can give no further financial or economic aid after March 31. Great Britain finds itself under the necessity of reducing or liquidating its commitments in several parts of the world, including Greece.

We have considered how the United Nations might assist in this crisis. But the situation is an urgent one requiring immediate action, and the United Nations and its related organizations are not in a position to extend help of the kind that is required.

It is important to note that the Greek Government has asked for our aid in utilizing effectively the financial and other assistance we may give to Greece, and in improving its public administration. It is of the utmost importance that we supervise the use of any funds made available to Greece, in such a manner that each dollar spent will count toward making Greece self-supporting, and will help to build an economy in which a healthy democracy can flourish.

No government is perfect. One of the chief virtues of a democracy, however, is that its defects are always visible and under democratic processes can be pointed out and corrected. The government of Greece is not perfect. Nevertheless it represents 85 percent of the members of the Greek Parliament who were chosen in an election last year. Foreign observers, including 692 Americans, considered this election to be a fair expression of the views of the Greek people.

The Greek Government has been operating in an atmosphere of chaos and extremism. It has made mistakes. The extension of aid by this country does not mean that the United States condones everything that the Greek Government has done or will do. We have condemned in the past, and we condemn now, extremist measures of the right or the left. We have in the past advised tolerance, and we advise tolerance now.

Greece's neighbor, Turkey, also deserves our attention.

The future of Turkey as an independent and economically sound state is clearly no less important to the freedom-loving peoples of the world than the future of Greece. The circumstances in which Turkey finds itself today are considerably different from those of Greece. Turkey has been spared the disasters that have beset Greece. And during the war, the United States and Great Britain furnished Turkey with material aid.

Nevertheless, Turkey now needs our support.

Since the war Turkey has sought additional financial assistance from Great Britain and the United States for the purpose of effecting that modernization necessary for the maintenance of its national integrity.

That integrity is essential to the preservation of order in the Middle East.

The British Government has informed us that, owing to its own difficulties, it can no longer extend financial or economic aid to Turkey.

As in the case of Greece, if Turkey is to have the assistance it needs, the United States must supply it. We are the only country able to provide that help.

I am fully aware of the broad implications involved if the United States extends assistance to Greece and Turkey, and I shall discuss these implications with you at this time.

One of the primary objectives of the foreign policy of the United States is the creation of conditions in which we and other nations will be able to work out a way of life free from coercion. This was a fundamental issue in the war with Germany and Japan. Our victory was won over countries which sought to impose their will, and their way of life, upon other nations.

To ensure the peaceful development of nations, free from coercion, the United States has taken a leading part in establishing the United Nations. The United Nations is designed to make possible lasting freedom and independence for all its members. We shall not realize our objectives, however, unless we are willing to help free peoples to maintain their free institutions and their national integrity against aggressive movements that seek to impose upon them totalitarian regimes. This is no more than a frank recognition that totalitarian regimes imposed upon free peoples, by direct or indirect aggression, undermine the foundations of international peace and hence the security of the United States.

The peoples of a number of countries of the world have recently had totalitarian regimes forced upon them against their will. The Government of the

United States has made frequent protests against coercion and intimidation, in violation of the Yalta agreement, in Poland, Rumania, and Bulgaria. I must also state that in a number of other countries there have been similar developments.

At the present moment in world history nearly every nation must choose between alternative ways of life. The choice is too often not a free one.

One way of life is based upon the will of the majority, and is distinguished by free institutions, representative government, free elections, guarantees of individual liberty, freedom of speech and religion, and freedom from political oppression.

The second way of life is based upon the will of a minority forcibly imposed upon the majority. It relies upon terror and oppression, a controlled press and radio, fixed elections and the suppression of personal freedoms.

I believe that it must be the policy of the United States to support free peoples who are resisting attempted subjugation by armed minorities or by outside pressures.

I believe that we must assist free peoples to work out their own destinies in their own way.

I believe that our help should be primarily through economic and financial aid which is essential to economic stability and orderly political processes.

The world is not static, and the *status quo* is not sacred. But we cannot allow changes in the *status quo* in violation of the Charter of the United Nations by such methods as coercion, or by such subterfuges as political infiltration. In helping free and independent nations to maintain their freedom, the United States will be giving effect to the principles of the Charter of the United Nations.

It is necessary only to glance at a map to realize that the survival and integrity of the Greek nation are of grave importance in a much wider situation. If Greece should fall under the control of an armed minority, the effect upon its neighbor, Turkey, would be immediate and serious. Confusion and disorder might well spread throughout the entire Middle East.

Moreover, the disappearance of Greece as an independent state would have a profound effect upon those countries in Europe whose peoples are struggling against great difficulties to maintain their freedoms and their independence while they repair the damages of war.

It would be an unspeakable tragedy if these countries, which have struggled so long against overwhelming odds, should lose that victory for which they sacrificed so much. Collapse of the free institutions and loss of independence would be disastrous not only for them but for the world. Discouragement and possibly failure would quickly be the lot of neighboring peoples striving to maintain their freedom and independence.

Should we fail to aid Greece and Turkey in this fateful hour, the effect will be far reaching to the West as well as to the East.

We must take immediate and resolute action.

I therefore ask the Congress to provide authority for assistance to Greece and Turkey in the amount of $400,000,000 for the period ending June 30, 1948. In requesting these funds, I have taken into consideration the maximum amount of relief assistance which would be furnished to Greece out of the $350,000,000 which I recently requested that the Congress authorize for the prevention of starvation and suffering in countries devastated by the war.

In addition to funds, I ask the Congress to authorize the detail of American civilian and military personnel to Greece and Turkey, at the request of those countries, to assist in the tasks of reconstruction, and for the purpose of supervising the use of such financial and material assistance as may be furnished. I recommend that authority also be provided for the instruction and training of selected Greek and Turkish personnel.

Finally, I ask that the Congress provide authority which will permit the speediest and most effective use, in terms of needed commodities, supplies, and equipment, of such funds as may be authorized.

If further funds, or further authority, should be needed for the purposes indicated in this message, I shall not hesitate to bring the situation before the Congress. On this subject the Executive and Legislative branches of the Government must work together.

This is a serious course upon which we embark.

I would not recommend it except that the alternative is much more serious.

The United States contributed $341,000,000,000 toward winning World War II. This is an investment in world freedom and world peace.

The assistance that I am recommending for Greece and Turkey amounts to little more than 1/10 of 1 percent of this investment. It is only common sense that we should safeguard this investment and make sure that it was not in vain.

The seeds of totalitarian regimes are nurtured by misery and want. They spread and grow in the evil soil of poverty and strife. They reach their full growth when the hope of the people for a better life has died.

We must keep that hope alive.

The free peoples of the world look to us for support in maintaining their freedoms.

If we falter in our leadership, we may endanger the peace of the world—and we shall surely endanger the welfare of this Nation.

Great responsibilities have been placed upon us by the swift movement of events.

I am confident that the Congress will face these responsibilities squarely.

President Truman's message marked a significant departure from traditional American foreign policy. No previous peacetime President had attempted to commit the United States openly to the support and the defense of a country outside of the western hemisphere. The enunciation of the open-ended principle of committing the United States "to support free peoples who are resisting attempted subjugation by armed minorities or by outside pressures," suggested a long-range policy, different in kind and in intent from any other foreign policy actively pursued over the course of American history. James Monroe had tentatively suggested such a principle in his first draft of the Monroe Doctrine, but John Quincy Adams was quick to seize upon it and persuade him that such a policy would be disastrous for the United States, and would tend to weaken the effect of the Monroe Doctrine in his own hemisphere. This new Truman Doctrine, as it came to be known, was also at opposite poles from Washington's eloquent plea in his Farewell Address, and in sharp contrast to the essentially isolationist history of this country. The implications of it were overwhelming and suggested a continuing role for the United States in the defense of independent sovereign nations all over the world.

Such an extension of American responsibility naturally required a corresponding expansion of the powers and responsibility of the President. Theodore Roosevelt had responded to several situations which brought the presidency into the international arena; he most certainly actively pursued what he considered to be American interests outside of the continental limits of the United States. As wartime Presidents both Woodrow Wilson and Franklin Roosevelt had assumed international military obligations and advocated American responsibility in the making and keeping of the peace, but the Truman Doctrine went considerably beyond those previous extensions of America's traditional "insular" foreign policy. The only paradigm in recent history for such global responsibility was the role of Great Britain during the previous two centuries, when she used her immense naval and mercantile influence to maintain a balance of power consistent with her national and imperialistic interests. The new American doctrine suggested a new definition of national interest, resting upon ideology, or at least upon the maintenance of the status quo and based upon the principle of self-determination of existing national states. Such a policy foreshadowed many complex and agonizing problems for the future, and some Americans were not happy over the prospects of attempting to carry out this policy.

The most sustained and articulate opposition came from the dean of American journalists, Walter Lippmann. In the summer of 1947 Lippmann wrote a series of discerning newspaper columns in which he analyzed what he considered to be a new and dangerous American foreign policy. At the focal point of his criticism was the so-called Truman Doctrine, but most of his complaints were directed at George Kennan, who had returned to this country to be in charge of a new planning staff in the State Department. There is no doubt that Kennan's informed and often brilliant messages from his former outpost in Moscow had contributed substantially to the development of a far greater awareness on the part of American policymakers of the roots and pattern of postwar Soviet political thinking and practice. It was also clear that he had helped stimulate a more sophisticated and more forceful American policy vis-à-vis the Soviet Union.

Between 1944 and 1947 Kennan wrote a number of key documents which were directed towards the education of American political leaders with respect to the operative principles of Soviet ideology, and the probable thrust of that ideology as it was being applied to the reality of the contemporary world situation. In an 8,000-word cable which Kennan wired back to the United States on Washington's birthday in 1946, he characterized the Soviet leaders as

> a political force committed fanatically to the belief that with US there can
> be no permanent modus vivendi, that it is desirable and necessary that the

internal harmony of our society be disrupted, our traditional way of life be destroyed, the international authority of our state be broken, if Soviet power is to be secure.[145]

Kennan did not consider this particular message one of his best. In fact, after reading it over with what he describes as "horrified amusement" 20 years later, he characterized much of it as reading "exactly like one of those primers put out by alarmed congressional committees or by the Daughters of the American Revolution, designed to arouse the citizenry to the dangers of the Communist conspiracy."[146] Nevertheless it established his reputation in Washington, was read by the President and numerous cabinet members and was printed and circulated among "hundreds, if not thousands, of higher officers in the armed services"[147] by Secretary of the Navy James Forrestal, who became a strong supporter of the chargé d'affairs in the American embassy in Moscow.

The following year Kennan sent Forrestal, at the secretary's request, a paper discussing the nature of Soviet power as a policy problem for the United States. Kennan indicates that it represented the "literary extrapolation of the thoughts which had been maturing in my mind, and which I had been expressing in private communications and speeches, for at least two years into the past."[148] American policy vis-á-vis the Soviet Union, Kennan advised in that paper, should be based upon an understanding that the Soviet ideology, which considers an irreconcilable conflict to exist between the historical mission of socialism and the dying system of western capitalism, remains the prevailing dynamic which guides the leaders of that nation. He pointed out that the Soviets had not abandoned that ideological principle, but on the contrary had developed an internal political structure and an external policy which was based upon that fundamental premise. It manifested itself in the absolute political control which Soviet leaders maintained within their society, protecting their leadership from any opposition and their society from internal weaknesses and disunity, and in a constant effort externally to hasten the ultimate collapse of western capitalism.

"Soviet policies," Kennan argued, "will reflect no abstract love of peace and stability, no real faith in the possibility of a permanent happy coexistence of the Socialist and capitalist worlds, but rather a cautious, persistent pressure toward the disruption and weakening of all rival influence and power."[149]

Kennan did not believe that the Kremlin was under any "ideological compunction to accomplish its purposes in a hurry."[150] Convinced of the historical validity of their ideology, the Soviet leaders, like the Church, were quite willing to pursue their ultimate objectives patiently and without taking any major risks which might seriously delay their inevitable triumph. Kennan did not anticipate an all-out Soviet military assault upon the West which might jeopardize that projected inevitable victory, but rather foresaw a long campaign, stimulated by the covert activities of the international communist apparatus and affiliated parties and constant diplomatic pressures, supported by the tremendous Soviet military machine.

The man who was about to become head of the State Department planning staff proposed two basic principles upon which American policy should be built.

The first of these principles subsequently became famous as the "policy of containment":

> In these circumstances it is clear that the main element of any United States policy toward the Soviet Union must be that of a long-term, patient but firm and vigilant containment of Russian expansive tendencies. . . . Soviet pressure against the free institutions of the western world is something that can be contained by the adroit and vigilant application of counter-force at a series of constantly shifting geographical and political points, corresponding to the shifts and maneuvers of Soviet policy, but which cannot be charmed or talked out of existence.[151]

The second principle which Kennan proposed as a general guideline for American policy towards the threat of world communism certainly did not receive the consideration in practice or even in discussion that the "containment" principle did:

> But in actuality the possibilities for American policy are by no means limited to holding the line and hoping for the best. It is entirely possible for the United States to influence by its actions the internal developments, both within Russia and throughout the international Communist movement, by which Russian policy is largely determined. This is not only a question of the modest measure of informational activity which this government can conduct in the Soviet Union and elsewhere, although that, too, is important. It is rather a question of the degree to which the United States can create among the peoples of the world generally the impression of a country which knows what it wants, which is coping successfully with the problems of its internal life and with the responsibilities of a World Power, and which has a spiritual vitality capable of holding its own among the major ideological currents of the time. To the extent that such an impression can be created and maintained, the aims of Russian Communism must appear sterile and quixotic, the hopes and enthusiasm of Moscow's supporters must wane, and added strain must be imposed on the Kremlin's foreign policies. For the palsied decrepitude of the capitalist world is the keystone of Communist philosophy. Even the failure of the United States to experience the early economic depression which the ravens of the Red Square have been predicting with such complacent confidence since hostilities ceased would have deep and important repercussions throughout the Communist world.[152]

This positive proposal to unleash the dynamic and creative forces of American society has been largely overlooked by critics of Kennan's containment policy. At the time his incisive analysis of the mainsprings of Soviet policy tended to reinforce less articulate but developing American antagonism and resistance to further Soviet territorial and political encroachments, while on the other hand his positive and creative thinking was a major influence in the development of the Marshall Plan.

When it leaked out that George Kennan was the author of the "X" article published in *Foreign Affairs*, however, Lippmann and others were convinced that he was the *eminence grise* of the Truman Doctrine, and they continued to identify him as such. This was unfortunate, as it most certainly was not true. Nevertheless the Lippmann arguments against the new American foreign policy were formidable. In a dozen pithy articles (later collected into a small book) he pointed out many of the glaring pitfalls and deficiencies in attempting to "contain" the Soviet Union. They represent a prophetic introduction to most of the major arguments which were later mounted against those who aggressively pursued the Truman Doctrine in the 1950s and the 1960s. Lippmann maintained that the United States was not capable militarily or economically of providing or sustaining a counterforce at "a series of constantly shifting geographical and political points, corresponding to the shifts and maneuvers of Soviet policy."[153] Another disadvantage to that policy, he pointed out, was that it would be handing the greatest strategic advantage to the enemy, for it would be allowing him to pick the battlefields at points where his military, geographical, political and economic advantages were obvious. He also argued that the policy of "containment" was unsuited to our constitutional background, for in order to be ready to maintain counterforces at a "series of constantly shifting geographical and political points," the executive branch would either have to usurp the appropriation function of the legislative branch in order to maintain a level of military and economic reserves capable of quickly responding to these thrusts, or be forced to go to the Congress each time with a request for authorization and funds, and in so doing, give the Soviets a tremendous tactical advantage.

The Lippmann critique continued in this devastating fashion. It would be impossible, he asserted, for the United States to oppose Soviet military forces at all the possible points of expansion, and so we would be dependent, in Eastern Europe and Asia, upon satellite troops and nations. American counterforces, Lippmann argued, would have to be made up of "Chinese, Afghans, Iranians, Turks, Kurds, Arabs, Greeks, Italians, Austrians, of anti-Soviet Poles, Czechoslovaks, Bulgars, Yugoslavs, Albanians, Hungarians, Finns and Germans."[154]

> The policy can be implemented only by recruiting, subsidizing and supporting a heterogeneous array of satellites, clients, dependents and puppets. The instrument of the policy of containment is therefore a coalition of disorganized, disunited, feeble or disorderly nations, tribes and factions around the perimeter of the Soviet Union.
>
> . . . To organize a coalition of disunited, feeble and immature states, and to hold it together for a prolonged diplomatic siege, which might last for ten or fifteen years, is, I submit, impossibly difficult.[155]

Lippmann went on to develop his central thesis that the United States should not involved itself in a worldwide campaign to wall in the Soviet Union, but rather should, through diplomatic means, negotiate a settlement of the outstanding conflicts between the two nations, and arrange a withdrawal of all Soviet, British, French and American troops from their occupying positions in Europe. The presence of Soviet troops in Germany, Austria, Poland, Czechoslovakia, Hungary, Rumania and Bulgaria constituted a serious threat to the country's natural allies in Western Europe, he maintained; and it was the future security and welfare of these natural allies (including the other nations in the Americas), that we tended to ignore. They would be the major losers in a cold war between the United States and the Soviet Union, and would be inclined to extricate themselves from a conflict which could only sap their strength and weaken the potential for their survival and development.

Towards the end of his analysis Lippmann acknowledged what he described as "serious competitors" in the field of foreign policy—the United Nations and the Marshall Plan. The United Nations, in his view, would become the instrument for maintaining peace "*after* a settlement of the Second World War has been arrived at."[156] Its councils would only be poisoned by the interjection of the cold war debate between the United States and the Soviet Union. The Marshall Plan, on the other hand, was the ideal approach which the United States should consistently pursue in its foreign policy. To those who identified the Marshall Plan as a mere extension of the Truman Doctrine, Lippmann said:

> The difference is fundamental. The Truman Doctrine treats those who are supposed to benefit by it as dependencies of the United States, as instruments of the American policy for "containing" Russia. The Marshall speech at Harvard treats the European governments as independent powers, whom we must help but cannot presume to govern, or to use as instruments of an American policy.[157]

Before leaving this question, Lippman directed a final blast at Mr. "X," the no-longer secret author of the containment article, as he reflected upon the distinction between the Truman Doctrine and the Marshall Plan:

> The real issue is hidden because the Truman Doctrine was promulgated shortly after General Marshall became Secretary of State, and because he made the decision to go to the support of Greece and Turkey, which was a concrete application of the Truman Doctrine. The issue is confused by the fact that Mr. Molotov and the Soviet propaganda abroad and many publicists here at home are representing the Marshall proposals to Europe as an application of the Truman Doctrine. The confusion is compounded still more because the Director of Secretary Marshall's Planning Staff is now known, through the publication of Mr. X's article, to have been the leading expert upon whose observations, predictions and hypotheses the Truman Doctrine is based.[158]

There is great irony in this comment in the light of what we now know of the protagonist, George Kennan. Kennan was still lecturing at the War College when the Truman Doctrine was drafted, but fortunately there exists a first-hand report of his reaction to it when it was first presented to him a few days before it was promulgated:

> To say that he found objections to it is to put it mildly. He objected strongly both to the tone of the message and the specific action proposed. He was in favor of economic aid to Greece, but he had hoped that military aid to Greece would be kept small, and he was opposed to aid of any kind to Turkey. It was nevertheless to the tone and ideological content of the

message, the portraying of two opposing ways of life, and the open-end commitment to aid free peoples that he objected most. The Russians might even reply by declaring war! Kennan voiced his objections to a number of people, including, finally, Acheson. It was too late. The decision had already been taken and widely approved.[159]

In his *Memoirs* Kennan provides further evidence from diary and lecture notes recorded at that time that he was strongly opposed to the critical passages in the Truman message which "placed our aid to Greece in the framework of a universal policy rather than in that of a specific decision addressed to a specific set of circumstances."[160] He, and Lippmann too, for that matter, was not opposed to granting aid to the Greeks at that time, but he drew the line on the Turkish aid program precisely because it was almost exclusively for military purposes. A detailed examination of his *Memoirs*, which are generously supplemented with diary notations and reports filed with the Department of State, makes it clear that Lippmann's monster image of the hard-line, anti-communist chief of the State Department's planning staff is highly inaccurate. There is no doubt that Kennan was a thoughtful student of the theory and reality of the communist state, and that his long tenure in Moscow had steeled him against the acceptance of simplistic solutions to the very complex relationship between the Soviets and the West. But the fact that he clearly perceived the aggressive political designs of the leaders in the Kremlin did not mean that he accepted a policy of universal and militaristic anticommunism as Lippmann inferred from the "X" article. Kennan did not feel, as the article plainly indicated, that the Soviets were willing to risk war to achieve their ends; the danger that he warned against was political in nature. The policy of containment that Kennan had in mind was political containment, and that policy was best served by creating political and economic strength in those areas not already dominated physically and politically by the Soviets. This is borne out not only by his recorded reactions at the time of the announcement of the Truman Doctrine, but by everything the man has done and said in his lifelong career as an extraordinary public servant.

In the postwar period Kennan set for himself the task of opposing the gross oversimplifications which characterized so much of American thinking about the Soviet Union. Many thought Americans were entering into a new period of history where the goodwill and cooperation which had seemed to permeate the wartime alliance would continue to create a climate of international cooperation in peacetime, a period where the United States and the Soviet Union would be able to accommodate each other's interests at the negotiation table and contribute towards each other's welfare by acts of generosity and friendship. As a realist Kennan could not accept such wishful thinking. His many years in Moscow, including a wartime stint, totally disabused him of any such notion, and he took pains to warn his superiors of falling into such erroneous thinking. He was extremely dubious about the Yalta agreements from the start, and firmly believed that there would be no method of dislodging the Soviets from the geographical areas they had captured through the advances of the Red Army. He wanted the United States to stop talking about democratic elections in those areas and disassociate itself from the totalitarian rule he predicted they were bound to fall prey to:

I felt that we were only deceiving ourselves and the Western public by clinging to the hope that what the foreseeable future held in store for most of these countries could be anything less than complete Communist domination and complete isolation from the West on the Communist pattern. This being so, I saw no reason why we should go out of our way to make things easier for the Russians in this area by aid programs of one sort or another or by sharing moral responsibility for what they were doing.[161]

Furthermore, Kennan felt that in deference to the "pipe dream of a general European collaboration, and out of fear, in particular, lest the Russians be offended if we took important action without them, we were neglecting positive undertakings for the reconstruction of a vigorous and hopeful state of affairs in the part of Europe which really was accessible to our influence.[162] Lippmann and many others missed the major thrust of Kennan's thinking and seized upon the term "containment" as if it were a vulgar plea for an anticommunist crusade. In reality Kennan and Lippmann were in substantial agreement on most of the major questions of American foreign policy. They were opposed to a universal, heavily militaristic program in support of nations willing to oppose communism, and they were in favor of a balance of power theory, where the United States put the major part of its resources into building up those countries in Western Europe which had the political stability to utilize them effectively, and were, like ourselves, experienced and dedicated to the democratic process. Where they were not in agreement was: 1) in their conflicting estimates regarding the effect the next 10 or 15 years would have upon the ability of Soviet totalitarianism to dominate the restless masses at home, and to control the increasing tensions which Kennan felt were sure to increase in the satellite regimes; and 2) Lippmann's bland assurance that it would be possible to negotiate a satisfactory peace treaty in Germany and bring about the withdrawal of all occupying troops from both Western and Eastern Europe. Lippmann considered that a *sine qua non* for the reconstruction of a friendly, vital Western European community; Kennan considered it desirable but highly improbable.

Kennan has since admitted certain deficiencies in the "X" article which led to much of the misunderstanding of it. The first was his failure to distinguish between the Soviet Union and its satellites, and then to emphasize that much of the weakness and internal tension he predicted would come about would be generated by the latter. A second flaw was not to stress that what he meant by containment was "the political containment of a political threat," and not "containment by military means of a military threat."[163] The third deficiency was his failure to define the proper economic and geographic limits of containment to be dictated by American interests and resources. The latter two have been grossly violated by later American policymakers, and it undoubtedly caused Kennan considerable remorse to have been identified with policies so greatly at variance with his views. Kennan admits that the experience "was a painful one," and he suffered particular "anguish" over Lippmann's confusion concerning his role in the development of the Truman Doctrine and the Marshall Plan:

To be held as the author of the former, and to have the latter held up to me as the mature correction of my youthful folly, hurt more than anything else.[164]

But a public explanation and/or a rebuttal were not the options of a career diplomat.

In reality, the criticism of the Truman Doctrine, particularly the open-ended commitment to aid any and all "free peoples," resulted rather quickly in administration spokesmen tempering its apparent potentially universal application. Testifying less than two weeks after the President's speech, Assistant Secretary of State Dean Acheson said in his opening statement:

> We have been asked whether this establishes a pattern for all future requests for American assistance. Any requests of foreign countries for aid will have to be considered according to the circumstances in each individual case. In another case we would have to study whether the country in question really needs assistance, whether its request is consistent with American foreign policy, whether the request for assistance is sincere, and whether assistance by the United States would be effective in meeting the problems of that country. It cannot be assumed, therefore, that this government would necessarily undertake measures in any other country identical or even closely similar to those proposed for Greece and Turkey.[165]

When questioned by Senator Smith of New Jersey, Secretary Acheson replied in a similar vein:

> I think that what the President said was much more limited than what you now suggest to me, and very clear indeed. He proposed that we should give this aid to Greece and Turkey. He pointed out that here were two countries which had constitutional systems which were founded on democratic principles which were struggling to maintain those systems. He said it was to our interest that all peoples who had free governments and democracies, that were moving toward human freedoms, should not be coerced into giving up those institutions, and that whatever help we could extend would be in accordance with our policy. I think that is what the President said quite clearly in his message.[166]

Both the misunderstandings and the real conflicts highlighted in this study of this critical dispute are significant, because they were the same misunderstandings and conflicts which characterized the almost schizoid foreign policy of the United States for the next 20 years. During most of the Truman administration the Marshall Plan thinking predominated, but with the advent of the administration of Dwight D. Eisenhower and particularly his secretary of state, John Foster Dulles, the Truman Doctrine was resurrected with a vengeance. In the Middle East, in Central America and Asia, American economic aid and military power (frequently covertly, e.g. Guatemala) were applied in situations which met the broad definitions laid down by the Truman Doctrine. They were initiated under the justification of protecting the sovereign independence of the countries involved, but in the final analysis they accomplished neither, and started a chain of commitments which sapped the country's strength and resources, making it difficult to deal with its own burgeoning problems, and damaged its prestige and relations in other parts of the world.

It is not the principle which is being challenged here, but the possibility that any single country could undertake such responsibilities under circumstances so disadvantageous and remote from its influence and control. The President naturally became the focal point of all of these situations, for he was confronted with the decision to act or not to act, and once having decided, he was burdened with all the lesser decisions which stemmed from the original action and the responsibility and political consequences (including blame) which the policy created. The office and the nation survived these experiences in the 1950s but there were ample indications even then that if similar situations continued in number and depth of commitment, they would impose too heavy a burden upon this country's resources, both human and economic, would preclude a serious attack upon problems of poverty, disease, urban blight and discrimination at home and would irreparably damage American prestige and alliances abroad. If it proved true, then that would suggest that the Truman Doctrine created problems by extending presidential power beyond its proper and legitimate limits.

Certainly Kennan was the principal architect of a policy which recognized the aggressive, antidemocratic force of communist ideology at a time when many in power wanted to overlook it. He argued for the necessity of resisting this thrust, at times even militarily, when there were no other alternatives and when the military arms of the East and the West came into an actual physical confrontation with one another. But the emphasis of his policy of containment was economic and political, and the Marshall Plan and the economic organization of Europe were far more representative of the thrust of his ideological cold war than were the military operations in Lebanon or the Eisenhower threat to China vis-â-vis the off-shore islands. Kennan saw time as the strongest advantage the West possessed, and he believed that if the western democracies could rehabilitate their broken and ailing political and economic systems, and remain firm in their resistance to the ideology of communism, in time the communist power and threat would weaken from within as the human appetite for freedom broke through the cold night of authoritarianism, thriving on oppression and militarism. That was the positive side of the cold war, a war, which the West, by and large, has won, despite its loss of confrontations like Vietnam, a country located a ridiculous distance from the tangible and real interests of the western democracies, where initial power bases were negligible and the democratic and political institutions of the country they were defending practically nonexistent.

The Truman Doctrine has plagued the United States since its inception, and although the aid plans for Greece and Turkey may have prevented a communist takeover in Greece and a Russian invasion or the increase of Russian influence in Turkey, the long-range results of the more general principle of military containment have not been impressive. The communists have not been contained by the threat of the use of counterforce, and when they have decided to attack, as they did in Korea and later in Vietnam, they have moved regardless of the possibility of American resistance. The doctrine's defenders claim victories not only in Korea, but in Guatemala and Lebanon, since by the actual use of force or its threat, the Soviet Union was prevented from gaining greater influence in those areas, and in Berlin where the Soviets were kept from dislodging the American army from its established bridgehead. The trouble with their argument is that whatever "victories" were achieved in those situations were brought about by the application or actual presence of armed force, which would have been available with or without the Truman Doctrine if the United States had decided to act. The universal threat of the application of such force hardly prevented the use of military force by the communists when they felt confident of winning, as for example in Korea; nor are there any clearly documented cases of the doctrine's actually discouraging other onslaughts from which the Soviets or their satellites withdrew because of the threat of American force.

While the Truman Doctrine's positive contributions are at least questionable, its negative effects are obvious. Over the past few decades the doctrine has been largely responsible for identifying the United States with an anticommunist crusade, interpreted by some to include offensive anti-Soviet action, such as the threatened wars of liberation in Eastern Europe, and by others to have led to a series of fundamentally anticommunist defense pacts with countries located around the perimeters of Soviet and Chinese communist power. Such threatened wars and defense pacts have not seriously weakened or discouraged Soviet or Chinese military aggression in Europe or Asia, but they have helped to poison the international diplomatic atmosphere and to strain our internal politics, our social fabric and our internal economy by the enormous military manpower and weapons drain that they have imposed for the past two decades.

This is not meant to be an affirmation of the cold war "revisionist" school of historians, who have blamed the United States almost exclusively for the existence of the conflict, and have glossed-over or justified the Soviet Union's actions, which, generally speaking, have triggered American overreaction. Moreover, American policy was not completely dominated by the Truman Doctrine during the late 1940s and 1950s, and it is clear that the creative and energizing impacts of the Marshall Plan and, later, Point Four, the Alliance for Progress, and even the Peace Corps, using an entirely different emphasis, have met with varying degrees of success and have helped to construct a different climate and image of American policy and American goals. Yet the Truman Doctrine syndrome has persisted for most of the last two decades; it has dominated the thinking of the American people and their policymakers, and has permeated America's actions in world affairs. It has accounted for much of the tremendous erosion of international goodwill which was directed towards the United States after World War II, and it has frequently undercut the positive and creative intentions of programs such as the Marshall Plan. On the whole it has tended to prop up dictators like Ngo Dinh Diem in Vietnam and Francisco Franco in Spain, without really encouraging any democratic social or political revolutions in the countries it has touched. In short, it has tended to identify the United States with a policy of reaction and militarism in a period of worldwide unrest and revolution, and has contributed towards making the actual imperialistic and totalitarian design of the Soviet Union appear like the blueprint for a democratic revolt of the masses.

In reviewing the events surrounding the drafting of the presidential message which enunciated the Truman Doctrine, President Truman and others who have described these events in detail, have provided an intimate glimpse of the institution of the modern presidency in the process of decision-making. The President was and is forced to rely heavily upon the work of his own personal staff and departmental assistants in preparing the extensive background work essential to such important policy statements. The process by which this critical document was transformed from an appeal to the Congress for economic and military aid for two specific countries threatened by internal and external pressures emanating from the Soviet Union into a universal policy of profound importance, is still not clear. The message itself was drafted by many hands, primarily those in the State Department, and was changed and redrafted several times before reaching its final form.

Although in complete agreement with the specific goal of immediate aid to Greece (although not to Turkey), George Kennan was one foreign policy advisor who recoiled at the thought of the broad implications of such a general policy statement being made by the country at that time. His reaction is particularly important in view of his later role as a policymaker in the State Department, and in the light of his well-known position as a person favoring firm political and diplomatic resistance to Soviet aggression. Kennan saw in that presidential message a commitment by this country to become involved politically, economically and ultimately militarily, if necessary, in every international situation in which Soviet influence could be detected as constituting a decisive influence. He realized, as many of his colleagues apparently did not, that such a policy, raised to the level of a universal principle, would undercut diplomatic freedom of maneuver and invite many negative reactions, reactions which a less truculent, more ambiguous and more sophisticated, quiet but unannounced resolution to resist Soviet power would not. Kennan's notes committed to paper at that time bear out his contention that he felt it was highly uncertain that "we would invariably find it in our interests or within our means to extend assistance to countries that found themselves in this extremity."[167] Subsequent events have proved the wisdom of this observation. The Truman Doctrine went beyond the limits within which the United States could maintain such a commitment on a universal basis, and at the same time preserve and support its own institutions, and meet the growing demands and needs of its own people.

In reflecting upon these events, President Truman, very typically and courageously, has assumed full responsibility for that aspect of the message. He stated that he was well aware of America's isolationist tradition and meant the doctrine's ringing challenge to signal an important departure from that policy and to enunciate a statement of this country's intention to establish its world leadership:

> This was the time to align the United States of America clearly on the side, and the head, of the free world. I knew that George Washington's spirit would be invoked against me, and Henry Clay's, and all other patron saints of the isolationists. But I was convinced that the policy I was about to proclaim was indeed as much required by the conditions of my day as was Washington's by the situation in his era and Monroe's doctrine by the circumstances which he then faced.[168]

Although cast in the future tense, the passage was written long after the event, and may reflect hindsight as well as foresight. But there is considerable evidence that

Truman was looking for an opportunity to assert America's new role in world affairs, to warn the Soviets in unequivocal language that America's patience had run out, and that the era of cooperation and good feeling was to be replaced by a tough and belligerent defense of our national interest, defined now in terms of the maintenance of international peace, order and the present boundaries of existing national states.

There is no doubt in my mind that some effective resistance to communist imperialism was necessary at that time, perhaps even much earlier; certainly later. In question was not the nature of the Soviet threat or the will of America to resist that reality, but the form and commitment of that resistance. The form selected by the President and his advisors established a firm commitment to a principle which went not only considerably beyond the limits of any previous American commitment, but considerably beyond the limits it would be possible to maintain. And despite future creative and constructive programs of economic and technical assistance, which helped to stimulate democracy and independence in most instances, the Truman Doctrine identified America's postwar role as that of a defender of the status quo. In the midst of a worldwide upheaval against colonialism, imperialism, capitalism and white domination, this proved to be an impossible position to maintain.

The impact of the Truman Doctrine upon the presidency was tremendous. Although Theodore Roosevelt was the first American President to seek a leadership role upon the world stage, the events of World War II and the wartime leadership of Franklin D. Roosevelt made it inevitable that his successors would inherit the mantle of world leadership, whether they sought it or not. The sheer power and wealth which America amassed clinched this leadership role for her; the relevant question was not whether the country would respond to its historical demand, but rather what the character of the response would be. Unfortunately the Truman Doctrine conveyed the notion that America's fundamental response to the complex challenge of world leadership was a military one, that is, the threat of military force to be used in response to communist aggression. The problem, however, was that communist aggression itself was a response to and not a cause of the crises, brought about by fear, ignorance, poverty and hunger. These could not be contained by an arms program, a series of defensive alliances or the threat of military forces used against internal revolutionary action or outside aggression. That was clearly foreseen by Kennan, Marshall and even Truman in the later formulation of the Marshall Plan and Point Four, but those constructive programs were frequently forced to vie with or take second place to the military response. That was to reach tragic proportions in the 1960s, but it was clearly foretold in a series of miscalculated steps taken during the 1950s, when the ringing military threat of the Truman Doctrine, particularly in the Eisenhower administration, overshadowed the patient economic, social and political responses necessary to deal with the real crises and not simply their outward manifestations.

The nature of the problem made it inevitable that it would be the President who would determine the fundamental character of the response. His constitutional role as foreign policy leader and Commander in Chief, and the wartime integration of those roles insured it, and in so doing enhanced the power of the presidential office.

(The cases that will be studied beyond this point will reflect this new institutional position of power, and some of the problems it created.) The United States and its presidential leaders could not have renounced these new responsibilities even if they had so desired, and whenever the quality of their response failed to rise to the challenge of leadership, not only this country, but now the world, would suffer the consequences.

New Problems in National Security

The extraordinary pressures of World War II brought about a de facto working unity between the military services which enabled them to get through the war without a serious breakdown of relationships. That is not to say, however, that all was smooth sailing, nor that there was sufficient and satisfactory coordination of their respective missions at all levels of command. There was, in fact, a great deal of infighting between the services, a tremendous amount of costly duplication of functions and many serious disagreements between them with respect to strategy and tactics. The firm but not obtrusive guiding hand of the wartime Commander in Chief, Franklin D. Roosevelt, prevented these disputes from reaching a point of paralysis, and the wise and tolerant leadership of General Marshall aided and abetted him. Without a degree of political genius put into operation there, the whole *ad hoc* arrangement might very well have broken down. But by the end of the war it was clear that this wartime administrative structure would not be satisfactory to handle peacetime problems, and there was general agreement that some form of unification of the services was necessary and desirable. A special committee created by the Joint Chiefs of Staff spent the best part of the last year of the war touring the service headquarters in Europe and the Pacific, interrogating military leaders and personnel. The committee came up with an endorsement for the creation of a single military department, supported by Generals Eisenhower and MacArthur, Admirals Nimitz and Halsey and a "substantial number of other commanders in the field and many officers in Washington."[169]

Still a number of important navy officials held back, and led by Admiral J. O. Richardson, they strongly opposed early schemes of unification, and even swung Nimitz and Halsey back into line with their views. But the imperatives for substantial change in the existing structure were too great to resist. The navy took the offensive and prepared its own plan of reorganization, which although forestalling organic integration of the services, contained many far-reaching ideas and proposals. Indeed, the problem of determining a viable military structure for the postwar world involved critical problems apart from unification. There was first of all the problem of the atomic bomb and atomic energy. Who was to control the future use, development and production of nuclear energy and all of its by-products? What was to be the military's role in that development? The wartime escalation of the political role of the top military leaders, and the growing recognition that security problems normally involved international political policy questions as well as military decisions, clearly indicated, as Samuel Huntington has pointed out, that some kind of a fundamental reorganization of the military establishment and reassessment of its relation to its Commander in Chief were very much overdue.[170]

The problem of the control and development of atomic energy was settled before an acceptable plan for reorganization of the services could be worked out. As early as October 1945 President Truman sent a message to Congress expressing his hope for international control of the atomic bomb, as well as the peaceful use of atomic energy, and requested legislation for its domestic control. The President had previously rejected a proposal made by retiring Secretary of War Henry Stimson in a cabinet meeting in September 1946, recommending that this country go directly to Moscow (along with the British) and approach the Russians with an agreement which would "limit the use of the atomic bomb as an instrument of war" and "encourage the development of atomic power for peaceful and humanitarian purposes." Stimson argued:

> For if we fail to approach them now and merely continue to negotiate with them, having this weapon rather ostentatiously on our hip, their suspicions . . . will increase. It will inspire them to . . . an all-out effort to solve the problem. If the solution is achieved in that spirit, it is much less likely that we will ever get the kind of covenant we may desperately need in the future.[171]

Instead of following Stimson's suggestion, the President joined with the British and the Canadians in a proposal to the United Nations asking that it create a commission for the control of atomic energy to ensure its use in peaceful undertakings. Unfortunately this proposal only generated a vindictive debate between the representatives of the East and West who got nowhere at all. In the meantime a dispute over military or civilian control of the atomic program on the home front developed. President Truman was in favor of civilian control, but the legislation then before the Congress, initially prepared by a special committee named by Secretary of War Stimson, seemed to many to be a continuation of the same military influence that had been in control of the "Manhattan Engineer District" which had produced the bomb. By the end of October the Senate decided to create a new committee to deal exclusively with the problem, and Senator Brien McMahon of Connecticut was made its chairman.

By that time the President had decided that the Johnson-May bill, the atomic energy measure then under consideration by the Congress, should be amended to provide clearly for civilian supremacy, and Senator McMahon agreed to sponsor such an amendment and later introduced a clean bill incorporating this principle into it. But the military refused to go along, and after patiently listening to their arguments and considering a memorandum on the question from the new secretary of war, Robert P. Patterson, the President directed the secretaries of both services and all military personnel to support the administration position of civilian control embodied in the McMahon bill.

Later, when the senator ran into serious opposition in the Congress, where attempts were made to weaken the provisions for civilian control, the President made public a strong letter to the senator in support of the measure. When

McMahon had trouble again in the spring shortly before the bill was passed, the President tried to help out again with a press conference statement aimed at discouraging amendments which might weaken or compromise the principle of civilian control. The McMahon bill passed both houses intact, and was signed by the President as the Atomic Energy Act of 1946 on August 1.

The significance of President Truman's strong insistence upon the principle of civilian control of atomic energy and, in effect, control of the bomb, cannot be overemphasized. It was one of the critical decisions in the postwar period, and the President's leadership never lagged. Truman had great respect for the military, but he was not in awe of the military leaders around him. After the top military leaders and their civilian service heads indicated their support for strong military influence in the control of atomic energy, the President *ordered*, not *requested* them to support this decision, which countermanded their own points of view.

President Harry S. Truman
Memorandum to the Secretaries of War and the Navy
On Civilian Control of Atomic Energy
January 23, 1946

Truman, II, 3-4.

I have read the Secretary of War's memorandum of December 27th, giving his view, together with those of certain members of the Interim Committee, on my proposals for specific amendments to the May-Johnson bill.

After careful consideration, it is my judgment that the recommendations contained in my memorandum of November 30th should be adhered to without modification.

I direct your attention to the following items of particular importance:

(1) A commission established by the Congress for the control of atomic energy should be exclusively composed of civilians. This is in accord with established American tradition and has found its way into statutory provisions which expressly prohibit members of the Armed Forces on active status from serving in other Governmental posts. These provisions the May-Johnson bill seeks to modify. In my judgment, the problem of atomic energy does not justify the departure.

I agree that in times of national emergency it may be desirable to call upon members of the Armed Forces to serve in administrative posts for which their experience peculiarly fits them. In such event, the Congress may, as it has in the past, pass specific enabling legislation. But I believe this to be an unusual step, to be invoked by the Congress only when the national interest or safety demands it.

(2) An absolute Government monopoly of ownership, production and processing of all fissionable materials appears to me imperative. *Fissionable* materials are, of course, to be distinguished from *source* materials from which fissionable materials may be derived. By fissionable materials, I mean such as U235, or Plutonium or any substance enriched in these beyond its natural state.

I recognize that administering close controls of fissionable materials may in some respects prove difficult. But the difficulty is small compared to the advantages of government monopoly in dealing with international problems—or compared to the danger of permitting anyone other than the Government to own or produce these crucial substances, the use of which affects the safety of the entire Nation. The benefits of atomic energy are the heritage of the people; they should be distributed as widely as possible. Government monopoly alone will assure both the material safety and the maximum utilization of atomic energy for the public welfare.

(3) Consistent with these principles I believe it essential that atomic energy devices be made fully available for private patents, and regulation of royalty fees to insure their reasonableness. These provisions will assure widespread distribution of the benefits of atomic energy while preserving the royalty incentive to maintain the interest of private enterprise.

While I have covered only three of the major points in my memorandum of November 30th, I deem adherence to all the recommendations in that memorandum to be essential.

The Chairman of the Military Affairs Committee of the House and the leaders in the House should be advised that the Administration desires recommitment of the May-Johnson bill for purposes of amendment or, failing this, that no steps be taken to alter the present status of the bill in the House.

It is my wish, furthermore, that in appearing before Congressional committees or in discussions with Members of Congress relative to atomic energy legislation officials of the Administration present views not inconsistent with the points given in my memorandum of November 30th and reaffirmed herein.

H. S. T.

President Harry S. Truman
Public Letter to Senator Brien McMahon
Supporting the Atomic Energy Bill
February 1, 1946

Truman, II, 4-5.

My dear Senator McMahon: You have requested my views on S. 1717, a bill for the domestic development and control of atomic energy. I wish to give you my thoughts at this time because I consider the subject of paramount importance and urgency, both from the standpoint of our welfare at home and that of achieving a durable peace throughout the world.

I appreciate the thorough and impartial manner in which atomic energy hearings have been held before your Committee. I believe that the hearings, in keeping with democratic tradition, have aided the people in obtaining a clearer insight into the problems which such legislation must meet.

You will recall that I sent a special message to the Congress on October 3, 1945, calling for legislation to fix a policy for the domestic control of atomic energy. Since then I have given considerable time to the further study of this most difficult subject. I have had the advantage of additional technical information and expressions of public opinion developed at the hearings. With this background I feel prepared to recommend in greater detail than before what I believe to be the essential elements of sound atomic energy legislation: [The letter then set forth in the same order the three points made in the foregoing memorandum to the Secretaries of War and Navy, in approximately the same language. It then continued:]

4. In my message of October 3rd, I wrote:

"Our science and industry owe their strength to the spirit of free inquiry and the spirit of free enterprise that characterize our country. . . . [This] is our best guaranty of maintaining the preeminence in science and industry upon which our national well-being depends."

Legislation in this field must assure genuine freedom to conduct independent research and must guarantee that controls over the dissemination of information will not stifle scientific progress.

Atomic energy legislation should also insure coordination between research activities of the Commission and those of the proposed National Science Foundation, now under consideration by the Congress.

5. Each of the foregoing provisions for domestic control of atomic energy will contribute materially to the achievement of a safe, effective international arrangement making possible the ultimate use of atomic energy for exclusively peaceful and humanitarian ends. The Commission should be in a position to carry out at once any international agreements relating to inspection, control of the production of fissionable materials, dissemination of information, and similar areas of international action.

I feel that it is a matter of urgency that sound domestic legislation on atomic energy be enacted with utmost speed. Domestic and international issues of the first importance wait upon this action.

To your Committee, pioneers in legislation of vast promise for our people and all people, there beckons a place of honor in history.

Sincerely,

Harry S. Truman

The navy plan for reorganization of the armed services, developed at the request of Secretary of the Navy James Forrestal by a committee headed by Ferdinand Eberstadt, addressed itself to the central issue of the reorganization debate, namely the essential military-political nature of most national security problems, and the necessity of coordinating the thinking, planning and execution of those departments of the executive branch of the government primarily involved. The Eberstadt committee proposed the continuation of the three separate services, but recommended that a National Security Council be created in which the State

Department and the three services would "interlock military with economic, intelligence and production planning."[172]

The army plan, presented by Lt. General J. Lawton Collins, actually proposed bona fide integration of the three services into "a single military department with a single Secretary and a single Chief of Staff of the Armed Forces, who would be not only an advisor to but an 'executive' for the Secretary." Under that proposal the air force, still a stepchild of the army, but a wartime full partner in the Joint Chiefs of Staff, would become an independent and coequal service, with primary responsibility for all "land-base combat aviation, other than that which is assigned to the Navy or to the Army for reconnaissance purposes or for the spotting of gunfire and for messenger service."[173] Of course this struck at the heart of the growing naval air force, an increasingly important element of contemporary and certainly future navy strategy and tactics. The obvious head-on clash between the army and navy proposals, and the real danger which the army plan constituted to the continued growth and independence of the navy was ominous. The navy desperately tried to delay any congressional action on a bill incorporating most of the army's proposals, and succeeded in getting the bill before the Senate Naval Affairs Committee, presided over by an old friend of the navy, Senator David I. Walsh of Massachusetts. That of course solved nothing, but it gave the navy some additional time to mount a defense. The struggle demanded presidential action, however, and after a number of months of interservice congressional maneuvering and appeals to the public for support of their respective approaches, President Truman submitted a message on unification to the Congress, which virtually endorsed the army program, although the President later wrote that he "endorsed fully the Navy's emphasis on the need for some means of more effectively meshing military planning with our foreign policy and agreed also that we needed to provide long-range plans for industrial mobilization consistent with the civilian economy."[174]

Congress responded by attempting to draft a bill which would incorporate the President's recommendations, and still be acceptable to both the army and the navy. A subcommittee of the Senate Military Affairs Committee prepared eight different drafts of the bill, but the navy continued to oppose all of them. The President finally called in the secretaries of both services, and asked them to sit down and to try and get together on the problem. "I knew it would work out better if I did not order the two branches of the services to reach an agreement, and I therefore suggested that they sit down together and work out their points of agreement and disagreement."[175] But President Truman removed one critical point from the controversy before the negotiations began; he had decided against a single chief of staff as reflecting too much of a "man on horseback" philosophy.

Truman was obviously a little too optimistic at that point, for although the secretaries did sit down and reach some accord,[176] they disappointed him by not being able to reach any agreement on four vital points: "a single military establishment; setting up three coordinate branches of the service; control of aviation; and administration of the Marine Corps." Commenting upon the situation in his *Memoirs*, the President wrote:

These four points were the basic issues which had always been the cause of conflict between the Army and the Navy. I was deeply disappointed that no substantial progress had been made toward resolving this traditional conflict, and I decided then that the only way in which unification could move forward was for me to settle personally each of four points of difference between the services. On June 15, after long and deliberate study, I made the decision in a letter to the Secretaries and to the heads of the congressional committees dealing with naval and military matters.

In this decision I supported the War Department's view that a single Department of National Defense was necessary to effective unification. I also supported the War Department's opinion that a separate Air Force should be established, and that the Air Force should take over all land-base aviation, including naval reconnaissance, anti-submarine patrol, and protection of shipping. It seemed to me that no one could give a valid reason for continuing the expensive duplication of land-based air services then existing.

I took the Navy's view that the function of the Marine Corps should continue undisturbed. I felt that if a Marine Corps were necessary, efforts to draw a hard and fast line as to the extent of its participation in amphibious operations and land fighting would be futile. I saw much justification in the Navy's position that the Marine Corps should be permitted to do those things essential to the success of a particular naval campaign.[177]

President Harry S. Truman
Letter to the Secretaries of War and the Navy
On the Unification of the Armed Forces
June 15, 1946

Public Papers of the Presidents: Harry S. Truman, 1946, 306-08.

Gentlemen: I have read with care your joint report of May 31, 1946. It was also helpful to me to have the full oral presentation of the points involved, which you and the members of your Departments made to me on June 4th.

I am pleased and gratified at the progress you have made. I feel that we have come a long way in narrowing the zone of disagreement which had previously existed between the services. The full understanding reached on eight vital aspects of unification is a significant accomplishment. These eight elements are Council of Common Defense, National Security Resources Board, Joint Chiefs of Staff, omission of single Military Chief of Staff, Central Intelligence Agency, Procurement and Supply, Research Agencies and Military Education and Training.

In addition to these eight points of agreement, I am advised also by representatives of both services that they are in accord in their attitude toward the provision in the Thomas Bill, S. 2044, which provides for four assistant secretaries in charge of Research, Intelligence, Procurement, and Training, respectively. They believe that such assistant secretaries are unnecessary. I agree with their position that the presence of these four assistant secretaries is undesirable because they would greatly complicate the internal administration of the services and that such a plan would deprive the secretaries of the respective services of functions which are properly theirs.

Your report of May 31st listed four items upon which you were unable to agree. An analysis of your comments contained in your report, and in the lengthy discussion which we had, discloses that the services are not nearly so far apart in their attitude toward these points as had been reported. It is my firm conviction that the determination of these questions in the manner which I present herein will result in a plan which incorporates the best features offered by the respective services.

With reference to the points upon which full agreement was not reached my position is as follows:

1. Single military department

There should be one Department of National Defense. It would be under the control of a civilian who would be a member of the cabinet. Each of the services would be headed by a civilian with the title of "Secretary." These secretaries would be charged with the internal administration within their own services. They would not be members of the cabinet. Each service would retain its autonomy, subject of course to the authority and overall control by the Secretary of National Defense. It is recognized that the services have different functions and different organizations and for these reasons the integrity of each service should be retained. The civilian secretaries of the services would be members of the Council of Common Defense and in this capacity they would have the further opportunity to represent their respective services to the fullest extent.

2. Three coordinated services

There should be three coordinate services—the Army, Navy and Air Force. The three services should be on a parity and should operate in a common purpose toward overall efficiency of the National Defense under the control and supervision of the Secretary of National Defense. The Secretaries of the three services should be known as Secretary for the Army, Secretary for the Navy, and Secretary for the Air Force.

3. Aviation

The Air Force shall have the responsibility for the development, procurement, maintenance and operation of the military air resources of the United States with the following exceptions, in which responsibility must be vested in the Navy:

(1) Ship, carrier and water-based aircraft essential to Naval operations, and aircraft of the United States Marine Corps.

(2) Land-type aircraft necessary for essential internal administration and for air transport over routes of sole interest to Naval forces and where the requirements cannot be met by normal air transport facilities.

(3) Land-type aircraft necessary for the training of personnel for the afore-mentioned purposes.

Land-based planes for Naval reconnaissance, anti-submarine warfare and protection of shipping can and should be manned by Air Force personnel. If the three services are to work as a team there must be close cooperation, with interchange of personnel and special training for specific duties.

Within its proper sphere of operation, Naval Aviation must not be restricted but must be given every opportunity to develop its maximum usefulness.

4. United States Marine Corps

There shall be maintained as a constituent part of the Naval service a balanced Fleet Marine Force including its supporting air component to perform the following functions:

(1) Service with the Fleet in the seizure or defense of Advance Naval Bases or for the conduct of such limited land operations as are essential to the prosecution of a Naval campaign.

(2) To continue the development of those aspects of amphibious operations which pertain to the tactics, technique, and equipment employed by the landing forces.

(3) To provide detachments and organizations for service on armed vessels of the Navy.

(4) To provide security detachments for protection of Naval property at Naval stations and bases.

It is important that the basic elements of the plan of unification be stated clearly. The eight fundamental points agreed upon and the four points which are herewith decided, constitute a total of twelve basic principles that should form the framework of the program for integration.

There is no desire or intention to affect adversely the integrity of any of the services. They should perform their separate functions under the unifying direction, authority and control of the Secretary of National Defense. The internal administration of the three services should be preserved in order that the high morale and esprit de corps of each service can be retained.

It was gratifying to have both of you and General Eisenhower and Admiral Nimitz assure me that you would all give your wholehearted support to a plan of unification no matter what the decision would be on those points upon which you did not fully agree. I know that I can count upon all of you for full assistance in obtaining passage in the Congress of a Bill containing the twelve basic elements set forth above.

Very sincerely yours,

Harry S. Truman

Note: The Secretaries' joint report, in the form of a letter dated May 31 and released with the Presidents reply, is published in the Congressional Record (vol. 92, p. 7425). The report outlines the eight points of agreement between Secretaries Patterson and Forrestal substantially as they are stated in the President's letter to the Committee Chairmen (Item 137). A summary of the positions taken on the four remaining points follows:

1. Single Military Department

War Department view. The military establishment should be set up as a single entity, headed by a civilian of Cabinet rank with authority and responsibility for the several services. The administration and supervision of the services should, however, so far as possible be delegated to their respective heads, in order that each service should have as much freedom of development as possible, and in order that the traditions and prestige of each should not be impaired.

Navy Department view. There was a need for unification, but in a less drastic and extreme form. Serious disadvantages would result from combining the services into one department. Such a step would involve sacrifices of administrative automony and service morale. Certain advantages would result from placing a Presidential Deputy with clearly defined powers of decision over specified matters at the head of the Council of Common Defense. From this as a starting point, it would be possible to move forward toward such further measures of unification as became advisable, based on further experience.

2. Three Coordinate Branches

War Department view. The military establishment should contain three coordinate branches—naval, ground, and air—each of which should have a civilian head and a military commander. These officials should have access to the President, but not Cabinet rank, since that would be in derogation of the position of the civilian head of the military establishment

Navy Department view. The national security required maintenance of the integrity of the Navy Department, headed by a civilian Secretary of Cabinet rank. Naval aviation, together with surface and subsurface components, had been integrated within the Navy, and similar integration by the Army of its air and ground forces would be in the best interest of national security. However, if the alternatives were three military departments or one, the Navy preferred three departments.

3. Aviation

War Department view. Responsibility for the development, procurement, maintenance, and operation of the military air resources of the United States should be a function of the Air Force, with exception of enumerated responsibilities which should be vested in the Navy.

Navy Department view. One reason for the Navy's strong conviction against a single department was the continued efforts of the Army air forces to restrict and limit naval aviation. To accomplish its fundamental purpose, the Navy needed a certain number of landplanes for naval reconnaissance, anti-submarine warfare, and protection of shipping. Landplanes, to be effective, must be manned by naval personnel trained in naval warfare. The Navy also required air transport essential to its needs.

4. United States Marine Corps

War Department view. There should be maintained as a constituent part of the naval service a balanced Fleet Marine Force including its supporting air component for (1) service with the fleet in the seizure of enemy positions not involving sustained land fighting, and (2) to continue the development of tactics, techniques, and equipment relating to those phases of amphibious warfare which pertain to waterborne aspects of landing operations.

Navy Department view. There should be maintained as a constituent part of the naval service a balanced Fleet Marine Force including its supporting air component for (1) service with the fleet in the seizure or defense of advance naval bases or for the conduct of such limited land operations as are essential to the prosecution of a naval campaign, and (2) to continue the development of those aspects of amphibious operations which pertain to the tactics, techniques, and equipment employed by land forces.

The President thought he had settled the dispute and expected compliance on the part of the army and navy, and quick action by the Congress. He got neither. Although he had attempted to arrive at a balanced compromise, the President's decisions were mostly against the navy, and the admirals held out for another six months before different positions and functions within the President's compromise structure could be clearly defined. It was one thing to create a secretary of defense, and quite another to put muscle into his power and responsibility. The navy reasoned that they could live with such a structure if the secretary had little or no power to interfere with their own operation; and they were largely able to get their own way. In the definitions of roles and missions of the services, language was finally worked out between the army and navy (with heavy emphasis upon the word coordinate) which did not really restrict what they considered to be their vital interests, but at the same time did not really solve any of the basic problems of integration. The document, which was later issued by the President as an executive order, was what Walter Millis has called an example of "semantic evasion," and the *Economist* described as "the remarkable structure of the agreement which conceals so many disagreements."[178] The following month President Truman submitted an entirely new bill to the Congress, incorporating the earlier agreements and decisions; six months later the National Security Act of 1947 became law.

The new law provided for a National Security Council (NSC), made up of the President, the secretary of defense, the secretary of state, the secretaries of the three services, the chairman of the new National Security Resources Board (also created in the new law) and such other department and/or agency heads as the President might add at a later date. The Central Intelligence Agency (CIA) was placed under jurisdiction of the council. In theory at least the council was expected to generate national security policy recommendations, based upon intelligence information supplied by the CIA and evaluated and analyzed by the heads of the agencies responsible for military, diplomatic and industrial planning and operations.

The "military establishment," as it was now officially designated, was to consist of the secretary of defense (a cabinet rank position), three independent departments, each with a civilian secretary (not of cabinet rank) as an administrative head and a chief of staff in command. The new secretary of defense would have three special civilian assistants and the War Council, made up of the three service department secretaries and the three chiefs of staff. But he was to have only "general direction, authority and control" over the service departments. He was also provided with several coordinating agencies: the Munitions Board to coordinate military procurement and the Research and Development Board to coordinate military research. His most significant responsibility was the power to "supervise and coordinate" the budget estimates.

What integrations of command functions there were in the new law were centered in the Joint Chiefs of Staff, at last authorized by statute (it had existed up to that time by informal action by the President) and transformed into a permanent agency with a secretariat and a staff, along with many joint committees. The Joint Chiefs (made up of the chiefs of staff of the three services, plus an optional chief of staff to the President) were still to serve as military advisors to the President as well as to the secretary of defense, and were also to transmit presidential military decisions to the service departments involved.

This extremely cursory review of the extended negotiations preparatory to the President's submittal of his final recommendations for the reorganization of the armed services after the war's end gives some indication of the complexity of the question and some hint to the extensive problems ahead for the President in his role as Commander in Chief in the future. For the previous 156 years the Presidents of the United States in peacetime had been able virtually to ignore any major responsibilities in this area. In the early period there was some activity against Indians, and later on sporadic problems on the borders and outside of the country, but until the twentieth century the President had needed to bring his powers as Commander in Chief into focus only during wartime. Some increase in that emphasis was noticeable during the Theodore Roosevelt and Wilson administrations, and later during the administration of Franklin D. Roosevelt, particularly in the Far East, but the change brought about by World War II was far out of proportion to anything else in our past history.

From 1945 on the peacetime military problems and commitments of the United States increased by a magnitude almost beyond the scope of finite imagination. Military government obligations in Italy, Japan and Germany, and the maintenance of military installations in the Pacific, in Europe, and other scattered parts of the world constituted the major source of this burden. Continuing or soon to develop struggles in Greece, China, the Philippines, the Middle East and elsewhere where American arms and economic support, if not military personnel, were called for, demanded immediate attention. It had already been made clear that a military establishment of that magnitude could not operate effectively under the limited parochial pattern of the prewar military and naval structures. The question was: How fundamental were the changes introduced by the National Security Act of 1947? Had it provided a rationalized (in the Weberian sense) structure for the military establishment? Did it restore to the Commander in Chief sufficient control through his secretary of defense to enable him to direct and control policies and planning in a coordinated military establishment?

Soon after the National Security Act went into effect it became apparent that the many compromises which went into its formulation had created a secretary of defense who lacked the power to coordinate the three branches of the armed forces. He was given only a handful of assistants and no department; he had only "general control" of the defense establishment. The three service secretaries maintained their positions on the Security Council, and the secretary of defense was particularly vulnerable to the cross pressures the three individual services could generate, especially on budget questions. And the weakness of the secretary of defense made it considerably more difficult, if not impossible, for the Commander in Chief to control those same forces once they were riding high in congressional committees, on the floor of Congress and even in the court of public opinion.

James Forrestal, who was elevated to the position of secretary of defense from the Navy Department he headed in the Truman administration, found himself being continually squeezed between the mounting demands of the individual services on the one hand, and the contracting budgets imposed by the President or other executive departments on the other. Forrestal tried to "sell" the services the concept of a balanced military force within the fiscal limits imposed by the President, but the generals and the admirals had strong allies on the armed services committees of both houses of Congress, and the defense secretary, despite his loyalty to the services and his unquestionable commitment to the strongest possible national defense posture based upon a hard line anti-communist point of view, was whipsawed by the conflicting parties in the struggle.

Before Forrestal resigned in a state of mental collapse, he had given much time to the problem and had worked closely with a task force of the first Hoover commission on governmental reorganization, headed by Ferdinand Eberstadt. The administration digested the task force's modest recommendations and in the spring of 1949 proposed an amendment to the National Security Act of 1947 aimed at achieving two basic purposes: "First, to convert the National Military Establishment into an executive department ... and, second, to provide the Secretary of Defense with appropriate responsibility and authority and with civil and military assistance adequate to fulfill his enlarged responsibility."[179] When the bill was finally signed in August, it implemented these objectives. A Defense Department was created, the secretary of defense having an unqualified "direction and control" of that department; the three services were downgraded from executive departments to military departments within the Defense Department; central fiscal controls were established through a Defense Department comptroller; and, finally, the secretary was given a deputy secretary and three assistants, with implicit understanding that the department was entitled to sufficient staff to carry out its responsibilities.[180]

The makeup of the National Security Council was also changed. The service secretaries were removed from the council, and the defense secretary thereafter represented the military in their plans and discussions, although the service secretaries and the Joint Chiefs of Staff sometimes attended at the invitation and at the discretion of the President. The Vice President of the United States was also made a statutory member of that body. The hope was that under this reorganization the secretary of defense would have sufficient power to develop real coordination and some essential integration of the armed forces, and also to implement the policies of the Commander in Chief. Within a very short time this new structure was tested in battle when the President was faced with the problem of not only imposing budgetary restrictions upon the armed services, but disciplining a military commander under actual wartime conditions.

The Commander in Chief Defends a Precarious Peace

As former President Harry Truman has written, prior to World War II "there were probably few Americans who knew or thought much about Korea other than that it was a strange land in far-off Asia."[181] In the early 1950s Korea became the scene of a shooting war which involved almost as many American casualties as World War I. And yet it was not a legal war in the constitutional sense, as the Congress did not vote a declaration of war, and on the record it remains a United Nations "police action." Our troops became initially involved on the basis of an executive action, later coming under the umbrella of the United Nations when the Security Council of that organization committed itself to the restoration of peace on the Korean peninsula.

The independent kingdom of Korea had fallen to the expanding imperialism of the Japanese in 1910, and was under Japanese rule until the end of World War II. After the war the Allied powers were generally committed to a four-power trusteeship, with ultimate independence a foreseeable goal. However, given the overwhelming number of critical situations to be dealt with at the end of the war, no specific decision was made about Korea by the Russians and the Americans, and as a consequence an *ad hoc* arrangement, dividing the country at the 38th parallel, with elements of the Russian army in the North and the American army in the South, was temporarily accepted by the two powers. The United States had no intention of agreeing to a permanent partition of the country, but the Russians continued to sabotage negotiations for a mutually satisfactory settlement based upon a united and independent Korea. Finally the United States turned to the United Nations and won the approval of the General Assembly for a U.N. commission to be sent to Korea to conduct free elections to establish a government which would later negotiate and supervise the withdrawal of Soviet and American troops. But the Russians would not permit the commission to penetrate beyond the 38th parallel, and as a result the elections were held only in the South, where the Republic of Korea came into existence in the spring of 1948. Six months later the Soviets countered these developments by creating the Democratic People's Republic of Korea. Shortly thereafter they unilaterally withdrew their occupation forces; the following spring the United States followed suit, with the exception of a group of officers left behind to serve as advisors in the training of the Korean army. The Russians did the same in the North.

The Americans' most serious problem in the South was Dr. Syngman Rhee, considered by some to be the "George Washington of Korea," and by many others to be a petty and ruthless tyrant. Rhee was chosen by the elected Korean National Assembly as the first President of the Republic of Korea. He had long been a champion of his country's independence, but at that time he was 75 years old and had been in exile for many years. In the American attempt to establish democratic institutions quickly and under rather unfavorable conditions, Rhee proved to be a real obstacle, as he tried to clamp down on any opposition to his extremely right-wing government, and created much dissension in the South. His continued threats to unify his country by force were also a considerable liability, and may well have touched off the determination of the communist government in the North to invade the Republic of Korea when they were ready.

And when they were ready on June 24, 1950, the North Koreans quite suddenly attacked the Republic in the South. The obviously careful preparations by the army of the Democratic People's Republic for such an attack—their heavier weapons and tanks and the element of great surprise accompanying their assault—made the lightly-armed South Koreans no real match for the armies of the North. They rapidly fell back in disarray and confusion, in many instances failing to put up any real battle at all. President Truman was visiting his family home in Independence, Missouri, at the time, and it was just before bedtime on Saturday evening when a call came through from Secretary of State Dean Acheson, informing him of the invasion. The President was ready to return to the capital that evening, but Acheson advised him not to because the information the State Department had at that time was so inadequate that there was little or nothing that could be done until more details were available. Truman flew back to Washington the following day, and met that evening at Blair House with the secretary of defense, the secretary of state, the Joint Chiefs of Staff, the service secretaries and several other high officials from the State Department.

The President was grim on arrival. He hurried off the plane and ignored his usual good-natured banter with reporters. In response to the familiar request from photographers for "just one more shot," Truman snapped back, "That's enough! We've got a job to do!"[182] Later he was overheard to state that he was not going to let "them" succeed, and that he planned to "hit them hard."[183] That was in keeping with Truman's conception of the presidency. In his fifth year in office, he was 66 years old. He had learned a great deal since that fateful day in 1945 when he was summoned to the White House and in the presence of the First Lady, Eleanor Roosevelt, informed that the President was dead. It was an awesome task at first, but Truman was a great student of American history, and from considerable study on his own, the President had been able to master the mechanics of the office, leaning heavily upon his historical background in developing his concept of the presidency and the larger problems with which he was confronted. When he arrived in Washington he was already prepared to act, but he was also prepared to await a thorough briefing by his advisors. The President's mood was best summarized by his own remark the following day: "This is the Greece of the Far East. If we are tough enough now there won't be any next step."[184]

Harry Truman was committed to the larger vision of presidential power and responsibility that his predecessors Franklin Roosevelt, Wilson, Theodore

Roosevelt, Lincoln, Jackson and Jefferson possessed. He saw the man in the White House as the center of a dynamic system which bogged down when the President refused to take hold and lead the nation. Inspired by the leadership of Roosevelt during the New Deal and the war. Truman saw himself, as Roosevelt had, as the champion of the common people, the inarticulate masses not heavily represented by the powerful interest groups in Washington. He never shrank from making tough decisions, and constantly amazed his colleagues by his ability to tackle the most complex problem, cut through the thicket of irrelevance and go right to the heart of the problem. He was not always right, but he refused "to pass the buck," and in crisis situations like Korea, he acted with remarkable speed and decisiveness, buoyed up by the considerable courage of his convictions. Truman had never fully revealed these qualities before assuming the presidency, nor was his performance distinguished once he was out of office. But while he remained in the White House and slept in Lincoln's bed, the little man with the bow tie from Independence gave the country strong leadership.

The President had requested that his secretary of state and secretary of defense prepare proposals for the Sunday evening meeting at Blair House, but there is little doubt that, flying back to Washington from Missouri, he had made up his own mind with respect to what his major decision would be:

> The plane left the Kansas City Municipal Airport at two o'clock, and it took just a little over three hours to make the trip to Washington. I had time to think aboard the plane. In my generation, this was not the first occasion when the strong had attacked the weak. I recalled some earlier instances: Manchuria, Ethiopia, Austria. I remembered how each time that the democracies failed to act it had encouraged the aggressors to keep going ahead. Communism was acting in Korea just as Hitler, Mussolini, and the Japanese had acted ten, fifteen, and twenty years earlier. I felt certain that if South Korea was allowed to fall Communist leaders would be emboldened to override nations closer to our own shores. If the Communists were permitted to force their way into the Republic of Korea without opposition from the free world, no small nation would have the courage to resist threats and aggression by stronger Communist neighbors. If this was allowed to go unchallenged it would mean a third world war, just as similar incidents had brought on the second world war. It was also clear to me that the foundations and the principles of the United Nations were at stake unless this unprovoked attack on Korea could be stopped.[185]

Acheson first reported to the gathering at the Blair House that Sunday evening that the United Nations Security Council (with the Russians absent, purely by accident) "had, by a vote of 9 to 0, approved a resolution declaring that a breach of the peace had been committed by the North Korean action and ordering the North Koreans to cease their action and withdraw their forces."[186] Then he introduced the proposals which President Truman had requested the State and Defense Departments to draw up. Those proposals included the evacuation of Americans from Korea, providing necessary air cover to defend the airports not in the hands of the North Koreans, in order to carry out such an evacuation, the airlift of supplies and ammunition to the South Koreans and the use of the Seventh Fleet in the Formosa Strait to prevent any spread of the fighting. There was agreement on the part of all present that all available American fighting units should be alerted for possible action in Korea in the event that the U.N. should decide to enforce its resolution.

The decisions made at the Blair House conference were immediately transmitted to General Douglas MacArthur, commander of American forces in the Far East, who was stationed in Japan. He was authorized to assist in the evacuation of American civilian personnel, to take naval and air action to prevent the Inchon-Kimpo-Seoul area from falling into North Korean hands and to dispatch any needed ammunition and equipment to the South. The Seventh Fleet was directed to proceed to Sasebo, Japan, and remain on the alert, and MacArthur was cautioned that although most of the measures referred to the protection of dependents and noncombatants, "further high level decisions may be expected as military and political situations develop."[187]

The following day, after conferring with his advisors, President Truman issued his first formal statement on the crisis.

President Harry S. Truman
Statement on the Violation of
The 38th Parallel in Korea
June 26, 1950

Public Papers of the Presidents: Harry S. Truman, 1950 (Washington, D.C., 1965), 491-92.

I conferred Sunday evening with the Secretaries of State and Defense, their senior advisers, and the Joint Chiefs of Staff about the situation in the Far East created by unprovoked aggression against the Republic of Korea.

The Government of the United States is pleased with the speed and determination with which the United Nations Security Council acted to order a withdrawal of the invading forces to positions north of the 38th parallel. In accordance with the resolution of the Security Council, the United States will vigorously support the effort of the Council to terminate this serious breach of the peace.

Our concern over the lawless action taken by the forces from North Korea, and our sympathy and support for the people of Korea in this situation, are being demonstrated by the cooperative action of American personnel in Korea, as well as by steps taken to expedite and augment assistance of the type being furnished under the Mutual Defense Assistance Program.

Those responsible for this act of aggression must realize how seriously the Government of the United States views such threats to the peace of the world. Willful disregard of the obligation to keep the peace cannot be tolerated by nations that support the United Nations Charter.

In Korea the military situation deteriorated rapidly, and the pressure for more active American intervention increased. Discussion on the floor of the Senate indicated that there was more criticism of the President for not taking stronger action than there was substantial opposition to American intervention. Ambassador Chang of South Korea visited the White House and presented the President with an urgent appeal from Syngman Rhee for assistance. When Truman met with his advisors for a second Blair House conference the following day, his secretary of state had already drafted proposals for more decisive American action. They included recommendations to instruct the American navy and air force to give the fullest support to the South Korean forces south of the 38th parallel, to order the Seventh Fleet into the Formosa Strait to prevent an attack on Formosa by China, or vice versa, to strengthen American forces in established Southeast Asian bases (for example, in the Philippines) and to report any actions taking place as a result of such instructions to the United Nations Security Council. No commitment of American ground forces was proposed or seriously considered at that meeting. The military was still wary of getting bogged down in a ground war in Asia, and was apprehensive about real Soviet and Chinese threats in other areas. The President and his advisors agreed to the Acheson proposals, and after conferring with congressional leaders the following day, Truman made a second and stronger statement on Korea. He read it first to the congressional leaders, and at that time there was no criticism of it.

President Harry S. Truman
Statement on the Korean Situation
June 27, 1950

Public Papers of the Presidents: Harry S. Truman, 1950, 492.

In Korea the Government forces, which were armed to prevent border raids and to preserve internal security, were attacked by invading forces from North Korea. The Security Council of the United Nations called upon the invading troops to cease hostilities and to withdraw to the 38th parallel. This they have not done, but on the contrary have pressed the attack. The Security Council called upon all members of the United Nations to render every assistance to the United Nations in the execution of this resolution. In these circumstances I have ordered United States air and sea forces to give the Korean Government troops cover and support.

The attack upon Korea makes it plain beyond all doubt that communism has passed beyond the use of subversion to conquer independent nations and will now use armed invasion and war. It has defied the orders of the Security Council of the United Nations issued to preserve international peace and security. In these circumstances the occupation of Formosa by Communist forces would be a direct threat to the security of the Pacific area and to United States forces performing their lawful and necessary functions in that area.

Accordingly I have ordered the 7th Fleet to prevent any attack on Formosa. As a corollary of this action I am calling upon the Chinese Government on Formosa to cease all air and sea operations against the mainland. The 7th Fleet will see that this is done. The determination of the future status of Formosa must await the restoration of security in the Pacific, a peace settlement with Japan, or consideration by the United Nations.

I have also directed that United States Forces in the Philippines be strengthened and that military assistance to the Philippine Government be accelerated.

I have similarly directed acceleration in the furnishing of military assistance to the forces of France and the Associated States in Indochina and the dispatch of a military mission to provide close working relations with those forces.

I know that all members of the United Nations will consider carefully the consequences of this latest aggression in Korea in defiance of the Charter of the United Nations. A return to the rule of force in international affairs would have far-reaching effects. The United States will continue to uphold the rule of law.

I have instructed Ambassador Austin, as the representative of the United States to the Security Council, to report these steps to the Council.

The next steps were almost inevitable. Discussions continued in both the Senate and the House, and although several Republican senators raised the question of the failure of the President to include Congress in the decision-making process, his actions were supported by speeches by his own party members and such Republican senators as Knowland of California, Smith and Hendrickson of New Jersey, Saltonstall and Lodge of Massachusetts, Morse of Oregon and others. In the House the members stood and cheered when the President's second statement was read by Majority Leader John McCormack. Late the same afternoon the Security Council of the United Nations in turn passed a stronger resolution which noted the failure of North Korea to respond to earlier appeals for a cease-fire and withdrawal; it called upon the member nations to respond to the appeal from the Republic of Korea for assistance and recommended that

> [m]embers of the United Nations furnish such assistance to the Republic of Korea as may be necessary to repel the armed attack and to restore international peace and security in the area.[188]

Rapid escalation of American armed forces activity was already taking place, however. By Thursday, June 29, General MacArthur, commander of American forces in the Far East, had been authorized to employ not only air and naval forces in support of South Korea, but also "Army combat and service units as to insure the retention of a port and air base in the general area of Pusan-Chinhae."[189] The next day, following an on-the-spot inspection of the military situation, General MacArthur requested authority to immediately move "a United States regimental combat team to the combat area in Korea as a nucleus of a possible buildup of two divisions from Japan for early offensive action in accordance with his mission of clearing South Korea of North Korean forces."[190]

When that request was conveyed to the President he agreed to immediately authorize the dispatch of the combat team, but wanted to meet again with his advisors before approving the rest of the request. They did meet again in the cabinet room of the White House early Friday morning, and after only 30 minutes' discussion, in which a number of topics were covered, they strongly supported MacArthur's request for utilizing the full number of troops available from his command. The President gave his instant approval to the recommendation. Later in the morning Truman met with a number of congressional leaders again, and indicated the scope of his decision. Only one member, Republican Senator Kenneth Wherry, was critical of the President for not bringing the question to the Congress before committing American troops to fight outside of the United States. That criticism would be heard again, but at that time the rest of the Republican and Democratic leaders present strongly approved of the President's action.

Within several days the American effort included infantrymen from the 24th Division who were rushed to the fighting front in Korea by sea and by air. Before long they were joined by many thousands more, on land, on the sea, and in the air. The President of the United States, acting under his authority as Commander in Chief, was directing military action in what amounted to a full-scale war against a foreign foe for the first time in the history of this country without congressional authorization. It was no arrogant action of a dictator, nor the decision of a man contemptuous of constitutional and democratic institutions. The world had changed since 1789, and particularly since 1945, and the nature of this country's commitment to the peace-keeping structure of the United Nations and to the protection of freedom in all parts of the world required this "police action" to help keep that peace. A congressional authorization of war in this instance would have interfered with, perhaps even destroyed, the principle which the United Nations was attempting to defend. But the lack of such a declaration of war was to limit the President in other areas in the days to come.

President Harry S. Truman
Designates General Douglas MacArthur
Commander of Allied Military Forces in Korea
July 8, 1950

Public Papers of the Presidents: Harry S. Truman, 1950, 520.

The Security Council of the United Nations in its resolution of July 7, 1950, has recommended that all members providing military forces and other assistance pursuant to the Security Council resolutions of June 25 and 27 make such forces and other assistance available to a unified command under the United States.

The Security Council resolution also requests that the United States designate the commander of such forces, and authorize the unified command at its discretion to use the United Nations flag in the course of operations against the North Korean forces concurrently with the flags of the various nations participating.

I am responding to the recommendation of the Security Council and have designated Gen. Douglas MacArthur as the Commanding General of the military forces which the members of the United Nations place under the unified command of the United States pursuant to the United Nations' assistance to the Republic of Korea in repelling the unprovoked armed attack against it.

I am directing General MacArthur, pursuant to the Security Council resolution, to use the United Nations flag in the course of operations against the North Korean forces concurrently with the flags of the various nations participating.

The "police action" in the Korean conflict provoked an extraordinary controversy which went to the very roots of the issue of the constitutional role of the President and his power as Commander in Chief. Robert A. Taft, the Republican leader in the Senate, led the forces critical of the President's actions. "The President," Senator Taft argued, "simply usurped authority, in violation of the laws and the Constitution, when he sent troops to Korea to carry out the resolution of the United Nations in an undeclared war."[191] At another point in the same speech Taft charged that the President "had no authority whatever to commit American troops to Korea without consulting Congress and without Congressional approval."[192] President Truman had not sought any additional authority for his action at the outbreak of hostilities, but he did request that a memorandum be prepared by the State Department which would assemble the documentation necessary to support his decision to go to the aid of the United Nations in its efforts to repel the attack in Korea.

Department of State Memorandum on The Authority of the President To Repel the Attack in Korea
July 3, 1950

The Department of State Bulletin, XXIII, 578, July 31, 1950, 173-79.

This memorandum is directed to the authority of the President to order the Armed Forces of the United States to repel the aggressive attack on the Republic of Korea.

As explained by Secretary Acheson to the press on June 28, as soon as word of the attack on Korea was received in Washington, it was the view of the President and of all his advisers that the first responsibility of the Government of the United States was to report the attack to the United Nations.

Accordingly, in the middle of the night of Saturday, June 24, 1950, Ambassador Gross, the United States deputy representative at the Security Council of the United Nations, notified Mr. Trygve Lie, the Secretary-General of the United

Nations, that armed forces from North Korea had commenced an unprovoked assault against the territory of the Republic of Korea.

The President, as Commander in Chief of the Armed Forces of the United States, has full control over the use thereof. He also has authority to conduct the foreign relations of the United States. Since the beginning of United States history, he has, upon numerous occasions, utilized these powers in sending armed forces abroad. The preservation of the United Nations for the maintenance of peace is a cardinal interest of the United States. Both traditional international law and article 39 of the United Nations Charter and the resolution pursuant thereto authorize the United States to repel the armed aggression against the Republic of Korea.

Constitutional Powers of the President

The President's control over the Armed Forces of the United States is based on article 2, section 2 of the Constitution which provides that he "shall be Commander in Chief of the Army and Navy of the United States."

In *United States* v. *Sweeny*, the Supreme Court said that the object of this provision was "evidently to vest in the President the supreme command over all the military forces,—such supreme and undivided command as would be necessary to the prosecution of a successful war." [157 U.S. (1895) 281, 284.]

That the President's power to send the Armed Forces outside the country is not dependent on Congressional authority has been repeatedly emphasized by numerous writers.

For example, ex-President William Howard Taft wrote:

The President is made Commander in Chief of the Army and Navy by the Constitution evidently for the purpose of enabling him to defend the country against invasion, to suppress insurrection and to take care that the laws be faithfully executed. If Congress were to attempt to prevent his use of the Army for any of these purposes, the action would be void. . . . Again, in the carrying on of war as Commander in Chief, it is he who is to determine the movements of the Army and of the Navy. Congress could not take away from him that discretion and place it beyond his control in any of his subordinates, nor could they themselves, as the people of Athens attempted to carry on campaigns by votes in the market-place. [*Our Chief Magistrate and His Powers*, 1916, pp. 128-129. Footnote in original.]

Professor Willoughby writes:

As to his constitutional power to send United States forces outside the country in time of peace when this is deemed by him necessary or expedient as a means of preserving or advancing the foreign interests or relations of the United States, there would seem to be equally little doubt, although it has been contended by some that the exercise of this discretion can be limited by congressional statute. That Congress has this right to limit or to forbid the sending of United States forces outside of the country in time of peace has been asserted by so eminent an authority as ex-Secretary Root. It would seem to author, however, that the President, under his powers as Commander in Chief of the Army and Navy, and his general control of the foreign relations of the United States, has this discretionary right constitutionally vested in him, and, therefore, not subject to congressional control. Especially, since the argument of the court in *Myers* v. *United States* with reference to the general character of the executive power vested in the President, and, apparently, the authority impliedly vested in him by reason of his obligation to take care that the laws be faithfully executed, it is reasonable to predict that, should the question be presented to it, the Supreme Court will so hold. Of course, if this sending is in pursuance of express provisions of a treaty, or for the execution of treaty provisions, the sending could not reasonably be subject to constitutional objection. [*The Constitutional Law of the United States*, 1929, vol. III, p. 1567. Footnote in original.]

In an address delivered before the American Bar Association in 1917 on the war powers under the Constitution, Mr. Hughes stated that "There is no limitation upon the authority of Congress to create an army and it is for the President as Commander-in-Chief to direct the campaigns of that Army wherever he may think they should be carried on." He referred to a statement by Chief Justice Taney in *Fleming* v. *Page* (9 How. 615) in which the Chief Justice said that as Commander in Chief the President "is authorized to direct the movements of the naval and military forces placed by law at his command." [S. doc. 105, 65th Cong., 1st sess., 7. Footnote in original.]

At the time the approval of the Treaty of Versailles was under consideration in the Senate, there was under discussion a reservation to article 10, presented by Senator Lodge, to the effect that "Congress . . . under the Constitution, has the sole power to declare war or authorize the employment of the military or naval forces of the United States." Senator Walsh of Montana stated in debate on November 10, 1919 that the statement was a recital of "What is asserted to be a principle of constitutional law." He said that if—

 . . . any declaration of that character should ever be made by the Senate of the United States, it would be singularly unfortunate. It is not true. It is not sound. It is fraught with the most momentous consequences, and may involve disasters the extent of which it is hardly possible to conceive.

The whole course of our history has been a refutation of such a declaration, namely, that the President of the United States, the Chief Executive of the United States, the Commander in Chief of the Army of the United States, has no power to employ the land or naval forces without any express authorization upon the part of Congress. Since the beginning of our Government, our Navy has been sent over the seven seas and to every port in the world. Was there ever any congressional act authorizing the President to do anything of that kind?

He stated that our Navy travels the sea "in order to safeguard and protect the rights of American citizens in foreign lands. Who can doubt that the President has no authority thus to utilize the naval and land forces of the United States?"

Mr. Borah stated:

I agree fully with the legal or constitutional proposition which the Senator states, and I hope this [reservation] will be stricken out. It is an act of supererogation to put it in. It does not amount to anything. It is a recital which is not true.

   It can not change the Constitution, and it ought not to be there. . . . It would simply be vain and futile and, if I may say so, with due respect to those who drew it, the doing of an inconsequential thing." [58 *Cong. Rec.*, pt. 8, p. 8195, Nov. 10, 1919, 66th Cong., 1st sess. Footnote in original.]

Not only is the President Commander in Chief of the Army and Navy, but he is also charged with the duty of conducting the foreign relations of the United States and in this field he "alone has the power to speak or listen as a representative of the Nation." [*United States* v. *Curtiss-Wright Export Corp. et al.* (299 U.S. (1936) 304, 319). Footnote in original.]

   Obviously, there are situations in which the powers of the President as Commander in Chief and his power to conduct the foreign relations of this country complement each other.

   The basic interest of the United States is international peace and security. The United States has, throughout its history, upon orders of the Commander in Chief to the Armed Forces and without congressional authorization, acted to prevent violent and unlawful acts in other states from depriving the United States and its nationals of the benefits of such peace and security. It has taken such action both unilaterally and in concert with others. A tabulation of 85 instances of the use of American Armed Forces without a declaration of war was incorporated in the *Congressional Record* for July 10, 1941,

Purposes for Sending American Troops Abroad

   It is important to analyze the purposes for which the President as Commander in Chief had authorized the despatch of American troops aborad. In many instances, of course, the Armed Forces have been used to protect specific American lives and property. In other cases, however, United States forces have been used in the broad interests of American foreign policy, and their use could be characterized as participation in international police action.

   The traditional power of the President to use the Armed Forces of the United States without consulting Congress was referred to in debates in the Senate in 1945. Senator Connally remarked:

The historical instances in which the President has directed armed forces to go to other countries have not been confined to domestic or internal instances at all. Senator Millikin pointed out that in many cases the President has sent troops into a foreign country to protect our foreign policy . . . notably in Central and South America. That was done, he continued, in order to keep foreign countries out of there—was not aimed at protecting any particular American citizen. It was aimed at protecting our foreign policy.

To his remark that he presumed that by the Charter of the United Nations we had laid down a foreign policy which we could protect, Senator Connally replied that that was absolutely correct. He added:

I was trying to indicate that fact by reading the list of instances of intervention on our part in order to keep another government out of territory in this hemisphere. That was a question of carrying out our international policy, and not a question involving the protection of some American citizen or American property at the moment. [*Cong. Rec.*, 79th Cong., 1st sess., vol. 91, pt. 8, Nov. 26, 1945. p. 10967. Footnote in original.]

During the Boxer Rebellion in China in 1900-1901, the President sent about 5,000 troops to join with British, Russian, German, French, and Japanese troops to relieve the siege of the foreign quarters in Peking and reestablish the treaty status. This was done without express congressional authority. In defining United States policy at the time Secretary of State Hay said:

. . . The purpose of the President is, as it has been heretofore, to act concurrently with the other powers; first, in opening up communication with Peking and rescuing the American officials, missionaries, and other Americans who are in danger; secondly, in affording all possible protection everywhere in China to American life and property; thirdly, in guarding and protecting all legitimate American interests; and, fourthly, in aiding to prevent a spread of the disorders to the other provinces of the Empire and a recurrence of such disasters. It is, of course, too early to forecast the means of attaining this last result; but the policy of the Government of the United States is to seek a solution which may bring about permanent safety and peace to China, preserve Chinese territorial and administrative entity, protect all rights guaranteed to friendly powers by treaty and international law, and safeguard for the world the principle of equal and impartial trade with all parts of the Chinese Empire. [John Bassett Moore, *A Digest of International Law*, vol. V, p. 482. See also Taft, *op. cit.* pp. 114-115; Rogers, *op. cit.* pp. 58-62. Footnote in original.]

After the opening up of Japan to foreigners in the 1850's through the conclusion of commercial treaties between Japan and certain Western powers, antiforeign disturbances occurred. In 1863, the American Legation was burned following previous attacks on the British Legation. The commander of the U. S. S. *Wyoming* was instructed to use all necessary force for the safety of the legation or of Americans residing in Japan. Secretary of State Seward said that the prime objects of the United States were:

First, to deserve and win the confidence of the Japanese Government and people, if possible, with a view to the common interest of all the treaty powers; secondly, to sustain and cooperate with the legations of these powers, in good faith, so as to render their efforts to the same end effective. [John Bassett Moore, *A Digest of International Law*, vol. V, pp. 747-748. Footnote in original.]

In 1864, the Mikado, not recognizing the treaties with the Western powers, closed the straits of Shimonoseki. At the request of the Tycoon's government (opposed to the Mikado), American, British, French, and Netherlands forces, in a joint operation, opened the straits by force. The object of the Western powers was the enforcement of treaty rights, with the approval of the government that granted them. [John Bassett Moore, *A Digest of International Law*, vol. V, p. 750; S. Ex. Doc. 58, 41 Cong. 2d sess. Footnote in original.]

Again, in 1868, a detachment of Japanese troops assaulted foreign residents in the streets of Hiogo. One of the crew of the *Oneida* was seriously wounded. The safety of the foreign population being threatened, naval forces of the treaty powers made a joint landing and adopted measures to protect the foreign settlement. [*Report of the Secretary of the Navy*, 1868, p. xi.]

Former Assistant Secretary of State James Grafton Rogers has characterized these uses of force as "international police action", saying:

> They amounted to executive use of the Armed Forces to establish our own and the world's scheme of international order. Two American Presidents used men, ships and guns on a large and expensive scale. [*World Policing and the Constitution*, published by the World Peace Foundation, 1945, pp. 66, 67. Footnote in original.]

In 1888 and 1889, civil war took place in Samoa where the United States, Great Britain, and Germany had certain respective treaty rights for the maintenance of naval depots. German forces were landed, and the German Government invited the United States to join in an effort to restore calm and quiet in the islands in the interest of all the treaty powers. The commander of the United States naval forces in the Pacific was instructed by the Secretary of the Navy that the United States was willing to cooperate in restoring order "on the basis of the full preservation of American treaty rights and Samoan authority, as recognized and agreed to by Germany, Great Britain, and the United States." He was to extend full protection and defense to American citizens and property, to protest the displacement of the native government by Germany as violating the positive agreement and understanding between the treaty powers, but to inform the British and German Governments of his readiness to cooperate in causing all treaty rights to be respected and in restoring peace and order on the basis of the recognition of the Samoan right to independence. [John Bassett Moore, *A Digest of International Law*, vol. I, pp. 545-546. Footnote in original.]

On July 7, 1941, the President sent to the Congress a message announcing that as Commander in Chief he had ordered the Navy to take all necessary steps to insure the safety of communications between Iceland and the United States as well as on the seas between the United States and all other strategic outposts and that American troops had been sent to Iceland in defense of that country. The United States, he said, could not permit "the occupation by Germany of strategic outposts in the Atlantic to be used as air or naval bases for eventual attack against the Western Hemisphere." For the same reason, he said, substantial forces of the United States had been sent to the bases acquired from Great Britain in Trinidad and British Guiana in the South to forestall any pincers movement undertaken by

Germany against the Western Hemisphere. [*Cong. Rec.,* 77th Cong., 1st sess., vol. 87, pt. 6, July 7, 1941, p. 5868. Footnote in original.]

Thus, even before the ratification of the United Nations Charter, the President had used the Armed Forces of the United States without consulting the Congress for the purpose of protecting the foreign policy of the United States. The ratification of the United Nations Charter was, of course, a landmark in the development of American foreign policy. As noted above, Senator Connally and Senator Millikin agreed that the President was entitled to use armed forces in protection of the foreign policy represented by the Charter. This view was also expressed in the Senate debates in connection with the ratification of the Charter. For example, Senator Wiley made the following pertinent statement:

It is my understanding, according to the testimony given before the Foreign Relations Committee of the Senate, that the terms "agreement or agreements" as used in article 43 are synonymous with the word "treaty." On the other hand, I recognize that Congress might well interpret them as agreements brought about by the action of the Executive and ratified by a joint resolution of both Houses. These agreements would provide for a police force and the specific responsibility of each nation. But outside of these agreements, there is the power in our Executive to preserve the peace, to see that the "supreme laws" are faithfully executed. When we become a party to this charter, and define our responsibilities by the agreement or agreements, there can be no question of the power of the Executive to carry out our commitments in relation to international policing. His constitutional power, however, is in no manner impaired. [*Cong. Rec.*, 79th Cong., 1st sess., vol. 91, July 27, 1945, p. 8127-8128. Footnote in original.]

An even fuller exposition of the point was made by Senator Austin, who stated:

Mr. President, I am one of those lawyers in the United States who believe that the general powers of the President—not merely the war powers of the President but the general authority of the President—are commensurate with the obligation which is imposed upon him as President, that he take care that the laws are faithfully executed. That means that he shall take all the care that is required to see that the laws are faithfully executed.

Of course, there are other specific references in the Constitution which show that he has authority to employ armed forces when necessary to carry out specific things named in the Constitution; but the great over-all and general authority arises from his obligation that he take care that the laws are faithfully executed. That has been true throughout our history, and the Chief Executive has taken care, and has sent the armed forces of the United States, without any act of Congress preceding their sending, on a great many occasions. I have three different compilations of those occasions. One of them runs as high as 150 times; another of them 72 times, and so forth. It makes a difference whether we consider the maneuvers which were merely shows of force as combined in the exercise of this authority—as I do—or whether we limit the count to those cases in which the armed forces have actually entered upon the territory of a peaceful neighbor. But there is no doubt in my mind of his obligation and authority to employ all the force that is necessary to enforce the laws.

It may be asked, How does a threat to international security and peace violate the laws of the United States? Perhaps, Mr. President, it would not have violated the laws of the United States previous to the obligations set forth in this treaty. Perhaps we have never before recognized as being true the fundamental doctrine with which I opened my remarks. But we are doing so now. We recognize that a breach of the peace anywhere on earth which threatens the security and peace of the world is an attack upon us; and after this treaty is accepted by 29 nations, that will be the express law of the world. It will be the law of nations, because according to its express terms it will bind those who are nonmembers, as well as members, and it will be the law of the United States, because we shall have adopted it in a treaty. Indeed, it will be above the ordinary statutes of the United States, because it will be on a par with the Constitution, which provides that treaties made pursuant thereto shall be the supreme law of the land.

So I have no doubt of the authority of the President in the past, and his authority in the future, to enforce peace. I am bound to say that I feel that the President is the officer under our Constitution in whom there is exclusively vested the responsibility for maintenance of peace. [*Cong. Rec.*, 79th Cong., 1st sess., vol. 91, July 26, 1945, p. 8064-8065. Footnote in original.]

Action contrary to the Charter of the United Nations is action against the interests of the United States. Preservation of peace under the Charter is a cornerstone of American foreign policy. President Truman said in his inaugural address in 1949:

In the coming years, our program for peace and freedom will emphasize four major courses of action.

First, we will continue to give unfaltering support to the United Nations and related agencies, and we will continue to search for ways to strengthen their authority and increase their effectiveness.

In the Korean situation, the resolution of the Security Council of June 25 determined, under article 39 of the Charter, that the action of the North Koreans constituted a breach of the peace and called upon "the authorities in North Korea (a) to cease hostilities forthwith; and (b) to withdraw their armed forces to the thirty-eighth parallel." It also called upon "all Members to render every assistance to the United Nations in the execution of this resolution." This is an application of the principles set forth in article 2, paragraph 5 of the Charter, which states: "All Members shall give the United Nations every assistance in any action it takes in accordance with the present Charter..." The Security Council resolution of June 27, passed after the North Korean authorities had disregarded the June 25 resolution, recommended "that Members of the United Nations furnish such assistance to the Republic of Korea as may be necessary to repel the armed attack and to restore international peace and security in the area." This recommendation was also made under the authority of article 39 of the Charter.

The President's action seeks to accomplish the objectives of both resolutions.

The continued defiance of the United Nations by the North Korean authorities would have meant that the United Nations would have ceased to exist as a serious instrumentality for the maintenance of international peace. The continued existence of the United Nations as an effective international organization is a paramount United States interest. The defiance of the United Nations is in clear violation of the Charter of the United Nations and of the resolutions adopted by the Security Council of the United Nations to bring about a settlement of the problem. It is a threat to international peace and security, a threat to the peace and security of the United States and to the security of United States forces in the Pacific.

These interests of the United States are interests which the President as Commander in Chief can protect by the employment of the Armed Forces of the United States without a declaration of war. It was they which the President's order of June 27 did protect. This order was within his authority as Commander in Chief.

Use of Land and Naval Forces
Of the United States
For Protection Purposes

The United States has used its land and naval forces in foreign territories during peacetime on many occasions during the past hundred years. They have been landed, *inter alia*, for the protection of American citizens and American territory, as in the instance of the Spanish Floridas in 1817; for the protection of American citizens located in disturbed areas; for the suppression of piracy; for meting out punishment (in an early day) to lawless bands who had murdered American citizens; for the suppression of local riots and the preservation of order; for the purpose of securing the payment of indemnity; and to prevent massacre.

Although there may have been earlier instances, the first instance that has been drawn to my attention of the landing of United States troops occurred in 1822 when President Monroe sent forces to expel freebooters who had taken possession in the name of the Governments of Buenos Aires and Venezuela of Amelia Island, off the coast of Florida. Although the island belonged to Spain the measure was not taken in concert with the Spanish Government or the local authorities of Florida. I find that as late as 1932 American forces were sent to Shanghai owing to the Sino-Japanese conflict as a measure of protection for the lives and property of American citizens in that area.

A list of various landings of American forces and the occasions therefor follows:

(1) Amelia Island, 1812, to protect Spanish island from foreign invasion or control. (2) Spanish Florida, 1814, to expel the British. (3) Cuba, 1823, to pursue and break up an establishment of pirates. (4) Puerto Rico, 1824, to atone for insult to the flag and procure apology. (5) Falkland Islands, 1831, to procure the release of certain vessels and their crews. (6) Island of Sumatra, 1832, to punish natives for attack and seizure of American ship and murder of crew. (7) Fiji Islands, 1840, to punish natives for an attack upon Americans. (8)

Samoa, 1841, to punish natives for the murder of a white man. (9) Island of Johanna, 1851, to collect indemnity (display of force). (10) Japan, 1853-54, to procure a commercial treaty. (11) China, 1854, American and British forces acted jointly during civil war in China to protect American and British nationals. (12) Greytown, 1854, to protect American property rights. (13) Fiji Islands, 1855, to protect American life. (14) Uruguay, 1855, to protect American consulate and American life and property. (15) China, 1856, to prevent injury to American interests. (16) Egypt, 1858, to secure protection of American citizens. (17) Uruguay, 1858, to protect life and property of foreign residents; action taken at request of regular Government in conjunction with forces of other powers. (18) Fiji Islands, 1858, to punish natives for murder of two Americans. (19) China, 1859, to restore order in Shanghai. (20) Kisembo, Africa, 1860, to prevent destruction of American property. (21) Panama, 1860, to restore order during insurrection. (22) Japan, 1863, to obtain redress for an unwarranted attack upon an American vessel. (23) Japan, 1864, to open the Straits of Shimonoseki in conjunction with other powers; action taken at request of the Tycoon's government. (24) Formosa, 1867, to punish natives who had murdered the crew of a wrecked American bark. (25) Japan, 1868, to protect American interests during local hostilities. (26) Uruguay, 1868, to protect American interests at request of local authorities. (27) Korea, 1871, to capture Korean forts after a surveying party which had been granted permission to make certain surveys and soundings in the interest of science and commerce had been treacherously attacked. (28) Honolulu, 1874, to suppress riotous proceedings at request of local authorities. (29) Mexico, 1876, to preserve order, pending arrival of regular Government forces after evacuation of revolutionists. (30) Egypt, 1882, to suppress riots and protect American interests. (31) Korea, 1888, to protect American residents. (32) Samoa, 1888, to establish a stable government; joint action by United States, Great Britain, and Germany. (33) Haiti, 1888, to obtain the release of an American merchant vessel captured by a Haitian war vessel. (34) Navassa Island, 1891, to protect American life and property. (35) Chile, 1891, to protect American consulate at Valparaiso. (36) Hawaii, 1893, to protect life and property at the time of the deposition of the Queen. (37) Brazil, 1893, to protect American commerce in Brazilian waters during a revolt of the Brazilian Navy; it was reported that the insurgents had the assistance of certain European powers. (38) Korea, 1894, to protect the American Legation. (39) Samoa, 1899, to assist in settling controversy over succession to Samoan throne. (40) Nicaragua, 1899, to protect life and property, upon petition of foreign merchants during insurrection. (41) China, 1900, to protect life and property at time of Boxer uprising. (42) Dominican Republic, 1903, to protect American interests. (43) Dominican Republic, 1903, to protect American lives and property and to prevent fighting within certain area. (44) Honduras, 1907, to protect American consulate and American interests during hostilities between Honduras and Nicaragua. (45) Nicaragua, 1910, to protect American life and property during revolution; to prevent the bombardment of Bluefields. (46) Honduras, 1910-11, to protect American interests during revolutionary disturbances. (47) China, 1911, to protect the consulate and property of American citizens of Foochow. (48) China, 1911, to protect American consulate and American citizens at Chinkiang. (49) China, 1911, to increase the guard of the American Legation at Peking. (50) China, 1912, to keep open the railroad from Peking to the sea. (51) China, 1912, to extend protection. (52) China, Swatow, 1912, to save a woman and some children and conduct them to safety. (53) Cuba, 1912, to quell uprising; to protect American life and property. (54) Honduras, 1912, to protect an American-owned railroad. (55) Nicaragua, 1912-13, to protect American property, at request of Government of Nicaragua. (56) Dominican Republic, 1912-14, to protect Dominican customshouses, in conformity with the provisions of the treaty of 1907. (57) China, Chapei, 1913, to prevent disorder and give protection. (58) China, Shanghai, 1913, for protection. (59) Paris, 1914, to act as a guard for the American Embassy. (60) Mexico, Veracruz, 1914, to enforce demands for amends for affronts and indignities to an officer of the U. S. S. *Dolphin* and the crew of the whaleboat of the *Dolphin*. (61) Haiti, 1914-1915, to protect American life and property during disturbed conditions. (62) China, Nanking, 1916, to quell a riot. (63) Mexico, 1916-17, to pursue Villa after his invasion of American territory. (64) Dominican Republic, 1916-24, to suppress revolution; to establish military government. (65) Cuba, 1917-19, to protect American consulate and American lives and property during insurrection and banditti fighting. (66) China, Chungking, 1918, for protection during a political crisis. (67) Honduras, 1919, to cooperate with the forces of Honduras in maintaining order in a neutral zone. (68) Panama, 1919, to extend protection, at request of Panamanian Government. (69) China, Kiukiang, 1920, to restore order during riot. (70) China, Youchow, 1920, to guard American property. (71) Guatemala, 1920, to protect the American Legation during local fighting. (72) Smyrna, 1922, to protect American life and property during the advance of

Turkish forces on that city. (73) China, Tungchow, 1922, to protect against possible violence by retreating Fengtien forces. (74) China, Foochow, 1922, to protect American nationals. (75) China, Masu Island, 1923, to protect Americans against brigandage. (76) Honduras, 1924, to protect American life and property during unsettled conditions; intermittent landing of forces. (77) Honduras, 1925, to protect American property. (78) Panama, 1925, to extend protection during unsettled conditions, at request of Panamanian Government. (79) Nicaragua, 1926, to protect life and property during revolution. (80) China, Hankow, 1927, to protect lives and interests of Americans during mob-riot disturbances. (81) China, Shanghai, 1927, to protect American lives and property. (82) China, Nanking, 1927, to afford protection against looting and general disorder. (83) China, Chinkiang, 1927, to extinguish fire on American property caused by gunfire. (84) China, Canton, 1927, to aid in evacuation. (85) China, Shanghai, 1932, to strengthen forces at Shanghai, as a measure of protection for the lives and property of American nationals. [Reprinted from H. Rept. 2495, 81st Cong., 2d sess., p. 67. Footnote in original.]

The State Department authors of that memorandum found a great deal in both theory and practice to support the President's action. They invoked constitutional authorities and historical precedents of previous Presidents, who from the days of the early nineteenth century had used the armed forces of the country to protect American lives, property and interests when they were threatened on foreign soil. In nearly every instance when American ships or troops were ordered to undertake such missions, they had done so without congressional debate or authorization. The rate of such incidents had greatly accelerated in the years since the turn of the century, when American interests and commitments to areas outside of the continental limits of the United States greatly increased.

The weakness of the memorandum was not simply its obviously hasty compilation, but more significantly, its failure to discern the differences in kind as well as degree among the types of cases it referred to—for example, the United States role in the Boxer Rebellion or the Samoan Revolution as distinguished from America's involvement in the Korean War. In the former situations the President had utilized the armed forces of the country in a more or less stand-by capacity, first to protect American lives and property in those areas, and second, to exert pressure to reestablish an orderly state of affairs consistent with American interests. In the Korean "police action" the United States committed hundreds of thousands of soldiers, naval personnel and airmen to an ongoing conflict of major proportions, against an enemy which was aided and abetted by two of the most powerful revolutionary nations in the world. Furthermore, the action was taken (at least formally) as a response to a United Nations resolution calling for resistance to the North Korean attack. That certainly introduced another major dimension into the situation, and distinguished it further from those discussed in the memorandum.

If indeed the United States involvement in the Chinese or the Samoan incidents had resulted in the outbreak of severe fighting on a rapidly increasing scale, it is clear that Presidents McKinley and Harrison would have gone to the Congress and asked for a declaration of war, as Polk did after goading Mexico into conflict. All of the previous situations referred to in the State Department document and its appended catalogue of 85 incidents, were really "police actions." Korea from the very start was a major military conflict, and as time went on it became more extensive than anyone would have predicted in 1950. What should have been recognized then, however, was that the precedents of the nineteenth century were not adequate to meet the problems of the atomic age. Too much had changed in the world for old rules to apply to an entirely new situation. A formula which succeeded in suppressing a riot, or even an insurrection in a backward area of the world which threatened an American consulate or legation, would not necessarily meet the problems of leading a United Nations military campaign against communist aggression on a peninsula jutting out of the Asian mainland.

This is not to suggest that President Truman should have either done nothing or gone to the Congress and called for an all-out declaration of war.[193] These were also outmoded alternatives for the atomic age. What was needed then and what is still needed now is nothing less than a new framework for dealing with such international crises, a framework which does not weaken the President's power as Commander in Chief or as a foreign policy leader, but which at the same time develops a role which the Congress can play in decisions that involve the deployment of hundreds of thousands of Americans in the armed forces, and in the appropriation and expenditure of billions of dollars to support their activity. A President who persists in ignoring or bypassing the Congress in decision-making of this magnitude jeopardizes the success of any such operation from the start, and also leaves himself and his administration vulnerable to later violent political attacks and very possibly to defeat, if the operation does not quickly achieve its objective. Truman found that out very quickly, and he also discovered that he would have to rely on the Congress at a later date for support of actions necessary to implement his original decisions. When that support was not forthcoming, vital aspects of his planning were jeopardized, and the Democratic presidential candidate ultimately suffered an ignominious political defeat in the election that followed.

In some senses Truman's predecessors in the twentieth century had been struggling with aspects of this problem (albeit half-heartedly and unsuccessfully) even before World War II and the advent of the atomic age. Theodore Roosevelt had cast the settlement of his intervention in the Dominican customs crisis in the form of a treaty (rather than an executive agreement) which he submitted to the Senate for approval, but failing to get their endorsement, he angrily and impatiently acted anyway. Woodrow Wilson followed suit in 1914, under far more reprehensible conditions, when he sought congressional approval for an outrageous punitive action against the Mexican government, an action which he initiated before the Senate had endorsed his request, and which brought about severe criticism throughout the world, anti-American riots in Central and South America and increased hostility in Mexico, even among those forces which the Wilson administration had been supporting against the existing governments.[194] The real key to an understanding of the affair was that Wilson was strongly opposed to the reactionary government then in power in Mexico, under the leadership of Victoriano Huerta, and he simply used that incident in a crude attempt to assist the revolutionary forces under Venuistiano Carranza and Pancho Villa to overthrow the Huerta regime. Wilson had been meddling outrageously in Mexican internal political affairs almost since he moved into the White House.

The incident which marked the opening scene of the Mexican incident took place when the paymaster and crew of a whaleboat of a United States warship anchored off the Mexican port of Tampico in the spring of 1914 were arrested by a Mexican colonel after the men from the whaleboat landed without permission behind the government troops' lines. When the circumstances of the arrest were brought to the attention of the Mexican authorities an apology was made to the commander of the American fleet and the men were immediately released. The admiral in command of the American squadron lying off Tampico, however, refused to accept the apology unless he received a guarantee that the officer who had made the arrest was severely punished, and the American flag hoisted to a prominent position on the shore and accorded a 21-gun salute by the Mexican government. Huerta went so far as to agree to punish the colonel if an investigation proved that the officer had acted improperly, and also agreed to accord the 21-gun salute to the American flag, if he in return received a guarantee that the American warship would respond to the salute.

President Wilson, intent upon scoring what he considered would be a victory over a political regime he wished to remove, refused to accept that minor condition. He broke off negotiations with the Huerta government, and began to design punitive action. He went before the Congress and requested open-ended support for his action, and ordered all American warships in the Atlantic to head for Tampico, and the Pacific fleet to sail immediately for the west coast of Mexico. In his speech to the Congress the President asked for authority to "use the armed forces of the United States in such ways and to such an extent as may be necessary to obtain from General Huerta and his adherents the fullest recognition of the rights and dignity of the United States, even amidst the distressing conditions now unhappily obtaining in Mexico."[195] Wilson assured the Mexican people that the United States did not seek war but only sought to maintain its dignity and influence unimpaired "for the use of liberty, both in the United States and wherever else it may be employed for the benefit of mankind."[196]

When informed of an impending large shipment of ammunition scheduled to arrive at Vera Cruz on a German vessel the day after he made his request, President Wilson ordered United States forces to seize the Mexican customhouse, and prevent the delivery of the war supplies to the Huerta government or anyone else. Although the House had voted the same day to authorize such action, the orders were given before the Senate had endorsed the President's request. The seizure resulted in a bloody battle which cost the lives of 126 Mexicans, while wounding another 195, and accounted for 19 American deaths with 71 wounded. Additional troops and warships were hurried to the scene as anti-American rioting and demonstrations broke out in Costa Rica, Guatemala, Chile, Ecuador and Uraguay. A riot was prevented in Buenos Aires only by severe police repression. Even Wilson's Mexican ally, Carranza, was disgusted by the turn of events, and both Mexican loyalist and opposition forces were extremely critical of the "Yankee Imperialism" demonstrated in that miserable affair.

During the episode, Wilson, like Roosevelt, was initially reluctant to act without congressional support, but, again like Roosevelt, he did not allow the lack of such approval to stop him from acting when he considered it necessary. Both instances are mentioned only to indicate some earlier presidential hesitations when

Presidents were forced to act independently and arbitrarily in the face of potentially serious consequences. President Truman, faced with decisions of far greater consequences, involving not simply a potential but an actual shooting war, with an enemy many times as powerful as the Dominicans or the Mexicans, chose not to make a request for congressional support for or approval (which would definitely have been forthcoming) of his action, and acted solely on the basis of his prerogative as Commander in Chief and as foreign policy leader to uphold American interests in the Pacific area and to carry out obligations which he believed the country had assumed on becoming a party to the treaty of the United Nations.

In his original criticism of President Truman for his failure to confer with the Congress and to seek its support in the Korean situation, Senator Taft, who was the Republican opposition leader, indicated that he would have supported a request for military assistance if it had come through what he outlined as the necessary statutory obligations under the enabling legislation underwriting America's commitment to the United Nations. In his speech Taft read from the statute governing the use of American armed forces in support of United Nations actions:

> The President is authorized to negotiate a special agreement or agreements with the Security Council which shall be subject to the approval of the Congress by appropriate act or joint resolution, providing for the numbers and types of armed forces, their degree of readiness and general location, and the nature of facilities and assistance, including rights of passage, to be made available to the Security Council on its call for the purpose of maintaining international peace and security in accordance with article 43 of said Charter. The President shall not be deemed to require the authorization of the Congress to make available to the Security Council on its call in order to take action under article 42 of said Charter and pursuant to such special agreement or agreements the armed forces, facilities, or assistance provided for therein: *Provided*, That nothing herein contained shall be construed as an authorization to the President by the Congress to make available to the Security Council for such purpose armed forces, facilities or assistance in addition to the forces, facilities, and assistance provided for in such special agreement or agreements.[197]

The senator continued to explain his interpretation of this law:

> So we have enacted the circumstances under which the President may use armed forces in support of a resolution of the Security Council of the United Nations. The first requisite is that we negotiate an agreement to determine what forces shall be used, and in what quantity, and that the agreement be approved by the Congress. No agreement has ever been negotiated, of course, and no agreement has been presented to Congress. So far as I can see, and so far as I have studied the matter, I would say that there is no authority to use armed forces in support of the United Nations in the absence of some previous action by Congress dealing with the subject and outlining the general circumstances and the amount of the forces that can be used.[198]

It has been suggested that President Truman was relieved from the obligation under the United Nations Participation Act cited by Senator Taft because the U.N. in its resolution of June 27, 1950, acted under Section 39 of the charter which recommends action, rather than under Section 43 which makes such decisions legally binding. I am unable to find any document of the Truman administration commenting on this aspect of the legal nature of the situation. Others have argued that such military agreements between the member countries and the Security Council would have been impossible once the Soviet Union returned to the council, and therefore the President decided to act on the basis of his general powers as Commander in Chief. What is important to the problem at hand is that the President avoided consulting the Congress before making his decision to assign the American armed forces in support of the U.N. action, and never thereafter requested congressional approval with regard to the decisions he made and the manner in which he implemented them.

A previous section of this study has demonstrated that at least from the mid-nineteenth century on, the war-making powers of Congress were negligible in comparison to the power and influence of the Chief Executive in that domain. Clinton Rossiter has written that "it is a matter of history that most of our wars were in full course before Congress could get around to declaring the fact."[199] Only the War of 1812 was preceded by substantial debate followed by a declaration of war. However Truman's handling of the Korean situation demonstrated the progressive erosion of congressional power in this area, an erosion which proved to be detrimental not only to the conduct of the war and the winning of the peace, but also to the balance and functioning of the American political system. Professor Edward S. Corwin raised the proper question at that time:

> What then is the answer? Futile and embittered debate between the holders of the powers that must be exercised in close cooperation if at all, or a decent consultation and accommodation of views between the two departments of government concerned? And surely, it is paradoxical in the extreme to reduce the legislative organ of government to the level of a mere rubber stamp of policies the professed purpose of which is the preservation of free institutions.[200]

Corwin's own solution was proposed before the Korean conflict erupted:

> The problem of keeping the President's role in foreign relations safely within the bounds of democratic processes is not to be solved by shutting our eyes to the facts of life, especially as they relate to the power and position of the United States in the contemporary world.
> The problem, in short, is one of domestic Constitutional reform. The diplomatic powers of the President cannot be substantially curtailed; but their exercise can be subjected to the counsel and the scrutiny of advisors some of whom acknowledge a primary allegiance not to the White House but to Capitol Hill.[201]

Truman's successor, Dwight David Eisenhower, made every effort to avoid the bind his Democratic predecessor had created for himself by appealing to the

Congress before critical international crises fully developed. Early in 1955, apprehensive about the steadily increasing aggressive actions by the Chinese communists against the off-shore islands, Eisenhower appealed to the Congress for authority "to employ the armed forces of this nation promptly and effectively" in order to discourage aggression and to "assure the security of Formosa and the Pescadores."[202] He was careful to point out that "authority for some of the actions which might be required would be inherent in the authority of the Commander in Chief."

> Until Congress can act I would not hesitate, so far as my Constitutional powers extend, to take whatever emergency action might be forced upon us in order to protect the rights and security of the United States.[203]

But his major point was that a firm and clear announcement of a united legislative-Executive determination to act in this situation would be the strongest guarantee of preventing conflict, and, in the case it developed, of insuring success.

> In the interest of peace, therefore, the United States must remove any doubts regarding our readiness to fight, if necessary, to preserve the vital stake of the free world in a free Formosa, and to engage in whatever operations may be required to carry out that purpose.
>
> To make this plain requires not only Presidential action but also Congressional action. In a situation as now confronts us, and under modern conditions of warfare, it would not be prudent to await the emergency before coming to the Congress. Then it might be too late. Already the warning signals are up.[204]

Eisenhower had matured since his early "Whigish" characterization of presidential power, and he not only asserted considerable executive independence with respect to military affairs, but he successfully fought off the Bricker constitutional amendment which would have weakened the President's treaty-making power.

Joint Congressional Resolution Authorizing President Eisenhower to Employ Armed Forces To Defend Formosa, the Pescadores and Related Areas
January 29, 1955

Public Law 4, 84th Cong. (69 Stat. 7).

Whereas the primary purpose of the United States, in its relations with all other nations, is to develop and sustain a just and enduring peace for all; and

Whereas certain territories in the West Pacific under the jurisdiction of the Republic of China are now under armed attack, and threats and declarations have been and are being made by the Chinese Communists that such armed attack is in aid of and in preparation for armed attack on Formosa and the Pescadores,

Whereas such armed attack if continued would gravely endanger the peace and security of the West Pacific Area and particularly of Formosa and the Pescadores; and

Whereas the secure possession by friendly governments of the Western Pacific Island chain, of which Formosa is a part, is essential to the vital interests of the United States and all friendly nations in or bordering upon the Pacific Ocean; and

Whereas the President of the United States on January 6, 1955, submitted to the Senate for its advice and consent to ratification a Mutual Defense Treaty between the United States of America and the Republic of China, which recognizes that an armed attack in the West Pacific area directed against territories, therein described, in the region of Formosa and the Pescadores, would be dangerous to the peace and safety of the parties to the treaty: Therefore be it

Resolved by the Senate and House of Representatives of the United States of America in Congress assembled, That the President of the United States be and he hereby is authorized to employ the Armed Forces of the United States as he deems necessary for the specific purpose of securing and protecting Formosa and the Pescadores against armed attack, this authority to include the securing and protection of such related positions and territories of that area now in friendly hands and the taking of such other measures as he judges to be required or appropriate in assuring the defense of Formosa and the Pescadores.

This resolution shall expire when the President shall determine that the peace and security of the area is reasonably assured by international conditions created by action of the United Nations or otherwise, and shall so report to the Congress.

President Eisenhower utilized that same procedure when a problem situation developed in the Middle East, and President Kennedy followed the precedent when the Cuban missile crisis arose. The divisive gap between the President and Congress was somewhat bridged by these efforts, and certainly relations between the two branches improved from their deteriorated condition in the Truman administration. I will return to this problem in greater detail in the final section, exploring the limits of presidential power, considering the issues of whether or not the 1955 resolution provided a sufficient paradigm for the solution to this complex and very vexing problem, and whether it was a formula generally applicable to the wide spectrum of crises that were bound to emerge during the 1960s and later in American history.

President Truman Survives the General's Challenge

The Korean "police action" produced one of the most serious crises of civilian-military relationships in the history of this country. There were incidents in the past when powerful generals had strongly disagreed with their Commander in Chief on matters of both military and political policy, and at least one incident where the officer in question allegedly took to the public press to assert his views. However never before in American history had a figure with the stature of Douglas MacArthur, in open violation of a written directive from his Commander in Chief, attempted to take a difference of opinion of a critical military and political policy question into the political arena, appealing outright for support from the party in opposition to the President.

A careful analysis of General Douglas MacArthur's military career prior to the Korean conflict produces considerable evidence to the effect that, if there ever was to be such a challenge to the authority of a President of the United States by any military officer in our history, MacArthur would be that man. Douglas MacArthur was born into the United States Army in almost the same sense that an heir to a ruling family is destined to succeed to the throne. His father was a famous military hero, and Douglas MacArthur entered West Point with the same ease and assurance that a member of a wealthy and aristocratic British family goes on to Eton or to Sandhurst. But from that point on his own ability and brilliance were responsible for his successes. He fought bravely and effectively in World War I, climbed rapidly to become chief of staff in the 1930s, planned and executed the extraordinary island-hopping campaign that recovered the Philippines and destroyed large sections of the Japanese army in World War II. Yet his career was marred with incidents of arrogance, or at least reported arrogance, and controversies with political superiors verging on insubordination. Even Franklin D. Roosevelt had difficulty in "managing" MacArthur, and at one point named him, along with Huey Long, as one of the two Americans he thought might have possibly become dictators in the United States.

Although his military career can be considered outstanding, there are also several notable flaws in the record, bad or questionable judgments in crisis situations, which indicate that his failures were probably of a magnitude equal to his successes. For example, the general was never able to adequately explain the reasons why, nine full hours after the Japanese raid on Pearl Harbor, the major part of the American air force in the Philippines was destroyed, having been lined up on Clark Field like rows of ducks waiting for the Japanese attack. The air force general in command in Manila, whom MacArthur blamed for the debacle, has stated that MacArthur repeatedly denied him permission to put his planes in the air to retaliate against the Japanese with an immediate bombing mission over Formosa.

During the Korean War MacArthur conducted several brilliant tactical operations. His last-ditch defense at Pusan, and his end-flank landing at Inchon, certainly rank with the best feats of leadership in American military history. But in keeping with his previous record, these successful operations must be balanced against his classic military blunder, the foolhardy advance to the Yalu River in the North, which led to setbacks which practically erased all of his previous gains, and constituted one of the most disastrous and humiliating defeats in American military history. MacArthur was that kind of general. When he was good, he was very, very good, and when he was bad, he was awful.

In the Korean "police action" Douglas MacArthur was the commander not of the American armed forces alone, but of the entire military force sponsored by the United Nations. Theoretically, he was subject to United Nations control in the ultimate sense; however, the practical arrangements of the military chain of command went through the United Nations to the cooperating nation-states, of which the United States was by far the major force, and then on through their regular civilian-military structure. This made MacArthur supreme commander in the field, but he was superseded in the total structure by the Joint Chiefs of Staff in Washington, the secretary of defense and the President acting as Commander in Chief. Such a command pattern was not normally too restricting, as historically the American military tradition afforded a reasonable amount of autonomy to the commander in the field, and when the field commander was a four-star general of the status and reputation of MacArthur, thousands of miles from the United States, he could expect a relatively free hand. And yet such a military leader was also expected to operate within the limits of the overall political and military policy established by the civilian leaders of the government, for that too was a tradition firmly rooted in the history of this country.

From almost the beginning of the Korean action both political and military misunderstandings and disagreements developed between General MacArthur in the field and his military and civilian chiefs in Washington. The first problem was over Formosa. Chiang Kai-shek, defeated on the Chinese mainland, had withdrawn to Formosa and was anxious to rekindle American friendship and military collaboration. At the outset of the North Korean attack upon South Korea, Chiang offered the immediate assistance of 33,000 of his troops to the South Koreans. Both the State Department and the Joint Chiefs had good reasons for refusing his offer. The State Department considered him a distinct political liability throughout the rest of Asia in the wake of his regime's collapse in China amid charges of corruption, the lack of a will to resist and very little popular support. To Asians who were in the process of throwing off the yoke of colonialism, Chiang represented poverty, incompetence and the old regime, and they wanted nothing to do with him. The Joint Chiefs argued that his proffered infantrymen would constitute a hindrance rather than a help. They would, in all probability, have to be refitted with equipment, trained or retrained, and would monopolize logistic transportation and equipment which American troops could make use of more effectively. The Truman administration had decided, however, to isolate Formosa from the mainland by patrolling the waters in between with the Seventh Fleet, in an effort to limit the war. They argued that such an action would prevent a communist invasion of Formosa as well as a landing on the mainland by Chiang. The American, and soon the United Nations', objective for that operation was to prevent the spread of more fighting into Korea.

MacArthur set the pattern of his future relations with Washington by his handling of the Formosa problem. Several days after the fighting broke out in Korea, he flew to Formosa for his first meeting with Chiang. It turned out to be something of a love feast between these two rather prepossessing mandarins, and when MacArthur returned to Tokyo, statements from both his headquarters and from that of Chiang caused immediate concern in Washington and in the world press. The statements from each camp heaped praise upon the other and intimated that arrangements had been agreed upon for future military cooperation.

President Truman was so concerned that a misconception of United Nations policy towards Formosa should not develop as a result of speculations concerning the MacArthur-Chiang meeting, that he quickly dispatched his special assistant for national security, Averell Harriman, to Tokyo to make certain that MacArthur understood the United States and U.N. policy towards Chiang and Formosa. Harriman wrote that in long talks with the general he made the administration's policy very clear, but he had apprehensions about MacArthur's willingness to appreciate the difficulties of the United States' worldwide commitments, and that the situation in the Far East was only one element in a very extended chain of situations in precarious and sensitive balance throughout the world. To make doubly sure that there would be no further outburst of conflicting policy from the American commander in the field, the Joint Chiefs of Staff again communicated to the general the main lines of American policy, with specific instructions to MacArthur not to make any commitment to Chiang which went beyond them.

Truman wrote that he "assumed that would be the last of it and that General MacArthur would accept the Formosa policy laid down by his Commander in Chief."[205] But this was not to be the case. Two weeks later the President obtained from the White House press room a copy of a statement sent by the general to the convention of the Veterans of Foreign Wars, which was, in effect, an attack on Truman's Formosa policy, and a plea for his own view that the oriental mind required "aggressive, resolute and dynamic leadership" rather than the "threadbare argument by those who advocate appeasement and defeatism in the Pacific that if we defend Formosa we alienate continental Asia."[206]

"It was my opinion that this statement could only serve to confuse the world as to just what our Formosa policy was, . . ." President Truman later wrote.

> Of course I would never deny General MacArthur or anyone else the right to differ with me in opinions. The official position of the United States, however, is defined by decisions and declarations of the President. There can be only one voice in stating the position of this country in the field of foreign relations. This is of fundamental constitutional significance. General MacArthur, in addition to being an important American Commander, was also the United Nations Commander in Korea. He was, in fact, acting for and on behalf of the United Nations. That body was then debating the question of Formosa, and its members—even those outside the Soviet block—differed sharply in their views regarding Formosa. It was hardly proper for the U.N.'s agent to argue a case then under discussion by that body.
>
> I realized that the damage had been done and that the MacArthur message was in the hands of the press.
>
> I gave serious thought to relieving General MacArthur as our Military Field Commander in the Far East and replacing him with General Bradley. I could keep MacArthur in command of the Japanese occupation, taking Korea and Formosa out of his hands. But after weighing it carefully I decided against such a step. It would have been difficult to avoid the appearance of a demotion, and I had no desire to hurt General MacArthur personally. My only concern was to let the world know that his statement was not official policy.[207]

The President directed the secretary of defense to wire the general immediately, ordering him to withdraw the statement. Truman followed the telegram with a long letter, explaining once again the American policy on Formosa and the reasoning behind it. The damage was done, however, as the complete text of the MacArthur statement in a national news magazine was already in the mails.

General MacArthur's brilliant Inchon landing caught the North Korean army by surprise and led to a quick reversal of the military situation in Korea. The following day the United Nations army broke through the perimeter behind which they had protected their beachhead at Pusan, and rapidly moved northward. Within four days the Tenth Army Corps, moving northeast from Inchon (and incidentally liberating Seoul, the capital of South Korea along the way) linked up with the Eighth Army, driving north from Pusan, to cut off, capture and destroy the better part of the North Korean army. There were few military achievements in history to equal this maneuver, but in due time that gain was cancelled out by the overextended drive to the North which provoked the Chinese armies to cross the Yalu and inflict upon the U.N. army a second serious defeat, shortly driving them back below the 38th parallel and out of the capital at Seoul once again.

The full burden of this second defeat should not be placed entirely upon the shoulders of Douglas MacArthur. It should be made clear that in advancing to the North MacArthur was not acting entirely on his own, but was supported by a United Nations directive, approved by the Joint Chiefs of Staff. At the same time it should be pointed out that this directive was drawn up on the basis of evaluations of intelligence reports made by MacArthur and his staff, and that the President, the U.N. and the Joint Chiefs were influenced by his considered opinion that neither the Russians nor the Chinese would move troops into Korea in any real strength.

A further difficulty can be found in the interpretation of the U.N. directive itself. From the start of the United Nations "police action" in Korea, President Truman, Averell Harriman, Secretary of State Dean Acheson, Secretary of Defense George Marshall and the Joint Chiefs of Staff had tried repeatedly to convince General MacArthur that they were fighting a "limited" war, and they wanted to keep it that way. The administration and the U.N. position was that they wanted to repulse communist aggression and destroy the North Korean army, if possible, but that they could not afford the danger of enlarging the conflict. American commitments extended from one end of the world to the other, and the Joint Chiefs were painfully aware that United States missions in Europe, Japan and other troubled areas were far below proper strength because of the drain of resources of men and arms going to Korea. Had the Russians decided to attack at any of those points the United States would hardly have been in a position to repulse them, short of dropping another atom bomb.

Moreover, considerable pressure was exerted upon the United Nations command by other countries whose armed forces and supporting civilian contingents were also active in Korea. The intelligence agencies of Australia, Sweden, Burma and the Netherlands had all decided that the Chinese communists were not bluffing in their threats to enter the war, but that point of view was contradicted and opposed by the United States Central Intelligence Agency.

When the U.N. army crossed the 38th parallel moving northward, MacArthur was instructed to pursue and destroy the enemy, but not to the extent that the pursuit risked the enlargement of the war. This last point was emphasized time and time again by the Commander in Chief in Washington and by members of the Joint Chiefs of Staff; and it was even suggested that only Korean troops be used in areas less than 150 miles from the boundaries of North Korea on the Yalu River. But MacArthur was convinced that neither the Russians nor the Chinese would, or could, strike back in force.

Yet Truman was so determined that there be no further misunderstandings between Washington and Tokyo that he flew to Wake Island for a meeting with the general on October 15. MacArthur was confident at the time, and he assured the President that victory had been won in Korea. When asked point blank about the chances of Russian or Chinese intervention, he discounted both. He saw no real possibility of the Russians being able or willing to move a sizeable number of troops into Korea, and he believed that since the Chinese had no real airpower, if they did try to get down into Korea, there would be the "greatest slaughter." So confident was he that the end of the war was in sight that he predicted that all resistance in North and South Korea would end by Thanksgiving Day, and that it was his hope to be able to withdraw the Eighth Army to Japan by Christmas. And in the glow of at least surface public satisfaction at the meeting, MacArthur told the President, according to the President's press secretary, "No commander in the history of war has had more complete and admirable support from the agencies in Washington than I have during the Korean operation."[208] It would not be long before that sentiment would change.

Soon all hell broke loose. The Chinese did cross the Yalu in great numbers, and in the course of the next few weeks they cut the United Nations army to ribbons. The U.N. troops were forced to retreat again below the 38th parallel, south of Seoul. The troops of the Tenth Army Corps were evacuated by a brilliant amphibious operation from Hungnam on the east coast, but the casualties along the total battlefront were very high, and most of the troops were frostbitten and badly battered.

As soon as it had become clear that contrary to his predictions the Chinese were pouring into Korea in great numbers, MacArthur wired Washington explaining that the nature of the war had changed, and requested permission to bomb the bridges of the Yalu River and the Chinese power installations in Manchuria. This was a direct invitation for a full-scale war with the Soviet Union as well as China, since a plausible argument could be made that Soviet territory and sovereignty were threatened by such raids. Permission was finally granted to bomb the Korean side of the bridges, for MacArthur felt he could not guarantee the safety of his troops without the bombing action, but in a matter of days the Yalu River froze over, and thousands of Chinese poured across the ice.

MacArthur was crestfallen by the turn of events; he blamed Truman and his advisors for restraining his hand, and for giving the Chinese what he termed a "sanctuary" beyond the Korean border. He had never accepted the general policy of trying to prevent a spread of the conflict in order to protect dwindling positions of American and free world strength in other critical areas, and now that his overoptimistic boasts had been crushed, he was anxious to pin the blame on somebody other than himself.

The final showdown between the general and the President came in the spring of 1951. By then the situation in South Korea had greatly improved, mostly due to the leadership of General Matthew Ridgway, who replaced General Walker after he was killed in a jeep accident after the Hungnam evacuation.

When General Ridgway assumed the field command in Korea, he found the retreating troops beaten, weary and at rock-bottom in morale. In a relatively short time he performed something of a miracle in reorganizing this beaten army into a force that retreated in good order to prepared positions south of Seoul, and once again began to savagely repulse the enemy attack. By March the United Nations armies had thrown the combined Chinese-North Korean forces out of Seoul, and in most cases beyond the 38th parallel. Another vital decision had to be made, and this time Truman and his military and political advisors in Washington were in no position or mood to risk any possible misinterpretation of their policy, which was meant to limit their military commitment in Korea and to end the conflict as soon as possible. President Truman picks up the thread of the tale at this point in his presidential memoirs.

President Harry S. Truman
Description of Events Leading to
The Dismissal of General MacArthur
January-April 1951

Truman, II, 438-50.

There is, of course, a difference between broad policy aims such as the President establishes and detailed applications of policy that have to be worked out on a day-by-day basis. On these details of application there normally are differences of opinion and discussions. Sometimes the details grow into proportions where the President must make the decision, but normally there are a great many conversations, conferences, study papers, etc., before a matter is placed before the President. Throughout the early months of 1951, Defense and State Department officials met repeatedly to plan possible courses of action in Korea and in Asia generally.

In March, as the tide of battle in Korea began to turn in our favor, both groups favored a new approach to a negotiated cease-fire. The reasoning was that, in the first place, since we had been able to inflict heavy casualties on the Chinese and were pushing them back to and beyond the 38th parallel, it would now be in their interest at least as much as ours to halt the fighting, and secondly, the invaders stood substantially ejected from the territory of the Republic of Korea.

The Department of State drew up a statement which they proposed I should issue. On March 19 Secretary Acheson, General Marshall, and the Joint Chiefs of Staff held a meeting at which they discussed this draft. They also agreed to inform General MacArthur that there was going to be a presidential announcement and to ask him to offer his recommendations.

I was just ending a brief vacation at the Little White House at Key West, Florida, where I kept in constant touch with Acheson and Marshall, when on

March 20 the Joint Chiefs of Staff, carrying out the agreement of the preceding day, sent this message to General MacArthur:

> State Department planning a Presidential announcement shortly that, with clearing of bulk of South Korea of aggressors, United Nations now preparing to discuss conditions of settlement in Korea. United Nations feeling exists that further diplomatic efforts toward settlement should be made before any advance with major forces north of 38th parallel. Time will be required to determine diplomatic reactions and permit new negotiations that may develop. Recognizing that parallel has no military significance, State has asked Joint Chiefs of Staff what authority you should have to permit sufficient freedom of action for next few weeks to provide security for United Nations forces and maintain contact with enemy. Your recommendation desired.

In his reply the following day General MacArthur recommended that no additional restrictions be imposed on his command. He pointed out that, with the forces at his command and operating under the limitations which had been placed on him, it was not practicable for him to attempt to clear North Korea of the enemy and that he felt for that reason his current directive covered the situation quite well.

Following the receipt of MacArthur's reply, the Joint Chiefs of Staff again met with the Secretary of Defense and the State Department, and further details of the proposed presidential announcement were worked out. Furthermore, State Department officials met with the Washington representatives of the other nations that had troops in Korea in order to obtain their approval to the proposed draft. This was the draft:

> I make the following statement as Chief Executive of the Government requested by the United Nations to exercise the Unified Command in Korea, and after full consultation with United Nations Governments contributing combat forces in support of the United Nations in Korea.
>
> United Nations forces in Korea are engaged in repelling the aggressions committed against the Republic of Korea and against the United Nations.
>
> The aggressors have been driven back with heavy losses to the general vicinity from which the unlawful attack was first launched last June.
>
> There remains the problem of restoring international peace and security in the area in accordance with the terms of the Security Council resolution of June 27, 1950. The spirit and principles of the United Nations Charter require that every effort be made to prevent the spread of hostilities and to avoid the prolongation of the misery and the loss of life.
>
> There is a basis for restoring peace and security in the area which should be acceptable to all nations which sincerely desire peace.
>
> The Unified Command is prepared to enter into arrangements which would conclude the fighting and ensure against its resumption. Such arrangements would open the way for a broader settlement for Korea, including the withdrawal of foreign forces from Korea.
>
> The United Nations has declared the policy of the world community

that the people of Korea be permitted to establish a unified, independent and democratic state.

The Korean people are entitled to peace. They are entitled to determine their political and other institutions by their own choice and in response to their own needs.

The Korean people are entitled to the assistance of the world community in repairing the ravages of war—assistance which the United Nations is ready to give and for which it has established the necessary machinery. Its member nations have already made generous offers of help. What is needed is peace, in which the United Nations can use its resources in the creative tasks of reconstruction.

It is regrettable that those who are opposing the United Nations in Korea have made so little response to the many opportunities which have been and continue to be afforded for a settlement in Korea.

A prompt settlement of the Korean problem would greatly reduce international tension in the Far East and would open the way for the consideration of other problems in that area by the processes of peaceful settlement envisaged in the Charter of the United Nations.

Until satisfactory arrangements for concluding the fighting have been reached, United Nations military action must be continued.

The thought behind this was that a suggestion of our willingness to settle, without any threats or recriminations, might get a favorable reply.

Unfortunately, the careful preparations were all in vain. The many hours spent to secure the approval of the other governments, the detailed discussions among the diplomats and defense leaders became useless when on March 24 General MacArthur released a statement that was so entirely at cross-purposes with the one I was to have delivered that it would only have confused the world if my carefully prepared statement had been made.

What General MacArthur said was this:

Operations continue according to schedule and plan. We have now substantially cleared South Korea of organized Communist forces. It is becoming increasingly evident that the heavy destruction along the enemy's lines of supply, caused by our round-the-clock massive air and naval bombardment, has left his troops in the forward battle area deficient in requirements to sustain his operations. This weakness is being brilliantly exploited by our ground forces. The enemy's human wave tactics have definitely failed him as our own forces have become seasoned to this form of warfare; his tactics of infiltration are but contributing to his piecemeal losses, and he is showing less stamina than our own troops under the rigors of climate, terrain and battle.

Of even greater significance than our tactical successes has been the clear revelation that this new enemy, Red China, of such exaggerated and vaunted military power, lacks the industrial capacity to provide adequately many critical items necessary to the conduct of modern war. He lacks the manufacturing base and those raw materials needed to produce, maintain and operate even moderate air and naval power, and he cannot provide the essentials for successful ground operations, such as tanks, heavy artillery and other refinements science has introduced into the conduct of military campaigns. Formerly his great numerical potential might well have filled this gap but with the development of existing methods of mass destruction, numbers alone do not offset the vulnerability inherent in such deficiencies. Control of the seas and the air, which in turn means control over supplies, communications, and transportation, are no less essential and decisive now than in the past. When this control exists as in our case, and is coupled with an inferiority of ground fire power as in the enemy's case, the resulting disparity is such that it cannot be overcome by bravery, however fanatical, or the most gross indifference to human loss.

These military weaknesses have been clearly and definitely revealed since Red China entered upon its undeclared war in Korea. Even under the inhibitions which now restrict the activity of the United Nations forces and the corresponding military advantages which accrue to Red China, it has been shown its complete inability to accomplish by force of arms the conquest of Korea. The enemy, therefore, must by now be painfully aware that a decision of the United Nations to depart from its tolerant effort to contain the war to the area of Korea, through an expansion of our military operations to its coastal areas and interior bases, would doom Red China to the risk of imminent military collapse. These basic facts being established, there should be no insuperable difficulty in arriving at decisions on the Korean problem if the issues are resolved on their own merits, without being burdened by extraneous matters not directly related to Korea, such as Formosa or China's seat in the United Nations.

The Korean nation and people, which have been so cruelly ravaged, must not be sacrificed. This is a paramount concern. Apart from the military area of the problem where issues are resolved in the course of combat, the fundamental questions continue to be political in nature and must find their answer in the diplomatic sphere. Within the area of my authority as the military commander, however, it would be needless to say that I stand ready at any time to confer in the field with the commander-in-chief of the enemy forces in the earnest effort to find any military means whereby realization of the political objectives of the United Nations in Korea, to which no nation may justly take exceptions, might be accomplished without further bloodshed.

This was a most extraordinary statement for a military commander of the United Nations to issue on his own responsibility. It was an act totally disregarding all directives to abstain from any declarations on foreign policy. It was an open defiance of my orders as President and as Commander in Chief. This was a challenge to the authority of the President under the Constitution. It also flouted the policy of the United Nations.

By this act MacArthur left me no choice—I could no longer tolerate his insubordination.

In effect, what MacArthur was doing was to threaten the enemy with an ultimatum—intimating that the full preponderance of Allied power might be brought to bear against Red China. To be sure, he said that this would be a political decision, but considering his high office, the world would assume that he had advance knowledge that such a decision would be made.

This was certainly the immediate effect among our allies. From capitals all over the world came rush inquiries: What does this mean? Is there about to be a shift in American policy?

There was more involved than the fate of a prepared statement that the President of the United States had intended to make, or even than the diplomatic furor created by this "pronunciamento," as the Norwegian Ambassador called it when he inquired at the State Department what it meant. What was much more important was that once again General MacArthur had openly defied the policy of his Commander in Chief, the President of the United States.

I held a conference with Dean Acheson, Robert Lovett, and Dean Rusk at noon that day, Saturday, and reviewed the order which had been sent to MacArthur on December 6, requiring that all public statements be cleared with the department concerned. I asked the others if there could be any doubt as to the meaning of this order, and they all agreed that it was a very clear directive.

I instructed Lovett to have a priority message sent to General MacArthur that would remind him of his duty under this order, for the main thing to do now was to prevent further statements by the general.

I was aware of the fact that in an earlier statement the same month General MacArthur had already issued a challenge to the policy of the President. On March 7 he had dictated a statement to reporters to the effect that unless I accepted his policy there would be "savage slaughter." However, he had then at least admitted that it was not his to make the decision. But now, by his statement, he had in a very real sense influenced the course of policy, and further statements like this could only do untold harm.

This message was therefore sent to him:

24 Mar 51

From JCS Personal for MacArthur   The President has directed that your attention be called to his order as transmitted 6 December 1950. In view of the information given you 20 March 1951 any further statements by you must be coordinated as prescribed in the order of 6 December.

The President has also directed that in the event Communist military leaders request an armistice in the field, you immediately report that fact to the JCS for instructions.

Bradley

I can only say that on that day I was deeply shocked. I had never underestimated my difficulties with MacArthur, but after the Wake Island meeting I had hoped that he would respect the authority of the President. I tried to place myself in his position, however, and tried to figure out why he was challenging the traditional civilian supremacy in our government.

Certainly his arguments and his proposals had always received full consideration by me and by the Joint Chiefs of Staff. If anything, they—and I—had leaned over backward in our respect for the man's military reputation. But all his statements since November—ever since the Chinese entry into Korea—had the earmarks of a man who performs for the galleries. It was difficult to explain this latest development unless it is assumed that it was of importance to the general to prevent any appearance that the credit for ending the fighting should go elsewhere.

I reflected on the similarities in the situation that had faced Abraham Lincoln in his efforts to deal with General McClellan. Carl Sandburg tells a story about Lincoln's relationship with McClellan: The general occasionally made political statements on matters outside the military field, and someone asked Lincoln what he would reply to McClellan. Lincoln's answer, so the story goes, was this: "Nothing—but it made me think of the man whose horse kicked up and struck his foot through the stirrup. He said to the horse: 'If you are going to get on, I will get off.' "

Lincoln had had great and continuous trouble with McClellan, though the policy differences in those days were the opposite of mine: Lincoln wanted McClellan to attack, and McClellan would not budge. The general had his own ideas on how the war, and even the country, should be run. The President would issue direct orders to McClellan, and the general would ignore them. Half the country knew that McClellan had political ambitions, which men in opposition to Lincoln sought to use. Lincoln was patient, for that was his nature, but at long last he was compelled to relieve the Union Army's principal commander. And though I gave this difficulty with MacArthur much wearisome thought, I realized that I would have no other choice myself than to relieve the nation's top field commander.

If there is one basic element in our Constitution, it is civilian control of the military. Policies are to be made by the elected political officials, not by generals or admirals. Yet time and again General MacArthur had shown that he was unwilling to accept the policies of the administration. By his repeated public statements he was not only confusing our allies as to the true course of our policies but, in fact, was also setting his policy against the President's.

I have always had, and I have to this day, the greatest respect for General MacArthur, the soldier. Nothing I could do, I knew, could change his stature as one of the outstanding military figures of our time—and I had no desire to diminish his stature. I had hoped, and I had tried to convince him, that the policy he was asked to follow was right. He had disagreed. He had been openly critical. Now, at last, his actions had frustrated a political course decided upon, in conjunction with its allies, by the government he was sworn to serve. If I allowed him to defy the civilian authorities in this manner, I myself would be violating my oath to uphold and defend the Constitution.

I have always believed that civilian control of the military is one of the strongest foundations of our system of free government. Many of our people are descended from men and women who fled their native countries to escape the oppression of militarism. We in America have sometimes failed to give the soldier and the sailor their due, and it has hurt us. But we have always jealously guarded the constitutional provision that prevents the military from taking over the government from the authorities, elected by the people, in whom the power resides.

It has often been pointed out that the American people have a tendency to choose military heroes for the highest office in the land, but I think the statement is misleading. True, we have chosen men like George Washington and Andrew Jackson, and even Ulysses S. Grant, as our Chief Executives. But only Grant among these three had been raised to be a professional soldier, and he had abandoned that career and been brought back into service, like thousands of other civilians, when war broke out. We have chosen men who, in time of war, had made their mark, but until 1952 we had never elevated to the White House any man whose entire life had been dedicated to the military [Dwight D. Eisenhower].

One reason that we have been so careful to keep the military within its own preserve is that the very nature of the service hierarchy gives military commanders little if any opportunity to learn the humility that is needed for good public service. The elected official will never forget—unless he is a fool—that others as well or better qualified might have been chosen and that millions remained unconvinced that the last choice made was the best one possible. Any man who has come up through the process of political selection, as it functions in our country, knows that success is a mixture of principles steadfastly maintained and adjustments made at the proper time and place—adjustments to conditions, not adjustment of principles.

These are things a military officer is not likely to learn in the course of his profession. The words that dominate his thinking are "command" and "obedience," and the military definitions of these words are not definitions for use in a republic.

That is why our Constitution embodies the principle of civilian control of the military. This was the principle that General MacArthur threatened. I do not believe that he purposefully decided to challenge civilian control of the military, but the result of his behavior was that this fundamental principle of free government was in danger.

It was my duty to act.

I wrestled with the problem for several days, but my mind was made up before April 5, when the next incident occurred.

On that day Representative Joseph W. Martin, the minority leader in the House, read a letter in the House which General MacArthur had addressed to him. Martin, an isolationist with a long record of opposition to forward-looking foreign policies, had written to MacArthur early in March and, among other things, had said that it was sheer folly not to use Chinese Nationalist troops in Korea. Then he had asked if this view paralleled the general's.

General MacArthur's reply, written on March 20, read as follows:

> I am most grateful for your note of the eighth forwarding me a copy of your address of February 12. The latter I have read with much interest, and find that with the passage of years you have certainly lost none of your old time punch.
>
> My views and recommendations with respect to the situation created by Red China's entry into war against us in Korea have been submitted to Washington in most complete detail. Generally these views are well

known and generally understood, as they follow the conventional pattern of meeting force with maximum counterforce as we have never failed to do in the past. Your view with respect to the utilization of the Chinese forces on Formosa is in conflict with neither logic nor this tradition.

It seems strangely difficult for some to realize that here in Asia is where the Communist conspirators have elected to make their play for global conquest, and that we have joined the issue thus raised on the battlefield; that here we fight Europe's war with arms while the diplomats there still fight it with words; that if we lose this war to Communism in Asia the fall of Europe is inevitable, win it and Europe most probably would avoid war and yet preserve freedom. As you point out, we must win. There is no substitute for victory.

The second paragraph of this letter was in itself enough of a challenge to existing national policy. MacArthur had been fully informed as to the reason why the employment of Chinese Nationalist forces was ruled out. He himself, only eight months earlier, had endorsed the merit of this decision. Later, when he had changed his position and reopened the subject, he had again been advised that this was part of the over-all policy on which the President had decided. So, in praising Mr. Martin's logic and traditional attitude, he was in effect saying that my policy was without logic and violated tradition.

Now, the tradition of which he wrote—that of meeting force with maximum counterforce—is in itself not one that exists outside military textbooks. To be sure, it is a good rule for the employment of troops, but it has no bearing on the relations between governments or between peoples. The American people have accomplished much and attained greatness not by the use of force but by industry, ingenuity, and generosity.

Of course the third paragraph of MacArthur's letter was the real "clincher." I do not know through what channels of information the general learned that the Communists had chosen to concentrate their efforts on Asia—and more specifically on his command. Perhaps he did not know just how much effort and how much sacrifice had been required to stem the Communist tide in Iran—in Greece—at Berlin. Perhaps he did not know how strenuously the Kremlin wished to block the emergence of a united front in western Europe. Actually, of course, my letter of January 13 had made it clear that Communism was capable of attacking not only in Asia but also in Europe and that this was one reason why we could not afford to extend the conflict in Korea. But then MacArthur added a belittling comment about our diplomatic efforts and reached his climax with the pronouncement that "there is no substitute for victory."

But there is a right kind and a wrong kind of victory, just as there are wars for the right thing and wars that are wrong from every standpoint.

As General Bradley later said: "To have extended the fighting to the mainland of Asia would have been the wrong war, at the wrong time and in the wrong place."

The kind of victory MacArthur had in mind—victory by the bombing of Chinese cities, victory by expanding the conflict to all of China—would have been the wrong kind of victory.

To some professional military men, victory—success on the battlefield alone—

becomes something of an end in itself. Napoleon, during his ill-fated Moscow campaign, said, "I beat them in every battle, but it does not get me anywhere."

The time had come to draw the line. MacArthur's letter to Congressman Martin showed that the general was not only in disagreement with the policy of the government but was challenging this policy in open insubordination to his Commander in Chief.

I asked Acheson, Marshall, Bradley, and Harriman to meet with me on Friday morning, April 6, to discuss MacArthur's action. I put the matter squarely before them. What should be done about General MacArthur? We discussed the question for an hour. Everyone thought that the government faced a serious situation.

Averell Harriman was of the opinion that I should have fired MacArthur two years ago. In the spring of 1949, as in 1948, MacArthur had pleaded that he could not come home because of the press of business in Tokyo, and it had been necessary for the Secretary of the Army, Kenneth Royall, to intervene urgently from Washington in order to get MacArthur to withhold his approval from a bill of the Japanese Diet which was completely contrary to the economic policy for the occupation as prescribed by the governmental authorities in Washington.

Secretary of Defense Marshall advised caution, saying he wished to reflect further. He observed that if I relieved MacArthur it might be difficult to get the military appropriations through Congress.

General Bradley approached the question entirely from the point of view of military discipline. As he saw it, there was a clear case of insubordination and the general deserved to be relieved of command. He did wish, however, to consult with the Chiefs of Staff before making a final recommendation.

Acheson said that he believed that General MacArthur should be relieved, but he thought it essential to have the unanimous advice of the Joint Chiefs of Staff before I acted. He counseled that the most careful consideration be given to this matter since it was of the utmost seriousness. He added, "If you relieve MacArthur, you will have the biggest fight of your administration."

We then joined the Cabinet for the regularly scheduled meeting. There was comment all around the table, of course, about the letter to Martin, but there was no discussion of the problem of what to do with MacArthur. After the Cabinet meeting, Acheson, Marshall, Bradley, and Harriman returned with me to my office, and we continued our discussion.

I was careful not to disclose that I had already reached a decision. Before the meeting adjourned, I suggested to Marshall that he go over all the messages in the Pentagon files that had been exchanged with General MacArthur in the past two years. Then I asked all four to return the following day at 9 A.M.

The next morning, Saturday, April 7, we met again in my office. This meeting was short. General Marshall stated that he had read the messages and that he had now concluded that MacArthur should have been fired two years ago. I asked General Bradley to make a final recommendation to me of the Joint Chiefs of Staff on Monday.

On Sunday, the eighth of April, I sent for Acheson to come to Blair House, and I discussed the situation further with him. I informed him that I had already that morning consulted with Snyder. I then told Acheson that I would prepare to act on

Monday when General Bradley made his report on the recommendations of the Joint Chiefs of Staff.

At nine o'clock Monday morning I again met with Marshall, Bradley, Acheson, and Harriman. General Bradley reported that the Joint Chiefs of Staff had met with him on Sunday, and it was his and their unanimous judgment that General MacArthur should be relieved.

General Marshall reaffirmed that this was also his conclusion. Harriman restated his opinion of Friday. Acheson said he agreed entirely to the removal of MacArthur.

It was only now that I answered that I had already made up my mind that General MacArthur had to go when he made his statement of March 24.

I then directed General Bradley to prepare the orders that would relieve General MacArthur of his several commands and replace him with Lieutenant General Matthew Ridgway, the commanding general of the Eighth Army in Korea. I instructed him to confer with Secretary of State Acheson, since the office of Supreme Commander, Allied Powers, was also involved.

The same group reported to me at the White House at three-fifteen on Monday afternoon with the drafted orders, which I signed.

It was decided that the notification of these orders should be given to General MacArthur through Secretary of the Army Pace, who was then in Korea. We understood that he was at Eighth Army Headquarters. I asked Acheson to transmit the orders to Pace through Ambassador Muccio and that Pace was to go to Tokyo and personally hand the orders to General MacArthur.

But our message was delayed in reaching Pace, first because of mechanical difficulties in transmission, and second because Pace was at the front with General Ridgway.

I requested Secretary Acheson to inform congressional leaders and to advise John Foster Dulles of our action regarding MacArthur, and to ask Dulles to go to Japan and assure the Yoshida government that the change in commander would not in any way affect our policy of pushing the Japanese peace treaty to a speedy conclusion. This Dulles agreed to do.

A change in plans became necessary, however, when late on the evening of April 10 General Bradley came rushing over to Blair House. He had heard, he said, that the story had leaked out and that a Chicago newspaper was going to print it the next morning. That was when I decided that we could not afford the courtesy of Secretary Pace's personal delivery of the order but that the message would have to go to General MacArthur in the same manner that relieving orders were sent to other officers in the service.

Under these new circumstances I felt compelled to have Joseph Short, my press secretary, call a special news conference for 1 A.M., April 11, which was as quickly as it was possible to have the orders, in their slightly changed form, reproduced.

The reporters were handed a series of papers, the first being my announcement of General MacArthur's relief.

"With deep regret," this announcement read, "I have concluded that General of the Army Douglas MacArthur is unable to give his wholehearted support to the policies of the United States Government and of the United Nations in matters pertaining to his official duties. In view of the specific responsibilities imposed upon me by the Constitution of the United States and the added responsibility which has been entrusted to me by the United Nations, I have decided that I must make a change of command in the Far East. I have, therefore, relieved General MacArthur of his commands and have designated Lieutenant General Matthew B. Ridgway as his successor.

"Full and vigorous debate on matters of national policy is a vital element in the constitutional system of our free democracy. It is fundamental, however, that military commanders must be governed by the policies and directives issued to them in the manner provided by our laws and Constitution. In time of crisis, the consideration is particularly compelling.

"General MacArthur's place in history as one of our greatest commanders is fully established. The Nation owes him a debt of gratitude for the distinguished and exceptional service which he had rendered his country in posts of great responsibility. For that reason I repeat my regret at the necessity for the action I feel compelled to take in his case."

The second document was the actual order of relief. It notified General MacArthur that he was relieved of his several commands and instructed him to turn over his authority to General Ridgway. There was a further document instructing General Ridgway to assume the functions formerly held by General MacArthur and informing him that Lieutenant General Van Fleet was on his way to Korea to take Ridgway's post as Eighth Army commander.

A number of background documents were also released. These included my order of December 6 concerning the clearance of public statements, the notification to MacArthur of the proposed presidential statement, his own counter-pronouncement, the reminder that followed it of the clearance-of-statements requirements, the letter to Congressman Martin, the message of the JCS to MacArthur on January 4 asking for his advice on the arming of additional ROK army units, and his reply of January 6.

The last two papers were included because of a new statement of MacArthur's that had just come to light. A periodical that had always been critical of administration policy had sent a series of questions to MacArthur. One of them had been aimed at the arming of South Koreans. The magazine said it had heard that South Koreans were eager to defend themselves but that "Washington" had refused them arms.

The principal reason, of course, that the Republic of Korea's request for additional arms had been denied was that General MacArthur had recommended against it in his message of January 6. But he had told this periodical that the matter was one that involved issues beyond his authority—implying that if it had been up to him the ROK's would have received the additional arms!

As far as I was concerned, these papers stated the case. The American people were still faced with Communist aggression in Korea; the Communist conspiracy was still threatening the West in Europe and in Asia. I went on the air on the evening of April 11 to restate the government's policy to the American people. I explained why we were in Korea and why we could not allow the Korean affair to become a general all-out war. I proclaimed our desire to arrive at a settlement along the lines of the statement that had been drafted in March and then not used. I explained why it had become necessary to relieve General MacArthur.

"The free nations," I told the radio audience, "have united their strength in an effort to prevent a third world war.

"That war can come if the Communist leaders want it to come. But this nation and its allies will not be responsible for its coming."

General McClellan had only speculated about marching on Washington; MacArthur returned to the capital in glory. But he made many stops on the way. An estimated 230,000 persons turned out to recognize his departure from Tokyo. In Hawaii 100,000 lined a 20-mile parade route. Approximately one-half million people greeted him in San Francisco, and New York City topped them all when thousands of out-of-towners from New Jersey, Connecticut and Massachusetts flocked to the city, swelling the reception mob to an estimated seven and one-half million people, who showered 2,850 tons of paper down from office buildings lining his parade route on to the conquering hero. And this welcome was not simply idle curiosity. Congressmen and senators indicated their mail ran 10 to 1 against the dismissal. House Republican Minority Leader Joseph Martin emerged from a conference of Senate and House Republican leaders, and raised the question of possible "impeachment" against the President.

The general finally moved on to Washington to address a joint session of the Senate and the House, where he delivered a speech that left millions in the television audience wiping tears from their eyes when it was over. MacArthur spoke only in generalities, identifying the administration position as one of appeasement, but suggested that the real patriot who wanted to carry the fight to the enemy was very rudely dismissed. MacArthur always presented a situation in that kind of a light. There were no greys, but only blacks and whites in his world, only good and bad, and of course he was always on the side of the angels. As he closed his speech, he spoke the phrase from the old barracks ballad which has now become associated with him:

> "Old soldiers never die; they just fade away." And like the old soldier of that ballad, I now close my military career and just fade away—an old soldier who tried to do his duty as God gave him the light to see that duty. Good-by.[209]

The fade-out did not come, however, until after a three-day appearance before the Senate Foreign Relations and Armed Services Committees, which sat in special joint session to investigate the general's dismissal. It is no exaggeration to say that not only the powers of the Commander in Chief, but the entire foundations of constitutional government, were at stake in this crisis. The public who supported General MacArthur and denounced President Truman hardly realized what the implications of their angry denunciations could lead to. The general had been dismissed, as John W. Spanier in his excellent study of the case concludes, because (1) he had failed to submit his statements for clearance as he had been ordered to by his Commander in Chief; (2) "because he had challenged the President's role as the nation's spokesman on foreign policy"; and (3) because he was not in sympathy with the administration's policy to limit the conflict in Korea, and could not be relied upon to carry out that policy.[210] To support General MacArthur in the persistence of his conflict with the President and to call for the restoration of his command, as Senator Richard Nixon did, or to raise vague threats of impeachment, as Representative Martin did, was to undermine the constitutional supremacy of the civilian head of the government over his subordinate military commander in the field.

This became all too clear to the senators and ultimately to the public during the course of the one-month investigation. In fact MacArthur's predilection to advance his position in the most glowing and euphoric manner really undid him. MacArthur testified before the committee for three days, arguing in favor of his policy of extending the war against Red China to the mainland, with bombing raids into Manchuria, a blockade of the coast and the release of Chiang Kai-shek's army. Anything short of that he labeled appeasement; in fact, he challenged the worldwide foreign and military policy of the Truman administration.

Clearly General MacArthur had not yet acclimated himself to the world of nuclear weapons, which imposed new rules of warfare upon those who possessed them. To talk as MacArthur did of "all out war," of applying "every available means to bring it to a swift end," or "that there is no substitute for victory," indicates that he failed to recognize the implications of living in the nuclear age. The result of applying such obsolete strategy was to invite the holocaust that reasonable men, military and civilian alike, were attempting to avoid. Nuclear weapons created the circumstances wherein conflicting nations or ideologies either agreed tacitly to limit their military efforts and weaponry or they faced mutual annihilation. This simple fact of life seemed to escape General MacArthur, although he argued boldly that the other side would not risk any such escalation, even in the face of his "all out attack."

The general's outlook was extremely parochial, concentrating upon his local theater of operations and totally ignoring other exposed areas of conflict. In the course of advancing that policy, he made two disastrous admissions which exposed his entire position. Under close examination by Senator Brien McMahon, he admitted that his responsibilities were confined to his theater of command, and that he lacked the proper information to make judgments on a global basis. "My responsibilities were in the Pacific," he testified, "and the Joint Chiefs of Staff and the various agencies of government are working day and night for an over-all solution to the global problem."[211]

"General, I think you make the point very well," the senator replied, ". . . that the Joint Chiefs and the President of the United States, the Commander in Chief, has to look at this thing on a global basis and a global defense."[212] Perhaps because of this earlier admission, MacArthur insisted throughout his testimony that the Joint Chiefs were on his side, and that it was only the political leaders who imposed limitations upon his military actions. He overstepped himself at that point because the Joint Chiefs followed him with testimony that they were in complete agreement with President Truman's policies, had indeed advised such a course of action from a purely military point of view and had continuously made those views clear to

General MacArthur in the field. In fact General Hoyt Vandenberg, chief of staff of the air force, testified that to follow MacArthur's policy of extending the air war against China, and possibly Russia, would seriously endanger the nation's ability to deter attack from another source. To accomplish what MacArthur wished, Vandenberg argued, would require an air force five to six times its present strength:

> While we can lay the industrial potential of Russia today [to] waste, in my opinion, or we can lay the Manchurian countryside [to] waste, as well as the principal cities of China, we cannot do both because we have a shoestring air force [87 wings].[213]

As the chairman of the Joint Chiefs, World War II hero General Omar Bradley summed up the feelings of the military and political administration. He warned that General MacArthur's policies in Korea would "involve us in the wrong war, at the wrong place, at the wrong time, and with the wrong enemy."[214]

President Truman, of course, made no appearance at the hearings, but his case was won by the able testimony of his military and political advisors. The presidency and the constitutional system had indeed survived their trial by fire, but their dependence upon the new military arm of the nation, the secretary of defense in the person of World War II army chief of staff, General George Catlett Marshall and the Joint Chiefs of Staff, was all too obvious. It would be difficult to predict the outcome of this crisis had these advisors turned the other way and failed to defend their Commander in Chief's decision as effectively and as brilliantly as they did.

Truman's temporary survival and MacArthur's demise did not terminate the awful travail of "limited war," however. The war continued, and with it the erosion of public trust and confidence in its leaders. Korea demonstrated that there are indeed limits to a "limited war," and those limits relate to the will of the societies caught up in such conflicts to sustain the inconvenience of war without the passionate emotional commitment that "total war" calls forth. In other words, it demonstrated that there are finite limits, of relatively short duration, in which the American people will tolerate the casualties, the tragedies and the hardships of even a limited effort, without rejecting the political leadership responsible for the situation and turning it out of office. MacArthur's support was rooted in the frustrations and impatience of those who were eager to end the war. They were drawn to his promise of a quick and somehow painless end to their troubles—an end to the war which in the beginning almost everyone, conservatives and liberals alike, supported with considerable enthusiasm. But without the frenetic pitch of emotions accompanying total commitment, this initial support quickly turned into sullen and tired resentment. Of course, the men in power were the victims; and the country would discover in the decade ahead how much stronger frustration and opposition could be with leaders who were responsible for involving the nation in a far less popular and justifiable "limited war."

But these inferences were obviously not drawn by those who succeeded the man from Missouri. The lesson that appears to have been learned by succeeding Presidents from both political parties and "the best and the brightest" who surround them, was that what should be avoided at all costs is an exposed position which holds the Chief Executive responsible for "limited war," without the recorded, formal support of the Congress. Truman had enjoyed the informal support of Congress and the American people in the initial stages of the Korean "police action," but once it disappeared there was no evidence of the former affirmative mood.

So, post-Korean Presidents attempted to avoid Truman's fate by seeking formal support of potential, as well as clear and present conflicts. Such prior commitments became broader as time went on and tended to chip away at what was left of the constitutional war-making powers of Congress. But while contributing to the erosion of the constitutional powers of the legislature, such broad delegations of the war-making powers did not protect the Chief Executive from the inevitable bitterness of a frustrated public, if it appeared that the initial grant of power was obtained under false pretenses. The failure of future Presidents and their advisors to grasp the implications of the first "limited war" led to the reenactment and further decline of public trust and confidence in their leader's ability to direct the nation when confronted with a war which demanded total sacrifice from some in a social environment which did not demand nor receive the full commitment of the rest of the society. Of course none of this applied if the limited military effort succeeded quickly and effectively without any real sacrifice or cost in human life.

Confrontation with the Soviets

In his third month in office President John Fitzgerald Kennedy experienced a traumatic defeat which haunted him for the rest of his days in the White House. In mid-April 1961 he authorized an invasion of Cuba by a brigade of approximately 1400 Cuban refugees, who had been trained and outfitted by the United States Central Intelligence Agency (CIA) in Guatemala. The refugee invasion force landed on the beach of Cochinos Bay (the Bay of Pigs) in the Zapata area of Cuba on April 17, 1961. The operation was a total failure; after 72 hours of furious fighting against overwhelming odds, the brigade surrendered to Fidel Castro, the greater number of its members having been taken prisoner.

Although American troops were not directly involved, the expedition had been planned and executed by the CIA; American pilots took part in air strikes; other Americans were involved in the landings; and American war vessels stood-by off Cuba, ready to evacuate the troops, or become involved in some other fashion if they received the "go ahead" signal. The United States could hardly conceal its conspiratory role in the whole matter, and was universally condemned by both friend and foe for having violated international law with its clandestine military activities, and compounding the error by failing miserably in this *opera bouffe* affair. The abortive invasion drew not only criticism but scorn, and shook world confidence in the ability of the young President, at the very beginning of his tenure, to wield power responsibly.

Kennedy, himself, often wondered aloud to his two close associates and later biographers, Theodore C. Sorensen and Arthur M. Schlesinger, jr., how he could have been drawn into such a hare-brained operation; during the rest of his two and one-half years as President, he never, despite his many triumphs, quite overcame his anguish over this debacle. Of course we now know that Kennedy had inherited the problem from the Eisenhower administration, which had planned the operation and had actually begun the training and preparations for it long before Kennedy was sworn into office. As a matter of fact it was Richard M. Nixon, Kennedy's 1960 presidential opponent, who first thought of the idea. Once underway it would have been difficult to cancel, for the members of the invasion force were determined to fulfill their sacred mission; in addition the President was inadequately briefed by the central intelligence officers who were in charge of the operation, and improperly advised by the military leaders who studied and evaluated the invasion plan.

But President Kennedy did not exonerate himself from responsibility for the fatal decision because of these inadequacies; he publicly and privately assumed the full blame for the disaster:

> "How could I have been so far off base?" he asked himself out loud. "All my life I've known better than to depend on the experts. How could I have been so stupid, to let them go ahead?"[215]

The President never came up with any satisfactory answer to his question, but during the remainder of his tenure in office, he made quite certain that the "experts" were never in control again, and that their advice and strategy would always be weighed and evaluated by those who bore the responsibility of considering factors quite beyond the range of mere technical expertise. The Bay of Pigs crisis developed so early in the young President's administration that he was simply not prepared to deal with it. A political analyst has observed:

> Every President needs about twelve months to get his executive team organized, to feel his way into the vast and dangerous machinery of the bureaucracy. . . . While [Kennedy] was still trying to move in the furniture, in effect, he found the roof falling in and the doors blowing off.[216]

Both the roof and the doors were firmly in place when the next Cuban crisis arose however. President Kennedy had effectively moved to master and direct the complex machinery of the foreign affairs and military powers with which mid-century Presidents from Franklin Roosevelt on had been confronted. The by-word of the Kennedy national security administrative apparatus was flexibility. Kennedy agreed with Professor Richard Neustadt that the President had to protect his options in decision-making, and had to free himself from the straightjacket into which simple adjustments to the existing power structure of the bureaucratic order would lead.

He wanted to be informed of all aspects and contingencies of a given situation, to maintain the freedom to invent new solutions to old problems, to be able to decide rapidly and to have confidence that his decisions would penetrate the labyrinth of civilian and military organizations that would have to carry out any policy. This necessitated that he and his deputies represented in the National Security Council (NSC) acquire control over the vast civilian-military complex of the nation, and that they mobilize this monolith to respond to their direction and to accomplish their goals. This was a large-scale undertaking in the 1960s.

President Kennedy decided quite early that the formal and very complex structure of the National Security Council and its subordinate units, the National Planning Board (NPB) and the Operations Coordinating Board (OCB), should be greatly simplified. He found that they were not tailored to his needs or objectives, to say nothing of his style. He eliminated the two sub-groups, and met less frequently with the full council (NSC), a pattern he also followed with his cabinet. He felt that these large, formal meetings frequently tended to discourage the free exchange of views, and to obscure rather than to illuminate problems and recommendations for alternative policies. He preferred to meet in smaller groups with NSC and cabinet members and other staff assistants directly responsible for the problem at hand. Anxious to obtain the full background and information upon which to base his judgments, he was also eager to benefit from the judgment of his department heads and aides.

Once final decisions were made, he was concerned that the lines of responsibility not be stretched too far, and that individuals known to him were held responsible for decisions they shared in formulating. This streamlined organizational structure, emphasizing flexible, direct and continuing contact with the Chief Executive, promised to achieve such an objective.

But it was also necessary for the line chiefs—the secretary of state, the secretary of defense, and others who might be concerned—to have full command and control of their organizations in order for the decisions to be carried out. Neither the simplified overall organizational structure described above, nor the secretaries' control over their departments were firm and complete at the time of the first Cuban crisis, and as a result lines of communication either broke down or were hopelessly confused. The flow of information to the President was abortive, inaccurate and incomplete; and the feedback from the White House to the ranks was also faulty. This combination obviously contributed considerably to the failure of the Bay of Pigs operation, quite apart from any of the venture's other irrational aspects.

The President never quite succeeded in overcoming the inertia of the State Department. His secretary of state, Dean Rusk, fit in to the style and tempo of "Foggy Bottom"[217] as if he had always belonged there, which, in truth, he had and did. Adlai Stevenson had warned Kennedy before his inauguration:

> [Beware of the] tremendous institutional inertial force [in the Department of State] which, unless manipulated forcefully from the outset, will overwhelm and dictate to the new regime. A similar institutional force in the Defense Department has systematically absorbed a series of Secretaries of Defense.[218]

Secretary Rusk quickly acquiesced and accommodated himself to the existing framework, and he could not become the driving wedge of a program of substantial reform. Rusk, as Arthur Schlesinger, jr. has pointed out, "was more than anything else, a man bred in the large organizations of mid-century America."

> But unlike McNamara [the secretary of defense], his organizational instinct was for service, not for mastery. Successively nurtured in the protective bosoms of the university, the Army, the government

department, the foundation, he drew reassurance from the solidity of the structure, the regularity of the procedures, the familiarity of the vocabulary.[219]

Consequently, the President came to rely heavily upon the small National Security Council (NSC) staff, housed in the White House basement and under the direction of McGeorge Bundy, former dean of the Harvard faculty. Bundy gathered together a brilliant group of assistants who considered it one of their most important functions to defend the interests of the President in the area of national security policy-making (which, of course, included foreign policy) from the foot-dragging inertia and narrower interests of the bureaucracies.

The NSC staff and its director demanded and received "the flow of raw intelligence from State, Defense and the CIA," and thus fortified could alert the President to developments and oversights which might not otherwise come to his attention. Bundy's group, together with presidential assistants such as Sorensen, Schlesinger, Richard Goodwin, et al., who spent at least part of their time on foreign policy and national security problems, raised the right questions and clarified alternatives in the policy-making area so that the President could decide and act, rather than be victimized by the flow of events as he had been in the Bay of Pigs disaster.

Furthermore Kennedy was the first post-World War II President to achieve command of the burgeoning military establishment. This was accomplished through the exceptional leadership of his Secretary of Defense, Robert S. McNamara. By 1960 the Defense Department had become an empire, or, better, a collection of empires, bigger in size than the total population of one-third of the nation-states which were members of the United Nations.

Defense operated enormous complexes of transport, communications, procurement, maintenance and distribution as well as of tanks, ships, planes and men. It made a multiplicity of fateful choices in the determination of strategy, the selection of weapons systems, the design of forces and the level of expenditure. Its decisions affected everything from the economy of San Diego to the destiny of mankind.[220]

Although there was no unity among the various relatively independent branches of the armed services, they were usually able to accomplish their frequently inflated objectives by organizing their powerful constituencies (veterans organizations, service connected families, military industrialists and professional military societies) to circumvent the President by appealing to their special champions in the Congress (particularly the armed services committees in both houses). During the Truman and Eisenhower administrations both Presidents found it increasingly difficult, if not impossible, to bring this colossus under control, and their civilian secretaries of defense became expendable (one even committed suicide) because they were whipsawed between the aggressive demands of their military subordinates and the requirements of the national administration.[221] McNamara broke this chain of power and reestablished civilian and presidential control over the military establishment.

After his appointment as secretary of defense, McNamara was asked by the President to respond to a series of searching questions with regard to overall military strategy, weapons and the state of the American defense posture. During Kennedy's first week in office the secretary reported back to the President, concluding that the strategy of massive retaliation had resulted in serious weaknesses in our conventional forces; that our nuclear force was vulnerable to surprise missile attack; that our nonnuclear forces were weak in combat-ready divisions, in airlift capacity and in tactical air support; that we possessed a weapons inventory completely devoid of certain major items; and that the United States had no counterinsurgency force in existence. McNamara further pointed out that an arbitrary budget ceiling for national security made "military strategy the stepchild of a predetermined budget." There were, he indicated,

> too many automatic decisions made in advance instead of in the light of an actual emergency, and too few Pentagon-wide plans for each kind of contingency. The Army was relying on airlift the Air Force could not supply. The Air Force was stockpiling supplies for a war lasting a few days while the Army stock-piles assumed a war of two years.[222]

To remedy these weaknesses McNamara initiated a sweeping reform program for the total military machinery. He brought to the Pentagon civilian scientists and economists (or upgraded those already there), military intellectuals or "whiz kids" as they were called, who all attempted to apply systematic quantitative analysis to strategic decisions. *The Times Literary Supplement* reported:

> The military intellectuals move freely through the corridors of the Pentagon and the State Department rather as the Jesuits through the courts of Madrid and Vienna three centuries ago.[223]

Arthur Schlesinger has described the rapid evolution of the "black" art of these professionals:

> Operations research, as it was called, had begun during the Second World War, and its first practitioners were mostly physicists, mathematicians, biologists and engineers. After the war, an invasion of economists gave operations research new scope and vitality. Where the scientists tended to accept the terms of the problem as presented to them, the economists, schooled in the search for the most efficient use of resources, accustomed to the "substitution" effect and trained in such concepts as "marginal utility" and "opportunity cost," were more audacious in the pursuit of alternatives. In this new phase, operations research was quick to demonstrate that there could be a variety of ways to achieve a desired end. . . .[224]

McNamara exploited the new techniques of systems analysis, linear and dynamic programming and game theory to test and evaluate the claims, the strategies and the performances of the individual services. When various army, air and naval weapons and operations could be "cost accounted," or reduced to quantitative equivalents with respect to both cost and efficiency, the secretary of defense could then decide between one weapons system and another. McNamara did just this, and in the process operationally scrambled the services to reconstruct the most efficient combined elements of a particular weapons system. This not only gave him a more effective and efficient defense system from the point of view of both cost and performance, but it also greatly weakened the power of the individual services to buck their civilian chief. As Schlesinger observed, "these techniques gave civil government the means of subjecting the anarchy of defense to a measure of order."[225]

When in the late summer of 1962 one of the Central Intelligence Agency's U-2 reconnaissance flights over Cuba revealed the presence of Soviet intermediate range missiles on the western end of the island, and construction underway to build launching pads for them, President Kennedy was in a far better position to deal with the problem than he had been 18 months earlier. By that time he had sufficient "on the job" training, and had established clear enough control over national security to guarantee a better performance than that in the first Cuban crisis. After receiving the first accurate reports of the presence of Russian missiles in Cuba, the President immediately set into motion the military, diplomatic, intelligence and communications machinery necessary to cope with such a situation. Although prepared, he and his advisors were surprised and shocked that the Soviets had taken this bold step. For more than a year the Russians had repeatedly renounced any intention to in any way shift or alter the balance of military power between the two nations. In April 1961 Chairman Nikita Khrushchev had assured the President:

> We do not have any bases in Cuba, and we do not intend to establish any.[226]

On September 6, 1962, President Kennedy's top assistant, Theodore Sorensen, was called to the Soviet embassy in Washington to receive an urgent message for the President from Chairman Khrushchev, who promised once again that the Soviets were not interested in jeopardizing the current *detente* between the two countries. Khrushchev assured the President:

> Nothing will be undertaken before the American Congressional elections [in November] that could complicate the international situation or aggravate the tension in the relations between our two countries . . . provided that no actions are taken on the other side which would change the situation.[227]

This last message was probably prompted by a flurry of rumors and charges that had come to the floor of the Congress hinting that the Russians had already established a nuclear missile beachhead in Cuba. In the United States Senate Republican Senator Kenneth B. Keating charged that Cuba was being prepared for offensive military action, and the Republican Senatorial and Congressional Campaign Committee announced that Cuba would be the dominant issue of the 1962 congressional election. These rumors and charges had been carefully checked out by American intelligence, and there was no factual evidence to support any of them.

Care should be taken in dealing with the prophetic reports of Senator Keating, in particular. Roberta Wohlsetter concludes that later investigation indicates that the senator from New York was "proceeding beyond the evidence in suggesting, as he did, that he had positive proof of the presence of medium range missiles, and of the capability for rapid transformation of surface-to-air missiles into medium range surface-to-ground missiles."[228] Furthermore, although Keating claimed that his public statements had been verified by official sources, those same sources have denied such verification, and Sorensen reports that Keating refused to reveal his sources, making it impossible for American intelligence to check their accuracy.[229] As Kennedy stated at a press conference at that time, "We cannot base the issue of war and peace on a rumor or report which is not substantiated, or which some member of Congress refuses to tell us where he heard it. . . . To persuade our allies to come with us, to hazard . . . the security . . . as well as the peace of the free world, we have to move with hard intelligence."[230]

But if Senator Keating's charges had not convinced the President, Republican hard-line conservative Senators Goldwater and Capehart, and South Carolina's turncoat Democrat, Strom Thurmond, were very impressed by his information; they attacked Kennedy's "do nothing" policy on the floor of the Senate. In campaign speeches across the country, in interviews and articles carried in the national press and on television, Republicans mounted a major effort demanding action on Cuba.

There had been recent hard evidence, however, of an extensive build-up of ground-to-air defensive missiles, and the presence of thousands of Russian military technicians in Cuba had been noted by the CIA. All of that had created such a highly charged preelection political atmosphere in the country that the President felt it necessary to issue a statement to the American people two days before Khrushchev's last assurance of Soviet innocence. He was assisted in drafting that statement by his brother, Attorney General Robert F. Kennedy and Deputy Attorney General Nicholas Katzenbach. Later Robert Kennedy pointed out that despite individual reports and rumors of the presence of intercontinental missiles in Cuba, the United States Intelligence Board had concluded as late as September 19, 1962, "that the Soviet Union would not make Cuba a strategic base."[231]

President John F. Kennedy
First Major Statement on
The Cuban Missile Crisis
September 4, 1962

David L. Larson, ed., *The "Cuban Crisis" of 1962: Selected Documents and Chronology* (Boston, 1963), 3-4.

All Americans, as well as all of our friends in this Hemisphere, have been concerned over the recent moves of the Soviet Union to bolster the military power of the Castro regime in Cuba. Information has reached this Government in the last four days from a variety of sources which establishes without doubt that the Soviets have provided the Cuban Government with a number of anti-aircraft defense missiles with a slant range of twenty-five miles which are similar to early models of our Nike. Along with these missiles, the Soviets are apparently providing the extensive radar and other electronic equipment which is required for their operation. We can also confirm the presence of several Soviet-made motor torpedo boats carrying ship-to-ship guided missiles having a range of fifteen miles. The number of Soviet military technicians now known to be in Cuba or en route— approximately 3,500—is consistent with assistance in setting up and learning to use this equipment. As I stated last week, we shall continue to make information available as fast as it is obtained and properly verified.

There is no evidence of any organized combat force in Cuba from any Soviet bloc country; of military bases provided to Russia; of a violation of the 1934 treaty relating to Guantanamo; of the presence of offensive ground-to-ground missiles; or of other significant offensive capability either in Cuban hands or under Soviet direction and guidance. Were it to be otherwise, the gravest issues would arise.

The Cuban question must be considered as a part of the worldwide challenge posed by Communist threats to the peace. It must be dealt with as a part of that larger issue as well as in the context of the special relationships which have long characterized the inter-American system.

It continues to be the policy of the United States that the Castro regime will not be allowed to export its aggressive purposes by force of the threat of force. It will be prevented by whatever means may be necessary from taking action against any part of the Western Hemisphere. The United States, in conjunction with other Hemisphere countries, will make sure that while increased Cuban armaments will be a heavy burden to the unhappy people of Cuba themselves, they will be nothing more.

The President ordered increased aerial surveillance of Cuba by U-2 overflights during September, and on September 7 he requested that Congress authorize him to call up members of the "ready reserve" to active duty, and also to extend enlistment, appointments and periods which reservists spend on active duty. A week later he opened his news conference with a second statement on Cuba in the light of increasingly belligerent statements emanating from Cuba and the Soviet Union; he warned that he would take whatever action was necessary if the security of the United States was threatened by aggressive acts or threats by Cuba towards any nation in the western hemisphere:

If at any time the Communist buildup in Cuba were to endanger or interfere with our security in any way, including our base at Guantanamo, our passage to the Panama Canal, our missile and space activities at Cape Canaveral, or the lives of American citizens in this country, or if Cuba should ever attempt to export its aggressive purposes by force or the threat of force against any nation in this hemisphere, or become an offensive military base of significant capacity for the Soviet Union, then this country will do whatever must be done to protect its own security and that of its allies.

We shall be alert, too, and fully capable of dealing swiftly with any such development. As President and Commander-in-Chief I have full authority now to take such action, and I have asked the Congress to authorize me to call up reserve forces should this or any other crisis make it necessary.[232]

A week later the Congress acted, passing a joint resolution which reiterated the warnings of the Monroe Doctrine to any European power against extending "their system to any portion of this Hemisphere," and reminded potential enemies of the Rio Treaty of 1947, which spelled out the principle that an attack against one American state should be considered "as an attack against all."[233] The resolution also threatened the use of military power to prevent Cuban aggression or the extension of subversive activities in the rest of the hemisphere, and "to prevent in Cuba the creation of or the use of an externally supported military capability endangering the security of the United States."[234] That resolution obviously strengthened the hand of the President in his future handling of the Cuban crisis.

Joint Congressional Resolution
On the Determination of the United States
With Respect to Cuba
September 1962

U.S. State Department, *Department of State Bulletin*, XLVII, No. 1217 (October 22, 1962), 597.

S. J. Res. 230; passed by the Senate on September 20, 1962 by a vote of 86 to 1 and by the House of Representatives on September 26, 1962 by a vote of 384 to 7.

Whereas President James Monroe, announcing the Monroe Doctrine in 1823, declared that the United States would consider any attempt on the part of European powers "to extend their system to any portion of this hemisphere as dangerous to our peace and safety"; and

Whereas in the Rio Treaty of 1947 the parties agreed that "an armed attack by any State against an American State shall be considered as an attack against all the American States, and, consequently, each one of the said contracting parties undertakes to assist in meeting the attack in the exercise of the inherent right of individual or collective self-defense recognized by article 51 of the Charter of the United Nations"; and

Whereas the Foreign Ministers of the Organization of American States at Punta del Este in January 1962 declared: "The present Government of Cuba has identified itself with the principles of Marxist-Leninist ideology, has established a political, economic, and social system based on that doctrine, and accepts military assistance from extracontinental Communist powers, including even the threat of military intervention in America on the part of the Soviet Union"; and

Whereas the International Communist movement has increasingly extended into Cuba its political, economic, and military sphere of influence: Now, therefore, be it

Resolved by the Senate and House of Representatives of the United States of America in Congress assembled, That the United States is determined—

(a) to prevent by whatever means may be necessary, including the use of arms, the Marxist-Leninist regime in Cuba from extending, by force or the threat of force, its aggressive or subversive activities to any part of this hemisphere;

(b) to prevent in Cuba the creation or use of an externally supported military capability endangering the security of the United States; and

(c) to work with the Organization of American States and with freedom-loving Cubans to support the aspirations of the Cuban people for self-determination.

The irony of the situation was that after the abortive Bay of Pigs episode, President Kennedy had attempted to play down the Cuban situation and had pursued a reasonable and subdued policy, attempting to dampen the emotional feeling in the country and gradually to relegate Cuba to a more realistic position within the overall framework of American policy. In defense of this position, however, and hoping to maintain a detached and cool equilibrium in the face of escalating Republican attacks, he had been forced to make a public declaration which placed his own credibility on the line if he failed to follow through once it was ascertained that Soviet missile bases were being constructed in Cuba.

President Kennedy continued to keep a wary eye on the Cuban situation, but the affairs of state were demanding, and in the course of the next four weeks he agonized over the civil rights crisis at the University of Mississippi, and finally dispatched troops to Oxford to quell the rioting that broke out there on the evening of October 1, 1962. He entertained and conferred with the President of Rwanda, the President of Pakistan, the Prime Minister of Burundi, the Crown Prince of Arabia, the President of Guinea and the Prime Minister of Algeria. He also attended the America's Cup races off Newport, Rhode Island; spoke at the United Steelworkers Convention in Miami, Florida; campaigned for the election of Democrats to the House and the Senate in Pennsylvania, Ohio, West Virginia, Minnesota, Kentucky, Michigan, Indiana, New Jersey, Maryland and New York; appointed Arthur Goldberg to the Supreme Court and Willard Wirtz to succeed him as secretary of labor; he created a Board of Inquiry in the east coast longshoremen's strike; appointed Maxwell D. Taylor chairman of the Joint Chiefs of Staff; congratulated Commander Walter Schirra on his return to earth after circling the globe six times in his space capsule; commemorated the centennial of the Emancipation Proclamation; sent a message to Pope John XXIII on the opening of the Second Vatican Council; signed the Drug Reform and the Trade Expansion Acts; urged restoration of cuts in the Foreign Aid Bill; and received reports of the outbreak of fighting in the Himalayas between Indian and Chinese army troops.

On the evening of October 15, 1962, CIA officials, who had interpreted the most recent U-2 pictures, notified McGeorge Bundy that they had definitely identified the crude beginnings of construction work on a medium-range missile base in the San Cristobal area of Cuba. Bundy did not notify the President until the following morning, waiting to check the veracity of this initial report, and also wishing to assure the President of a good night's sleep. After conferring with Bundy and personally inspecting the aerial views, Kennedy at 11:45 that same morning called together a group that would later be referred to as the Executive Committee of the National Security Council (the EXCOM). Those present at the first meeting from the State Department were: Secretary Dean Rusk, Under Secretary George Ball, Latin-American Assistant Secretary Edwin Martin, Deputy Under Secretary Alexis Johnson and Soviet expert Llewellyn Thompson. (Participating until departing for his new post as ambassador to France the following night was Charles "Chip" Bohlen.) Those present from the Defense Department were: Secretary Robert McNamara, Deputy Secretary Roswell Gilpatric, Assistant Secretary Paul Nitze and General Maxwell Taylor (newly appointed chairman of the Joint Chiefs of Staff). On the first day Deputy Director Carter represented the CIA; thereafter (upon his return to Washington) Director John McCone was in attendance.

Other government officials who were also involved in these meetings were: Attorney General Robert Kennedy, Secretary of the Treasury Douglas Dillon and White House aides Bundy and Sorensen. (Also sitting in on the earlier and later meetings were Vice President Lyndon Johnson and Kenneth O'Donnell. Others— such as Dean Acheson, Adlai Stevenson and Robert Lovett—sat in from time to time; and six days later USIA Deputy Director Donald Wilson, acting for the ailing Edward R. Murrow, was officially added.)[235]

Several accounts by President Kennedy's advisors and others document well what went on at the meetings of this critically important committee, perhaps one of the most important committees in history.[236] For almost a week they met around the clock, conjecturing first about Soviet motives, and then about the wide range of possible American responses to this reckless challenge. As Robert Kennedy disarmingly pointed out, "It is no reflection on them that none was consistent in his opinion from the very beginning to the end."[237] They conferred in the White House cabinet room and in Assistant Secretary Ball's conference room in the State Department, and as they weighed alternatives, they successfully brought to bear the full range of the tremendous resources of intellect and experience which they represented. Few would question today the final decision which the President, with their help, came to at the end of this agonizing week, but at the time other alternatives appeared to be more feasible, at least until they were thrashed out at length and explored for their full implications by this astute and experienced group of advisors.

In a superficial way the Executive Committee reflected almost perfectly the social and institutional origins assigned to the "power elite" by the sociologist, C. Wright Mills. These men were leaders in the social "class" groups, which, Mills argues, alone have decision-making power in this country—the military, the large corporations and the executive branch of the government. Only two of those present at the meeting had any real background in the legislative branch of the federal government—the President and the Vice President. In Kennedy's case, however, his power began to radiate only after he left the legislature, while the Vice President was unable to transpose very much of his tremendous congressional standing and power to the office he then held.

Moreover, a large percentage of the group had graduated from the same universities (Harvard and Yale could claim 13 of the 23 members of the group and at least 7 were members of either the Century or the Metropolitan Club, or both).[238] Even the member of the Irish mafia (the name applied by Washington newsmen to President Kennedy's White House aides of Irish descent) who was privileged to sit in on the Executive Committee sessions, Kenneth O'Donnell, was a Harvard graduate.

But when one takes a more penetrating look at the Mills thesis as applied to this group, it topples under its own weight. Power is never totally divorced from institutions or from social classes, but most of the men in the room owed their presence in this select but troubled company to their independent abilities and records and in many cases to their success in rising to the top, in spite of or even against the countervailing obstacles imposed by their institutional and social backgrounds. In most cases they were not at all representative of the institutions or social classes from which they emerged, and their success and the positions they held were frequently the result of their opposition to prevailing opinions and practices within their own "reference" groups. Take, for example, the military man present at the meeting. It is true that General Taylor was a career military officer, but he owed both his presence at the meeting, and his position as chairman of the Joint Chiefs of Staff mainly to his opposition to prevailing theories held by the military establishment, from which he had, for all practical purposes, recently been expelled. He came to the attention of the President, and was brought back from "voluntary" retirement, only because he had written a brilliant critique of the state of military practice and theory in the Pentagon at that time. The other representatives of the military establishment, Secretaries McNamara, Gilpatrick and Nitze, were drawn not from the military class but from business or career service in the government. But even then they were not in any sense representative of the institutions from which they came, any more than of the establishment which they now served.

McNamara was, it is true, president of one of the largest corporations in America before coming to Washington. He achieved that pinnacle, however, not by the standard corporation executive route, but because of his highly technical knowledge and competence in a period when the corporations were undergoing a technical revolution. He was a manager more than a businessman, and the managerial revolution thesis of Burnham which can be traced back to Berle and Means, fits the case of the secretary of defense far more accurately than does the power elite argument of Mills.

Cutting through the verbiage of ideological sociology, Taylor and McNamara, or even Dillon and Lovett, were part of a select company at that moment, not as representatives of the military or corporate power structure, but because the President of the United States had confidence in their judgment. I would certainly not argue, however, that they were originally selected for cabinet positions without consideration to their former business, military, or executive department connections. Dillon was initially brought into the President's executive family because he enjoyed the confidence of the business and the Republican party leaders, but he earned the respect and confidence of the President (who had been taught at the knee of his anti-establishment father not to trust "those sons-of-bitches") in spite of, rather than because of, his former connections. Anyone taking the trouble to study their careers, opinions and relationships to President Kennedy from any but the most sterile ideological perspective, will ferret out such obvious facts. And this applied to corporation lawyers Acheson, Stevenson and Ball, as well as to career diplomats Bohlen, Johnson and Thompson.

The revelations of Kennedy's extremely intimate biographers reveal that the Executive Committee, which functioned during the Cuban missile crisis as an important advisory panel to the President, was a group that could trace the career lines of its members back to the institutional power centers of American life, but neither the individual members nor the group as a whole was particularly representative of the "class" interests of such institutional power centers. They would not have been able to survive on the Kennedy "team" if they had not earned the confidence of the young President, more by the quality of their minds and the experience of their varied careers than by their present or former institutional or "class" attachments.

It would make more sense to view these individuals as representatives of the various bureaucratic institutions which they had come to represent, in Don K. Price's phrase: "Where you stand depends upon where you sit." Secretary McNamara represented the rational national security requirements of the defense establishment, where he had to reconcile the interests and objectives of the various military services with the overall policies he had set in motion. Rusk and the State Department participants in the Executive Committee meetings had to consider at all times the impact of decisions made about Cuba with foreign policy requirements in other areas of interest (eg. NATO and the Organization of American States—OAS). The military services obviously had their own axes to grind, and their continuing representative at the meetings, the new chairman of the Joint Chiefs of Staff (JCS), General Maxwell D. Taylor, reported that there were conflicting points of view among his constitutents in the JCS; there were even suspicions among the Joint Chiefs that he was not representing their views aggressively enough. Attorney General Robert Kennedy and presidential aide Theodore Sorensen were particularly sensitive to the interests of the President at these meetings, protecting his power and options, while working to bring greater harmony, agreement and consensus among the group. These were the real interests which had to be reconciled in making the final decision, not the abstract class interests in which sociologists like Mills placed so much faith.

The magnitude of the Soviet arms build-up in Cuba was a major undertaking on their part. When intelligence reports had collected all the information available, the potential threat appeared to be significant. Graham Allison has detailed the statistics of the hardware and manpower in a comprehensive summary:[239] it included 42 medium-range ballistic missiles (MRBMs), 12 intermediate-range ballistic missiles (IRBMs), 42 Ilyushin IL-28 medium range jet bombers, 144 surface-to-air anti-aircraft missiles (SAMs), launchers with related equipment and 4 missiles per launcher, 42 high performance MIG-21 fighter aircraft, assorted cruise missiles and missile-carrying patrol boats and 22,000 Soviet troops for construction, operation and defense of those weapons. The men and equipment arrived on 100 Soviet cargo vessels and 42 more were on their way at the time of the quarantine.

The missiles alone doubled the first strike strength of the Soviet Union vis à vis the United States, for these missiles would have been far short of the range of this country if based in the Soviet Union. That is why McNamara's early remarks in the EXCOM were puzzling when he said: "A missile is a missile. It makes no great difference if you are killed by a missile from the Soviet Union or from Cuba." But of course it did make a difference, because these medium-range and intermediate-range missiles would not have been able to kill any Americans if they had been based in the Soviet Union and not 90 miles from the U.S. mainland.

The Executive Committee tackled their critical advisory role with a vengeance. The President requested that they put all other duties and problems aside, and concentrate upon making an intensive survey of the dangers and all possible courses of action until the crisis was resolved. Because of his already planned and announced campaign appearances, Kennedy alone had to keep up a public facade in order to prevent the country from speculating wildly about his mysterious disappearance from the campaign trail. The President and his advisors considered it essential to maintain absolute secrecy about their discovery until they came to a definite decision about what action the United States would take. This preserved some of the options available to them during those difficult days, and kept the Russians in ignorance of both the American discovery and the projected reprisals while they were still under discussion. Before the end of the week sophisticated Washingtonians realized something was "up," but, perhaps because of the President's previous assurances, they were more prone to suspect a Berlin crisis than a Soviet-American showdown in the Caribbean.

After McNamara and the Joint Chiefs of Staff had alerted the armed forces for any possible military contingency, the first afternoon of meetings was largely taken up with unsuccessful attempts to agree upon the motives of the Soviet leaders in initiating such a risky gambit. Sorensen outlined five different hypotheses, none of which was found to be completely satisfactory in explaining the Soviets' behavior. The first explanation, and the one which John F. Kennedy in the final analysis tended to favor more than the others, was what Sorensen has called "cold war politics."

Theory 1. Cold War Politics. Khrushchev believed that the American people were too timid to risk nuclear war and too concerned with legalisms to justify any distinction between our overseas missile bases and his—that once we were actually confronted with the missiles we would do nothing but protest—that we would thereby appear weak and irresolute to the world, causing our allies to doubt our word and to seek accommodations with the Soviets, and permitting increased Communist sway in Latin America in particular. This was a probe, a test of America's will to resist. If it succeeded, he could move in a more important place—In West Berlin or with new pressure on our overseas bases—with missiles staring down our throats from Cuba. A Lenin adage, said Bohlen in one of our first meetings, compared national expansion to a bayonet drive: if you strike steel, pull back; if you strike mush, keep going. Khrushchev, having invested considerable money and effort in nuclear hardware he hoped never to use in battle, at least wanted one more try at using it for blackmail purposes.

Theory 2. Diverting Trap. If the United States did respond, presumably by attacking "little" Cuba, the Allies would be divided, the UN horrified, the Latin Americans more anti-American than ever, and our forces and energies diverted while Khrushchev moved swiftly in on Berlin. (Some speculated that Khrushchev also calculated that any strong U.S. reaction would help him prove to the Stalinists and Chinese that the West was no "paper tiger.")

Theory 3. Cuban Defense. A Soviet satellite in the Western Hemisphere was so valuable to Khrushchev—in both his drive for expansion and his contest with Red China—that he could not allow it to fall; and thus, in his view, an invasion from the United States or hostile Latin-American states, which seemed inevitable if Cuba collapsed internally, had to be prevented at all costs. The Castro brothers, requesting military aid, could cite the Bay of Pigs and the constant invasion talk in Congress and the Cuban refugee community. Although they reportedly had expected no more than a firm Soviet pledge, the presence of Soviet missiles looked to them like an even tighter guarantee of their security. (It should be noted that the Soviet Union struck throughout to this position. Mikoyan claimed in a conversation with the President weeks after it was all over that the weapons were purely defensive, that they had been justified by threats of invasion voiced by Richard Nixon and Pentagon generals, and that the Soviets intended to inform the United States of these weapons immediately after the elections to prevent the matter from affecting the American political campaign.)

Theory 4. Bargaining Barter. Well aware of Cuba's sensitive role in domestic American politics, Khrushchev intended to use these bases in a summit or UN confrontation with Kennedy as effective bargaining power—to trade them off for his kind of Berlin settlement, or for a withdrawal of American overseas bases.

Theory 5. Missile Power. The Soviets could no longer benefit from the fiction that the missile gap was in their favor. To close it with ICBMs (intercontinental ballistic missiles) and submarine-based missiles was too expensive. Providing Cuban bases for their existing MRBMs and IRBMs (medium- and intermediate-range ballistic missiles) gave them a swift and comparatively inexpensive means of adding sharply to the total number of missiles targeted on the United States, positioned to by-pass most of our missile warning system and permitting virtually no tactical warning time between their launch and their arrival on target. The fifteen-minute ground alert on which our nuclear bombers stood by on runways would no longer be sufficient. To be sure, these Cuban missiles alone, in view of all the other megatonnage the Soviets were capable of unleashing upon us, did not substantially alter the strategic balance *in fact*—unless these first installations were followed by so many more that Soviet military planners would have an increased temptation to launch a pre-emptive first strike. But that balance would have been substantially altered *in appearance*; and in matters of national will and world leadership, as the President said later, such appearances contribute to reality.

His own analysis regarded the third and fifth theories as offering likely but insufficient motives and he leaned most strongly to the first. But whichever theory was correct, it was clear that the Soviet move, if successful, would "materially . . . and politically change the balance of power" in the entire cold war, as he would later comment. Undertaken in secrecy, accompanied by duplicity, the whole effort was based on confronting Kennedy and the world in November with a threatening *fait accompli*, designed perhaps to be revealed by Khrushchev personally, we speculated, in a bristling UN speech, to be followed by a cocky demand for a summit on Berlin and other matters. With these somber thoughts in mind, our Tuesday morning meeting ended; and I went down the hall to my office with a sense of deep foreboding and heavy responsibility.[240]

The evening meeting and those that followed were devoted to exploring possible American responses to the Soviet challenge, and carefully weighing the detailed implications of each alternative. The President was not a participant in most of those meetings, for it was agreed that in order not to alert public concern and possible hysteria, he should continue his regular state duties and his active political campaigning for congressional candidates. Also his absence from most of the discussions induced a degree of candor which might not have been possible if he had been present. He was kept accurately and currently informed of the nature of the continuing discussion, however, and around-the-clock aerial surveillance by the U-2s kept the committee and the President fully aware of almost hour-to-hour construction developments at the missile bases in Cuba.

Sorensen has summarized the major categories of possible alternative actions or inactions which were discussed at the meetings. The proposals were:

1. Do nothing.
2. Bring diplomatic pressures and warnings to bear upon the Soviets. Possible forms included an appeal to the UN or OAS for an inspection team, or a direct approach to Khrushchev, possibly at a summit conference. The removal of our missile bases in Turkey in exchange for the removal of the Cuban missiles was also listed in our later discussions as a possibility which Khrushchev was likely to suggest if we did not.

3. Undertake a secret approach to Castro, to use this means of splitting him off from the Soviets, to warn him that the alternative was his island's downfall and that the Soviets were selling him out.

4. Initiate indirect military action by means of a blockade, possibly accompanied by increased aerial surveillance and warnings. Many types of blockades were considered.

5. Conduct an air strike—pinpointed against the missiles only or against other military targets, with or without advance warning. (Other military means of directly removing the missiles were raised—bombarding them with pellets that would cause their malfunctioning without fatalities, or suddenly landing paratroopers or guerillas—but none of these was deemed feasible.)

6. Launch an invasion—or, as one chief advocate of this course put it: "Go in there and take Cuba away from Castro."[241]

It is clear that much of the discussion at the meetings resolved itself into a debate over the virtues of alternatives four and five, that is, a blockade or quarantine as opposed to an air strike pinpointed against the missile sights. The other alternatives were also carefully considered, but the major support at the meetings gradually clustered about variations of these last two strategies. Those who favored an immediate air strike argued that the Soviets had already breached the balance of power between the two countries by their covert and daring move. They had broken their publicly pledged word and violated the long-standing and almost sacred Monroe Doctrine, to say nothing of the Punta del Este Agreement. If permitted to make the missiles operative, the Soviets would have irreparably damaged world confidence in the willingness and ability of the United States to defend its own and/or its allies' interests, and eliminated by one stroke whatever advantage our advanced weapons technology, strategic bases (both land bases and polaris submarines), and industrial production lead had given us in previous years. An immediate surgical air strike, destroying both missiles and missile sites, was the only sure way of responding to this thus far successful Soviet move, and correcting the shifting balance of military power.

The blockade defenders did not challenge any of these arguments, except the contention that an immediate air strike was the only method of protecting the nation's security. An effective naval blockade could prevent vital armaments from reaching Cuba, could prevent the missile sites from becoming operative, and would precipitate a showdown with the Soviet Union in a theater of military operations where the United States had all the advantages. Outside of a submarine fleet, the Soviets' naval strength was negligible, and the blockade would be put into effect in unfamiliar waters thousands of miles from Soviet territory. If a blockade failed, the options of an air strike to stop the Soviets' missile preparations and an invasion would still be available to them. Furthermore, and most importantly, both Robert Kennedy and Secretary McNamara argued that an air strike destroying Soviet weapons and killing Soviet citizens deployed in the Cuban bases would present the Soviets with a challenge from which they could not easily back off, and to which they could retaliate only by launching a full-scale nuclear war.

The air strike initially had very strong support. According to correspondent

Elie Abel, who interviewed practically all of the participants in these meetings, Dean Acheson was totally convinced that the air strike was the right step to take, and he was joined in the beginning of the discussions by General Taylor, John McCone, Douglas Dillon, Paul Nitze and McGeorge Bundy. Former Secretary of State Acheson argued that "the President of the United States had the responsibility for the security of the people of the United States and of the whole free world, and that it was his obligation to take the only action which could protect that security, and that meant destroying the missiles."[242] Ironically, these arguments were supported by Senator William Fulbright, chairman of the Senate Foreign Relations Committee, and Senator Richard Russell, chairman of the Armed Services Committee, when they were consulted by the President.

The Joint Chiefs of Staff were also consulted by the President and they were unanimous in calling for an air strike. When questioned by Kennedy as to what the Russian reaction would be to such an attack, General Curtis LeMay, air force chief of staff, assured him that there would be no reaction. The President was skeptical. The latest aerial photographs revealed the presence of a minimum of 16 and possibly 32 missiles with a range of 1,000 miles. American intelligence estimated that their atomic warhead potential equalled one-half the entire ICBM capacity of the Soviet Union, and that 80 million Americans would be dead a few minutes after the missiles aimed at principal American cities within that 1000-mile radius had been fired. One member of the Joint Chiefs of Staff advocated that the United States Air Force drop an atomic bomb on the Cuban missile sites. But the President was convinced that such an attack would lead to a nuclear war between the Soviet Union and the United States:

> They, no more than we, can't let these things go by without doing something. They can't, after all their statements, permit us to take out their missiles, kill a lot of Russians, and then do nothing. If they don't take action in Cuba, they certainly will in Berlin.[243]

The air strike supporters were very effectively opposed by Robert Kennedy, Secretary McNamara, Roswell Gilpatric, Alexis Johnson, George Ball, Robert Lovett and Theodore Sorensen. Adlai Stevenson, who returned to the United Nations before the end of the week, had initially sought a diplomatic solution, but supported the blockade as opposed to an air strike. Both groups presented their positions as forcefully and persuasively as possible in order to try to create a majority consensus, and also to provide the President with the clearest and most valid arguments for each strategy. Dillon and Bundy were finally won over to the blockade idea, presumably on the basis of the persuasiveness of the arguments presented by Robert Kennedy and Robert McNamara, particularly the fact that the decision to invoke the blockade did not negate the possibility of utilizing the other options if the first attempt failed to accomplish the desired objective.

In arguing against the air strike proposal Robert Kennedy was at his best:

> With some trepidation, I argued that, whatever validity the military and political arguments were for an attack in preference to a blockade, America's traditions and history would not permit such a course of action. Whatever military reasons he [Acheson] and others could marshal, they

were nevertheless, in the last analysis, advocating a surprise attack by a very large nation against a very small one. This, I said, could not be undertaken by the U.S. if we were to maintain our moral position at home and around the globe. Our struggle against Communism throughout the world was far more than physical survival—it had as its essence our heritage and our ideals, and these we must not destroy.[244]

President Kennedy had made it clear from the beginning that whatever strategy was adopted, the objective was to remove the missiles and the bases from Cuba, and there was no disagreement between the two groups about this. The disagreement arose over the assessment of the imminent danger involved, the risks of a more general conflict and the probabilities involved in determining the effectiveness of a blockade. The argument that finally won the day with the President, as well as with the majority of his advisors, was that the options of an air strike or even an invasion were still available in the event that the blockade failed. Of course that theory could have been exploded by a surprise missile attack from the Soviet Union or Cuba, or an incident on the high seas which would lead to nuclear retaliation by the Soviets. Nevertheless, there were risks in any choice, and fewer risks in attempting the blockade than in any other alternative. Khrushchev could avoid an open clash by ordering his ships back or directing them to different ports without a total loss of face, but he could not absorb an air strike against Soviet personnel without retaliating.

By Thursday night of the same week in which the missile sites were discovered and throughout which the Executive Committee met, the President had tentatively decided in favor of the blockade. He had not yet, however, ruled out the possibility of an air strike, and he met again with the Joint Chiefs of Staff and several air force generals to hear their urgent arguments. At that meeting the President heard nothing he had not heard before, and the analysis and the debate in the Executive Committee had clarified the implications of each alternative in his mind. At the end of the meeting with the military, he ordered the staff to proceed posthaste to put the blockade plan into operation. Consideration was given to preparations for Soviet retaliation short of nuclear attack in other areas like Berlin. Military, air and naval alerts were put into effect, mobilizing nearly all of the ready manpower available to the military establishment, and preparing them for any contingencies. The President continued his campaigning on Friday to keep up the front and to discourage the rumors in Washington and elsewhere, which by now were assuming major proportions.

On Saturday, October 20, he returned to Washington, giving the excuse that he had a developing cold (which he had); after arriving there he quickly convened the National Security Council for the first time in the crisis. The final decision was announced and the details agreed upon at that meeting. The secrecy which had held up so extremely well during the week was beginning to crumble, the press was aware an important crisis was in the works, and one newspaper had pieced together sufficient information and intended to break the story. Because of all of these factors, the President wanted to go on radio and television the next day and speak to the American people, but he was persuaded to delay his talk for 24 hours so that congressional leaders and America's allies could be informed of his decision and strategy before it was put into effect. President Kennedy delivered his message on Monday evening, October 22, 1962.

President John F. Kennedy
Address to the Nation on
The Cuban Missile Crisis
October 22, 1962

Larson, 41-46.

Good evening, my fellow citizens. This Government, as promised, has maintained the closest surveillance of the Soviet military build-up on the island of Cuba. Within the past week unmistakable evidence has established the fact that a series of offensive missile sites is now in preparation on that imprisoned island. The purposes of these bases can be none other than to provide a nuclear strike capability against the Western Hemisphere.

Upon receiving the first preliminary hard information of this nature last Tuesday morning (October 16) at 9:00 a.m., I directed that our surveillance be stepped up. And having now confirmed and completed our evaluation of the evidence and our decision on a course of action, this Government feels obliged to report this new crisis to you in fullest detail.

The characteristics of these new missile sites indicate two distinct types of installations. Several of them include medium-range ballistic missiles capable of carrying a nuclear warhead for a distance of more than 1,000 nautical miles. Each of these missiles, in short, is capable of striking Washington, D.C., the Panama Canal, Cape Canaveral, Mexico City, or any other city in the southeastern part of the United States, in Central America, or in the Caribbean area.

Additional sites not yet completed appear to be designed for intermediate-range ballistic missiles capable of traveling more than twice as far—and thus capable of striking most of the major cities in the Western Hemisphere, ranging as far north as Hudson Bay, Canada, and as far south as Lima, Peru. In addition, jet bombers, capable of carrying nuclear weapons, are now being uncrated and assembled in Cuba, while the necessary air bases are being prepared.

This urgent transformation of Cuba into an important strategic base—by the presence of these large, long-range, and clearly offensive weapons of sudden mass destruction—constitutes an explicit threat to the peace and security of all the Americas, in flagrant and deliberate defiance of the Rio Pact of 1947, the traditions of this nation and Hemisphere, the Joint Resolution of the 87th Congress, the Charter of the United Nations, and my own public warnings to the Soviets on September 4 and 13.

This action also contradicts the repeated assurances of Soviet spokesmen, both publicly and privately delivered, that the arms build-up in Cuba would retain its original defensive character and that the Soviet Union had no need or desire to station strategic missiles on the territory of any other nation.

The size of this undertaking makes clear that it has been planned for some months. Yet only last month, after I had made clear the distinction between any introduction of ground-to-ground missiles and the existence of defensive antiaircraft missiles, the Soviet Government publicly stated on September 11 that, and I quote, "The armaments and military equipment sent to Cuba are designed exclusively for defensive purposes," and, I quote the Soviet Government, "There is no need for the Soviet Government to shift its weapons for a retaliatory blow to any other country, for instance Cuba," and that, and I quote the Government, "The Soviet Union has so powerful rockets to carry these nuclear warheads that there is no need to search for sites for them beyond the boundaries of the Soviet Union." That statement was false.

Only last Thursday, as evidence of this rapid offensive build-up was already in my hand, Soviet Foreign Minister Gromyko told me in my office that he was instructed to make it clear once again, as he said his Government had already done, that Soviet assistance to Cuba, and I quote, "pursued solely the purpose of contributing to the defense capabilities of Cuba," that, and I quote him, "training by Soviet specialists of Cuban nationals in handling defensive armaments was by no means offensive," and that "if it were otherwise," Mr. Gromyko went on, "the Soviet Government would never become involved in rendering such assistance." That statement also was false.

Neither the United States of America nor the world community of nations can tolerate deliberate deception and offensive threats on the part of any nation, large or small. We no longer live in a world where only the actual firing of weapons represents a sufficient challenge to a nation's security to constitute maximum peril. Nuclear weapons are so destructive and ballistic missiles are so swift that any substantially increased possibility of their use or any sudden change in their deployment may well be regarded as a definite threat to peace.

For many years both the Soviet Union and the United States, recognizing this fact, have deployed strategic nuclear weapons with great care, never upsetting the precarious status quo which insured that these weapons would not be used in the absence of some vital challenge. Our own strategic missiles have never been transferred to the territory of any other nation under a cloak of secrecy and deception; and our history, unlike that of the Soviets since the end of World War II, demonstrates that we have no desire to dominate or conquer any other nation or impose our system upon its people. Nevertheless, American citizens have become adjusted to living daily on the bull's eye of Soviet missiles located inside the U.S.S.R. or in submarines.

In that sense missiles in Cuba add to an already clear and present danger— although it should be noted the nations of Latin America have never previously been subjected to a potential nuclear threat.

But this secret, swift, and extraordinary build-up of Communist missiles—in an area well known to have a special and historical relationship to the United States and the nations of the Western Hemisphere, in violation of Soviet assurances, and in defiance of American and hemispheric policy—this sudden, clandestine decision to station strategic weapons for the first time outside of Soviet soil—is a deliberately provocative and unjustified change in the status quo which cannot be accepted by this country if our courage and our commitments are ever to be trusted again by either friend or foe.

The 1930's taught us a clear lesson: Aggressive conduct, if allowed to grow unchecked and unchallenged, ultimately leads to war. This nation is opposed to war. We are also true to our word. Our unswerving objective, therefore, must be to prevent the use of these missiles against this or any other country and to secure their withdrawal or elimination from the Western Hemisphere.

Our policy has been one of patience and restraint, as befits a peaceful and powerful nation, which leads a worldwide alliance. We have been determined not to be diverted from our central concerns by mere irritants and fanatics. But now further action is required—and it is underway; and these actions may only be the beginning. We will not prematurely or unnecessarily risk the costs of worldwide nuclear war in which even the fruits of victory would be ashes in our mouth—but neither will we shrink from that risk at any time it must be faced.

Acting, therefore, in the defense of our own security and of the entire Western Hemisphere, and under the authority entrusted to me by the Constitution as endorsed by the resolution of the Congress, I have directed that the following initial steps be taken immediately:

First: To halt this offensive build-up, a strict quarantine on all offensive military equipment under shipment to Cuba is being initiated. All ships of any kind bound for Cuba from whatever nation or port will, if found to contain cargoes of offensive weapons, be turned back. This quarantine will be extended, if needed, to other types of cargo and carriers. We are not at this time, however, denying the necessities of life as the Soviets attempted to do in their Berlin blockade of 1948.

Second: I have directed the continued and increased close surveillance of Cuba and its military build-up. The Foreign Ministers of the Organization of American States in their communique of October 3 rejected secrecy on such matters in this Hemisphere. Should these offensive military preparations continue, thus increasing the threat to the Hemisphere, further action will be justified. I have directed the Armed Forces to prepare for any eventualities; and I trust that in the interests of both the Cuban people and the Soviet technicians at the sites, the hazards to all concerned of continuing this threat will be recognized.

Third: It shall be the policy of this nation to regard any nuclear missile launched from Cuba against any nation in the Western Hemisphere as an attack by the Soviet Union on the United States, requiring a full retaliatory response upon the Soviet Union.

Fourth: As a necessary military precaution I have reinforced our base at Guantanamo, evacuated today the dependents of our personnel there, and ordered additional military units to be on a standby alert basis.

Fifth: We are calling tonight for an immediate meeting of the Organ of Consultation, under the Organization of American States, to consider this threat to hemispheric security and to invoke articles six and eight of the Rio Treaty in support of all necessary action. The United Nations Charter allows for regional security arrangements—and the nations of this Hemisphere decided long ago against the military presence of outside powers. Our other allies around the world have also been alerted.

Sixth: Under the Charter of the United Nations, we are asking tonight that an emergency meeting of the Security Council be convoked without delay to take action against this latest Soviet threat to world peace. Our resolution will call for the prompt dismantling and withdrawal of all offensive weapons in Cuba, under the supervision of United Nations observers, before the quarantine can be lifted.

Seventh and finally: I call upon Chairman Khrushchev to halt and eliminate this clandestine, reckless, and provocative threat to world peace and to stable relations between our two nations. I call upon him further to abandon this course of world domination and to join in an historic effort to end the perilous arms race and transform the history of man. He has an opportunity now to move the world back from the abyss of destruction—by returning to his Government's own words that it had no need to station missiles outside its own territory, and withdrawing these weapons from Cuba—by refraining from any action which will widen or deepen the present crisis—and then by participating in a search for peaceful and permanent solutions.

This nation is prepared to present its case against the Soviet threat to peace, and our own proposals for a peaceful world, at any time and in any forum in the Organization of American States, in the United Nations, or in any other meeting that could be useful—without limiting our freedom of action.

We have in the past made strenuous efforts to limit the spread of nuclear weapons. We have proposed the elimination of all arms and military bases in a fair and effective disarmament treaty. We are prepared to discuss new proposals for the removal of tensions on both sides—including the possibilities of a genuinely independent Cuba, free to determine its own destiny. We have no wish to war with the Soviet Union, for we are a peaceful people who desire to live in peace with all other peoples.

But it is difficult to settle or even discuss these problems in an atmosphere of intimidation. That is why this latest Soviet threat—or any other threat which is made either independently or in response to our actions this week—must and will be met with determination. Any hostile move anywhere in the world against the safety and freedom of peoples to whom we are committed—including in particular the brave people of West Berlin—will be met by whatever action is needed.

Finally, I want to say a few words to the captive people of Cuba, to whom this speech is being directly carried by special radio facilities. I speak to you as a friend, as one who knows of your deep attachment to your fatherland, as one who shares your aspirations for liberty and justice for all. And I have watched and the American people have watched with deep sorrow how your nationalist revolution was betrayed and how your fatherland fell under foreign domination. Now your leaders are no longer Cuban leaders inspired by Cuban ideals. They are puppets and agents of an international conspiracy which has turned Cuba against your friends and neighbors in the Americas—and turned it into the first Latin American country to become a target for nuclear war, the first Latin American country to have these weapons on its soil.

These new weapons are not in your interest. They contribute nothing to your peace and well being. They can only undermine it. But this country has no wish to cause you to suffer or to impose any system upon you. We know that your lives and land are being used as pawns by those who deny you freedom.

Many times in the past Cuban people have risen to throw out tyrants who destroyed their liberty. And I have no doubt that most Cubans today look forward to the time when they will be truly free—free from foreign domination, free to choose their own leaders, free to select their own system, free to own their own land, free to speak and write and worship without fear or degradation. And then shall Cuba be welcomed back to the society of free nations and to the associations of this Hemisphere.

My fellow citizens, let no one doubt that this is a difficult and dangerous effort on which we have set out. No one can foresee precisely what course it will take or what costs or casualties will be incurred. Many months of sacrifice and self-discipline lie ahead—months in which both our patience and our will will be tested, months in which many threats and denunciations will keep us aware of our dangers. But the greatest danger of all would be to do nothing.

The path we have chosen for the present is full of hazards, as all paths are; but it is the one most consistent with our character and courage as a nation and our commitments around the world. The cost of freedom is always high—but Americans have always paid it. And one path we shall never choose, and that is the path of surrender or submission.

Our goal is not the victory of might but the vindication of right—not peace at the expense of freedom, but both peace and freedom, here in this Hemisphere and, we hope, around the world. God willing, that goal will be achieved

---

The quarantine went into effect on October 24 at 2 p.m. Greenwich time. A flotilla of American naval vessels, Task Force 136, made up of 16 destroyers, 3 cruisers, an antisubmarine aircraft carrier and 6 utility ships took up positions in a great arc extending 500 miles from Cape Maysi, on the tip of eastern Cuba. The navy was instructed to stop and board all ships which appeared to be carrying offensive weapons, and to prevent them from continuing to Cuba, if, indeed, they did carry such weapons. They were carefully warned that

> force shall not be used except in case of failure or refusal to comply with directions . . . after reasonable efforts have been made to communicate them to the vessel or craft, or in case of self-defense. In any case force shall be used only to the extent necessary.[245]

The President and his advisors emphasized firmness and restraint in all of their preparations, not only for the blockade, but also for the other actions held in abeyance—the aerial bombing and the invasion. Originally a decision had been made to retaliate by an air strike if one of the unarmed U-2 planes was shot down, but the President had not given the air force such blanket authority, so when Major

Rudolf Anderson, jr., who had flown the mission which had made the original discovery photographs, was shot down, Kennedy delayed the strike but ordered fighter escorts for all further flights, with instructions to respond in the event of any attack.

The pressures on the President and the EXCOM were tremendous during that period, each day, each hour, even each minute was pregnant with the possibility of disastrous news. It was a real testing period, a serious game of "Russian roulette" with the stakes so high that neither side could contemplate the results of an error in judgment or a miscalculation. Relaxing one evening after waiting impatiently for word from the blockading fleet, President Kennedy talked with his brother and his old friend, Kenny O'Donnell, of the dangers inherent in such a crisis:

> "The great danger and risk in all of this," he [the President] said, "is a miscalculation—a mistake in judgment." A short time before, he had read Barbara Tuchman's book *The Guns of August*, and he talked about the miscalculations of the Germans, the Russians, the Austrians, the French, and the British. They somehow seemed to tumble into war, he said, through stupidity, individual idiosyncracies, misunderstandings, and personal complexes of inferiority and grandeur. We talked about the miscalculation of the Germans in 1939 and the still unfulfilled commitments and guarantees that the British had given to Poland.
>
> Neither side wanted war over Cuba, we agreed, but it was possible that either side could take a step that—for reasons of "security" or "pride" or "face"—would require a response by the other side, which, in turn, for the same reasons of security, pride, or face, would bring about a counter-response and eventually an escalation into armed conflict. That was what he wanted to avoid. He did not want anyone to be able to write, at a later date, a book on "The Missiles of October" and say that the U.S. had not done all it could to preserve the peace. We were not going to misjudge, or miscalculate, or challenge the other side needlessly, or precipitously push our adversaries into a course of action that was not intended or anticipated.[246]

President Kennedy and his advisors believed that the heaviest pressure was on the Russians, and that the United States was in a position to tighten the screw as open preparations for the air strike and/or invasion continued in Florida and in the Gulf ports, a short distance from the island of Cuba. The American case had been fortified by a unanimous resolution passed by 20 member nations of the Organization of American States, denouncing the Soviet ploy and threatening military reprisal if the "missiles and other weapons with offensive capability" were not withdrawn. Adlai Stenenson's brilliant performance in the United Nations, where he exposed to the world the Soviet deceit in concealing the missile bases by producing the photographic evidence, both vindicated the humiliation he had suffered at the American deceit during the Bay of Pigs crisis and enhanced world sympathy for American actions now.

But with all of this, the results of the showdown remained uncertain, and four nervous days went by as the Executive Committee met every day in the White

House, intently scanning intelligence reports and continuing to analyze minute-to-minute and hour-to-hour developments. As of yet there had been no public communication between Chairman Khrushchev and the President, although indirect messages were exchanged through United Nations Secretary General U Thant and also through the British philosopher Bertrand Russell.[247] Khrushchev and Kennedy had, however, according to Theodore Sorensen, exchanged private letters (by wireless teletype) on Tuesday and Wednesday, in which the Soviet leader appeared to have been caught off-balance, and reflected a somewhat bewildered mood of rhetorical denunciation of the United States "piracy," following the line of the official Soviet governmental denunciation of the blockade introduced at the U.N. on Tuesday, October 23.[248] President Kennedy replied immediately to these communications with firm restatements of the United States position. Bertrand Russell's appeal for peace condemned the "desperate" American action, which, he informed Kennedy, had "no conceivable justification," and he praised Khrushchev's "continued forebearance." Because of its obviously biased attitude the peace appeal had no affect on the Americans, yet Khrushchev used it as a springboard for a broad propaganda appeal to bolster his dangerous and weakened position.

U Thant's exchange with the two heads of state had more positive results. The secretary general proposed to Khrushchev that in order to avoid a rapidly developing conflict, the Soviets ought to suspend "all arms shipments to Cuba," and to Kennedy that he suspend "the quarantine measures involving the searching of ships *bound* for Cuba," so that tensions could be eased and serious negotiations begun. This effort, although not successful in initiating negotiations between the two powers, in many ways broke the ice, and induced replies which stimulated further communication between U Thant and his two correspondents, and then between the two heads of state directly. Answering the following day, Khrushchev indicated his general agreement with U Thant's suggestions and President Kennedy replied that he had authorized Ambassador Stevenson to discuss any possibly mutual arrangements. Thant quickly dispatched a second message to both the Soviet Premier and the American President, attempting to nail down their agreements, and hoping they would follow his specific proposals aimed at avoiding a showdown. By that time the United States Navy had already stopped and boarded a Soviet vessel, but after ascertaining that there were no arms aboard, allowed it to proceed to Cuba.

Both Kennedy and Khrushchev replied to U Thant the same day, the President indicating that American ships would do everything possible to avoid direct confrontation with Soviet vessels if the Russians, in turn, would direct their ships to "stay away from the interception area" as U Thant had requested them to do. Something of a detente was accomplished when the secretary general received assurances from Khrushchev that he would respect the request and direct all ships not yet in the American interception zones to stay out. But in his reply, President Kennedy emphasized that the United States was primarily concerned with the removal of the offensive Soviet weapons from Cuba, and that at present "work on these systems [was] continuing."[249]

The following day Chairman Khrushchev sent another message directly to

President Kennedy. Made public for the first time last year, earlier accounts had described it as reading "like the nightmare outcry of a frightened man." Some thought Khrushchev must have been so anguished and unstable when he wrote it that it was almost incoherent.[250] Robert Kennedy derided that characterization, indicating that it was anything but incoherent; rather, it represented the belated recognition that the destructive collision course onto which the two nations had catapulted themselves must be avoided at all costs.[251] The attorney general acted upon that understanding, and by virtue of his resourceful contributions to the crisis decision-making process, the conflict was ultimately resolved.

Premier Nikita S. Khrushchev
Personal Message to President Kennedy
On Resolving the Cuban Missile Crisis
October 26, 1962

Arthur M. Schlesinger, jr., ed., *Dynamics of World Power: Documentary History of United States Foreign Policy, 1945-1973* (New York, 1973) II, 699-703.

I have received your letter of October 25. From your letter, I got the feeling that you have some understanding of the situation which has developed and [some] sense of responsibility. I value this.

Now we have already publicly exchanged our evaluations of the events around Cuba and each of us has set forth his explanation and his understanding of these events. Consequently, I would judge that, apparently, a continuation of an exchange of opinions at such a distance, even in the form of secret letters, will hardly add anything to that which one side has already said to the other.

I think you will understand me correctly if you are really concerned about the welfare of the world. Everyone needs peace: both capitalists, if they have not lost their reason, and still more, Communists, people who know how to value not only their own lives but, more than anything, the lives of the peoples. We, Communists, are against all wars between states in general and have been defending the cause of peace since we came into the world. We have always regarded war as a calamity, and not as a game nor as a means for the attainment of definite goals, nor, all the more, as a goal in itself. Our goals are clear, and the means to attain them is labor. War is our enemy and a calamity for all the peoples.

It is thus that we, Soviet people, and, together with us, other peoples as well, understand the questions of war and peace. I can, in any case, firmly say this for the peoples of the Socialist countries, as well as for all progressive people who want peace, happiness, and friendship among peoples.

I see, Mr. President, that you too are not devoid of a sense of anxiety for the fate of the world, of understanding, and of what war entails. What would a war give you? You are threatening us with war. But you well know that the very least which you would receive in reply would be that you would experience the same consequences as those which you sent us. And that must be clear to us, people invested with authority, trust, and responsibility. We must not succumb to intoxication and petty passions, regardless of whether elections are impending in this or that country, or not impending. These are all transient things, but if indeed war should break out, then it would not be in our power to stop it, for such is the logic of war. I have participated in two wars and know that war ends when it has rolled through cities and villages, everywhere sowing death and destruction.

In the name of the Soviet Government and the Soviet people, I assure you that your conclusions regarding offensive weapons on Cuba are groundless. It is apparent from what you have written me that our conceptions are different on this score, or rather, we have different estimates of these or those military means. Indeed, in reality, the same forms of weapons can have different interpretations.

You are a military man and, I hope, will understand me. Let us take for example a simple cannon. What sort of means is this: offensive or defensive? A cannon is a defensive means if it is set up to defend boundaries or a fortified area. But if one concentrates artillery, and adds to it the necessary number of troops, then the same cannons do become an offensive means, because they prepare and clear the way for infantry to attack. The same happens with missile-nuclear weapons as well, with any type of this weapon.

You are mistaken if you think that any of our means on Cuba are offensive. However, let us not quarrel now. It is apparent that I will not be able to convince you of this. But I say to you: You, Mr. President, are a military man and should understand: can one attack, if one has on one's territory even an enormous quantity of missiles of various effective radiuses and various power, but using only these means? These missiles are a means of extermination and destruction. But one cannot attack with these missiles, even nuclear missiles of a power of 100 megatons because only people, troops, can attack. Without people, any means however powerful cannot be offensive.

How can one, consequently, give such a completely incorrect interpretation as you are now giving, to the effect that some sort of means on Cuba are offensive? All the means located there, and I assure you of this, have a defensive character, are on Cuba solely for the purposes of defense, and we have sent them to Cuba at the request of the Cuban Government. You, however, say that these are offensive means. But, Mr. President, do you really seriously think that Cuba can attack the United States and that even we together with Cuba can attack you from the territory of Cuba? Can you really think that way? How is it possible? We do not understand this. Has something so new appeared in military strategy that one can think that it is possible to attack thus? I say precisely attack, and not destroy.

I believe that you have no basis to think this way. You can regard us with distrust, but, in any case, you can be calm in this regard, that we are of sound mind and understand perfectly well that if we attack you, you will respond the same way. But you too will receive the same that you hurl against us. And I think that you also understand this. My conversation with you in Vienna gives me the right to talk to you this way.

This indicates that we are normal people, that we correctly understand and correctly evaluate the situation. Consequently, how can we permit the incorrect actions which you ascribe to us? Only lunatics or suicides, who themselves want to perish and to destroy the whole world before they die, could do this.

We, however, want to live and do not at all want to destroy your country. We want something quite different: to compete with your country on a peaceful basis. We quarrel with you, we have differences on ideological questions. But our view of the world consists in this, that ideological questions, as well as economic problems, should be solved not by military means, they must be solved on the basis of peaceful competition, i.e., as this is understood in Capitalist society, on the basis of competition. We have proceeded and are proceeding from the fact that the peaceful co-existence of the two different social-political systems, now existing in the world, is necessary, that it is necessary to assure a stable peace. That is the sort of principle we hold.

You have now proclaimed piratical measures, which were employed in the Middle Ages, when ships proceeding in international waters were attacked, and you have called this "a quarantine" around Cuba. Our vessels, apparently, will soon enter the zone which your navy is patrolling. I assure you that these vessels, now bound for Cuba, are carrying the most innocent peaceful cargoes. Do you really think that we only occupy ourselves with the carriage of so-called offensive weapons, atomic and hydrogen bombs? Although perhaps your military people imagine that these cargoes are some sort of special type of weapon, I assure you that they are the most ordinary peaceful products.

Consequently, Mr. President, let us show good sense. I assure you that on those ships, which are bound for Cuba, there are no weapons at all. The weapons which were necessary for the defense of Cuba are already there. I do not want to say that there were not any shipments of weapons at all. No, there were such shipments, but now Cuba has already received the necessary means of defense.

I don't know whether you can understand me and believe me. But I should like to have you believe in yourself and to agree that one cannot give way to passions; it is necessary to control them. And in what direction are events now developing? If you stop the vessels, then, as you yourself know, that would be piracy. If we started to do that with regard to your ships, then you would also be as indignant as we and the whole world now are. One cannot give another interpretation to such actions, because one cannot legalize lawlessness. If this were permitted, then there would be no peace, there would also be no peaceful co-existence. We should then be forced to put into effect the necessary measures of a defensive character to protect our interests in accordance with international law. Why should this be done? To what would all this lead?

Let us normalize relations. We have received an appeal from the Acting Secretary General of the U.N., U Thant, with his proposals. I have already answered him. His proposals come to this, that our side should not transport armaments of any kind to Cuba during a certain period of time, while negotiations are being conducted—and we are ready to enter such negotiations—and the other side should not undertake any sort of piratical actions against vessels engaged in navigation on the high seas. I consider these proposals reasonable. This would be a way out of the situation which has been created, which would give the peoples the possibility of breathing calmly. You have asked what happened, what evoked the delivery of weapons to Cuba? You have spoken about this to our Minister of Foreign Affairs. I will tell you frankly, Mr. President, what evoked it.

We were very grieved by the fact—I spoke about it in Vienna—that a landing took place, that an attack on Cuba was committed, as a result of which many Cubans perished. You yourself told me then that this had been a mistake. I respected that explanation. You repeated it to me several times, pointing out that not everybody occupying a high position would acknowledge his mistakes as you had done. I value such frankness. For my part, I told you that we too possess no less courage; we also acknowledged those mistakes which had been committed during the history of our state, and not only acknowledged, but sharply condemned them.

If you are really concerned about the peace and welfare of your people, and this is your responsibility as President, then I, as the Chairman of the Council of Ministers, am concerned for my people. Moreover, the preservation of world peace should be our joint concern, since if, under contemporary conditions, war should break out, it would be a war not only between the reciprocal claims, but a world wide cruel and destructive war.

Why have we proceeded to assist Cuba with military and economic aid? The answer is: we have proceeded to do so only for reasons of humanitarianism. At one time, our people itself had a revolution, when Russia was still a backward country. We were attacked then. We were the target of attack by many countries. The U.S.A. participated in that adventure. This has been recorded by participants in the aggression against our country. A whole book has been written about this by General Graves, who, at that time, commanded the U.S. Expeditionary Corps. Graves called it "The American Adventure in Siberia."

We know how difficult it is to accomplish a revolution and how difficult it is to reconstruct a country on new foundations. We sincerely sympathize with Cuba and the Cuban people, but we are not interfering in questions of domestic structure, we are not interfering in their affairs. The Soviet Union desires to help the Cubans build their life as they themselves wish and that others should not hinder them.

You once said that the United States was not preparing an invasion. But you also declared that you sympathized with the Cuban counter-revolutionary emigrants, that you support them and would help them to realize their plans against the present Government of Cuba. It is also not a secret to anyone that the threat of armed attack, aggression, has constantly hung, and continues to hang over Cuba. It is only this which impelled us to respond to the request of the Cuban Government to furnish it aid for the strengthening of the defensive capacity of this country.

If assurances were given by the President and the Government of the United States that the U.S.A. itself would not participate in an attack on Cuba and would restrain others from actions of this sort, if you would recall your fleet, this would immediately change everything. I am not speaking for Fidel Castro, but I think that he and the Government of Cuba, evidently, would declare demobilization and would appeal to the people to get down to peaceful labor. Then, too, the question of armaments would disappear, since, if there is no threat, then armaments are a burden for every people. Then, too, the question of the destruction, not only of the armaments which you call offensive, but of all other armaments as well, would look different.

I spoke in the name of the Soviet Government in the United Nations and introduced a proposal for the disbandment of all armies and for the destruction of all armaments. How then can I now count on those armaments?

Armaments bring only disasters. When one accumulates them, this damages the economy, and if one puts them to use, then they destroy people on both sides. Consequently, only a madman can believe that armaments are the principal means in the life of society. No, they are an enforced loss of human energy, and what is more are for the destruction of man himself. If people do not show wisdom, then in the final analysis they will come to a clash, like blind moles, and then reciprocal extermination will begin.

Let us therefore show statesmanlike wisdom. I propose: We, for our part, will declare that our ships, bound for Cuba, will not carry any kind of armaments. You would declare that the United States will not invade Cuba with its forces and will not support any sort of forces which might intend to carry out an invasion of Cuba. Then the necessity for the presence of our military specialists in Cuba would disappear.

Mr. President, I appeal to you to weigh well what the aggressive, piratical action, which you have declared the U.S.A. intends to carry out in international waters, would lead to. You yourself know that any sensible man simply cannot agree with this, cannot recognize your right to such actions.

If you did this as the first step towards the unleashing of war, well then, it is evident that nothing else is left to us but to accept this challenge of yours. If, however, you have not lost your self-control and sensibly conceive what this might lead to, then, Mr. President, we and you ought not now to pull on the ends of the rope in which you have tied the knot of war, because the more the two of us pull, the tighter that knot will be tied. And a moment may come when that knot will be tied so tight that even he who tied it will not have the strength to untie it, and then it will be necessary to cut that knot, and what that would mean is not for me to explain to you, because you yourself understand perfectly of what terrible forces our countries dispose.

Consequently, if there is no intention to tighten that knot and thereby to doom the world to the catastrophe of thermonuclear war, then let us not only relax the forces pulling on the ends of the rope, let us take measures to untie that knot. We are ready for this.

We welcome all forces which stand on positions of peace. Consequently, I expressed gratitude to Mr. Bertrand Russell, too, who manifests alarm and concern for the fate of the world, and I readily responded to the appeal of the Acting Secretary General of the U.N., U Thant.

There, Mr. President, are my thoughts, which, if you agreed with them could put an end to that tense situation which is disturbing all peoples.

These thoughts are dictated by a sincere desire to relieve the situation, to remove the threat of war.

Several other messages from Soviet officials in this country and Europe indicated an effort to probe the possibilities of a settlement without the complete loss of Soviet face. Earlier that same afternoon, John Scali, a radio and television news correspondent in Washington, was approached by a consul at the Soviet embassy who begged him for an immediate luncheon engagement, and then proposed a settlement based on terms very similar to, but more specific than, the Khrushchev letter. This informal Soviet proposal suggested that the missile sites would be dismantled and shipped back to the Soviet Union under United Nations supervision, and that Castro would pledge not to accept offensive weapons in the future if the United States would promise not to invade Cuba. The Soviet official suggested that if Ambassador Stevenson were to propose this settlement at the United Nations, he would discover that the Soviet representative would be "interested." Scali was urged to carry this message to the State Department. Meanwhile various attempts were made in Great Britain, through high and clandestine channels, to bring about a British proposal for a summit conference.[252]

The President and his advisors viewed these signals hopefully, and met on Saturday morning, October 27, prepared to consider the possibility of negotiations. Reports indicated that all of the Soviet ships seeming to carry additional offensive weapons had either stopped or veered off their course, and by Thursday and Friday they appeared to have turned around and were heading back to their Russian ports. But a new and public Khrushchev letter to the President again dashed hopes of an immediate settlement, as the Soviet leader appeared to have upped the ante. The tone of this fresh communication was still conciliatory, but Khrushchev now suggested as the basis for a *detente*, a *quid pro quo* arrangement whereby the Russians would remove what the Americans "considered offensive weapons" if the United States would "evacuate its analogous weapons from Turkey."[253]

Ambassador Stevenson had suggested a somewhat similar exchange in the early meetings of the Executive Committee, and President Kennedy had been annoyed then to realize that his decision two months earlier to remove what he considered to be obsolete missiles from Turkey, had not yet been carried out. But to hedge now on the original demand to remove the missiles from Cuba before any further discussions could take place, and to accept new conditions imposed by the Russians, would, in a sense, be to give in to Soviet blackmail and to agree to what they might well have intended by the missile ploy from the very beginning. This is apparently how the President and his advisors looked at it, although it appears that the crisis could have been resolved at this point if President Kennedy had acceded to Khrushchev's terms.

There were other difficulties with this latter solution, however. Not only would it have been a real psychological victory for the Soviets, for they would have gained a concession they never were in a position to demand before, but they would have strengthened their position vis à-vis the United States, by weakening the confidence of our allies in any future showdown where vital interests were at stake. It might have avoided war, but at the cost of transforming a potential diplomatic triumph, which would have strengthened the United States' hand in preventing future crises of this kind and perhaps future thermonuclear wars, into a humiliating defeat in which the Soviets forced the United States to back down in the face of their firm resistance.

Premier Nikita S. Khrushchev
Public Message (Extract) to President Kennedy
On Resolving the Cuban Missile Crisis
October 27, 1962

Schlesinger, *Dynamics of World Power*, II, 703-05.

It is with great satisfaction that I studied your reply to Mr. U Thant on the adoption of measures in order to avoid contact by our ships and thus avoid irreparable fatal consequences. This reasonable step on your part persuades me that you are showing solicitude for the preservation of peace, and I note this with satisfaction. . . .

Our purpose has been and is to help Cuba, and no one can challenge the humanity of our motives aimed at allowing Cuba to live peacefully and develop as its people desire. You want to relieve your country from danger and this is understandable. However, Cuba also wants this. All countries want to relieve themselves from danger. But how can we, the Soviet Union and our government, assess your actions which, in effect, mean that you have surrounded the Soviet Union with military bases, surrounded our allies with military bases, set up military bases literally around our country, and stationed your rocket weapons at them? This is no secret. High-placed American officials demonstratively declare this. Your rockets are stationed in Britain and in Italy and pointed at us. Your rockets are stationed in Turkey.

You are worried over Cuba. You say that it worries you because it lies at a distance of 90 miles across the sea from the shores of the United States. However, Turkey lies next to us. Our sentinels are pacing up and down and watching each other. Do you believe that you have the right to demand security for your country and the removal of such weapons that you qualify as offensive, while not recognizing this right for us?

You have stationed devastating rocket weapons, which you call offensive, in Turkey literally right next to us. How then does recognition of our equal military possibilities tally with such unequal relations between our great states? This does not tally at all. . . .

This is why I make this proposal: We agree to remove those weapons from Cuba which you regard as offensive weapons. We agree to do this and to state this commitment in the United Nations. Your representatives will make a statement to the effect that the United States, on its part, bearing in mind the anxiety and concern of the Soviet state, will evacuate its analogous weapons from Turkey. Let us reach an understanding on what time you and we need to put this into effect. . . .

We, having assumed this commitment in order to give satisfaction and hope to the peoples of Cuba and Turkey and to increase their confidence in their security, will make a statement in the Security Council to the effect that the Soviet Government gives a solemn pledge to respect the integrity of the frontiers and the sovereignty of Turkey, not to intervene in its domestic affairs. . . .

The U.S. Government will make the same statement in the Security Council with regard to Cuba.

Why would I like to achieve this? Because the entire world is now agitated and expects reasonable actions from us. . . . I attach a great importance to such understanding because it might be a good beginning and, specifically, facilitate a nuclear test ban agreement. The problem of tests could be solved simultaneously, not linking one with the other, because they are different problems. However, it is important to reach an understanding to both these problems in order to make a good gift to the people, to let them rejoice in the news that a nuclear test ban agreement has also been reached and thus there will be no further contamination of the atmosphere. Your and our positions on this issue are very close.

All this, possibly, would serve as a good impetus to searching for mutually acceptable agreements on other disputed issues, too, on which there is an exchange of opinion between us. These problems have not yet been solved, but they wait for an urgent solution which would clear the international atmosphere. We are ready for this.

The young American President, as the poet Robert Frost had advised, was at that point perhaps more Irish than Harvard, and he elected to stand firm on his original demands. It was Robert Kennedy, apparently, who suggested the solution to the impasse; he advised that the most recent Khrushchev note be ignored, and that the President respond to the proposal outlined in the previous day's letter, which had been underscored by the Soviet embassy's approach to the Washington correspondent. This suggestion met with strong approval in the Executive Committee, and a reply was drafted and delivered to the Soviet embassy for transmittal to Khrushchev by 8 o'clock that same evening, October 27. At the suggestion of his brother, Robert Kennedy personally sought out Soviet Ambassador Anatoly Dobrynin that same evening, informing him in no uncertain terms that unless the United States received Soviet assurances within 24 hours that work had halted on the bases and they had begun removing them immediately from Cuba, military action would commence on Tuesday morning.

President John F. Kennedy
First Letter to Premier Khrushchev
During the Cuban Missile Crisis
October 27, 1962

Schlesinger, *Dynamics of World Power*, II, 705-06.

I have read your letter of October 26th with great care and welcomed the statement of your desire to seek a prompt solution to the problem. The first thing that needs to be done, however, is for work to cease on offensive missile bases in Cuba and for all weapons systems in Cuba capable of offensive use to be rendered inoperable, under effective United Nations arrangements.

Assuming this is done promptly, I have given my representatives in New York instructions that will permit them to work out this weekend—in cooperation with the Acting Secretary General and your representative—an arrangement for a permanent solution to the Cuban problem along the lines suggested in your letter of October 26th. As I read your letter, the key elements of your proposals—which seem generally acceptable as I understand them—are as follows:

1. You would agree to remove these weapons systems from Cuba under appropriate United Nations observation and supervision; and undertake, with suitable safeguards, to halt the further introduction of such weapons systems into Cuba.

2. We, on our part, would agree—upon the establishment of adequate arrangements through the United Nations to ensure the carrying out and continuation of these commitments—to remove promptly the quarantine measures now in effect and to give assurances against an invasion of Cuba. I am confident that other nations of the Western Hemisphere would be prepared to do likewise.

If you will give your representative similar instructions, there is no reason why we should not be able to complete these arrangements and announce them to the world within a couple of days. The effect of such a settlement on easing world tensions would enable us to work toward a more general arrangement regarding "other armaments," as proposed in your second letter which you made public. I would like to say again that the United States is very much interested in reducing tensions and halting the arms race; and if your letter signifies that you are prepared to discuss a detente affecting NATO and the Warsaw Pact, we are quite prepared to consider with our allies any useful proposals.

But the first ingredient, let me emphasize, is the cessation of work on missile sites in Cuba and measures to render such weapons inoperable, under effective international guarantees. The continuation of this threat, or a prolonging of this discussion concerning Cuba by linking these problems to the broader questions of European and world security, would surely lead to an intensified situation on the

Cuban crisis and a grave risk to the peace of the world. For this reason I hope we can quickly agree along the lines outlined in this letter and in your letter of October 26th.

John F. Kennedy

The fat was in the fire, and during the next 24 hours the committee would decide upon one of the alternative solutions to the problem at hand. They broke for a short dinner in the White House cafeteria at 8 o'clock Saturday evening. Nerves were frayed and tempers short, Sorensen reports, after the superhuman pressures of the previous two weeks. But preparation continued for any contingency, and when the meeting broke up at 10 o'clock, everything was in readiness for the execution of any of the planned alternatives.[254]

Early the next morning the crisis was over. A quick reply from Chairman Khrushchev indicated his complete willingness to halt work on the missile bases (he indicated such an order was already in effect), and to begin dismantling them on the assurance of the President that

> there would be no attack, no invasion of Cuba, and not only on the part of the United States, but also on the part of other nations of the Western Hemisphere, as you said in your same message. Then the motives which induced us to render assistance of such a kind to Cuba disappear.[255]

The President was given the Soviet leader's message on his way to mass, and the Executive Committee met with him when he returned at 11 a.m. in the White House cabinet room, as they had done so many times during the previous two weeks. The participants were exhilarated by the turn of events, and noisily exchanged personal accounts of where they were and what they had been doing when the news of Khrushchev's reply reached them. The members of the committee rose when the President walked in, and perhaps some of those who had been present at the meetings following the Bay of Pigs debacle could not prevent themselves from making comparisons. How different the circumstances, how much brighter the prospects, how much more confident the participants! Both the President and the presidency had significantly changed in the interim, and the satisfactory outcome of the missile crisis was indeed tangible evidence of the great transformation that had taken place.[256]

The President was relieved that the worst was over, but he was all business, and had no time for rejoicing or gloating. Tactical plans had been produced, troops mobilized, planes held in readiness, and without supreme care some mistake or oversight could still have ignited this tinder box into a great conflagration. Sorensen has given us a graphic picture of the President in action in his moment of triumph:

> Displaying the same caution and precision with which he had determined for thirteen days exactly how much pressure to apply, he quickly and quietly organized the machinery to work for a UN inspection and reconnaissance effort. He called off the Sunday overflights and

ordered the Navy to avoid halting any ships on that day. (The one ship previously approached had stopped.) He asked that precautions be taken to prevent Cuban exile units from upsetting the agreement through one of their publicity-seeking raids. He laid down the line we were all to follow—no boasting, no gloating, not even a claim of victory. We had won by enabling Khrushchev to avoid complete humiliation—we should not humiliate him now. If Khrushchev wanted to boast that he had won a major concession and proved his peaceful manner, that was the loser's prerogative. Major problems of implementing the agreement still faced us. Other danger spots in the world remained. Soviet treachery was too fresh in our memory to relax our vigil now.[257]

Kennedy vetoed the idea of a dramatic radio and television appearance and issued instead a short statement hailing Khrushchev's "constructive contribution to peace," and responding to the Soviet leader's expression that the resolution of this crisis could lead to the solution of other basic conflicts between the two great powers.

President John F. Kennedy
Statement on the Resolution
Of the Cuban Missile Crisis
October 28, 1962

Schlesinger, *Dynamics of World Power*, II, 708-09.

I welcome Chairman Khrushchev's statesmanlike decision to stop building bases in Cuba, dismantling offensive weapons and returning them to the Soviet Union under United Nations verification. This is an important and constructive contribution to peace.

We shall be in touch with the Secretary General of the United Nations with respect to reciprocal measures to assure peace in the Caribbean area.

It is my earnest hope that the governments of the world can, with a solution of the Cuban crisis, turn their urgent attention to the compelling necessity for ending the arms race and reducing world tensions. This applies to the military confrontation between the Warsaw Pact and NATO countries as well as to other situations in other parts of the world where tensions lead to the wasteful diversion of resources to weapons of war.

The President also replied immediately by letter to Chairman Khrushchev, even before the official translation of Khrushchev's letter was in his hands; again he used exemplary restraint and exhibited gracious courtesy.

President John F. Kennedy
Reply to Premier Khrushchev's Agreement
To Resolve the Cuban Missile Crisis
October 28, 1962

Schlesinger, *Dynamics of World Power*, II, 709-10.

Dear Mr. Chairman: I am replying at once to your broadcast message of October twenty-eight, even though the official text has not yet reached me, because of the great importance I attach to moving forward promptly to the settlement of the Cuban crisis. I think that you and I, with our heavy responsibilities for the maintenance of peace, were aware that developments were approaching a point where events could have become unmanageable. So I welcome this message and consider it an important contribution to peace.

The distinguished efforts of Acting Secretary General U Thant have greatly facilitated both our tasks. I consider my letter to you of October twenty-seventh and your reply of today as firm undertakings on the part of both governments which should be promptly carried out. I hope that the necessary measures can at once be taken through the United Nations, as your message says, so that the United States in turn will be able to remove the quarantine measures now in effect. I have already made arrangements to report all these matters to the Organization of American States, whose members share a deep interest in a genuine peace in the Caribbean area.

You referred in your letter to a violation of your frontier by an American aircraft in the area of the Chukotsk Peninsula. I have learned that this plane, without arms or photographic equipment, was engaged in an air-sampling mission in connection with your nuclear tests. Its course was direct from Eielson Air Force Base in Alaska to the North Pole and return. In turning south, the pilot made a serious navigational error which carried him over Soviet territory. He immediately made an emergency call on open radio for navigational assistance and was guided back to his home base by the most direct route. I regret this incident and will see to it that every precaution is taken to prevent recurrence.

Mr. Chairman, both of our countries have great unfinished tasks and I know that your people as well as those of the United States can ask for nothing better than to pursue them free from the fear of war. Modern science and technology have given us the possibility of making labor fruitful beyond anything that could have been dreamed of a few decades ago.

I agree with you that we must devote urgent attention to the problem of disarmament, as it relates to the whole world and also to critical areas. Perhaps now, as we step back from danger, we can together make real progress in this vital field. I think we should give priority to questions relating to the proliferation of nuclear weapons, on earth and in outer space, and to the great effort for a nuclear test ban. But we should also work hard to see if wider measures of disarmament can be agreed and put into operation at an early date. The United States government will be prepared to discuss these questions urgently, and in a constructive spirit, at Geneva or elsewhere.

John F. Kennedy

The crisis was not yet over, and there would be much pulling and tugging before all of the Soviet weapons (both missiles and bombers) were on their way back to Russia. But the climax had passed, and the die was now cast for peace and conciliation between the two great powers. It had been a great performance from beginning to end. The young President had earned his place in history by this one act alone, as the Prime Minister of Great Britain, Harold Macmillan, put it.

In his White House office Theodore Sorensen, the President's assistant and long-time advisor, plucked a copy of *Profiles in Courage* from the shelf and read to his secretary part of the introductory quotation that Kennedy, then a senator, had selected from Edmund Burke's eulogy of Charles James Fox:

He may live long, he may do much. But here is the summit. He never can exceed what he does this day.[258]

Alone with his brother in the White House office after the worst was over, the President revealed that curious mixture of irony and wit, touched with a Gaelic sense of brooding foreknowledge of the tragedy in store for him. "This is the night I should go to theater," the President told his brother, obviously referring to the Lincoln assassination. "If you go, I want to go with you,"[259] Bobby replied, with an ironic twist of his own.

In the Bay of Pigs crisis which had developed several months after President Kennedy was inaugurated, the young Chief Executive was inexperienced, largely unfamiliar with the planning of the operation, poorly informed, and badly advised about many aspects of the affair. He felt frustrated as he was caught up in the flow of events, and was incapable of even controlling his own executive departments as the situation developed. Just the opposite was true in the missile crisis. The circumstances of the two situations were obviously different, but even more striking was the vast difference between the decision-making structure of the executive branch in the second crisis as opposed to the first. By the late summer of 1962 Kennedy had transformed the presidency from a chief of staff operation, presiding over frequently warring and largely independent power centers—which was the condition of the office when he inherited it from Eisenhower—into a tightly knit, functionally strong Executive.

The new structure was organized to expedite the rapid and accurate flow of information to the President from his department and bureau chiefs, and correspondingly, enhance the flow of executive and administrative direction from the President to his subordinate departments and their executive officers. Some very early Presidents, such as Washington, Jefferson and Jackson, had been able to organize their administrations to achieve somewhat the same results, but the technological and political revolutions of the twentieth century, and the changes brought about by two world wars created new problems of a magnitude never before faced by an American President. The rapid changes in the military establishment and the fantastic increase in its size accounted for a large part of the problem. The formal statutory reorganization which the Congress enacted in 1947 (and later amended), which had created the Department of Defense, offered a formal but not a real solution to the problem. Kennedy was convinced by his failure in the Bay of Pigs adventure that he would have to gain control over his own executive family in order to achieve organic direction in his administration. Through the efforts of McNamara he succeeded in accomplishing his goal in the Defense Department, and where he did not succeed, for example in the State Department, he created a new instrument for obtaining information and coordinating national security planning and operations (the Bundy operation).

When the missile crisis exploded he was ready. His own executive house was in order, and he could rely on the information given to him by his chief subordinates, as well as rest assured that his final decisions would be implemented on the various administrative levels under his jurisdiction as President and Commander in Chief. It is true that many material factors favored the United States in this critical international showdown: the proximity of the United States and its military, naval and air force bases to the targets in question; the great distance and wide cultural gulf separating the Soviet Union from Cuba and the Cubans; and the overwhelming power of the United States in the air, on the sea, and even on land if it came to a military showdown in this hemisphere. But without the cool, clear and comprehensive leadership that Kennedy brought to this critical decision and the equally critical diplomacy that followed, these other factors would have been to no avail.

The President and his advisors considered the erection of the missile bases in Cuba not as a humanitarian gesture on the part of the Soviet Union to provide its weak ally, Cuba, with weapons to defend itself, but rather as a calculated risk on the part of an extremely strong adversary to narrow or perhaps even eliminate the United States' military superiority over them. For this reason the President, acting in his capacity as Commander in Chief, had to act, and to act decisively, to protect the security of the United States. For the first time in history two nuclear powers went to the brink and both survived, but it is clear that in the process both realized there might not be a happy outcome in the case of another such confrontation.

In this sense, the missile crisis was perhaps fortunate, not only in the sense that the United States succeeded in protecting itself from Soviet intrigue, and maintaining, at least for the time being, its clear superiority in military power; but because this first real showdown came early in the nuclear age, when one power had sufficient strength and advantage to be able to force the other to back down. This alone would not have had constructive results and might easily have produced such great humiliation and desire for revenge that it might have been only the prelude to a great disaster. However, the manner in which the young American President handled the crisis throughout prevented such a reaction, and produced none of the latent causes for a revengeful return engagement. From the beginning President

Kennedy acted with firmness but with admirable restraint in deed as well as in words, always addressing his counterpart in the Soviet Union with respect and with great concern to protect Chairman Khrushchev's prestige and reputation with his own people. There was not a reckless action or remark on the part of the President during the 13 days of the crisis, and his obvious sensitivity and grace in dealing with his powerful adversary had positive results, not only with respect to the crisis at hand, but in the realization by the leaders of both countries that neither one could afford to risk this kind of a showdown again.

At the beginning of the crisis President Kennedy had implored his fellow Americans not to lose their nerve or their heads, but some did not follow his advice, or his splendid example. At the height of the crisis many American college and university students were in an uproar, not because they were irate against the Soviet Union for initiating this stellar piece of brinkmanship, but because their President had the wisdom and the courage to force the Russian's hand. Thousands of students met at rallies to denounce the President, and were addressed by some of their professors who outdid them in their attack upon the administration and their praise for Khrushchev and Castro. One of my colleagues congratulated the demonstrators outside of the American embassy in London, who cried: "Viva Fidel! Kennedy to hell!" A famous American writer in whose company I was during those trying days kept pointing out to me (erroneously) that the United States base at Guantanamo Bay was the only place on the island of Cuba where Blacks were segregated from whites. Some even argued that the existence of missile bases in Cuba was a step in the direction of peace. Arthur Schlesinger reports that the followers of a Harvard professor who headed an independent political movement in Massachusetts advocating peace prayed for American acceptance of the missiles. Michael Foot's left-wing British Labor party magazine, the *Tribune*, argued that "It may well be that Kennedy is risking blowing the world to hell in order to sweep a few Democrats into office.[260] But the majority of Americans stood behind their President during the crisis, and were inspired by his brilliant leadership.

Some recognition ought to be given to Nikita Khrushchev, who has been generally denounced for his role in the missile crisis. It unquestionably cost him his political career, and transformed what once looked like a promising new chapter in Soviet history to a life of domestic exile and failure. Some of the historical downgrading of Khrushchev is certainly legitimate. The wild scheme of attempting to redress the balance of power in the cold war between Russia and the United States by erecting missile bases in Castro's Cuba was the action of a reckless adventurer and not of the leader of a major world power. His frequently colorful but often outrageous statements and performances on the world stage give further support to such an evaluation. Yet there were extenuating circumstances in the Cuban situation. American policy towards Cuba during the period was also inexcusable, and was guilty of equally irresponsible actions like the Bay of Pigs campaign. The overwhelming military power of the United States was a constant source of alarm to Fidel Castro, and he probably exerted considerable pressure upon his ally in Moscow to provide him with some security against another and more disastrous American invasion. Cuba and the Soviet Union had legitimate grievances against the general drift of American policy or nonpolicy towards Cuba, and although their solution was even more irresponsible and hazardous, it was prompted by legitimate fear and uncertainty about Cuba's survival.

But once the missile bases were discovered, and President Kennedy made it very clear to the Soviet leader that he considered the legitimate interests of the United States to be endangered by their continued presence, Khrushchev played a very constructive role in the ultimate resolution of the problem. The tone of his first letter was not hysterical, and there were many sobering thoughts in it. He very graphically reminded President Kennedy of what the consequences of a head-on nuclear collision between the two countries would be, and pleaded for restraint. He offered a perfectly reasonable solution to a rather complex problem—a solution which Kennedy accepted.

Contrary to general belief, the arrangement was not entirely unfavorable to the Soviet Union. The Soviets lost their missile bases in Cuba, of course, but they received for the first time the assurance of the American President that if they honored their end of the bargain, the United States would promise not to invade Cuba. This not only saved the Soviets' face with Castro, but it was one of the things that both Castro and Khrushchev were aiming for in the first place. Furthermore, the crisis assisted the United States in developing a more reasonable policy towards the Castro government in Cuba. Without compromising its strong opposition to the Castro regime and many of its policies, the United States eliminated, as it should have, the threat of a massive invasion of Cuba as a possible resolution of the conflict. Khrushchev's earthy and effective style, and most certainly his responsible diplomacy in the shadow of a nuclear holocaust, contributed significantly to the solution of the crisis.

A recent interview with the deposed and now domestically exiled Soviet leader emphasizes his interpretation and evaluation of the outcome of that terrifying crisis.

Nikita S. Khrushchev
Comments on the Cuban Missile Crisis
July 30, 1967

"Mr. K Looks Back," in *Boston Sunday Globe*, July 30, 1967, A-7.

Mr. Kennedy made a very strong impression on me, both as a man and as a statesman. I like the way he, unlike Eisenhower, had his personal opinion on all questions we discussed ... Kennedy was entirely different from Eisenhower and had a precisely formulated answer to every question. Apparently he had thought them out before and they corresponded to his main line of thought, to his personal point of view.

I liked his face, sometimes stern and at other times lightened by a really good-natured smile.

Kennedy was a real statesman. Unfortunately, I did not have a chance to meet him in the United States nor in our country.

Kennedy had a talent for solving international conflicts by negotiation. I had proof of this during the so-called Cuban crisis.

I think if Kennedy had been alive today we would have had an excellent relationship with the United States because he would never have let his country get into such a sticky situation as it is now in Vietnam.

The American press made a lot of fuss about the Russians bringing rockets to Cuba and planning to capture the United States. Perhaps we shouldn't have done it. But if rockets had not been installed, would there be a Cuba now? No, it would have been wiped out. And if that is true, it means that our transportation of rockets was justified. It cost us money but we did not lose a single man.

We took our rockets and bombers away in exchange for President Kennedy's promise not to invade Cuba.

And I am not ashamed that, as the newspapers wrote, I made concessions to the American President and ordered the removal of the rockets from Cuba.

We must give credit to the United States, and first of all to President Kennedy who also showed sense and coolheadedness. He gave us his promise to carry his part and we carried out ours. And that's the way we liquidated the possibility of beginning a nuclear war.

After President Kennedy's death, President Johnson who took over, assured us that he would stick to the promises made by President Kennedy. So far, they have not been violated.

Later, in his book, *Khrushchev Remembers*, the former Soviet Premier reflected further on the episode, attempting to make the best of the situation and portray it as a victory for Soviets who remained calm while the free world leaders trembled. But as bizarre as his description of the incident was, he continued to present John F. and Robert Kennedy in an heroic light.

Nikita S. Khrushchev
Later Reflections on the Cuban Missile Crisis
1970

Nikita S. Khrushchev, *Khrushchev Remembers* (Boston, 1970), 500.

In our negotiations with the Americans during the crisis, they had, on the whole, been open and candid with us, especially Robert Kennedy. The Americans knew that if Russian blood were shed in Cuba, American blood would surely be shed in Germany. The American government was anxious to avoid such a development. It had been, to say the least, an interesting and challenging situation. The two most powerful nations of the world had been squared off against each other, each with its finger on the button. You'd have thought that war was inevitable. But both sides showed that if the desire to avoid war is strong enough, even the most pressing dispute can be solved by compromise. And a compromise over Cuba was indeed found. The episode ended in a triumph of common sense. I'll always remember the late President with deep respect because, in the final analysis, he showed himself to be sober-minded and determined to avoid war. He didn't let himself become frightened, nor did he become reckless. He didn't overestimate America's might, and he left himself a way out of the crisis. He showed real wisdom and statesmanship when he turned his back on right-wing forces in the United States who were trying to goad him into taking military action against Cuba. It was a great victory for us, though, that we had been able to extract from Kennedy a promise that neither America nor any of her allies would invade Cuba.

President Kennedy's widow put the situation in its proper perspective in a personal note she wrote to Chairman Khrushchev after her husband's tragic assassination:

> You and he were adversaries, but you were allied in a determination that the world should not be blown up. You respected each other and could deal with each other. . . .
>
> The danger which troubled my husband was that war might be started not so much by the big men as by the little ones.
>
> While big men know the needs for self-control and restraint—little men are sometimes moved more by fear and pride. If only in the future the big men can continue to make the little ones sit down and talk, before they start to fight   [261]

It is clear that no other President of the United States had ever wielded the power which was in the hands of John Fitzgerald Kennedy during the missile crisis. He drew together the full military might of this country (including its nuclear power) to enforce a presidential decision dictated by a concern for the country's national security. Not even great wartime Presidents like Lincoln and Roosevelt had been forced to make decisions in which so many lives hung in the balance. No nuclear age President has been so close to the brink of a world holocaust, has been so firmly in control of the instruments of both power and destruction, and no President ever acquitted himself with greater courage and modesty, or with more restraint than he. When it was all over, the office of the presidency loomed more powerful and, in a sense, more frightening than ever before in its 185-year history. Mrs. Kennedy quite rightly pointed to the dangers implicit in the possession of such overwhelming power by men of lesser stature, thus raising many serious and perhaps even insurmountable problems for both the office of the presidency and the men who would assume its reins of power in the future.

NOTES

1. Edwin S. Corwin defines "total war" as a "functional totality, by which I mean, the politically ordered participation in the war effort of all personal and social forces, the scientific, the mechanical, the commercial, the economic, the moral, the literary and artistic, and the psychological." (See Edwin S. Corwin, *Total War and the Constitution* (New York, 1947), 4.)
2. Bernard M. Baruch, *The Public Years* [New York, 1960], 24.
3. Baruch, 44.
4. Benedict Crowell and Robert Forrest Wilson, *The Giant Hand: Our Mobilization and Control of Industry and Natural Resources, 1917-1918* (New Haven, Connecticut, 1921), 34.
5. Baruch, 55.
6. Baruch, 55.
7. Quoted in Ray Stannard Baker, *Woodrow Wilson: Life and Letters* (New York, 1937) VI, 309.
8. Baruch, 74.
9. Clinton Rossiter, *Constitutional Dictatorship: Crisis Government in the Modern Democracies* (Princeton, New Jersey, 1948), 243.
10. Rossiter, *Constitutional Dictatorship*, 243.
11. Baker, VII, 185.
12. Baker, VII, 185-86.
13. Baker, VII, 191.
14. Samuel P. Huntington, *The Soldier and the State* (Cambridge, Massachusetts, 1957), 144.
15. Arthur S. Link, *Wilson: The New Freedom* (Princeton, New Jersey, 1956), 298.
16. Link, 299.
17. Baker, VII, 85.
18. Baker, VII, 85.
19. Baker, VII, 89.
20. General Peyton C. March, *The Nation at War* (New York, 1932), 113.
21. Baker, VII, 354. The text of the telegram is taken from the President's shorthand notes made upon decoding Colonel House's message.
22. Baker, VII, 363.
23. March, 50.
24. Ernest R. May, "Wilson," in Ernest R. May, ed., *The Ultimate Decision: The President as Commander in Chief* (New York, 1960), 131.
25. *United States* v. *Curtiss-Wright Export Corporation*, 299 U.S. 304 (1936).
26. See the discussion in William Leuchtenburg, "The Contentious Commissioner: *Humphrey's Executor* v. *United States*," in Harold M. Hyman and Leonard W. Levy, eds., *Freedom and Reform: Essays in Honor of Henry Steele Commager* (New York, 1967), 297-302.
27. George Sutherland, "The Internal and External Powers of the Government," Senate Doc. No. 417, 61st Cong., 2nd sess. (1909). Justice Sutherland's biographer traces this point of view back still further to the influence of an important teacher, Judge James V. Campbell at the University of Michigan Law School. See Joel Frances Paschal, *Mr. Justice Sutherland: A Man Against the State* (Princeton, New Jersey, 1951).
28. Quoted in David M. Levitan, "The Foreign Relations Power: An Analysis of Mr. Justice Sutherland's Theory," in *Yale Law Journal*, LV, No. 3 (April 1946), 473-74.
29. *U.S.* v. *Curtiss-Wright Export Corporation*, 299 U.S. 319 (1936).
30. *U.S.* v. *Curtiss-Wright Export Corporation*, 299 U.S. 319 (1936).
31. *U.S.* v. *Curtiss-Wright Export Corporation*, 299 U.S. 320 (1936).
32. *U.S.* v. *Curtiss-Wright Export Corporation*, 299 U.S. 316 (1936).
33. Henry Steele Commager, ed., *Documents of American History* (New York, 1949) I, 106.
34. *U.S.* v. *Curtiss-Wright Export Corporation*, 299 U.S. 319 (1936).
35. *U.S.* v. *Curtiss-Wright Export Corporation*, 299 U.S. 319 (1936).
36. *U.S.* v. *Curtiss-Wright Export Corporation*, 299 U.S. 320 (1936).
37. *U.S.* v. *Curtiss-Wright Export Corporation*, 299 U.S. 320 (1936).
38. Quoted from a letter from Harlan Stone to Edwin Borchard, February 14, 1942, in Alpheus Thomas Mason, *Harlan Fiske Stone: Pillar of the Law* (New York, 1956), 650 footnote.
39. *United States* v. *Belmont*, 301 U.S. 330-31 (October 1936).

40. Quoted in Charles A. Beard, *American Foreign Policy in the Making, 1932-1940* (New Haven, Connecticut, 1946), 29.
41. Quoted in Beard, 165.
42. Quoted in Beard, 165.
43. Samuel I. Rosenman, ed., *The Public Papers and Addresses of Franklin D. Roosevelt* (New York, 1941) VII, 410.
44. Cordell Hull, *The Memoirs of Cordell Hull* (New York, 1948) I, 545.
45. William L. Langer and Everett S. Gleason, *The Challenge to Isolationism, 1937-1940* (New York, 1952) I, 19.
46. Langer and Gleason, I, 19.
47. Langer and Gleason, I, 19.
48. Rosenman, VIII, 2-4.
49. Beard, 35.
50. Beard, 38.
51. Rosenman, VIII, xxxiv-xxxv.
52. Senator Robert La Follette of Wisconsin, Progressive candidate for President in 1924, Senator William E. Borah of Idaho, Burton K. Wheeler of Montana and Senator Gerald P. Nye of North Dakota.
53. Langer and Gleason, I, 79-82; 136-47.
54. Langer and Gleason, I, 144.
55. U.S. Department of State, *Foreign Relations of the United States, 1940* (Washington, D.C., 1958) III, 49-50.
56. Harold Ickes, *The Secret Dairy of Harold Ickes* (New York, 1954) III, 188.
57. Ickes, III, 188.
58. Rosenman, IX, 261.
59. Rosenman, IX, 263.
60. Mark Lincoln Chadwin, *The Hawks of World War II* (Chapel Hill, North Carolina, 1968), 33.
61. Without a doubt the most important members of the Century group were the small but extremely influential band of journalists, editors and publishers who not only had access to the key members of the administration and to the British ambassador, but who could also support their objectives in newspapers and magazines which were read by millions of Americans. Joseph Alsop was probably the most active and enthusiastic member of the group, but Walter Lippmann, Henry Luce (publisher of *Time, Life* and *Fortune*), Barry Bingham, publisher of the Louisville *Courier Journal* and three other members of his staff (Mark Ethridge, Herbert Agar and Ulric Bell), Geoffrey Parsons, chief editorial writer for the New York *Herald Tribune*, Major George Fielding Eliot, military affairs columnist for the *Tribune*, Elmer Davis, popular Washington news commentator with the Columbia Broadcasting System, all played significant roles.

    The universities were represented by James B. Conant, president of Harvard University and Ernest M. Hopkins, president of Dartmouth; among the educators were Stringfellow Barr, president of St. John's College in Annapolis, Maryland and William Agar, headmaster of the Newman School in Lakewood, New Jersey. The church was represented by Henry W. Hobson, Episcopal bishop of Cincinnati, Dr. Henry Sloan Coffin, president of Union Theological Center in New York City and one of its future presidents, Dr. Henry Pitt Van Dusen. Other prominent Century group members were Harold Guinzburg, publisher of Viking Press, Robert Sherwood, the playwright, corporation lawyers Dean Acheson and Allan Dulles, motion picture producer Walter Wanger, Lewis W. Douglas, a wealthy Arizona insurance executive who was Franklin Roosevelt's first budget director, but who had become a confirmed anti-New Deal Republican and a close advisor to that party's presidential candidate, Wendell Willkie, and a handful of businessmen like Ward Cheyney, a silk manufacturer, the banker James P. Warburg, and Will Clayton, a leading cotton broker and a member of the Export-Import Bank. The only outstanding military figure in the group was Admiral William H. Stanley, but General Pershing was also persuaded to make a radio address on behalf of the group.

    The membership of the group, in terms of their social backgrounds, was representative of what could be loosely termed the "American establishment." Most were highly competent professional leaders in their respective fields, had been well educated in the country's most elite educational institutions and in many cases had taken advanced work abroad in major institutions like Oxford and Heidelburg. Of the original 28 members of the group, 22 were white, Anglo-Saxon Protestants; a handful of Jews and Catholics were well-integrated into the system. A large percentage of the group had been active for many years in the elitist foreign policy advisory group, the Foreign Policy Association, which would play an increasingly influential role in the postwar world. (This information is compiled from Chadwin's study.)

62. See Chadwin.
63. Langer and Gleason, II, 746-49.
64. Quoted in Chadwin, 95.
65. Langer and Gleason, II, 754.
66. Benjamin V. Cohen, "The Presidency As I Have Seen It," in Emmet John Hughes, *The Living Presidency* (Baltimore, Maryland, 1973), 324.
67. From a letter signed by Charles C. Burlingham, Thomas D. Thatcher, George Rubless and Dean Acheson, in *The New York Times*, August 11, 1940, Section four, 9.
68. Quoted from Stimon's diary (MS) in Langer and Gleason, II, 757.
69. *Foreign Relations, 1940*, III, 68.
70. Winston S. Churchill, *The Second World War* (London, 1949) I, 408-09.
71. *Foreign Relations*, 1940, III, 72.
72. *Foreign Relations*, 1940, III, 72.
73. Langer and Gleason, II, 766-76. See also Rosenman, IX, 392-94, for the exchange of notes between Hull and Lothian.
74. *United States Reports*, 299 U.S. 320 (1939).
75. Rosenman, IX, 405.
76. Quincy Wright, "The Transfer of Destroyers to Great Britain," in *American Journal of International Law*, XXXIV, No. 4 (October 1940), 680. The Jackson opinion was also supported by Professor Alexander N. Sack in letters to *The New York Times*, October 27, November 17 and December 20, 1940. Cited in Langer and Gleason, II, 772-73.
77. Edwin Borchard, "The Attorney General's Opinion on the Exchange of Destroyers for Naval Bases," in *American Journal of International Law*, XXXIV, No. 4 (October 1940), 690. He was joined by Professor Herbert W. Briggs, "Neglected Aspects of the Destroyer Deal," in the same issue, 569-87; and by Professor Herbert Wright in a letter to *The New York Times*, December 15, 1940 and Professor Lawrence Preuss, "The Concepts of Neutrality and Non-Belligerency," in *Annals*, November 1941, 97-109. Also cited in Langer and Gleason, II.
78. Langer and Gleason, II, 773.
79. Edwin S. Corwin, "Some Aspects of the Presidency," in *Annals of the American Academy of Political and Social Science*, CCXVIII, November 1941.
80. From a letter by Edward S. Corwin in *The New York Times*, October 13, 1940.
81. Churchill, II, 367.
82. William R. Emerson, "FDR," in May, 139.
83. Churchill, III, 573.
84. Churchill, III, 576.
85. Robert E. Sherwood, *Roosevelt and Hopkins: An Intimate History* (New York, 1948), 332.
86. Sherwood, 583.
87. Sherwood, 589-90.
88. Francis Biddle, *In Brief Authority* (Garden City, New York, 1962), 213.
89. James MacGregor Burns, *Roosevelt: The Soldier of Freedom* (New York, 1970), 213.
90. Morton Grodzins, *Americans Betrayed: Politics and the Japanese Evacuation* (Chicago, 1949).
91. Biddle, 215.
92. Biddle, 215.
93. Quoted in Carey McWilliams, *Prejudice: Japanese Americans: Symbol of Racial Intolerance* (Boston, 1945), 115.
94. McWilliams, 116.
95. Biddle reports that a confidential survey of opinion outside of southern California conducted by the Office of Facts and Figures indicated that only 14 percent of those interviewed favored internment of persons of Japanese ancestry. Biddle, 224.
96. Biddle, 218.
97. Biddle, 218.
98. Dorothy Swaine Thomas and Richard S. Nishimoto, *The Spoilage* (Berkeley, California, 1946).
99. McWilliams, 2.
100. Rosenman, VIII, 174-76. These orders were supplemented by 108 separate orders issued by General De Witt.
101. Biddle, 218.
102. Biddle, 219.
103. *Korematsu* v. *United States*, 323 U.S. 223 (1944).
104. *Korematsu* v. *United States*, 323 U.S. 223-24 (1944).
105. *Korematsu* v. *United States*, 323 U.S. 226 (1944).

106. *Korematsu* v. *United States*, 323 U.S. 233-35 (1944).
107. *Korematsu* v. *United States*, 323 U.S. 241-42 (1944).
108. *Korematsu* v. *United States*, 323 U.S. 245-47 (1944).
109. *Korematsu* v. *United States*, 323 U.S. 248 (1944).
110. Clinton Rossiter, *The Supreme Court and the Commander in Chief* (Ithaca, New York, 1951), 52-53.
111. Quoted from testimony given by Anna Rosenberg Hoffman in Arthur M. Schlesinger, jr., "Origins of the Cold War," in *Foreign Affairs*, XLVI, No. 1 (October 1967), 40 footnote. The remark, of course, referred to Averell Harriman, the American ambassador to the Soviet Union, who had developed a rather hard and critical point of view with respect to Soviet moves in Eastern Europe.
112. Churchill, VI, 227-28.
113. Churchill, VI, 572-74.
114. Schlesinger, "Origins of the Cold War," 26-28.
115. Walter Millis, ed., *The Forrestal Diaries*, (New York, 1951), 36-37.
116. Millis, *Forrestal Diaries*.
117. Schlesinger, "Origins of the Cold War," 22.
118. Robert James Maddox, *The New Left and the Origins of the Cold War* (Princeton, New Jersey, 1973), 4.
119. Quoted in Schlesinger, "Origins of the Cold War," 24 footnote. Revisionist theory largely stems from the teaching and writings of William Appleman Williams, *The Tragedy of American Diplomacy* (New York, 1959); Williams, ed., *The Shaping of American Diplomacy*, rev. ed. (Chicago, 1960); and the elaborate but not very illuminating two-volume work by Denna Frank Fleming, *The Cold War and Its Origins* (Garden City, New York, 1961). See also Gar Alperovitz, *Atomic Diplomacy: Hiroshima and Potsdam* (New York, 1965); David Horowitz, *The Free World Colossus* (New York, 1965); and Carl Oglesby and Richard Shaull, *Containment and Change* (New York, 1967); Gabriel Kolko, *The Politics of War: The World and United States Foreign Policy, 1943-1945* (New York, 1968) and *The Limits of Power: The World and United States Foreign Policy, 1945-1954* (New York, 1972); Diane Shaver Clemens, *Yalta* (New York, 1970); Lloyd C. Gardner, *Architects of Illusion: Men and Ideas in American Foreign Policy, 1941-1949* (Chicago, 1970), Richard M. Freeland, *The Truman Doctrine and the Origins of McCarthyism* (New York, 1972); Martin Herz, *Beginnings of the Cold War* (Bloomington, Indiana, 1966).
120. Truman, *Memoirs*, I, 72. (My emphasis.)
121. Maddox, 4-5.
122. Quoted in Millis, *Forrestal Diaries*, 40.
123. Schlesinger, "Origins of the Cold War," 46.
124. Schlesinger, "Origins of the Cold War," 46-47.
125. Schlesinger, "Origins of the Cold War," 47.
126. Maddox, 10-11.
127. Maddox, 10-11.
128. Maddox, 10-11.
129. Maddox, 10-11.
130. Charles S. Maier, "Revisionism and Interpretation of Cold War Origins," in *Perspectives in American History* (1970), IV, 345-46.
131. J. L. Richardson, "Cold War Revisionism: A Critique," in *World Politics*, XXIV, No. 1 (October-July 1972), 608.
132. Robert W. Tucker, *The Radical Left and American Foreign Policy* (Baltimore, Maryland, 1971), 151-52.
133. Schlesinger, "Origins of the Cold War," 47.
134. Schlesinger, "Origins of the Cold War," 47.
135. George F. Kennan, *Memoirs, 1925-1950* (Boston, 1967), 225.
136. Kennan, "Russia—Seven Years Later," in *Memoirs*, Annex A, 519.
137. Kennan, "Russia—Seven Years Later," 530-31.
138. Williams, *The Tragedy of American Diplomacy*, 158.
139. Joseph Marion Jones, *The Fifteen Weeks (February 21-June 5, 1947)* (New York, 1964), 136.
140. Schlesinger, "Origins of the Cold War," 46-47.
141. *Public Papers of the Presidents: Harry S. Truman, 1947* (Washington, D.C., 1963), 178.
142. *Public Papers, Harry Truman, 1947*, 178.
143. *Public Papers, Harry Truman, 1947*, 178.

144. *Public Papers, Harry Truman, 1947*, 178.
145. Kennan, "Excerpts from Telegraphic Message from Moscow of February 22, 1946," in *Memoirs*, Annex C, 557.
146. Kennan, *Memoirs*, 294.
147. Kennan, *Memoirs*, 295.
148. Kennan, *Memoirs*, 354-55.
149. *Foreign Affairs*, XXV, No. 4 (July 1947), 580-81. This citation and that following it appeared in "The Sources of Soviet Conduct," the author of which was listed as "X," but who was later identified as George Kennan. The article in *Foreign Affairs* was an edited version of the original memorandum prepared for Secretary Forrestal.
150. Kennan, "The Sources of Soviet Conduct," 574.
151. Kennan, "The Sources of Soviet Conduct," 575-76.
152. Kennan, "The Sources of Soviet Conduct," 581.
153. Quoted from Kennan, "The Sources of Soviet Conduct," 13.
154. Walter Lippmann, *The Cold War* (New York, 1947), 21.
155. Lippmann, 21-22.
156. Lippmann, 58.
157. Lippmann, 54.
158. Lippmann, 52-53.
159. Jones, 155.
160. Kennan, *Memoirs*, 320.
161. Kennan, *Memoirs*, 253.
162. Kennan, *Memoirs*, 256.
163. Kennan, *Memoirs*, 358.
164. Kennan, *Memoirs*, 361.
165. Quoted in Jones, 190.
166. Quoted in Jones, 191.
167. Kennan, *Memoirs*, 320.
168. Truman, II, 102.
169. Walter Millis, *Arms and the State* (New York, 1958), 146.
170. Huntington, Chapters 12-15.
171. Henry L. Stimson and McGeorge Bundy, *On Active Service in Peace and War* (New York, 1947), 644.
172. Millis, *Arms and the State*, 151.
173. Millis, *Arms and the State*, 153.
174. Millis, *Arms and the State*, 154.
175. Truman, II, 50.
176. Millis reports that the army accepted most of the navy's plan for the National Security Council, National Security Resources Board and the Central Intelligence Agency. They also agreed to three autonomous departments—army, navy and air force—which would each have its own secretary (with reduced power), and that there should be a secretary of defense, although no Defense Department. (Millis, *Arms and the State*, 171-72.)
177. Truman, II, 50-51.
178. Quoted in Millis, *Arms and the State*, 176.
179. Quoted in Millis, *Arms and the State*, 233.
180. Millis, *Arms and the State*, 233.
181. Truman, II, 316.
182. Glenn D. Paige, *The Korean Decision* (New York, 1968), 124.
183. Paige, 124.
184. Paige, 148.
185. Truman, II, 332-33.
186. Truman, II, 334.
187. Paige, 142.
188. Paige, 204-05.
189. Paige, 250-51.
190. Paige, 254.
191. *Congressional Record*, XCVII, Part I (82nd Cong., 1st sess.), 57.
192. *Congressional Record*, XCVII, Part I (82nd Cong., 1st sess.), 57.
193. The author of a very elaborate study of the Korean decision has very little to say with regard to the considerations of the President in making his judgment. The chairman of the Senate Foreign Relations Committee responded to Truman's inquiry concerning his own authority to commit troops in Korea:

If a burglar breaks into your house you can shoot him without going down to the police station and getting permission. You might run into a long debate in Congress which would tie your hands completely. You have the right to do it as Commander in Chief and under the U.N. Charter. (Paige, 149.)

Later on this same author cites an interview with Secretary Acheson, who was convinced that the President acted on the basis of his advice in not asking Congress for a joint resolution supporting his decisions. Acheson did not want to risk affecting the morale of American combat troops by exposing the decisions to possible attacks in Congress, or to precipitate prolonged debate on the ultimate costs or consequences of military intervention. (Paige, 187.)

In an interview with the author of Truman's oral biography sometime later, Acheson granted that this might have been an erroneous decision, He added, however:

I don't think so myself. But it can be argued that it was wrong. If the Congress had promptly and without debate passed a resolution endorsing vigorously what had happened, this, of course, would have been fine, and it would have nipped in the bud all the statements about the Korean War being Mr Truman's war and so on.

But that is hindsight, and I have said that I think hindsight is nonsense. It proves nothing. (Quoted in Merle Miller, *Plain Speaking: An Oral Biography of Harry S. Truman* [New York, 1973], 284.)

194. Link 347-416.
195. Quoted in Link, 398.
196. Link, 398.
197. Speech to the Senate, June 28, 1950. *Congressional Record*, XCVI, Part 7 (81st Cong., 2nd sess.), 9323.
198. *Congressional Record*, XCVI, Part 7 (81st Cong., 2nd sess.), 9323.
199. Clinton Rossiter, *The Supreme Court*, 66.
200. Edward S. Corwin, "The President's Power," in the *New Republic*, January 29, 1951, 16.
201. Edwin S. Corwin, "Who Has the Power to Make War?" in *The New York Times Magazine*, July 31, 1949, 14.
202. "Special Message to the Congress Regarding United States Policy for the Defense of Formosa, January 24, 1955," in *Public Papers of the Presidents: Dwight D. Eisenhower, 1955* (Washington, D.C., 1959), 210.
203. "Special Message on Formosa," 209.
204. "Special Message on Formosa," 210.
205. Truman, II, 354.
206. Truman, II, 354.
207. Truman, II, 355-56. Recalling the incidents years later, the feisty ex-President said that he wanted to fire MacArthur at that time, but his top advisors (Acheson, Secretary of Defense Louis Johnson and the Joint Chiefs of Staff) talked him out of it:

I told them I wanted to fire him and I wanted to send over General Bradley to take his place. But they talked me out of it. They said it would cause too much of an uproar, and so I didn't do it, and I was wrong.
... The only thing I learned out of the whole MacArthur deal is that when you feel there's something you have to do and you know in your gut you have to do it, the sooner you get it over with, the better off everybody is. (Miller, 292.)

208. Quoted in Louis Koenig, *The Chief Executive* (New York, 1964), 243.
209. Koenig, 247.
210. John W. Spanier, *The Truman-MacArthur Controversy and the Korean War* (Cambridge, Massachusetts, 1959). MacArthur later revealed an understanding of the relationship of a military officer to his civilian Commander in Chief totally foreign to the American tradition:

I find in existence a new and heretofore unknown and dangerous concept that the members of the Armed Forces owe their primary allegiance to and loyalty to those who temporarily exercise the authority of the executive branch of the government, rather than to the country, and its Constitution they are sworn to defend. No proposition could cast greater doubt on the integrity of the Armed Forces. (Quoted in Haynes, 259.)

211. From the Senate hearings quoted in Spanier, 226.
212. Spanier, 226.
213. Spanier, 241.
214. Trumbull Higgins, *Korea and the Fall of MacArthur* (New York, 1960), 163.
215. Theodore C. Sorensen, *Kennedy* (New York, 1965), 309.
216. From an article by John Fischer in *Harper's Magazine*; quoted in Sorensen, 291.
217. The land area where the new State Department building was erected, and which later became its familiar appellation.

218. Arthur M. Schlesinger, jr., *A Thousand Days* (Boston, 1965), 408.
219. Schlesinger, *A Thousand Days*, 434.
220. Schlesinger, *A Thousand Days*, 312.
221. A fascinating, although at times overly imaginative, account of this process as it affected the life and fortunes of Secretary of Defense James Forrestal has been written by Arnold A. Rogow, *James Forrestal: A Study of Personality, Politics and Policy* (New York, 1963).
222. Quoted in Sorensen, 603.
223. Quoted in Schlesinger, *A Thousand Days*, 315.
224. Schlesinger, *A Thousand Days*, 313.
225. Schlesinger, *A Thousand Days*, 314.
226. Elie Abel, *The Missile Crisis* (New York, 1966), 16.
227. Sorensen, 667.
228. Roberta Wohlsetter, *Cuba and Pearl Harbor: Hindsight and Foresight*, a Rand Corporation Memorandum prepared for the Office of the Assistant Secretary of Defense for International Security Affairs (Santa Monica, California, 1965), 9.
229. Sorensen, 670.
230. Sorensen, 670.
231. Quoted in Robert F. Kennedy, "Thirteen Days: The Story About How the World Almost Ended," in *McCall's*, November 1968, 8.
232. Harold W. Chase and Allen H. Lerman, eds., *Kennedy and the Press* (New York, 1965), 318.
233. David L. Larson, ed., *The "Cuban Crisis" of 1962: Selected Documents and Chronology* (Boston, 1963), 19.
234. Larson, 19.
235. Sorensen, 674-75.
236. See Schlesinger, Sorensen, Abel and Kennedy; also Henry M. Pachter, *Collision Course: The Cuban Missile Crisis and Coexistence* (New York, 1963).
237. Kennedy, "Thirteen Days," 9.
238. *Who's Who: An Annual Biographical Dictionary* (New York, 1973).
239. Graham T. Allison, *Essence of Decision: Explaining the Cuban Missile Crisis* (Boston, 1971), 104-5. I have borrowed Abram Chayes summary of this material, Abram Chayes, *The Cuban Missile Crisis: International Crises and the Role of Law* (New York, 1974), 6.
    Both volumes give illuminating treatments of the Missile Crisis, the latter of which came to my attention after completion of my chapter on the subject. The first volume is particularly useful in probing the motives of the Soviet move, and Chayes's study stresses the significance of the evolving policy adhering to a framework of international law in working through the structure of the Organization for American States.
240. Sorensen, 676-78.
241. Sorensen, 682.
242. Kennedy, "Thirteen Days," 148.
243. Kennedy, "Thirteen Days," 9.
244. Kennedy, "Thirteen Days," 148.
245. Quoted from a "Proclamation of Interdiction of the Delivery of Offensive Weapons to Cuba," in Sorensen, 708.
246. Kennedy, "Thirteen Days," 152.
247. This correspondence along with the Kennedy-Khrushchev exchanges (with the exception of the missing Khrushchev letter) can be found in Larson.
248. Sorensen, 709.
249. Larson, 146.
250. Abel, 179-83.
251. Abel, 179.
252. Kennedy, "Thirteen Days," 86.
253. Abel, 146-47.
254. Larson, 156-57.
255. Sorensen, 716.
256. Larson, 162.
257. Sorensen, 717.
258. Sorensen, 718.
259. Kennedy, "Thirteen Days," 170.
260. Quoted in Schlesinger, *A Thousand Days*, 817.
261. Quoted in William Manchester, *The Death of a President* (New York, 1967), 653.

Bibliography

Abel, Elie. *The Missile Crisis*. New York: Bantam Books, 1966.

Allison, Graham T. *Essence of Decision: Explaining the Cuban Missile Crisis*. Boston: Little Brown and Company, 1971.

Alperovitz, Gar. *Atomic Diplomacy: Hiroshima and Potsdam*. New York: Simon and Schuster, 1965.

Baker, Ray Stannard. *Woodrow Wilson: Life and Letters*. Vols. VI, VII. New York: Doubleday, Doran and Company, Inc., 1937.

Baruch, Bernard M. *The Public Years*. New York: Pocket Books, Inc., 1962.

Beard, Charles A. *American Foreign Policy in the Making, 1932-1940*. New Haven, Connecticut: Yale University Press, 1946.

Biddle, Francis. *In Brief Authority*. Garden City, New York: Doubleday and Company, Inc., 1962.

Borchard, Edwin. "The Attorney General's Opinion on the Exchange of Destroyers for Naval Bases." *American Journal of International Law*. XXXIV. No. 4 (October 1940).

Briggs, Herbert W. "Neglected Aspects of the Destroyer Deal." *American Journal of International Law*. XXXIV. No. 4 (October 1940).

Burlingham, Charles C., Thomas D. Thatcher, George Rublee, and Dean Acheson. Letter to *New York Times*, August 11, 1940, Section IV.

Burns, James MacGregor. *Roosevelt: The Soldier of Freedom*. New York: Harcourt Brace and World, Inc., 1970.

Chadwin, Mark Lincoln. *The Hawks of World War II*. Chapel Hill, North Carolina: University of North Carolina Press, 1968.

Chase, Harold W., and Lerman, Allen H., eds. *Kennedy and the Press*. New York: Thomas Y. Crowell Company, 1965.

Chayes, Abram. *The Cuban Missile Crisis: International Crises and the Role of Law*. New York: Oxford University Press, 1974.

Churchill, Winston S. *The Second World War*. Vols. II-VI. London: Cassell and Company, 1954.

Cohen, Benjamin V. "The Presidency As I Have Seen It." Emmet, John Hughes. *The Living Presidency*. Baltimore, Maryland: Penguin Books, 1973.

Commager, Henry Steele, ed. *Documents of American History*. Fifth ed. New York: Appleton-Century-Crofts, Inc., 1949.

Congressional Record. XCVI, Part 7 (81st Cong., 2nd sess.). Senate, June 28, 1950.

. XCVII, Part 1 (81st Cong., 2nd sess.). Senate, January 5, 1951.

Corwin, Edward S. "The President's Power." *The New Republic*. January 29, 1951.

. "Who Has the Power to Make War?" *The New York Times Magazine*. July 31, 1949.

. "Some Aspects of the Presidency." *The Annals of the American Academy of Political and Social Science*. November 1941.

. *Total War and the Constitution*. First ed. New York: Alfred A. Knopf, 1947.

. Letter to *The New York Times*. October 13, 1940.

Crowell, Benedict, and Wilson, Robert Forrest. *The Giant Hand: Our Mobilization and Control of Industry and Natural Resources, 1917-1918*. New Haven, Connecticut: Yale University Press, 1921.

FitzSimons, Louise. *The Kennedy Doctrine*. New York: Random House, 1972.

Fleming, Denna Frank. *The Cold War and Its Origins*. 2 vols. Garden City, New York: Doubleday and Company, 1961.

Grodzins, Morton. *Americans Betrayed: Politics and the Japanese Evacuation*. Chicago: University of Chicago Press, 1949.

Higgins, Trumbull. *Korea and the Fall of MacArthur*. New York: Oxford University Press, 1960.

Hilsman, Roger. *To Move a Nation: The Politics of Foreign Policy in the Administration of John F. Kennedy*. Garden City, New York: Doubleday and Company, Inc., 1967.

Horowitz, David. *The Free World Colossus*. New York: Hill and Wang, 1965.

Hull, Cordell. *The Memoirs of Cordell Hull.* Vol. I. New York: The Macmillan Company, 1948.

Huntington, Samuel P. *The Soldier and the State.* Cambridge, Massachusetts: The Belknap Press of Harvard University Press, 1957.

Ickes, Harold. *The Secret Diary of Harold Ickes.* Vol. III, *The Lowering Clouds: 1939-1941.* New York: Simon and Schuster, 1954.

Jones, Joseph Marion. *The Fifteen Weeks.* New York: Harcourt, Brace and World (Harbinger), 1964.

Kennan, George F. *Memoirs, 1925-1950.* Boston: Atlantic-Little, Brown, 1967.

⸻. "The Sources of Soviet Conduct," by X. *Foreign Affairs.* XXV. No. 4 (July 1947).

Kennedy, Robert F. "Thirteen Days: The Story About How the World Almost Ended." *McCall's.* XCVI. No. 2 (November 1968).

Khrushchev, Nikita S. *Khrushchev Remembers: The Last Testament.* Boston: Little, Brown and Company, 1974.

Koenig, Louis. *The Chief Executive.* New York: Harcourt, Brace and World, 1964.

Langer, William L., and S. Everett Gleason. *The Challenge to Isolation, 1937-1940.* New York: Harper and Brothers, 1952.

Larson, David L., ed. *The "Cuban Crisis" of 1962: Selected Documents and Chronology.* Boston: Houghton Mifflin Company, 1963.

Leuchtenburg, William E. "The Contentious Commissioner: *Humphrey's Executor* v. *United States.*" In Harold M. Hyman and Leonard W. Levy, eds., *Freedom and Reform: Essays in Honor of Henry Steele Commager.* New York: Harper and Row, 1957.

Levitan, David M. "The Foreign Relations Power: An Analysis of Mr. Justice Sutherland's Theory." *Yale Law Journal.* LV. No. 3 (April 1946).

Link, Arthur S. *Wilson: The New Freedom.* Princeton, New Jersey: Princeton University Press, 1956.

Lippmann, Walter. *The Cold War.* New York: Harper and Brothers, 1947.

McWilliams, Carey. *Prejudice: Japanese Americans: Symbol of Racial Intolerance.* Boston: Little, Brown and Company, 1945.

1948

Maddox, Robert James. *The New Left and the Origins of the Cold War*. Princeton, New Jersey: Princeton University Press, 1973.

Manchester, William. *The Death of a President*. New York: Harper and Row, 1967.

March, General Peyton C. *The Nation at War*. Garden City, New York: Doubleday, Doran and Company, Inc., 1932.

Mason, Alpheus Thomas. *Harlan Fiske Stone: Pillar of the Law*. New York: The Viking Press, 1956.

May, Ernest R. "Wilson." In Ernest R. May, ed., *The Ultimate Decision: The President as Commander in Chief*. New York: George Braziller, 1960.

Millis, Walter. *Arms and the State*. New York: The Twentieth Century Fund, 1958.

_____, ed. *The Forrestal Diaries*. New York: The Viking Press, 1951.

"Mr. K. Looks Back." *Boston Sunday Globe*, July 30, 1967.

Oglesby, Carl and Shaull, Richard. *Containment and Change*. New York: The Macmillan Company, 1967.

Pachter, Henry. *Collision Course: The Cuban Missile Crisis and Coexistence*. New York: Frederick A. Praeger, 1963.

Paige, Glenn D. *The Korean Decision*. New York: Free Press, 1968.

Paschal, Joel Francis. *Mr. Justice Sutherland: A Man Against the State*. Princeton, New Jersey: Princeton University Press., 1951.

Pershing, John J. *My Experiences in the World War*. New York: Frederick A. Stokes, 1961.

Preuss, Lawrence. "The Concepts of Neutrality and Non-Belligerency." *Annals of the American Academy of Political and Social Science* (November, 1941).

Public Papers of the Presidents: Dwight D. Eisenhower, 1955. Washington, D.C.: U.S. Government Printing Office, 1959.

Public Papers of the Presidents: Harry S. Truman, 1946. Washington, D.C.: U.S. Government Printing Office, 1962.

Public Papers of the Presidents: Harry S. Truman, 1947. Washington, D.C.: U.S. Government Printing Office, 1963.

Public Papers of the Presidents: Harry S. Truman, 1950. Washington, D.C.: U.S. Government Printing Office, 1959.

Rogow, Arnold A. *James Forrestal: A Study of Personality, Politics and Policy*. New York: The Macmillan Company, 1963.

Roosevelt, Elliott, ed. *F.D.R.: His Personal Letters, 1928-1945*. Vol. II. New York: Duell, Sloan and Pearce, 1950.

Rosenman, Samuel I., ed. *The Public Papers and Addresses of Franklin D. Roosevelt*. Vol. VII-IX. New York: The Macmillan Company, 1941.

Rossiter, Clinton. *Constitutional Dictatorship: Crisis Government in the Modern Democracies*. Princeton, New Jersey: Princeton University Press, 1948.

        . *The Supreme Court and the Commander in Chief*. Ithaca, New York: Cornell University Press, 1951.

Sack, Alexander N. Letters to *New York Times*. October 27, November 17 and December 20, 1940.

Schlesinger, Arthur M., jr. *A Thousand Days*. Boston: Houghton Mifflin, Company, 1965.

        , ed. *The Dynamics of World Power: A Documentary History of United States Foreign Policy, 1945 1973*. New York: Chelsea House/McGraw-Hill, 1973.

        . *The Imperial Presidency*. Boston: Houghton Mifflin Company, 1973.

        . "The Origins of the Cold War." *Foreign Affairs*. XLVI. No. 1 (October 1967).

Sorensen, Theodore C. *Kennedy*. New York: Harper and Row, 1965.

Spanier, John W. *The Truman-MacArthur Controversy and the Korean War*. Cambridge, Massachusetts. The Belknap Press of Harvard University Press, 1959.

Stimson, Henry L. and Bundy, McGeorge. *On Active Service*. New York: Harper Press, 1947.

Sutherland, George. "The Internal and External Powers of the Government." Senate Doc. No. 417, 61st Cong., 2nd sess. (1909).

Taylor, Maxwell D. *Swords and Plowshares*. New York: W. W. Norton and Company, Inc., 1972.

Thomas, Dorothy Swaine, and Nishimoto, Richard S. *The Spoilage*. Berkeley, California: University of California Press, 1946.

Truman, Harry S. *Memoirs*. Vol. I, *Year of Decisions*. Garden City, New York, Doubleday and Company, 1955.

———. *Memoirs,* Vol. II, *Years of Trial and Hope*. Garden City, New York: Doubleday and Company, 1956.

Tucker, Robert W. *The Radical Left and American Foreign Policy*. Baltimore, Maryland: The Johns Hopkins Press, 1971.

United States Department of State. *Foreign Relations of the United States, 1940*. Vol. III. Washington, D.C.: U.S. Government Printing Office, 1958.

United States v. *Belmont*, 301 U.S. 324 (1936).

United States v. *Curtiss-Wright Export Corporation*, 299 U.S. 304 (1936).

Walton, Richard J. *Cold War and Counter-Revolution: The Foreign Policy of John F. Kennedy*. Baltimore, Maryland: Penguin Books, 1973.

Williams, William Appleman, ed. *The Shaping of American Diplomacy*. Revised ed. Chicago: Rand McNally, 1960.

———. *The Tragedy of American Diplomacy*. Cleveland and New York: World Publishing Company, 1959.

Wohlsetter, Roberta. "Cuba and Pearl Harbor: Hindsight and Foresight." A Rand Corporation Memorandum prepared for the Office of the Assistant Secretary of Defense for International Security Affairs. Santa Monica, California, 1965.

Wright, Herbert. Letter to *New York Times*. December 15, 1940.

Wright, Quincy. "The Transfer of Destroyers to Great Britain." *American Journal of International Law*. XXXIV. No. 4 (October, 1940).

VI. Limits of
Presidential Power
Reexamined

LIMITS OF PRESIDENTIAL
POWER REEXAMINED

The Supreme Court versus the New Deal

The American people elected Franklin Delano Roosevelt as their President in 1932 because he represented a hope, the desperate hope that he would provide the quality of leadership necessary to recover the equilibrium which the country had lost after 12 years of Republican administrations and 3 years of the worst economic depression in its history. In the election of 1936 things were quite different. By then the American people were quite familiar with Roosevelt; they had experienced his New Deal for four years, they had heard him talk and explain his actions and programs to them on the radio in their homes; most of them, whether they were farmers in the midwest, automotive workers in Detroit, or stockbrokers on Wall Street, had felt the impact of his legislative and executive efforts to pull the country out of the Depression and put it back onto the road to recovery.

They observed that process begin with the "bank holiday" of 1933 and watched it continue for the next four years with an almost ceaseless chain of dynamic executive initiatives touching the very roots of agricultural, industrial and economic power and organization in the country. Deflated prices in agriculture were attacked with a national program aimed at inducing farmers to embrace crop restrictions by accepting government payments for curtailing their regular production; industry was encouraged to regulate itself by restricting price-cutting and maintaining minimum wages and working conditions for employees; regulations were introduced into investment banking and the stock market in order to protect the interests of the investors; and vast programs of public works were begun to put millions of idle men and women back to work. The first four years of the New Deal did not overcome the Depression nor did they restore the economic stability of former years, but an impressive beginning was made—a beginning that held the promise that the economic and political character of the nation that would ultimately emerge from the Depression would be a very different one from that of the 1920s.

The measures that the President and Congress had already taken gave clear warning that under Roosevelt's leadership the New Deal was not simply interested in restoring the status quo, but was intent upon developing a new and more economically and politically egalitarian foundation for American society. The people who would benefit most directly from this shift of economic and political power sensed the value of this movement and in most instances supported it, while those who perceived it as a threat to their special privileges and already advantageous positions (privileges and advantages that, for the most part, failed to protect them from the ravages of the Great Depression) were frightened by this prospect and began to fight back against Roosevelt and his New Deal philosophy. The Republican party was the center of gravity for most of those opposed to the New Deal, but other organizations, such as the Liberty League and the National Committee to Uphold Constitutional Government, were organized with the specific objective of alerting the American people to the dangerous threat of the collectivism of Franklin Roosevelt and the New Deal.

During Roosevelt's first term none of these groups had developed substantial support in Congress. The Republicans had been able to elect only 5 senators and 117 members to the House in the 1932 elections. That gave the President a wide margin of support in the House, but votes in the Senate were considerably much closer. The National Industrial Recovery Act squeezed through the Senate with a margin of only 7 votes (46-39), meaning that many in the President's own party were opposed to his economic plans for American industry. But there were many other manifestations of latent Senate opposition to his more extreme ideas on basic economic reform.

Although those who felt threatened by the New Deal appeared to make no headway with Congress and certainly gained no strong allies in the congressional elections of 1934 and 1936, they were increasingly heartened by the growing opposition—one might more properly say hostility—of the Supreme Court to the broad legislative enactments of the New Deal. The Court, during the latter part of the nineteenth century, and for most of the first 30 years of the twentieth century, generally pursued a course favorable to the business and industrial interests of the country. This was reflected in a number of important decisions protecting the railroads from state regulation, in the application of the due process clause of the 14th Amendment to protect the rights of corporations; in the Court's opposition to the rights of organized labor and to any state or federal attempts to establish minimum rates of pay for workers, or to eliminate child labor, and even in its unsuccessful struggle to prevent a graduated income tax. Some people considered these attitudes of the Court as strictly unbiased interpretations of the letter of the Constitution, but many others saw them as an effort to protect the powerful economic interests of the country against legislative regulation, state or federal. Ex-President and later Chief Justice William Howard Taft on several occasions clearly indicated the significant role of the Court as a last ditch bastion in the protection of the country's major economic interests. When Taft left the White House in 1913 after his overwhelming defeat by Woodrow Wilson in the 1912 election, he told newspapermen that above all other things he was most proud of having named six of the nine members of the Supreme Court. "And I have said to them," Taft continued, "Damn you, if any of you die, I'll disown you."[1]

Taft reiterated the strong implication behind his humorous remark later in the 1920 election, when he campaigned for Warren G. Harding, the Republican candidate for President. Taft charged that President Wilson had been subservient to labor union domination, and had appointed "many persons of socialistic tendency to office and power. . . . Mr. Wilson is in favor of a latitudinarian construction of the Constitution. . . ."[2] Then the future chief justice went on to his most incautious revelation:

> Four of the incumbent Justices are beyond the *retiring age of seventy,* and the next President will probably be called upon to appoint their successors. There is no greater domestic issue in this election than the maintenance of the Supreme Court as *the bulwark to enforce the guaranty that no man shall not be deprived of his property without due process of law.*[3]

Taft was appointed to the Court when Harding was elected, and he remained there until he died, defending the old order from what he considered threats from the collectivist left. Even Republican President Herbert Hoover was suspect of intermittent liberal deviations. In his declining years Taft wrote:

> I am older and slower and less acute and more confused. However, as long as things continue as they are, and I am able to answer in my place, I must stay on the court in order to prevent the Bolsheviki from getting control. . . . [T]he only hope we have of keeping a consistent declaration of constitutional law is for us to live as long as we can. . . .[4]

Most of the Taft Court, excluding the chief justice, continued on into the New Deal, and in Roosevelt they were confronted with a more serious "Bolsheviki" than anything they had faced in the Hoover administration.

During the election campaign of 1932 Roosevelt indicated that he was quite prepared for the possible opposition of the Supreme Court. In one of his barnstorming speeches he said that he was well aware that the Republicans had been in complete control of all branches of the federal government for the past four years, "the Executive, the Senate, the House of Representatives, and I might as well add for good measure, the Supreme Court as well."[5] Observing Chief Justice Charles Evans Hughes swear in the President on January 20, 1937, and obtain from him his commitment to protect and defend the Constitution of the United States, the secretary of the interior, Harold Ickes, confided in his diary that "what . . . the Constitution [was] to the Chief Justice was not the Constitution to the President, at least in some very vital particulars."[6]

But in the early days of the New Deal the Supreme Court was not in the forefront of the Chief Executive's or his "brain trust" advisors' minds. They were confronted with a series of economic and social crises unparalleled in American history, and as they went to work writing presidential proclamations, drafting legislation and creating new emergency agencies, their minds were focused primarily on the problems they faced rather than on the technical limitations of constitutional law which would cripple their efforts at a later date. It takes a reasonable period of time before a litigant can bring a case before the Supreme Court, and it took two and three years before major New Deal legislation came before the highest court in the land for critical examination.

The Court with which the New Deal would ultimately have to come to terms consisted largely of holdovers from previous Republican administrations. Only two of the nine members, James C. McReynolds and Louis D. Brandeis, had been appointed by a Democratic President, Woodrow Wilson, but after his appointment McReynolds forsook the "New Freedom" of his mentor and developed into one of the most hardshell reactionaries on the Court. Wilson considered the appointment of McReynolds the greatest mistake of his two administrations. A native of Tennessee who had been attorney general in Wilson's first cabinet, it was never quite clear how McReynolds went as far as he did on the little he had to recommend of himself. He was an embittered bachelor, a man who had great difficulty in relating to people, almost any kind of people, and was a confirmed anti-Semite. Time and again he went out of his way to insult Justice Brandeis, and his hostility was so great that Chief Justice Hughes had to divide the Court in half in order to entertain both men for dinner.

George Sutherland, a former senator, was probably the most powerful intellectual force among the four conservatives on the Court, and during his long tenure he wrote some powerful and significant decisions—among them the strong defense of the President's broad powers in the area of foreign affairs (U.S. *v.* Curtiss-Wright) and in defense of the rights of Blacks, by repudiating the clear discrimination in the impaneling of an all-white jury in one of the Scottsboro trials. On economic issues, however, he was immovable, and lined up with McReynolds, Butler and Van Devanter on every anti-New Deal opinion they wrote. Pierce Butler, the third member of the quartet, a former railroad attorney and a Catholic from Maryland, was also a last-ditch defender of nineteenth-century laissez faire. He was alleged to have been a stronger but more discrete anti-Semite than McReynolds, and was reported to have pleaded with Hoover at the time of the appointment of Justice Benjamin N. Cardozo "not to inflict the Court with another Jew."[7] By the mid-thirties Justice Willis Van Devanter had been on the Court for a quarter of a century, and his failure or inability to share his load of the decision-writing chores made him a distinct liability, increasing the workload of his colleagues.

Three of the remaining five judges constituted the so-called "liberal" faction of the Court; they normally voted together on cases where the powers of the Congress were held to be inadequate to deal with economic problems critical to the public welfare. The oldest of the trio and indeed a legend in his own time, was Louis D. Brandeis. Even before joining the Court in 1916, Brandeis had made tremendous contributions to the country which had welcomed his parents from Germany in 1849. From the time he passed through Harvard Law School, establishing a scholastic record which has never been equaled,[8] Brandeis made a significant mark on every activity with which he was associated. He was sufficiently successful as a corporation lawyer in Boston to have amassed a comfortable fortune before he was 50, and then he devoted most of his time to carving out a unique role in American public life as the "people's advocate." Brandeis went into the courts and appeared before city, state and national legislative committees, representing the people's interests in a wide range of problems, from fighting for the restriction of the working hours of women, to exposing the monopolistic practices of railroad and insurance companies in cheating the public through their arbitrarily fixed rates and fraudulent elimination of competition. A key advisor to Woodrow Wilson and the architect of the "New Freedom" presidential campaign of 1912, Brandeis had inspired and, in fact, helped to draft much of the antitrust and banking legislation of the early

Wilson administration. When Brandeis was finally appointed to the Court, after a protracted fight against him, led by the more influential members of the same economic interests he had so ably exposed and fought against, he teamed up with Justice Oliver Wendell Holmes in writing a number of brilliant decisions which stoutly defended individual civil liberties and freedom of expression in a world which was becoming all too inhospitable to those values.

Brandeis' two closest associates were also outstanding men and jurists. Harlan Fiske Stone had been Calvin Coolidge's attorney general, a successful corporation lawyer and a dean of Columbia University Law School. Stone possessed one of the best minds and most contentious pens of any justice who ever sat on the Court. He was appointed by Herbert Hoover, and after the Court fight had died down, he became chief justice of one of the most active and controversial Courts in American history. The third member of the trio, Benjamin Cardozo, was a brilliant legal scholar, a shy and diffident man who had an outstanding career on the important New York Court of Appeals before being appointed by Hoover. Brandeis, Stone and Cardozo did not always see eye to eye on the wide range of complex legal problems that came before the Court, but they did agree on the major cases that came to the Court challenging the right of the Congress to use the commerce clause of the Constitution or its clear taxing power to regulate business, agriculture and industry.

The remaining two judges, Chief Justice Charles Evans Hughes and Associate Justice Owen J. Roberts, both Hoover appointees, could not properly be placed in either of the previous two groups. By the mid-1930s the chief justice had captured all of the prizes American politics had to offer except the presidency itself. He had been appointed to the Court twice, by Taft in 1910 and by Hoover in 1930. He had also been governor of New York, secretary of state under Harding, had resigned from the Court in 1916 to run for the presidency (which he came very close to winning), and had been elected as United States Representative to the World Court in 1928. Justice Roberts was a distinguished Philadelphia Main Line lawyer who had forcefully prosecuted the Teapot Dome scandals before his appointment.

Before returning to the Court as chief justice in 1930, Hughes had developed a theory of the role of the Supreme Court in the American political system, which he revealed in a series of lectures at Columbia University in 1928. One of the significant and more ironic aspects of his theory was the proposition "that the Court has found its fortress in public opinion."[9] What he meant by that he explained later in his lectures. The Constitution grants complete independence to the Court only in the area of original jurisdiction, Hughes pointed out, "while the critical appellate jurisdiction (which incorporates the function of constitutional or judicial review) is subject to 'such exceptions' and 'such regulations' as the Congress shall make."[10] In order then for the Court to maintain its independence and integrity, Hughes argued, particularly in relation to the Congress, which has jurisdiction over some of its important functions, it must be responsive to the will of the American people. The future chief justice pointed out three occasions when the Court had violated this principle: the *Dred Scott* decision before the Civil War, the legal tender cases in 1870 and, 25 years later, the decisions ruling the income tax unconstitutional. Hughes argued that by violating strong public opinion in these three instances "the

Court has suffered severely from self-inflicted wounds."[11] Much of Hughes' behavior during the crisis over the Court in the mid-thirties can be explained by his obvious attempt to prevent another traumatic loss of public confidence in the wisdom and integrity of the Court.

The chief justice more often voted with the liberals than against them, but the opposite was true of Justice Roberts. Hughes had the difficult job of attempting to hold together this badly divided Court on a minimal level of civility to one another, as the justices went their separate ways politically, socially and in terms of constitutional theory. It was an impossible task. Hughes was an irreconcilable civil libertarian and a moderate on questions of governmental regulation. He voted with the liberals on some of their key dissents, but his efforts to moderate conflicts of law and theory particularly affronted Stone's strong sense of intellectual superiority, and much harsh feeling simmered close to the surface. Roberts, although initially welcomed by the Democrats who remembered his persistent prosecution of the Teapot Dome scandals, turned out to be much more of a conservative than they anticipated. Up until the end of the 1937 term he regularly voted with the neanderthal wing of the Court. His was the fifth vote in the 5-4 decisions against New Deal legislation, and when he later shifted significantly in his opinions during the 1937 term, the conservatives no longer had a majority.

The literature on the Supreme Court is a growing one, and there are a number of accounts which very adequately discuss the series of decisions the Court handed down in 1935 and 1936, which succeeded in seriously jeopardizing the New Deal and inhibiting its further development.[12] Beginning with the "hot oil" decision of January 7, 1935,[13] the justices found a series of New Deal statutes unconstitutional. In that case the Court decided that Congress had made an unconstitutional delegation of power to the President in authorizing him to prosecute oil companies engaged in the interstate sale of oil, which had been produced in violation of restrictive codes set up by the states, but which was in accordance with provisions of the National Industrial Recovery Act. To make matters even worse, the government admitted in court that criminal penalties for violation of the codes had been inadvertently left out of the official printed version of the executive regulation, and the Court decided that no prosecutions under the statute would be legal until that was remedied.

The "hot oil" case was followed by another unfavorable decision of the Court—the invalidation of the Railroad Retirement Act.[14] In another 5 to 4 division by the Court, the chief justice sided with Brandeis, Stone and Cardozo in the dissent. The law was not a critical piece of New Deal legislation, but the decision of the majority gave fair warning of things to come. Chief Justice Hughes pointed out in his dissent that it would have been understandable had the Court objected to certain features of the law (e.g., the inclusion of questionable categories of employees, basis of payments, conditions imposed, etc.), but after reviewing these "the majority finally raised a barrier against all legislative action of this nature by declaring that the subject matter itself lies beyond the reach of the congressional authority to regulate interstate commerce."

That is a conclusion of such serious and far-reaching importance that it overshadows all other questions raised by the Act. Indeed, it makes their discussion superfluous. The final objection goes, as the opinion states, "to the heart of the law, even if it could survive the loss of the unconstitutional features" which the opinion perceives. I think that the conclusion thus reached is a departure from sound principles and places an unwarranted limitation upon the commerce clause of the Constitution.[15]

The chief justice was attempting valiantly to avoid the fate the Court suffered in the three cases he had cited in his Columbia address, but his own Court was not responding to his efforts. Several weeks later the Court got even more ambitious. In the course of one morning, it struck three times against the New Deal and Roosevelt. To begin with, it negated the Frazier-Lemke Act, a law designed to bring badly needed relief to farm mortgagors.[16] The second decision was a humiliating blow although it did not declare any New Deal laws unconstitutional; in Humphrey's Executor v. United States the Court decided that the President did not have the power to remove a member of the Federal Trade Commission if he was not being dismissed for reasons clearly set forth by Congress in the enabling statute. The decision upset the Court's position in the *Myers* case and left the removal power of the President vis-à-vis the regulatory commissions very much up in the air. Furthermore, the Court failed to cite the fact that in removing Humphrey, the President had been acting in accordance with the only guiding opinion of the Court, Chief Justice Taft's extremely broad decision in the *Myers* case. In its final decision that day the Court ruled the entire National Industrial Recovery Act unconstitutional.[17] In that decision once again the Court did not confine itself to the rather narrow question before it, but roamed far and wide; Justice Hughes suggested in the majority decision that the commerce clause of the Constitution was inadequate to deal with regulations imposed upon hours, wages and working conditions in industry. The Court was particularly disturbed at the fact that the NRA codes reached down into small industries like poultry, with dubious interstate implications, and was thoroughly alarmed at the broad nature of the authority delegated to the President in the act.

This last decision undermined much of the recovery machinery the New Deal had enacted, and introduced an element of chaos into the problems of developing a sound and steady course to economic stability. Robert Jackson, then assistant to the attorney general of the United States, but who was later named to the Supreme Court, wrote in retrospect that " 'hell broke loose' in the lower courts." Sixteen hundred injunctions restraining officers of the federal government from carrying out acts of Congress were granted by federal judges. At that time a single district judge could grant an injunction nullifying a federal law passed by the House of Representatives and the Senate, and approved by the President.[18] Little wonder that the President in his news conference following the decision complained: "We have been relegated to the horse-and-buggy definition of interstate commerce."[19]

In the election year of 1936 the Supreme Court continued to hammer away at the New Deal, but some resolution of the judicial attack upon the decisions of a representative government appeared inevitable. One of the statutes struck down during the 1936 term was the Bituminous Coal Conservation Act, sponsored by Senator Joseph Guffey of Pennsylvania; it attempted to recover for that beleaguered industry some semblance of the regulation of prices, wages and working conditions of which it had been stripped since the overthrow of the NRA.[20] The industry, which for more than two decades had been plagued by violent strikes and abject poverty among its workers, had made a remarkable recovery under the codes created by the NRA, and the Guffey bill was an attempt to salvage that recovery by eliminating the Chief Executive's role in the regulation procedures, which the Court had held as unconstitutional. The Court directed its attention to the wage regulations of the labor section of the law and declared the entire document unconstitutional by a 5 to 4 vote, with the chief justice voting once again with the minority. The Court also rejected a law designed to relieve the hardship of municipalities' bankruptcies.[21] At the time of the decision 2,019 municipalities' improvement districts and other taxing agencies throughout the country were in default of their obligations. The New York Minimum Wage Law for women was also declared unconstitutional by the same 5-4 majority.[22]

But the major blow to the New Deal came at the very beginning of the session when the Court invalidated the Agricultural Adjustment Act, the key Roosevelt measure affecting over 40 percent of the population who lived in rural areas of the country.[23] The AAA had attempted to bring relief to that desperate sector of the population whose money income was reduced during the Depression to under one-third of what it had been previously. The AAA, a major government program, was a broad effort to raise farm prices, which had skidded to starvation levels, by inducing crop reduction through subsidy payments. The Court rejected the program on the grounds that it constituted a violation of the taxing power of the Constitution:

> Congress has no power to enforce its commands on the farmer to the ends sought by the Agricultural Adjustment Act. . . . It does not help to declare the local conditions throughout the nation have created a situation of national concern; for this is but to say that whenever there is a widespread similarity of local conditions, Congress may ignore constitutional limitations upon its own powers and usurp those reserved to the states.[24]

This smug statement drew a justifiably sharp dissent from Justice Stone, who was joined by Justice Brandeis and Justice Cardozo. In concluding his attack upon the majority opinion, Justice Stone called it a "tortured construction of the Constitution." He reminded his brothers "that while unconstitutional exercise of power by the executive and legislative branches of the government is subject to judicial restraint, the only check upon our own exercise of power is our own sense of self-restraint." The proper method, he warned, for removing unwise laws from the statute books was to "appeal . . . not to the courts but to the ballot and to the processes of democratic government."[25]

> Courts are not the only agency of government that must be assumed to have capacity to govern. Congress and the courts both unhappily may falter or be mistaken in the performance of their constitutional duty. But interpretation of our great charter of government which proceeds on any assumption that the responsibility for the preservation of our institutions is the exclusive concern of any one of the three branches of government, or that it alone can save them from destruction is far more likely, in the long

run, "to obliterate the constituent members" of "an indestructible union of indestructible states" than the frank recognition that language, even of a constitution may mean what it says: that the power to tax and spend includes the power to relieve a nation-wide economic maladjustment by conditional gifts of money.[26]

It was a harsh dissent, but throughout the session, with respect to the other laws it voided, the Court continued to demonstrate its need of such a lecture. The New Deal was stymied by those decisions. The President bided his time, however. He faced an election campaign during the summer and fall of 1936, and although he made the New Deal the issue between him and his opponent, Alfred M. Landon, the Supreme Court or any plans he had for changing it were not brought forward during the campaign. The Republicans, on the other hand, claimed the Court as their ally, and attempted to exploit its prestige to the utmost.

The President Tries to Fight Back

Franklin Roosevelt naturally considered the overwhelming victory in the 1936 election[27] a clear endorsement of his New Deal, and soon after his second inauguration he announced what his plans for the future would be. After the unfortunate decision on the AAA the previous spring, Roosevelt had asked his attorney general, Homer S. Cummings, together with the solicitor general, Stanley Reed, to make a study of alternative actions which were open to the President in dealing with the Court. A number of strong Presidents—Jefferson, Jackson and Lincoln— had all had running battles with the Court at one time or another during their terms in the White House. In some cases those battles led to changes in the personnel of the Court itself, for there is nothing in the Constitution which specifies the number of justices who should serve on the Court. Moreover, the appellate jurisdiction is subject to such exceptions and regulations as the Congress shall make. John Adams was the first President to tamper with the number of justices who would sit on the Court. He convinced Congress to pass a law reducing the number of judges from six (as it then was) to five, the law to take effect when the next vacancy occurred, thus hopefully depriving Thomas Jefferson of an appointment. Jefferson circumvented that problem easily by using his own influence with the Congress to have the number of judges increased first to six and later to seven. During the Civil War the number was increased to ten in order to prevent the Court from attempting to block Lincoln's war policies; after the assassination Congress cut the number back to eight in order to preclude Andrew Johnson's filling any vacancies.

President Roosevelt had a number of options open to him. He could, of course, increase the number of justices, as some of his predecessors had done. Retirement for a member of the Court could be made more attractive. Hatton Sumners, chairman of the House Judiciary Committee, favored that idea, and his bill proposing retirement with full-salary pensions was passed while the Court fight was on; this very probably influenced some of the later resignations. Another idea was to raise the number of justices required to invalidate a law from the majority of five to possibly six or seven of a nine-man Court. An important presidential advisor, Ben Cohen, proposed that Congress be given the right to supersede a Supreme Court decision by voting for a measure a second time (after one election had passed) if it had been invalidated by the Court. Many members of the Senate and of the House went on record with their own suggestions for changing the personnel or procedures of the Court. Senator Joseph O'Mahoney from Montana wanted to strip the Court of its power to review the constitutionality of a law. Congressman Emanuel Celler of New York, a prominent member of the House Judiciary Committee, stated that Congress had no other alternative than to pack the Court. Many of these proposals would have required or at least would have been strengthened, if they were incorporated into a constitutional amendment. But whether or not to propose such an amendment was one of the decisions the President had to make. Senators Burton K. Wheeler, leader of the opposition to the President's Court plan, Hiram Johnson and even William Borah all favored some kind of reform of the Court power of constitutional review at one time or another, yet all of the members of Congress mentioned above opposed the President's plan once it was announced. Why?

President Roosevelt announced his Court reform plan on February 5, 1937. He presented it to the Congress in a special message, after first reading it to a meeting of cabinet members and congressional leaders. There was no general discussion following this meeting, and the President had not consulted any of them previously, with the exception of his attorney general, who had drawn up the plan. The secret was so well kept that even the President's key political advisor and campaign manager, Jim Farley, was not informed before any of the others. The President worked with Attorney General Cummings and Solicitor General Reed for weeks on the proposal, and extraordinary care was taken that the plan did not leak out. Secrecy was carried to such lengths that mimeographed copies of the President's message and a draft of the bill were not run off until the morning that the plan was to be announced; on that day the President summoned his White House secretarial staff at 6:30 a.m. so they could have the job completed by midmorning.

Farley was not the only one left in the dark. The President had not even mentioned the proposal to his inner circle of advisors and assistants, men like Harry Hopkins, Harold Ickes, Tom Corcoran, Ben Cohen and Felix Frankfurter. Needless to say he left the congressional leaders of the Democratic party (including Vice President Garner) out of his confidence.

The President unquestionably felt himself to be at the pinnacle of his power and, in the light of his past record of success in getting the Congress to accept his legislative recommendations and his recent overwhelming endorsement by a large majority of the American people, he expected to have his own way once again. He introduced his reform plan in characteristic dramatic Rooseveltian fashion, and he obviously did not envision serious opposition to its passage.

Several books have been written which record the history of the Court fight, and several more are in the offing.[28] It would be folly to attempt in the course of a few short pages to provide a detailed account of these significant events. More to the point would be a careful analysis of why the President failed in his effort to translate his proposal into law, and an assessment of his claim that he really won the battle anyway. But first the specifics of the plan itself.

President Roosevelt introduced his plan for reorganizing the federal judicary of the United States to the Congress on February 5, 1937. The proposal did not mention the struggle between the President and the Court. It concentrated on the increasingly heavy burden of the large number of cases the Court was required to review each term; it pointed out that the Court refused to review almost nine times as many cases as it heard; and finally it emphasized the fact that close to 10 percent of the 237 federal judges were over the retirement age of 70 years but refused to retire and in some instances were incapable of carrying their share of the workload. To remedy this condition and to inject new blood into the entire court system, the President proposed appointing an additional judge for every one of the present judges over 70 years of age who refused to retire.

Nothing was said specifically about restructuring the Supreme Court in the proposal, but since the Supreme Court was part of the federal system and 6 of its members were over the retirement age, it would clearly have given Roosevelt the power to appoint as many as six new justices if no one retired. The President's plan also contained more detailed suggestions for administrative reform of some of the procedures of the federal court system, particularly prohibiting the lower courts from issuing injunctions or decrees on constitutional questions, without previous and ample notice to the attorney general and an opportunity for the United States to present evidence and be heard. The President also suggested that there should be direct and immediate appeal to the Supreme Court in any cases where a court of the first instance determined the constitutionality of the question.

President Franklin D. Roosevelt
Presents a Reorganization Plan for the Judiciary
February 5, 1937

Rosenman, VIII, 51-66.

To the Congress:
I have recently called the attention of the Congress to the clear need for a comprehensive program to reorganize the administrative machinery of the Executive Branch of our Government. I now make a similar recommendation to the Congress in regard to the Judicial Branch of the Government, in order that it also may function in accord with modern necessities.

The Constitution provides that the President "shall from time to time give to the Congress information of the State of the Union, and recommend to their consideration such measures as he shall judge necessary and expedient." No one else is given a similar mandate. It is therefore the duty of the President to advise the Congress in regard to the Judiciary whenever he deems such information or recommendation necessary.

I address you for the further reason that the Constitution vests in the Congress direct responsibility in the creation of courts and judicial offices and in the formulation of rules of practice and procedure. It is, therefore, one of the definite duties of the Congress constantly to maintain the effective functioning of the Federal Judiciary.

The Judiciary has often found itself handicapped by insufficient personnel with which to meet a growing and more complex business. It is true that the physical facilities of conducting the business of the courts have been greatly improved, in recent years, through the erection of suitable quarters, the provision of adequate libraries and the addition of subordinate court officers. But in many ways these are merely the trappings of judicial office. They play a minor part in the processes of justice.

Since the earliest days of the Republic, the problem of the personnel of the courts has needed the attention of the Congress. For example, from the beginning, over repeated protests to President Washington, the Justices of the Supreme Court were required to "ride Circuit" and, as Circuit Justices, to hold trials throughout the length and breadth of the land—a practice which endured over a century.

In almost every decade since 1789, changes have been made by the Congress whereby the numbers of judges and the duties of judges in federal courts have been altered in one way or another. The Supreme Court was established with six members in 1789; it was reduced to five in 1801; it was increased to seven in 1807; it was increased to nine in 1837; it was increased to ten in 1863; it was reduced to seven in 1866; it was increased to nine in 1869.

The simple fact is that today a new need for legislative action arises because the personnel of the Federal Judiciary is insufficient to meet the business before them. A growing body of our citizens complain of the complexities, the delays, and the expense of litigation in United States Courts.

A letter from the Attorney General, which I submit herewith, justifies by reasoning and statistics the common impression created by our overcrowded federal dockets—and it proves the need for additional judges.

Delay in any court results in injustice.

It makes lawsuits a luxury available only to the few who can afford them or who have property interests to protect which are sufficiently large to repay the cost. Poorer litigants are compelled to abandon valuable rights or to accept inadequate or unjust settlements because of sheer inability to finance or to await the end of a long litigation. Only by speeding up the processes of the law and thereby reducing their cost, can we eradicate the growing impression that the courts are chiefly a haven for the well-to-do.

Delays in the determination of appeals have the same effect. Moreover, if trials of original actions are expedited and existing accumulations of cases are reduced, the volume of work imposed on the Circuit Courts of Appeals will further increase.

The attainment of speedier justice in the courts below will enlarge the task of the Supreme Court itself. And still more work would be added by the recommendation which I make later in this message for the quicker determination of constitutional questions by the highest court.

Even at the present time the Supreme Court is laboring under a heavy burden. Its difficulties in this respect were superficially lightened some years ago by authorizing the court, in its discretion, to refuse to hear appeals in many classes of cases. This discretion was so freely exercised that in the last fiscal year, although 867 petitions for review were presented to the Supreme Court, it declined to hear 717 cases. If petitions in behalf of the Government are excluded, it appears that the court permitted private litigants to prosecute appeals in only 108 cases out of 803 applications. Many of the refusals were doubtless warranted. But can it be said that full justice is achieved when a court is forced by the sheer necessity of keeping up with its business to decline, without even an explanation, to hear 87 percent of the cases presented to it by private litigants?

It seems clear, therefore, that the necessity of relieving present congestion extends to the enlargement of the capacity of all the federal courts.

A part of the problem of obtaining a sufficient number of judges to dispose of cases is the capacity of the judges themselves. This brings forward the question of aged or infirm judges– a subject of delicacy and yet one which requires frank discussion.

In the federal courts there are in all 237 life tenure permanent judgeships. Twenty-five of them are now held by judges over seventy years of age and eligible to leave the bench on full pay. Originally no pension or retirement allowance was provided by the Congress. When after eighty years of our national history the Congress made provision for pensions, it found a well-entrenched tradition among judges to cling to their posts, in many instances far beyond their years of physical or mental capacity. Their salaries were small. As with other men, responsibilities and obligations accumulated. No alternative had been open to them except to attempt to perform the duties of their offices to the very edge of the grave.

In exceptional cases, of course, judges, like other men, retain to an advanced age full mental and physical vigor. Those not so fortunate are often unable to perceive their own infirmities. "They seem to be tenacious of the appearance of adequacy." The voluntary retirement law of 1869 provided, therefore, only a partial solution. That law, still in force, has not proved effective in inducing aged judges to retire on a pension.

This result had been foreseen in the debates when the measure was being considered. It was then proposed that when a judge refused to retire upon reaching the age of seventy, an additional judge should be appointed to assist in the work of the court. The proposal passed the House but was eliminated in the Senate.

With the opening of the twentieth century, and the great increase of population and commerce, and the growth of a more complex type of litigation, similar proposals were introduced in the Congress. To meet the situation, in 1913, 1914, 1915 and 1916, the Attorneys General then in office recommended to the Congress that when a district or a circuit judge failed to retire at the age of seventy, an additional judge be appointed in order that the affairs of the court might be promptly and adequately discharged.

In 1919 a law was finally passed providing that the President "may" appoint additional district and circuit judges, but only upon a finding that the incumbent judge over seventy "is unable to discharge efficiently all the duties of his office by reason of mental or physical disability of permanent character." The discretionary and indefinite nature of this legislation has rendered it ineffective. No President should be asked to determine the ability or disability of any particular judge.

The duty of a judge involves more than presiding or listening to testimony or arguments. It is well to remember that the mass of details involved in the average of law cases today is vastly greater and more complicated than even twenty years ago. Records and briefs must be read; statutes, decisions, and extensive material of a technical, scientific, statistical and economic nature must be searched and studied; opinions must be formulated and written. The modern tasks of judges call for the use of full energies.

Modern complexities call also for a constant infusion of new blood in the courts, just as it is needed in executive functions of the Government and in private business. A lowered mental or physical vigor leads men to avoid an examination of complicated and changed conditions. Little by little, new facts become blurred through old glasses fitted, as it were, for the needs of another generation; older men, assuming that the scene is the same as it was in the past, cease to explore or inquire into the present or the future.

We have recognized this truth in the civil service of the nation and of many states by compelling retirement on pay at the age of seventy. We have recognized it in the Army and Navy by retiring officers at the age of sixty-four. A number of states have recognized it by providing in their constitutions for compulsory retirement of aged judges.

Life tenure of judges, assured by the Constitution, was designed to place the courts beyond temptations or influences which might impair their judgments: it was not intended to create a static judiciary. A constant and systematic addition of younger blood will vitalize the courts and better equip them to recognize and apply the essential concepts of justice in the light of the needs and the facts of an ever-changing world.

It is obvious, therefore, from both reason and experience, that some provision must be adopted, which will operate automatically to supplement the work of older judges and accelerate the work of the court.

I, therefore, earnestly recommend that the necessity of an increase in the number of judges be supplied by legislation providing for the appointment of additional judges in all federal courts, without exception, where there are incumbent judges of retirement age who do not choose to retire or to resign. If an elder judge is not in fact incapacitated, only good can come from the presence of an additional judge in the crowded state of the dockets; if the capacity of an elder judge is in fact impaired, the appointment of an additional judge is indispensable. This seems to be a truth which cannot be contradicted.

I also recommend that the Congress provide machinery for taking care of sudden or long-standing congestion in the lower courts. The Supreme Court should be given power to appoint an administrative assistant who may be called a Proctor. He would be charged with the duty of watching the calendars and the business of all the courts in the federal system. The Chief Justice thereupon should be authorized to make a temporary assignment of any circuit or district judge hereafter appointed in order that he may serve as long as needed in any circuit or district where the courts are in arrears.

I attach a carefully considered draft of a proposed bill, which, if enacted, would, I am confident, afford substantial relief. The proposed measure also contains a limit on the total number of judges who might thus be appointed and also a limit on the potential size of any one of our federal courts.

These proposals do not raise any issue of constitutional law. They do not suggest any form of compulsory retirement for incumbent judges. Indeed, those who have reached the retirement age, but desire to continue their judicial work, would be able to do so under less physical and mental strain and would be able to play a useful part in relieving the growing congestion in the business of our courts. Among them are men of eminence and great ability whose services the Government would be loath to lose. If, on the other hand, any judge eligible for retirement should feel that his court would suffer because of an increase in its membership, he may retire or resign under already existing provisions of law if he wishes so to do. In this connection let me say that the pending proposal to extend to the Justices of the Supreme Court the same retirement privileges now available to other federal judges, has my entire approval.

One further matter requires immediate attention. We have witnessed the spectacle of conflicting decisions in both trial and appellate courts on the constitutionality of every form of important legislation. Such a welter of uncomposed differences of judicial opinion has brought the law, the courts, and, indeed, the entire administration of justice dangerously near to disrepute.

A federal statute is held legal by one judge in one district; it is simultaneously held illegal by another judge in another district. An act valid in one judicial circuit is invalid in another judicial circuit. Thus rights fully accorded to one group of citizens may be denied to others. As a practical matter this means that for periods running as long as one year or two years or three years—until final determination can be made by the Supreme Court—the law loses its most indispensable element—equality.

Moreover, during the long processes of preliminary motions, original trials, petitions for rehearings, appeals, reversals on technical grounds requiring re-trials, motions before the Supreme Court and the final hearing by the highest tribunal—during all this time labor, industry, agriculture, commerce and the Government itself go through an unconscionable period of uncertainty and embarrassment. And it is well to remember that during these long processes the normal operations of society and government are handicapped in many cases by differing and divided opinions in the lower courts and by the lack of any clear guide for the dispatch of business. Thereby our legal system is fast losing another essential of justice—certainty.

Finally, we find the processes of government itself brought to a complete stop from time to time by injunctions issued almost automatically, sometimes even without notice to the Government, and not infrequently in clear violation of the principle of equity that injunctions should be granted only in those rare cases of manifest illegality and irreparable damage against which the ordinary course of the law offers no protection. Statutes which the Congress enacts are set aside or suspended for long periods of time, even in cases to which the Government is not a party.

In the uncertain state of the law, it is not difficult for the ingenious to devise novel reasons for attacking the validity of new legislation or its application. While these questions are laboriously brought to issue and debated through a series of courts, the Government must stand aside. It matters not that the Congress has enacted the law, that the Executive has signed it and that the administrative machinery is waiting to function. Government by injunction lays a heavy hand upon normal processes; and no important statute can take effect—against any individual or organization with the means to employ lawyers and engage in wide-flung litigation—until it has passed through the whole hierarchy of the courts. Thus the judiciary, by postponing the effective date of Acts of the Congress, is assuming an additional function and is coming more and more to constitute a scattered, loosely organized and slowly operating third house of the National Legislature.

This state of affairs has come upon the nation gradually over a period of decades. In my annual message to this Congress I expressed some views and some hopes.

Now, as an immediate step, I recommend that the Congress provide that no decision, injunction, judgment or decree on any constitutional question be promulgated by any federal court without previous and ample notice to the Attorney General and an opportunity for the United States to present evidence and be heard. This is to prevent court action on the constitutionality of Acts of the Congress in suits between private individuals, where the Government is not a party to the suit, without giving opportunity to the Government of the United States to defend the law of the land.

I also earnestly recommend that in cases in which any court of first instance determines a question of constitutionality, the Congress provide that there shall be a direct and immediate appeal to the Supreme Court, and that such cases take precedence over all other matters pending in that court. Such legislation will, I am convinced, go far to alleviate the inequality, uncertainty and delay in the disposition of vital questions of constitutionality arising under our fundamental law.

My desire is to strengthen the administration of justice and to make it a more effective servant of public need. In the American ideal of government the courts find an essential and constitutional place. In striving to fulfill that ideal, not only the judges but the Congress and the Executive as well, must do all in their power to bring the judicial organization and personnel to the high standards of usefulness which sound and efficient government and modern conditions require.

This message has dealt with four present needs:

First, to eliminate congestion of calendars and to make the judiciary as a whole less static by the constant and systematic addition of new blood to its personnel; second, to make the judiciary more elastic by providing for temporary transfers of circuit and district judges to those places where federal courts are most in arrears; third, to furnish the Supreme Court practical assistance in supervising the conduct of business in the lower courts; fourth, to eliminate inequality, uncertainty and delay now existing in the determination of constitutional questions involving federal statutes.

If we increase the personnel of the federal courts so that cases may be promptly decided in the first instance, and may be given adequate and prompt hearing on all appeals; if we invigorate all the courts by the persistent infusion of new blood; if we grant to the Supreme Court further power and responsibility in maintaining the efficiency of the entire federal judiciary; and if we assure government participation in the speedier consideration and final determination of all constitutional questions, we shall go a long way toward our high objectives. If these measures achieve their aim, we may be relieved of the necessity of considering any fundamental changes in the powers of the courts or the constitution of our Government—changes which involve consequences so far-reaching as to cause uncertainty as to the wisdom of such course.

The Attorney General's Letter of February 2, 1937, to the President, inclosed with the foregoing message, follows:

My dear Mr. President: Delay in the administration of justice is the outstanding defect of our federal judicial system. It has been a cause of concern to practically every one of my predecessors in office. It has exasperated the bench, the bar, the business community and the public.

The litigant conceives the judge as one promoting justice through the mechanism of the Courts. He assumes that the directing power of the judge is exercised over its officers from the time a case is filed with the clerk of the court. He is entitled to assume that the judge is pressing forward litigation in the full recognition of the principle that "justice delayed is justice denied." It is a mockery of justice to say to a person when he files suit, that he may receive a decision years later. Under a properly ordered system rights should be determined promptly. The course of litigation should be measured in months and not in years.

Yet in some jurisdictions, the delays in the administration of justice are so interminable that to institute suit is to embark on a life-long adventure. Many persons submit to acts of injustice rather than resort to the courts. Inability to secure a prompt judicial adjudication leads to improvident and unjust settlements. Moreover, the time factor is an open invitation to those who are disposed to institute unwarranted litigation or interpose unfounded defenses in the hopes of forcing an adjustment which could not be secured upon the merits. This situation frequently results in extreme hardships. The small business man or the litigant of limited means labors under a grave and constantly increasing disadvantage because of his inability to pay the price of justice.

Statistical data indicate that in many districts a disheartening and unavoidable interval must elapse between the date that issue is joined in a pending case and the time when it can be reached for trial in due course. These computations do not take into account the delays that occur in the preliminary stages of litigation or the postponements after a case might normally be expected to be heard.

The evil is a growing one. The business of the courts is continually increasing in volume, importance, and complexity. The average case load borne by each judge has grown nearly fifty percent since 1913, when the District Courts were first organized on their present basis. When the courts are working under such pressure it is inevitable that the character of their work must suffer.

The number of new cases offset those that are disposed of, so that the Courts are unable to decrease the enormous back-log of undigested matters. More than fifty thousand pending cases (exclusive of bankruptcy proceedings) overhang the federal dockets—a constant menace to the orderly processes of justice. Whenever a single case requires a protracted trial, the routine business of the court is further neglected. It is an intolerable situation and we should make shift to amend it.

Efforts have been made from time to time to alleviate some of the conditions that contribute to the slow rate of speed with which causes move through the Courts. The Congress has recently conferred on the Supreme Court the authority to prescribe rules of procedure after verdict in criminal cases and the power to adopt and promulgate uniform rules of practice for civil actions at law in the District Courts. It has provided terms of Court in certain places at which federal Courts had not previously convened. A small number of judges have been added from time to time.

Despite these commendable accomplishments, sufficient progress has not been made. Much remains to be done in developing procedure and administration, but this alone will not meet modern needs. The problem must be approached in a more comprehensive fashion, if the United States is to have a judicial system worthy of the nation. Reason and necessity require the appointment of a sufficient number of judges to handle the business of the federal

Courts. These additional judges should be of a type and age which would warrant us in believing that they would vigorously attack their dockets, rather than permit their dockets to overwhelm them.

The cost of additional personnel should not deter us. It must be borne in mind that the expense of maintaining the judicial system constitutes hardly three-tenths of one percent of the cost of maintaining the federal establishment. While the estimates for the current fiscal year aggregate over $23,000,000 for the maintenance of the legislative branch of the government, and over $2,100,000,000 for the permanent agencies of the executive branch, the estimated cost of maintaining the judiciary is only about $6,500,000. An increase in the judicial personnel, which I earnestly recommend, would result in a hardly perceptible percentage of increase in the total annual budget.

This result should not be achieved, however, merely by creating new judicial positions in specific circuits or districts. The reform should be effectuated on the basis of a consistent system which would revitalize our whole judicial structure and assure the activity of judges at places where the accumulation of business is greatest. As congestion is a varying factor and cannot be foreseen, the system should be flexible and should permit the temporary assignment of judges to points where they appear to be most needed. The newly created personnel should constitute a mobile force, available for service in any part of the country at the assignment and direction of the Chief Justice. A functionary might well be created to be known as Proctor, or by some other suitable title, to be appointed by the Supreme Court and to act under its direction, charged with the duty of continuously keeping informed as to the state of federal judicial business throughout the United States and of assisting the Chief Justice in assigning judges to pressure areas.

I append hereto certain statistical information, which will give point to the suggestions I have made. [Statistics omitted. Ed.]

These suggestions are designed to carry forward the program for improving the processes of justice which we have discussed and worked upon since the beginning of your first administration.

The time has come when further legislation is essential.

To speed justice, to bring it within the reach of every citizen, to free it of unnecessary entanglements and delays are primary obligations of our government.

Respectfully submitted,

Homer S. Cummings, Attorney General

. . . The foregoing figures indicate that the number of cases terminated each year approximately equals the number of new cases filed, so that the courts are making no substantial gain in disposing of arrears.

The Draft of the Proposed Bill follows:

Be it enacted by the Senate and the House of Representatives of the United States of America in Congress assembled, That

(a) When any judge of a court of the United States, appointed to hold his office during good behavior, has heretofore or hereafter attained the age of seventy years and has held a commission or commissions as judge of any such court or courts at least ten years, continuously or otherwise, and within six months thereafter has neither resigned nor retired, the President, for each such judge who has not so resigned or retired, shall nominate, and by and with the advice and consent of the Senate, shall appoint one additional judge to the court to which the former is commissioned. Provided, That no additional judge shall be appointed hereunder if the judge who is of retirement age dies, resigns or retires prior to the nomination of such additional judge.

(b) The number of judges of any court shall be permanently increased by the number appointed thereto under the provisions of subsection (a) of this section. No more than fifty judges shall be appointed thereunder, nor shall any judge be so appointed if such appointment would result in (1) more than fifteen members of the Supreme Court of the United States, (2) more than two additional members so appointed to a circuit court of appeals, the Court of Claims, the United States Court of Customs and Patent Appeals, or the Customs Court, or (3) more than twice the number of judges now authorized to be appointed for any district or, in the case of judges appointed for more than one district, for any such group of districts.

(c) That number of judges which is at least two-thirds of the number of which the Supreme Court of the United States consists, of three-fifths of the number of which the United States Court of Appeals for the District of Columbia, the Court of Claims or the United States Court of Customs and Patent Appeals consists, shall constitute a quorum of such court.

(d) An additional judge shall not be appointed under the provisions of this section when the judge who is of retirement age is commissioned to an office as to which Congress has provided that a vacancy shall not be filled.

Sec. 2. (a) Any circuit judge hereafter appointed may be designated and assigned from time to time by the Chief Justice of the United States for service in the circuit court of appeals for any circuit. Any district judge hereafter appointed may be designated and assigned from time to time by the Chief Justice of the United States for service in any district court, or, subject to the authority of the Chief Justice, by the senior circuit judge of his circuit for service in any district court within the circuit. A district judge designated and assigned to another district hereunder may hold court separately and at the same time as the district judge in such district. All designations and assignments made hereunder shall be filed in the office of the clerk and entered on the minutes of both the court from and to which a judge is designated and assigned, and thereafter the judge so designated and assigned shall be authorized to discharge all the judicial duties (except the power of appointment to a statutory position or of permanent designation of a newspaper or depository of funds) of a judge of the court to which he is designated and assigned. The designation and assignment of a judge shall not impair his authority to perform such judicial duties of the court to which he was commissioned as may be necessary or appropriate. The designation and assignment of any judge may be terminated at any time by order of the Chief Justice or the senior circuit judge, as the case may be.

(b) After the designation and assignment of a judge by the Chief Justice, the senior circuit judge of the circuit in which such judge is commissioned may certify to the Chief Justice any consideration which such senior circuit judge believes to make advisable that the designated judge remain in or return for service in the court to which he was commissioned. If the Chief Justice deems the reasons sufficient he shall revoke, or designate the time of termination of, such designation and assignment.

(c) In case a trial or hearing has been entered upon but has not been concluded before the expiration of the period of service of a district judge designated and assigned hereunder, the period of service shall, unless terminated under the provisions of subsection (a) of this section, be deemed to be extended until the trial or hearing has been concluded. Any designated and assigned district judge who has held court in another district than his own shall have power, notwithstanding his absence from such district and the expiration of any time limit in his designation, to decide all matters which have been submitted to him within such district, to decide motions for new trials, settle bills of exceptions, certify or authenticate narratives of testimony, or perform any other act required by law or the rules to be performed in order to prepare any case so tried by him for review in an appellate court; and his action thereon in writing filed with the clerk of the court where the trial or hearing was had shall be as valid as if such action had been taken by him within that district and within the period of his designation. Any designated and assigned circuit judge who has sat on another court than his own shall have power, notwithstanding the expiration of any time limit in his designation, to participate in the decision of all matters submitted to the court while he was sitting and to perform or participate in any act appropriate to the disposition or review of matters submitted while he was sitting on such court, and his action thereon shall be as valid as if it had been taken while sitting on such court and within the period of his designation.

Sec. 3 (a) The Supreme Court shall have power to appoint a Proctor. It shall be his duty: (1) to obtain and, if deemed by the Court to be desirable, to publish information as to the volume, character, and status of litigation in the district courts and circuit courts of appeals, and such other information as the Supreme Court may from time to time require by order, and it shall be the duty of any judge, clerk or marshal of any court of the United States promptly to furnish such information as may be required by the Proctor; (2) to investigate the need of assigning district and circuit judges to other courts and to make recommendations thereon to the Chief Justice; (3) to recommend, with the approval of the Chief Justice, to any court of the United States methods for expediting cases pending on its dockets; and (4) to perform such other duties consistent with his office as the Court shall direct.

(b) The Proctor shall, by requisition upon the Public Printer, have any necessary printing and binding done at the Government Printing Office and authority is conferred upon the Public Printer to do such printing and binding.

(c) The salary of the Proctor shall be $10,000 per annum, payable out of the Treasury in monthly installments, which shall be in full compensation for the services required by law. He shall also be allowed, in the discretion of the Chief Justice, stationery, supplies, travel expenses, equipment, necessary professional and clerical assistance and miscellaneous expenses appropriate for performing the duties imposed by this section. The expenses in connection with the maintenance of his office shall be paid from the appropriation of the Supreme Court of the United States.

Sec. 4. There is hereby authorized to be appropriated, out of any money in the Treasury not otherwise appropriated, the sum of $100,000 for the salaries of additional judges and the other purposes of this Act during the fiscal year 1937.

Sec. 5. When used in this Act—

(a) The term "judge of retirement age" means a judge of a court of the United States, appointed to hold his office during good behavior, who has attained the age of seventy years and has held a commission or commissions as judge of any such court or courts at least ten years, continuously or otherwise, and within six months thereafter, whether or not he is eligible for retirement, has neither resigned nor retired.

(b) The term "circuit court of appeals" includes the United States Court of Appeals for the District of Columbia; the term "senior circuit judge" includes the Chief Justice of the United States Court of Appeals for the District of Columbia; and the term "circuit" includes the District of Columbia.

(c) The term "district court" includes the District Court of the District of Columbia but does not include the district court in any territory or insular possession.

(d) The term "judge" includes justice.

Sec. 6. This Act shall take effect on the thirtieth day after the date of its enactment.

Counterattack: The Court Reform Plan Defeated

Five and one-half months later the proposal was dead, killed in a vote by the Senate to recommit the measure to the judiciary committee, with the understanding that any provision dealing with the Supreme Court be deleted from the bill if and when it returned to the Senate floor. It amounted to a complete and humiliating defeat for the President. In the final vote only 20 loyal supporters voted against the motion, which had already been agreed upon by the Democratic leaders of the senior body. How was it that a President at the pinnacle of his power and popularity, and with such wide party support in both houses of Congress, could suffer such a humiliating defeat?

There are, of course, no simple answers to this difficult question. Roosevelt's surprising defeat in the Court battle came about for a number of complex reasons. One of the first things that hurt the President and prevented him from mobilizing his maximum strength in this struggle was the manner in which he introduced the proposal. In 1936 and 1937 the Court was on the minds of everyone who was involved in politics in Washington, and there was general feeling among a large majority that something would have to be done about the Court's persistence in invalidating New Deal legislation, passed by both houses of Congress and signed by the President. There was, however, a great deal of uncertainty about the best method of preventing the Court from continually vetoing the people's will, but at the same time no one wanted to do violence to one of the great American myths— the separation of powers of the three major branches of government.

Any solution to the problem called for consultation with a number of people who could have provided the President with some expert guidance on the subject, guidance which sensed the political realities of his move, not only from the point of view of the professional politicians and congressmen, but also of the legal profession, the Court itself (particularly its liberal members) and the American people as a whole. If the President had consulted his chosen advisors, he might have discovered how far it was possible to go and at what point he would run into really stiff opposition. He chose rather to hold his own counsel and listen only to his attorney general and solicitor general. He did not even consult his close personal friend and frequent advisor, Felix Frankfurter, a professor at the Harvard Law School. Although Frankfurter kept in close touch with the President on a wide range of subjects, particularly those dealing with law and the Supreme Court, which was his major interest, he was utterly unprepared for the February 5 announcement. He wrote to the President two days later that it had blown him "off the top of Vesuvius where you sat me some weeks ago. Yes, you 'shocked' me by the deftness of the general scheme for dealing with the mandate for national action which you received three times, in '32, and '34, and '36, and each time with increasing emphasis. You 'shocked' me no less by the dramatic untarnished secrecy with which you kept your scheme until you took the whole nation into your confidence."[29]

Two years earlier Frankfurter had written to the President on this subject and had outlined his strategy as to how to deal with the Court. It is worth reprinting in its entirety, for, in retrospect, it represents the soundest judgment rendered by anyone on the subject.

Felix Frankfurter
Letter to President Franklin D. Roosevelt
On How to Deal with the Court
May 29, 1935

Max Freedman, ed., *Roosevelt and Frankfurter, Their Correspondence 1928-1945* (Boston, 1967), 272-73.

Cambridge, Massachusetts
May 29, 1935

Dear Mr. President: In the interest of clarity may I put in a few words on paper the gist of my thoughts on the issues of the Supreme Court vs. The President.

1. Postponement of fighting out that issue at the present time does not rule the issue out as one on which you may later go to the country. I assume that a strategist like you will select time and circumstances most favorable for victory. I suspect that events may give you better conditions for battle than you have even now.

Decisions in other cases may accumulate popular grievances against the Court on issues so universally popular that the Borahs, the Clarks, the Nyes and all the current of opinion they represent will be with you in addition to the support you have today. That is why I think it so fortunate that the Administration has pending before Congress measures like the Social Security bill, the Holding Company bill, the Wagner bill, the Guffey bill. Go on with these. Put *them* up to the Supreme Court. Let the Court strike down any or all of them next winter or spring, especially by divided Court. *Then* propose a Constitutional amendment giving the national Government adequate power to cope with national economic and industrial problems. That will give you an overwhelming issue of a positive character arising at the psychological time for the '36 campaign, instead of mere negative issue of being "agin" the Court which, rising now, may not be able to sustain its freshness and dramatic appeal until election time.

2. That approach has these advantages:

(a) It defines a sharp issue—of the increase of Congressional power on industrial and economic problems—instead of attacking the Supreme Court's vague general powers. A general attack on the Court, unlimited in the changes it *may* cause, would give opponents a chance to play on vague fears of a leap in the dark and upon the traditionalist loyalties the Court is still able to inspire.

(b) It cuts across all technicalities of law and presents an issue which the common man can understand and which he can feel means something personally important to him.

I am, be assured, as anxious as you are that you should not try to fool the American people into believing that you can do more than the Supreme Court permits you to do. But I also know how much you still can do, how the Supreme Court can eat its words, and what a difference it makes in the Court's application of "the law" how statutes are drawn, how they are administered, how they are tested by the right selection of cases, how these cases are treated in lower courts by judges, district attorneys and government counsel, how they are handled and argued before the Supreme Court itself.

All of which is respectfully and affectionately submitted.

F.F.

That was unquestionably the best advice the President received on the issue, but he did not take it. Frankfurter remained loyal to the President in spite of this, but Roosevelt's failure to confer with others like Vice President Garner and the chairman of the Senate and House Judiciary Committees, Senator Henry F. Ashurst from Arizona and Congressman Hatton Sumners from Texas, was disastrous. Ignoring fellow Democrats like Senator Burton K. Wheeler, senior senator from Montana and Senator Joseph C. O'Mahoney of Wyoming, both of whom had expressed dissatisfaction with the Court and wanted to do something about it, drove them into the hands of the opposition, whereas earlier discussions with them might have won their support for a different court reform proposal.

The President also had informal access to leading members of the Court itself, particularly Brandeis and Stone, and if he had attempted to sound them out on the proposal before it was set, he might have avoided his difficulties. Prior consultation with such individuals would not necessarily have swung them into line as powerful advocates for the plan, but it might have led to modifications they would accept, or might have helped at least to neutralize their overt or covert opposition. As it turned out they (and many more) had very strong feelings on the subject, and Roosevelt's failure to consult with them or at least indirectly obtain their views on the subject was a tactical error of considerable magnitude. As far as the Democrats were concerned, however, it released them from the position in which they would have found themselves if it had been a real party issue, and allowed them to take a stand different from that of their President without considering it a breach of party loyalty.

Another major reason for the defeat of the court bill was the transparent hypocrisy of the plan itself. Initially masking its intent to pack the Court was "too clever by half," as Professor Leuchtenburg has put it, and the plan led to a certain confusion and later resentment.[30] No doubt the entire federal court system needed basic reform, but the President's plan was designed essentially to circumvent the present majority of the Supreme Court which had been nullifying the New Deal, slowly but surely.

Not to come out and say this, but rather to cloak his motive in broad general statements about the federal court system, was so transparently "phony" that it encouraged the false picture that many of the diehard opponents of the President were trying to promote, namely that of a power-hungry, dishonest manipulator, who was trying to undermine the American system, gain control of the Supreme Court and make himself a dictator. This point of view was even reflected by some responsible critics like Walter Lippmann who wrote:

> My feeling is that if Mr. Roosevelt's attempt to enhance his power by the judiciary bill, the reorganization bill, and the wages and hours bill is not checked here and now, we shall see actions that will astonish us even more than the scheme to pack the Court.[31]

The surprise and "tricky quality" of the proposal also worked to its detriment. In his research Attorney General Cummings had made the amazing discovery that in 1913 when McReynolds was attorney general in the Wilson administration, he had submitted a memorandum to the President proposing a plan whereby the President would appoint an additional judge to every federal district court where existing judges over the retiring age refused to quit. Cummings and later Roosevelt were tickled by the irony of their discovery, and it was one of the important reasons why they both warmed up so to a very similar plan (although this time they included the Supreme Court), which Cummings worked up into the President's proposal. They placed greater value on such aspects of the proposal as secrecy and irony, than on the political sensitivities of their party leaders and the people whom they represented.

There were many indications of the immediate unpopularity of the plan. Roosevelt's secretary of the treasury and personal friend, Henry Morgenthau, wrote that he had not met anyone who thought well of it.[32] Moreover, the initial message failed to capitalize upon the major complaints the President, and presumably his supporters, held against the attitude of the Court. In a book defending the President's grievances against the Court, and otherwise devoid of any criticism of his tactics, Robert Jackson has concluded that in the message

> the fighting issues, ready-made for the President, were not seized. There was not a word about the usurpation, the unwarranted interferences with lawful governmental activities, and the tortured construction of the Constitution, all of which could be proved against the Court from the words of its most respected members. It lacked the simplicity and clarity

which was the President's genius and, to men not learned in the procedures of the Court, much of it seemed technical and confusing.[33]

"Opponents of his plan," Professor Leuchtenburg has written, "had no difficulty in proving that Court inefficiency was a bogus issue and showing what the President really wanted was a more responsive Court":

> The over-age argument made little sense since one of the President's most consistent supporters had been the eighty-year-old Louis Brandeis, and the President's message offended many of the Justice's admirers. Septuagenarian senators put little stock in the argument that faculties of septuagenarian judges may be impaired. The seventy-nine-year-old Carter Glass pointed out that Littleton had written his great treatise on property law at the age of seventy-eight and that Lord Coke had been eighty-one when he produced his masterpiece "Coke Upon Littleton."[34]

The President, recognizing after the first month went by that his initial message had gotten the fight off on the wrong foot, tried to recover lost ground with a speech at a Washington victory dinner and several days later in a fireside chat on the subject. In both instances he argued that the Supreme Court was blocking the social and economic reforms necessary for recovery and for the further development of democracy in America; that, he continued, had been one of the situations the reform plan had been meant to correct. Although both speeches were quite successful efforts and probably won some doubtful supporters back to the fold, considerable damage had already been done by the dishonesty and the subterfuge of the original approach.

President Franklin D. Roosevelt Fireside Chat Discussing the Reorganization of the Judiciary
March 9, 1937

Rosenman, VI, 122-33.

Last Thursday I described in detail certain economic problems which everyone admits now face the Nation. For the many messages which have come to me after that speech, and which it is physically impossible to answer individually, I take this means of saying "thank you."

Tonight, sitting at my desk in the White House, I make my first radio report to the people in my second term of office.

I am reminded of that evening in March, four years ago, when I made my first radio report to you. We were then in the midst of the great banking crisis.

Soon after, with the authority of the Congress, we asked the Nation to turn over all of its privately held gold, dollar for dollar, to the Government of the United States.

Today's recovery proves how right that policy was.

But when, almost two years later, it came before the Supreme Court its constitutionality was upheld only by a five-to-four vote. The change of one vote would have thrown all the affairs of this great Nation back into hopeless chaos. In effect, four Justices ruled that the right under a private contract to exact a pound of flesh was more sacred than the main objectives of the Constitution to establish an enduring Nation.

In 1933 you and I knew that we must never let our economic system get completely out of joint again—that we could not afford to take the risk of another great depression.

We also became convinced that the only way to avoid a repetition of those dark days was to have a government with power to prevent and to cure the abuses and the inequalities which had thrown that system out of joint.

We then began a program of remedying those abuses and inequalities—to give balance and stability to our economic system—to make it bomb-proof against the causes of 1929.

Today we are only part-way through that program—and recovery is speeding up to a point where the dangers of 1929 are again becoming possible, not this week or month perhaps, but within a year or two.

National laws are needed to complete that program. Individual or local or state effort alone cannot protect us in 1937 any better than ten years ago.

It will take time—and plenty of time—to work out our remedies administratively even after legislation is passed. To complete our program of protection in time, therefore, we cannot delay one moment in making certain that our National Government has power to carry through.

Four years ago action did not come until the eleventh hour. It was almost too late.

If we learned anything from the depression we will not allow ourselves to run around in new circles of futile discussion and debate, always postponing the day of decision.

The American people have learned from the depression. For in the last three national elections an overwhelming majority of them voted a mandate that the Congress and the President begin the task of providing that protection—not after long years of debate, but now.

The Courts, however, have cast doubts on the ability of the elected Congress to protect us against catastophe by meeting squarely our modern social and economic conditions.

We are at a crisis in our ability to proceed with that protection. It is a quiet crisis. There are no lines of depositors outside closed banks. But to the far-sighted it is far-reaching in its possibilities of injury to America.

I want to talk with you very simply about the need for present action in this crisis—the need to meet the unanswered challenge of one-third of a Nation ill-nourished, ill-clad, ill-housed.

Last Thursday I described the American form of Government as a three horse team provided by the Constitution to the American people so that their field might be plowed. The three horses are, of course, the three branches of government—the

Congress, the Executive and the Courts. Two of the horses are pulling in unison today; the third is not. Those who have intimated that the President of the United States is trying to drive that team, overlook the simple fact that the President, as Chief Executive, is himself one of the three horses.

It is the American people themselves who are in the driver's seat.

It is the American people themselves who want the furrow plowed.

It is the American people themselves who expect the third horse to pull in unison with the other two.

I hope that you have re-read the Constitution of the United States in these past few weeks. Like the Bible, it ought to be read again and again.

It is an easy document to understand when you remember that it was called into being because the Articles of Confederation under which the original thirteen States tried to operate after the Revolution showed the need of a National Government with power enough to handle national problems. In its Preamble, the Constitution states that it was intended to form a more perfect Union and promote the general welfare; and the powers given to the Congress to carry out those purposes can be best described by saying that they were all the powers needed to meet each and every problem which then had a national character and which could not be met by merely local action.

But the framers went further. Having in mind that in succeeding generations many other problems then undreamed of would become national problems, they gave to the Congress the ample broad powers "to levy taxes . . . and provide for the common defense and general welfare of the United States."

That, my friends, is what I honestly believe to have been the clear and underlying purpose of the patriots who wrote a Federal Constitution to create a National Government with national power, intended as they said, "to form a more perfect union . . . for ourselves and our posterity."

For nearly twenty years there was no conflict between the Congress and the Court. Then Congress passed a statute which, in 1803, the Court said violated an express provision of the Constitution. The Court claimed the power to declare it unconstitutional and did so declare it. But a little later the Court itself admitted that it was an extraordinary power to exercise and through Mr. Justice Washington laid down this limitation upon it: "It is but a decent respect due to the wisdom, the integrity and the patriotism of the legislative body, by which any law is passed, to presume in favor of its validity until its violation of the Constitution is proved beyond all reasonable doubt."

But since the rise of the modern movement for social and economic progress through legislation, the Court has more and more often and more and more boldly asserted a power to veto laws passed by the Congress and State Legislatures in complete disregard of this original limitation.

In the last four years the sound rule of giving statutes the benefit of all reasonable doubt has been cast aside. The Court has been acting not as a judicial body, but as a policy-making body.

When the Congress has sought to stabilize national agriculture, to improve the conditions of labor, to safeguard business against unfair competition, to protect our national resources, and in many other ways, to serve our clearly national needs, the majority of the Court has been assuming the power to pass on the wisdom of these Acts of the Congress—and to approve or disapprove the public policy written into these laws.

That is not only my accusation. It is the accusation of most distinguished Justices of the present Supreme Court. I have not the time to quote to you all the language used by dissenting Justices in many of these cases. But in the case holding the Railroad Retirement Act unconstitutional, for instance, Chief Justice Hughes said in a dissenting opinion that the majority opinion was "a departure from sound principles," and placed "an unwarranted limitation upon the commerce clause." And three other Justices agreed with him.

In the case holding the A.A.A. unconstitutional, Justice Stone said of the majority opinion that it was a "tortured construction of the Constitution." And two other Justices agreed with him.

In the case holding the New York Minimum Wage Law unconstitutional, Justice Stone said that the majority were actually reading into the Constitution their own "personal economic predilections," and that if the legislative power is not left free to choose the methods of solving the problems of poverty, subsistence and health of large numbers in the community, then "government is to be rendered impotent." And two other Justices agreed with him.

In the face of these dissenting opinions, there is no basis for the claim made by some members of the Court that something in the Constitution has compelled them regretfully to thwart the will of the people.

In the face of such dissenting opinions, it is perfectly clear, that as Chief Justice Hughes has said: "We are under a Constitution, but the Constitution is what the Judges say it is."

The Court in addition to the proper use of its judicial functions has improperly set itself up as a third House of the Congress—a super-legislature, as one of the justices has called it—reading into the Constitution words and implications which are not there, and which were never intended to be there.

We have, therefore, reached the point as a Nation where we must take action to save the Constitution from the Court and the Court from itself. We must find a way to take an appeal from the Supreme Court to the Constitution itself. We want a Supreme Court which will do justice under the Constitution—not over it. In our Courts we want a government of laws and not of men.

I want—as all Americans want—an independent judiciary as proposed by the framers of the Constitution. That means a Supreme Court that will enforce the Constitution as written—that will refuse to amend the Constitution by the arbitrary exercise of judicial power—amendment by judicial say-so. It does not mean a judiciary so independent that it can deny the existence of facts universally recognized.

How then could we proceed to perform the mandate given us? It was said in last year's Democratic platform, "If these problems cannot be effectively solved within the Constitution, we shall seek such clarifying amendment as will assure the power to enact those laws, adequately to regulate commerce, protect public health and safety, and safeguard economic security." In other words, we said we would seek an amendment only if every other possible means by legislation were to fail.

When I commenced to review the situation with the problem squarely before me, I came by a process of elimination to the conclusion that, short of amendments, the only method which was clearly constitutional, and would at the same time carry out other much needed reforms, was to infuse new blood into all our Courts. We must have men worthy and equipped to carry out impartial justice. But, at the same time, we must have Judges who will bring to the Courts a present-day sense of the Constitution—Judges who will retain in the Courts the judicial functions of a court, and reject the legislative powers which the courts have today assumed.

In forty-five out of the forty-eight States of the Union, Judges are chosen not for life but for a period of years. In many States Judges must retire at the age of seventy. Congress has provided financial security by offering life pensions at full pay for Federal Judges on all Courts who are willing to retire at seventy. In the case of Supreme Court Justices, that pension is $20,000 a year. But all Federal Judges, once appointed, can, if they choose, hold office for life, no matter how old they may get to be.

What is my proposal? It is simply this: whenever a Judge or Justice of any Federal Court has reached the age of seventy and does not avail himself of the opportunity to retire on a pension, a new member shall be appointed by the President then in office, with the approval, as required by the Constitution, of the Senate of the United States.

That plan has two chief purposes. By bringing into the judicial system a steady and continuing stream of new and younger blood, I hope, first, to make the administration of all Federal justice speedier and, therefore, less costly; secondly, to bring to the decision of social and economic problems younger men who have had personal experience and contact with modern facts and circumstances under which average men have to live and work. This plan will save our national Constitution from hardening of the judicial arteries.

The number of Judges to be appointed would depend wholly on the decision of present Judges now over seventy, or those who would subsequently reach the age of seventy.

If, for instance, any one of the six Justices of the Supreme Court now over the age of seventy should retire as provided under the plan, no additional place would be created. Consequently, although there never can be more than fifteen, there may be only fourteen, or thirteen, or twelve. And there may be only nine.

There is nothing novel or radical about this idea. It seeks to maintain the Federal bench in full vigor. It has been discussed and approved by many persons of high authority ever since a similar proposal passed the House of Representatives in 1869.

Why was the age fixed at seventy? Because the laws of many States, the practice of the Civil Service, the regulations of the Army and Navy, and the rules of many of our Universities and of almost every great private business enterprise, commonly fix the retirement age at seventy years or less.

The statute would apply to all the courts in the Federal system. There is general approval so far as the lower Federal courts are concerned. The plan has met opposition only so far as the Supreme Court of the United States itself is concerned. If such a plan is good for the lower courts it certainly ought to be equally good for the highest Court from which there is no appeal.

Those opposing this plan have sought to arouse prejudice and fear by crying that I am seeking to "pack" the Supreme Court and that a baneful precedent will be established.

What do they mean by the words "packing the Court"?

Let me answer this question with a bluntness that will end all *honest* misunderstanding of my purposes.

If by that phrase "packing the Court" it is charged that I wish to place on the bench spineless puppets who would disregard the law and would decide specific cases as I wished them to be decided, I make this answer: that no President fit for his office would appoint, and no Senate of honorable men fit for their office would confirm, that kind of appointees to the Supreme Court.

But if by that phrase the charge is made that I would appoint and the Senate would confirm Justices worthy to sit beside present members of the Court who understand those modern conditions, that I will appoint Justices who will not undertake to override the judgment of the Congress on legislative policy, that I will appoint Justices who will act as Justices and not as legislators—if the appointment of such Justices can be called "packing the Courts," then I say that I and with me the vast majority of the American people favor doing just that thing—now.

Is it a dangerous precedent for the Congress to change the number of the Justices? The Congress has always had, and will have, that power. The number of Justices has been changed several times before, in the Administrations of John Adams and Thomas Jefferson—both signers of the Declaration of Independence—Andrew Jackson, Abraham Lincoln and Ulysses S. Grant.

I suggest only the addition of Justices to the bench in accordance with a clearly defined principle relating to a clearly defined age limit. Fundamentally, if in the future, America cannot trust the Congress it elects to refrain from abuse of our Constitutional usages, democracy will have failed far beyond the importance to it of any kind of precedent concerning the Judiciary.

We think it so much in the public interest to maintain a vigorous judiciary that we encourage the retirement of elderly Judges by offering them a life pension at full salary. Why then should we leave the fulfillment of this public policy to chance or make it dependent upon the desire or prejudice of any individual Justice?

It is the clear intention of our public policy to provide for a constant flow of new and younger blood into the Judiciary. Normally every President appoints a large number of District and Circuit Judges and a few members of the Supreme Court. Until my first term practically every President of the United States had appointed at least one member of the Supreme Court. President Taft appointed five members and named a Chief Justice; President Wilson, three; President Harding, four, including a Chief Justice; President Coolidge, one; President Hoover, three, including a Chief Justice.

Such a succession of appointments should have provided a Court well-balanced as to age. But chance and the disinclination of individuals to leave the Supreme bench have now given us a Court in which five Justices will be over seventy-five years of age before next June and one over seventy. Thus a sound public policy has been defeated.

I now propose that we establish by law an assurance against any such ill-balanced Court in the future. I propose that hereafter, when a Judge reaches the age of seventy, a new and younger Judge shall be added to the Court automatically. In this way I propose to enforce a sound public policy by law instead of leaving the composition of our Federal Courts, including the highest, to be determined by chance or the personal decision of individuals.

If such a law as I propose is regarded as establishing a new precedent, is it not a most desirable precedent?

Like all lawyers, like all Americans, I regret the necessity of this controversy. But the welfare of the United States, and indeed of the Constitution itself, is what we all must think about first. Our difficulty with the Court today rises not from the Court as an institution but from human beings within it. But we cannot yield our constitutional destiny to the personal judgment of a few men who, being fearful of the future, would deny us the necessary means of dealing with the present.

This plan of mine is no attack on the Court; it seeks to restore the Court to its rightful and historic place in our system of Constitutional Government and to have it resume its high task of building anew on the Constitution "a system of living law." The Court itself can best undo what the Court has done.

I have thus explained to you the reasons that lie behind our efforts to secure results by legislation within the Constitution. I hope that thereby the difficult process of constitutional amendment may be rendered unnecessary. But let us examine that process.

There are many types of amendment proposed. Each one is radically different from the other. There is no substantial group within the Congress or outside it who are agreed on any single amendment.

It would take months or years to get substantial agreement upon the type and language of an amendment. It would take months and years thereafter to get a two-thirds majority in favor of that amendment in *both* Houses of the Congress.

Then would come the long course of ratification by three-fourths of all the States. No amendment which any powerful economic interests or the leaders of any powerful political party have had reason to oppose has ever been ratified within anything like a reasonable time. And thirteen States which contain only five percent of the voting population can block ratification even though the thirty-five States with ninety-five percent of the population are in favor of it.

A very large percentage of newspaper publishers, Chambers of Commerce, Bar Associations, Manufacturers' Associations, who are trying to give the impression that they really do want a constitutional amendment would be the first to exclaim as soon as an amendment was proposed, "Oh! I was for an amendment all right, but this amendment that you have proposed is not the kind of an amendment that I was thinking about. I am, therefore, going to spend my time, my efforts and my money to block that amendment, although I would be awfully glad to help get some other kind of amendment ratified."

Two groups oppose my plan on the ground that they favor a constitutional amendment. The first includes those who fundamentally object to social and economic legislation along modern lines. This is the same group who during the campaign last Fall tried to block the mandate of the people.

Now they are making a last stand. And the strategy of that last stand is to suggest the time-consuming process of amendment in order to kill off by delay the legislation demanded by the mandate.

To them I say: I do not think you will be able long to fool the American people as to your purposes.

The other group is composed of those who honestly believe the amendment process is the best and who would be willing to support a reasonable amendment if they could agree on one.

To them I say: we cannot rely on an amendment as the immediate or only answer to our present difficulties. When the time comes for action, you will find that many of those who pretend to support you will sabotage any constructive amendment which is proposed. Look at these strange bed-fellows of yours. When before have you found them really at your side in your fights for progress?

And remember one thing more. Even if an amendment were passed, and even if in the years to come it were to be ratified, its meaning would depend upon the kind of Justices who would be sitting on the Supreme Court bench. An amendment, like the rest of the Constitution, is what the Justices say it is rather than what its framers or you might hope it is.

This proposal of mine will not infringe in the slightest upon the civil or religious liberties so dear to every American.

My record as Governor and as President proves my devotion to those liberties. You who know me can have no fear that I would tolerate the destruction by any branch of government of any part of our heritage of freedom.

The present attempt by those opposed to progress to play upon the fears of danger to personal liberty brings again to mind that crude and cruel strategy tried by the same opposition to frighten the workers of America in a pay-envelope propaganda against the Social Security Law. The workers were not fooled by that propaganda then. The people of America will not be fooled by such propaganda now.

I am in favor of action through legislation:

First, because I believe that it can be passed at this session of the Congress.

Second, because it will provide a reinvigorated, liberal-minded Judiciary necessary to furnish quicker and cheaper justice from bottom to top.

Third, because it will provide a series of Federal Courts willing to enforce the Constitution as written, and unwilling to assert legislative powers by writing into it their own political and economic policies.

During the past half century the balance of power between the three great branches of the Federal Government, has been tipped out of balance by the Courts in direct contradiction of the high purposes of the framers of the Constitution. It is my purpose to restore that balance. You who know me will accept my solemn assurance that in a world in which democracy is under attack, I seek to make American democracy succeed. You and I will do our part.

Both the nature of the proposal and its timing were also harmful to the President's objectives. Many critics of the Court, besides Frankfurter, favored a constitutional amendment which would either give impetus to the retirement of overaged members of the Court or would give the Congress explicit power to legislate in the areas then restricted by the Court. Roosevelt rejected that approach because he was uncertain that a two-thirds vote could be obtained in Congress, or that its members could agree on broad enough language to cover necessary social and economic legislation. Furthermore, he was doubtful whether such an amendment could obtain the endorsement of the required number of states in a reasonable period of time. He wrote Frankfurter:

> Supposing such an amendment had passed at the close of this session, every state legislature would have adjourned for the year. In 1938, only about one-third of the legislatures meet and because of the Congressional elections in 1938 the issue would, in all probability, be delayed in enough states to make ratification in 1938 impossible.
>
> That brings us to 1939. The chances are that quite aside from the issue an unwieldy Democratic majority in both Houses will be slightly reduced as a result of the 1938 elections. Any such reduction would be used as an argument against ratification thus, in all probability, leaving the amendment unratified up to and through the 1940 national election.[35]

Roosevelt then went on to make a point which revealed a sense of true political cynicism that many would not have believed of him:

> If I were in private practice and without a conscience, I would gladly undertake for a drawing account of fifteen or twenty million dollars (easy enough to raise) to guarantee that an amendment would not be ratified prior to the 1940 elections. In other words, I think I could withhold ratification in thirteen states and I think you will agree with my judgment on this.[36]

The point that Roosevelt missed in his extremely acute analysis of the difficulties in getting an amendment to the Constitution ratified was that ratification of the amendment might not have been necessary to accomplish his objective. The Court was teetering precariously on its (usually) one-vote majority against the New Deal, and the psychological impact of a threatened amendment limiting its power or affecting its structure might well have been all that was needed to bring the Court around. Actually, such a reversal was already in the offing, and the threat of a constitutional amendment would have enhanced its probability.

But the timing of a drive for an amendment or any other method of changing the power of the Court to veto progressive legislation was critically important. Roosevelt apparently never seriously considered raising the Court issue during the 1936 election campaign, but that was when the issue should properly have been joined. Franklin D. Roosevelt and the New Deal were the issues of the 1936 elections, but in endorsing them overwhelmingly the people had not underwritten any changes in the Court or in the Constitution which the President might see fit to make. It would have taken a much more powerful campaign than the President and his supporters mounted, and it would have had to have drawn the major issue very sharply, stating explicitly that the continuation of the New Deal and all that it implied would be impossible if the Court were not restructured.

Roosevelt could have used all of his tremendously effective techniques of persuasion in driving home this point, but in failing to utilize the election as a means of obtaining a specific mandate for changing either the Court or its point of view, he lost a golden opportunity which might have insured an orderly change immediately following the election. The fact that the Republican leadership realized that the President would move on the Court issue after the election does not at all mean that the people understood this, or that they were not surprised and shocked when they heard of the President's plan. They should have been given an opportunity to vote on this question; they were not, and that was one of the vital weaknesses of Roosevelt's attempt to reform the Court.

These were decisions of a strategic nature over which the President had full control. Yet there were a number of other factors which also contributed significantly to the defeat of the Court plan over which Roosevelt had little or no influence. Probably heading the list in this category was the role of the Supreme Court justices themselves. Each of them was opposed to the plan, and Chief Justice Hughes and Justice Brandeis were quite active in contributing to its defeat. The President's young troubleshooter, Tom Corcoran, who was close to Brandeis, got permission to sound out the 79-year-old justice on the proposal just before its announcement, and Brandeis quickly indicated that he was completely opposed to it.[37] Later when the leader of the Senate's opposition forces, Senator Burton K. Wheeler, came to him and requested that the justice sign a statement defending the Court against the President's charge of inefficiency and delay, Brandeis put Wheeler in touch with Hughes, who had originally turned down the judiciary committee's invitation to testify on the proposal. Hughes agreed to write a letter to the committee, probably upon Brandeis' urging, dealing with the charges of inefficiency and delay contained in the President's initial proposal. Brandeis and Van Devanter signed the letter. It was made public just about one and a half months after the proposal was announced, and it had a devastating influence upon the public's reaction to the Court plan. The black-robed justices of the Supreme Court had an aura of mystery and majesty about them, and a statement from three of its most revered members, covering a full range of the Court's divided opinions, had considerable impact upon the public.

The letter began by refuting the arguments contained in the President's proposal which charged that the Supreme Court was congested and "by sheer necessity of keeping up with its business," was forced to "decline, without even an explanation to hear 87% of the cases presented to it by private litigants."[38] Replying to this charge, Justice Hughes argued:

> The Supreme Court is fully abreast of its work. . . . There is no congestion of cases upon our calendar.
>
> This gratifying condition has obtained for several years. We have been able for several terms to adjourn after disposing of all cases which are ready to be heard.[39]

The President and the chief justice were talking right past each other with respect to this charge, because Roosevelt was criticizing the practice of the Court's failure to grant *certiorari* in a large percentage of cases submitted to it (between 80 and 90 percent), and Chief Justice Hughes was talking about the much smaller number of cases which the Court actually heard and ruled upon. This dispute was far too technical for the public to follow, and the chief justice's tactics of responding to it by citing a completely different but effective statistic might have been "dirty pool," but it was a brilliant debating point and won the argument with the public. In a more detailed explanation of how the Court works, Hughes dismissed the President's criticism that the procedure did not properly serve the ends of justice because so many petitions for *certiorari* were denied by simply stating that the Court only considered those cases which it judged to be in the public interest.

Then the chief justice turned with devastating logic to the proposal that an increase in the number of judges would improve the efficiency of the Court:

> An increase in the number of Justices of the Supreme Court, apart from any question of policy, which I do not discuss, would not promote the efficiency of the Court. It is believed that it would impair the efficiency so long as the Court acts as a unit. There would be more judges to hear, more judges to confer, more judges to discuss, more judges to be convinced and to decide.[40]

With respect to the suggestion that such an enlarged Court might divide itself in hearing cases, Hughes sharply replied that a decision by a part of the Court would not be satisfactory, in addition to the fact that the Constitution authorized only "one Supreme Court."[41]

There could be no denying that the chief justice had the better of the argument, or that the letter had a considerable impact upon the general public. Vice President Garner immediately called the President at Warm Springs, Georgia, where he was vacationing, and told him simply: "We're licked."[42] Presidential supporter and later Supreme Court Justice Jackson considered the letter to be the most significant factor in the defeat of the Court plan. Hughes was pleased with his handiwork, and later wrote:

> This letter appears to have had a devastating effect by destroying the specious contention as to the need of additional justices to expedite the work of the Court. It had the effect of focusing attention on the real purpose of the bill.[43]

Another factor which contributed to the downfall of the Court plan was that it provided the Congress, which had for some time been bridling under its eclipse by the President, with an opportunity to assert its own position on a public question. Roosevelt made it all the easier by making this an exclusive presidential proposal (complete with drafted bill), and directing it against a revered target—the Supreme Court. During the dark days of his first term and well into its third and fourth year, Congress offered the President the greatest degree of cooperation. Urgent bills, drafted in the executive branch, were hustled through the Congress, sometimes in a few days, occasionally in a few hours. During the New Deal the President had become the center of the decision-making process, not only in his capacity as Chief of Foreign Affairs and administrative head of the government, but in the legislative field as well.

Over the years many members of Congress, particularly important public figures like Wheeler, Garner and Speaker Bankhead, began to resent their loss of power and prestige, and they also began to become concerned about the general philosophy and direction of the New Deal. The President was quite aware that he led a united party only by virtue of a combination of extremely tenuous conditions which forced lifelong conservatives into a coalition with militant liberals. That coalition was forced together by the pressures of the Great Depression, but as those pressures eased somewhat and the programs of the New Deal began to foster the growth of labor unions in the North, minimum wages and federal housing, etc., many of the southern and border-state conservative Democrats became restless and privately more estranged from their leader.

Roosevelt was very conscious of the fragile nature of his New Deal alliance in the Congress. Frankfurter recorded a conversation he had with the President and Ferdinand Pecora in the Oval Room of the White House in the summer of 1935, which reflected this awareness. The three were discussing a row which had broken out between conservative Democratic Senator Millard Tydings from Maryland and Harold Ickes. Two very powerful figures in the Senate, Senator Pat Harrison from Mississippi and Majority Leader Joseph Robinson of Arkansas, had taken up the cudgels for Tydings and were demanding Ickes' scalp. Commenting on the general situation, Roosevelt was reported to have said:

> Moreover, at bottom, the leaders like Joe Robinson, though he has been loyal, and Pat Harrison are troubled about the whole New Deal. They just wonder where the man in the White House is taking the old Democratic party. During their long public life, forty years or so, they knew it was the old Democratic party. They were safe and when the Republicans got into trouble, the old Democratic party won nationally. But in any event they, and in the South without opposition, were all right and old-fashioned. But now they just wonder where that fellow in the White House is taking the good old Democratic party. They are afraid there is going to be a new Democratic party which they will not like. That's the basic fact in all these controversies and that explains why I will have trouble with my own Democratic party from this time on in trying to carry out further programs of reform and recovery. I know the problem inside my party but I intend to appeal from it to the American people and to go steadily forward with all I have.[44]

When the Court battle developed it provided a perfect outlet for these latent but strong feelings. The President had not consulted these men in determining his course of action. Moreover, he was trampling on an institution for which they still had a great deal of respect. The Supreme Court's reversal of many New Deal measures bothered the White House more than it did Pat Harrison, Vice President Garner or Millard Tydings, who thought much of the legislation was too socialistic anyway. Furthermore, the Court's rejection of New Deal legislation on constitutional grounds did not enhance the prestige of the Congress, for the statutes had been imposed upon the legislature by the executive branch to begin with. Legislators were quite aware that Congress had earned the reputation of being merely a "rubber stamp" for Roosevelt and the New Deal, and they were not pleased one bit. This was a Congress in which the President's party possessed a better than 4 to 1 majority in the House and an almost 5 to 1 advantage in the Senate, and yet there appeared to be nothing Roosevelt could do to stem the revolt. As one historian observed: "Men who had feared to oppose his economic policies, because they anticipated popular disapproval, now had the perfect justification for breaking with the President and going to the people."[45]

Vice President Garner, who presided over the Senate and was a powerful figure in the Congress, was seen to hold his fingers to his nose with one hand and his thumb pointing downward with the other hand the first time he heard of the Court plan. Garner did not openly oppose the President, but he left Washington for a protracted period during the middle of the battle, and he did nothing to work for its success. In the House both Speaker Bankhead and Majority Leader Sam Rayburn were opposed to the Court plan, along with powerful figures like Congressman Sumners, chairman of the judiciary committee, and Celler of New York, ranking Democrat on the committee. Oldline southern Democrats like Harry Byrd and Carter Glass of Virginia were both in opposition, and so was the normally strong Roosevelt supporter, Senator Tom Connally from Texas. The President also lacked the support he frequently had from the Progressives, George Norris[46] and Hiram Johnson, and farmer-laborite Henrik Shipstead. He was opposed by western Democrats like Senators O'Mahoney, Wheeler and Burke. Roosevelt was able to maintain the support of liberals like Senators Robert F. Wagner and Hugo Black, but he was deserted by other liberals like Governor Herbert Lehman of New York.

Senate Majority Leader Robinson, although personally lukewarm to the scheme, went down the line for the President, expecting to be named as Roosevelt's first appointee to the Court, but after his unexpected death in the middle of the floor fight on the Court bill, any chances for it collapsed and Garner was pulled in to work out as graceful an administration withdrawal as possible. Robinson's death was the climactic event which brought tumbling down whatever tenuous majority the President's plan might have had. Robinson was a solid member of the Senate establishment, and he had been able to pledge a number of votes on the strength of the argument (probably unspoken) that if the President's plan went through, he would realize his lifelong ambition by being the President's first choice for the Court. Some members would have voted for the Court bill on this basis alone, but when Robinson was stricken with a fatal heart attack just as the debate on the Court bill was moving into high gear, these same individuals felt no obligation to support the measure in his absence.

Two other events referred to earlier were also decisive in turning the tide against the President's Court plan. They undoubtedly had considerable impact upon the public's view of the whole business, and convinced many that the proposed change was now totally unnecessary. The first was the reversal of the Court's position, or more specifically, Justice Roberts' position, on the right of a state to pass a minimum wage law. In the 1920s the Supreme Court had ruled that Congress could not establish a minimum wage law in the District of Columbia,[47] and ten months before the President proposed his plan, the Court had declared unconstitutional a New York State statute fixing a minimum wage for women.[48]

Justice Roberts had voted with the majority in the New York decision, but soon after the election in 1936 he told the chief justice that he was prepared to vote to uphold yet another minimum wage law passed in the State of Washington. Hughes was delighted with this information, yet he bided his time before announcing the majority decision in the case.[49]

For one thing, it was necessary to await the return of the ailing Justice Stone in order to round out the majority, and for another, the chief justice wanted to delay the decision until a decent period of time had elapsed after the President announced his plan, taking care that it would not look like the Court was simply responding to pressure from the other branch. It would, of course, be mere conjecture to speculate that the chief justice also timed the decision so that it would have the most dramatic impact on the course of the Court battle then going on. A New Deal lawyer remarked at the time of the *West Coast Hotel* decision that "a switch in time saved nine."[50] In his opinion for the majority (Justices Hughes, Roberts, Brandeis, Stone and Cardozo), the chief justice bore heavily on former Chief Justice Taft's dissent in the 1920 minimum wage case, overruling this decision and endorsing the right of the states to engage in wage regulation legislation. He also elaborated upon the reasons for Roberts' shift of position. In the New York minimum wage case where Roberts had taken a different position, the litigant had not challenged the validity of the 1920 (Adkins) case, and if that decision stood, then the precedents were clearly in favor of overruling any minimum wage law. If the Court's previous decision was to be overturned, however, then Roberts was free to make a fresh judgment on the principle involved. If their reasoning appears confusing, much of what the Court has done in its previous history partakes of this same doubletalk.

The opponents of the Court plan were greatly encouraged by the *West Coast Hotel* decision because they felt that it would pull some of the wavering props out from under the President's already shaky position. Roosevelt and his last-ditch supporters, on the other hand, were somewhat perplexed by this new turn of events. They could not be (at least publicly) critical of the decision, for the majority of the Court had now swung around to their point of view. This became more evident when two weeks later the same majority upheld the National Labor Relations Act with its guarantees of the rights of workers to organize into unions of their own choosing,[51] and six weeks later when the Court decided that the Social Security Act fell within the constitutional jurisdiction of the general welfare clause.[52]

However, the margin of victory was slim and still very precarious. No one could psyche out Roberts' basic position at that point, and feelings were that it might very well be that in the next case he would return to the neanderthal wing of the Court, and the New Deal would be right back where it had always been. In this sense the new development was of very dubious value to the President, for it really gave him no real assurance about the future. By indicating to the public that the Court had finally "come around," it further weakened Roosevelt's chances of getting his Court bill through the Senate. Robinson was disturbed. He told a White House aide:

> The thing to do Joe [Keenan], is to settle the thing right now. This bill's raising hell in the Senate. Now it's going to be worse than ever, but if the

President wants to compromise I can get him a couple of extra justices tomorrow. What he ought to do is say he's won, which he has, agree to compromise to make the thing sure, and wind the whole business up.[53]

But again Attorney General Cummings' opinion prevailed:

It is not a wholesome situation when an administration, under a mandate to carry out a progressive program, must face a court of nine with four votes lost to it in advance. The margin is too narrow and the risk is too great.[54]

What Cummings and the President failed to understand was that they were prepared to take an even greater risk—a defeat of the Court bill—rather than jeopardize the complete revolution. The President was still overconfident and badly informed of the sentiment in the country at that time.

But things were to get still worse. Roosevelt failed to rally support among the two largest organized groups in the country which had benefited most from the New Deal, the farm organizations and organized labor, both of which had supported the New Deal up to that point.[55] Two of the major farm organizations (the Grange and the American Farm Bureau) were strongly opposed to the Court plan, and despite their gratitude to Roosevelt for his continued support of their interests, they refused to give even formal endorsement to the proposal. On the other hand, both the major labor organizations, the American Federation of Labor (A.F. of L.) and the Congress of Industrial Organizations (CIO), formally endorsed the bill, but did very little more than that. The CIO was distracted by massive organizing drives, and its leader, John L. Lewis, was disappointed in the failure of the President to come to labor's defense during the sit-down strikes and other violent labor-management confrontations then going on. Labor's Non-Partisan League, under the leadership of Major Berry, did try to lobby for the measure on Capitol Hill, with very meager success. There was much opposition to the Court bill among many of the Republican conservative-oriented A.F. of L. leaders, and the CIO people were too preoccupied with their own troubles to do much at all.

After the Court's favorable decision on the National Labor Relations Act, the labor movement was less interested in the Court bill than ever, and a senator or congressman could oppose it with impunity as far as union members were concerned. It should also be noted that this was almost ten years before the labor movement started to organize its political potential effectively, and although Roosevelt and the New Deal received overwhelming electoral support from union members, the appeal was made and won on an individual rather than an organizational basis. Roosevelt demonstrated this in the election of 1940 when union members ignored John L. Lewis' appeal to vote against Roosevelt and for Wendell Willkie.

As if the Court's reversal of its earlier minimum wage decision and its approval of the National Labor Relations Act and the Social Security Act were not enough, towards the end of the session the aging Justice Van Devanter wrote to the President asking him to accept his resignation at the end of the spring term of the Court. This, of course, increased the President's new majority on the Court and prompted even his staunch supporter from South Carolina, Senator James F. Byrnes, to ask: "Why run for a train after you've caught it?"[56] But the President apparently felt that he was too far committed to back up an inch and the fight droned on until the middle of the summer. The President's dander was up and he was convinced that the people were behind him on this issue. He was wrong, and that misjudgment betrayed him into plowing ahead into the oncoming defeat and the consequences which followed from it.

The combination of the Court's reversal, Van Devanter's resignation and finally Majority Leader Robinson's sudden and tragic death forced the Senate to move to kill the President's proposal much more quickly and with less subtlety than it would have normally. Vice President Garner went to Arkansas from Texas to attend Joe Robinson's funeral and then returned to Washington for the first time in weeks to attempt to engineer a face-saving *coup de grace* for the Court bill. He saw the President on July 19 and asked him if he wanted it "with the bark on or the bark off." Roosevelt replied: "With the bark off."[57] Garner then proceeded to tell him that he was beaten and asked for and received authorization to make the best deal possible under the circumstances to resolve the problem. The result was several hurried meetings and finally an agreement between both sides to recommit the bill to the Judiciary Committee of the Senate, which would report out a new Court bill within ten days. Private agreement had already been reached that the new Court bill would be introduced without the sections dealing with the Supreme Court and several other undesirable provisions. The Senate voted in favor of this motion on July 21, and the President's plan to "pack" the Supreme Court was dead.

The list of reasons previously advanced as an explanation of how and why the Court bill was killed is closely related to the pervasive role of public opinion. It is certainly true that many members of the Senate had already broken with Roosevelt, in spirit if not in flesh, and the bill merely provided them with the opportunity of doing what they had long wanted to do, but had not dared. The public's attitude provided them with a kind of smokescreen of impunity, for the public would not necessarily interpret their vote against the bill as a vote against the President. The public did not think of the Court bill in those terms. Many sympathized with Roosevelt's opposition to the Court without supporting his method of correcting the situation. Public opinion also figured prominently in Justice Hughes' strategy. He realized as well as anyone the unpopularity of his Court's earlier decisions against the New Deal, and he also understood how vulnerable the Court was to public opinion if the attitude prevailed. The President had assisted him immeasurably by his mismanagement in presenting the proposal and the content of the plan itself. Then when the Court switched its opinion in the minimum wage case and Van Devanter resigned, the public saw no further reason for Court reform and tended to side with the Court against the President.

Public opinion research at that time clearly confirms this conclusion. Sampling respondents to a rather wide range of questions scheduled before, during and after the Court struggle indicate that it is clear that the public strongly opposed the President's efforts. In response to the very direct question of whether or not they supported the President's Court reform plan, Dr. Gallup and his associates at the American Institute of Public Opinion found that an increasing majority were opposed to it as the months rolled on.

POLLS CONDUCTED BY
THE AMERICAN INSTITUTE OF PUBLIC OPINION
(Gallup Poll) Princeton, New Jersey

Question: "Should Congress pass the President's Supreme Court Plan?"[58]

	Yes	No
April 5, 1937	47%	53%
April 26, 1937	46%	54%
May 17, 1937[59]	42%	58%
May 24, 1937	41%	59%
June 7, 1937[60]	40%	60%

In a series of questions of a somewhat wider scope, Dr. Gallup obtained evidence of even greater opposition to specifics of the President's plan and his tactics involved in it:

Would you favor curbing the power of the Supreme Court to declare acts of Congress unconstitutional?
(Dec. '36)   No 59%

Would you favor a constitutional amendment requiring Supreme Court Justices to retire at some age between 70 and 75?
(Apr. '37)   Yes 64%

Would you favor a compromise on the Court Plan which would permit the President to appoint two new judges instead of six?
(May '37)   No 62%

Would you like to have President Roosevelt continue his fight to enlarge the Supreme Court?
(Sept. '37)   No 68%

Do you believe the Roosevelt administration should try to defeat the reelection of Democratic congressmen who opposed the Supreme Court plan?
(Sept. '37)   No 73%[61]

Elmo B. Roper, jr. conducted a poll for *Fortune* magazine during the last week in March and the first week in April of 1937, and also questioned his respondents with respect to their support or opposition to the President's Court proposal. Roper discovered that 28 percent of the people he polled were in favor of the proposed law, 36 percent were solidly against it and another 22 percent did not know. But still a fourth group, representing 14 percent of the sample, were strongly opposed to the President's solution to the problem, but were almost as firmly convinced that something "should be done about the Supreme Court."[62]

Roper was anxious to find out from the 28 percent who strongly supported the President's proposal what their reasons were for agreeing with the President. His answers confirmed several of my earlier conclusions. Less than 1 percent of the group cited Roosevelt's initial specious argument that his plan would speed up the work of the Court, and only 13 percent favored the "retirement-at-70" principle contained in his bill. The remaining 86 percent felt that the Court was blocking the will of the majority of the American people. Although Roper pointed out that the size and character of his sample precluded absolute accuracy, he did argue that his results were accurate enough to indicate "which way the wind was blowing."[63]

> They are accurate enough to warrant the conclusion that a majority of the people who have an opinion on the issue feel that something should be done to the Court; that it has too often blocked the will of the people, but that the President's proposal does not properly solve the question.[64]

It is clear then that behind the revolts of Congress during the embargo case in 1809 (see Volume I of this series) and 1937 there was a groundswell of public opinion that would have made any other action impossible. The people may have been badly informed in both instances, and lacked the proper information for forming an intelligent opinion of either the embargo or the Court plan, but they clearly developed strong opinions on the subject, and their senators and congressmen knew where they stood. Unfortunately, only fragmentary evidence of this kind of activity is available in either situation, but the little we do have does give some indication of "which way the wind was blowing." In Jefferson's papers there were discovered, from the State of Massachusetts alone, 31 different petitions with 5571 signatures protesting the embargo.[65] Countless violations of the embargo were recorded in every border and coastal state, and frequent violence marked encounters between the law enforcement agents and American citizens asserting what they considered their freedom to trade as they saw fit.[66] Opposition to the Court plan was less violent than the flagrant violations of the embargo, but a great deal more systematic.

There is no doubt that although the forces supporting Roosevelt's proposals were uncharacteristically quiet and ineffective during the struggle, organized groups of opposition were singularly active and apparently successful in crystallizing opinion against the plan. Central to these efforts was the work of the National Committee to Uphold Constitutional Government, which was initially organized to fight the Court bill.[67] Frank Gannett, a wealthy publisher of 18 newspapers with a total circulation of 665,000 (the third largest chain in the country), poured time, energy, newsprint and money into the committee's fight. He personally advanced $49,000 into the coffers of the committee to get it off to a good start, and in the course of a little more than a year, $320,000 was collected. Working closely with a number of different opposition leaders in the Senate and the House, the committee exploited the free franking privileges of members of Congress and spent less than $200,000 distributing over 15,000,000 pieces of literature, all of which presented urgent appeals of a nonpartisan nature against the bill.

The mailing was highly selective, concentrating on opinion and community leaders, professional men and business leaders.[68] In all instances the committee urged the recipients of its correspondence to write to their representatives, urging the defeat of the bill. The committee also supplied 2000 daily newspapers with press releases and 300 radio stations carried its packaged talks. At a critical moment during the Senate debate over the Court bill, one of the opposition leaders informed Gannett that a modified version of the Court bill had an eight-vote majority and that its fate would be decided by 12 senators who favored the plan but were wavering. Gannett immediately sent 30,000 telegrams to voters in those 12 states, and the senators' offices were bombarded with protests. The committee was convinced that their activity was successful, for several days later 8 of the 12 senators came out against the bill.[69] Another senator who announced his opposition to the bill admitted that out of 30,000 letters he received with regard to the Court bill, only a few hundred approved the measure.[70] William Allen White provided the clue to how powerful middle-class opinion was largely molded by the "leaders' whom the Committee deluged with material":

> [T]he day after election the middle-class moves in and runs the show through its various organizations of public expression, the newspapers, the churches, the lodges, the clubs, the public corridors—from the pullman's observation car on down to the filling station. The middle class for one hundred fifty years has organized itself to rule by public expression in these various outlets. The only way the proletariat makes its will public is in the mob and riot which are soon suppressed and generally remains echoes. Any President is powerless before middle class opinion. . . .[71]

The defeat proved to be costly for the New Deal, for it strengthened the anti-Roosevelt coalition in both houses of Congress and presented a serious obstacle to the passage of further New Deal measures. Leuchtenburg argues that the Court defeat "destroyed the unity of the Democratic party. . . . The new Court might be willing to uphold new laws, but an angry and divided Congress would pass few of them for the justices to consider."[72] In August of that same year, economic disaster recurred and the nation plunged into a serious recession before it had fully recovered. *The New York Times* business index dropped 25 points, and steel production fell from 80 percent of capacity to 19 percent. In the next four months two million people lost their jobs. WPA and relief rolls sky-rocketed and once again hunger stalked the land. Not until the war economy of the 1940s was underway did the economy right itself again.[73]

Though he suffered a critical strategic setback, Roosevelt had not really lost his fight against the Court's restrictive views. Van Devanter's retirement and Robert's "switch in time" had undercut the determined anti-New Deal majority, and despite the fact that the Court "packing" plan failed, Roosevelt's philosophy of government intervention to protect the public interest prevailed. Benjamin F. Wright noted in 1942:

> No event, or series of events, has ever before produced so many changes in constitutional doctrine within such a short time. In the four subsequent terms of the Court the reversals and distinctions have been so numerous and so sweeping that today much of the constitutional law of 1936 appears to belong to a different constitution.[74]

Leuchtenburg pointed out that "from 1937 to 1946, the Court reversed thirty-two of its earlier decisions. Eight of the precedents had been adopted unanimously."[75]

> The Constitutional Revolution of 1937 altered fundamentally the character of the Court's business, the nature of its decisions, and the alignment of its friends and foes. From the Marshall Court to the Hughes Court the tribunal had been largely concerned with questions of property

rights. After 1937 its agenda concentrated on matters of civil liberties and other personal rights. For more than a century before 1937, the Court had been inclined to safeguard corporations and other property interests from reform-minded legislatures. But after the Constitutional Revolution, Robert McCloskey has observed, "The businessman, so long the Court's darling, was shorn of his constitutional fleece and now faced popular sovereignty protected by nothing save his own ample resources. While from 1800 to 1937 the principal critics of the Supreme Court were social reformers and the main defenders the propertied groups who were the chief beneficiaries of the Court's decisions, after 1937 roles were reversed with reformers commending and conservatives censuring the Court."[76]

Roosevelt had won his revolution but at a cost he had not expected to pay.

FDR's Impact

It has recently become fashionable to minimize the accomplishments of Franklin D. Roosevelt and the New Deal. New Left critics in particular have taken him to task for not having utilized the opportunity which presented itself at the depth of the Depression in 1933 to transform American society into a dynamic new social and economic community, eliminating inequality and poverty, redistributing income and bringing opportunity and happiness to all Americans. Judged by these standards the New Deal was a failure and Franklin D. Roosevelt was a political opportunist, persuading millions of Americans that he was salvaging their lives and protecting democratic institutions, when in reality he was actually rescuing the capitalist system, expanding the middle class and establishing the foundations of the corporate state.

The Nestor of the New Deal critics is Howard Zinn, a beautiful human being whose initial dissatisfaction probably arose when he went to the South to teach in a Black college, where he was fully exposed to the fruits of 300 years of insufferable racial domination in this country; the experience produced in him a restless antagonism to the drift of American society. He became a senior counselor to, and the historian of, the "new abolitionists," the generation of young Blacks and whites who rejected the patterns of segregated life in America and struck out, initially non-violently, but later violently, to correct long neglected injustices. Zinn's own social and political odyssey and the American involvement in Vietnam heightened his sense of alienation from the mainstream of American society, manifesting itself in an angry attack on what were considered to be the roots of contemporary American life and liberal politics. The New Deal fell directly within the purview of his sense of frustration and dissatisfaction. After enumerating some of the accomplishments of the New Dealers and noting the enthusiasm of many Americans who looked back with pride to that period, Zinn chided:

> Yet when it was over, the fundamental problem remained—and still remains—unsolved: how to bring the blessings of immense natural wealth and staggering productive potential to every person in the land. Also

unsolved was the political corollary of that problem: how to organize ordinary people to convey to national leadership something more subtle than the wail of crisis (which speaks for itself); how to communicate the day to day pains felt, between emergencies, in garbage-strewn slums, crowded schools, grimy bus stations, inadequate hospital wards, Negro ghettos, and rural shacks—the environment of millions of Americans clawing for subsistence in the richest country in the world.

When the reform energies of the New Deal began to wane around 1939 and the depression was over, the nation was back to its normal state: a permanent army of unemployed; twenty or thirty million poverty-ridden people effectively blocked from public view by a huge, prosperous, and fervently consuming middle class; a tremendously efficient yet wasteful productive apparatus that was efficient because it could produce limitless supplies of what it decided to produce, and wasteful because what it decided to produce was not based upon what was most needed by society but on what was most profitable to business.

What the New Deal did was to refurbish middle-class America, which had taken a dizzying fall in the depression, to restore jobs to half the jobless, and to give just enough to the lowest classes (a layer of public housing, a minimum of social security) to create an aura of good will. Through it all, the New Dealers moved in an atmosphere thick with suggestions, but they accepted only enough of these to get the traditional social mechanism moving again, plus just enough more to give a taste of what a truly-far reaching reconstruction might be.[77]

Another critic echoed some of the same complaints, singling out the conservative nature of New Deal reforms:

The liberal reforms of the New Deal did not transform the American system; they conserved and protected American corporate capitalism, occasionally by absorbing parts of threatening programs. There was no significant redistribution of power in American society, only limited recognition of other organized groups, seldom of unorganized peoples. Neither the bolder programs advanced by the New Dealers nor the final legislation greatly extended the beneficence of government beyond the middle classes or drew upon the wealth of the few for the needs of the many. Designed to maintain the American system, liberal activity was directed toward essentially conservative goals. Experimentalism was most frequently limited to means, it operated within safe channels, far short of Marxism or even native American radicalisms that offered structural critiques and structural solutions.

All of this is not to deny the changes wrought by the New Deal—the extension of welfare programs, the growth of federal power, the strengthening of the Executive, even the narrowing of property rights. But it is to assert that the elements of continuity are stronger, that the magnitude of change has been exaggerated. The New Deal failed to solve the problem of depression, it failed to raise the impoverished, it failed to redistribute income, it failed to extend equality and generally countenanced racial discrimination and segregation. It failed generally to make business more responsible to the social welfare or to threaten business' pre-eminent political power. In this sense, the New Deal, despite the shifts in tone and spirit from the earlier decade, was profoundly conservative and continuous with the 1920's.[78]

The author of *The Greening of America*, Charles A. Reich, is another formidable critic of the New Deal, and he too despaired of its failure to redirect the regressive forces in American life:

The New Deal did succeed in coping with the Depression emergency, which might have brought down the whole system, but the system's problems were preserved along with it.

Far greater doubt about reform arises not from lag, but from the shallowness of the New Deal's accomplishments and its failure to follow through. Such radical efforts as redistribution of income, greater public ownership and planning, and programs aimed at improving the quality of life were soon abandoned. The evils that crept into the American political system—urban disenfranchisement, disenfranchisement of blacks, gerrymandering, bosses and undemocratic political conventions, oligarchical control of Congress, and newspaper domination of the channels of public opinion—were all left to grow worse. The Black was allowed to remain in his outcast status. The tendency of American culture to crass and garish materialism was not checked. It is true that the period of reform was brief and shortly interrupted by international events; Dr. New Deal became Dr. Win-the-War. But it is clear that the New Deal never touched the deeper problems of American life, which continued to grow worse all through the 1930's.[79]

Certainly not a "New Leftist," Jacob Cohen provides a more balanced assessment of the New Deal in his review of Schlesinger's *Age of Roosevelt*, yet he too questioned the depth of Roosevelt's response to the crisis with which he was confronted:

He [Schlesinger's Roosevelt] was the perfect democratic leader, heroic in stature, yet committed to the task of leadership through persuasion and education rather than coercion. One cannot doubt from reading the *Age of Roosevelt* that America would have been a different place under a different President. In this sense Schlesinger's conviction that the President is the center of freedom in a democratic system stands as proven.

But for me the most remarkable thing I learn from Roosevelt from these books was his ignorance of the moment in which he lived, of the forces he governed, and the future he was entering. No man, of course, can know the entire truth of his time. What are historians for, except to remind us of this? Lincoln did not fully understand the forces of incipient capitalism with which he was allied, though these forces had emerged and were there to be known. Yet Lincoln understood with clarity and depth, the nature of the crisis of democracy and of the nation in which he was involved.

Roosevelt over and over impresses us with his ignorance in these matters. America had more to fear than fear itself: it had an economic system addicted to cycles of boom and bust to fear; it had a world movement of totalitarianism to fear; it had the complications which attend mass society to fear and it had much that could be stated explicitly to accomplish as well. . . .

What could Roosevelt have accomplished that he didn't? That is the question we should ask. To what further use could he have put the dextrous powers of his office?[80]

These are serious complaints and disturbing questions, and they cannot be lightly shrugged off. A President must ultimately be evaluated by the success or failure of his policies; a judgment must be made as to how effectively the inhabitant of the White House responds to the challenges with which his administration is confronted. But in making this or any other judgment, serious consideration must be given to what he did accomplish, as well as to what he did not. In the final analysis the one has to be weighed against the other.

Roosevelt came to power at one of the most critical moments in all of American history. Not only the presidency, but the total American political system, was being tested by a series of converging problems and destructive forces as overwhelming as any that had emerged in any period in our national life, with the exception of the Civil War. Men's faith in the possibilities of democratic institutions was as sorely tested in 1933 as was their faith in the Union in 1861. To have come to power and restored faith in the constitutional processes of the American political system in a period of history when democracy was in retreat all over the world was an achievement in itself. Totalitarianism was on the march in an increasingly large area of the world, and where democratic governments were not overthrown, they appeared to be incapable of engaging the support and loyalty of their citizens.

Franklin D. Roosevelt arrested this debilitating social and political erosion in the United States. He assisted millions of Americans in recapturing their individual pride and self confidence, prevented outright starvation and rampant economic and social disorder and gradually reconstructed the people's faith in their government and their willingness to hope and dream that they could once again determine, if not their own destinies, their children's and their grandchildren's futures. It was no small undertaking, no compromised objective. Roosevelt was entrusted with this task by the American people, in part because of the superb courage and will power he demonstrated in rehabilitating his own broken physical condition into a vibrant and quite effective posture. Not only did thousands of handicapped persons and polio victims take heart from Roosevelt's triumph of will, but millions of Americans who were fortunate enough to be physically well, marvelled at his inspiring example. He had succeeded in arresting many of their worst fears and restored the integrity of government, convincing them that all was not hopeless, that men of good will could yet seize control of the ebb and flow of disastrous events and recover the will to survive.

This achievement must stand next to Lincoln's as one of the truly great exercises in political leadership in American history. The New Left critics of the

New Deal, for the most part, do not deny this contribution, but neither do they recognize it or credit it fully for the significant historical phenomenon that it was. Lurking behind their frustration and dissatisfaction with the present is the somewhat frantic and despairing complaint that it all could have been otherwise, if only Roosevelt had demonstrated the wisdom and determination to act differently than he did. But is such criticism reasonable? Was the necessary understanding of the nature of the problems which Roosevelt and the New Dealers confronted possible, or the knowledge even available at that time, to have yielded solutions, the nature and magnitude of which these critics would have found satisfactory? What is usually left out of their critiques is not only an alternative model of constructive policies which might have been pursued, but more important, the identification of the creative source of political leadership, leaders not of ideological, peripheral movements and parties, but leaders of men and ideas in touch with the American people, men who might have done otherwise and done better. Theoretical criticisms based upon speculative fantasy are interesting, but hardly the stuff of which history is made.

The most creative and far-reaching advocate of social and economic change among all of the New Dealers, Rexford Guy Tugwell, has provided an interesting series of studies of Roosevelt and the men around him, which radiate a sense of the very personal and first-hand experiences which they shared. Tugwell, who pushed for more decisive policies from the very beginning, was a frustrated advisor, an unrequited lover on the scene, but he was not a Monday-morning historian, second-guessing the decisions which the men of power and history made. He described what he thinks were Roosevelt's real objectives:

> I am certain that he had intentions which were quite definite and not at all so loosely held that they could be called wide. They were simple, too, in his mind, I believe. In fact one of the clues to his character was that, however devious and seemingly confused his own methods or those he allowed to be used by his subordinates, the ends he sought were easily and quite securely carried in his mind, clear as precepts are to a child. He wanted all Americans to grow up healthy and vigorous and to be practically educated; he wanted workers to have jobs for which they were fairly paid and he wanted them to give a decent day's work for the pay; he wanted businessmen to work within a set of rules which seemed to him easily defined and, if adhered to, capable of righting most commercial wrongs; he wanted everyone free to vote, to worship, to behave as he wished within an accepted national scheme; he wanted officeholders to behave as though office were a public trust. It is easy to be speciously profound about President Roosevelt, and no doubt many historians will be; but it is my belief that everything he ever did or allowed to be done was, in the circumstances and in his view of them, calculated to bring about one of these simple and admirable ends.[81]

There appears to have been no way American society could have avoided the New Deal, for Roosevelt's leadership was the best available during this dim period of history, and was better by far than any of the possible alternatives. His critics are quite right in asserting that much more could have been achieved if other ideas and other leaders had been available. The total breakdown of the national economic system at the end of the 1920s and the agonizing experience of four years of inept Republican leadership totally incapable of coming to grips with any aspect of major national problems, really did present a unique opportunity for fundamental reforms which could have changed the character of the future of the society far more radically than did the New Deal. There can be no quarrel with this contention. What is equally incontrovertible is that the knowledge, the understanding, the capacity to go beyond the frequently temporary and sometimes feeble but well-intentioned efforts of the New Deal were simply not present in the society at that time. Roosevelt knew what objectives he wanted to succeed, but he never discovered the social and economic formula for achieving them.

Keynesian economics was still an unwritten, undeveloped and as yet untested series of speculative propositions. Socialism was presented to the American people by the charming rhetoric of Norman Thomas and communism by the less charming wing of that party which had survived the Stalinist purge and had tied itself to the Kremlin kite. Doctrines of the far right were rumbling through the nation in the radio speeches of Father Coughlin and in the regional populism of Huey Long. These were not solutions, however, but rather caricatures of reality, and the American people, or at least most of them, rejected them, if they even got to the point of seriously considering them at all.

Basic change in the fundamental values and structure of a society requires not only conditions which cry out for such change, but also the ideas, the policies, the theories of change and the ideological commitment of a strong leadership, if not a movement, capable of bringing ideologies and policies to the forefront of the consciousness of the masses of society. With such developments change is certainly possible, probably inevitable, although the outcome of that change can only be determined by the quality of the ideas and leadership which bring it about.

But it is obvious that those ingredients for basic social and economic change were not at hand in the America of the 1930s. Perhaps it was a golden opportunity to reconstruct the values and goals of the society, but if those goals and values had not yet emerged or in any sense crystallized in the form of a social and political movement or awareness, it is idle to continue to speculate and to grieve over what might have been. Far more useful is the careful analysis of these same problems and the construction of viable solutions to them, in an exercise to prepare for future crises when basic changes might once again be possible.

This is not to minimize the enormous contribution made by Franklin D. Roosevelt and the New Deal to American life and to the growth and shaping of the American presidency. Roosevelt rekindled the spirits of the American people when they were probably at their lowest ebb in their 300-year history. He sent major portions of the society back to work again; the wheels began to turn and the crops were harvested. In so doing he strengthened the public domain, invigorated the public services, built roads, dams, schools and other public buildings; through the TVA he helped to develop an entire region of the country, introducing flood control and the prevention of soil erosion, making available maximum power at reasonable rates, and reinforcing the economic and social sinews of the area. He helped immeasurably in the creation of a strong labor movement and in returning agriculture to the profit columns once again.

> The hungry were fed; the jobless were at work; fear no longer haunted men who ought to be free from its compulsions; children went to school decently fed and clothed. And the men who had been greedy, irresponsible, and careless had had a terrible lesson. Also a watch would be put on them now, and if they became greedy again the government would interfere. This was all simple. It amounted to security, freedom and decency. And President Roosevelt was one of those who knew well enough that these were not values which may be established once and for all. They were administered virtues, requiring leadership, which he was prepared to go on giving, a trust which he knew the people would thenceforth yield him as their protector.[82]

Of course there were great dangers in avoiding the basic flaws in the economic and social system, and the development of the welfare or corporate state and all the paternalism and the loss of real freedom and individuality which accompanies it may be the price we now pay. But these were desperate days and there were far worse alternatives close at hand. Throughout the turmoil Roosevelt preserved the democratic process, a process capable of transforming a society at any moment in which that society is ready to be transformed. Yet transformation is not accomplished by hindsight; it cannot be achieved with the stroke of a revisionist's pen. It must emerge out of the drama of the nation's political life, in the political consciousness of its people. Roosevelt preserved that possibility as an option for a future day by salvaging a desperate situation and keeping the country's spirit alive through it all. It was a great achievement, and to continually fault him for what it was impossible for him or any other American political leader on the horizon at that moment in history to accomplish is to engage in a form of self-deception which is more appropriate to fantasy than to the writing of history.

As President, Roosevelt demonstrated powers and capacities which none of his predecessors had ever discovered, let alone utilized. His wife's uncle, who was also his sixth cousin, Theodore Roosevelt, had, in his own words very effectively used the White House as a bully pulpit to enlist the support of the American people in many of his more favored crusades. Cousin Franklin went him one better by eliminating the stiff formality of the pulpit, with its clear implication of talking down to the people, and communicated in a number of ways which reached his audience in their homes and in their hearts more directly than had any President before or in the forseeable future. It was not only the fireside chat that Franklin Roosevelt—FDR, as he was more affectionately called—so effectively and eloquently utilized; but this President was successful at dramatizing to good effect nearly everything he did or said. His press conferences, his trips, his personal appearances in Congress, even his vacations, were all carefully and skillfully orchestrated to call attention to one critical point or another.

Tugwell relates the story of the cruise of the *Myth II*, a 40-foot yawl that Roosevelt had leased for a week's cruise that took him up the New England coast on the Long Island Sound, through the Cape Cod Canal and up the Atlantic coast to

Portsmouth. It was to be FDR's last vacation before the rigors of the first national campaign. At the appointed time the yawl was towed out to deeper waters from her berth on Long Island, and the candidate with his four six-foot plus stalwart sons set out for their cruise with several boatloads of newspapermen, cameramen and political celebrities following in their wake. Roosevelt was at the helm and amazed most of the observers and millions of other Americans by his expertise in controlling the vessel. He was, of course, a master at that, having sailed all of his life; what was particularly astonishing to all but the most intimate was that this polio victim, with his spindly, steel-braced legs upon which he could hardly walk, was hearty enough to command the helm of this sturdy vessel and every evening maneuver her successfully to her designated mooring in port with the finesse of an international cup racer. And the presence of his tanned and athletic sons was not lost upon his eager national audience either.

Of course the future President was off on an enjoyable cruise and there was no one who appreciated the sheer ecstasy of the communion with the sea more than he. But at the end of the week when he was lifted, tanned and relaxed, from the dinghy onto the dock in Portsmouth, New Hampshire, millions of Americans had learned something about their future President which he wanted them very much to know. There was no question that he was a physical invalid, but there was no longer any doubt in anyone who had followed that journey that he was a rugged invalid—a man capable of sailing a vessel of this nature up the New England coast without any professional assistance must know what he was doing. And he did. He was conveying an important message to many who still harbored doubts about putting a man without functioning legs into the White House. He capitalized on his infirmity and transformed it into an asset. He assured his fellow Americans that he could go the distance, as he most certainly could. And on the side he was healing some political wounds, interviewing Democratic politicians as he proceeded up the coast, monopolizing the front page of most newspapers and being featured in the newsreels. And as the country soon discovered, he was exploiting his presence to convey ideas and objectives which could not be communicated in any other way. This was the first of many subsequent and successful voyages.

Franklin D. Roosevelt's career was extraordinarily similar to that of Theodore Roosevelt. Both attended Groton and Harvard and studied law at Columbia University. Both were elected to the New York state legislature while in their twenties, both served as governor of New York State, as assistant secretary of the navy, both ran as vice presidential candidates and both, of course, were elected President of the United States. Perhaps their differences were more important than their similarities, however, although they shared certain personality traits and even agreed on some public questions. In their personal relations, they were both outgoing; politically, both were classical Progressives and probably of the greatest importance of all, both triumphed over physical disabilities, experiences which were significant in molding their characters and toughening the fiber of their wills.

Theodore Roosevelt was a weak and sickly child, a "delicate boy" as he described himself, suffering from rather violent attacks of asthma and burdened with poor eyesight. During one of his asthma attacks he was sent off by himself to Moosehead Lake for a cure; on the stagecoach ride to the lake he encountered two boys about his own size and age. Realizing young Roosevelt's frailty and his inability to defend himself, the other two boys made life miserable for him on the journey, and when he attempted to fight back they handled him easily and made him look ridiculous. When Theodore returned home he asked his father to help him to learn how to box, and his father outfitted a gym for him on the top floor of their East Twentieth Street house in New York City, and provided him with a boxing instructor. Roosevelt admitted that he was an awkward pupil, but after two or three years of hard work and training he could handle himself well, and he boxed and wrestled at Groton and Harvard. The confidence this initial training gave him, combined with his natural love for the outdoors, made a sports and nature fanatic out of him for the rest of his life, and certainly his exploits in the "Wild West" and in the Spanish-American War can be linked to these early experiences.

Franklin Roosevelt had no severe physical handicaps to overcome in his early youth, although he tended to be too light and inept to ever become proficient at the various team sports in which he attempted to participate. His mother was more influential in his life than his father, which was the opposite experience to that of his cousin, who greatly admired his strong and influential father. Franklin's father was a much older man, who died when he was relatively young, and his mother was the dominant influence in his life. Perhaps nothing would have come of his very modest early talents if he had not suffered the catastrophic attack of polio in the summer of 1921 at the midpoint of his career. His recovery and courageous struggle to regain his physical prowess and to reestablish his political career is one of the great legends of America. There is no question that this long, lonely and at times even humiliating experience not only strengthened Roosevelt's character and determination, but it also probably matured a newly discovered compassion for others in need, a compassion which he demonstrated so eloquently and effectively time and time again as President.

Like many of the critics of the New Deal, I think that in terms of coming to grips with the ultimate problems which confronted the society in the 1930s, the New Deal was a failure. Roosevelt failed to chart a new course for the American economy, to correct the major shortcomings in American life, or to give new direction to the thrust of the dynamic technology which had been developing for the previous 50 years. In this sense Roosevelt failed to insure a better American future which would protect the American dream of individual freedom and liberty and personal fulfillment for every American. But neither Roosevelt nor any of his contemporaries were capable of accomplishing such an objective at that time. In feeding the hungry, in rehabilitating the spirit, in preserving the institutions of democracy—particularly the presidency—Franklin D. Roosevelt fulfilled an important historical role, nonetheless, and insured for society the opportunity to rise to the greater challenges of the future.

Harry Truman and the Steel Crisis of 1952

Both examples of the limits of presidential power analyzed have focused on Presidents of extraordinary popularity acting at the height of their public acclaim. Thomas Jefferson and Franklin D. Roosevelt were Presidents who sought and used power effectively; they were skilled Executives as well as consummate politicians. If these two giants could have fallen from grace because their policies and methods were rejected by the citizens of their country, then surely executive power temporarily commanded by Presidents of considerably lesser stature may disappear more rapidly, particularly when negative circumstances begin to converge within the ambience of their administrations. Such was the case of Harry S. Truman, a good and effective President, but a man who enjoyed significant peaks of strong public approval, and who at other times, fell to rather dismal levels of public rebuke.

Truman had many remarkable assets which contributed to his success in the presidency. He was a man of high moral character, honest, direct and loyal. He possessed a quick mind, worked easily with details, was a great student of history and of the presidency, and he brought to his first and "accidental" presidency (when he succeeded Franklin D. Roosevelt upon his death), a sense of humility and awe at having reached the highest position of power in the land. He was a fortunate man, with the knack of appearing at the right moment in the right place. While these qualities partially accounted for his rise to fame and preeminence, what was more important was that he tackled every duty and problem with which he was confronted with the same grim determination to do the best that he could, and that was usually good enough to get the job done quickly and decisively.

Truman never brooded over problems. He liked to make a decision, and after considering the alternatives, he made up his mind and never agonized over it further. From his own testimony, this even included such momentous decisions as the dropping of the atomic bomb and the initiation of the "police action" in Korea. He bore the responsibility for making these judgments without flinching. Truman indicates that he never regretted either action; moreover, he slept soundly every night in the White House before and after.

In the spring of 1952, however, Harry Truman's presidency was in difficulty. There were numerous reasons for his troubled situation. One was that the country had been run by Democrats for the previous 20 years. There is a certain rhythm in the ebb and flow of politics, and it was clear in 1952 that there was more ebb than flow in the condition of the presidential party. In periods of adversity, the people often tire of their leaders. While Truman was a good President, perhaps far too advanced for his time, he struggled to bring about some of the unachieved objectives of his distinguished predecessor, as well as introducing many innovations of his own.

As an accidental President, he had to take over the command of the armed forces in the midst of the war, bring that war to a successful conclusion and then face all the pent-up frustrations among the population that such a prolonged period of war always brings out. Once the voluntary army was mustered out of service, millions of jobs were needed; consumer goods were required overnight to meet the demand which four years of denial called forth. On every level of the society—jobs, consumer goods, inflation, to say nothing of the vastly increased commitments abroad to the Allies—the problems of world starvation, of nuclear control, of peace and a stable world order were escalating. As Clinton Rossiter indicates, "History may record that it was no mean achievement simply to have gone through the motions of being President in these eight years."[83] Continuing, Rossiter also points out that although the Truman White House was tainted with the scandals of a number of his close palace guard feathering their own nests at the public expense, it should also be remembered that Truman mobilized some of the most impressive talent to serve in governmental posts in recent years—"names like Marshall, Lovett, Forrestal, Acheson, Bedell Smith, Hoffman, Bohlen, Symington, Foster, Bradley, Clay, Lewis Douglas, Kennan, Draper, Jessup, Harriman, Finletter, Patterson McCloy and Eisenhower and Dulles."[84]

But Harry Truman was surviving in the presidency and in fact accomplishing many unique historical achievements, like the Marshall Plan, when he ran into the frustrated backlash of the Korean War. Every war produces frustrations among the civilian population, but the virtue of a total war, in this sense, is its command of the total commitment of the population to the war's objectives, and its willingness to put up with hardships and deprivations until the victory sought has been won. This was generally characteristic of the American people in World War II. Their resentments were reflected after the war was over, but not during it. Truman was able to ride out many of these problems, and in a rather stirring political comeback, he became President in his own right in the upset victory of 1948. But soon afterwards, Truman was confronted with increasing criticism from an anti-New and Fair Deal-dominated Congress, not only on spending issues, but, justified or not, for the fall of China to the communists. The latter was particularly reflected in the rise of Senator Joe McCarthy and the issue of domestic communism. The continuing problem of inflation and the frustrations and increasing discontent of both labor and business only added to the deteriorating climate. All of this was exaggerated by the outbreak of the Korean War, when a limited emergency was called, but the measures passed proved inadequate to control the disruptive elements of a runaway war economy.

Although the Congress and the American people applauded what they considered to be the courageous and forthright decision of President Truman to come to the aid of South Korea, as the war dragged on and as the United States suffered humiliating defeats in the field, the people became frustrated, and they began to oppose what they now referred to as "Mr. Truman's War." They were annoyed by the failure of the government to control inflation, the inability of wages to keep pace with prices, and finally, the removal of the popular General MacArthur was more than they could stand. The latter proved especially costly to the President. When Harry Truman faced the possibility of a prolonged strike in the steel industry in the second debilitating year of the Korean War, he was confronted with a series of problems over and beyond the issue at hand which weakened his ability to deal effectively with it. Fed up with sacrificing, fed up with waiting, fed up with suffering if they had friends or relatives directly involved in the war, the American people had to blame someone, and the man they identified most clearly with their condition was the President of the United States. Many of them became fed up with Harry Truman, too.

In a total war, the President is far better able to absorb the undercurrents of resentment which accompany sacrifices and sufferings on the part of the general population. Total war binds the country together, at least for the duration. But the Korean War was not a total war. It did not demand the total mobilization of the society, although perhaps it should have, and neither governmental control nor citizen commitment, was substantial. It was the first modern "limited war" which this country fought, and it should have taught us that such wars are difficult and as time goes on, impossible to sustain. They are difficult from a military point of view, because they demand a restricted military response and an approach to war under which some commanders cannot operate effectively, as the MacArthur crisis clearly indicated (see section five of this volume). Other global commitments and problems which may themselves break out into shooting wars require that the nation's efforts be restrained, restricted and controlled as much as possible. There are many who maintain that a free and open democratic society does not possess the discipline to support a limited war for long. Certainly the Korean experience provided a good deal of evidence for that point of view.

That was the background and the mood of the people when the country was threatened with an industry-wide steel strike in the winter of 1951. Both labor and industry by that time were girdling under the frustrating restrictions of a limited war economy. The labor movement had grown considerably in strength during World War II, due mostly to the sympathetic assistance of the War Labor Board, which operated under the principle that it could deal more effectively with organized workers in a disciplined trade union than it could with uncontrollable and anarchic demands of unorganized groups. Labor was represented in many wartime agencies, and many of the unions made considerable strides in collective bargaining during this period. There were wage and price controls and also excess profits taxes.

Governmental machinery to control wages, prices and production were created during the Korean War also. At Truman's instigation, Congress passed the Defense Production Act, but insisted that the responsibilities for controlling wages and prices be integrated into one agency, to avoid the whip-saw effect experienced by separate wage and price control agencies in World War II. Forced to comply with this requirement of the law, Truman created the Economic Stabilization Agency, which had general responsibilities for economic mobilization of the entire economy. However, within this overall agency, a separate wage control board was created which had the tripartite representation of labor, industry and the public, just as it had in World War II. Eventually it ran into the same problems the earlier agency had faced, where a decision to grant an increase in wages necessarily was dependent upon the decision to grant an increase in prices to cover its costs.

In the early months of the war, particularly when the American forces were enjoying successes in the Inchon landing and the subsequent march to the North, the wage and price control agencies sufficed. They engaged in so-called "jaw-boning" activities; that is, they attempted to convince labor and industry to hold the line on wages and prices. But with the Yalu disaster facing him and the threat of a prolonged and discouraging war, Truman created, by Executive Order (10193), the Office of Defense Mobilization, with the powerful president of the General Electric Corporation, Charles E. Wilson, at its head. Labor was unhappy with this move, however, for Wilson's anti-union predilections were well known to the labor movement. They felt they were being downgraded by being placed under the jurisdiction of a top management representative. On the other hand, the scandals in the Truman administration made it difficult to attract high quality personnel, and Wilson's prestige was sorely needed to bolster the war production program.

The history of economic mobilization during the Korean War is such a complicated development that it would detract from the purpose of this study of presidential power if it were delineated here. Grant McConnell has done an excellent and highly detailed study of the step-by-step developments of the mobilization machinery in the steel case, which can be consulted for further background.[85] What is important, however, is that a major labor-management conflict was in the making in the midst of a war effort, and the man in the White House found himself increasingly frustrated in his attempts to resolve it. Truman was extremely sympathetic to the arguments of the steelworkers. As he wrote in his *Memoirs*:

> The industry was making more money, while the workers in the plants found that the increases in the cost of living had cut down the purchasing power of their pay. The cost of food and clothing and similar basic items had gone up.[86]

The President went on to express his support of the historical claims of the trade union movement and the important role that many of the unions played in the lives of their members.

Now it was true that most union members supported Truman and the Democratic party, and the unions contributed heavily to his campaign for the presidency. Such considerations were not irrelevant to the President. On the other hand, Harry Truman's sympathy and support were obviously not for sale; his opinions about the trade union movement and the basic validity of the steelworkers' case were genuine expressions of solidarity with many of his fellow citizens with whom he felt a close bond. The President was also greatly irritated at the arrogance of the steel industry's refusal to bargain in good faith with the union, and to respect the governmental machinery for settling wage and price disputes. The profits in the steel industry were considerably in excess of what they were the previous year, and the President was convinced that the industry could absorb a wage increase without a corresponding inflationary increase in the price of steel. His problem was, however, that he was powerless to render such a decision or even to expedite its progress. A President in a declining period of public and congressional support is virtually powerless to impose his will even upon the bureaucratic agencies and officials of his own administration. Although he fought stubbornly against the tide which eroded his presidential power and thwarted his objectives, he was unable to check its momentum.

The power of the presidency does not flow automatically from the constitutional definition of the responsibilities of the office or even from the precedents that previous Presidents have established. Each President has to establish his claim to these powers anew, to fight for the public and congressional support that are necessary to make them valid. The election of a President is merely the beginning, albeit an important and sometimes a strong beginning, but once in office he must seek and protect his power consciously and wisely, as Richard Neustadt has argued, in order to insure his ability to shape and enforce policy and to provide leadership in responding to the needs of the country. When a President has lost the support which makes his policy role possible, he is crippled in office and will fail in any effort to impose his will upon a fundamentally hostile political environment. This was Harry Truman's tragic plight towards the end of his second term in office in 1952. He had lost the confidence, and thus the power, to lead the country.

Truman's objectives were, in my opinion, appropriate in 1952, when he attempted to prevent a dangerous national steel strike by supporting the basically justifiable demands of the steelworkers and refusing to pass on the cost of their wage increase to a much abused and virtually helpless taxpayer and consumer. Whatever it was called, there was a war in progress, and the President correctly invoked the machinery of the Defense Production Act to attempt to settle this labor-management dispute, without disrupting war production and possibly hurting the armies in the field. The Congress, on the other hand, wanted the President to invoke the procedures of the Taft-Hartley Act, which provided for an 80-day injunction to prevent a strike which would jeopardize the national interests. When collective bargaining broke down almost immediately between the United Steelworkers Union, CIO, and the United States Steel Company, the wage policy committee representing all the members of the union under contract in the steel industry set a deadline of December 31, 1951, for a strike throughout the industry. The President recorded that he was informed by Secretary of Defense Robert Lovett:

> [A]ny stoppage of steel production, for even a short time, would increase the risk we had taken in the "stretch-out" of the armament program. He [Lovett] also pointed out that our entire combat technique in all three services depended on the fullest use of our industrial facilities. Stressing the situation in Korea, he said that "we are holding the line with ammunition, and not with the lives of our troops." Any curtailment of steel production, he warned, would endanger the lives of our fighting men.[87]

In reality Truman had no choice at that point, if he wanted to continue the production of steel, but to refer the dispute to the Wage Stabilization Board, as outlined in the Defense Production Act. But many in Congress and in the nation persisted in urging him to invoke the emergency injunction procedure of the Taft-Hartley Act. This action might have prevented the strike for the next 80 days, but it could not guarantee that it could be prevented after that period. It contained no provision for mandating collective bargaining, and when the cooling-off period expired, the President and the country would probably still have been confronted with the same problem. The procedure was an anathema to labor, and given its already resentful attitudes, the steelworkers might have disobeyed such an injunction, or if they complied, failed to cooperate with any other governmental machinery in settling the dispute. It appeared to the President that the referral of the dispute to the Wage Stabilization Board was the only realistic alternative to endless strife and, ultimately, to the loss of essential steel production. But his judgment, proved to be wrong.

Under different circumstances the President would, in all probability, have been able to bring the dispute to a settlement through the method he selected. His influence and the absence of any other suitable alternatives probably would have led the union to accept the recommendations of the WSB and the steel industry to accept the reasonable price increase which the Office of Price Stabilization granted (the director of OPS actually offered the steel industry the highest possible price increase under his interpretation of existing statutes). But the difficulty with these speculations is that they assume the back-up of a strong and influential Chief Executive. They also assume that once such final offers were on the table, the parties would accept them because they really would be aware at that point there were no other alternatives.

But that was not the case in this situation. The steel companies conjectured that other alternatives did exist because the President was not strong enough to impose his will upon all the participants involved in reaching such a settlement. But the President lacked the strength to accomplish this because he did not have sufficient public or congressional support to make his decisions binding. The steel companies were gambling in order to achieve greater profits; it proved a costly gamble for them in the end, for they lost heavily during the shut-down, but they suspected correctly that Truman would not be able to make them accept the wage increase recommended by the Wage Stabilization Board, if the price increase offered by the OPS was not satisfactory to them. It was not satisfactory and the struggle continued.

It became an incredibly complicated field of force, particularly as the power vectors were decentralized by the President's loss of influence. The steel companies realized that Congress was up-in-arms at the President for failing to impose the Taft-Hartley Act; the public was disgusted because they knew whatever the settlement, it only meant higher prices for them; and many of the various members of the governmental bureaucracy were balking because they realized that the President was no longer strong enough to back them up and they had to be prepared to defend their positions on their own. As one studies this case, this mood descends upon all of those involved like a murky fog settling over a bustling city. It clouds up the familiar profile of the buildings etched against the sky, and rearranges the pattern of spatial relationships. The loss of presidential power and influence changes the "rules of the game" within the interstices of the executive branch of the government, and the participants fail to respond in quite the same way as they might normally.

The first man to break ranks with the President was his head of domestic wartime mobilization—Charles E. Wilson. Unlike the President, Wilson was more sympathetic to the steel industry than he was to the union. When the Wage Stabilization Board handed down a recommendation for a wage increase, generous but far less than the union was demanding, Wilson attacked it and then insisted that the steel companies be given the price increase they requested to cover what they estimated the wage increase would cost them. When the President (and his price stabilization officials) refused to go along with that deal, Wilson resigned, stating simply that he did not think the WSB recommendations and the government's price policy met "the principles of equity. . . ."[88] The principle of equity which the steel industry was demanding was an exorbitant figure ($12.00 a ton) to cover the cost of the wage increase. (WSB statisticians claimed that was considerably in excess of the amount necessary to cover their recommendations.)

This was a severe blow to the President. It further weakened his influence in the situation for, from the outside, it looked very much that this internal squabble was prompted by Truman's clear favoritism to labor, and neither the Congress nor the public would stand for that. Furthermore, it looked as if Wilson had been badly treated by the President, and the press took up the cause, pointing to the continued mess in Washington and the anarchy which prevailed in the emergency stabilization program. The President's ability to bring any kind of order to the crumbling situation was rapidly disappearing.

The steel industry, sensing they had the government on the run, refused to consider the WSB wage recommendation after it became apparent that the President and the OPS would hold out against the price increase which the industry demanded. They were playing for bigger stakes than an immediate settlement of their dispute; the possibility of striking a blow against the strong arm of government acting in labor disputes in the future, a position the steel industry favored at this stage of its development was apparent to all. It almost seemed as if the steel companies were forcing the President to act in such a fashion as to further weaken his position and perhaps the role of the presidency itself in the long run. And Truman, with his determined self assurance and strong will, was moving ahead to accomplish precisely the objective which would hurt him the most.

The rest of the story is quite well known. Faced with the limited alternative of invoking a Taft-Hartley injunction, something the President refused to do because he considered it doubly unfair to the steelworkers' union at this stage of the dispute, since they had already been forced to delay the strike over 80 days in compliance with the wage stabilization procedures, Truman decided that the government should take over the steel plants and operate them until a settlement could be worked out by the two parties in the dispute. Although this has a totalitarian ring to it, the procedure is not that horrendous, for nothing really changes hands; the government does not march troops in and operate the plants, but rather requires both management and the union to stay on their jobs and encourages them to continue bargaining until a settlement is reached. It is essentially a legal transfer of control, but it was a step which most of the American people, the Congress of the United States and the Supreme Court were not prepared to accept. Harry Truman had exceeded the limits of presidential power, and he was ordered by a court of law, and ultimately by the Supreme Court of the United States, to cease and desist from his takeover of the steel mills. In the final analysis the President fell back upon his last resort, his undefined and "inherent" powers to act in the national interest, and it was at that point that one of the opinions of the justices voting with the majority offered the most illuminating definition of the limits of presidential power that had yet been rendered.

Last minute negotiations failed to bring about a settlement and the steelworkers' union called a national strike to begin at 12:01 a.m., April 9, 1952. The union was willing to accept the WSB wage recommendations, but the price demands of the steel companies were so exorbitant ($12.00 increase per ton, whereas the highest offer of the government was $4.50 a ton) that no settlement could be worked out. One hour and a half before the strike was to begin the President went on radio and spoke to the nation, explaining that he was taking over the steel plants and appealing for public support in his effort to hold the line on inflation, while guaranteeing continued production of steel to meet the demands of the war in Korea. But the hour was too late. A large segment of the public had already made up its mind, most of the press was howling for the President's head, and he had few allies who defended his conduct throughout the crisis. The appeal to the country was the right move, because it was only through mobilizing public support that he could hope to be sustained in his action, but it was too late: the future indeed looked bleak.

President Harry S. Truman
Executive Order Directing the
Government Seizure of the Steel Mills
April 8, 1952

Youngstown Sheet & Tube Co. et al. v. *Sawyer*, 343 U.S. 579, 589-92 (1952).

EXECUTIVE ORDER

Directing the Secretary of Commerce to Take Possession of and Operate the Plants and Facilities of Certain Steel Companies

Whereas on December 16, 1950, I proclaimed the existence of a national emergency which requires that the military, naval, air, and civilian defenses of this country be strengthened as speedily as possible to the end that we may be able to repel any and all threats against our national security and to fulfill our responsibilities in the efforts being made throughout the United Nations and otherwise to bring about a lasting peace; and

Whereas American fighting men and fighting men of other nations of the United Nations are now engaged in deadly combat with the forces of aggression in Korea, and forces of the United States are stationed elsewhere overseas for the purpose of participating in the defense of the Atlantic Community against aggression; and

Whereas the weapons and other materials needed by our armed forces and by those joined with us in the defense of the free world are produced to a great extent in this country, and steel is an indispensable component of substantially all of such weapons and materials; and

Whereas steel is likewise indispensable to the carrying out of programs of the Atomic Energy Commission of vital importance to our defense efforts; and

Whereas a continuing and uninterrupted supply of steel is also indispensable to the maintenance of the economy of the United States, upon which our military strength depends; and

Whereas a controversy has arisen between certain companies in the United States producing and fabricating steel and the elements thereof and certain of their workers represented by the United Steel Workers of America, CIO, regarding terms and conditions of employment; and

Whereas the controversy has not been settled through the processes of collective bargaining or through the efforts of the Government, including those of the Wage Stabilization Board, to which the controversy was referred on December 22, 1951, pursuant to Executive Order No. 10233, and a strike has been called for 12:01 A.M., April 9, 1952; and

Whereas a work stoppage would immediately jeopardize and imperil our national defense and the defense of those joined with us in resisting aggression, and would add to the continuing danger of our soldiers, sailors, and airmen engaged in combat in the field; and

Whereas in order to assure the continued availability of steel and steel products during the existing emergency, it is necessary that the United States take possession of and operate the plants, facilities, and other property of the said companies as hereinafter provided:

Now, Therefore, by virtue of the authority vested in me by the Constitution and laws of the United States, and as President of the United States and Commander in Chief of the armed forces of the United States, it is hereby ordered as follows:

1. The Secretary of Commerce is hereby authorized and directed to take possession of all or such of the plants, facilities, and other property of the companies named in the list attached hereto, or any part thereof, as he may deem necessary in the interests of national defense; and to operate or to arrange for the operation thereof and to do all things necessary for, or incidental to, such operation.

2. In carrying out this order the Secretary of Commerce may act through or with the aid of such public or private instrumentalities or persons as he may designate; and all Federal agencies shall cooperate with the Secretary of Commerce to the fullest extent possible in carrying out the purposes of this order.

3. The Secretary of Commerce shall determine and prescribe terms and conditions of employment under which the plants, facilities, and other properties possession of which is taken pursuant to this order shall be operated. The Secretary of Commerce shall recognize the rights of workers to bargain collectively through representatives of their own choosing and to engage in concerted activities for the purpose of collective bargaining, adjustment of grievances, or other mutual aid or protection, provided that such activities do not interfere with the operation of such plants, facilities, and other properties.

4. Except so far as the Secretary of Commerce shall otherwise provide from time to time, the managements of the plants, facilities, and other properties

possession of which is taken pursuant to this order shall continue their functions, including the collection and disbursement of funds in the usual and ordinary course of business in the names of their respective companies and by means of any instrumentalities used by such companies.

5. Except so far as the Secretary of Commerce may otherwise direct, existing rights and obligations of such companies shall remain in full force and effect, and there may be made, in due course, payments of dividends on stock, and of principal, interest, sinking funds, and all other distributions upon bonds, debentures, and other obligations, and expenditures may be made for other ordinary corporate or business purposes.

6. Whenever in the judgment of the Secretary of Commerce further possession and operation by him of any plant, facility, or other property is no longer necessary or expedient in the interest of national defense, and the Secretary has reason to believe that effective future operation is assured, he shall return the possession and operation of such plant, facility, or other property to the company in possession and control thereof at the time possession was taken under this order.

7. The Secretary of Commerce is authorized to prescribe and issue such regulations and orders not inconsistent herewith as he may deem necessary or desirable for carrying out the purposes of this order; and he may delegate and authorize subdelegation of such of his functions under this order as he may deem desirable.

Harry S. Truman

President Harry S. Truman
Radio and Television Address on
Government Operation of the Steel Mills
April 8, 1952

Public Papers of the Presidents: Harry S. Truman, 1952-53, VIII, 246-50.

My fellow Americans: Tonight, our country faces a grave danger. We are faced by the possibility that at midnight tonight the steel industry will be shut down. This must not happen.

Steel is our key industry. It is vital to the defense effort. It is vital to peace.

We do not have a stockpile of the kinds of steel we need for defense. Steel is flowing directly from the plants that make it into defense production.

If steel production stops, we will have to stop making the shells and bombs that are going directly to our soldiers at the front in Korea. If steel production stops, we will have to cut down and delay the atomic energy program. If steel production stops, it won't be long before we have to stop making engines for the Air Force planes.

These would be the immediate effects if the steel mills close down. A prolonged shutdown would bring defense production to a halt and throw our domestic economy into chaos.

These are not normal times. These are times of crisis. We have been working and fighting to prevent the outbreak of world war. So far we have succeeded. The most important element in this successful struggle has been our defense program. If that is stopped, the situation can change overnight.

All around the world, we face the threat of military action by the forces of aggression. Our growing strength is holding these forces in check. If our strength fails, these forces may break out in renewed violence and bloodshed.

Our national security and our chances for peace depend on our defense production. Our defense production depends on steel.

As your President, I have to think about the effects that a steel shutdown here would have all over the world.

I have to think about our soldiers in Korea, facing the Chinese Communists, and about our soldiers and allies in Europe, confronted by the military power massed behind the Iron Curtain. I have to think of the danger to our security if we are forced, for lack of steel, to cut down on our atomic energy program.

I have no doubt that if our defense program fails, the danger of war, the possibility of hostile attack, grows that much greater.

I would not be faithful to my responsibilities as President if I did not use every effort to keep this from happening.

With American troops facing the enemy on the field of battle, I would not be living up to my oath of office if I failed to do whatever is required to provide them with the weapons and ammunitions they need for their survival.

Therefore, I am taking two actions tonight.

First, I am directing the Secretary of Commerce to take possession of the steel mills, and to keep them operating.

Second, I am directing the Acting Director of Defense Mobilization to get the representatives of the steel companies and the steelworkers down here to Washington at the earliest possible date in a renewed effort to get them to settle their dispute.

I am taking these measures because it is the only way to prevent a shutdown and to keep steel production rolling. It is also my hope that they will help bring about a quick settlement of the dispute.

I want you to understand clearly why these measures are necessary, and how this situation in the steel industry came about.

In normal times—if we were not in a national emergency—this dispute might not have arisen. In normal times, unions are entitled to whatever wages they can get by bargaining, and companies are entitled to whatever prices they can get in a competitive market.

But today, this is different. There are limitations on what wages employees can get, and there are limitations on what prices employers can charge.

We must have these limitations to prevent a wage-price spiral that would send prices through the roof, and wreck our economy and our defense program.

For more than a year we have prevented any such runaway inflation. We have done it by having rules that are fair to everyone—that require everyone to sacrifice some of his own interests to the national interest. These rules have been laid down under laws enacted by Congress, and they are applied by fair, impartial Government boards and agencies.

These rules have been applied in this steel case. They have been applied to the union, and they have been applied to the companies. The union has accepted these rules. The companies have not accepted them. The companies insist that they must have price increases that are out of line with the stabilization rules. The companies have said that unless they can get those increases they will not settle with the union. The companies have said, in short, that unless they can have what they want, the steel industry will shut down. That is the plain, unvarnished fact of the matter.

Let me tell you how this situation came about.

The steel companies and the steelworkers union had a contract that ran until December 31, 1951.

On November 1, 1951, the union gave notice that in view of the higher cost of living, and the wage increases already received by workers in other industries, the steelworkers wanted higher wages and better working conditions in their new contract for 1952.

The steel companies met with the union but the companies never really bargained. The companies all took the same position. They said there should be no changes in wages and working conditions—in spite of the fact that there had been substantial changes in many other industries, and in spite of the fact that the steel industry is making very high profits.

No progress was made, and a strike was threatened last December 31.

Before that happened, I sent the case to the Wage Stabilization Board. I asked them to investigate the facts and recommend a settlement that would be fair to both parties, and would also be in accordance with our rules for preventing inflation. Meanwhile, I asked both sides to keep the steel industry operating, and they did.

The Wage Board went into the facts very thoroughly. About 3 weeks ago, on March 20, the Wage Board recommended certain wage increases and certain changes in working conditions.

The Wage Board's recommendations were less than the union thought they ought to have. Nevertheless, the union accepted them as a basis for settlement.

There has been a lot of propaganda to the effect that the recommendations of the Wage Board were too high, that they would touch off a new round of wage increases, and that a new wage-price spiral would set in.

The facts are to the contrary. When you look into the matter, you find that the Wage Board's recommendations were fair and reasonable. They were entirely consistent with what has been allowed in other industries over the past 18 months. They are in accord with sound stabilization policies.

Under these recommendations, the steelworkers would simply be catching up with what workers in other major industries are already receiving.

The steelworkers have had no adjustment in their wages since December 1, 1950. Since that time the cost of living has risen, and workers in such industries as automobiles, rubber, electrical equipment, and meatpacking have received increases ranging from 13 to 17 cents an hour.

In the steel case the Wage Board recommended a general wage increase averaging 13¾ cents an hour in 1952. Obviously, this sets no new pattern and breaks no ceiling. It simply permits the steelworkers to catch up to what workers in other industries have already received.

The Board also recommended a 2½ cent wage increase to go into effect next January, if the union would agree to an 18-month contract. In addition, the Board recommended certain other provisions concerning such matters as paid holidays and extra pay for Sunday work. The steel industry has been lagging behind other industries in these matters, and the improvements suggested by the Board are moderate.

When you look at the facts, instead of the propaganda, it is perfectly plain that the Wage Board's recommendations in the steel case do provide a fair and reasonable basis for reaching a settlement on a new management-labor contract—a settlement that is consistent with our present stabilization program. Of course, neither party can ever get everything it thinks it deserves; and, certainly, the parties should bargain out the details. But in the present circumstances, both the companies and the union owe it to the American people to use these recommendations as a basis for reaching a settlement.

The fact of the matter is that the settlement proposed by the Board is fair to both parties and to the public interest. And what's more, I think the steel companies know it. They can read figures just as well as anybody else—just as well as I can or anybody in the business. I think they realize that the Board's recommendations on wages are reasonable, and they are raising all this hullabaloo in an attempt to force the Government to give them a big boost in prices.

Now, what about the price side? Is it true that the steel companies need a big increase in prices in order to be able to raise wages?

Here are the facts.

Steel industry profits are now running at the rate of about $2½ billion a year. The steel companies are now making a profit of about $19.50 on every ton of steel they produce. On top of that, they can get a price increase of close to $3 a ton under the Capehart amendment to the price control law. They don't need this, but we are going to have to give it to them, because the Capehart amendment requires it.

Now add this to the $19.50 a ton they are already making and you have profits of better than $22 a ton.

Now, what would the Wage Board's recommendations do to steel profits? To hear the steel companies talk, you would think the wage increase recommended by the Board would wipe out their profits altogether. Well, the fact of the matter is that if all the recommendations of the Wage Board were put into effect, they would cost the industry about $4 or $5 a ton.

In other words, if the steel companies absorbed every penny of the wage increase, they would still be making profits of $17 or $18 a ton on every ton of steel they made.

Now, a profit of $17 or $18 a ton for steel is extremely high. During 1947, 1948, and 1949, the 3 years before the Korean outbreak, steel profits averaged a little better than $11 a ton. The companies could absorb this wage increase entirely out of profits, and still be making higher profits than they made in the 3 prosperous years before Korea.

The plain fact is, though most people don't realize it, the steel industry has never been so profitable as it is today—at least not since the "profiteering" days of World War I.

And yet, in the face of these facts, the steel companies are now saying they ought to have a price increase of $12 a ton, giving them a profit of $26 or $27 a ton. That's about the most outrageous thing I ever heard of. They not only want to raise their prices to cover any wage increase; they want to double their money on the deal.

Suppose we were to yield to these demands. Suppose we broke our price control rules, and gave the steel companies a big price increase. That would be a terrible blow to the stability of the economy of the United States of America.

A big boost in steel prices would raise the prices of other things all up and down the line. Sooner or later, prices of all the products that use steel would go up—tanks and trucks and buildings, automobiles and vacuum cleaners and refrigerators, right on down to canned goods and egg beaters.

But even worse than this, if we broke our price control rules for steel, I don't see how we could keep them for any other industry.

There are plenty of other industries that would like to have big price increases. Our price control officials meet every day with industries that want to raise their prices. For months they have been turning down most of these requests, because most of the companies have had profits big enough to absorb cost increases and still leave a fair return.

The paper industry has been turned down. So has the brass industry, the truck industry, the auto parts industry, and many others.

All these industries have taken "no" for an answer, and they have gone home and kept right on producing. That's what any law abiding person does when he is told that what he'd like to do is against the rules.

But not the steel companies—not the steel companies. The steel industry doesn't want to come down and make its case, and abide by the decision like everybody else. The steel industry wants something special, something nobody else can get.

If we gave in to the steel companies on this issue, you could say goodby to stabilization. If we knuckled under to the steel industry, the lid would be off. Prices would start jumping up all around us—not just prices of things using steel, but prices of many other things we buy, including milk and groceries and meat.

You may think this steel dispute doesn't affect you. You may think it's just a matter between the Government and a few greedy companies. But it is not. If we granted the outrageous prices the steel industry wants, we would scuttle our whole price control program. And that comes pretty close to home for everybody in the country.

It is perfectly clear, from the facts I have cited, that the present danger to our stabilization program comes from the steel companies' insistence on a big jump in steel prices.

The plain fact of the matter is that the steel companies are recklessly forcing a shutdown of the steel mills. They are trying to get special, preferred treatment, not available to any other industry. And they are apparently willing to stop steel production to get it.

As President of the United States it is my plain duty to keep this from happening. And that is the reason for the measures I have taken tonight.

At midnight the Government will take over the steel plants. Both management and labor will then be working for the Government. And they will have a clear duty to heat up their furnaces again and go on making steel.

When management and labor meet down here in Washington they will have a chance to go back to bargaining and settle their dispute. As soon as they do that, we can turn the steel plants back to their private owners with the assurance that production will continue.

It is my earnest hope that the parties will settle without delay—tomorrow, if possible. I don't want to see the Government running the steel plants one minute longer than is absolutely necessary to prevent a shutdown.

A lot of people have been saying I ought to rely on the procedures of the Taft-Hartley Act to deal with this emergency.

This has not been done because the so-called emergency provisions of the Taft-Hartley Act would be of no help in meeting the situation that confronts us tonight.

That act provides that before anything else is done, the President must first set up a board of inquiry to find the facts on the dispute and report to him as to what they are. We would have to sit around a week or two for this board to report before we could take the next step. And meanwhile, the steel plants would be shut down.

Now there is another problem with the Taft-Hartley procedure. The law says that once a board of inquiry has reported, the Government can go to the courts for an injunction requiring the union to postpone a strike for 80 days. This is the only provision in the law to help us stop a strike. But the fact is that in the present case, the steelworkers' union has already postponed its strike since last December 31—99 days. In other words, the union has already done more, voluntarily, than it could be required to do under the Taft-Hartley Act. We do not need further delay and a prolonging of the crisis. We need a settlement and we need it fast.

Consequently, it is perfectly clear that the emergency provisions of the Taft-Hartley Act do not fit the needs of the present situation. We have already had the benefit of an investigation by one board. We have already had more delay than the Taft-Hartley Act provides.

But the overriding fact is that the Taft-Hartley procedure could not prevent a steel shutdown of at least a week or two.

We must have steel. We have taken the measures that are required to keep the steel mills in operation. But these are temporary measures and they ought to be ended as soon as possible.

The way we want to get steel production—the only way to get it in the long run—is for management and labor to sit down and settle their dispute. Sooner or later that's what will have to be done. So it might just as well be done now as any time.

There is no excuse for the present deadlock in negotiations. Everyone concerned knows what ought to be done. A settlement should be reached between the steel companies and the union. And the companies should then apply to the Office of Price Stabilization for whatever price increase they are entitled to under the law.

That is what is called for in the national interest.

On behalf of the whole country, I ask the steel companies and the steelworkers' union to compose their differences in the American spirit of fair play and obedience to the law of the land.

The morning after the President's speech, he sent a message to the Congress, somewhat ambiguous in content, suggesting that Congress might want to consider different actions than he had taken. He was quite ready to cooperate in such an undertaking if a new proposal was forthcoming. This puzzled many congressmen, for it appeared to be more of an argument for the record than anything else. Throughout the crisis, the President had come in for sharp criticism in both houses, some congressmen going as far as to propose impeachment, while others from time to time proposed other harassing efforts. On the whole, although Congress was quite unhappy about the turn of events and filled the *Congressional Record* with criticism and denunciations of the President, no clear line of policy emerged from either house as to how to resolve the dispute other than to invoke a Taft-Hartley injunction.

To make matters worse for the President he was without an attorney general at the time, and when the steel companies went into the courts the following day to obtain a restraining order to prevent the takeover of their property, the President had to rely upon the weak defense of the assistant attorney general, who bungled the arguments in the government's behalf. The district court judge, however, refused to grant the temporary injunction requested, not on the merits of the argument, but because he found that such a court order was not necessary. Whatever harm or loss might be inflicted upon the owners was not irreparable from a legal point of view, and there were adequate remedies under the law to protect their interests. The 13 experienced corporation lawyers representing the various steel companies then filed motions for a permanent injunction, and hearings were set for approximately two weeks from that date, the steel company attorneys failing to persuade the government to waive its right to a reasonable period to prepare a defense of its position. That meant the government remained in control of the steel mills for the next two weeks, and possibly longer.

The formal takeover of the steel plants was not the major worry of the steel companies, because they went on operating without any loss of revenue. What they were apprehensive about, however, was the possibility of the government's engaging in collective bargaining with the union in the meantime, acting, of course, in its new capacity as their legal employer. Richard Neustadt, who was on the White House staff at that time, has revealed that the President and his advisors had something like that very much in mind:

> Having seized the mills in desperation to avert production losses, the White House wanted to be rid of them as fast as possible—which meant as fast as it could gain assurance that production would continue once they were returned to private hands. This called for some settlement of the labor dispute whose lack of settlement had led to seizure in the first place.

The circle could be broken only if continued government control were made so unattractive in the eyes of both disputants that they would prefer agreement with each other. To that end a tactic was devised: the Secretary of Commerce, as administrator of the mills, was to put into effect a *portion* of the union's wage demands to which the men were automatically entitled under the existing rules of wage control (a so-called cost-of-living adjustment). At the same time, he was to ask the price controllers for the amount of price relief to which the companies were automatically entitled under "pass through" provisions of existing legislation (the so-called Capehart Amendment). Secretary Sawyer then was to announce that he would do no more. Management and labor would be faced with a *fait accompli* that satisfied neither the union's wage demands nor the company's price demands but put some things beyond dispute and foreclosed better terms for the duration. With this prospect before them, both sides might conclude that more was to be gained from settlement than from continued government direction. So, at least, the White House hoped.[89]

Much can be learned from understanding why this rather extraordinary plot failed. Sawyer was the stumbling block. He refused to act, or rather he stalled, and the President lacked the power to force him to put the strategy into motion. Sawyer was a businessman and was under certain pressures from his own "reference group," as the sociologists would put it. He had no taste for the takeover in the first place, and he was unwilling to be the one to put his signature to the wage order. He did not refuse to respond to the orders of the President in so many words, but he busied himself with preparations, delaying any overt activity for four weeks, when by that time the Supreme Court prevented any such action.

During this interim period the matter was working its way through the courts towards a final determination. The district court granted the permanent injunction the steel companies sought on the grounds that the President of the United States had no authority under the Constitution for such a seizure. The government's argument that the President possessed a "broad residuum of power" under the Constitution to take such an action to protect the public interest in an emergency was rejected by the Court in unequivocal language:

> There is no express grant of power in the Constitution authorizing the President to direct this seizure. There is no grant of power from which it reasonably can be implied. There is no enactment of Congress authorizing it. On what, then, does defendant rely to sustain his acts? According to his brief, reiterated in oral argument, he relies upon the President's "broad residuum of power" sometimes referred to as "inherent" power under the Constitution, which, as I understand his counsel, is not to be confused with "implied" powers as that term is generally understood, namely, those which are reasonably appropriate to the exercise of a granted power.
>
> This contention requires a discussion of basic fundamental principles of constitutional government, which I have always understood are immutable, absent [sic] a change in the framework of the Constitution

itself in the manner provided therein. The Government of the United States was created by the ratification of the Constitution. It derives its authority wholly from the powers granted to it by the Constitution, which is the only source of power authorizing action by any branch of Government. It is a government of limited, enumerated, and delegated powers. The office of President of the United States is a branch of the Government, namely, that branch where the executive power is vested, and his powers are limited along with the powers of the two other great branches or departments of Government, namely, the legislative and judicial.

The President therefore must derive this broad "residuum of power" or "inherent" power from the Constitution itself, more particularly Article II thereof, which contains that grant of Executive power. . . .

The non-existence of this "inherent" power in the President has been recognized by eminent writers, and I cite in this connection the unequivocal language of the late Chief Justice Taft in his treatise entitled "Our Chief Magistrate and His Powers" (1916) wherein he says: "The true view of the Executive function is, as I conceive it, that the President can exercise no power which cannot be fairly and reasonably traced to some specific grant of power or justly implied and included within such express grant as proper and necessary to its exercise. Such specific grant must be either in the Federal Constitution or in an Act of Congress passed in pursuance thereof. There is no undefined residuum of power which he can exercise because it seems to him to be in the public interest, and there is nothing in the Neagle case and its definition of a law of the United States, or in other precedents, warranting such an inference. The grants of executive power are necessarily in general terms in order not to embarrass the Executive within the field of action plainly marked for him, but his jurisdiction must be justified and vindicated by affirmative constitutional or statutory provision, or it does not exist."

I stand on that as a correct statement of the law. . . .

Enough has been said to show the utter and complete lack of authoritative support for defendant's position. That there may be no doubt as to what it is, he states it unequivocally when he says in his brief that he does "not perceive how Article II [of the Constitution] can be read . . . so as to limit the Presidential power to meet all emergencies," and he claims that the finding of the emergency is "not subject to judicial review." To my mind this spells a form of government alien to our constitutional government of limited powers. I therefore find that the acts of defendant are illegal and without authority of law.[90]

The government appealed the decision in the district court of appeals, which overruled Judge Pine's ruling in the lower court and granted a stay of the injunction. The steel companies then applied for a *writ of certiorari* in the Supreme Court, knowing that that body could review the question of the President's power to seize the mills and settle the matter once and for all. The Court granted *certiorari* and agreed to review the matter, setting the stage for the dramatic events of the next few weeks. The President was now in danger not only of being prevented from seizing the steel mills, but of permanently impairing or restricting the President's powers to act in the public interest in an emergency. The Court is normally reluctant to pass on such so-called "political questions," holding with Marshall:

> The province of the court is, solely, to decide on the rights of individuals, not to enquire how the executive, or executive officers, perform duties in which they have a discretion. Questions, in their nature political, or which are, by the constitution and laws submitted to the executive, can never be made by this court.[91]

By agreeing to review the constitutional questions involved, there was every indication that the Court would make an important ruling. The oral arguments were presented the second week in May, 1952, and the decision was handed down two and one-half weeks later. The steel companies were represented by no less than 40 distinguished lawyers, but the oral presentation was made by just one, John W. Davis, then an extremely successful Wall Street corporation lawyer, and formerly solicitor general of the United States and the Democratic party candidate for President in 1924. The government was ably represented by its solicitor general, Philip Perlman. Davis argued persuasively that the President could not seize the steel mills while ignoring a statute (Taft-Hartley) which provided a remedy for just such an emergency. Perlman asserted that the President had the option of employing the procedures of the Defense Production Act rather than Taft-Hartley, and that when all else had failed, he had adequate power under the Constitution to act in the face of a serious national emergency.

On June 2, 1952 the Court handed down its decision. Six different opinions were filed by the justices, in addition to the opinion of the Court written by Justice Black. They ranged far and wide on the subject of presidential power. Five of the justices agreed with Black that the President had exceeded his authority in seizing the steel mills, but the majority expressed their opinions in four additional opinions. The minority opinion was written by Justice Vinson and concurred in by Justice Reed and Justice Minton. The decision of the Court was, of course, most significant in resolving the particular problem, but Justice Jackson's brilliant opinion must also be included here because it speaks so eloquently and wisely to the question of the limits of presidential power in terms so forceful that they clarify an ambiguous area that had not received such careful and serious attention in all of its previous history, or in any of the previous decisions of the Supreme Court.

Justice Hugo Black
Majority Opinion of the Supreme Court in
Youngstown Sheet & Tube Co. *v.* Sawyer
June 2, 1952

Youngstown Sheet & Tube Co. et al. v. *Sawyer*, 343 U.S. 579, 582-89 (1952).

We are asked to decide whether the President was acting within his constitutional power when he issued an order directing the Secretary of Commerce to take possession of and operate most of the Nation's steel mills. The mill owners argue that the President's order amounts to lawmaking, a legislative function which the Constitution has expressly confided to the Congress and not to the President. The Government's position is that the order was made on findings of the President that his action was necessary to avert a national catastrophe which would inevitably result from a stoppage of steel production, and that in meeting this grave emergency the President was acting within the aggregate of his constitutional powers as the Nation's Chief Executive and the Commander in Chief of the Armed Forces of the United States. The issue emerges here from the following series of events:

In the latter part of 1951, a dispute arose between the steel companies and their employees over terms and conditions that should be included in new collective bargaining agreements. Long-continued conferences failed to resolve the dispute. On December 18, 1951, the employees' representative, United Steelworkers of America, C.I.O., gave notice of an intention to strike when the existing bargaining agreements expired on December 31. The Federal Mediation and Conciliation Service then intervened in an effort to get labor and management to agree. This failing, the President on December 22, 1951, referred the dispute to the Federal Wage Stabilization Board [This Board was established under Executive Order 10233, 16 Fed. Reg. 3503. Footnote in original.] to investigate and make recommendations for fair and equitable terms of settlement. This Board's report resulted in no settlement. On April 4, 1952, the Union gave notice of a nation-wide strike called to begin at 12:01 a.m. April 9. The indispensability of steel as a component of substantially all weapons and other war materials led the President to believe that the proposed work stoppage would immediately jeopardize our national defense and that governmental seizure of the steel mills was necessary in order to assure the continued availability of steel. Reciting these considerations for his action, the President, a few hours before the strike was to begin, issued Executive Order 10340, a copy of which is attached as an appendix, *post*, p. 589. [sic] The order directed the Secretary of Commerce to take possession of most of the steel mills and keep them running. The Secretary immediately issued his own possessory orders, calling upon the presidents of the various seized companies to serve as operating managers for the United States. They were directed to carry on their activities in accordance with regulations and directions of the Secretary. The next morning the President sent a message to Congress reporting his action. Cong. Rec., April 9, 1952, p. 3962. Twelve days later he sent a second message. Cong. Rec., April 21, 1952, p. 4192. Congress has taken no action.

Obeying the Secretary's orders under protest, the companies brought proceedings against him in the District Court. Their complaints charged that the seizure was not authorized by an act of Congress or by an constitutional provisions. The District Court was asked to declare the orders of the President and the Secretary invalid and to issue preliminary and permanent injunctions restraining their enforcement. Opposing the motion for preliminary injunction, the United States asserted that a strike disrupting steel production for even a brief period would so endanger the well-being and safety of the Nation that the President had "inherent power" to do what he had done—power "supported by the Constitution, by historical precedent, and by court decisions." The Government also contended that in any event no preliminary injunction should be issued because the companies had made no showing that their available legal remedies were inadequate or that their injuries from seizure would be irreparable. Holding against the Government on all points, the District Court on April 30 issued a preliminary injunction restraining the Secretary from "continuing the seizure and possession of the plants . . . and from acting under the purported authority of Executive Order No. 10340." 103 F. Supp. 569. On the same day the Court of Appeals stayed the District Court's injunction. 90 U.S. App. D.C.——, 197 F. 2d 582. Deeming it best that the issues raised be promptly decided by this Court, we granted certiorari on May 3 and set the cause for argument on May 12. 343 U.S. 937.

Two crucial issues have developed: *First.* Should final determination of the constitutional validity of the President's order be made in this case which has proceeded no further than the preliminary injunction stage? *Second.* If so, is the seizure order within the constitutional power of the President?

I

It is urged that there were non-constitutional grounds upon which the District Court could have denied the preliminary injunction and thus have followed the customary judicial practice of declining to reach and decide constitutional questions until compelled to do so. On this basis it is argued that equity's extraordinary injunctive relief should have been denied because (a) seizure of the companies' properties did not inflict irreparable damages, and (b) there were available legal remedies adequate to afford compensation for any possible damages which they might suffer. While separately argued by the Government, these two contentions are here closely related, if not identical. Arguments as to both rest in large part on the Government's claim that should the seizure ultimately be held unlawful, the companies could recover full compensation in the Court of Claims for the unlawful taking. Prior cases in this Court have cast doubt on the right to recover in the Court of Claims on account of properties unlawfully taken by government officials for public use as these properties were alleged to have been. See *e.g., Hooe v. United States,* 218 U.S. 322, 335-336; *United States v. North American Co.,* 253 U.S. 330, 333. But see *Larson v. Domestic & Foreign Corp.,* 337 U.S. 682, 701-702. Moreover, seizure and governmental operation of these going businesses were bound to result in many present and future damages of such nature as to be difficult, if not incapable, of measurement. Viewing the case this way, and in the light of the facts presented, the District Court saw no reason for delaying decision of the constitutional validity of the orders. We agree with the District Court and can see no reason why that question was not ripe for determination on the record presented. We shall therefore consider and determine that question now.

II

The President's power, if any, to issue the order must stem either from an act of Congress or from the Constitution itself. There is no statute that expressly authorizes the President to take possession of property as he did here. Nor is there any act of Congress to which our attention has been directed from which such a power can fairly be implied. Indeed, we do not understand the Government to rely on statutory authorization for this seizure. There are two statutes which do authorize the President to take both personal and real property under certain conditions. [The Selective Service Act of 1948, 62 Stat. 604, 625-627, 50 U.S.C. App. (Supp. IV) § 468; the Defense Production Act of 1950, Tit. II, 64 Stat. 798, as amended, 65 Stat. 132. Footnote in original.] However, the Government admits that these conditions were not met and that the President's order was not rooted in either of the statutes. The Government refers to the seizure provisions of one of these statutes (§ 201 (b) of the Defense Production Act) as "much too cumbersome, involved, and time-consuming for the crisis which was at hand."

Moreover, the use of the seizure technique to solve labor disputes in order to prevent work stoppages was not only unauthorized by any congressional enactment; prior to this controversy, Congress had refused to adopt that method of settling labor disputes. When the Taft-Hartley Act was under consideration in 1947, Congress rejected an amendment which would have authorized such governmental seizures in cases of emergency. [93 Cong. Rec. 3637-3645. Footnote in original.] Apparently it was thought that the technique of seizure, like that of compulsory arbitration, would interfere with the process of collective bargaining. [93 Cong. Rec. 3835-3836. Footnote in original.] Consequently, the plan Congress adopted in that Act did not provide for seizure under any circumstances. Instead, the plan sought to bring about settlements by use of the customary devices of mediation, conciliation, investigation by boards of inquiry, and public reports. In some instances temporary injunctions were authorized to provide cooling-off periods. All this failing, unions were left free to strike after a secret vote by employees as to whether they wished to accept their employers' final settlement offer. [Labor Management Relations Act, 1947, 61 Stat. 136, 152-156, 29 U.S.C. (Supp. IV) §§ 141, 171-180. Footnote in original.]

It is clear that if the President had authority to issue the order he did, it must be found in some provision of the Constitution. And it is not claimed that express constitutional language grants this power to the President. The contention is that presidential power should be implied from the aggregate of his powers under the Constitution. Particular reliance is placed on provisions in Article II which say that "The executive Power shall be vested in a President . . ."; that "he shall take Care that the Laws be faithfully executed"; and that he "shall be Commander in Chief of the Army and Navy of the United States."

The order cannot properly be sustained as an exercise of the President's military power as Commander in Chief of the Armed Forces. The Government attempts to do so by citing a number of cases upholding broad powers in military commanders engaged in day-to-day fighting in a theater of war. Such cases need not concern us here. Even though "theater of war" be an expanding concept, we cannot with faithfulness to our constitutional system hold that the Commander in Chief of the Armed Forces has the ultimate power as such to take possession of private property in order to keep labor disputes from stopping production. This is a job for the Nation's lawmakers, not for its military authorities.

Nor can the seizure order be sustained because of the several constitutional provisions that grant executive power to the President. In the framework of our Constitution, the President's power to see that the laws are faithfully executed refutes the idea that he is to be a lawmaker. The Constitution limits his functions in the lawmaking process to the recommending of laws he thinks wise and the vetoing of laws he thinks bad. And the Constitution is neither silent nor equivocal about who shall make laws which the President is to execute. The first section of the first article says that "All legislative Powers herein granted shall be vested in a Congress of the United States. . . ." After granting many powers to the Congress, Article I goes on to provide that Congress may "make all Laws which shall be necessary and proper for carrying into Execution the foregoing Powers, and all other Powers vested by this Constitution in the Government of the United States, or in any Department or Officer thereof."

The President's order does not direct that a congressional policy be executed in a manner prescribed by Congress—it directs that a presidential policy be executed in a manner prescribed by the President. The preamble of the order itself, like that of many statutes, sets out reasons why the President believes certain policies should be adopted, proclaims these policies as rules of conduct to be followed, and again, like a statute, authorizes a government official to promulgate additional rules and regulations consistent with the policy proclaimed and needed to carry that policy into execution. The power of Congress to adopt such public policies as those proclaimed by the order is beyond question. It can authorize the taking of private property for public use. It can make laws regulating the relationships between employers and employees, prescribing rules designed to settle labor disputes, and fixing wages and working conditions in certain fields of our economy. The Constitution does not subject this lawmaking power of Congress to presidential or military supervision or control.

It is said that other Presidents without congressional authority have taken possession of private business enterprises in order to settle labor disputes. But even if this be true, Congress has not thereby lost its exclusive constitutional authority to make laws necessary and proper to carry out the powers vested by the Constitution "in the Government of the United States, or any Department or Officer thereof."

The Founders of this Nation entrusted the lawmaking power to the Congress alone in both good and bad times. It would do no good to recall the historical events, the fears of power and the hopes for freedom that lay behind their choice. Such a review would but confirm our holding that this seizure order cannot stand,

The judgment of the District Court is

Affirmed

Justice Robert Jackson
Concurring Opinion in Youngstown Sheet & Tube Co. *v.* Sawyer
June 2, 1952

Youngstown Sheet & Tube Co. et al. v. *Sawyer*, 343 U.S. 579, 634-55 (1952).

Mr. Justice Jackson, concurring in the judgment and opinion of the Court.

That comprehensive and undefined presidential powers hold both practical advantages and grave dangers for the country will impress anyone who has served as legal adviser to a President in time of transition and public anxiety. While an interval of detached reflection may temper teachings of that experience, they probably are a more realistic influence on my views than the conventional materials of judicial decision which seem unduly to accentuate doctrine and legal fiction. But as we approach the question of presidential power, we half overcome mental hazards by recognizing them. The opinions of judges, no less than executives and publicists, often suffer the infirmity of confusing the issue of a power's validity with the cause it is invoked to promote, of confounding the permanent executive office with its temporary occupant. The tendency is strong to emphasize transient results upon policies—such as wages or stabilization—and lose sight of enduring consequences upon the balanced power structure of our Republic.

A judge, like an executive adviser, may be surprised at the poverty of really useful and unambiguous authority applicable to concrete problems of executive power as they actually present themselves. Just what our forefathers did envision, or would have envisioned had they foreseen modern conditions, must be divined from materials almost as enigmatic as the dreams Joseph was called upon to interpret for Pharaoh. A century and a half of partisan debate and scholarly speculation yields no net result but only supplies more or less apt quotations from respected sources on each side of any question. They largely cancel each other. [A Hamilton may be matched against a Madison. 7 The Works of Alexander Hamilton, 76-117; 1 Madison, Letters and Other Writings, 611-654. Professor Taft is counterbalanced by Theodore Roosevelt. Taft, Our Chief Magistrate and His Powers, 139-140; Theodore Roosevelt, Autobiography, 388-389. It even seems that President Taft cancels out Professor Taft. Compare his "Temporary Petroleum Withdrawal No. 5" of September 27, 1909, *United States* v. *Midwest Oil Co.,* 236 U.S. 459, 467, 468, with his appraisal of executive power in "Our Chief Magistrate and His Powers" 139-140. Footnote in original.] And court decisions are indecisive because of the judicial practice of dealing with the largest questions in the most narrow way.

The actual art of governing under our Constitution does not and cannot conform to judicial definitions of the power of any of its branches based on isolated clauses or even single Articles torn from context. While the Constitution diffuses power the better to secure liberty, it also contemplates that practice will integrate the dispersed powers into a workable government. It enjoins upon its branches separateness but interdependence, autonomy but reciprocity. Presidential powers are not fixed but fluctuate, depending upon their disjunction or conjunction with those of Congress. We may well begin by a somewhat over-simplified grouping of practical situations in which a President may doubt, or others may challenge, his powers, and by distinguishing roughly the legal consequences of this factor of relativity.

1. When the President acts pursuant to an express or implied authorization of Congress, his authority is at its maximum, for it includes all that he possesses in his own right plus all that Congress can delegate. [It is in this class of cases that we find the broadest recent statements of presidential power, including those relied on here. *United States* v. *Curtiss-Wright Corp.,* 299 U.S. 304, involved, not the question of the President's power to act without congressional authority, but the question of his right to act under and in accord with an Act of Congress. The constitutionality of the Act under which the President had proceeded was assailed on the ground that it delegated legislative powers to the President. Much of the Court's opinion is *dictum,* but the *ratio decidendi* is contained in the following language:

> When the President is to be authorized by legislation to act in respect of a matter intended to affect a situation in foreign territory, the legislator properly bears in mind the important consideration that the form of the President's action—or, indeed, whether he shall act at all—may well depend, among other things, upon the nature of the confidential information which he has or may thereafter receive, or upon the effect which his action may have upon our foreign relations. This consideration, in connection with what we have already said on the subject, discloses the unwisdom of requiring Congress in this field of governmental power to lay down narrowly definite standards by which the President is to be governed. As this court said in *Mackenzie* v. *Hare,* 239 U.S. 299, 311, As a government, the United States is invested with all the attributes of sovereignty. As it has the character of nationality it has the powers of nationality, especially those which concern its relations and intercourse with other countries. *We should hesitate long before limiting or embarrassing such powers.* (Italics supplied.) *Id.,* at 321-322.

That case does not solve the present controversy. It recognized internal and external affairs as being in separate categories, and held that the strict limitation upon congressional delegations of power to the President over internal affairs does not apply with respect to delegations of power in external affairs. It was intimated that the President might act in external affairs without congressional authority, but not that he might act contrary to an Act of Congress.

Other examples of wide definition of presidential powers under statutory authorization are *Chicago & Southern Air Lines, Inc.* v. *Waterman Steamship Corp.,* 333 U.S. 103, and *Hirabayashi* v. *United States,* 320 U.S. 81. But see, *Jecker* v. *Montgomery,* 13 How. 498, 515; *United States* v. *Western Union Telegraph Co.,* 272 F. 311; aff'd, 272 F. 893; rev'd on consent of the parties, 260 U.S. 754; *United States Harness Co.* v. *Graham,* 288 F. 929. Footnote in original.] In these circumstances, and in these only, may he be said (for what it may be worth) to personify the federal sovereignty. If his act is held unconstitutional under these circumstances, it usually means that the Federal Government as an undivided whole lacks power. A seizure executed by the President pursuant to an Act of Congress would be supported by the strongest of presumptions and the widest latitude of judicial interpretation, and the burden of persuasion would rest heavily upon any who might attack it.

2. When the President acts in absence of either a congressional grant or denial of authority, he can only rely upon his own independent powers, but there is a zone of twilight in which he and Congress may have concurrent authority, or in which its distribution is uncertain. Therefore, congressional inertia, indifference or quiescence may sometimes, at least as a practical matter, enable, if not invite, measures on independent presidential responsibility. In this area, any actual test of power is likely to depend on the imperatives of events and contemporary imponderables rather than on abstract theories of law. [Since the Constitution implies that the writ of habeas corpus may be suspended in certain circumstances but does not say by whom, President Lincoln asserted and maintained it as an executive function in the face of judicial challenge and doubt. *Ex parte Merryman,* 17 Fed. Cas. 144; *Ex parte Milligan,* 4 Wall. 2, 125; see *Ex parte Bollman,* 4 Cranch 75, 101. Congress eventually ratified his action. Habeas Corpus Act of March 3, 1863, 12 Stat. 755. See Hall, Free Speech in War Time, 21 Col. L. Rev. 526. Compare *Myers* v. *United States,* 272 U.S. 52, with *Humphrey's Executor* v. *United States,* 295 U.S. 602; and *Hirabayashi* v. *United States,* 320 U.S. 81, with the case at bar. Also compare *Ex parte Vallandigham,* 1 Wall. 243, with *Ex parte Milligan, supra.*

3. When the President takes measures incompatible with the expressed or implied will of Congress, his power is at its lowest ebb, for then he can rely only upon his own constitutional powers minus any constitutional powers of Congress over the matter. Courts can sustain exclusive presidential control in such a case only by disabling the Congress from acting upon the subject. [President Roosevelt's effort to remove a Federal Trade Commissioner was found to be contrary to the policy of Congress and impinging upon an area of congressional control, and so his removal power was cut down accordingly. *Humphrey's Executor* v. *United States,* 295 U.S. 602. However, his exclusive power of removal in executive agencies, affirmed in *Myers* v. *United States,* 272 U.S. 52, continued to be asserted and maintained. *Morgan* v. *Tennessee Valley Authority,* 115 F. 2d 990, cert. denied, 312 U.S. 701; *In re Power to Remove Members of the Tennessee Valley Authority,* 39 Op. Atty. Gen. 145; President Roosevelt's Message to Congress of March 23, 1938, *The Public Papers and Addresses of Franklin D. Roosevelt,* 1938 (Rosenman), 151. Footnote in original.] Presidential claim to a power at once so conclusive and preclusive must be scrutinized with caution, for what is at stake is the equilibrium established by our constitutional system.

Into which of these classifications does this executive seizure of the steel industry fit? It is eliminated from the first by admission, for it is conceded that no congressional authorization exists for this seizure. That takes away also the support of the many precedents and declarations which were made in relation, and must be confined to this category. [The oft-cited Louisiana Purchase had nothing to do with the separation of powers as between the President and Congress, but only with state and federal power. The Louisiana Purchase was subject to rather academic criticism, not upon the ground that Mr. Jefferson acted without authority from Congress, but that neither had express authority to expand the boundaries of the United States by purchase or annexation. Mr. Jefferson himself had strongly opposed the doctrine that the States' delegation of powers to the Federal Government could be enlarged by resort to implied powers. Afterwards in a letter to John Breckenridge, dated August 12, 1803, he declared:

> The Constitution has made no provision for our holding foreign territory, still less for incorporating foreign nations into our Union. The executive in seizing the fugitive occurrence which so much advances the good of their country, have done an act beyond the Constitution. The Legislature in casting behind them metaphysical subtleties, and risking themselves like faithful servants, must ratify and pay for it, and throw themselves on their country for doing for them unauthorized, what we know they would have done for themselves had they been in a situation to do it. 10 The Writings of Thomas Jefferson 407, 411. Footnote in original.]

Can it then be defended under flexible tests available to the second category? It seems clearly eliminated from that class because Congress has not left seizure of private property an open field but has covered it by three statutory policies inconsistent with this seizure. In cases where the purpose is to supply needs of the Government itself, two courses are provided: one, seizure of a plant which fails to comply with obligatory orders placed by the Government; [Selective Service Act of 1948, § 18, 62 Stat. 625, 50 U.S.C. App. (Supp. IV) § 468 (c).] another, condemnation of facilities, including temporary use under the power of eminent domain. [Defense Production Act of 1950, § 201, 64 Stat. 799, amended, 65 Stat. 132, 50 U.S.C. App. (Supp. IV) § 2081. For the latitude of the condemnation power which underlies this Act, see *United States* v. *Westinghouse Co.*, 339 U.S. 261, and cases therein cited. Footnote in original.] The third is applicable where it is the general economy of the country that is to be protected rather than exclusive governmental interests. [Labor Management Relations Act, 1947, §§ 206-210, 61 Stat. 136, 155, 156, 29 U.S.C. (Supp. IV) §§ 141, 176-180. The analysis, history and application of this Act are fully covered by the opinion of the Court, supplemented by that of Mr. Justice Frankfurter and of Mr. Justice Burton, in which I concur. Footnote in original.] None of these were invoked. In choosing a different and inconsistent way of his own, the President cannot claim that it is necessitated or invited by failure of Congress to legislate upon the occasions, grounds and methods for seizure of industrial properties.

This leaves the current seizure to be justified only by the severe tests under the third grouping, where it can be supported only by any remainder of executive power after subtraction of such powers as Congress may have over the subject. In short, we can sustain the President only by holding that seizure of such strike-bound industries is within his domain and beyond control by Congress. Thus, this Court's first review of such seizures occurs under circumstances which leave presidential power most vulnerable to attack and in the least favorable of possible constitutional postures.

I did not suppose, and I am not persuaded, that history leaves it open to question, at least in the courts, that the executive branch, like the Federal Government as a whole, possesses only delegated powers. The purpose of the Constitution was not only to grant power, but to keep it from getting out of hand. However, because the President does not enjoy unmentioned powers does not mean that the mentioned ones should be narrowed by a niggardly construction. Some clauses could be made almost unworkable, as well as immutable, by refusal to indulge some latitude of interpretation for changing times. I have heretofore, and do now, give to the enumerated powers the scope and elasticity afforded by what seem to be reasonable, practical implications instead of the rigidity dictated by a doctrinaire textualism.

The Solicitor General seeks the power of seizure in three clauses of the Executive Article, the first reading, "The executive Power shall be vested in a President of the United States of America." Lest I be thought to exaggerate, I quote the interpretation which his brief puts upon it: "In our view, this clause constitutes a grant of all the executive powers of which the Government is capable." If that be true, it is difficult to see why the forefathers bothered to add several specific items, including some trifling ones. [". . . he may require the Opinion, in writing, of the principal Officer in each of the executive Departments, upon any Subject relating to the Duties of their respective Offices. . . ." U.S. Const., Art. II, § 2. He ". . . shall Commission all the Officers of the United States." U.S. Const., Art. II, § 3. Matters such as those would seem to be inherent in the Executive if anything is. Footnote in original.]

The example of such unlimited executive power that must have most impressed the forefathers was the prerogative exercised by George III, and the description of its evils in the Declaration of Independence leads me to doubt that they were creating their new Executive in his image. Continental European examples were no more appealing. And if we seek instruction from our own times, we can match it only from the executive powers in those governments we disparagingly describe as totalitarian. I cannot accept the view that this clause is a grant in bulk of all conceivable executive power but regard it as an allocation to the presidential office of the generic powers thereafter stated.

The clause on which the Government next relies is that "The President shall be Commander in Chief of the Army and Navy of the United States. . . ." These cryptic words have given rise to some of the most persistent controversies in our constitutional history. Of course, they imply something more than an empty title. But just what authority goes with the name has plagued presidential advisers who would not waive or narrow it by nonassertion yet cannot say where it begins or ends. It undoubtedly puts the Nation's armed forces under presidential command. Hence, this loose appellation is sometimes advanced as support for any presidential action, internal or external, involving use of force, the idea being that it vests power to do anything, anywhere, that can be done with an army or navy.

That seems to be the logic of an argument tendered at our bar—that the President having, on his own responsibility, sent American troops abroad derives from that act "affirmative power" to seize the means of producing a supply of steel for them. To quote, "Perhaps the most forceful illustration of the scope of Presidential power in this connection is the fact that American troops in Korea, whose safety and effectiveness are so directly involved here, were sent to the field by an exercise of the President's constitutional powers." Thus, it is said, he has invested himself with "war powers."

I cannot foresee all that it might entail if the Court should indorse this argument. Nothing in our Constitution is plainer than that declaration of a war is entrusted only to Congress. Of course, a state of war may in fact exist without a formal declaration. But no doctrine that the Court could promulgate would seem to me more sinister and alarming than that a President whose conduct of foreign affairs is so largely uncontrolled, and often even is unknown, can vastly enlarge his mastery over the internal affairs of the country by his own commitment of the Nation's armed forces to some foreign venture. [How widely this doctrine espoused by the President's counsel departs from the early view of presidential power is shown by a comparison. President Jefferson, without authority from Congress, sent the American fleet into the Mediterranean, where it engaged in a naval battle with the Tripolitan fleet. He sent a message to Congress on December 8, 1801, in which he said:

Tripoli, the least considerable of the Barbary States, had come forward with demands unfounded either in right or in compact, and had permitted itself to denounce war on our failure to comply before a given day. The style of the demand admitted but one answer. I sent a small squadron of frigates into the Mediterranean with orders to protect our commerce against the threatened attack. . . . Our commerce in the Mediterranean was blockaded and that of the Atlantic in peril. . . . One of the Tripolitan cruisers having fallen in with and engaged the small schooner *Enterprise*, . . . was captured, after a heavy slaughter of her men. . . Unauthorized by the Constitution, without the sanction of Congress, to go beyond the line of defense, the vessel, being disabled from committing further hostilities, was liberated with its crew. The Legislature will doubtless consider whether, by authorizing measures of offense also, they will place our force on an equal footing with that of its adversaries. I communicate all material information on this subject, that in the exercise of this important function confided by the Constitution to the Legislature exclusively their judgment may form itself on a knowledge and consideration of every circumstance of weight. I Richardson, *Messages and Papers of the Presidents*, 314. Footnote in original.] I do not, however, find it necessary or appropriate to consider the legal status of the Korean enterprise to discountenance argument based on it.

Assuming that we are in a war *de facto*, whether it is or is not a war *de jure*, does that empower the Commander in Chief to seize industries he thinks necessary to supply our army? The Constitution expressly places in Congress power "to raise and *support* Armies" and "to *provide* and *maintain* a Navy." (Emphasis supplied.) This certainly lays upon Congress primary responsibility for supplying the armed forces. Congress alone controls the raising of revenues and their appropriation and may determine in what manner and by what means they shall be spent for military and naval procurement. I suppose no one would doubt that Congress can take over war supply as a Government enterprise. On the other hand, if Congress sees fit to rely on free private enterprise collectively bargaining with free labor for support and maintenance of our armed forces, can the Executive, because of lawful disagreements incidental to that process, seize the facility for operation upon Government-imposed terms?

There are indications that the Constitution did not contemplate that the title Commander in Chief *of the Army and Navy* will constitute him also Commander in Chief of the country, its industries and its inhabitants. He has no monopoly of "war powers," whatever they are. While Congress cannot deprive the President of the command of the army and navy, only Congress can provide him an army or navy to command. It is also empowered to make rules for the "Government and Regulation of land and naval Forces," by which it may to some unknown extent impinge upon even command functions.

That military powers of the Commander in Chief were not to supersede representative government of internal affairs seems obvious from the Constitution and from elementary American history. . . .

We should not use this occasion to circumscribe, much less to contract, the lawful role of the President as Commander in Chief. I should indulge the widest latitude of interpretation to sustain his exclusive function to command the instruments of national force, at least when turned against the outside world for the security of our society. But, when it is turned inward, not because of rebellion but because of a lawful economic struggle between industry and labor, it should have no such indulgence. His command power is not such an absolute as might be implied from that office in a militaristic system but is subject to limitations consistent with a constitutional Republic whose law and policy-making branch is a representative Congress. The purpose of lodging dual titles in one man was to insure that the civilian would control the military, not to enable the military to subordinate the presidential office. No penance would ever expiate the sin against free government of holding that a President can escape control of executive powers by law through assuming his military role. What the power of command may include I do not try to envision, but I think it is not a military prerogative, without support of law, to seize persons or property because they are important or even essential for the military and naval establishment.

The third clause in which the Solicitor General finds seizure powers is that "he shall take Care that the Laws be faithfully executed. . . ." [U.S. Const., Art. II, § 3.] That authority must be matched against words of the Fifth Amendment that "No person shall be . . . deprived of life, liberty or property, without due process of law. . . ." One gives a governmental authority that reaches so far as there is law, the other gives a private right that authority shall go no farther. These signify about all there is of the principle that ours is a government of laws, not of men, and that we submit ourselves to rulers only if under rules.

The Solicitor General lastly grounds support of the seizure upon nebulous, inherent powers never expressly granted but said to have accrued to the office from the customs and claims of preceding administrations. The plea is for a resulting power to deal with a crisis or an emergency according to the necessities of the case, the unarticulated assumption being that necessity knows no law.

Loose and irresponsible use of adjectives colors all non-legal and much legal discussion of presidential powers. "Inherent" powers, "implied" powers, "incidental" powers, "plenary" powers, "war" powers and "emergency" powers are used, often interchangeably and without fixed or ascertainable meanings.

The vagueness and generality of the clauses that set forth presidential powers afford a plausible basis for pressures within and without an administration for presidential action beyond that supported by those whose responsibility it is to defend his actions in court. . . .

In the practical working of our Government we already have evolved a technique within the framework of the Constitution by which normal executive powers may be considerably expanded to meet an emergency. Congress may and has granted extraordinary authorities which lie dormant in normal times but may be called into play by the Executive in war or upon proclamation of a national emergency. In 1939, upon congressional request, the Attorney General listed ninety-nine such separate statutory grants by Congress of emergency or wartime executive powers. [39 Op. Atty. Gen. 348.] They were invoked from time to time as need appeared. Under this procedure we retain Government by law—special, temporary law, perhaps, but law nonetheless. The public may know the extent and limitations of the powers that can be asserted, and persons affected may be informed from the statute of their rights and duties.

In view of the ease, expedition and safety with which Congress can grant and has granted large emergency powers, certainly ample to embrace this crisis, I am quite unimpressed with the argument that we should affirm possession of them without statute. Such power either has no beginning or it has no end. If it exists, it need submit to no legal restraint. I am not alarmed that it would plunge us straightway into dictatorship, but it is at least a step in that wrong direction.

As to whether there is imperative necessity for such powers, it is relevant to note the gap that exists between the President's paper powers and his real powers. The Constitution does not disclose the measure of the actual controls wielded by the modern presidential office. That instrument must be understood as an Eighteenth-Century sketch of a government hoped for, not as a blueprint of the Government that is. Vast accretions of federal power, eroded from that reserved by the States, have magnified the scope of presidential activity. Subtle shifts take place in the centers of real power that do not show on the face of the Constitution. . . .

But I have no illusion that any decision by this Court can keep power in the hands of Congress if it is not wise and timely in meeting its problems. A crisis that challenges the President equally, or perhaps primarily, challenges Congress. It not good law, there was worldly wisdom in the maxim attributed to Napoleon that "The tools belong to the man who can use them." We may say that power to legislate for emergencies belongs in the hands of Congress, but only Congress itself can prevent power from slipping through its fingers. . . .

Although six justices of the Court had determined that the President had acted unconstitutionally, their divided opinions on the subject gave no clear consensus with regard to future presidential seizures. Justice Black's opinion for the Court was terse and could be construed to limit its application to cases when the President acted without statutory authority. Others in the majority based their judgments on evidence of strong congressional opposition to seizure, reflected in the debates and the provisions of the Taft-Hartley Act. They refused to state that the President lacked the power of seizure in a real emergency, even if he did not have congressional authorization to do so. The unity of the three dissenters was in marked contrast to this chorus of conflicts. The chief justice emphasized the critical nature of the emergency and asserted that the prerogative of the President to cope with it fell within his responsibilities as Chief Executive and Commander in Chief. John P. Roche suggests:

> The legal arguments between the two divisions of the Court were consequently of little significance; the vital disagreement was over premises. Granted the assumption that no emergency existed, the majority view fell into the tradition of limitation. Granted the assumption that an emergency existed, the minority opinion fell into an equally well-defined tradition of judicial restraint. It is submitted that this argument over premises is not one that can be solved by the process of legal ratiocination; rather, it must be determined through judicial insight into the attitudes and opinions of the American community—particularly as reflected in the views of congressmen. It is essentially a problem in social psychology, not in law. An emergency is—like the middle class—more state of mind than an objective sociopolitical phenomenon.[92]

There is no doubt, however, that Truman's failure to succeed in this policy was rooted in the strong opposition of the press and his critical loss of popular support as a result of the prolonged duration of the war. A Gallup poll taken a week after the seizure showed his popularity at a very low figure, although it had even been lower several months earlier. Fifty-nine percent of the individuals interviewed disapproved of the way he was handling his job as President, while only 28 percent approved. Several weeks later when a poll was taken on the question of approval or disapproval of his action in the strike, only 35 percent approved and 43 percent disapproved. Moreover, among better informed citizens, the ratio was 38 percent approving, 51 percent disapproving.[93] A survey of the nation's press indicated that not a single major newspaper supported the seizure; *The New York Times, Washington Post, Atlanta Constitution, Chicago Tribune*, Chicago *Daily News* and *the Sun-Times*, Cleveland *Plain Dealer*, St. Louis *Post Dispatch* and the St. Louis *Globe Democrat*, The San Francisco *Chronicle*, the Hearst papers and others wrote editorials opposing the government's take-over.[94] The Congress and the Court had substantial support in their restraint of the President, and they did not shirk what they considered to be their responsibility.

The Jackson opinion came closest to providing some guidance for considering the future emergency powers of the President. Roche suggests that his three-part distinction replaced the mechanistic conception of the "separation of powers" with one that established the responsibility of the Court to maintain the "ground rules" of "government by discussion":

Cutting through the legalistic arguments of both parties, the Justice suggested that presidential actions might be placed in one of three categories: first, where the President acts on the basis of delegated congressional authority; second, where the President takes unauthorized action which does not run counter to the wishes of Congress; and, third, where the President "takes measures incompatible with the expressed or implied will of Congress." Actions of the first category would have a strong presumption of legitimacy; actions of the second would have to be judged "on the imperatives of events and contemporary imponderables rather than abstract theories of law," while actions in the third must be subjected to strong judicial scrutiny, for there the President's "power is at its lowest ebb" and what is at stake is the equilibrium established by our constitutional system.[95]

The Dialectic of Public Discourse

In examining the limits of presidential power through the use of three significant cases in American history—the embargo during Jefferson's second administration, the Court-packing case of Franklin D. Roosevelt and Harry Truman's seizure of the steel mills—analysis reveals conclusions which indicate both the vulnerability and accessibility of presidential powers. It shows clearly that in each case supremely confident national leaders suffered policy defeats as ignominious as those suffered by less popular and less qualified men. They had forgotten what Richard Neustadt asserts is the *sine qua non* of presidential power—"the power to persuade."[96] They failed to persuade their constituents that what they had decided was right, and when a President acts without the support of the people, in fact in the face of their growing opposition, whatever power he might think he possesses evaporates into thin air, and it is only a question of time before the checks and balances of the system begin to negate his policy.

This matter of persuasion is not simply a rhetorical *tour de force*, however. Such major policies must, as Schlesinger points out, correspond to the "balance of administrative power."[97] The President calculates this balance by his own political sensitivity. "And because the President's own frame of reference is at once so all-encompassing and so political," Professor Neustadt writes, "what he sees as a balance for himself is likely to be close to what is viable in terms of public policy. Viability requires three ingredients."[98]

First is a purpose that moves with the grain of history, a direction consonant with coming needs. Second is an operation that proves manageable to the men who must administer it, acceptable to those who must support it, tolerable to those who must put up with it, in Washington and out. Timing can be crucial for support and acquiescence; proper timing is the third ingredient. The President who sees his power stakes sees something very much like the ingredients that make for viability in policy.[99]

Other examples might have been used, but in every other case the President involved was neither as powerful nor as popular as Jefferson and Roosevelt, nor was the policy in question as significant to the history of presidential politics. Jefferson is certainly one of the two or three most revered of all American Presidents, and his power and influence in the country and in the Congress have rarely if ever been matched. And yet in the course of 14 months his major policy lay in ruins, and his administration suffered such a substantial blow that his successor's regime was never able to recover from it. In crushing the embargo, Congress regained most of the power and prestige it had lost during Jefferson's two terms of dominant leadership, and Madison was humiliated and ignored by the rising giants of both houses of Congress from the very beginning of his administration.

Roosevelt's struggle over the Supreme Court was another inevitable and compelling choice in explaining the limits of presidential power. No President in the history of the office has exerted more power or maintained greater popular support than he. But he lost his struggle to reform the structure of the Supreme Court, and although the defeat was blunted by changes emanating from the Court itself, the political cost of the struggle divided his party and generally killed what hopes he had for continuing New Deal reforms and initiating new programs during his remaining years in the White House. A leading historian of the New Deal has written that after the Court battle

> Congress granted the President one final reform, a federal wages and hours law, but it required almost every parliamentary weapon in the administration's arsenal to get it through. . . . By 1939, Congress was moving aggressively to dismantle the New Deal. It slashed relief appropriations, killed Roosevelt appointments and, in a deliberate slap at the Keynesians, eliminated what was left of an undistributed profits tax.[100]

How mistaken both of these great Presidents were. There is no doubt that they both possessed the confidence of the overwhelming majority of the American people as they launched their respective policies, but the people rapidly became confused about those policies and later resented them. And the latent opposition, although greatly weakened as both the 1808 Federalists and the 1937 Republicans were, rapidly reformed their ranks and exploited every opportunity that was given to them. But in Jefferson's case and in Roosevelt's, too, they were really beaten within their own party, where they possibly could have won their battles if they had taken the issues to the people, explained them carefully and honestly and then fought for their support.

If the real or outer limits of the President's power are the negative voices of the court of public opinion, then it is clear that if Presidents in our era want to insure against that limitation being imposed upon them, they must go to the people and convince them they are right. The presidential press conference, the fireside chat, the in depth interview on television or in the newspaper and the formal speech are different ways in which a President tries to accomplish this objective. Such communication, however, involves great sensitivity and considerable artistry in knowing when to speak, just what to say and what issues to save for such priority treatment. Overexposure for a President, too much pleading, can also hurt his standing with the public and weaken his ability to persuade the people to favor his policies. It was clear that when President Harry Truman spoke to the American people during the steel seizure crisis of 1952, he appealed to them once too often, and his capital was drained to the point where he could no longer command the public support he had once been able to rally and needed to uphold his decision.

There are other sophisticated ways by which a President can induce a favorable climate of opinion among his constituents, for example, by utilizing the administrative and political powers of the presidency to apply federal spending and patronage in a critical area, or in a slow economic period, by proclaiming relief for the taxpayers by cutting governmental expenditures and proposing reductions in taxes. Within the interstices of specific statutes and appropriations there is usually some flexibility or yardage in executive discretion which a skillful President can use to his political advantage. Of course the maintenance of good and close relations with the fourth estate is always to his advantage, and in fact is essential for his survival. But in the final analysis, if he wants public support on a specific issue, he must take his case to the people and fight for it.

But if it is true that public opinion, or better, strong public opposition, is the high watermark of presidential power, what guarantee is there that the public will be alerted and well enough informed to determine when a President's actions threaten to or actually overstep the proper limits of his power? Obviously there can be no such guarantee if the limit of presidential power is the public will itself. The real danger lies in the atrophy of that will. The public can be and frequently is indolent, apathetic, badly informed or not informed at all. But if the public will is the only real barrier against the inordinate use or misuse of presidential power, then the state of public information, of public interest in the affairs of state, of public understanding of the issues and of the political process in all of its complexities, is the most essential prerequisite for a healthy body politic in a democratic state.

Public opinion then emerges as the critical force in the restraint of presidential power. In a far more realistic sense than the theoretical "checks and balances" of constitutional arrangements, public acceptance or rejection of presidential policies is the court of last appeal, and a President whose objectives are frustrated by either the Court or the Congress must first win general support among his constituents, if he expects to prevail. And even if he has the support of Congress initially, and his policies do not run into the constitutional opposition of the Court, he must maintain the support and confidence of the majority of the people in order to insure the continued approval of the other two branches. But if the public will is such a decisive factor in restraining presidential power and validating presidential leadership, is there an institutional force within the American political system which attempts to insure that the public is well enough informed and sufficiently enlightened so as to render a reasonable opinion? Did the Founding Fathers seriously consider this problem, and devise any institutional basis for its solution?

The answer, of course, is no. The Founding Fathers created a republic, founded upon the basic concept of democratic rule, without seriously considering the problem of how citizens who would make up the body politic would develop the wisdom and understanding to implement that rule properly. Delegates to the Constitutional Convention like Alexander Hamilton attempted to temper the democratic principle with oligarchical safeguards, but they arrived at no successful conclusion finally as to who would inform and enlighten the ultimate guardians of liberty. Some gave voice to the fear of "the tyranny of the many," but no one proposed a solution as to how the many or even the few would obtain the requisite knowledge to rule successfully.

The argument that the government they created was a representative republic with a limited franchise is not an adequate explanation, for the foundation of representative government is still the citizen, and no effort to limit the franchise by educational qualifications can be found in the Constitution. Any subsequent restrictions (property, education, etc.) were established by states and they certainly were not aimed at protecting intellectual virtue. The fact is that no serious thought was given as to how citizens would acquire the enlightenment and experience to govern wisely and humanely. It was an article of faith or reasoning with Madison, and probably with many others, that the institutions of popular government would blunt the selfish force of special interests and produce a public interest that would work for the general welfare of all. Madison argued in Federalist No. 10 that the representative character of the government and the great number and extensive range of its citizens would tend to both "refine and enlarge the public views. . . ."[101]

That is merely an hypothesis, however, and although it has much in theory and actually some later evidence in experience in its support, it does not create on a sustaining basis the institutional foundation for the enlightenment of the electorate on public issues. No attention was given or has been given since to the exploration of any institutional methods for developing the public wisdom to insure the quality of our representative form of government. But that is, after all, the fundamental problem of self-government. The quality of democratic government and policies can be no better than the quality of the public decisions which create and control them. If there is no sustaining institutional force within the body politic for developing such understanding among its ultimate decision-makers, then the whole polity suffers, and eludes the quality and effectiveness necessary for greatness.

This was a major oversight, of course, and although free public education was initiated at a much later date to partially compensate for this deficiency, education per se has never fulfilled this vague mission, Greek in origin, that the state has an obligation to educate all citizens for their role as a governing class. Educational theory has never resolved the dilemma of how much and what kind and quality of education is essential for the responsibilities of citizenship, and although examinations of this problem by enumerable committees, boards and study commissions have reached desperately for answers (including the famous *Harvard Report on General Education* of 1946), no universally satisfactory solution, curriculum or other program has yet been discovered.

In the twentieth century the presidency attempted to overcome this problem by using the office as a "bully pulpit" to educate and to appeal to the people. Theodore

Roosevelt, Woodrow Wilson and Franklin Delano Roosevelt were masters of this art; they succeeded in building support for legislative programs, executive actions and even for backing efforts in the diplomatic realm through their skillful use of the office. At the turn of the century Theodore Roosevelt took the initiative in establishing this new relationship with the public, a relationship which Elmer Cornwell, jr. has argued has given the presidential office much of "its power and importance":

> The leverage the President has acquired in the lawmaking process has been . . . based on use of the arts of persuasion, and ultimately grounded in the popular support he can claim or mobilize.[102]

Roosevelt called the reporters covering the White House in off the street and established a press room for them inside the official presidential residence. He introduced such techniques as the White House briefing, the trial balloon and official leak, revealing information confidentially to representatives of the press but exacting their promise not to divulge its source. He attempted to centralize the news of his administration within the White House, advising his cabinet members to consult him before issuing statements to the press. He resurrected the presidential tour or "swing around the circuit" as a newsmaking device, creating attention in the parts of the country in which he spoke, and making news of the presidency in other sections where he was not able to travel. During his fight for railroad regulations in the Hepburn Act, "he went all out . . . to mobilize public opinion to force Congressional passage. . . ."[103]

Wilson took up where Roosevelt left off, and although nowhere near as effusive as his predecessor, he held regular press conferences twice a week, and managed through his administration to make the White House and the presidency the central focus of Washington and the nation. Franklin Roosevelt went beyond his two brilliant predecessors in establishing a human bond between himself and the people and also with representatives of the press. When he wanted to, he used this relationship to his advantage more effectively than any inhabitant of the White House in its long history.

But all of those methods served as instruments for expanding the President's influence, and if they can be characterized as "educational," they are educational only along lines acceptable to the President. The enlightened citizen deserves and needs more than the usually able and persuasive presentation of one side of a question in order to render a reasonable opinion. If, indeed, public opinion does and should play the important role that I am ascribing to it, and if it does represent the major, and in many instances the only, effective, countervailing force to the constantly growing power of the President, then there must be some institutional means of countering the President's influence and developing other and more critical views on public policy.

Both houses of Congress, working without executive guidance and support, have on several occasions brought about important national compromises, like the Missouri Compromise in 1820, and generated temporary solutions to several major problems, such as the institution of the Interstate Commerce Commission in 1887 and the Sherman Anti-Trust Act in 1890. For extended periods of time they have dominated the politics of the country. As sounding boards for particular interests, regional, economic and social, they have reflected in the councils of government important and necessary representative views on major questions and brought to the governmental process extraordinary legislative skill and experience with which they have on a few occasions initiated and on many others analyzed, studied and improved measures that have come before them. But they have never brought a definitive solution to any significant national problem without the energy and leadership of a strong President.

The Congress has sometimes filled vacuums, as it did after the Civil War; it has sometimes followed the direction of an exceptional leader. It has nurtured important national figures itself. When the national current has been moving upstream, Congress has marched along with incredible energy and enthusiasm, as it did with Woodrow Wilson in 1913 and 1914 when it passed the Federal Reserve Act, enacted a greatly reduced tariff and tightened the Sherman Anti-Trust Act. But when the SOS sign was really up, when the problems reached a certain magnitude at the national level and when presidential leadership was absent, the Congress has either abdicated, marked time, or produced more heat than light until the problem came to a boil. Fortunately our political system has almost always, at such times, produced strong executive leadership willing to shoulder these responsibilities, initiate proposals and provide the moral inspiration needed to unite the country and move ahead. But that is not to argue that the protracted delays that have been involved in many instances have not been very costly to the welfare and progress of the country. We can only be thankful that reforms were not delayed interminably, and that the institution of the presidency has time and time again produced the vigorous and imaginative leadership which has finally brought these long overdue problems to a workable solution.

The American system has only worked effectively when it has been able to find, or perhaps to create, such leadership. Without it the situation stagnates or, far worse, festers. Of course we have been able to muddle through some extended periods of history without strong presidential leadership, but these have been periods of marking time, not periods where problems have been solved, policies initiated or programs and ideas tested. The 1850s was such a period, as was the late nineteenth century, the period from 1920 to 1932 and most recently the dismal, lackluster 1950s. Each one of these periods was costly for the United States. During each one the clock of effective government virtually stopped while the problems heated up to such a degree that solutions had to be found if things were to proceed.

I would argue that the modern presidency has developed over the last 185 years through a series of unique responses to the major challenges history has placed in its path. It has not developed according to any single man's theory or any single President's actions. It has been an evolutionary growth, bit by bit, little by little. And it has by no means been a steady, organic development. There have been periods of striking growth, periods of slow, stultifying paralysis, and also times of retrogression, perhaps something like taking two steps forward, one step backward. Along with Washington, Jefferson, Jackson, Lincoln, Wilson and the Roosevelts, there have also been Pierce, Buchanan, Grant, Harding and Coolidge occupying the White House. The overall pattern, however, has been positive, assertive, one of forward movement, gathering more power and more responsibility along the way. But within that pattern there have been periods, sometimes prolonged periods, when the prerogatives of the President, his power and prestige, have been whittled down to considerably lesser dimensions.

The presidential responses which have accounted for the extraordinary growth of power in this office and which have been described throughout this book sketch the profile of the political history of this country. The response has not always been immediate, but as the magnitude of the problem developed, as it began to rub against the raw nerves of existing institutions and large sections of our population, solutions have become necessary and essential, and delay has only prolonged the agony.

Before the picture of presidential leadership becomes too euphoric, however, it is necessary to remember that the presidency has never moved faster than the country was willing to go. This is the lesson that the embargo and the Court-packing cases drive home. If the country is going to move, if the machinery of government is going to function in the interests of its citizens, then these same citizens must support and in some cases demand the kind of policies that will accomplish their objectives. The public will can strengthen as well as limit presidential power. Without it the Chief Executive is crippled, despite the powers he has wielded beforehand, but with the people solidly behind him, as Woodrow Wilson put it, no other combination of forces is strong enough to resist him. This assumes, of course, that the President is acting in a situation where there has been no expressed determination of the will of Congress. If Congress has already made a determination, then it can be quite a different question. As Supreme Court Justice Robert H. Jackson wrote in his separate but concurring opinion in the steel seizure case.

> When the President takes measures incompatible with the expressed or implied will of Congress, his power is at its lowest ebb, for then he can rely only upon his own constitutional powers minus any constitutional powers of Congress over the matter. Courts can sustain exclusive presidential control in such a case only by disabling the Congress from acting on the subject.[104]

If the President has to undermine the authority of either Congress or the Court to achieve a policy objective, however, then the cost may be too great even if the possibility of public support seems feasible. The Court-packing case certainly underscored this principle.

The growth of presidential power has usually been in the interest of the nation at large, and any move to weaken the powers we have been analyzing would be, in my opinion, a disaster. But it would also be extremely unwise not to clarify some proper limitation of presidential power, especially since the country and the world have entered into a period when the number, complexity and importance of the problems which find their way to the President's desk increase hourly, and when the existing system appears so willing to transfer so much of its constantly expanding responsibilities in the President's direction, but frequently denies him the resources to deal with them. Although there are many instances where the presidential office could be enhanced by changes readily available, there is also a real need to establish the ground rules, the outer limits or the political context within which those changes can be made.

Rather than weaken or emasculate the President's present powers as some have suggested, the office needs considerably more power, at least in domestic affairs, to carry out mandates directed by the majority of the people. I have dealt with many of these proposals in the appropriate sections of these volumes. The question that we are dealing with here is the ultimate limit of such change or development, for it cannot be unlimited, nor should it be in conflict with the political equilibrium of the system. In other words, the proper limits of presidential power for which we are searching can best be found in viewing the system as a whole, and demanding of it a limited role for the President in keeping with the dynamic principles of representative democratic government.

On the other hand, there is considerable danger in the virtually unchallenged and perhaps unchallengeable power which the American President sometimes appears to possess. Perhaps some of the fear that Professor Bartlett and Senators Fulbright and McCarthy have expressed is justified, for there is a vast difference between persuasion and enlightenment, and the President when operating from his "bully pulpit" usually persuades and does not enlighten. Danger is constantly present in a relationship between an artful persuader and an inadequately informed object of persuasion. In hard political terms, the American public is hardly equipped to make judgments in the areas of tax policy, nuclear arms, urban poverty programs and welfare legislation almost simultaneously, with inadequate or at best superficial knowledge and understanding of viable alternatives to the policies it is asked to support.

Neither the opposition party nor the Congress itself has mastered the arts of mass communication and persuasion; they are hardly a match for a popular President who goes to the people with an eloquent plea for action. James MacGregor Burns has argued that "a great society needs not consensus but creative leadership and *creative opposition*—hence it needs the sting of challenge in a society rich in diversity and in a politics rich in dissent."[105] The clash of issues and points of view in a continuing national debate might provide the best possible political education for an apathetic citizenry, and generate not only heat, but hopefully some light on questions that are now hopelessly outside the area of intelligibility for the average citizen. Why should not the leaders of the opposition party, most of whom are based in Congress or in the state gubernatorial offices, perform this function, the role of a shadow cabinet, advancing their own interests as well as raising the level of public discussion and public understanding? Why not?

Such a dialectical structure of the discussion of public issues might be just what this country needs to bring new light and wisdom to its politics, and also to restore vitality and relevance to the functions of Congress. When the President goes to the people on an issue of great importance, there is very little political resonance in the atmosphere, his message bounces off the veils of indifference which shroud the body politic. The Constitution provided a series of checks and balances at the center of the government to regulate the excessive power of any one of the three branches, but it failed to define or to create the dynamic educational machinery necessary to illuminate public opinion, without which the body politic can hardly aspire to the qualitative greatness which it so much admires and covets.

In fact there is danger, particularly in our times, that the potential virility of public opinion can be hypnotized or mesmerized by the manipulations of the mass communications media. Used with such effectiveness by many Presidents and their supporters, the media need not tip the scales in favor of presidential power, however. For, as it frequently does, it has often almost ignored its responsibility to enlighten public opinion on critical questions and has tranquilized the public into an inert mass by its penchant for "entertainment" motivated by its desire to sell a product. C. Wright Mills draws a frightening picture of what can happen if this persists in his comparison of an alert public or publics and an inert mass society:

> In a *public*, as we may understand the term, (1) virtually as many people express opinions as receive them. (2) Public communications are so organized that there is a chance immediately and effectively to answer back any opinion expressed in public. Opinion formed by such discussion (3) readily finds an outlet in effective action, even against—if necessary— the prevailing system of authority. And (4) authoritative institutions do not penetrate the public, which is thus more or less autonomous in its operations. When these conditions prevail, we have the working model of a community of publics, and this model fits closely the several assumptions of classic democratic theory.
>
> At the opposite extreme, in a *mass*, (1) far fewer people express opinions than receive them; for the community of publics becomes an abstract collection of individuals who receive impressions from the mass media. (2) The communications that prevail are so organized that it is difficult or impossible for the individual to answer back immediately or with any effect. (3) The realization of opinion in action is controlled by authorities who organize and control the channels of such action. (4) The mass has no autonomy from institutions; on the contrary, agents of authorized institutions penetrate this mass, reducing any autonomy it may have in the formation of opinion by discussion.[106]

The growth of presidential power which has been described in the pages of these volumes is a phenomenon essential to the progress and well being of the republic. However, without an adequate countervailing force which can restrain the excesses of power which are bound to develop in the presidency, and a countervailing source of information and opinion which can match the President's extraordinary resources and opportunities for molding public sentiment, the country will never move towards the greatness it seeks. The healthy clash of these forces in the mass communications media can create the basis for public enlightenment on political issues, and produce the essential intellectual and political ferment necessary to achieve public wisdom in national affairs. This could bring about the restoration of the real dialectic of reason first developed by Plato and Aristotle and the Greek city states, not the corrupted form of the dialectic of history invented by Hegel and distorted by Marx. The power that men have discovered within the presidential office is not an evil, but rather a necessary functional response to the needs of a developing democratic society; yet it will be best preserved and enhanced if it is forced to defend its actions and policies in the crucible of an intellectually and politically resonant public discussion, stung by criticism and challenged by the broad opposition of intelligent and resourceful dissent.

The objective is, of course, a stronger and healthier body politic, and a presidency sure in its reserves of power, adequate to its responsibilities, but always measured in terms of its potential limitations. What has not been stressed enough, however, but which may appear as a welcome byproduct of this development and is perhaps an objective more important than a governmental balance of power, is the ultimate effect of the new political dialectic on the role of the citizen. The Greeks understood this when they defined man as a political as well as a rational animal; they understood that the realization of one was essential to the development of the other. The political community is not only a necessary accommodation to man's social and economic needs, but it is indeed a means to man's social and intellectual development. Aristotle did not recognize as a man anyone who existed outside the political community. Rousseau considered the moment when the social contract was first affirmed as a sacred one, creating in effect a new being, a citizen with a moral as well as a physical dimension. Mill argued that when the sphere of men's political action is circumscribed, "their sentiments are narrowed and dwarfed in the same proportion."[107] We can only hope that the definition of the proper limits of presidential power by means of a creative and dynamic dialectic of public discussion and political resonance will achieve for the citizens of this republic a higher dimension of citizenship and by virtue of this, a new birth of freedom.

NOTES

1. Quoted in Robert Jackson, *The Struggle for Judicial Supremacy* (New York, 1941), 183.
2. Jackson, 183.
3. Jackson, 183-84.
4. Jackson, 185.
5. Quoted in Leonard Baker, *Back to Back: The Duel Between FDR and the Supreme Court* (New York, 1967), 108.
6. Harold L. Ickes, *The Secret Diary of Harold L. Ickes* (New York, 1954) II, 52.
7. Quoted in Baker, 121.
8. At least not until 1941, according to James M. Landis, then dean of the Harvard Law School. See Alpheus T. Mason, *Brandeis, A Free Man's Life* (New York, 1946).
9. Charles Evans Hughes, *The Supreme Court of the United States* (New York, 1928), 24.
10. Hughes, 25.
11. Hughes, 50.
12. A highly selective list ought to include the following: Robert H. Jackson, *The Struggle for Judicial Supremacy*, Chapters IV and V; Carl Brent Swisher, *American Constitutional Development* (Boston, 1943), Chapters 35 and 36; Alpheus T. Mason, *The Supreme Court: Vehicle of Revealed Truth or Power Group, 1930-1937* (Boston, 1953); Alpheus T. Mason, *Harlan Fiske Stone: Pillar of the Law* (New York, 1956), Part IV; Irving Brant, *Storm Over the Constitution* (Princeton, New Jersey, 1938), and *The Twilight of the Supreme Court* (New Haven, Connecticut, 1947); and Merlo J. Pusey, *Charles Evans Hughes* (New York, 1951) II, Chapters 69, 70 and 71.
13. *Panama Refining Co.* v. *Ryan; Amazon Petroleum Corp.* v. *Ryan*, 293 U.S. 389.
14. *Retirement Board* v. *Alton Railroad Co.*, 295 U.S. 330, 374.

15. Quoted in Jackson, 105-06.
16. *Louisville Bank* v. *Radford*, 295 U.S. 555.
17. *A. L. A. Schecter Poultry Corp.* v. *United States*, 295 U.S. 495.
18. *A. L. A. Schecter Poultry Corp.* v. *United States*, 295 U.S. 495.
19. Samuel I. Rosenman, ed., *The Public Papers and Addresses of Franklin D. Roosevelt* (New York, 1938) IV, 221.
20. *Carter* v. *Carter Coal Co.*, 298 U.S. 238.
21. *Ashton* v. *Cameron County District*, 298 U.S. 513.
22. *Morehead* v. *New York ex rel. Tipaldo*, 298 U.S. 587.
23. *United States* v. *Butler*, 297 U.S. 1.
24. Quoted in Jackson, 133.
25. Quoted in Jackson, 134-35.
26. Quoted in Jackson, 135.
27. Roosevelt carried 46 of the existing 48 states and rolled up over 7,000,000 more popular votes than his opponent.
28. The best book and the most lively account is a journalistic report entitled *The 168 Days*, written by two Washington newspaper correspondents, Joseph Alsop and Turner Catledge (Garden City, New York, 1938). A more recent account is Leonard Baker, *Back to Back*, which contains some new material gleaned from interviews with the participants and from a perusal of FDR's papers. There are also William R. Barnes and A. W. Littlefield, *The Supreme Court Issues and the Constitution* (New York, 1937); and Alfred Haines Cope and Fred Krinsky, eds., *Franklin D. Roosevelt and the Supreme Court* (Boston, 1952). An unpublished dissertation, "The President's Supreme Court Proposal: A Study in Presidential Leadership and Public Opinion" (University of California at Los Angeles, 1953) was written by E. Kinback MacColl and is correctly described by James MacGregor Burnes as the "fullest and most authoritative source for the court fight." William Leuchtenburg has what will undoubtedly be the magisterial account under preparation.
29. Max Freedman, ed., *Roosevelt and Frankfurter, Their Correspondence, 1928-1945* (Boston, 1967), 380.
30. William E. Leuchtenburg, *Franklin D. Roosevelt and the New Deal, 1932-1940* (New York, 1963), 233.
31. Quoted in Baker, 48.
32. Baker, 47.
33. Jackson, 189.
34. Leuchtenburg, *FDR and the New Deal*, 233.
35. Freedman, 381-82.
36. Freedman, 382.
37. Baker, 33-35.
38. Baker, 33-35.
39. Pusey, II, 756.
40. Pusey, II, 756.
41. Pusey, II, 756.
42. Quoted in Baker, 159.
43. Baker, 160.
44. Freedman, 282-83.
45. Leuchtenburg, *FDR and the New Deal*, 234.
46. Norris had spoken out against the bill, but in the end he gave it his lukewarm support and his vote. There was no question, however, that he did nothing whatsoever to work for its approval.
47. *Adkins* v. *Children's Hospital*, 261 U.S. 525.
48. *Morehead* v. *New York ex rel. Tipaldo*, 298 U.S. 587.
49. *West Coast Hotel Co.* v. *Parish*, 300 U.S. 379.
50. Abe Fortas as quoted in Baker, 182.
51. *National Labor Relations Board* v. *Jones and Laughlin*, 301 U.S. 1.
52. *Steward Machine Co.* v. *Davis*, 301 U.S. 548; *Helvering* v. *Davis*, 301 U.S. 619.
53. Quoted in Alsop and Catledge, 153.
54. Quoted in Baker, 181.
55. There is some discussion of this, though not very detailed, in Alsop and Catledge, 115-19; 164-76; and Baker, 202-05.
56. Quoted in Leuchtenburg, *FDR and the New Deal*, 237.
57. Quoted in Alsop and Catledge, 279.
58. Hadley Cantril, ed., *Public Opinion, 1935-1936* (Princeton, New Jersey, 1951), 150.

59. In May the question was changed to: "Should Congress pass the President's Supreme Court proposal?"
60. In June the question was changed to: "Should Congress pass the President's plan to enlarge the Supreme Court?"
61. George Gallup and Claude Robinson, "Public Opinion Surveys, 1935-1938," in *Public Opinion Quarterly*, July 1938, 378-79.
62. Elmo B. Roper, jr., "Neutral Opinion on the Court Proposal," in *Public Opinion Quarterly*, July 1937, 18-20.
63. Roper, 20.
64. Roper, 20.
65. Louis Martin Sears, *Jefferson and the Embargo* (Durham, North Carolina, 1927), 153.
66. Adams, Levy and Sears record dozens of such incidents, and there were hundreds of others the records of which exist only in the court and Treasury files and have gone unheralded.
67. Most of this background material on the committee and its campaign against the Court bill is drawn from Richard Polenberg, *Reorganizing Roosevelt's Government: The Controversy Over Executive Reorganization, 1936-1939* (Cambridge, Massachusetts, 1966), 55-63.
68. The Gannett Committee lists included officials from every farm organization, editors of every agricultural publication and 23,000 individual and presumably wealthy farmers. The list also contained the names of 161,000 lawyers, 121,000 doctors, 68,000 business leaders, 137,000 clergymen of all faiths, influential women and numerous politicians.
69. Polenberg, 63.
70. Baker, 78.
71. Baker, 85.
72. Leuchtenburg, *FDR and the New Deal*, 239.
73. Leuchtenburg, *FDR and the New Deal*, 243-44.
74. Quoted in William E. Leuchtenburg, "The Constitutional Revolution of 1937," in *The Great Depression: Essays and Memoirs from Canada and the United States* (Vancouver, British Columbia, 1969), 61.
75. Leuchtenburg, "The Constitutional Revolution," 63.
76. Leuchtenburg, "The Constitutional Revolution," 64.
77. Howard Zinn, ed., *New Deal Thought* (Indianapolis, Indiana, 1966), xvi-xvii.
78. Barton J. Bernstein, "The New Deal: Conservative Achievements of Liberal Reform," in Barton J. Bernstein and Allen J. Matusow, eds., *Twentieth Century America: Recent Interpretations* (New York, 1972), 245-46.
79. Charles A. Reich, *The Greening of America* (New York, 1970), 50.
80. Jacob Cohen, "Schlesinger and the New Deal," in *Dissent,* VIII (Autumn 1961), 472.
81. Rexford Guy Tugwell, "The Experimental Roosevelt," in William E. Leuchtenburg, ed., *Franklin D. Roosevelt: A Profile* (New York, 1967), 69.
82. Tugwell, "The Experimental Roosevelt," 72.
83. Clinton Rossiter, *The American Presidency* (New York, 1956), 121.
84. Rossiter, 124.
85. Grant McConnell, *The President Seizes the Steel Mills* (Inter-University Case Program, University, Alabama), 1960.
86. Quoted in Alan F. Westin, *The Anatomy of a Constitutional Law Case* (New York, 1958), 8.
87. Harry S. Truman, *Memoirs* (New York, 1958) II, *Years of Trial and Hope*, 469.
88. Westin, 7.
89. Richard Neustadt, *Presidential Power: The Politics of Leadership* (New York, 1960), 22-23.
90. From the opinion of Judge David Pine, April 29, 1952, in Westin, 69-70.
91. *Marbury* v. *Madison*, 1 Cranch 137 (1803).
92. John P. Roche, *Shadow and Substance* (New York, 1964), 154.
93. George Gallup, *The Gallup Poll: Public Opinion, 1935-1971* (New York, 1972) II, 1062; 1065.
94. Roche, 160, footnote 78.
95. Roche, 152.
96. Neustadt, 10.
97. Quoted in Neustadt, 184.
98. Neustadt, 184.
99. Neustadt, 184.
100. Leuchtenburg, *FDR and the New Deal*, 261; 272-73.
101. Benjamin Fletcher Wright, ed., *The Federalist* (Cambridge, Massachusetts, 1961). See James Madison, Federalist No. 10, "The Size and Variety of the Union as a Check on Faction," 134.

102. Elmer E. Cornwell, jr., *Presidential Leadership of Public Opinion* (Bloomington, Indiana, 1965), 3-4.
103. Cornwell, 24.
104. *Youngstown Sheet & Tube Co. et al.* v. *Sawyer*, 343 U.S. 637-38.
105. James MacGregor Burns, *Presidential Government: The Crucible of Leadership* (Boston, 1966), 351. (My emphasis.)
106. C. Wright Mills, *The Power Elite* (New York, 1951), 303-04.
107. John Stuart Mill, *Utilitarianism: Liberty, and Representative Government* (London, 1944), 204.

Bibliography

Alsop, Joseph and Catledge, Turner. *The One Hundred Sixty-Eight Days.* New York: DaCapo Press, 1938.

Baker, Leonard. *Back to Back: The Duel Between FDR and the Supreme Court.* New York: The Macmillan Company, 1967.

Bernstein, Barton J. and Matusow, Allen J., eds. *Twentieth Century America: Recent Interpretations.* New York: Harcourt, Brace Jovanovich, 1972.

Brant, Irving. *Storm Over the Constitution.* Princeton, New Jersey: Princeton University Press, 1938.

_____. *The Twilight of the Supreme Court.* New Haven, Connecticut: Yale University Press, 1947.

Burns, James MacGregor. *Presidential Government: The Crucible of Leadership.* Boston: Houghton Mifflin Company, 1966.

Cantril, Hadley, ed. *Public Opinion, 1935-1936.* Princeton, New Jersey: Princeton University Press, 1951.

Cohen, Jacob. "Schlesinger and the New Deal." *Dissent.* VIII (Autumn 1961).

Cope, Alfred Hanes and Krinsky, Fred, eds. *Franklin D. Roosevelt and the Supreme Court.* Boston: D. C. Heath and Company, 1952.

Cornwell, Elmer E., jr. *Presidential Leadership of Public Opinion.* Bloomington, Indiana: Indiana University Press, 1965.

Freedman, Max, ed. *Roosevelt and Frankfurter, Their Correspondence, 1928-1945.* Boston: Little, Brown and Company, 1968.

Gallup, George. *The Gallup Poll: Public Opinion, 1935-1971.* Vol. II. New York: Random House, 1972.

Hughes, Charles Evans. *The Supreme Court of the United States.* New York: Columbia University Press, 1928.

Ickes, Harold L. *The Secret Diary of Harold L. Ickes.* Vol. II. New York: Simon and Schuster, 1954.

Jackson, Robert. *The Struggle for Judicial Supremacy*. New York: Vintage Books, 1941.

Leuchtenburg, William E. *Franklin D. Roosevelt and the New Deal, 1932-1940*. New York: Harper and Row, 1963.

McConnell, Grant. *The President Seizes the Steel Mills*. University, Alabama: University of Alabama Press, 1960.

Mason, Alpheus T. *Brandeis, A Free Man's Life*. New York: Viking Press, 1956.

. *Harlan Fiske Stone: Pillar of the Law*. New York: Viking Press, 1956.

. *The Supreme Court: Vehicle of Revealed Truth or Power Group, 1930-1937*. Boston: Houghton Mifflin Company, 1947.

Mill, John Stuart. *Utilitarianism: Liberty and Representative Government*. New York: E. P. Dutton and Company, 1944.

Mills, C. Wright. *The Power Elite*. New York: Oxford University Press, 1951.

Neustadt, Richard. *Presidential Power: The Politics of Leadership*. New York: John Wiley and Sons, 1960.

Polenberg, Richard. *Reorganizing Roosevelt's Government; The Controversy Over Executive Reorganization, 1936-1939*. Cambridge, Massachusetts: Harvard University Press, 1966.

Pusey, Merlo J. *Charles Evans Hughes*. 2 vols. New York: Columbia University Press, 1951.

Reich, Charles A. *The Greening Of America*. New York: Random House, 1970.

Roche, John P. *Shadow and Substance*. New York: The Macmillan Company, 1964.

Rosenman, Samuel I., ed. *The Public Papers and Addresses of Franklin D. Roosevelt*. Vols. IV, V, VI, VIII. New York: Russell and Russell Publishers, 1938.

Rossiter, Clinton. *The American Presidency*. New York: Harcourt, Brace and World, Inc., 1956.

Swisher, Carl Brent. *American Constitutional Development*. Boston: Houghton Mifflin Company, 1943.

Truman, Harry S. *Memoirs.* Vol. II., *Years of Trial and Hope.* New York: Doubleday and Company, 1958.

Tugwell, Rexford Grey. "The Experimental Roosevelt." William E. Leuchtenburg, ed., *Franklin D. Roosevelt: A Profile.* New York: Hill and Wang, 1967.

Westin, Alan F. *The Anatomy of a Constitutional Law Case.* New York: The Macmillan Company, 1958.

Wright, Benjamin Fletcher, ed. *The Federalist.* Cambridge, Massachusetts: Harvard University Press, 1961.

Zinn, Howard, ed. *New Deal Thought.* Indianapolis, Indiana: The Bobbs-Merrill Company, Inc., 1966.

VII. The Future of Presidential Power

**Including a Dialogue
on Major Aspects of the Presidency
with Professors Arthur M. Schlesinger, Jr. and Leon Friedman**

THE FUTURE OF
PRESIDENTIAL POWER

The Imperial Presidency

After almost 200 years of dynamic if not always continuous growth and development, the American presidency is in real trouble, in a manner and to a degree never before approached in the span of its turbulent history. Throughout these three volumes, I have tried to trace the growth of presidential power, to pinpoint the important benchmarks which signaled critical advances in its development and to explain, to justify and even to question its advisability, when such a challenge was required. On the whole this development has been necessary, as Arthur Schlesinger has argued, "to overcome the tendency toward inertia" which exists in the division of power at the center of our political system and to enable "the American republic to meet the great crises of its history."[1] During the first 150 years of the republic this development was not inordinate; it did not destroy the delicate balance of power so essential to the active heartbeat of the system, nor did it come about because of ill-advised abuses of the office by its inhabitants. It was a natural, organic development—a series of responses to critical problems which could not be resolved without dynamic executive leadership.

The growth of the power of the presidency since World War II has been of an entirely different character. The range of problems confronting this country at the end of that terrifying human struggle went far beyond anything approached in our previous history. The United States emerged as the most powerful military and economic power in the world, and the Executive leader of the American people became the most important statesman on the world scene. During the Truman, Eisenhower and Kennedy administrations, the response to this new challenge was not characterized by any individual lust for power or inability to discipline its application. Rather, it was the attempt by self-controlled individuals to guide their own ways through very dangerous and relatively unexplored seas of international and domestic crises.

This has been one of the worst years in the history of the American presidency. Never before has the prestige and power of the office fallen into such disrepute. There have been presidential scandals and lackluster Chief Executives in the past, but the country has never experienced anything approaching the degradation of the White House which we have witnessed during the past few years. The American presidency has served the republic admirably, sometimes brilliantly, over the course of its almost 200 years of existence. There has been an ebb and flow of power just as there has been a rise and fall of particularly talented leadership. Volume II of this series has documented the long post-Civil War period when the Executive office was overshadowed by an arrogant and at times corrupt legislature. But in the twentieth century, American Presidents recovered their footing and provided more effective leadership to the nation than any inhabitants of the White House since the days of Jackson. But during this entire period, no President has so clearly abused the prerogatives of his office as Richard Milhous Nixon. It will not be easy to recover from this experience.

How did this come about, why did it develop at this particular moment in history, and what can it foretell for the future of the office? One cannot end a study of the growth of presidential power without responding to these questions. In fact some reasonable answers to such questions may alone justify the over 2000 pages which precede this final section. For if history cannot cast some light upon the present, provide a perspective in which current flaws are illuminated by comparisons with the trials and errors of the past, it becomes a futile and irrelevant exercise, perhaps a proper enterprise for encyclopedists or folklorists but not particularly germane to the discourse of serious men and women who are struggling to discover truth.

At the outset it should be emphasized that in this last section I will not attempt to maintain the format established previously. History is written every day in the newspapers and journals, and some of it will stand the test of time. But most contemporary journalism serves only as a partial source for future historical analysis, which will be written when all of the evidence is in and can be properly evaluated. To attempt to write the history of the American presidency in the past decade, with its extraordinary turmoil and dislocations, without first tapping the widest range of sources, many of which have yet to be revealed, would not simply be risky, but foolhardy and historically unsound. Much of what has transpired during these years has not yet been disclosed; in some cases it has not even been recorded. There are many secret documents not yet declassified, presidential papers (indeed tapes) unexamined, memoirs still unwritten and testimony, reflection and interrogation still untapped. It would be impossible and foolish to pass judgment on the Johnson and the Nixon administrations with finality.

That does not mean that nothing of any significance can be said of their administrations, however, or that some tentative conclusions cannot be reached. There is an overwhelming record accumulating day by day, and living so close to the period itself, while being bombarded with information, it is certainly possible to begin to put the pieces together. We must try, for the problems at hand will not await the final judgment of history. Men must choose, they must act, they must attempt to determine the course of events. Even a somewhat hazy and indistinct set of guidelines is better than no direction whatsoever. But the caution and reserve with which one approaches contemporary problems and events must be even greater than that applied to the study and reconstruction of the past, although frequently the sources available are more adequate and potentially more revealing of the circumstances involved.

The parameters of any discussion of the contemporary presidency have already been established by Arthur Schlesinger, jr. in his recent study, *The Imperial Presidency*. The very language of his work will provide the terms of future discourse on the subject, and though Schlesinger is bound to encounter his own revisionists in due time, his study provides the touchstone for all serious discussion of the appalling transformation of the office in the last decade.

It is ironic that the 1960s dawned with such great hopes for the presidency. Eloquently expressed by John F. Kennedy as he announced his candidacy for that office, he reviewed the history of the presidency, touching upon both its great and its not so great moments and asserting finally that the 1960s called for a revitalized quality of presidential leadership:

> It will demand that the President place himself in the very thick of the fight, that he care passionately about the fate of the people he leads, that he is willing to serve them at the risk of incurring their momentary displeasure.[2]

He went on to define the various areas of leadership the President would have to assume—executive, legislative, party and moral—in order to provide the inspiration and direction the challenges facing the country required (see section four of this volume). This high flown rhetoric has been criticized by Henry Fairlie as constituting the false hopes engendered in the "politics of expectation," but Fairlie fails to note the extent to which Kennedy rose on several brilliant occasions to meet the high standards he had himself enunciated. If the Progressive program of the Theodore Roosevelt and Wilson years provided the skeletal outline of the unfulfilled agenda for our times, Kennedy's announcement speech set the proper tone for the expectations of presidential leadership in our period.

The first major tragedy of the 1960s was Kennedy's assassination, just as he was about to make major breakthroughs in foreign and domestic policies. With the missile crisis behind him, Kennedy, in a speech at the American University the following summer, showed a new determination and confidence in achieving a *detente* with the Soviet Union. In the fall of 1963 he was actively pursuing the passage of a tax cut and a new civil rights bill, along with longer-range plans for advanced legislation dealing with compensatory education and a program to combat poverty in the United States. Kennedy was optimistic about his reelection in 1964 and hopeful of a mandate for creative political action, a luxury denied him in 1960 in the wake of his marginal electoral victory over Nixon. At the same time the President was aware of the constraints imposed upon any Executive in the White House. He considered this problem in the introduction he wrote to Theodore Sorensen's Gino Speranza lectures:

> Many things have been written about the conditions of presidential decisions. The President, for example, is rightly described as a man of extraordinary powers. Yet it is true that he must wield these powers under extraordinary limitations—and it is these limitations which so often give the problem of choice its complexity and even poignancy. Lincoln, Franklin Roosevelt once remarked, "was a sad man because he couldn't get it all at once. And nobody can." Every President must endure a gap between what he would like and what is possible.[3]

Kennedy was succeeded by Lyndon Baines Johnson, an experienced legislator and Democratic party leader for three decades. Johnson immediately won the acclaim of the country for his masterful and effective transition during one of the most trying periods in this country's history. He quickly took up the unfinished struggle for Kennedy's legislative program and drove it through to a successful conclusion. Johnson not only achieved Kennedy's unfulfilled legislative goals, but he developed a wide range of social and economic legislation of his own and provided the political clout to push them through Congress. In finishing out Kennedy's unexpired term and in winning a landslide victory over Senator Barry Goldwater in 1964, Lyndon Johnson continued to demonstrate his political acuity and established a firm reputation as a President capable of leading his party and the American people to a higher level of national prosperity and a broadened sense of social responsibility.

Johnson also accomplished another stunning achievement in national leadership. The first President to come from a southern state in over 100 years, he was determined to act forcefully to bring about a greater level of equality for Black citizens in this country. Johnson's refusal to equivocate on this issue accounted for continued progress, particularly in the South, in bringing many hundreds of thousands of Black Americans into the electoral process and in extending equality of education in southern communities to a degree that shamed "integrated" communities in the North. Without Johnson's leadership these advances could not have been made. When a southern-born Democratic President of the United States could stand before both houses of Congress, and in appealing for additional voting rights legislation declare "We shall overcome," it was a symbolic victory for the democratic principle of equality that the Constitution demands, but which has been for so long denied to Black citizens in this country.

Unfortunately Johnson's tenure in the White House was flawed by his excessive use of his power as foreign policy leader and Commander in Chief. In time this overshadowed his significant domestic achievements and ultimately drove him from the White House. During this period Johnson initiated one of the most tragic interludes in American history, a disastrous war which brought nothing but untold grief to all who were closely involved and misfortune to the rest of the country. Later, in the Nixon administration, the excesses of the power of the President as a world leader were extended to include outrageous violations of constitutional rights on the domestic level, plunging the nation into its most regressive and politically damaging crisis in this century, perhaps in its entire history.

The Vietnam War and Presidential War Powers

Arthur Schlesinger has defined ours as the age of the "Imperial Presidency," a time in which "a conception of presidential power" prevailed, "so spacious and peremptory as to imply a radical transformation of the traditional polity. In the last years presidential primacy so indispensable to the political order, has turned into presidential supremacy."[4] This development has nowhere been so clearly documented as in the continuing aggrandizement of the powers of the President in the area of war and peace—when the foreign policy and military powers have been fused into a comprehensive and now quite threatening concept of world leadership. In Volume II, I traced the roots of this development in the administrations of McKinley and Theodore Roosevelt, and again in this volume (section five) in the war tenures of Wilson, Franklin Roosevelt and Harry Truman, spurred on in the latter two cases by the remarkable *Curtiss-Wright* decision of the Supreme Court in 1936.

We have observed that powers, in most cases legitimately sought by Presidents struggling with very real and threatening challenges from the outside, have gradually been incorporated into the armor of their peacetime successors, so that in the 1960s and 1970s they are assertions so "spacious and peremptory" as to overwhelm the balance of power which has served as the fulcrum of the constitutional protection of our liberties. There was ample warning of this possibility during World War II and the Korean "police action," but during the administrations of Johnson and Nixon, this concept of the war and peace powers has been asserted with renewed vigor, frequently enshrouded beneath a veil of presidential secrecy that is more than alarming; it is also very dangerous.

Of critical importance is the clear identification of the situations in which this dangerous expansion of presidential power took place. Schlesinger points out:

> Lyndon Johnson came to the Presidency with an old and honest belief in spacious presidential authority to deploy forces abroad in the service of American foreign policy. He had defended Truman's decision in 1950; and, while he had come to believe that Truman made a mistake in not asking for a congressional resolution, *he saw this as (a) political, not (a) constitutional, error.* A resolution could protect an administration's flanks, but the President already had the legal power.[5]

This was certainly not a new doctrine. It had been espoused not only by Acheson and Truman, but by a number of previous Presidents as well. But its incremental application to relatively minor operations in the nineteenth century, like the dispatch of a company of marines to protect an American legation from a native revolt on the Fiji Islands or dealing with pirates on the high seas to Truman's actions in Korea and Johnson's in Vietnam, constituted what might best be described as the transformation that takes place when a difference of degree becomes a difference in kind. Johnson's decision to increase the 16,000 military "advisors" (who lost only 100 dead) in South Vietnam to over a half million troops engaged in a war which resulted in thousands of deaths and hundreds of thousands of casualties was a significant difference in kind, as opposed to degree, or better, a "quantum leap" into the vast and unpredictable unknown.

I prefer, however, to avoid any detailed discussion of the Vietnam War, and to concentrate upon the decisions which precipitated our engagement in this second "police action" or undeclared war. Johnson had the foresight to circumvent the bind in which Truman found himself when he was left with an unpopular war on his hands. In failing to obtain a congressional commitment, the early enthusiasts for his policies in Korea were later able to withdraw their support and refer to the war as "Truman's war." Johnson, on the contrary, succeeded in nailing Congress to the cross of his future policies in Vietnam by the catch-all Southeast Asia Resolution, more commonly referred to as the "Gulf of Tonkin" resolution.

In the summer of 1964 Lyndon Johnson had not yet unleashed America's full military power in the jungles of Vietnam. There were, however, substantial numbers of American personnel and increasing American concern and activity there. Shortly after noon on August 2, the American destroyer, U.S.S. *Maddox* was cruising in the Tonkin Gulf when three North Vietnamese PT boats were sighted. Although the *Maddox* was 30 miles from the mainland, she was close to the nearest Vietnamese island off the coast, Hon Vat (5.1 nautical miles), and 11 miles from the island of Hon Me, which was attacked by South Vietnamese high-powered attack ships within 48 hours of the time when the PT boats were sighted. The American ship attempted to head out to sea, but the smaller and faster PT boats continued their pursuit. When they were approximately 5 miles from the destroyer, she fired three warning shots; when they were ignored and the PT boats failed to veer off, the *Maddox* opened up her five-inch batteries and blew one of the boats out of the water. The other two were hit by U.S. aircraft from the carrier U.S.S. *Ticonderoga*. The *Maddox* successfully avoided torpedoes launched by the Vietnamese and no one on board was injured.

The North Vietnamese version of that encounter differs considerably from the American account. On the same day, August 2, 1964, the Vietnamese People's Army liaison mission addressed a telegram to the International Control Commission, alleging an American attack upon North Vietnam:

> At 24:30 hours on 30 July, the Americans and their henchmen in South Vietnam sent two warships to bombard Hon Ngu Island off Gua Hoi Hoi, Nghe Am Province. This island is four kilometers from the coast. At the same time another warship was sent to bombard Hon Me Island off Ba Lang, Thanh Hoa Province. This island is twelve kilometers from the coast. . . . Obviously these are not individual acts, but part of the premeditated common plan of the Americans and their henchmen to carry out schemes to intensify the provocative and destructive acts against the DRV [Democratic Republic of Vietnam] while striving to step up their aggressive war in South Vietnam.[6]

Another North Vietnamese report of the incident carried on Hanoi radio emphasized the defensive nature of the Vietnam action:

> . . . [T]he enemy had brazenly violated our territorial waters. We had to show them the brave (words indistinct). Because the U.S. navy destroyer has the strength of long-range firepower, we had to move in close to it. Lively, mobile, witty and courageous, we were determined to fulfill our duty to protect the tranquil waters of our fatherland.[7]

Granting the propaganda nature of both reports and the bravado indulged, they indicate that the North Vietnamese connected the activities of the *Maddox* and other members of the "De Soto Patrol" (the code name of the operation) with simultaneous raids upon the offshore islands by the South Vietnamese navy. The previous week the head of the South Vietnamese government had threatened to carry the war to the North, and the commander of that nation's air force had threatened bombing raids which would destroy Hanoi, if not all of North Vietnam.[8] With the presence of American advisors in South Vietnam, training and supporting South Vietnamese military and naval operations, what else were the North Vietnamese to think when they observed American ships of war a few miles off their coastline at the same time that raids were being conducted on military and naval bases in that area. The South Vietnamese raiding craft passed so close to the *Maddox* that they were observable to the crew of the destroyer.

The two most controversial points surrounding the presence of the American patrol in these waters were the dispute between the United States and North Vietnam as to what constituted the legitimate North Vietnamese territorial waters, and, secondly, what was the mission of the American "De Soto Patrol" in the Tonkin Gulf. The North Vietnamese, as many other communist countries do, claimed territorial waters 12 miles off their coastline, while the United States only recognized the international limit of 3 miles. Secretary of Defense Robert McNamara maintained that the American patrol was on a "routine" assignment in international waters at the time of the attack. The North Vietnamese accused the American ship of violating their territorial waters and operating in support of the South Vietnamese navy, which was conducting raids on military and naval installations in North Vietnam. The top secret equipment installed on the *Maddox* and operated by special personnel who were not part of her regular crew, clearly indicated that the ship's mission was not purely routine. This highly sophisticated electronic equipment was being used to obtain information that would at an absolute minimum be useful to South Vietnam and injurious to the North. There was also considerable question, raised by subsequent investigations by the Senate Foreign Relations Committee, whether the equipment on the *Maddox* was used in an attempt to confuse the North Vietnamese during raids by the South Vietnamese navy and to lure defense operations into another area.

United States officials have frequently and heatedly denied any connection between the South Vietnamese raids on the islands of Hon Me and Hon Ngu, but there is substantial evidence to the contrary. Captain John J. Herrick, an experienced navy veteran of many years service, was in command of the American patrol. He cabled the Seventh Fleet commander after the attack:

> (a) Evaluation of info from various sources indicated that the DRV considers patrol directly involved with 34-A operations [34-A was the code name for the South Vietnamese raids on North Vietnam installations]. DRV considers US ships present as enemies because of these operations and have already indicated readiness to treat us in that category.
> (b) DRV are very sensitive about Hon Me. Believes this is PT operating base and that the cove there presently contains many numerous patrol and PT craft which have been repositioned from northerly bases.[9]

The secretary of defense later denied that Captain Herrick had any basis for making such a statement and the captain later admitted as much, but the cable clearly suggests that the commander on the scene made precisely that judgment. In addition, Captain Herrick subsequently recommended that the patrol be withdrawn since its continued presence in that area of the Gulf of Tonkin constituted an "unnecessary risk." He was overruled by the commander of the United States forces in the Pacific, Admiral Ulysses Grant Sharp, who felt that such a withdrawal would jeopardize the American "resolve to assert our legitimate rights in these international waters."[10]

At any rate, there was no question that the North Vietnam PT boats attacked the *Maddox* 28 miles off the North Vietnamese coastline and 11 miles from the island under siege. The United States immediately protested the attack and warned the North Vietnamese of grave consequences if it was repeated. Two days later a second attack was reported by the *Maddox* and her sister destroyer, the *Turner Joy*. The attackers were reported to have been driven off by the destroyers' guns, and no casualties and no damage were reported to either ship. Later investigation by independent studies of the affair revealed that there was considerable doubt, even at that time, that such an attack had ever taken place. Some objects appeared on the radar screen, but it was a miserably dark and rainy night with a very rough sea and the possibility of error was great. In fact, after carefully examining members of the crew who had manned the radar equipment and the batteries and then checking on possible evidence of the sightings, Captain Herrick was very uncertain himself as to just what took place. In his first cable after the alleged attack he warned:

> Entire action leaves many doubts except for apparent attempted ambush at beginning. Suggest thorough reconnaissance in daylight by aircraft.[11]

A later warning, after more reflection, was stated in even stronger language:

> Review of action makes many reported contacts and torpedoes fired appear doubtful. . . . Freak weather effects and overeager sonarmen may have accounted for many reports. No actual visual sightings by Maddox. Suggest complete evaluation before any further action.[12]

An Annapolis graduate and career naval officer, Herrick was a decorated veteran of World War II and the Korean War and had held numerous previous commands at sea. He was no one to panic or vacillate. A serious warning from an officer of his experience ought to have eliminated any possibility of precipitate action. But Washington was impatient and ready to go. Reports coming to the President from Vietnam for the past year had been routinely pessimistic, indicating that with all our aid and advice, the South Vietnamese were losing the war. Johnson and his military advisors were anxious for a dramatic reversal, but the veteran politician was also cautious, especially during an election year, of tipping his full hand. A decisive but surgical response to the present challenge was necessary, but then further inaction would follow, at least until the election was over. He would preserve his image as a responsible leader under fire. Campaigning as the safe and sane candidate of peace against the gun-slinging, irresponsible senator from

Arizona who was anxious to end the stalemate, Johnson issued almost self-executioning orders, commanding a retaliation if there was another serious challenge by the North Vietnamese:

> Johnson had announced that he had issued new instructions regarding future patrols and engagements with enemy craft: The Navy was to continue the patrol in the Gulf of Tonkin, with the Turner Joy joining the Maddox, and a combat air patrol was to be maintained over both vessels. Both the planes and the destroyers had orders "(a) to attack any force which attacked them in international waters, and (b) to attack with the objective of not only driving off the force, but of destroying it."[13]

Since there was no real evidence that the attackers in the second alleged incident had been "destroyed," there remained unfinished business. After a day of frantic meetings and messages across the Pacific demanding confirmation of the attack, Captain Herrick, pressured by his superiors to maintain his patrol in enemy waters infested with small enemy craft capable of sinking the destroyers, was required to conduct an on-the-spot investigation and interrogation of all members of the crew. Only one crew member of the *Maddox* claimed to have seen the enemy craft. The chief gunnery officer did not think any North Vietnamese boats had come within range and many sonarmen were skeptical about the reported sightings. Reports from the *Turner Joy* were equally indecisive, although several aboard claimed to have sighted a searchlight. Despite continuous badgering from at least three admirals in the top command of the navy, Herrick sent off a final reply which arrived in Washington after the retaliatory air strike was underway. It hardly provided sufficient evidence upon which to base such a raid:

> Maddox scored no known hits and never positively identified a boat as such. . . . Weather was overcast with limited visibility. . . . Air support not successful in locating targets. . . . There were no stars or moon resulting in almost total darkness throughout action. . . . No known damage or personnel casualties to either ship. . . . Turner Joy claims sinking one boat and damaging another. . . . The first boat to close Maddox probably fired torpedo at Maddox which was heard but not seen. All subsequent Maddox torpedo reports were doubtful in that it is supposed that sonarman was hearing ship's own propeller beat.[14]

On such evidence men are forced to act or not to act. Washington was convinced by the evaluation of the top naval commander in the area that an attack had been made, and a strong air strike was authorized by the President, in an attempt to wipe out the bases from which the torpedo boats emerged. Sixty-four air sorties were conducted, destroying 25 of the boats known to be based at the target sites. An oil storage facility which supplied the torpedo boats was all but wiped out. It was not exactly a restrained response, given the conflicting and uncertain reports of an attack which caused no damage to either American ship and might very well not have taken place at all. North Vietnam continued to maintain that no such attack took place. After the American air strike was underway, President Johnson went on radio and television to report the unconfirmed American version of the attack which his naval chiefs had accepted. "Repeated acts of violence," the President said, "must be met not only with alert defense but with positive reply."[15]

It was only after the action was taken that the President called the leaders of Congress together and requested a special resolution which would reflect the unity of the country in its moment of crisis and provide him with congressional support for any further use of the armed forces in Vietnam as required. The resolution, prepared by the executive branch, provided Johnson with carte blanche approval for any further military or naval actions he deemed necessary; but for the time being, things were quiet and the election campaign proceeded apace.

The Gulf of Tonkin Resolution
August 10, 1964

78 Stat. 384 (August 10, 1964).

JOINT RESOLUTION

To promote the maintenance of international peace and security in southeast Asia.

Whereas naval units of the Communist regime in Vietnam, in violation of the principles of the Charter of the United Nations and of international law, have deliberately and repeatedly attacked United States naval vessels lawfully present in international waters, and have thereby created a serious threat to international peace; and

Whereas these attacks are part of a deliberate and systematic campaign of aggression that the Communist regime in North Vietnam has been waging against its neighbors and the nations joined with them in the collective defense of their freedom; and

Whereas the United States is assisting the peoples of southeast Asia to protect their freedom and has no territorial, military or political ambitions in that area, but desires only that these peoples should be left in peace to work out their own destinies in their own way: Now, therefore, be it

Resolved by the Senate and House of Representatives of the United States of America in Congress assembled, That the Congress approves and supports the determination of the President, as Commander in Chief, to take all necessary measures to repel any armed attack against the forces of the United States and to prevent further aggression.

Sec. 2. The United States regards as vital to its national interest and to world peace the maintenance of international peace and security in southeast Asia. Consonant with the Constitution of the United States and the Charter of the United Nations and in accordance with its obligations under the Southeast Asia Collective Defense Treaty, the United States is, therefore, prepared, as the President determines, to take all necessary steps, including the use of armed force, to assist any member or protocol state of the Southeast Asia Collective Defense Treaty requesting assistance in defense of its freedom.

Sec. 3. This resolution shall expire when the President shall determine that the peace and security of the area is reasonably assured by international conditions created by action of the United Nations or otherwise, except that it may be terminated earlier by concurrent resolution of the Congress.

Approved August 10, 1964.

This resolution was introduced by the chairman of the Senate Foreign Relations Committee, J. William Fulbright, who lived to regret his action. There is question whether or not President Johnson and Secretary of Defense Robert S. McNamara were entirely candid with Senator Fulbright or other House and Senate leaders when they proposed the resolution to them. The record is not yet complete on this murky episode, but subsequent investigation by Senator Fulbright's committee indicated that there is serious doubt whether the members of Congress were provided with all of the information available at that time, or that the incident was presented in the full context of other critical facts affecting it. On the occasion of this important reexamination of the Southeast Asia Resolution, Senator Fulbright protested to Secretary of Defense McNamara, who was testifying at the time:

> I think this committee, and certainly no chairman of the committee, I think it was very unfair to ask us to vote upon a resolution when the state of the evidence was as uncertain as I think it is now. . . .
>
> We have taken what is called the functional equivalent of a declaration of war upon evidence of this kind, and action as precipitate as this was. Even the commander, that is one of the crucial cablegrams from the commander of the task force, recommended that nothing be done until the evidence was further evaluated. . . .
>
> But that alone almost, if I had known of that one telegram, if that had been before me on the 6th of August, I certainly don't believe that I would have rushed into action.
>
> We met, if you will recall for 1 hour and 40 minutes, in a joint meeting with the Armed Services and this committee and we accepted your statement completely without doubt. I went on the floor to urge passage of the resolution. You quoted me, as saying these things on the floor. Of course all my statements were based upon your testimony. I had no independent evidence, and now I think I did a great disservice to the Senate. I feel guilty for not having enough sense at that time to have raised these questions and asked for evidence. I regret it.
>
> I have publicly apologized to my constituents and to the country for the unwise action I took, without at least inquiring into the basis. It never occurred to me that there was the slightest doubt, certainly on the part of Commander Herrick, who was in charge of the task force, that this attack took place. He obviously had doubts, for his own cablegram so states.

That is the reason for it. I feel a very deep responsibility and I regret it more than anything I have ever done in my life, that I was the vehicle which took that resolution to the floor and defended it in complete reliance upon information which, to say the very least, is somewhat dubious at this time.

Well, I just wanted to make that for the record.[16]

This certainly is one of the more remarkable statements ever made by a chairman of a congressional committee. Secretary McNamara argued that Captain Herrick did not state that he doubted the attack had taken place, yet surely this is a mere technicality, for he doubted the validity of almost every piece of evidence of an attack and he put that into teletype communication to Washington at least three times during the decision-making period. McNamara also pointed out that Herrick was convinced that the attack had taken place after reevaluating the evidence, but the secretary failed to mention the degree of top-level naval pressure which encouraged that evaluation.

Clearly Senator Fulbright and his colleagues in Congress were not fully apprised of the circumstances surrounding the attack on August 2, 1964 or the alleged attack on August 4, nor were they aware of all the doubts and contradictory reports surrounding them. They were persuaded, without having been adequately informed, to endorse the Southeast Asia Resolution, which, incidentally, had been prepared weeks in advance by the State Department, in anticipation of precisely this kind of crisis. The entire episode indicates the degree of control of a situation which a President possesses by his command of sources of information. He can release just as much or as little as he sees fit under the circumstances, and can even exaggerate or distort the facts if there is no check upon him. This is not to say that the latter was true in this situation, but simply defines the range of possibilities available under this setup.

After Congress rushed through the resolution in two days time, President Johnson did not press any further military, naval or air attacks against the North Vietnamese. This was an election year, and the Democrats renominated Johnson by acclamation at the party meeting in Atlantic City. The manner in which he now conducted himself, his total orchestration of the convention, the way in which he exploited his staff and all of those around him, clearly indicated that as President in his own right, he would perform further ostentatious displays of unbridled power. There was little evidence, as he warmed up to the responsive crowds in several frenetic campaign tours, that this President would recognize the inherent limits of the office and the fickleness of the national approval he had so obviously earned through his effective transition in office. The setting for a dramatic and tragic turnabout of the consensus was implicit in the relish with which he strutted in the warming sunlight of public approval.

Johnson had a rare, political homespun quality about him, and when he got going on the hustings, he did not freeze up as he did in Uncle Dudley fashion on television; he grabbed hold of his audiences and would not let go. At these moments, there was no one in American politics who could touch him. Theodore White records Johnson in one of those magic moments. In a speech delivered to a crowd in

Los Angeles six days before the election, Johnson was 100 percent genuine, cornpone and brilliant politician.

Just because we are powerful, we can't just mash a button and tell an independent country to go to——because they don't want to go to—— and we don't get very far rattling our rockets or lobbing them into the men's rooms or bluffing with our bombs.

I saw President Kennedy in the Cuban crisis in thirty-eight different meetings, and we got up to the last hours. Khrushchev had his missiles trained on this country that would completely wipe out San Francisco and Los Angeles. There would be no life left. Those men stood there, one speaking for the United States and the free world, and the other speaking for the Communist world. They got eyeball to eyeball, and I saw the generals with their stars come into the room [the great hand reached up and stroked the shoulders where the stars had been] and the admirals with their braid [the great hand stroked the sleeve crusted with Navy braid] and the Secretary of State with all of his diplomatic experience. [Sometimes he would talk about the Secretary of State, who was a Rhodes scholar at Oxford, you know, and the Secretary of Defense, who was President of the Ford Motor Company, making half a million dollars a year.]

I listened to every word. I never left home in the morning, a single morning that I knew I would get back that night to see Lady Bird and those daughters. So, as a little boy in my country used to say, we were doing some pretty heavy thinking, because we were right up to the gun. But Mr. Kennedy put his knife right there in his ribs and held it, Khrushchev put his there and held it, and neither one of them shook, trembled or developed palsy; neither one of them wobbled. Our planes were in the air. They had their bombs in them. Our Navy was on the seas; they were ready. But Mr. Khrushchev finally decided rather than to see three hundred million people killed and the Soviet Union wiped out—and they could wipe out America too—that, humiliating as it was, it might be a little wiser to wrap up his missiles in those tarpaulins [here the hands bundled and wrapped the missiles] and put them on those ships and take them back home, and that is what he did.

. . . [the] first responsibility, the only real issue in this campaign, the only thing that you ought to be concerned about at all, is who can best keep the peace? In the nuclear age the President doesn't get a second chance to make a second guess. If he mashes that button [here the big thumb mashed and squirmed as it pressed an imaginary button]—that is it.

So we cannot make a foreign policy, we cannot keep the peace by bluff and bluster and by threats and ultimatums. We can keep the peace and we can only keep the peace by two methods: first, with a strong defense, and we are today, I tell you as your Commander in Chief, the mightiest nation in all the world; and second, we can keep the peace, in the words of the Prophet Isaiah, by reasoning together, by responsibility, by negotiation.[17]

Soon after his victory as the peace candidate, Johnson turned to considerations of war. During the campaign he had virtually forgotten about Vietnam, but now that his overwhelming popular victory had renewed his hold on the White House, the President was forced to review the policy proposals of his advisors, who had not been idle. David Halberstam has drawn the picture of this period so perceptively that one cannot do better than to repair to his account for as accurate a description as is likely to be presented until more incriminating information surfaces (if it ever does). Nevertheless, elements of the classic tragedy were present throughout.

Johnson was a more than life-size hero in the Aristotelian sense, consumed with his own ambitions for American society—ambitions that may well have been generous and well intentioned, but were not shaped to the sensitive contours of reality and the human material with which he had to work. As his one-time press secretary, George Reedy, put it:

> Lyndon Johnson was a man who thought that all of the world's problems could be solved by giving people greater access to electric power, by placing an adequate floor under farm prices, by assuring everyone an equal right to a job, and by giving everyone an education. I think education was his principal fascination. The man was almost superstitious about education. I believe he thought it would cure chilblains.[18]

Nicholas von Hoffman caught something of his overreach in his loving eulogy to Johnson:

> Lyndon you were immoderate and greedy. You outdid all the rest of us hungry Americans for reaching out and grabbing, fingers always stretched for grasping. . . .[19]

Von Hoffman went on to praise Johnson for his great and redeeming stand for civil rights, but no eulogy could cover up his lack of restraint in pursuit of frequently unrealistic objectives.

After the election Johnson's key military and civilian advisors on Vietnam continued to press him for a substantial American military commitment. It had become clear to General Maxwell Taylor, the new American ambassador to South Vietnam, to McGeorge Bundy, Robert McNamara and others that the South Vietnamese were being beaten; without greater American military support the situation was hopeless for them. Johnson was cautious and continued to resist, but elaborate plans were prepared for pinpoint massive bombings in the North. Yet, Taylor came back from Saigon to plead for "plans to drive Hanoi out of its supporting role to the guerrilla insurgency," but the Johnson administration was apparently not ready to move.

> My audience in Washington was generally sympathetic to such ideas but still not ready to bite the bullet and face the inevitability of either taking military action against North Vietnam or running the very real risk of failing disastrously in Southeast Asia. . . . But I did return to Saigon with authority to plan military action against the North with our allies but with the understanding that the United States was not committed to execute the plans.[20]

It was the decision in Washington that execution was still not "politically feasible."

Then the second major Vietnamese "incident" occurred on February 7, 1965. The United States Air Force barrack at Pleiku was attacked by mortar fire and hand grenades from a raiding party, killing 8 Americans and wounding 126. Bundy, on an inspection tour in Saigon, Ambassador Taylor and Commanding General William Westmoreland all recommended instant retaliation in strength and the President gave his approval to massive bombing raids in areas north of the 17th parallel. These were followed by a sustained bombing campaign, appropriately code named Rolling Thunder. Subsequently, marine units were landed as security forces and the inevitable decision to use combat troops was made in July of that year. The war rapidly escalated. Johnson continued to press for peace negotiations, but in the light of their failure he was determined to press for an all-out military victory. Despite intermittent bombing halts, the magnitude of the war continued to increase and by the end of the year close to 200,000 military personnel were involved in Southeast Asia.

Lyndon Johnson should not be singled out exclusively for blame in the Vietnam debacle. The United States had become involved in Southeast Asia before his administration, and many of his advisors, who he inherited from his predecessor—those David Halberstam has referred to as the "best and the brightest"—were still in the White House when the critical decisions to escalate the war were made. Many of them were, in fact, more aggressive advocates for those actions than Johnson himself. But as Harry Truman has reminded us, the buck stops at the President's desk, and although the Vietnam War was a national tragedy in which in some sense the whole nation shared responsibility, Johnson was the President when the crucial decisions were made. History will judge him severely because of this. He had the power to reverse the drift of events, and he failed to do so.

As the furor of the war increased, criticism on the home front became more pronounced and a number of former supporters of the Tonkin Gulf resolution began to attack the war and the failure of the President to achieve a quick peace settlement. Uneasy about the tenuous state of the authority for military action under the resolution (it could be withdrawn at any time), the Johnson administration presented a legal defense of its actions in Vietnam, arguing that the President had full authority under the Constitution to authorize "the actions of the United States currently undertaken in Vietnam."[21] However, the argument continued, it was "not necessary to rely on the Constitution alone as the source of the President's authority, since the SEATO [Southeast Asia Treaty Organization] treaty—advised and consented to by the Senate and forming part of the law of the land—sets forth a United States commitment to defend South Vietnam against armed attack, and since the Congress—in the joint resolution of August 10, 1964, and in the authorization and appropriations acts for support of the U.S. military effort in Vietnam—has given its approval and support to the President's actions."[22]

The State Department's memorandum setting forth these arguments stated that the President had sufficient constitutional power to act independently of the Tonkin Gulf resolution and the SEATO treaty, but it was unnecessary to press that point since he was operating under their combined authority. But the major thrust of the document was directed to demonstrating the constitutional authority of the

President, which conceivably might have to stand alone to authorize his continued action.

The essence of this argument was characterized by Schlesinger as the most expansive ever made in defense of the President's war powers:

> In 1787, when the Founding Fathers reserved for the President the power to repel sudden attacks, "the world was a far larger place, and the framers probably had in mind attacks upon the United States." Now the world has grown much smaller. In the twentieth century, "an attack on a country far from our shores can impinge directly on the nation's security. . . ." The Constitution leaves the President the judgment to determine whether the circumstances of a particular armed attack are so urgent and the potential consequences so threatening to the security of the United States that he should act without formally consulting the Congress. In short, warfare anywhere on earth could, if the President so judged, constitute an attack on the United States and thereby authorize him to wage 'defensive' war without congressional consent. Under this theory it was hard to see why any future President would ever see any legal need to go to Congress before leading the nation into war.[23]

The following year another representative of the State Department just about buried Congress's power to declare war. In testimony before Senator Fulbright's Foreign Relations Committee, Under-Secretary of State Nicholas Katzenbach, a distinguished lawyer and former attorney general of the United States, argued that declaring war was "an outmoded phraseology," and would serve no useful purpose in Vietnam. He also asserted that the President had full constitutional authority to act in situations like Vietnam without congressional approval.[24]

Under-Secretary of State Nicholas Katzenbach Testimony (Extract) before the Senate Foreign Relations Committee on U.S. Commitments to Foreign Powers
August 17, 1967

U.S. Congress, Senate, Foreign Relations Committee, *U.S. Commitments to Foreign Powers*, Hearings, 90th Cong., 1st sess., 79-83; 141.

THE CHAIRMAN. Let us see if we can develop a few of the specific points. You make a statement that in speaking of the President—

> His is a responsibility borne of the need for speed and decisiveness in an emergency. His is the responsibility of controlling and directing all the external aspects of the Nation's power.

How do you fit this in with the constitutional provision as to the declaration of war by the Congress?

Yesterday we had one of the Nation's leading authorities, Professor Bartlett before us. He interprets the Constitution as meaning that the Congress has the exclusive power to initiate war. He used the word "initiate" rather than "declare" but "to declare" are the words of the Constitution. He feels this has been eroded by practice, particularly beginning about the turn of the century. Do you agree with his interpretation as to the meaning of the Constitution on the question of declaration of war?

MR. KATZENBACH. I believe that the Constitution makes it very clear that a declaration of war is the function of Congress. I believe our history has been that the wars we have declared have been declared at the initiative and instance of the Executive.

The function of the Congress is one to declare. It is not one to wage, not one to conduct, but one simply to declare. That is the function of Congress as expressed in the Constitution.

THE CHAIRMAN. To declare the war and to authorize the war, I guess.

MR. KATZENBACH. To declare it.

THE CHAIRMAN. Not to conduct it.

MR. KATZENBACH. That is true.

THE CHAIRMAN. You refer to the President as "the voice of policy."

MR. KATZENBACH. Yes.

THE CHAIRMAN. I gathered from the discussion yesterday, citing Jefferson and others who were involved in the creation of the Constitution, Jefferson referred to the Presidential power as the power to "transact the business." That refers to the conduct of the policies, but the conduct of it is not the same as the making of policy or the formulation of the overall policy, is it? They are two different things.

MR. KATZENBACH That is correct, and Congress has, as I noted, participated in the formulation of our policies, and many of the specific powers of Congress come into play in their conduct and operation. The Executive acts in accordance with the Constitution and in accordance with laws that are passed. I think he does so scrupulously. When I say that the voice of policy is the voice of the Presidency, I mean, Mr. Chairman, that it is he who speaks for the United States in foreign affairs; for who else can do so if it is not the President?

THE CHAIRMAN. The voice of policy, it seems to me, is the Congress in the crucial matter of declaring war or carrying on a war, as opposed, for example, to the repelling of an attack, which is quite different, or of rescuing citizens who are stranded in a place which is in a state of emergency, and usually contemplates a limited participation. These latter actions are opposed to the kind of war that we are now engaged in that has been going on for a number of years. That is a full-fledged war. It seems to me there is a very important distinction between whether or not we go to war or whether or not we respond to an emergency. There is a real difference between the conduct, that is the carrying out of the policy and the creation, the formulation of policy. I am trying to develop your views about the nature of this problem. I think the Constitution contemplated that the Congress should make the decision of whether or not we should engage in war. Don't you agree to that?

MR. KATZENBACH. Yes, Mr. Chairman, I agree that the Congress should, except in the case of emergencies, participate in major decisions of that kind.

Let me say, that indeed in the war to which you refer it did participate. It did participate in that. Now, let me elaborate my statement in that regard and see if I can make myself clear, because I think it is important. And, Mr. Chairman, I think this issue is a difficult one, one on which I think the Congress and the Executive should work together, as indeed I think they have.

The point is this. The use of the phrase "to declare war" as it was used in the Constitution of the United States had a particular meaning in terms of the events and the practices which existed at the time it was adopted and which existed really until the United Nations was organized. The phrase came from a context that recognized "war" to be an instrument of implementing the acceptable policy, but which is not acceptable in the climate today, which rejects the idea of aggression, which rejects the idea of conquest. The phrase came from the earlier context.

Now, it came for a function. As you rightly say, it was recognized by the Founding Fathers that the President might have to take emergency action to protect the security of the United States, but that if there was going to be another use of the armed forces of the United States, that was a decision which Congress should check the Executive on, which Congress should support. It was for that reason that the phrase was inserted in the Constitution.

Now, over a long period of time, and indeed the distinguished witness yesterday I think made the point very well, there have been many uses of the military forces of the United States for a variety of purposes without a congressional declaration of war. But it would be fair to say that most of these were relatively minor uses of force, although indeed in one case a landing of the Marines to protect property, I think, led the Marines to remain in a foreign country really in effect as an American Government, for some 20 years, which I would scarcely call minor. The reason for this was that there was a reluctance to describe these as acts of war and to use a formulation of declaring war, when war even in those days had the context of the use of military forces in another country in pursuit of national policy to acquire territory or to do various other things as an instrument of national policy.

And so there were several acts, they were called acts less than war, and called by a variety of other names. They were not submitted to the Congress to declare war because of the feeling for many, many years, that this would immediately mislead people with respect to what the objectives of the United States in these limited instances were.

Now, with the abolition of the use of force for all but a small number of purposes, by the commitment expressed in the U.N. Charter with respect to aggression, the question arises as to how the Congress can and should participate in the decision to use force; (1) where there is an emergency, and (2) beyond that, in a matter such as Korea where I think there was a genuine need for speed, or in the current instance in Vietnam?

A declaration of war would not, I think, correctly reflect the very limited objectives of the United States with respect to Vietnam. It would not correctly reflect our efforts there, what we are trying to do, the reasons why we are there, to use an outmoded phraseology, to declare war.

THE CHAIRMAN. You think it is outmoded to declare war?

MR. KATZENBACH. In this kind of a context I think the expression of declaring a war is one that has become outmoded in the international arena.

But I think there is, Mr. Chairman, an obligation on the part of the Executive to give Congress the opportunity, which that language was meant to reflect in the Constitution of the United States, to express its views with respect to this. In this instance, in the instance, if you will, of Vietnam, Congress had an opportunity to participate in these decisions. Congress ratified the SEATO treaty by an overwhelming vote, which expressed the security concerns and the general obligation of the United States in accordance with its constitutional process to attempt to preserve order and peace and defense against aggression in Southeast Asia. That was debated, that was discussed, and it was affirmed by two-thirds of the Senate, and in fact confirmed by an overwhelming vote.

THE CHAIRMAN. You are talking about the SEATO treaty?

MR. KATZENBACH. I am talking about the SEATO treaty. That is not all that happened.

THE CHAIRMAN. You mentioned that as a basis for the Tonkin Gulf resolution?

MR. KATZENBACH. Congress participated in that. Congress made important decisions with respect to the interests of the United States in Southeast Asia and undertook important obligations to other signatories of that treaty. That is not all that happened.

As the situation there deteriorated, as American ships were attacked in the Tonkin Gulf, the President of the United States came back to Congress to seek the views of Congress with respect to what should be done in that area and with respect to the use of the military of the United States in that area, and on those resolutions Congress had the opportunity to participate and did participate, as you well remember, Mr. Chairman. The views of the Congress I think were very clearly expressed. That resolution authorized the President of the United States, by an overwhelming vote, with only two dissents in both Houses of Congress, two together, to use the force of the United States in that situation. The combination of the two, it seems to me, fully fulfills the obligation of the Executive in a situation of this kind to participate with the Congress to give the Congress a full and effective voice, the functional equivalent of the constitutional obligation expressed in the provision of the Constitution with respect to declaring war. Beyond that Mr. Chairman——

THE CHAIRMAN. They did not ask for a declaration of war. They do not have one yet.

MR. KATZENBACH. That is true in the very literal sense of the word.

THE CHAIRMAN. It is quite true, not only literally, but in spirit. You haven't requested and you don't intend to request a declaration of war, as I understand it.

MR. KATZENBACH. As I explained—that is correct, Mr. Chairman, but didn't that resolution authorize the President to use the armed forces of the United States in whatever way was necessary? Didn't it? What could a declaration of war have done that would have given the President more authority and a clearer voice of the Congress of the United States than that did?

THE CHAIRMAN. This is exactly one of the principal criticisms of Professor Bartlett yesterday about the imprecision of the resolution. It was presented as an emergency situation; the repelling of an attack which was alleged to have been unprovoked upon our forces in the high seas. It looked at the moment as if it was a wholly unprovoked, unjustified, and an unacceptable attack upon our armed forces. He criticized the language of that resolution yesterday as a mistake, but he went on to say that "the conditions in which it was submitted to the Congress" made it, I believe he said, enormously difficult to resist it.

The circumstances partook of an emergency, as an attack upon the United States which would fall within the procedures or the principles developed in the last century of repelling attacks temporarily as opposed to a full-fledged war like the one which we are in. And he was, I thought, quite critical of that, and the circumstances were such that we were asked to act upon this resolution very quickly. As a matter of fact, the President had already responded, before the resolution was approved, to the attack upon the sources of the PT boats.

It has been interpreted as equivalent to a declaration of war. I think it is a very critical difference as to how we regard it.

I had a debate on the floor with Senator Russell about whether or not this kind of resolution is now accepted as a substitute for a declaration of war. I don't think it is properly such, especially having been made under conditions of great emergency. It wasn't a deliberate decision by the Congress to wage war in that full-fledged sense against a foreign government. I think that has been one of the difficulties now, that we are not quite sure which government we are waging the war against although it seems to me it is fairly evident. . . .

THE CHAIRMAN. Let me ask the original question more precisely. I read the first part. Maybe this can tie down at least your views, aside from Senator Morse's or mine or others. Would the President, if there were no resolution, be with or without constitutional authority to send U.S. soldiers to South Vietnam in the numbers that are there today?

MR. KATZENBACH. It would be my view, as I indicated, Mr. Chairman, that he does have that authority. I think there would be others both inside and outside of the Government who would not agree with that. It was precisely that reason——

THE CHAIRMAN. On what basis?

MR. KATZENBACH. We have been exploratory about this over the years; an effort has been made to avoid disputes of that kind or to have disputes of that kind become important in the conduct of foreign policy.

THE CHAIRMAN. Would you say the same with regard to the authority to bomb North Vietnam, as opposed to repelling an attack in South Vietnam?

MR. KATZENBACH. Well, I do not see it as opposed to it, Senator.

THE CHAIRMAN. Well, in contrast?

MR. KATZENBACH. The objectives, the reasons we are in there have been made repeatedly clear.

THE CHAIRMAN. The answer is "Yes," then, is it; is that it?

MR. KATZENBACH. I cannot answer a question, Senator, that characterizes the two as different. I will answer the question by saying yes, I think it includes the authority to bomb North Vietnam.

THE CHAIRMAN. Yes.

MR. KATZENBACH. As part of the defense against the aggression. I think that, but not as distinguished from it.

THE CHAIRMAN. In short, did the Gulf of Tonkin resolution give the President authority which otherwise under the Constitution he would not have had and if so what was it?

MR. KATZENBACH. In my judgment, Senator, he already had constitutionally that authority. But I would think as a matter of history and precedent it would be extremely difficult, in this kind of a situation for a President to exercise that authority on his own when, one, the authority would be disputed, and the fact of the authority would be disputed, and secondly, when he wanted and needed, needed very much, the sense of Congress in this respect. He knew as a constitutional matter that he would have to depend upon the Congress if he were to exercise the policy in that way, and he wanted in a sense an indication that the Congress would support that exercise of his authority. He also wanted to avoid the constitutional questions that had come up at the time of Korea.

Leonard C. Meeker, State Department Advisor
Memorandum on the Legality of American
Participation in the Defense of South Vietnam
March 4, 1966

State Department Bulletin 474 (1966). Reprinted in John Norton Moore, *Law and the Indo-China War* (Princeton, New Jersey, 1972), 603-32.

I. THE UNITED STATES AND SOUTH VIET-NAM HAVE THE RIGHT UNDER INTERNATIONAL LAW TO PARTICIPATE IN THE COLLECTIVE DEFENSE OF SOUTH VIET-NAM AGAINST ARMED ATTACK

In response to requests from the Government of South Viet-Nam, the United States has been assisting that country in defending itself against armed attack from the Communist North. This attack has taken the forms of externally supported subversion, clandestine supply of arms, infiltration of armed personnel, and most recently the sending of regular units of the North Vietnamese army into the South.

International law has long recognized the right of individual and collective self-defense against armed attack. South Viet-Nam and the United States are engaging in such collective defense consistently with international law and with United States obligations under the United Nations Charter.

A. South Viet-Nam is being Subjected to
Armed Attack by Communist North Viet-Nam

The Geneva accords of 1954 established a demarcation line between North

Viet-Nam and South Viet-Nam. They provided for withdrawals of military forces into the respective zones north and south of this line. The accords prohibited the use of either zone for the resumption of hostilities or to "further an aggressive policy."

During the 5 years following the Geneva conference of 1954, the Hanoi regime developed a covert political-military organization in South Viet-Nam based on Communist cadres it had ordered to stay in the South, contrary to the provisions of the Geneva accords. The activities of this covert organization were directed toward the kidnaping and assassination of civilian officials—acts of terrorism that were perpetrated in increasing numbers.

In the 3-year period from 1959 to 1961, the North Viet-Nam regime infiltrated an estimated 10,000 men into the South. It is estimated that 13,000 additional personnel were infiltrated in 1962, and, by the end of 1964, North Viet-Nam may well have moved over 40,000 armed and unarmed guerrillas into South Viet-Nam.

The International Control Commission reported in 1962 the findings of its Legal Committee:

> . . . there is evidence to show that arms, armed and unarmed personnel, munitions and other supplies have been sent from the Zone in the North to the Zone in the South with the objective of supporting, organizing and carrying out hostile activities, including armed attacks directed against the Armed Forces and Administration of the Zone in the South.
>
> . . . there is evidence that the PAVN [People's Army of Viet-Nam] has allowed the Zone in the North to be used for inciting, encouraging and supporting hostile activities in the Zone in the South, aimed at the overthrow of the Administration in the South.

Beginning in 1964, the Communists apparently exhausted their reservoir of Southerners who had gone North. Since then the greater number of men infiltrated into the South have been native-born North Vietnamese. Most recently, Hanoi has begun to infiltrate elements of the North Vietnamese army in increasingly larger numbers. Today, there is evidence that nine regiments of regular North Vietnamese forces are fighting in organized units in the South.

In the guerrilla war in Viet-Nam, the external aggression from the North is the critical military element of the insurgency, although it is unacknowledged by North Viet-Nam. In these circumstances, an "armed attack" is not as easily fixed by date and hour as in the case of traditional warfare. However, the infiltration of thousands of armed men clearly constitutes an "armed attack" under any reasonable definition. There may be some question as to the exact date at which North Viet-Nam's aggression grew into an "armed attack," but there can be no doubt that it had occurred before February 1965.

B. International Law Recognizes the Right of Individual and Collective Self-Defense Against Armed Attack

International law has traditionally recognized the right of self-defense against armed attack. This proposition has been asserted by writers on international law through the several centuries in which the modern law of nations has developed.

The proposition has been acted on numerous times by governments throughout modern history. Today the principle of self-defense against armed attack is universally recognized and accepted. [See, *e.g.*, Jessup, *A Modern Law of Nations,* 163 ff. (1948); Oppenheim, *International Law,* 297 ff. (8th ed., Lauterpacht, 1955). And see, generally, Bowett, *Self-Defense in International Law* (1958). Footnote in original.]

The Charter of the United Nations, concluded at the end of World War II, imposed an important limitation on the use of force by United Nations members. Article 2, paragraph 4, provides:

> All Members shall refrain in their international relations from the threat or use of force against the territorial integrity or political independence of any state, or in any other manner inconsistent with the Purposes of the United Nations.

In addition, the charter embodied a system of international peacekeeping through the organs of the United Nations. Article 24 summarizes these structural arrangements in stating that the United Nations members:

> . . . confer on the Security Council primary responsibility for the maintenance of international peace and security, and agree that in carrying out its duties under this responsibility the Security Council acts on their behalf.

However, the charter expressly states in article 51 that the remaining provisions of the charter—including the limitation of article 2, paragraph 4, and the creation of United Nations machinery to keep the peace—in no way diminish the inherent right of self-defense against armed attack. Article 51 provides:

> Nothing in the present Charter shall impair the inherent right of individual or collective self-defense if an armed attack occurs against a Member of the United Nations, until the Security Council has taken the measures necessary to maintain international peace and security. Measures taken by Members in the exercise of this right of self-defense shall be immediately reported to the Security Council and shall not in any way affect the authority and responsibility of the Security Council under the present Charter to take at any time such action as it deems necessary in order to maintain or restore international peace and security.

Thus, article 51 restates and preserves, for member states in the situations covered by the article, a long-recognized principle of international law. The article is a "saving clause" designed to make clear that no other provision in the charter shall be interpreted to impair the inherent right of self-defense referred to in article 51.

Three principal objections have been raised against the availability of the right of individual and collective self-defense in the case of Viet-Nam: (1) that this right applies only in the case of an armed attack on a United Nations member; (2) that it does not apply in the case of South Viet-Nam because the latter is not an independent sovereign state; and (3) that collective self-defense may be undertaken only by a regional organization operating under chapter VIII of the United Nations Charter. These objections will now be considered in turn.

C. The Right of Individual and Collective Self-Defense Applies in the Case of South Viet-Nam Whether or Not That Country is a Member of the United Nations

1. South Viet-Nam Enjoys the Right of Self-Defense

The argument that the right of self-defense is available only to members of the United Nations mistakes the nature of the right of self-defense and the relationship of the United Nations Charter to international law in this respect. As already shown, the right of self-defense against armed attack is an inherent right under international law. The right is not conferred by the charter, and, indeed, article 51 expressly recognizes that the right is inherent.

The charter nowhere contains any provision designed to deprive nonmembers of the right of self-defense against armed attack. [While nonmembers, such as South Viet-Nam, have not formally undertaken the obligations of the United Nations Charter as their own treaty obligations, it should be recognized that much of the substantive law of the charter has become part of the general law of nations through a very wide acceptance by nations the world over. This is particularly true of the charter provisions bearing on the use of force. Moreover, in the case of South Viet-Nam, the South Vietnamese Government has expressed its ability and willingness to abide by the charter, in applying for United Nations membership. Thus it seems entirely appropriate to appraise the actions of South Viet-Nam in relation to the legal standards set forth in the United Nations Charter. Footnote in original.] Article 2, paragraph 6, does charge the United Nations with responsibility for insuring that nonmember states act in accordance with United Nations "Principles so far as may be necessary for the maintenance of international peace and security." Protection against aggression and self-defense against armed attack are important elements in the whole charter scheme for the maintenance of international peace and security. To deprive nonmembers of their inherent right of self-defense would not accord with the principles of the organization, but would instead be prejudicial to the maintenance of peace. Thus article 2, paragraph 6—and, indeed, the rest of the charter—should certainly not be construed to nullify or diminish the inherent defensive rights of nonmembers.

2. The United States has the Right to Assist in the Defense of South Viet-Nam although the Latter is not a United Nations Member

The cooperation of two or more international entities in the defense of one or both against armed attack is generally referred to as collective self-defense. United States participation in the defense of South Viet-Nam at the latter's request is an example of collective self-defense.

The United States is entitled to exercise the right of individual or collective self-defense against armed attack, as that right exists in international law, subject only to treaty limitations and obligations undertaken by this country.

It has been urged that the United States has no right to participate in the collective defense of South Viet-Nam because article 51 of the United Nations Charter speaks only of the situation "if an armed attack occurs *against a Member of the United Nations.*" This argument is without substance.

In the first place, article 51 does not impose restrictions or cut down the otherwise available rights of United Nations members. By its own terms, the article preserves an inherent right. It is, therefore, necessary to look elsewhere in the charter for any obligation of members restricting their participation in collective defense of an entity that is not a United Nations member.

Article 2, paragraph 4, is the principal provision of the charter imposing limitations on the use of force by members. It states that they:

> . . . shall refrain in their international relations from the threat or use of force against the territorial integrity or political independence of any state, or in any other manner inconsistent with the Purposes of the United Nations.

Action taken in defense against armed attack cannot be characterized as falling within this proscription. The record of the San Francisco conference makes clear that article 2, paragraph 4, was not intended to restrict the right of self-defense against armed attack. [See 6 UNCIO Documents 459. Footnote in original.]

One will search in vain for any other provision in the charter that would preclude United States participation in the collective defense of a nonmember. The fact that article 51 refers only to armed attack "against a Member of the United Nations" implies no intention to preclude members from participating in the defense of nonmembers. Any such result would have seriously detrimental consequences for international peace and security and would be inconsistent with the purposes of the United Nations as they are set forth in article 1 of the charter. [In particular, the statement of the first purpose: "To maintain international peace and security, and to that end: to take effective collective measures for the prevention and removal of threats to the peace, and for the suppression of acts of aggression or other breaches of the peace, and to bring about by peaceful means, and in conformity with the principles of justice and international law, adjustment or settlement of international disputes or situations which might lead to a breach of the peace. . . ." Footnote in original.] The right of members to participate in the defense of nonmembers is upheld by leading authorities on international law. [Bowett, *Self-Defense in International Law,* 193-195 (1958); Goodhart, "The North Atlantic Treaty of 1949," 79 *Recueil Des Cours,* 183, 202-204 (1951, vol. II), quoted in 5 *Whiteman's Digest of International Law,* 1067-1068 (1965); Kelsen, *The Law of the United Nations,* 793 (1950); see Stone, *Aggression and World Order,* 44 (1958). Footnote in original.]

D. The Right of Individual and Collective Self-Defense Applies Whether or Not South Viet-Nam is Regarded As an Independent Sovereign State

1. South Viet-Nam Enjoys the Right of Self-Defense

It has been asserted that the conflict in Viet-Nam is "civil strife" in which foreign intervention is forbidden. Those who make this assertion have gone so far as to compare Ho Chi Minh's actions in Viet-Nam with the efforts of President Lincoln to preserve the Union during the American Civil War. Any such characterization is an entire fiction disregarding the actual situation in Viet-Nam. The Hanoi regime is anything but the legitimate government of a unified country in which the South is rebelling against lawful national authority.

The Geneva accords of 1954 provided for a division of Viet-Nam into two zones at the 17th parallel. Although this line of demarcation was intended to be temporary, it was established by international agreement, which specifically forbade aggression by one zone against the other.

The Republic of Viet-Nam in the South has been recognized as a separate international entity by approximately 60 governments the world over. It has been admitted as a member of a number of the specialized agencies of the United Nations. The United Nations General Assembly in 1957 voted to recommend South Viet-Nam for membership in the organization, and its admission was frustrated only by the veto of the Soviet Union in the Security Council.

In any event there is no warrant for the suggestion that one zone of a temporarily divided state—whether it be Germany, Korea, or Viet-Nam—can be legally overrun by armed forces from the other zone, crossing the internationally recognized line of demarcation between the two. Any such doctrine would subvert the international agreement establishing the line of demarcation, and would pose grave dangers to international peace.

The action of the United Nations in the Korean conflict of 1950 clearly established the principle that there is no greater license for one zone of a temporarily divided state to attack the other zone than there is for one state to attack another state. South Viet-Nam has the same right that South Korea had to defend itself and to organize collective defense against an armed attack from the North, A resolution of the Security Council dated June 25, 1950, noted "with grave concern the armed attack upon the Republic of Korea by forces from North Korea," and determined "that this action constitutes a breach of the peace."

2. The United States is Entitled to Participate in the Collective Defense of South Viet-Nam Whether or Not the Latter is Regarded as an Independent Sovereign State

As stated earlier, South Viet-Nam has been recognized as a separate international entity by approximately 60 governments. It has been admitted to membership in a number of the United Nations specialized agencies and has been excluded from the United Nations Organization only by the Soviet veto.

There is nothing in the charter to suggest that United Nations members are precluded from participating in the defense of a recognized international entity against armed attack merely because the entity may lack some of the attributes of an independent sovereign state. Any such result would have a destructive effect on the stability of international engagements such as the Geneva accords of 1954 and on internationally agreed lines of demarcation. Such a result, far from being in accord with the charter and the purposes of the United Nations, would undermine them and would create new dangers to international peace and security.

E. The United Nations Charter Does Not Limit
the Right of Self-Defense to Regional Organizations

Some have argued that collective self-defense may be undertaken only by a regional arrangement or agency operating under chapter VIII of the United Nations Charter. Such an assertion ignores the structure of the charter and the practice followed in the more than 20 years since the founding of the United Nations.

The basic proposition that rights of self-defense are not impaired by the charter—as expressly stated in article 51—is not conditioned by any charter provision limiting the application of this proposition to collective defense by a regional arrangement or agency. The structure of the charter reinforces this conclusion. Article 51 appears in chapter VII of the charter, entitled "Action With Respect to Threats to the Peace, Breaches of the Peace, and Acts of Aggression," whereas chapter VIII, entitled "Regional Arrangements," begins with article 52 and embraces the two following articles. The records of the San Francisco conference show that article 51 was deliberately placed in chapter VII rather than chaper VIII, "where it would only have a bearing on the regional system." [17 UNCIO Documents 288. Footnote in original.]

Under article 51, the right of self-defense is available against any armed attack, whether or not the country attacked is a member of a regional arrangement and regardless of the source of the attack. Chapter VIII, on the other hand, deals with relations among members of a regional arrangement or agency, and authorizes regional action as appropriate for dealing with "local disputes." This distinction has been recognized ever since the founding of the United Nations in 1945.

For example, the North Atlantic Treaty has operated as a collective security arrangement, designed to take common measures in preparation against the eventuality of an armed attack for which collective defense under article 51 would be required. Similarly, the Southeast Asia Treaty Organization was designed as a collective defense arrangement under article 51. Secretary of State Dulles emphasized this in his testimony before the Senate Foreign Relations Committee in 1954.

By contrast, article 1 of the Charter of Bogota (1948), establishing the Organization of American States, expressly declares that the organization is a regional agency within the United Nations. Indeed, chapter VIII of the United Nations Charter was included primarily to take account of the functioning of the inter-American system.

In sum, there is no basis in the United Nations Charter for contending that the right of self-defense against armed attack is limited to collective defense by a regional organization.

F. The United States has Fulfilled
its Obligations to the United Nations

A further argument has been made that the members of the United Nations have conferred on United Nations organs—and, in particular, on the Security

Council—exclusive power to act against aggression. Again, the express language of article 51 contradicts that assertion. A victim of armed attack is not required to forego individual or collective defense of its territory until such time as the United Nations organizes collective action and takes appropriate measures. To the contrary, article 51 clearly states that the right of self-defense may be exercised "*until* the Security Council has taken the measures necessary to maintain international peace and security." [An argument has been made by some that the United States, by joining in the collective defense of South Viet-Nam, has violated the peaceful settlement obligation of article 33 in the charter. This argument overlooks the obvious proposition that a victim of armed aggression is not required to sustain the attack undefended while efforts are made to find a political solution with the aggressor. Article 51 of the charter illustrates this by making perfectly clear that the inherent right of self-defense is impaired by "Nothing in the present Charter," including the provisions of article 33. Footnote in original.]

As indicated earlier, article 51 is not literally applicable to the Viet-Nam situation since South Viet-Nam is not a member. However, reasoning by analogy from article 51 and adopting its provisions as an appropriate guide for the conduct of members in a case like Viet-Nam, one can only conclude that United States actions are fully in accord with this country's obligations as a member of the United Nations.

Article 51 requires that:

> Measures taken by Members in the exercise of this right of self-defense shall be immediately reported to the Security Council and shall not in any way affect the authority and responsibility of the Security Council under the present Charter to take at any time such action as it deems necessary in order to maintain or restore international peace and security.

The United States has reported to the Security Council on measures it has taken in countering the Communist aggression in Viet-Nam. In August 1964 the United States asked the Council to consider the situation created by North Vietnamese attacks on United States destroyers in the Tonkin Gulf. The Council thereafter met to debate the question, but adopted no resolutions. Twice in February 1965 the United States sent additional reports to the Security Council on the conflict in Viet-Nam and on the additional measures taken by the United States in the collective defense of South Viet-Nam. In January 1966 the United States formally submitted the Viet-Nam question to the Security Council for its consideration and introduced a draft resolution calling for discussions looking toward a peaceful settlement on the basis of the Geneva accords.

At no time has the Council taken any action to restore peace and security in Southeast Asia. The Council has not expressed criticism of United States actions. Indeed, since the United States submission of January 1966, the members of the Council have been notably reluctant to proceed with any consideration of the Viet-Nam question.

The conclusion is clear that the United States has in no way acted to interfere with United Nations consideration of the conflict in Viet-Nam. On the contrary, the

United States has requested United Nations consideration, and the Council has not seen fit to act.

G. International Law Does Not Require a Declaration of War as a Condition Precedent to Taking Measures of Self-Defense Against Armed Attack

The existence or absence of a formal declaration of war is not a factor in determining whether an international use of force is lawful as a matter of international law. The United Nations Charter's restrictions focus on the manner and purpose of its use and not on any formalities of announcement.

It should also be noted that a formal declaration of war would not place any obligations on either side in the conflict by which that side would not be bound in any event. The rules of international law concerning the conduct of hostilities in an international armed conflict apply regardless of any declaration of war.

H. Summary

The analysis set forth above shows that South Viet-Nam has the right in present circumstances to defend itself against armed attack from the North and to organize a collective self-defense with the participation of others. In response to requests from South Viet-Nam, the United States has been participating in that defense, both through military action within South Viet-Nam and actions taken directly against the aggressor in North Viet-Nam. This participation by the United States is in conformity with international law and is consistent with our obligations under the Charter of the United Nations.

II. THE UNITED STATES HAS UNDERTAKEN COMMITMENTS TO ASSIST SOUTH VIET-NAM IN DEFENDING ITSELF AGAINST COMMUNIST AGGRESSION FROM THE NORTH

The United States has made commitments and given assurances, in various forms and at different times, to assist in the defense of South Viet-Nam.

A. The United States Gave Undertakings at the End of the Geneva Conference in 1954

At the time of the signing of the Geneva accords in 1954, President Eisenhower warned "that any renewal of Communist aggression would be viewed by us as a matter of grave concern," at the same time giving assurance that the United States would "not use force to disturb the settlement." And the formal declaration made by the United States Government at the conclusion of the Geneva conference stated that the United States "would view any renewal of the aggression in violation of the aforesaid aggreements with grave concern and as seriously threatening international peace and security."

B. The United States Undertook an International
Obligation to Defend South Viet-Nam in the SEATO Treaty

Later in 1954 the United States negotiated with a number of other countries and signed the Southeast Asia Collective Defense Treaty. The treaty contains in the first paragraph of article IV the following provision:

> Each Party recognizes that aggression by means of armed attack in the treaty area against any of the Parties or against any State or territory which the Parties by unanimous agreement may hereafter designate, would endanger its own peace and safety, and agrees that it will in that event act to meet the common danger in accordance with its constitutional processes. Measures taken under this paragraph shall be immediately reported to the Security Council of the United Nations.

Annexed to the treaty was a protocol stating that:

> The Parties to the Southeast Asia Collective Defense Treaty unanimously designate for the purposes of Article IV of the Treaty the States of Cambodia and Laos and the free territory under the jurisdiction of the State of Vietnam.

Thus, the obligations of article IV, paragraph 1, dealing with the eventuality of armed attack, have from the outset covered the territory of South Viet-Nam. The facts as to the North Vietnamese armed attack against the South have been summarized earlier, in the discussion of the right of self-defense under international law and the Charter of the United Nations. The term "armed attack" has the same meaning in the SEATO treaty as in the United Nations Charter.

Article IV, paragraph 1, places an obligation on each party to the SEATO treaty to "act to meet the common danger in accordance with its constitutional processes" in the event of an armed attack. The treaty does not require a collective determination that an armed attack has occurred in order that the obligation of article IV, paragraph 1, become operative. Nor does the provision require collective decision on actions to be taken to meet the common danger. As Secretary Dulles pointed out when transmitting the treaty to the President, the commitment in article IV, paragraph 1, "leaves to the judgment of each country the type of action to be taken in the event an armed attack occurs."

The treaty was intended to deter armed aggression in Southeast Asia. To that end it created not only a multilateral alliance but also a series of bilateral relationships. The obligations are placed squarely on "each Party" in the event of armed attack in the treaty area—not upon "the Parties," a wording that might have implied a necessity for collective decision. The treaty was intended to give the assurance of United States assistance to any party or protocol state that might suffer a Communist armed attack, regardless of the views or actions of other parties. The fact that the obligations are individual, and may even to some extent differ among the parties to the treaty, is demonstrated by the United States understanding, expressed at the time of signature, that its obligations under article IV, paragraph 1, apply only in the event of *Communist* aggression, whereas the other parties to the treaty were unwilling so to limit their obligations to each other.

Thus, the United States has a commitment under article IV, paragraph 1, in the event of armed attack, independent of the decision or action of other treaty parties. A joint statement issued by Secretary Rusk and Foreign Minister Thanat Khoman of Thailand on March 6, 1962, reflected this understanding:

> The Secretary of State assured the Foreign Minister that in the event of such aggression, the United States intends to give full effect to its obligations under the Treaty to act to meet the common danger in accordance with its constitutional processes. The Secretary of State reaffirmed that this obligation of the United States does not depend upon the prior agreement of all other parties to the Treaty, since this Treaty obligation is individual as well as collective.

Most of the SEATO countries have stated that they agreed with this interpretation. None has registered objection to it.

When the Senate Committee on Foreign Relations reported on the Southeast Asia Collective Defense Treaty, it noted that the treaty area was further defined so that the "Free Territory of Vietnam" was an area "which, if attacked, would fall under the protection of the instrument." In its conclusion the committee stated:

> The committee is not impervious to the risks which this treaty entails. It fully appreciates that acceptance of these additional obligations commits the United States to a course of action over a vast expanse of the Pacific. Yet these risks are consistent with our own highest interests.

The Senate gave its advice and consent to the treaty by a vote of 82 to 1.

C. The United States has Given Additional Assurances to the Government of South Viet-Nam

The United States has also given a series of additional assurances to the Government of South Viet-Nam. As early as October 1954 President Eisenhower undertook to provide direct assistance to help make South Viet-Nam "capable of resisting attempted subversion or aggression through military means." On May 11, 1957, President Eisenhower and President Ngo Dinh Diem of the Republic of Viet-Nam issued a joint statement which called attention to "the large build-up of Vietnamese Communist military forces in North Viet-Nam" and stated.

> Noting that the Republic of Viet-Nam is covered by Article IV of the Southeast Asia Collective Defense Treaty, President Eisenhower and President Ngo Dinh Diem agreed that aggression or subversion threatening the political independence of the Republic of Viet-Nam would be considered as endangering peace and stability.

On August 2, 1961, President Kennedy declared that "the United States is determined that the Republic of Viet-Nam shall not be lost to the Communists for lack of any support which the United States Government can render." On December 7, of that year President Diem appealed for additional support. In his reply of December 14, 1961, President Kennedy recalled the United States declaration made at the end of the Geneva conference in 1954, and reaffirmed that the United States was "prepared to help the Republic of Viet-Nam to protect its people and to preserve its independence." This assurance has been reaffirmed many times since.

III. ACTIONS BY THE UNITED STATES AND SOUTH VIET-NAM ARE JUSTIFIED UNDER THE GENEVA ACCORDS OF 1954

A. Description of the Accords

The Geneva accords of 1954 [These accords were composed of a bilateral cease-fire agreement between the "Commander-in-Chief of the People's Army of Viet Nam" and the "Commander-in-Chief of the French Union forces in Indo-China," together with a Final Declaration of the Conference, to which France adhered. However, it is to be noted that the South Vietnamese Government was not a signatory of the cease-fire agreement and did not adhere to the Final Declaration. South Viet-Nam entered a series of reservations in a statement to the conference. This statement was noted by the conference, but by decision of the conference chairman it was not included or referred to in the Final Declaration. Footnote in original.] established the date and hour for a cease-fire in Viet-Nam, drew a "provisional military demarcation line" with a demilitarized zone on both sides, and required an exchange of prisoners and the phased regroupment of Viet Minh forces from the south to the north and of French Union forces from the north to the south. The introduction into Viet-Nam of troop reinforcements and new military equipment (except for replacement and repair) was prohibited. The armed forces of each party were required to respect the demilitarized zone and the territory of the other zone. The adherence of either zone to any military alliance, and the use of either zone for the resumption of hostilities or to "further an aggressive policy," were prohibited. The International Control Commission was established, composed of India, Canada and Poland, with India as chairman. The task of the Commission was to supervise the proper execution of the provisions of the cease-fire agreement. General elections that would result in reunification were required to be held in July 1956 under the supervision of the ICC.

B. North Viet-Nam Violated
The Accords from the Beginning

From the very beginning, the North Vietnamese violated the 1954 Geneva accords. Communist military forces and supplies were left in the South in violation of the accords. Other Communist guerrillas were moved north for further training and then were infiltrated into the South in violation of the accords.

C. The Introduction of United States Military
Personnel and Equipment was Justified

The accords prohibited the reinforcement of foreign military forces in Viet-Nam and the introduction of new military equipment, but they allowed replacement of existing military personnel and equipment. Prior to late 1961 South Viet-Nam had received considerable military equipment and supplies from the United States, and the United States had gradually enlarged its Military Assistance Advisory Group to slightly less than 900 men. These actions were reported to the ICC and were justified as replacements for equipment in Viet-Nam in 1954 and for French training and advisory personnel who had been withdrawn after 1954.

As the Communist aggression intensified during 1961, with increased infiltration and a marked stepping up of Communist terrorism in the South, the United States found it necessary in late 1961 to increase substantially the numbers of our military personnel and the amounts and types of equipment introduced by this country into South Viet-Nam. These increases were justified by the international law principle that a material breach of an agreement by one party entitles the other to withhold compliance with an equivalent, corresponding, or related provision until the defaulting party is prepared to honor its obligations. [This principle of law and the circumstances in which it may be invoked are most fully discussed in the Fourth Report on the Law of Treaties by Sir Gerald Fitzmaurice, articles 18, 20 (U.N. doc. A/CN.4/120 (1959)) II Yearbook of the International Law Commission 37 (U.N. doc. A/CN.4/SER.A/1959/Add.1) and in the later report by Sir Humphrey Waldock, article 20 (U.N. doc. A/CN 4/156 and Add. 1-3 (1963)) II Yearbook of the International Law Commission 36 (U.N. doc. A/CN.4/SER.A/1963/Add.1). Among the authorities cited by the fourth report for this proposition are: II Oppenheim, *International Law* 136, 137 (7th ed. Lauterpacht 1955); I Rousseau, *Principes generaux du droit international public* 365 (1944); II Hyde, *International Law* 1660 et seq. (2d ed. 1947); II Guggenheim, *Traite de droit international public* 84, 85 (1935); Spiropoulos, *Traite theorique et pratique de droit international public* 289 (1933); Verdross, *Völkerrecht*, 328 (1950); Hall, *Treatise* 21 (8th ed. Higgins 1924); 3 Accioly, *Tratado de Direito Internacional Publico* 82 (1956-57). See also draft articles 42 and 46 of the Law of Treaties by the International Law Commission, contained in the report on the work of its 15th session (General Assembly, Official Records, 18th Session, Supplement No. 9 (A/5809)). Footnote in original.]

In accordance with this principle, the systematic violation of the Geneva accords by North Viet-Nam justified South Viet-Nam in suspending compliance with the provision controlling entry of foreign military personnel and military equipment.

D. South Viet-Nam was Justified in Refusing to
Implement the Election Provisions of the Geneva Accords

The Geneva accords contemplated the reunification of the two parts of Viet-

Nam. They contained a provision for general elections to be held in July 1956 in order to obtain a "free expression of the national will." The accords stated that "consultations will be held on this subject between the competent representative authorities of the two zones from 20 July 1955 onwards."

There may be some question whether South Viet-Nam was bound by these election provisions. As indicated earlier, South Viet-Nam did not sign the cease-fire agreement of 1954, nor did it adhere to the Final Declaration of the Geneva conference. The South Vietnamese Government at that time gave notice of its objection in particular to the election provisions of the accords.

However, even on the premise that these provisions were binding on South Viet-Nam, the South Vietnamese Government's failure to engage in consultations in 1955, with a view to holding elections in 1956, involved no breach of obligation. The conditions in North Viet-Nam during that period were such as to make impossible any free and meaningful expression of popular will.

Some of the facts about conditions in the North were admitted even by the Communist leadership in Hanoi. General Giap, currently Defense Minister of North Viet-Nam, in addressing the Tenth Congress of the North Vietnamese Communist Party in October 1956, publicly acknowledged that the Communist leaders were running a police state where executions, terror, and torture were commonplace. A nationwide election in these circumstances would have been a travesty. No one in the North would have dared to vote except as directed. With a substantial majority of the Vietnamese people living north of the 17th parallel, such an election would have meant turning the country over to the Communists without regard to the will of the people. The South Vietnamese Government realized these facts and quite properly took the position that consultations for elections in 1956 as contemplated by the accords would be a useless formality. [In any event, if North Viet-Nam considered there had been a breach of obligation by the South, its remedies lay in discussion with Saigon, perhaps in an appeal to the cochairmen of the Geneva conference, or in a reconvening of the conference to consider the situation. Under international law, North Viet-Nam had no right to use force outside its own zone in order to secure its political objectives. Footnote in original.]

IV. THE PRESIDENT HAS FULL AUTHORITY TO COMMIT UNITED STATES FORCES IN THE COLLECTIVE DEFENSE OF SOUTH VIET-NAM

There can be no question in present circumstances of the President's authority to commit United States forces to the defense of South Viet-Nam. The grant of authority to the President in article II of the Constitution extends to the actions of the United States currently undertaken in Viet-Nam. In fact, however, it is unnecessary to determine whether this grant standing alone is sufficient to authorize the actions taken in Viet-Nam. These actions rest not only on the exercise of Presidential powers under article II but on the SEATO treaty—a treaty advised and consented to by the Senate—and on actions of the Congress, particularly the joint resolution of August 10, 1964. When these sources of authority are taken together—

article II of the Constitution, the SEATO treaty, and actions by the Congress—there can be no question of the legality under domestic law of United States actions in Viet-Nam.

A. The President's Power Under Article II of the Constitution Extends to the Actions Currently Undertaken in Viet-Nam

Under the Constitution, the President, in addition to being Chief Executive, is Commander in Chief of the Army and Navy. He holds the prime responsibility for the conduct of the United States foreign relations. These duties carry very broad powers, including the power to deploy American forces abroad and commit them to military operations when the President deems such action necessary to maintain the security and defense of the United States.

At the Federal Constitutional Convention in 1787, it was originally proposed that Congress have the power "to make war." There were objections that legislative proceedings were too slow for this power to be vested in Congress; it was suggested that the Senate might be a better repository. Madison and Gerry then moved to substitute "to declare war" for "to make war," "leaving to the Executive the power to repel sudden attacks." It was objected that this might make it too easy for the Executive to involve the nation in war, but the motion carried with but one dissenting vote.

In 1787 the world was a far larger place, and the framers probably had in mind attacks upon the United States. In the 20th century, the world has grown much smaller. An attack on a country far from our shores can impinge directly on the nation's security. In the SEATO treaty, for example, it is formally declared that an armed attack against Viet-Nam would endanger the peace and safety of the United States.

Since the Constitution was adopted there have been at least 125 instances in which the President has ordered the armed forces to take action or maintain positions abroad without obtaining prior congressional authorization, starting with the "undeclared war" with France (1798-1800). For example, President Truman ordered 250,000 troops to Korea during the Korean war of the early 1950's. President Eisenhower dispatched 14,000 troops to Lebanon in 1958.

The Constitution leaves to the President the judgment to determine whether the circumstances of a particular armed attack are so urgent and the potential consequences so threatening to the security of the United States that he should act without formally consulting the Congress.

B. The Southeast Asia Collective Defense Treaty Authorizes the President's Actions

Under article VI of the United States Constitution, "all Treaties made, or which shall be made, under the Authority of the United States, shall be the supreme Law of the Land." Article IV, paragraph 1, of the SEATO treaty establishes as a matter of law that a Communist armed attack against South Viet-Nam endangers the peace and safety of the United States. In this same provision the United States has undertaken a commitment in the SEATO treaty to "act to meet the common danger in accordance with its constitutional processes" in the event of such an attack.

Under our Constitution it is the President who must decide when an armed attack has occurred. He has also the constitutional responsibility for determining what measures of defense are required when the peace and safety of the United States are endangered. If he considers that deployment of U.S. forces to South Viet-Nam is required, and that military measures against the source of Communist aggression in North Viet-Nam are necessary, he is constitutionally empowered to take those measures.

The SEATO treaty specifies that each party will act "in accordance with its constitutional processes."

It has recently been argued that the use of land forces in Asia is not authorized under the treaty because their use to deter armed attack was not contemplated at the time the treaty was considered by the Senate. Secretary Dulles testified at that time that we did not intend to establish (1) a land army in Southeast Asia capable of deterring Communist aggression, or (2) an integrated headquarters and military organization like that of NATO; instead, the United States would rely on "mobile striking power" against the sources of aggression. However, the treaty obligation in article IV, paragraph 1, to meet the common danger in the event of armed aggression, is not limited to particular modes of military action. What constitutes an adequate deterrent or an appropriate response, in terms of military strategy, may change; but the essence of our commitment to act to meet the common danger, as necessary at the time of an armed aggression, remains. In 1954 the forecast of military judgment might have been against the use of substantial United States ground forces in Viet-Nam. But that does not preclude the President from reaching a different military judgment in different circumstances, 12 years later.

C. The Joint Resolution of Congress of August 10, 1964, Authorizes United States Participation in the Collective Defense of South Viet-Nam

As stated earlier, the legality of United States participation in the defense of South Viet-Nam does not rest only on the constitutional power of the President under article II—or indeed on that power taken in conjunction with the SEATO treaty. In addition, the Congress has acted in unmistakable fashion to approve and authorize United States actions in Viet-Nam.

Following the North Vietnamese attacks in the Gulf of Tonkin against United States destroyers, Congress adopted, by a Senate vote of 88-2 and a House vote of 416-0, a joint resolution containing a series of important declarations and provisions of law.

Section 1 resolved that "the Congress approves and supports the determination of the President, as Commander in Chief, to take all necessary measures to repel any armed attack against the forces of the United States and to prevent further aggression." Thus, the Congress gave its sanction to specific actions by the

President to repel attacks against United States naval vessels in the Gulf of Tonkin and elsewhere in the western Pacific. Congress further approved the taking of "all necessary measures . . . to prevent further aggression." This authorization extended to those measures the Presidemt might consider necessary to ward off further attacks and to prevent further aggression by North Viet-Nam in Southeast Asia.

The joint resolution then went on to provide in section 2:

> The United States regards as vital to its national interest and to world peace the maintenance of international peace and security in southeast Asia. Consonant with the Constitution of the United States and the Charter of the United Nations and in accordance with its obligations under the Southeast Asia Collective Defense Treaty, the United States is, therefore, prepared, as the President determines, to take all necessary steps, including the use of armed force, to assist any member or protocol state of the Southeast Asia Collective Defense Treaty requesting assistance in defense of its freedom.

Section 2 thus constitutes an authorization to the President, in his discretion, to act—using armed force if he determines that is required—to assist South Viet-Nam at its request in defense of its freedom. The identification of South Viet-Nam through the reference to "protocol state" in this section is unmistakable, and the grant of authority "as the President determines" is unequivocal.

It has been suggested that the legislative history of the joint resolution shows an intention to limit United States assistance to South Viet-Nam to aid, advice, and training. This suggestion is based on an amendment offered from the floor by Senator [Gaylord] Nelson which would have added the following to the text:

> The Congress also approves and supports the efforts of the President to bring the problem of peace in Southeast Asia to the Security Council of the United Nations, and the President's declaration that the United States, seeking no extension of the present military conflict, will respond to provocation in a manner that is "limited and fitting." Our continuing policy is to limit our role to the provision of aid, training assistance, and military advice, and it is the sense of Congress that, except when provoked to a greater response, we should continue to attempt to avoid a direct military involvement in the Southeast Asian conflict. [110 *Cong. Rec.* 18459 (Aug. 7, 1964). Footnote in original.]

Senator [J. W.] Fulbright, who had reported the joint resolution from the Foreign Relations Committee, spoke on the amendment as follows:

> It states fairly accurately what the President has said would be our policy, and what I stated my understanding was as to our policy; also what other Senators have stated. In other words, it states that our response should be appropriate and limited to the provocation, which the Senator states as "respond to provocation in a manner that is limited and fitting," and so forth. We do not wish any political or military bases there. We are not seeking to gain a colony. We seek to insure the capacity of these people

to develop along the lines of their own desires, independent of domination by communism.

The Senator has put into his amendment a statement of policy that is unobjectionable. However, I cannot accept the amendment under the circumstances. I do not believe it is contrary to the joint resolution, but it is an enlargement. I am informed that the House is now voting on this resolution. The House joint resolution is about to be presented to us. I cannot accept the amendment and go to conference with it, and thus take responsibility for delaying matters.

I do not object to it as a statement of policy. I believe it is an accurate reflection of what I believe is the President's policy, judging from his own statements. That does not mean that as a practical matter I can accept the amendment. It would delay matters to do so. It would cause confusion and require a conference, and present us with all the other difficulties that are involved in this kind of legislative action. I regret that I cannot do it, even though I do not at all disagree with the amendment as a general statement of policy.

Senator Nelson's amendment related the degree and kind of U.S. response in Viet-Nam to "provocation" on the other side; the response should be "limited and fitting." The greater the provocation, the stronger are the measures that may be characterized as "limited and fitting." Bombing of North Vietnamese naval bases was a "limited and fitting" response to the attacks on U.S. destroyers in August 1964, and the subsequent actions taken by the United States and South Viet-Nam have been an appropriate response to the increased war of aggression carried on by North Viet-Nam since that date. Moreover, Senator Nelson's proposed amendment did not purport to be a restriction on authority available to the President but merely a statement concerning what should be the continuing policy of the United States.

Congressional realization of the scope of authority being conferred by the joint resolution is shown by the legislative history of the measure as a whole. The following exchange between Senators Cooper and Fulbright is illuminating:

MR. COOPER [John Sherman Cooper]. . . . The Senator will remember that the SEATO Treaty, in article IV, provides that in the event an armed attack is made upon a party to the Southeast Asia Collective Defense Treaty, or upon one of the protocol states such as South Vietnam, the parties to the treaty, one of whom is the United States, would then take such action as might be appropriate, after resorting to their constitutional processes. I assume that would mean, in the case of the United States, that Congress would be asked to grant the authority to act.

Does the Senator consider that in enacting this resolution we are satisfying that requirement of article IV of the Southeast Asia Collective Defense Treaty? In other words, are we now giving the President advance authority to take whatever action he may deem necessary respecting South Vietnam and its defense, or with respect to the defense of any other country included in the treaty?

MR. FULBRIGHT. I think that is correct.

MR. COOPER. Then, looking ahead, if the President decided that it was necessary to use such force as could lead into war, we will give that authority by this resolution?

MR. FULBRIGHT. That is the way I would interpret it. If a situation later developed in which we thought the approval should be withdrawn it could be withdrawn by concurrent resolution. [110 *Cong. Rec.* 18409 (Aug. 6, 1964). Senator [Wayne] Morse, who opposed the joint resolution, expressed the following view on August 6, 1964, concerning the scope of the proposed resolution: "Another Senator thought, in the early part of the debate, that this course would not broaden the power of the President to engage in a land war if he decided that he wanted to apply the resolution in that way.

"That Senator was taking great consolation in the then held belief that, if he voted for the resolution, it would give no authority to the President to send many troops into Asia. I am sure he was quite disappointed to finally learn, because it took a little time to get the matter cleared, that the resolution places no restriction on the President in that respect. If he is still in doubt, let him read the language on page 2, lines 3 to 6, and page 2, lines 11 to 17. The first reads:

> The Congress approves and supports the determination of the President, as Commander in Chief, to take all necessary measures to repel any armed attack against the forces of the United States and to prevent further aggression.

It does not say he is limited in regard to the sending of ground forces. It does not limit that authority. That is why I have called it a predated declaration of war, in clear violation of article I, section 8, of the Constitution, which vests the power to declare war in the Congress, and not in the President.

"What is proposed is to authorize the President of the United States, without a declaration of war, to commit acts of war." (110 *Cong. Rec.* 18426-7 (Aug. 6, 1964)). Footnote in original.]

The August 1964 joint resolution continues in force today. Section 2 of the resolution provides that it shall expire "when the President shall determine that the peace and security of the area is reasonably assured by international conditions created by action of the United Nations or otherwise, except that it may be terminated earlier by concurrent resolution of the Congress." The President has made no such determination, nor has Congress terminated the joint resolution. [On March 1, 1966, the Senate voted, 92-5, to table an amendment that would have repealed the joint resolution. Footnote in original.]

Instead, Congress in May 1965 approved an appropriation of $700 million to meet the expense of mounting military requirements in Viet-Nam. (Public Law 89-18, 79 Stat. 109.) The President's message asking for this appropriation stated that this was "not a routine appropriation. For each Member of Congress who supports this request is also voting to persist in our efforts to halt Communist aggression in South Vietnam." The appropriation act constitutes a clear congressional endorsement and approval of the actions taken by the President.

On March 1, 1966, the Congress continued to express its support of the President's policy by approving a $4.8 billion supplemental military authorization by votes of 392-4 and 93-2. An amendment that would have limited the President's authority to commit forces to Viet-Nam was rejected in the Senate by a vote of 94-2.

D. No Declaration of War by the Congress is Required
To Authorize United States Participation in
The Collective Defense of South Viet-Nam

No declaration of war is needed to authorize Americans actions in Viet-Nam. As shown in the preceding sections, the President has ample authority to order the participation of United States armed forces in the defense of South Viet-Nam.

Over a very long period in our history, practice and precedent have confirmed the constitutional authority to engage United States forces in hostilities without a declaration of war. This history extends from the undeclared war with France and the war against the Barbary pirates at the end of the 18th century to the Korean war of 1950-53.

James Madison, one of the leading framers of the Constitution, and Presidents John Adams and Jefferson all construed the Constitution, in their official actions during the early years of the Republic, as authorizing the United States to employ its armed forces abroad in hostilities in the absence of any congressional declaration of war. Their views and actions constitute highly persuasive evidence as to the meaning and effect of the Constitution. History has accepted the interpretation that was placed on the Constitution by the early Presidents and Congresses in regard to the lawfulness of hostilities without a declaration of war. The instances of such action in our history are numerous.

In the Korean conflict, where large-scale hostilities were conducted with an American troop participation of a quarter of a million men, no declaration of war was made by the Congress. The President acted on the basis of his constitutional responsibilities. While the Security Council, under a treaty of this country—the United Nations Charter—recommended assistance to the Republic of Korea against the Communist armed attack, the United States had no treaty commitment at that time obligating us to join in the defense of South Korea. In the case of South Viet-Nam we have the obligation of the SEATO treaty and clear expressions of congressional support. If the President could act in Korea without a declaration of war, *a fortiori* he is empowered to do so now in Viet-Nam.

It may be suggested that a declaration of war is the only available constitutional process by which congressional support can be made effective for the use of United States armed forces in combat abroad. But the Constitution does not insist on a rigid formalism. It gives Congress a choice of ways in which to exercise its powers. In the case of Viet-Nam the Congress has supported the determination of the President by the Senate's approval of the SEATO treaty, the adoption of the joint resolution of August 10, 1964, and the enactment of the necessary authorizations and appropriations.

V. CONCLUSION

South Viet-Nam is being subjected to armed attack by Communist North Viet-Nam, through the infiltration of armed personnel, military equipment, and regular combat units. International law recognizes the right of individual and collective self-defense against armed attack. South Viet-Nam, and the United States upon the request of South Viet-Nam, are engaged in such collective defense of the South. Their actions are in conformity with international law and with the Charter of the United Nations. The fact that South Viet-Nam has been precluded by Soviet veto from becoming a member of the United Nations and the fact that South Viet-Nam is a zone of temporarily divided state in no way diminish the right of collective defense of South Viet-Nam.

The United States has commitments to assist South Viet-Nam in defending itself against Communist aggression from the North. The United States gave undertakings to this effect at the conclusion of the Geneva conference in 1954. Later that year the United States undertook an international obligation in the SEATO treaty to defend South Viet-Nam against Communist armed aggression. And during the past decade the United States has given additional assurances to the South Vietnamese Government.

The Geneva accords of 1954 provided for a cease-fire and regroupment of contending forces, a division of Viet-Nam into two zones, and a prohibition on the use of either zone for the resumption of hostilities or to "further an aggressive policy." From the beginning, North Viet-Nam violated the Geneva accords through a systematic effort to gain control of South Viet-Nam by force. In the light of these progressive North Vietnamese violations, the introduction into South Viet-Nam beginning in late 1961 of substantial United States military equipment and personnel, to assist in the defense of the South, was fully justified; substantial breach of an international agreement by one side permits the other side to suspend performance of corresponding obligations under the agreement. South Viet-Nam was justified in refusing to implement the provisions of the Geneva accords calling for reunification through free elections throughout Viet-Nam since the Communist regime in North Viet-Nam created conditions in the North that made free elections entirely impossible.

The President of the United States has full authority to commit United States forces in the collective defense of South Viet-Nam. This authority stems from the constitutional powers of the President. However, it is not necessary to rely on the Constitution alone as the source of the President's authority, since the SEATO treaty—advised and consented to by the Senate and forming part of the law of the land—sets forth a United States commitment to defend South Viet-Nam against armed attack, and since the Congress—in the joint resolution of August 10, 1964, and in authorization and appropriations acts for support of the U.S. military effort in Viet-Nam—has given its approval and support to the President's actions. United States actions in Viet-Nam, taken by the President and approved by the Congress, do not require any declaration of war, as shown by a long line of precedents for the use of United States armed forces abroad in the absence of any congressional declaration of war.

During a press conference in August 1967, Johnson reaffirmed this point of view in a lengthy answer he gave to Sarah McClendon, a reporter for a group of Texas newspapers. She asked the President why he had not gone to the Congress to ask for a declaration of war against North Vietnam. Johnson replied that he had already obtained the agreement of Congress "on the course that the government followed in its commitments abroad."[24] He suggested that gradually the declaration of war has been replaced by the request for a joint resolution from the Congress in support of recommended policies—a resolution which Congress could withdraw at any time. This mode of "declaring war," or substituting for an individual declaration, had been suggested by Senator Taft during the Korean crisis, he said, and had been adopted by both his predecessors at one time or another. But, the President insisted,

> we stated then and we repeat now, we did not think the resolution was necessary to do what we did and what we are doing. But we thought it was desirable. We thought if we were going to ask them to stay the whole route, and if we expected them to be there on the landing, we ought to ask them to be there on the takeoff.[25]

Arthur Schlesinger observes that at the same time Johnson was overriding the formal constitutional checks on the power of the President, he also "began to liquidate unwritten checks, especially those operating at other times within the executive branch itself."[26] What he is referring to, of course, is the atmosphere of controversy and opposition that most Presidents are either forced to accept because of political circumstances they inherit with the office, or, as in the case of the more secure leaders like Franklin Roosevelt and John F. Kennedy, invited because they thrived on the dialectic of conflict. Their own maturity allowed them to tolerate, even at times to encourage, criticism and conflicting ideas among their subordinates because they realized how much they profited from them. One sees in Johnson, and in his successor, a gnawing sense of insecurity and an inability to tolerate having close to the throne, advisors and subordinates who challenged in any serious way the prevailing policies, attitudes and even premises from which policies were derived. In Johnson's case there was one exception, Under-Secretary of State George Ball, a loyal and astute statesman who "called them as he saw them" throughout the Vietnam War. Unfortunately, when an advisor of this calibre is so out of tune with the White House entourage, his contributions are liable to be minimal and his role ineffective; he becomes an in-house devil's advocate who is listened to politely but generally ignored when serious decisions are made.

Presidents need a clarification of their options, an opportunity to observe the impact of their policies and ideas upon others and the sharp interplay of conflict in order to prevent myopic policy fixations. In some cases, and this was particularly true of FDR, this lively ambience gave him contact with constituencies and groups from whom he was normally isolated and provided him with a wider set of choices in any given situation and a more democratic sensitivity to the ebb and flow of opinion outside the White House. A President has to guard against the isolation which his role frequently imposes upon him. Johnson and Nixon fell prey to or trapped themselves in a false reality. George Reedy warns:

From the President's standpoint, the greatest staff problem is that of maintaining his contact with the world's reality that lies outside of the White House walls. Very few have succeeded in doing so. They start their administrations fresh from political wars, which have a tendency to keep men closely tied to the facts of life, but it is only a matter of time until White House assistants close in like a pretorian guard. Since they are the only people that a President sees on a day-to-day basis, they become to him the voice of the people. They represent the closest approximation that he has of outside contacts, and it is inevitable that he comes to regard them as humanity itself.

Even the vision of so earthy a politician as Lyndon Johnson became blurred as the years went by.[27]

A former member of his administration has described President Johnson as "sustained by a shrinking circle of true believers, still . . . confident that his goals and methods will be ultimately vindicated."[28] George Kennan was not quite as gentle. He thought the President and his inner circle were "like men in a dream, seemingly insensitive to outside opinion, seemingly unable to arrive at any realistic assessment of the effects of their own acts."[29]

The expanded concept of the President's war powers underwent further stretching by Richard Milhous Nixon. Lyndon Johnson, exercising the scope of his own war powers, was unable to achieve either peace or victory in Vietnam. He left office rather than face defeat in the election campaign of 1968. The morass of Vietnam sapped Johnson's confidence and energy, and he retired to his ranch in Texas to live out his few remaining years, bitter over the events which had thrust him from the height of his popularity to the ignominy of a tortured existence in which he could hardly appear in public without being subjected to attack and insult from the swelling ranks of the anti war movement. The more balanced evaluation of his contributions will come as the memory of war recedes; Johnson's important role in stabilizing the badly shaken institutions of the republic in 1963 and his later legislative triumphs will win him a more respected place in history, balancing his domestic performance against the catastrophe of his wartime leadership. But all of this will do little to ease the personal wounds inflicted by his anti-war critics.

Nixon, too, was a peace candidate, and he eventually did negotiate a withdrawal of American armed forces from Vietnam, but not before he had in turn escalated the tempo of the war and nearly doubled American casualties. Nixon stretched the already expanded sinews of presidential war powers almost beyond their constitutional recognition. In reaching for arguments to justify his temporary expansion of the war into the neighboring country of Cambodia, Nixon and his advisors argued that such measures were necessary to protect the lives of the American armed forces if they were threatened from outside of the war zones.

As Commander in Chief, I had no choice but to act to defend those men. And as Commander in Chief, if I am faced with that decision again, I will exercise that power to defend these men.[30]

Congress was not informed of these bombings, nor did it learn until July 16, 1973 that intensive periodic bombing had been going on in Cambodia since March

1969. There was no authorization for these bombings, it was not covered by the Southeast Asia Resolution, nor was Congress informed about them. In fact, Defense Department records were falsified to conceal the bombing raids, and government officials and President Nixon himself concealed this situation and even misrepresented it to the Congress and the American people. During the 14 months after March 19, 1969, before the Cambodian incursion and bombing was announced, American B-52s dropped 105,837 tons of bombs on Cambodia in 3,695 sorties. Only 13 members of Congress were supposedly informed of these raids, but of that number, according to ten members of the House Judiciary Committee who investigated this situation, three are deceased, three others deny having been informed, and of the four who acknowledge such a briefing, the most important one, Senator Stennis, chairman of the Senate Armed Forces Committee, has indicated in the only public statement by any of the 13 that he had "no indication of the massiveness of the bombing."[31]

The President continued to refer to his responsibilities as Commander in Chief and reiterated that he would act in any situation, regardless of the political sacrifice, to protect the lives of American troops. This position compounded the retreat from constitutional restraints within which the Founding Fathers expected the American President to function. The Vietnam War or "police action" had already defied normal constitutional practice in its inception and subsequent escalation; now the Commander in Chief suggested that to protect the first unconstitutional decision, he would ignore any other constitutional restraints to protect the lives of American servicemen. "Peace with honor" might have been achieved without the cost of additional lives lost and casualties inflicted by terminating American involvement in the war. It could not be won by any reasonable calculation, its continuance brought untold suffering and destruction to both North and South Vietnam and it created such bitter division in the United States that its destructive implications were already far beyond control. But peace was not forthcoming.

Nixon's subsequent defense of the Cambodian invasion, or incursion as it was referred to by the administration, and its legal defense by the appointed representative of the President's advisors, the assistant attorney general and later Supreme Court justice, William H. Rehnquist, made nonsense of most of the history described in these volumes. They built a defense of the war-making powers of the President not simply upon a broad constitutional interpretation, but rather by compounding all the previous situations in which Presidents have violated constitutional restraints. Rehnquist hopped from case to case, extrapolating a bit of *obiter dicta* from a Supreme Court decision (Little v. Barreme) which had nothing to do with the legal precedent the case established (it restrained rather than enlarged the power of the Commander in Chief) and using what is perhaps the most extreme example of the violation of constitutional restraints—the case of Polk's unconstitutional actions in ordering army units into the sovereign territory of another country, in violation of existing treaty arrangements and without consultation with or the approval of Congress. Rehnquist even found solace in the principal mid-century Court decision restraining the powers of the President as Commander in Chief—Youngstown Sheet and Tube Co. v. Sawyer, again lifting a bit of *obiter dictum* not germane to the decision rendered by the Court. Their entire argument was stitched together out of misrepresentations and misinterpretations of historical precedents, drawing inferences dramatically at variance with a balanced evaluation of their real substance and meaning. Many of the facts were misstated, the citation of one Supreme Court decision was inaccurate and the inferences drawn from this hodge-podge of precedents and irrelevancies was without historical perspective. But it was offered by the Nixon administration as its only legal defense of the Cambodian venture.

President Richard M. Nixon
Address on "Military Action in Cambodia"
April 30, 1970

Public Papers of the Presidents: Richard Nixon, 1970 (Washington, D.C., 1971), 405-10.

Good evening my fellow Americans.

Ten days ago in my report to the nation on Vietnam I announced a decision to withdraw an additional 150,000 Americans from Vietnam over the next year. I said then that I was making that decision despite our concern over increased enemy activity in Laos, in Cambodia and in South Vietnam.

And at that time, I warned that if I concluded that increased enemy activity in any of these areas endangered the lives of Americans remaining in Vietnam, I would not hesitate to take strong and effective measures to deal with that situation.

Despite that warning, North Vietnam has increased its military aggression in all these areas, and particularly in Cambodia.

After full consultation with the National Security Council, Ambassador Bunker, General Abrams and my other advisers, I have concluded that the actions of the enemy in the last 10 days clearly endanger the lives of Americans who are in Vietnam now and would constitute an unacceptable risk to those who will be there after withdrawal of another 150,000.

To protect our men who are in Vietnam, and to guarantee the continued success of our withdrawal and Vietnamization program, I have concluded that the time has come for action.

Tonight, I shall describe the actions of the enemy, the actions I have ordered to deal with that situation, and the reasons for my decision.

Cambodia, a small country of seven million people, has been a neutral nation since the Geneva Agreement of 1954—an agreement, incidentally, which was signed by the Government of North Vietnam.

American policy since then has been to scrupulously respect the neutrality of the Cambodian people. We have maintained a skeleton diplomatic session of fewer than 15 in Cambodia's capital, and that only since last August. For the previous 4 years, from 1965 to 1969 we did not have any diplomatic mission whatever in Cambodia. And for the past 5 years we have provided no military assistance whatever and no economic assistance to Cambodia.

North Vietnam, however, has not respected that neutrality.

For the past 5 years—as indicated on this map that you see here—North Vietnam has occupied military sanctuaries all along the Cambodian frontier with South Vietnam. Some of these extend up to 20 miles into Cambodia. The sanctuaries are in red, and as you note they are on both sides of the border. They are used for hit and run attacks on American and South Vietnamese forces in South Vietnam. These Communist-occupied territories contain major base camps, training sites, logistics facilities, weapons and ammunition factories, airstrips and prisoner of war compounds.

For 5 years neither the United States nor South Vietnam has moved against these enemy sanctuaries because we did not wish to violate the territory of a neutral nation. Even after the Vietnamese Communists began to expand these sanctuaries 4 weeks ago, we counseled patience to our South Vietnamese allies and imposed restraints on our own commanders.

In contrast to our policy the enemy in the past 2 weeks has stepped up his guerrilla actions and he is concentrating his main force in these sanctuaries that you see on this map, where they are building up the large massive attacks on our forces and those of South Vietnam.

North Vietnam in the last 2 weeks has stripped away all pretence of respecting the sovereignty or the neutrality of Cambodia. Thousands of their soldiers are invading the country from the sanctuaries; they are encircling the capital of Pnom Penh. Coming from these sanctuaries as you see here, they have moved into Cambodia and are encircling the capital.

Cambodia, as a result of this, has sent out a call to the United States, to a number of other nations, for assistance. Because if this enemy effort succeeds, Cambodia would become a vast enemy staging area and a springboard for attacks on South Vietnam along 600 miles of frontier—a refuge where enemy troops could return from combat without fear of retaliation.

North Vietnamese men and supplies could then be poured into that country, jeopardizing not only the lives of our men but the people of South Vietnam as well.

Now confronted with this situation we had three options.

First, we can do nothing. Now, the ultimate result of that course of action is clear. Unless we indulge in wishful thinking, the lives of Americans remaining in Vietnam after our next withdrawal of 150,000 would be gravely threatened.

Let us go to the map again. Here is South Vietnam. Here is North Vietnam. North Vietnam already occupies this part of Laos. If North Vietnam also occupied this whole band in Cambodia, or the entire country, it would mean that South Vietnam was completely outflanked and the forces of Americans in this area, as well as the South Vietnamese, would be in an untenable military position.

Our second choice is to provide massive military assistance to Cambodia itself. Now, unfortunately, while we deeply sympathize with the plight of 7 million Cambodians whose country has been invaded, massive amounts of military assistance could not be rapidly and effectively utilized by this small Cambodian Army against the immediate threat. With other nations we shall do our best to provide the small arms and other equipment which the Cambodian Army of 40,000 needs and can use for its defense. But the aid we will provide will be limited for the purpose of enabling Cambodia to defend its neutrality and not for the purpose of making it an active belligerent on one side or the other.

Our third choice is to go to the heart of the trouble. That means cleaning out major North Vietnamese- and Vietcong-occupied territories, these sanctuaries which serve as bases for attacks on both Cambodia and American and South Vietnamese forces in South Vietnam. Some of these, incidentally, are as close to Saigon as Baltimore is to Washington. This one, for example, is called the Parrot's Beak. It is only 33 miles from Saigon.

Now faced with these three options, this is the decision I have made. In cooperation with the armed forces of South Vietnam, attacks are being launched this week to clean out major enemy sanctuaries on the Cambodian-Vietnam border.

A major responsibility for the ground operations is being assumed by South Vietnamese forces. For example, the attacks in several areas, including the Parrot's Beak that I referred to a moment ago, are exclusively South Vietnamese ground operations, under South Vietnamese command, with the United States providing air and logistical support.

There is one area, however, immediately above the Parrot's Beak, where I have concluded that a combined American and South Vietnamese operation is necessary.

Tonight, American and South Vietnamese units will attack the headquarters for the entire Communist military operation in South Vietnam. This key control center has been occupied by the North Vietnamese and Vietcong for 5 years in blatant violation of Cambodia's neutrality.

This is not an invasion of Cambodia. The areas in which these attacks will be launched are completely occupied and controlled by North Vietnamese forces. Our purpose is not to occupy the areas. Once enemy forces are driven out of these sanctuaries and once their military supplies are destroyed, we will withdraw.

These actions are in no way directed to security interests of any nation. Any government that chooses to use these actions as a pretext for harming relations with the United States will be doing so on its own responsibility and on its own initiative, and we will draw the appropriate conclusions.

Now, let me give you the reasons for my decision.

A majority of the American people, a majority of you listening to me are for the withdrawal of our forces from Vietnam. The action I have taken tonight is indispensable for the continuing success of that withdrawal program.

A majority of the American people want to end this war rather than to have it drag on interminably. The action I have taken tonight will serve that purpose.

A majority of the American people want to keep the casualties of our brave men in Vietnam at an absolute minimum. The action I take tonight is essential if we are to accomplish that goal.

We take this action not for the purpose of expanding the war into Cambodia but for the purpose of ending the war in Vietnam and winning the just peace we all desire. We have made—we will continue to make every possible effort to end this war through negotiation at the conference table rather than through more fighting in the battlefield.

Let us look again at the record. We have stopped the bombing of North

Vietnam. We have cut air operations by over 20 per cent. We have announced the withdrawal of over 250,000 of our men. We have offered to withdraw all of our men if they will withdraw theirs. We have offered to negotiate all issues with only one condition—and that is that the future of South Vietnam be determined, not by North Vietnam, and not by the United States, but by the people of South Vietnam themselves.

The answer of the enemy has been intransigence at the conference table, belligerence at Hanoi, massive military aggression in Laos and Cambodia, and stepped-up attacks in South Vietnam, designed to increase American casualties.

This attitude has become intolerable. We will not react to this threat to American lives merely by plaintive diplomatic protests. If we did, the credibility of the United States would be destroyed in every area of the world where only the power of the United States deters aggression.

Tonight, I again warn the North Vietnamese that if they continue to escalate the fighting when the United States is withdrawing its forces, I shall meet my responsibility as Commander in Chief of our Armed Forces to take the action I consider necessary to defend the security of our American men.

The action I have announced tonight puts the leaders of North Vietnam on notice that we will be patient in working for peace; we will be conciliatory at the conference table, but we will not be humiliated. We will not be defeated. We will not allow American men by the thousands to be killed by an enemy from privileged sanctuaries.

The time came long ago to end this war through peaceful negotiations. We stand ready for those negotiations. We have made major efforts, many of which must remain secret. I say tonight: All the offers and approaches made previously remain on the conference table whenever Hanoi is ready to negotiate seriously.

But if the enemy response to our most conciliatory offers for peaceful negotiation continues to be to increase its attacks and humiliate and defeat us, we shall react accordingly.

My fellow Americans, we live in an age of anarchy, both abroad and at home. We see mindless attacks on all the great institutions which have been created by free civilizations in the last 500 years. Even here in the United States, great universities are being systematically destroyed. Small nations all over the world find themselves under attack from within and from without.

If when the chips are down, the world's most powerful nation, the United States of America, acts like a pitiful, helpless giant, the forces of totalitarianism and anarchy will threaten free nations and free institutions throughout the world.

It is not our power but our will and character that is being tested tonight. The question all Americans must ask and answer tonight is this: Does the richest and strongest nation in the history of the world have the character to meet a direct challenge by a group which rejects every effort to win a just peace, ignores our warning, tramples on solemn agreements, violates the neutrality of an unarmed people, and uses our prisoners as hostages?

If we fail to meet this challenge, all other nations will be on notice that despite its overwhelming power the United States when a real crisis comes will be found wanting.

During my campaign for the Presidency, I pledged to bring Americans home from Vietnam. They are coming home.

I promised to end this war. I shall keep that promise.

I promised to win a just peace. I shall keep that promise.

We shall avoid a wider war, but we are also determined to put an end to this war.

In this room, Woodrow Wilson made the great decision which led to victory in World War I. Franklin Roosevelt made the decision which led to our victory in World War II. Dwight D. Eisenhower made decisions which ended the war in Korea and avoided war in the Middle East. John F. Kennedy, in his finest hour, made the great decision which removed Soviet nuclear missiles from Cuba and the Western Hemisphere.

I have noted that there has been a great deal of discussion with regard to this decision that I have made and I should point out that I do not contend that it is in the same magnitude as these decisions that I have just mentioned. But between those decisions and this decision, there is a difference that is very fundamental. In those decisions the American people were not assailed by counsels of doubt and defeat from some of the most widely known opinion leaders of the nation.

I have noted, for example, that a Republican Senator has said that this action I have taken means that my party has lost all chance of winning the November elections. And others are saying today that this move against enemy sanctuaries will make me a one-term President.

No one is more aware than I am of the political consequences of the action I have taken. It is tempting to take the easy political path, to blame this war on previous administrations and to bring all of our men home immediately— regardless of the consequences, even though that would mean defeat for the United States; to desert 18 million South Vietnamese people who have put their trust in us; to expose them to the same slaughter and savagery which the leaders of North Vietnam inflicted on hundreds of thousands of North Vietnamese who chose freedom when the Communists took over North Vietnam in 1954; to get peace at any price now, even though I know that a peace of humiliation for the United States would lead to a bigger war or surrender later.

I have rejected all political considerations in making this decision.

Whether my party gains in November is nothing compared to the lives of 400,000 brave Americans fighting for our country and for the cause of peace and freedom in Vietnam. Whether I may be a one-term President is insignificant compared to whether by our failure to act in this crisis the United States proves itself to be unworthy to lead the forces of freedom in this critical period in world history. I would rather be a one-term president and do what I believe was right than to be a two-term President at the cost of seeing America become a second-rate power and to see this nation accept the first defeat in its proud 190-year history.

I realize in this war there are honest, deep differences in this country about whether we should have become involved, that there are differences to how the war should have been conducted. But the decision I announce tonight transcends those differences. For the lives of American men are involved. The opportunity for 150,000 Americans to come home in the next 12 months is involved. The future of 18 million people in South Vietnam and 7 million people in Cambodia is involved. The possibility of winning a just peace in Vietnam and in the Pacific is at stake.

It is customary to conclude a speech from the White House by asking support for the President of the United States. Tonight, I depart from that precedent. What I ask is far more important. I ask for your support for our brave men fighting tonight halfway around the world—not for territory—not for glory—but so that their younger brothers and their sons and your sons can have a chance to grow up in a world of peace and freedom and justice.

Thank you and good night.

Assistant Attorney General William H. Rehnquist
The Constitutional Issues—Administration Position
On the American Incursion into Cambodia
June 1970

William H. Rehnquist, "The Consitutional Issues—Administration Position," *New York University Law Review,* XLVIII (June 1970), 163-74.

I am pleased to avail myself of the opportunity of discussing the legal basis for the President's recent action in ordering American Armed Forces to attack Communist sanctuaries inside the border of Cambodia. So much of the discussion surrounding these recent events has been emotional that I think the Association of the Bar performs a genuine public service in encouraging reasoned debate of the very real issues involved.

I wish in these remarks to develop answers to several questions which I believe lie at the root of the matter under discussion. After having explored these questions in their historical context, I will make an effort to apply to the Cambodian incursion what seem to me to be the lessons of both history and constitutional law.

First, may the United States lawfully engage in armed hostilities with a foreign power in the absence of a congressional declaration of war? I believe that the only supportable answer to this question is "yes" in the light of our history and of our Constitution.

Second, is the constitutional designation of the President as Commander-in-Chief of the Armed Forces a grant of substantive authority, which gives him something more than just a seat of honor in a reviewing stand? Again, I believe that this question must be answered in the affirmative.

Third, what are the limits of the President's power as Commander-in-Chief, when that power is unsupported by congressional authorization or ratification of his acts? One would have to be bold indeed to assert a confident answer to this question. But I submit to you that one need not approach anything like the outer limits of the President's power, as defined by judicial decision and historical practice, in order to conclude that it supports the action that President Nixon took in Cambodia.

Before turning to a more detailed discussion of these three questions, let me advert briefly to the provisions of the Constitution itself with respect to the war power and to the debates of the Framers on this subject. Article I, section 8 provides that Congress shall have the power "to declare war." Article II, section 2 designates the President as Commander-in-Chief of the Armed Forces. This textual allocation of authority readily suggests that a division of the nation's war power between the President and Congress was intended. An examination of the proceedings of the Constitutional Convention as found in the Madison notes confirms that suggestion. [J. Madison, Notes of Debates in the Federal Convention of 1787, at 475-77 (Ohio Univ. Press. ed. 1966) Footnote in original.] The Framers did not intend to precisely delimit the boundary between the power of the executive branch and that of the legislative branch any more than they did in any of the other broad areas they considered. While rejecting the traditional power of kings to commit unwilling nations to war, they at the same time recognized the need for quick executive response to rapidly developing international situations.

It is interesting to note that the question before the Convention on Friday, August 17, 1787, was a motion to approve the language of the draft as it then read conferring upon Congress the power "to make war," rather than "to declare war." [Id. Footnote in original.] During the debate, Charles Pinckney urged that the warmaking power be confined to the Senate alone, while Pierce Butler asked that the power be vested in the President. James Madison and Elbridge Gerry then jointly moved to substitute the word "declare" for the word "make," thus in their words "leaving to the Executive the power to repel sudden attacks." Rufus King supported the substitution of the word "declare," urging that the word "make" might be understood to mean to "conduct war," which he believed to be an executive function.

After this brief debate with only New Hampshire dissenting, it was agreed that the grant to Congress should be of the power to "declare" war. Pinckney's motion to strike out the whole clause, and thereby presumably leave the way open to vest the entire warmaking power in the Executive, was then defeated by a voice vote. [Id. Footnote in original.]

The Framers here, as elsewhere in the Constitution, painted with a broad brush, and it has been left to nearly two hundred years of interpretation by each of the three coordinate branches of the National Government to define with somewhat more precision the line separating that which the President may do alone from that which he may do only with the assent of Congress.

It has been recognized from the earliest days of the Republic by the President, by Congress, and by the Supreme Court, that the United States may lawfully engage in armed hostilities with a foreign power without a congressional declaration of war. Our history is replete with instances of "undeclared wars," from the war with France in 1798 through 1800, to the Vietnamese war. The Fifth Congress passed a law contained in the first book of the *Statutes at Large,* authorizing President Adams to "instruct the commanders of the public armed vessels which are, or which shall be employed in the service of the United States, to subdue, seize and take any armed French vessel, which shall be found within the jurisdictional limits of the United States, or elsewhere, on the high seas. [Act of July 9, 1798, ch. 67, 1 Stat. 578.

Footnote in original.] Now this is clearly an act of war, engaging American ships in armed hostilities, and yet Congress authorized it without feeling at all obligated to declare war on France.

The President proceeded to carry out congressional instructions, and such naval seizures were not uncommon during the period of the undeclared war with France. The Supreme Court, in a case arising out of this undeclared war, recognized the differences between what it called "solemn" war, which required a declaration by Congress, and "imperfect" war, which did not. [*Bas v. Tingy,* 4 U.S. (4 Dall.) 36, 39-40 (1800). Footnote in original.]

Other examples abound of congressional authorization for armed military action without Congress having declared war. This does not answer the question, obviously, as to what the President may do without congressional authorization. The fact that the United States can engage in armed hostilities without congressional declaration of war does not mean that it can do so without congressional authorization. But it focuses on substance rather than form, and I think history simply will not admit any other conclusion than that a declaration of war by Congress is not necessary to legitimize the engagement of American Armed Forces in conflict.

What power does the designation of the President as Commander-in-Chief confer upon him? This type of question is one that for obvious reasons has not been the subject of a lot of judicial precedents so one has to pick his way among historical actions and among occasional observations by Supreme Court Justices in order to get some idea of what was intended. Chief Justice Marshall, writing for the Court in *Little v. Barreme,* [6 U.S. (2 Cranch) 170 (1804). Footnote in original.] in 1804 spoke of the power of the President to order the seizure of a ship on the high seas in a situation where Congress has not specified the procedure:

> It is by no means clear, that the President of the United States, whose high duty it is to "take care that the laws be faithfully executed," and who is commander-in-chief of the armies and navies of the United States, might not, without any special authority for that purpose, in the then existing state of things, have empowered the officers commanding the armed vessels of the United States, to seize and send into port for adjudication, American vessels which were forfeited, by being engaged in this illicit commerce. [Id. at 176. Footnote in original.]

Justice Grier, speaking for the Supreme Court in its famous decision in the *Prize Cases,* [67 U.S. (2 Black) 635 (1862.) Footnote in original.] likewise viewed the President's designation as Commander-in-Chief as being a substantive source of authority on which he might rely:

> Whether the President in fulfilling his duties, as Commander-in-chief, in suppressing an insurrection, has met with such armed hostile resistance, and a civil war of such alarming proportions as will compel him to accord to them the character of belligerents, is a question to be decided by *him,* and this Court must be governed by the decisions and acts of the political department of the Government to which this power was entrusted. "He

must determine what degree of force the crisis demands." [Id. at 670. Footnote in original.]

Lest it be thought that Chief Justice Marshall and Justice Grier are not relevant to the twentieth century, Justice Johnson, concurring in *Youngstown Sheet & Tube Co. v. Sawyer,* [343 U.S. 579, 643 (1952). Footnote in original.] expressed a similar thought:

> We should not use this occasion to circumscribe, much less to contract, the lawful role of the President as Commander-in-Chief. I should indulge the widest latitude of interpretation to sustain his exclusive function to command the instruments of national force, at least when turned against the outside world for the security of our society. [Id. at 645. Footnote in original.]

Presidents throughout the history of our country have exercised this power as Commander-in-Chief as if it did confer upon them substantive authority. They have deployed American Armed Forces outside of the United States. They have sent American Armed Forces into conflict with foreign powers on their own initiative. Presidents have likewise exercised the widest sort of authority in conducting armed conflicts already authorized by Congress.

These are actually, I believe, three separate facets of the President's power as Commander-in-Chief. They are the power to commit American Armed Forces to conflict where it hasn't previously existed, the power to deploy American Armed Forces throughout the world, frequently in a way which might invite retribution from unfriendly powers, and the power to determine how a war that's already in progress will be conducted.

Congress has on some of these occasions acquiesced in the President's action without formal ratification; on others it has ratified the President's action; and on still others it has taken no action at all. On several of the occasions, individual members of Congress, and, at the close of the Mexican War, one House of Congress on a preliminary vote, have protested executive use of the Armed Forces. While a particular course of executive conduct to which there was no opportunity for the legislative branch to effectively object cannot conclusively establish a constitutional precedent in the same manner as it would be established by an authoritative judicial decision, a long continued practice on the part of the Executive, acquiesced in by the Congress, is itself some evidence of the existence of constitutional authority to support such a practice. As stated by Justice Frankfurter in his concurring opinion in the *Youngstown Steel* case:

> The Constitution is a framework for government. Therefore the way the framework has consistently operated fairly establishes that it has operated according to its true nature. Deeply embedded traditional ways of conducting government cannot supplant the Constitution or legislation, but they give meaning to the words of the text or supply them. [Id. at 610. Footnote in original.]

The historical examples have been marshalled in numerous recent studies of the President's power, and I will but summarize some of them briefly. President Jefferson, in 1801, sent a small squadron of American naval vessels into the Mediterranean to protect United States commerce against the Barbary pirates. He was of the view that for these ships to take offensive, as opposed to defensive, action, congressional action would be necessary.

In 1845 President Polk ordered military forces to the coast of Mexico and to the western frontier of Texas in order to prevent any interference by Mexico with the proposed annexation of Texas to the United States. Following annexation, Polk ordered General Zachary Taylor to march from the Nueces River which Mexico claimed as the southern border of Texas, to the Rio Grande River, which Texas claimed as her southern boundary, and beyond. While so engaged, Taylor's forces encountered Mexican troops, and hostilities between the two nations commenced on April 25, 1846. [1 S. Morison & H. Commager, The Growth of the American Republic 591-93 (4th ed. 1950). Footnote in original.]

There had been no prior authorization by Congress for Taylor's march south of the Nueces. Justice Grier, in his opinion in the *Prize Cases,* commented on the fact, stating: "The battles of Palo Alto and Resaca de la Palma had been fought before the passage of the Act of Congress of May 13, 1846, which recognized '*a state of war as existing by the act of the Republic of Mexico.*' " [67 U.S. (2 Black) at 668. Footnote in original.]

In 1854 President Pierce approved the action of the naval officer who bombarded Greytown, Nicaragua, in retaliation against a revolutionary government that refused to make reparations for damage and violence to United States citizens. This action was upheld by Judge Samuel Nelson, then a judge in the Southern District of New York and later a Justice of the Supreme Court of the United States, in *Durand v. Hollis.* [8 F. Cas. 111 (No. 4186) (C.C.S.D.N.Y. 1860). Footnote in original.] In his opinion in that case, Judge Nelson said:

> The question whether it was the duty of the president to interpose for the protection of the citizens at Greytowwn against an irresponsible and marauding community that had established itself there, was a public political question, in which the government, as well as the citizens whose interests were involved, was concerned, *and which belonged to the executive to determine*; and his decision is final and conclusive, and justified the defendant in the execution of his orders given through the secretary of the navy. [Id. at 112 (emphasis added). Footnote in original.]

In April 1861 President Lincoln called for 75,000 volunteers to suppress the rebellion by the Southern States, [Morison & Commager, supra, at 649. Footnote in original.] and proclaimed a blockade of the Confederacy. [Id. at 668-69. Footnote in original.] These actions were taken prior to their later ratification by Congress in July 1861. [Id at 669. Footnote in original.] The Supreme Court upheld the validity of the President's action in proclaiming a blockade in the *Prize Cases.* [67 U.S. (2 Black) 635 (1862). Footnote in original.]

In 1900 President McKinley sent an expedition of 5000 United States troops as a component of an international force during the Boxer Rebellion in China. [J. Rhodes, The McKinley & Roosevelt Administrations 127 (1922). Footnote in original.] While Congress recognized the existence of the conflict by providing for combat pay, [Id. Footnote in original.] it neither declared war nor formally ratified the President's action.

Similar incidents in Central America took place under the administrations of President Theodore Roosevelt, [Morison & Commager, supra, at 403-04. Footnote in original.] Taft [M. Rodriguez, Central America 119 (1965). Footnote in original.] and Wilson. [Morison & Commager, supra, at 442-43. Footnote in original.] Naval or armed forces were sent to Panama, [Id. at 403-04. Footnote in original.] Nicaragua, [Id. at 438-39. Footnote in original.] and twice to Mexico [Id. at 442-43. Footnote in original.] in the first two decades of the twentieth century. On none of these occasions was there prior congressional authorization.

Prior to the Vietnam conflict, the most recent example of Presidential combat use of American forces without congressional declaration of war was President Truman's intervention in the Korean conflict. In many senses, this is undoubtedly the high water mark of executive exercise of the power of Commander-in-Chief to commit American forces to hostilities.

Following the invasion of South Korea by the North Koreans in June 1950 and a request for aid by the United Nations Security Council, President Truman ordered air and sea forces to give South Korean troops cover and support and ordered the Seventh Fleet to guard Formosa. [R. Morris, Great Presidential Decisions 400 (1965). Footnote in original.] Ultimately 250,000 troops were engaged in the Korean War which lasted for more than three years.

President Truman relied upon the United Nations Charter as a basis for his action, as well as his power as Commander-in-Chief. The fact that his actions were authorized by the United Nations Charter, however, does not reduce the value of the incident as a precedent for executive action in committing United States Armed Forces to extensive hostilities without a formal declaration of war by Congress. The United Nations Charter was ratified by the Senate and has the status of a treaty, but it does not by virtue of this fact override any constitutional provision. [See Reid v. Covert, 351 U.S. 487 (1956); Geofroy v. Riggs, 133 U.S. 258 (1890). Footnote in original.] If a congressional declaration of war would be required in other circumstances to commit United States forces to hostilities to the extent and nature of those undertaken in Korea, the ratification of the United Nations Charter would not obviate a like requirement in the case of the Korean conflict.

Presidents have likewise used their authority as Commander-in-Chief to deploy United States forces throughout the world. Critics of President Wilson claimed that his action in arming American merchant vessels in early 1917 precipitated our entry into the First World War. Similarly, President Roosevelt's critics have asserted that various actions he took to aid the Allies in the year 1941 played a part in our involvement in the Secold World War. Whatever substance there may be to these criticisms, these Presidential actions stand as the constructions placed by these two Presidents on their power as Commander-in-Chief of the Armed Forces.

The third facet of the power of Commander-in-Chief is the right and obligation to determine how hostilities, once lawfully begun, shall be conducted. This aspect of the President's power is one which is freely conceded by even those students who read the Commander-in-Chief provision least expansively. Indeed, it has seldom, if ever, been seriously challenged. Chief Justice Chase, concurring in *Ex parte Milligan*, [71 U.S. (4 Wall.) 2 (1866). Footnote in original.] said:

> Congress has the power not only to raise and support and govern armies but to declare war. It has, therefore, the power to provide by law for carrying on war. This power necessarily extends to all legislation essential to the prosecution of war with vigor and success, *except such as interferes with the command of the forces and the conduct of campaigns. That power and duty belongs to the President as commander-in-chief.* [Id. at 139 (emphasis added). Footnote in original.]

And if we look back at several of our armed engagements in the past, whether declared wars or otherwise, this type of decision has been freely and frequently engaged in by the Commander-in-Chief. In the First World War, for example, it was necessary to make the tactical decision whether the United States troops in France would fight as a separate command under a United States general or whether United States divisions should be incorporated in existing groups or armies commanded by French or British generals. President Wilson and his military advisors decided that United States forces would fight as a separate command.

In the Second World War similar military decisions on a global scale were required—decisions that partook as much of political strategy as they did of military strategy. For example, should the United States concentrate its military and material resources on either the Atlantic or Pacific fronts to the exclusion of the other, or should it pursue the war on both fronts simultaneously? Where should the reconquest of Allied territories in Europe and Africa begin? What should be the goal of the Allied powers? It will readily be recalled by many of us that decisions such as these were reached by the Allied commanders and chief executive officers of the Allied nations without any formal congressional participation. The series of conferences attended by President Roosevelt and President Truman ultimately established the Allied goals in fighting the Second World War, including the demand for unconditional surrender on the part of the Axis nations.

Similar strategic and tactical decisions were involved in the undeclared Korean War. Decisions such as whether the United States forces should pursue Korean forces into North Korea and as to whether United States Air Force planes should pursue Communist planes north of the Yalu River into China were made by the President as Commander-in-Chief without formal congressional participation.

While these examples help outline the contours of the President's power as Commander-in-Chief in the absence of congressional authorization, they do not, of course, mark a sharp boundary. It is abundantly clear, however, that Congress can by authorizing Presidential action remove any doubt as to its constitutional validity. Thus, when the Gulf of Tonkin Resolution was enacted, [Act of Aug. 10, 1964, Pub. L. No. 88-408, 78 Stat. 384. See Documentary Supplement infra. Footnote in original.] Congress noted that whatever the limits of the President's authority in acting alone might be, whenever the Congress and the President act together "there can be no doubt" of his consitutional authority. [H.R. Rep. No. 1708, 88th Cong., 2d Sess. 4 (1965). Footnote in original.]

Congress may, of course, authorize Presidential action by declaration of war, but its authorization may also take other forms. From the example of the Fifth Congress' delegation to President Adams of the power to stop French vessels on the high seas, [See text accompanying note 4 supra. Footnote in original.] through the legislative acts authorizing President Eisenhower to use troops in Lebanon [Act of Mar. 9, 1957, Pub. L. No. 85-7, 71 Stat. 5. Footnote in original.] and in Formosa [Act of Jan. 29, 1955, Pub. L. No. 84-4, 69 Stat. 5. Footnote in original.] and authorizing President Kennedy to use Armed Forces in connection with the Cuban Missile crisis, [Act of Oct. 3, 1962, Pub. L. No. 87-733, 75 Stat. 697. Footnote in original.] to the Gulf of Tonkin Resolution in 1964, [Act of Aug. 10, 1964, Pub. L. No. 88-408, 78 Stat. 384. See Documentary Supplement infra. Footnote in original.] both Congress and the President have made it clear that it is the substance of congressional authorization, and not the form which that authorization takes, which determines the extent to which Congress has exercised its portion of the war power.

It has been suggested that there may be a question of unlawful delegation of powers here, and that Congress is not free to give a blank check to the President. Whatever may be the answer to that abstract question in the domestic field, I think it is plain from *United States v. Curtiss-Wright Export Corp.,* [299 U.S. 304 (1936). Footnote in original.] which was decided only a year after *Schechter Poultry Corp. v. United States,* [295 U.S. 495 (1935). In that case the Supreme Court had declared that Congress was not permitted to abdicate or to delegate to the President its domestic economic powers under the Constitution. Id. at 529. Footnote in original.] that the principle of unlawful delegation of powers does not apply in the field of external affairs. The Supreme Court in *Curtiss-Wright* made this clear:

> Whether, if the Joint Resolution had related solely to internal affairs it would be open to the challenge that it constituted an unlawful delegation of legislative power to the Executive, we find it unnecessary to determine. The whole aim of the resolution is to affect a situation entirely external to the United States, and falling within the category of foreign affairs. . . .
>
> It results that the investment of the federal government with the powers of external sovereignty did not depend upon the affirmative grants of the Constitution. The powers to declare and wage war, to conclude peace, to make treaties, to maintain diplomatic relations with other sovereignties, if they had never been mentioned in the Constitution, would have vested in the federal government as necessary concomitants of nationality. [299 U.S. at 315, 318. Footnote in original.]

The situation confronting President Nixon in Viet Nam in 1970 must be evaluated against almost two centuries of historical construction of the constitutional division of the war power between the President and Congress. It must also be evaluated against the events which had occurred in the preceding six years. In August 1964 at the request of President Johnson following an attack on American naval vessels in the Gulf of Tonkin, Congress passed the so-called Gulf of Tonkin Resolution. That resolution approved and supported the determination of the President "to take all necessary measures to repel any armed attack against the forces of the United States and to prevent further aggression." It also provided that the United States is "prepared as the President determines, to take all necessary steps, including the use of armed force, to assist any member or protocol state of the Southeast Asia Collective Defense Treaty requesting assistance in defense of its freedom." [Act of Aug. 10, 1964, Pub. L. No. 88-408, 78 Stat. 384. See Documentary Supplement infra. Footnote in original.]

While the legislative history surrounding the Gulf of Tonkin Resolution may be cited for a number of varying interpretations of exactly what Congress was authorizing, it cannot be fairly disputed that substantial military operations in support of the South Vietnamese were thereby authorized. Steadily increasing number of United States Armed Forces were sent into the Vietnamese combat during the years following the passage of the Gulf of Tonkin Resolution. United States Air Force planes bombed not only South Viet Nam, but North Viet Nam. When President Nixon took office in January 1969, he found nearly half a million combat and supporting troops engaged in the field in Viet Nam. His predecessor, acting under the authorization of the Gulf of Tonkin Resolution, had placed these troops in the field, and I for one have no serious doubt that Congress and the President together had exercised their shared war power to lawfully bring about this situation.

President Nixon continued to maintain United States troops in the field in South Viet Nam in pursuance of his policy to seek a negotiated peace which will protect the right of the South Vietnamese people to self-determination. He has begun troop withdrawals, but hostile engagements with the enemy continue. The President feels, and I believe rightfully, that he has an obligation as Commander-in-Chief to take what steps he deems necessary to assure the safety of American Armed Forces in the field. On the basis of the information available to him, he concluded that the continuing build-up of North Vietnamese troops in sanctuaries across the Cambodian border posed an increasing threat both to the safety of American forces and to the ultimate success of the Vietnamization program. He also determined that, from a tactical point of view, combined American-South Vietnamese strikes at these sanctuaries had a very substantial likelihood of success. He, therefore, ordered them to be made.

The President's determination to authorize incursion into these Cambodian border areas is precisely the sort of tactical decision traditionally confided to the Commander-in-Chief in the conduct of armed conflict. From the time of the drafting of the Constitution it has been clear that the Commander-in-Chief has authority to take prompt action to protect American lives in situations involving hostilities. Faced with a substantial troop commitment to such hostilities made by the previous Chief Executive, and approved by successive Congresses, President Nixon had an obligation as Commander-in-Chief of the Armed Forces to take what steps he deemed necessary to assure their safety in the field. A decision to cross the Cambodian border, with at least the tacit consent of the Cambodian Government, in order to destroy sanctuaries being utilized by North Vietnamese in violation of Cambodia's neutrality, is wholly consistent with that obligation. It is a decision made during the course of an armed conflict already commenced as to how that conflict will be conducted, rather than a determination that some new and previously unauthorized military venture will be taken.

By crossing the Cambodian border to attack sanctuaries used by the enemy, the United States has in no sense gone to "war" with Cambodia. United States forces are fighting with or in support of Cambodian troops, and not against them. Whatever protest may have been uttered by the Cambodian Government was obviously the most perfunctory, formal sort of declaration. The Cambodian incursion has not resulted in a previously uncommitted nation joining the ranks of our enemies, but instead has enabled us to more effectively deter enemy aggression heretofore conducted from the Cambodian sanctuaries.

Since even those authorities least inclined to a broad construction of the executive power concede that the Commander-in-Chief provision does confer substantive authority over the manner in which hostilities are conducted, the President's decision to invade and destroy the border sanctuaries in Cambodia was clearly authorized under even a narrow reading of his power as Commander-in-Chief.

President Richard M. Nixon
Report on the Conclusion of
The Cambodian Operation
June 30, 1970

Public Papers of the Presidents: Richard Nixon, 1970, 529-41.

Together with the South Vietnamese, the armed forces of the United States have just completed successfully the destruction of enemy base areas along the Cambodian—South Viet-Nam frontier. All American troops have withdrawn from Cambodia on the schedule announced at the start of the operation.

The allied sweeps into the North Vietnamese and Viet Cong base areas along the Cambodian-South Vietnamese border:

—will save American and allied lives in the future;

—will assure that the withdrawal of American troops from South Viet-Nam can proceed on schedule;

—will enable our program of Vietnamization to continue on its current timetable;

—should enhance the prospects for a just peace.

At this time, it is important to review the background for the decision, the results of the operation, their larger meaning in terms of the conflict in Indochina—and to look down the road to the future.

It is vital to understand at the outset that Hanoi left the United States no reasonable option but to move militarily against the Cambodian base areas. The purpose and significance of our operations against the Cambodian sanctuaries can only be understood against the backdrop of what we are seeking to accomplish in Viet-Nam—and the threat that the Communist bases in Cambodia posed to our objectives. Nor can that military action of the last 2 months be divorced from its cause—the threat posed by the constant expansion of North Vietnamese aggression throughout Indochina.

America's purpose in Viet-Nam and Indochina remains what it has been—a peace in which the peoples of the region can devote themselves to development of their own societies, a peace in which all the peoples of Southeast Asia can determine their own political future without outside interference.

When this administration took office, the authorized strength of American troops in South Viet-Nam was 549,500—the high-water mark of American military presence in Southeast Asia. The United States had been negotiating at Paris for 10 months, but nothing had been agreed upon other than the shape of the bargaining table. No comprehensive allied peace proposal existed. There was no approved plan to reduce America's involvement in the war—in the absence of a negotiated settlement.

Since January of 1969, we have taken steps on all fronts to move toward peace. Along with the Government of South Viet-Nam, we have put forward a number of concrete and reasonable proposals to promote genuine negotiations. These proposals were first outlined by me 13 months ago, on May 14, 1969, and by President Thieu on July 11, 1969. Through both public and private channels, our proposals have been repeated and amplified many times since.

These proposals are designed to secure the removal of all foreign military forces from South Viet-Nam and to establish conditions in which all political forces can compete freely and fairly in the future of the country. Our principal goal has been to enable the people of South Viet-Nam to determine their future free of outside interference.

To indicate our good faith, to improve the climate for negotiations, we changed the orders to our commanders in South Viet-Nam. This has helped to reduce casualties. We have cut tactical air operations in South Viet-Nam by more than 20 percent. We initiated a troop withdrawal program which, during the course of next spring, will bring American troop strength 265,000 men below the level authorized when this administration took office.

These are not the actions of a government pursuing a military solution. They are the decisions of a government seeking a just peace at the conference table.

But Hanoi has ignored our unilateral gestures and rejected every offer of serious negotiations. Instead it has insisted that—as a precondition to talks—we pledge unconditionally to withdraw all American forces from South Viet-Nam and to overthrow the elected government.

These proposals are not a basis for negotiation; they are a demand for surrender. For the United States to accept these conditions would make the negotiations meaningless. Acceptance of such conditions would assure in advance Communist domination of South Viet-Nam.

With Hanoi's intransigence on the negotiating front, this administration was faced with essentially three options.

We could have continued the maximum existing level of American involvement in Viet-Nam. But this was incompatible with the Nixon doctrine of increasing responsibilities for the Asian countries; and it was unacceptable to the American people.

We could have begun the immediate withdrawal for all our forces. We rejected this course of capitulation which would have only won temporary respite at the price of graver crises later. We also rejected that course as both incompatible with America's commitments and tradition, and disastrous in terms of its long-range consequences for peace in the Pacific and peace in the world.

We selected instead a third option—that of gradually shifting the total combat burden to the South Vietnamese.

Since the beginning of this administration 17 months ago, it has been our policy to train and equip the South Vietnamese to take over the burden of their own defense from American troops. Even in the absence of progress at the peace table in Paris, and despite continued enemy pressures in South Viet-Nam, this policy of "Vietnamization" has permitted us to carry out repeated withdrawals of American troops.

As our policy has been tested, more and more Americans have been brought home. By June of 1969, we could announce the pullout of 25,000 American troops. They came home. In September of 1969, we announced the withdrawal of an additional 35,000 American troops. They came home.

In December of 1969, we announced the withdrawal of 50,000 more American troops. They were home by spring of this year. On April 20, I announced the forthcoming withdrawal of an additional 150,000 Americans to be completed during next spring—50,000 of them will be home or on their way home by the 15th of October.

This transfer of primary responsibility for self-defense from American forces to Asian forces reflects our approach to foreign policy. Increasingly, the United States will look to the countries of the region to assume the primary responsibility for their own security—while America moves gradually from a leading to a supporting role.

To be successful this policy requires the striking of a careful balance—whether in South Viet-Nam or elsewhere in Asia. While the growing strength of our allies, and the growing measure of their regional cooperation, allows for a reduction in American presence—they could not survive a sudden and precipitous American withdrawal from our responsibilities. This would lead to a collapse of local strength in the transition period between the old era of principal U.S. involvement to the new era of partnership and emphasis on local and regional cooperation.

Doing too much for an allied people can delay their political maturity, promote a sense of dependency, and diminish that nation's incentive to stand on its own feet. But doing too little for an ally can induce a sense of despair, endanger their right of self-determination, and invite their defeat when confronted by an aggressor.

As we have proceeded with Vietnamization it has been with these principles in mind.

Looking at American policy in Viet-Nam these 17 months, this administration—in the generosity of its negotiating offers, in the limitations on its military actions, and in the consistency of its troop withdrawals—has written a record of restraint. The response from the enemy over those same 17 months has been intransigence in Paris, belligerence from Hanoi, and escalation of the war throughout Indochina.

Enemy attacks in Viet-Nam increased during April.

This past winter Hanoi launched a major offensive against the legitimate government of Laos which they themselves had helped to establish under the 1962

Geneva accords. For years, in violation of those accords, North Vietnamese troops have occupied Laotian territory and used its eastern regions as a highway for the export of aggression into South Viet-Nam.

In March and April of this year, Communist troops used their long-held bases in Cambodia to move against the Government of Cambodia in a way which increased the long-term threat to allied forces in South Viet-Nam as well as to the future of our Vietnamization and withdrawal programs. These new violations, too, took place against a backdrop of years of Communist disregard of the neutrality and territorial integrity of Cambodia—guaranteed in the 1954 Geneva agreements to which Hanoi was a signatory.

In assessing the April 30 decision to move against the North Vietnamese and Viet Cong sanctuaries in Cambodia, four basic facts must be remembered.

It was North Viet-Nam—not we—which brought the Viet-Nam war into Cambodia.

For 5 years, North Viet-Nam has used Cambodian territory as a sanctuary from which to attack allied forces in South Viet-Nam. For 5 years, American and allied forces—to preserve the concept of Cambodian neutrality and to confine the conflict in Southeast Asia—refrained from moving against those sanctuaries.

It was the presence of North Vietnamese troops on Cambodian soil that contributed to the downfall of Prince Sihanouk. It was the indignation of the Cambodian people against the presence of Vietnamese Communists in their country that led to riots in Phnom Penh which contributed to Prince Sihanouk's ouster—an ouster that surprised no nation more than the United States. At the end of Sihanouk's rule, the United States was making efforts to improve relations with his government and the Prince was taking steps against the Communist invaders on his national soil.

It was the government appointed by Prince Sihanouk and ratified by the Cambodian National Assembly—not a group of usurpers—which overthrew him with the approval of the National Assembly. The United States had neither connection with, nor knowledge of, these events.

It was the major expansion of enemy activity in Cambodia that ultimately caused allied troops to end 5 years of restraint and attack the Communist base areas.

The historical record is plain.

Viet Cong and North Vietnamese troops have operated in eastern Cambodia for years. The primary objective of these Communist forces has been the support of Hanoi's aggression against South Viet-Nam. Just as it has violated the 1962 Geneva accords on Laos, North Viet-Nam has consistently ignored its pledge, in signing the 1954 Geneva accords, to respect Cambodian neutrality and territorial integrity.

In a May 1967 Phnom Penh radio broadcast, Prince Sihanouk's following remarks were reported to the Cambodian people:

> I must tell you that the Vietnamese communists and the Viet Cong negotiated with us three or four times but that absolutely nothing comes out of the negotiations. . . . After I expelled the French and after the

French troops left Cambodia, Viet Minh remained in our country in order to conquer it. How can we have confidence in the Viet Minh? . . . If we side with the Viet Minh we will lose our independence.

Late in 1969, Prince Sihanouk ordered Cambodia's underequipped and weak armed forces to exercise some measure of control over North Vietnamese and Viet Cong Communist forces occupying Cambodian territory.

At the same time, the Communist forces were actively preparing in their base areas for new combat in South Viet-Nam. These areas—on the Cambodian side of the Viet-Nam-Cambodian border—have for years served as supply depots and base camps for enemy troops infiltrated through Laos into South Viet-Nam. They have also served as sanctuaries for North Vietnamese and Viet Cong headquarters elements and for combat troops to rest, refit, and resupply on their return from South Viet-Nam.

Our screening of more than 6 tons of documents captured in the Cambodian operations has provided conclusive proof of Communist reliance on Cambodia as a logistic and infiltration corridor and as a secure area from which Communist designs on Viet-Nam as well as in Cambodia itself could be carried out.

On January 6, 1970, Prince Sihanouk departed on vacation in France. His Prime Minister, Lon Nol, and Deputy Prime Minister, Sirik Matak, were left in charge. In early March, with Sihanouk still in power, there were public demonstrations, first in the eastern provinces of Cambodia and later in Phnom Penh, against flagrant North Vietnamese violation of Cambodia's territorial integrity.

On March 13, Prince Sihanouk left Paris for Moscow and Peking, avowedly to seek Soviet and Chinese assistance in persuading the Vietnamese Communists to reduce the presence of North Vietnamese and Viet Cong forces in Cambodia.

Then, on March 18, the Cambodian National Assembly by unanimous vote declared that Prince Sihanouk was no longer Chief of State. Cheng Heng was retained as Acting Chief of State. Lon Nol and Sirik Matak kept their positions. Reasons for Sihanouk's ouster included growing objections to his mishandling of the economy and to his bypassing of the Cabinet and National Assembly; but resentment over North Viet-Nam's flagrant misuse of Cambodian territory certainly contributed. Sihanouk arrived in Peking the same day and met with the Peking leadership as well as with the North Vietnamese Prime Minister, who had hastened to Peking to greet him. Thereafter Sihanouk has increasingly identified himself with the Communist cause in Indochina.

This Government had no advance warning of the ouster of Sihanouk, with whom we had been attempting to improve relations. Our initial response was to seek to preserve the status quo with regard to Cambodia and to try to prevent an expansion of Communist influence. The immunity of the Cambodian sanctuaries had been a serious military handicap for us for many years. But we had refrained from moving against them in order to contain the conflict. We recognized both the problems facing Sihanouk and the fact that he had exercised some measure of control over Communist activities, through regulation of the flow of rice and military supplies into the sanctuaries from coastal ports. We considered that a neutral Cambodia outweighed the military benefits of a move against the base areas.

This is why diplomatically our first reaction to Sihanouk's overthrow was to encourage some form of accommodation in Cambodia. We spoke in this sense to interested governments. And we made clear through many channels that we had no intention of exploiting the Cambodian upheaval for our own ends.

These attempts ran afoul of Hanoi's designs. North Viet-Nam and the Viet Cong withdrew their representation from Phnom Penh. North Vietnamese and Viet Cong forces began to expand their base areas along the border.

By April 3, they were beginning to launch attacks against Cambodian forces in Svay Rieng Province. Later these attacks were extended to other outposts in eastern Cambodia, forcing Cambodian troops to evacuate border positions in the Parrot's Beak area by April 10. Communist attacks were also directed against Mekong River traffic.

By April 16, the North Vietnamese and Viet Cong troops began to launch isolated attacks deep into Cambodia including an attack on the capital of Takeo Province south of Phnom Penh.

Despite escalating Communist activity in Cambodia, we continued to exercise restraint. Though the implications of the Communist actions for our efforts in Viet-Nam were becoming increasingly ominous, Communist intentions in Cambodia were still not absolutely clear. The military moves by the North Vietnamese and Viet Cong in Cambodia could still be interpreted as temporary actions to secure their base camps in light of the uncertainties following Sihanouk's removal.

When I made my April 20 speech announcing the withdrawal of 150,000 troops over the next year, I knew that we might be at a crossroads in Cambodia. I nevertheless made the announcement because it would leave no doubt about our intention to deescalate the conflict.

I also used the occasion to restate very forthcoming political principles for a negotiated peace. At the same time I described the pattern of North Vietnamese aggression in Indochina and acknowledged that my withdrawal decision involved some risks when viewed against this enemy escalation. I therefore reiterated my determination to take strong and effective measures if increased enemy action in Laos, Cambodia, or South Viet-Nam jeopardized the security of our remaining forces in Viet-Nam.

Within days of my April 20 speech, Communist intentions became painfully and unamibiguously clear. In the face of our restraint and our warnings, the North Vietnamese continued to expand their territorial control, threatening to link up their base areas. From a series of isolated enclaves, the base areas were rapidly becoming a solid band of self-sustaining territory stretching from Laos to the sea from which any pretense of Cambodian sovereignty was rapidly being excluded.

—On April 20, North Vietnamese forces temporarily captured Saang, only 18 miles south of Phnom Penh.

—On April 22, Communist forces assaulted the town of Snuol east of Phnom Penh.

—On April 23, they attacked the town of Mimot and an important bridge linking the town of Snuol and the capital of Kratie Province on Route 13.

—On April 24, they moved on the resort city of Kep.

—On April 26, they attacked some ships on the Mekong and occupied the town of Angtassom, a few miles west of Takeo.

—They then attacked the city of Chhlong, on the Mekong River north of Phnom Penh, and the port city of Kampot.

—During this same period, they cut almost every major road leading south and east out of Phnom Penh.

The prospect suddenly loomed of Cambodia's becoming virtually one large base area for attack anywhere into South Viet-Nam along the 600 miles of the Cambodian frontier. The enemy in Cambodia would have enjoyed complete freedom of action to move forces and supplies rapidly across the entire length of South Viet-Nam's flank to attack our forces in South Viet-Nam with impunity from well-stocked sanctuaries along the border.

We thus faced a rapidly changing military situation from that which existed on April 20.

The possibility of a grave new threat to our troops in South Viet-Nam was rapidly becoming an actuality.

This pattern of Communist action prior to our decision of April 30 makes it clear the enemy was intent both on expanding and strengthening its military position along the Cambodian border and overthrowing the Cambodian Government. The plans were laid, the orders issued, and already being implemented by Communist forces.

Not only the clear evidence of Communist actions—but supporting data screened from more than 6 tons of subsequently captured Communist documents—leaves no doubt that the Communists' move against the Cambodian Government preceded the U.S. action against the base areas.

On April 30, before announcing our response, I outlined the three basic choices we had in the face of the expanding Communist threat.

First, we could do nothing. This would have eroded an important restraint on the loss of American lives. It would have run the risk of Cambodia's becoming one vast enemy staging area, a springboard for attacks on South Viet-Nam without fear of retaliation. The dangers of having done nothing would not have fully materialized for several months, and this Government might have been commended for exercising restraint. But, as withdrawals proceeded, our paralysis would have seriously jeopardized our forces in Viet-Nam and would have led to longer lists of American casualties. The United States could not accept the consequences of inaction in the face of this enemy escalation. The American men remaining in South Viet-Nam after our withdrawal of 150,000 would have been in severe jeopardy.

Our second choice was to provide massive assistance to Cambodia. This was an unrealistic alternative. The small Cambodian army of 30,000 could not effectively utilize any massive transfusion of military assistance against the immediate enemy threat. We also did not wish to get drawn into the permanent direct defense of Cambodia. This would have been inconsistent with the basic premises of our foreign policy.

After intensive consultations with my top advisers, I chose the third course. With the South Vietnamese we launched joint attacks against the base areas so long occupied by Communist forces.

Our military objectives were to capture or destroy the arms, ammunition, and supplies that had been built up in those sanctuaries over a period of years and to disrupt the enemy's communication network. At the least this would frustrate the impact of any Communist success in linking up their base areas if it did not prevent this development altogether.

I concluded that, regardless of the success of Communist assaults on the Cambodian Government, the destruction of the enemy's sanctuaries would:

—remove a grave potential threat to our remaining men in South Viet-Nam, and so reduce future American casualties.

—give added assurance of the continuance of our troop withdrawal program.

—ensure the timetable for our Vietnamization program.

—increase the chances of shortening the war in South Viet-Nam.

—enhance the prospects of a negotiated peace.

—emphasize to the enemy whether in Southeast Asia or elsewhere that the word of the United States—whether given in a promise or a warning—was still good.

Ten major operations were launched against a dozen of the most significant base areas with 32,000 American troops and 48,000 South Viet-Namese participating at various times. As of today, all Americans, including logistics personnel and advisers, have withdrawn, as have a majority of the South Vietnamese forces.

Our military response to the enemy's escalation was measured in every respect. It was a limited operation for a limited period of time with limited objectives.

We have scrupulously observed the 21-mile limit on penetration of our ground combat forces into Cambodian territory. These self-imposed time and geographic restrictions may have cost us some military advantages, but we knew that we could achieve our primary objectives within these restraints. And these restraints underscored the limited nature of our purpose to the American people.

My June 3 interim report pointed up the success of these operations and the massive amounts of supplies we were seizing and destroying. We have since added substantially to these totals. A full inventory is attached as an appendix to the report. Here are some highlights.

According to latest estimates from the field, we have captured:

—22,892 individual weapons—enough to equip about 74 full-strength North Vietnamese infantry battalions—and 2,509 big crew-served weapons—enough to equip about 25 full-strength North Vietnamese infantry battalions;

—More than 15 million rounds of ammunition, or about what the enemy has fired in South Viet-Nam during the past year;

—14 million pounds of rice, enough to feed all the enemy combat battalions estimated to be in South Viet-Nam for about 4 months;

—143,000 rockets, mortars, and recoilless-rifle rounds, used against cities and bases. Based on recent experience, the number of mortars, large rockets, and recoilless-rifle rounds is equivalent to what the enemy shoots in about 14 months in South Viet-Nam;

—Over 199,552 antiaircraft rounds, 5,482 mines, 62,022 grenades, and 83,000 pounds of explosives, including 1,002 satchel charges;

—Over 435 vehicles, and destroyed over 11,688 bunkers and other military structures.

And while our objective has been supplies rather than personnel, the enemy has also taken a heavy manpower loss—11,349 men killed and about 2,328 captured and detainees.

Significant Enemy Losses in Cambodia

I.	*Ammunition*	
	Machine Rounds	4,067,177
	Rifle Rounds	10,694,990
	Total Small Arms (Machinegun and Rifle Rounds)	14,762,167
	Antiaircraft Rounds	199,552
	Mortar Rounds	68,539
	Large Rocket Rounds	2,123
	Small Rocket Rounds	43,160
	Recoilless-Rifle Rounds	29,185
	Grenades	62,022
	Mines	5,482
II.	*Weapons*	
	Individual	22,892
	Crew-served	2,509
III.	*Food*	
	Rice (lbs.)	14,046,000
	Man-Months of Rice	309,012
	Total Food (lbs.)	14,518,000
IV.	*Facilities*	
	Bunkers / Structures destroyed	11,688
V.	*Transportation*	
	Vehicles	435
	Boats	167
VI.	*Examples of Other Equipment*	
	Radios	248
	Generators	49
	Total Communications Equipment (lbs.)	58,600
	Miscellaneous Explosives (lbs.)	83,000
	(including 1,002 satchel charges)	
	Medical Supplies (lbs.)	110,800
	Documents (lbs.)	12,400
VII.	*Personnel*	
	Enemy Killed in Action	11,349
	POW's (includes detainees)	2,328

These are impressive statistics. But what is the deeper meaning of the piles of enemy supplies and the rubble of enemy installations?

We have eliminated an immediate threat to our forces and to the security of

South Viet-Nam—and produced the prospect of fewer American casualties in the future.

We have inflicted extensive casualties and very heavy losses in material on the enemy—losses which can now be replaced only from the North during a monsoon season and in the face of counteraction by South Vietnamese ground and U.S. air forces.

We have ended the concept of Cambodian sanctuaries, immune from attack, upon which the enemy military had relied for 5 years.

We have dislocated supply lines and disrupted Hanoi's strategy in the Saigon area and the Mekong Delta. The enemy capacity to mount a major offensive in this vital populated region of the South has been greatly diminished.

We have effectively cut off the enemy from resupply by the sea. In 1969, well over half of the munitions being delivered to the North Vietnamese and Viet Cong in Cambodia came by sea.

We have, for the time being, separated the Communist main-force units—regular troops organized in formal units similar to conventional armies—from the guerrillas in the southern part of Viet-Nam. This should provide a boost to pacification efforts.

We have guaranteed the continuance of our troop withdrawal program. On June 3, I reaffirmed that 150,000 more Americans would return home within a year and announced that 50,000 would leave Viet-Nam by October 15.

We have bought time for the South Vietnamese to strengthen themselves against the enemy.

We have witnessed visible proof of the success of Vietnamization as the South Vietnamese performed with skill and valor and competence far beyond the expectation of our commanders or American advisers.

The morale and self-confidence of the Army of South Viet-Nam is higher than ever before.

These then are the major accomplishments of the operations against the Cambodian base areas. Americans can take pride in the leadership of General Abrams [Gen. Creighton W. Abrams, Commander, U.S. Military Assistance Command, Viet-Nam] and in the competence and dedication of our forces.

There is another way to view the success of these operations. What if we had chosen the first option—and done nothing?

The enemy sanctuaries by now would have been expanded and strengthened. The thousands of troops he lost, in killed or captured, would be available to attack American positions and with the enormous resources that we captured or destroyed still in his hands.

Our Vietnamization program would be in serious jeopardy; our withdrawals of troops could only have been carried out in the face of serious threat to our remaining troops in Viet-Nam.

We would have confronted an adversary emboldened by our timidity, an adversary who had ignored repeated warnings.

The war would be a good deal further from over than it is today.

Had we stood by and let the enemy act with impunity in Cambodia—we would be facing a truly bleak situation.

The allied operations have greatly reduced these risks and enhanced the prospects for the future. However, many difficulties remain and some setbacks are inevitable. We still face substantial problems, but the Cambodian operations will enable us to pursue our goals with greater confidence.

When the decision to go into Cambodia was announced on April 30, we anticipated broad disagreement and dissent within the society. Given the divisions on this issue among the American people, it could not have been otherwise.

But the majority of the Americans supported that decision—and now that the Cambodian operation is over, I believe there is a wide measure of understanding of the necessity for it.

Although there remains disagreement about its long-term significance, about the cost to our society of having taken this action—there can be little disagreement now over the immediate military success that has been achieved. With American ground operations in Cambodia ended, we shall move forward with our plan to end the war in Viet-Nam and to secure the just peace on which all Americans are united.

Now that our ground forces and our logistic and advisory personnel have all been withdrawn, what will be our future policy for Cambodia?

The following will be the guidelines of our policy in Cambodia:

1. There will be no U.S. ground personnel in Cambodia except for the regular staff of our Embassy in Phnom Penh.

2. There will be no U.S. advisers with Cambodian units.

3. We will conduct—with the approval of the Cambodian Government—air interdiction missions against the enemy efforts to move supplies and personnel through Cambodia toward South Viet-Nam and to reestablish base areas relevant to the war in Viet-Nam. We do this to protect our forces in South Viet-Nam.

4. We will turn over material captured in the base areas in Cambodia to the Cambodian Government to help it defend its neutrality and independence.

5. We will provide military assistance to the Cambodian Government in the form of small arms and relatively unsophisticated equipment in types and quantities suitable for their army. To date we have supplied about $5 million of these items, principally in the form of small arms, mortars, trucks, aircraft parts, communications equipment, and medical supplies.

6. We will encourage other countries of the region to give diplomatic support to the independence and neutrality of Cambodia. We welcome the efforts of the Djakarta group of countries [Australia, Indonesia, Japan, Korea, Laos, Malaysia, New Zealand, the Philippines, Singapore, South Viet-Nam, Thailand. Footnote in original.] to mobilize world opinion and encourage Asian cooperation to this end.

7. We will encourage and support the efforts of third countries who wish to furnish Cambodia with troops or material. We applaud the efforts of Asian nations to help Cambodia preserve its neutrality and independence.

I will let the Asian governments speak for themselves concerning their future policies. I am confident that two basic principles will govern the actions of those nations helping Cambodia:

—They will be at the request of, and in close concert with, the Cambodian Government.

—They will not be at the expense of those nations' own defense—indeed they will contribute to their security, which they see bound up with events in Cambodia.

The South Vietnamese plan to help. Of all the countries of Southeast Asia,

South Viet-Nam has most at stake in Cambodia. A North Vietnamese takeover would, of course, have profound consequences for its security. At the same time, the leaders of South Viet-Nam recognize that the primary focus of their attention must be on the security of their own country. President Thieu has reflected these convictions in his major radio and TV address of June 27. Our understanding of Saigon's intentions is as follows:

1. South Vietnamese forces remain ready to prevent reestablishment of base areas along South Viet-Nam's frontier.

2. South Vietnamese forces will remain ready to assist in the evacuation of Vietnamese civilians and to respond selectively to appeals from the Cambodian Government should North Vietnamese aggression make this necessary.

3. Most of these operations will be launched from within South Viet-Nam. There will be no U.S. air or logistics support. There will not be U.S. advisers on these operations.

4. The great majority of South Vietnamese forces are to leave Cambodia.

5. The primary objective of the South Vietnamese remains Vietnamization within their country. Whatever actions are taken in Cambodia will be consistent with this objective.

In this June 27 speech President Thieu emphasized that his government will concentrate on efforts within South Viet-Nam. He pledged that his country will always respect the territory, borders, independence, and neutrality of Cambodia and will not interfere in its internal politics. His government does not advocate stationing troops permanently in Cambodia or sending the South Vietnamese army to fight the war for the Cambodian army.

Under the foreign policy guidelines first outlined at Guam a year ago, I stressed that a threatened country should first make maximum efforts in its own self-defense. The Cambodian people and soldiers are doing that against the superior forces of the North Vietnamese and Viet Cong invaders. The majority of the Cambodian people support the present government against the foreign intruders. Cambodian troops have remained loyal and have stood up well in the face of great pressures from a better armed and experienced foe.

Secondly, our policy stresses there should be regional cooperation where a country is not strong enough to defend herself. Cambodia's neighbors are providing that cooperation by joining with her in a collective effort. Each of them is a target of Communist aggression; each has a stake in Cambodia's neutrality and independence.

Third, the United States will assist such self-help and regional actions where our participation can make a difference. Over the long term, we expect the countries of Asia to provide increasingly for their own defense. However, we are now in a transitional phase when nations are shouldering greater responsibilities but when U.S. involvement, while declining, still plays an important role.

In this interim period, we must offset our lower direct involvement with increased military and economic assistance. To meet our foreign policy obligations while reducing our presence will require a redirection—both quantitatively and qualitatively—in our assistance programs.

Prince Sihanouk wrote in December 1969 about the Communist threat to his country and the balance presented by American forces in Southeast Asia. In a generally anti-American article in the official Cambodian government party newspaper, he stated:

> On the diplomatic and political plane, the fact that the U.S. remains in our region and does not yet leave it allows us maneuverings . . . to assure on the one hand our more than honorable presence in the concert of nations . . . this presence (and this is an irony of fate for the anti-imperialists that we are) is an essential condition for the "respect," the "friendship" and even for the aid of our socialist "friends." When the U.S. has left these regions, it is certain that the Cambodia of the Sangkum will be the objective of the shellings of the heavy Communist guns: unfriendliness, subversion, aggressions, infiltrations and even occupations.

The Search for Peace

In our search for a lasting peace in Southeast Asia, we are applying the three basic principles of our foreign policy which are set forth in the foreign policy report to Congress last February: partnership, strength, and willingness to negotiate.

—The partnership of our Vietnamization program and of our support for regional defense efforts.

—The strength of our action against the Communist bases in Cambodia and the steadfastness of the American people to see the war through to an honorable conclusion.

—The willingness to negotiate expressed in our generous proposals for a settlement and in our flexibility once Hanoi agrees to serious negotiations.

All three elements are needed to bring peace in Southeast Asia. The willingness to negotiate will prove empty unless buttressed by the willingness to stand by just demands. Otherwise negotiations will be a subterfuge for capitulation. This would only bring a false and transitory peace abroad and recrimination at home.

While we search for genuine negotiation we must continue to demonstrate resolution both abroad and at home and we must support the common defense efforts of threatened Asian nations.

To the leaders in Hanoi, I say the time has come to negotiate. There is nothing to be gained in waiting. There is never an ideal moment when both sides are in perfect equilibrium.

The lesson of the last 2 months has reinforced the lessons of the last 2 years—the time has come to negotiate a just peace.

In Cambodia, the futility of expanded aggression has been demonstrated. By its actions in Cambodia, North Viet-Nam and the Viet Cong provoked the destruction of their sanctuaries and helped to weld together the independent states of Southeast Asia in a collective defense effort, which will receive American support.

The other side cannot impose its will through military means. We have no intention of imposing ours. We have not raised the terms for a settlement as a result of our recent military successes. We will not lower our minimum terms in response to enemy pressure. Our objective remains a negotiated peace with justice for both sides and which gives the people of South Viet-Nam the opportunity to shape their own future.

With major efforts the North Vietnamese can perhaps rebuild or readjust Cambodian supply areas over a period of months. They can pursue their war against South Viet-Nam and her neighbors. But what end would a new round of conflict serve? There is no military solution to this conflict. Sooner or later, peace must come. It can come now, through a negotiated settlement that is fair to both sides and humiliates neither. Or it can come months or years from now, with both sides having paid the further price of protracted struggle.

We would hope that Hanoi would ponder seriously its choice, considering both the promise of an honorable peace and the costs of continued war.

We repeat: All our previous proposals, public and private, remain on the conference table to be explored, including the principles of a just political settlement that I outlined on April 20.

We search for a political solution that reflects the will of the South Vietnamese people and allows them to determine their future without outside interference.

We recognize that a fair political solution should reflect the existing relationship of political forces.

We pledge to abide by the outcome of the political process agreed upon by the South Vietnamese.

For our part, we shall renew our efforts to bring about genuine negotiations both in Paris and for all of Indochina. As I said in my address last September to the United Nations General Assembly:

"The people of Viet-Nam, North and South alike, have demonstrated heroism enough to last a century. . . . The people of Viet-Nam, North and South, have endured an unspeakable weight of suffering for a generation. And they deserve a better future."

We call on Hanoi to join us at long last in bringing about that better future.

All of this adds up to the imperial presidency, as Schlesinger has so accurately observed:

> Both Johnson and Nixon had indulged in presidential war-making beyond the boldest dreams of their predecessors. Those who had stretched the executive war power to what had seemed its "outer limits" in the past had done so in the face of visible and dire threat to national survival: Lincoln confronted by rebellion, Roosevelt by Hitler. Neither had pretended to be exercising routine powers of the Commander in Chief. Johnson and Nixon had surpassed all their predecessors in claiming that inherent and exclusive presidential authority, unaccompanied by emergencies threatening the life of the nation, unaccompanied by the authorization of Congress or the blessing of an international organization, permitted a President to order troops into battle at his unilateral pleasure.[32]

Another interesting distinction which Schlesinger makes between the Johnson and Nixon theories of the presidential war power is that Johnson's theory was more sweeping in principle but more confined in practice, while the opposite was true for Nixon. He made his appeal on narrower grounds, but indicated no restraint in curtailing his actions.

> Now in justifying the commitment of American troops to battle in neutral states with no gesture at all toward (in the words of Andrew Jackson) previous understanding with that body by whom war could alone be declared and by whom all the provisions for sustaining its perils must be furnished—in doing this, Nixon cited no emergency that denied time for congressional action, expressed no doubt about the perfect legality of his personal extension of the war into two new countries, and showed no interest in retrospective congressional ratification. The authority claimed by Nixon appeared indefinitely extensible so long as a President could declare American forces anywhere in the world in danger of attack. It appeared extinguishable only when an American military withdrawal ended the hazard of such attack.[33]

The full hypocrisy of the Nixon position was revealed when there were no longer American troops in Vietnam whose protection could justify (in his terms) the bombing of Cambodia. Nevertheless, after March 28, 1973 when American troops were withdrawn from that beleaguered country, the secret and intensive bombing of Cambodia continued for weeks, and there were even threats of a renewal of bombing in Vietnam. It is time we turn back to Lincoln's warning against presidential war-making:

> Allow the President to invade a neighboring nation, whenever he shall deem it necessary to repel an invasion . . . and you allow him to make war at pleasure. Study to see if you can fix any limit to his power in this respect. . . .[34]

That remains our most critical problem today. Indeed, what resources does the body politic possess to resist this dangerous manifestation of the imperial presidency? To explore this critical question, I sat down with Arthur M. Schlesinger, jr., the distinguished American historian and biographer and the Albert Schweitzer professor of humanities at the City University of New York, and Leon Friedman, author and editor of many volumes dealing with legal and judicial problems and a professor at the Hofstra School of Law. Mr. Friedman is a man who has been involved in the fight against presidential usurpation of power, particularly as it may curb the rights of individuals, as an attorney for the American Civil Liberties Union.

I began my inquiry by asking Professor Schlesinger whether or not there are present within the Johnson-Nixon concepts of the imperial presidency manifestations of institutional flaws or historical examples from the early history of the presidency, which might have been restrained if they had been properly understood and effectively checked at the time. I then asked him to distinguish his concept of the imperial presidency, which I have been discussing above, from that of the revolutionary presidency, a term which he has asserted to characterize the domestic rule of Richard Nixon.

ARTHUR M. SCHLESINGER, JR.: Well, obviously everything has historical antecedents. The Founding Fathers who gathered in Philadelphia had two things in mind in regard to their new government. One was to establish a strong and effective national government, with an energetic Executive, and the second was to make sure that the Executive operated within a strong and effective system of accountability. They provided for certain formal modes of accountability in the Constitution itself—the President's accountability to Congress and to the courts—and there evolved very rapidly in the republic various informal modes of accountability: the President's accountability to his colleagues in the cabinet and the executive branch, to his political party, once parties began to crystallize, to the press and the media of opinion and to public opinion in general, even to international opinion—after all, the Declaration of Independence spoke of a decent respect for the opinions of mankind. And so, there evolved a system of accountability to match the powers which the Constitution bestowed on the presidency.

The system of accountability had one great weakness, however, and this was in the realm of foreign affairs. In the realm of foreign affairs, the Congress, the courts, the people, felt much less sure of their ground, much less confident of their information and their judgment, and therefore were much less inclined to challenge and check and balance the presidency than they were ready to do in domestic affairs. So, in addition to the ambiguous state in which the Constitution left the conduct of foreign affairs, the more critical foreign affairs seemed, the more power flowed to the presidency. War was a particular example of this, but international crisis in general meant an increase in presidential power. What I have called the imperial presidency seems to me essentially a product of the fact that the United States was in a situation of protracted international crisis from 1939 to the present. This period, therefore, brought about a steady transfer of power to the presidency—a transfer assisted by the fact that Congress, having done so deplorably in foreign affairs, even in its own eyes, in the period from the rejection of the Treaty of Versailles to the passage of the rigid neutrality legislation of the 1930s, and having acquired an inferiority complex by these experiences, was more than ready to let the President take the initiative and the responsibility. What I would call the imperial presidency is a situation where the balance between presidential power and presidential accountability has been gravely disturbed. Nixon's effort to consolidate and institutionalize this imbalance and to establish the presidency on a plebiscitary basis could only be called the revolutionary presidency.

WILLIAM M. GOLDSMITH: Would you find that in any of the earlier periods of the presidency there was what one might call a slippage of this area? If, for example, the President had been held accountable for actions beyond the pale of the Constitution before this period that you have described as the era of the imperial presidency, where the great emphasis on foreign affairs, actually in war powers, takes place, might perhaps the results have been different?

Take the conduct of President Tyler prior to the Mexican War. Now here, it seems to me, is an example where we have a clear manifestation of the accountability system not working effectively. Tyler and his secretary of state, John C. Calhoun, actually negotiated an agreement secretly with the Republic of Texas which the Congress was not aware of, and in fact, with a great deal of effort for an attenuated period of time, could not even pry out of the State Department and the presidential office. Information regarding this commitment was withheld, and the commitment was a serious one because it put the government of the United States on record with an agreement to transfer a certain number of troops, a certain number of naval ships—

SCHLESINGER: Or essentially to come to the military aid of Texas in case Mexico invaded, which, for a couple of strict constructionists like Tyler and Calhoun, was an astonishing development.

GOLDSMITH: Well, one finds that, as you point out in your book, continually, in the history of comparing ideology with performance, that the actual political concerns of the moment seem to have an overwhelming effect on—

SCHLESINGER: They dissolve scruples very quickly.

GOLDSMITH: Right, but now in this instance (and of course Polk came on very hard after Tyler and compounded the lack of accountability by actually issuing orders to carry out this commitment by moving the troops into an area which was literally sovereign territory of another state—a state with which we had perfectly normal and peaceful relations), Tyler was able to get away with this. Polk succeeded by virtue of a quick manipulation of a declaration of war by Congress which effected a *fait accompli* in this situation. In both instances these Presidents were not held properly accountable to the Congress and they were able to exert their will in a situation and neither the Congress nor the Constitution restrained them. Now the question I am really raising is, if one puts together a series of such instances, both in the nineteenth and twentieth centuries, is there some kind of cumulative or gradual erosion of the ability of the Congress to restrain a President, and does this not establish a certain kind of precedent where we see, in one instance after another, Presidents who have not been restrained who serve as examples for successive Presidents who feel under even less compunction than their predecessors?

SCHLESINGER: Well, I suppose that's so. I would agree that the system of accountability has decayed under the pressure of international crises. I think that the examples from the 1840s are symptomatic rather than compulsory. Tyler failed in his effort to get a treaty annexing Texas because a senator broke the secrecy in the manner of later patriots and disclosed secret papers to the newspapers.

GOLDSMITH: The first Ellsberg case.

SCHLESINGER: Well, an early Ellsberg case; the first, I suppose, was the time of the Jay treaty, but in any case the treaty was defeated. And though Polk brought war about through his deployment of troops, he observed the constitutional formality, he got a declaration of war. He did not suppose, in the modern fashion, that his power as Commander in Chief gave him the authority to wage a war without congressional authorization. But I do think, in general, that the pressure of international crisis on the system of accountability opened a large gap in the system, a breach which weakened the system dangerously and permitted the President to acquire exceptional powers in foreign affairs. The resultant imbalance between presidential power and presidential accountability eventually tempted Presidents of that inclination to use their excessive power not only to meet international crisis, but also for their own purposes at home. So I say what you have today is a combination: on the one hand, certain long-running structural tendencies, partly the consequence of certain unsolved problems in the Constitution, and partly the consequence of America's entry into the world and the increasing weight of foreign affairs on national policy; and on the other hand, certain personalities with a psychic need for the unilateral exercise of authority. I think if Hubert Humphrey had been elected in 1968 or George McGovern had been elected in 1972, we would not have had the attempt to transform the imperial presidency, that is, the presidency out of balance, into the revolutionary presidency, in which the imbalance in the traditional Constitution would be made the basis for a new order.

LEON FRIEDMAN: If I could try and answer one of Professor Goldsmith's earlier questions, and to put at least one optimistic note in all this. You asked whether the specific instances of presidential overreaching might not create a precedent for further and further overreaching later on. If anything, there seems to be a kind of a one-free-shot by the President in which other institutions, whether it is Congress, the public, or the courts, permit the President to do it once, but the second time around, in effect, they suddenly see it's not just an aberration, and they are willing to try to deal with it on an institutional level.

I can give you a few examples of this. In the Truman steel seizure case, the government argued before the Supreme Court that President Roosevelt had seized a number of steel mills during WW II and no one said anything about it. It had not been challenged in the courts; it had not been challenged in Congress. Eventually Congress did pass a law permitting certain kinds of presidential seizures, in effect, but it did not sanction what had happened before. Nevertheless, there were at least some situations that the solicitor general could point to as examples of what President Roosevelt had done, and he argued this was all that Harry Truman was trying to do.

But the Court wouldn't buy that. In effect they said just because the Constitution has been violated once before, that does not create a precedent for the future. And there is some explicit language to that effect in Powell v. McCormack, involving congressional overreaching rather than presidential overreaching. This may be the case in the impoundment situation also, where, in fact, Congress allowed certain Presidents to impound some funds in a limited situation, but the minute there was an attempt to do it on a large scale, for other purposes, then suddenly they stopped and said, "We won't permit this to happen anymore." And perhaps the whole war-power situation is another example. Harry Truman got away with it once in Korea, but when it was attempted on a much larger scale in Vietnam, Congress decided perhaps that it was time to stop this.

SCHLESINGER: The difference was that we were losing the war in Vietnam. I fear the Congress wouldn't have done a damn thing about it if we had the relative success in Vietnam that we had had in Korea.

FRIEDMAN: Well, it just may be that some of these overreachings in effect created an awareness, in other words, that the first time it was done, a President can get away with it, until the rest of the polity get the sense that this is going to be a practice that is going too far.

GOLDSMITH: It seems to me this raises several other rather important questions, particularly the example that you bring up of the Korean War. I think it is important to dwell on this for a minute, to see, in effect, what was really happening the "second time around," as you put it.

Clearly, there was some discomfort on the part of a number of people at the invasion of South Korea by the North Koreans, when the President mobilized substantial military and naval resources to come to the aid of South Korea in support of a United Nations resolution. There was discomfort on the part of people like Senator Taft and some strict constructionists in Congress, but as Professor Schlesinger points out, one of the things that modified, at least for the time being, that feeling of disapproval was that first of all, generally speaking, the American people and Congress itself approved of the President's action. In other words, I think that the country was sympathetic to the support of South Korea. Secondly, it was a war that, at least in the final analysis, we were coming close to winning.

But the two points I want to make regarding this are that what you referred to as the second-time-around may be not simply a second shot, but a real difference, using the medieval distinction, where a difference of degree becomes a difference in kind, when it becomes large enough. And maybe a second incident or a second situation becomes a substantial or large enough breach so that something has to be done about it. The second point I want to make, and for me it is the more important, is to raise the question of the reaction to the situation. What, indeed, was ultimately the lesson, if one wants to put it in these terms, the historical lesson learned from the Truman incident in the Youngstown steel seizure case?

It was clear in the last months, and even in the last few years of Truman's administration, that the war became a very unpopular war, as limited wars usually do, and this weakened the power and strength of the President. It occurred to many that if Truman had called upon the Congress at an earlier period for a declaration of war or some resolution supporting his actions in coming to the assistance of the United Nations that he would have been in a stronger position in the steel case, and in a stronger position generally.

And so I think the reading that was given in that incident was that it was politically not feasible to act without some kind of recorded congressional approval or support. But here again, it seems to me that what Arthur was addressing himself to earlier, namely the checks and balances in the system and the openness of the system, were not operating effectively in any of the subsequent situations where approval was given, because, in effect, Congress was not really aware of what was going on. It was not participating fully; it was not informed; information was not freely flowing; and the President simply in a moment of need, or projecting what future needs would be, came to the Congress and asked for support. And twice in the Eisenhower administration and once in the Kennedy administration, he got that support, substantial support. But in no way does this eliminate the problem of the system not operating effectively enough to keep the presidential office or the presidential powers within constitutional harness under these circumstances. If one tries to examine that situation and the lessons drawn from it, one concludes that a President is safe if he gets general approval from Congress before acting.

SCHLESINGER: I think that's right. I think that the reaction to Korea was the resort to joint resolutions in the future. In other words, the implication of Congress in war situations came to seem a political necessity. The question whether it was a constitutional necessity is something which only a few people went into, like Taft, and most people did not think very hard about it, including, I am ashamed to say, myself, and other historians at the time.

FRIEDMAN: I think that the Middle East resolution for example, when Eisenhower asked for a resolution when he sent some troops into—

SCHLESINGER: Well, oddly enough, Eisenhower did get a Middle East resolution, but when he sent the troops into Lebanon, he did not cite the Middle East resolution as justification for it. He had been persuaded by the reaction of the Senate Foreign Relations Committee, led by Senator Fulbright, that he didn't need such a resolution—that it was within his own presidential power to act. But I think it is symptomatic of the whole business. What you had in that situation was really not so much presidential rapacity for power, as congressional abdication of power. Congress, during this period, had it seen its congressional responsibilities, could have affected the situation rather considerably. But people like Rayburn and Johnson, when the question of Formosa resolution came up, said they didn't think the President needed the resolution. Constitutionally they didn't think it was necessary. And it was this situation which helped freeze everybody into a position which, I think, betrayed the Constitution, in the sense that the Constitution asserted that all these decisions should be shared decisions. And then Congress, for whatever reasons, wanted these to be presidential decisions. Partly, I suppose, because it was less of a political risk for them. I mean, there is much less risk in supporting what a President, with his alleged superior information and so on, wants to do with foreign affairs, than in opposing him. And they wanted to get out of the zone of risk.

FRIEDMAN: When we get to the Tonkin Gulf resolution, that really is a significant change from even the Formosa resolution. Because there, first, the resolution was prepared in May 1964, months before there was a Tonkin Gulf episode; and secondly, there was a series of steps which the United States government had taken in that area, in the Tonkin area, by supplying the South Vietnamese with PT boats and helping them with certain raids, which, in effect, provoked the episode and led to the resolution which was prepared months before. So Congress was, in effect, doubly fooled at that time, and went along by overwhelming majorities to give the President exactly the resolution he was asking for. The whole system of accountability, granted the fact that if they had known everything they probably would have given the resolution anyhow, still they did not want to know; they were not told, and something was slipped by them in a very calculating way in order to give the President as much of a free hand as he wanted.

SCHLESINGER: To get back to Bill's initial question, I think that this, therefore, was the situation; the system of accountability was breached by the alleged or real necessities of foreign policy, and in consequence, the President acquired a larger role in foreign affairs than the Constitution originally envisaged, but which people accepted for one reason or another as inescapable. Once that happened, once you breach the system of accountability in foreign policy, then various crises and developments gave the presidency, or specific Presidents, the feeling that the initiative they enjoyed out of necessity in foreign policy could be used at home. That's really what began to happen in the last few years, with the idea of national security serving as the bridge between foreign affairs and domestic affairs. And there again you have an interesting point: powers that go to the presidency to meet domestic crises do not spill over into foreign affairs. Roosevelt received, during the 1930s, considerable power delegated by Congress to deal with the Depression. At the same time Congress was giving this exceptionally popular President all these domestic powers it was tying him hand and foot in foreign affairs, and removing vital areas of foreign policy from presidential discretion through the neutrality acts.

On the other hand, President Truman was far less popular than Roosevelt. At the nadir of his popularity in early 1952, he was almost as unpopular in the polls as President Nixon in 1974. Nonetheless, the power which he enjoyed in foreign affairs emboldened him to take the steps of seizing the steel mills on national security grounds. So there is a spill over from the power acquired for foreign purposes into domestic purposes, while there does not seem to be a spill over from the power to meet domestic crises into foreign crises.

GOLDSMITH: I'm trying to see what the stepping stones of this process are just a little more clearly, because one can experience in the period prior to the imperial presidency a sense in the Congress, a willingness in a number of situations—the State Department has documented them time and time again   of the use of American troops to protect a foreign embassy or to deal with some situation involving the lives of American citizens in foreign country. But in the 1950s and the 1960s this is sharply graduated into very large scale operations—the Mideast situation in Lebanon involved something like 14,000 troops. Half a million troops or more were involved in the Korean situation. There is, certainly, a great difference in magnitude, and it seems to me that the difference in magnitude transforms it really into a difference in kind. Because you are doing something very different when you send a half million men to fight an enemy in a foreign country, then when you dispatch a company of marines on a rescue operation.

SCHLESINGER: One difference, of course, is that in one case you're doing a rescue operation, and in the other case you're taking on a sovereign state.

GOLDSMITH: Now I'm just a little curious about when this shift really took place in terms of the attitudes of people you mentioned, like Johnson and Rayburn and Fulbright and members of the Congress? It seems to me in the earlier part of the twentieth century they would have been appalled at the thought of a commitment of that degree. Is this simply a change?

SCHLESINGER: Not altogether, I think. It really began, one could argue, when McKinley sent 5,000 troops to China during the Boxer rebellion. China declared war on the U.S., a forgotten fact. The U.S. did not declare war on China. But we did send 5,000 troops in an expeditionary force which we tried to assimilate to the previous precedents; that is we were rescuing and defending American citizens in danger in a case of internal turbulence and anarchy. We did not feel that we were taking on a sovereign state. We were entering a situation where there was no law and/or order, and therefore we had to save our own. But that went through with surprisingly little criticism. When Congress came into session, no one questioned it very much. But I really think that you show very interestingly in your book the extent to which Theodore Roosevelt established a lot of the precedents in foreign affairs, and particularly the presidential commitments, without knowledge of Congress or even without much knowledge in the executive branch itself. But I suppose the Korean War was the real turning point.

GOLDSMITH: This is the threshold where the erosion of the accountability of the President becomes so large, so massive, that the President now operates in a field that is quite new and quite different.

FRIEDMAN: After Professor Schlesinger's question, there was a carry over from foreign affairs into domestic affairs and, I think this may also reflect on why the change took place in the cold war period in the 50s. And I think one big area which Professor Schlesinger talks about in his book is control of information—secrecy. There are some things that the President knows that no one else knows. And if they don't know, if it is Congress or the public—if they don't know everything that he knows, then their opinions are of no value.

SCHLESINGER:—or so they are given to understand.

FRIEDMAN: That's right. I was at a conference a while back where Philip Morrison, a professor from MIT, told us that he would argue with Edward Teller all the time about some phase of scientific policy, and Teller would always end the argument with "Well, if you knew what I know, you wouldn't take that position." And Morrison, five years later, found out what Teller knew, and he still thought that Teller was wrong. It is that kind of control, that sense of tremendous power over information, over secrecy, that has infiltrated a large part of the presidential establishment over the last 20 years. And I think the Nixon administration has just brought this to a head. The most serious offense that anyone could commit is to leak a secret. Because secrecy is power; information is power; and the whole Kissinger tape episode, the Huston plan itself, was an effort to get information about supposed enemies. Even the Watergate break-in was an attempt to get information, because information is power.

SCHLESINGER: It is odd when you consider the Kissinger press conference where he went on about his honor and all that, and in which he said that there was a real situation of national security caused by the publication of the story in *The New York Times* in 1969 that the United States was bombing Cambodia. He implied in 1974 that he still considered this a secret that had to be kept and he had no regrets for having reacted in a very strong way to the publication of the story. Who was this a secret from? It obviously wasn't a secret from the Cambodians, who were being bombed; it wasn't a secret from the North Vietnamese, who were in close touch with the Cambodians; it wasn't a secret from the Chinese or the Russians, who knew all about it. The only ones this was a secret from were the United States Congress and the American people. And Henry Kissinger, to this day, still contends it was a matter of national security to keep this fact from the American Congress and the American people.

FRIEDMAN: To get back to the development from Korea on. After the Gulf of Tonkin resolution was passed, Congress went along with the President in what was happening in Vietnam. Each year there were huge appropriations—$20 billion appropriations for Vietnam. And one or two senators, Wayne Morse and Ernest Gruening, would say if you vote for appropriations, you are voting to continue this terrible war. And Congress, year after year would say, "Well, what can we do? The troops are in the field, there's nothing we can do about it once they're there." And after a period of time, when his policy became so disastrous, we had the whole '68 anti-war effort by Gene McCarthy. Congress suddenly decided that something had to be done. What they had done, passing the war powers resolution, may or may not have been the best solution, but what else could Congress do in this situation? I mean what other ways are there to control the President in this particular area? But if you try and trace the development from 1964 on, when the basic Vietnam policy was more and more under challenge, it is hard to say that Congress or the public's reaction had any effect until the presidential year came up.

SCHLESINGER: Or until the draft began to hit the middle class as well as the poor people.

GOLDSMITH: It seems to me, we ought to approach this question of accountability in some fashion in which we could arrive at some institutional resolution of the problem, namely, how can the political process be strengthened to reinforce the sense of accountability of the President? It seems to me that we are moving so rapidly through the 1950s and the 1960s that we are not going to be able to sense and clearly identify where the specific erosion of the ability of the Congress to restrain the President took place. Maybe, in fact, that power never existed— though theoretically it exists within the framework of the Constitution. And the question is how, in terms of government, can it be made effective?

I want to get back for a moment to the Korean situation, because I am not fully satisfied with the resolution of that problem. It seems that the discussion and the reaction to Truman's preemptory leadership in Korea was that the American public is not going to support an action of this kind for a long period of time. It was considered politically unwise for a President to extend himself to such a degree, because, in effect, when you get into these things, they may last for a protracted period and before too long the public loses faith. The lesson that is drawn from the Korean situation, then, is that so-called "limited wars" are politically unwise and unfeasible.

If the constitutional issue had been more seriously raised in the very beginning of that situation, and if there had been an awareness and a sense of agreement between Congress and its constituents that a President had to be accountable to the extent that he had to obtain permission in order to make decisions like Korea, wouldn't that have strengthened the sinews of accountability or at least established or reinforced some institutionalization of accountability in the system?

SCHLESINGER: I think it would have. I think you are quite right— that those who should have been sensitive were not. I can remember Henry Steele Commager and I, and other historians, using these lists of prior unilateral presidential military interventions without distinguishing an intervention to save a missionary who was about to be eaten by a cannibal from a war against a sovereign state. I think the scholars were at fault; I think the lawyers were at fault. Afterall, President Truman decided not to ask for a joint resolution after consultation with his secretary of state, who had been a law clerk to Justice Brandeis, and who walked to work every day with Justice Frankfurter. Obviously Dean Acheson told him that this is what the Constitution said.

FRIEDMAN: And the courts fell down too, didn't they? There were a couple of soldiers who were sent to Korea who came in and objected saying "We don't want to be sent there," and the court gave the very short shrift. There was a fellow out in Tennessee, Fyke Farmer, who said this was an unconstitutional war, and he didn't get to first base. So in terms of presenting the constitutional argument, to whom do you present it? And how is the Constitution to be interpreted; who hears the constitutional argument? In Korea, I think you are probably right. The basic policy was popular enough so that none of the organs that could and should have raised the questions were willing to do it. Now the second time around, in Vietnam, there were law suits trying to have the Vietnam War declared unconstitutional in 1966 and 1967 down in the District of Columbia and in a place out in Kansas, a law professor brought a suit out there, but they had absolutely no success at all. The courts would not take a look at it. Then when we [the American Civil Liberties Union] brought a law suit here in New York right after the Cambodian invasion in 1970, the courts were willing to take another look at it. As far as the judges were concerned, the undercurrent of feeling was that Cambodia was a significant escalation, they were not quite sure how far it was going to go, but they were willing to take a look at it. And I think maybe the Cambodian invasion was a crossing point. But it was only then that the other institutions of government that could exercise some oversight were willing to even look at the problem, let alone do anything about it.

SCHLESINGER: Well, I think it's generally the way Congress and the courts operate, anyway. Of course, it would be very difficult for the courts to stop a war in progress. They pronounce against these things generally after they are over. Congress has now tried to pull itself together. You know it's odd on the Tonkin Gulf resolution. The last section of that resolution, you will remember, provided for the possibility of repealing the resolution through concurrent resolution.

FRIEDMAN: Which they did do.

SCHLESINGER: Well, they finally *did* repeal it when the Nixon administration said it didn't need the resolution anymore. But the Congress has now passed the War Powers bill over President Nixon's veto, a piece of legislation which I find and which Congress seems to find enormously puzzling. Some members of Congress have opposed it, like Senator Goldwater, on the ground that it represents intolerable restriction of presidential power. Others have opposed it, like Senator Eagleton, on the ground that it represents an intolerable expansion of presidential power. So clearly, it is not one of the more unambiguous pieces of legislation. In effect, it empowers the President to wage war on his own for a period of from 90 to 120 days. Thereafter, to continue the war, he must get specific congressional approval, and Congress can take action to stop the war through concurrent resolution, before the period of time is already underway.

I, myself, find it is a very unconvincing piece of legislation. On the other hand, a lot of people who have thought long and hard about it think it's a great gain. I was wondering how you gentlemen felt about this as a structural attempt to restore congressional authority to Congress. I might add that I think it is unconvincing in the first place because it does give the President power which he does not now have to wage war on his own for 90 to 120 days, and secondly, if he succeeds in doing that, it seems to be most improbable that Congress could call off a war that the President wanted to continue.

GOLDSMITH: I think there are both good and bad things about the War Powers resolution, but perhaps more important, there are both good and bad things that one can read into it. On the good side, it records the intent of the Congress to restore its critical constitutional role in the decision to declare war, but moreover, it reflects an understanding that the erosion of its powers in this area has come about because the Congress delegated this power to the President in too many situations. There is no constitutional authorization for such a delegation, and the development of this trend in recent years has been alarming.

In the beginning Congress stood by and watched the President act in situations where its constitutional responsibilities should have prompted at least its joint efforts. Later, when the independent action of the President backfired in the Korean War, and when public opinion turned sharply against the war, succeeding Presidents attempted to avoid this embarrassment by going to the Congress prior to acting and requesting open-ended delegations of power to act with congressional approval, while at the same time asserting the constitutional power to act without such approval. Dwight D. Eisenhower was the first President to engage in this serious departure from historical practice, for such actions were cloaked in the rhetorical justification of a "Whig" President attempting to include the Congress in what would otherwise be an independent executive decision.

But this was a faulty interpretation of the problem. By delegating these broad and virtually open-ended grants of war-making power to the President, the Congress was excluding itself from the critical decisions that would have to be made further along the way, and, in fact, abrogating its constitutional responsibilities as the body designated by the Constitution "to declare war." Senator Wayne Morse pointed this out time and time again in the debates over the Formosa and Mid-East resolutions, but he was overwhelmed by bipartisan support for these resolutions, encouraged by the eloquence and prestige of the 77-year old Democratic chairman of the Senate Foreign Relations Committee, Senator Walter George of Georgia. He argued that the President had done a courageous thing in coming to Congress and eliciting its support. This constitutionally abortive practice became almost standard operating procedure for Eisenhower's successors, and we have seen its disastrous effect in the Vietnam situation.

This, then, points up the negative aspects of the present resolution which you have emphasized, Arthur. Insofar as the War Powers resolution restores Congress to its constitutional role as the body responsible for making the decision to go to war it is of value, but the whole procedure which it introduces is a complicated one, and contains still a large measure of the sense of delegating this responsibility—if only for 30 or 60 days to the President. This is the responsibility of the Congress, and there is no way to avoid it. In the final analysis, it will depend upon how Congress interprets its role under this new legislation. If it jealously guards its powers and demands that the President come to it before asserting his role as Commander in Chief, then the resolution will be a great improvement over the present ambiguous situation. If, on the other hand, it allows the initiative to be seized by the President, who can interpret the resolution as at least a conditional delegation of the war-making power, then it will be a disaster. It depends more upon the political climate and the understanding of the constitutional roles of the respective branches than upon the letter of any particular resolution. If this is to be a government of laws and not men, men must enforce the principles of those laws.

SCHLESINGER: Yes, that's quite true. For example, the Formosa resolution authorized President Eisenhower, and I quote the language, "to employ the armed forces of the United States as he deems necessary" in defense of Formosa, the Pescadores and related positions and so on. Whereas earlier resolutions, like the resolutions against Tripoli in 1802 and Algeria in 1815, named an enemy in order to specify an action. This was an open-ended resolution which represented a delegation of the war-making authority to the President, though it still maintained the fascade, so to speak, of congressional authorization.

GOLDSMITH: You also refer in your book to a situation when James Madison refused in 1810 a delegation of authority from the Congress when it wanted to delegate such power to him. Madison felt very strongly that this was a very serious constitutional breach, and refused to accept the delegation.

FRIEDMAN: But to get back to Professor Schlesinger's question, I have a lot of qualms about the War Powers resolution, too. But perhaps in terms of accountability, perhaps as a symbol or metaphor for congressional participation in these decisions, it can serve a useful purpose. In other words, if the President says to himself, "I must go to Congress: I must report to Congress within 48 hours: I must give another report within another period, I must get something from them within 120 days—"

SCHLESINGER: The reporting provisions are very lax. I think you have to report once every six months.

FRIEDMAN: I appreciate that, but just the sense of "I've got to go to Congress to do something" could be helpful. It will encourage a sense of self-restraint on the part of the President.

SCHLESINGER: I shouldn't say this to a lawyer, but I don't regard statutes as metaphors. I mean a statute is a statute. This statute seems to me to give power to the President to get us into war and to create a momentum which makes it unlikely that Congress is going to recall the war. I don't think Congress should pass symbols and metaphors. I think if it passes a law, it should be construed as a law.

FRIEDMAN: Well, then it is an example of how impossible it is to institutionalize the control of presidential foreign policy. It really is quite difficult. Congress passed a national commitments resolution in 1969 saying that if the President makes a commitment that is less than a war, a treaty sending troops abroad, that it should do so only under congressional approval. It was a resolution, but it didn't have any binding effect. No one has paid attention to it since. If that were the form of legislation, how would you enforce it?

Congress's ability to control the war power is really limited to appropriations, and when it finally wanted to do something about the Cambodian bombing, it simply passed a law saying no more dollars for the Cambodian bombing—and that stopped it. Now maybe that is its only power in this situation. Maybe the War Powers resolution doesn't mean anything. I was following the debate as it went along, and everyone argued 30-60-90 days, and they were concerned about the kind of enabling legislation that Congress would need. But there was no particular consensus on how to deal with this problem, other than just to stop the money from going. Maybe that's the ultimate power that Congress has here. That, and the fact that wars get stopped in election years, or immediately after elections years, if you are voted into office on that basis.

SCHLESINGER: I do think there are things that can be done. If there is a statute or resolution which contains effective provisions for the recall of hostilities or the termination of hostilities through concurrent resolutions, for example, plus really stringent reporting provisions, it would be good. I think those parts would be useful. I'm not sure authorizing the President to fight wars on his own, for 90 days or 120 days if he needs 30 more days to disengage, adds very much to it. However, I agree with you in general that this is a very hard problem to solve structurally. And I think many of the problems of presidential power have fallen into this category—mechanical solutions seem improbable. I think we have to face the fact that there is no fail safe mechanism that is going to contain presidential power, and that in the end the solution is going to lie, if I can borrow that invaluable phrase from women's liberation, in the process of national consciousness raising—raising the consciousness of future Presidents so that they will remember and respect the system of accountability, and raising the consciousness of future Congresses so that they will meet some of their own responsibilities which they have so dismally failed to meet. And the restoration of some of the sense that these decisions have to be shared decisions, and there has to be give and take between the executive and legislative branches. I hope that this experience is going to educate the electorate to elect as Presidents people who have a high degree of constitutional sensitivity and will also understand that no foreign policy is going to be much good if Congress does not understand it and accept it.

GOLDSMITH: I would like to take a crack at Schlesinger's suggestion and perhaps propose a more radical solution. Looking historically at Congress's power to appropriate funds and to withdraw that power, it has not been a very effective weapon in restricting the President or restricting warfare throughout our history. I doubt that it ever will be, because it seems to me that in the one instance that you cite when it was successful, that was the period when the troops really were withdrawn. The war had literally been closed down, and the Congress was at that point willing to go along. But when there are substantial numbers of troops involved, and a substantial commitment on the part of the country, to expect the Congress to withdraw the economic support for that operation and possibly to endanger the lives of those individuals who are involved, I think it is a fairly weak reed as an effective or viable restraint on the power of the President in war making.

Regarding the new legislation, I agree with you, Arthur, in your assertion that no mechanical solution is really going to resolve this problem, and particularly a mechanical solution that is so open-ended and so loose and has so many problems of its own. I don't think it is going to do any harm; and I don't think that it is going to encourage the war-making power of the President or induce him to act in a more aggressive manner than normally, because it does remind him that he has at some point to report back and sustain his operation with the approval of Congress. But it seems to me that if we are left at this point in our history with the possibility of

Congress' cutting off the funds and failing to appropriate support for armies in the field, or with the application of this new statute, then we are limited by these modes of operation in restraining the clear and unmistakable evolution of the war-making power of the President. These have led not only to aggressive war-making power on the part of the President, but all of these other difficulties that we are subsequently going to get to; if this is so, then we are in a pretty bad way.

It seems to me that the raising of consciousness is an important solution to the problem, but one asks the question of how does one raise consciousness? We are really raising a fundamental question about the state of the polity. How can we develop, through the institutions of government, a greater sense of responsibility on the part of the citizens and Congress, and a greater sense of their role and participation in all phases of the political process? Unless we come up with some substantial answer to this question, any mechanical or even any constitutional or statutory solution is in the final analysis not going to work. This is a theme I touch upon in all three volumes. For want of a better name, I call it a sense of development or a restoration of a dialectical tension at the center of the system. It is Wilson's old idea of government as an educator. I think that the Congress assumes that its lawmaking role is its primary and sometimes its exclusive function. I think that what all of this past experience demonstrates to me is that the government really has to be a teacher; government has to be a source of information. What we have lost is that kind of interesting, exciting dialectical tension at the center—that opposition between the parties that makes issues and government come alive. We are talking here of institutions—what is the Congress going to do; what is the President going to do? But in some sense Congress doesn't act as Congress. The party can act in Congress as a powerful educational force, and the opposition party, or the President, as the head of the party with supporters in Congress, can get some interplay between these two. This is certainly not a new idea, and it isn't one that even in terms of the British system today reveals itself as a very successful idea, but it seems to me that our system of checks and balances is peculiarly well adapted to this function if we can develop a more responsible party system with a dynamic concept of its role as a politically educational force in the society. I think that this is the way you get at the consciousness problem.

SCHLESINGER: I agree.

GOLDSMITH: People aren't interested in government on a day-to-day basis. They are not concerned with these problems until they become crises that hit them in the face. To talk in general terms just of education, we know that better educated people are not necessarily the more politically aware people, that education as a concept is simply not going to be a solution to this problem. It certainly is not going to restrain the President. We really do have to develop a political process that is more viable, that is more exciting, where you have greater tension, greater debate, greater confrontation.

For example, the President delivers his State of the Union Message before both houses of Congress, we listen for a half hour to Mike Mansfield tediously tick off the opposition party's program. That is symptomatic of the way which Congress views, or the opposition party views, its functional responsibility. They are not in the age of McLuhan; they are in the dark ages in terms of offering any alternative response.

Through television, through the media of communication, through the sense of development of greater party responsibility, greater party organization, we can find the way out of these dilemmas, not simply problems of foreign policy and war, but also domestic questions. But we have to get back to the reinvigoration of the political process.

I feel very strongly that it is not a question of the President becoming too powerful. The President, in most of these instances, has walked into a situation, has been sucked up into a vacuum, because there is an absolute vacuum in the system and the President has literally been forced to act. Now some Presidents by virtue of personality, by virtue of interest in policies, even flaws in their character, have abused this opportunity, have acted more forcefully and more aggressively than other Presidents. But it seems to me that the real slack in the system is not simply in Congress, but comes about because Congress doesn't have any idea of what its proper function is in this consciousness raising process. If we had political parties in Congress that were far more aware of their function as educational forces—

Well, the theory of the limits of presidential power that emerges in these three volumes is the sense that public opinion has ultimately been the only real check on executive power. The only instances where powerful Presidents, at the apex of their power and popularity, have been restrained is when the public was determined to limit that power. In the first volume there is the embargo with Jefferson, and in this last volume the court packing case and ultimately the steel seizure cases. And it seems to me that in these three instances, it isn't the Court, it isn't the Congress, but it is really the public that has supported the Court or supported the Congress, that has stopped the President in his tracks.

If, then, the public is the only real check or restraint upon presidential power, then to leave the problem of how the public consciousness or the public awareness is developed to the point where it plays this kind of role, to leave that to pure accident, is to allow the system to drift to where it has drifted today. No one can design this; no one can manipulate it. But if you are going to make an institutional change, an institutional change that would be most exemplary is one in which Congress began to conceive of an entirely different role than it now plays in the system. It should be understood that, by and large, mechanical solutions or appropriations are two really awkward weapons to restrain a President in the full-blown power of the modern period. Congress always needs this kind of supporting backstop, a higher consciousness level or a heightened public opinion. And if this isn't one of the objectives of the system, and if you have the President or the one party led by a President, or the opposition party led by an organized and effective group that is communicating continually with the public and pressing its position, then it seems to me that you have the institutional basis for really achieving a higher level of consciousness or leverage in the system that is ultimately going to be able to restrain the President when necessary.

FRIEDMAN: Let me just throw in one thing. Sometimes you don't need that, and for a number of reasons which maybe we should explore. I'm thinking about the whole episode relating to the resignation of Richardson and Ruckelshaus—the Saturday night massacre. The President made an attempt on the Friday of that week to establish his office as not being subject to a court order. That was, in effect, the thesis that he was advancing. And on Saturday he fired Cox and Richardson, and Ruckelshaus resigned. The storm that met the White House on Saturday, Sunday, and Monday led, on Tuesday of that week, to the President's giving up that attempt. It didn't have to be institutionalized: Congress was not taking the lead in that case. There was something that the President had done that the public-at-large was simply not willing to go along with.

GOLDSMITH: I don't think the exception proves the rule. This crisis was two years or more in the making, and the so-called Saturday night massacre came after a crescendo had been reached in public exposure, investigations, trials, and so on. I don't think one can normally count on this kind of a reaction to restrain the excesses of presidential power, and I think we are in real trouble if we sit back and assume that such countervailing power will readily materialize. Furthermore, I'm not confident that the public was accurately informed, even in this instance, as to all of the complex questions involved.

SCHLESINGER: May I bring the conversation back to the larger point. I think that we have a situation now where you have the imbalance between presidential power and presidential accountability, which we have called the imperial presidency, and you have the effort to make that imbalance a permanent feature of the system, which is the revolutionary presidency. Then you have the effort to try to restore the constitutional balance.

We have this imbalance between power and accountability, and there are two ways of getting it back into balance. One is to cut back presidential power, and the other is to build up presidential accountability. And I think we are all more or less in agreement. I take it that on the whole, through most of American history, the presidency is an office which has served the public well, and that you don't overreact to a particular situation by taking actions which may do permanent damage to what has been on the whole a useful office. Though there are certain marginal things that can be done by statute to contain the presidency, the basic question is not one so much of cutting back presidential power as of rehabilitating, strengthening and enforcing the system of accountability.

It seems to me that there are two parts of it. One is the part that Bill Goldsmith was talking about a moment ago, with such eloquence. And that is the importance which we tend to forget of politics as an educational process, and the extent to which debate, discussion and action are means of engaging public interest in the issues of government, and therefore renewing a sense of the limits, which in a constitutional system must restrain all the branches of government. I think that is half of it. I think the other half of it is to make it clear to the Presidents who abuse their power, that they cannot place themselves above the law and the Constitution—that they can't get away with it.

I think that, for example, I suppose the most effective way to raise the consciousness of future Presidents is through the impeachment process. The successful impeachment and removal of President Nixon will do more to restrain future Presidents and future White House staffs from overstepping their constitutional bounds than anything else, just as the decision not to impeach President Nixon can only convince his successors, I suppose, that they have a license to do more or less the things that he did, which Congress did not deem worthy of impeachment. So I think that there is both the educational side of it and, so to speak, the punitive side of it, to produce this full raising of consciousness.

GOLDSMITH: Does the punitive side also have a substantial educational side?

SCHLESINGER: Yes. Punishment can be a very effective form of education.

GOLDSMITH: Before we leave this question of the abuse of the war-making powers in the age of the imperial presidency, I think it is important that we point out that in each instance one of the critical problems and disadvantages both the Congress and the public were operating under was a clear lack of information of what was really taking place. I think both of you pointed out earlier that information and knowledge are frequently equivalent to power, and without such information the Congress and the public are powerless to act. This was true in the Tyler administration with regard to the President's commitments to Texas and Polk's orders to the armed forces, and it was certainly true in the Tonkin Gulf and Cambodian situations, when not even the leaders of Congress were informed of the real circumstances of the incidents.

There simply has to be a better way of first informing the Congress and ultimately the public regarding even sensitive questions of national security. Of course there is national security information which cannot be immediately communicated to the public, but certainly there ought to be carefully designed procedures whereby the leaders of Congress—the party leaders in both houses, along with the chairmen of the foreign affairs and military affairs committees in both houses, would be able to sit in on National Security Council meetings and be as fully informed as any of the top members of the President's cabinet or staff. Funds ought be provided for staff personnel to assist them in these functions, and guidelines developed as to how such procedures can be implemented, both to protect sensitive data and to reflect the serious and important nature of this information in the selection of chairmen to head these committees, and the parties in Congress.

This change could be brought about without amending the Constitution or without destroying the concept of the division of power among the various branches, as an underlying principle of our political system. In fact this principle has been undermined by not instituting such a procedure long ago, for the lack of adequate information regrading national security developments has prevented Congress from fulfilling its constitutional role of declaring war or preventing war from being declared. All that would be necessary would be a brief amendment to the National Security Act, which has been amended before to change the statutory composition of the National Security Council. No President or no administration can be or should be entrusted with the exclusive possession of information which could result in the life or death of the republic. Such a monopoly of secret data does not really strengthen an independent Executive, but rather has proved to make him ultimately vulnerable to attack, defeat and even disgrace when secrets are finally revealed, in changed circumstances. The security of the nation with regard to decisions of war and peace was entrusted by the Founding Fathers to both Congress and the President, and the information necessary to make such decisions must be fully available to both branches of government entrusted with the authority to make such decisions.

It was recently disclosed by Representative Michael Harrington of Massachusetts, a member of the House Armed Services Committee, that the Central Intelligence Agency (CIA) had spent somewhere between 8 and 11 million dollars over a period of three years (1970-73) in an attempt to undermine the Marxist Allende government in Chile. This is the most recent exposé of such undercover CIA operations. The money was apparently spent bribing candidates in the national election and supporting the campaigns of those running in opposition to the ruling local and national Marxist leadership. Other information brought to light by *The New York Times* revealed that the policies that were developed cut off all United States funds from Chile and also loans from the World Bank, and considerably weakened the Chilean economy and contributed to bringing the government to the brink of economic disaster.

These decisions were apparently made by the high-level, top secret Forty Committee, consisting of the director of the National Security Council (who at present is also the secretary of state), the deputy secretary of state, the deputy secretary of defense, the chairman of the Joint Chiefs of Staff and the director of the CIA. This committee reviews and authorizes all CIA covert operations and operates under general mandate of the National Security Council. All of its recommendations are ultimately authorized by the President of the United States. Members of this committee have publicly denied such policies with regard to Chile in testimony before congressional committees, but this recent information was obtained by Congressman Harrington who, as a member of the Armed Services Committee, demanded and was granted the opportunity of reading a copy of the secret testimony of the director of the CIA before a subcommittee of the Armed Services Committee.

This certainly describes secret government, and although those involved would probably testify that such operations are in the interest of the United States and must remain secret to be effective, they are a product of a dangerous phase of the era of the imperial presidency. Secret level government and secret foreign policies are now conducted by the President and his advisors without the knowledge and authorization of Congress. I would remedy this situation by making the same congressional leaders who are statutory members of the National Security Council, statutory members of a counterintelligence review committee. This measure would at least make such policies known and accountable to Congress and then through Congress to the American people. The idea of the President conducting secret foreign policies and supporting them with secret governmental funds is destructive to the ends of democratic government in this country.

War Powers Resolution
November 7, 1973

Laws of 93rd Cong.—1st sess., Public Law 93-148; 87 Stat. 555, 614-19.

JOINT RESOLUTION CONCERNING
THE WAR POWERS OF CONGRESS AND THE PRESIDENT

Resolved by the Senate and House of Representatives of the United States of American in Congress assembled, That:

Short Title

Section 1

This joint resolution may be cited as the "War Powers Resolution".

Sec. 2

(a) It is the purpose of this joint resolution to fulfill the intent of the framers of the Constitution of the United States and insure that the collective judgment of both the Congress and the President will apply to the introduction of United States Armed Forces into hostilities, or into situations where imminent involvement in hostilities is clearly indicated by the circumstances, and to the continued use of such forces in hostilities or in such situations.

(b) Under article I, section 8, of the Constitution, it is specifically provided that the Congress shall have the power to make all laws necessary and proper for carrying into execution, not only its own powers but also all other powers vested by the Constitution in the Government of the United States, or in any department or officer thereof.

(c) The constitutional powers of the President as Commander-in-Chief to introduce United States Armed Forces into hostilities, or into situations where imminent involvement in hostilities is clearly indicated by the circumstances, are exercised only pursuant to (1) a declaration of war, (2) specific statutory authorization, or (3) a national emergency created by attack upon the United States, its territories or possessions, or its armed forces.

Consultation

Sec. 3

The President in every possible instance shall consult with Congress before introducing United States Armed Forces into hostilities or into situations where imminent involvement in hostilities is clearly indicated by the circumstances, and after every such introduction shall consult regularly with the Congress until United

States Armed Forces are no longer engaged in hostilities or have been removed from such situations.

Reporting

Sec. 4

(a) In the absence of a declaration of war, in any case in which United States Armed Forces are introduced—

(1) into hostilities or into situations where imminent involvement in hostilities is clearly indicated by the circumstances;

(2) into the territory, airspace or waters of a foreign nation, while equipped for combat, except for deployments which relate solely to supply, replacement, repair, or training of such forces; or

(3) in numbers which substantially enlarge United States Armed Forces equipped for combat already located in a foreign nation;

the President shall submit within 48 hours to the Speaker of the House of Representatives and to the President pro tempore of the Senate a report, in writing, setting forth—

(A) the circumstances necessitating the introduction of United States Armed Forces;

(B) the constitutional and legislative authority under which such introduction took place; and

(C) the estimated scope and duration of the hostilities or involvement.

(b) The President shall provide such other information as the Congress may request in the fulfillment of its constitutional responsibilities with respect to committing the Nation to war and to the use of United States Armed Forces abroad.

(c) Whenever United States Armed Forces are introduced into hostilities or into any situation described in subsection (a) of this section, the President shall, so long as such armed forces continue to be engaged in such hostilities or situation, report to the Congress periodically on the status of such hostilities or situation as well as on the scope and duration of such hostilities or situation, but in no event shall he report to the Congress less often than once every six months.

Congressional Action

Sec. 5

(a) Each report submitted pursuant to section 4(a)(1) shall be transmitted to the Speaker of the House of Representatives and to the President pro tempore of the Senate on the same calendar day. Each report so transmitted shall be referred to the Committee on Foreign Affairs of the House of Representatives and to the Committee on Foreign Relations of the Senate for appropriate action. If, when the report is transmitted, the Congress has adjourned sine die or has adjourned for any period in excess of three calendar days, the Speaker of the House of Representatives and the President pro tempore of the Senate, if they deem it advisable (or if petitioned by at least 30 percent of the membership of their respective Houses) shall jointly request the President to convene Congress in order that it may consider the report and take appropriate action pursuant to this section.

(b) Within sixty calendar days after a report is submitted or is required to be submitted pursuant to section 4(a)(1), whichever is earlier, the President shall terminate any use of United States Armed Forces with respect to which such report was submitted (or required to be submitted), unless the Congress (1) has declared war or has enacted a specific authorization for such use of United States Armed Forces, (2) has extended by law such sixty-day period, or (3) is physically unable to meet as a result of an armed attack upon the United States. Such sixty-day period shall be extended for not more than an additional thirty days if the President determines and certifies to the Congress in writing that unavoidable military necessity respecting the safety of United States Armed Forces requires the continued use of such armed forces in the course of bringing about a prompt removal of such forces.

(c) Notwithstanding subsection (b), at any time that United States Armed Forces are engaged in hostilities outside the territory of the United States, its possessions and territories without a declaration of war or specific statutory authorization, such forces shall be removed by the President if the Congress so directs by concurrent resolution.

Congressional Priority Procedures for
Joint Resolution or Bill

Sec. 6

(a) Any joint resolution or bill introduced pursuant to section 5(b) at least thirty calendar days before the expiration of the sixty-day period specified in such section shall be referred to the Committee on Foreign Affairs of the House of Representatives or the Committee on Foreign Relations of the Senate, as the case may be, and such committee shall report one such joint resolution or bill, together with its recommendations, not later than twenty-four calendar days before the expiration of the sixty-day period specified in such section, unless such House shall otherwise determine by the yeas and nays.

(b) Any joint resolution or bill so reported shall become the pending business of the House in question (in the case of the Senate the time for debate shall be equally divided between the proponents and the opponents), and shall be voted on within three calendar days thereafter, unless such House shall otherwise determine by yeas and nays.

(c) Such a joint resolution or bill passed by one House shall be referred to the committee of the other House named in subsection (a) and shall be reported out not later than fourteen calendar days before the expiration of the sixty-day period specified in section 5(b). The joint resolution or bill so reported shall become the pending business of the House in question and shall be voted on within three calendar days after it has been reported, unless such House shall otherwise determine by yeas and nays.

(d) In the case of any disagreement between the two Houses of Congress with respect to a joint resolution or bill passed by both Houses, conferees shall be promptly appointed and the committee of conference shall make and file a report with respect to such resolution or bill not later than four calendar days before the expiration of the sixty-day period specified in section 5(b). In the event the conferees are unable to agree within 48 hours, they shall report back to their respective Houses in disagreement. Notwithstanding any rule in either House concerning the printing of conference reports in the Record or concerning any delay in the consideration of such reports, such report shall be acted on by both Houses not later than the expiration of such sixty-day period.

Congressional Priority Procedures for
Concurrent Resolution

Sec. 7

(a) Any concurrent resolution introduced pursuant to section 5(c) shall be referred to the Committee on Foreign Affairs of the House of Representatives or the Committee on Foreign Relations of the Senate, as the case may be, and one such concurrent resolution shall be reported out by such committee together with its recommendations within fifteen calendar days, unless such House shall otherwise determine by the yeas and nays.

(b) Any concurrent resolution so reported shall become the pending business of the House in question (in the case of the Senate the time for debate shall be equally divided between the proponents and the opponents) and shall be voted on within three calendar days thereafter, unless such House shall otherwise determine by yeas and nays.

(c) Such a concurrent resolution passed by one House shall be referred to the committee of the other House named in subsection (a) and shall be reported out by such committee together with its recommendations within fifteen calendar days and shall thereupon become the pending business of such House and shall be voted upon within three calendar days, unless such House shall otherwise determine by yeas and nays.

(d) In the case of any disagreement between the two Houses of Congress with respect to a concurrent resolution passed by both Houses, conferees shall be promptly appointed and the committee of conference shall make and file a report with respect to such concurrent resolution within six calendar days after the legislation is referred to the committee of conference. Notwithstanding any rule in either House concerning the printing of conference reports in the Record or concerning any delay in the consideration of such reports, such report shall be acted on by both Houses not later than six calendar days after the conference report is filed. In the event the conferees are unable to agree within 48 hours, they shall report back to their respective Houses in disagreement.

Interpretation of Joint Resolution

Sec. 8

(a) Authority to introduce United States Armed Forces into hostilities or into situations wherein involvement in hostilities is clearly indicated by the circumstances shall not be inferred—

(1) from any provision of law (whether or not in effect before the date of the enactment of this joint resolution), including any provision

contained in any appropriation Act, unless such provision specifically authorizes the introduction of United States Armed Forces into hostilities or into such situations and states that it is intended to constitute specific statutory authorization within the meaning of this joint resolution; or

(2) from any treaty heretofore or hereafter ratified unless such treaty is implemented by legislation specifically authorizing the introduction of United States Armed Forces into hostilities or into such situations and stating that it is intended to constitute specific statutory authorization within the meaning of this joint resolution.

(b) Nothing in this joint resolution shall be construed to require any further specific statutory authorization to permit members of United States Armed Forces to participate jointly with members of the armed forces of one or more foreign countries in the headquarters operations of high-level military commands which were established prior to the date of enactment of this joint resolution and pursuant to the United Nations Charter or any treaty ratified by the United States prior to such date.

(c) For purposes of this joint resolution, the term "introduction of United States Armed Forces" includes the assignment of members of such armed forces to command, coordinate, participate in the movement of, or accompany the regular or irregular military forces of any foreign country or government when such military forces are engaged, or there exists an imminent threat that such forces will become engaged, in hostilities.

(d) Nothing in this joint resolution—

(1) is intended to alter the constitutional authority of the Congress or of the President, or the provisions of existing treaties; or

(2) shall be construed as granting any authority to the President with respect to the introduction of United States Armed Forces into hostilities is clearly indicated by the circumstances which authority he would not have had in the absence of this joint resolution.

Separability Clause

Sec. 9

If any provision of this joint resolution or the application thereof to any person or circumstance is held invalid, the remainder of the joint resolution and the application of such provision to any other person or circumstance shall not be affected thereby.

Effective Date

Sec. 10

This joint resolution shall take effect on the date of its enactment.
Passed over Presidential veto Nov. 7, 1973.

Domestic Policy and the
Threat to Individual Rights

Our attention then turned to the domestic area where presidential power had been so abused in recent years under the administration of Richard Nixon. The record is not closed on any of these questions, and the testimony and information is still far from complete. The public record is overflowing with material which frames the issue, but I would like to call attention to some of these materials before continuing the dialogue.

In recent years there has been much reference made to the style that has been reflected by the various Presidents who have served in our time. Styles vary greatly among Presidents; some are gregarious while others are shy and retiring, some are charismatic, while others are not. What is important about any presidential style is how it serves the purposes of the President and to what extent these purposes are consistent with the values and aims of the society over which the President presides.

Richard Nixon's style has been a matter of controversy ever since he entered politics in the postwar period, running for Congress against Jerry Voorhis. Nixon invoked the wrath of liberals at that time by misrepresenting Voorhis' political record and objectives and suggesting his affinity for communist causes. Nixon adopted and refined these same campaign techniques in running against Helen Gahagan Douglas several years later for the Senate. In a period of frantic anti-communism, Richard Nixon systematically exploited this issue against every political opponent he faced, none of whom were by any stretch of the imagination sympathetic to communism. In truth, they were all militant and effective anti-communists in their own spheres of influence, even though Nixon misrepresented their records in his appeal to the general anti-communist hysteria running rampant across the land. As Arthur Schlesinger put it:

> He is the only major American politician in our history, who came to prominence by techniques which, if generally adopted, would destroy the whole fabric of mutual confidence on which our democracy rests.[35]

It was never really a question of communism or anti-communism, but rather of truth and objectivity, neither of which the Nixon style appeared to have much room for. Nixon's retrospective self-image during this period emphasized his role in the Hiss case, which was a perfectly legitimate and perhaps even remarkable performance of congressional investigation. Alistair Cooke called it *A Generation On Trial,* and perhaps this was true, but this was not the same generation that Richard Nixon attempted to taint. Adlai Stevenson, Helen Gahagan Douglas and Jerry Voorhis fought the communists within the liberal movement where it counted. The investigation of Hiss was one thing, but the politically self-serving attack on the liberals was quite another. Nixon's attempt to tar and feather those who were both anti-McCarthy and anti-communist for his own ends was characteristic of his rise to power and notoriety in one of the more dismal periods of American history.

The importance of this aspect of the Nixon style cannot be overlooked in ferreting out the flaws of his tenure as Chief Executive. When Nixon finally became President, anti-communism had long since been a dead issue, and ironically, he made great progress in his conduct of foreign affairs by burying many of the old anti-communist fears of the past through reestablishing relations with Communist China and in nursing *detente* with the Soviet Union. But that did not mean that the deviousness which had characterized his political career from the very beginning had been discarded; it had merely found new levels of application. Nixon no longer berated lifelong anti-communists for being "soft on communism," but his style of distorting reality became imbedded within the heart of the internal operation of the office of the presidency.

It is now clear that the Nixon era has been a tragic experience for the presidency and for the country, but since the very essence of tragedy is to experience catharsis by identifying with the horrors of the unfolding events, and through such identification, experience pity and fear which cleanses the spirit, we can only hope that the bolting insight which can produce a high level of understanding of the human predicament, will emerge among us. Let us hope that the national tragedy of Watergate will have some of this effect upon the country. We were all spectators, though at the same time participants, or better, victims. The events were really happening to us, because it was our President, our political system and our country, not something taking place on a stage in which we had only passing identification. It is important to understand that when we are passing judgment upon Watergate, we are also passing judgment upon ourselves, regardless of how remote our connections to Washington and the government might be. In fact, that very remoteness is in itself part of this national tragedy.

It is conceivable but probably unrealistic to speculate that when Richard Nixon finally achieved his lifelong ambition to become President of the United States, he might have abandoned his political style, secure in the White House and triumphant over the legions whose hatred and contempt he had earned during his climb to power. But, the continuing existence of the unpopular Vietnam War during his first term in the White House provided a new *cause célèbre* in which he would seek "peace with honor," while continuing to absorb mounting casualties in Asia and serious domestic turmoil at home. Far from developing a balanced and stable administration in Washington, Nixon and the small group of political operatives he gathered around him isolated themselves from the sources of criticism and opposition in the country, developing a "state of siege" mentality which provided armor against the outside world and freedom to pursue their own strategy within their own circle.

There is some evidence that Nixon's first term did not start out this way. In the dawn of victory a certain degree of euphoria and goodwill usually prevails. There is, first of all, the time of speculation about whom the President will appoint to his cabinet and to other influential positions in his new administration; then, an interim period after the inauguration when administration policies are being born and when the administration line is not so thoroughly taut and so irrevocably established that it becomes a daily target for the opposition party and a hostile press. Henry Kissinger once remarked in a graduate seminar which I attended that there is only a short period in any administration in which basic changes in policy can be made. These are the few golden months at the very beginning, when new faces take over the reins of government and the bureaucracy has to tread water until the new lines of policy are made clear. While this is the normal pattern of events, the Nixon administration was not a normal one, and one cannot assume that it enjoyed as long or as free a breathing spell as many of its predecessors.

The adversary relationship that had long existed between Nixon and the liberal community spilled over into the opinion-making centers of the nation—not necessarily into the editorial pages in Dallas, Dubuque and Cleveland, or among the owners and publishers of the country's newspapers, radio and television networks, but rather into the influential Washington press corps, the major universities, the network news departments and their nightly newscasters, all of whom independently developed their own ideas and reflected their own opinions, and of course the national journals of opinion, most of which were centered in New York City. Though no one could expect a prolonged honeymoon between these influential opinion-makers and the President, any newly-elected President gets some grace period before he becomes fair game for the press, and this was only partially true for Richard Nixon.

The problems that his administration confronted were not new—American society had been burdened with the war, racism and severe economic and social dislocations long before Nixon ever entered the White House. The presence of a new array of advisors—dominated by Henry Kissinger in the field of foreign policy and Daniel Patrick Moynihan in the domestic urban areas—added an increment of hopeful speculation about possible shifts in emphasis from what the liberal community might expect of its perennial antagonist. There were some new ideas and fresh beginnings, and the early months of the Nixon administration were not completely dominated by total hostility on the part of its normal opinion-making enemies. Nixon himself had over the years developed the psychological armor which, for the most part, protected or immunized him from his critics, but it was not apparent at the beginning that that armor would also envelop his White House staff and totally short-circuit two-way communication with the opinion centers outside. This was to come sometime later. In a perceptive piece in the *Washington Post*, Lou Cannon wrote:

> The first occupants of the Nixon White House do not remember it as a government citadel under siege. The White House of their memory is a happier place than that, a good place to work and to govern. They are gone now, these men (gone, too, the men who replaced them) but they look back at the springtime of 1969 as the halcyon time when bright ideas abounded and the dialogue had yet to disappear.
>
> *"It wasn't just a place of extreme paranoia then," Stephen Hess, the one time Eisenhower speechwriter who is now at the Brookings Institution, pointed out. "If anything the model would have been early Roosevelt.*

Moynihan had a shop of young bubbling intellectuals. Arthur Burns and his people were different but very, very good. There was a clash of ideas."

The first stirrings of trouble were with the Congress. "At first it all sounded great," says Sen. Bob Dole of Kansas, who would become the administration point man in some of the President's toughest Senate battles. "We went down to the White House for a reception with the early birds, those who worked for Nixon before the nomination. We thought we were in clover. But nothing happened."[36]

The first six months of the Nixon administration produced no startling surprises. The President travelled to Europe early in 1969 and made a favorable impression upon European statesmen whom President Johnson had not been able to charm in five years of trying. In France, President Charles de Gaulle offered the longest and warmest toast to the American President that he had ever accorded to a visiting head of state, and in Britain, President Nixon met with equal success. At a private dinner at Number 10 Downing Street, Prime Minister Harold Wilson passed him a note commenting on a gracious remark Nixon had made, relieving the British Foreign Office of a ticklish and embarrassing situation:

> That was one of the kindest and most generous acts I have known in a quarter century in politics. Just proves my point. You can't guarantee being born a lord. It is possible—you've shown it—to be born a gentleman.[37]

This was heady wine for a President who had aspired to a grandiose role in world leadership, who patterned himself after Woodrow Wilson. He made his priorities clear to an interviewer in 1967 when he suggested:

> I've always thought this country could run itself domestically, without a President. All you need is a competent Cabinet to run the country at home. You need a President for foreign policy.[38]

Seven tragic years later Richard Nixon would discover how wrong that concept of the presidency was. In fact, Nixon began running into trouble with Congress early in his first term. He had been elected by a slim margin and had not brought many Republicans along with him into Congress, where the Democrats controlled both houses. Angered by the successful Republican campaign to force the resignation of Lyndon Johnson's friend and advisor, Supreme Court Justice Abe Fortas, the Democrats carefully scrutinized Nixon's replacement nominee, Clement F. Haynesworth, jr., chief judge of the Fourth Circuit Court of Appeals, from Greenville, South Carolina. The President had promised to appoint strict constructionists to the Court during the 1968 campaign, and the appointment of a southern judge was in keeping with his strategy to appeal to that region for their support in exchange for his support for such policies as the slowdown of civil rights activities. Haynesworth was bitterly opposed by organized labor and liberal Democrats on the grounds of his hostility to the labor movement and his evasiveness on civil rights questions. Extraordinary pressure built up on both sides, the White House leaning on all Republicans and southern Democrats to support the nomination, and the AFL-CIO, liberal and civil rights organizations attempting to persuade Democratic and Republican liberals to defeat the nomination. Three months after his name was brought forward by the President, Haynesworth's nomination was rejected by the Senate, 55 to 45. Seventeen Republicans voted against the White House nominee, including Hugh Scott, the Republican minority leader in the Senate, and his assistant, Senator Robert Griffin.

The administration defeat marked the real beginning of a serious breach between the executive and legislative branches of the government. The inexperience of many of the President's top assistants had a great deal to do with this, for there were many members of the President's party in both houses who felt the President's staff was sealing him off from normal contact with them. The President was furious at what he considered a humiliating defeat, but he indicated he would not back off from appointing a southern strict constructionist in spite of his first setback, and he did do it again, nominating Judge G. Harold Carswell of Tallahassee, Florida, a member of the Fifth Circuit Court of Appeals.

Carswell turned out to be a far inferior candidate to Haynesworth. He not only had a poor civil rights record, but he was also not highly regarded as a technician of the law; his decisions had a higher rate of reversal on appeal than all but 6 of 67 judges in his circuit. Of his 84 published decisions, nearly 60 percent had been reversed, more than twice the average of the judges in his circuit. In the end his appointment was opposed by the deans of the Harvard, Yale, Pennsylvania and UCLA Law Schools, and a number of leading members of the Bar, for his not possessing the high calibre of qualifications necessary for service on the Supreme Court of the United States. In Carswell's case, he had a long and damaging record of active support for segregation, both on the bench and as a private attorney. After a long and even more bitter struggle between the White House and the Senate, Carswell's nomination was also defeated. This act provoked Nixon into one of the strongest public attacks upon the Senate by a President in this century:

> I have reluctantly concluded, with the Senate presently constituted, I cannot successfully nominate to the Supreme Court any federal appellate judge from the South who believes as I do in the strict construction of the Constitution.
>
> Judges Carswell and Haynesworth have endured with admirable dignity vicious assaults on their intelligence, their honesty and their character. They have been falsely charged with being racist. But when all the hypocrisy is stripped away, the real issue was their philosophy of strict construction of the Constitution, a philosophy that I share—and the fact that they had the misfortune of being born in the South. After the rejection of Judge Carswell and Judge Haynesworth, this conclusion is inescapable.[39]

Nixon went on to argue that the only criteria he had for his selection were (1) strict construction of the Constitution to help restore the balance of the Court; (2) that they be experienced members of the judiciary from the Court of Appeals; and (3) that they be from the South. He emphasized that one quarter of the American people live in that area of the country and that they should have adequate representation on the Court.

With yesterday's action, the Senate has said that no Southern appellate judge who believes in a strict interpretation of the Constitution can be elevated to the Supreme Court. As long as the Senate is constituted the way it is today, I will not nominate another Southerner and let him be subjected to the kind of malicious character assassination accorded both Judges Haynesworth and Carswell.[40]

The President indicated that the next candidate would come from outside the South:

I understand the bitter feeling of millions of Americans who live in the South about the act of regional discrimination that took place in the Senate yesterday. They have my assurance that the day will come when men like Judges Carswell and Haynesworth can and will sit on the high Court.[41]

Of course, such an attack upon the Senate created a wave of bitterness against the President, many senators believing that the statement was simply a politically self-serving piece of rhetoric, another example of the Nixon style, but one prominent lawyer who was deeply involved in the Carswell fight, according to Richard Harris, warned,

He meant it. Those of us who raised our heads out of the trenches in this fight will never be forgiven. As far as the President is concerned, anyone who was against him on this one is just plain against him.[42]

This turned out to be more truth than poetry. It would seem that if we are looking for a significant benchmark of when the Nixon administration really began to develop the "state of siege" mentality, it was after the Carswell defeat. Nixon had long been critical of and uneasy with the divided and at times chaotic form of the American political system. It offended his sense of order, for one thing, and it interfered with his effort to direct coherent policies for another. And yet, by the rules of the game, presiding over a divided government where the opposition party and its allies controlled a majority in both houses of the legislature, he would have to face the prospect of frequent defeats or find some other way of overcoming this obstacle. The accepted pattern was to go to the people and to appeal to them over the heads of Congress, creating sufficient support to bring pressure on enough members of Congress to change. Nixon tried this on many occasions, but he did not succeed enough times to satisfy his own demands. A better way would have to be found.

Nixon had inherited the power and the trappings of the imperial presidency from Lyndon Johnson. Even more than Johnson, he responded to the pageantry of the office and embellished it at every opportunity, going to the extreme of dressing the White House police force in elegant ceremonial uniforms with stove pipe hats and patent leather visors, as if they were members of a European court. He even introduced trumpeters to announce the coming and going of the President at official gatherings. A man so addicted to the outward manifestations of power is not likely to be sympathetic to forces which tend to whittle that power down to life-size. So the war with Congress was more or less inevitable, given the nature of the system and the personality of the President. But this conflict was exacerbated by the Court showdown and the impatience of an increasing number of senators and congressmen with the pace of Nixon's policy to wind down the war. His initial decision to gradually withdraw American personnel from Vietnam as the negotiations dragged on in Paris was accepted, even if not enthusiastically, with at least some degree of forebearance. But as the months dragged on and the war continued into the second, third and fourth years of his administration, the protest marches emerged again to haunt Nixon as they had bedeviled Johnson, and Executive-congressional relations did not improve.

In the first week of May 1970, on the heels of the President's announcement of the Cambodian incursion, the nation's campuses exploded once again, this time with even greater violence and disruption than on previous occasions. Waiting years for the war to end and even half believing President Nixon when he promised to wind it down, it now appeared to students as if the war was both widening and intensifying. They felt that they could not stand by and let it happen further. At Kent State University in Ohio, four students were killed and eleven were wounded by the rifles of a company of the Ohio National Guard called to the campus to suppress the demonstration. This action embittered students throughout the country, and broadened the scope of their protest.

The President first ignored their pleas, condemning the protesters as "bums" who were "blowing up the campuses."[43] Two weeks later when two more students were killed and eleven more wounded at Jackson State College in Mississippi, the President backed-off from his hard-line position and met with the presidents of a number of colleges and universities to talk some of the problems out. He also appointed the Presidential Commission on Campus Unrest and made other conciliatory moves to calm the troubled waters. None of these efforts had that effect, however, and as the summer lengthened into fall, resentment on both sides continued without any noticeable improvement.

There are positive things that can be said about the first Nixon term in the White House. There was the untiring diplomatic skill of Henry Kissinger, who persisted in the long negotiations with the Vietnamese in Paris; there was the high style and brilliance of Pat Moynihan, who nurtured a revolutionary family assistance plan that, under somewhat different circumstances, might well have made a revolutionary breakthrough in social legislation; there was the bulldog persistence of Secretary of Defense Melvin Laird, who persisted over the opposition of the military in winding down the war and shipping the troops home. There was also the breakthrough with China, which took courage and imagination and represented a diplomatic move that a Democratic administration probably could not have made. There were also some very useful and constructive proposals advanced by the Ash Council on Executive Organization. But the positive gains were not really conducive to winning political support in Congress, and they were accompanied by intermittent crises in Vietnam and at home, continuing and worsening inflation, greater alienation on the part of the young, the Blacks and other minorities, and the continuing hostility of labor and the liberal establishment. Nixon, his closest advisors and White House staff, shielded themselves more and more from public confrontations in which they always came out second best. The White House became more isolated as two-way communication was discouraged, and appeals to the silent majority were juxtaposed to the very vocal minority who marched on Washington and assailed his administration.

The President, who was initially concerned about somehow appeasing if not pleasing the liberal elements of his own party, moved further to the right and found consolation in the conservative wing of his own party and the more conservative members of the opposition party. Liberals, like Moynihan and Finch, with somewhat conflicting views began to disappear from the administration, and individuals who were "rocking the boat," such as Secretary of the Interior Walter Hickel and his entire staff and civil rights enthusiasts in the Department of Health, Education and Welfare, were eased out of the picture so that hard-line loyalists could take over. The Nixon group, which had usurped power in the Republican party, built its own political organization outside the party. It grew to its logical fulfillment in the establishment of the Committee to Reelect the President, which was operated and staffed by White House loyalists almost independent of the core of the Republican party.

The overwhelming Nixon victory in 1972 eradicated the pessimistic mood of the President and his advisors in 1970, 1971 and early 1972. Although they put up a brave front for the media, the impact of his frantic and intensive campaigning in the election of 1970 was minimal at best, and the situation went downhill after the election. Negotiations in Paris appeared to be stalled indefinitely; Nixon felt forced to apply new pressures on North Vietnam after a full-scale invasion south of the demilitarized zone by the North Vietnamese army, and he ordered the long-postponed mining of Haiphong Harbor and massive bombing of the North in the spring of 1972. The real Nixon upswing occurred after the Moscow summit in the summer of 1972, with the confusions of the McGovern campaign at home and the agreement with North Vietnam just before the election. It appeared that Nixon was really the man in charge and knew what he was doing, he radiated confidence, but previous to this, confidence in the electorate was anything but the real mood of the Nixon White House. It was an administration in a "state of siege." In fact, most of the Watergate plans and activities were set in motion during that period.

Perhaps the years 1970-72 are an arbitrary period, but there are indications from materials which came to light in the Watergate investigation that during this period the Nixon administration was in panic and moved in a dozen different directions to subvert the political process and the office of the presidency. There was no question that the President greatly resented his humiliation by the Congress in the Haynesworth and Carswell defeats and in other major legislative losses he sustained, and also objected to the continued hostility of the press and the liberal establishment. He was apparently convinced, however, that he could do nothing overtly to change this, and his only hope of reelection and ultimate historical restitution would lie in ignoring the political process and using the considerable powers of the presidency to his own ends. He would not allow mounting criticism in Congress and in the nation to deter him from his game plan in Vietnam. He would withdraw from all further confrontations with the opposition, see as little of the press as possible and communicate directly only with the American people, when he had something of great importance to convey. Furthermore, he would use every covert instrument at his disposal to hinder, obstruct and injure "enemies" of the administration, relying upon the secrecy of his inner circle and their loyalty to him and his objectives to carry such a program through.

What Schlesinger has characterized as "the structural forces tending to transfer power to the presidency" that were inherent in the imperial presidency, "were now reinforced by compulsive internal drives—a sense of life as a battlefield, a belief that the nation was swarming with personal enemies, a flinching from face-to-face argument, an addiction to seclusion, a preoccupation with response to crisis, an insistence on a controlled environment for decision."

> For a man so constituted, the Imperial Presidency was the perfect shield and refuge. But Nixon not only had an urgent psychological need for exemption from the democratic process. He also boldly sensed an historical opportunity to transform the Presidency—to consolidate within the White House all the powers, as against Congress, as against the electorate, as against the rest of the executive branch itself, that a generation of foreign and domestic turbulence had chaotically delivered to the Presidency.[44]

I am not suggesting that such a calculated and organized effort was anywhere written down or even conceived of by its prime operatives as a plebiscitary attack upon the American political process. Nor was it ever systematically developed as a theory of presidential power and performance. Rather, it was adopted as a strategy of desperation by a President and his staff who had failed to accomplish their objectives in the demanding and chaotic arena of checks and balances that characterize the American political system. It revealed a willingness to circumvent that system, to avoid the use of regular institutional channels when systematic circumvention would protect the administration and its policies from careful scrutiny and review by other branches of the government or outside independent sources. It seems clear that by 1970-72, and maybe long before that, to Richard Nixon it appeared that he could not win reelection by adhering to the "rules of the game" and that he would have to thoroughly rely upon the Nixon style of politics and write his own rules.

What evidence can be presented to support this theory of a Nixon-inspired plebiscitary—what Arthur Schlesinger has termed a "revolutionary" presidency? What indications are there that during the Nixon administration the phenomena of the imperial presidency which we discussed earlier and which developed during the post-World War II period, would be transformed into an office which attempted to reach beyond even these greatly expanded limits, a presidency quite threatening to the values upon which our political system rests? It is best to summarize the areas where the most critical abuses of power took place. The first thing to disappear in the Nixon White House under siege was the invigorating clash of opinions that had characterized its early months. The major contestants in those days were Arthur Burns, the experienced and able conservative economist and Pat Moynihan, but there was initially a sprinkling of more liberal-minded members of the Nixon entourage who challenged the hard-line thinking and instinctive reactions of his principal advisors. By the time the siege set in, however, Moynihan, Finch, Hickel (and all of his top assistants), Jim Farmer, James Allen, Stephen Hess, Leon

Panetta—not all liberals with a small or large "L," but independent-minded men of integrity who did not exactly fit into the new pattern—had all departed. It was smoother sailing after they left, but unfortunately they were the last link with reality the Nixon administration had. Thereafter the rigid and hard-line H. R. Haldeman, John D. Ehrlichman and Charles W. Colson took over, and the White House became a fortress against any critical voice within the government.

In the early part of the century, Theodore Roosevelt and later Woodrow Wilson established a new relationship with the press, Roosevelt inviting reporters from off the street inside the White House and Wilson establishing regular press conferences. Franklin D. Roosevelt institutionalized this open, informal and two-way form of communication between the President and the rest of the country. He held 1011 press conferences during his 12 years in the White House, and they were always warm, fascinating and usually informative sessions. By Nixon's time, the presidential press conference had become, as James MacGregor Burns put it, "as much a White House fixture as the cabinet meeting."[45] Richard Nixon practically did away with both, rarely meeting with his cabinet and holding only 28 press conferences during his first four years in office, and fewer during his second term. This was his second critical abuse of his power.

The almost total absence of these regular meetings, which had informed the country in a way in which no formal address or press release could hope to convey, deprived Americans of hearing and sensing their President's reactions to the kinds of problems that were in their minds and further enveloped the mysterious administration into a deeper pall of silence and secrecy. The President, too, was deprived of his only essential contact with the conduits of public opinion, and he was forced to rely exclusively upon digests of news and opinion prepared by a staff which was accountable only to him and not to the public. As a result, they told him essentially what he wanted to hear. But the press conference,

> as most Presidents rapidly discovered, was a forum in which they not only told things but learned things. Preparation for the conference required the President to acquaint himself with matters of public business that might be far from his own immediate concern. And the questions asked at the conference often disclosed to him things about the government and the country that his own executive establishment, consciously or not, had been keeping from him.[46]

The series of disastrous encounters with Congress had convinced President Nixon that there must be a better way of controlling its spendthrift habits and forcing it to conform more rigidly to administration policies. Theodore White points out how much that problem bothered the inner circle of the Nixon administration in 1971 in the report of a dinnertable conversation with Casper Weinberger, then deputy director of the budget, budget director George Schultz and Bob Haldeman:

> The mood was relaxed and convivial, but there was a somber undertone to the pleasant evening. Two qualities were apparent: these men were under siege—and they were calm. They agreed that this was the low point of their administration; their story was not getting across. Over and over again

there was the problem: how to come to grips with the government. How could they *control* a Democratic Congress which denounced Pentagon expenditures, yet according to them, appropriated $1.4 billion *more* for the Pentagon than the President wanted? A Highway Administration that was piling up more money than could possibly—or wisely—be spent on highways?[47]

They finally discovered a way to control these expenditures by impounding the funds appropriated by Congress. Other Presidents had used this device, but only in contingency circumstances; for example when Thomas Jefferson did not spend $50,000 appropriated for gunboats on the Mississippi, because the threat of war had been relieved by treaties with France and Spain. Later Presidents have made discretionary judgments with respect to the quality and quantity of the production of national defense armaments (e.g., Truman and Kennedy), and Lyndon Johnson impounded a whopping $5,000,000,000 in appropriated funds, but only after receiving the approval of congressional leaders. He later released some of these funds because of local and state pressures. Moreover, it was clearly an economy measure, for the cuts and impoundments went right across the board in almost every area. No one particular program or policy was singled out to be eliminated by the President. Nonetheless, the fact that Jefferson, Truman, Kennedy and Johnson had done it (albeit under very different circumstances) did not necessarily make impoundment a constitutional act.

Legislation in the early part of the century (the Anti-Deficiency Acts of 1905 and 1906, amended in 1951) encouraged executive discretion in spending appropriated funds in order to effect savings and to establish reserves for contingencies, thus avoiding deficiency appropriations, a particularly obnoxious ordeal for Congress. Nixon, as he did in so many other cases, simply used these precedents as a point of departure to misrepresent their real intent and implications. In fact he used impoundment as an instrument of selective law enforcement, deciding from among a wide range of statutes and their subsequent appropriations which programs he would fund and which he would not. Dr. Louis Fisher of the Congressional Research Service of the Library of Congress has pointed out:

> In the spring of 1971, the Nixon Administration announced that it was withholding more than $12 billion, most of which consisted of highway money and funds for various urban programs. When Secretary Romney appeared before a Senate committee in March, he explained that funds were being held back from various urban programs because there was no point in accelerating programs that were "scheduled for termination." He was referring to the fact that Congress had added funds to grant-in-aid programs which the Administration wanted to consolidate and convert into its revenue-sharing proprosal. To impound funds in this prospective sense—holding on to money in anticipation that Congress will enact an Administration bill—is a new departure for the impoundment technique. Impoundment is not being used to avoid deficiencies, or to effect savings, or even to fight inflation, but rather to shift the scale of priorities from one Administration to the next, *prior to congressional action.*[48]

Senator Edmund S. Muskie charged President Nixon with "twisting . . . the Constitution in order to deny the Congress the final say over the spending of public funds."

The case of the water pollution control funds is a particularly clear instance. Last year we amended the original act precisely in order to mandate a reliable allotment and assured funding procedure. Because of past failures to deliver Federal funds on a timely basis, communities had lost their ability to plan the financing of needed water treatment facilities. Conscious of a backlog of state projects eligible for Federal assistance and based on an administration determination of need we specifically directed the Environmental Protection Administration to allot $11 billion in this fiscal year and the next, and I repeat, we didn't authorize, we specifically directed the allotments of these funds.

Explaining the new provisions to the Senate before it overrode the veto, I said that we were willing "to give the administration some flexibility concerning the obligation of construction grant funds" under the program. But that flexibility was meant only to avoid waste. It never extended to the 3-year authorization of $18 billion, and it is the authorization which the administration, by limiting allotments, has effectively attempted to reduce and emasculate.

May I repeat that, the President undertook to use his constitutional power of the veto to disagree with the Congress and perhaps undercut the bill. The Congress overrode the veto and now the President has undertaken to reduce the authorization bill by refusing to execute a direction of the Congress and the effect is to rewrite the authorization bill in a way that cannot be recaptured by the Executive or by Congress except by reenactment of the legislation which has already been reenacted over the President's veto.

The audacity of the act almost takes one's breath away. And it should force the Congress to consider honestly what a President capable of such abuse of power might do next.[49]

Congress, and particularly the Senate, was up in arms over the Nixon impoundments. The most prized and precious function of the Congress was being challenged by such actions, for in effect the President was refusing to carry out laws that had been passed over his veto and to spend appropriations duly mandated by Congress. Even the President's assistant attorney general and Supreme Court appointee, William H. Rehnquist, was on record as arguing that there was no constitutional basis for impoundment.

It is in our view extremely difficult to formulate a constitutional theory to justify a refusal by the President to comply with a Congressional directive to spend. It may be argued that the spending of money is inherently an executive function, but the execution of any law is, by definition, an executive function, and it seems an anomalous proposition that because the Executive branch is bound to execute the laws, it is free to decline to execute them.[50]

Believing that it had a strong case against the President, and infuriated that Nixon was poaching on its sacred territory of lawmaking and appropriations, Congress hit back on two fronts. Individual members of the Senate and the House joined together to file a brief in support of the State Highway Commission of Missouri against the secretary of transportation and the Office of Management and the Budget (the transformed Bureau of the Budget in the Nixon administration), seeking injunctive and *mandamus* relief to pry loose funds initially allocated to Missouri from the Highway Trust Fund and impounded by the Nixon administration. Congress also drafted legislation which severely restricted the ability of the President to impound legally appropriated funds designated by Congress for specific purposes.[51]

The decision of the circuit court of appeals was favorable to the State Highway Commission of Missouri and its supporting members of Congress. The Department of Justice decided not to contest the decision, and the government released the impounded funds.[52] Some 29 other cases against the government had been decided by the fall of 1973, all but 5 against the government.

Progress on the legislative level was not that rapid. Both the Senate and House passed strong measures drastically limiting the power of the President to impound, but they encountered some delay in the final stages of the legislative process. There were also significant differences between the Senate and House bills, the former requiring the President to submit notice of all impoundments to the Congress and prohibiting them if they did not receive the approval of a joint resolution within 60 days. In the milder House version the opposite procedure was proposed, namely, action by joint resolution of the Congress was required to prevent the impoundment within the same period.

The final resolution was the incorporation of the anti-impoundment provisions into the important Budget Reform Act, which was passed in the summer of 1974. This measure was long overdue and introduced a wide range of changes to the procedures with which Congress deals with the federal budget. During the impoundment debates earlier in 1973, the argument was pressed that the archaic methods used by the Congress in reviewing the federal budget had led to the general chaos of which, in appropriations procedures and general budgetary review, the Executive was able to take advantage. In revamping its budget review procedures, the Congress took a giant step forward in restricting the improper role of the Executive in his constitutional responsibilities and was the first major reassertion of the constitutional role of the Congress in this crisis period.

The impoundment procedures incorporated into the new budget law split the difference between the Senate and House versions of the initial proposal. In cases where presidential impoundment merely delayed spending appropriated funds, the House proposal of requiring a joint Senate-House resolution to negate the impoundment was necessary. But in impoundments involving termination of programs or total cuts for fiscal reasons, a joint resolution would be required to sustain the impounding 45 days after it had been submitted (as it must be) to the Congress. In other words, if no action were to be taken by the Congress, the impoundment would be null and void. The law also contained provisions to amend the clause in the Anti-Deficiency Act of 1950, which had been used by the administration in defense of its actions. Provision in this law was also made for the comptroller general to go into the courts and compel the compliance of the executive branch, if the President were to ignore such action or inaction by the Congress.[53]

Unquestionably the most blatant abuse of executive power during this period was the assault upon the privacy and rights of individuals through illegal acts by members of the Nixon administration, and their frequent use of government agencies to abet and implement their actions. It would be impossible in this section to even begin to catalogue and analyze all of these significant transgressions. Volumes of congressional testimony and reports, grand jury proceedings, trials and hearings in the courts, have just begun to document the extent of this assault upon constitutional liberties and the protection of laws governing the activities of the executive branch. It is important to emphasize here, however, the major areas in which these transgressions occurred, for it helps one in one's search for legal and constitutional remedies to these abuses of presidential power.

Much of what took place emanated from a growing fear within the executive establishment of the ability of outside influences to pierce the curtain of secrecy that shrouded the White House and its operations. The President's special counsel, Charles W. Colson, told a reporter of the Detroit *News*:

> The thing that is completely misunderstood about Watergate is that everybody thinks the people surrounding President Nixon were drunk with power. . . . It was insecurity. That insecurity began to breed a form of paranoia. We overreacted to the attacks against us and to a lot of things.[54]

In the very beginning several critical national security "leaks" triggered very real concern on the part of the Nixon administration and immediate steps were taken to remedy this situation. Whether these efforts to determine the source of the leaks were effective or the methods used legitimate exercises of presidential power is quite another question. Early in 1969 President Nixon authorized a wiretapping program in the hope of securing information on the security leaks, and that program remained in effect for almost two years. During that period national security wiretaps authorized by the attorney general were placed by the FBI on the telephones of 17 individuals, including members of the staff of the National Security Council (some for an extended period of time and others for only a few weeks), members of the Washington press corps, members of the White House staff and several other government officials.

Another wiretap at the home of newspaper columnist Joseph Kraft was installed without the specific authorization of the President (as far as one now knows). Rather, his assistant, John Ehrlichman, instructed another White House employee, John Caulfield, to install the tap, although not through the FBI, which Ehrlichman described as a "sieve." Caulfield arranged to have the tap made by the former chief of security of the Republican National Committee, with the aid of a secret service employee. The instruction was discontinued shortly thereafter on Ehrlichman's orders. In the meantime it had been learned that Kraft was not in Washington but in Paris. The attorney general then authorized an FBI physical "spot" check on Kraft, which was supervised by Deputy FBI Director William

Sullivan. It included "bugging" Kraft's hotel room in Paris. Despite all their measures, no evidence was obtained to indicate any unauthorized disclosure of classified materials.[55]

Alarmed by the campus protests and riots in the spring of 1970 (after the Cambodian incursion), the President called a meeting at the White House in June of 1970 to duscuss the need for btter1domestic intelligence. In addition to presidential assistants H. R. Haldeman and John Ehrlichman and staff assistant Tom Charles Huston, also present at the meeting were FBI director, J. Edgar Hoover, Defense Intelligence Agency director, General Donald Bennett, National Security Agency director, Admiral Noel Gayler and Central Intelligence Agency director, Richard Helms. The President acquainted this group with the problem of developing better domestic intelligence operations in the light of the recent escalation of bombings and other acts of violence. He appointed Hoover, General Bennett, Admiral Gayler and Helms as an *ad hoc* committee to study intelligence needs and restraints. Hoover was asked to serve as chairman of this committee and Huston as the liaison officer at the White House.

Apparently this group met regularly for several weeks, and on June 25, 1970 they completed a report for the White House entitled "Special Report: Interagency Committee on Intelligence (Ad Hoc)," later known as the Huston plan. The report surveyed the current internal security threat, analyzed the status of the various radical, student, antiwar and Black militant groups and proceeded to note certain inadequacies in present intelligence gathering procedures, coverage and interpretation. It outlined a number of possible expanded and intensified efforts to improve those procedures.

The arguments for and against adopting such measures ranged from leaving present restrictions in effect to removing restrictions and expanding both activities and coverage. The committee did not make a decision with regard to which alternative to adopt, but it noted the objections of the FBI (and in one instance the military) to making any substantial changes in the existing restrictions. Hoover was opposed to any expansion of the present limited system involving highly-selective electronic surveillance to include the implementation of covert mail coverage, surreptitious entry, encouraging campus observers and informers, the use of military undercover agents (here the military also objected) and was even against the creation of a permanent interagency intelligence committee, which could provide periodic evaluations of domestic intelligence.

It is useless to speculate in regard to Hoover's reluctance to go along with these proposals. He may have considered the alarm of the Nixon administration unwarranted; he may have been reacting as a bureaucrat, seeing the proposed expansion of domestic intelligence gathering to these other groups (NSC, CIA) as an improper invasion of his exclusive jurisdiction; he may have anticipated the predictable bungling and exposure which was sure to follow such hastily conceived plans for expansion and realized that this would be damaging to the work of the FBI; or he just may have been a better constitutionalist (perhaps even of recent vintage) than he was reputed to have been and took exception to the illegal and unconstitutional nature of these methods. In any case, he was strongly opposed, and he was the only one consulted who was against the changes being made. Huston's version of his objections is amusing and perhaps accurate:

He knew he wasn't going to be around a hell of a lot longer, and he didn't want any kind of scandal that would blemish his waning years. He was worried about his legend. And so he refused to do certain things that twenty years before he'd have done without "batting an eye." Hoover would not, for example, let his agents do second story jobs or search the mails. Likewise he forbade the recruitment of campus informers under twenty-one years of age, a policy that drastically reduced the FBI's ability to penetrate the New Left. Not that such techniques offended his principles; he never said they were wrong or illegal or unconstitutional. "He'd just sit there and moan about the 'jackals of the press' and how you had to be careful because, if you weren't, the 'jackals of the press' and the civil liberties people would jump down your back and raise hell."[56]

If J. Edgar Hoover and the FBI were reluctant to engage in these illegal intelligence gathering activities, Tom Charles Huston and the President were of the opposite inclination. Each time that Hoover, the veteran, the most honored and at the same time most feared crime and political radical hunter in the nation, said no, Huston and the President said yes.

But Hoover warned the White House that the actions proposed were in violation of the law, would not be effective and they would be exposed and attacked in the press. Huston was not moved by Hoover's objections. In a very revealing memorandum to Haldeman, Huston characterized Hoover's objections to the illegal intelligence gathering methods he was so anxious to introduce as "inconsistent and frivolous," stressing "the possible embarrassment to the intelligence community from public disclosure of clandestine operations."[57] In an earlier memorandum to Haldeman (and presumably the President) Huston argued:

> There is no valid argument against the use of legal mail covers except Mr. Hoover's concern that the civil liberties of people may become upset. This risk is surely an acceptable one and hardly serious enough to justify denying ourselves a valuable and legal intelligence tool.[58]

Huston's use of the word "legal" is significant. The top law enforcement officer of the nation was attempting to explain to him that surreptitious entry, unlimited electronic surveillance and mail covers were illegal, but apparently to this young Indiana lawyer, anything the President of the United States authorized was considered legal. The irony is overwhelming. It seems that throughout the whole Watergate episode the only consistently strong voice raised against these illegal and unconstitutional methods which the Nixon administration, through their own groups of "plumbers," eventually adopted and practiced was that of J. Edgar Hoover, who could have protected the White House from its eventual exposure and downfall if its inhabitants had heeded his experienced advice.

Interagency Committee on Intelligence (Ad Hoc)
Special Report—Parts Two and Three
June 25, 1970

U.S., Congress, House, Committee on the Judiciary, *Statement of Information,* Hearings, 93rd Cong., 2nd sess., May-June 1974 (Washington, D.C., 1974), Book VII, Part I, 411-31.

[Note: The text which appears on pages 411-431 of the *Statement of Information* is reprinted here in full, including notes. However, asterisks have been inserted where blank spaces indicating deletions appear in the *Statement* text.— Ed.]

TOP SECRET

PART TWO
RESTRAINTS ON INTELLIGENCE COLLECTION

The Committee noted that the President had made it clear that he desired full consideration be given to any regulations, policies, or procedures which tend to limit the effectiveness of domestic intelligence collection. The Committee further noted that the President wanted the pros and cons of such restraints clearly set forth so that the President will be able to decide whether or not a change in current policies, practices, or procedures should be made.

During meetings of the Committee, a variety of limitations and restraints were discussed. All of the agencies involved, Defense Intelligence Agency (DIA), the three military counterintelligence services, the Central Intelligence Agency (CIA), the National Security Agency (NSA), and the Federal Bureau of Investigation (FBI), participated in these considerations.

In the light of the directives furnished to the Committee by the White House, the subject matters hereinafter set forth were reviewed for the consideration and decision of the President.

I. Specific Operational Restraints

A. Interpretive Restraint on Communications Intelligence

Preliminary Discussion

      *   *   *

Note: Page 24 has been deleted by the Chairman and Ranking Minority Member prior to public release of this document.

Note: Page 25 has been deleted by the Chairman and Ranking Minority Member prior to public release of this document.

B. Electronic Surveillances and Penetrations

Preliminary Discussion
The limited number of electronic surveillances and penetrations substantially restricts the collection of valuable intelligence information of material importance to the entire intelligence community.

*   *   *

Nature of Restrictions
Electronic surveillances have been used on a selective basis. Restrictions, initiated at the highest levels of the Executive Branch, arose as a result of the condemnation of these techniques by civil rights groups, Congressional concern for invasion of privacy, and the possibility of their adverse effect on criminal prosecutions.

Advantages of Maintaining Restrictions
1. Disclosure and embarrassment to the using agency and/or the United States is always possible since such techniques often require that the services or advice of outside personnel be used in the process of installation.
2.   *   *   *
3. Certain elements of the press in the United States and abroad would undoubtedly seize upon disclosure of electronic coverage in an effort to discredit the United States.
4. The monitoring of electronic surveillances requires considerable manpower and, where foreign establishments are involved, the language resources of the agencies could be severely taxed.

Advantages of Relaxing Restrictions
1. The U.S. Government has an overriding obligation to use every available scientific means to detect and neutralize forces which pose a direct threat to the Nation.
2. Every major intelligence service in the world, including those of the communist bloc, use such techniques as an essential part of their operations, and it is believed the general public would support their use by the United States for the same purpose.
3. The President historically has had the authority to act in matters of national security. In addition, Title III of the Omnibus Crime Control and Safe Streets Act of 1968 provides a statutory basis.
4. Intelligence data from electronic coverage is not readily obtainable from other techniques or sources. Such data includes information which might assist in formulating foreign policy decisions, information leading to the identification of intelligence and/or espionage principals and could well include the first indication of intention to commit hostile action against the United States.
5. Acquisition of such material from COMINT without benefit of the assistance which electronic surveillance techniques can provide, if possible at all, would be extremely expensive. Therefore, this approach could result in considerable dollar savings compared to collection methods.

Decision: Electronic Surveillances and Penetrations
   _____ Present procedures on electronic coverage should continue.

   _____ Present procedures should be changed to permit intensification of coverage of individuals and groups in the United States who pose a major threat to the internal security.

   _____ Present procedures should be changed to permit intensification of coverage   *   *   *   of interest to the intelligence community.

   _____ More information is needed.

Note: The FBI does not wish to change its present procedure of selective coverage on major internal security threats as it believes this coverage is adequate at this time. The FBI would not oppose other agencies seeking authority of the Attorney General for coverage required by them and thereafter instituting such coverage themselves.

C. Mail Coverage

Preliminary Discussion
   The use of mail covers can result in the collection of valuable information relating to contacts between U.S. nationals and foreign governments and intelligence services. CIA and the military investigative agencies have found this information particularly helpful in the past. Essentially, there are two types of mail coverage: routine coverage is legal, while the second—covert coverage—is not. Routine coverage involves recording information from the face of envelopes. It is available, legally, to any duly authorized Federal or state investigative agency submitting a written request to the Post Office Department and has been used frequently by the military intelligence services. Covert mail coverage, also known as "sophisticated mail coverage," or "flaps and seals," entails surreptitious screening and may include opening and examination of domestic or foreign mail. This technique is based on high-level cooperation of top echelon postal officials.

           *   *   *

Nature of Restrictions
   Covert coverage has been discontinued while routine coverage has been reduced primarily as an outgrowth of publicity arising from disclosure of routine mail coverage during legal proceedings and publicity afforded this matter in Congressional hearings involving accusations of governmental invasion of privacy.

Advantages of Maintaining Restrictions

Routine Coverage:
   1. Although this coverage is legal, charges of invasion of privacy, no matter how ill-founded, are possible.

2. This coverage depends on the cooperation of rank-and-file postal employees and is, therefore, more susceptible to compromise.

Covert Coverage:
1. Coverage directed against diplomatic establishments, if disclosed, could have adverse diplomatic repercussions.
2. This coverage, not having sanction of law, runs the risk of any illicit act magnified by the involvement of a Government agency.
3. Information secured from such coverage could not be used for prosecutive purposes.

Advantages of Relaxing Restrictions

Routine Coverage:
1. Legal mail coverage is used daily by both local and many Federal authorities in criminal investigations. The use of this technique should be available to permit coverage of individuals and groups in the United States who pose a threat to the internal security.

Covert Coverage:
1. High-level postal authorities have, in the past, provided complete cooperation and have maintained full security of this program.
2. This technique involves negligible risk of compromise. Only high echelon postal authorities know of its existence, and personnel involved are highly trained, trustworthy, and under complete control of the intelligence agency.
3. This coverage has been extremely successful in producing hard-core and authentic intelligence which is not obtainable from any other source.

Decision: Mail Coverage
_____ Present restrictions on both types of mail coverage should be continued.

_____ Restrictions on legal coverage should be removed.

_____ Present restrictions on covert coverage should be relaxed on selected targets of priority foreign intelligence and internal security interest.

_____ More information is needed.

Note: The FBI is opposed to implementing any covert mail coverage because it is clearly illegal and it is likely that, if done, information would leak out of the Post Office to the press and serious damage would be done to the intelligence community. The FBI has no objection to legal mail coverage providing it is done on a carefully controlled and selective basis in both criminal and security matters.

D. Surreptitious Entry

Preliminary Discussion

*   *   *

Nature of Restrictions

Use of surreptitious entry, also referred to as "anonymous" sources: and "black bag jobs," has been virtually eliminated.

*   *   *

Advantages of Maintaining Restrictions

1. The activity involves illegal entry and trespass.
2. Information which is obtained through this technique could not be used for prosecutive purposes.
3. The public disclosure of this technique would result in widespread publicity and embarrassment. The news media would portray the incident as a flagrant violation of civil rights.

Advantages of Relaxing Restrictions

1. Operations of this type are performed by a small number of carefully trained and selected personnel under strict supervision. The technique is implemented only after full security is assured. It has been used in the past with highly successful results and without adverse effects.
2. Benefits accruing from this technique in the past have been innumerable.

*   *   *

3. In the past this technique, when used against subversives, has produced valuable intelligence material.

Decision: Surreptitious Entry

_____ Present restrictions should be continued.

_____ Present restrictions should be modified to permit procurement.   *   *   *

_____ Present restrictions should also be modified to permit selective use of this technique against other urgent and high priority internal security targets.

_____ More information is needed.

Note: The FBI is opposed to surreptitious entry   *   *   *

E. Development of Campus Sources

Preliminary Discussion

Public disclosure of CIA links with the National Student Association and the subsequent issuance of the Katzenbach Report have contributed to a climate adverse to intelligence-type activity on college campuses and with student-related groups. It should be noted that the Katzenbach Report itself does not specifically restrain CIA from developing positive or counterintelligence sources to work on targets abroad.

Restrictions currently in force limit certain other elements of the intelligence community access to some of the most troublesome areas: campuses, college faculties, foreign and domestic youth groups, leftist journalists, and black militants.

*   *   *

Nature of Restrictions

The need for great circumspection in making contacts with students, faculty members, and employees of institutions of learning is widely recognized. However, the requirements of the intelligence community for increased information in this area is obvious from the concern of the White House at the absence of hard information about the plans and programs of campus and student-related militant organizations. At the present time no sources are developed among secondary school students and, with respect to colleges and universities, sources are developed only among individuals who have reached legal age, with few exceptions. This policy is designed to minimize the possibility of embarrassment and adverse publicity, including charges of infringement of academic freedom.

Advantages of Maintaining Restrictions

1. Students, faculty members, and others connected with educational institutions are frequently sensitive to and hostile towards any Government activity which smacks of infringement on academic freedom. They are prone to publicize inquiries by governmental agencies and the resulting publicity can often be misleading in portraying the Government's interest.

2. Students are frequently immature and unpredictable. They cannot be relied on to maintain confidences or to act with discretion to the same extent as adult sources.

Advantages of Relaxing Restrictions

1. To a substantial degree, militant New Left and antiwar groups in the United States are comprised of students, faculty members, and others connected with educational institutions. To a corresponding degree, effective coverage of these groups and activities depends upon development of knowledgeable sources in the categories named. In this connection, the military services have capabilities which could be of value to the FBI.

2. Much of the violence and disorders which have occurred on college campuses have been of a hastily planned nature. Unless sources are available within the student bodies, it is virtually impossible to develop advance information concerning such violence.

3. The development of sources among students affiliated with New Left elements affords a unique opportunity to cultivate informant prospects who may rise to positions of leadership in the revolutionary movement or otherwise become of great long-range value.

4. The extraordinary and unprecedented wave of destruction which has swept U.S. campuses in the past several months and which in some respects represents a

virtual effort to overthrow our system provides a clear justification for the development of campus informants in the interest of national security.

5. Contacts with students will make it possible to obtain information about travel abroad by U.S. students and about attendance at international conferences.

Decision: Development of Campus Sources

_____ Present restrictions on development of campus and student-related sources should be continued.

_____ Present restrictions should be relaxed to permit expanded coverage of violence-prone campus and student-related groups.

_____ CIA coverage of American students (and others) traveling abroad or living abroad should be increased.

_____ More information is needed.

Note: The FBI is opposed to removing any present controls and restrictions relating to the development of campus sources. To do so would severely jeopardize its investigations and could result in leaks to the press which would be damaging and which could result in charges that investigative agencies are interfering with academic freedom.

F. Use of Military Undercover Agents

Preliminary Discussion

The use of undercover agents by the military services to develop domestic intelligence is currently limited to penetration of organizations whose membership includes military personnel and whose activities pose a direct threat to the military establishment. For example, although the Navy has approximately 54 Naval ROTC units and numerous classified Government contract projects on various campuses across the country, the Naval Investigative Service conducts no covert collection on college campuses. The same is true of the other military services.

Nature of Restrictions

The use of undercover agents by the military investigative services to develop domestic intelligence among civilian targets is believed beyond the statutory intent of the Congress as expressed in Title 10, U.S. Code, and in current resource authorizations. The Delimitations Agreement (1949 agreement signed by the FBI, Army, Navy and Air Force which delimits responsibility for each agency with regard to investigations of espionage, counterespionage, subversion and sabotage) reflects the current missions of the FBI and the military services. Further, there is a lack of assets to undertake this mission unless essential service-related counter-intelligence missions are reduced. There is also concern for morale and disciplinary reactions within the services should the existence of such covert operations become known.

Advantages of Maintaining Restrictions

1. If the utilization of military counterintelligence in this mission is contrary to

the intent of the Congress, discovery of employment may result in unfavorable legislation and further reductions in appropriations.

2. Lacking direct statutory authority, the use of the military services in this mission could result in legal action directed against the Executive Branch.

3. The use of military personnel to report on civilian activities for the benefit of civilian agencies will reduce the ability of the military services to meet service-connected intelligence responsibilities.

4. If expansion of the mission of the military services with regard to college campuses is to provide coverage of any significance, it will require corollary increases in resources.

5. Prosecutions for violations of law discovered in the course of military penetration of civilian organizations must be tried in civil courts. The providing of military witnesses will require complicated interdepartmental coordination to a much greater extent than the present and will serve, in the long run, to reduce security.

6. Disclosure that military counterintelligence agencies have been furnishing information obtained through this technique to nonmilitary investigative agencies with respect to civilian activities would certainly result in considerable adverse publicity. The Army's recent experience with former military intelligence personnel confirms this estimate. Since obligated service officers, first enlistees and draftees are drawn from a peer group in which reaction is most unfavorable, morale and disciplinary problems can be anticipated.

Advantages of Relaxing Restrictions

1. Lifting these restrictions would expand the scope of domestic intelligence collection efforts by diverting additional manpower and resources for the collection of information on college campuses and in the vicinity of military installations.

2. The use of undercover agents by the military counterintelligence agencies could be limited to localized targets where the threat is great and the likelihood of exposure minimal. Moreover, controlled use of trusted personnel leaving the service to return to college could expand the collection capabilities at an acceptable risk.

3. The military services have a certain number of personnel pursuing special academic courses on campuses and universities. Such personnel, who in many instances have already been investigated for security clearance, would represent a valuable pool of potential sources for reporting on subversive activities of campus and student-related groups.

Decision: Use of Military Undercover Agents
_____ Present restrictions should be retained.

_____ The counterintelligence mission of the military services should be expanded to include the active collection of intelligence concerning student-related dissident activities, with provisions for a close coordination with the FBI.

_____ No change should be made in the current mission of the military counter-intelligence services; however, present restrictions should be relaxed to permit the use of trusted military personnel as FBI assets in the collection of intelligence regarding student-related dissident activities.

_____ More information is needed.

Note: The FBI is opposed to the use of any military undercover agents to develop domestic intelligence information because this would be in violation of the Delimitations Agreement. The military services, joined by the FBI, oppose any modification of the Delimitations Agreement which would extend their jurisdiction beyond matters of interest to the Department of Defense.

II. Budget and Manpower Restrictions

The capability of member agencies, NSA, CIA, DIA, FBI, and the military counterintelligence services, to collect intelligence data is limited by available resources, particularly in terms of budget and/or qualified manpower. For some agencies fiscal limitations or recent cutbacks have been acute. Budgetary requirements for some agencies, other than the FBI, are reviewed and passed upon by officials who, in some instances, may not be fully informed concerning intelligence requirements.

* * *

The military services noted that cuts in budget requirements for counter-intelligence activities have the effect of severely hampering the ability of these services to accomplish missions relating to coverage of threats to the national security. Budgetary deficiencies have occurred at a time when investigative work loads are increasing significantly.

Manpower limitations constitute a major restriction on the FBI's capabilities in the investigation of subversive activities. The problem is further complicated by the fact that, even if substantial numbers of Agents could be recruited on a crash basis, the time required to conduct background investigations and to provide essential training would mean several months' delay in personnel being available for use against the rapidly escalating subversive situation.

* * *

In the event, as a result of this report, additional collection requirements should be levied on the agencies involved it would be necessary to provide for essential funding.

Decision: Budget and Manpower Restrictions
_____ Each agency should submit a detailed estimate as to projected manpower needs and other costs in the event the various investigative restraints herein are lifted.

_____ Each agency must operate within its current budgetary or manpower limitations, irrespective of action required as result of this report.

_____ More information is needed.

PART THREE
EVALUATION OF INTERAGENCY COORDINATION

I. Current Procedures to Effect Coordination

There is currently no operational body or mechanism specifically charged with the overall analysis, coordination, and continuing evaluation of practices and policies governing the acquisition and dissemination of intelligence, the pooling of resources, and the correlation of operational activities in the domestic field.

Although a substantial exchange of intelligence and research material between certain of the interested agencies already exists, much remains to be done in the following areas: (1) the preparation of coordinated intelligence estimates in a format useful for policy formulation; (2) the coordination of intelligence collection resources of the member agencies and the establishment of clear-cut priorities for the various agencies; and (3) the coordination of the operational activities of member agencies in developing the required intelligence.

II. Suggested Measures to Improve the Coordination of Domestic Intelligence Collection

It is believed that an interagency group on domestic intelligence should be established to effect coordination between the various member agencies. This group would define the specific requirements of the various agencies, provide regular evaluations of domestic intelligence, develop recommendations relative to policies governing operations in the field of domestic intelligence, and prepare periodic domestic intelligence estimates which would incorporate the results of the combined efforts of the entire intelligence community.

Membership in this group should consist of the principal officers responsible for domestic intelligence collection activities of the Federal Bureau of Investigation, the Central Intelligence Agency, the National Security Agency, the Defense Intelligence Agency, and the counterintelligence agencies of the Departments of the Army, Navy, and Air Force. In addition, an appropriate representative of the White House would have membership. The committee would report periodically to the White House, and a White House staff representative would coordinate intelligence originating with this committee in the same manner as Dr. Henry Kissinger, Assistant to the President, coordinates foreign intelligence on behalf of the President. The chairman would be appointed by the President.

This interagency group would have authority to determine appropriate staff requirements and to implement these requirements, subject to the approval of the President, in order to meet the responsibilities and objectives described above.

Decision: Permanent Interagency Group

_____ An ad hoc group consisting of the FBI, CIA, NSA, DIA, and the military counterintelligence agencies should be appointed and should serve as long as the President deems necessary, to provide evaluations of domestic intelligence, prepare periodic domestic intelligence estimates, and carry out the other objectives indicated above.

_____ A permanent committee consisting of the FBI, CIA, NSA, DIA, and the military counterintelligence agencies should be appointed to provide evaluations of domestic intelligence, prepare periodic domestic intelligence estimates, and carry out the other objectives indicated above.

_____ No further action required.

_____ More information is needed.

Note: The FBI is opposed to the creation of a permanent committee for the purpose of providing evaluations of domestic intelligence, however the FBI would approve of preparing periodic domestic intelligence estimates.

Tom Charles Huston
Memorandum and Recommendations to H. R. Haldeman
Accompanying the Special Report of the
Interagency Committee on Intelligence
July 1970

New York Times Staff, eds., *The Watergate Hearings: Break-in and Cover-up* (New York, 1973), 748-55.

TOP SECRET
Memorandum for: H. R. Haldeman
From: Tom Charles Huston
Subject: Domestic intelligence review

1. Background

A working group consisting of the top domestic intelligence officials of the FBI, CIA, DIA, NAS, and each of the military services met regularly throughout June to discuss the problems outlined by the President and to draft the attached report. The discussions were frank and the quality of work first-rate. Cooperation was excellent, and all were delighted that an opportunity was finally at hand to address themselves jointly to the serious internal security threat which exists.

I participated in all meetings, but restricted my involvement to keeping the committee on the target the President established. My impression that the report would be more accurate and the recommendations more helpful if the agencies were allowed wide latitude in expressing their opinions and working out arrangements which they felt met the President's requirements consistent with the resources and missions of the member agencies.

2. Mr. Hoover

I went into this exercise fearful that C.I.A. would refuse to cooperate. In fact, Dick Helms [Director of Central Intelligence] was most cooperative and helpful, and the only stumbling block was Mr. Hoover. He attempted at the first meeting to divert the committee from operational problems and redirect its mandate to the preparation of another analysis of existing intelligence. I declined to acquiesce in this approach, and succeeded in getting the committee back on target.

When the working group completed its report, Mr. Hoover refused to go along with a single conclusion drawn or support a single recommendation made. His position was twofold:

(1) Current operations are perfectly satisfactory and (2) No one has any business commenting on procedures he has established for the collection of intelligence by the F.B.I. He attempted to modify the body of the report, but I successfully opposed it on the grounds that the report was the conclusion of all the agencies, not merely the F.B.I. Mr. Hoover then entered his objections as footnotes to the report. Cumulatively, his footnotes suggest that he is perfectly satisfied with current procedures and is opposed to any changes whatsoever. As you will note from the report, his objections are generally inconsistent and frivolous—most express concern about possible embarrassment to the intelligence community (i.e., Hoover) from public disclosure of clandestine operations.

Admiral Gaylor and General Bennett were greatly displeased by Mr. Hoover's attitude and his insistence on footnoting objections. They wished to raise a formal protest and sign the report only with the understanding that they opposed the footnotes. I prevailed upon them not to do so since it would only aggravate Mr. Hoover and further complicate our efforts. They graciously agreed to go along with my suggestion in order to avoid a nasty scene and jeopardize the possibility of positive action resulting from the report. I assured them that their opinion would be brought to the attention of the President.

3. Threat Assessment

The first 23 pages of the report constitute an assessment of the existing internal security threat, our current intelligence coverage of this threat, and areas where our coverage is inadequate. All agencies concurred in this assessment, and it serves to explain the importance of expanded intelligence collection efforts.

4. Restraints on Intelligence Collection

Part Two of the report discusses specific operational restraints which currently restrict the capability of the intelligence community to collect the types of information necessary to deal effectively with the internal security threat. The report explains the nature of the restraints and sets out the arguments for and against modifying them. My concern was to afford the President the strongest arguments on both sides of the question so that he could make an informed decision as to the future course of action to be followed by the intelligence community.

I might point out that of all the individuals involved in the preparation and consideration of this report, only Mr. Hoover is satisfied with existing procedures.

Those individuals within the F.B.I. who have day-to-day responsibilities for domestic intelligence operations privately disagree with Mr. Hoover and believe that it is imperative that changes in operating procedures be initiated at once.

I am attaching to this memorandum my recommendations on the decision the President should make with regard to these operational restraints. Although the report sets forth the pros and cons on each issue, it may be helpful to add my specific recommendations and the reasons therefore in the event the President has some doubts on a specific course of action.

5. Improvement in Interagency Coordination

All members of the committee and its working group, with the exception of Mr. Hoover, believe that it is imperative that a continuing mechanism be established to effectuate the coordination of domestic intelligence efforts and the evaluation of domestic intelligence data. In the past there has been no systematic effort to mobilize the full resources of the intelligence community in the internal security area and there has been no mechanism for preparing community-wide domestic intelligence estimates such as is done in the foreign intelligence area by the United States Intelligence Board. Domestic intelligence information coming into the White House has been fragmentary and unevaluated. We have not had for example, a community-wide estimate of what we might expect short- or long-term in the cities or on the campuses or within the military establishment.

Unlike most of the bureaucracy, the intelligence community welcomes direction and leadership from the White House. There appears to be agreement, with the exception of Mr. Hoover, that effective coordination within the community is possible only if there is direction from the White House. Moreover, the community is pleased that the White House is finally showing interest in their activities and an awareness of the threat which they so acutely recognize.

I believe that we will be making a major contribution to the security of the country if we can work out an arrangement which provides for institutionalized coordination within the intelligence community and effective leadership from the White House.

6. Implementation of the President's Decisions

If the President should decide to lift some of the current restrictions and if he should decide to authorize a formalized domestic intelligence structure, I would recommend the following steps:

(A) Mr. Hoover should be called in privately for a stroking session at which the President explains the decision he has made, thanks Mr. Hoover for his candid advice and past cooperation, and indicates he is counting on Edgar's cooperation in implementing the new decisions.

(B) Following this Hoover session, the same individuals who were present at the initial session in the Oval Office should be invited back to meet with the President. At that time, the President should thank them for the report, announce his decisions, indicate his desires for future activity, and present each with an autographed copy of the photo of the first meeting which Ollie took.

(C) An official memorandum setting forth the precise decisions of the President should be prepared so that there can be no misunderstanding. We should also incorporate a review procedure which will enable us to ensure that the decisions are fully implemented.

I hate to suggest a further imposition on the President's time, but think these steps will be necessary to pave over some of the obvious problems which may arise if the President decides, as I hope he will, to overrule Mr. Hoover's objections to many of the proposals made in this report. Having seen the President in action with Mr. Hoover, I am confident that he can handle this situation in such a way that we can get what we want without putting Edgar's nose out of joint. At the same time, we can capitalize on the goodwill the President has built up with the other principals and minimize the risk that they may feel they are being forced to take a back seat to Mr. Hoover.

7. Conclusion

I am delighted with the substance of this report and believe it is a first-rate job. I have great respect for the integrity, loyalty, and competence of the men who are operationally responsible for internal security matters and believe that we are on the threshold of an unexcelled opportunity to cope with a very serious problem in its germinal stages when we can avoid the necessity for harsh measures by acting swift, discreetly, and decisively to deflect the threat before it reaches alarming proportions.

I might add, in conclusion, that it is my personal opinion that Mr. Hoover will not hesitate to accede to any decision which the President makes, and the President should not, therefore, be reluctant to overrule Mr. Hoover's objections. Mr. Hoover is set in his ways and can be bull-headed as hell, but he is a loyal trooper. Twenty years ago he would never have raised the type of objections he has here, but he's getting old and worried about his legend. He makes life tough in this area, but not impossible—for he'll respond to direction by the President and that is all we need to set the domestic intelligence house in order.

OPERATIONAL RESTRAINTS ON INTELLIGENCE COLLECTION

A. Interpretive Restraint on Communications Intelligence

Recommendation:
Present interpretation should be broadened to permit and program for coverage by N.S.A. [National Security Agency] of the communications of U.S. citizens using international facilities.

Rationale:

The F.B.I. does not have the capability to monitor international communications. N.S.A. is currently doing so on a restricted basis, and the information is particularly useful to the White House and it would be to our disadvantage to allow the F.B.I. to determine what N.S.A. should do in this area without regard to our own requirements. No appreciable risk is involved in this course of action.

B. Electronic Surveillance and Penetrations

Recommendation:

Present procedures should be changed to permit intensification of coverage of individuals and groups on the United States who pose a major threat to the internal security.

Also, present procedures should be changed to permit intensification of coverage of foreign nationals and diplomatic establishments in the United States of interest to the intelligence community.

At the present time, less than [unclear] electronic penetrations are operative. This includes coverage of the C.P.U.S.A. [Communist Party, U.S.A.] and organized crime targets, with only a few authorized against subject of pressing internal security interest.

Mr. Hoover's statement that the F.B.I. would not oppose other agencies seeking approval for the operating electronic surveillances is gratuitous since no other agencies have the capability.

Everyone knowledgeable in the field, with the exception of Mr. Hoover, concurs that existing coverage is grossly inadequate. C.I.A. and N.S.A. note that this is particularly true of diplomatic establishments, and we have learned at the White House that it is also true of New Left groups.

C. Mail Coverage

Recommendation:

Restrictions on legal coverage should be removed.

Also, present restrictions on covert coverage should be relaxed on selected targets of priority foreign intelligence and internal security interest.

Rationale:

There is no valid argument against use of legal mail covers except Mr. Hoover's concern that the civil liberties people may become upset. This risk is surely an acceptable one and hardly serious enough to justify denying ourselves a valuable and legal intelligence tool.

Covert coverage is illegal and there are serious risks involved. However, the advantages to be derived from its use outweigh the risks. This technique is particularly valuable in identifying espionage agents and other contacts of foreign intelligence services.

D. Surreptitious Entry

Recommendation:

Present restrictions should be modified to permit procurement of vitally needed foreign cryptographic material.

Also, present restrictions should be modified to permit selective use of this technique against other urgent security targets.

Rationale:

Use of this technique is clearly illegal: it amounts to burglary. It is also highly risky and could result in great embarrassment if exposed. However, it is also the most fruitful tool and can produce the type of intelligence which cannot be obtained in any other fashion.

The F.B.I., in Mr. Hoover's younger days, used to conduct such operations with great success and with no exposure. The information secured was invaluable.

N.S.A. has a particular interest since it is possible by this technique to secure material with which N.S.A. can break foreign cryptographic codes. We spend millions of dollars attempting to break these codes by machine. One successful surreptitious entry can do the job successfully at no dollar cost.

Surreptitious entry of facilities occupied by subversive elements can turn up information about identities, methods of operation, and other invaluable investigative information which is not otherwise obtainable. This technique would be particularly helpful if used against the Weathermen and Black Panthers.

The deployment of the executive protector force has increased the risk of surreptitious entry of diplomatic establishments. However, it is the belief of all except Mr. Hoover that the technique can still be successfully used on a selective basis.

E. Development of Campus Sources

Recommendation:

Present restrictions should be relaxed to permit expanded coverage of violence-prone campus and student-related groups.

Also, C.I.A. coverage of American students (and others) traveling or living abroad should be increased.

Rationale:

The F.B.I. does not currently recruit any campus sources among individuals below 21 years of age. This dramatically reduces the pool from which sources may be drawn. Mr. Hoover is afraid of a young student surfacing in the press as an F.B.I. source, although the reaction in the past to such events has been minimal. After all, everyone assumes the F.B.I. has such sources.

The campus is the battleground of the revolutionary protest movement. It is impossible to gather effective intelligence about the movement unless we have campus sources. The risk of exposure is minimal, and where exposure occurs the adverse publicity is moderate and short-lived. It is a price we must be willing to pay for effective coverage of the campus scene. The intelligence community, with the exception of Mr. Hoover, feels strongly that it is imperative the [unclear] increase the number of campus sources this fall in order to forestall widespread violence.

C.I.A. claims there are not existing restraints on its coverage of overseas activities of U.S. nationals. However, this coverage has been grossly inadequate since 1965 and an explicit directive to increase coverage is required.

F. Use of Military Undercover Agents

Recommendation:
Present restrictions should be retained.

Rationale:
The intelligence community is agreed that the risks of lifting these restraints are greater than the value of any possible intelligence which would be acquired by doing so.

BUDGET AND MANPOWER RESTRICTIONS

Recommendation:
Each agency should submit a detailed estimate as to projected manpower needs and other costs in the event the various investigative restraints herein are lifted.

Rationale:
In the event that the above recommendations are concurred in, it will be necessary to modify existing budgets to provide the money and manpower necessary for their implementation. The intelligence community has been badly hit in the budget squeeze. (I suspect the foreign intelligence operations are in the same shape) and it maybe will be necessary to make some modifications. The projected figures should be reasonable, but will be subject to individual review if this recommendation is accepted.

MEASURES TO IMPROVE
DOMESTIC INTELLIGENCE OPERATIONS

Recommendation:
A permanent committee consisting of the F.B.I., C.I.A., N.S.A., D.I.A. [Defense Intelligence Agency] and the military counterintelligence agencies should be appointed to provide evaluations of domestic intelligence estimates, and carry out the other objectives specified in the report.

Rationale:
The need for increased coordination, joint estimates, and responsiveness to the White House is obvious to the intelligence community. There are a number of

operational problems which need to be worked out since Mr. Hoover is fearful of any mechanism which might jeopardize his autonomy. C.I.A. would prefer an ad hoc committee to see how the system works, but other members believe that this would merely delay the establishment of effective coordination and joint operations. The value of lifting intelligence collection restraints is proportional to the availability of joint operations and evaluation, and the establishment of this interagency group is considered imperative.

A top secret memorandum to Huston from Haldeman on July 14, 1970 indicated that the President had approved his recommendations, with the exception of his proposals for implementing the decisions. Huston had suggested that Hoover be called to the Oval Office personally by the President for a "stroking session," so that "we can get what we want without putting Edgar's nose out of joint."[59] He also asserted at the end of his memorandum that Hoover would fall in line if the President insisted, because he believed that 20 years ago Hoover would not have raised his objections, "but he's getting old and worried about his legend."[60] It should be noted that not only Nixon, but the head of the CIA and the general and admiral in charge of intelligence in the Defense Department and the National Security Council were all strongly in favor of this gestapo-like operation, according to Huston.

H. R. Haldeman
Memorandum to Tom Charles Huston on his
Domestic Intelligence Gathering Recommendations
July 14, 1970

Statement of Information, Book VII, Part 1, 447.

TOP SECRET
Memorandum for: Mr. Huston
Subject: Domestic Intelligence Review

The recommendations you have proposed as a result of the review have been approved by the President.

He does not, however, want to follow the procedure you outlined on page 4 of your memorandum regarding implementation. He would prefer that the thing simply be put into motion on the basis of this approval.

The formal official memorandum should, of course, be prepared and that should be the device by which to carry it out.

I realize this is contrary to your feeling as to the best way to get this done. If you feel very strongly that this procedure won't work you had better let me know and we'll take another stab at it. Otherwise let's go ahead.

H. R. Haldeman

Nixon may have made a mistake in not inviting J. Edgar Hoover in for Huston's suggested "stroking session." Following the President's directions, Huston sent to each member of the Interagency Intelligence Committee a copy of a decision memorandum, suggested and approved by the President, which incorporated Huston's recommendations as final decisions, despite Hoover's objections to lifting existing restraints on intelligence gathering. This was done without approaching Hoover individually or reconvening the committee, as Huston had suggested.

Tom Charles Huston
Decision Memorandum to Members of the
Interagency Committee on Intelligence
July 23, 1970

The Watergate Hearings, 756-59.

TOP SECRET
Handle via Comint Channels Only
Subject: Domestic Intelligence

The President has carefully studied the special report of the Interagency Committee on Intelligence (ad hoc) and made the following decisions:

1. Interpretive Restraint on Communications Intelligence

National Security Council Intelligence Directive Number 6 (NSCID-6) is to be interpreted to permit N.S.A. to program for coverage and communications of U.S. citizens using international facilities.

2. Electronic Surveillances and Penetrations

The intelligence community is directed to intensify coverage of individuals and groups in the United States who pose a major threat to the internal security. Also, coverage of foreign nationals and diplomatic establishments in the United States of interest to the intelligence community is to be intensified.

3. Mail Coverage

Restrictions on legal coverage are to be removed, restrictions on covert coverage are to be relaxed to permit use of this technique on selected targets of priority foreign intelligence and internal security interest.

4. Surreptitious Entry

Restraints on the use of surreptitious entry are to be removed. The technique is to be used to permit procurement of vitally needed foreign cryptographic material and against other urgent and high priority internal security targets.

5. Development of Campus Sources

Coverage of violence-prone campus and student-related groups is to be increased. All restraints which limit this coverage are to be removed. Also, C.I.A. coverage of American students (and others) traveling or living abroad is to be increased.

6. Use of Military Undercover Agents

Present restrictions are to be retained.

7. Budget and Manpower

Each agency is to submit a detailed estimate as to projected manpower needs and other costs required to implement the above decisions.

8. Domestic Intelligence Operations

A committee consisting of the directors or other appropriate representatives appointed by the directors, of the F.B.I., C.I.A., N.S.A., D.I.A., and the military counterintelligence agencies is to be constituted effective August 1, 1970, to provide evaluations of domestic intelligence, prepare periodic domestic intelligence estimates, carry out the other objectives specified in the report, and perform such other duties as the President shall, from time to time, assign. The director of the F.B.I. shall serve as chairman of the committee. Further details on the organization and operations of this committee are set forth in an attached memorandum.

The President has directed that each addressee submit a detailed report, due on September 1, 1970, on the steps taken to implement these decisions. Further such periodic reports will be requested as circumstances merit.

The President is aware that procedural problems may arise in the course of implementing these decisions. However, he is anxious that such problems be resolved with maximum speed and minimum misunderstanding. Any difficulties which may arise should be brought to my immediate attention in order that an appropriate solution may be found and the President's directives implemented in a manner consistent with his objectives.

Tom Charles Huston

ORGANIZATION AND OPERATIONS OF THE INTERAGENCY GROUP ON DOMESTIC INTELLIGENCE AND INTERNAL SECURITY (IAG)

1. Membership

The membership shall consist of representatives of the F.B.I., C.I.A., D.I.A., N.S.A., and the counterintelligence agencies of the Departments of the Army, Navy, and Air Force. To insure the high level consideration of issues and problems which the President expects to be before the group, the directors of the respective agencies should serve personally. However, if necessary and appropriate, the director of a member agency may designate another individual to serve in his place.

2. Chairman

The director of the F.B.I. shall serve as chairman. He may designate another individual from his agency as the F.B.I. representative on the group.

3. Observers

The purpose of the group is to effectuate community-wide coordination and secure the benefits of community-wide analysis and estimating. When problems arise which involve areas of interest to agencies or departments not members of the group, they shall be invited, at the discretion of the group, to join the group as observers and participants in those discussions of interest to them. Such agencies and departments include the Departments of State (I & R, Passport); Treasury (I.R.S., Customs); Justice (B.N.D.D., Community Relations Service); and such other agencies which may have investigative or law enforcement responsibilities touching on domestic intelligence or internal security matters.

4. White House Liaison

The President has assigned to Tom Charles Huston staff responsibility for domestic intelligence and internal security affairs. He will participate in all activities of the group as the personal representative of the President.

5. Staffing

The group will establish such subcommittee or working groups as it deems appropriate. It will also determine and implement such staffing requirements as it may deem necessary to enable it to carry out its responsibilities, subject to the approval of the President.

6. Duties

The group will have the following duties:

(A) Define the specific requirements of member agencies of the intelligence community.

(B) Effect close, direct coordination between member agencies.

(C) Provide regular evaluations of domestic intelligence.

(D) Review policies governing operations in the field of domestic intelligence and develop recommendations.

(E) Prepare periodic domestic intelligence estimates which incorporate the results of the combined efforts of the intelligence community.

(F) Perform such other duties as the President may from time to time assign.

7. Meetings

The group shall meet at the call of the chairman, a member agency, or the White House representative.

8. Security

Knowledge of the existence and purposes of the group shall be limited on a strict "need to know" basis. Operations of, and papers originating with, the group shall be classified "top secret handle via Comint channels only."

9. Other Procedures

The group shall establish such other procedures as it believes appropriate to the implementation of the duties set forth above.

All of these discussions and passing of memoranda had bypassed the attorney general, and when he was informed of the President's decisions he joined with Hoover in requesting a reconsideration. As a result, the decision memorandum was quickly withdrawn by the White House and Huston was shortly thereafter removed as the liaison person and replaced by John Dean. Dean decided upon a much lower profile for the whole operation and with Huston out of the picture, he was able to smooth things over. Relegated to the sidelines, Huston continued to struggle for a *1984*-type intelligence unit. In a final memorandum to Haldeman, he castigated J. Edgar Hoover for being able to veto the President's initial decision to go along with his recommendations. What is interesting about this and other Huston memoranda is how accurately they reflect the real attitudes of the Nixon administration and how, regardless of the formal disposition of Huston's recommendations and his own position in the White House, in the end his advice prevailed. Nixon, Haldeman, Ehrlichman and Colson later gave up on the FBI and mounted their own intelligence operations, uninhibited by the restraints which J. Edgar Hoover had wanted to apply. Tom Charles Huston proved a prophet unhonored in his own administration.

Huston's thinking on this problem is fascinating. He was a young conservative idealogue from Logansport, Indiana, a former president of the Young Americans for Freedom, who served his army time as an intelligence officer in the Pentagon. In retrospect, he views Hoover's opposition to and influence in overthrowing his extensive counterintelligence plan as the critical event leading to Watergate. Had Nixon fought for the Huston plan, which would have authorized this frightening secret police operation under the cloak of the powerful heads of the four agencies— the FBI, the CIA, the Defense Department and the National Security Council— Huston argues, he would never have had to create his own undercover agency to conduct the break-ins and leave himself open to the exposure of Watergate.[61]

Tom Charles Huston
Memorandum to H. R. Haldeman on
Domestic Intelligence Gathering
August 5, 1970

Statement of Information, Book VII, Part 1, 480-84.

TOP SECRET
Handle via Comint Channels Only
Eyes Only
Memorandum for: H. R. Haldeman
From: Tom Charles Huston
Subject: Domestic Intelligence

In anticipation of your meeting with Mr. Hoover and the Attorney General, I would like to pass on these thoughts:

1. More than the FBI is involved in this operation. NSA, DIA, CIA, and the military services all have a great stake and a great interest. All of these agencies supported the options selected by the President. For your private information, so did all the members of Mr. Hoover's staff who worked on the report (he'd fire them if he knew this).

3. We are not getting the type of hard intelligence we need at the White House. We will not get it until greater effort is made through community-wide coordination to dig out the information by using all the resources potentially available. It is, of course, a matter of balancing the obvious risks against the desired results. I thought we balanced these risks rather objectively in the report, and Hoover is escalating the risks in order to cloak his determination to continue to do business as usual.

4. At some point, Hoover has to be told who is President. He has become totally unreasonable and his conduct is detrimental to our domestic intelligence operations. In the past two weeks, he has terminated all FBI liaison with NSA, DIA, the military services, Secret Service—everyone except the White House. He terminated liaison with CIA in May. This is bound to have a crippling effect upon the entire community and is contrary to his public assurance to the President at the meeting that there was close and effective coordination and cooperation within the intelligence community. It is important to remember that the entire intelligence

community knows that the President made a positive decision to go ahead and Hoover has now succeeded in forcing a review. If he gets his way it is going to look like he is more powerful than the President. He had his say in the footnotes and RN decided against him. That should close the matter and I can't understand why the AG is a party to reopening it. All of us are going to look damn silly in the eyes of Helms, Gayler, Bennett, and the military chiefs if Hoover can unilaterally reverse a Presidential decision based on a report that many people worked their asses off to prepare and which, on its merits, was a first-rate, objective job.

5. The biggest risk we could take, in my opinion, is to continue to regard the violence on the campus and in the cities as a temporary phenomenon which will simply go away as soon as the Scranton Commission files its report. The one statement that Rennie Davis made at HEW which I thought made sense was that the Attorney General was kidding himself when he said the campuses would be quiet this fall. Davis predicted that at least 30 would be closed down in September. I don't like to make predictions, but I am not at all convinced, on the basis of the intelligence I have seen, that we are anywhere near over the hump on this problem, and I am convinced that the potential for even greater violence is present, and we have a positive obligation to take every step within our power to prevent it.

6. Hoover can be expected to raise the following points in your meeting:

(a) "Our present efforts are adequate." The answer is, bullshit! This is particularly true with regard to FBI campus coverage.

(b) "The risks are too great; these folks are going to get the President into trouble and RN had better listen to me." The answer is that we have considered the risks, we believe they are acceptable and justified under the circumstances. We are willing to weigh each exceptionally sensitive operation on its merits, but the Director of the FBI is paid to take risks where the security of the country is at stake. Nothing we propose to do has not been done in the past—and in the past it was always done successfully.

(c) "I don't have the personnel to do the job the President wants done." The answer is (1) he has the people and/or (2) he can get them.

(d) "I don't object to NSA conducting surreptitious entry if they want to." The answer is that NSA doesn't have the people, can't get them, has no authority to get them, and shouldn't have to get them. It is an FBI job.

(e) "If we do these things the 'jackels of the press' and the ACLU will find out; we can't avoid leaks." Answer: We can avoid leaks by using trained, trusted agents and restricting knowledge of sensitive operations on a strict need to know basis. We do this on other sensitive operations every day.

(f) "If I have to do these things, the Attorney General will have to approve them in writing." This is up to the AG, but I would tell Hoover that he has been instructed to do them by the President and he is to do them on that authority. He needn't look for a scape goat. He has his authority from the President and he doesn't need a written memo from the AG. To maintain security, we should avoid written communications in this area.

(g) "We don't need an Inter-Agency Committee on Intelligence Operations because (1) we're doing fine right now—good coordination, etc.—and (2) there are other existing groups which can handle this assignment." The answer is that we are doing lousy right now and there aren't other groups which can do the job we have in mind because: (1) they don't meet; (2) they don't have the people on them we want or have some people we don't want; (3) they don't have the authority to do what we want done; (4) ultimately this new operation will replace them; and (5) they aren't linked to the White House staff.

There are doubtless another dozen or so specious arguments that Hoover will raise, but they will be of similar quality. I hope that you will be able to convince the AG of the importance and necessity of getting Hoover to go along. We have worked for nearly a year to reach this point; others have worked far longer and had abandoned hope. I believe we are talking about the future of this country, for surely domestic violence and disorder threaten the very fabric of our society. Intelligence is not the cure, but it can provide the diagnosis that makes a cure possible. More importantly, it can provide us with the means to prevent the deterioration of the situation. Perhaps lowered voices and peace in Vietnam will defuse the tense situation we face, but I wouldn't want to rely on it exclusively.

There is this final point. For eighteen months we have watched people in this government ignore the President's orders, take actions to embarrass him, promote themselves at his expense, and generally make his job more difficult. It makes me fighting mad, and what Hoover is doing here is putting himself above the President. If he thought the Attorney General's advice should be solicited, he should have done so before the report was sent to the President. After all, Hoover was chairman of the committee and he could have asked the AG for his comments. But no, he didn't do so for it never occurred to him that the President would not agree with his footnoted objections. He thought all he had to do was put in a footnote and the matter was settled. He had absolutely no interest in the views of NSA, CIA, DIA, and the military services, and obviously he has little interest in our views, or apparently even in the decisions of the President. I don't see how we can tolerate this, but being a fatalist, if not a realist, I am prepared to accept the fact that we may have to do so.

Tom Charles Huston

Finally emerging after many weeks of weaving and dodging, President Nixon set forth the facts described above in an accurate fashion. However, he failed to note that he personally had approved the recommendations which Hoover turned down, or that these same intelligence methods which were declared illegal and vetoed by the FBI were used by members of his White House staff in cases not for the protection of legitimate national security interests, but rather the political objective of keeping the Nixon administration in power.

In the face of growing resentment and opposition to the war, it became more difficult for the Nixon administration to maintain an undeviating course in Vietnam. Concerned first about the presidential elections in 1972, the administration became almost paranoid in its efforts to protect itself from criticism and perhaps weakening or destroying any credibility of its opponents. President Nixon was correct in asserting that the Huston plan was never put into effect (although he had approved it), but that means little when one discovers that its recommendations were finally implemented, not by the Federal Bureau of Investigation, the police arm of the government, but by a group of patriotic ex-FBI and -CIA agents, who operated virtually without restraint and used methods and techniques common to the secret police of totalitarian regimes. They acted not merely to protect the national security interests of the United States, but rather to protect and advance the political interests of the Nixon administration.

The most flagrant example of these undercover intelligence techniques was in the pre-Watergate break-in of the office of Dr. Daniel Ellsberg's psychiatrist, Dr. Lewis Fielding. His files were ransacked in search of psychiatric material relating to Dr. Ellsberg. Ellsberg was, of course, the man who made the Pentagon Papers available to the press. In a long formal statement issued to the press in May 1973, Nixon cited national security concerns as the basis for creating the special investigations unit within the White House which staged the break-in, and he assumed overall responsibility for its activities; however, he denied any knowledge of "any illegal means to be used" in pursuit of its mission. His denial of any specific authorization of the break-in must be judged in relation to his earlier approval of general authority for investigative units to engage in surreptitious entry, in the face of the FBI's opposition to such methods.

President Richard M. Nixon
Statement on the Watergate Inquiry and
The Special Investigations Unit
May 22, 1973

The New York Times, May 23, 1973, 28,

Allegations surrounding the Watergate affair have so escalated that I feel a further statement from the President is required at this time.

A climate of sensationalism has developed in which even second- or third-hand hearsay charges are headlined as fact and repeated as fact.

Important national security operations which themselves had no connection with Watergate have become entangled in the case.

As a result, some national security information has already been made public through court orders, through the subpoenaing of documents and through testimony witnesses have given in judicial and Congressional proceedings. Other sensitive documents are now threatened with disclosure; continued silence about those operations would compromise rather than protect them, and would also serve to perpetuate a grossly distorted view—which recent partial disclosures have given—of the nature and purpose of those operations.

The purpose of this statement is threefold:

First, to set forth the facts about my own relationship to the Watergate matter.

Second, to place in some perspective some of the more sensational—and inaccurate—of the charges that have filled the headlines in recent days, and also some of the matters that are currently being discussed in Senate testimony and elsewhere.

Third, to draw the distinction between national security operations and the Watergate case. To put the other matters in perspective, it will be necessary to describe the national security operations first.

In citing these national security matters, it is not my intention to place a national security "cover" on Watergate, but rather to separate them out from Watergate—and at the same time to explain the context in which certain actions took place that were later misconstrued or misused.

Long before the Watergate break-in, three important national security operations took place which have subsequently become entangled in the Watergate case.

The first operation, begun in 1969, was a program of wiretaps. All were legal, under the authorities then existing. They were undertaken to find and stop serious national security leaks.

The second operation was a reassessment, which I ordered in 1970, of the adequacy of internal security measures. This resulted in a plan and a directive to strengthen our intelligence operations. They were protested by Mr. Hoover, and as a result of his protest they were not put into effect.

The third operation was the establishment, in 1971, of a special investigations unit in the White House. Its primary mission was to plug leaks of vital security information. I also directed this group to prepare an accurate history of certain crucial national security matters which occurred under prior Administrations, on which the Government's records were incomplete.

Here is the background of these three security operations initiated by my Administration.

By mid-1969, my Administration had begun a number of highly sensitive foreign policy initiatives. They were aimed at ending the war in Vietnam, achieving a settlement in the Middle East, limiting nuclear arms, and establishing new relationships among the great powers. These involved highly secret diplomacy. They were closely interrelated. Leaks of secret information about any one could endanger all.

Exactly that happened. News accounts appeared in 1969, which were obviously based on leaks—some of them extensive and detailed—by people having access to the most highly classified security materials.

There was no way to carry forward these diplomatic initiatives unless further leaks could be prevented. This required finding the source of the leaks.

In order to do this, a special program of wiretaps was instituted in mid-1969 and terminated in February, 1971. Fewer than 20 taps, of varying duration, were involved. They produced important leads that made it possible to tighten the security of highly sensitive materials.

I authorized this entire program. Each individual tap was undertaken in accordance with procedures legal at the time and in accord with long-standing precedent.

The persons who were subject to these wiretaps were determined through coordination among the director of the F.B.I., my assistant for national security affairs, and the Attorney General. Those wiretapped were selected on the basis of access to the information leaked, material in security files, and evidence that developed as the inquiry proceeded.

Information thus obtained was made available to senior officials responsible for national security matters in order to curtail further leaks.

In the spring and summer of 1970, another security problem reached critical proportions. In March a wave of bombings and explosions struck college campuses, and cities. There were 400 bomb threats in one 24-hour period in New York City. Rioting and violence on college campuses reached a new peak after the Cambodian operation and the tragedies at Kent State and Jackson State. The 1969-70 school year brought nearly 1,800 campus demonstrations, and nearly 250 cases of arson on campus. Many colleges closed. Gun battles between guerrilla-style groups and police were taking place. Some of the disruptive activities were receiving foreign support.

Complicating the task of maintaining security was the fact that, in 1966, certain types of undercover F.B.I. operations that had been conducted for many years had been suspended. This also had substantially impaired our ability to collect foreign intelligence information. At the same time, the relationships between the F.B.I. and other intelligence agencies had been deteriorating. By May, 1970, F.B.I. Director Hoover shut off his agency's liasion with the C.I.A. altogether.

On June 5, 1970, I met with the director of the F.B.I. (Mr. Hoover), the director of the Central Intelligence Agency (Mr. Richard Helms), the director of the Defense Intelligence Agency (Gen. Donald V. Bennett) and the director of the National Security Agency (Adm. Noel Gayler). We discussed the urgent need for better intelligence operations. I appointed Director Hoover as chairman of an interagency committee to prepare recommendations.

On June 25, the committee submitted a report which included specific options for expanded intelligence operations, and on July 23 the agencies were notified by memorandum of the options approved. After reconsideration, however, prompted by the opposition of Director Hoover, the agencies were notified five days later, on July 28, that the approval had been rescinded. The options initially approved had included resumption of certain intelligence operations which had been suspended in 1966. These in turn had included authorization for surreptitious entry—breaking and entering, in effect—on specified categories of targets in specified situations related to national security.

Because the approval was withdrawn before it had been implemented, the net result was that the plan for expanded intelligence activities never went into effect.

The documents spelling out this 1970 plan are extremely sensitive. They include—and are based upon—assessments of certain foreign intelligence capabilities and procedures, which of course must remain secret. It was this unused plan and related documents that John Dean removed from the White House and placed in a safe deposit box, giving the keys to Judge Sirica. The same plan, still unused, is being headlined today.

Coordination among our intelligence agencies continued to fall short of our national security needs. In July, 1970, having earlier discontinued the F.B.I.'s liaison with the C.I.A., Director Hoover ended the F.B.I.'s normal liaison with all other agencies except the White House. To help remedy this, an Intelligence Evaluation Committee was created in December, 1970. Its members included representatives of the White House, C.I.A., F.B.I., N.S.A., the Departments of Justice, Treasury, and Defense, and the Secret Service.

The Intelligence Evaluation Committee and its staff were instructed to improve coordination among the intelligence community and to prepare evaluations and estimates of domestic intelligence. I understand that its activities are now under investigation. I did not authorize nor do I have any knowledge of any illegal activity by this committee. If it went beyond its charter and did engage in any illegal activities, it was totally without my knowledge or authority.

On Sunday, June 13, 1971, The New York Times published the first installment of what came to be known as "the Pentagon papers." Not until a few hours before publication did any responsible Government official know that they had been stolen. Most officials did not know they existed. No senior official of the Government had read them or knew with certainty what they contained.

All the Government knew, at first, was that the papers comprised 47 volumes and some 7,000 pages, which had been taken from the most sensitive files of the Departments of State and Defense and the C.I.A., covering military and diplomatic moves in a war that was still going on.

Moreover, a majority of the documents published with the first three installments in The Times had not been included in the 47-volume study—raising serious questions about what and how much else might have been taken.

There was every reason to believe this was a security leak of unprecedented proportions.

It created a situation in which the ability of the Government to carry on foreign relations even in the best of circumstances could have been severely compromised. Other governments no longer knew whether they could deal with the United States in confidence. Against the background of the delicate negotiations the United States was then involved in on a number of fronts—with regard to Vietnam, China, the Middle East, nuclear arms limitations, U.S.-Soviet relations, and others—in which the utmost degree of confidentiality was vital, it posed a threat so grave as to require extraordinary actions.

Therefore during the week following the Pentagon papers publication, I approved the creation of a special investigations unit within the White House—which later came to be known as the "plumbers." This was a small group at the White House whose principal purpose was to stop security leaks and to investigate other sensitive security matters. I looked to John Ehrlichman for the supervision of this group.

Egil Krogh, Mr. Ehrlichman's assistant, was put in charge. David Young was added to this unit, as were E. Howard Hunt and G. Gordon Liddy.

The unit operated under extremely tight security rules. Its existence and functions were known only to a very few persons at the White House. These included Messrs. Haldeman, Ehrlichman and Dean.

At about the time the unit was created, Daniel Ellsberg was identified as the person who had given the Pentagon papers to The New York Times. I told Mr. Krogh that as a matter of first priority, the unit should find out all it could about

Mr. Ellsberg's associates and his motives. Because of the extreme gravity of the situation, and not then knowing what additional national secrets Mr. Ellsberg might disclose, I did impress upon Mr. Krogh the vital importance to the national security of his assignment. I did not authorize and had no knowledge of any illegal means to be used to achieve this goal.

However, because of the emphasis I put on the crucial importance of protecting the national security, I can understand how highly motivated individuals could have felt justified in engaging in specific activities that I would have disapproved had they been brought to my attention.

Consequently, as President, I must and do assume responsibility for such actions despite the fact that I, at no time approved or had knowledge of them.

I also assigned the unit a number of other investigatory matters, dealing in part with compiling an accurate record of events related to the Vietnam war, on which the Government's records were inadequate (many previous records having been removed with the change of Administrations) and which bore directly on the negotiations then in progress. Additional assignments included tracing down other national security leaks, including one that seriously compromised the United States negotiating position in the SALT talks.

The work of the unit tapered off around the end of 1971. The nature of its work was such that it involved matters that, from a national security standpoint, were highly sensitive then and remain so today.

These intelligence activities had no connection with the break-in of the Democratic headquarters, or the aftermath.

I considered it my responsibility to see that the Watergate investigation did not impinge adversely upon the national security area. For example, on April 18th, 1973, when I learned that Mr. Hunt, a former member of the special investigations unit at the White House, was to be questioned by the U.S. Attorney, I directed Assistant Attorney General Petersen to pursue every issue involving Watergate but to confine his investigation to Watergate and related matters and to stay out of national security matters. Subsequently, on April 25, 1973, Attorney General Kleindienst informed me that because the Government had clear evidence that Mr. Hunt was involved in the break-in of the office of the psychiatrist who had treated Mr. Ellsberg, he, the Attorney General, believed that despite the fact that no evidence had been obtained from Hunt's acts, a report should nevertheless be made to the court trying the Ellsberg case. I concurred, and directed that the information be transmitted to Judge Byrne immediately.

The burglary and bugging of the Democratic National Committee head-quarters came as a complete surprise to me. I had no inkling that any such illegal activities had been planned by persons associated with my campaign; if I had known, I would not have permitted it. My immediate reaction was that those guilty should be brought to justice and, with the five burglars themselves already in custody, I assumed that they would be.

Within a few days, however, I was advised that there was a possibility of C.I.A. involvement in some way.

It did seem to me possible that, because of the involvement of former C.I.A. personnel, and because of some of their apparent associations, the investigation could lead to the uncovering of covert C.I.A. operations totally unrelated to the Watergate break-in.

In addition, by this time, the name of Mr. Hunt had surfaced in connection with Watergate, and I was alerted to the fact that he had previously been a member of the special investigations unit in the White House. Therefore, I was also concerned that the Watergate investigation might well lead to an inquiry into the activities of the special investigations unit itself.

In this area, I felt it was important to avoid disclosure of the details of the national security matters with which the group was concerned. I knew that once the existence of the group became known, it would lead inexorably to a discussion of these matters, some of which remain, even today, highly sensitive.

I wanted justice done with regard to Watergate; but in the scale of national priorities with which I had to deal—and not at that time having any idea of the extent of political abuse which Watergate reflected—I also had to be deeply concerned with insuring that neither the covert operations of the C.I.A. nor the operations of the special investigations unit should be compromised. Therefore, I instructed Mr. Haldeman and Mr. Ehrlichman to insure that the investigation of the break-in not expose either an unrelated covert operation of the C.I.A. or the activities of the White House investigations unit—and to see that this was personally coordinated between General Walters, the deputy director of the C.I.A., and Mr. Gray of the F.B.I. It was certainly not my intent, nor my wish, that the investigation of the Watergate break-in or of related acts be impeded in any way.

On July 6, 1972, I telephoned the acting director of the F.B.I., L. Patrick Gray, to congratulate him on his successful handling of the hijacking of a Pacific Southwest Airlines plane the previous day. During the conversation Mr. Gray discussed with me the progress of the Watergate investigation, and I asked him whether he had talked with General Walters. Mr. Gray said that he had, and that General Walters had assured him that the C.I.A. was not involved. In the discussion, Mr. Gray suggested that the matter of Watergate might lead higher. I told him to press ahead with his investigation.

It now seems that later, through whatever complex of individual motives and possible misunderstandings, there were apparently wide-ranging efforts to limit the investigation or to conceal the possible involvement of members of the Administration and the campaign committee.

I was not aware of any such efforts at the time. Neither, until after I began my own investigation, was I aware of any fund-raising for defendants convicted at the break-in at Democratic headquarters, much less authorize any such fund-raising. Nor did I authorize any offer of executive clemency for any of the defendants.

In the weeks and months that followed Watergate, I asked for, and received, repeated assurances that Mr. Dean's own investigation (which included reviewing files and sitting in on F.B.I. interviews with White House personnel) had cleared everyone then employed by the White House of involvement.

In summary, then:

(1) I had no prior knowledge of the Watergate bugging operation, or of any illegal surveillance activities for political purposes.

(2) Long prior to the 1972 campaign, I did set in motion certain internal security measures, including legal wiretaps, which I felt were necessary from a national security standpoint and, in the climate then prevailing, also necessary from a domestic security standpoint.

(3) People who had been involved in the national security operations later, without my knowledge or approval, undertook illegal activities in the political campaign of 1972.

(4) Elements of the early post-Watergate reports led me to suspect, incorrectly, that the C.I.A. had been in some way involved. They also led me to surmise, correctly, that since persons originally recruited for covert national security activities had participated in Watergate, an unrestricted investigation of Watergate might lead to and expose those covert national security operations.

(5) I sought to prevent the exposure of these covert national security activities, while encouraging those conducting the investigation to pursue their inquiry into the Watergate itself. I so instructed my staff, the Attorney General and the acting director of the F.B.I.

(6) I also specifically instructed Mr. Haldeman and Mr. Ehrlichman to insure that the F.B.I. would not carry its investigation into areas that might compromise these covert national security activities or those of the C.I.A.

(7) At no time did I authorize or know about any offer of executive clemency for the Watergate defendants. Neither did I know, until the time of my own investigation, of any efforts to provide them with funds.

With hindsight, it is apparent that I should have given more heed to the warning signals I received along the way about a Watergate cover-up and less to the reassurances.

With hindsight, several other things also become clear:

With respect to campaign practices, and also with respect to campaign finances, it should now be obvious that no campaign in history has ever been subjected to the kind of intensive and searching inquiry that has been focused on the campaign waged in my behalf in 1972.

It is clear that unethical, as well as illegal, activities took place in the course of that campaign.

None of these took place with my specific approval or knowledge. To the extent that I may in any way have contributed to the climate in which they took place, I did not intend to; to the extent that I failed to prevent them, I should have been more vigilant.

It was to help insure against any repetition of this in the future that last week I proposed the establishment of a top-level, bipartisan, independent commission to recommend a comprehensive reform of campaign laws and practices. Given the priority I believe it deserves, such reform should be possible before the next Congressional elections in 1974.

It now appears that there were persons who may have gone beyond my directives, and sought to expand on my efforts to protect the national security operations in order to cover up any involvement they or certain others might have had in Watergate. The extent to which this is true, and who may have participated and to what degree, are questions that it would not be proper to address here. The proper forum for settling these matters is in the court.

To the extent that I have been able to determine what probably happened in the tangled course of this affair, on the basis of my own recollections and of the conflicting accounts and evidence that I have seen, it would appear that one factor at work was that at critical points various people, each with his own perspective and his own responsibilities, saw the same situation with different eyes and heard the same words with different ears. What might have seemed insignificant to one seemed significant to another; what one saw in terms of public responsibility, another saw in terms of political opportunity; and mixed through it all, I am sure, was a concern on the part of many that the Watergate scandal should not be allowed to get in the way of what the Administration sought to achieve.

The truth about Watergate should be brought out in an orderly way, recognizing that the safeguards of judicial procedure are designed to find the truth, not to hide the truth.

With his selection of Archibald Cox—who served both President Kennedy and President Johnson as Solicitor General—as the special supervisory prosecutor for matters related to the case, Attorney General-designate Richardson has demonstrated his own determination to see the truth brought out. In this effort he has my full support.

Considering the number of persons involved in this case whose testimony might be subject to a claim of executive privilege, I recognize that a clear definition of that claim has become central to the effort to arrive at the truth.

Accordingly, executive privilege will not be invoked as to any testimony concerning possible criminal conduct or discussions of possible criminal conduct, in the matters presently under investigation, including the Watergate affair and the alleged cover-up.

I want to emphasize that this statement is limited to my own recollections of what I said and did relating to security and to the Watergate. I have specifically avoided any attempt to explain what other parties may have said and done. My own information on those other matters is fragmentary, and to some extent contradictory. Additional information may be forthcoming of which I am unaware. It is also my understanding that the information which has been conveyed to me has also become available to those prosecuting these matters. Under such circumstances, it would be prejudicial and unfair of me to render my opinions on the activities of others; those judgments must be left to the judicial process, our best hope for achieving the just result that we all seek.

As more information is developed, I have no doubt that more questions will be raised. To the extent that I am able, I shall also seek to set forth the facts as known to me with respect to those questions.

The "plumbers unit" which conducted the break-in of Dr. Fielding's office was indicted by the Watergate grand jury and the case came before Judge Gerhard A. Gesell. On May 24, 1974 Judge Gesell handed down the following decision. It is a ringing defense of the fourth amendment of the Constitution and a decisive document in the history of Watergate.

District Judge Gerhard A. Gesell
Decision of the Court in
United States *v*. John Ehrlichman, et al.
May 24, 1974

376 F. Supp. 29 (D.D.C. 1974).

Five defendants stand indicted for conspiring to injure a Los Angeles psychiatrist in the enjoyment of his Fourth Amendment rights by entering his offices without a warrant for the purpose of obtaining the doctor's medical records relating to one of his patients, a Daniel Ellsberg, then under Federal indictment for revealing top secret documents. They now claim that broad pretrial discovery into the alleged national security aspects of this case is essential to the presentation of their defense, in that it will establish (1) that the break-in was legal under the Fourth Amendment because the President authorized it for reasons of national security, and (2) that even in the absence of such authorization the national security information available to the defendants at that time led them to the good-faith, reasonable belief that the break-in was legal and justified in the national interest. The Court has carefully considered these assertions, which have been fully briefed and argued over a two-day period, and finds them to be unpersuasive as a matter of law. [The Court also rejects the claim that this indictment must be dismissed because the judiciary has no right to risk the public disclosure of the sensitive national security information required for the prosecution and defense of the case. Totten v. United States, 92 U.S. 105, 23 L.Ed. 605 (1875), cited by defendants, is inapplicable to criminal actions and has been modified by a century of legal experience, which teaches that the courts have broad authority to inquire into national security matters so long as proper safeguards are applied to avoid unwarranted disclosures. Nixon v. Sirica, 487 F.2d 700, 713 (D.C. Cir. 1973). *See also* United States v. Reynolds, 345 U.S. 1, 73 S.Ct. 528, 97 L.Ed. 727 (1953). Footnote in original.]

In approaching these issues, it is well to recall the origins of the Fourth Amendment and the crucial role that it has played in the development of our constitutional democracy. That Amendment provides:

The right of the people to be secure in their persons, houses, papers, and effects, against unreasonable searches and seizures, shall not be violated, and no Warrants shall issue, but upon probable cause, supported by Oath or affirmation, and particularly describing the place to be searched, and the persons or things to be seized.

The Fourth Amendment protects the privacy of citizens against unreasonable and unrestrained intrusion by Government officials and their agents. It is not theoretical. It lies at the heart of our free society. As the Supreme Court recently remarked, "no right is held more sacred." Terry v. Ohio, 392 U.S. 1, 9, 88 S.Ct. 1868, 1873, 20 L.Ed. 2d 889 (1968), quoting from Union Pacific R. Co. v. Botsford, 141 U.S. 250, 251, 11 S.Ct. 1000, 35 L.Ed. 734 (1891). Indeed, the American Revolution was sparked in part by the complaints of the colonists against the issuance of writs of assistance, pursuant to which the King's revenue officers conducted unrestricted, indiscriminate searches of persons and homes to uncover contraband. James Otis' famous argument in *Lechmere's Case*, challenging the writ as a "monster of oppression" and a "remnant of Star Chamber tyranny," [Otis' argument was abstracted by John Adams. *See* Legal Papers of John Adams 134-44 Footnote in original.] sowed one of the seeds of the coming rebellion. The Fourth Amendment was framed against this background; and every state in the Union, by its own constitution, has since reinforced the protections and the security which that Amendment was designed to achieve.

Thus the security of one's privacy against arbitrary intrusion by governmental authorities has proven essential to our concept of ordered liberty. When officials have attempted to justify law enforcement methods that ignore the strictures of this Amendment on grounds of necessity, such excuses have proven fruitless, for the Constitution brands such conduct as lawless, irrespective of the end to be served. Throughout the years the Supreme Court of the United States, regardless of changes in its composition or contemporary issues, has steadfastly applied the Amendment to protect a citizen against the warrantless invasion of his home or office, except under carefully delineated emergency circumstances. Coolidge v. New Hampshire, 403 U.S. 443, 91 S.Ct. 2022, 29 L. Ed.2d 564 (1971); Warden v. Hayden, 387 U.S. 294, 87 S.Ct. 1642, 18 L.Ed.2d 782 (1967); Agnello v. United States, 269 U.S. 20, 46 S.Ct. 4, 70 L.Ed. 145 (1925). No right so fundamental should now, after the long struggle against governmental trespass, be diluted to accommodate conduct of the very type the Amendment was designed to outlaw.

The break-in charged in this indictment involved an unauthorized entry and search by agents of the Executive branch of the Federal Government. It is undisputed that no warrant was obtained and no Magistrate gave his approval. Moreover, none of the traditional exceptions to the warrant requirement are claimed and none existed; however desirable the break-in may have appeared to its instigators, there is no indication that it had to be carried out quickly, before a warrant could have been obtained. On the contrary, it had been meticulously planned over a period of more than a month. The search of Dr. Fielding's office was therefore clearly illegal under the unambiguous mandate of the Fourth Amendment. *See* Wolf v. People, 117 Colo. 279, 187 P.2d 926 (1947), aff'd sub nom., Wolf v. Colorado, 338 U.S. 25, 69 S.Ct. 1359, 93 L.Ed. 1782 (1949).

Defendants contend that even though the Fourth Amendment would ordinarily prohibit break-ins of this nature, the President has the authority, by reason of his special responsibilities over foreign relations and national defense, to suspend its requirements, and that he did so in this case. Neither assertion is accurate. Many of the landmark Fourth Amendment cases in this country and in England concerned citizens accused of disloyal or treasonous conduct, for history teaches that such suspicions foster attitudes within a government that generate conduct inimical to individual rights. *See* United States v. United States District Court, 407 U.S. 297, 314, 92 S.Ct. 2125, 32 L.Ed.2d 752 (1972). The judicial response to such Executive overreaching has been consistent and emphatic: the Government must comply with the strict constitutional and statutory limitations on trespassory searches and arrests even when known foreign agents are involved. *See, e. g.,* Abel v. United States, 362 U.S. 217, 226, 80 S.Ct. 683, 4 L.Ed.2d 668 (1960); United States v. Coplon, 185 F.2d 629 (2d Cir. 1950), cert. denied, 342 U.S. 920, 72 S.Ct. 362, 96 L.Ed. 688 (1952). To hold otherwise, except under the most exigent circumstances, would be to abandon the Fourth Amendment to the whim of the Executive in total disregard of the Amendment's history and purpose.

Defendants contend that, over the last few years, the courts have begun to carve out an exception to this traditional rule for purely intelligence-gathering searches deemed necessary for the conduct of foreign affairs. However, the cases cited are carefully limited to the issue of wiretapping, a relatively nonintrusive search, United States v. Butenko, 494 F.2d 593 (3d Cir. 1974); United States v. Brown, 484 F.2d 418 (5th Cir. 1973); Zweibon v. Mitchell, 363 F.Supp. 936 (D.D.C.1973), and the Supreme Court has reserved judgment in this unsettled area. United States v. United States District Court, 407 U.S. 297, 322 n. 20, 92 S.Ct. 2125, 32 L.Ed.2d 752 (1972). [While the Fourth Amendment undoubtedly encompasses nontrespassory surveillance, "physical entry of the home is the chief evil against which the wording of the Fourth Amendment is directed. . . ." United States v. United States District Court, *supra*, at 313. Footnote in original.] The Court cannot find that this recent, controversial judicial response to the special problem of national security wiretaps indicates an intention to obviate the entire Fourth Amendment whenever the President determines that an American citizen, personally innocent of wrongdoing, has in his possession information that may touch upon foreign policy concerns [The doctrine of the President's inherent authority as "the sole organ of the nation in its external relations," 10 Annals of Cong. 613 (1800) (remarks of John Marshall), has been developed by a series of Supreme Court decisions dealing with the President's power to enter into international agreements and to prohibit commercial contracts which impede American foreign policy. Chicago & So. Air Lines, Inc. v. Waterman Steamship Corp., 333 U.S. 103, 68 S.Ct. 431, 92 L.Ed. 568 (1948); United States v. Pink, 315 U.S. 203, 62 S.Ct. 552, 86 L.Ed. 796 (1942); United States v. Belmont, 301 U.S. 324, 57 S.Ct. 758, 81 L.Ed. 1134 (1937); United States v. Curtiss-Wright Export Corp., 299 U.S. 304, 57 S.Ct. 216, 81 L.Ed. 255 (1936). None of these cases purport to deal with the constitutional rights of American citizens or with Presidential action in defiance of congressional legislation. When such issues have arisen, Executive assertions of inherent authority have been soundly rejected. *See* Kent v. Dulles, 357 U.S. 116, 78 S.Ct. 1113, 2 L.Ed.2d 1204 (1958); Youngstown Sheet & Tube Co. v. Sawyer, 343 U.S. 579, 72 S.Ct. 863, 96 L.Ed. 1153 (1952). Footnote in original.] Such a doctrine, even in the context of purely information-gathering searches, would give the Executive a blank check to disregard the very heart and core of the Fourth Amendment and the vital privacy interests that it protects. Warrantless criminal investigatory searches—which this break-in may also have been [This possibility is strongly suggested by that portion of the President's letter to the Court set forth at p. 34, *infra*. Footnote in original.]—would, in addition, undermine vital Fifth and Sixth Amendment rights.

The facts presented pretrial lead the Court to conclude as a matter of law that the President not only lacked the authority to authorize the Fielding break-in but also that he did not in fact give any specific directive permitting national security break-ins, let alone this particular intrusion. The President has repeatedly and publicly denied prior knowledge or authorization of the Fielding break-in, and the available transcripts of the confidential tape recordings support that claim. [The President has called the break-in "illegal, unauthorized, as far as I am concerned, and completely deplorable" (Presidential news conference, August 22, 1973), and has repeatedly insisted that he gave no approval and had no prior knowledge of that incident (*see, e. g.,* President's letter to the Court, *infra*, p. 34; President's Statements of May 22, 1973, and August 15, 1973). On March 21, 1973, while discussing the break-in long after the fact, the President stated, "I don't know what the hell we did that for," and the possibility of claiming a national security justification was thereafter considered (Tape Transcript of March 21, 1973, meeting between the President, John Dean and H. R. Haldeman). Footnote in original.] No defendant has presented any evidence to the contrary, and neither Ehrlichman nor Colson, the two defendants who had the greatest access to the President, contend that such specific authorization was given to anyone. The Special Prosecutor has uncovered nothing to the contrary. Although there is no recording of the crucial San Clemente meeting between the President, Ehrlichman and Krogh, their similar accounts of that conversation reflect intense Presidential concern with the need to plug the national security leaks and a belief that Dr. Ellsberg might be involved, but no specific reference either to Dr. Fielding or to trespassory searches. The President described that meeting in the following terms:

> I considered the problem of such disclosures most critical to the national security of the United States and it was my intent, which I believe I conveyed, that the fullest authority of the President under the Constitution and the law should be used if necessary to bring a halt to these disclosures. I considered the successful prosecution of anyone responsible for such unauthorized disclosures a necessary part of bringing to an end this dangerous practice of making such unauthorized disclosures.
>
> I did not have prior knowledge of the break-in of Dr. Fielding's office, nor was I informed of it until March 17, 1973. [Letter to the Court from President Richard M. Nixon, dated April 29, 1974. Footnote in original.]

Such comments simply cannot be interpreted to direct a break-in in violation of the Fourth Amendment.

Defendants adopt the fall-back position that even if the President did not specifically authorize the Fielding break-in, he properly delegated to one or more of the defendants or unindicted co-conspirators the authority to approve national security break-ins. Of course, since the President had no such authority in the first place, he could not have delegated it to others. Beyond this, however, the Court rejects the contention that the President could delegate his alleged power to suspend constitutional rights to non-law enforcement officers in the vague, informal, inexact terms noted above. Even in the wiretap cases the courts have stressed the fact that the President had specifically delegated the authority over "national security" wiretaps to his chief legal officer, the Attorney General, who approved each such tap. *See, e. g.,* Katz v. United States, 389 U.S. 347, 364, 88 S.Ct. 507, 19 L.Ed. 2d 576 (1967) (White, J., concurring). *Cf.* United States v. Chavez, —— U.S. ——, 94 S.Ct. 1849, 40 L.Ed.2d 380, 42 U.S.L.W. 4660 (1974). Whatever accommodation is required between the guarantees of the Fourth Amendment and the conduct of foreign affairs, it cannot justify a casual, ill-defined assignment to White House aides and part-time employees granting them an uncontrolled discretion to select, enter and search the homes and offices of innocent American citizens without a warrant. *Cf.* Ex parte Milligan, 71 U.S. (4 Wall.) 2, 18 L.Ed. 281 (1866); Ex parte Merryman, 17 Fed. Cas. p. 144, 151 (No. 9,487) (C.C.Md. 1861).

Defendants contend that, even if the break-in was illegal, they lacked the specific intent necessary to violate section 241 because they reasonably *believed* that they had been authorized to enter and search Dr. Fielding's office. As explained above, however, such authorization was not only factually absent but also legally insufficient, and it is well established that a mistake of law is no defense in a conspiracy case to the knowing performance of acts which, like the unauthorized entry and search at issue here, are *malum in se. See, e. g.,* Hamburg-American Steam Packet Co. v. United States, 250 F. 747, 758-759 (2d Cir.), cert. denied, 246 U.S. 662, 38 S.Ct. 333, 62 L.Ed. 927 (1918); Chadwick v. United States, 141 F. 225, 243 (6th Cir. 1905); United States v. DePietro, 36 F.Supp. 389 (W.D.N.Y. 1941); Commonwealth v. O'Rourke, 311 Mass. 213, 40 N.E.2d 883, 887 (1942); People v. McLaughlin, 111 Cal.App.2d 781, 245 P.2d 1076 (1952); G. Williams, Criminal Law 288 n. 4 (2d ed. 1961). As the Supreme Court said in Screws v. United States, 325 U.S. 91, 106, 65 S.Ct. 1031, 1037, 89 L.Ed. 1495 (1945), "[t]he fact that the defendants may not have been thinking in constitutional terms is not material [to a charge under § 242, a related specific intent statute,] where their aim was not to enforce local law but to deprive a citizen of a right and that right was protected by the Constitution." Here, defendants are alleged to have intended to search Dr. Fielding's office without a warrant, and their mistaken belief that such conduct did not offend the Constitution would not protect them from prosecution under section 241. *See also* Williams v. United States, 341 U.S. 97, 101-102, 71 S.Ct. 576, 95 L.Ed. 774 (1951).

The cases cited by the defendants are not to the contrary. United States v. Guest, 383 U.S. 745, 86 S.Ct. 1170, 16 L.Ed.2d 239 (1966), requires only that the acts which violate federal rights must have been the primary purpose of the conspiracy rather than an incidental side effect. And United States v. Murdock, 290 U.S. 389, 54 S.Ct. 223, 78 L.Ed. 381 (1933), merely reflects the rule that mistake of law often *is* a defense to *malum prohibitum* crimes requiring specific intent, such as those created by the federal tax laws. *See also* Commonwealth v. Rudnick, 318 Mass. 45, 60 N.E.2d 353 (1945). *But see* Chadwick v. United States, *supra,* at 243.

Mistake of law may also excuse an act if it resulted from good faith reliance upon a court order or decision, United States v. Mancuso, 139 F.2d 90 (3d Cir. 1943); State v. O'Neil, 147 Iowa 513, 126 N.W. 454 (1910), or upon the legal advice of an executive officer charged with interpreting or enforcing the law in question. *See* Cox v. Louisiana, 379 U.S. 559, 85 S.Ct. 476, 13 L.Ed. 2d 487 (1965); Raley v. Ohio, 360 U.S. 423, 79 S.Ct. 1257, 3 L.Ed.2d 1344 (1959). This principle however, cannot be stretched to encompass a mistake based upon the assurances of an alleged co-conspirator with regard to the criminality of acts that are *malum in se. See* United States v. Konovsky, 202 F.2d 721, 730-731 (7th Cir. 1953) (obedience to the orders of a superior does not necessarily negate the specific intent requirement set forth in *Screws*).

Defendants nonetheless are entitled to present factual material that negatives the claim that they conspired to break in. This will, of course, permit them to explain contacts and activities which may imply collaboration as to the break-in but which they contend was collaboration in pursuit of different, more legitimate efforts to tighten security and prevent leaks within the Government establishment. This material, of course, will necessarily also reflect upon the underlying questions of intent and apparently will require the presentation of some evidence bearing on the defendant's knowledge and authority in national security areas. Discovery to this end—within strict limits—should be permitted by specific, particularized documentary discovery adequate to corroborate their factual contentions as to the legitimate reasons for their association.

To the extent that the Special Prosecutor has not already produced all material relevant to these limited issues within the possession of his office, the Department of Justice and the F.B.I., defendants may demand such production under Brady v. Maryland, 373 U.S. 83, 83 S.Ct. 1194, 10 L.Ed.2d 215 (1963), and Rule 16 of the Federal Rules of Criminal Procedure. Defendants may pursue such material in the possession of other government agencies or private parties by means of tightly framed subpoenas *duces tecum*, in accordance with Rule 17 of the Federal Rules of Criminal Procedure. These subpoenas must be confined to documents the defendants wrote, received, or read, and a strict rule of relevance and materiality will be applied. Cumulative material will be rejected. These subpoenas should give adequate notice and be returnable in open court on June 6, 1974, at 9:30 a. m. At that time the Court will hear any objections and make rulings, document-by-document, following such *in camera* inspection as may be necessary. All documents subpoenaed shall be produced in court.

Defendants, while expressing some willingness to go along with this procedure, claim that the Special Prosecutor is required by *Brady* to obtain all of this material himself and disclose it to the defendants. Although the issue is unsettled, there is some support for the contention that the prosecutor's duty of production under *Brady* applies not only to documents in the possession of any federal investigative agency, United States v. Bryant, 142 U.S.App.D.C. 132, 439 F.2d 642, 650 (1971), but also to those held by any agency closely connected to the allegations in the indictment. United States v. Deutsch, 475 F.2d 55, 57 (5th Cir. 1973). While this rule would undoubtedly be reasonable in most federal prosecutions, it cannot be applied to the instant case. Here the Government is prosecuting itself, and those in the Government who have evidence needed by the defense are in an adversary position toward the Special Prosecutor and perhaps in some instance toward the defendants as well. Under such circumstances, in which the customary informal requests within the Government would be to no avail, the subpoena approach set forth above best serves the purposes of *Brady* by providing a prompt, orderly and enforceable procedure for obtaining the necessary disclosures prior to trial.

While the Court is thus limiting the Prosecutor's duty to demand exculpatory evidence from other government agencies, it is not limiting the Government's ultimate duty to produce such material: if evidence relevant and material to the defense is suppressed despite a sufficiently specific demand from one of the defendants, the Court will use the full range of its sanctions, including dismissal, if necessary, to insure that defendants received a fair trial. *See* United States v. Coplon, 185 F.2d 629 (2d Cir. 1950), cert. denied, 342 U.S. 920, 72 S.Ct. 362, 96 L.Ed. 688 (1952); United States v. Andolschek, 142 F.2d 503 (2d Cir. 1944).

Defendants' motions for discovery are granted to the extent set forth above and are denied in all other respects. The motion for dismissal because of the danger of exposing national security information is denied.

So ordered.

Some of this was frightening, other aspects of it ludicrous and pathetic. Unable to trust and control the intelligence machinery of the FBI, the CIA and the intelligence divisions of the National Security Council and the Defense Department, the White House went out and hired a couple of ex-New York City gum shoes, a crew of ex-CIA and -FBI men and an assortment of other "patriots" to wage war on various elements of the society who were opposed to the administration and its policies. The drama wavered between tragedy and comedy, but in either direction it was destructive to the interests of democratic institutions and to values in this country. They made our national interests no more secure, apprehended no traitors, but they violated the law and the Constitution and disgraced legitimate government. Huston summed up the predicament of these frightened and desperate men when he complained,

> No one who had been in the White House could help but feel he was in a
> state of siege. They were dumping on you from all sides. It seemed that no
> one ever liked what was done in Vietnam.[62]

Perhaps that was the real answer. The administration insisted upon asserting its own game plan in Vietnam and it was unwilling to subject its policy, or lack of it, to the checks and balances of the democratic process. It was not absolutely clear that it would not have won in such a confrontation, because until the very end there was indecision, doubt and lack of an alternative policy on the part of its opponents. There was no real leadership, and the democratic process was faltering. But the Nixon administration was taking no chances, and surreptitious entry, the use of government agencies like the Bureau of Internal Revenue to assist friends and to punish enemies, were all part of the game plan.

The climax to this sordid chapter in American history came in the attempt by the Nixon administration to manipulate the electoral process in the presidential sweepstakes of 1972. Millions of dollars were raised by the Committee to Reelect the President (CRP) and poured into many of these illegal efforts. Examples of "high jinks" and campaign stunts, many initiated by the Democratic party's court jester, Dick Tuck, were elevated to the level of systematic campaign strategy. Even before the campaign got underway, the Committee to Reelect was extremely active in the Democratic primaries, attempting to damage the chances of its frontrunner, Senator Edmund Muskie of Maine, who was consistently outscoring Nixon in the early public opinion polls. Nixon and his advisors realized that if they could eliminate Muskie, Senator George McGovern of South Dakota, the candidate of the left and "peace" wings of the Democratic party, would be easier to defeat in November.

Members of the White House staff bombarded two different commissioners of Internal Revenue to obtain information from IRS returns which would assist certain "friends" of the White House like Reverend Billy Graham and film star John Wayne and damage the reputations and careers of "enemies" like Lawrence O'Brien, chairman of the Democratic party and Gerald Wallace, brother of George Wallace, governor of Alabama, whose plans to run an independent campaign for the presidency would be a threat to Nixon's "southern strategy." The White House also struggled unsuccessfully to obtain the tax returns of all of McGovern's financial backers. The following affidavits filed by two former tax commissioners graphically reveal the extent of the use of these private governmental records by the Nixon administration to further its own ends.

Johnnie M. Walters,
Former Commissioner of Internal Revenue
Affidavits on Political Use of the IRS
May and June 1974

Statement of Information, Book VIII, 231-35,238-41.

AFFIDAVIT, MAY 6, 1974

1. I served as Commissioner of Internal Revenue from August 6, 1971, through April 30, 1973.

2. On September 11, 1972, I met with John W. Dean, III, pursuant to his request, in his office at the Old Executive Office Building. At that meeting he gave me a list of names, and requested that IRS undertake examinations or investigations of the people named on the list. The list appeared to contain names of persons on the 1972 Presidential campaign staff of Senator George McGovern and of contributors to that campaign.

3. Mr. Dean stated that he had been directed to give the list to me. It was my impression at the time of the September 11, 1972 meeting that John D. Ehrlichman was the one who had given Mr. Dean his directions, but I do not recollect on what my impression was based. Mr. Dean stated that he had not been asked by the

President to have this done and that he did not know whether the President had asked that any of this activity be undertaken. Mr. Dean expressed the hope that the IRS could do this in such a manner that would "not cause ripples." He indicated that he was not yet under pressure with respect to this matter.

4. I advised Mr. Dean that compliance with the request would be disastrous for the IRS and for the Administration and would make the Watergate affair look like a "Sunday school picnic." I asked whether he had discussed the matter with Secretary Shultz, and he said no. I advised him that I would discuss the matter with Secretary Shultz, and that I would recommend to Secretary Shultz that we do nothing on the request.

5. On September 13, 1972, at the earliest opportunity, I discussed the matter with Secretary Shultz, showed him the list, and advised him that I believed that we should not comply with Mr. Dean's request. Mr. Shultz looked briefly at the list, and said do nothing with respect to it. I placed the list in a sealed envelope and placed it in my office safe. I believe I may have informed Mr. Dean of the decision, but do not specifically recall doing so.

6. On or about September 25, 1972, I received a telephone call from Mr. Dean. He inquired as to what progress I had made with respect to the list. I told him that no progress had been made. He asked if it might be possible to develop information on fifty-sixty-seventy of the names. I again told him that, although I would reconsider the matter with Secretary Shultz, any activity of this type would be inviting disaster.

7. Thereafter, on or about September 29, 1972 and again at the earliest opportunity, I discussed the matter again with Secretary Shultz. We again agreed that nothing would be done with respect to the list. I have no recollection of any further discussions about the matter during my tenure as IRS Commissioner, except the possibility of mentioning (without showing) it to the present Commissioner, Donald C. Alexander, as he was in the process of being named Commissioner.

8. At no time did I furnish any name or names from the list to anyone, nor did I request any IRS employee or official to take any action with respect to the list.

9. I removed the list from the safe when I left IRS and thereafter personally kept it in the sealed envelope and locked in my present office.

10. On July 11, 1973, upon written request, I submitted the list, along with my handwritten notes of the September 11, 1972 meeting, to the Joint Committee on Internal Revenue Taxation in connection with that Committee's investigation of allegations that the IRS took enforcement actions for political purposes.

Johnnie M. Walters

AFFIDAVIT, JUNE 10, 1974

1. This statement is made upon my best recollection of the facts as they occurred, without my having had the benefit of reference to files and other materials

in the possession of the Internal Revenue Service (IRS) which might permit a more precise statement.

2. I served as Commissioner of Internal Revenue from August 6, 1971 through April 30, 1973.

3. Beginning late in 1971 or early in 1972 the IRS began an intensive investigation of the Howard Hughes organizations and operations. During the course of that investigation, IRS learned that some fairly substantial amounts of money had been paid by the Hughes organization to Lawrence O'Brien and his associates. Sensitive case reports with respect to the Hughes investigation reflected the O'Brien payments. (Sensitive case reports are sent to the Commissioner from the field each month to keep him and the Secretary of the Treasury advised of IRS investigations or proceedings relating to prominent persons or sensitive matters.) A Special Assistant to the Commissioner (during my tenure as Commissioner, Roger Barth) regularly delivered to the Secretary of the Treasury the monthly sensitive case reports.

4. During the summer of 1972, Secretary Shultz informed me that someone in the White House (subsequently identified as John Ehrlichman) had information that Mr. O'Brien had received large amounts of income which might not have been reported properly. The Secretary asked whether IRS could check on the matter, and I advised that IRS could.

5. I thereupon requested Assistant Commissioner Hanlon (Compliance) to determine whether Mr. O'Brien had filed returns which reflected substantial amounts of income. After a few days, he reported orally that Mr. O'Brien had filed returns which reported large amounts of income during the preceding years, that IRS had examined the returns for 1970 and 1971, that Mr. O'Brien had paid a small deficiency for one year, and that the examinations were closed. I reported this to Secretary Shultz.

6. Thereafter, from Secretary Shultz I learned that Mr. Ehrlichman was not satisfied with the report on the status of Mr. O'Brien's returns. I informed Secretary Shultz that Mr. O'Brien would be interviewed in connection with the Hughes investigation. I do not recall specifically whether scheduling of the interview of Mr. O'Brien originated in the Field investigation independently of Secretary Shultz's inquiries or as a result of Secretary Shultz's inquiries, but, in any case, IRS needed the interview and would have scheduled it. During 1972, however, it was IRS policy to postpone investigations involving sensitive cases, to the extent possible without loss of position or revenue, until after the election. In line with that policy, IRS probably would not have interviewed Mr. O'Brien prior to the election; however, because of the indicated inquiries, IRS did interview Mr. O'Brien during the summer of 1972.

7. To the best of my recollection, the IRS field personnel had some difficulty in scheduling an interview with Mr. O'Brien and at one point they agreed to interview his son instead (who had informed the IRS agents that he had information about his father's financial matters). Before that interview took place, however, I was informed by Secretary Shultz that Mr. Ehrlichman thought IRS should interview Mr. O'Brien, not his son. I agreed with that and directed that IRS

interview Mr. O'Brien rather than his son. I do not know how Mr. Ehrlichman learned of some of the details of which he had knowledge.

8. IRS interviewed Mr. O'Brien on or about August 17, 1972. Mr. O'Brien was cooperative although the interview was limited timewise, and Mr. O'Brien suggested that any further interview be postponed until after the election. My recollection is that IRS furnished a copy of the Conference Report to Secretary Shultz. A short time thereafter, Secretary Shultz informed me that Mr. Ehrlichman was not satisfied and that he needed further information about the matter. I advised the Secretary that IRS had checked the filing of returns and the examination status of those returns (closed) and that there was nothing else IRS could do.

9. On or about August 29, 1972, at the request of Secretary Shultz, I went to his office with Roger Barth so that we could conclude review of the O'Brien matter and dispose of it. Secretary Shultz, Mr. Barth and I discussed the matter and agreed that IRS could do no more. We then jointly telephoned Mr. Ehrlichman. Scretary Shultz informed Mr. Ehrlichman of that; I stated that IRS had verified that Mr. O'Brien had filed returns, that those returns reflected large amounts of income, that IRS already had examined and closed the returns, and that we (Shultz, Walters and Barth) all agreed that there was nothing further for IRS to do. Mr. Ehrlichman indicated disappointment, and said to me "I'm goddamn tired of your foot dragging tactics." I was offended and very upset but decided to make no response to that statement. Following the telephone conversation, I told Secretary Shultz that he could have my job any time he wanted it.

10. The meeting with the Secretary and telephone conversation with Mr. Ehrlichman stand out in my recollections as the final incidents in the O'Brien matter, however, in concluding the matter, I may have furnished some data with respect to Mr. O'Brien's returns to Secretary Shultz shortly after (5 or 6 days) that encounter (some questions posed seem to indicate this).

Johnnie M. Walters

Randolph W. Thrower,
Former Commissioner of Internal Revenue
Affidavit on Political Use of the IRS
May 24, 1974

Statement of Information, Book VIII, 40-42.

This statement is made upon the basis of my best recollection of the facts and the sequence in which they occurred, without my having had the benefit of reference to files and other materials in the possession of the Internal Revenue Service which would permit a more precise statement.

In the summer of 1970, Clark Mollenhoff, Special Assistant to the President, telephoned me to inquire about an extensive field examination which the IRS was conducting into the possible diversion of political contributions for the benefit of private individuals in the 1968 campaign of George Wallace of Alabama. A brief statement as to the current status of the investigation had been included in our most recent "Sensitive Case Report." For many years reports on the status of sensitive cases within the IRS had been given a very limited and controlled distribution within the Commissioner's staff and a copy had customarily been sent by special courier to the Secretary of the Treasury. I understand that customarily the Secretary of the Treasury would advise the President of any matters in the sensitive case report about which the President, by reason of his official duties and responsibilities, should be advised.

As I recall, Mr. Mollenhoff advised me that the report on the Wallace campaign was desired by or on behalf of the President and in connection with his official responsibilities. In earlier discussions over the disclosure of confidential information in the possession of the IRS, Mr. Mollenhoff and I had reached an understanding that this would constitute a legal justification for the disclosure.

Pursuant to Mr. Mollenhoff's request, I asked the office of the Assistant Commissioner—Compliance to prepare for the White House a summarization of the Wallace investigation in the form of a memorandum from me. A memorandum was prepared which I reviewed and, after a few modifications, sent to Mr. Mollenhoff at the White House.

A few days later a column by Jack Anderson described the IRS investigation of charges of diversion of contributions in the 1968 Wallace campaign. It appeared to me that the Jack Anderson report came directly out of my memorandum. I called in the Assistant Commissioner—Inspection, Vernon D. Acree, and asked him to investigate the possibility of an unlawful disclosure of confidential tax information. I asked him, in particular, to study carefully my memorandum in relation to other factual summaries in the IRS files, in order to determine whether we could identify any possible source for the Jack Anderson report other than my own memorandum, such as other reports in the hands of the IRS or taxpayers' counsel. I also asked him to investigate the possibility of a leak in the movement of my memorandum within the IRS or the Treasury Department. At the time I was leaving the city on official business and asked that he attempt to have a report available on my return.

On my return Mr. Acree advised that my memorandum was clearly the source of the Jack Anderson column. He advised further that he had traced the movement of my memorandum within the Service and the Treasury Department and found nothing to suggest that the leak had occurred in these offices. Thereupon I called Mr. Mollenhoff who, before I could state my complaint, announced that he knew what I was calling about and wanted to assure me that he had not breached the operating procedures which he and I had developed and that he was in no way responsible for the leak. I told him that while it was a very serious breach of the laws against disclosure, I had felt confident that he was not responsible. I stated, nevertheless, that I was greatly disturbed by it and wanted to know how it possibly could have occurred. Mr. Mollenhoff replied that the responsibility was at a higher level. I asked, "How high?" His response was to the effect that it occurred at the highest level or at the very top. While I do not recall the precise language used, I received the impression that he was referring to Mr. Haldeman or possibly Messrs. Haldeman and Ehrlichman [sic].

Thereafter I telephoned Mr. Ehrlichman to discuss the disclosure and arranged for a meeting at the White House with him and Mr. Haldeman which was attended by the Chief Counsel of the IRS, K. Martin Worthy, and myself. In the conference Mr. Worthy and I discussed the seriousness of the leak and the fact that an unauthorized disclosure constituted a criminal act. I did not make any accusations as Mr. Mollenhoff had asked me to hold in confidence what he had told me as to the apparent source of the leak. Messrs. Haldeman and Ehrlichman did not indicate to Mr. Worthy and me the source of the leak but did take our complaint seriously and assured us that they would cooperate in undertaking to prevent such incidents in the future and would call the gravity of the situation to the attention of those in the White House who might from time to time have access to such information.

Randolph W. Thrower

Nothing like that campaign had ever occurred before in an American presidential election. Systematic efforts were made to misrepresent the views of candidates like Muskie on such key issues as busing in the South and ethnic minorities in the North, schedules were tampered with, spies were introduced into campaign headquarters and finally several major break-ins into the central headquarters of the Democratic party were conducted by a group of hired "cloak and dagger men," who were caught in the act of installing highly sophisticated electronic equipment in the telephones of the office and rifling through party files in search of information that could be used to denigrate or blackmail its candidates. No words can adequately admonish the depravity of these actions, yet the President and his top advisors continued to dismiss them as minor irregularities and mistakes of subordinates.

The decisive document which succinctly indicts all of this activity, is the articles of impeachment, submitted by the Committee on the Judiciary of the United States House of Representatives. The second article is the most important of the three articles voted by the committee because it goes to the heart of the quintessential impeachable crime—the abuse of the powers of the office entrusted to the President by the constitutional oath and the violation of the constitutional rights of the citizens of the republic.

House of Representatives
Committee on the Judiciary
Articles of Impeachment
August 4, 1974

The New York Times, August 4, 1974, Sec. 4,2.

ARTICLE I

In his conduct of the office of President of the United States, Richard M. Nixon, in violation of his constitutional oath faithfully to execute the office of President of the United States and, to the best of his ability, preserve, protect and defend the Constitution of the United States, and in violation of his constitutional duty to take care that the laws be faithfully executed, has prevented, obstructed, and impeded the administration of justice, in that:

On June 17, 1972, and prior thereto, agents of the Committee for the Re-election of the President:

Committed unlawful entry of the headquarters of the Democratic National Committee in Washington, District of Columbia, for the purpose of securing political intelligence. Subsequent thereto, Richard M. Nixon, using the powers of his high office, engaged personally and through his subordinates and agents in a course of conduct or plan designed to delay, impede, and obstruct the investigation of such unlawful entry; to cover up, conceal and protect those responsible; and to conceal the existence and scope of other unlawful covert activities.

The means used to implement this course of conduct or plan have included one or more of the following:

[1]

Making or causing to be made false or misleading statements to lawfully authorized investigative officers and employes of the United States.

[2]

Withholding relevant and material evidence or information from lawfully authorized investigative officers and employes of the United States.

[3]

Approving, condoning, acquiescing in, and counseling witnesses with respect to the giving of false or misleading statements to lawfully authorized investigative officers and employes of the United States and false or misleading testimony in duly instituted judicial and Congressional proceedings.

[4]

Interfering or endeavoring to interfere with the conduct of investigations by the Department of Justice of the United States, the Federal Bureau of Investigation, the office of Watergate Special Prosecution Force, and Congressional committees.

[5]

Approving, condoning and acquiescing in the surreptitious payment of substantial sums of money for the purpose of obtaining the silence or influencing the testimony of witnesses, potential witnesses or individuals who participated in such illegal entry and other illegal activities.

[6]

Endeavoring to misuse the Central Intelligence Agency, an agency of the United States.

[7]

Disseminating information received from officers of the Department of Justice of the United States to subjects of investigations conducted by lawfully authorized investigative officers and employes of the United States, for the purpose of aiding and assisting such subjects in their attempts to avoid criminal liability.

[8]

Making false or misleading public statements for the purpose of deceiving the people of the United States into believing that a thorough and complete investigation had been conducted with respect to allegations of misconduct on the part of personnel of the executive branch of the United States and personnel of the Committee for the Reelection of the President, and that there was no involvement of such personnel in such misconduct; or

[9]

Endeavoring to cause prospective defendants, and individuals duly tried and convicted, to expect favored treatment and consideration in return for their silence or false testimony, or rewarding individuals for their silence or false testimony.

In all of this, Richard M. Nixon has acted in a manner contrary to his trust as President and subversive of constitutional government, to the great prejudice of the cause of law and justice and to the manifest injury of the people of the United States.

Wherefore Richard M. Nixon, by such conduct, warrants impeachment and trial, and removal from office.

ARTICLE II

Using the powers of the office of President of the United States, Richard M. Nixon, in violation of his constitutional oath faithfully to execute the office of President of the United States, and to the best of his ability preserve, protect and defend the Constitution of the United States, and in disregard of his constitutional duty to take care that the laws be faithfully executed, has repeatedly engaged in conduct violating the constitutional right of citizens, impairing the due and proper administration of justice in the conduct of lawful inquiries, of contravening the law of governing agencies of the executive branch and the purposes of these agencies.

This conduct has included one or more of the following:

[1]

He has, acting personally and through his subordinates and agents, endeavored to obtain from the Internal Revenue Service in violation of the constitutional rights of citizens, confidential information contained in income tax returns for purposes not authorized by law; and to cause, in violation of the constitutional rights of citizens, income tax audits or other income tax investigations to be initiated or conducted in a discriminatory manner.

[2]

He misused the Federal Bureau of Investigation, the Secret Service and other executive personnel in violation or disregard of the constitutional rights of citizens by directing or authorizing such agencies or personnel to conduct or continue electronic surveillance or other investigations for purposes unrelated to national security, the enforcement of laws or any other lawful function of his office.

He did direct, authorize or permit the use of information obtained thereby for purposes unrelated to national security, the enforcement of laws or any other lawful function of his office. And he did direct the concealment of certain records made by the Federal Bureau of Investigation of electronic surveillance.

[3]

He has, acting personally and through his subordinates and agents, in violation or disregard of the constitutional rights of citizens, authorized and permitted to be maintained a secret investigative unit within the office of the President, financed in part with money derived from campaign contributions, which unlawfully utilized the resources of the Central Intelligence Agency, engaged in covert and unlawful activities, and attempted to prejudice the constitutional right of an accused to a fair trial.

[4]

He has failed to take care that the laws were faithfully executed by failing to act when he knew or had reason to know that his close subordinates endeavored to impede and frustrate lawful inquiries by duly constituted executive, judicial and legislative entities concerning the unlawful entry into the headquarters of the Democratic National Committee and the cover-up thereof and concerning other unlawful activities including those relating to the confirmation of Richard Kleindienst as Attorney General of the United States, the electronic surveillance of private citizens, the break-in into the offices of Dr. Lewis Fielding and the campaign financing practices of the Committee to Re-elect the President.

[5]

In disregard of the rule of law he knowingly misused the executive power by interfering with agencies of the executive branch including the Federal Bureau of Investigation, the Criminal Division and the office of Watergate special prosecution force of the Department of Justice, and the Central Intelligence Agency, in violation of his duty to take care that the laws be faithfully executed.

In all of this Richard M. Nixon has acted in a manner contrary to his trust as President and subversive of constitutional government to the great prejudice of the cause of law and justice and to the manifest injury of the people of the United States.

Wherefore, Richard M. Nixon by such conduct warrants impeachment and trial and removal from office.

ARTICLE III

In his conduct of the office of President of the United States, Richard M. Nixon, contrary to his oath faithfully to execute the office of President of the United States and to the best of his ability to preserve, protect and defend the Constitution of the United States, and in violation of his constitutional duty to take care that the laws be faithfully executed, has failed without lawful cause or excuse to produce papers and things, as directed by duly authorized subpoenas issued by the Committee on the Judiciary of the House of Representatives on April 11, 1974, May 15, 1974, May 30, 1974, and June 24, 1974, and willfully disobeyed such subpoenas.

The subpoenaed papers and things were deemed necessary by the committee in order to resolve by direct evidence fundamental factual questions relating to Presidential direction, knowledge or approval of actions demonstrated by other evidence to be substantial grounds for impeachment of the President.

In refusing to produce these papers and things Richard M. Nixon, substituting his judgment as to what materials were necessary for the inquiry, interposed the powers of the Presidency against the lawful subpoenas of the House of Representatives, thereby assuming for himself functions and judgments necessary to the exercise of the sole power of impeachment vested by the Constitution in the House of Representatives.

In all this, Richard M. Nixon has acted in a manner contrary to his trust as President and subversive of constitutional government, to the great prejudice of the cause of law and justice, and to the manifest injury of the people of the United States.

Wherefore, Richard M. Nixon, by such conduct warrants impeachment and trial and removal from office.

Returning once again to our discussion, I asked Professor Schlesinger and Mr. Friedman to add their views to this brief synopsis of the Nixon, or perhaps better, the Watergate legacy to the problem of presidential power and its abuse. How, do you think, will the Watergate, impeachment, resignation and pardon controversies effect the future of the presidency?

FRIEDMAN: Let me stress what I consider to be one of the most critical problems of the future presidency. If you think about the most serious offenses of the President, or the ones that have given rise to the greatest concern, they relate in a very direct way to the control of information, and to the President's control of information in a way so that others will not have access to it. For example, the Kissinger leaks, the 17 wiretaps on newsmen and other people in the government in order to find out if they were the sources of certain leaks to the outside. The government was willing to put taps on people's phones for 21 months, long after some of them left the government, in order to find out what they were doing, find out what they were saying, and to use this information for their own—for political intelligence purposes. The Huston plan itself, which consisted of mail covers, break-ins and extensive wiretaps, was an attempt to find out information about their enemies. And finally the Watergate break-in itself—the attempt to put a wiretap on their direct political foes—was an attempt to gather information, to gather secret information about the other side in order to protect their own position. So, in effect, a large part of the offenses of the last five years has been in the area of collecting, gathering and keeping secret information which the government feels, or the executive department felt, would maintain its position.

Now this is an area in which Congress can act, and in fact, has started to act. There are a number of bills which are now pending that would alter the classification system, so that the government could not put a classification stamp on a document, and try, without legal basis, to say it is a crime if you disseminate this to the public. This of course was the attempt in the Ellsberg case, and there are at least threats that it is being done in other areas. But to the extent that classification itself, marking something secret or top secret, can be controlled in some kind of rational and sensible way, that itself would restrict the President's unreviewable authority in this area.

The second thing that Congress is trying to do is to amend the Freedom of Information Act. And the whole theory of the Freedom of Information Act is that there are documents and information, beyond those classified for security purposes, which the public should be entitled to get as a matter of course. And there have been a number of very dramatic lawsuits which have been won and certain policies of the government have necessarily been changed because certain information is now made public, and certain ways of doing things cannot be hidden behind a bureaucratic screen. So attempts to institutionalize this, and to clarify the area in which the public has the right to know, is one of the most important things that Congress can do, and, in fact, is trying to do, in this area.

SCHLESINGER: In addition to which, Congress can do things itself to improve its access to information. There have been proposals, for example, to transform the congressional research service, which presently spends most of its time writing term papers for constituents or doing short-term research for congressmen, into a genuine research institute, a kind of RAND for Congress, to serve, in effect, as a sort of counterpart to the Bureau of the Budget, as we used to call it. Such an institute could provide congressmen both with information and analyses and assessments and alternative policies. In addition, Congress could do very much more than it does in seeking information about foreign affairs from the public domain. There's quite as much knowledge about most countries of the world in the universities or among journalists or writers or businessmen as there is in the State Department or the CIA. If Congress wanted to, it could inform itself and the electorate much more than it does by asking witnesses to testify before congressional committees.

I do think, though, that the question of information is, to a degree, an alibi. Congress likes to exercise its own evasion of responsibility by saying, in effect, "We can't oppose the President because we don't have enough information." One advantage of giving Congress all the information it can handle is to destroy that particular alibi. If Congress had the will, it could assert itself, with or without information. Legislators in recent years have put forward the notion that, if only, for example, Congress had more computers, then it could argue with the executive branch. But Congress had no computers in the 1830s or the 1870s, or the 1930s. Instead, it had strong-willed members, people whom Presidents had to take into account, whether or not their information was accurate. Congress is better educated today; it has more information, but it has less will. The provision of information will, as I say, undermine the alibi, but it won't guarantee the will to make Congress a more effective partner.

GOLDSMITH: Have these two developments gone hand in hand, and in some sense fed or compounded the problem of presidential power? In other words, as the imbalance between the two branches became greater in the recent period, has the President tended to shore up and defend his imperial status by his monopoly on certain information and by virtually keeping secret, or deceiving the Congress and the public, with respect to many of his activities?

SCHLESINGER: Well I think he did. Presidents on the whole don't resist power. They enjoy power, or, if they don't enjoy it, at least they feel it is safer in their hands than in the hands of Congress. Even Eisenhower, who came in as a Whig determined to restore constitutional balance, promulgated the most sweeping version of executive privilege up to his time, and it was Eisenhower who turned the CIA into an instrument of intervention overseas, safe from any form of legislative accountability. So even Eisenhower, who in theory was going to roll back presidential power, increased it in practice—because Congress was perfectly willing to let him do it.

Then the process becomes cumulative. The executive bureaucracy perceives that secrecy is a great protection for itself; it's a great way of turning off criticism and burying mistakes. And the longer these habits exist, the more accepted they are. By the 1950s you even found congressmen denouncing the executive because it didn't keep things secret enough. Remember all the talk about security risks in the executive branch. "Security risks" were very often people who told things to newspapermen in order to increase the information available to the Congress and to the American people.

FRIEDMAN: Well, are we coming to at least one conclusion, that impeachment is a double answer in the sense that it eliminated a particular President who has abused the power and will serve as a lesson for future Presidents? Or, is it the institution itself? I mean what other institutional notions are possible? Is there some kind of parliamentary system as Thomas Finletter's idea about a joint conference, institutionalizing Congress and the presidency? The President will then answer, in effect, to a high council in Congress. Is that a possibility? Are we subject to further drift no matter who the President is simply because of the nature of world politics? Will Congress necessarily defer to Gerald Ford or some other President in other instances and may we not find some of these problems minimized but the institutional drift continuing?

SCHLESINGER: I think the institutional drift is very strong and is going to require a great assertion of will to arrest it and a great sensitivity and responsibility on the part of the new President. I don't find the parliamentary solution very convincing. The Finletter argument is ingenious and incisive; but, of course, he does not really advocate a parliamentary solution. Some do—Charles M. Hardin, for example. What they overlook is that the parliamentary system, in practice, increases the power of the Executive. Woodrow Wyatt, who served for 20 years as a Labor member of Parliament, has recently written a book, *Turn Again, Westminster*, in which he argues the only way to save Parliament from total impotence is to introduce the separation of powers into England; only by doing this can Parliament stop being a total creature of the Executive. Nor do I think that the parliamentary requirement of centralized and disciplined parties and so on is compatible with the genius of American politics. The structural tendencies carrying power to the presidency are very strong. That is why I could not share the view of Richard Nixon or of Professor Charles Black of the Yale Law School that giving up a paper or a tape would destroy the office of the presidency forever. The office of the presidency is a powerful and, I believe, indestructible one.

But I do think that a certain number of statutory reforms would be helpful. You have both mentioned the question of the congressional overhaul of the secrecy system. I think this is essential. I think that Congress ought to discharge its supervisory and its oversight responsibilities with regard to intelligence and law enforcement agencies. Senator Mike Mansfield, as long ago as 1954, suggested setting up a joint committee on the CIA; Congress could have set it up at any time. It has only come to a vote once in 20 years. I think that such procedures as having executive agreements registered with the House and Senate Committees on Foreign Affairs are important. It may be that Congress would want to pay a certain amount of attention to the White House staff. I'm note sure that I agree with the notion of statutory limits on the size of that staff, though there may even be merit in that. Certainly all members of the White House staff who are not just advisors, but who actually issue orders to the departments and to the bureaus, should, it seems to me, be confirmed by the Senate and available for interrogation before congressional committees. Congress can do things of this sort, which will be useful, though not decisive, in restoring the constitutional balance.

GOLDSMITH: I think that the context of presidential power is more important than what happens exclusively to the President or the presidency as an institution, because I think the President responds to the political and social environment in which he operates. If I were to write a hopeful scenario of the outcome of the impeachment process it would, first of all, clear the air; this is essential and important. Yet I don't think that impeachment can necessarily provide the sinew, the muscle, the direction, to begin creatively to reconstruct a more viable process.

I come back again to one of my favorite themes: in order to find more balance in the system, Congress has to discover that it too can have access to policy formulation, that it too can reach the public. The President, starting with Theodore Roosevelt, certainly in modern times, has successfully bridged the gap between the office and the public. He has found ways and means of effectively communicating with the public. Congress still has not made any such discovery or resolved the communication gap successfully. It seems to me that is its weakness and contributes to the imbalance at the center of the system. I think Congress has to find a way, and not simply Congress, but the parties in Congress, to organize themselves and begin to take issues to the people, as the President frequently does. This is the proper role for an opposition party, particularly, but it is one that has been rarely utilized in American history.

There is no question in my mind that the reconstruction of a viable political process has to involve the development and regeneration of the political party operating through Congress, as well as the political parties restraining the President. One of the hats the President wears, as Clinton Rossiter used to refer to it, is that of party leader; but the opposition party has not imposed any restraining force on the President. We can see in the revolutionary or Nixon presidency, a President disengaging himself almost entirely from the party, operating in isolation from the party, and surrounding himself with a veritable corporal's guard of non-party advisors and non-party figures, who, in fact, prevented many of the stronger influences in his party, members of his own cabinet, from reaching and advising him.

It is both outrageous and absurd for the Republican party to be able to wash its hands of the actions and policies of the Republican President and say to the American people that most Republicans in Congress had no more to do with Watergate or any of the other abuses of power by the President than the Democrats did. Nevertheless, it is probably true. Recent Presidents have not been accountable to or acted as leaders of their parties in Congress, and this may be one of the weakest links in our chain of government.

I think that this has been a very dangerous development in the presidency and a very dangerous development in American politics. If impeachment clears the air, the reconstruction of the political environment can mean that Congress can begin to concern itself in a very different way than it ever has in the past, with finding ways and means by which parties, operating within the context of Congress, can communicate with, reach, inform, and even dramatize issues and excite the American people. This would be a very vigorous development that could lead to a healthier political environment.

Take the problem of secrecy. I quite agree with Arthur when he points to the fact that Congress has abdicated and avoided all kinds of opportunities and potential for a cutting through that heavy curtain. It may be true that the President, and particularly the recent Presidents, have attempted to shield themselves and to restrict information, but Congress has access to the universities and many other institutions within the society which have a great ability to obtain information and to translate it into the framework of the political process.

On the question of the staffing of the presidency, there are many things that the most recent President, Richard Nixon, has done to organize or reorganize the Executive office of the presidency that, logically, or in terms of public administration expertise, have a logical ring to them. In some cases these have been things that political scientists and public administration experts have been asking for many years, for many decades. But rather than directed towards opening up the system and increasing the flow of accountability and information within the executive branch and between the two branches of government, however, in the Nixon administration, they have been used to enclose and to isolate the President from the political process, from members of his own party, from the Congress and from the American people. This is a misuse of administrative reform and has expanded the staff and the expenditure of the Executive office of the President not to make it more responsive and accountable to its constituents, but less responsive and accountable instead.

FRIEDMAN: Well, I would also just add that in terms of Congress serving a function as public educator, certainly the Ervin committee hearings on Watergate served a very useful function in reminding people what the fourth amendment was all about. I think particularly of Senator Ervin's exchange about a break-in into someone's house, which was a very eloquent and very forceful presentation of what the constitutional amendments are about. And so congressional investigations can serve that particular kind of function—the educative function that we have been talking about.

Bill, could I just ask you to develop that one last theme about the kind of reorganization of the executive branch which you say, from a public administration point might have been desirable. What kind of changes do you refer to?

GOLDSMITH: That is a difficult concept to deal with briefly. The initial reorganization of the Executive office of the President in the late 1930s was directed towards assisting the President to handle an ever increasing and complex set of responsibilities, enhancing accountability by centralizing lines of authority and giving the President a small staff to expedite the flow of information and reporting into the White House and to assist in clarifying policy directives which emanated from the Oval Office. All the specific reforms proposed at that time were not adopted, but this was the general theme of the suggested changes. During the next 20 years these reforms blossomed through the work of the Hoover Commissions, which tackled specific areas of administrative confusion and the mushrooming complexity of responsibilities which developed as the bureaucracy of the executive branch grew.

President Kennedy attempted to simplify operations at the White House by eliminating major staff members who stood between the President and his administrative subordinates, *major-domos* like Sherman Adams under Eisenhower. He also tried to meet with selected members of his cabinet and with presidential assistants assigned to specific problem areas in order to work out policies and plans for implementing them, rather than meeting regularly with his entire cabinet. This worked fairly well, for it did not diminish the role and responsibilities of the heads of important departments, but at the same time it strengthened and clarified the policymaking machinery.

President Nixon's reforms have not had such striking success. They appear to have been gleaned from the "tables of organization" of advanced business management theory, but proved to be not readily adaptable to an executive branch administering to a country of over 200 million citizens. The principles Nixon announced when introducing his reforms sounded good on paper, but produced a contrary effect in practice. For example, in his message accompanying Reorganization Plan No. 2, the President argued:

> A President whose programs are carefully coordinated, whose information system keeps him adequately informed, and whose organizational assignments are plainly set out, can delegate authority with security and confidence. A President whose office is deficient in these respects will be inclined, instead, to retain close control of operating responsibilities which he cannot and should not handle.[63]

There is much that can be said for this noble statement of intentions, but the reforms and their implementation during the next few years were at odds with these objectives. In fact the Nixon system in practice produced something very close to what the President had warned against.

Although the White House staff mushroomed to gigantic proportions during this period, it is impossible to seriously entertain the thought that the "President was adequately informed."[64] He was counselled almost exclusively by a staff who tailored information according to what they thought he wanted to hear. The extraordinary revelations of presidential ignorance in certain areas, which the infamous tapes reveal, and the amount of information kept back from the President by his closest aides is frightening. But even more threatening is the manner in which the inner circle of the White House was organized to produce just such results. President Nixon delegated a great deal of authority to his staff, based upon the assumption that he was fully informed about everything taking place in his administration. It is clear that this was not the case. The same staff charged with the responsibility of informing was also expected to administer. They obviously informed along lines which would strengthen their own power.

Another fatal flaw in the President's internal operating procedure in the White House was that he drained power from his constitutional advisors and the heads of the operating departments of the government and concentrated it in the White House. Then, he liberally delegated many of these same powers to his immediate staff, who did not hold a formally responsible, constitutional function or role; they were not responsible to an operating department or its constituency, but were total creatures of the President. As such, they were committed (in practice anyway) to *his* interests as distinguished from the interests of the public at large. The result was the politicization of the White House in the worst sense, for it was not organic politics, integrated in a balanced fashion in a give and take relationship with the operating and administrative responsibilities of the government, but rather a personal court of subjects who flattered the President as they misinformed him and interposed their delegated authority over the authority and opinions of those who had real responsibilities and points of reference outside of the Executive office itself. There are other aspects, both good and bad, to the Nixon organizational reforms in the White House, but this was their most critical deficiency. It completely short-circuited the democratic process, and made a mockery of responsible government and effective administration.

Reviewing and evaluating these developments, a special panel appointed by the National Academy of Public Administration at the request of the chairman (and senior minority member) of the Senate Select Committee on Presidential Campaign Activities, said this:

> [T]he structure which was designed to provide the President with staff assistance and advice has been gradually fashioned into an instrument of control—not unlike that of a modern corporation. None of this was done in secret, but openly and proudly, building vigorously upon trends in organization of the Presidency first noted over a decade ago, and pursued in the name of efficient, effective and responsive government. Increasingly, though not consciously, access to the President was shut out. The principal officers of the executive departments and agencies and the leadership (both majority and minority) of the Congress met with more and more difficulty in seeing him. Equally important, the free flow and competition of ideas and interests were cut off.
>
> What emerges is a picture of the centralization of power in the White House and the concomitant confusion of roles and responsibilities by placing operating authority in personal and advisory staff who make the key decisions but are shielded from public view and public access. The President needs adequate staff assistance and sufficient flexibility to serve his personal style in meeting his constitutional responsibilities; yet the full bloom of a monocratic Presidency cannot fulfill the best interests of the Republic.
>
> . . . Our Constitutional system is based upon the principle of the unity of executive power and the premise that "the executive power is more easily

confined when it is one." The concept of the assistant Presidents sharing by delegation or otherwise in the powers exclusively vested in the President by the Constitution cannot be reconciled with this principle.[65]

A recent study of the administrative behavior of the last six presidential administrations attributes much of the difficulty in Nixon's White House to the shortcomings of what it calls "the formalistic approach" to the problem of running the government.[66] Such an approach, the author argues, purports to establish an orderly process of decision-making through thorough analysis and to conserve the decision-maker's time for the large decisions a President has to confront. The very tidiness of the system, however, tends to hide its great potential drawbacks. The coordinated and screened flow of information may be distorted by the screeners; there is a tendency to eliminate the legitimate political interests of conflicting groups and the sentiments of the public at large, and there is a constant tendency to delay responses to vital problems. When one adds to this list of deficiencies the point that the later years of the Nixon administration were characterized by the "state of siege" mentality in the White House, and that there was an explicit lack of serious concern for domestic problems, one can more easily provide some explanation for the Nixon downfall. What was produced was a "presidency insulated from the information and pressures which stimulate imagination, feed inspiration, foster insight and develop sensitivity."[67]

A very astute presidential scholar has pointed out other serious problems resulting from the expanded White House staff responsibility:

> Perhaps the most disturbing aspect of the expansion of the Presidential Establishment is that it has become a powerful inner sanctum of government, isolated from traditional constitutional checks and balances. It is common practice today for anonymous, unelected and unratified aides to negotiate sensitive international commitments by means of executive agreements that are free from congressional oversight. Other aides in the Presidential Establishment wield fiscal authority over billions of dollars in funds that Congress has assigned to one purpose and the administration routinely redirects to another—all with no semblance of public scrutiny.[68]

A former cabinet member in the Nixon administration complained that the centralization of control in the Executive office has downgraded the executive departments and created doubts and uncertainties regarding their policy responsibilities.

> There is an isolation of thought developing [in the Nixon presidency]. In early 1970, I was conscious of a deepening malaise inside the Administration—a sense of vague uneasiness. Others in the cabinet shared my feelings that some of the White House staff were stepping up their efforts to filter contacts between the Cabinet and the President. It appeared that an effort was being made to centralize control of all executive branch activities of the government immediately within the White House, utilizing the various departments—represented by

secretaries at the cabinet level—merely as clearinghouses for White House policy, rather than as action agencies.

Should a department—for example, Interior—develop policy for those activities under its control, submit those ideas to the White House for approval or disapproval, then follow through at the administrative level? Or, as some of the White House personnel seemed to want it, should a department wait only for marching orders to be issued by the Executive Mansion?[69]

That veteran British observer of American politics, Henry Fairlie, has compared the Nixon White House to the courts of the emperors of Turkey and China, who relied heavily upon eunuchs "whom they had raised from poverty and obscurity, partly because their backgrounds ensured that they would not become rivals, and partly because they could not generate a line of succession of their own."[70]

> The alacrity with which thousands of young men pleaded to be castrated, so they might enter the service of the emperor, was the cause in some periods of such a superfluity of them that they became an aggrieved minority of the unemployed, and even of the unemployable. . . .
>
> Party government is the opposite of eunuch rule. The parties have backgrounds and continuity; the politicians, sustained in public life by the parties, have pasts and futures. If either of them, party or politician, wishes to continue, they must each use the political process in all its resourcefulness, have their ears to the ground, gather in smoke-filled rooms, meet in the washrooms on Capitol Hill, and studiously obey a score of other conventions of party politics. In this way, they are kept in touch with what they need to know, not least with the limits as well as the resources of the political process. They do not think they can just do anything.
>
> But none of this is true of the eunuch rule of the personal entourages which now move into the White House. Many of the convicted or indicted members of the personal staff of Nixon have said that their main error was that they were willing to do for their President whatever it seemed necessary to do. That attitude could not have prevailed if the President's men had had some close association with the party of which he is supposed to be at least the titular head. At some point, someone would have said to them, "But we don't do it like that—we didn't do it like that in the days of President Harding, rest his soul."[71]

GOLDSMITH: I would like to ask you, Dr. Schlesinger, what you think the impact of the impeachment investigations of President Nixon have had upon the problem of presidential power? In the aftermath of impeachment and resignation, where is the presidency today, and what can we expect of it in the future?

SCHLESINGER: A century ago, the impeachment of Andrew Johnson, though Johnson escaped conviction and removal, unquestionably contributed to the weakness of the presidency. Even *with* Johnson's acquittal, the republic entered into a period of presidential subordination and congressional domination. Yet there were limits beyond which the presidency could not be diminished.

One reason for the presidential eclipse after 1868 was that foreign affairs were issues of secondary concern. Once foreign policy became a prime consideration at the turn of the century, the presidency was bound to revive if only as a matter of functional necessity. Even the most powerful of Congresses could not conduct the foreign relations of the country. And even before the Spanish-American War the presidency, responding to other and subtler, functional necessities, was on the way back. For Congress can act as a united body only under extreme duress. It is centrifugal by nature, always tending to disperse power. It is amenable to special interests, and special interests through most of American history have been conservative interests.

The presidency thus began to emerge—Henry Jones Ford acutely noted it at the time—as the agency of popular control, as the means by which the democratic and progressive impulses of the nation could find voice and power. The fact that in our own time the strong presidency has also shown a potentiality for anti-democratic purposes must not lead us to forget that presidential leadership has been the means by which the nation has been moved ahead to achieve such progress as it has achieved in the humanization of industrial society, in the struggle for racial justice, in the protection of resources and the environment, in the defense of labor organization, in the support of the Bill of Rights.

In short, the weakness of the presidency after the Civil War was caused less by the revulsion against Lincoln's Jacksonian presidency and by the impeachment of Johnson than by the absence of issues imperatively demanding presidential leadership (or, to put it more precisely, for by contemporary standards such issues existed in abundance, by the absence of popular expectations that the presidency was supposed to do anything about these issues). A century later these issues exist in far greater intensity and are regarded as within the scope and obligation of presidential action. It is inconceivable to me that the presidency will fade away in a time when, quite apart from pressing international questions, the domestic problems of race, poverty, inflation, crime and urban decay are straining the bonds of national cohesion and demanding, quite as much as in the 1930s, a strong domestic presidency to hold the nation together. In short, I would say that the near-impeachment of Nixon will not weaken the presidency in any serious way. What it will do is to restore to Presidents and, one trusts, to Congresses and citizens, a sense of the constitutional limits within which a strong presidency must operate.

GOLDSMITH: I agree. For my part, I think the constitutional process has given a good account of itself. The House Judiciary Committee has conducted its investigations and hearings with remarkable thoroughness and superb concentration upon the essential abuses of power involved. Their only flaw was in failing to cite the secret bombing of Cambodia as an impeachable offense. Our representatives in Congress, politicians if you will, often come under substantial abuse and criticism. Perhaps they deserve it; but in this instance they distinguished themselves by the restraint they demonstrated in the conduct of the hearings and the dignity which they brought to these proceedings. The leaks that occurred from executive sessions were the only instances which marred this record.

Another positive contribution to emerge from this tragic and costly affair was the clear and coherent answer to the ambiguous question of what constitutes an impeachable offense. John Doar's memorandum on this question is undoubtedly the most comprehensive and informative contribution to a working definition of "high crimes and misdemeanors" to be advanced since the brief discussions of the terms at the Constitutional Convention. James St. Clair's responding brief for the government does not approach it in legal and historical depth and clarity.

Impeachment Judiciary Staff of the House Judiciary Committee
Constitutional Grounds for Presidential Impeachment
February 20, 1974

Committee on the Judiciary, House of Representatives, 93rd Cong., 2nd sess. (1974).

I
INTRODUCTION

The Constitution deals with the subject of impeachment and conviction at six places. The scope of the power is set out in Article II, Section 4:

> The President, Vice President and all civil Officers of the United States, shall be removed from Office on Impeachment for, and Conviction of, Treason, Bribery, or other high Crimes and Misdemeanors.

Other provisions deal with procedures and consequences. Article I, Section 2 states:

> The House of Representatives . . . shall have the sole Power of Impeachment.

Similarly, Article I, Section 3, describes the Senate's role:

> The Senate shall have the sole Power to try all Impeachments. When sitting for that Purpose, they shall be on Oath or Affirmation. When the President of the United States is tried, the Chief Justice shall preside: And no Person shall be convicted without the Concurrence of two thirds of the Members present.

The same section limits the consequences of judgment in cases of impeachment:

> Judgment in Cases of Impeachment shall not extend further than to removal from Office, and disqualification to hold and enjoy any Office of honor, Trust or Profit under the United States: but the Party convicted shall nevertheless be liable and subject to Indictment, Trial, Judgment and Punishment, according to law.

Of lesser significance, although mentioning the subject, are: Article II, Section 2:

> The President . . . shall have Power to grant Reprieves and Pardons for Offences against the United States, except in Cases of Impeachment.

Article III, Section 2:

> The Trial of all Crimes, except in Cases of Impeachment, shall be by Jury. . . .

Before November 15, 1973 a number of Resolutions calling for the impeachment of President Richard M. Nixon had been introduced in the House of Representatives, and had been referred by the Speaker of the House, Hon. Carl Albert, to the Committee on the Judiciary for consideration, investigation and report. On November 15, anticipating the magnitude of the Committee's task, the House voted funds to enable the Committee to carry out its assignment and in that regard to select an inquiry staff to assist the Committee.

On February 6, 1974, the House of Representatives by a vote of 410 to 4 "authorized and directed" the Committee on the Judiciary "to investigate fully and completely whether sufficient grounds exist for the House of Representatives to exercise its constitutional power to impeach Richard M. Nixon, President of the United States of America."

To implement the authorization (H. Res. 803) the House also provided that "For the purpose of making such investigation, the committee is authorized to require . . . by subpoena or otherwise . . . the attendance and testimony of any person . . . and . . . the production of such things; and . . . by interrogatory, the furnishing of such information, as it deems necessary to such investigation."

This was but the second time in the history of the United States that the House of Representatives resolved to investigate the possibility of impeachment of a President. Some 107 years earlier the House had investigated whether President Andrew Johnson should be impeached. Understandably, little attention or thought has been given the subject of the presidential impeachment process during the intervening years. The Inquiry Staff, at the request of the Judiciary Committee, has prepared this memorandum on constitutional grounds for presidential impeachment. As the factual investigation progresses, it will become possible to state more specifically the constitutional, legal and conceptual framework within which the staff and the Committee work.

Delicate issues of basic constitutional law are involved. Those issues cannot be defined in detail in advance of full investigation of the facts. The Supreme Court of the United States does not reach out, in the abstract, to rule on the constitutionality of statutes or of conduct. Cases must be brought and adjudicated on particular facts in terms of the Constitution. Similarly, the House does not engage in abstract, advisory or hypothetical debates about the precise nature of conduct that calls for the exercise of its constitutional powers; rather, it must await full development of the facts and understanding of the events to which those facts relate.

What is said here does not reflect any prejudgment of the facts or any opinion or inference respecting the allegations being investigated. This memorandum is written before completion of the full and fair factual investigation the House directed be undertaken. It is intended to be a review of the precedents and available interpretive materials, seeking general principles to guide the Committee.

This memorandum offers no fixed standards for determining whether grounds for impeachment exist. The framers did not write a fixed standard. Instead they adopted from English history a standard sufficiently general and flexible to meet future circumstances and events, the nature and character of which they could not foresee.

The House has set in motion an unusual constitutional process, conferred solely upon it by the Constitution, by directing the Judiciary Committee to "investigate fully and completely whether sufficient grounds exist for the House of Representatives to exercise its constitutional power to impeach." This action was not partisan. It was supported by the overwhelming majority of both political parties. Nor was it intended to obstruct or weaken the presidency. It was supported by Members firmly committed to the need for a strong presidency and a healthy executive branch of our government. The House of Representatives acted out of a clear sense of constitutional duty to resolve issues of a kind that more familiar constitutional processes are unable to resolve.

To assist the Committee in working toward that resolution, this memorandum reports upon the history, purpose and meaning of the constitutional phrase, "Treason, Bribery, or other high Crimes and Misdemeanors."

II

THE HISTORICAL ORIGINS
OF THE IMPEACHMENT PROCESS

The Constitution provides that the President ". . . shall be removed from Office on Impeachment for, and Conviction of, Treason, Bribery, or other high Crimes and Misdemeanors." The framers could have written simply "or other crimes"—as indeed they did in the provision for extradition of criminal offenders from one state to another. They did not do that. If they had meant simply to denote seriousness, they could have done so directly. They did not do that either. They adopted instead a unique phrase used for centuries in English parliamentary impeachments, for the meaning of which one must look to history.

The origins and use of impeachment in England, the circumstances under which impeachment became a part of the American constitutional system, and the American experience with impeachment are the best available sources for developing an understanding of the function of impeachment and the circumstances in which it may become appropriate in relation to the presidency.

A. The English Parliamentary Practice

Alexander Hamilton wrote, in No. 65 of *The Federalist*, that Great Britain had served as "the model from which [impeachment] has been borrowed." Accordingly, its history in England is useful to an understanding of the purpose and scope of impeachment in the United States.

Parliament developed the impeachment process as a means to exercise some measure of control over the power of the King. An impeachment proceeding in England was a direct method of bringing the King's ministers and favorites—men who might otherwise have been beyond reach—to account. Impeachment, at least in its early history, has been called "the most powerful weapon in the political armory, short of civil war."[1] It played a continuing role in the struggles between King and Parliament that resulted in the formation of the unwritten English constitution. In this respect impeachment was one of the tools used by the English Parliament to create more responsive and responsible government and to redress imbalances when they occurred.[2]

The long struggle by Parliament to assert legal restraints over the unbridled will of the King ultimately reached a climax with the execution of Charles I in 1648 and the establishment of the Commonwealth under Oliver Cromwell. In the course of that struggle, Parliament sought to exert restraints over the King by removing those of his ministers who most effectively advanced the King's absolutist purposes. Chief among them was Thomas Wentworth, Earl of Strafford. The House of Commons impeached him in 1640. As with earlier impeachments, the thrust of the charge was damage to the state.[3] The first article of impeachment alleged[4]

> That he . . . hath traiterously endeavored to subvert the Fundamental Laws and Government of the Realms . . . and in stead thereof, to introduce Arbitrary and Tyrannical Government against Law. . . .

The other articles against Strafford included charges ranging from the allegation that he had assumed regal power and exercised it tyrannically to the charge that he had subverted the rights of Parliament.[5]

Characteristically, impeachment was used in individual cases to reach offenses, as perceived by Parliament, against the system of government. The charges, variously denominated "treason," "high treason," "misdemeanors," "malversations," and "high Crimes and Misdemeanors," thus included allegations of misconduct as various as the Kings (or their ministers) were ingenious in devising means of expanding royal power.

At the time of the Constitutional Convention the phrase "high Crimes and Misdemeanors" had been in use for over 400 years in impeachment proceedings in Parliament.[6] It first appears in 1386 in the impeachment of the King's Chancellor, Michael de la Pole, Earl of Suffolk.[7] Some of the charges may have involved common law offenses.[8] Others plainly did not: de la Pole was charged with breaking a promise he made to the full Parliament to execute in connection with a parliamentary ordinance the advice of a committee of nine lords regarding the improvement of the estate of the King and the realm; "this was not done, and it was the fault of himself as he was then chief officer." He was also charged with failing to expend a sum that Parliament had directed be used to ransom the town of Ghent, because of which "the said town was lost."[9]

The phrase does not reappear in impeachment proceedings until 1450. In that year articles of impeachment against William de la Pole, Duke of Suffolk (a descendant of Michael), charged him with several acts of high treason, but also with "high Crimes and Misdemeanors,"[10] including such various offenses as "advising the King to grant liberties and privileges to certain persons to the hindrance of the due execution of the laws," "procuring offices for persons who were unfit, and unworthy of them" and "squandering away the public treasure."[11]

Impeachment was used frequently during the reigns of James I (1603-1625) and Charles I (1628-1648). During the period from 1620 to 1640 over 100 impeachments were voted by the House of Commons.[12] Some of these impeachments charged high treason, as in the case of Strafford; others charged high crimes and misdemeanors. The latter included both statutory offenses, particularly with respect to the Crown monopolies, and non-statutory offenses. For example, Sir Henry Yelverton, the King's Attorney General, was impeached in 1621 of high crimes and misdemeanors in that he failed to prosecute after commencing suits, and exercised authority before it was properly vested in him.[13]

There were no impeachments during the Commonwealth (1649-1660). Following the end of the Commonwealth and the Restoration of Charles II (1660-1685) a more powerful Parliament expanded somewhat the scope of "high Crimes and Misdemeanors" by impeaching officers of the Crown for such things as negligent discharge of duties[14] and improprieties in office.[15]

The phrase "high Crimes and Misdemeanors" appears in nearly all of the comparatively few impeachments that occurred in the Eighteenth Century. Many of the charges involved abuse of official power or trust. For example, Edward, Earl of Oxford, was charged in 1701 with "violation of his duty and trust" in that, while a member of the King's privy council, he took advantage of the ready access he had to the King to secure various royal rents and revenues for his own use, thereby greatly diminishing the revenues of the crown and subjecting the people of England to "grievous taxes."[16] Oxford was also charged with procuring a naval commission for William Kidd, "known to be a person of ill fame and reputation," and ordering him "to pursue the intended voyage, in which Kidd did commit diverse piracies . . . , being thereto encouraged through hopes of being protected by the high station and interest of Oxford, in violation of the law of nations, and the interruption and discouragement of the trade of England."[17]

The impeachment of Warren Hastings, first attempted in 1786 and concluded in 1795,[18] is particularly important because comtemporaneous with the American Convention debates. Hastings was the first Governor-General of India. The articles indicate that Hastings was being charged with high crimes and misdemeanors in the form of gross maladministration, corruption in office, and cruelty toward the people of India.[19]

Two points emerge from the 400 years of English parliamentary experience with the phrase "high Crimes and Misdemeanors." First, the particular allegations of misconduct alleged damage to the state in such forms as misapplication of funds, abuse of official power, neglect of duty, encroachment on Parliament's prerogatives, corruption, and betrayal of trust.[20] Second, the phrase "high Crimes and Misdemeanors" was confined to parliamentary impeachments; it had no roots in the ordinary criminal law,[21] and the particular allegations of misconduct under that heading were not necessarily limited to common law or statutory derelictions or crimes. [My emphasis]

B. The Intention of the Framers

The debates on impeachment at the Constitutional Convention in Philadelphia focus principally on its applicability to the President. The framers sought to create a responsible though strong executive; they hoped, in the words of Elbridge Gerry of Massachusetts, that "the maxim would never be adopted here that the chief Magistrate could do no wrong."[22] Impeachment was to be one of the central elements of executive responsibility in the framework of the new government as they conceived it.

The constitutional grounds for impeachment of the President received little direct attention in the Convention; the phrase "other high Crimes and Misdemeanors" was ultimately added to "Treason" and "Bribery" with virtually no debate. There is evidence, however, that the framers were aware of the technical meaning the phrase had acquired in English impeachments.

Ratification by nine states was required to convert the Constitution from a proposed plan of government to the supreme law of the land. The public debates in the state ratifying conventions offer evidence of the contemporaneous understanding of the Constitution equally as compelling as the secret deliberations of the delegates in Philadelphia. That evidence, together with the evidence found in the debates during the First Congress on the power of the President to discharge an executive officer appointed with the advice and consent of the Senate, shows that the framers intended impeachment to be a constitutional safeguard of the public trust, the powers of government conferred upon the President and other civil officers, and the division of powers among the legislative, judicial and executive departments.

1. *The Purpose of the Impeachment Remedy*

Among the weaknesses of the Articles of Confederation apparent to the delegates to the Constitutional Convention was that they provided for a purely legislative form of government whose ministers were subservient to Congress. One of the first decisions of the delegates was that their new plan should include a separate executive, judiciary, and legislative.[23] However, the framers sought to avoid the creation of a too-powerful executive. The Revolution had been fought against the tyranny of a king and his council, and the framers sought to build in safeguards against executive abuse and usurpation of power. They explicity rejected a plural executive, despite arguments that they were creating "the foetus of monarchy,"[24] because a single person would give the most responsibility to the office.[25] For the same reason, they rejected proposals for a council of advice or privy council to the executive.[26]

The provision for a single executive was vigorously defended at the time of the state ratifying conventions as a protection against executive tyranny and wrongdoing. Alexander Hamilton made the most carefully reasoned argument in Federalist No. 70, one of the series of *Federalist Papers* prepared to advocate the ratification of the Constitution by the state of New York. Hamilton criticized both a plural executive and a council because they tend "to conceal faults and destroy responsibility." A plural executive, he wrote, deprives the people of "the two greatest securities they can have for the faithful exercise of any delegated power"—"[r]esponsibility . . . to censure and to punishment." When censure is divided and responsibility uncertain, "the restraints of public opinion . . . lose their efficacy" and "the opportunity of discovering . . . with facility and clearness the misconduct of the persons [the public] trust, in order either to their removal from office, or to their actual punishment in cases which admit of it" is lost.[27] A council, too, "would serve to destroy, or would greatly diminish, the intended and necessary responsibility of the Chief Magistrate himself."[28] It is, Hamilton concluded, "far more safe that there should be a single object for the jealousy and watchfulness of the people; . . . all multiplication of the Executive is rather dangerous than friendly to liberty."[29]

James Iredell, who played a leading role in the North Carolina ratifying convention and later became a justice of the Supreme Court, explained that under the proposed Constitution the President "is of a very different nature from a monarch. He is to be . . . personally responsible for any abuse of the great trust reposed in him."[30] In the same convention, William R. Davie, who had been a delegate in Philadelphia, explained that the "predominant principle" on which the Convention had provided for a single executive was "the more obvious responsibility of one person." When there was but one man, said Davie, "the public were never at a loss" to fix the blame.[31]

James Wilson, in the Pennsylvania convention, described the security furnished by a single executive as one of its "very important advantages":

> The executive power is better to be trusted when it has no screen. Sir, we have a responsibility in the person of our President; he cannot act improperly, and hide either his negligence or inattention; he cannot roll upon any other person the weight of his criminality; no appointment can take place without his nomination; and he is responsible for every nomination he makes. . . . Add to all this, that officer is placed high, and is possessed of power far from being contemptible, yet not a *single privilege* is annexed to his character; far from being above the laws, he is amenable to them in his private character as a citizen, and in his public character by *impeachment*.[32]

As Wilson's statement suggests, the impeachability of the President was considered to be an important element of his responsibility. Impeachment had been included in the proposals before the Constitutional Convention from its beginning.[33] A specific provision, making the executive removable from office on impeachment and conviction for "malpractice or neglect of duty," was unanimously adopted even before it was decided that the executive would be a single person.[34] The only major debate on the desirability of impeachment occurred when it was moved that the provision for impeachment be dropped, a motion that was defeated by a vote of eight states to two.[35]

One of the arguments made against the impeachability of the executive was that he "would periodically be tried for his behaviour by his electors" and "ought to be subject to no intermediate trial, by impeachment."[36] Another was that the executive could "do no criminal act without coadjutors [asssistants] who may be punished." Without his subordinates, it was asserted, the executive "can do nothing of consequence," and they would "be amenable by impeachment to the public justice."[37]

This latter argument was made by Gouverneur Morris of Pennsylvania, who abandoned it during the course of the debate, concluding that the executive should be impeachable.[38] Before Morris changed his position, however, George Mason had replied to his earlier argument:

> Shall any man be above justice? Above all shall that man be above it, who can commit the most extensive injustice? When great crimes were committed he was for punishing the principal as well as the Coadjutors.[39]

James Madison of Virginia argued in favor of impeachment stating that some provision was "indispensible" to defend the community against "the incapacity, negligence or perfidy of the chief magistrate." With a single executive, Madison argued, unlike a legislature whose collective nature provided security, "loss of capacity or corruption was more within the compass of probable events, and either of them might be fatal to the Republic."[40] Benjamin Franklin supported impeachment as "favorable to the executive"; where it was not available and the chief magistrate had "rendered himself obnoxious," recourse was had to assassination. The Constitution should provide for the "regular punishment [of the executive] when his misconduct should deserve it, and for his honorable acquittal when he should be unjustly accused."[41] Edmund Randolph also defended "the propriety of impeachment":

> The Executive will have great opportunitys of abusing his power; particularly in time of war when the military force, and in some respects the public money will be in his hands. Should no regular punishment be provided it will be irregularly inflicted by tumults and insurrections.[42]

The one argument made by the opponents of impeachment to which no direct response was made during the debate was that the executive would be too dependent on the legislature—that, as Charles Pinckney put it, the legislature would hold impeachment "as a rod over the Executive and by that means effectually destroy his independence."[43] That issue, which involved the forum for trying impeachments and the mode of electing the executive, troubled the Convention until its closing days. Throughout its deliberations on ways to avoid executive subservience to the legislature, however, the Convention never reconsidered its early decision to make the executive removable through the process of impeachment.[44]

2. *Adoption of "high Crimes and Misdemeanors"*

Briefly, and late in the Convention, the framers addressed the question how to describe the grounds for impeachment consistent with its intended function. They did so only after the mode of the President's election was settled in a way that did not make him (in the words of James Wilson) "the Minion of the Senate."

The draft of the Constitution then before the Convention provided for his removal upon impeachment and conviction for "treason or bribery." George Mason objected that these grounds were too limited:

> Why is the provision restrained to Treason and Bribery only? Treason as defined in the Constitution will not reach many great and dangerous offenses. Hastings is not guilty of Treason. Attempts to subvert the Constitution may not be Treason as above defined. As bills of attainder which have saved the British Constitution are forbidden, it is the more necessary to extend the power of impeachments.[45]

Mason then moved to add the word "maladministration" to the other two grounds. Maladministration was a term in use in six of the thirteen state constitutions as a ground for impeachment, including Mason's home state of Virginia.[46]

When James Madison objected that "so vague a term will be equivalent to a tenure during pleasure of the Senate," Mason withdrew "maladministration" and substituted "high crimes and misdemeanors agst the State," which was adopted eight states to three, apparently with no further debate.[47]

That the framers were familiar with English parliamentary impeachment proceedings is clear. The impeachment of Warren Hastings, Governor-General of India, for high crimes and misdemeanors was voted just a few weeks before the beginning of the Constitutional Convention and George Mason referred to it in the debates.[48] Hamilton, in the *Federalist* No. 65, referred to Great Britain as "the model from which [impeachment] has been borrowed." Furthermore, the framers were well-educated men. Many were also lawyers. Of these, at least nine had studied law in England.[49]

The Convention had earlier demonstrated its familiarity with the term "high misdemeanor."[50] A draft constitution had used "high misdemeanor" in its provision for the extradition of offenders from one state to another.[51] The Convention, apparently unanimously, struck "high misdemeanor" and inserted "other crime" "in order to comprehend all proper cases: it being doubtful whether 'high misdemeanor' had not a technical meaning too limited."[52]

The "technical meaning" referred to is the parliamentary use of the term high misdemeanor. Blackstone's *Commentaries on the Laws of England*—a work cited by delegates in other portions of the Convention's deliberations and which Madison later described (in the Virginia ratifying convention) as "a book which is in every man's hand"[53]—included "high misdemeanors" as one term for positive offenses "against the king and government." The "first and principal" high misdemeanor, according to Blackstone, was "mal-administration of such high officers, as are in public trust and employment," "usually punished by the method of parliamentary impeachment."[54]

"High Crimes and Misdemeanors" has traditionally been considered a "term of art," like such other constitutional phrases as "levying war" and "due process." The Supreme Court has held that such phrases must be construed, not according to modern usage, but according to what the framers meant when they adopted them. Chief Justice Marshall wrote of another such phrase:

It is a technical term. It is used in a very old statute of that country whose language is our language, and whose laws form the substratum of our laws. It is scarcely conceivable that the term was not employed by the framers of our constitution in the sense which had been affixed to it by those from whom we borrowed it.[55]

3. *Grounds for Impeachment*

Mason's suggestion to add "maladministration," Madison's objection to it as "vague," and Mason's substitution of "high Crimes and Misdemeanors agst the State" are the only comments in the Philadelphia convention specifically directed to the constitutional language describing the grounds for impeachment of the President. Mason's objection to limiting the grounds to "Treason and Bribery" was that treason would "not reach many great and dangerous offences" including "[a]ttempts to subvert the Constitution."[56] His willingness to substitute "high Crimes and Misdemeanors," especially given his apparent familiarity with the English use of the term as evidenced by his reference to the Warren Hastings impeachment, suggests that he believed "high Crimes and Misdemeanors" would cover the offenses about which he was concerned.

Contemporary comments on the scope of impeachment are persuasive as to the intention of the framers. In *Federalist* No. 65, Alexander Hamilton described the subject of impeachment as:

> ... those offences which proceed from the misconduct of public men, or, in other words, from the abuse or violation of some public trust. They are of a nature which may with peculiar propriety be denominated *Political*, as they relate chiefly to injuries done immediately to the society itself.[57]

Comments in the state ratifying conventions also suggest that those who adopted the Constitution viewed impeachment as a remedy for usurpation or abuse of power or serious breach of trust. Thus, Charles Cotesworth Pinckney of South Carolina stated that the impeachment power of the House reaches "those who behave amiss, or betray their public trust."[58] Edmund Randolph said in the Virginia convention that the President may be impeached if he "misbehaves."[59] He later cited the example of the President's receipt of presents or emoluments from a foreign power in violation of the constitutional prohibition of Article I, section 9.[60] In the same convention George Mason argued that the President might use his pardoning power to "pardon crimes which were advised by himself" or, before indictment or conviction, "to stop inquiry and prevent detection." James Madison responded:

> [I]f the President be connected, in any suspicious manner, with any person, and there be grounds to believe he will shelter him, the House of Representatives can impeach him; they can remove him if found guilty; . . .[61]

In reply to the suggestion that the President could summon the Senators of only a few states to ratify a treaty, Madison said,

> Were the President to commit any thing so atrocious . . . he would be

impeached and convicted, as a majority of the states would be affected by his misdemeanor.[62]

Edmund Randolph referred to the checks upon the President:

> It has too often happened that powers delegated for the purpose of promoting the happiness of a community have been perverted to the advancement of the personal emoluments of the agents of the people; but the powers of the President are too well guarded and checked to warrant this illiberal aspersion.[63]

Randolph also asserted, however, that impeachment would not reach errors of judgment: "No man ever thought of impeaching a man for an opinion. It would be impossible to discover whether the error in opinion resulted from a wilful mistake of the heart, or an involuntary fault of the head."[64]

James Iredell made a similar distinction in the North Carolina convention, and on the basis of this principle said, "I suppose the only instances, in which the President would be liable to impeachment, would be where he had received a bribe, or had acted from some corrupt motive or other."[65] But he went on to argue that the President:

> . . . must certainly be punishable for giving false information to the Senate. He is to regulate all intercourse with foreign powers, and it is his duty to impart to the Senate every material intelligence he receives. If it should appear that he has not given them full information, but has concealed important intelligence which he ought to have communicated, and by that means induced them to enter into measures injurious to their country, and which they would not have consented to had the true state of things been disclosed to them,—in this case, I ask whether, upon an impeachment for a misdemeanor upon such an account, the Senate would probably favor him.[66]

In short, the framers who discussed impeachment in the state ratifying conventions, as well as other delegates who favored the Constitution,[67] implied that it reached offenses against the government, and especially abuses of constitutional duties. The opponents did not argue that the grounds for impeachment had been limited to criminal offenses.

An extensive discussion of the scope of the impeachment power occurred in the House of Representatives in the First Session of the First Congress. The House was debating the power of the President to remove the head of an executive department appointed by him with the advice and consent of the Senate, an issue on which it ultimately adopted the position, urged primarily by James Madison, that the Constitution vested the power exclusively in the President. The discussion in the House lends support to the view that the framers intended the impeachment power to reach failure of the President to discharge the responsibilities of his office.[68]

Madison argued during the debate that the President would be subject to impeachment for "the wanton removal of meritorious officers."[69] He also contended, that the power of the President unilaterally to remove subordinates was "absolutely necessary" because "it will make him in a peculiar manner, responsible for [the] conduct" of executive officers. It would, Madison said:

> . . . subject him to impeachment himself, if he suffers them to perpetrate with impunity high crimes or misdemeanors against the United States, or neglects to superintend their conduct, so as to check their excesses.[70]

Elbridge Gerry of Massachusetts, who had also been a framer though he had opposed the ratification of the Constitution, disagreed with Madison's contentions about the impeachability of the President. He could not be impeached for dismissing a good officer, Gerry said, because he would be "doing an act which the Legislature has submitted to his discretion."[71] And he should not be held responsible for the acts of subordinate officers, who were themselves subject to impeachment and should bear their own responsibility.[72]

Another framer, Abraham Baldwin of Georgia, who supported Madison's position on the power to remove subordinates, spoke of the President's impeachability for failure to perform the duties of the executive. If, said Baldwin, the President "in a fit of passion" removed "all the good officers of the Government" and the Senate were unable to choose qualified successors, the consequence would be that the President "would be obliged to do the duties himself; or, if he did not, we would impeach him, and turn him out of office, as he had done others."[73]

Those who asserted that the President had exclusive removal power suggested that it was necessary because impeachment, as Elias Boudinot of New Jersey contended, is "intended as a punishment for a crime, and not intended as the ordinary means of re-arranging the Departments."[74] Boudinot suggested that disability resulting from sickness or accident "would not furnish any good ground for impeachment; it could not be laid as treason or bribery, nor perhaps as a high crime or misdemeanor."[75] Fisher Ames of Massachusetts argued for the President's removal power because "mere intention [to do a mischief] would not be cause for impeachment" and "there may be numerous causes for removal that do not amount to a crime."[76] Later in the same speech Ames suggested that impeachment was available if an officer "misbehaves"[77] and for "mal-conduct."[78]

One further piece of contemporary evidence is provided by the *Lectures on Law* delivered by James Wilson of Pennsylvania in 1790 and 1791. Wilson described impeachments in the United States as "confined to political characters, to political crimes and misdemeanors, and to political punishments."[79] And, he said:

> The doctrine of impeachments is of high import in the constitutions of free states. On one hand, the most powerful magistrates should be amenable to the law. On the other hand, elevated characters should not be sacrificed merely on account of their elevation. No one should be secure while he violates the constitution and the laws: every one should be secure while he observes them. . . .[80]

From the comments of the framers and their contemporaries, the remarks of the delegates to the state ratifying conventions, and the removal power debate in the First Congress, it is apparent that the scope of impeachment was not viewed narrowly. It was intended to provide a check on the President through impeachment, but not to make him dependent on the unbridled will of the Congress.

Impeachment, as Justice Joseph Story wrote in his *Commentaries on the Constitution* in 1833, applies to offenses of "a political character":

> Not but that crimes of a strictly legal character fall within the scope of the power . . . ; but that it has a more enlarged operation, and reaches, what are aptly termed political offenses, growing out of personal misconduct, or gross neglect, or usurpation, or habitual disregard of the public interest in the discharge of the duties of political office. These are so various in their character, and so indefinable in their actual involutions, that it is almost impossible to provide systematically for them by positive law. They must be examined upon very broad and comprehensive principles of public policy and duty. They must be judged of by the habits, and rules, and principles of diplomacy, or departmental operations and arrangements, or parliamentary practice, of executive customs and negotiations, of foreign, as well as domestic political movements; and in short, by a great variety of circumstances, as well those, which aggravate, as those, which extenuate, or justify the offensive acts, which do not properly belong to the judicial character in the ordinary administration of justice, and are far removed from the reach of municipal jurisprudence.[81]

C. The American Impeachment Cases

Thirteen officers have been impeached by the House since 1787: one President, one cabinet officer, one United States Senator, and ten Federal judges.[82] In addition there have been numerous resolutions and investigations in the House not resulting in impeachment. However, the action of the House in declining to impeach an officer is not particularly illuminating. The reasons for failing to impeach are generally not stated, and may have rested upon a failure of proof, legal insufficiency of the grounds, political judgment, the press of legislative business, or the closeness of the expiration of the session of Congress. On the other hand, when the House has voted to impeach an officer, a majority of the Members necessarily have concluded that the conduct alleged constituted grounds for impeachment.[83]

Does Article III, Section 1 of the Constitution, which states that judges "shall hold their Offices during good Behaviour," limit the relevance of the ten impeachments of judges with respect to presidential impeachment standards as has been argued by some? It does not. The argument is that "good behavior" implies an additional ground for impeachment of judges not applicable to other civil officers. However, the only impeachment provision discussed in the Convention and included in the Constitution is Article II, Section 4, which, by its express terms, applies to all civil officers, including judges, and defines impeachment offenses as "Treason, Bribery, and other high Crimes and Misdemeanors."

In any event, the interpretation of the "good behavior" clause adopted by the House in deciding to impeach a judge has not been made clear in any of them.

Whichever view is taken, the judicial impeachments have involved as assessment of the conduct of the officer in terms of the constitutional duties of his office. In this respect, the impeachments of judges are consistent with the three impeachments of non-judicial officers.

Each of the thirteen American impeachments involved charges of misconduct incompatible with the official position of the officeholder. This conduct falls into three broad categories: (1) exceeding the constitutional bounds of the powers of the office in derogation of the powers of another branch of government; (2) behaving in a manner grossly incompatible with the proper function and purpose of the office; and (3) employing the power of the office for an improper purpose or for personal gain.[84]

1. *Exceeding the Powers of the Office in Derogation of Another Branch of Government*

The first American impeachment, of Senator William Blount in 1797, was based on allegations that Blount attempted to incite the Creek and Cherokee Indians to attack the Spanish settlers of Florida and Louisiana, in order to capture the territory for the British. Blount was charged with engaging in a conspiracy to compromise the neutrality of the United States, in disregard of the constitutional provisions for conduct of foreign affairs. He was also charged, in effect, with attempting to oust the President's lawful appointee as principal agent for Indian affairs and replace him with a rival, thereby intruding upon the President's supervision of the executive branch.[85]

The impeachment of President Andrew Johnson in 1868 also rested on allegations that he had exceeded the power of his office and had failed to respect the prerogatives of Congress. The Johnson impeachment grew out of a bitter partisan struggle over the implementation of Reconstruction in the South following the Civil War. Johnson was charged with violation of the Tenure of Office Act, which purported to take away the President's authority to remove members of his own cabinet and specifically provided that violation would be a "high misdemeanor," as well as a crime. Believing the Act unconstitutional, Johnson removed Secretary of War Edwin M. Stanton and was impeached three days later.

Nine articles of impeachment were originally voted against Johnson, all dealing with his removal of Stanton and the appointment of a successor without the advice and consent of the Senate. The first article, for example, charged that President Johnson

> . . . unmindful of the high duties of his office, of his oath of office, and of the requirement of the Constitution that he should take care that the laws be faithfully executed, did unlawfully, and in violation of the Constitution and laws of the United States, order in writing the removal of Edwin M. Stanton from the office of Secretary for the Department of War.[86]

Two more articles were adopted by the House the following day. Article Ten charged that Johnson, "unmindful of the high duties of his office, and the dignity and proprieties thereof," had made inflammatory speeches that attempted to ridicule and disgrace the Congress.[87] Article Eleven charged him with attempts to prevent the execution of the Tenure of Office Act, an Army appropriations act, and a Reconstruction act designed by Congress "for the more efficient government of the rebel states." On its face, this article involved statutory violations, but it also reflected the underlying challenge to all of Johnson's post-war policies.

The removal of Stanton was more a catalyst for the impeachment than a fundamental cause.[88] The issue between the President and Congress was which of them should have the constitutional—and ultimately even the military—power to make and enforce Reconstruction policy in the South. The Johnson impeachment, as did the British impeachments of great ministers, involved issues of state going to the heart of the constitutional division of executive and legislative power.

2. Behaving in a Manner Grossly Incompatible with the Proper Function and Purpose of the Office

Judge John Pickering was impeached in 1803, largely for intoxication on the bench.[89] Three of the articles alleged errors in a trial in violation of his trust and duty as a judge; the fourth charged that Pickering, "being a man of loose morals and intemperate habits," had appeared on the bench during the trial in a state of total intoxication and had used profane language. Seventy-three years later another judge, Mark Delahay, was impeached for intoxication both "on and off" the bench but resigned before articles of impeachment were adopted.

A similar concern with conduct incompatible with the proper exercise of judicial office appears in the decision of the House to impeach Associate Supreme Court Justice Samuel Chase in 1804. The House alleged that Justice Chase had permitted his partisan views to influence his conduct of two trials held while he was conducting circuit court several years earlier. The first involved a Pennsylvania farmer who had led a rebellion against a Federal tax collector in 1789 and was later charged with treason. The articles of impeachment charged that "unmindful of the solemn duties of his office, and contrary to the sacred obligation" of his oath, Chase "did conduct himself in a manner highly arbitrary, oppressive, and unjust," citing procedural rulings against the defense.

Similar language appeared in articles relating to the trial of a Virginia printer indicted under the Sedition Act of 1798. Specific examples of Chase's bias were alleged, and his conduct was characterized as "an indecent solicitude . . . for the conviction of the accused, unbecoming even a public prosecutor but highly disgraceful to the character of a judge, as it was subversive of justice." The eighth article charged that Chase, "disregarding the duties . . . of his judicial character, . . . did . . . pervert his official right and duty to address the grand jury" by delivering "an intemperate and inflammatory policial harangue." His conduct was alleged to be a serious breach of his duty to judge impartially and to reflect on his competence to continue to exercise the office.

Judge West H. Humphreys was impeached in 1862 on charges that he joined the Confederacy without resigning his federal judgeship.[90] Judicial prejudice against Union supporters was also alleged.

Judicial favoritism and failure to give impartial consideration to cases before him was also among the allegations in the impeachment of Judge George W. English in 1926. The final article charged that his favoritism had created distrust of the disinterestedness of his official actions and destroyed public confidence in his court.[91]

3. Employing the Power of the Office for an Improper Purpose or for Personal Gain

Two types of official conduct for improper purposes have been alleged in past impeachments. The first type involves vindictive use of their office by federal judges; the second, the use of office for personal gain.

Judge James H. Peck was impeached in 1826 for charging with contempt a lawyer who had publicly criticized one of his decisions, imprisoning him, and ordering his disbarment for 18 months. The House debated whether this single instance of vindictive abuse of power was sufficient to impeach, and decided that it was, alleging that the conduct was unjust, arbitrary, and beyond the scope of Peck's duty.

Vindictive use of power also constituted an element of the charges in two other impeachments. Judge George W. English was charged in 1926, among other things, with threatening to jail a local newspaper editor for printing a critical editorial and with summoning local officials into court in a non-existent case to harangue them. Some of the articles in the impeachment of Judge Charles Swayne (1903) alleged that he maliciously and unlawfully imprisoned two lawyers and a litigant for contempt.

Six impeachments have alleged the use of office for personal gain or the appearance of financial impropriety while in office. Secretary of War William W. Belknap was impeached in 1876 of high crimes and misdemeanors for conduct that probably constituted bribery and certainly involved the use of his office for highly improper purposes—receiving substantial annual payments through an intermediary in return for his appointing a particular post trader at a frontier military post in Indian territory.

The impeachments of Judges Charles Swayne (1903), Robert W. Archbald (1912), George W. English (1926), Harold Louderback (1932) and Halsted L. Ritter (1936) each involved charges of the use of office for direct or indirect personal monetary gain.[92] In the Archbald and Ritter cases, a number of allegations of improper conduct were combined in a single, final article, as well as being charged separately.

In drawing up articles of impeachment, the House has placed little emphasis on criminal conduct. Less than one-third of the eighty-three articles the House has adopted have explicitly charged the violation of a criminal statute or used the word "criminal" or "crime" to describe the conduct alleged, and ten of the articles that do were those involving the Tenure of Office Act in the impeachment of President Andrew Johnson. The House has not always used the technical language of the criminal law even when the conduct alleged fairly clearly constituted a criminal offense, as in the Humphreys and Belknap impeachments. Moreover, a number of articles, even though they may have alleged that the conduct was unlawful, do not seem to state criminal conduct—including Article Ten against President Andrew Johnson (charging inflammatory speeches), and some of the charges against all of the judges except Humphreys.

Much more common in the articles are allegations that the officer has violated his duties or his oath or seriously undermined public confidence in his ability to perform his official functions. Recitals that a judge has brought his court or the judicial system into disrepute are commonplace. In the impeachment of President Johnson, nine of the articles allege that he acted "unmindful of the high duties, or of his oath of office," and several specifically refer to his constitutional duty to take care that the laws be faithfully executed.

The formal language of an article of impeachment, however, is less significant than the nature of the allegations that it contains. All have involved charges of conduct incompatible with continued performance of the office; some have explicitly rested upon a "course of conduct" or have combined disparate charges in a single, final article. Some of the individual articles seem to have alleged conduct that, taken alone, would not have been considered serious, such as two articles in the impeachment of Justice Chase that merely alleged procedural errors at trial. In the early impeachments, the articles were not prepared until after impeachment had been voted by the House, and it seems probable that the decision to impeach was made on the basis of all the allegations viewed as a whole, rather than each separate charge. Unlike the Senate, which votes separately on each article after trial, and where conviction on but one article is required for removal from office, the House appears to have considered the individual offenses less significant than what they said together about the conduct of the official in the performance of his duties.

Two tendencies should be avoided in interpreting the American impeachments. The first is to dismiss them too readily because most have involved judges. The second is to make too much of them. They do not all fit neatly and logically into categories. That, however, is in keeping with the nature of the remedy. It is intended to reach a broad variety of conduct by officers that is both serious and incompatible with the duties of the office.

Past impeachments are not precedents to be read with an eye for an article of impeachment identical to allegations that may be currently under consideration. The American impeachment cases demonstrate a common theme useful in determining whether grounds for impeachment exist—that the grounds are derived from understanding the nature, functions and duties of the office.

III. THE CRIMINALITY ISSUE

The phrase "high Crimes and Misdemeanors" may connote "criminality" to some. This likely is the predicate for some of the contentions that only an indictable crime can constitute impeachable conduct. Other advocates of an indictable-offense requirement would establish a criminal standard of impeachable conduct because that standard is definite, can be known in advance and reflects a contemporary legal view of what conduct should be punished. A requirement of criminality would require resort to familiar criminal laws and concepts to serve as standards in the impeachment process. Furthermore, this would pose problems concerning the applicability of standards of proof and the like pertaining to the trial of crimes.[93]

The central issue raised by these concerns is whether requiring an indictable offense as an essential element of impeachable conduct is consistent with the purposes and intent of the framers in establishing the impeachment power and in setting a constitutional standard for the exercise of that power. This issue must be considered in light of the historical evidence of the framers' intent.[94] It is also useful to consider whether the purposes of impeachment and criminal law are such that indictable offenses can, consistent with the Constitution, be an essential element of grounds for impeachment. The impeachment of a President must occur only for reasons at least as pressing as those needs of government that give rise to the creation of criminal offenses. But this does not mean that the various elements of proof, defenses, and other substantive concepts surrounding an indictable offense control the impeachment process. Nor does it mean that state or federal criminal codes are necessarily the place to turn to provide a standard under the United States Constitution. *Impeachment is a constitutional remedy. The framers intended that the impeachment language they employed should reflect the grave misconduct that so injures or abuses our constitutional institutions and form of government as to justify impeachment.* [My emphasis.]

This view is supported by the historical evidence of the constitutional meaning of the words "high Crimes and Misdemeanors." That evidence is set out above.[95] It establishes that the phrase "high Crimes and Misdemeanors"—which over a period of centuries evolved into the English standard of impeachable conduct—has a special historical meaning different from the ordinary meaning of the terms "crimes" and "misdemeanors."[96] "High misdemeanors," referred to a category of offenses that subverted the system of government. Since the fourteenth century the phrase "high Crimes and Misdemeanors" had been used in English impeachment cases to charge officials with a wide range of criminal and non-criminal offenses against the institutions and fundamental principles of English government.[97]

There is evidence that the framers were aware of this special, non-criminal meaning of the phrase "high Crimes and Misdemeanors" in the English law of impeachment.[98] Not only did Hamilton acknowledge Great Britain as "the model from which [impeachment] has been borrowed," but George Mason referred in the debates to the impeachment of Hastings, then pending before Parliament. Indeed, Mason, who proposed the phrase "high Crimes and Misdemeanors," expressly stated his intent to encompass "[a]ttempts to subvert the Constitution."[99]

The published records of the state ratifying conventions do not reveal an intention to limit the grounds of impeachment to criminal offenses.[100] James Iredell said in the North Carolina debates on ratification:

> the person convicted is further liable to a trial at common law, and may receive such common-law punishment as belongs to a description of such offences *if it be punishable by that law*. [Emphasis added.][101]

Likewise, George Nicholas of Virginia distinguished disqualification to hold office from conviction for criminal conduct:

> If [the President] deviates from his duty, he is responsible to his constituents. . . . He will be absolutely disqualified to hold any place of

profit, honor, or trust, and liable to further punishment *if he has committed such high crimes as are punishable at common law.* [Emphasis added.][102]

The post-convention statements and writings of Alexander Hamilton, James Wilson, and James Madison—each a participant in the Constitutional Convention—show that they regarded impeachment as an appropriate device to deal with offenses against constitutional government by those who hold civil office, and not a device limited to criminal offenses.[103] Hamilton, in discussing the advantages of a single rather than a plural executive, explained that a single executive gave the people "the opportunity of discovering with facility and clearness the misconduct of the persons they trust, in order either to their removal from office, or to their actual punishment in cases which admit of it."[104] Hamilton further wrote: "Man, in public trust, will much oftener act in such a manner as to render him unworthy of being any longer trusted, than in such a manner as to make him obnoxious to legal punishment."[105]

The American experience with impeachment, which is summarized above, reflects the principle that impeachable conduct need not be criminal. Of the thirteen impeachments voted by the House since 1789, at least ten involved one or more allegations that did not charge a violation of criminal law.[106]

Impeachment and the criminal law serve fundamentally different purposes. Impeachment is the first step in a remedial process—removal from office and possible disqualification from holding future office. The purpose of impeachment is not personal punishment;[107] its function is primarily to maintain constitutional government. Furthermore, the Constitution itself provides that impeachment is no substitute for the ordinary process of criminal law since it specifies that impeachment does not immunize the officer from criminal liability for his wrongdoing.[108] [My emphasis.]

The general applicability of the criminal law also makes it inappropriate as the standard for a process applicable to a highly specific situation such as removal of a President. The criminal law sets a general standard of conduct which all must follow. It does not address itself to the abuses of presidential power. In an impeachment proceeding a President is called to account for abusing powers which only a President possesses.

Other characteristics of the criminal law make criminality inappropriate as an essential element of impeachable conduct. While the failure to act may be a crime, the traditional focus of criminal law is prohibitory. *Impeachable conduct, on the other hand, may include the serious failure to discharge the affirmative duties imposed on the President by the Constitution.* [My emphasis.] Unlike a criminal case, the cause for the removal of a President may be based on his entire course of conduct in office. In particular situations, it may be a course of conduct more than individual acts that has a tendency to subvert constitutional government.

To confine impeachable conduct to indictable offenses may well be to set a standard so restrictive as not to reach conduct that might adversely affect the system of government. Some of the most grievous offenses against our constitutional form of government may not entail violations of the criminal law.

If criminality is to be the basic element of impeachable conduct, what is the standard of criminal conduct to be? Is it to be criminality as known to the common law, or as divined from the Federal Criminal Code, or from an amalgam of State criminal statutes? If one is to turn to State statutes, then which of those of the States is to obtain? If the present Federal Criminal Code is to be the standard, then which of its provisions is to apply? If there is to be new Federal legislation to define the criminal standard, then presumably both the Senate and the President will take part in fixing that standard. How is this to be accomplished without encroachment upon the constitutional provision that "the sole power" of impeachment is vested in the House of Representatives?

A requirement of criminality would be incompatible with the intent of the framers to provide a mechanism broad enough to maintain the integrity of constitutional government. Impeachment is a constitutional safety valve; to fulfill this function, it must be flexible enough to cope with exigencies not now foreseeable. Congress has never undertaken to define impeachable offenses in the criminal code. Even respecting bribery, which is specifically identified in the Constitution as grounds for impeachment, the federal statute establishing the criminal offense for civil officers generally was enacted over seventy-five years after the Constitutional Convention.[109]

In sum, to limit impeachable conduct to criminal offenses would be incompatible with the evidence concerning the constitutional meaning of the phrase "high Crimes and Misdemeanors" and would frustrate the purpose that the framers intended for impeachment. [My emphasis.] State and federal criminal laws are not written in order to preserve the nation against serious abuse of the presidential office. But this is the purpose of the constitutional provision for the impeachment of a President and that purpose gives meaning to "high Crimes and Misdemeanors."

IV. CONCLUSION

Impeachment is a constitutional remedy addressed to serious offenses against the system of government. The purpose of impeachment under the Constitution is indicated by the limited scope of the remedy (removal from office and possible disqualification from future office) and by the stated grounds for impeachment (treason, bribery and other high crimes and misdemeanors). It is not controlling whether treason and bribery are criminal. More important, they are constitutional wrongs that subvert the structure of government, or undermine the integrity of office and even the Constitution itself, and thus are "high" offenses in the sense that word was used in English impeachments.

The framers of our Constitution consciously adopted a particular phrase from the English practice to help define the constitutional grounds for removal. The content of the phrase "high Crimes and Misdemeanors" for the framers is to be related to what the framers knew, on the whole, about the English practice—the broad sweep of English constitutional history and the vital role impeachment had played in the limitation of royal prerogative and the control of abuses of ministerial and judicial power.

Impeachment was not a remote subject for the framers. Even as they labored in Philadelphia, the impeachment trial of Warren Hastings, Governor-General of India, was pending in London, a fact to which George Mason made explicit reference in the Convention. Whatever may be said on the merits of Hastings' conduct, the charges against him exemplified the central aspect of impeachment—the parliamentary effort to reach grave abuses of governmental power.

The framers understood quite clearly that the constitutional system they were creating must include some ultimate check on the conduct of the executive, particularly as they came to reject the suggested plural executive. While insistent that balance between the executive and legislative branches be maintained so that the executive would not become the creature of the legislature, dismissable at its will, the framers also recognized that some means would be needed to deal with excesses by the executive. Impeachment was familiar to them. They understood its essential constitutional functions and perceived its adaptability to the American context.

While it may be argued that some articles of impeachment have charged conduct that constituted crime and thus that criminality is an essential ingredient, or that some have charged conduct that was not criminal and thus that criminality is not essential, the fact remains that in the English practice and in several of the American impeachments the criminality issue was not raised at all. *The emphasis has been on the significant effects of the conduct—undermining the integrity of office, disregard of constitutional duties and oath of office, arrogation of power, abuse of the governmental process, adverse impact on the system of government.* [My emphasis.] Clearly, these effects can be brought about in ways not anticipated by the criminal law. Criminal standards and criminal courts were established to control individual conduct. Impeachment was evolved by Parliament to cope with both the inadequacy of criminal standards and the impotence of courts to deal with the conduct of great public figures. It would be anomalous if the framers, having barred criminal sanctions from the impeachment remedy and limited it to removal and possible disqualification from office, intended to restrict the grounds for impeachment to conduct that was criminal.

The longing for precise criteria is understandable; advance, precise definition of objective limits would seemingly serve both to direct future conduct and to inhibit arbitrary reaction to past conduct. In private affairs the objective is the control of personal behavior, in part through the punishment of misbehavior. In general, advance definition of standards respecting private conduct works reasonably well. However, where the issue is presidential compliance with the constitutional requirements and limitations on the presidency, the crucial factor is not the intrinsic quality of behavior but the significance of its effect upon our constitutional system or the functioning of our government.

It is useful to note three major presidential duties of broad scope that are explicitly recited in the Constitution: "to take Care that the Laws be faithfully executed," to "faithfully execute the Office of President of the United States" and to "preserve, protect, and defend the Constitution of the United States" to the best of his ability. [My emphasis.] The first is directly imposed by the Constitution; the second and third are included in the constitutionally prescribed oath that the

President is required to take before he enters upon the execution of his office and are, therefore, also expressly imposed by the Constitution.

The duty to take care is affirmative. So is the duty faithfully to execute the office. [My emphasis.] A President must carry out the obligations of his office diligently and in good faith. The elective character and political role of a President make it difficult to define faithful exercise of his powers in the abstract. A President must make policy and exercise discretion. This discretion necessarily is broad, especially in emergency situations, but the constitutional duties of a President impose limitations on its exercise.

The "take care" duty emphasizes the responsibility of a President for the overall conduct of the executive branch, which the Constitution vests in him alone. He must take care that the executive is so organized and operated that this duty is performed.

The duty of a President to "preserve, protect, and defend the Constitution" to the best of his ability includes the duty not to abuse his powers or transgress their limits—not to violate the rights of citizens, such as those guaranteed by the Bill of Rights, and not to act in derogation of powers vested elsewhere by the Constitution.

Not all presidential misconduct is sufficient to constitute grounds for impeachment. *There is a further requirement—substantiality.* In deciding whether this further requirement has been met, the facts must be considered as a whole in the context of the office, not in terms of separate or isolated events. *Because impeachment of a President is a grave step for the nation, it is to be predicated only upon conduct seriously incompatible with either the constitutional form and principles of our government or the proper performance of constitutional duties of the presidential office.* [My emphasis.]

NOTES

1. Plucknett, "Presidential Address" reproduced in 3 *Transactions, Royal Historical Society*, 5th Series, 145 (1952).
2. See generally C. Roberts, *The Growth of Responsible Government in Stuart England* (Cambridge 1966).
3. Strafford was charged with treason, a term defined in 1352 by the Statute of Treasons, 25 Edw. 3, stat. 5, c.2 (1352). The particular charges against him presumably would have been within the compass of the general, or "salvo," clause of that statute, but did not fall within any of the enumerated acts of treason. Strafford rested his defense in part on that failure; his eloquence on the question of retrospective treasons ("Beware you do not awake these sleeping lions, by the searching out [of] some neglected moth-eaten records, they may one day tear you and your posterity in pieces: it was your ancestors' care to chain them up within the barricadoes of statutes; be not you ambitious to be more slikful and curious than your forefathers in the art of killing." *Celebrated Trials* (Phila. 1837) 518) may have dissuaded the Commons from bringing the trial to a vote in the House of Lords; instead they caused his execution by bill of attainder.
4. J. Rushworth, *The Tryal of Thomas Earl of Strafford*, in 8 Historical Collections 8 (1686).
5. Rushworth, *supra* n. 4, at 8-9. R. Berger, *Impeachment: The Constitutional Problems* 30 (1973), states that the impeachment of Strafford "... constitutes a great watershed in English constitutional history of which the Founders were aware."
6. *See generally* A. Simpson, *A Treatise on Federal Impeachments* (Philadelphia, 1916) 81-190 (Appendix of English Impeachment Trials); M.V. Clarke, "The Origin of Impeachment" in

Oxford Essays in Medieval History, 164 (Oxford, 1934). Reading and analyzing the early history of English impeachments is complicated by the paucity and ambiguity of the records. The analysis that follows in this section has been drawn largely from the scholarship of others, checked against the original records where possible.

The basis for what became the impeachment procedure apparently originated in 1341, when the King and Parliament alike accepted the principle that the King's ministers were to answer in Parliament for their misdeeds. C. Roberts, *supra* n. 2, at 7. Offenses against Magna Carta, for example, were failing for technicalities in the ordinary courts, and therefore Parliament provided that offenders against Magna Carta be declared in Parliament and judged by their peers. *Id.*, at 173.

7. Simpson, *supra* n. 6, at 86; Berger, *supra* n. 5, at 61; Adams and Stevens, *Select Documents of English History* (London 1927) 148.
8. For example, de la Pole was charged with purchasing property of great value from the King while using his position as Chancellor to have the lands appraised at less than they were worth, all in violation of his oath, in deceit of the King and in neglect of the need of the realm. Adams and Stevens, *supra* n. 7, at 148.
9. Adams and Stevens, *supra* n. 7, at 148-150.
10. 4 Hatsell (Shannon, Ireland, 1971, reprint of London 1796, 1818) 67.
11. 4 Hatsell, *supra* n. 10, at 67, charges 2, 6 and 12.
12. Roberts, *supra* n. 2, at 133.
13. 2 Howell *State Trials* 1136, 1137. *See generally* Simpson, *supra* n. 6, 91-127; Berger, *supra* n. 5, 67-73.
14. Peter Pett, Commissioner of the Navy, was charged in 1668 with negligent preparation for an invasion by the Dutch, and negligent loss of a ship. The latter charge was predicated on alleged willful neglect in failing to insure that the ship was brought to a mooring. 6 Howell *State Trials* 865, 866-67.
15. Chief Justice Scroggs was charged in 1680, among other things, with brow beating witnesses and commenting on their credibility, and with cursing and drinking to excess, thereby bringing "the highest scandal on the public justice of the kingdom." 8 Howell *State Trials* 200.
16. Simpson, *supra* n. 6, at 144.
17. Simpson, *supra* n. 6, at 144.
18. *See generally* Marshall, *The Impeachment of Warren Hastings* (Oxford, 1965).
19. Of the original resolutions proposed by Burke in 1786 and accepted by the House as articles of impeachment in 1787, both criminal and non-criminal offenses appear. The fourth article, for example, charging that Hastings had confiscated the landed income of the Begums of Oudh, was described by Pitt as that of all others that bore the strongest marks of criminality. Marshall, *supra* n. 19, at 53.

   The third article, on the other hand, known as the Benares charge, claimed that circumstances imposed upon the Governor-General a duty to conduct himself "on the most distinguished principles of good faith, equity, moderation and mildness." Instead, continued the charge, Hastings provoked a revolt in Benares, resulting in "the arrest of the rajah, three revolutions in the country and great loss, whereby the said Hastings is guilty of a high crime and misdemeanor in the destruction of the country aforesaid." The Commons accepted this article, voting 119-79 that these were grounds for impeachment. Simpson, *supra* n. 6, at 168-170; Marshall, *supra* n. 19, at XV, 46.
20. *See, e.g.* Berger, *supra* n. 5 at 70-71.
21. Berger, *supra* n. 5, at 62.
22. 2 *The Records of the Federal Convention* 66 (M. Farrand ed. 1911) (hereinafter cited as Farrand).
23. 1 Farrand 322.
24. 1 Farrand 66.
25. This argument was made by James Wilson of Pennsylvania, who also said that he preferred a single executive "as giving most energy dispatch and responsibility to the office." 1 Farrand 65.
26. A number of suggestions for a Council to the President were made during the Convention. Only one was voted on, and it was rejected three states to eight. This proposal, by George Mason, called for a privy council of six members—two each from the eastern, middle, and southern states—selected by the Senate for staggered six-year terms, with two leaving office every two years. 2 Farrand 537, 542.

   Gouverneur Morris and Charles Pinckney, both of whom spoke in opposition to other proposals for a council, suggested a privy council composed of the Chief Justice and the heads of executive departments. Their proposal, however, expressly provided that the President "shall in all cases exercise his own judgment, either conform to [the] opinion [of the council] or not as he may think proper." Each officer who was a member of the council would "be responsible for his opinion on the affairs relating to his particular Department" and liable to impeachment and removal from office "for neglect of duty, malversation, or corruption." 2 Farrand 342-44.

Morris and Randolph's proposal was referred to the Committee on Detail, which reported a provision for an expanded privy council including the President of the Senate and the Speaker of the House. The council's duty was to advise the President "in all matters respecting the execution of his office, which he shall think proper to lay before them: But their advice shall not conclude him, nor affect his responsibility for the measures he shall adopt." 2 Farrand 367. This provision was never brought to a vote or debated in the Convention.

Opponents of a council argued that it would lessen executive responsibility. A council, said James Wilson, "oftener serves to cover, than prevent malpractices." 1 Farrand 97. And the Committee of Eleven, consisting of one delegate from each state, to which proposals for a council to the President as well as other questions of policy were referred, decided against a council on the ground that the President, "by persuading his council, to concur in his wrong measures, would acquire their protection for them." 2 Farrand 542.

Some delegates thought the responsibility of the President to be "chimerical": Gunning Beford because "he would not be punished for mistakes," 2 Farrand 43; Elbridge Gerry, with respect to nomination for offices, because the President could "always plead ignorance." 2 Farrand 539. Benjamin Franklin favored a Council because it "would not only be a check on a bad President but be a relief to a good one." He asserted that the delegates had "too much . . . fear of cabals in appointment by a number," and "too much confidence in those of single persons." Experience, he said, showed that "caprice, the intrigues of favorites and mistresses, etc." were "the means most prevalent in monarchies." 2 Farrand 542.

27. *The Federalist* No. 70, at 459-60 (Modern Library ed.) (A. Hamilton) (hereinafter cited as *Federalist*). The "multiplication of the Executive," Hamilton wrote, adds "to the difficulty of detection":
> The circumstances which may have led to any national miscarriage of misfortune are sometimes so complicated that, where there are a number of actors who may have had different degrees and kinds of agency, though we may clearly see on the whole that there has been mismanagement, yet it may be impracticable to pronounce to whose account the evil which may have been incurred is truly chargeable.

If there should be "collusion between the parties concerned, how easy it is to clothe the circumstances with so much ambiguity, as to render it uncertain what was the precise conduct of any of those parties?" *Id.* at 461.

28. *Federalist* No. 70 at 461. Hamilton stated:
> A council to a magistrate, who is himself responsible for what he does, are generally nothing better than a clog upon his good intentions, are often the instruments and accomplices of his bad, and are almost always a cloak to his faults. *Id.* at 462-63.

29. *Federalist* No. 70 at 462.
30. 4 J. Elliot, *The Debates in the Several State Conventions on the Adoption of the Federal Constitution* 74 (reprint of 2d ed.) (hereinafter cited as Elliot).
31. 4 Elliot 104.
32. 2 Elliot 480 (emphasis in original).
33. The Virginia Plan, fifteen resolutions proposed by Edmund Randolph at the beginning of the Convention, served as the basis of its early deliberations. The ninth resolution gave the national judiciary jurisdiction over "impeachments of any National officers." 1 Farrand 22.
34. 1 Farrand 88. Just before the adoption of this provision, a proposal to make the executive removable from office by the legislature upon request of a majority of the state legislatures had been overwhelmingly rejected. *Id.* 87. In the course of debate on this proposal, it was suggested that the legislature "should have the power to remove the Executive at pleasure"—a suggestion that was promptly criticized as making him "the mere creature of the Legislature" in violation of "the fundamental principle of good government," and was never formally proposed to the Convention. *Id.* 85-86.
35. 2 Farrand 69.
36. Farrand 67 (Rufus King). Similarly, Gouverneur Morris contended that if an executive charged with a criminal act were re-elected, "that will be sufficient proof of his innocence." *Id.* 64.

It was also argued in opposition to the impeachment provision, that the executive should not be impeachable "whilst in office"—an apparent allusion to the constitutions of Virginia and Delaware, which then provided that the governor (unlike other officers) could be impeached only after he left office. *Id.* See 7 Thorpe, *The Federal and State Constitutions* 3812 (1909). In response to this position, it was argued that corrupt elections would result, as an incumbent sought to keep his office in order to maintain his immunity from impeachment. He will "spare no means whatever to get himself re-elected," contended William R. Davie of North Carolina. *Id.* George Mason asserted that the danger of corrupting electors "furnished a peculiar reason in favor of impeachment whilst in office': "Shall the man who has practised corruption and by that means procured his appointment in the first instance, be suffered to escape punishment, by repeating his guilt?" *Id.* 65.

37. 2 Farrand 54.
38. "This Magistrate is not the King but the prime-Minister. The people are the King." 2 Farrand 69.
39. 2 Farrand 65.
40. 2 Farrand 65-66.
41. 2 Farrand 65.
42. 2 Farrand 67.
43. 2 Farrand 66.
44. See Appendix B for a chronological account of the Convention's deliberations on impeachment and related issues.
45. 2 Farrand 550.
46. The grounds for impeachment of the Governor of Virginia were "maladministration, corruption, or other means, by which the safety of the State may be endangered." 7 Thorpe, *The Federal and State Constitutions* 3812 (1909).
47. 2 Farrand 550. Mason's wording was unanimously changed later the same day from "agst the State" to "against the United States" in order to avoid ambiguity. This phrase was later dropped in the final draft of the Constitution prepared by the Committee on Style and Revision, which was charged with arranging and improving the language of the articles adopted by the Convention without altering its substance.
48. *Supra*, n.1.
49. R. Berger, *Impeachment: The Constitutional Problems* 87, 89 and accompanying notes (1973).
50. As a technical term, a "high" crime signified a crime against the system of government, not merely a serious crime. "This element of injury to the commonwealth—that is, to the state itself and to its constitution—was historically the criterion for distinguishing a 'high' crime of misdemeanor from an ordinary one. The distinction goes back to the ancient law of treason, which differentiated 'high' from 'petit' treason." Bestor, Book Review, 49 Wash. L. Rev. 255, 263-64 (1973). *See* 4. W. Blackstone, Commentaries* (Quoted in Bestor, *supra*).
51. The provision (article XV of Committee draft of the Committee on Detail) orginally read: "Any person charged with treason, felony or high misdemeanor in any State, who shall flee from justice, and shall be found in any other State, shall, on demand of the Executive power of the State from which he fled, be delivered up and removed to the State having jurisdiction of the offence." 2 Farrand 187-88.

    This clause was virtually identical with the extradition clause contained in article IV of the Articles of Confederation, which referred to "any Person guilty of, or charged with treason, felony, or other high misdemeanor in any state. . . ."
52. 2 Farrand 443.
53. 3 Elliott 501.
54. 4 Blackstone's Commentaries* 121 (emphasis omitted).
55. *U.S. v. Burr*, 25 Fed. Cas. 1, 159 (No. 14, 693) (C.C.D. Va. 1807).
56. 2 Farrand 550.
57. *The Federalist* No. 65 at 423-24 (Modern Library ed.) (A. Hamilton).
58. 4 Elliot 281.
59. 3 Elliot 201.
60. 3 Elliot 486.
61. 3 Elliot 497-98. Madison went on to say, contrary to his position in the Philadelphia convention, that the President could be suspended when suspected, and his powers would devolve on the Vice President, who could likewise be suspended until impeached and convicted, if he were also suspected. *Id.*, 498.
62. 3 Elliot 500. John Rutledge of South Carolina made the same point, asking "whether gentlemen seriously could suppose that a President, who has a character at stake, would be such a fool and knave as to join with ten others [two-thirds of a minimal quorum of the Senate] to tear up liberty by the roots, when a full Senate were competent to impeach him." 4 Elliot 268.
63. 3 Elliot 117.
64. 3 Elliot 401.
65. 4 Elliot 126.
66. 4 Elliot 127.

67. For example, Wilson Nicholas in the Virginia convention asserted that the President "is personally amenable for his maladministration" through impeachment, 3 Elliot 17; George Nicholas in the same convention referred to the President's impeachability if he "deviates from his duty," *Id.* 240. Archibald MacLaine in the South Carolina convention also referred to the President's impeachability for "any mal-administration in his office," 4 Elliot 47; and Reverend Samuel Stillman of Massachusetts referred to his impeachability for "malconduct," asking, "With such a prospect, who will dare to abuse the powers vested in him by the people?" 2 Elliot 169.

68. Chief Justice Taft wrote with reference to the removal power debate in the opinion for the Court in *Myers* v. *United States*, that constitutional decisions of the First Congress "have always been regarded, as they should be regarded, as of the greatest weight in the interpretation of that fundamental instrument." 272 U.S. 52, 174-75 (1926).

69. 1 Annals of Cong. 498 (1789).

70. *Id.* 372-73.

71. *Id.* 502.

72. *Id.* 535-36. Gerry also implied, perhaps rhetorically, that a violation of the Constitution was grounds for impeachment. If, he said, the Constitution failed to include provision for removal of executive officers, an attempt by the legislature to cure the omission would be an attempt to amend the Constitution. But the Constitution provided procedures for its amendment, and "an attempt to amend it in any other way may be a high crime or misdemeanor, or something worse." *Id.* 503.

73. *Id.* 559. John Vining of Deleware commented:

   The President. What are his duties? To see the laws faithfully executed; if he does not do this effectually, he is responsible. To whom? To the people. Have they the means of calling him to account, and punishing him for neglect? They have secured in the Constitution, by impeachment, to be presented by their immediate representatives; if they fail here, they have another check when the time of election comes round. *Id.* 572.

74. *Id.* 375.

75. *Id.*

76. *Id.* 474.

77. *Id.* 475.

78. *Id.* 477. The proponents of the President's removal power were careful to preserve impeachment as a supplementary method of removing executive officials. Madison said impeachment will reach a subordinate "whose bad actions may be connived at or overlooked by the President." *Id.* 372. Abraham Baldwin said:

   The Constitution provides for   what? That no bad man should come into office. But suppose that one such could be got in, he can be got out again in despite of the President. We can impeach him, and drag him from his place. . . . *Id.* 558.

79. Wilson, *Lectures on Law*, in 1 *The Works of James Wilson*, 426 (R. McCloskey ed. 1967).

80. *Id.* 425.

81. 1 *J. Story Commentaries on the Constitution of the United States*, Sec. 764, at 531 (3d. ed. 1858).

82. Eleven of these officers were tried in the Senate. Articles of impeachment were presented to the Senate against a twelfth (Judge English), but he resigned shortly before trial. The thirteenth (Judge Delahay) resigned before articles could be drawn. See Appendix C for a brief synopsis of each impeachment.

83. Only four of the thirteen impeachments—all involving judges—have resulted in conviction in the Senate and removal from office. While conviction and removal show that the Senate agreed with the House that the charges on which conviction occurred stated legally sufficient grounds for impeachment, acquittals offer no guidance on this question, as they may have resulted from a failure of proof, other factors, or a determination by more than one third of the Senators (as in the Blount and Belknap impeachments) that trial or conviction was inappropriate for want of jurisdiction.

84. A procedural note may be useful. The House votes both a resolution of impeachment against an officer and articles of impeachment containing the specific charges that will be brought to trial in the Senate. Except for the impeachment of Judge Delahay, the discussion of grounds here is based on the formal articles.

85. After Blount had been impeached by the House, but before trial of the impeachment, the Senate expelled him for "having been guilty of a high misdemeanor, entirely inconsistent with his public trust and duty as a Senator."

86. Article one further alleged that Johnson's removal of Stanton was unlawful because the Senate had earlier rejected Johnson's previous suspension of him.

87. Quoting from speeches which Johnson had made in Washington, D.C., Cleveland, Ohio, and St.

Louis, Missouri, article ten pronounced these speeches "censurable in any, [and] peculiarly indecent and unbecoming in the Chief Magistrate of the United States." By means of these speeches, the article concluded, Johnson had brought the high office of the Presidency "into contempt, ridicule, and disgrace, to the great scandal of all good citizens."

88.   The Judiciary Committee had reported a resolution of impeachment three months earlier, charging President Johnson in its report with omissions of duty, usurpations of power, violations of his oath of office, the laws and the Constitution in his conduct of Reconstruction. The House voted down the resolution.

89.   The issue of Pickering's insanity was raised at trial in the Senate, but was not discussed by the House when it voted to impeach or to adopt articles of impeachment.

90.   Although some of the language in the articles suggested treason, only high crimes and misdemeanors were alleged, and Humphrey's offenses were characterized as a failure to discharge his judicial duties.

91.   Some of the allegations against Judges Harold Louderback (1932) and Halsted Ritter (1936) also involved judicial favoritism affecting public confidence in their courts.

92.   Judge Swayne was charged with falsifying expense accounts and using a railroad car in the possession of a receiver he had appointed. Judge Archbald was charged with using his office to secure business favors from litigants and potential litigants before his court. Judges English, Louderback, and Ritter were charged with misusing their power to appoint and set the fees of bankruptcy receivers for personal profit.

93.   See A. Simpson, *A Treatise on Federal Impeachments* 28-29 (1916). It has also been argued that because Treason and Bribery are crimes, "other high Crimes and Misdemeanors" must refer to crimes under the *ejusdem generis* rule of construction. But *ejusdem generis* merely requires a unifying principle. The question here is whether that principle is criminality or rather conduct subversive of our constitutional institutions and form of government.

94.   The rule of construction against redundancy indicates an intent not to require criminality. If criminality is required, the word "misdemeanor" would add nothing to "high Crimes."

95.   See part II.B. *supra.*

96.   See part II.B.2. *supra.*

97.   See part II.A. *supra*, n. 6 to n. 21 and accompanying text.

98.   See part II.B.2. *supra*, n. 4 to n. 10 accompanying text.

99.   See *Id.*, n. 1 to n. 3 and accompanying text.

100.   See part II.B.3. *supra*, text accompanying n. 3 to n. 10.

101.   4 Elliot 114.

102.   3 Elliot 240.

103.   See part II.B.1., text accompanying n. 11, part II.B.3., text accompanying n. 2, 6, 7, 14, 15, 24 and 25.

104.   *Federalist* No. 70, at 461.

105.   *Id.* at 459.

106.   See Part II.C. *supra.*

107.   It has been argued that "[i]mpeachment is a special form of punishment for crime," but that gross and willful neglect of duty would be a violation of the oath of office and "[s]uch violation, by criminal acts of commission or omission, is the only nonindictable offense for which the President, Vice President, judges or other civil officers can be impeached." I. Brant, *Impeachment, Trials and Errors*, at 13, 20, 23 (1972). While this approach might in particular instances lead to the same results as the approach to impeachment as a constitutional remedy for action incompatible with constitutional government and the duties of constitutional office, it is, for the reasons stated in this memorandum, the latter approach that best reflects the intent of the framers and the constitutional function of impeachment. At the time the Constitution was adopted, "crime" and "punishment for crime" were terms used far more broadly than today. The seventh edition of Samuel Johnson's dictionary, published in 1785, defines "crime" as "an act contrary to right, an offense; a great fault; an act of wickedness." To the extent that the debates on the Constitution and its ratification refer to impeachment as a form of "punishment" it is punishment in the sense that today would be thought a non-criminal sanction, such as removal of a corporate officer for misconduct breaching his duties to the corporation.

108.   It is sometimes suggested that various provisions in the Constitution exempting cases of impeachment from certain provisions relating to the trial and punishment of crimes indicate an intention to require an indictable offense as an essential element of impeachable conduct. In addition to the provision referred to in the text (Article I, Section 3), cases of impeachment are exempted from the power of pardon and the right to trial by jury in Article II, Section 2 and

Article III, Section 2 respectively. These provisions were placed in the Constitution in recognition that impeachable conduct *may* entail criminal conduct and to make it clear that even when criminal conduct is involved, the trial of an impeachment was not intended to be a criminal proceeding. The sources quoted at notes 8-13, *supra*, show the understanding that impeachable conduct may, but need not, involve criminal conduct.

109. It appears from the annotations to the Revised Statutes of 1873 that bribery was not made a federal crime until 1790 for judges, 1853 for Members of Congress, and 1863 for other civil officers. *U.S. Rev. Stat.*, Title LXX, Ch. 6, §§ 5499-502. This consideration strongly suggests that conduct not amounting to statutory bribery may nonetheless constitute the constitutional "high Crime and Misdemeanor" of bribery.

Much was made of the problem of "executive privilege" during the Watergate drama. At various times the President invoked executive privilege to deny the Ervin committee the right to compel the testimony of his administrative subordinates. It was also invoked against efforts by the grand jury, the courts, the Congress and finally the House Committee on the Judiciary sitting to consider impeachment, to secure and subpoena recorded transcripts of conversations which took place in the office of the President and other papers related to such conversations. The argument over the legitimacy of executive privilege went on for more than a year and was subject to detailed analysis and controversy, not only by the President and the attorneys representing him and the legislative and judicial bodies attempting to obtain such testimony, papers and electronic tapes, but also by members of the press and the academy, who relentlessly pursued the argument for many months.

The President's claim to absolute executive privilege had little or no basis in historical precedent. In fact there are few if any absolutes in the broad spectrum of rights and privileges established by the Constitution and enacted throughout almost 200 years of lawmaking. In the case of the division of powers, however, even the Supreme Court tries to avoid entering this "political thicket," and usually leaves it up to the executive and legislative branches to resolve their own conflicts. The removal power of the President is such an instance, and the battle over this power raged between the two branches for almost 100 years before Chief Justice Taft and the Court intervened in the first quarter of his century (see Volume II, section three and Volume III, section two of this series). In short, the constitutional process has frequently been the scene of battles in which thoughtful arguments and powerful claims have been advanced on more than one side of a controversy. The road to settled and satisfactory consensus, particularly regarding matters which are only implicit in the Constitution, is often stormy and rugged, and it may take decades, perhaps even centuries, to resolve satisfactorily.

Until very recently, the principle of executive privilege has been far less controversial than the removal power. It was first invoked by Washington, supported by Jefferson and Madison, and used by Presidents from Jackson to Nixon when it appeared to be in their interest to employ it.[72] Even Chief Justice John Marshall, who appeared, albeit unsuccessfully, to challenge Thomas Jefferson's use of this discretionary power in the Burr trial, defended the President's power and independence from the legislature or the judiciary "in his political character" in his famous Marbury v. Madison decision:

> By the Constitution of the United States, the President is invested with certain important political powers, in the exercise of which he is to use his own discretion, and is accountable only to his country in his political character, and to his own conscience.[73]

Marshall did not spell out what these political powers were, but obviously the President's role as Commander in Chief in wartime was one, and when exercising the command function he is not accountable to the Congress. This does not, however, invite him to ignore constitutionally guaranteed rights and privileges, but as we have observed, resistance to the President, even on these grounds, is very dubious while the battle is being joined.

Implicit in all of this is the distinction between a parliamentary form of government, where the Executive is continuously answerable and accountable to Parliament for his actions both during war and peace, and our very different divided or, as some would still have it, system of separation of powers, in the United States. It is nowhere stated in the Constitution, but was inferred from the broader interpretation of that document by Washington, Jefferson, Madison and Jackson and others who defended the principle which we now call "executive privilege," that such discretionary power was necessary and essential to the Chief Executive of the nation in the independent conduct of the presidency. This discretionary power was also recognized by the early Congresses, which normally included in their demands for presidential documents a recognition of his right to withhold from them any document or such information which, in his discretionary judgment, might compromise the public interest. Confidentiality between the President and his advisors has always had to be maintained in order that he may be free to hear all points of view on critical and sensitive problems, like those of national security, and be assured that such counsel is fully protected from disclosure.

No absolute claim of privilege, however, was made by earlier Presidents nor was it argued that such a privilege should be extended to a President's subordinates as well. Neither had it invariably been recognized above other privileges when in conflict with the rights and/or privileges advanced by other branches of the government or individual citizens. It was always an ambiguous grey area, not clarified by any single decision of the Court. In such an ambiguous state, its limits were normally prescribed by the balance of political power which existed at the time it was invoked and the integrity of those involved.

The claim of President Nixon and his attorneys to *unreviewable* executive privilege, covering all confidential discussions and papers of the President, even in the face of the demand by the Watergate special prosecutor for an examination by a special investigating grand jury, and later in a criminal trial against certain presidential assistants and advisors, went beyond any precedent previously established. Confronting this exhorbitant claim was an equally unfounded argument advanced primarily by Raoul Berger of Harvard, a leading authority in the field, that there was no constitutional basis for the principle of executive privilege, and in fact it is an historical "myth."[74] Fortunately neither position was upheld by the Supreme Court which reviewed the question when Nixon attempted to deny the special prosecutor access to tapes, memoranda, transcripts or other writings which Leon Jaworski argued were essential to his criminal prosecution of the President's subordinates. The Court denied that the President's claim of absolute or unqualified executive privilege can "prevail over the demands of due process of law in the fair administration of criminal justice."[75] On the other hand the Court affirmed the constitutional basis for the principle of "executive privilege":

> Whatever the nature of the privilege of confidentiality of presidential communications in the exercise of Art. II powers the privilege can be said to derive from the supremacy of each branch within its own assigned area of constitutional duties. Certain powers and privileges flow from the nature of enumerated powers; the protection of the confidentiality of presidential communications has similar constitutional underpinnings.[76]

Further:

> A President and those who assist him must be free to explore alternatives in the process of shaping policies and making decisions and to do so in a way many would be unwilling to express except privately. These are the considerations justifying a presumptive privilege for presidential communications. The privilege is fundamental to the operation of government and inextricably rooted in the separation of powers under the Constitution.[77]

To those like the special prosecutor and Berger who argued that such a principle is not authorized by the Constitution, the unanimous Court responded by stating:

> The silence of the Constitution on this score is not dispositive. "The rule of constitutional interpretation announced in McCulloch v. Maryland, 4 Wheat. 316, that that which was reasonably appropriate and relevant to the exercise of a granted power was considered as accompanying the grant, has been so universally applied it suffices merely to state it." Marshall v. Gordon, 243 U.S. 521, 537 (1917).[78]

But the Court did not stop there. It attempted to narrow the application of the decision.

> We are not here concerned with the balance between the President's generalized interest in confidentiality and the need for relevant evidence in civil litigation, nor with that between the confidentiality interest and congressional demands for information, nor with the President's interest in preserving state secrets. We address only the conflict between the President's assertion of a *generalized* privilege of confidentiality against the constitutional need for relevant evidence to criminal trials.[79]

Opening the door even wider, the Court suggested that when the claim advanced for executive privilege or confidentiality was based upon "military, diplomatic or national security considerations," and not the "broad, undifferentiated claim of public interest," it might be upheld by the courts, even in the face of demands of a criminal prosecution.[80] Allan Westin, an outstanding authority on constitutional law, argues that the decision affirms that "the President has a constitutional basis for asserting privilege and can have this enforced by the courts."[81] The eagerness of the champions of the historical "myth" thesis to bring the question before the Supreme Court may have led, and I hope I am wrong in this conjecture, to the establishment of a broader conception of executive privilege than existed before the decision. The result in the future may be its more frequent and contrived application. If this turns out to be true, it will only demonstrate once again that judicial review is not always the ideal solution to our most agonizing constitutional questions and that such considerations are sometimes overlooked by intellectuals when they pontificate from the protected and sometimes unrealistic atmosphere of their academic studies.

If the public discussion of this question had been more reasonable, objective and historically accurate, the issue might have been resolved without a unanimous decision by the Supreme Court. Of course it may well have been necessary to go to the Supreme Court to force Nixon to yield the tapes, but it is conceivable that his stance might have been different had the concept of executive privilege not been attacked so stridently and wrongly by his opponents. This alone probably accounted for his legal advisors initially believing that he had a good chance of being upheld in the courts. Of course this is sheer speculation. But, whereas in the past most Presidents have pressed the claims of executive privilege quite modestly and relatively infrequently, they have also been restrained by the subtle interplay of the three branches as they confront each other in the political process. The Court has now succeeded in fastening down a unanimous decision which may lead to the more expanded and improper development of the concept of executive privilege when the memory of Watergate recedes into history.[82]

Chief Justice Warren Burger
Supreme Court Decision in
U.S. *v.* Nixon, Nixon *v.* U.S.
July 24, 1974

The United States Law Week, Vol. 42, Sec. 4 (July 23, 1974), 5237-47.

Mr. Chief Justice Burger delivered the opinion of the Court.

These cases present for review the denial of a motion, filed on behalf of the President of the United States, in the case of *United States* v. *Mitchell et al.* (D.C. Crim. No. 74-110), to quash a third-party subpoena *duces tecum* issued by the United States District Court for the District of Columbia, pursuant to Fed. Rule Crim. Proc. 17 (c). The subpoena directed the President to produce certain tape recordings and documents relating to his conversations with aides and advisers. The court rejected the President's claims of absolute executive privilege, of lack of jurisdiction, and of failure to satisfy the requirements of Rule 17 (c). The President appealed to the Court of Appeals. We granted the United States' petition for certiorari before judgment, [See 28 U.S.C.§§ 1254 (1) and 2101 (e) and our Rule 20.

See, *e.g., Youngstown Sheet & Tube Co.* v. *Sawyer,* 343 U.S. 937, 579, 584 (1952); *United States* v. *United Mine Workers,* 329 U.S. 708, 709, 710 (1946); 330 U.S. 258, 269 (1947); *Carter* v. *Carter Coal Co.,* 298 U.S. 238 (1936); *Rickert Rice Mills* v. *Fontenot,* 297 U.S. 110 (1936); *Railroad Retirement Board* v. *Alton R. Co.,* 295 U.S. 330, 344 (1935); *United States* v. *Bankers Trust Co.,* 294 U.S. 240, 243 (1935). Footnote in original.] and also the President's responsive cross-petition for certiorari before judgment [The cross-petition in No. 73-1834 raised the issue whether the grand jury acted within its authority in naming the President as a coconspirator. Since we find resolution of this issue unnecessary to resolution of the question whether the claim of privilege is to prevail, the cross-petition for certiorari is dismissed as improvidently granted and the remainder of this opinion is concerned with the issues raised in No. 73-1766. On June 19, 1974, the President's counsel moved for disclosure and transmittal to this Court of all evidence presented to the grand jury relating to its action in naming the President as an unindicted coconspirator. Action on this motion was deferred pending oral argument of the case and is now denied. Footnote in original.] because of the public importance of the issues presented and the need for the prompt resolution.——U.S.——,—— (1974.)

On March 1, 1974, a grand jury of the United States District Court for the District of Columbia returned an indictment charging seven named individuals [The seven defendants were John N. Mitchell, H. R. Haldeman, John D. Ehrlichman, Charles W. Colson, Robert C. Mardian, Kenneth W. Parkinson, and Gordon Strachan. Each had occupied either a position of responsibility on the White House staff or the Committee for the Re-Election of the President. Colson entered a guilty plea on another charge and is no longer a defendant. Footnote in original.] with various offenses, including conspiracy to defraud the United States and to obstruct justice. Although he was not designated as such in the indictment, the grand jury named the President, among others, as an unindicted coconspirator. [The President entered a special appearance in the District Court on June 6 and requested that court to lift its protective order regarding the naming of certain individuals as coconspirators and to any additional extent deemed appropriate by the Court. This motion of the President was based on the ground that the disclosures to the news media made the reasons for continuance of the protective order no longer meaningful. On June 7, the District Court removed its protective order and, on June 10, counsel for both parties jointly moved this Court to unseal those parts of the record which related to the action of the grand jury regarding the President. After receiving a statement in opposition from the defendants, this Court denied that motion on June 15, 1974, except for the grand jury's immediate finding relating to the status of the President as an unindicted coconspirator.——U.S.—— (1974). Footnote in original.] On April 18, 1974, upon motion of the Special Prosecutor, see n. 8, *infra,* a subpoena *duces tecum* was issued pursuant to Rule 17 (c) to the President by the United States District Court and made returnable on May 2, 1974. This subpoena required the production, in advance of the September 9 trial date, of certain tapes, memoranda, papers, transcripts, or other writings relating to certain precisely identified meetings between the President and others. [The specific meetings and conversations are enumerated in a schedule attached to the subpoena.

42a-46a of the App. Footnote in original.] The Special Prosecutor was able to fix the time, place and persons present at these discussions because the White House daily logs and appointment records had been delivered to him. On April 30, the President publicly released edited transcripts of 43 conversations; portions of 20 conversations subject to subpoena in the present case were included. On May 1, 1974, the President's counsel, filed a "special appearance" and a motion to quash the subpoena, under Rule 17 (c). This motion was accompanied by a formal claim of privilege. At a subsequent hearing, [At the joint suggestion of the Special Prosecutor and counsel for the President, and with the approval of counsel for the defendants, further proceedings in the District Court were held *in camera.* Footnote in original.] further motions to expunge the grand jury's action naming the President as an unindicted coconspirator and for protective orders against the disclosure of that information were filed or raised orally by counsel for the President.

On May 20, 1974, the District Court denied the motion to quash and the motions to expunge and for protective orders.——F. Supp.——(1974). It further ordered "the President or any subordinate officer, official or employee with custody or control of the documents or objects subpoenaed," *id.*, at ——, to deliver to the District Court, on or before May 31, 1974, the originals of all subpoenaed items, as well as an index and analysis of those items, together with tape copies of those portions of the subpoenaed recordings for which transcripts had been released to the public by the President on April 30, The District Court rejected jurisdictional challenges based on a contention that the dispute was nonjusticiable because it was between the Special Prosecutor and the Chief Executive and hence "intra-executive" in character; it also rejected the contention that the judiciary was without authority to review as assertion of executive privilege by the President. The court's rejection of the first challenge was based on the authority and powers vested in the Special Prosecutor by the regulation promulgated by the Attorney General; the court concluded that a justiciable controversy was presented. The second challenge was held to be foreclosed by the decision in *Nixon* v. *Sirica,*——U.S. App. D.C.——, 487 F. 2d 700 (1973).

The District Court held that the judiciary, not the President, was the final arbiter of a claim of executive privilege. The court concluded that, under the circumstances of this case, the presumptive privilege was overcome by the Special Prosecutor's prima facie "demonstration of need sufficiently compelling to warrant judicial examination in chambers. . . ."——F. Supp., at——. The court held, finally, that the Special Prosecutor had satisfied the requirements of Rule 17 (c). The District Court stayed its order pending appellate review on condition that review was sought before 4 p.m., May 24. The court further provided that matters filed under seal remained under seal when transmitted as part of the record.

On May 24, 1974, the President filed a timely notice of appeal from the District Court order, and the certified record from the District Court was docketed in the United States Court of Appeals for the District of Columbia Circuit. On the same day, the President also filed a petition for writ of mandamus in the Court of Appeals seeking review of the District Court order.

Later on May 24, the Special Prosecutor also filed, in this Court, a petition for a writ of certiorari before judgment. On May 31, the petition was granted with an expedited briefing schedule.——U.S.——(1974). On June 6, the President filed, under seal, a cross-petition for writ of certiorari before judgment. This cross-petition was granted June 15, 1974,——U.S.——(1974), and the case was set for argument on July 8, 1974.

I
JURISDICTION

The threshold question presented is whether the May 20, 1974, order of the District Court was an appealable order and whether this case was properly "in," 28 U.S.C. § 1254, the United States Court of Appeals when the petition for certiorari was filed in this Court. Court of Appeals jurisdiction under 28 U.S.C. § 1291 encompasses only "final decisions of the district courts." Since the appeal was timely filed and all other procedural requirements were met, the petition is properly before this Court for consideration if the District Court order was final. 28 U.S.C. § 1254 (1); 28 U.S.C. § 2101 (e).

The finality requirement of 28 U.S.C. § 1291 embodies a strong congressional policy against piecemeal reviews, and against obstructing or impeding an ongoing judicial proceeding by interlocutory appeals. See, *e.g.*, *Cobbledick* v. *United States*, 309 U.S. 323, 324-326 (1940). This requirement ordinarily promotes judicial efficiency and hastens the ultimate termination of litigation. In applying this principle to an order denying a motion to quash and requiring the production of evidence pursuant to a subpoena duces tecum, it had been repeatedly held that the order is not final and hence not appealable, *United States* v. *Ryan*, 402 U.S. 530, 532 (1971); *Cobbledick* v. *United States*, 309 U.S. 322 (1940); *Alexander* v. *United States*, 201 U.S. 117 (1906). This Court has

> consistently held that the necessity for expedition in the administration of the criminal law justifies putting one who seeks to resist the production of desired information to a choice between compliance with a trial court's order to produce prior to any review of that order, and resistance to that order with the concomitant possibility of an adjudication of contempt if his claims are rejected on appeal. *United States* v. *Ryan*, 402 U.S. 530, 533 (1971).

The requirement of submitting to contempt, however, is not without exception and in some instances the purposes underlying the finality rule require a different result. For example, in *Perlman* v. *United States*, 247 U.S. 7 (1918), a subpoena had been directed to a third party requesting certain exhibits; the appellant, who owned the exhibits, sought to raise a claim of privilege. The Court held an order compelling production was appealable because it was unlikely that the third party would risk a contempt citation in order to allow immediate review of the appellant's claim of privilege. *Id.*, at 12-13. That case fell within the "limited class of cases where denial of immediate review would render impossible any review whatsoever of an individual's claims," *United States* v. *Ryan, supra,* at 533.

Here too the traditional contempt avenue to immediate appeal is peculiarly inappropriate due to the unique setting in which the question arises. To require a President of the United States to place himself in the posture of disobeying an order of a court merely to trigger the procedural mechanism for review of the ruling would be unseemly, and present an unnecessary occasion for constitutional confrontation between two branches of the Government. Similarly, a federal judge should not be placed in the posture of issuing a citation to a President simply in order to invoke review. The issue whether a President can be cited for contempt could itself engender protracted litigation, and would further delay both review on the merits of his claim of privilege and the ultimate termination of the underlying criminal action for which his evidence is sought. These considerations lead us to conclude that the order of the District Court was an appealable order. The appeal from that order was therefore properly "in" the Court of Appeals, and the case is now properly before this Court on the writ of certiorari before judgment. 28 U.S.C. § 1254; 28 U.S.C. § 2101 (e). *Gay* v. *Ruff,* 292 U.S. 25, 30 (1934). [The parties have suggested this Court has jurisdiction on other grounds. In view of our conclusion that there is jurisdiction under 28 U.S.C. § 1254 (1) because the District Court's order was appealable, we need not decide whether other jurisdictional vehicles are available. Footnote in original.]

II

JUSTICIABILITY

In the District Court, the President's counsel argued that the court lacked jurisdiction to issue the subpoena because the matter was in intra-branch dispute between a subordinate and superior officer of the Executive Branch and hence not subject to judicial resolution. That argument has been renewed in this Court with emphasis on the contention that the dispute does not present a "case" or "controversy" which can be adjudicated in the federal courts. The President's counsel argues that the federal courts should not intrude into areas committed to the other branches of Government. He views the present dispute as essentially a "jurisdictional" dispute within the Executive Branch which he analogizes to a dispute between two congressional committees. Since the Executive Branch has exclusive authority and absolute discretion to decide whether to prosecute a case, *Confiscation Cases,* 7 Wall. 454 (1869), *United States* v. *Cox,* 342 F. 2d 167, 171 (CA5), cert. denied, 381 U.S. 935 (1965), it is contended that a President's decision is final in determining what evidence is to be used in a given criminal case. Although his counsel concedes the President has delegated certain specific powers to the Special Prosecutor, he has not "waived nor delegated to the Special Prosecutor the President's duty to claim privilege as to all materials . . . which fall within the President's inherent authority to refuse to disclose to any executive officer." Brief for the President 47. The Special Prosecutor's demand for the items therefore presents, in the view of the President's counsel, a political question under *Baker* v.

Carr, 369 U.S. 186 (1962), since it involves a "textually demonstrable" grant of power under Art. II.

The mere assertion of a claim of an "intra-branch dispute," without more, has never operated to defeat federal jurisdiction; justiciability does not depend on such a surface inquiry. In *United States* v. *ICC*, 337 U.S. 426 (1949), the Court observed, "courts must look behind names that symbolize the parties to determine whether a justiciable case or controversy is presented." *Id.*, at 430. See also: *Powell* v. *McCormack*, 395 U.S. 486 (1969); *ICC* v. *Jersey City*, 322 U.S. 503 (1944); *United States ex rel. Chapman* v. *FPC*, 345 U.S. 153 (1953); *Secretary of Agriculture* v. *United States*, 347 U.S. 645 (1945); *FMB* v. *Isbrandsten Co.*, 356 U.S. 481, 482 n. 2 (1958); *United States* v. *Marine Bank Corp.*,——U.S.——(1974), and *United States* v. *Connecticut National Bank*,——U.S.——(1974).

Our starting point is the nature of the proceeding for which the evidence is sought—here a pending criminal prosecution. It is a judicial proceeding in a federal court alleging violation of federal laws and is brought in the name of the United States as sovereign. *Berger* v. *United States*, 295 U.S. 78, 88 (1935). Under the authority of Art. II, § 2, Congress has vested in the Attorney General the power to conduct the criminal litigation of the United States Government. 28 U.S.C. § 516. It has also vested in him the power to appoint subordinate officers to assist him in the discharge of his duties. 28 U.S.C. §§509, 510, 515, 533. Acting pursuant to those statutes, the Attorney General has delegated the authority to represent the United States in these particular matters to a Special Prosecutor with unique authority and tenure. [The regulation issued by the Attorney General pursuant to his statutory authority, vests in the Special Prosecutor plenary authority to control the course of investigations and litigation related to "all offenses arising out of the 1972 Presidential Election for which the Special Prosecutor deems it necessary and appropriate to assume responsibility, allegations involving the President, members of the White House staff, or Presidential appointees, and any other matters which he consents to have assigned to him by the Attorney General." 38 Fed. Reg. 30739, as amended by 38 Fed. Reg. 32805. In particular, the Special Prosecutor was given full authority, *inter alia*, "to contest the assertion of 'Executive Privilege' . . . and handl[e] all aspects of any cases within his jurisdiction." *Ibid*. The regulations then go on to provide:

> In exercising this authority, the Special Prosecutor will have the greatest degree of independence that is consistent with the Attorney-General's statutory accountability for all matters falling within the jurisdiction of the Department of Justice. The Attorney General will not countermand or interfere with the Special Prosecutor's decisions or actions. The Special Prosecutor will determine whether and to what extent he will inform or consult with the Attorney General about the conduct of his duties and responsibilities. In accordance with assurances given by the President to the Attorney General that the President will not exercise his Constitutional powers to effect the discharge of the Special Prosecutor or to limit the independence he is hereby given, the Special Prosecutor will not be removed from his duties except for extraordinary improprieties on

his part and without the President's first consulting the Majority and Minority Leaders and Chairman and ranking Minority Members of the Judiciary Committees of the Senate and House of Representatives and ascertaining that their consensus is in accord with his proposed action. Footnote in original.]

The regulation gives the Special Prosecutor explicit power to contest the invocation of executive privilege in the process of seeking evidence deemed relevant to the performance of these specially delegated duties. [That this was the understanding of Acting Attorney General Robert Bork, the author of the regulations establishing the independence of the Special Prosecutor, is shown by his testimony before the Senate Judiciary Committee:

> Although it is anticipated that Mr. Jaworski will receive cooperation from the White House in getting any evidence he feels he needs to conduct investigations and prosecutions, it is clear and understood on all sides that he has the power to use judicial processes to pursue evidence if disagreement should develop.

Hearings before the Senate Judiciary Committee on the Special Prosecutor, 93d Cong., 1st Sess., pt. 2, at 470 (1973). Acting Attorney General Bork gave similar assurances to the House Subcommittee on Criminal Justice. Hearings before the House Judiciary Subcommittee on Criminal Justice on H. J. Res. 784 and H. R. 10937, 93d Cong., 1st Sess. 266 (1973). At his confirmation hearings, Attorney General Willian Saxbe testified that he shared Acting Attorney General Bork's views concerning the Special Prosecutor's authority to test any claim of executive privilege in the courts. Hearings before the Senate Judiciary Committee on the nomination of William B. Saxbe to be Attorney General, 93d Cong., 1st Sess. 9 (1973). Footnote in original.] 38 Fed. Reg. 30739.

So long as this regulation is extant it has the force of law. In *Accardi* v. *Shaughnessy*, 347 U.S. 260 (1953), regulations of the Attorney General delegated certain of his discretionary powers to the Board of Immigration Appeals and required that Board to exercise its own discretion on appeals in deportation cases. The Court held that so long as the Attorney General's regulations remained operative, he denied himself the authority to exercise the discretion delegated to the Board even though the original authority was his and he could reassert it by amending the regulations. *Service* v. *Dulles*, 354 U.S. 363, 388 (1957), and *Vitarelli* v. *Seaton*, 359 U.S. 535 (1959), reaffirmed the basic holding of *Accardi*.

Here, as in *Accardi*, it is theoretically possible for the Attorney General to amend or revoke the regulation defining the Special Prosecutor's authority. But he has not done so. [At his confirmation hearings Attorney General William Saxbe testified that he agreed with the regulations adopted by Acting Attorney General Bork and would not remove the Special Prosecutor except for "gross impropriety." Hearings, Senate Judiciary Committee on the nomination of William B. Saxbe to be Attorney General, 93d Cong., 1st Sess., 5-6, 8-10 (1973). There is no contention here that the Special Prosecutor is guilty of any such impropriety. Footnote in original.] So long as this regulation remains in force the Executive Branch is bound by it, and indeed the United States as the sovereign composed of the three branches is bound to respect and to enforce it. Moreover, the delegation of authority to the Special Prosecutor in this case is not an ordinary delegation by the Attorney General to a subordinate officer: with the authorization of the President, the Acting Attorney General provided in the regulation that the Special Prosecutor was not to be removed without the "consensus" of eight designated leaders of Congress. Note 8, *supra*.

The demands of and the resistance to the subpoena present an obvious controversy in the ordinary sense, but that alone is not sufficient to meet constitutional standards. In the constitutional sense, controversy means more than disagreement and conflict; rather it means the kind of controversy courts traditionally resolve. Here at issue is the production or nonproduction of specified evidence deemed by the Special Prosecutor to be relevant and admissible in a pending criminal case. It is sought by one official of the Government within the scope of his express authority; it is resisted by the Chief Executive on the ground of his duty to preserve the confidentiality of the communications of the President. Whatever the correct answer on the merits, these issues are "of a type which are traditionally justiciable." *United States* v. *ICC*, 337 U.S., at 430. The independent Special Prosecutor with his asserted need for the subpoenaed material in the underlying criminal prosecution is opposed by the President with his steadfast assertion of privilege against disclosure of the material. This setting assures there is "that concrete adverseness which sharpens the presentation of issues upon which the court so largely depends for illumination of difficult constitutional questions." *Baker* v. *Carr*, 369 U.S., at 204. Moreover, since the matter is one arising in the regular course of a federal criminal prosecution, it is within the traditional scope of Art. III power. *Id.*, at 198.

In light of the uniqueness of the setting in which the conflict arises, the fact that both parties are officers of the Executive Branch cannot be viewed as a barrier to justiciability. It would be inconsistent with the applicable law and regulation, and the unique facts of this case to conclude other than that the Special Prosecutor has standing to bring this action and that a justiciable controversy is presented for decision.

III
RULE 17 (c)

The subpoena *duces tecum* is challenged on the ground that the Special Prosecutor failed to satisfy the requirements of Fed. Rule Crim. Proc. 17 (c), which governs the issuance of subpoenas *duces tecum* in federal criminal proceedings. If we sustained this challenge, there would be no occasion to reach the claim of privilege asserted with respect to the subpoenaed material. Thus we turn to the question whether the requirements of Rule 17 (c) have been satisfied. See *Arkansas-Louisiana Gas Co.* v. *Dept. of Public Utilities*, 304 U.S. 61, 64 (1938); *Ashwander* v. *Tennessee Valley Authority*, 297 U.S. 288, 346-347 (1936). (Brandeis, J., concurring.)

Rule 17 (c) provides:

A subpoena may also command the person to whom it is directed to produce the books, papers, documents or other objects designated therein. The court on motion made promptly may quash or modify the subpoena if compliance would be unreasonable or oppressive. The court may direct that books, papers, documents or objects designated in the subpoena be produced before the court at a time prior to the trial or prior to the time when they are to be offered in evidence and may upon their production permit the books, papers, documents or objects or portions thereof to be inspected by the parties and their attorneys.

A subpoena for documents may be quashed if their production would be "unreasonable or oppressive," but not otherwise. The leading case in this Court interpreting this standard is *Bowman Dairy Co.* v. *United States*, 341 U.S. 214 (1950). This case recognized certain fundamental characteristics of the subpoena *duces tecum* in criminal cases: (1) it was not intended to provide a means of discovery for criminal cases. *Id.*, at 220; (2) its chief innovation was to expedite the trial by providing a time and place *before* trial for the inspection of subpoenaed materials. [The Court quoted a statement of a member of the advisory committee that the purpose of the Rule was to bring documents into court "in advance of the time that they are offered in evidence, so that they may then be inspected in advance, for the purpose . . . of enabling the party to see whether he can use [them] or whether he wants to use [them]." 341 U.S., at 220 n. 5. The Manual for Complex and Multidistrict Litigation published by the Administrative Office of the United States Courts recommends that Rule 17 (c) be encouraged in complex criminal cases in order that each party may be compelled to produce its documentary evidence well in advance of trial and in advance of the time it is to be offered. P. 142, CCH Ed. Footnote in original.] *Ibid.* As both parties agree, cases decided in the wake of *Bowman* have generally followed Judge Weinfeld's formulation in *United States* v. *Iozia*, 13 F. R. D. 335, 338 (SDNY 1952), as to the required showing. Under this test, in order to require production prior to trial, the moving party must show: (1) that the documents are evidentiary [The District Court found here that it was faced with "the more unusual situation . . . where the subpoena, rather than being directed to the government by the defendants, issues to what, as a practical matter, is a third party." *United States* v. *Mitchell*,——F. Supp.——(D.C. 1974). The Special Prosecutor suggests that the evidentiary requirement of *Bowman Dairy Co.* and *Iozia* does not apply in its full vigor when the subpoena *duces tecum* is issued to third parties rather than to government prosecutors. Brief for the United States 128-129. We need not decide whether a lower standard exists because we are satisfied that the relevance and evidentiary nature of the subpoenaed tapes were sufficiently shown as a preliminary matter to warrant the District Court's refusal to quash the subpoena. Footnote in original.] and relevant; (2) that they are not otherwise procurable reasonably in advance of trial by exercise of due diligence; (3) that the party cannot properly prepare for trial without such production and inspection in advance of trial and that the failure to obtain such inspection may tend unreasonably to delay the trial; (4) that the application is made in good faith and is not intended as a general "fishing expedition."

Against this background, the Special Prosecutor, in order to carry his burden, must clear three hurdles: (1) relevancy; (2) admissibility; (3) specificity. Our own review of the record necessarily affords a less comprehensive view of the total situation than was available to the trial judge and we are unwilling to conclude that the District Court erred in the evaluation of the Special Prosecutor's showing under Rule 17 (c). Our conclusion is based on the record before us, much of which is under seal. Of course, the contents of the subpoenaed tapes could not at that stage be described fully by the Special Prosecutor, but there was a sufficient likelihood that each of the tapes contains conversations relevant to the offenses charged in the indictment. *United States* v. *Gross*, 24 F. R. D. 138 (SDNY 1959). With respect to many of the tapes, the Special Prosecutor offered the sworn testimony or statements of one or more of the participants in the conversations as to what was said at the time. As for the remainder of the tapes, the identity of the participants and the time and place of the conversations, taken in their total context, permit a rational inference that at least part of the conversations relate to the offenses charged in the indictment.

We also conclude there was a sufficient preliminary showing that each of the subpoenaed tapes contains evidence admissible with respect to the offenses charged in the indictment. The most cogent objection to the admissibility of the taped conversations here at issue is that they are a collection of out-of-court statements by declarants who will not be subject to cross-examination and that the statements are therefore inadmissible hearsay. Here, however, most of the tapes apparently contain conversations to which one or more of the defendants named in the indictment were party. The hearsay rule does not automatically bar all out-of-court statements by a defendant in a criminal case. [Such statements are declarations by a party defendant that "would surmount all objections based on the hearsay rule . . ." and, at least as to the declarant himself "would be admissible for whatever inferences" might be reasonably drawn. *United States* v. *Matlock*, ——U.S.—— (1974). *On Lee* v. *United States*, 343 U.S. 747, 757 (1953). See also McCormick on Evidence, § 270, at 651-652 (1972 ed.). Footnote in original.] Declarations by one defendant may also be admissible against other defendants upon a sufficient showing, by independent evidence, [As a preliminary matter, there must be substantial, independent evidence of the conspiracy, at least enough to take the question to the jury. *United States* v. *Vaught*, 385 F. 2d 320, 323 (CA4 1973); *United States* v. *Hoffa*, 349 F. 2d 20, 41-42 (CA6 1965), aff'd on other grounds, 385 U.S. 293 (1966); *United States* v. *Santos*, 385 F. 2d 43, 45 (CA7 1967), cert. denied, 390 U.S. 954 (1968); *United States* v. *Morton*, 483 F. 2d 573, 576 (CA8 1973); *United States* v. *Spanos*, 462 F. 2d 1012, 1014 (CA9 1972); *Carbo* v. *United States*, 314 F. 2d 718, 737 (CA9 1963), cert denied, 377 U.S. 953 (1964). Whether the standard has been satisfied is a question of admissibility of evidence to be decided by the trial judge. Footnote in original.] of a conspiracy among one or more other defendants and the declarant and if the declarations at issue were in furtherance of that conspiracy. The same is true of declarations of coconspirators who are not defendants in the case on trial. *Dutton* v. *Evans*, 400 U.S. 74, 81 (1970). Recorded conversations may also be admissible for the limited purpose of impeaching the credibility of any defendant who testifies or any other coconspirator who testifies. Generally, the need for evidence to impeach witnesses is insufficient to require its production in advance of trial. See, *e.g., United States* v. *Carter*, 15 F. R. D. 367, 371 (D. D. C. 1954). Here, however, there are other valid potential evidentiary uses for the same material and the analysis and possible transcription of the tapes may take a significant period of time. Accordingly, we cannot say that the District Court erred in authorizing the issuance of the subpoena *duces tecum*.

Enforcement of a pretrial subpoena *duces tecum* must necessarily be committed to the sound discretion of the trial court since the necessity for the subpoena most often turns upon a determination of factual issues. Without a determination of arbitrariness or that the trial court finding was without record support, an appellate court will not ordinarily disturb a finding that the applicant for a subpoena complied with Rule 17 (c). See, *e.g., Sue* v. *Chicago Transit Authority*, 279 F. 2d 416, 419 (CA7 1960); *Shotkin* v. *Nelson*, 146 F. 2d 402 (CA10 1944).

In a case such as this, however, where a subpoena is directed to a President of the United States, appellate review, in deference to a coordinate branch of government, should be particularly meticulous to ensure that the standards of Rule 17 (c) have been correctly applied. *United States* v. *Burr*, 25 Fed. Cas. 30, 34 (No. 14,692d) (1807). From our examination of the materials submitted by the Special Prosecutor to the District Court in support of his motion for the subpoena, we are persuaded that the District Court's denial of the President's motion to quash the subpoena was consistent with Rule 17 (c). We also conclude that the Special Prosecutor has made a sufficient showing to justify a subpoena for production *before* trial. The subpoenaed materials are not available from any other source, and their examination and processing should not await trial in the circumstances shown. *Bowman Dairy Co., supra; United States* v. *Iozia, supra.*

IV
THE CLAIM OF PRIVILEGE

A

Having determined that the requirements of Rule 17 (c) were satisfied, we turn to the claim that the subpoena should be quashed because it demands "confidential conversations between a President and his close advisors that it would be inconsistent with the public interest to produce." App. 48a. The first contention is a broad claim that the separation of powers doctrine precludes judicial review of a President's claim of privilege. The second contention is that if he does not prevail on the claim of absolute privilege, the court should hold as a matter of constitutional law that the privilege prevails over the subpoena *duces tecum*.

In the performance of assigned constitutional duties each branch of the Government must initially interpret the Constitution, and the interpretation of its powers by any branch is due great respect from the others. The President's counsel, as we have noted, reads the Constitution as providing an absolute privilege of confidentiality for all presidential communications. Many decisions of this Court, however, have unequivocally reaffirmed the holding of *Marbury* v. *Madison*, 1 Cranch 137 (1803), that "it is emphatically the province and duty of the judicial department to say what the law is." *Id.*, at 177.

No holding of the Court has defined the scope of judicial power specifically relating to the enforcement of a subpoena for confidential presidential communications for use in a criminal prosecution, but other exercises of powers by the Executive Branch and the Legislative Branch have been found invalid as in conflict with the Constitution. *Powell* v. *McCormack, supra; Youngstown, supra*. In a series of cases, the Court interpreted the explicit immunity conferred by express provisions of the Constitution on Members of the House and Senate by the Speech or Debate Clause, U.S. Const. Art. I § 6. *Doe* v. *McMillan*, 412 U.S. 306 (1973); *Gravel* v. *United States*, 408 U.S. 606 (1973); *United States* v. *Brewster*, 408 U.S. 501 (1972); *United States* v. *Johnson*, 383 U.S. 169 (1966). Since this Court has consistently exercised the power to construe and delineate claims arising under express powers, it must follow that the Court has authority to interpret claims with respect to powers alleged to derive from enumerated powers.

Our system of government "requires that the federal courts on occasion interpret the Constitution in a manner at variance with the construction given the document by another branch." *Powell* v. *McCormack, supra*, 549. And in *Baker* v. *Carr*, 369 U.S., at 211, the Court stated:

> [d]eciding whether a matter has in any measure been committed by the Constitution to another branch of government, or whether the action of that branch exceeds whatever authority has been committed, is itself a delicate exercise in constitutional interpretation, and is a responsibility of this Court as ultimate interpreter of the Constitution.

Notwithstanding the deference each branch must accord the others, the "judicial power of the United States" vested in the federal courts by Art. III, § 1 of the Constitution can no more be shared with the Executive Branch than the Chief Executive, for example, can share with the Judiciary the veto power, or the Congress share with the Judiciary the power to override a presidential veto. Any other conclusion would be contrary to the basic concept of separation of powers and the checks and balances that flow from the scheme of a tripartite government. The Federalist, No. 47, p. 313 (C. F. Mittel ed. 1938). We therefore reaffirm that it is "emphatically the province and the duty" of this Court "to say what the law is" with respect to the claim of privilege presented in this case. *Marbury* v. *Madison, supra*, at 177.

B

In support of his claim of absolute privilege, the President's counsel urges two grounds one of which is common to all governments and one of which is peculiar to our system of separation of powers. The first ground is the valid need for protection of communications between high government officials and those who advise and assist them in the performance of their manifold duties; the importance of this confidentiality is too plain to require further discussion. Human experience teaches that those who expect public dissemination of their remarks may well temper candor with a concern for appearances and for their own interests to the detriment of the decisionmaking process. [There is nothing novel about governmental confidentiality. The meetings of the Constitutional Convention in 1787 were conducted in complete privacy. 1 Farrand. The Records of the Federal Convention of 1787, xi-xxv (1911). Moreover, all records of those meetings were sealed for more than 30 years after the Convention. See 3 U.S. Stat. At Large, 15th Cong., 1st Sess., Res. 8 (1818). Most of the Framers acknowledged that without secrecy no constitution of the kind that was developed could have been written. Warren. The Making of the Constitution, 134-139 (1937) Footnote in original.] Whatever the nature of the privilege of confidentiality of presidential communications in the exercise of Art. II powers the privilege can be said to derive from the supremacy of each branch within its own assigned area of constitutional duties. Certain powers and privileges flow from the nature of enumerated powers; [The Special Prosecutor argues that there is no provision in the Constitution for a presidential privilege as to his communications corresponding to the privilege of Members of Congress under the Speech or Debate Clause. But the silence of the Constitution on this score is not dispositive. "The rule of constitutional interpretation announced in *McCulloch* v. *Maryland*. 4 Wheat. 316, that that which was reasonably appropriate and relevant to the exercise of a granted power was considered as accompanying the grant, has been so universally applied that it suffices merely to state it." *Marshall* v. *Gordon*, 243 U.S. 521, 537 (1917). Footnote in original.] the protection of the confidentiality of presidential communications has similar constitutional underpinnings.

The second ground asserted by the President's counsel in support of the claim of absolute privilege rests on the doctrine of separation of powers. Here it is argued that the independence of the Executive Branch within its own sphere. *Humphrey's Executor* v. *United States*, 295 U.S. 602, 629-630; *Kilbourn* v. *Thompson*, 103 U.S. 168, 190-191 (1880), insulates a president from a judicial subpoena in an ongoing criminal prosecution, and thereby protects confidential presidential communications.

However, neither the doctrine of separation of powers, nor the need for confidentiality of high level communications, without more, can sustain an absolute, unqualified presidential privilege of immunity from judicial process under all circumstances. The President's need for complete candor and objectivity from advisers calls for great deference from the courts. However, when the privilege depends solely on the broad, undifferentiated claim of public interest in the confidentiality of such conversations, a confrontation with other values arises. Absent a claim of need to protect military, diplomatic or sensitive national security secrets, we find it difficult to accept the argument that even the very important interest in confidentiality of presidential communications is significantly diminished by production of such material for *in camera* inspection with all the protection that a district court will be obliged to provide.

The impediment that an absolute, unqualified privilege would place in the way of the primary constitutional duty of the Judicial Branch to do justice in criminal prosecutions would plainly conflict with the function of the courts under Art. III. In designing the structure of our Government and dividing and allocating the sovereign power among three coequal branches, the Framers of the Constitution sought to provide a comprehensive system, but the separate powers were not intended to operate with absolute independence.

> "While the Constitution diffuses power the better to secure liberty, it also contemplates that practice will integrate the dispersed powers into a workable government. It enjoins upon its branches separateness but interdependence, autonomy but reciprocity." *Youngstown Sheet & Tube Co.* v. *Sawyer*, 343 U.S. 579, 635 (1952) (Jackson, J., concurring).

To read the Art. II powers of the President as providing an absolute privilege as against a subpoena essential to enforcement of criminal statutes on no more than a generalized claim of the public interest in confidentiality of nonmilitary and nondiplomatic discussions would upset the constitutional balance of "a workable government" and gravely impair the role of the courts under Art. III.

C

Since we conclude that the legitimate needs of the judicial process may outweigh presidential privilege, it is necessary to resolve those competing interests in a manner that preserves the essential functions of each branch. The right and indeed the duty to resolve that question does not free the judiciary from according high respect to the representations made on behalf of the President. *United States* v. *Burr*, 25 Fed. Cas. 187, 190, 191-192 (No. 14,694) (1807).

The expectation of a President to the confidentiality of his conversations and correspondence, like the claim of confidentiality of judicial deliberations, for example, has all the values to which we accord deference for the privacy of all citizens and added to those values the necessity for protection of the public interest in candid, objective, and even blunt or harsh opinions in presidential decision-making. A President and those who assist him must be free to explore alternatives in the process of shaping policies and making decisions and to do so in a way many would be unwilling to express except privately. These are the considerations justifying a presumptive privilege for presidential communications. The privilege is fundamental to the operation of government and inextricably rooted in the separation of powers under the Constitution. ["Freedom of communication vital to fulfillment of wholesome relationships is obtained only by removing the specter of compelled disclosure . . . [G]overnment . . . needs open but protected channels for the kind of plain talk that is essential to the quality of its functioning." *Carl Zeiss Stiftung* v. *V. E. B. Carl Zeiss, Jena*, 40 F. R. D. 318, 325 (D.C. 1966). See *Nixon* v. *Sirica*,——U.S. App. D.C.——, ——487 F. 2d 700, 713 (1973); *Kaiser Aluminum & Chem. Corp.* v. *United States*, 157 F. Supp. 939 (Ct. Cl. 1958) (*per* Reed, J.); The Federalist No. 64 (S. F. Mittel ed. 1938). Footnote in original.] In *Nixon* v.

Sirica,——U.S. App. D.C.——, 487 F. 2d 700 (1973), the Court of Appeals held that such presidential communications are "presumptively privileged," *id.*, at 717, and this position is accepted by both parties in the present litigation. We agree with Mr. Chief Justice Marshall's observation, therefore, that "in no case of this kind would a court be required to proceed against the President as against an ordinary individual." *United States* v. *Burr*, 25 Fed. Cas. 187, 191 (No. 14,694) (CCD Va. 1807).

But this presumptive privilege must be considered in light of our historic commitment to the rule of law. This is nowhere more profoundly manifest than in our view that "the twofold aim [of criminal justice] is that guilt shall not escape or innocence suffer." *Berger* v. *United States*, 295 U.S. 78, 88 (1935). We have elected to employ an adversary system of criminal justice in which the parties contest all issues before a court of law. The need to develop all relevant facts in the adversary system is both fundamental and comprehensive. The ends of criminal justice would be defeated if judgments were to be founded on a partial or speculative presentation of the facts. The very integrity of the judicial system and public confidence in the system depend on full disclosure of all the facts, within the framework of the rules of evidence. To ensure that justice is done, it is imperative to the function of courts that compulsory process be available for the production of evidence needed either by the prosecution or by the defense.

Only recently the Court restated the ancient proposition of law, albeit in the context of a grand jury inquiry rather than a trial,

> that the public . . . has a right to every man's evidence' except for those persons protected by a constitutional, common law, or statutory privilege, *United States* v. *Bryan*, 339 U.S., at 331 (1949); *Blackmer* v. *United States*, 284 U.S. 421, 438; *Branzburg* v. *United States*, 408 U.S. 665, 688 (1973).

The privileges referred to by the Court are designed to protect weighty and legitimate competing interests. Thus, the Fifth Amendment to the Constitution provides that no man "shall be compelled in any criminal case to be a witness against himself." And, generally, an attorney or a priest may not be required to disclose what has been revealed in professional confidence. These and other interests are recognized in law by privileges against forced disclosure, established in the Constitution, by statute, or at common law. Whatever their origins, these exceptions to the demand for every man's evidence are not lightly created nor expansively construed, for they are in derogation of the search for truth. [Because of the key role of the testimony of witnesses in the judicial process, courts have historically been cautious about privileges. Justice Frankfurter, dissenting in *Elkins* v. *United States*, 364 U.S. 206, 234 (1960), said of this: "Limitations are properly placed upon the operation of this general principle only to the very limited extent that permitting a refusal to testify or excluding relevant evidence has a public good transcending the normally predominant principle of utilizing all rational means for ascertaining truth." Footnote in original.]

In this case the President challenges a subpoena served on him as a third party requiring the production of materials for use in a criminal prosecution on the claim that he has a privilege against disclosure of confidential communications. He does not place his claim of privilege on the ground they are military or diplomatic secrets. As to these areas of Art. II duties the courts have traditionally shown the utmost deference to presidential responsibilities. In *C. & S. Air Lines* v. *Waterman Steamship Corp.*, 333 U.S. 103, 111 (1948), dealing with presidential authority involving foreign policy considerations, the Court said:

> The President, both as Commander-in-Chief and as the Nation's organ for foreign affairs, has available intelligence services whose reports are not and ought not to be published to the world. It would be intolerable that courts, without the relevant information, should review and perhaps nullify actions of the Executive taken on information properly held secret. *Id.*, at 111.

In *United States* v. *Reynolds*, 345 U.S. 1 (1952), dealing with a claimant's demand for evidence in a damage case against the Government the Court said:

> It may be possible to satisfy the court, from all the circumstances of the case, that there is a reasonable danger that compulsion of the evidence will expose military matters which, in the interest of national security, should not be divulged. When this is the case, the occasion for the privilege is appropriate, and the court should not jeopardize the security which the privilege is meant to protect by insisting upon an examination of the evidence, even by the judge alone, in chambers.

No case of the Court, however, has extended this high degree of deference to a President's generalized interest in confidentiality. Nowhere in the Constitution, as we have noted earlier, is there any explicit reference to a privilege of confidentiality, yet to the extent this interest relates to the effective discharge of a President's powers, it is constitutionally based.

The right to the production of all evidence at a criminal trial similarly has constitutional dimensions. The Sixth Amendment explicitly confers upon every defendant in a criminal trial the right "to be confronted with the witnesses against him" and "to have compulsory process for obtaining witnesses in his favor." Moreover, the Fifth Amendment also guarantees that no person shall be deprived of liberty without due process of law. It is the manifest duty of the courts to vindicate those guarantees and to accomplish that it is essential that all relevant and admissible evidence be produced.

In this case we must weigh the importance of the general privilege of confidentiality of presidential communications in performance of his responsibilities against the inroads of such a privilege on the fair administration of criminal justice. [We are not here concerned with the balance between the President's generalized interest in confidentiality and the need for relevant evidence in civil litigation, nor with that between the confidentiality interest and congressional demands for information, nor with the President's interest in preserving state secrets. We address only the conflict between the President's assertion of a generalized privilege of confidentiality against the constitutional need for relevant evidence to criminal trials. Footnote in original.] The interest in preserving confidentiality is weighty indeed and entitled to great respect. However we cannot conclude that advisers will be moved to temper the candor of their remarks by the infrequent occasions of disclosures because of the possibility that such conversations will be called for in the context of a criminal prosecution. [Mr. Justice Cardozo made this point in an analogous context. Speaking for a unanimous Court in *Clark* v. *United States*, 289 U.S. 1 (1933), he emphasized the importance of maintaining the secrecy of the deliberations of a petit jury in a criminal case. "Freedom of debate might be stifled and independence of thought checked if jurors were made to feel that their arguments and ballots were to be freely published in the world." *Id.*, at 13. Nonetheless, the Court also recognized that isolated inroads on confidentiality designed to serve the paramount need of the criminal law would not vitiate the interests served by secrecy:

> A juror of integrity and reasonable firmness will not fear to speak his mind if the confidences of debate are barred to the ears of mere impertinence or malice. He will not expect to be shielded against the disclosure of his conduct in the event that there is evidence reflecting upon his honor. The chance that now and then there may be found some timid soul who will take counsel of his fears and give way to their repressive power is too remote and shadowly to shape the course of justice. *Id.*, at 16. Footnote in original.]

On the other hand, the allowance of the privilege to withhold evidence that is demonstrably relevant in a criminal trial would cut deeply into the guarantee of due process of law and gravely impair the basic function of the courts. A President's acknowledged need for confidentiality in the communications of his office is general in nature, whereas the constitutional need for production of relevant evidence in a criminal proceeding is specific and central to the fair adjudication of a particular criminal case in the administration of justice. Without access to specific facts a criminal prosecution may be totally frustrated. The President's broad interest in confidentiality of communications will not be vitiated by disclosure of a limited number of conversations preliminarily shown to have some bearing on the pending criminal cases.

We conclude that when the ground for asserting privilege as to subpoenaed materials sought for use in a criminal trial is based only on the generalized interest in confidentiality, it cannot prevail over the fundamental demands of due process of law in the fair administration of criminal justice. The generalized assertion of privilege must yield to the demonstrated, specific need for evidence in a pending criminal trial.

D

We have earlier determined that the District Court did not err in authorizing the issuance of the subpoena. If a president concludes that compliance with a subpoena would be injurious to the public interest he may properly, as was done here, invoke a claim of privilege on the return of the subpoena. Upon receiving a claim of privilege from the Chief Executive, it became the further duty of the District Court to treat the subpoenaed material as presumptively privileged and to require the Special Prosecutor to demonstrate that the presidential material was "essential to the justice of the [pending criminal] case." *United States* v. *Burr, supra,* at 192. Here the District Court treated the material as presumptively privileged, proceeded to find that the Special Prosecutor had made a sufficient showing to rebut the presumption and ordered an *in camera* examination of the subpoenaed material. On the basis of our examination of the record we are unable to conclude that the District Court erred in ordering the inspection. Accordingly we affirm the order of the District Court that subpoenaed materials be transmitted to that court. We now turn to the important question of the District Court's responsibilities in conducting the *in camera* examination of presidential materials or communications delivered under the compulsion of the subpoena *duces tecum.*

E

Enforcement of the subpoena *duces tecum* was stayed pending this Court's resolution of the issues raised by the petitions for certiorari. Those issues now having been disposed of, the matter of implementation will rest with the District Court. "[T]he guard, furnished to [President] to protect him from being harassed by vexatious and unnecessary subpoenas, is to be looked for in the conduct of the [district] court after the subpoenas have issued; not in any circumstances which is to precede their being issued." *United States* v. *Burr, supra,* at 34. Statements that meet the test of admissibility and relevance must be isolated; all other material must be excised. At this stage the District Court is not limited to representations of the Special Prosecutor as to the evidence sought by the subpoena; the material will be available to the District Court. It is elementary that *in camera* inspection of evidence is always a procedure calling for scrupulous protection against any release or publication of material not found by the court, at that stage, probably admissible in evidence and relevant to the issues of the trial for which it is sought. That being true of an ordinary situation, it is obvious that the District Court has a very heavy responsibility to see to it that presidential conversations, which are either not relevant or not admissible, are accorded that high degree of respect due the President of the United States. Mr. Chief Justice Marshall sitting as a trial judge in the *Burr* case, *supra,* was extraordinarily careful to point out that:

> [I]n no case of this kind would a Court be required to proceed against the President as against an ordinary individual. *United States* v.. *Burr,* 25 Fed. Cases 187, 191 (No. 14,694).

Marshall's statement cannot be read to mean in any sense that a President is above the law, but relates to the singularly unique role under Art. II of a President's communications and activities, related to the performance of duties under that Article. Moreover, a President's communications and activities encompass a vastly wider range of sensitive material than would be true of any "ordinary individual." It is therefore necessary [When the subpoenaed material is delivered to the District Judge *in camera* questions may arise as to the excising of parts and it lies within the discretion of that court to seek the aid of the Special Prosecutor and the President's counsel for *in camera* consideration of the validity of particular excisions, where the basis of excision is relevancy or admissibility or under such cases as *Reynolds, supra* or *Waterman Steamship, supra.* Footnote in original.] in the public interest to afford presidential confidentiality the greatest protection consistent with the fair administration of justice. The need for confidentiality even as to idle conversations with associates in which casual reference might be made concerning political leaders within the country or foreign statesmen is too obvious to call for further treatment. We have no doubt that the District Judge will at all times accord to presidential records that high degree of deference suggested in *United States* v. *Burr, supra,* and will discharge his responsibility to see to it that until released to the Special Prosecutor no *in camera* material is revealed to anyone. This burden applies with even greater force to excised material; once the decision is made to excise, the material is restored to its privileged status and should be returned under seal to its lawful custodian.

Since this matter came before the Court during the pendency of a criminal prosecution, and on representations that time is of the essence, the mandate shall issue forthwith.

Affirmed.

Mr. Justice Rehnquist took no part in the consideration or decision of these cases.

Leon Jaworski, Special Prosecutor, and *Philip A. Lacovara,* Counsel to the Special Prosecutor, for petitioner in No. 73-1766 and respondent in No. 73-1834; *James D. St. Clair,* Attorney for the President (*Michael A. Sterlacci, Jerome J. Murphy, Loren A. Smith, James R. Prochnow, Eugene R. Sullivan, Jean A. Staudt, Theodore J. Garrish, James J. Tansey* and *Larry G. Gutterridge,* with him on the brief) for respondent in No. 73-1766 and petitioner in No. 73-1834; *Norman Dorsen, Melvin L. Wulf* and *John H. F. Shattuck* filed brief for American Civil Liberties Union, as amicus curiae, seeking affirmance, in No. 73-1766.

The demise of Richard Nixon's political career came shortly after the impeachment vote of the House Judiciary Committee, which followed on the heels of the Supreme Court decision on the tapes. The chances of the President's surviving a Senate trial, which was certain to follow after the bipartisan vote in the judiciary committee were dealt another stunning blow when the President issued a statement a few days later indicating that among the new tapes he had been ordered to hand over to the courts was one which clearly implicated him in the post-Watergate cover-up, a charge to which the House Judiciary Committee had found him guilty. This announcement eliminated the last Nixon supporters on the judiciary committee, who then joined with their colleagues in unanimously voting to impeach the President.

Three days later President Nixon sadly announced his resignation in a speech to the nation. He left for his compound in California the following day. Vice President Gerald R. Ford, who had only served in that capacity for ten months, was sworn in as President of the United States at 12:03 p.m. on August 9, 1974. One month later President Ford granted Richard Nixon "a full, free, and absolute pardon . . . for all offenses against the United States which he . . . has committed or may have committed or taken part in during the period from January 20, 1969, through August 9, 1974."[83]

President Richard M. Nixon
Resignation Address
August 8, 1974

The New York Times, August 9, 1974, 2.

[Note: Following is a transcript of President Nixon's address . . . as recorded by *The New York Times*—Ed.]

Good evening.

This is the 37th time I have spoken to you from this office in which so many decisions have been made that shape the history of this nation.

Each time I have done so to discuss with you some matters that I believe affected the national interest. And all the decisions I have made in my public life I have always tried to do what was best for the nation.

Throughout the long and difficult period of Watergate, I have felt it was my duty to persevere; to make every possible effort to complete the term of office to which you elected me.

In the past few days, however, it has become evident to me that I no longer have a strong enough political base in the Congress to justify continuing that effort.

As long as there was such a base, I felt strongly that it was necessary to see the constitutional process through to its conclusion; that to do otherwise would be unfaithful to the spirit of that deliberately difficult process, and a dangerously destabilizing precedent for the future.

But with the disappearance of that base, I now believe that the constitutional purpose has been served. And there is no longer a need for the process to be prolonged.

I would have preferred to carry through to the finish whatever the personal agony it would have involved, and my family unanimously urged me to do so.

But the interests of the nation must always come before any personal considerations. From the discussions I have had with Congressional and other leaders I have concluded that because of the Watergate matter I might not have the support of the Congress that I would consider necessary to back the very difficult decisions and carry out the duties of this office in the way the interests of the nation will require.

I have never been a quitter.

To leave office before my term is completed is opposed to every instinct in my body. But as President I must put the interests of America first.

America needs a full-time President and a full-time Congress, particularly at this time with problems we face at home and abroad.

To continue to fight through the months ahead for my personal vindication would almost totally absorb the time and attention of both the President and the Congress in a period when our entire focus should be on the great issues of peace abroad and prosperity without inflation at home.

Therefore, I shall resign the Presidency effective at noon tomorrow.

Vice President Ford will be sworn in as President at that hour in this office.

As I recall the high hopes for American with which we began this second term, I feel a great sadness that I will not be here in this office working on your behalf to achieve those hopes in the next two and a half years.

But in turning over direction of the Government to Vice President Ford I know, as I told the nation when I nominated him for that office 10 months ago, that the leadership of America will be in good hands.

In passing this office to the Vice President I also do so with the profound sense of the weight of responsibility that will fall on his shoulders tomorrow, and therefore of the understanding, the patience, the cooperation he will need from all Americans.

As he assumes that responsibility he will deserve the help and the support of all of us. As we look to the future, the first essential is to begin healing the wounds of this nation. To put the bitterness and divisions of the recent past behind us and to rediscover those shared ideals that lie at the heart of our strength and unity as a great and as a free people.

By taking this action, I hope that I will have hastened the start of that process of healing which is so desperately needed in America.

I regret deeply any injuries that may have been done in the course of the events that led to this decision. I would say only that if some of my judgments were wrong—and some were wrong—they were made in what I believed at the time to be the best interests of the nation.

To those who have stood with me during these past difficult months, to my family, my friends, the many others who've joined in supporting my cause because they believed it was right, I will be eternally grateful for your support.

And to those who have not felt able to give me your support, let me say I leave with no bitterness toward those who have opposed me, because all of us in the final analysis have been concerned with the good of the country however our judgments might differ.

So let us all now join together in affirming that common commitment and in helping our new President succeed for the benefit of all Americans.

I shall leave this office with regret at not completing my term but with gratitude for the privilege of serving as your President for the past five and a half years.

These years have been a momentous time in the history of our nation and the world. They have been a time of achievement in which we can all be proud—

achievements that represent the shared efforts of the administration, the Congress and the people. But the challenges ahead are equally great.

And they, too, will require the support and the efforts of a Congress and the people, working in cooperation with the new Administration.

We have ended America's longest war. But in the work of securing a lasting peace in the world, the goals ahead are even more far-reaching and more difficult. We must complete a structure of peace, so that it will be said of this generation—our generation of Americans—by the people of all nations, not only that we ended one war but that we prevented future wars.

We have unlocked the doors that for a quarter of a century stood between the United States and the People's Republic of China. We must now insure that the one-quarter of the world's people who live in the People's Republic of China will be and remain, not our enemies, but our friends.

In the Middle East, 100 million people in the Arab countries, many of whom have considered us their enemies for nearly 20 years, now look on us as their friends. We must continue to build on that friendship so that peace can settle at last over the Middle East and so that the cradle of civilization will not become its grave.

Together with the Soviet Union we have made the crucial breakthroughs that have begun the process of limiting nuclear arms. But we must set as our goal not just limiting but reducing and finally destroying these terrible weapons so that they cannot destroy civilization.

And so that the threat of nuclear war will no longer hand over the world and the people, we have opened a new relation with the Soviet Union. We must continue to develop and expand that new relationship so that the two strongest nations of the world will live together in cooperation rather than confrontation.

Around the world—in Aisa, in Africa, in Latin America, in the Middle East— there are millions of people who live in terrible poverty, even starvation. We must keep as our goal turning away from production for war and expanding production for peace so that people everywhere on this earth can at last look forward, in their children's time, if not in our time, to having the necessities for a decent life.

Here in America we are fortunate that most of our people have not only the blessings of liberty but also the means to live full and good, and by the world's standards, even abundant lives.

We must press on, however, toward a goal not only of more and better jobs but of full opportunity for every man, and of what we are striving so hard right now to achieve—prosperity, without inflation.

For more than a quarter of a century in public life, I have shared in the turbulent history of this evening.

I have fought for what I believe in. I have tried, to the best of my ability, to discharge those duties and meet those responsibilities that were entrusted to me.

Sometimes I have succeeded. And sometimes I have failed. But always I have taken heart from what Theodore Roosevelt said about the man in the arena whose face is married by dust and sweat and blood, who strives valiantly, who errs and comes short again and again because there is not effort without error and short-coming, but who does actually strive to do the deed, who knows the great

2278

enthusiasm, the great devotion, who spends himself in a worthy cause, who at the best knows in the end the triumphs of high achievements and with the worst if he fails, at least fails while daring greatly.

I pledge to you tonight that as long as I have a breath of life in my body I shall continue in that spirit. I shall continue to work for the great causes to which I have been dedicated throughout my years as a Congressman, a Senator, Vice President and President, the cause of peace—not just for America but among all nations—prosperity, justice and opportunity for all of our people.

There is one cause above all to which I have been devoted and to which I shall always be devoted for as long as I live.

When I first took the oath of office as President five and a half years ago, I made this sacred commitment to consecrate my office, my energies and all the wisdom I can summon to the cause of peace among nations.

I've done my very best in all the days since to be true to that pledge.

As a result of these efforts, I am confident that the world is a safer place today, not only for the people of America but for the people of all nations, and that all of our children have a better chance than before of living in peace rather than dying in war.

This, more than anything, is what I hoped to achieve when I sought the Presidency. This, more than anything, is what I hope will be my legacy to you, to our country, as I leave the Presidency.

To have served in this office is to have felt a very personal sense of kinship with each and every American. In leaving it, I do so with this prayer: May God's grace be with you in all the days ahead.

President Gerald R. Ford
Proclamation of Pardon
September 8, 1974

The New York Times, September 9, 1974, 1.

Richard Nixon became the thirty-seventh President of the United States on January 20, 1969, and was re-elected in 1972 for a second term by the electors of forty-nine of the fifty states. His term in office continued until his resignation on August 9, 1974.

Pursuant to resolutions of the House of Representatives, its Committee on the Judiciary conducted an inquiry and investigation on the impeachment of the President extending over more than eight months. The hearings of the committee and its deliberations, which received wide national publicity over television, radio, and in printed media, resulted in votes adverse to Richard Nixon on recommended Articles of Impeachment.

As a result of certain acts or omissions occurring before his resignation from the office of President, Richard Nixon has become liable to possible indictment and trial for offenses against the United States. Whether or not he shall be prosecuted depends on findings of the appropriate grand jury and on the discretion of the authorized prosecutor. Should an indictment ensue, the accused shall then be entitled to a fair trial by an impartial jury, as guaranteed to every individual by the Constitution.

It is believed that a trial of Richard Nixon, if it became necessary, could not fairly begin until a year or more has elapsed. In the meantime, the tranquility to which this nation has been restored by the events of recent weeks could be irreparably lost by the prospects of bringing to trial a former President of the United States. The prospects of such trial will cause prolonged and divisive debate over the propriety of exposing to further punishment and degradation a man who has already paid the unprecedented penalty of of relinquishing the highest elective office in the United States.

Now, therefore, I, Gerald R. Ford, President of the United States, pursuant to the pardon power conferred upon me by Article II, Section 2, of the Constitution, have granted and by these presents do grant a full, free, and absolute pardon unto Richard Nixon for all offenses against the United States which he, Richard Nixon, has committed or may have committed or taken part in during the period from January 20, 1969, through August 9, 1974.

In witness whereof, I have hereunto set my hand this 8th day of September in the year of our Lord nineteen hundred seventy-four, and of the independence of the United States of America the 199th.

Gerald R. Ford

In the course of our conversation we touched upon a number of pressure points in the political bloodstream which badly need attention, perhaps radical therapy. Certainly much can be done to reharness the war powers of the President so they can again fit into the constitutional scheme which the Founding Fathers outlined. The War Powers Joint Resolution passed by the Congress in November 1973, over the President's veto, is a beginning, but presents problems which Schlesinger and others have pointed out, will create more restrictive circumstances in which the President is forced to act and may discourage some of the deception and independent decision-making that has taken place in the past.

Several suggestions have been made to enhance the level of information from which Congress must make its decisions. There is no reason why the leaders of Congress, which has the constitutional responsibility to declare war, should not be instantly apprised of all information available to the National Security Council. With its leaders sitting on that council and provided with a staff which can assimilate the incoming intelligence data available to the NSC staff (including information regarding CIA activities), the leaders of Congress will be as well informed on national security situations as the President, the Department of Defense and other top military or political agencies dealing with any critical area of activity. It is up to Congress to select individuals for these assignments who are representative of the best, not merely the oldest and most experienced in Congress, to work out procedures as to how such leaders can inform the House and Senate of essential background information for making national security decisions to protect the public interest. Machinery for congressional examination and effective use of the veto power over executive agreements in the foreign policy field is long overdue. The distinction between such agreements and congressionally approved treaties has become too indistinct in recent years.

But despite the institutional reorganization and changes that must take place, the decisions about whether to go to war or remain at peace, whether or not to send troops or armaments to supplicant countries, in short, how to utilize and also to restrict the use of our tremendous war-making powers, will ultimately rest on the sentiment of the electorate, which is the benefactor or victim of such policies. Formal changes and reforms can contribute just so much to raising the level and improving the quality of political life, but real and basic change can only come about when the political environment is conducive to such developments.

It seems that in the final analysis, raising the level of political consciousness is the real bulwark against Executive war-making and other abuses of presidential power. Our previous analysis has demonstrated that severe limits upon popular Presidents have only been imposed in those rare instances when the level of political consciousness required it. Otherwise, a resourceful President can exploit his charisma, his access to "top secret" information, his constitutional powers as Commander in Chief and foreign policy leader to mobilize the country and commit its destiny to military adventures from which it becomes virtually impossible to withdraw. Realistically, to be able to restrain such activities a more open system of government is necessary—a system in which the opposition party based in Congress can always examine and publicly discuss the drift of affairs and offer opposition to such developments if it feels that such policies are not in the public interest. This is the classical role of the opposition party, and our political institutions should be shaped in such a manner as to provide an opportunity for performing this vital function. The reaction of the public will be the decisive factor, the ultimate decision-maker, but in the meantime the Executive's position and peculiar access to both information and specialized power will not be able to prevent discussion of the course he is proposing and alternative policies to it. Of course this is not a new idea, but in the recent past the institutional framework of our national government has not functioned in such a manner to make democratic checks and balances possible. We must do something to remedy this.

The presidency has not been the only source of the abuse of power in our political history. The supremacy of Congress in the latter half of the nineteenth century and the misuse of the power of the Supreme Court in the 1930s were two instances when the balance of power in the system was badly distorted. A more open and dialectical process at the decision-making centers of government would have the effect of checking such abuses and keeping any inordinate grasp for power on the part of all branches within reasonable limits. If informed and enlightened, the public will not quickly succumb to the transient emotions of the moment, but will be better equipped to evaluate policy proposals in the light of its perception of its own interests. Of course this is a rationalist hope, but what else have we?

Some long-range decentralization of power at the center of the system, as many conservatives have long been advocating, would also be exemplary when indeed possible. But the difficulties and accompanying disadvantages of transfers of power should not be minimized. We should be more imaginative in designing policies and practices that allow for a maximum of local control and decision-making within the context of national standards and policies. The early history of the Tennessee Valley Authority provides a dynamic example of such a policy working quite effectively. The absence of standards or guidelines in the new revenue-sharing legislation provides too much leeway for local departures from essential national norms. More experience and careful study can improve such a situation. However, in an increasingly interdependent and shrinking universe, and in a nation honeycombed by various networks of electronic communication systems and related interdependent industries—commerce, agriculture, education, law and social and economic problems—it is hardly realistic to ignore the influence and pressures of national imperatives.

A rational and dialectical politics based upon national issues requires the dynamics of a party system in order to sustain its effectiveness—both on the initiating and the receiving ends. I am not describing a frenetic campaign, a one-shot, all-out effort, but rather strong sustaining centers of ideas, policies, personnel and organization which can capitalize upon proposed media reforms, take advantage of such opportunities and carry on a consistent and continuing dialogue between the party leaders in government and the body politic throughout the nation. This is the only realistic and viable political process that can survive, and it is the only way in which an alert, informed and educated public opinion can elevate the standards of government and continue to insist upon those standards in its yearly performance.

But it is one thing to suggest a more responsible role for the opposition party in Congress and quite another to consider practical steps with which this could be brought about. The trend in the nation and in Congress itself seems to be in the other direction. One hears so much glorification, particularly in the new suburban political reform movements, of the independent voter and ticket splitting, that one wonders whether any substantial thought is ever given to the *political* consequences of such behavior. The intentions of its practitioners are, of course, quite honorable as they try to bestow a higher moral tone and sense of responsibility upon their vote in general elections, but they completely overlook the damage which that intermittent and basically anarchic activity does to the only logical instrument for imposing responsible political behavior upon elected officeholders—that is a well-organized and responsive political party. Without the existence of such parties (and we have lingered in the twilight of such a condition for quite some time), the presentation of rational alternatives to policy decisions becomes virtually impossible. The incoherent babble of independent voices, undisciplined by any feeling of allegiance to party principle, platform or leadership, weakens the dialogue of reason in political life and renders public participation in national policymaking a figment of the earnest and committed reformer's imagination.

It is not only the new suburban reformers who seem to nourish this development of "independent" politics, but many of the practitioners of the dismal "science" of politics appear to view it with enthusiasm or at least resignation. It provides rich pastures for more useless behavorial research and endless sterile articles in academic journals. It is impervious to the resonant echoes of history; its persistence and growth takes place at the expense of the quality of political life in this country. Encouraging the divorce of party and government, in its ultimate *reductio ad absurdium* it produces a nightmare like Watergate. Perhaps if these students of government discarded their tenuous labels as "scientists" and got close enough to the reality of politics to get their feet wet, they would assume a leadership role in this debate, instead of continuing docilely and endlessly to identify voting trends and correlate political phenomena that have little or no substantive value.

I view the exploitation of national prime time television as one of the most hopeful means of breaking through the log jam which blocks meaningful public participation in critical national policy decision-making. It also has the most promising hope of strengthening the political party system. According to a recent study sponsored by the Twentieth Century Fund on *Presidential Television*, 97 percent of the American people now possess or have access to at least one television receiver, which operates on an average of more than seven hours every day.[84] A member of the Federal Communications Commission has estimated that "the average male viewer, between his second and sixty-fifth year will watch television for 3,000 entire days—roughly nine full years of his life. During the average weekday winter evening nearly half of the American people are to be found silently seated with fixed gaze upon a phospherescent screen."[85] I cannot attest to the accuracy of these figures, nor do I wish to engage in discussion of their cultural implications. But it is clear that prime time evening television presents the greatest opportunity for creating a vital and effective system of political communication which could have a profound impact upon the presidency and the total political process.

In a sense this has already happened. The "bully pulpit" of the presidency has been a significant political factor since the days of Theodore Roosevelt, but only in the age of radio and television has the tremendous weapon of presidential communications influence been fully exploited. Franklin D. Roosevelt was the supreme presidential artist and master of communication, but recent Presidents have exploited television and radio increasingly to capture public attention and to attempt to influence public opinion. Prior to Watergate, a lackluster President like Richard Nixon, although he discouraged and almost eliminated the two-way communication system of press conferences, televised or not, utilized radio and television to a much greater extent than any of his predecessors. The comparative figures are staggering:

> In his first eighteen months in office, President Nixon appeared on prime-time television as many times as the *combined* appearances of Presidents Eisenhower, Kennedy and Johnson in their first eighteen months in office. During his first forty months in office prior to his Moscow trip, President Nixon had made thirty-two special appearances in prime time, compared to twenty-four by President Johnson in over five years, ten by President

Kennedy in under three years and twenty-three by President Eisenhower in eight years.[86]

Nixon was aggressive in his use of prime time television in situations where he was able to preempt all three networks, but he lagged way behind his predecessors with regard to his willingness to submit himself to the cross examination of the press:

> In his three terms and one month in office, Franklin Delano Roosevelt held 998 presidential news conferences; Truman 324 in under eight years; Eisenhower 193 in eight years; Kennedy 64 in three years; Johnson 126 in six years; and Richard Nixon, in his first four years, only 28. In the last two years, Nixon permitted only 10.[87]

The inference is clear that Richard Nixon exploited the electronic media to attempt (quite successfully) to influence American public opinion, but avoided systematic examination of his policies by the press. In fact, Nixon considered the press his enemy and avoided it like the plague. This proved to be a very unhealthy experience for both Nixon and the American people, but he did achieve certain short-term political advantages from his manipulative use of the media. In one television appearance President Nixon spoke to an estimated 72 million Americans, several million more than the number of voters who cast their ballots for him and his opponent, Hubert Humphrey, in 1968. There is evidence that such television appearances have a significant impact upon public opinion:

> Polls have disclosed, for example, that public support for a Kennedy tax proposal rose by 4 percent after his television address on the subject; that support for President Johnson's position on Vietnam issues rose by 30 percent after one of his television addresses; and that support for President Nixon's Vietnam policies rose by 18 percent after one of his television addresses. Louis Harris reports a definite "correlation between televised presidential speeches and increased public acceptance of the president's positions.[88]

It seems clear that such domination, almost a political monopoly of the electronic mass communications media, is a potentially dangerous aspect of the growth of presidential power, a threatening potential weapon in the abuse of such power. Our representative institutions can never be safe or even very effective in such a political environment. It has contributed immeasurably in recent years to a tilt in favor of the President, as opposed to Congress, of the prized balance of power. It tends to overwhelm the opposition party, which usually has little success in gaining access to the media to respond.

> At the end of the first year of his administration, President Nixon had made four television addresses carried in prime time simultaneously by all three networks, had held eight televised news conferences, and had been supported by more than fifty network appearances of his political allies, including Vice President Agnew, Attorney General Mitchell, and the Republican National Committee chairman. Not once during this period

had the Democratic National Committee (DNC) obtained access to network television under its own control. The DNC's views had been expressed only through the occasional appearance of its chairman, Senator Fred Harris of Oklahoma, on non-prime-time interview programs.[89]

The Democratic National Committee was even unable to buy time on two of the networks for fund raising appeals, and it lost its case when it went before the Supreme Court. The time is ripe and long overdue for the redress of this deplorable situation. The democratic process can only thrive in an atmosphere of meaningful freedom, where all sides of critical national issues can be fully expressed. The political process can only be effectively protected from the abuse of presidential or congressional power if both institutions are accorded equal and ample time to express their points of view. It is essential that the opposition party, whether it constitutes a majority or a minority in Congress, play the role of congressional spokesman. This would be the only way of developing the necessary intellectual and political tension which the system presently lacks. It could become the means of redeeming a disintegrating party system, which has grown tired and nearly functionless from lack of meaningful activity. The very challenge of exciting the media could generate new leadership in the parties in Congress, which are frequently led by the oldest members of the inner club.

There are obviously problems which can be identified and objections offered against the development of a media-oriented dialectic of national politics. Television can be easily abused or used ineffectively; there can be overexposure as well as underexposure; there are always minority parties to consider and many other questions. But none of these arguments is strong enough to discourage serious experimentation in this area and immediate consideration of legislation that will make such programming not only possible but mandatory. The radio and television airwaves, Herbert Hoover told us back in the twenties, belong to the American people, and any time the Congress decides to mandate the use of prime time television and radio for regular political discussion and education, it can legislate regulations to which the networks will have to adhere. Considerable thought should be given to the matter before jumping at instant solutions, but the authors of *Presidential Television* have provided very sensible proposals which can at least open up the discussion.

CONGRESS: Congress, in consultation with the television networks, should permit television cameras on the floor of the House and Senate for the broadcast of specially scheduled prime-time evening sessions at which the most important matters before it each term are discussed, debated, and voted on. The sessions should be scheduled and broadcast at least four times per year and carried simultaneously by all three networks. These broadcasts should be exempt from the "equal time" law and the fairness and political party doctrines.

THE OPPOSITION PARTY: (1) *Response Time:* Presidential television and opposition party television should be de-regulated—taken out of the hands of the FCC. The national committee of the opposition party should be given by law an automatic right of response to any presidential radio or television address made during the ten months preceding a presidential election or within the ninety days preceding a congressional election in nonpresidential years. Section 315 of the Communications Act of 1934—the equal time provision—should be amended to provide that every radio or television broadcaster or CATV system that carries an address of the president within that response period must, upon request, provide equal broadcast opportunities to the national committee of the political party whose nominee for president has received the second-highest number of popular votes in the most recent election for that office. Only those presidential appearances in documentaries or newscasts in which the president's appearance is only incidental, and appearances which already give rise to "equal time" for an opposition candidate, should be exempt from this requirement. "Equal broadcast opportunities" would mean free time when the president's time has been free, at an equally desirable time of day in terms of potential audience (for example, prime time if the president has appeared in prime time). The national committee should control format if the president has had control of his format. The national committee would not be limited to addressing only those issues raised by the president in his appearance. When a presidential appearance has been carried simultaneously by all three net-works, the national committee response should also be carried simultaneously by the networks. The national committee should choose its spokesman or spokesmen. The opposition response should be exempt from the "equal time" law and the fairness and political party doctrines.

(2) *National Debates:* Between elections, the national committee of the opposition party, the national committee of the president's party, and the commercial and public television networks should together develop a plan to present live debates—"The National Debates"—between spokesmen for the two major parties with agreed topics and formats quarterly each year (but only twice in federal election years). All debates should be scheduled during prime time and broadcast simultaneously by all net-works. This proposal should be carried out voluntarily by the parties and networks rather than be required by legislation. Minor parties would participate in "The National Debates" according to the guidelines set forth in *Voters' Time* (the 1969 report of the nonpartisan Commission on Campaign Costs in the Electronic Era, sponsored by The Twentieth Century Fund, Inc.). "The National Debates" should be exempt from the "equal time" law and the fairness and political party doctrines.

(3) *Voters' Time:* The reforms proposed in *Voters' Time* should be adopted to ensure all significant presidential candidates a minimum amount of free, simultaneous television time. The two major party candidates would receive six thirty-minute prime-time program periods in the thirty-five days preceding a presidential election; candidates of minor

parties of sufficient size (based on a formula contained in the *Voters' Time* report) would receive one or two half-hour periods depending on their party's relative strength.

THE SUPREME COURT: Various steps should be taken to improve the coverage of the Court's decisions, but the justices of the Court should remain outside the television spotlight.

OTHER PARTIES: These reforms, taken together, should redress the balance now heavily tilted toward the president. But in the world of politics and government the unexpected regularly occurs. In such circumstances, balance can evaporate and the public's right to receive differing views or to gauge the personality of all significant candidates can be impeded despite the balancing mechanism. It is not always the party or the Congress that can speak for the opposition. To allow for the unexpected and to add flexibility, responsible spokesmen of any kind should not be prevented from purchasing a reasonable amount of time. Broadcasters should set aside a portion of commercial advertising time for purchase by responsible spokesmen on a first-come, first served basis. This would enable the opposition party, a minor party, or members of Congress to buy additional time. . . .[90]

All of this hinges on the acceptance of responsible roles on the part of the major political parties in the future. Implicit of this is the need for a reassertion of the power and performance of Congress, which it has certainly abandoned over the past few decades. The key to making the President accountable and restricted to his constitutional limits is a Congress alert to its responsibilities, willing to and capable of asserting its own prerogatives in the give and take of our constitutional balance of powers. But Congress is not an entity which moves as a might host. It is made up of 535 independent and frequently quarreling senators and congressmen, who respond to the interests and demands of different constituencies, who view problems from different perspectives, who are committed to different principles and viewpoints and who even reflect different ideologies and values. In rare instances, perhaps when challenged regarding its own special privileges and powers, Congress can unite and mobilize its full arsenal of powers to direct them towards the accomplishment of some objective. But these occasions are rare indeed. Congress is an institution which rarely acts in its own right. It is not even organized to do so. It is divided into two legislative houses, and further divided into political parties which, although considerably fragmented and divided themselves, more nearly approach homogeneity than the legislative chambers in which they operate.

The controversy over the legitimacy of political parties in our system is not of recent origin. We have been fighting with it ever since Jefferson and Madison went into active opposition to the Federalists during the 1790s. It has been argued that the American people will not and cannot develop a strong party commitment and discipline, and there is substantial evidence in our almost 200-year history to bear this out. What is suggested here, however, is that there really are no other reasonable alternatives. We either subject our individual wills to the discipline of working with others within the framework of a political party, or we continue to be impotent and anarchic, dominated by small, well-disciplined groups which usually operate outside of the disciplining limits of party (like Nixon and his White House "palace guard"), or we resign ourselves to the paralysis, the *immobilisme*, of extreme pluralistic politics where "nothing is done, or not much is done," as that great student of urban politics, Edward C. Banfield, has put it.[91] I think it is clear that the mounting problems and the confused priorities which have brought most progress in our society to a halt are the result of this chaos, and cannot be remedied by anything short of the most radical political surgery.

I have been amused by the disclaimers of practically every national Republican leader that he or she had nothing to do with the "mess" in the White House. Most were *persona non grata* in those circles, it is true, and were just about excluded from Nixon's Committee to Reelect the President, which served as the "Politburo" for Watergate activities, apart from directing the campaign for Nixon's landslide victory in 1972. For the most part their claims of estrangement from the man the Republican party nominated to head its national ticket in 1968 and 1972 (not to mention 1960, as well) are probably true, but also tragic and absurd. What meaning can political party symbols and platforms have if the standardbearer of the party is permitted total autonomy to ignore the influential members of the party and its elected structure, both in running for office and administering that office once elected? Does a political party have no accountability at all for a man it has thrice nominated for the presidency? Under these circumstances the role of the party is meaningless and is simply a symbolic trap to seduce voters, who remain loyal to symbols long after they have lost their meaning.

Not to be partisan about the matter, in my own state of Massachusetts the candidate of my party (who happens to be a first-rate individual) who ran for governor, along with the rest of the statewide slate, has never been instructed by a convention or any other agent with regard to the policies which the party favors. Under these circumstances, what level of accountability, what control or influence will the party and its members have upon the governor and his slate if they are elected? Conversely, what claim will the governor have upon the representatives of the party in the legislature to support policies and programs which they played no role in drafting? The disintegration of political parties in American life has reached absurd levels of development.

We may make wise choices among individual candidates for specific offices, but without a political party, what broader agreement, what possibilities exist for the support of policies which were presumably the basis for choosing the candidate in the first place? The contradictions and absurdities in our present political behavior arise from this irrational and chaotic pattern.

The restrictions upon presidential power so loudly demanded at the moment will have no long-range impact until the more basic flaws in the political process are recognized and remedied. Watergate never could have happened if a properly disciplined and responsible party system had been in operation. If, by some circumstance, it had, the responsible party would probably have suffered such an ignominious defeat at the polls that it would be in limbo for years to come. But at present many authorities are already predicting a brilliant recovery for Nixon's "party" in the 1976 elections. And why not, if it can successfully shrug off any responsibility for the Watergate crimes?

Of course there are steps that can be taken; some have already been initiated to restrict the abuses of presidential power we have experienced in the past decade. The War Powers resolution is a first step in this area, and the amendment to the new budget legislation which controls the presidential impoundment of funds is another step in the right direction. In fact the Budget Reform Act is itself a major reassertion of congressional power. Congress is presently considering actions to repeal lingering emergency legislation which provide Presidents with extraordinary peace-time power; such things as executive agreements, the cloak-and-dagger operations of the CIA and the destructive secrecy that enshrouds many of the foreign policy decisions of the government are also being examined. Secrecy in government is being attacked from many different quarters, and legislation has been introduced to prevent the President from tampering with agencies like the Bureau of Internal Revenue and the Federal Bureau of Investigation. Some members of Congress even contemplate segregating the Department of Justice from the executive branch or even making the attorney general an elective office, although in my judgment these are very bad ideas, reflecting a basic ignorance of the problem they attempt to address.

Of a different and quite dangerous nature are the more extreme proposals emanating from the prophets of disaster, who would throw the baby out with the bath water. In the nineteenth century Henry C. Lockwood argued that the presidency was "disguised monarchy," and proposed that it should be abolished.[92] He suggested:

> The evils of the presidential system are already widely acknowledged to have within them the potency of danger to the public weal, and it seems to us that the time has arrived for the people to act directly and bravely and by intelligent, sustained, and peaceful opposition, put an end to this department of government.[93]
>
> Our conclusion is that the Presidency should be abolished and the following amendments to the Constitution be adopted: The supreme power of legislating and executing all laws of the United States shall be vested in Congress, which body shall be the final judge of its own powers, subject, nevertheless, to the right of the Executive Council, hereinafter, provided for, at any time they shall elect, to dissolve Congress upon an issue framed and appeal to the people.[94]

He then went on to outline the makeup of his executive council of six members (the secretaries of state, war, navy, interior, attorney general and postmaster), who were to head up their respective departments, to be appointed by Congress and subject to removal by the same body.[95]

Reminiscent of this now forgotten proposal is the most extreme recent attack on the presidency by a brilliant historian who is more at home on the European continent in the pre-World War I period than she is in her own political culture. In several articles published in the op-ed page of *The New York Times,* Barbara Tuchman, author of the Pulitzer prize-winning, *The Guns of August,* has again called for the abolition of the presidency and its replacement with what she calls "cabinet government." The term itself is improperly used because it is normally employed to describe the parliamentary form of government, where the ruling party or coalition in parliament selects a group of its leaders to conduct the executive responsibilities of the government as long as they continue to enjoy a majority. Ms. Tuchman does not want to go that far, being aware, I imagine, that it might be rather difficult to convince the American people to make such a total transformation of their political system after almost 200 years in existence. Ms. Tuchman would be satisfied to eliminate the President and substitute for him a committee or cabinet which could rule collectively.

We could substitute true cabinet government by a directorate of six to be nominated as a slate by each party and elected as a slate for a single six-year term with a rotating chairman, each to serve for a year as in the Swiss system. The Chairman's vote would carry the weight of two to avoid a tie. (Although a five-man Cabinet originally seemed preferable when I first proposed the plan in 1968.) I find that the main departments of Government, one for each member of the Cabinet to administer, cannot be rationally arranged under fewer than six headings—(1) Foreign, including military and CIA. (2) Financial, including Treasury, taxes, budget and tariffs. (3) Judicial. (4) Business (or Production or Trade). (5) Physical Resources, including Interior, Parks, Forests, Conservation and Environment Protection. (6) Human Affairs, including HEW, Labor and cultural endowment.[96]

I thought I was having a bad dream when I read Ms. Tuchman's first article, but apparently not, for the following year she was back at it again, just as disappointed with Mr. Ford as she had been Mr. Nixon.

The only way to diffuse the Presidency and minimize the risk of a knave, a simpleton or a despot exercising supreme authority without check or consultation is to divide the power and spread the responsibility. Constitutional change is not beyond our capacity.[97]

Probably the most effective response to this argument for a plural Executive was made by Alexander Hamilton in Federalist No. 70 almost 200 years ago:

Wherever two or more persons are engaged in any common enterprise or pursuit, there is always danger of difference of opinion. If it be a public trust or office, in which they are clothed with equal dignity and authority, there is peculiar danger of personal emulation and even animosity. From either, and especially from all these causes, the most bitter dissensions are apt to spring. Whenever these happen, they lessen the respectability, weaken the authority, and distract the plans and operations of those whom they divide. If they should unfortunately assail the supreme executive magistracy of a country, consisting of a plurality of persons, they might impede or frustrate the most violent and irreconcilable factions, adhering differently to the different individuals who composed the magistracy.[98]

Hamilton was wise enough to understand that such a proposal was bound to render more difficult, if not impossible, precisely the problem which we are attempting to resolve—presidential accountability:

> Man, in public trust, will much oftener act in such a manner as to render him unworthy of being any longer trusted, than in such a manner as to make him obnoxious to legal punishment. But the multiplication of the executive adds to the difficulty of detection in either case. It often becomes impossible, amidst mutual accusations, to determine on whom the blame or punishment of pernicious measure, or a series of pernicious measures ought really to fall. It is shifted from one to another with so much dexterity, and under such plausible appearances, that public opinion is in suspense about the real author. The circumstances which may have led to any national miscarriage of misfortune are sometimes so complicated that, where there are a number of actors who may have had different degrees and kinds of agency, though we may clearly see upon the whole that there has been mismanagement, yet it may be impracticable to pronounce to whose account the evil which may have been incurred is truly chargeable.[99]

If there was one overwhelming and encouraging aspect of the Watergate scandal, it was that the House Judiciary Committee knew to impeach once it concluded that the constitutional powers of the President had actually been abused. What if a cabinet had been at the head of our government and one member turned to the other with an accusing finger, saying "It was not I."

It is interesting that Ms. Tuchman makes no case for the vitality or equality of cabinet government at this moment of history in the countries which enjoy its full advantages. Cabinet government in Italy is practically bankrupt, France had to reject it after decades of *immobilisme* and it is not altogether clear whether other countries on the continent and elsewhere that enjoy the virtues of collective leadership are particularly happy with their present form of government. Despite this obvious deficiency of presenting a positive case for a radical alternative to our present system, the historian from Cos Cob, Connecticut, would abolish the presidency—an institution which has served this nation brilliantly for most of the past 200 years, a longer time span than any executive office in the age of democracy.

Such a foolish proposal deserves scant attention except that it is probably symptomatic of what we will be hearing from various and surprising quarters for some time to come. In moments of deep national crisis, many who should know better lose their heads and suggest remedial action completely out of keeping with our traditions and political culture. The Founding Fathers decided against the principle of cabinet government almost two centuries ago and in its place developed the presidential system, which has carried us through our history, on the whole, rather exceptionally. At the sign of a major failure in its operation, surgery is proposed which would totally transform the nature of our political system, the good with the bad. The proposal is based upon superficial and emotional reactions to Watergate and its aftermath, which are bound to be shared by other unhappy and irate Americans, but what is needed at this moment of doubt and uncertainty is the balanced perspective of history to protect us from such dubious adventures.

If history teaches us anything, it cautions us to distrust instant and total remedies to correct deep and long-standing flaws in the operation of our political institutions. Watergate was not simply a nightmarish aberration which appeared suddenly on the political landscape and will disappear from our national life once the guilty are discovered and punished, as many have already been. To this extent, Ms. Tuchman is right in sensing that the problem is so pervasive, so deep set, so reflective of unfortunate lapses in moral and responsible conduct that the Watergate syndrome extends far beyond the limits of the Executive office in Washington and touches much of our every day existence in society. This cannot be changed overnight. The persistent resistance to any change, not only at the center of our political system, but also in the entrenched institutions and behaviors of nongovernmental activity, will not yield to gimmicks or respond to radical surgery of the character that Ms. Tuchman and others will recommend. It will first require a deeper understanding of the causes of such behavior and a sensitivity to the obvious failure of the political process and our other institutions to correct such flaws long before a cancer of the magnitude of Watergate develops again.

It is my intention that this historical examination of the growth of presidential power will make a contribution to this understanding. It has been cast in the perspective of history because I cannot conceive of understanding the true depth of the problems without analyzing the institution of the presidency, its strengths and its weaknesses, in their historical context and focusing particularly upon the question of power, its evolution and its proper limits. The very resiliency of the office, its ability to shoulder so much of the burden of our historical past, should at a very minimum argue against radical surgery. The presidency has been at the center of almost every exciting moment of national growth and development; it has been the lever that has raised effective resistance to national political fragmentation and disorder, has been the focal point of the protection we have created to preserve our national resources, has led us in justifiable wars in defense of our national integrity, as well as into mistaken episodes. Before the scalpel of emotional reaction performs what could be considered a lobotomy upon our national political system, grave consideration should be accorded to the dynamic and creative role which the American presidency has performed in our history. More than the flag or the national anthem, *it* has been the symbol of our national unity and has dramatized the heroic aspects of the nation's history. One cannot cut away the critical focal point of the country's proudest traditions without rendering irreparable damage to the body politic.

There are other arguments for not abolishing or even crippling the presidency. Any understanding of the way our political system operates recognizes that further fragmentation of the singlemost source of leadership in our divided political system would be a disaster from which it would be difficult, if not impossible, to recover. If Watergate and its larger political and moral contexts have any meaning or lessons to teach us, they would be that the country and the political system need *more* political leadership rather than *less*. As Nelson Polsby and Aaron Wildavsky have argued so tellingly,

> The institutional lesson to be learned from these events [Watergate], we believe, is not that the Presidency should be diminished, but that other

institutions should grow in stature. The first order of priority should go to rebuilding our political parties, because they are most in need of help and could do most to bring Presidents in line with strong sentiments in the country. Had there been Republican elders of sufficient size and weight, the President representing their party could not have so readily strayed in his perception of the popular will. Whatever its other defects, a party provides essential connective tissue between people and Presidents.[100]

Henry Fairlie has pointed out, "this is a voice that has not been heard for a long time in the political science or political journalism of the country."[101] But it is a warning that must be heeded if we are to keep our President within the constitutional limits of the office and at the same time keep from destroying the political system, which by any relevant standards of comparison has served the interests of this country so well. Nixon and Watergate were not the products of an office so corrupted and drunk with power that no other behavior was possible, but rather the result of a flawed political character who had been fully exposed to the nation for a quarter of a century. Nixon secured the highest office in the nation because neither of the major political parties was capable of resisting his unscrupulous onslought nor virile enough to control or oppose him effectively.

Our problem is not simply Richard Nixon, who is a sad reflection of the weaknesses and evils which still thrive in the nation and permeate and cripple its political process. The remedy for Watergate is not the abolition or castration of the office—the natural source of much of the vitality of the system when it is properly accountable to other sources of power in the body politic—the courts, the Congress, the political parties and the constituencies. Disciplined and enforced accountability is the remedy for the imperial presidency and the further degeneration of it into the revolutionary or unrestrained Executive, who is permitted to overrun the constitutional limits of his office. Such accountability cannot be enforced without the impetus of a political party system which will educate through the dialectic of meaningful political discourse to generate a level of public opinion, which, in the final analysis, can be the political sovereign of the nation.

That wise student of the presidency, James MacGregor Burns, has warned us not to abstract the presidency from history, politics and ideology, and overreact to the present crisis:

> The Johnson and Nixon Administrations are not representative of the American Presidency. Both were a response to political disarray in this country, which had its roots immediately in Vietnam, and more fundamentally in such long-term developments as the demoralization of our party system. . . . We must ask ourselves to what extent the failures of the last few years have been political rather than presidential or institutional failures. . . . We should maintain the strength of the Executive, perhaps even augment it in domestic matters, not simply so it can respond to crisis more quickly, but to anticipate and plan against crisis, which is one of the great potential strengths of the Executive.[102]

He is absolutely right. I have already discussed various steps that have been taken, are contemplated or should be taken to curtail presidential activity, and it is quite proper to suggest several areas where presidential power should be enhanced. In section two of this volume it was suggested that the President be given the power to adjust tax rates, upwards and downwards within certain specified limits, in order to provide more flexible fiscal control of the economy. It is arguable that any administration, regardless of whether it commands a majority or a minority in both houses of Congress, should have the assurance that its critical legislative proposals will get by the appropriate committees for an examination by the full compliment of both the Senate and the House. In section three I discussed the use and misuse of presidential commissions, which frequently fall all over themselves vying for an opportunity for access to the public. The President should have access to and be able to underwrite support for the best minds in the country in every critical area of national concern requiring study and analysis; and he should be able to appoint such study and research commissions without interference from Congress, with at least limited funds at his disposal for their support. He should not, however, as a matter of strategy, pile one commission or commission report upon another, but should provide time, attention and access to the mass communications media for adequate presentation to the public and subsequent discussion and analysis of each case.

Government and the academy have much in common and they should be able to use each other's expertise and experience more effectively than they have in the past. This does not mean, however, that academicians who are not responsible to party or constituencies should live privileged and autonomous lives in government. A better way must be found to exchange knowledge and experience, valuable in both directions, without giving academic "experts" immunity from the political process. At the same time their usefulness must be respected and their cooperation expected in providing mechanisms for its application in situations where government information, understanding and experience are weak and where strong leadership is essential. The complex field of education is one area where substantially broader understanding is necessary and available, if the searchers know where to look and how to interpret and use the information.

Burns points out another reason why we should think twice before dismantling the presidency. He argues:

> . . . [T]he Presidency has represented, on the whole, the egalitarian and libertarian thrust in this country. We ought to be very careful about threatening this institution, not because we have had egalitarian and libertarian Presidents, but because the very structure of the Presidency, with its electoral, institutional, and behavorial aspects, has made it the kind of institution it is [103]

But perhaps one of the problems with the presidency in the past was that the high level of expectations of so many placed too large a burden upon its shoulders. This is counterproductive in the long run, because when the expectations are not immediately or completely realized, or even not realized at all, disillusionment develops and apathy emerges. This is a familiar cycle, with the young particularly, but it is also quite observable among minority groups rightfully seeking full equality under the law, special interest groups and regional interests in search of national support. The universe is not always instantly malleable, and the President, like other political decision-makers, must weigh and balance many pressures and interests before determining a proper course of action.

Another familiar attack on the presidency these days involves a great deal of talk about demythologizing the office. Americans are being reminded that they should not approach their President as if he were a king, an emperor, one who can perform no evil act or entertain anything but the highest thoughts. Indeed, my problem is that I have never met anyone who thought he was. My reading of history indicates that this has always been true. Jefferson, Jackson, Lincoln, FDR and Truman were among the most maligned Presidents in our history—yet they survived the ordeal and found an honored resting place in history.

I do not believe Americans are in any real danger of deifying their President. I think many of my fellow countrymen, thankfully, are inclined to think well of him until proven otherwise. Would we want it to be any different? Is there not some value, even in a democratic society, in having some respected leaders who are admired for particular virtues which they possess? We are in trouble when we approach the point where children no longer admire national leaders and can find nothing in their lives or conduct to inspire ambition or interest in a career of public service. The symbolic importance of leadership has value, although limited by reason and reality, in a republic, and we would diminish much that is useful and unifying in our nation if we become premature sceptics, thinking only the worst of our leaders, guarding against the weakness of recognizing what indeed may be the superior qualities which bring them to our attention.

A nation without myths is a country without soul. If much of the greatness of our early history as a nation is embodied in the qualities of our foremost leaders, most of whom were Presidents, let us not destroy those memories but continue to honor them intelligently, critically and with respect. Too much respect for leaders is not the source of some of our troubles but rather the lack of leaders in whom we have sufficient respect. It is time we set about the task of restoring the political and moral environment in which such leaders can emerge.

The wonder and good fortune of this country is that outstanding leaders have emerged at precisely those moments when we needed them most. Sometimes they were late in arriving (an earlier appearance might have salvaged more hope), but the important point is that they did arrive, they provided strong leadership so that in its most critical crises the country, its political institutions and its people survived and made progress when the future had looked so dismal. The Presidents we call great are the leaders who grasped the nature of the problem at hand and provided the direction and the energy for the country to move forward. Our political system would be lost without this dynamic source of energy and leadership.

Without Jefferson's devotion to liberty, his concept of national unity and growth; without Jackson's assertion of national priority and the public welfare; Lincoln's defense of the Union; Theodore Roosevelt's reinvigoration of the office of the President in defense of the public interest and the natural environment; Franklin Roosevelt's inspiring leadership in restoring public confidence in democratic institutions and in his wartime leadership in the struggle for freedom; John F. Kennedy's brilliant beginning and courage in the face of crisis; without such exhilarating benchmarks, the history of this country, in fact its very existence as a nation, would certainly be questionable. Watergate should not be permitted to overshadow our pride in these historical moments of greatness. Yet energy and leadership can get out of hand. In addition to strong constitutional checks and balances there must be an informed public, a strong and alert Congress and a courageous but restrained Court to keep the President within bounds. It is the character and quality of the political environment which provides these necessary constraints upon power, and when that environment becomes polluted, its products suffer.

The country desperately needs to recover lost values, invigorate its institutions, heal its social divisions and set new goals. Leadership—presidential leadership—is central but certainly not exclusively responsible for such a national agenda. Many of these problems are concrete—the rebuilding of our cities, the rescue of our natural environment, the improvement of our systems of public transportation— but there is also a symbolic level of leadership which is just as essential. Black Americans have waited three centuries for a symbolic act of sufficient magnitude to atone for America's original sin of racism to convince this gifted part of our population that this is their homeland and that the American dream is their rightful legacy as Americans. Of course they seek more than symbolism, but they also have a right to expect the symbolic recognition of past errors and the future commitment to full retribution. A great and wise President will understand this and act accordingly.

The most eloquent and balanced definition of the true limits of presidential power came from the stylish pen of my friend and former colleague, the late Clinton Rossiter, who was not only a scholar steeped in a profound understanding of the presidency and American history, but also a master of prose:

> . . . [T]he President is not a Gulliver immobilized by ten thousand tiny cords, nor even a Prometheus chained to a rock of frustration. He is, rather, a kind of magnificent lion who can roam widely and do great deeds so long as he does not try to break loose from his broad reservation. Our pluralistic system of restraints is designed to keep him from going out of bounds, not to paralyze him in the field that has been reserved for his use. He will feel few checks upon his power if he uses that power as he should. This may well be the final definition of the strong and successful President: the one who knows just how far he can go in the direction he wants to go. If he cannot judge the limits of his power, he cannot call upon its strength. If he cannot sense the possible, he will exhaust himself attempting the impossible. The power of the President moves as a mighty host only with the grain of liberty and morality.[104]

Let us keep it that way. A renewed consciousness of our own sense of liberty and public morality is bound to reflect itself in more responsible presidential leadership.

NOTES

1. Arthur M. Schlesinger, jr., *The Imperial Presidency* (Boston, 1973), viii.
2. Arthur M. Schlesinger, jr., and Fred L. Israel, eds., *History of American Presidential Elections, 1789-1968* (New York, 1971) IV, 3537. The entire speech is reprinted in section four of this volume, 1621ff.
3. Theodore C. Sorensen, *Decision-Making in the White House* (New York, 1963), xii.
4. Schlesinger, *The Imperial Presidency,* viii.
5. Schlesinger, *The Imperial Presidency,* 177-78.
6. Quoted in Joseph C. Goulden, *Truth Is the First Casualty: The Tonkin Gulf Affair—Illusion and Reality* (Chicago, 1969), 26.
7. Quoted in Anthony Austin, *President's War: The Story of the Tonkin Gulf Resolution and How the Nation Was Trapped in Vietnam* (New York, 1971), 263.
8. Quoted in Duane Lockard, *The Perverted Priorities of American Politics* (New York, 1971), 246.
9. U.S., Congress, Senate, Foreign Relations Committee, *The Gulf of Tonkin: The 1964 Incidents,* Hearings, 90th Cong., 2nd sess., February 20, 1968 (Washington, D.C., 1968), 33.
10. Goulden, 140.
11. Quoted in Goulden, 151.
12. Quoted in Goulden, 152.
13. Goulden, 28.
14. Goulden, 156.
15. Austin, 47.
16. *The Gulf of Tonkin: The 1964 Incidents,* 80. The entire hearing ought to be read by anyone interested in the major points in contention, along with the Goulden and Austin studies.
17. Theodore H. White, *The Making of the President 1964* (New York, 1965), 373-74.
18. George E. Reedy, *The Presidency in Flux* (New York, 1973), 93.
19. Nicholas von Hoffman, *Washington Post,* January 24, 1973.
20. Maxwell D. Taylor, *Swords and Plowshares* (New York, 1972), 327.
21. Memorandum by the State Department legal advisor, Leonard C. Meeker, "The Legality of the United States Participation in the Defense of Viet-Nam," March 4, 1966. Reprinted from *State Department Bulletin 474* (1966) in John Norton Moore, *Law and the Indo-China War* (Princeton, New Jersey, 1972), 622.
22. Meeker, 632.
23. Schlesinger, *The Imperial Presidency,* 183-84.
24. U.S., Congress, Senate, Foreign Relations Committee, *U.S. Commitments to Foreign Powers,* Hearings, 90th Cong., 1st sess., August 17, 1967 (Washington, D.C., 1967), 125.
25. *U.S. Commitments to Foreign Powers,* 126.
26. Schlesinger, *The Imperial Presidency,* 185.
27. George E. Reedy, *The Twilight of the Presidency* (New York, 1970), 95.
28. Townsend Hoopes, *The Limits of Intervention* (New York, 1970), 203.
29. Hoopes, 203.
30. Quoted in Schlesinger, *The Imperial Presidency,* 187-88.
31. From the dissenting views of Congresswoman Elizabeth Holtzman, joined by Congressmen Kastenmeir, Edwards, Hungate, Conyers, Waldie, Drinan, Rangel, Owens, Mezvinsky, to the "Report on the Impeachment of Richard M. Nixon, President of the United States," printed in the *Congressional Record,* CXX, H9051 (Daily edition, August 22, 1974).
32. Schlesinger, *The Imperial Presidency,* 193.
33. Schlesinger, *The Imperial Presidency,* 193-94.
34. Lincoln to Herndon, February 15, 1848, in Roy P. Basler, ed., *The Collected Works of Abraham Lincoln* (New Brunswick, New Jersey, 1953) I, 451-52.
35. Schlesinger, *The Imperial Presidency,* 217.
36. Lou Cannon, "The Siege Psychology and How It Grew," in *Washington Post,* July 29, 1973. Reprinted in *Year of Scandal: How the Washington Post Covered the Watergate and the Agnew Crisis* (Washington, D.C., 1973).
37. Quoted in Rowland Evans, jr., and Robert D. Novak, eds., *Nixon in the White House: The Frustration of Power* (New York, 1972), 170-71.

38. Quoted in Theodore H. White, *The Making of the President 1968* (New York, 1969), 417.
39. Quoted in Evans and Novak, 170-71.
40. Evans and Novak, 171.
41. Evans and Novak, 171.
42. Quoted in Richard Harris, *Decision* (New York, 1971), 209.
43. Evans and Novak, 275.
44. Schlesinger, *The Imperial Presidency,* 216-17.
45. Quoted in Schlesinger, *The Imperial Presidency,* 225.
46. Schlesinger, *The Imperial Presidency,* 224-25.
47. Theodore H. White, *The Making of the President 1972* (New York, 1973), 75.
48. Louis Fisher, *President and Congress: Power and Policy* (New York, 1972), 125-26.
49. U.S., Congress, *Impoundment of Appropriated Funds by the President,* Joint Hearings of the Ad Hoc Subcommittee on Impoundment of Funds of the Committee on Government Operations, and Subcommittee on the Separation of Powers of the Committee on the Judiciary, 93rd Cong., 1st sess., January 31, 1973 (Washington, D.C., 1973), 150-51.
50. *Impoundment of Appropriated Funds by the President,* 394.
51. The list of senators and congressmen joining with Senator Sam Ervin in submitting the *amicus curiae* brief is virtually a roster of the Senate Democratic leadership:

> In addition to several states, the following also submitted an *amicus curiae* brief on behalf of the appellee: Senator Samuel J. Ervin, Jr., chairman, Government Operations Committee; Senator James O. Eastland, President Pro Tempore, chairman, Judiciary Committee; Senator Michael J. Mansfield, majority leader; Senator Robert C. Byrd, assistant majority leader; Senator Jennings Randolph, chairman, Public Works Committee; Senator John L. McClellan, chairman, Appropriations Committee; Senator Howard W. Cannon, chairman, Aeronautical and Space Sciences Committee; Senator Thomas F. Eagleton, chairman, District of Columbia Committee; Senator J. W. Fulbright, chairman, Foreign Relations Committee; Senator Vance Hartke, chairman, Veterans' Affairs Committee; Senator Henry M. Jackson, chairman, Interior and Insular Affairs Committee; Senator Gale W. McGee, chairman, Post Office and Civil Service Committee; Senator Warren G. Magnuson, chairman, Commerce Committee; Senator Lee Metcalf, chairman, Joint Committee on Congressional Organization; Senator John Sparkman, chairman, Banking, Housing and Urban Affairs Committee; Senator Stuart Symington; Senator Harrison A Williams, Jr., chairman, Labor and Public Welfare Committee; Representative J. J. Pickle; Representative Benjamin Rosenthal; Representative Morris K. Udall; Senator John A. Stennis, chairman, Armed Services Committee; Senator Herman E. Talmadge, chairman, Agriculture and Forestry Committee; Senator Frank E. Moss, chairman, Aeronautical and Space Sciences Committee; Senator Hubert H. Humphrey; Senator John V. Tunney; Representative William V. Alexander, Jr.; Representative Robert F. Drinan; and Public Citizen, Inc. (Cited in *State Highway Commission of Missouri* v. *John A. Volpe,* No. 72-1512, U.S. Court of Appeals [8th Cir., April 2, 1973] in 479 F.2d 1099.)

52. The decision of the court stated:

> . . . For although a general appropriation act may be viewed as not providing a specific mandate to expend *all* of the funds appropriated, this does not *a fortiori* endow the Secretary with the authority to use unfettered discretion as to when and how the monies may be used. The act circumscribes that discretion and only an analysis of the act itself can dictate the latitude of the questioned discretion.
> . . . We conclude that the statutory provisions of the Federal-Aid Highway Act of 1956, as amended, 23 U.S.C. #101 et seq. (1970), do not expressly or impliedly authorize the Secretary to withhold the authority to obligate apportioned funds where the only reasons are those advanced by the Secretary in this case. (*State Highway Commission of Missouri* v. *Volpe,* 479 F.2d 1099, 1109, 1118).

53. For further information describing the legislative history of the anti-impoundment measures, see *1973 Congressional Almanac* (Washington, D.C., 1974); and for detailed analysis of the new Budget Reform procedures and legislation, see *Congressional Quarterly,* June 15, 1974, 1590-94.
54. Quoted in Cannon, C4.
55. U.S., Congress, House, Committee on the Judiciary, *Statement of Information,* Hearings, 93rd Cong., 2nd sess., May-June 1974 (Washington, D.C., 1974), Book VII, Part 1, 142-356.
56. Tom Charles Huston quoted in an interview by Bo Burlingham, "Paranoia in Power," in *Harpers Magazine,* October 1974, 32.

57. Tom Charles Huston, Memorandum on Domestic Intelligence Review, to H. R. Haldeman, July 1970. Reprinted in New York Times Staff, eds., *The Watergate Hearings: Break-in and Cover-up* (New York, 1973), 753.

58. Tom Charles Huston, "Operational Restraints on Intelligence Collection," Memorandum to H. R. Haldeman, July 1970. Reprinted in *Statement of Information*, VII, Part 1, 439.

59. Huston, Memorandum on Domestic Intelligence Review, 754.

60. Huston, Memorandum on Domestic Intelligence Review, 755.

61. Quoted in Burlingham, 36.

62. Quoted in Burlingham, 36.

63. U.S., Congress, House, *Reorganization Plan No. 2 of 1970* (Office of Management and Budget; Domestic Council), Hearings before a Subcommittee on Government Operations, 91st Cong., 2nd sess., April 28, 1970 (Washington, D.C., 1970), 2.

64. A study conducted several years ago by Congress' research arm, the Congressional Research Service, compiled a count of the employees working in and attached to the White House; it found that "between 1954 and 1971 the number of presidential advisers has grown from 25 to 45, the White House staff from 266 to 600, and the Executive Office staff from 1,175 to 5,395." Quoted from Thomas E. Cronin's interesting article, "The Swelling of the Presidency," in *Saturday Review of the Society*, I, No. 1 (February 1973), 30.

65. U.S., Congress, Senate, *Watergate: Its Implications for Responsible Government*, report prepared by a panel of the National Academy of Public Administration at the request of Senate Select Committee on Presidential Campaign Activities (March 1974), 27, 33.

66. Richard Tanner Johnson, *Managing the White House: An Intimate View of Six Presidents* (New York, 1974).

67. Johnson, 91.

68. Cronin, "The Swelling of the Presidency," 33.

69. Thomas E. Cronin, "Presidents as Chief Executives," in Rexford Guy Tugwell and Thomas E. Cronin, eds., *The Presidency Reappraised* (New York, 1974), 254-55.

70. Henry Fairlie, "The Lessons of Watergate; Or the Possibility of Morality in Politics," in *Encounter*, XLIII, No. 4 (October 1974), 21.

71. Fairlie, 21.

72. A listing of such refusals by 17 Presidents of the United States, from George Washington to Harry S. Truman, was prepared by President Truman and his staff in response to an abortive effort by the Republican-controlled Congress in 1948 to pass a law requiring the President to produce confidential material on the demand of Congress, even if the President thought it was not in the public interest to do so. Truman considered the measure unconstitutional. The list is reprinted in Justice McKinnon's dissent in the decision of the U.S. Court of Appeals for the District of Columbia in *Nixon* v. *Sirica*, 487 F.2d 700, 732 (D.C. Cir. 1973).

73. *Marbury* v. *Madison*, 1 Cranch 165 (1803).

74. Raoul Berger, *Executive Privilege: A Constitutional Myth* (Cambridge, Massachusetts, 1974), 1.

75. *United States* v. *Nixon*, 42 LW 5237 (1974), reprinted in Leon Friedman, ed., *United States v. Nixon* (New York, 1974), 616.

76. Friedman, *United States v. Nixon*, 611.

77. Friedman, *United States v. Nixon*, 613.

78. Friedman, *United States v. Nixon*, 611, n. 16.

79. Friedman, *United States v. Nixon*, 616, n. 19. (My emphasis).

80. Friedman, *United States v. Nixon*, 612.

81. Friedman, *United States v. Nixon*, xxi.

82. This question requires more detailed analysis than these pages can tolerate. I hope to develop this analysis at a later date.

83. "Proclamation of Pardon," *The New York Times*, September 9, 1974, 1.

84. Newton N. Minow, John Bartlow Martin and Lee M. Mitchell, eds., *Presidential Television: A Twentieth Century Fund Report* (New York, 1973), v.

85. Commissioner Nicholas Johnson quoted in Minow, et al., v.

86. Minow, et al., ix.

87. Minow, et al., ix.

88. Minow, et al., 19.

89. Minow, et al., 134.

90. Minow, et al., 161-63.

91. Edward C. Banfield, *Political Influence* (New York, 1966), 341.

92. Henry C. Lockwood, *The Abolition of the Presidency* (New York, 1884), 315.

93. Lockwood, 16.

94. Lockwood, 303.
95. Lockwood, 302-03.
96. *New York Times,* February 13, 1973, 35.
97. *New York Times,* September 30, 1974, 39.
98. Jacob Cooke, ed., *The Federalist Papers* (Cleveland, Ohio, 1961), 474.
99. Cooke, 476-77.
100. Aaron Wildavesky and Nelson W. Polsby, "The Legitimacy of the Presidency," in *The Washington Post: Outlook,* October 28, 1973, C5.
101. Fairlie, 16.
102. James MacGregor Burns, "Don't Go Too Far," in *The Center Magazine,* September-October 1974, 56.
103. Burns, 56.
104. Clinton Rossiter, *The American Presidency* (New York, 1960), 72-73.

Bibliography

Austin, Anthony. *President's War: The Story of the Tonkin Gulf Resolution and How the Nation Was Trapped in Vietnam.* New York: J. B. Lippincott and Company, 1971.

Banfield, Edward C. *Political Influence.* New York: The Free Press, Macmillan, 1966.

Berger, Raoul. *Executive Privilege: A Constitutional Myth.* Cambridge, Massachusetts: Harvard University Press, 1974.

Burlingham, Bo. "Paranoia in Power." *Harpers Magazine,* October 1974.

Burns, James MacGregor. "Don't Go Too Far." *The Center Magazine,* September-October 1974.

Cannon, Lou. "The Siege Psychology and How It Grew." *Washington Post,* July 29, 1973.

Cooke, Jacob, ed. *The Federalist Papers.* Cleveland, Ohio: Wesleyan University Press, 1961.

Cronin, Thomas E. "The Swelling of the Presidency." *Saturday Review of the Society.* I. No. 1 (February 1973).

Evans, Rowland, jr., and Novak, Robert D., eds. *Nixon in the White House: The Frustration of Power.* New York: Random House, 1972.

Fairlie, Henry. "The Lessons of Watergate: Or the Possibility of Morality in Politics." *Encounter.* XLIII. No. 4 (October 1974).

Fisher, Louis. *President and Congress: Power and Policy.* New York: The Free Press, Collier Macmillan, 1972.

Friedman, Leon, ed. *United States v. Nixon.* New York: Chelsea House Publishers/R. R. Bowker Company, 1974.

Goulden, Joseph C. *Truth Is the First Casualty: The Tonkin Gulf Affair—Illusion and Reality.* Chicago: Rand McNally and Company, 1969.

Harris, Richard. *Decision.* New York: E. P. Dutton and Company, 1971.

Hoopes, Townsend. *The Limits of Intervention.* New York: David McKay Company, Inc., 1970.

Johnson, Richard Tanner. *Managing the White House: An Intimate View of Six Presidents*. New York: Harper and Row, 1974.

Lockard, Duane. *The Perverted Priorities of American Politics*. New York: The Macmillan Company, 1971.

Lockwood, Henry C. *The Abolition of the Presidency*. New York: R. Worthington, 1884.

Meeker, Leonard C. "The Legality of the United States Participation in Defense of Viet-Nam." Memorandum of March 4, 1966. *State Department Bulletin 474*. Washington, D.C.: U.S. Government Printing Office, 1966. Reprinted in John Norton Moore, *Law and the Indo-China War*. Princeton, New Jersey: Princeton University Press, 1972.

Minow, Newton N.; Martin, John Bartlow; and Mitchell, Lee M. *Presidential Television: A Twentieth Century Fund Report*. New York: Basic Books, Inc., 1973.

New York Times Staff, eds. *The Watergate Hearings: Break-in and Cover-up*. New York: Bantam Books, Inc., 1973.

Nixon v. *Sirica,* 487 F.2d 700 (D.C. Cir. 1973).

Reedy, George E. *The Presidency in Flux*. New York: Columbia University Press, 1973.

_____. *The Twilight of the Presidency*. New York: W.W. Norton and Company, 1970.

Rehnquist, William H. "The Constitutional Issues—Administration Position." *New York University Law Review*. XLVIII (June 1970).

Rossiter, Clinton. *The American Presidency*. New York: Harcourt, Brace and Company, 1960.

Schlesinger, Arthur M., jr. *The Imperial Presidency*. Boston: Houghton Mifflin Company, 1973.

_____, and Israel, Fred L., eds. *History of American Presidential Elections, 1789-1968*. New York: Chelsea House Publishers/McGraw-Hill, 1971.

Sorensen, Theodore C. *Decision-Making in the White House*. New York: Columbia University Press, 1963.

State Highway Commission of Missouri v. *John A. Volpe*. 479 F.2d 1099.

Taylor, Maxwell D. *Swords and Plowshares.* New York: W.W. Norton and Company, Inc., 1972.

Tugwell, Rexford Guy, and Cronin, Thomas E., eds. *The Presidency Reappraised.* New York: Praeger Publishers, 1974.

United States. Congress. House. Committee on the Judiciary. *Report on the Impeachment of Richard M. Nixon, President of the United States.* 93rd Cong., 2nd sess. Washington, D.C.: U.S. Government Printing Office, 1974.

⎯⎯⎯. House. Committee on the Judiciary. *Statement of Information.* Hearings, 93rd Cong., 2nd sess., May-June 1974. Washington, D.C.: U.S. Government Printing Office, 1974.

⎯⎯⎯. House. *Reorganization Plan No. 2 of 1970* (Office of Management and Budget; Domestic Council). Hearings before a Subcommittee on Government Operations, 91st Cong., 2nd sess., April 28, 1970. Washington, D.C.: U.S. Government Printing Office, 1970.

⎯⎯⎯. *Impoundment of Appropriated Funds by the President.* Joint Hearings of the Ad Hoc Subcommittee on Impoundment of Funds of the Committee on Government Operations, and Subcommittee on the Separation of Powers of the Committee on the Judiciary, 93rd Cong., 1st sess., January 31, 1973. Washington, D.C.: U.S. Government Printing Office, 1968.

⎯⎯⎯. Senate. Foreign Relations Committee. *The Gulf of Tonkin: The 1964 Incidents.* Hearings, 90th Cong., 2nd sess., February 20, 1968. Washington, D.C.: U.S. Government Printing Office, 1968.

⎯⎯⎯. Senate. Foreign Relations Committee. *U.S. Commitments to Foreign Powers.* Hearings, 90th Cong., 1st sess., August 17, 1967. Washington, D.C.: U.S. Government Printing Office, 1967.

United States v. *Nixon,* 42 LW 5237 (1974).

White, Theodore H. *The Making of the President 1964.* New York: Atheneum Publishers, 1965.

⎯⎯⎯. *The Making of the President 1968.* New York: Atheneum Publishers, 1969.

⎯⎯⎯. *The Making of the President 1972.* New York: Atheneum Publishers, 1973.

Wildavesky, Aaron, and Polsby, Nelson W. "The Legitimacy of the Presidency." *The Washington Post: Outlook,* October 28, 1973.

SOURCES AND ACKNOWLEDGEMENTS

The task of selecting the critical experiences and documents which marked the growth of presidential power over the past 185 years has not been an easy one. I have no doubt that my decisions will meet with very legitimate criticisms and differences of opinion. One cannot expect it to be otherwise, particularly when dealing with many of the critical turning points in American history and the Presidents who played such an important role in them. The reader should bear in mind that this is not a history of the American presidency nor of the men who filled that office, but rather an historical analysis, with ample documentation, of the creation and growth of the power of that office. Some striking presidential experiences, for example, Woodrow Wilson's unsuccessful attempt to bring this country into the League of Nations was an extremely important presidential event, but it was not an occasion which enhanced the power of the Chief Executive nor was it the best example to use to illustrate the limits of presidential power. Such criteria have been the basis for my selection process.

It was my hope and secret design that these volumes not only serve as a source of documents, but that even those coming to search out and analyze a particular presidential paper or speech will tarry long enough to read something of the context of the events surrounding its emergence and perhaps reflect along with me as to its significance in the development of the office. Americans have fashioned an extra-ordinarily resilient political system among the great powers of the world, and nothing within the framework of our political process has been more dynamic or more complex than the office of the presidency. At present it faces its most important crisis in its long and stormy history, but certainly a thoroughgoing under-standing of its past crises and their historical resolutions is a *sine qua non* to thinking creatively about its future. I hope that the documents in their historical context, in as close to their original form as possible, along with the analysis supplied, will illuminate this undertaking.

Some may find the placement of the documents in the midst of their narrative context a bit unusual and perhaps disconcerting. It is my conviction that if the particular document was critical to the decision or action of the President at that time, it belonged right where I have put it, in the belief that it should be read and possibly interpreted differently. This kind of interest and concern will mark the success of this study, rather than any wholesale agreement with the arguments presented in these pages.

I have tried to hold the number of source citations to a minimum in order to allow for an uncluttered flow of the narrative, limiting them to the acknowlegment of direct quotations and paraphrases where the identification of a source was deemed essential. For the most part, I considered published collections of presidential papers, correspondence and public documents and made no effort to go beyond those sources, because plunging into the unpublished papers of 37 Presidents of the United States and their close governmental associates would have required more time and expense than I was able to command. The interest in and thoroughgoing study of nearly every presidential administration has, however, uncovered and presented much of value in already published works, memoirs and reflections of previous events and men. At the end of each section I included a selected bibliography which though not complete, represents the more important and rewarding sources in any particular area.

The editors and I assume full responsibility for any inconsistencies which may appear within the text and the documented materials. In an effort to remain as true as possible to the original source, archaic spellings, punctuation and grammatical usage have been retained where appropriate. In the rare instances when modifications were necessary to facilitate matters of space or readability, they have been duly noted within the text. I have relied heavily upon James D. Richardson's *Messages and Papers of the Presidents of the United States* and other public documents, particularly collections of papers, letters, diaries and memoirs of Presidents and their close associates, in compiling useful presidential documents. First-rate biographies such as Arthur Link's multi-volume study of Woodrow Wilson and others too numerous to mention have been invaluable. Although I have often been critical of his views on certain aspects of presidential power, I am, like any other student of the presidency, greatly indebted to that superb scholar, Edward S. Corwin, who has taught us all so much and has set such high standards of scholarship in this area. Biographers and analysts of the presidency, particularly Arthur M. Schlesinger, jr., James MacGregor Burns, Allan Nevins, Carl Sandburg, Clinton Rossiter, Richard E. Neustadt, Louis Koenig, Richard Hofstadter and many others have provided profound insights into both the character and problems of the office.

If there was any single source of intellectual inspiration in my formative years, it came from Scott Buchanan, who took the time to encourage my stumbling efforts as a student and opened up levels of my mind I would have never discovered independently. Ever since those wonderful years at St. John's, he has continued to inspire me enough to produce a work which I would not be ashamed to place in his hands. I owe a great deal to other teachers also, particularly Stringfellow Barr, Mark Van Doren, Sidney Hook, William Gorman, John Otto Neustadt, David B. Truman, Julien Franklin, William E. Leuchtenburg and Zbigniew K. Brzezinski. I would have faltered early as a teacher myself without the encouragement and support of my colleagues John P. Roche and I. Milton Sacks.

Throughout my years at Brandeis, I have enjoyed the warm friendship and support of Lawrence Fuchs, and in recent years, when at times my faith in the integrity of the academy has been jolted, I have been reassured by the principled and courageous example of my friend and colleague, John Mathews. Henry David Aiken and Peter Diamondopoulos have kept me from losing my philosophical bearings and have also proved their friendship time and again. Two very close friends, Philip Camponeschi and Jerry Cohen have often opened my eyes to my own inconsistencies and oversights and have encouraged me through the years to keep plodding ahead. Gail Frances Sullivan has regularly lifted my spirits and inspired me by her loyalty and confidence in the 'old man.' And, I am indeed grateful for the encouragement and faith in this project of my sister, Jane Elizabeth Tenney and my dear friends and in-laws, Tony and Clara Lovink.

In the writing and production of these three volumes, I owe particular thanks to Arthur M. Schlesinger, jr., who from the beginning recognized whatever merit they possess and helped me immeasurably in improving their quality. Harold Steinberg and Leon Friedman have assisted me in the difficult task of bringing this enterprise to a successful conclusion, and Debbie Weiss, with the able assistance of Kathy Hammell, was an invaluable editor, helping me to put the manuscript into its final form. In the early stages of the undertaking Albert S. Chappell and Lawrence Josephs assisted with research and editing; Grace Short typed many of my illegible first drafts and helped in many other ways to bring order to my erratic behavior. Also assisting in that respect were Barbara Sachar, Carol Smith and Rosalie Gurin. By patiently waiting for delayed comments on papers and by their provoking questions and comments in seminars, my students have cooperated and contributed to my analysis and understanding of the presidency. Many years ago the members of one of my presidency seminars participated in much of the research that went into section two of this volume.

I owe a particular vote of thanks to a number of patient librarians at Brandeis, in my home town of Concord, Massachusetts and in the deep caverns of the magnificent Widner Library at Harvard University. All have been tolerant of my wayward habits and always cooperative. Among those who I mention for special attention are Marcia Morse, Ivon B. Mills, Rosalie Archer, Edna Dolber, Florence Lever, Virginia Massey, Daniel Lurie and Victor Berch.

Finally a word of appreciation to my three wonderful children—Suzy, Michael and Cricket—who have postponed many vacations and weekend family safaris, and cooperated in innumerable ways so Dad could finish the books and get back again to being a father. I hope it has all been worth it. My dedication to my wife in Volume I very inadequately expresses my gratitude for the support and strength she has always provided.

W.M.G.

PERMISSIONS

INDEX

B

F

I

J

L

X

Y

Z